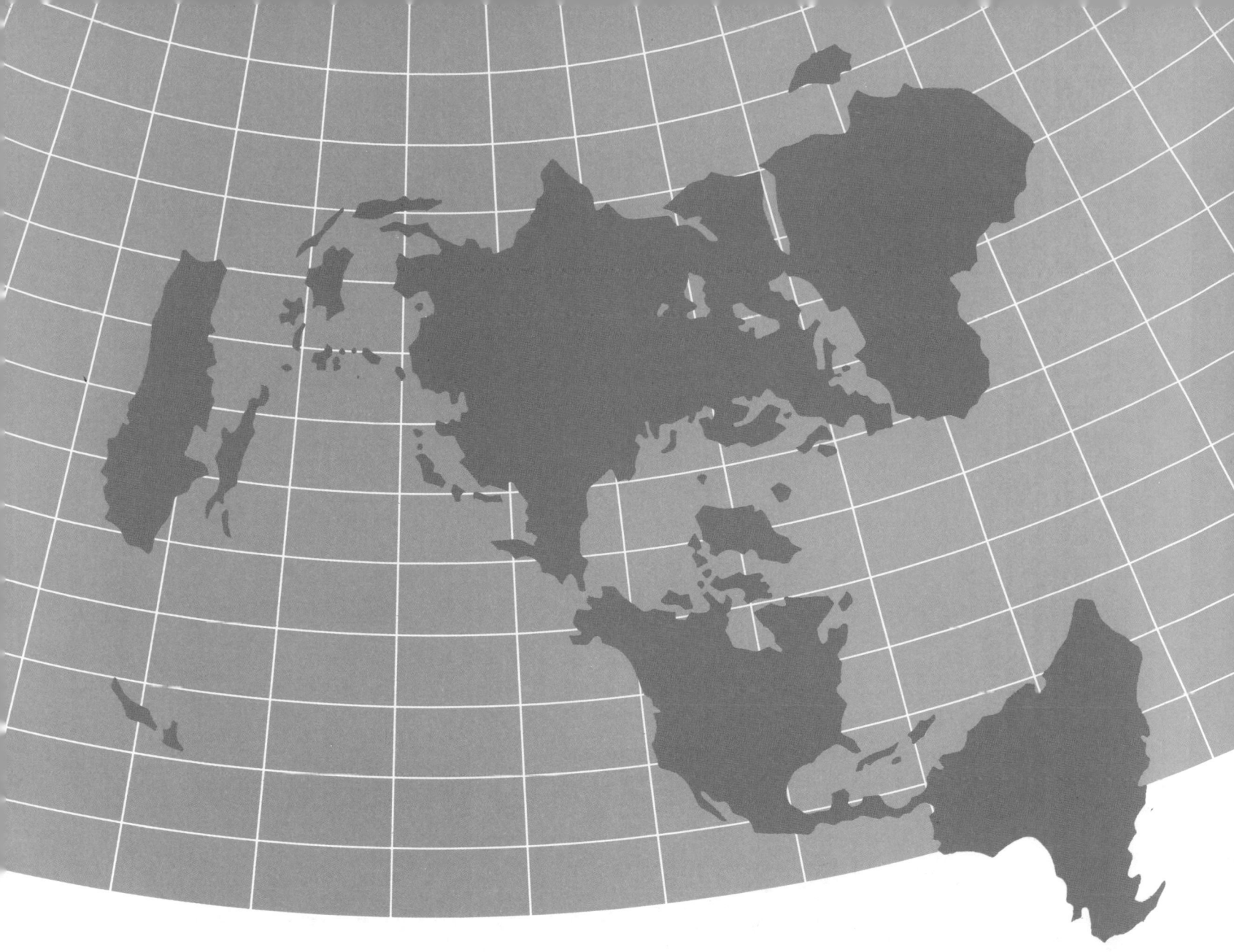

Rand McNally
World Atlas

Rand McNally & Company

Chicago / New York / San Francisco

Contents

Using the Atlas

Using the Atlas 3A

Today's World in Maps

Europe
Global View 6A
Annual Rainfall 8A
Vegetation 8A
Population 9A
Minerals 9A
Energy 10A
Natural Hazards 10A

Asia
Annual Rainfall 11A
Population 11A
Global View 12A
Vegetation 14A
Economic/Minerals 14A
Energy 15A
Natural Hazards 15A

Africa
Global View 16A
Annual Rainfall 18A
Vegetation 18A
Population 18A
Economic/Minerals 18A
Political Change 19A
Peoples 19A
Natural Hazards 19A
Landforms 19A

Australia, New Zealand, Oceania
Global View 20A
Annual Rainfall 22A
Vegetation 22A
Population 22A
Economic/Minerals 22A
Energy 23A
Natural Hazards 23A

South America
Global View 24A
Annual Rainfall 26A
Vegetation 26A
Population 26A
Economic/Minerals 26A
Energy 27A
Peoples 27A
Natural Hazards 27A
Landforms 27A

North America
Global View 28A
Annual Rainfall 30A
Vegetation 30A
Population 30A
Economic/Minerals 30A
Energy 31A
Water Resources 31A
Natural Hazards 31A
Landforms 31A

Time Zones 32A

Copyright © 1986, 1984 by Rand McNally & Company
All rights reserved
Printed in the U.S.A. by Rand McNally & Company
Sixth printing, May 1987
Library of Congress Catalog Card No.: 84-60927

The Political World in Maps

The World
Polar Map of the World 1
The World 2

Europe
Europe 3
British Isles 4
France and the Low Countries 5
Germany, Austria and Switzerland 6
Poland and Czechoslovakia 7
Spain and Portugal 8
Italy 9
Yugoslavia, Hungary, Romania
and Bulgaria 10
Norway, Sweden and Finland 11
Western Soviet Union 12
Soviet Union 13
Eastern Mediterranean 14

Asia
Israel and Arabia 15
Eurasia 16
China, Mongolia, Korea, Japan and Taiwan ... 17
Japan and Korea 18
Indonesia and the Philippines 19
India, Pakistan, Bangladesh, Burma
and Sri Lanka 20

Africa
Africa 21
Northwestern Africa 22
Northeastern Africa 23
Central and Southern Africa 24

Australia and New Zealand
Australia 25
Southeastern Australia and New Zealand ... 26

South America
South America 27
Central and Southern Argentina and Chile ... 28
Bolivia, Paraguay, Northern Argentina
and Chile 29
Uruguay and Southern Brazil 30
Peru and Ecuador 31
Colombia and Venezuela 32

North America
North America 33
Mexico 34
West Indies 35
Canada 36
  British Columbia 37
  Alberta 38
  Saskatchewan 39
  Manitoba 40
  Ontario 41
  Quebec 42
  Maritime Provinces 43
  Newfoundland 44
United States 45
  Alabama 46
  Alaska 47
  Arizona and New Mexico 48
  Arkansas 49
  California 50
  Colorado 51
  Connecticut and Rhode Island 52
  Delaware and Maryland 53
  Florida 54
  Georgia 55
  Hawaii 56
  Idaho 57
  Illinois 58
  Indiana 59
  Iowa 60
  Kansas 61
  Kentucky 62
  Louisiana 63
  Maine 64
  Massachusetts 65
  Michigan 66
  Minnesota 67
  Mississippi 68
  Missouri 69
  Montana 70
  Nebraska 71
  Nevada and Utah 72
  New Hampshire and Vermont 73
  New Jersey 74
  New York 75
  North Carolina 76
  North Dakota and South Dakota 77
  Ohio 78
  Oklahoma 79
  Oregon 80
  Pennsylvania 81
  South Carolina 82
  Tennessee 83
  Texas 84
  Virginia 85
  Washington 86
  West Virginia 87
  Wisconsin 88
  Wyoming 89

World Tables and Facts

World Political Information Table 90
World Facts and Comparisons 95
  Movements, Measurements, Inhabitants,
  Surface, Extremes of Temperature
  and Rainfall 95
  The Continents 95
  Approximate Population of the World,
  1650-1984 95
  Largest Countries of the World
  in Population 95
  Largest Countries of the World in Area 95
  Principal Mountains of the World 96
  Great Oceans and Seas of the World 97
  Principal Lakes of the World 97
  Principal Rivers of the World 97
  Principal Islands of the World 97
Population of Foreign Cities and Towns, Countries
and Important Political Divisions 98

United States Tables and Facts

United States City and County Populations
and ZIP Codes 115
Geographical Facts about the
United States 147
Historical Facts about the United States 147
State Areas and Populations 147
U.S. State General Information 148

Abbreviations 149

Index 150

Maps and Atlases

Since ancient times, maps have played a unique role in presenting information about the world, and maps defining territory and ownership are almost as old as the human territorial instinct itself. Dating from the second and first millenia B.C., the rock-carving map of the Val Camonica, Italy, in figure 1 shows stepped square fields, paths, rivers, and houses. Elegant as well as useful maps have been produced by many cultures. In figure 2, the Mexican map of the Tepetlaoztoc Valley, drawn in 1583, marks hills with wavy lines and roads with footprints between parallel lines. The methods and materials used to create these maps were dependent upon the technology available, and their accuracy suffered considerably, whereas modern maps are highly accurate, benefiting from our ever-increasing technological knowledge. Satellite imagery, shown in figure 3, now furnishes current, highly precise material from which maps such as that in figure 4 may be created or updated.

In the 1500s Gerardus Mercator, a Flemish cartographer, coined the word *atlas* to describe

Using the Atlas

a collection of maps. The atlas is unique among reference publications because only it, with its maps, actually shows *where* things are located in the world. As a dictionary defines words, as an encyclopedia defines things, an atlas graphically defines the world. Only on a map can the countries, cities, roads, rivers, and lakes covering a vast area be simultaneously viewed in their relative locations. Routes between places can be traced, trips planned, boundaries of neighboring states and countries examined, distances between places measured, the meandering of streams and the sizes of lakes visualized—and remote places imagined.

This atlas brings together not only a variety of maps but also an assortment of tables and other reference material, with topics ranging from the world's size and population to the countries' political status. To get the most out of the atlas, it is necessary to have a general idea of the arrangement of the information.

Sequence of the Maps

The world is made up of seven major land-masses: the continents of Europe, Asia, Africa, Australia, South America, North America, and Antarctica (figure 5). To allow for the inclusion of detail, each continent is broken down into a series of maps, and this grouping is arranged so that as consecutive pages are turned, a continuous and successive part of the continent is shown. Larger-scale maps are used for regions of greater detail (having many cities, for example) or for areas of global significance.

The continental sequence of the maps is as follows: Europe (traditionally first in atlases), Asia (connected to Europe and forming the Eurasian landmass), Africa, Australia and Oceania, South America, and North America.

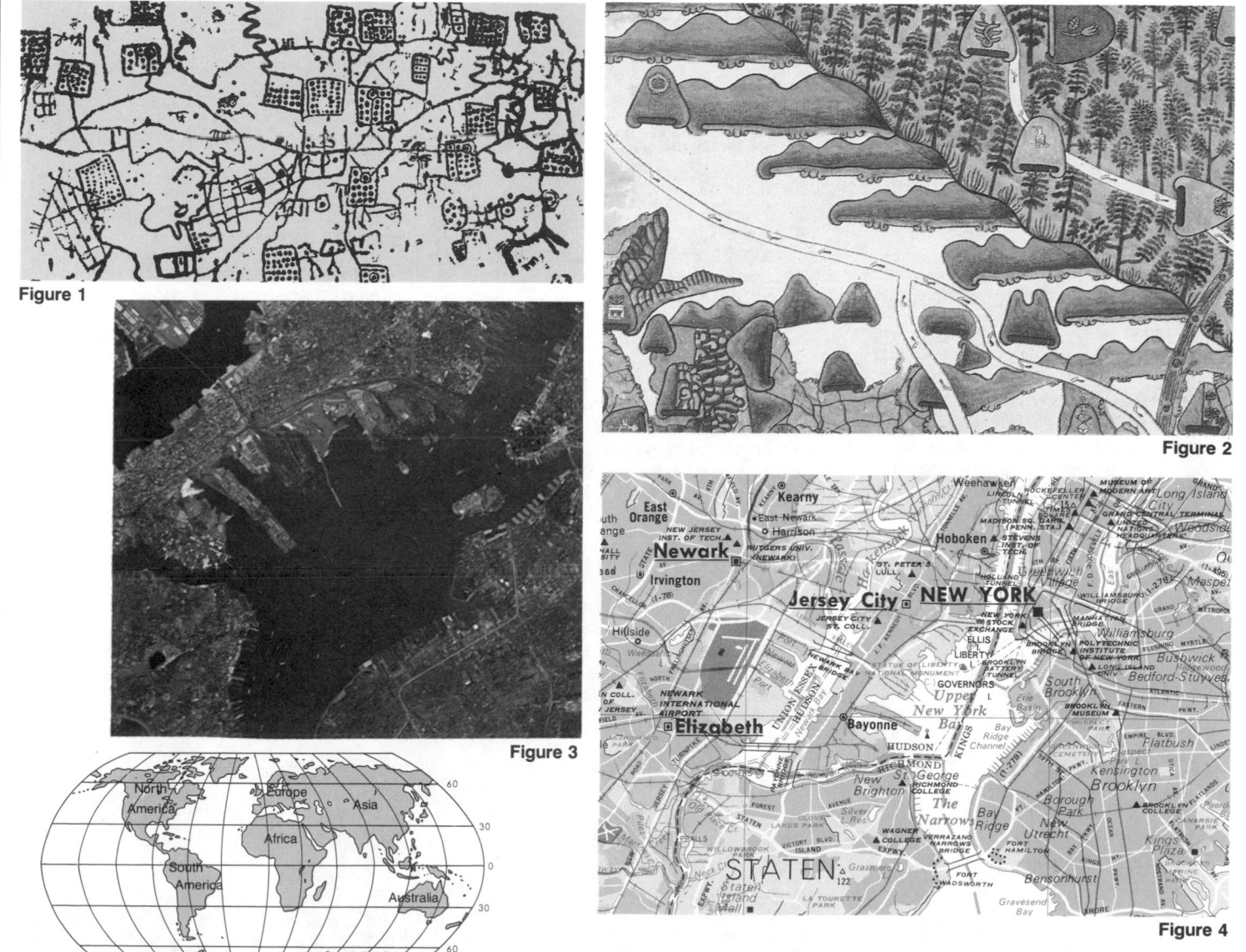

Figure 1

Figure 2

Figure 3

Figure 4

Figure 5

Getting the Information

An atlas can be used for many purposes, from planning a trip to finding hot spots in the news and supplementing world knowledge. But to realize the full potential of an atlas, the user must be able to:

1. Find places on the maps
2. Measure distances
3. Determine directions
4. Understand map symbols

Finding Places

One of the most common and important tasks facilitated by an atlas is finding the *location* of a place in the world. A river's name in a book, a city mentioned in the news, or a vacation spot may prompt your need to know where the place is located. The illustrations and text below explain how to find Benguela, Angola.

1. Look up the place-name in the index at the back of the atlas. Benguela, Angola, can be found on the map on page 24, and it can be located on the map by the letter-number key *C2* (figure 6).

Bay-Ber		**155**
Benewah, Idaho	B2	57
Benewah, co., Idaho	B2	57
Bengal, reg., Bngl., India	D8	20
Bengasi (Banghāzī), Libya	B2	23
Bengbu, China	E8	17
Bengkulu, Indon.,	F2	19
Benguela, Ang.	C2	24
Benguela, dist., Ang.	C3	24
Benham, Ky.	D7	62
Ben Hill, co., Ga.	D3	55

Figure 6

2. Turn to the map of Central and Southern Africa on page 24. Note that the letters A through H and the numbers 1 through 10 appear in the margins of the maps.

3. To find Benguela on the map, place your left index finger on C and your right index finger on 2. Move your left finger across the map and your right finger down the map. Your fingers will meet in the area in which Benguela is located (figure 7).

Figure 7

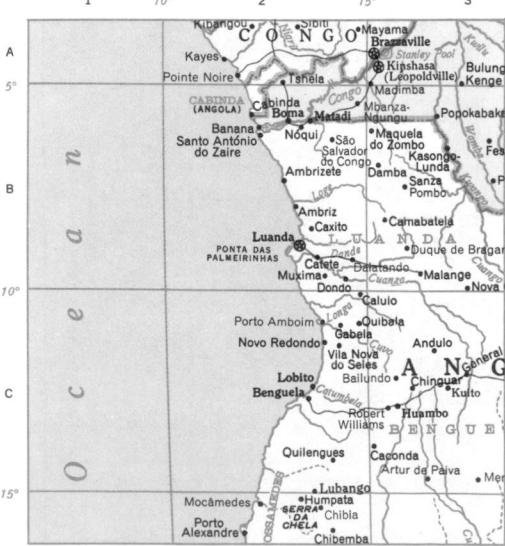

Measuring Distances

In planning trips, determining the distance between two places is essential, and an atlas can help in travel preparation. For instance, to determine the approximate distance between Paris and Rouen, France, follow these three steps:

1. Lay a slip of paper on the map on page 5 so that its edge touches the two cities. Adjust the paper so one corner touches Rouen. Mark the paper directly at the spot where Paris is located (figure 8).

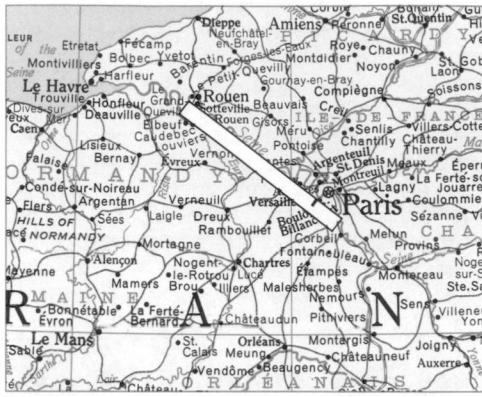

Figure 8

2. Place the paper along the scale of statute miles beneath the map. Position the corner at 0 and line up the edge of the paper along the scale. The pencil mark on the paper indicates Rouen is between 50 and 75 miles from Paris (figure 9).

Figure 9

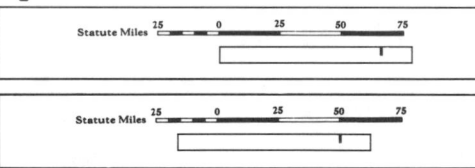

Figure 10

3. To find the exact distance, move the paper to the left so that the pencil mark is at 50 on the scale. The corner of the paper stands in the fourth 5-mile unit on the scale. This means that the two towns are 50 plus 15 plus 2, or 67 miles, apart (figure 10).

Determining Directions

Most of the maps in the atlas are drawn so that when oriented for normal reading north is at the top of the map, south is at the bottom, west is at the left, and east is at the right. Most maps have a series of lines drawn across them—the lines of latitude and longitude. Lines of latitude, or parallels of latitude, are drawn east and west.

Figure 11

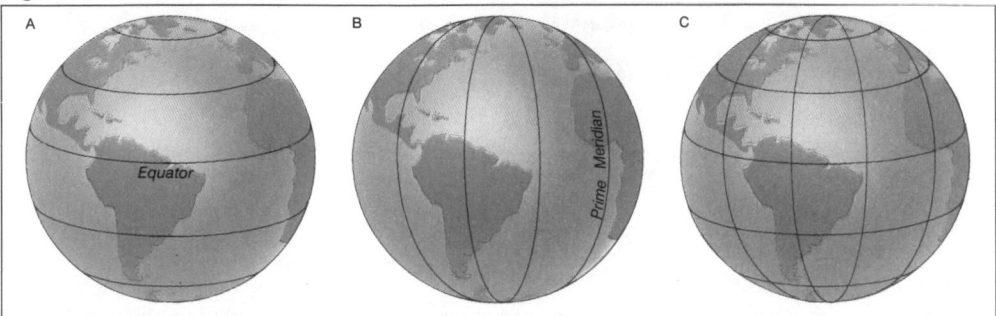

Lines of longitude, or meridians of longitude, are drawn north and south (figure 11).

Parallels and meridians appear as either curved or straight lines. For example, in the section of the map of Europe in figure 12, the parallels of latitude appear as curved lines. The meridians of longitude are straight lines that come together toward the top of the map.

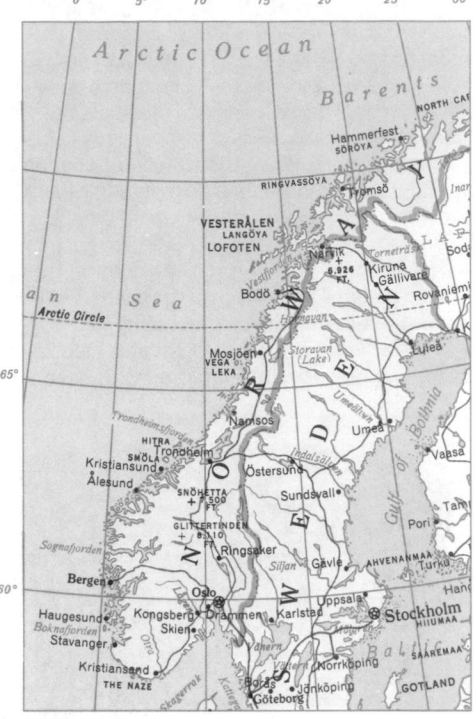

Figure 12

Latitude and longitude lines help locate places on maps. Parallels of latitude are numbered in degrees north and south of the *Equator*. Meridians of longitude are numbered in degrees east and west of a line called the *Prime Meridian*, running through Greenwich, England, near London. Any place on earth can be located by the latitude and longitude lines running through it.

To determine directions or locations on maps, you must use the parallels and meridians. For example, suppose you want to know which city is farther north, Bergen, Norway, or Stockholm, Sweden. The map in figure 12 shows that Stockholm is south of the 60° parallel of latitude and Bergen is north of it. This means that Bergen is farther north than Stockholm. By looking at the meridians of longitude, you can determine which city is farther east. Bergen is approximately 5° east of the 0° meridian (Prime Meridian), and Stockholm is almost 20° east of it. This means that Stockholm is farther east than Bergen.

Map Symbols (Legend)
For maps pages 1–89

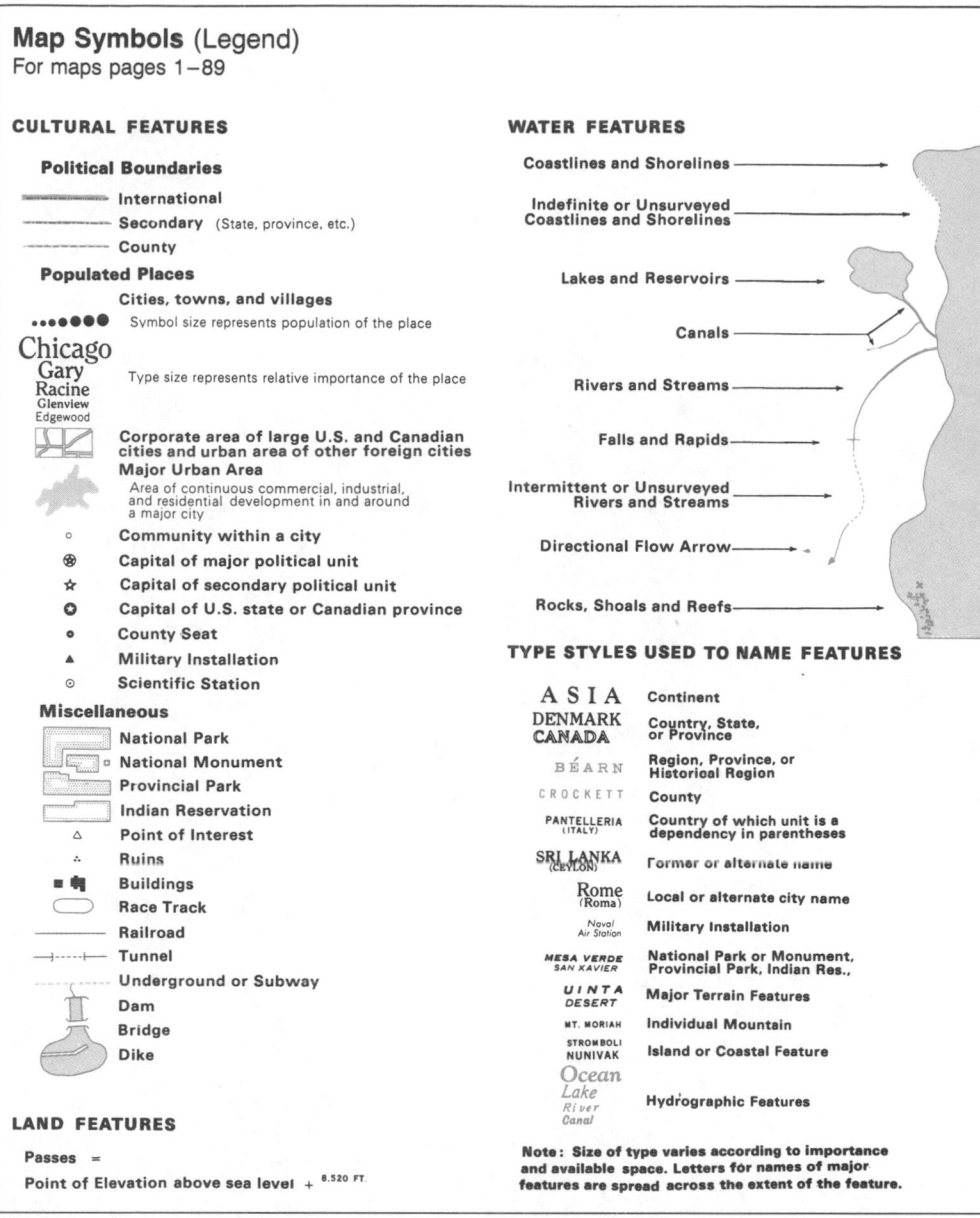

CULTURAL FEATURES

Political Boundaries

━━━━━━ International

———— Secondary (State, province, etc.)

············ County

Populated Places

Cities, towns, and villages

····•••● Symbol size represents population of the place

Chicago
Gary
Racine
Glenview
Edgewood

Type size represents relative importance of the place

Corporate area of large U.S. and Canadian cities and urban area of other foreign cities
Major Urban Area
Area of continuous commercial, industrial, and residential development in and around a major city

○ Community within a city

⊛ Capital of major political unit

☆ Capital of secondary political unit

◉ Capital of U.S. state or Canadian province

◦ County Seat

▲ Military Installation

⊙ Scientific Station

Miscellaneous

National Park

National Monument

Provincial Park

Indian Reservation

△ Point of Interest

∴ Ruins

■ ◉ Buildings

⬭ Race Track

———— Railroad

—┼—┼— Tunnel

---------- Underground or Subway

Dam

Bridge

Dike

LAND FEATURES

Passes =

Point of Elevation above sea level + 8,520 FT.

Figure 13

WATER FEATURES

Coastlines and Shorelines ⟶

Indefinite or Unsurveyed Coastlines and Shorelines ⟶

Lakes and Reservoirs ⟶

Canals ⟶

Rivers and Streams ⟶

Falls and Rapids ⟶

Intermittent or Unsurveyed Rivers and Streams ⟶

Directional Flow Arrow ⟶

Rocks, Shoals and Reefs ⟶

TYPE STYLES USED TO NAME FEATURES

A S I A — Continent

DENMARK CANADA — Country, State, or Province

BÉARN — Region, Province, or Historical Region

CROCKETT — County

PANTELLERIA (ITALY) — Country of which unit is a dependency in parentheses

SRI LANKA (CEYLON) — Former or alternate name

Rome (Roma) — Local or alternate city name

Naval Air Station — Military Installation

MESA VERDE SAN XAVIER — National Park or Monument, Provincial Park, Indian Res.,

U I N T A DESERT — Major Terrain Features

MT. MORIAH — Individual Mountain

STROMBOLI NUNIVAK — Island or Coastal Feature

Ocean Lake River Canal — Hydrographic Features

Note: Size of type varies according to importance and available space. Letters for names of major features are spread across the extent of the feature.

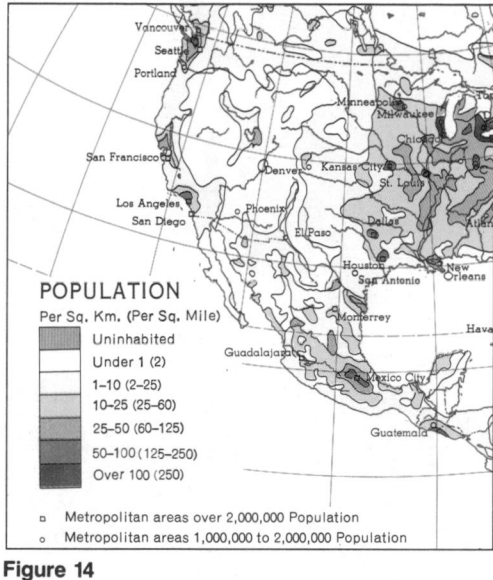

POPULATION
Per Sq. Km. (Per Sq. Mile)

- Uninhabited
- Under 1 (2)
- 1–10 (2–25)
- 10–25 (25–60)
- 25–50 (60–125)
- 50–100 (125–250)
- Over 100 (250)

▫ Metropolitan areas over 2,000,000 Population
◦ Metropolitan areas 1,000,000 to 2,000,000 Population

Figure 14

Figure 15

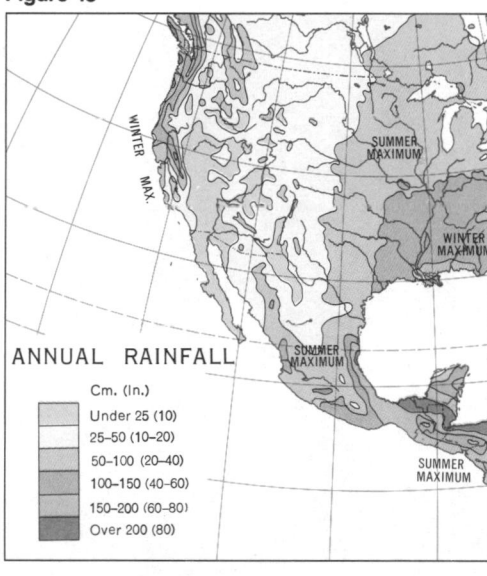

ANNUAL RAINFALL
Cm. (In.)

- Under 25 (10)
- 25–50 (10–20)
- 50–100 (20–40)
- 100–150 (40–60)
- 150–200 (60–80)
- Over 200 (80)

Understanding Map Symbols

In a very real sense, the whole map is a symbol, representing the world or a part of it. It is a reduced representation of the earth; each of the world's features—cities, rivers, etc.—is represented on the map by a symbol. Map symbols may take the form of points, such as dots or stars (often used for cities, capital cities, or points of interest), or lines (roads, rivers, railroads). Symbols may also occupy an area, showing extent of coverage (states, forests, deserts). They seldom look like the feature they represent and therefore must be identified and interpreted. For instance, the maps in this atlas show and differentiate political units (countries, states) with color. The political units are further defined by a heavy line depicting their boundaries. Neither the colors nor the boundary lines are actually found on the surface of the earth, but because countries and states are such important political components of the world, strong symbols are used to represent them.

The legend in figure 13 identifies the symbols used in this atlas.

Thematic Maps and Tables

The reference maps and index provide the source of much of the information in the atlas. Supplementing these are thematic maps and tables.

Thematic Maps

A thematic map is a special-topic map that uses symbols to show certain characteristics of, generally, one class of geographical information. For instance, the map in figure 14, presenting the theme of *population*, shows the pattern of where people live. Likewise the *rainfall* theme map shows where the greatest and least amounts of precipitation are distributed.

The thematic map's primary concern is to communicate visually the major impressions of the distribution of the theme. For example, the most populated areas in North America, as shown in the map in figure 14, are in central and eastern United States, contrasting with the very low densities of most of the West. One of the most important aspects of the thematic map section is the use of different maps to show

comparisons and relationships between the various distributions. For example, people tend to inhabit areas of plentiful rainfall, and the close relationship between dense population and heavy rainfall patterns is made evident by comparing figures 14 and 15.

Tables

The tables in the atlas supplement the information found on the maps, providing statistical data about the world.

For each political unit, the World Political Information Table specifies area in square miles, latest estimated population, population density, capital, largest city, and principal languages. In addition, the table describes form of government and political or administrative status. Another world table shows the population of major foreign cities and towns.

A table of United States cities and towns lists the latest estimated population and the ZIP code of major cities. Geographical and historical facts about the United States are also included in the tabular section.

Global View
Europe

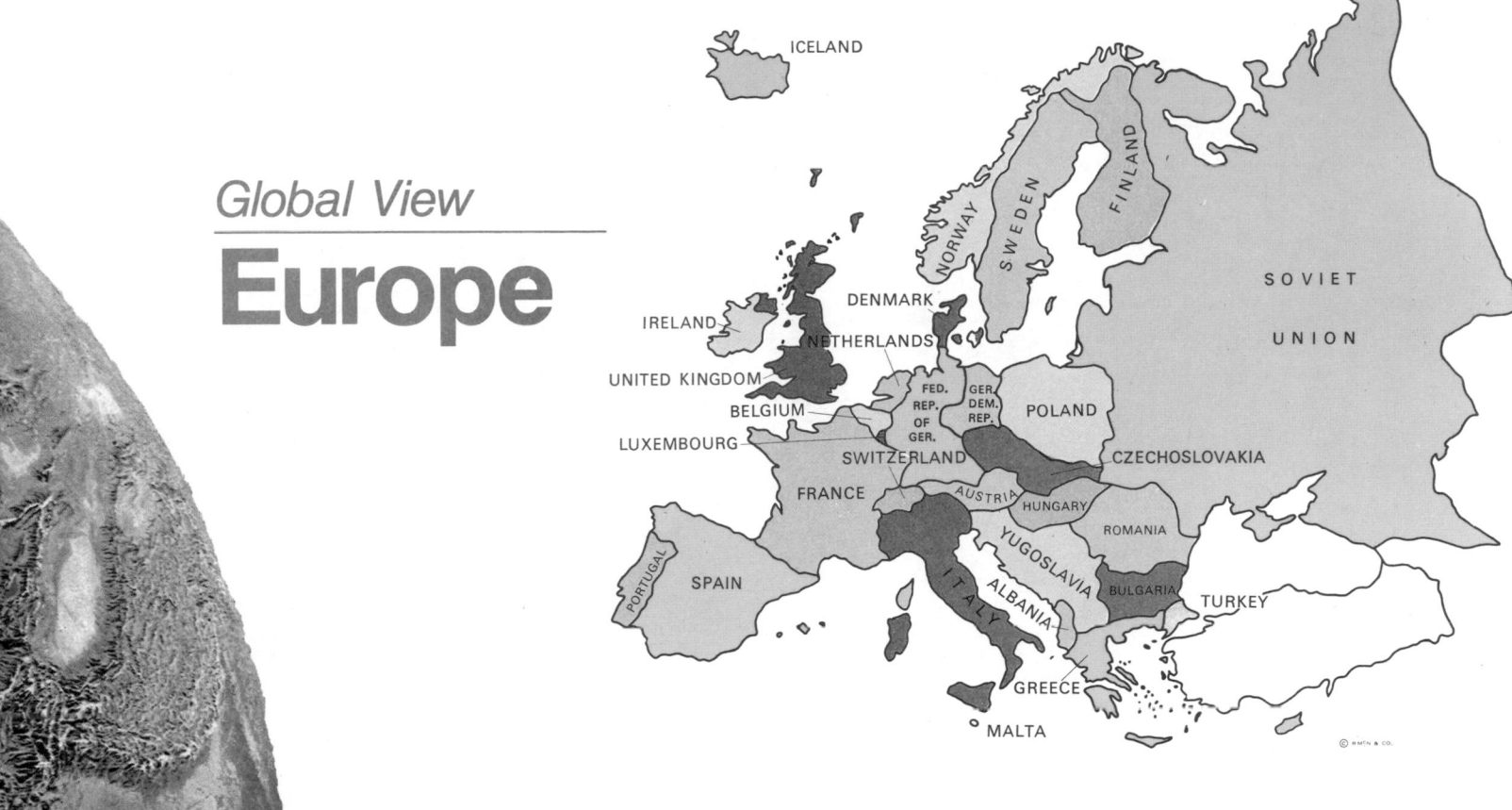

This global view centers on the western extension of Asia, the region the world knows as the continent of Europe. Often the two are linked together under the name Eurasia. This peninsula, or arm, of the great Asian landmass, itself is comprised of numerous peninsulas—those of Scandinavia, Iberia, Italy, and the Balkans—and many offshore islands, the most important group being the British Isles.

The thrust of this arm of Asia into the Atlantic Ocean, the North and Mediterranean seas provides a clear-cut western terminus. But the limits of Europe are not so clearly defined on its eastern flank where no natural barriers exist. For the sake of a "boundary" geographers have come to recognize the low Ural Mountains and the Ural River, the Caspian Sea, the Caucasus Mountains, and the Black Sea as the eastern and southeastern border.

From Europe's eastern limits, where the north to south dimension is approximately 2,500 miles, the irregularly shaped continent tapers toward the southwest and the surrounding bodies of water. Through Europe's history its miles of coastline encouraged contact with the other continents, and the seas became avenues of exchange for culture, politics, and technology with other regions of the world.

Internally Europe embraces a varied landscape comparable to no other region of its size in the world: In a total area of only 3,825,000 square miles are found extremes from zero winters and dry steppes in the east to year-round humid, mild climates in the west; extremes in elevation from the heights of the Alps to the below-sea-level Belgian and Netherlands coasts; and a variation in the distribution of inhabitants from the densely populated, industrialized northwest to the sparsely peopled areas in the agricultural south and east. Thirty-three independent nations, each with its own national, religious, cultural, and political heritage, add to this variegated landscape.

Because much of Europe is neither too hot or cold, or too high or low, a great extent of its land has been developed, aided by an impressive river-canal system, dominated by the Rhine and Danube. Its natural and cultural wealth has made possible an economic-social-political system which has long influenced the economic, political, and social structure of the rest of the world.

Today, because of its density of population, strategic location, politics, history, economic strength, and cultural tradition, Europe still may rightfully and strongly claim to be one of the hubs of the world.

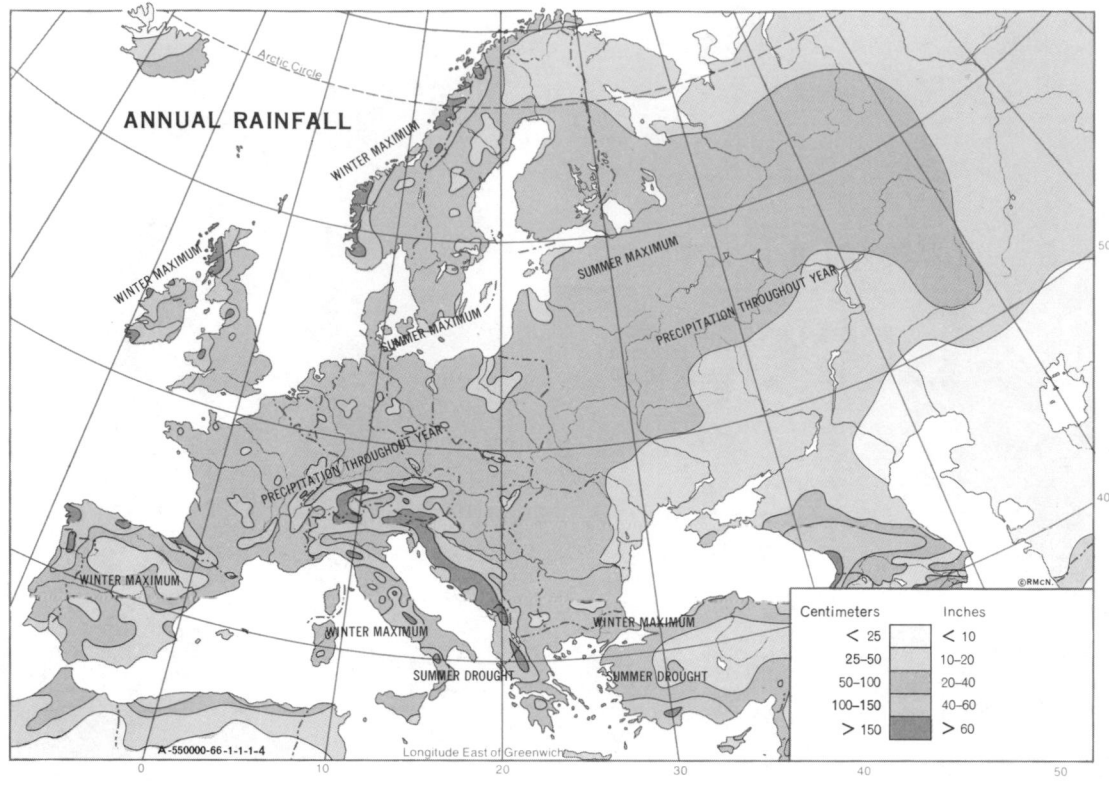

ANNUAL RAINFALL

Centimeters	Inches
< 25	< 10
25–50	10–20
50–100	20–40
100–150	40–60
> 150	> 60

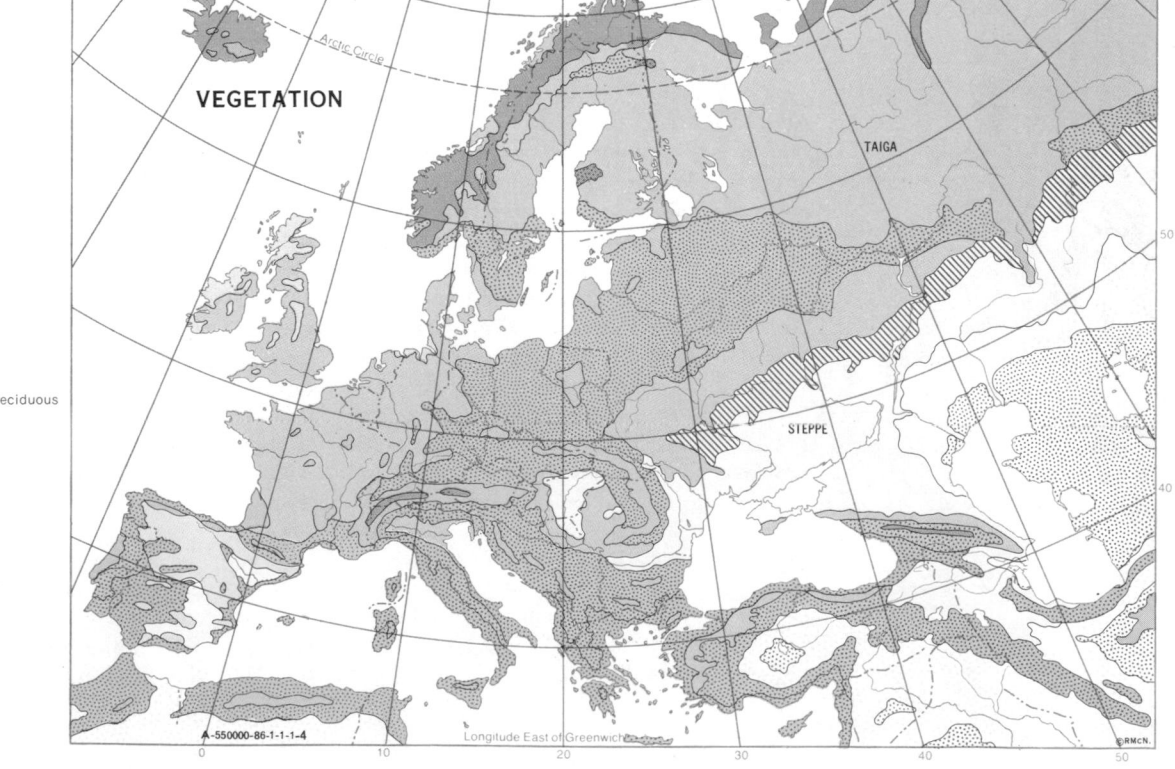

VEGETATION

VEGETATION

- Coniferous forest
- Mediterranean vegetation
- Mixed forest: coniferous-deciduous
- Semi-deciduous forest
- Deciduous forest
- Wooded steppe
- Grass (steppe)
- Short grass
- Desert shrub
- Heath and moor
- Alpine vegetation, tundra
- Little or no vegetation

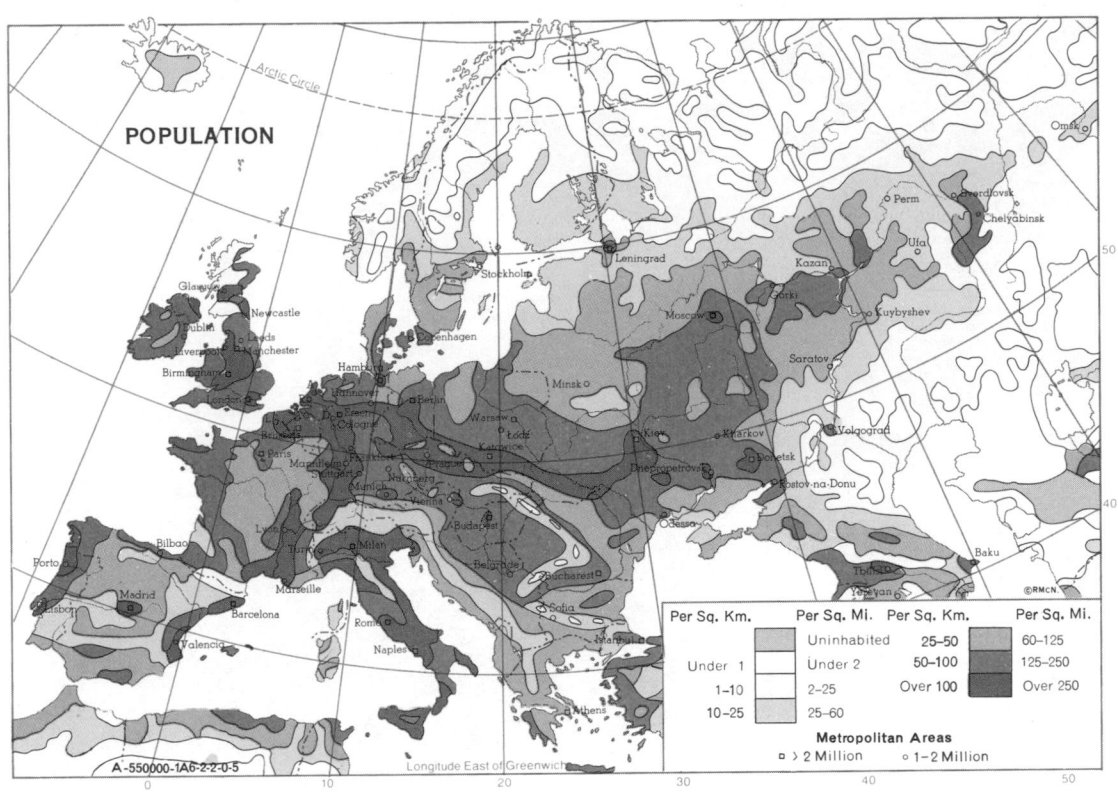

POPULATION

Per Sq. Km.	Per Sq. Mi.	Per Sq. Km.	Per Sq. Mi.
	Uninhabited	25–50	60–125
Under 1	Under 2	50–100	125–250
1–10	2–25	Over 100	Over 250
10–25	25–60		

Metropolitan Areas
□ > 2 Million   ○ 1–2 Million

A-550000-1A6-2-2-0-5   Longitude East of Greenwich

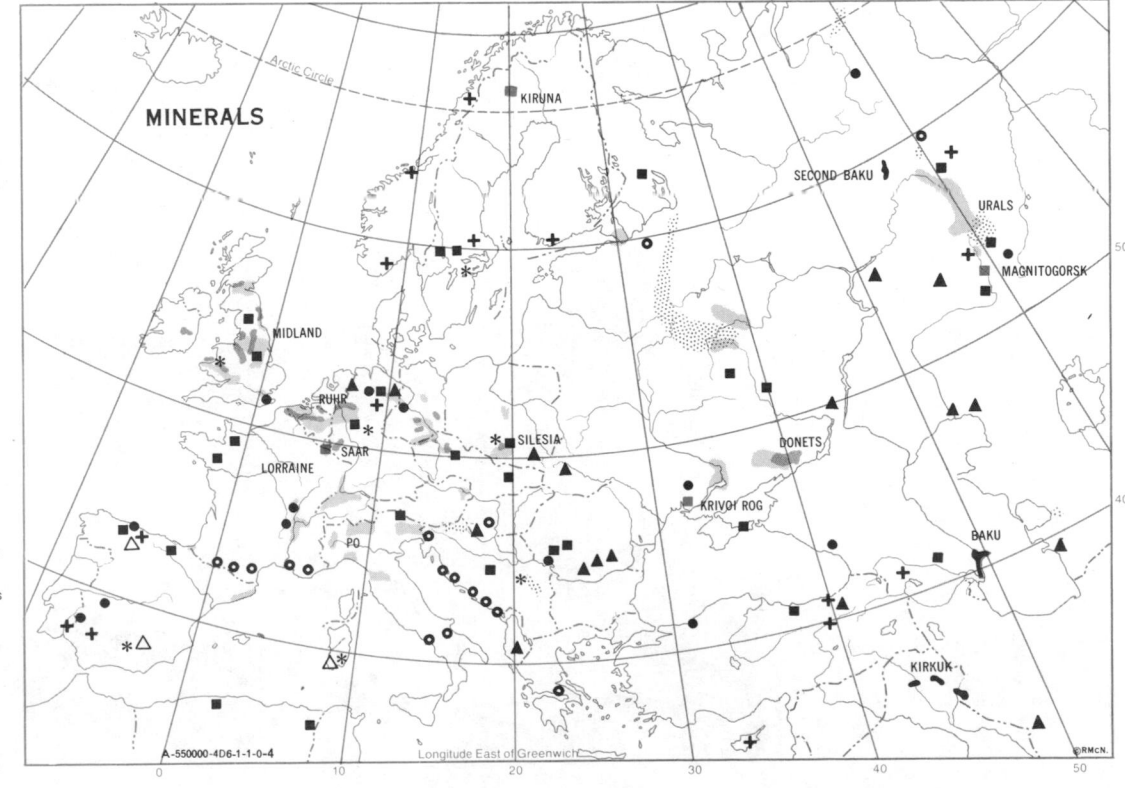

MINERALS

	Industrial areas
	Major coal deposits
●	Major petroleum deposits
	Lignite deposits
▲	Minor petroleum deposits
●	Minor coal deposits
■	Major iron ore
■	Minor iron ore
✳	Lead
⊙	Bauxite
△	Zinc
✚	Copper

A-550000-4D6-1-1-0-4   Longitude East of Greenwich   ©RMcN.

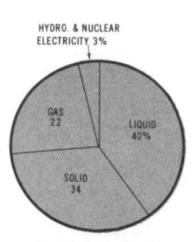

HYDRO. & NUCLEAR
ELECTRICITY 3%

GAS
22

LIQUID
40%

SOLID
34

Energy Consumption
3,699,305 metric tons
coal equivalent-1979

ENERGY

Energy Producing Plants

▽ Geothermal
• Hydroelectric
■ Nuclear

Mineral Fuel Deposits

• Uranium: major deposit
△ Natural Gas: major field
▲ Petroleum: major field
• Petroleum: minor field
   Petroleum: major producing area
   Coal: major bituminous and anthracite
   Coal: minor bituminous and anthracite
   Coal: lignite

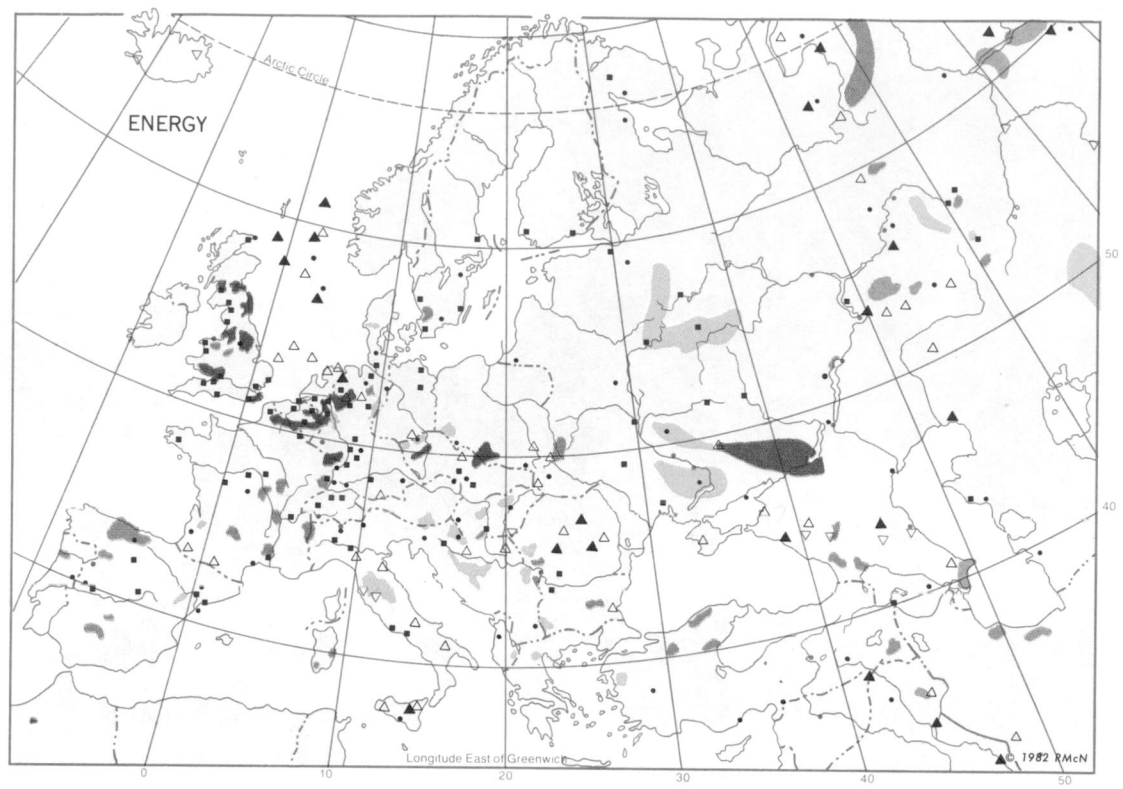

ENERGY

Longitude East of Greenwich

© 1982 RMcN

NATURAL HAZARDS

○ Volcanoes*
● Earthquakes*
● Major flood disasters*
   Tsunamis
   Limit of iceberg drift

   Temporary pack ice
   Areas subject to desertification

   *Twentieth Century occurrences

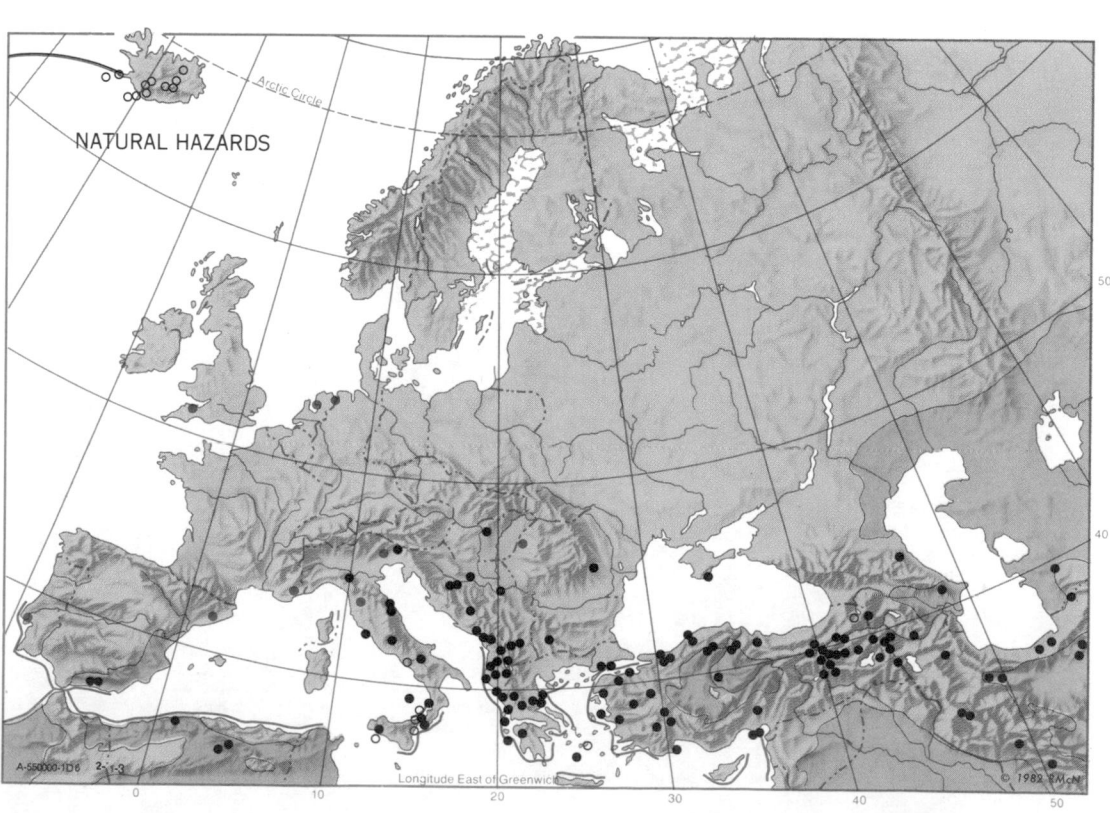

NATURAL HAZARDS

A-550000-1D6 2 1 3

Longitude East of Greenwich

© 1982 RMcN

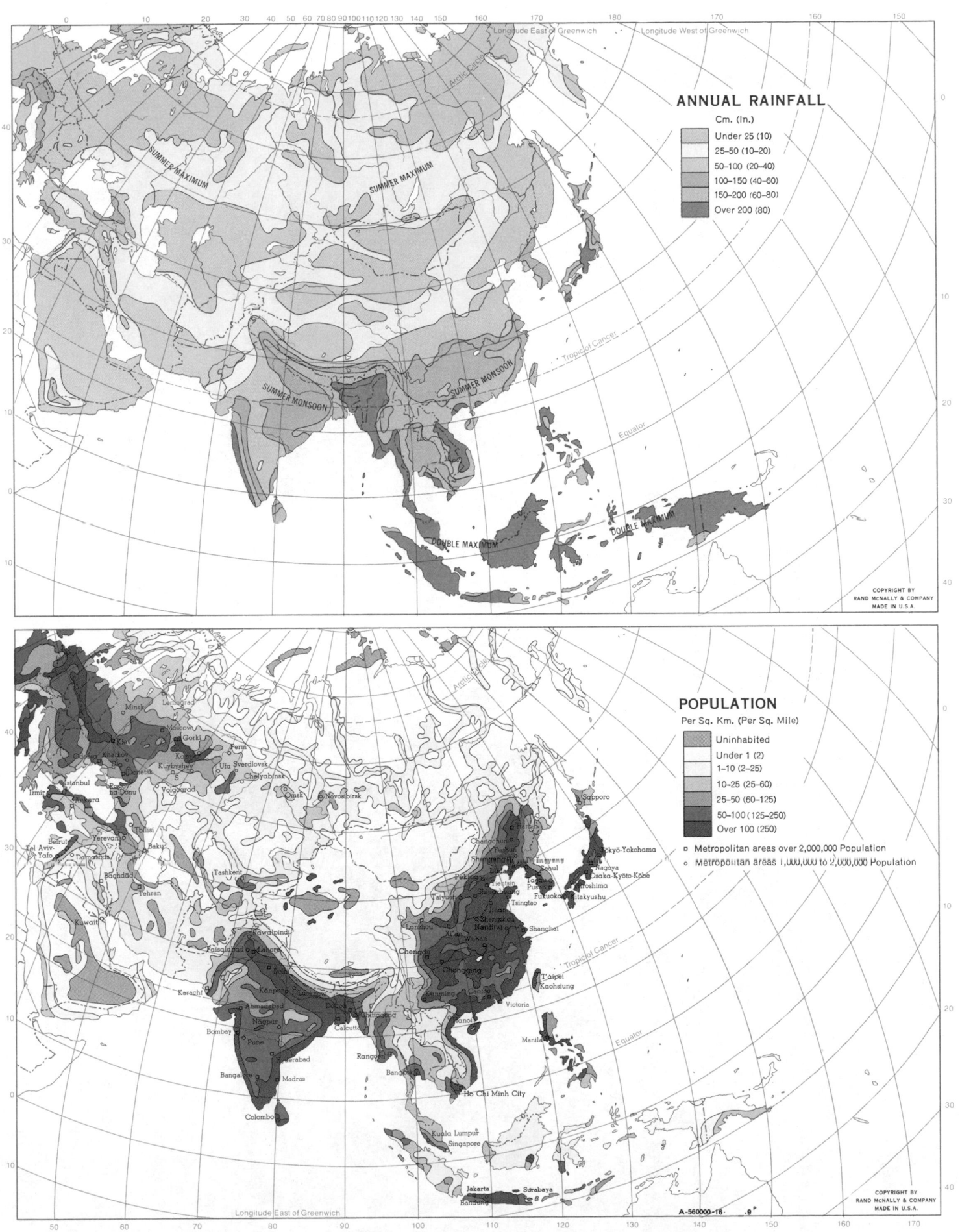

ANNUAL RAINFALL
Cm. (In.)
Under 25 (10)
25–50 (10–20)
50–100 (20–40)
100–150 (40–60)
150–200 (60–80)
Over 200 (80)

POPULATION
Per Sq. Km. (Per Sq. Mile)
Uninhabited
Under 1 (2)
1–10 (2–25)
10–25 (25–60)
25–50 (60–125)
50–100 (125–250)
Over 100 (250)
□ Metropolitan areas over 2,000,000 Population
○ Metropolitan areas 1,000,000 to 2,000,000 Population

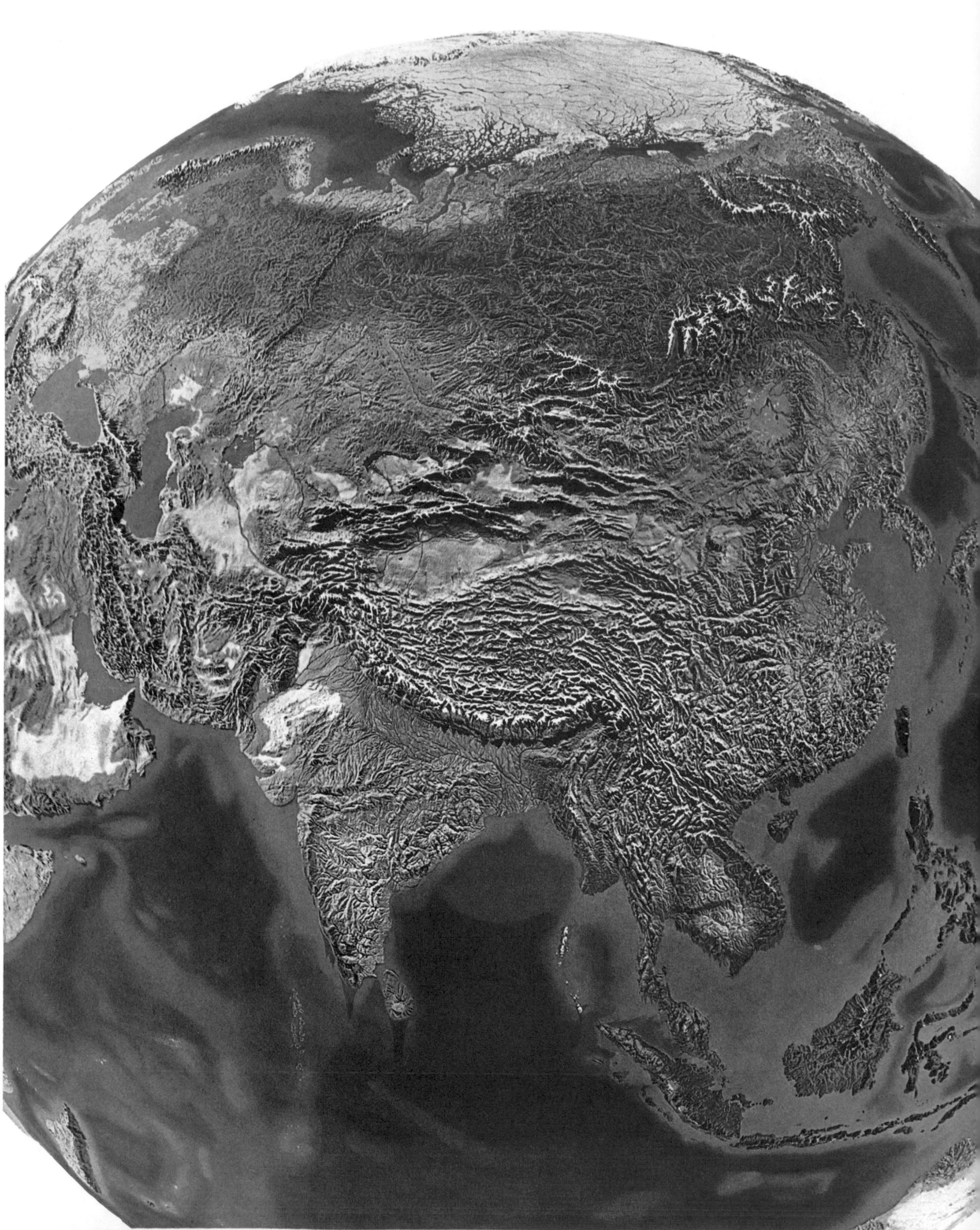

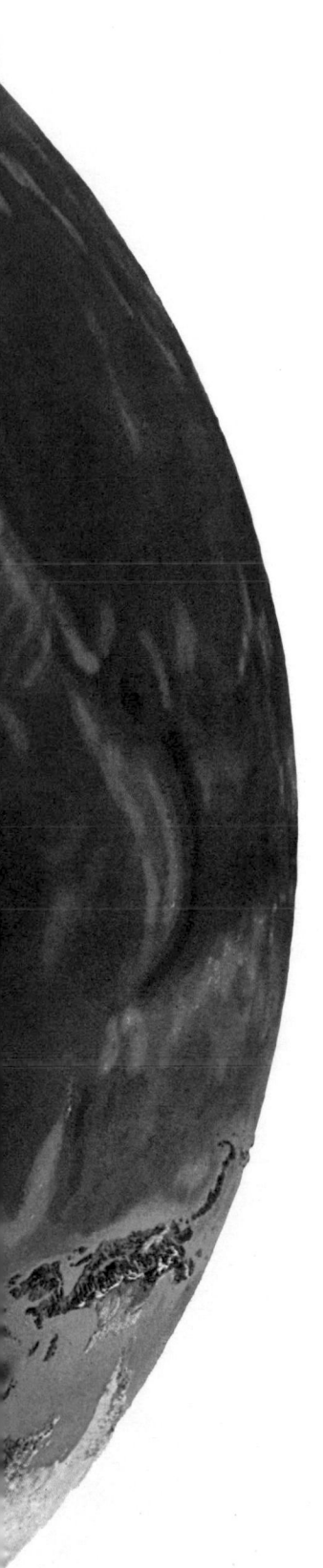

Global View
Asia

Asia, the massive giant of continents, spreads its 17,085,000 square miles from polar wastes to regions of tropical abundance, and from Oriental to Occidental hearthlands. Much of Asia's vastness, however, is occupied by deserts, steppes, and by frozen and near-frozen wastes. Rugged upland areas stretch from Turkey and Iran, through the two-mile-high Tibetan Plateau, to the Bering Strait, leaving only one-third of Asia suitable for human habitation. These barriers also separate the two dominant, sharply contrasting parts of Asia—the realm made up of Southwest, South, and Southeast Asia from that of "European" Asia.

Rimming the south and east coasts of the continent are the most densely populated regions of the world, each dominated by a life-giving river system—the Tigris-Euphrates, the Indus and Ganges, the Brahmaputra, the Irrawaddy and Salween, the Menam and Mekong, the Yangtze and Hwang Ho, as well as innumerable small river valleys, plains, and islands. Separated from one another by deserts, massifs, and seas these regions account for over one-half of the world's population.

The civilizations associated with this population (where rural densities frequently may exceed 1,000 people per square mile) were developed largely upon the strength of intensive agricultural systems. Today these systems still occupy more than 60 percent of the populace, who manage only to win a bare subsistence. Changeover from subsistence agricultural economic systems to industrialized economies has been successful only in Japan and parts of the U.S.S.R.

North of the great Gobi Desert and the mountain barriers of the interior is the second Asia which, on almost every hand, differs from the southern portion of the continent. In the far north severe climatic elements send temperatures to −90°F., and permanently frozen ground impedes growth of vegetation. Only the scattered settlements next to the Trans-Siberian Railway give the area an indication of development. The activities of most of the populace are clearly directed toward Europe rather than Asia.

These two realms of the Asian continent do share two common characteristics. One is vast, yet generally inaccessible, natural resources—extensive forests, minerals, and hydroelectric potential—and the second is the drive to industrialize in order to "catch up" to the general material well-being of the Western World.

In the future, as the common characteristics, resources and drive, are developed, Asia's two realms may witness a change. A material way of life may result consistent with their heritage and historic contributions to the world.

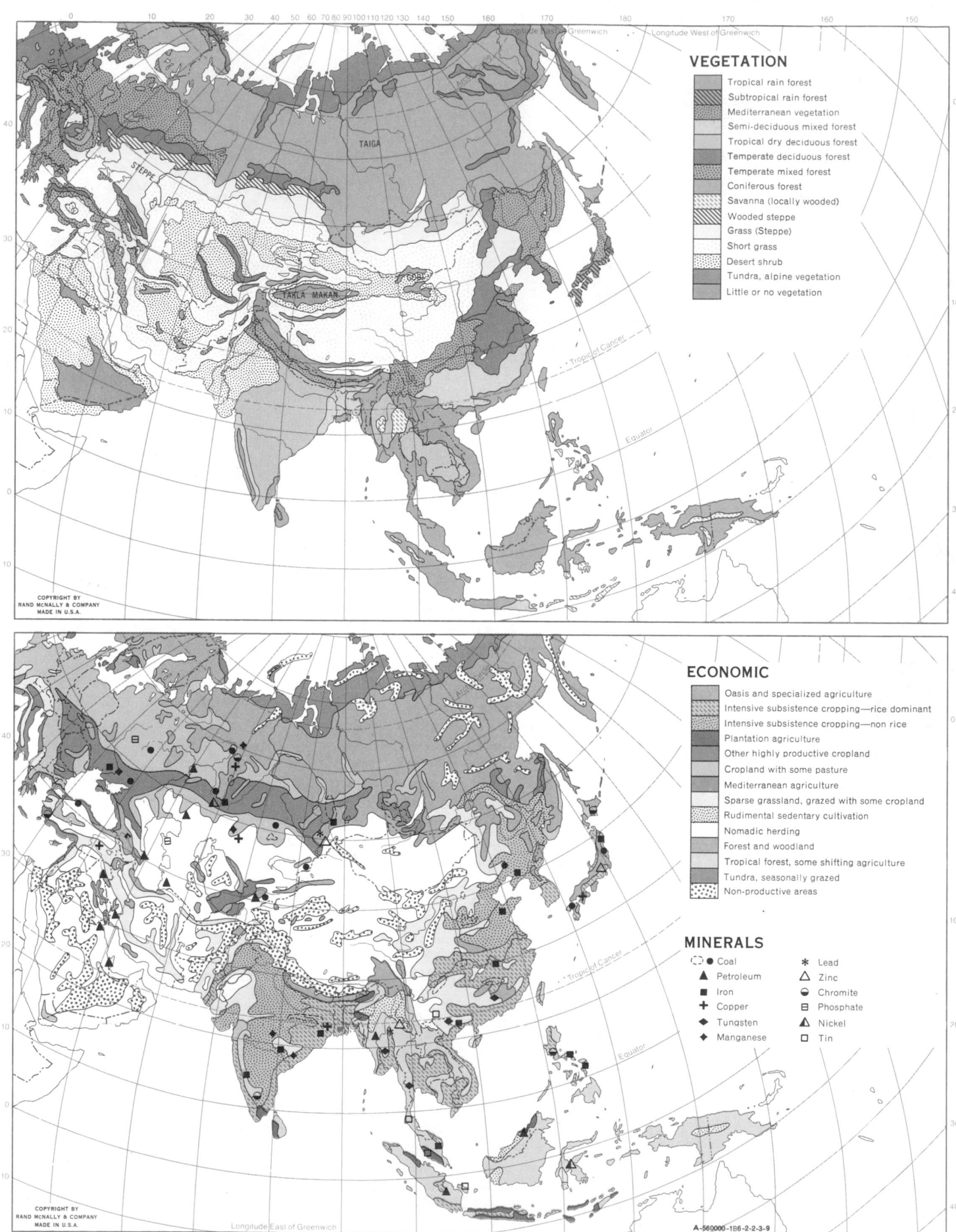

VEGETATION

Tropical rain forest
Subtropical rain forest
Mediterranean vegetation
Semi-deciduous mixed forest
Tropical dry deciduous forest
Temperate deciduous forest
Temperate mixed forest
Coniferous forest
Savanna (locally wooded)
Wooded steppe
Grass (Steppe)
Short grass
Desert shrub
Tundra, alpine vegetation
Little or no vegetation

ECONOMIC

Oasis and specialized agriculture
Intensive subsistence cropping—rice dominant
Intensive subsistence cropping—non rice
Plantation agriculture
Other highly productive cropland
Cropland with some pasture
Mediterranean agriculture
Sparse grassland, grazed with some cropland
Rudimental sedentary cultivation
Nomadic herding
Forest and woodland
Tropical forest, some shifting agriculture
Tundra, seasonally grazed
Non-productive areas

MINERALS

⬡● Coal   ✳ Lead
▲ Petroleum   △ Zinc
■ Iron   ⊖ Chromite
✛ Copper   ⊟ Phosphate
◆ Tungsten   ◮ Nickel
◆ Manganese   ▢ Tin

COPYRIGHT BY
RAND McNALLY & COMPANY
MADE IN U.S.A.

COPYRIGHT BY
RAND McNALLY & COMPANY
MADE IN U.S.A.

A-560000-186-2-2-3-9

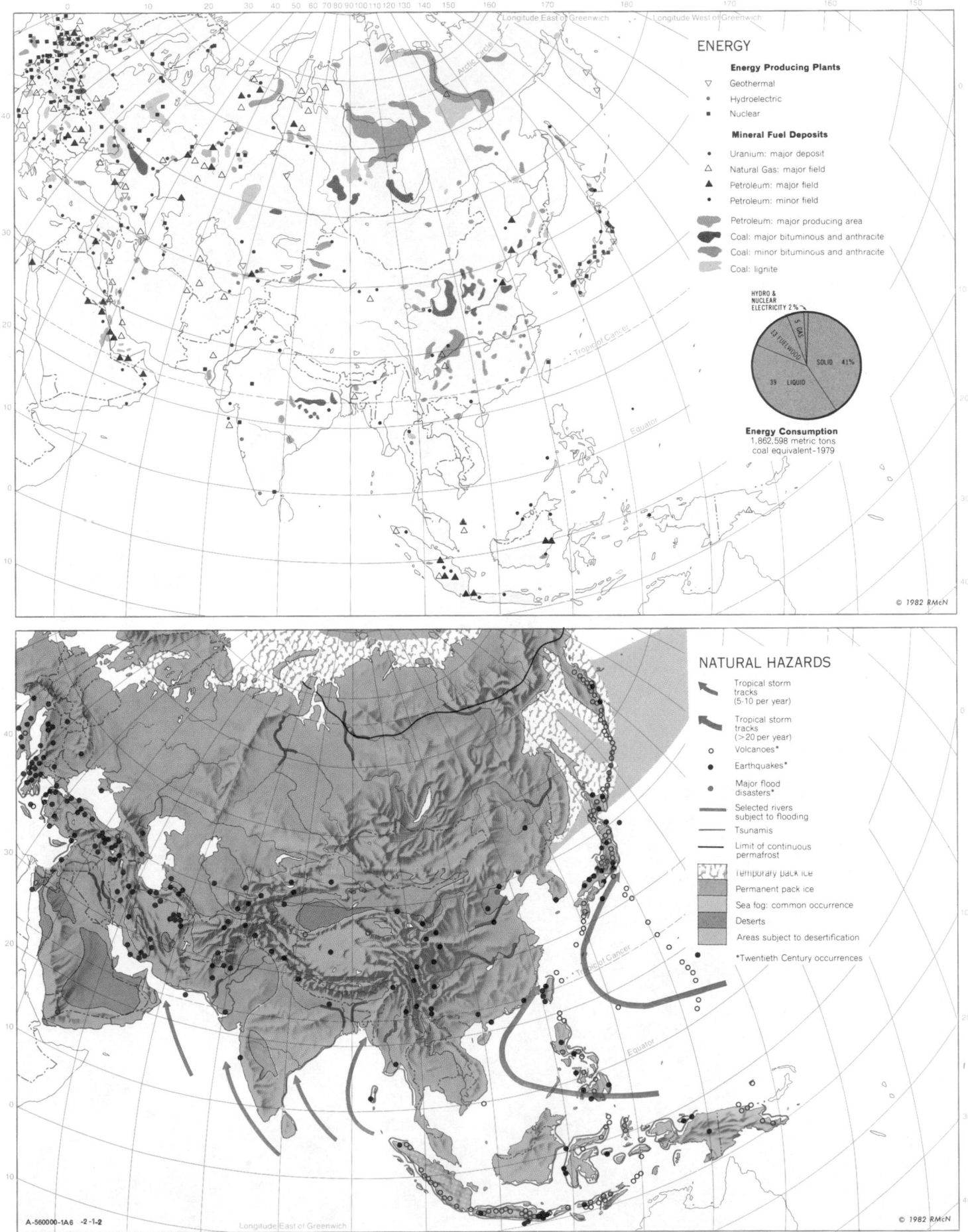

ENERGY

Energy Producing Plants

▽ Geothermal

• Hydroelectric

■ Nuclear

Mineral Fuel Deposits

• Uranium: major deposit

△ Natural Gas: major field

▲ Petroleum: major field

• Petroleum: minor field

Petroleum: major producing area

Coal: major bituminous and anthracite

Coal: minor bituminous and anthracite

Coal: lignite

HYDRO & NUCLEAR ELECTRICITY 2%

5 GAS

13 FUELWOOD

SOLID 41%

39 LIQUID

Energy Consumption
1,862,598 metric tons
coal equivalent-1979

© 1982 RMcN

NATURAL HAZARDS

Tropical storm tracks (5-10 per year)

Tropical storm tracks (>20 per year)

○ Volcanoes*

● Earthquakes*

● Major flood disasters*

Selected rivers subject to flooding

Tsunamis

Limit of continuous permafrost

Temporary pack ice

Permanent pack ice

Sea fog: common occurrence

Deserts

Areas subject to desertification

*Twentieth Century occurrences

A-560000-1A6 -2-1-2

Longitude East of Greenwich

© 1982 RMcN

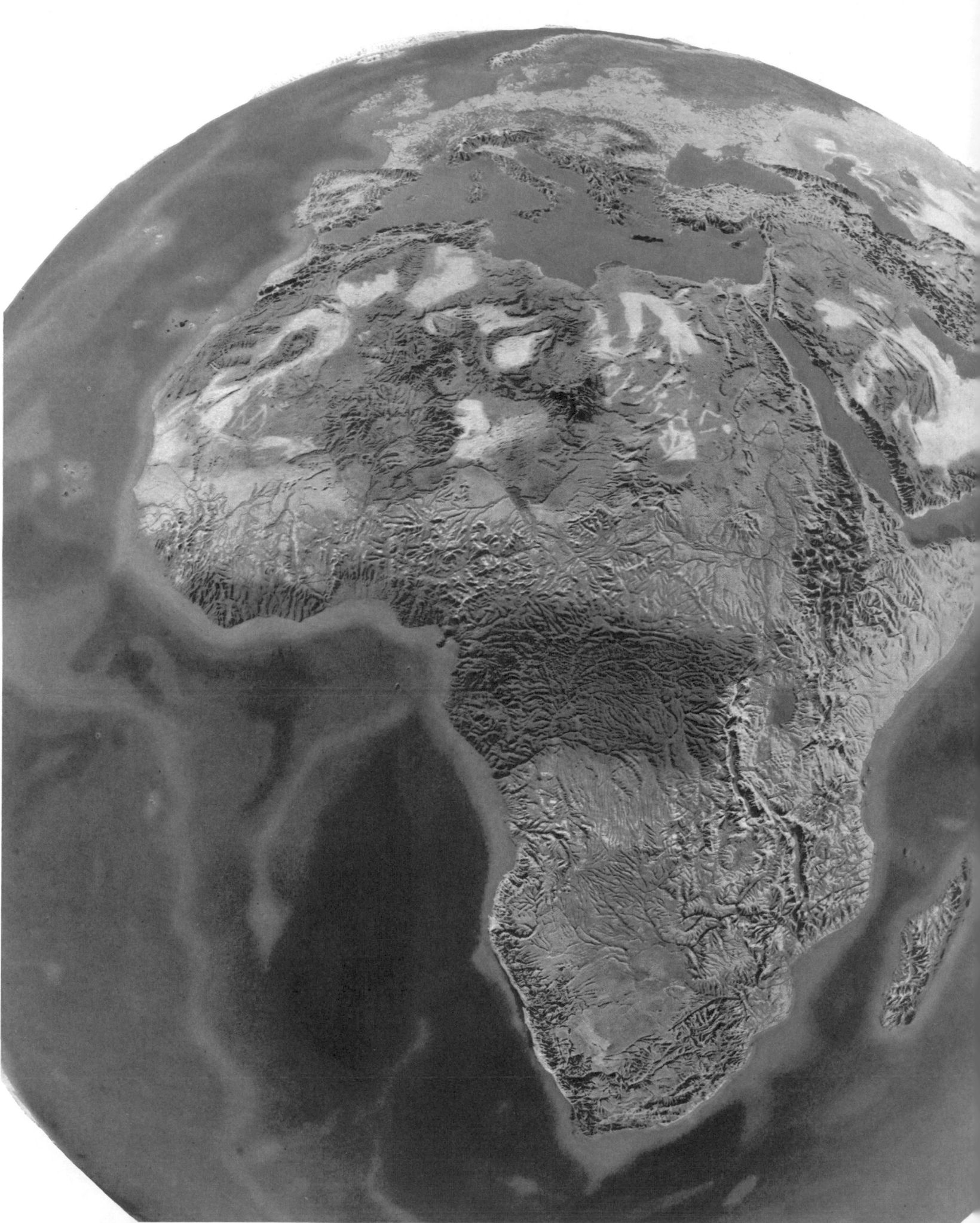

Global View
Africa

For centuries most of Africa's 11,685,000 square miles was unknown to outsiders. Access by one available avenue, the Nile, was impeded by the cataracts above Aswan. Since much of the interior is upland or plateau, usually dropping off rather sharply near the coasts, most of Africa's great rivers have rapids or falls close to the seaboard and so have not provided convenient routes to the interior. Moreover, the coastline is very regular, with few of the natural harbors of the other continents.

Once penetrated, much of the interior proved inhospitable to man. In the north, the world's largest desert, the immense expanse of the Sahara, blocks Africa's north rim from the central and southern portions. Near the other end of Africa, the Kalahari Desert helps separate the pleasant southernmost portion from the rest of the continent. In the center, the vast Congo Basin, humid, thinly settled, and unattractive, runs from the Atlantic seaboard east to the foot of the rugged highlands of East Africa, marked by the Rift Valley, which can be identified by the string of elongated lakes.

Africa's most important internal boundary is the Sahara. North of it the Mediterranean coastal countries are Moslem in tradition and have had close connections with Europe and the Near East. South of the Sahara are the many rich and varied cultures of Negroid tribal Africa. Unlike in many ways though they are, Mediterranean and Black Africa have until recently shared a common history of domination by non-African colonial powers. As late as 1945 there were only four independent nations in the entire continent. Now, spurred by the forces of nationalism, one new nation after another has emerged.

Past developments in communications, transport, education, and agricultural and industrial techniques, though limited, have formed a legacy from the old colonial powers on which the new African nations can build. Resources of iron ore, gold, oil, copper, timber, and a host of other vital raw materials are available. And there are many areas where climate and soil conditions are conducive to commercial agriculture particularly for peanuts and cacao.

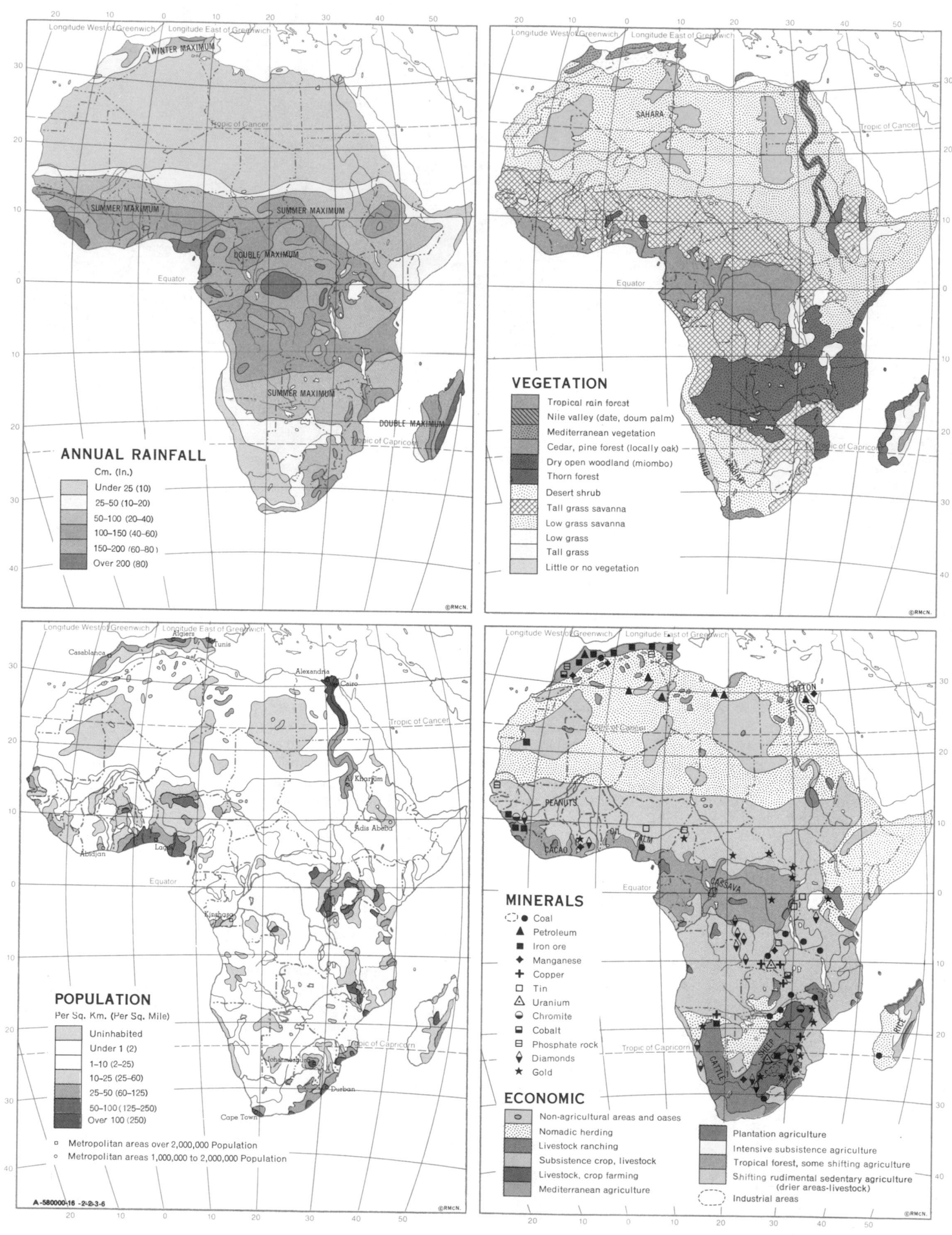

ANNUAL RAINFALL

Cm. (In.)

	Under 25 (10)
	25–50 (10–20)
	50–100 (20–40)
	100–150 (40–60)
	150–200 (60–80)
	Over 200 (80)

VEGETATION

- Tropical rain forest
- Nile valley (date, doum palm)
- Mediterranean vegetation
- Cedar, pine forest (locally oak)
- Dry open woodland (miombo)
- Thorn forest
- Desert shrub
- Tall grass savanna
- Low grass savanna
- Low grass
- Tall grass
- Little or no vegetation

POPULATION

Per Sq. Km. (Per Sq. Mile)

	Uninhabited
	Under 1 (2)
	1–10 (2–25)
	10–25 (25–60)
	25–50 (60–125)
	50–100 (125–250)
	Over 100 (250)

□ Metropolitan areas over 2,000,000 Population
○ Metropolitan areas 1,000,000 to 2,000,000 Population

A-580000-16 -2-2-3-6

MINERALS

- ◖● Coal
- ▲ Petroleum
- ■ Iron ore
- ◆ Manganese
- ✛ Copper
- □ Tin
- △ Uranium
- ◓ Chromite
- ▣ Cobalt
- ⊟ Phosphate rock
- ◈ Diamonds
- ★ Gold

ECONOMIC

- Non-agricultural areas and oases
- Nomadic herding
- Livestock ranching
- Subsistence crop, livestock
- Livestock, crop farming
- Mediterranean agriculture
- Plantation agriculture
- Intensive subsistence agriculture
- Tropical forest, some shifting agriculture
- Shifting rudimental sedentary agriculture (drier areas-livestock)
- Industrial areas

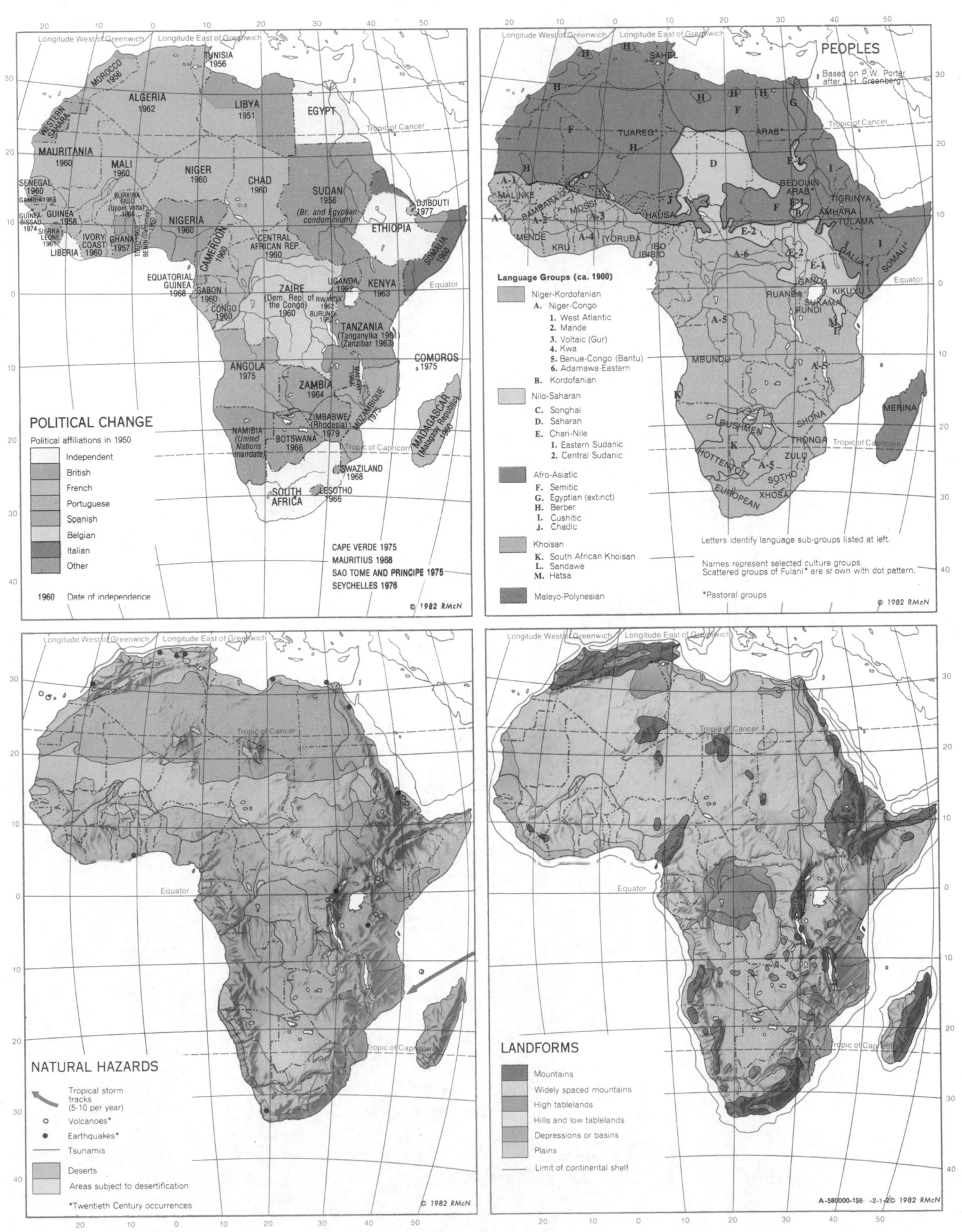

POLITICAL CHANGE

Political affiliations in 1950

- Independent
- British
- French
- Portuguese
- Spanish
- Belgian
- Italian
- Other

1960   Date of independence

CAPE VERDE 1975
MAURITIUS 1968
SAO TOME AND PRINCIPE 1975
SEYCHELLES 1976

© 1982 RMcN

PEOPLES

Based on P. W. Porter
after J. H. Greenberg

Language Groups (ca. 1900)

Niger-Kordofanian
  A. Niger-Congo
    1. West Atlantic
    2. Mande
    3. Voltaic (Gur)
    4. Kwa
    5. Benue-Congo (Bantu)
    6. Adamawa-Eastern
  B. Kordofanian

Nilo-Saharan
  C. Songhai
  D. Saharan
  E. Chari-Nile
    1. Eastern Sudanic
    2. Central Sudanic

Afro-Asiatic
  F. Semitic
  G. Egyptian (extinct)
  H. Berber
  I. Cushitic
  J. Chadic

Khoisan
  K. South African Khoisan
  L. Sandawe
  M. Hatsa

Malayo-Polynesian

Letters identify language sub-groups listed at left.

Names represent selected culture groups.
Scattered groups of Fulani* are shown with dot pattern.

*Pastoral groups

© 1982 RMcN

NATURAL HAZARDS

Tropical storm tracks (5-10 per year)
○ Volcanoes*
● Earthquakes*
— Tsunamis

Deserts
Areas subject to desertification

*Twentieth Century occurrences

© 1982 RMcN

LANDFORMS

- Mountains
- Widely spaced mountains
- High tablelands
- Hills and low tablelands
- Depressions or basins
- Plains

— Limit of continental shelf

A-580000-1S6 -2-1-2 © 1982 RMcN

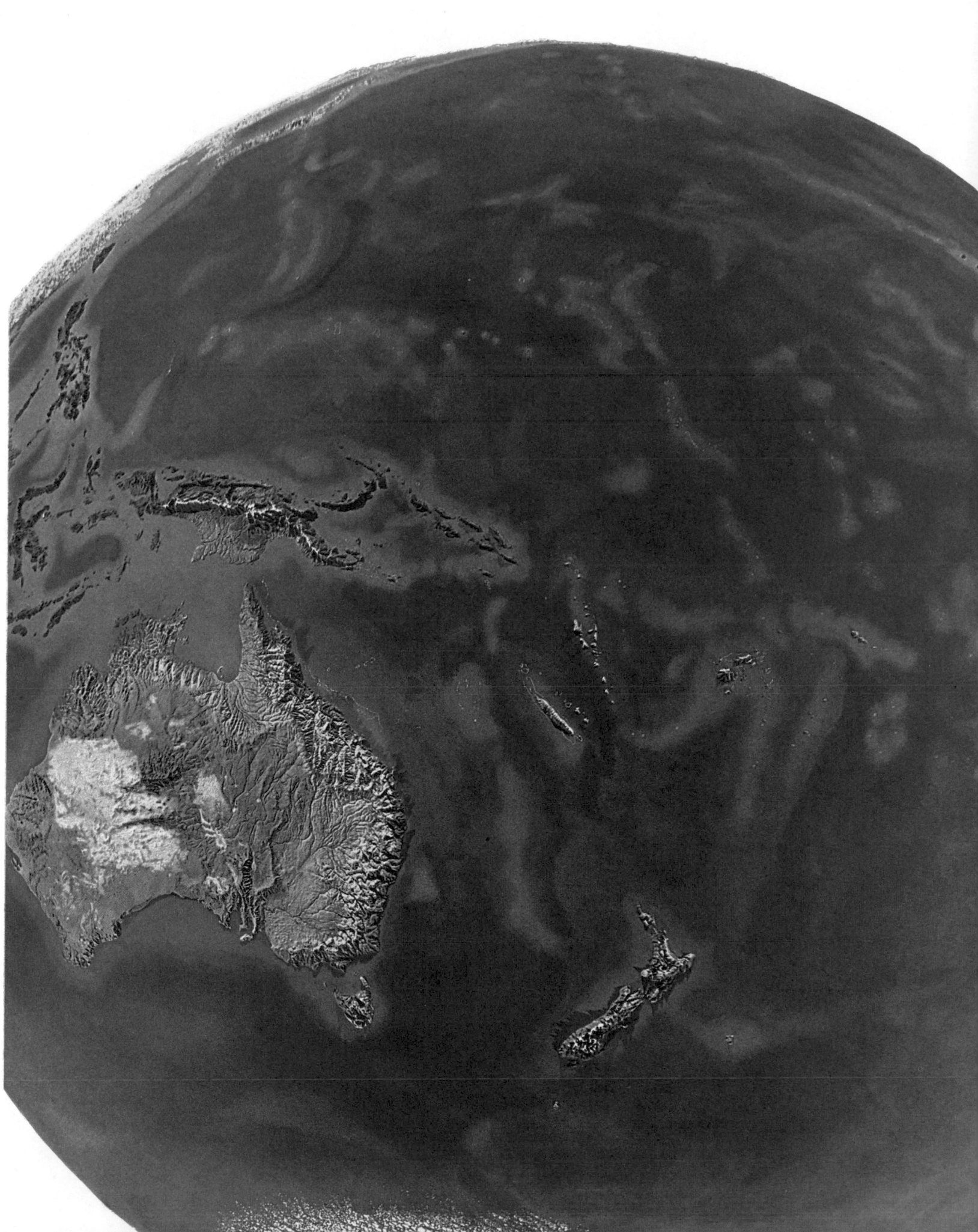

Australia, New Zealand, Oceania

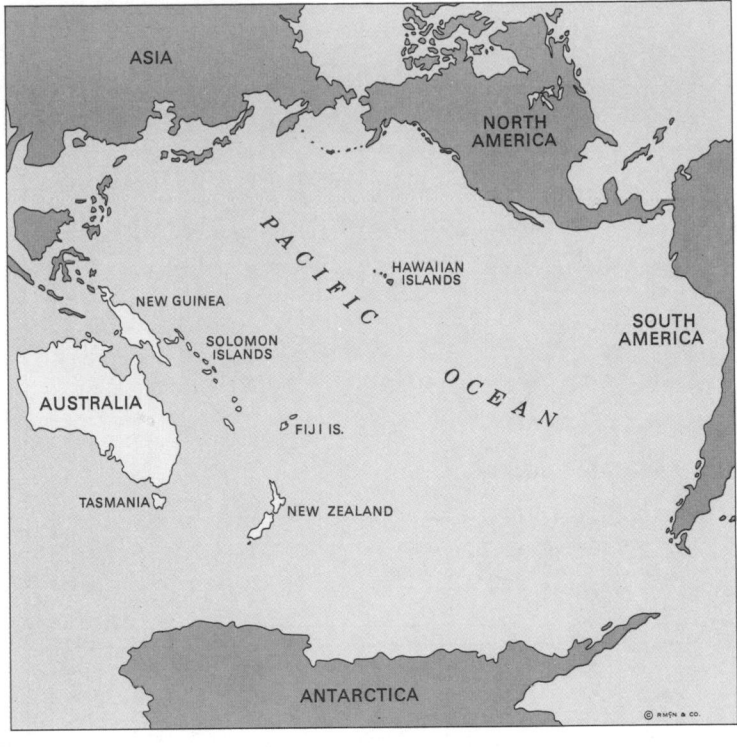

This region of the world is composed of the island continent of Australia, the substantial islands of New Zealand and New Guinea, clusters of smaller islands, and the many pinpoint atolls scattered throughout the expanse of the central and southern Pacific. Extreme isolation and their island nature are common characteristics held by these realms, but other similarities are few.

Australia's size compares with that of the forty-eight conterminous United States. Dry air masses sweep across the western interior from the west, creating the largest desert outside of the Sahara. Along the eastern coast higher temperatures and humidity have combined to produce climates conducive to a varied agricultural system, and therefore, the population is concentrated along this favorable coastal strip. The mountains of the east tend to isolate the population in a number of distinct clusters. Sydney, Melbourne, Brisbane, and Adelaide are the four principal centers, acting as chief exporters of the wool and wheat, and the importers, manufacturers, and distributors for the continent.

New Zealand, like Australia, is an enclave of a European settlement in the Pacific. Upon the vegetation of this climatically mild area the descendants of European settlers have established a thriving economy based upon the exportation of butter, beef, and mutton. The mountainous spine running the length of New Zealand provides some magnificent scenery and the gamut of climatic types.

New Guinea is closely related to both Indonesia and Melanesia, and so links Southeast Asia with Oceania. Although much larger, it typifies the larger islands of the Southwestern Pacific. Like New Guinea, these islands have a mountainous core and narrow, alluvial coastal plains. Upon the plains, under tropical heat and humidity, a variety of tropical agricultural products are raised and some of the islands, such as Fiji, have well developed commercial economies.

Unlike New Guinea and the larger islands are the speck-like atolls scattered throughout the central and southern Pacific. These South Sea Islands are famed for isolation, mild climate, and scenic beauty. But their size, limited resources, and small population, keep their economies at a subsistence level.

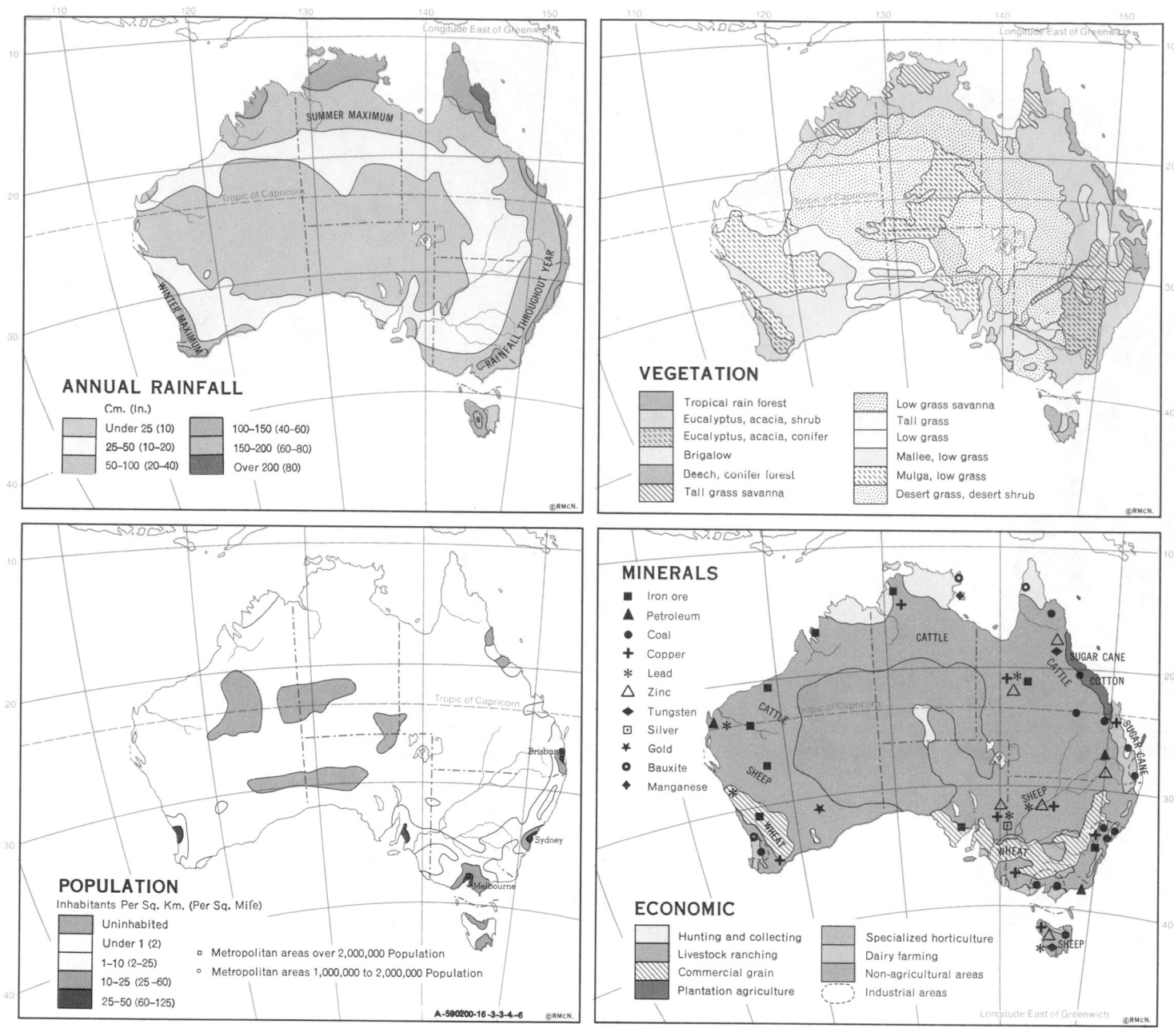

ANNUAL RAINFALL

Cm. (In.)

- Under 25 (10)
- 25–50 (10–20)
- 50–100 (20–40)
- 100–150 (40–60)
- 150–200 (60–80)
- Over 200 (80)

©RMcN.

VEGETATION

- Tropical rain forest
- Eucalyptus, acacia, shrub
- Eucalyptus, acacia, conifer
- Brigalow
- Beech, conifer forest
- Tall grass savanna
- Low grass savanna
- Tall grass
- Low grass
- Mallee, low grass
- Mulga, low grass
- Desert grass, desert shrub

©RMcN.

POPULATION

Inhabitants Per Sq. Km. (Per Sq. Mile)

- Uninhabited
- Under 1 (2)
- 1–10 (2–25)
- 10–25 (25–60)
- 25–50 (60–125)

- □ Metropolitan areas over 2,000,000 Population
- ○ Metropolitan areas 1,000,000 to 2,000,000 Population

A-590200-16-3-3-4-6   ©RMcN.

MINERALS

- ■ Iron ore
- ▲ Petroleum
- ● Coal
- + Copper
- ✳ Lead
- △ Zinc
- ◆ Tungsten
- ⊡ Silver
- ✴ Gold
- ⊙ Bauxite
- ◆ Manganese

ECONOMIC

- Hunting and collecting
- Livestock ranching
- Commercial grain
- Plantation agriculture
- Specialized horticulture
- Dairy farming
- Non-agricultural areas
- Industrial areas

©RMcN.

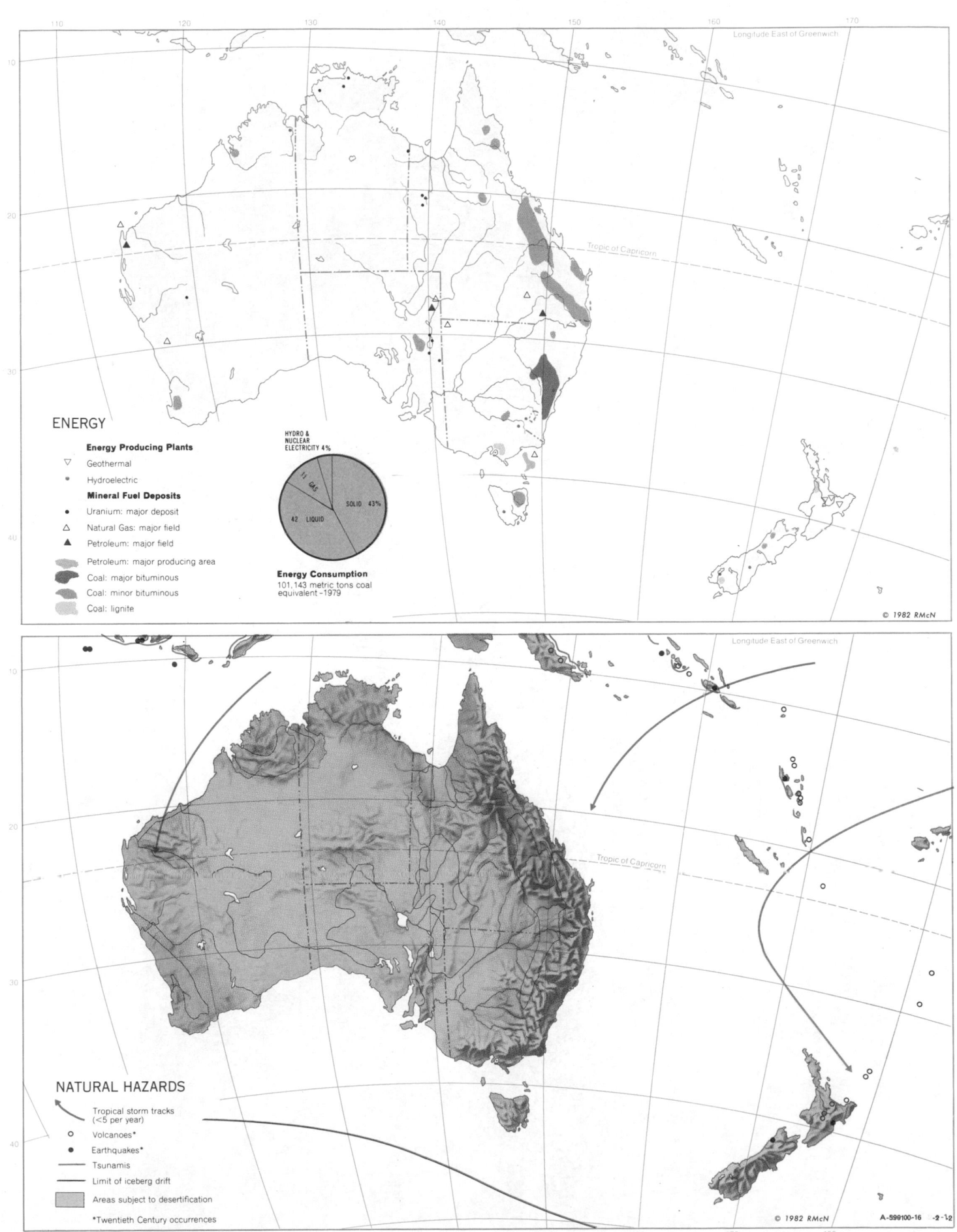

ENERGY

Energy Producing Plants

▽ Geothermal

• Hydroelectric

Mineral Fuel Deposits

• Uranium: major deposit

△ Natural Gas: major field

▲ Petroleum: major field

    Petroleum: major producing area

    Coal: major bituminous

    Coal: minor bituminous

    Coal: lignite

HYDRO &
NUCLEAR
ELECTRICITY 4%

11 GAS

SOLID 43%

42 LIQUID

Energy Consumption
101,143 metric tons coal
equivalent -1979

© 1982 RMcN

NATURAL HAZARDS

↗ Tropical storm tracks
    (<5 per year)

○ Volcanoes*

● Earthquakes*

— Tsunamis

— Limit of iceberg drift

    Areas subject to desertification

*Twentieth Century occurrences

© 1982 RMcN   A-599100-16 -2-12

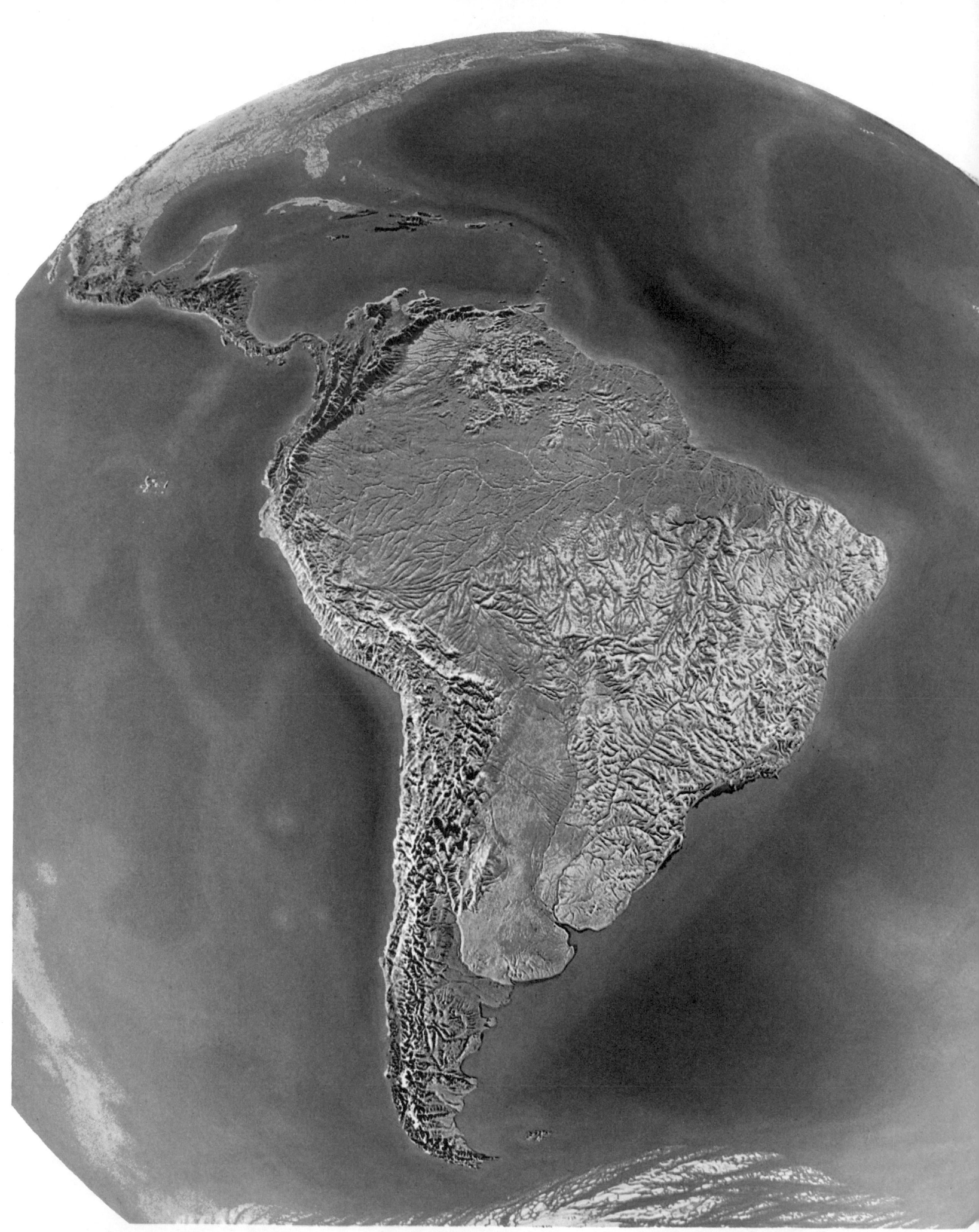

Global View
South America

Triangularly shaped South America is surrounded by water except at the narrow Isthmus of Panama. No great peninsulas extend into its seas or oceans, and its outlines are more regular than those of most other continents.

The Andes Mountains rise like a wall along the western shores, and this formidable chain runs the entire length of the continent, rising to altitudes of over 20,000 feet. It is the longest continuous mountain chain in the world.

The bulk of the continent slopes eastward from the eastern face of the Andes. From north to south, landforms include plains drained by the Orinoco and the eroded plateau areas of the Guiana and Brazilian highlands, the tropical lowlands of the Amazon Basin, savanna called the Gran Chaco, which is drained by the Paraná-Paraguay-Plata river systems, the pampas, and the plains of Patagonia.

The shape of the continent, its position astride the Equator, the water surrounding it, and the mountainous terrain have resulted in a variety of climates. The area east of the Andes from Venezuela to Northern Argentina, is dominated by moisture-laden air masses of the Atlantic. This two-thirds of the continent has a tropical or subtropical environment. Most of the remaining portion is under the influence of the relatively dry, cool Pacific air masses, which create the driest region in the world—the Atacama Desert of Chile. These cool Pacific air masses, too, on crossing the Andes in the narrow southern portion of the continent, create the Patagonian Desert of Argentina. In the higher altitudes of the mountain chain climates familiar to mid and upper latitudes are found.

Much of the interior of South America is still inaccessible, owing to extensive regions of mountains or jungle. Most of the settlement has been around the periphery of the continent. Spanish and Portuguese settlers, and later Germans and Italians, have developed highly specialized commercial economies in certain of the peripheral areas. Around Buenos Aires, São Paulo, Santiago, Bogotá economies based on agricultural products have been developed—wheat, beef, coffee, citrus fruit to name a few. Exported minerals—oil from Venezuela, tin from Bolivia, and copper from Chile—are economic mainstays of other countries.

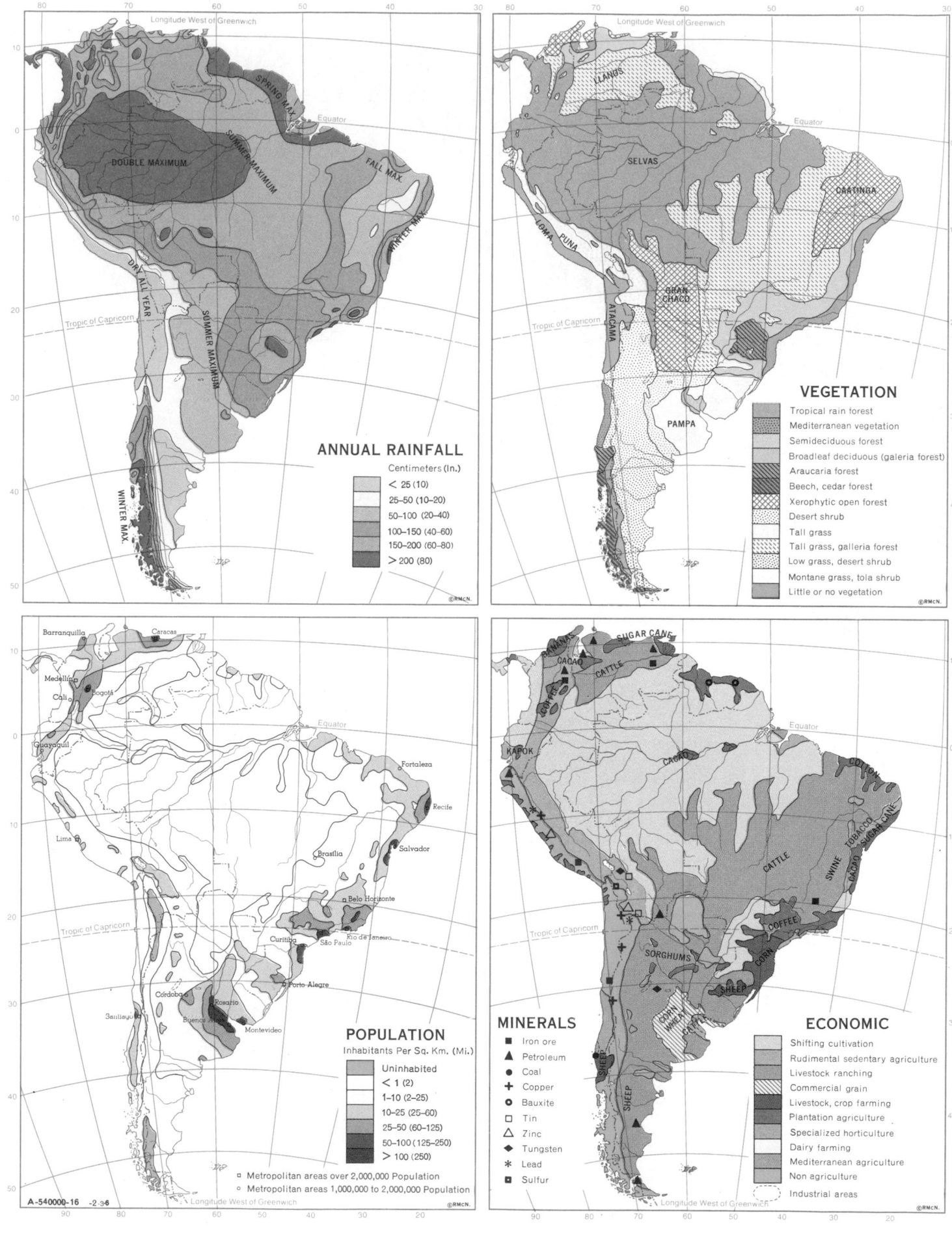

ANNUAL RAINFALL

Centimeters (In.)

	< 25 (10)
	25–50 (10–20)
	50–100 (20–40)
	100–150 (40–60)
	150–200 (60–80)
	> 200 (80)

VEGETATION

Tropical rain forest
Mediterranean vegetation
Semideciduous forest
Broadleaf deciduous (galeria forest)
Araucaria forest
Beech, cedar forest
Xerophytic open forest
Desert shrub
Tall grass
Tall grass, galleria forest
Low grass, desert shrub
Montane grass, tola shrub
Little or no vegetation

POPULATION

Inhabitants Per Sq. Km. (Mi.)

	Uninhabited
	< 1 (2)
	1–10 (2–25)
	10–25 (25–60)
	25–50 (60–125)
	50–100 (125–250)
	> 100 (250)

□ Metropolitan areas over 2,000,000 Population
○ Metropolitan areas 1,000,000 to 2,000,000 Population

A-540000-16   -2-3-6

MINERALS

■ Iron ore
▲ Petroleum
● Coal
✛ Copper
◉ Bauxite
□ Tin
△ Zinc
◆ Tungsten
✳ Lead
▣ Sulfur

ECONOMIC

Shifting cultivation
Rudimental sedentary agriculture
Livestock ranching
Commercial grain
Livestock, crop farming
Plantation agriculture
Specialized horticulture
Dairy farming
Mediterranean agriculture
Non agriculture
Industrial areas

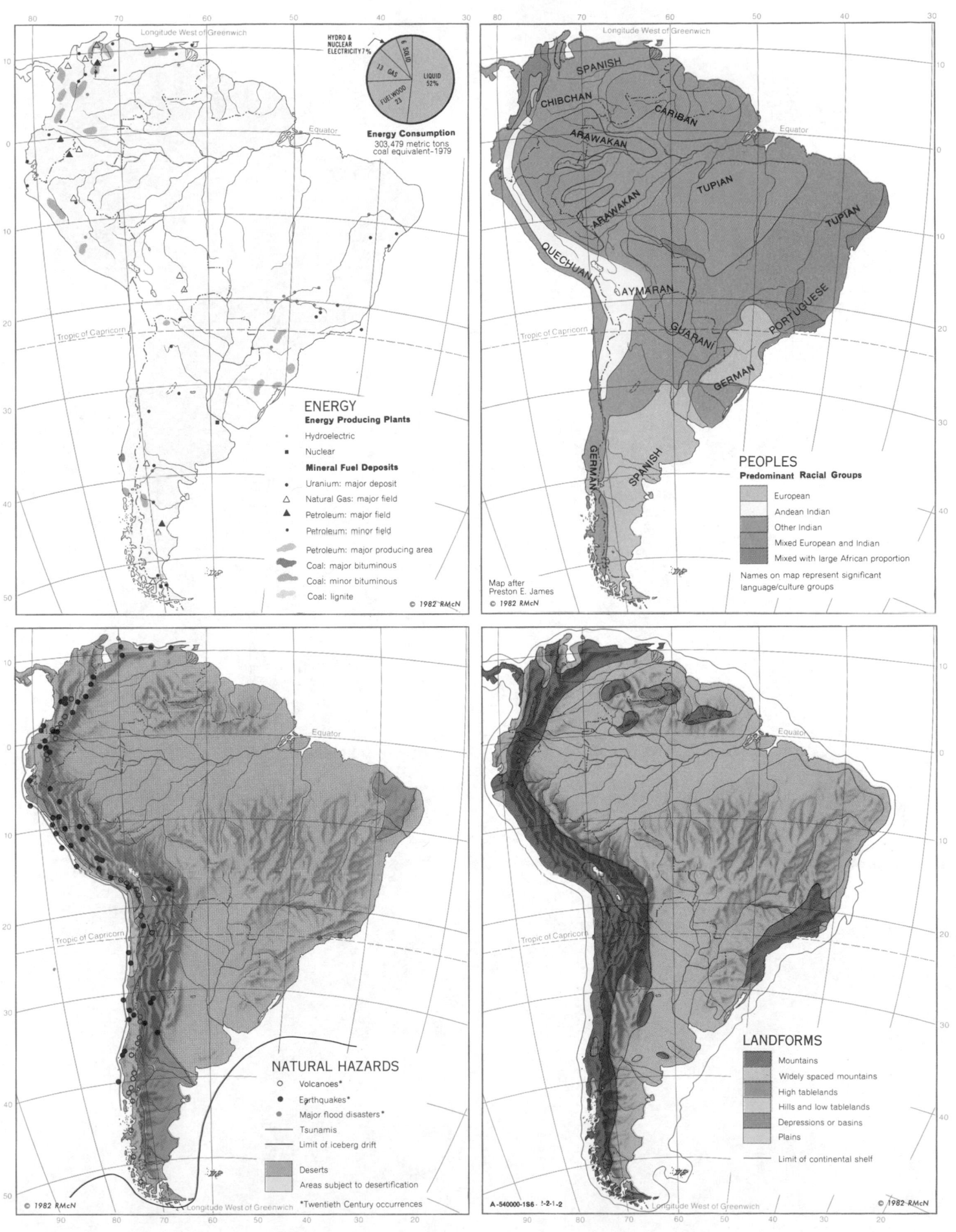

ENERGY

Energy Producing Plants

- • Hydroelectric
- ■ Nuclear

Mineral Fuel Deposits

- • Uranium: major deposit
- △ Natural Gas: major field
- ▲ Petroleum: major field
- • Petroleum: minor field
- Petroleum: major producing area
- Coal: major bituminous
- Coal: minor bituminous
- Coal: lignite

© 1982 RMcN

HYDRO & NUCLEAR ELECTRICITY 7%
6 SOLID
13 GAS
LIQUID 52%
FUELWOOD 23

Energy Consumption
303,479 metric tons
coal equivalent–1979

PEOPLES

Predominant Racial Groups

- European
- Andean Indian
- Other Indian
- Mixed European and Indian
- Mixed with large African proportion

Names on map represent significant
language/culture groups

Map after
Preston E. James
© 1982 RMcN

SPANISH
CHIBCHAN
ARAWAKAN
ARAWAKAN
QUECHUAN
AYMARAN
CARIBAN
TUPIAN
TUPIAN
GUARANI
PORTUGUESE
GERMAN
GERMAN
SPANISH

NATURAL HAZARDS

- ○ Volcanoes*
- ● Earthquakes*
- ● Major flood disasters*
- Tsunamis
- Limit of iceberg drift
- Deserts
- Areas subject to desertification

*Twentieth Century occurrences

© 1982 RMcN

LANDFORMS

- Mountains
- Widely spaced mountains
- High tablelands
- Hills and low tablelands
- Depressions or basins
- Plains
- Limit of continental shelf

A-540000-1S6-1-2-1-2

© 1982 RMcN

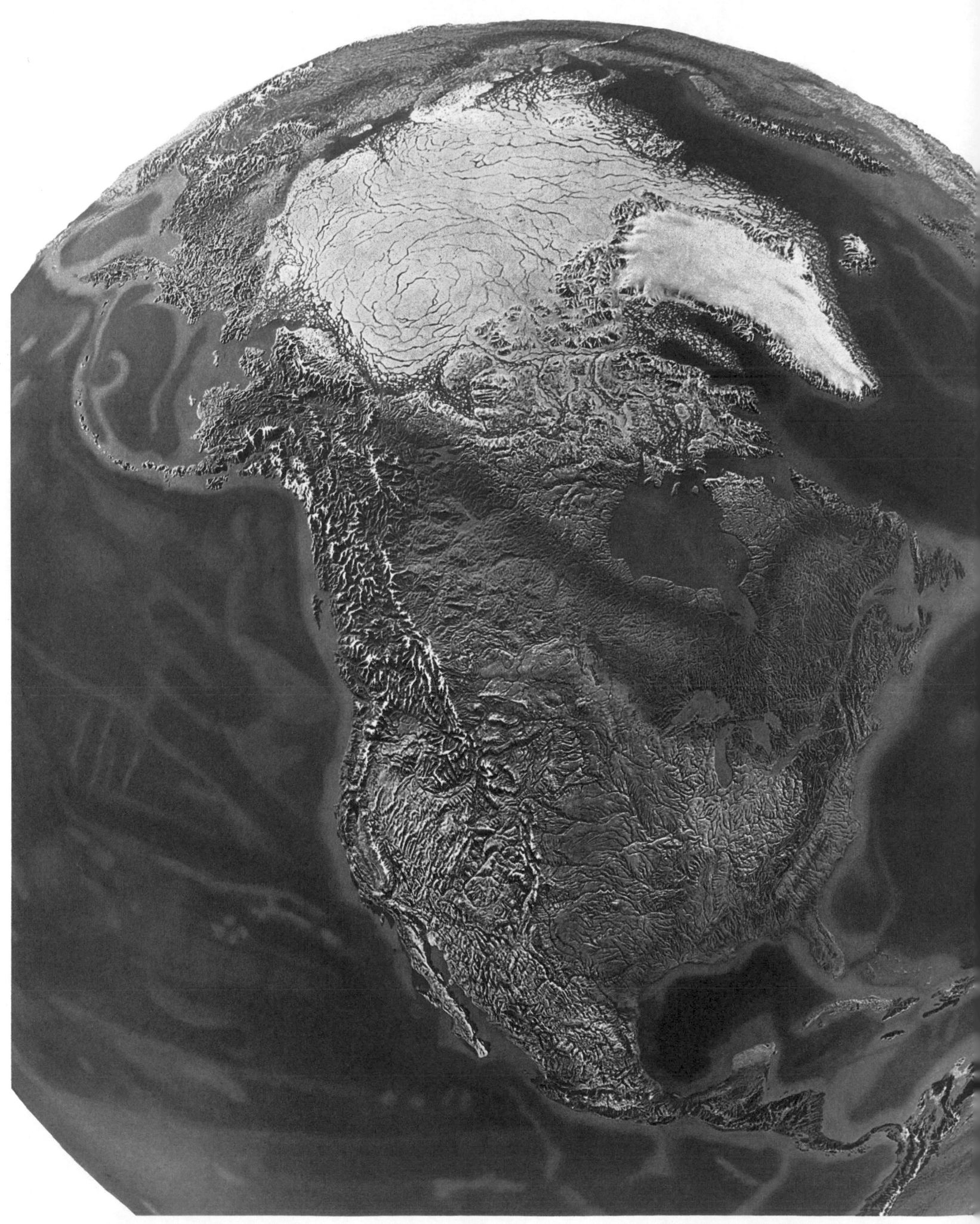

Global View
North America

Physically the North American continent extends from the ice-covered Arctic Ocean in the north to the tropical Isthmus of Panama in the south. North America, like Africa and South America, tapers from north to south. Canada, the United States, and Mexico occupy over 85 per cent of its total area of nearly 9,500,000 square miles. Central America, the West Indies, and Greenland make up the remainder.

Within this vast area, differences, rather than similarities, abound. All major types of climate can be found in North America ranging from the cold, perpetual ice cap of Greenland to the hot, moist tropical rain forests of Central America. Landforms vary from the towering chain of the Rocky Mountains, through the high plateau of Mexico, the relatively low Appalachian Highland, the featureless expanses of the Arctic tundra, the regularity of the Great Plains, and the fertile fields of the interior lowlands and coastal plains. Soils, vegetation, temperature, precipitation—all reflect the differences that can be expected over such an area.

Similarly, the development of agriculture and industry has varied considerably over the North American continent. Modern methods and the extensive use of machinery characterize agriculture in the flat to gently rolling areas of Midwestern United States and the Prairie Provinces of Canada. Stock-grazing is prevalent in the more arid areas of the continent. Agriculture in Middle America is characterized by the extensive use of hand labor. Here subtropical crops are important, for instance, bananas in Central America and sugar cane in the West Indies.

Early settlement, access to raw materials, a well developed transportation network, and a density of population providing both labor and markets have led to a heavy concentration of industrial development in the northeast quarter of the United States and the southeastern rim of Canada. Other industrial development has taken place in scattered locations in southern and western United States and in the largest cities of Middle America.

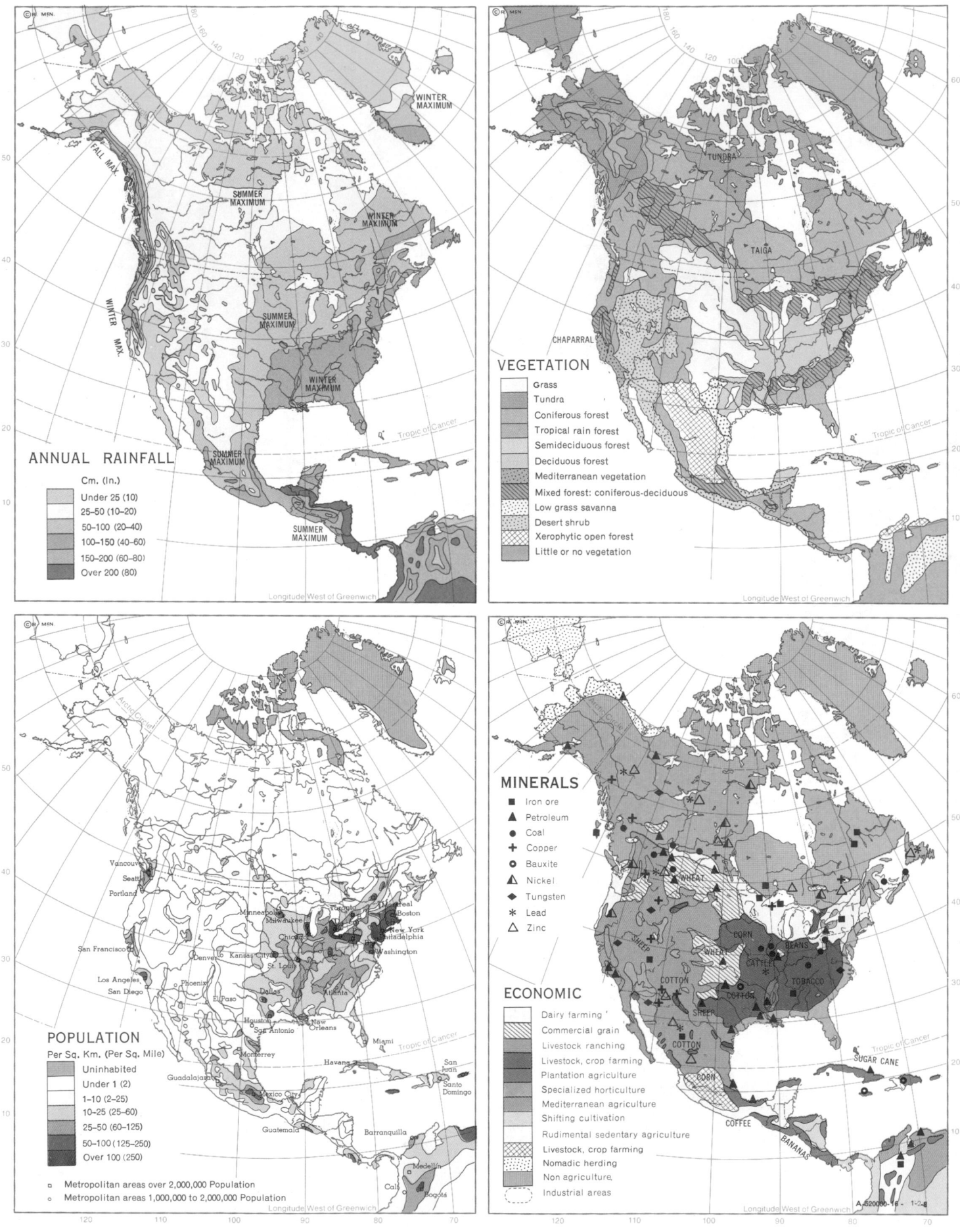

ANNUAL RAINFALL

Cm. (In.)

	Under 25 (10)
	25–50 (10–20)
	50–100 (20–40)
	100–150 (40–60)
	150–200 (60–80)
	Over 200 (80)

WINTER MAXIMUM

FALL MAX.

SUMMER MAXIMUM

WINTER MAXIMUM

WINTER MAX.

SUMMER MAXIMUM

WINTER MAXIMUM

SUMMER MAXIMUM

SUMMER MAXIMUM

VEGETATION

	Grass
	Tundra
	Coniferous forest
	Tropical rain forest
	Semideciduous forest
	Deciduous forest
	Mediterranean vegetation
	Mixed forest: coniferous-deciduous
	Low grass savanna
	Desert shrub
	Xerophytic open forest
	Little or no vegetation

TUNDRA

TAIGA

CHAPARRAL

POPULATION

Per Sq. Km. (Per Sq. Mile)

	Uninhabited
	Under 1 (2)
	1–10 (2–25)
	10–25 (25–60)
	25–50 (60–125)
	50–100 (125–250)
	Over 100 (250)

▫ Metropolitan areas over 2,000,000 Population

◦ Metropolitan areas 1,000,000 to 2,000,000 Population

MINERALS

■	Iron ore
▲	Petroleum
●	Coal
+	Copper
◉	Bauxite
△	Nickel
◆	Tungsten
✳	Lead
△	Zinc

ECONOMIC

	Dairy farming
	Commercial grain
	Livestock ranching
	Livestock, crop farming
	Plantation agriculture
	Specialized horticulture
	Mediterranean agriculture
	Shifting cultivation
	Rudimental sedentary agriculture
	Livestock, crop farming
	Nomadic herding
	Non agriculture
	Industrial areas

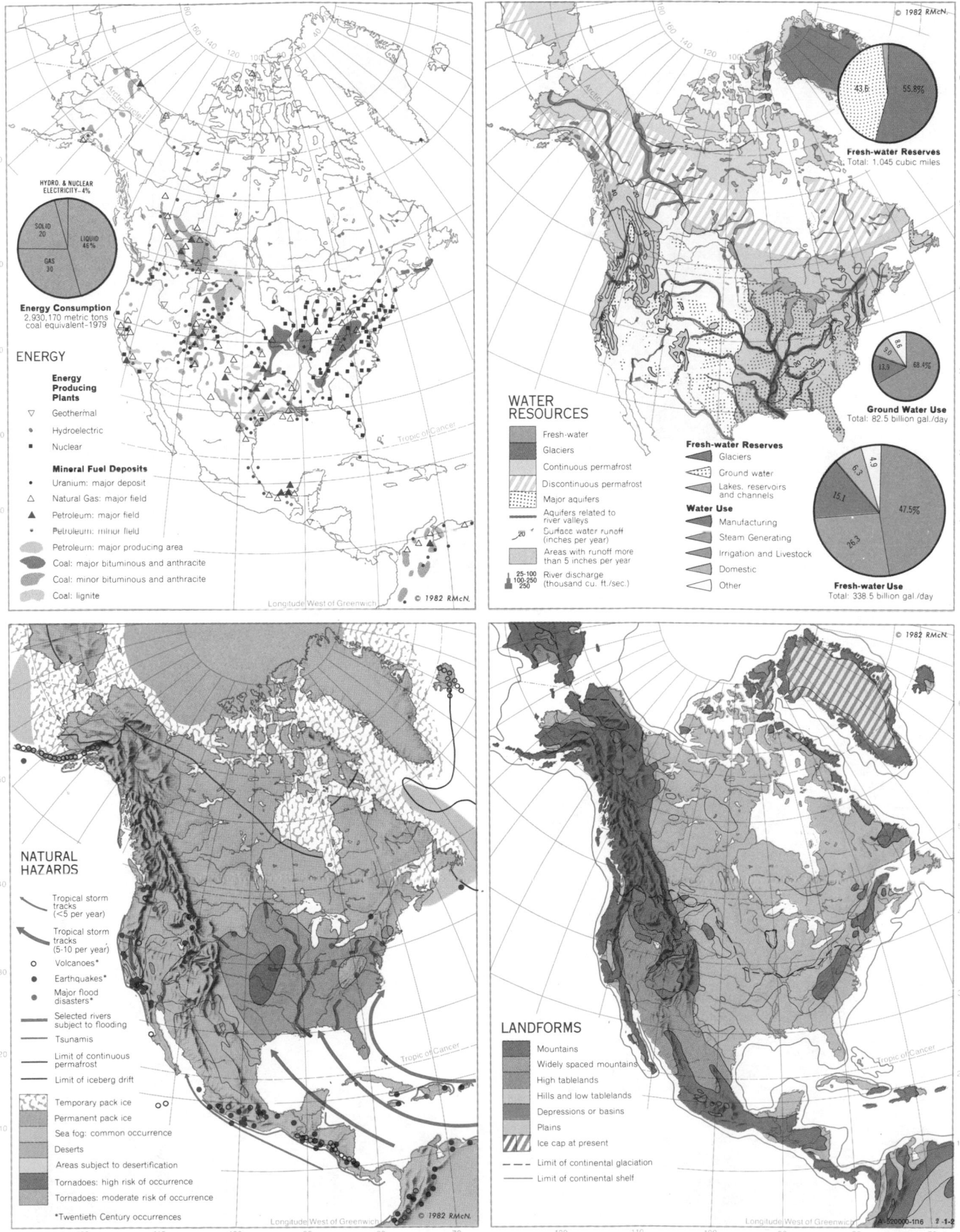

© 1982 RMcN.

ENERGY

HYDRO. & NUCLEAR
ELECTRICITY–4%

SOLID
20

LIQUID
46%

GAS
30

Energy Consumption
2,930,170 metric tons
coal equivalent–1979

**Energy
Producing
Plants**

▽ Geothermal

● Hydroelectric

■ Nuclear

Mineral Fuel Deposits

● Uranium: major deposit

△ Natural Gas: major field

▲ Petroleum: major field

• Petroleum: minor field

Petroleum: major producing area

Coal: major bituminous and anthracite

Coal: minor bituminous and anthracite

Coal: lignite

WATER RESOURCES

Fresh-water

Glaciers

Continuous permafrost

Discontinuous permafrost

Major aquifers

Aquifers related to
river valleys

Surface water runoff
(inches per year)

Areas with runoff more
than 5 inches per year

25-100
100-250
250
River discharge
(thousand cu. ft./sec.)

Fresh-water Reserves

Glaciers

Ground water

Lakes, reservoirs
and channels

Water Use

Manufacturing

Steam Generating

Irrigation and Livestock

Domestic

Other

43.6   55.8%

Fresh-water Reserves
Total: 1,045 cubic miles

8.6
9.6
13.5   68.4%

Ground Water Use
Total: 82.5 billion gal./day

4.9
6.3
15.1
26.3   47.5%

Fresh-water Use
Total: 338.5 billion gal./day

NATURAL HAZARDS

Tropical storm
tracks
(<5 per year)

Tropical storm
tracks
(5-10 per year)

○ Volcanoes*

● Earthquakes*

● Major flood
disasters*

Selected rivers
subject to flooding

Tsunamis

Limit of continuous
permafrost

Limit of iceberg drift

Temporary pack ice

Permanent pack ice

Sea fog: common occurrence

Deserts

Areas subject to desertification

Tornadoes: high risk of occurrence

Tornadoes: moderate risk of occurrence

*Twentieth Century occurrences

LANDFORMS

Mountains

Widely spaced mountains

High tablelands

Hills and low tablelands

Depressions or basins

Plains

Ice cap at present

Limit of continental glaciation

Limit of continental shelf

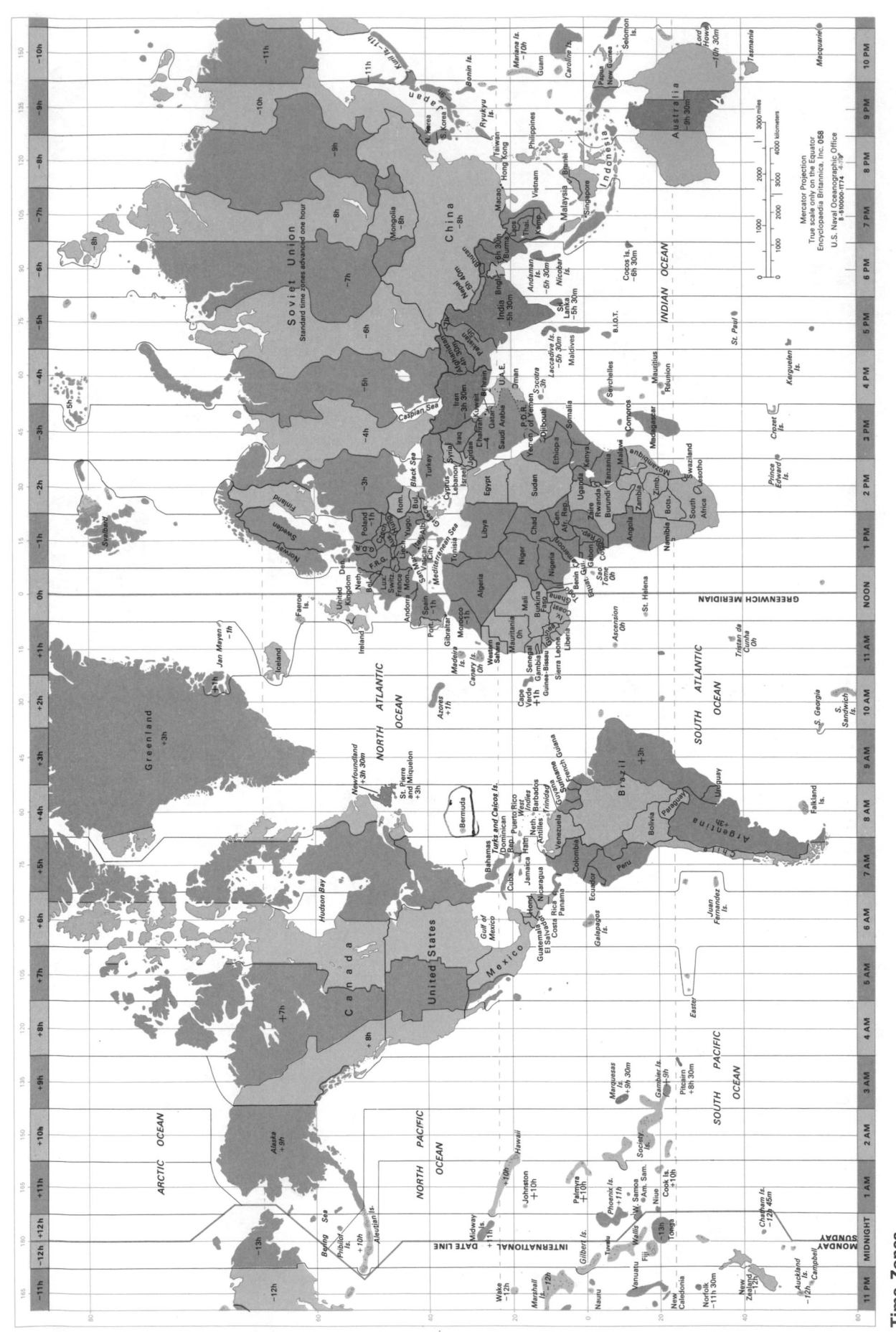

The standard time zone system, fixed by international agreement and by law in each country, is based on a theoretical division of the globe into 24 zones of 15° longitude each. The mid-meridian of each zone fixes the hour for the entire zone. The zero time zone extends 7½° east and 7½° west of the Greenwich meridian, 0° longitude. Since the earth rotates toward the east, time zones to the west of Greenwich are earlier, to the east, later. Plus and minus hours at the top of the map are added to or subtracted from local time to find Greenwich time. Local standard time can be determined for any area in the world by adding one hour for each time zone counted in an easterly direction from one's own, or by subtracting one hour for each zone counted in a westerly direction. To separate one day from the next, the 180th meridian has been designated as the international date line. On both sides of the line the time of day is the same, but west of the line it is one day later than it is to the east. Countries that adhere to the international zone system adopt the zone applicable to their location. Some countries, however, establish time zones based on political boundaries, or adopt the time zone of a neighboring unit. For all or part of the year some countries also advance their time by one hour, thereby utilizing more daylight hours each day.

Time Zones

Standard time zone of even-numbered hours from Greenwich time

Standard time zone of odd-numbered hours from Greenwich time

Time varies from the standard time zone by half an hour

Time varies from the standard time zone by other than half an hour

| h m | hours, minutes

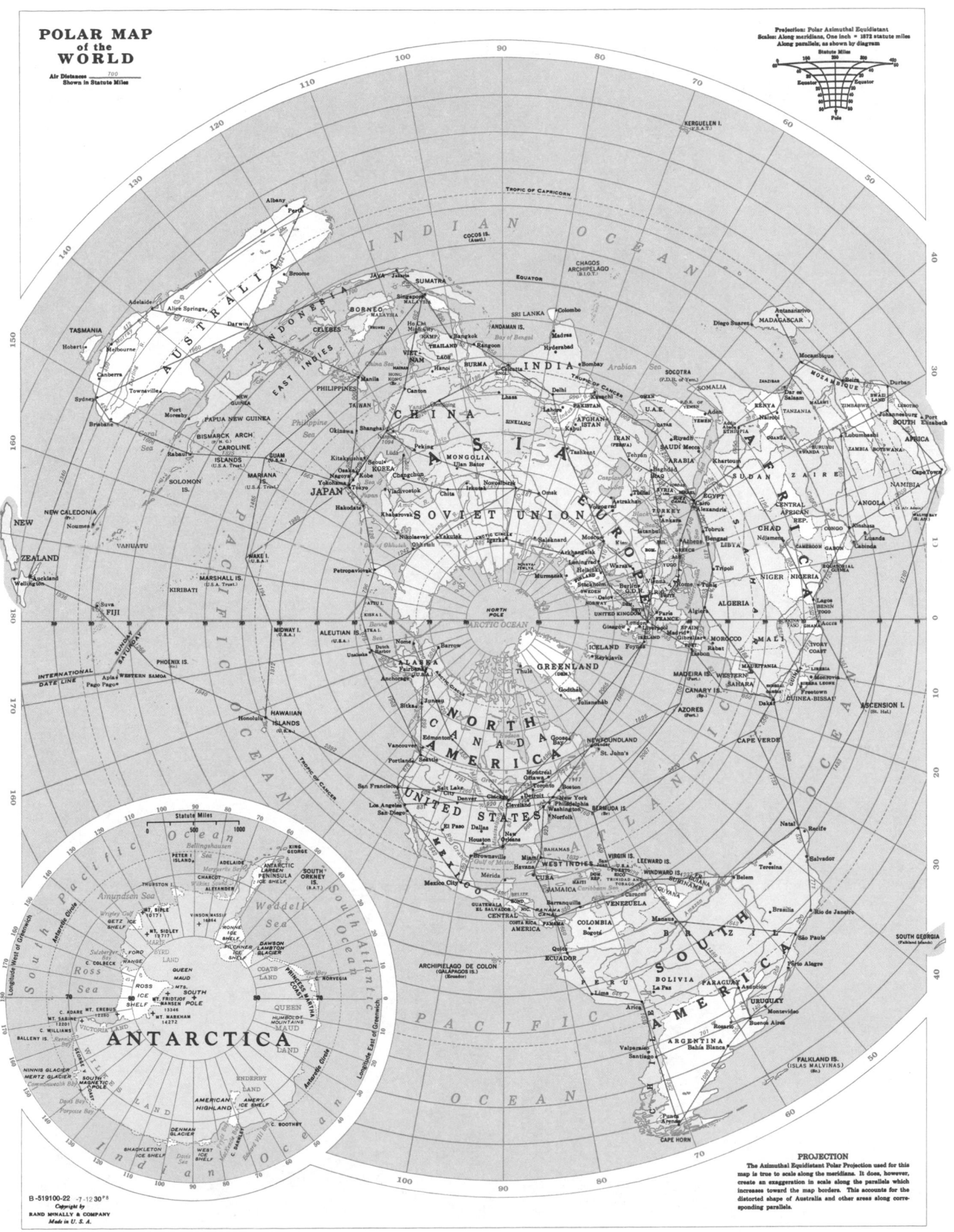

POLAR MAP
of the
WORLD

Air Distances _700_
Shown in Statute Miles

Projection: Polar Azimuthal Equidistant
Scales: Along meridians, One inch = 1872 statute miles
Along parallels, as shown by diagram

PROJECTION

The Azimuthal Equidistant Polar Projection used for this map is true to scale along the meridians. It does, however, create an exaggeration in scale along the parallels which increases toward the map borders. This accounts for the distorted shape of Australia and other areas along corresponding parallels.

Graphic Linear Scale

Scale on the Equator 1:33,000,000

Statute Miles

Miller Cylindrical Projection

RAND McNALLY & COMPANY

COSMO SERIES WORLD

Made in U.S.A.

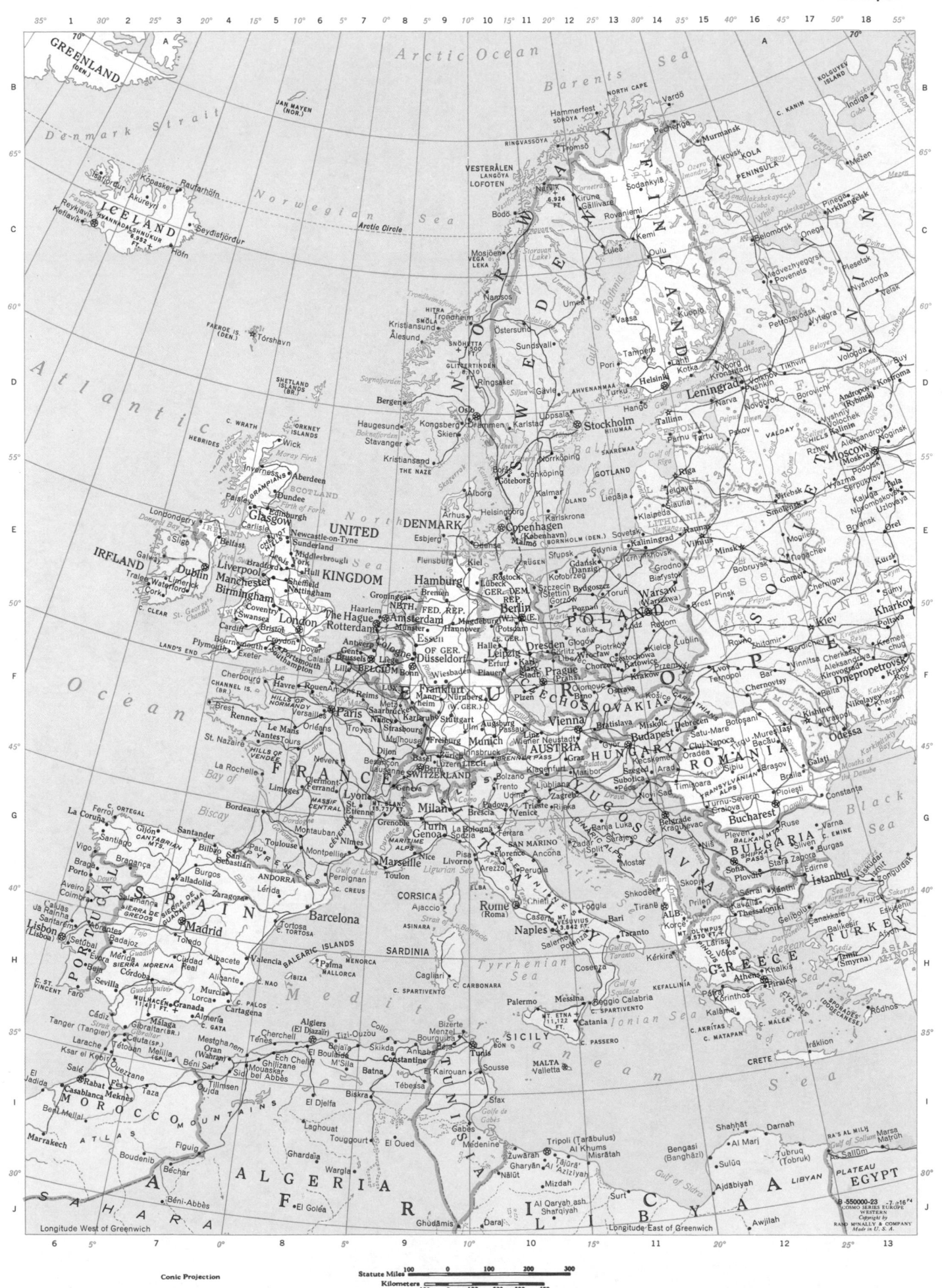

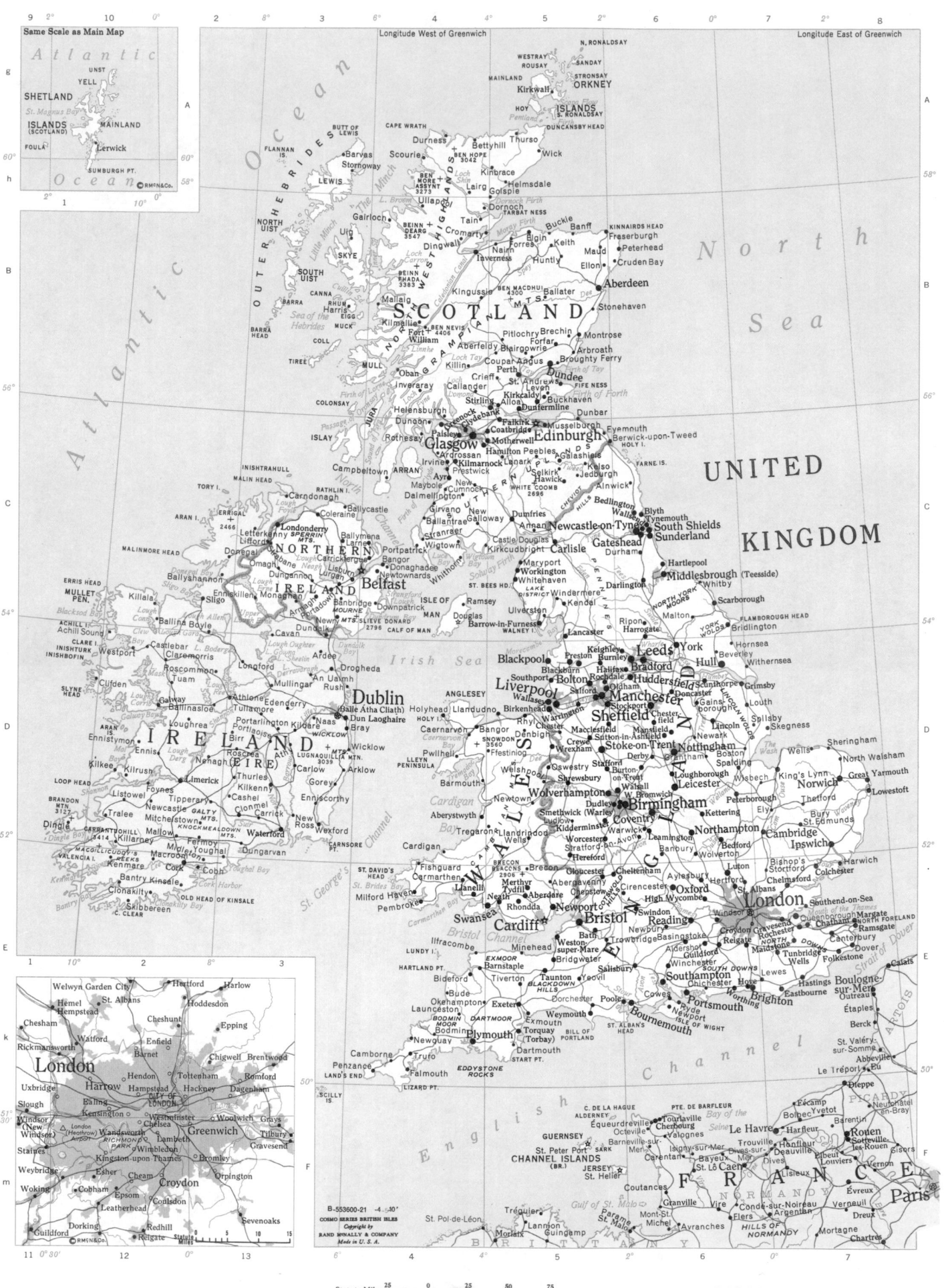

Same Scale as Main Map

Longitude West of Greenwich

Longitude East of Greenwich

SCOTLAND

UNITED KINGDOM

NORTHERN IRELAND

IRELAND (EIRE)

WALES

ENGLAND

North Sea

Atlantic Ocean

Irish Sea

English Channel

FRANCE

NORMANDY

BRITTANY

PICARDY

London

CHANNEL ISLANDS (BR.)

Statute Miles   25   0   25   50   75

Kilometers   25   0   25   50   100

Conic Projection

B-553600-21 -4-5-30°
COSMO SERIES BRITISH ISLES
Copyright by
RAND M9NALLY & COMPANY
Made in U.S.A.

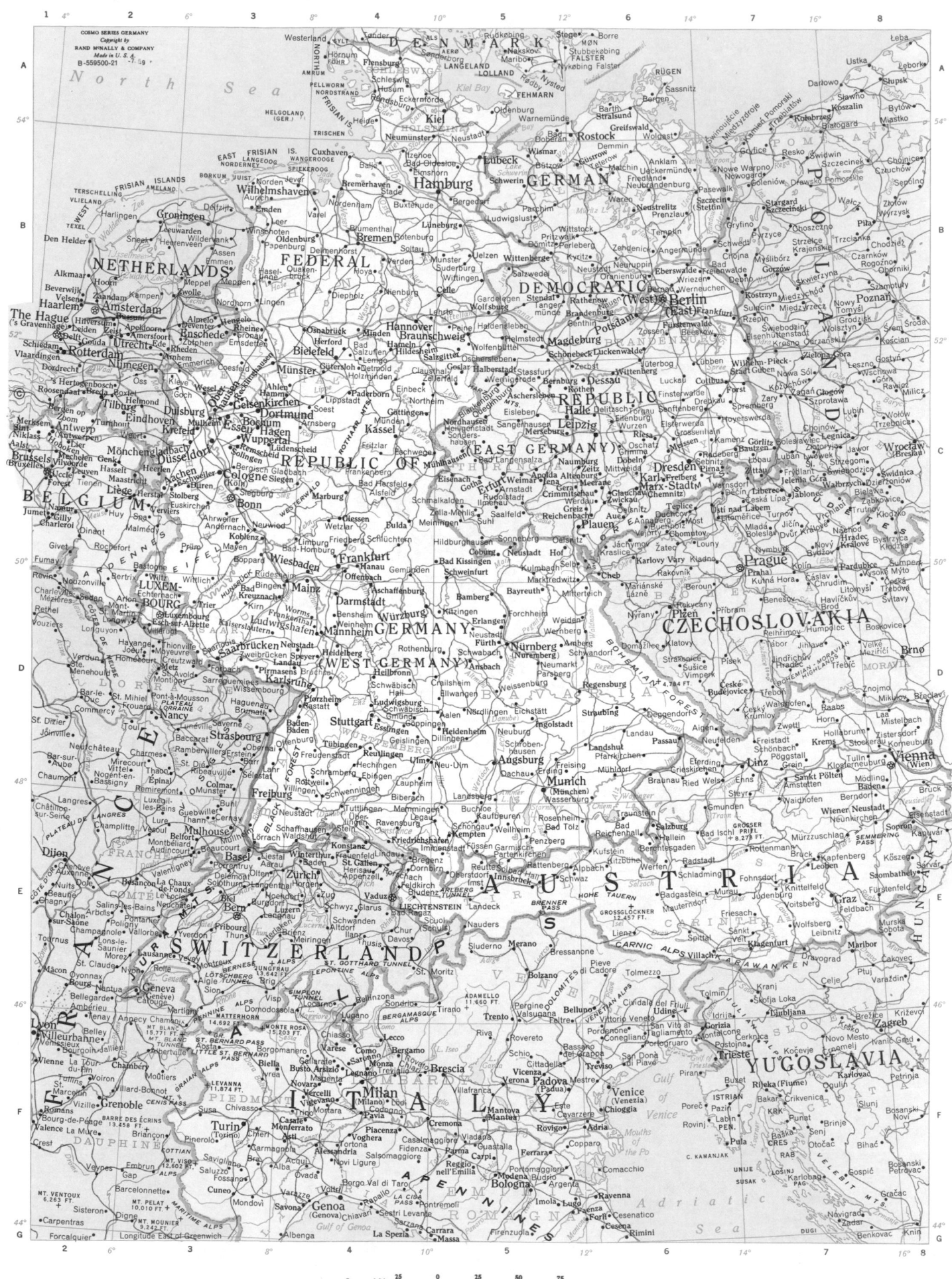

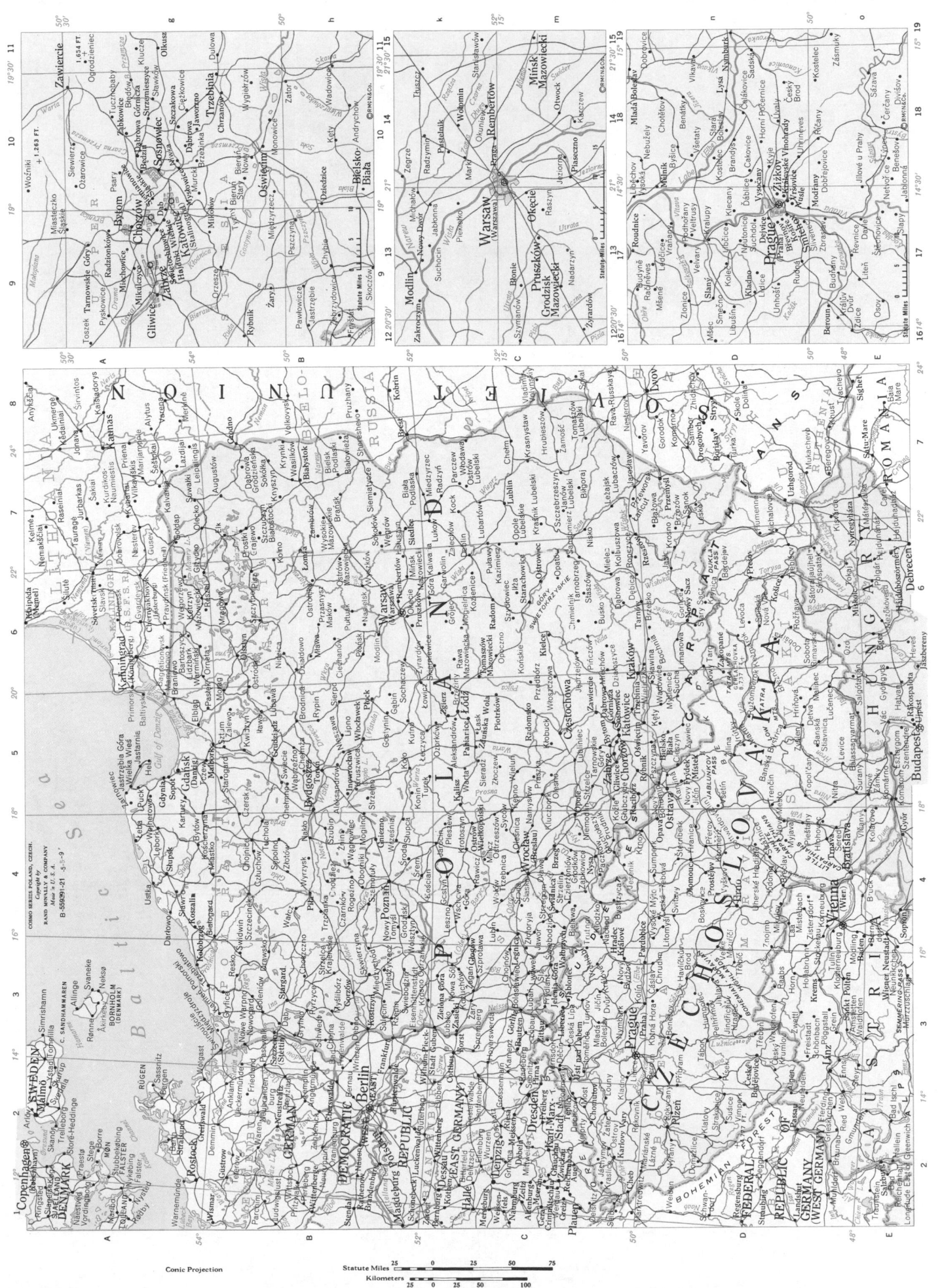

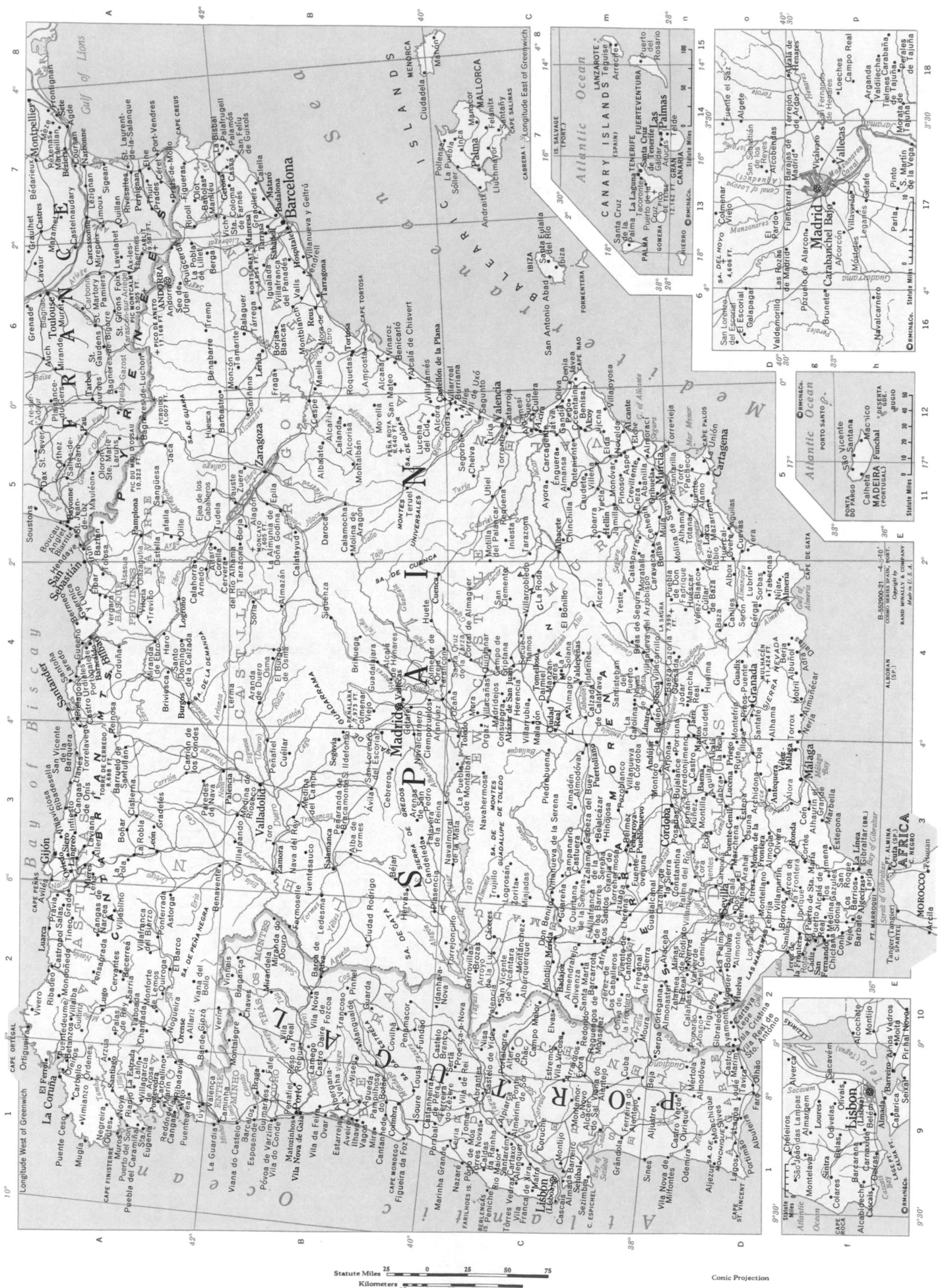

Statute Miles
Kilometers

Conic Projection

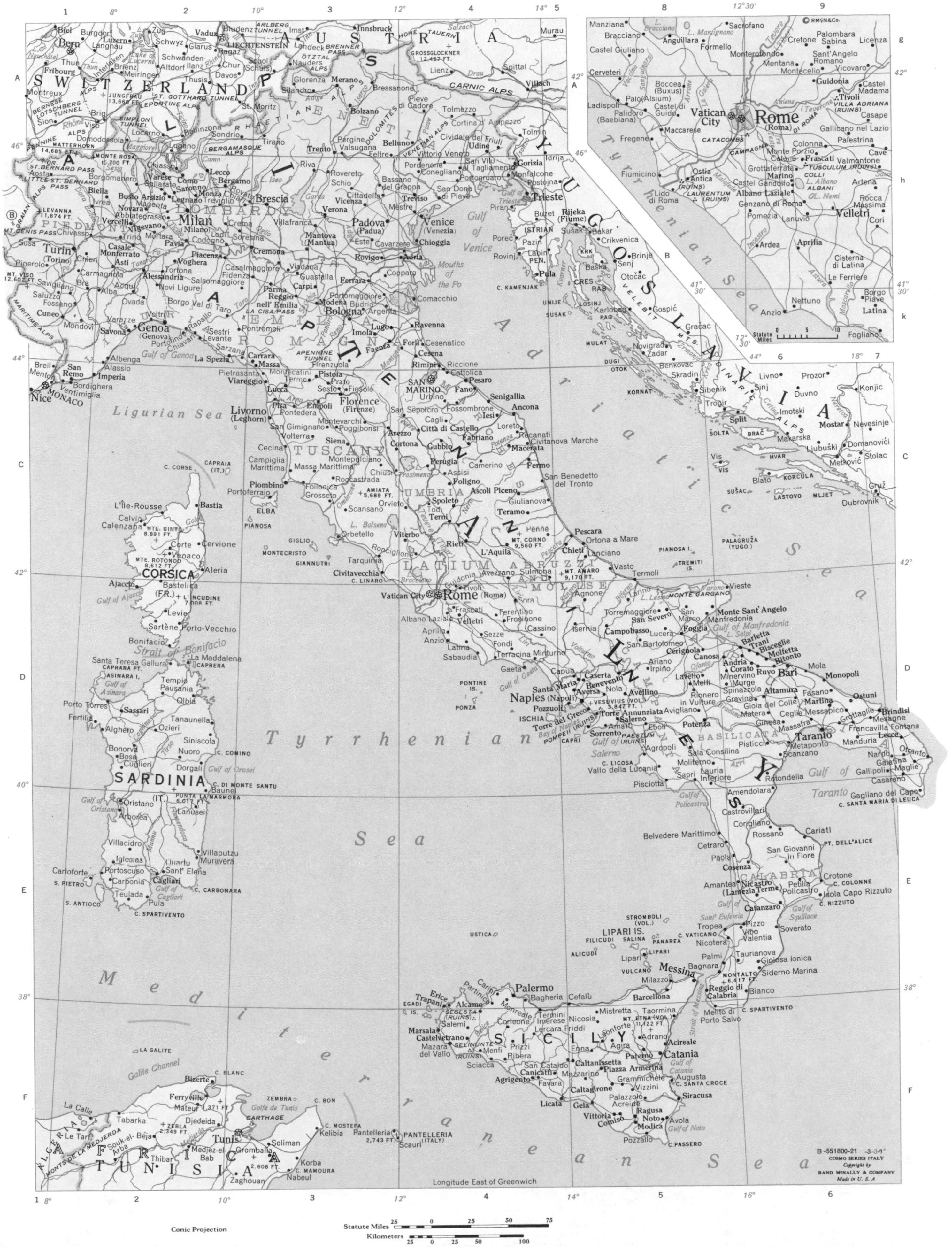

SWITZERLAND
AUSTRIA
YUGOSLAVIA
TUNISIA
AFRICA

SARDINIA
CORSICA (FR.)
SICILY
CALABRIA
BASILICATA
APULIA
CAMPANIA
LATIUM
TUSCANY
UMBRIA
ABRUZZI
MOLISE
LOMBARDY
PIEDMONT
EMILIA
ROMAGNA

Ligurian Sea
Tyrrhenian Sea
Mediterranean Sea
Adriatic Sea
Gulf of Venice
Gulf of Genoa
Gulf of Taranto
Gulf of Manfredonia
Gulf of Gallipoli
Strait of Bonifacio
Strait of Messina
Galite Channel

Major cities:
Bern, Turin (Torino), Milan (Milano), Genoa (Genova), Venice (Venezia), Padova (Padua), Verona, Brescia, Bergamo, Bologna, Parma, Modena, Ferrara, Ravenna, Trieste, Rijeka (Fiume), Florence (Firenze), Pisa, Livorno (Leghorn), Siena, Arezzo, Perugia, Ancona, Pescara, Rome (Roma), Vatican City, Naples (Napoli), Salerno, Foggia, Bari, Brindisi, Taranto, Lecce, Potenza, Cosenza, Catanzaro, Reggio di Calabria, Messina, Palermo, Catania, Siracusa, Marsala, Trapani, Agrigento, Cagliari, Sassari, Nice, Monaco, Tunis

Inset (upper right): Rome (Roma) / Vatican City
Rome, Vatican City, Tivoli, Frascati, Ostia Antica, Anzio, Nettuno, Latina, Velletri, Albano Laziale, Bracciano

Conic Projection
Statute Miles 25 0 25 50 75
Kilometers 25 0 25 50 100
Longitude East of Greenwich

B-551800-21 -3-3-1*
COSMO SERIES ITALY
Copyright by
RAND M?NALLY & COMPANY
Made in U.S.A

Statute Miles

Kilometers

Conic Projection

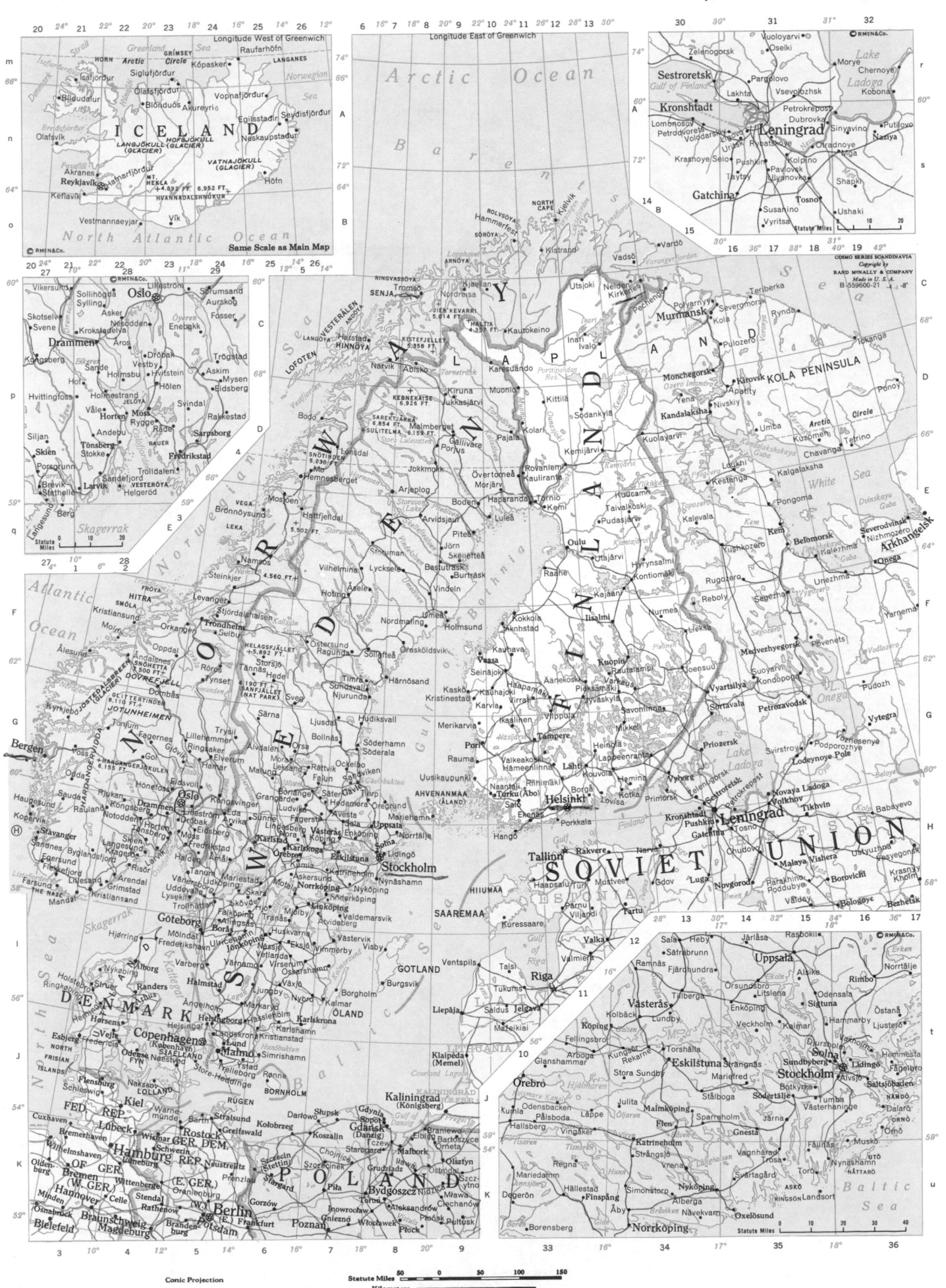

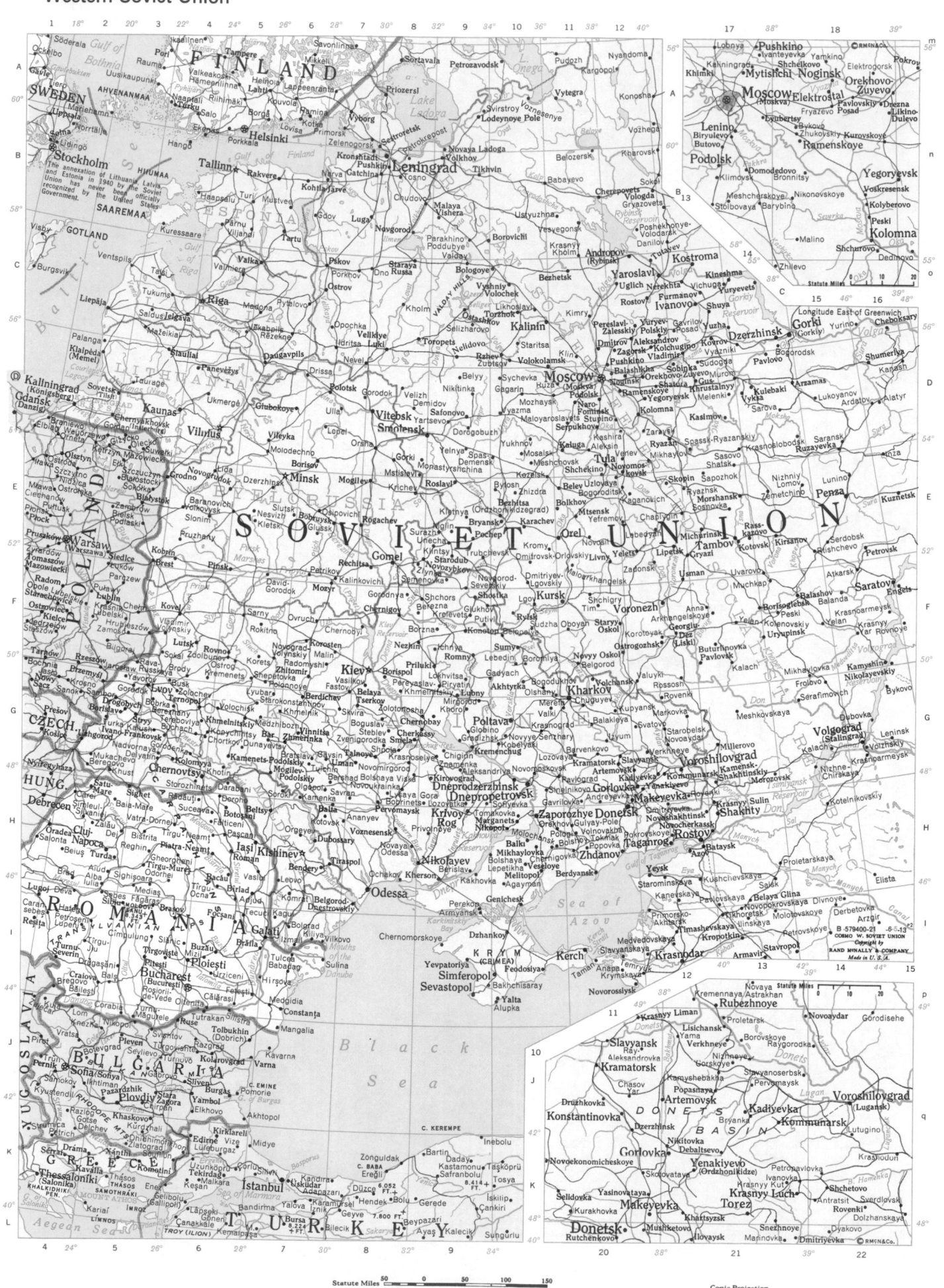

Lambert Azimuthal Equal Area Projection

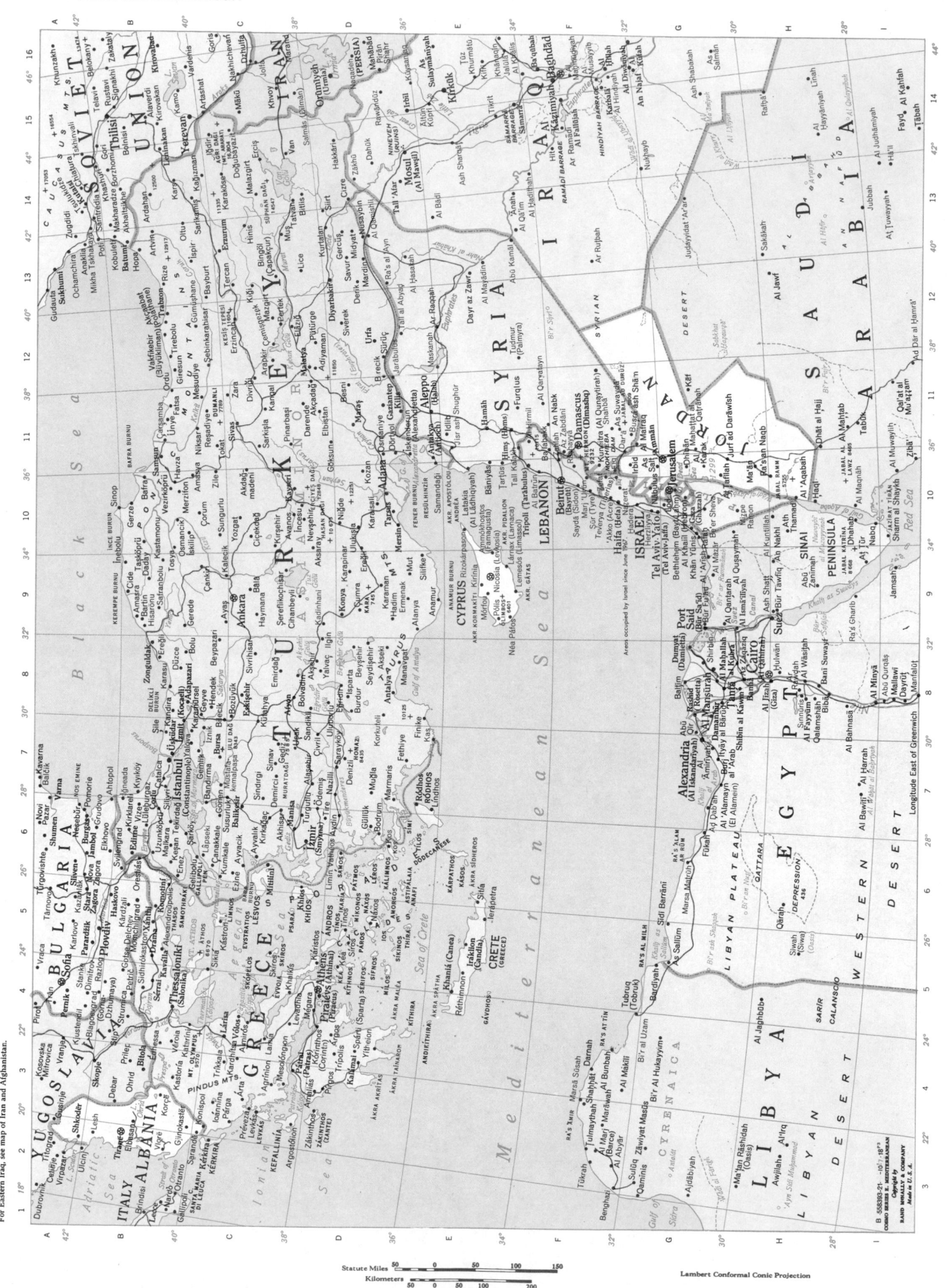

For Eastern Iraq, see map of Iran and Afghanistan.

B 556393-21-
COSMO SERIES E. MEDITERRANEAN
Copyright by
RAND McNALLY & COMPANY
Made in U.S.A.

Statute Miles
Kilometers

Lambert Conformal Conic Projection

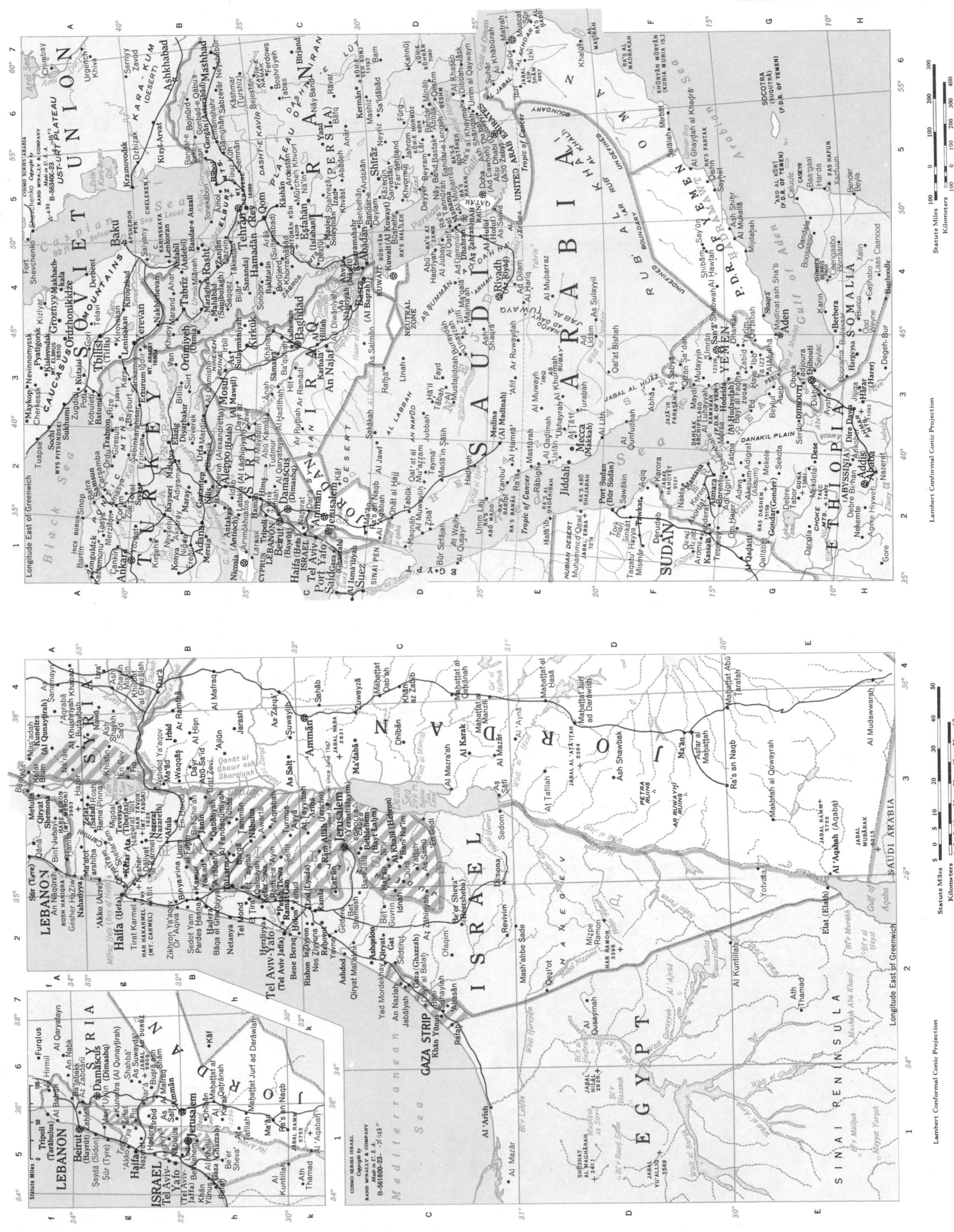

Lambert Conformal Conic Projection

Statute Miles
Kilometers

Lambert Conformal Conic Projection

Statute Miles
Kilometers

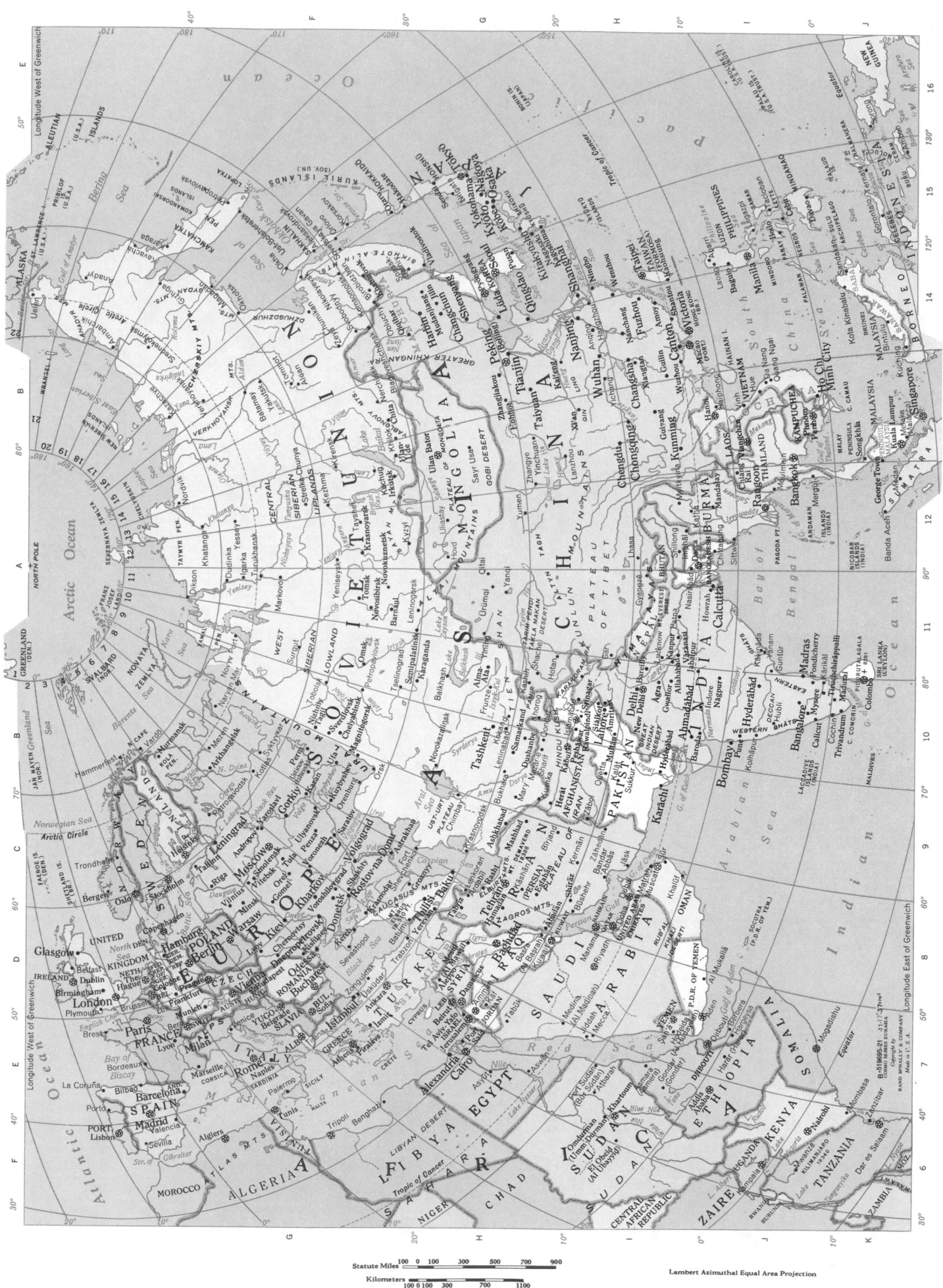

Statute Miles

Kilometers

Lambert Azimuthal Equal Area Projection

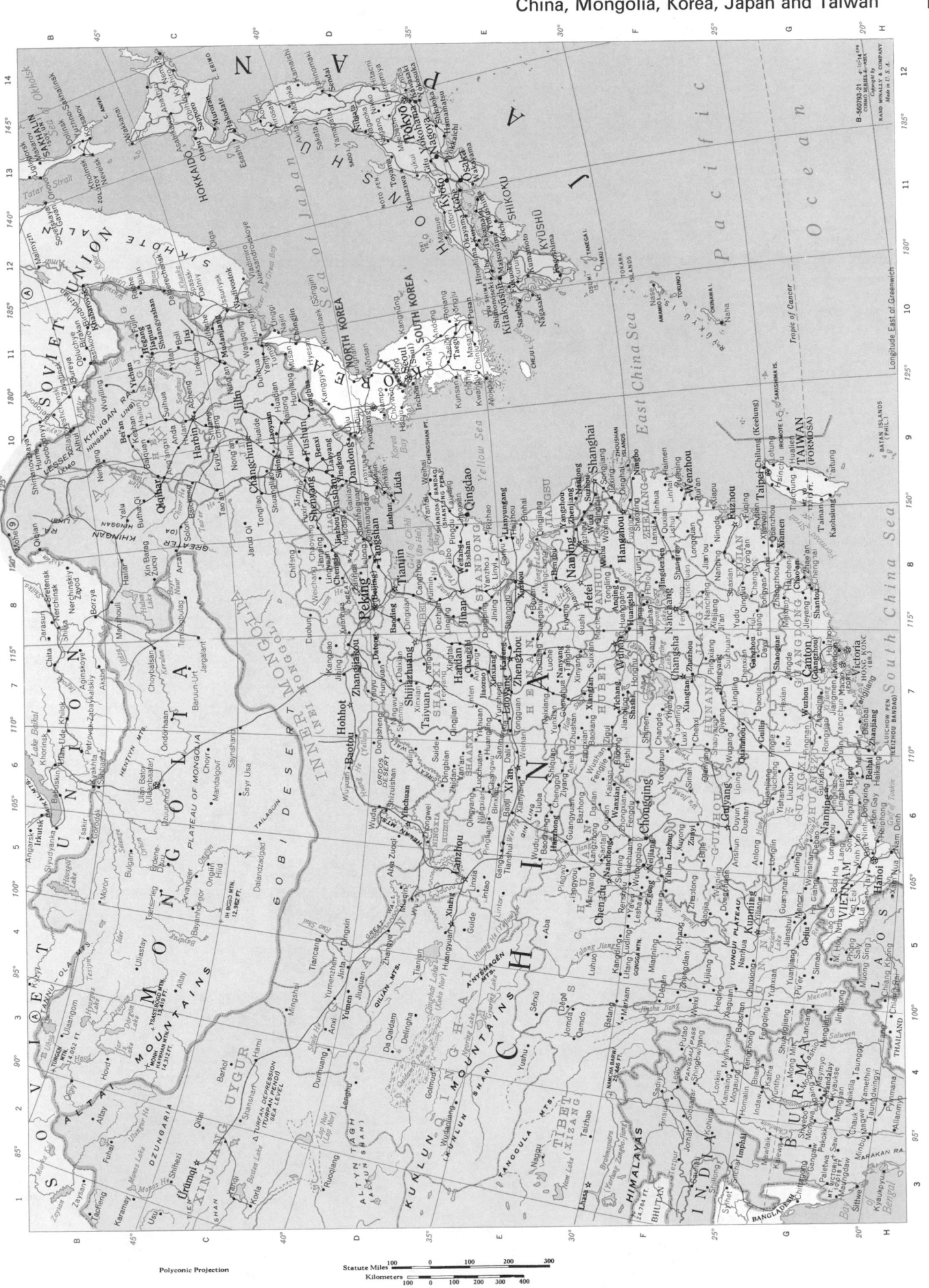

Statute Miles
100   0   100   200   300

Kilometers
100   0   100   200   300   400

Statute Miles

Kilometers

Lambert Conformal Conic Projection

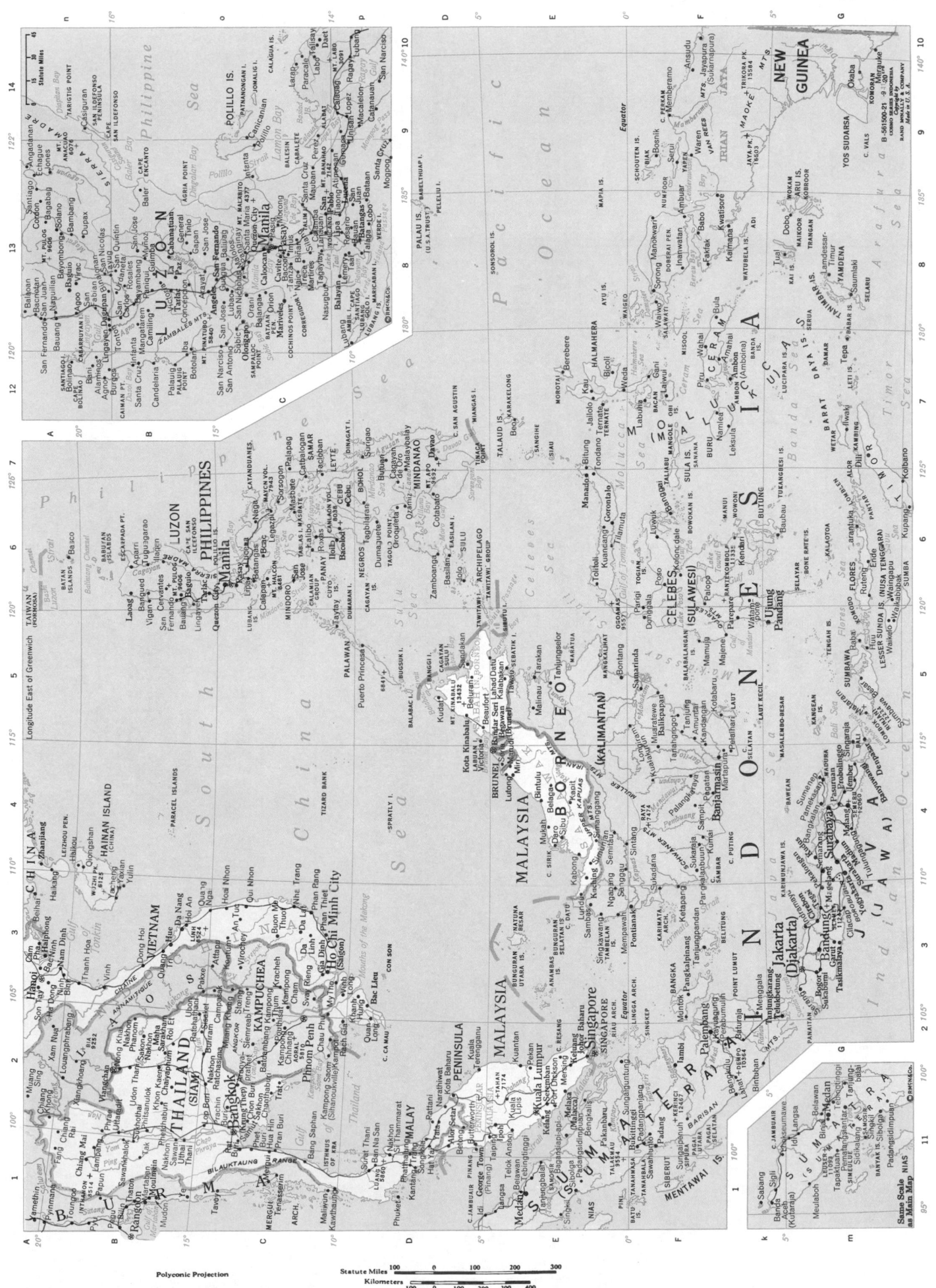

Polyconic Projection

Statute Miles

Kilometers

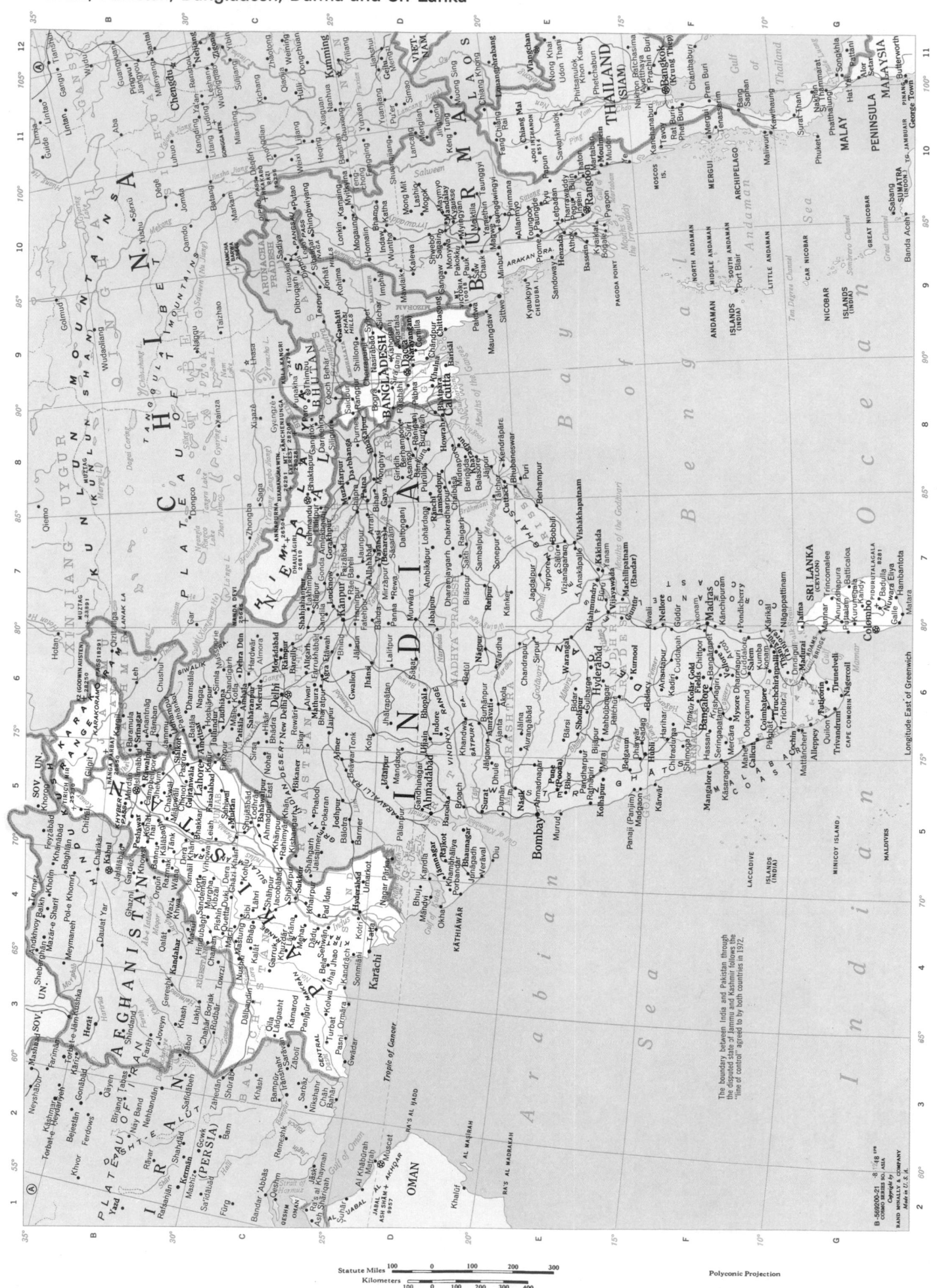

Statute Miles

Kilometers

Polyconic Projection

The boundary between India and Pakistan through the disputed state of Jammu and Kashmir follows the "line of control" agreed to by both countries in 1972.

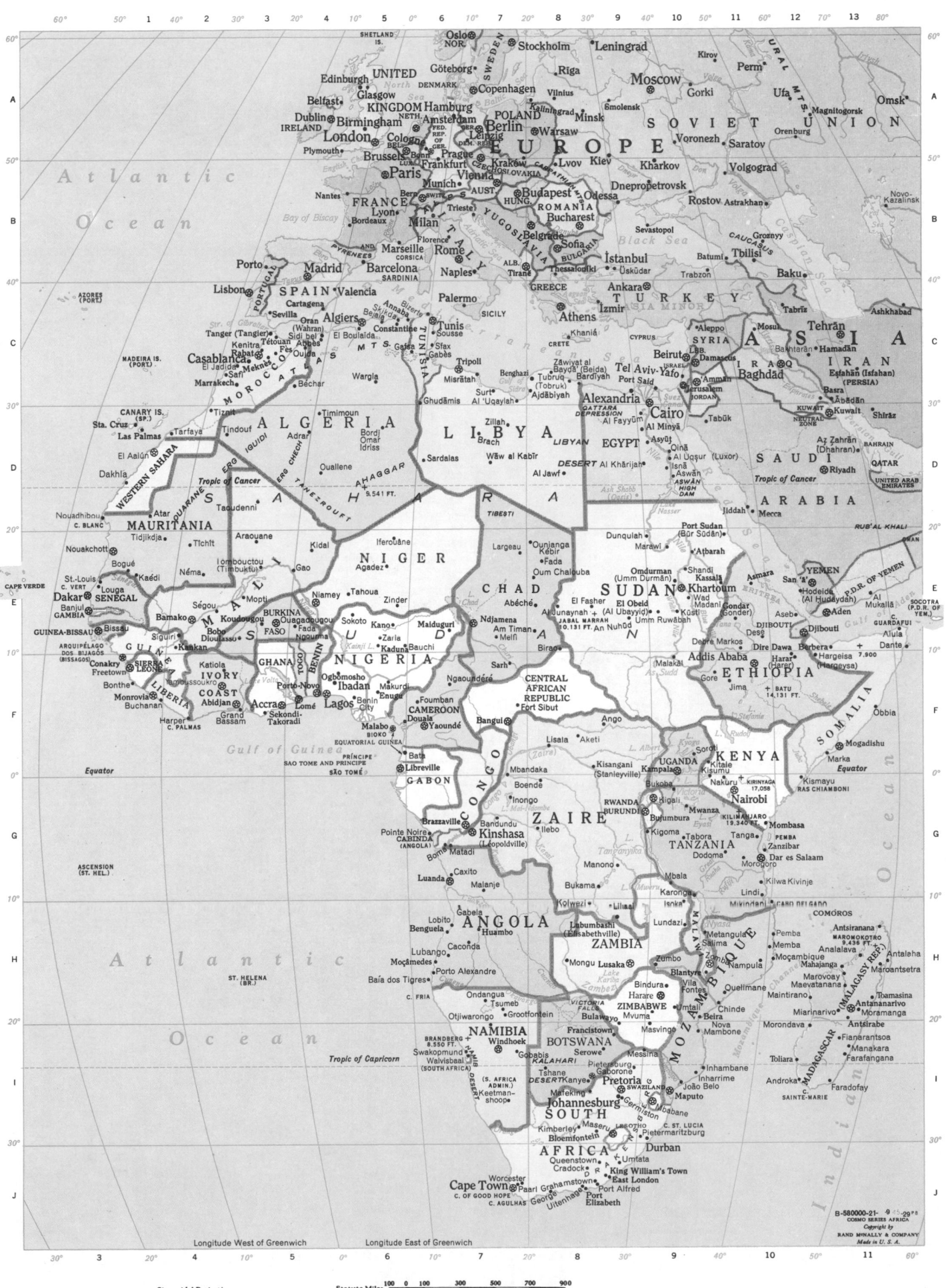

Oslo
NOR.
Stockholm
Leningrad
Kirov
Perm

Edinburgh UNITED Göteborg
Riga
Moscow
Gorki
Ufa
Omsk

Belfast Glasgow
Copenhagen
Vilnius
Smolensk
SOVIET UNION
Magnitogorsk

Dublin Birmingham KINGDOM Hamburg Amsterdam
Minsk
Orenburg
Novo-
Kazalinsk

IRELAND London
Brussels
Berlin
Warsaw
Voronezh
Saratov

Plymouth Cologne Leipzig
Prague
Lvov Kiev
Kharkov
Volgograd

Paris Frankfurt
EUROPE
Dnepropetrovsk
Rostov Astrakhan

Nantes Munich Vienna
Budapest
ROMANIA
Odessa
Sevastopol
Groznyy

FRANCE Lyon Bern
Trieste HUNG.
Bucharest
Black Sea
CAUCASUS
Tbilisi

Bordeaux Milan YUGOSLAVIA
Belgrade
Sofia
Batumi
Baku

Bay of Biscay Florence
Rome
Thessaloníki
İstanbul
Trabzon

Porto Marseille ITALY
Naples GREECE Athens
Ankara
TURKEY
Tabrīz
Ashkhabad

Madrid Barcelona SARDINIA
Palermo
İzmir
ASIA MINOR
Tehrān
Hamadān

Lisbon Valencia
SICILY
CRETE
CYPRUS
SYRIA
Mosul
IRAN

SPAIN
Palermo
Aleppo
Beirut
Damascus
Baghdad
Eşfahān (Isfahan)
(PERSIA)

Sevilla Algiers Tunis
Tripoli
Tel Aviv-Yafo
Amman IRAQ
Basra
Abādān
Shīrāz

Casablanca MOROCCO
Benghazi
Alexandria
Cairo
Kuwait
KUWAIT
QATAR

ALGERIA
LIBYA
EGYPT
SAUDI
Riyadh
UNITED ARAB EMIRATES

Tropic of Cancer
LIBYAN DESERT
ARABIA
RUB 'AL KHALI

WESTERN SAHARA
S A H A R A
Port Sudan
Mecca
Jiddah
YEMEN

MAURITANIA
NIGER
SUDAN
Khartoum
Asmara
ETHIOPIA
SOMALIA

Nouakchott
MALI
CHAD
Omdurman
Addis Ababa
DJIBOUTI

Dakar SENEGAL
BURKINA
NIGERIA
CENTRAL AFRICAN REPUBLIC
KENYA
Nairobi

GAMBIA GUINEA
GHANA
IVORY COAST
CAMEROON
UGANDA
Mogadishu

SIERRA LEONE LIBERIA
Lagos
EQUATORIAL GUINEA
GABON
CONGO
ZAIRE
TANZANIA

Gulf of Guinea
SAO TOME AND PRINCIPE
Brazzaville Kinshasa
RWANDA
BURUNDI

Equator
GABON
ANGOLA
ZAMBIA
Dar es Salaam

ASCENSION
(ST. HEL.)
ANGOLA
MALAWI
COMOROS

Atlantic
Ocean
ST. HELENA (BR.)
NAMIBIA
ZIMBABWE
MOZAMBIQUE
MADAGASCAR

Tropic of Capricorn
BOTSWANA
Pretoria
SWAZILAND

SOUTH
Johannesburg
LESOTHO

AFRICA
Cape Town
Durban

Sinusoidal Projection

Statute Miles 100 0 100   300   500   700   900
Kilometers 100 0 100 300 500 700 900 1100 1300

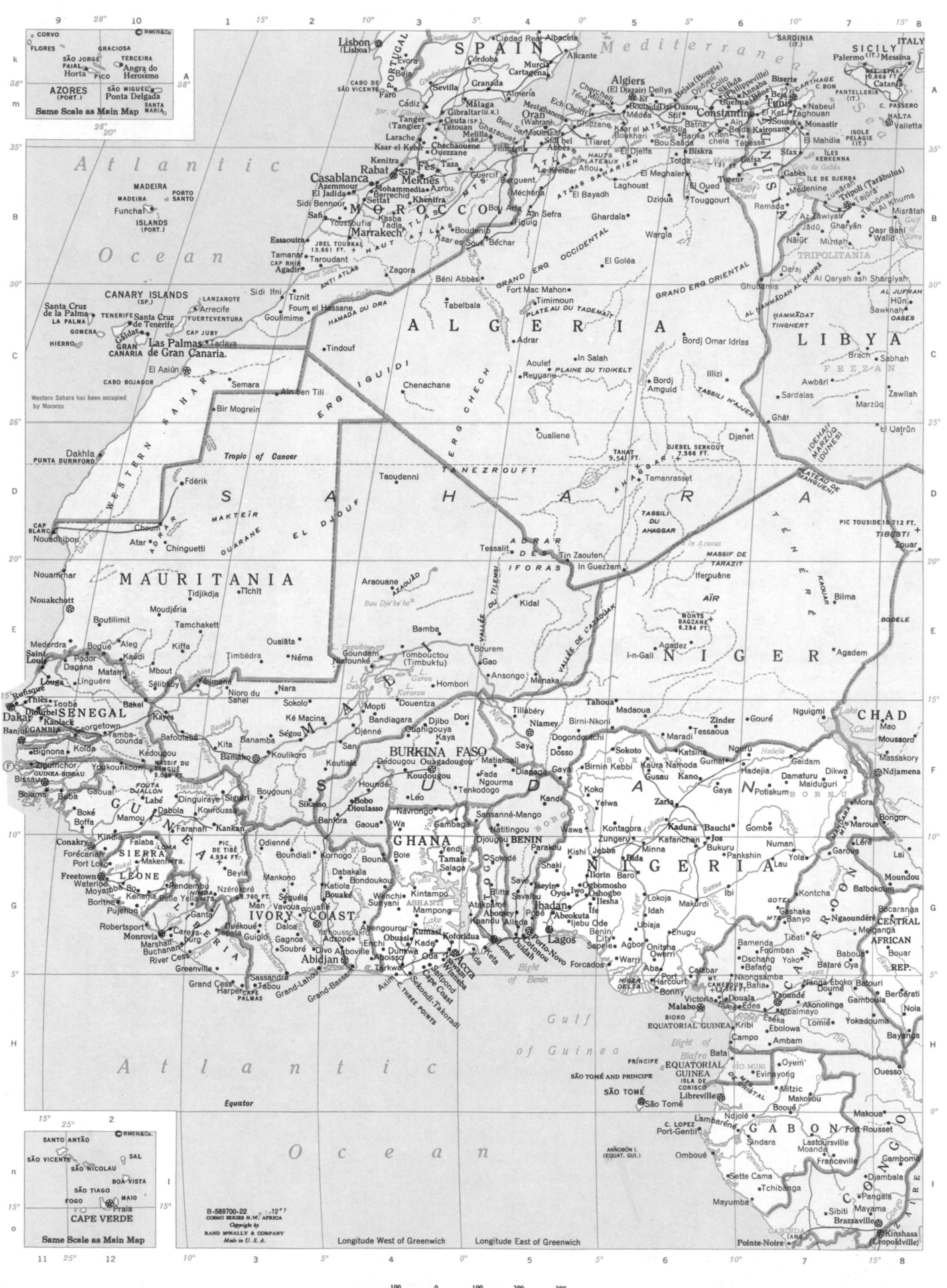

Longitude West of Greenwich   Longitude East of Greenwich

Statute Miles
Kilometers

Sinusoidal Projection

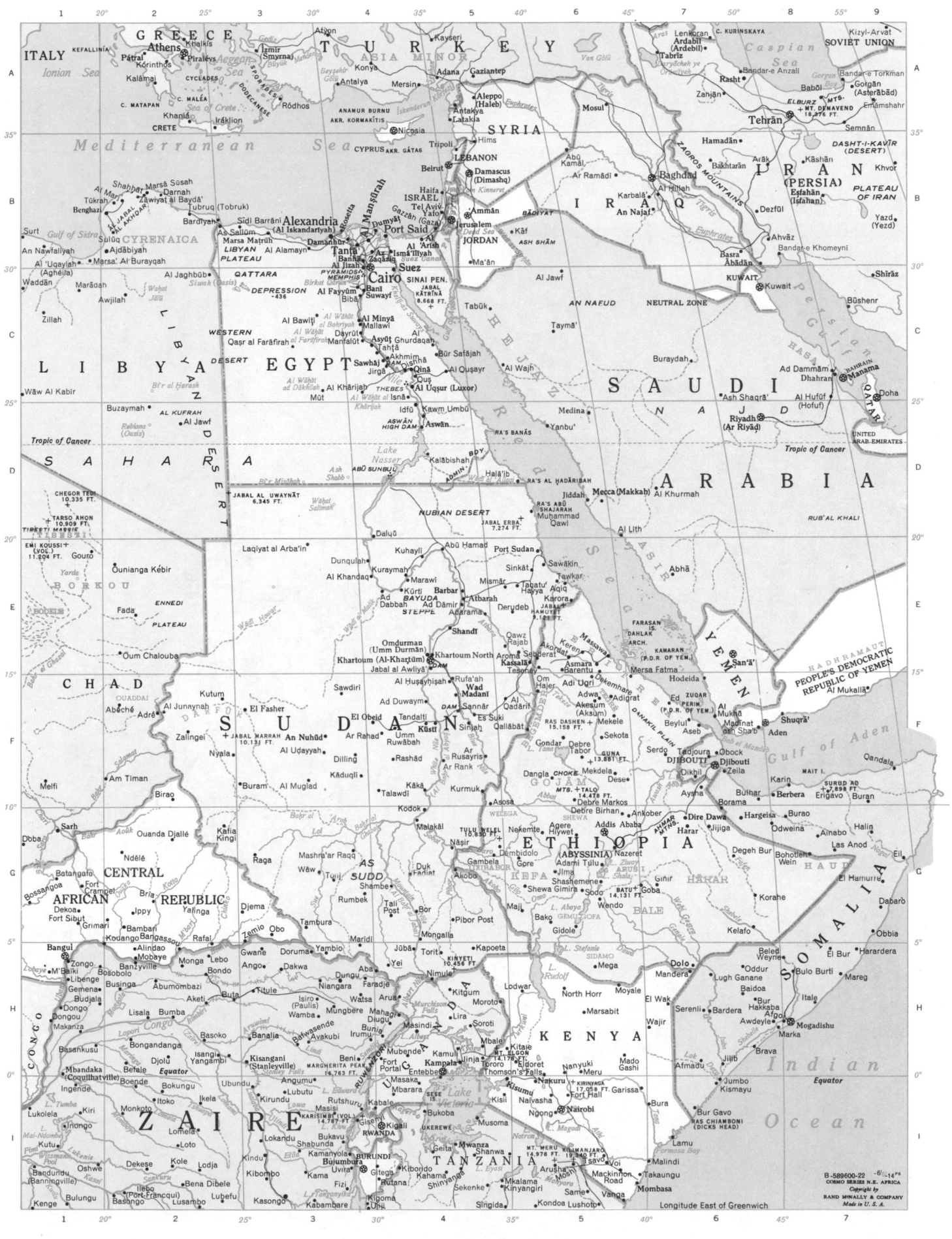

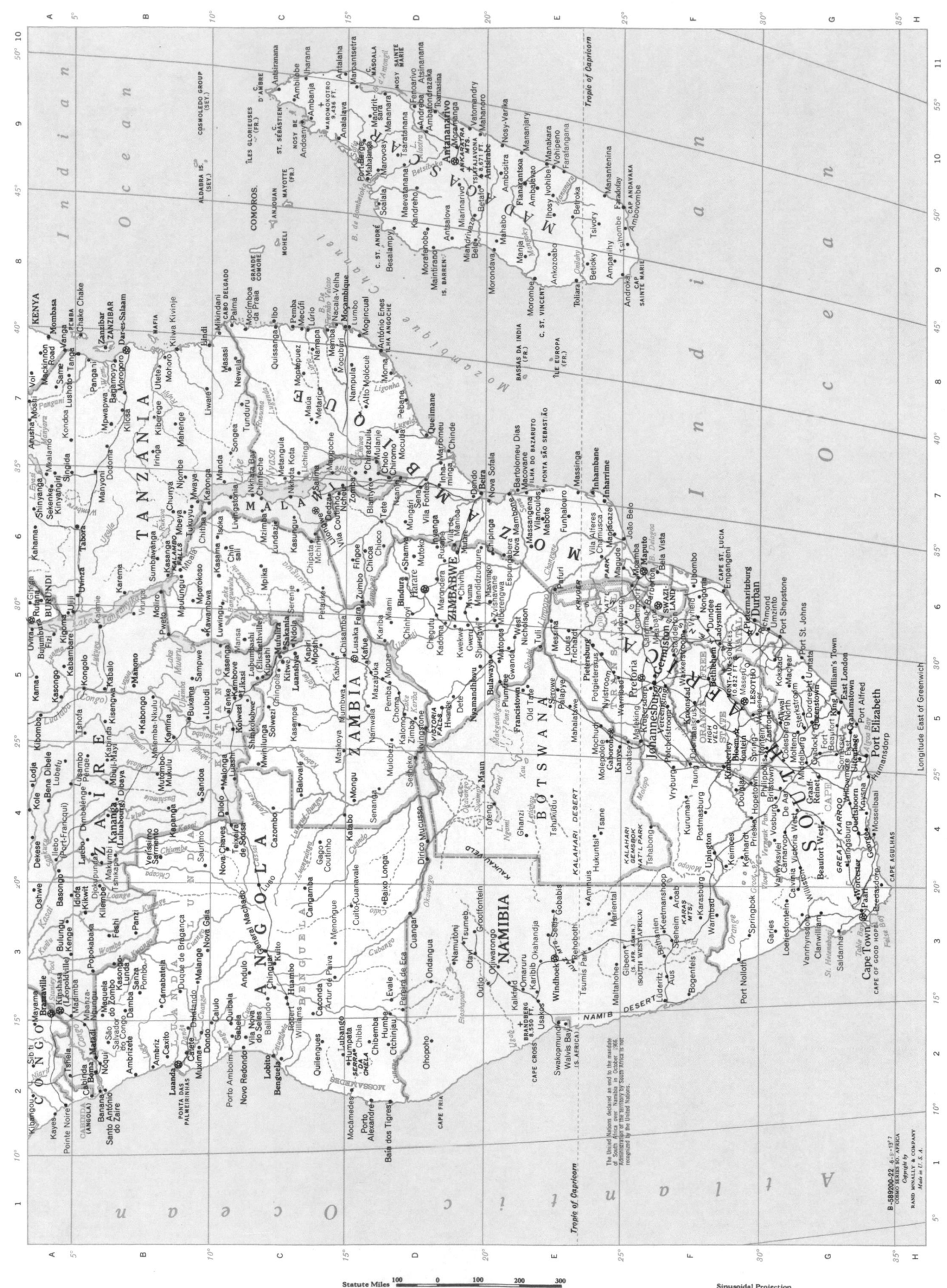

Statute Miles

Kilometers

Sinusoidal Projection

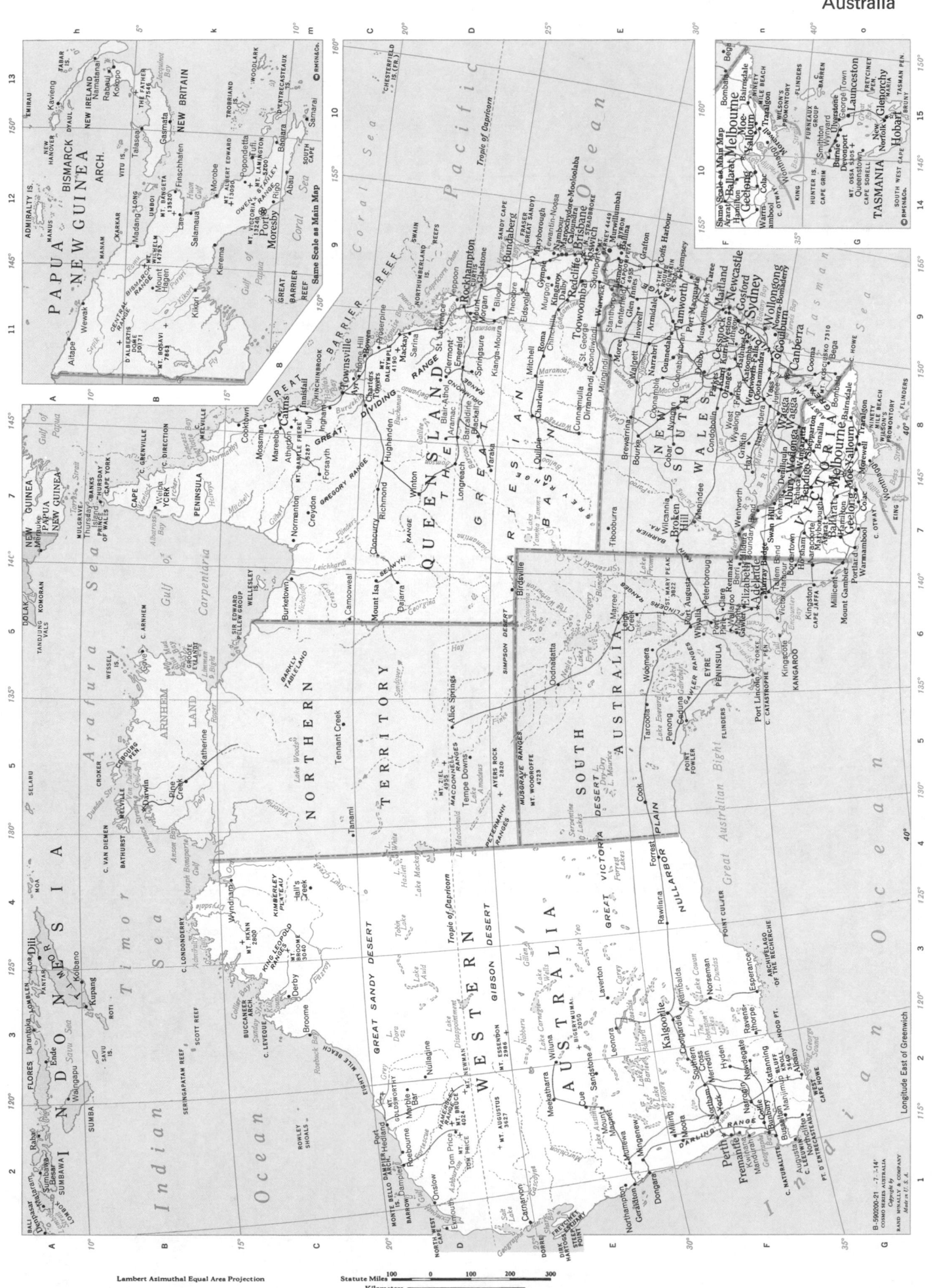

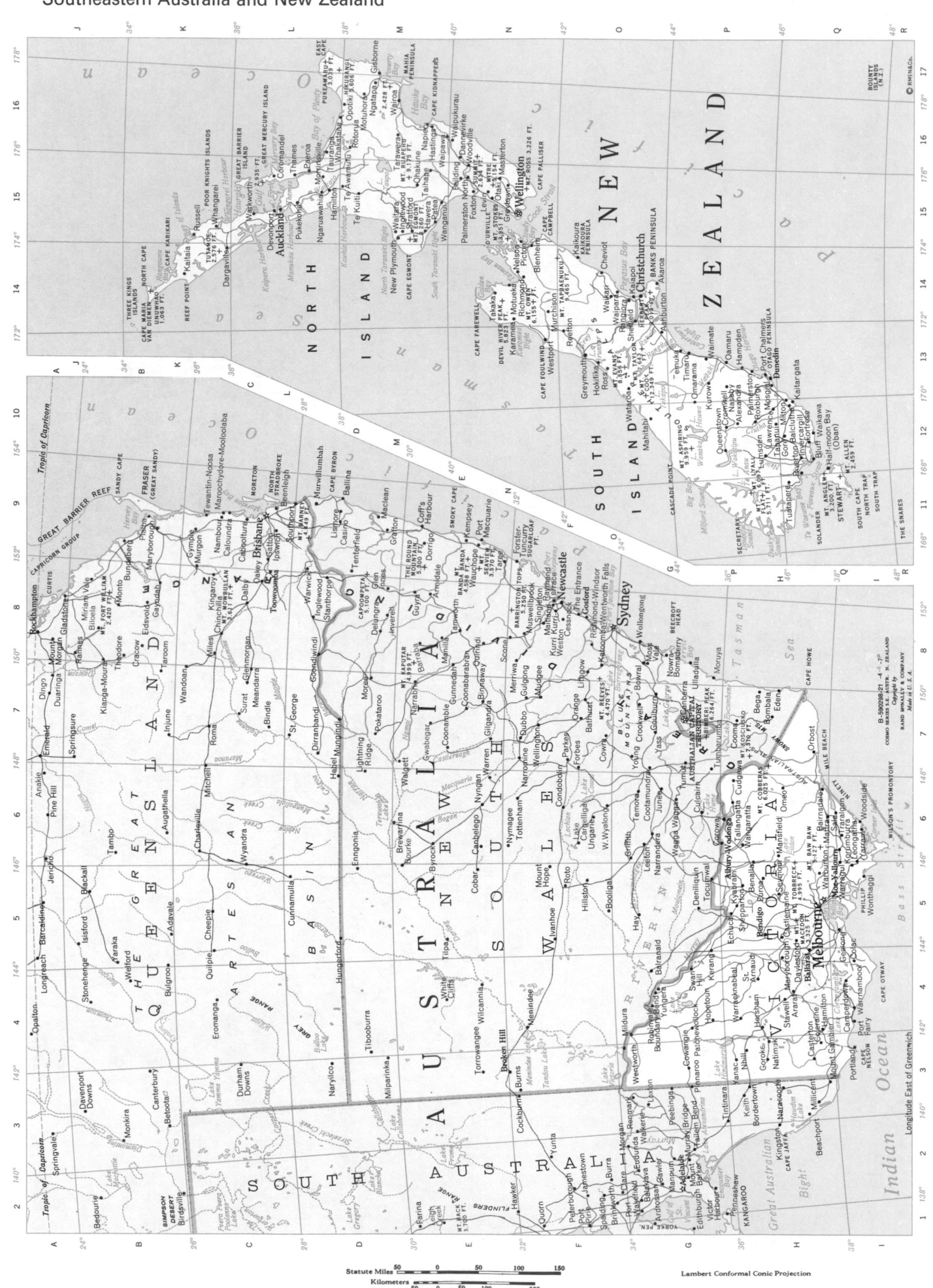

Statute Miles

Kilometers

Lambert Conformal Conic Projection

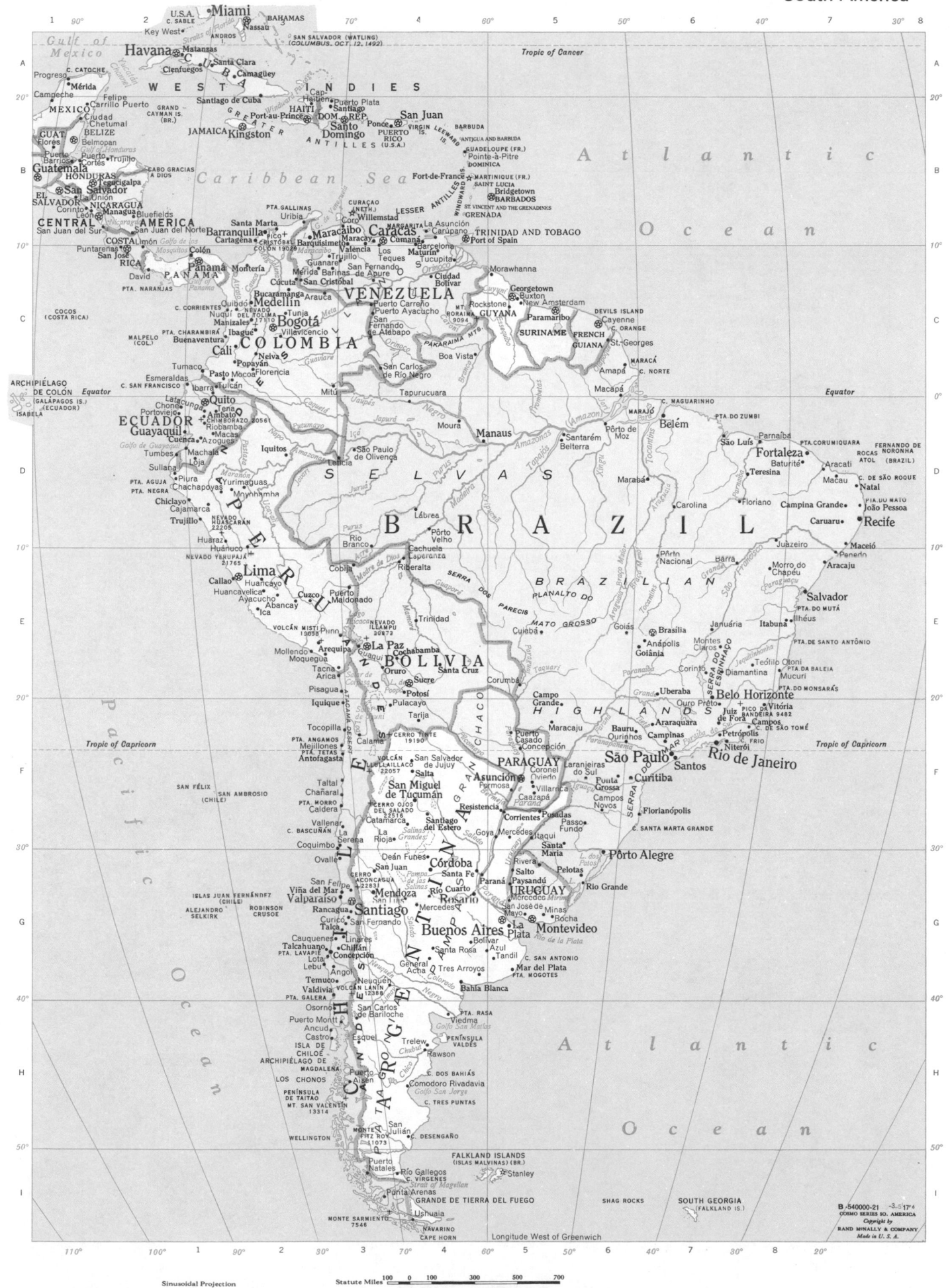

Sinusoidal Projection

Statute Miles
100   0   100   300   500   700

Kilometers
100 0 100   300   500   700   900   1100

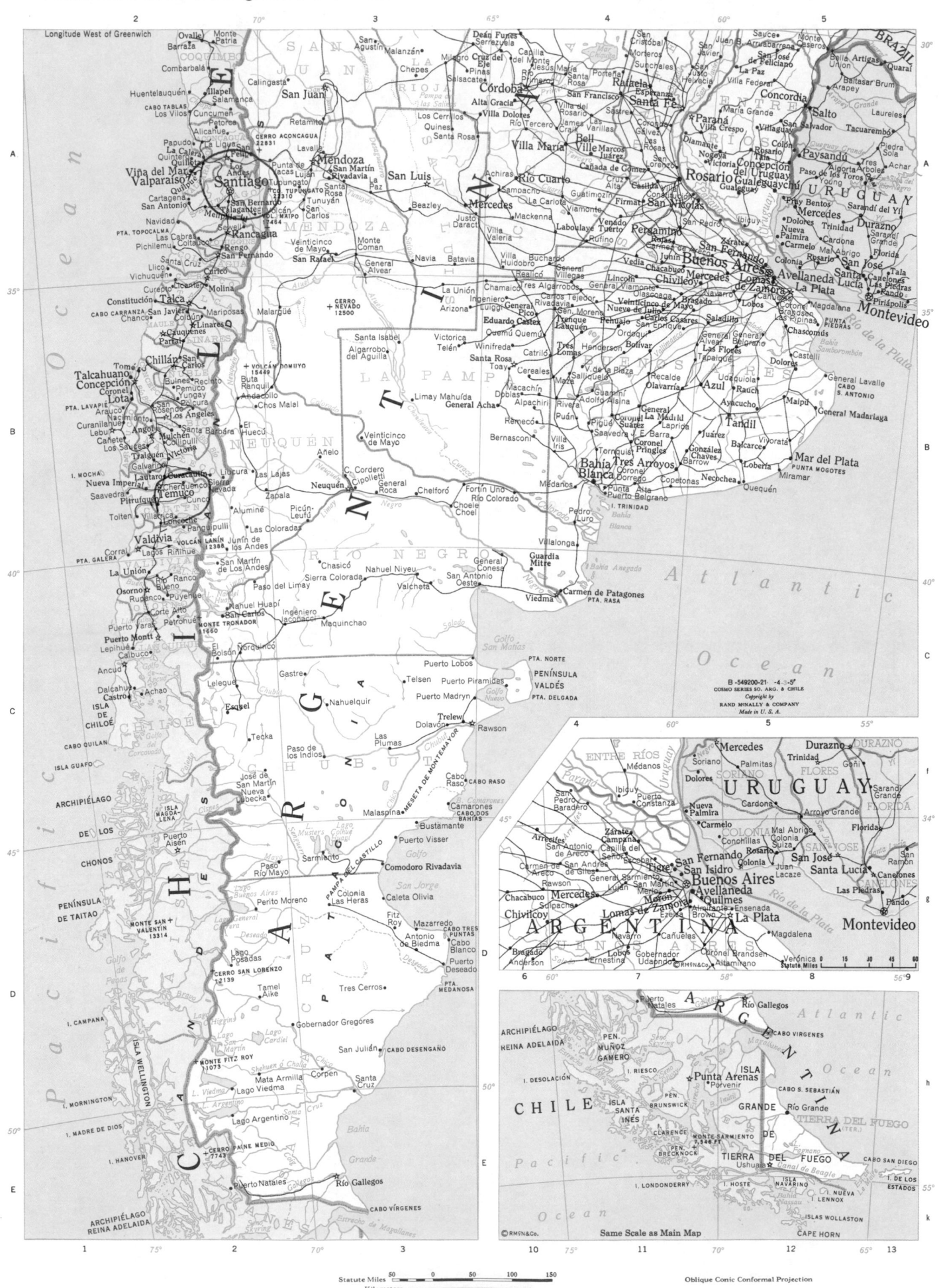

Statute Miles

Kilometers

Oblique Conic Conformal Projection

Same Scale as Main Map

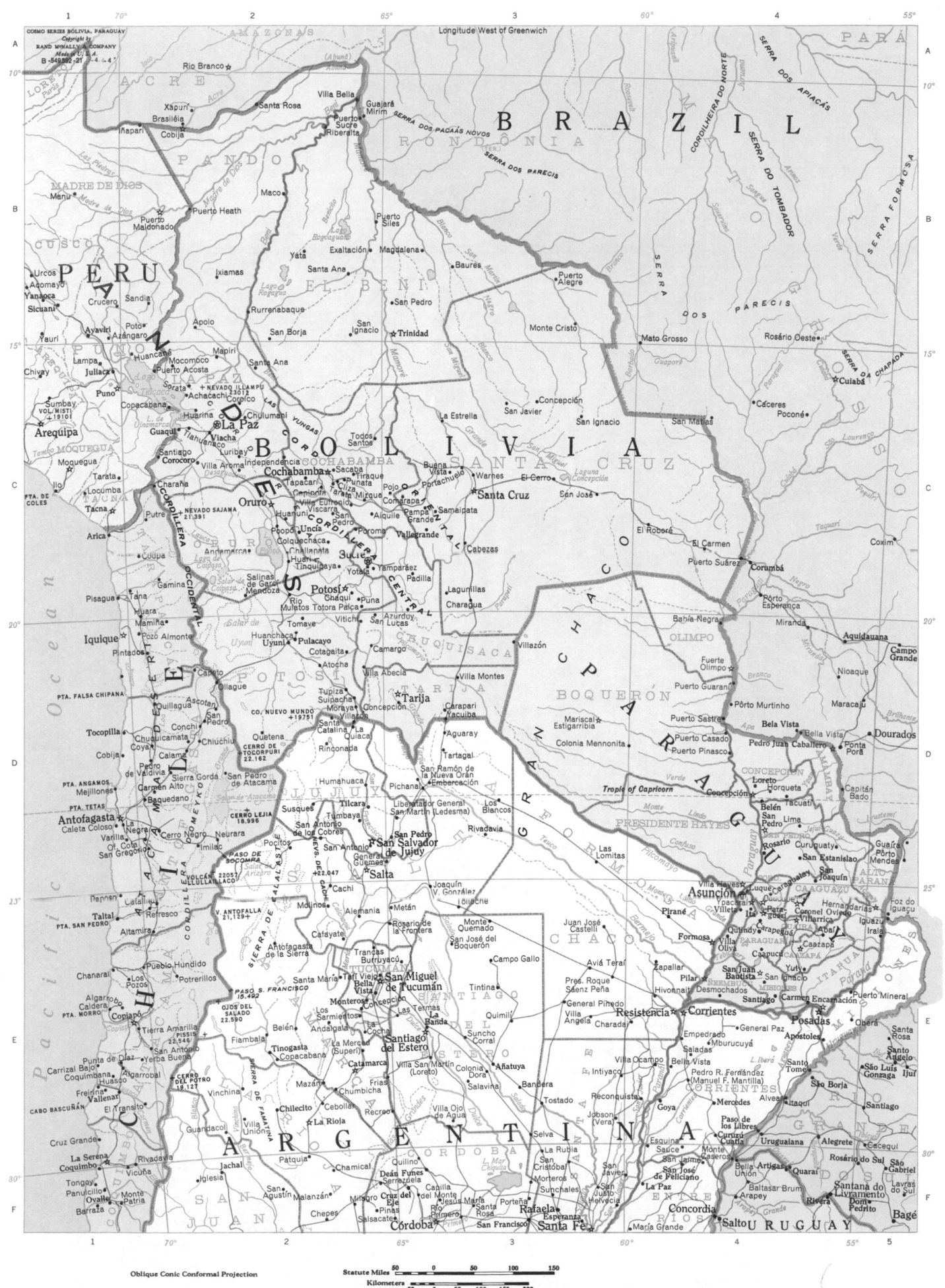

COSMO SERIES BOLIVIA, PARAGUAY
Copyright by
RAND McNALLY & COMPANY
Made in U.S.A.
B-549582-21

Oblique Conic Conformal Projection

Statute Miles

Kilometers

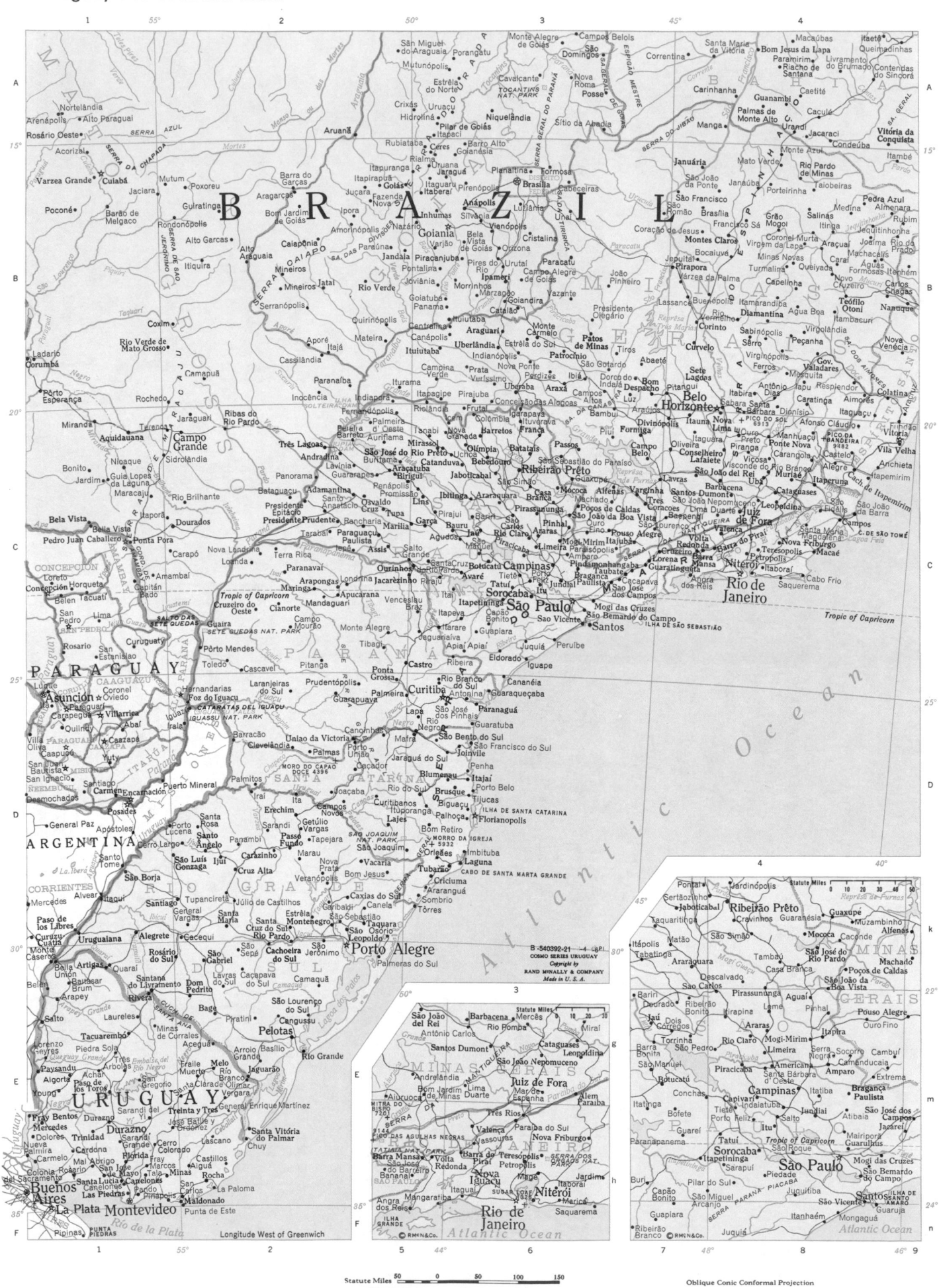

Statute Miles

Kilometers

Oblique Conic Conformal Projection

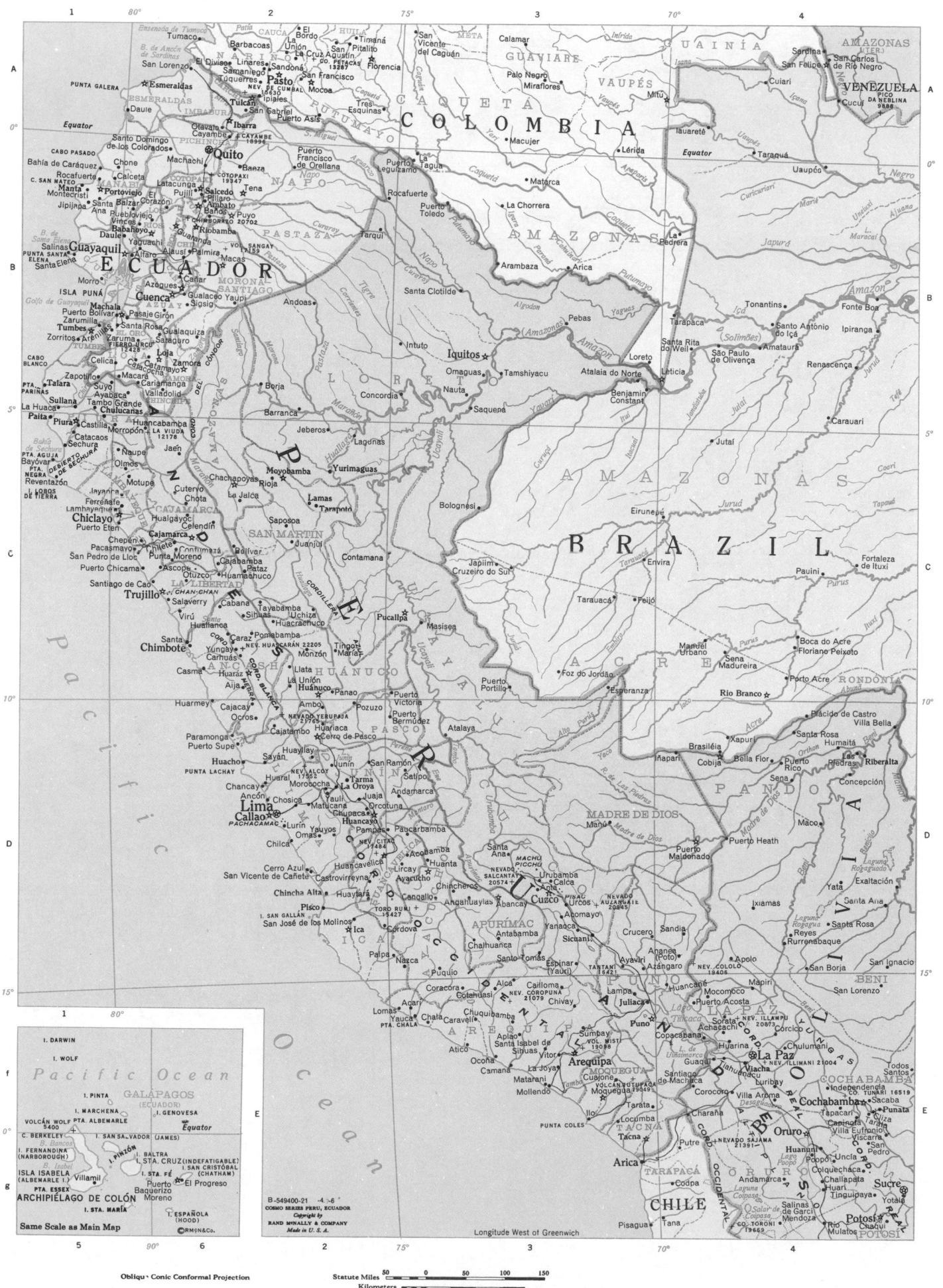

Obliqu^ Conic Conformal Projection

Longitude West of Greenwich

Statute Miles

Kilometers

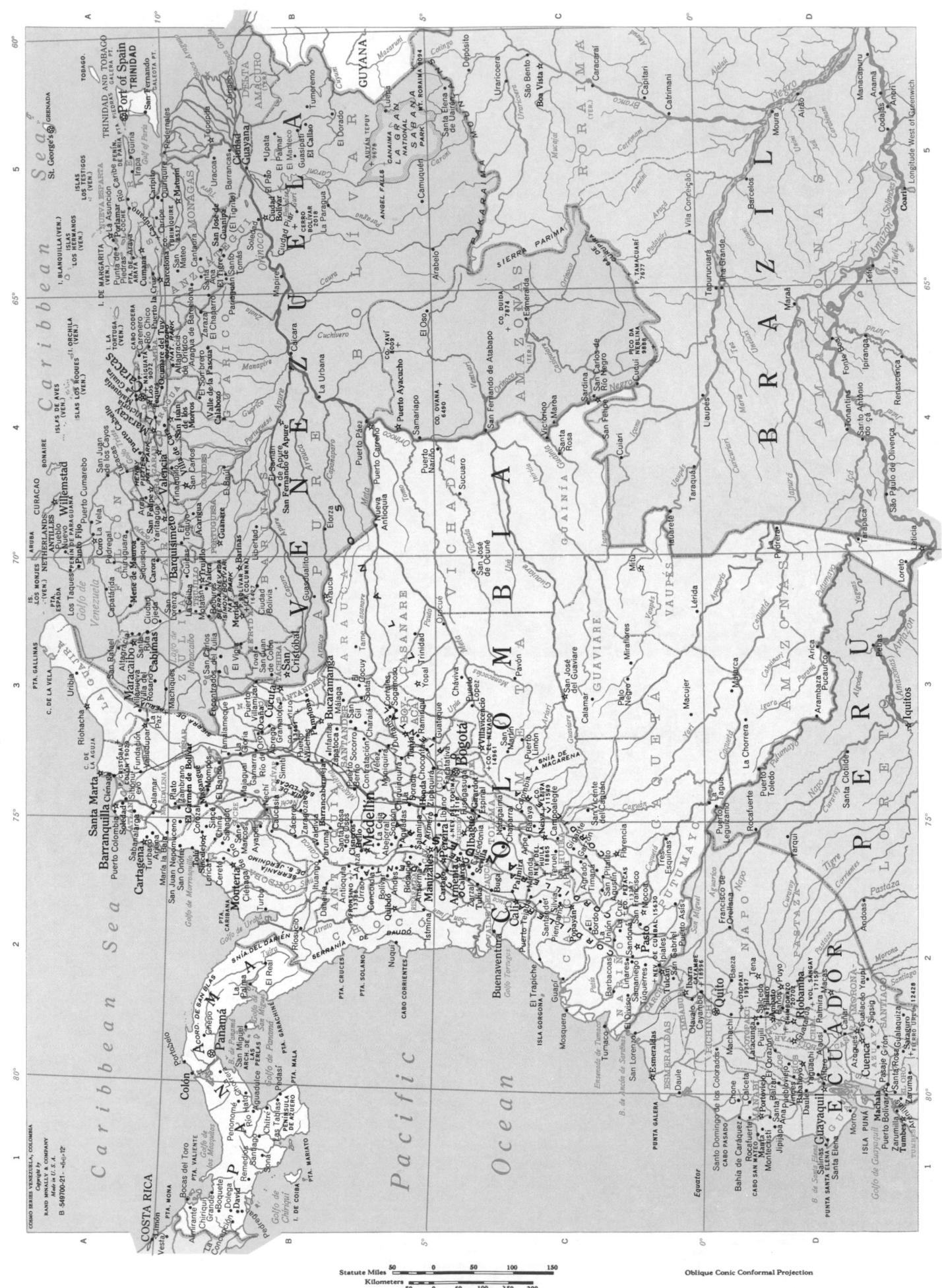

Statute Miles

Kilometers

Oblique Conic Conformal Projection

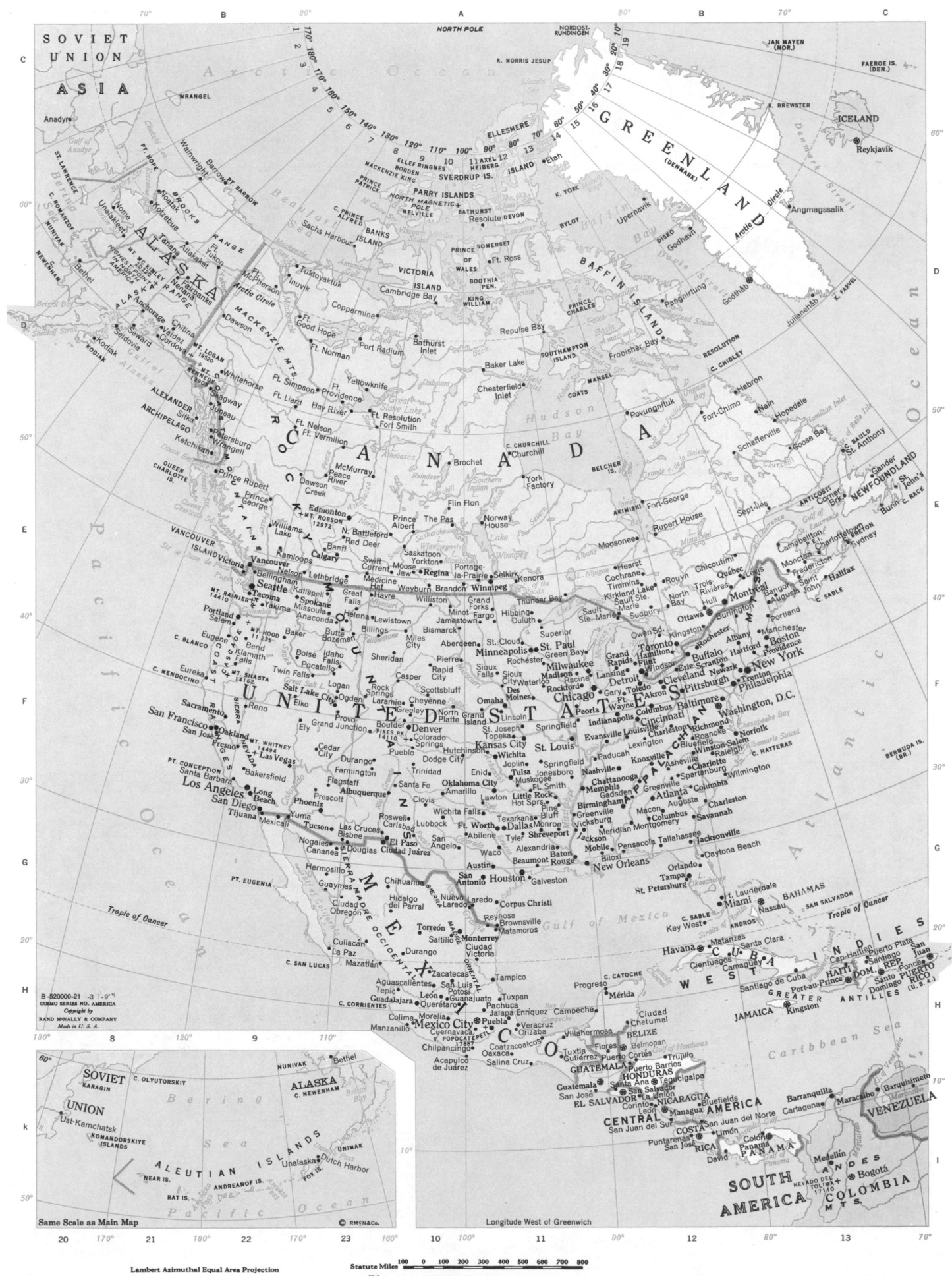

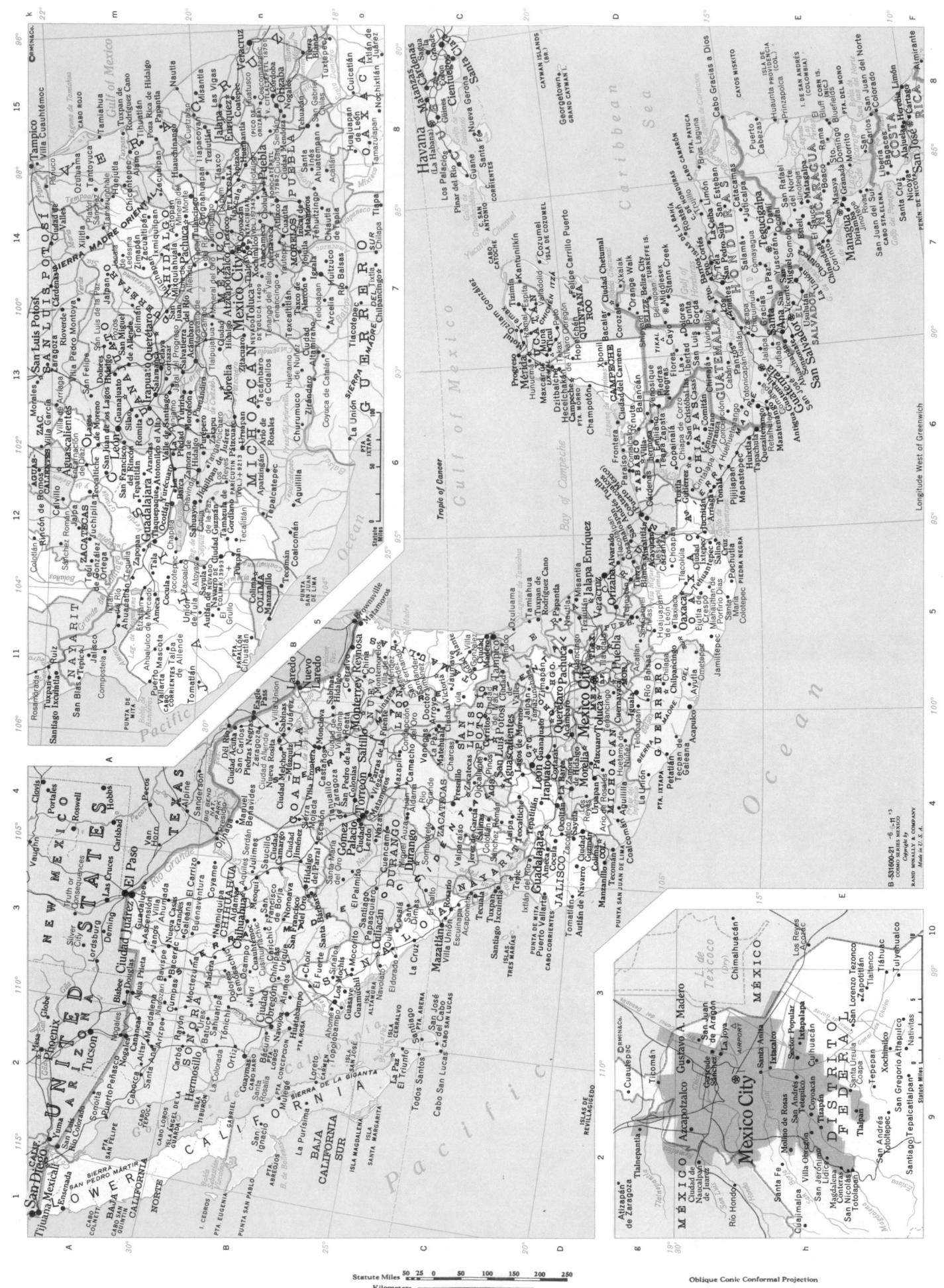

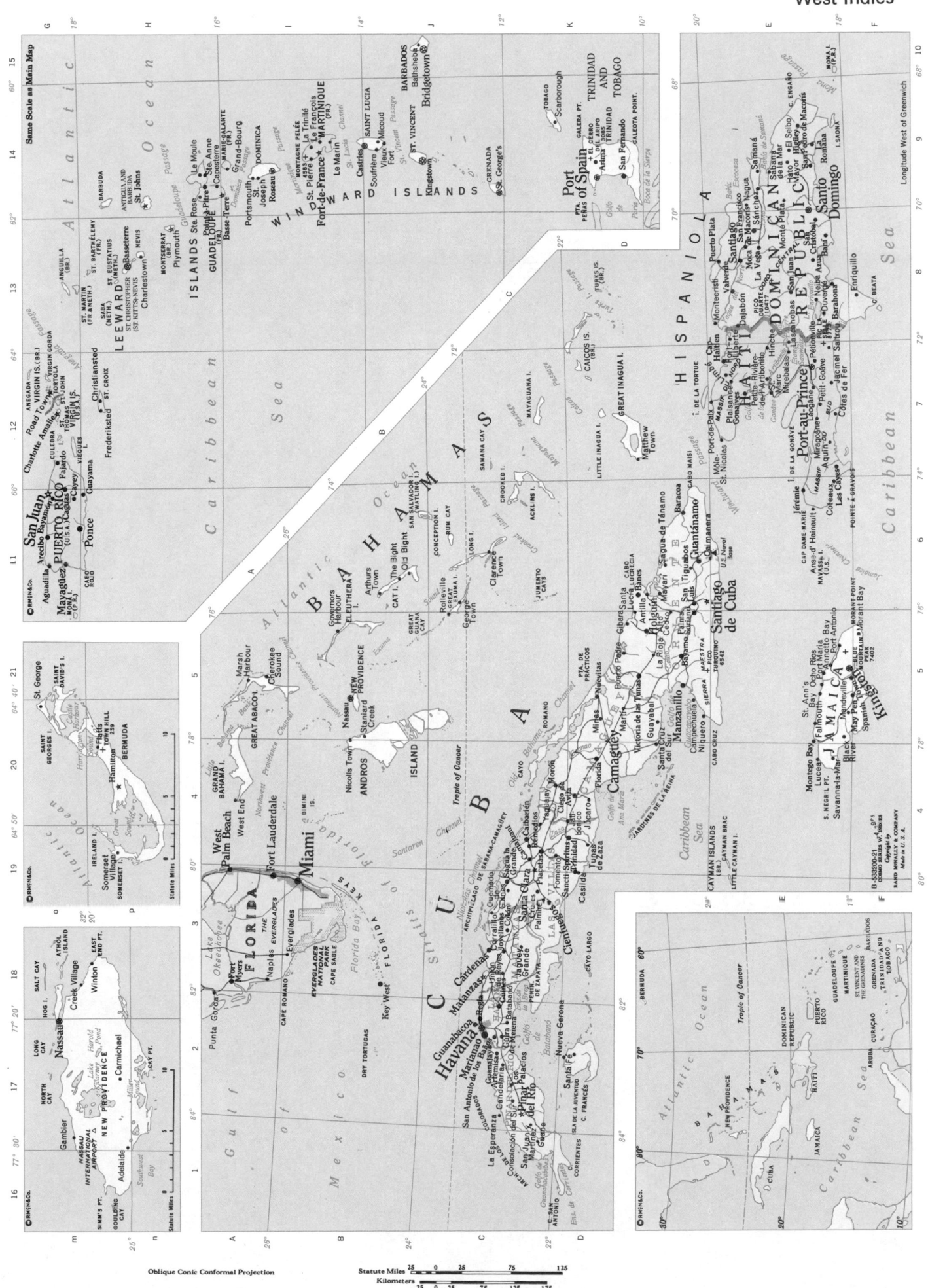

Oblique Conic Conformal Projection

Statute Miles

Kilometers

Statute Miles 100 0 100 200 300

Kilometers 100 0 100 200 300 400

Lambert Conformal Conic Projection

CONOCO SERIES CANADA B

Copyright by
RAND McNALLY & COMPANY
Made in U.S.A.
B-520000-22 -5 -11"

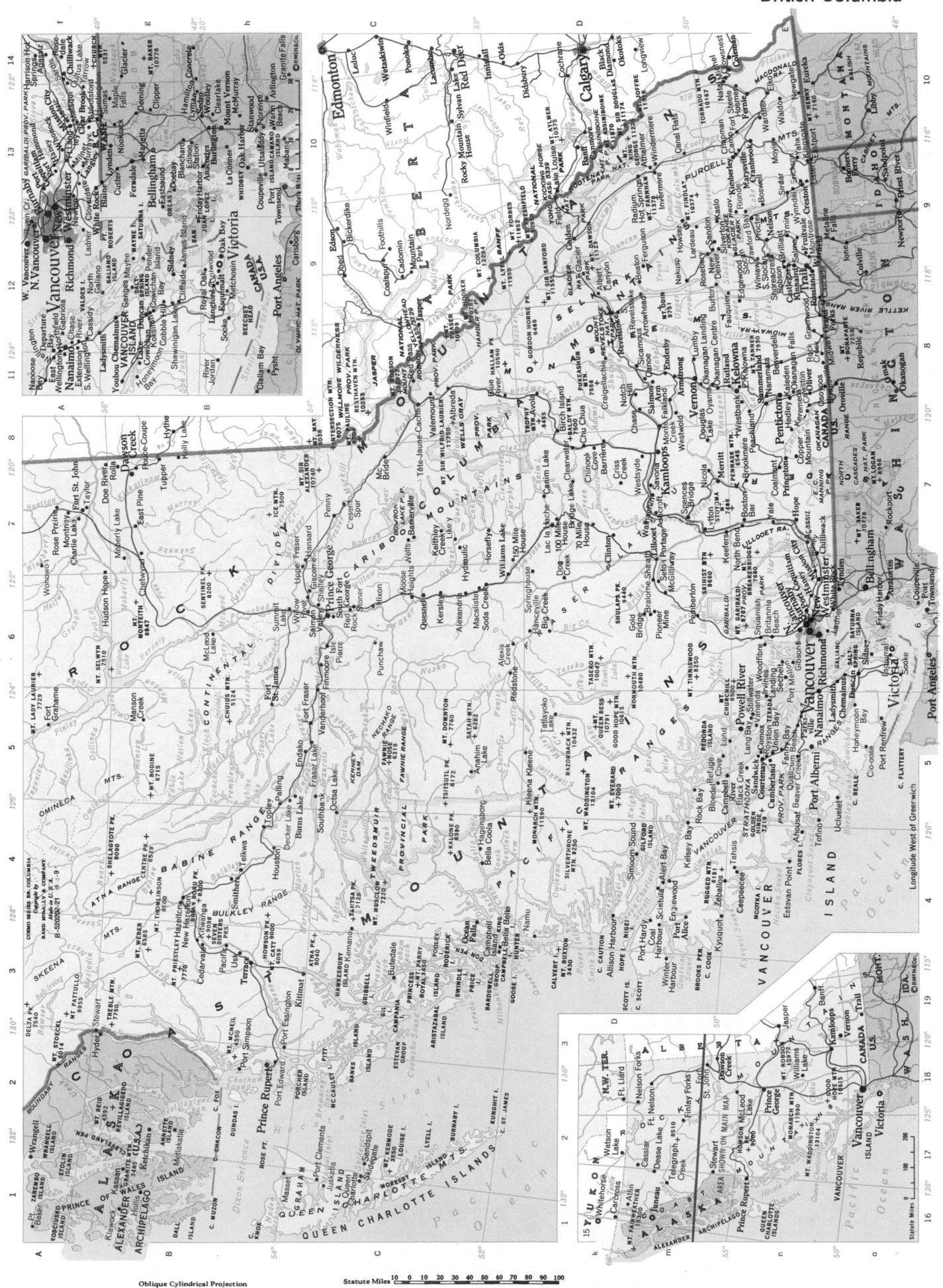

Oblique Cylindrical Projection

Statute Miles

Kilometers

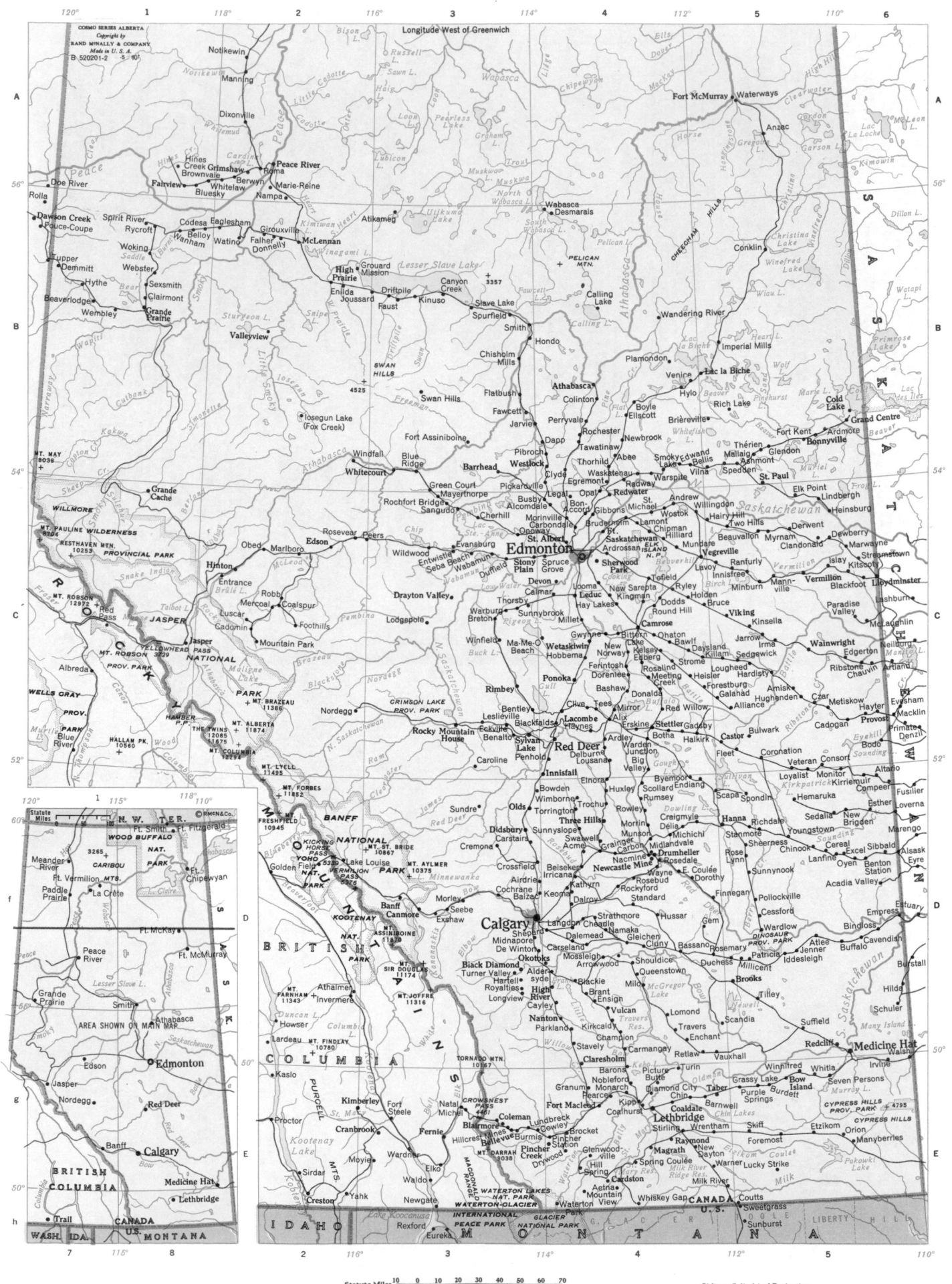

Statute Miles 10 0 10 20 30 40 50 60 70

Kilometers 10 0 10 20 40 60 80 100

Oblique Cylindrical Projection

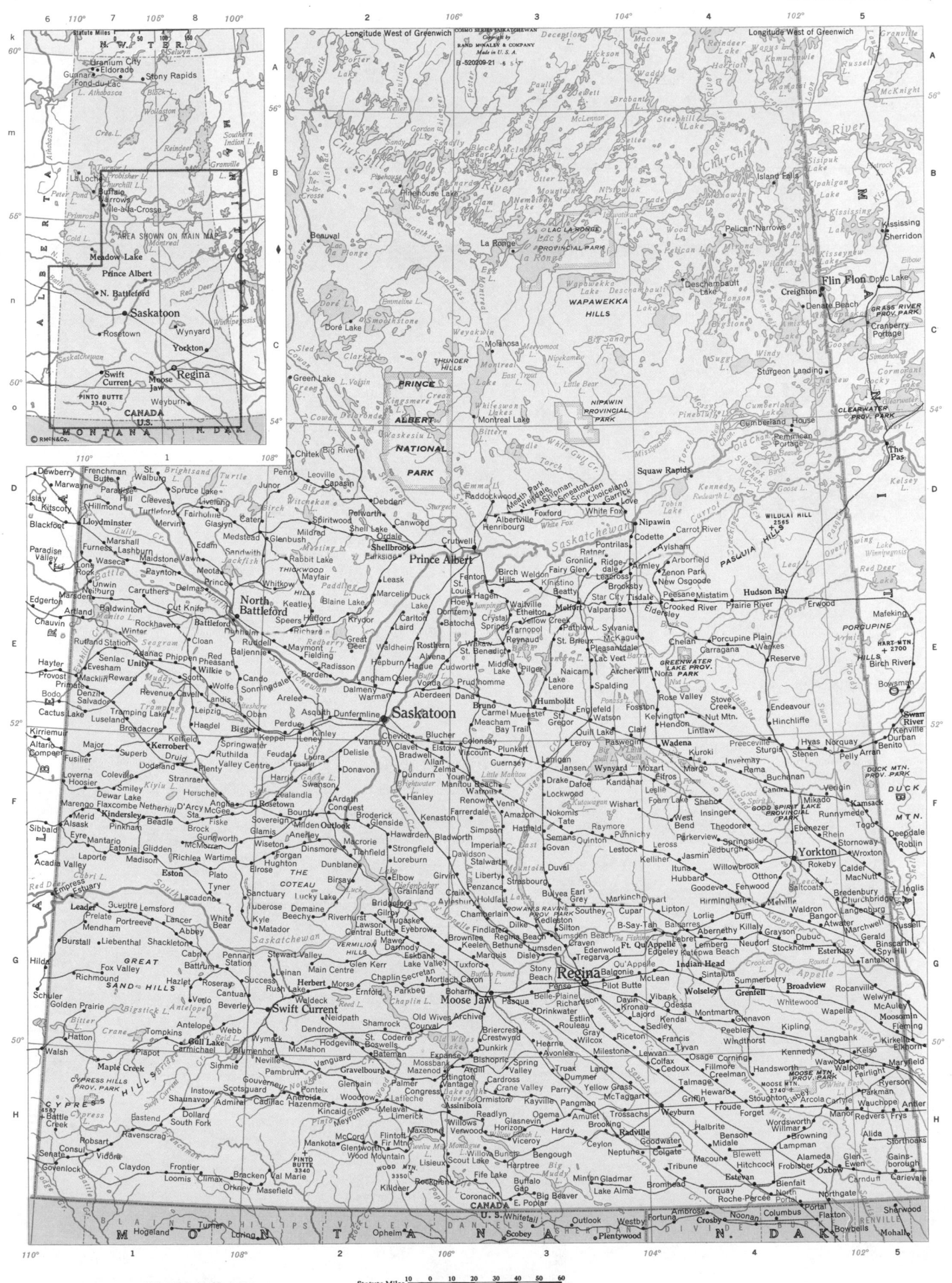

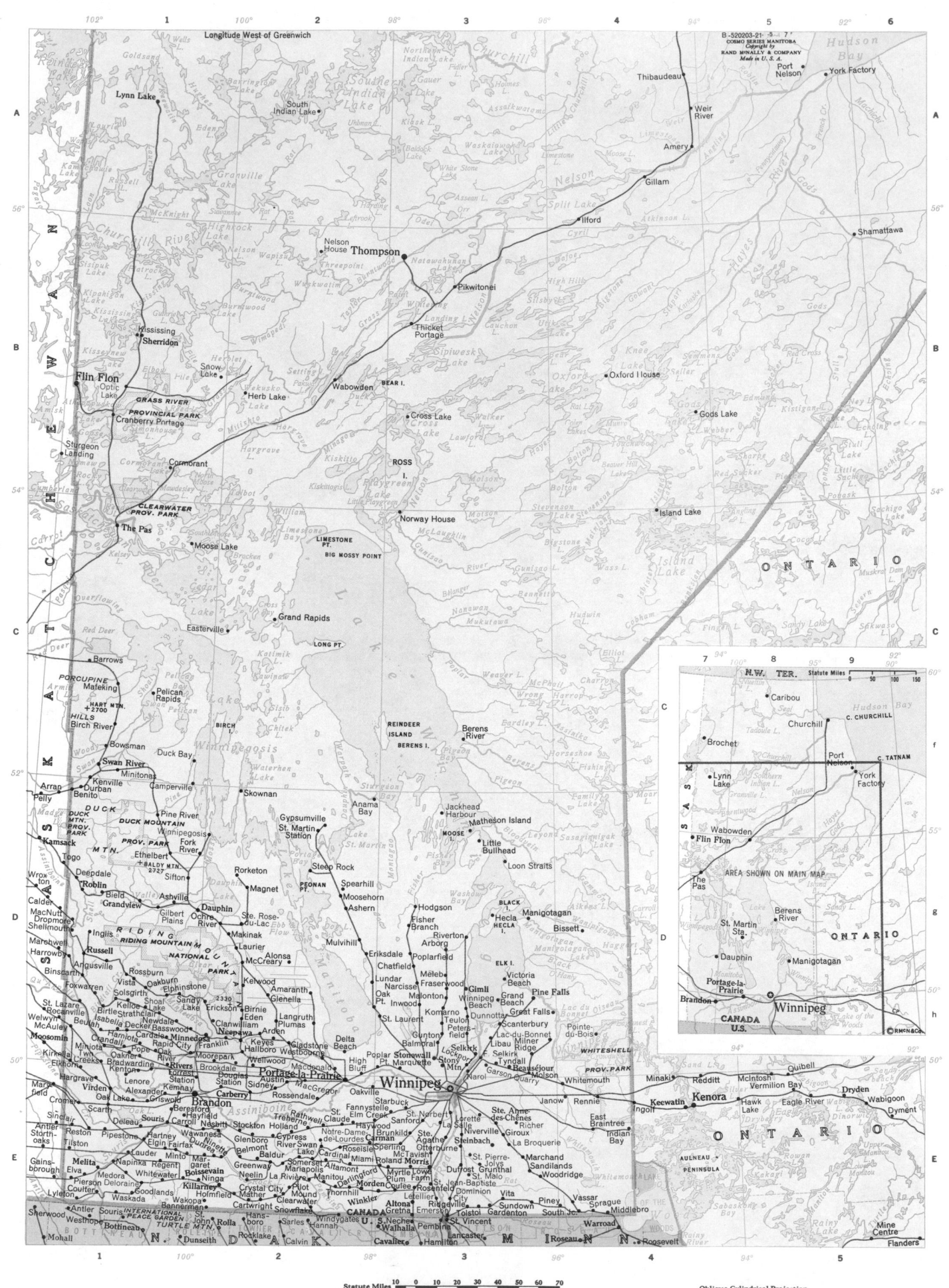

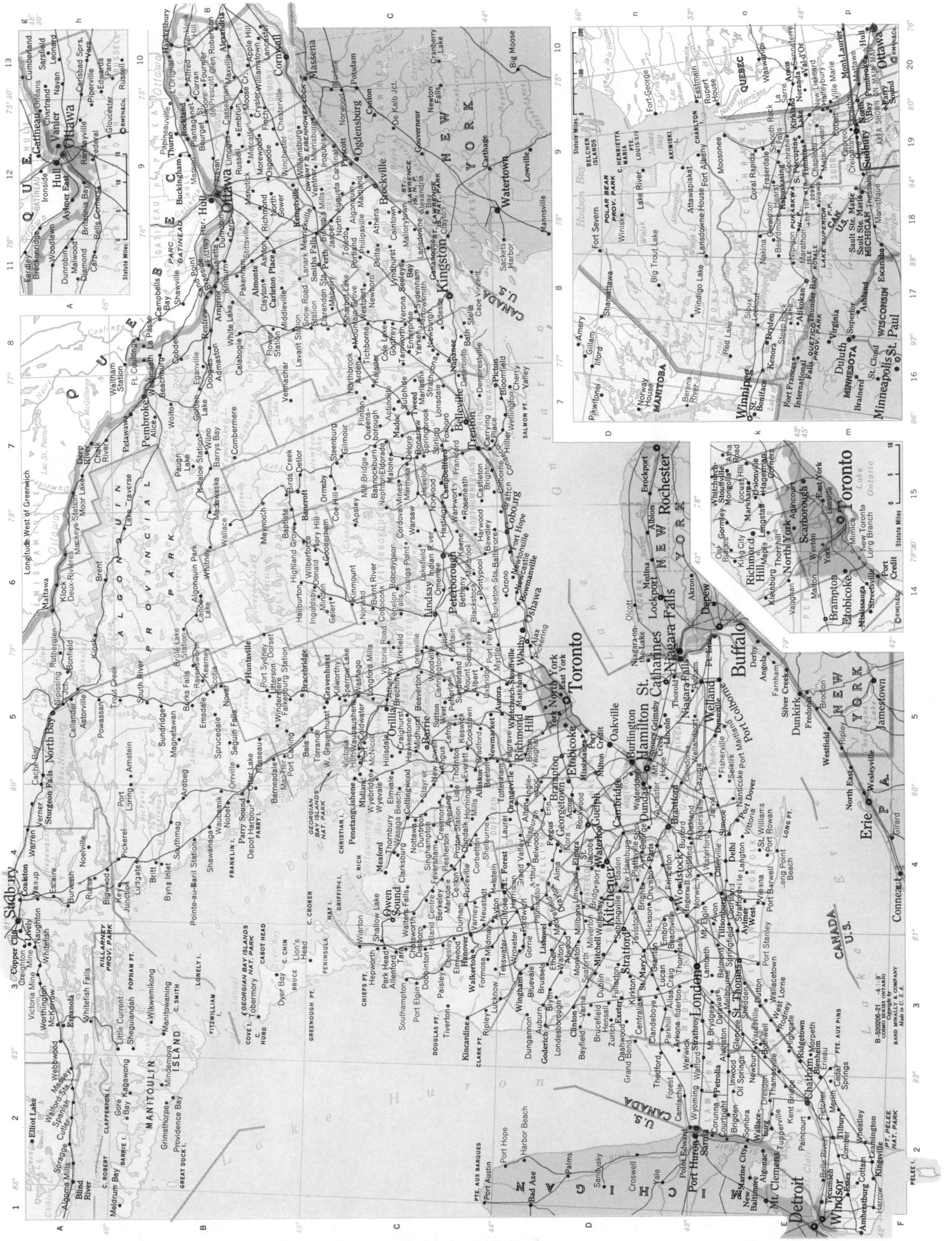

QUEBEC

ALGONQUIN PROVINCIAL PARK

NEW YORK

CANADA
U.S.

Sudbury

North Bay

Ottawa
Hull

Kingston

Brockville

Cornwall

Watertown

Owen Sound

Toronto

Hamilton

St. Catharines

Niagara Falls

Buffalo

London

Kitchener

Stratford

Sarnia

Port Huron

Windsor

Detroit

Lake Huron

Lake Ontario

Lake Erie

MANITOULIN ISLAND

GEORGIAN BAY

MICHIGAN

PENNA.

Longitude West of Greenwich

Oblique Cylindrical Projection

Statute Miles
5 0 5 10 20 30 40 50

Kilometers
5 0 5 15 25 35 45 55 65 75

B-520206-21 -4-.9'
COSMO SERIES ONTARIO
Copyright by
RAND McNALLY & COMPANY
Made in U.S.A.

QUEBEC

MANITOBA

ONTARIO

MINNESOTA

WISCONSIN

Hudson Bay

James Bay

Lake Superior

Winnipeg

Duluth

Minneapolis St. Paul

Sault Ste. Marie

Sudbury

Ottawa

POLAR BEAR PROV. PARK

QUETICO PROV. PARK

Rochester

NEW YORK

Toronto

Scarborough

North York

Etobicoke

Mississauga

Brampton

Markham

Statute Miles
0 5 10

Lake Ontario

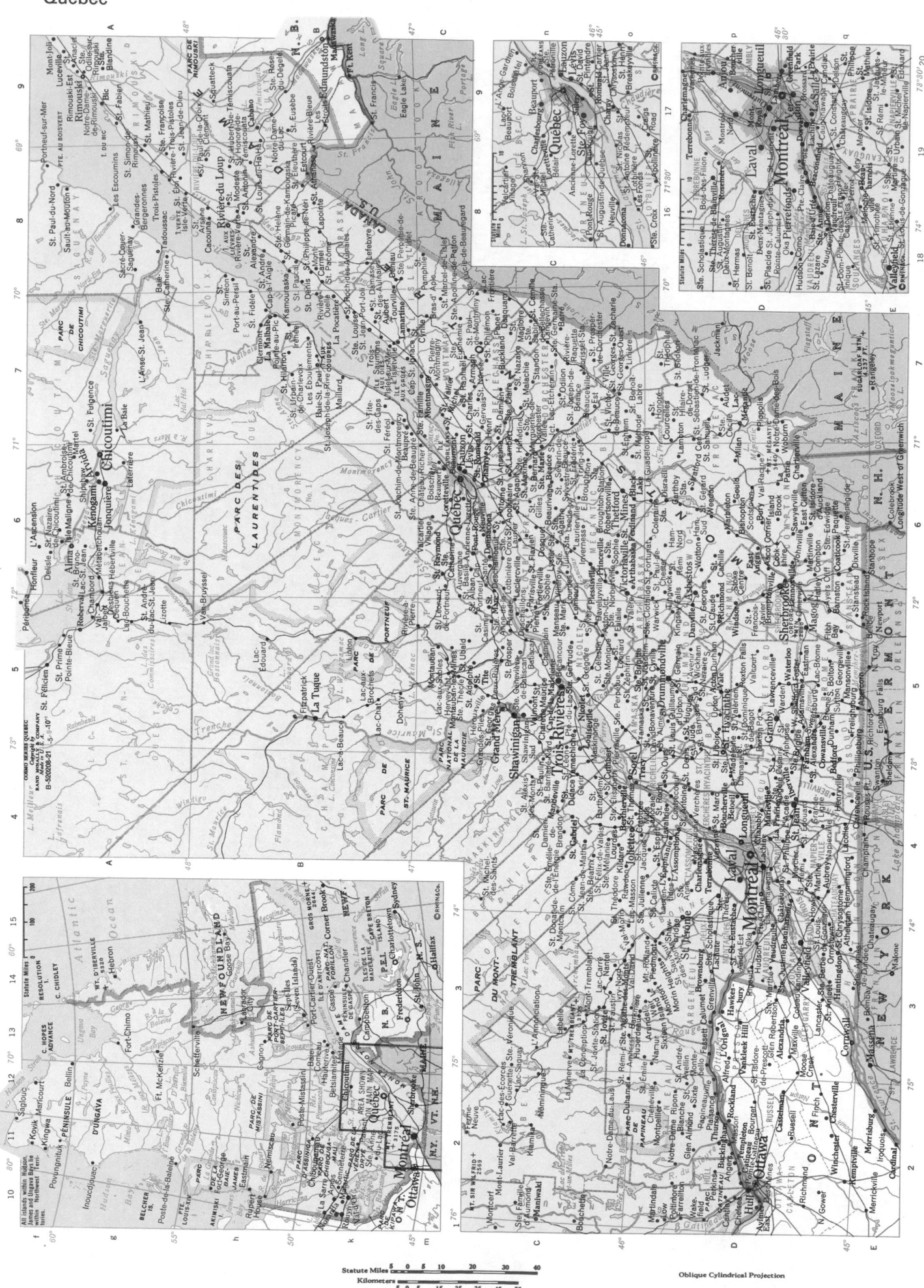

Statute Miles

Kilometers

Oblique Cylindrical Projection

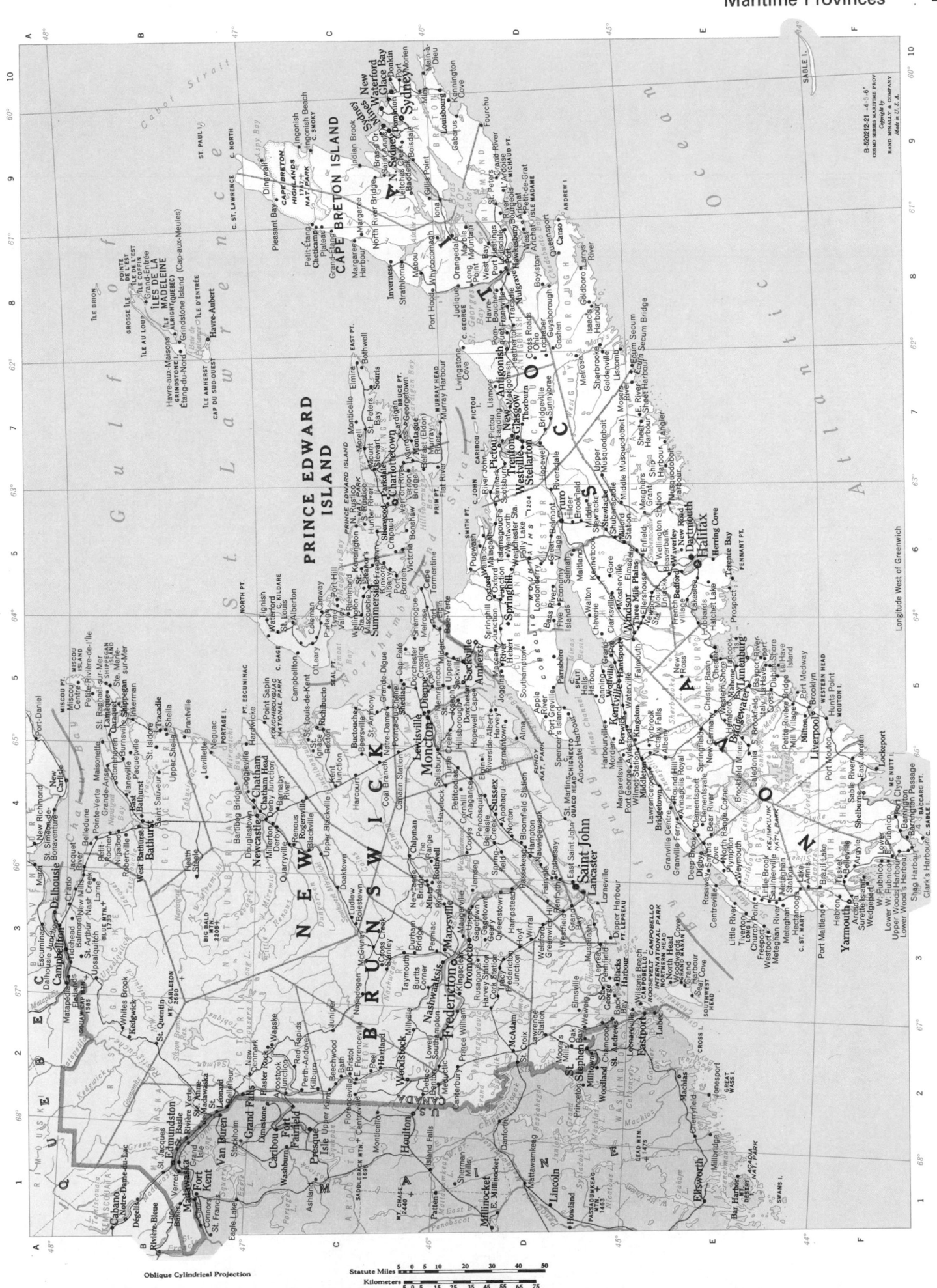

Oblique Cylindrical Projection

Statute Miles

Kilometers

B-500212-21 -4 -6'
COSMO SERIES MARITIME PROV.
Copyright by
RAND M9NALLY & COMPANY
Made in U.S.A.

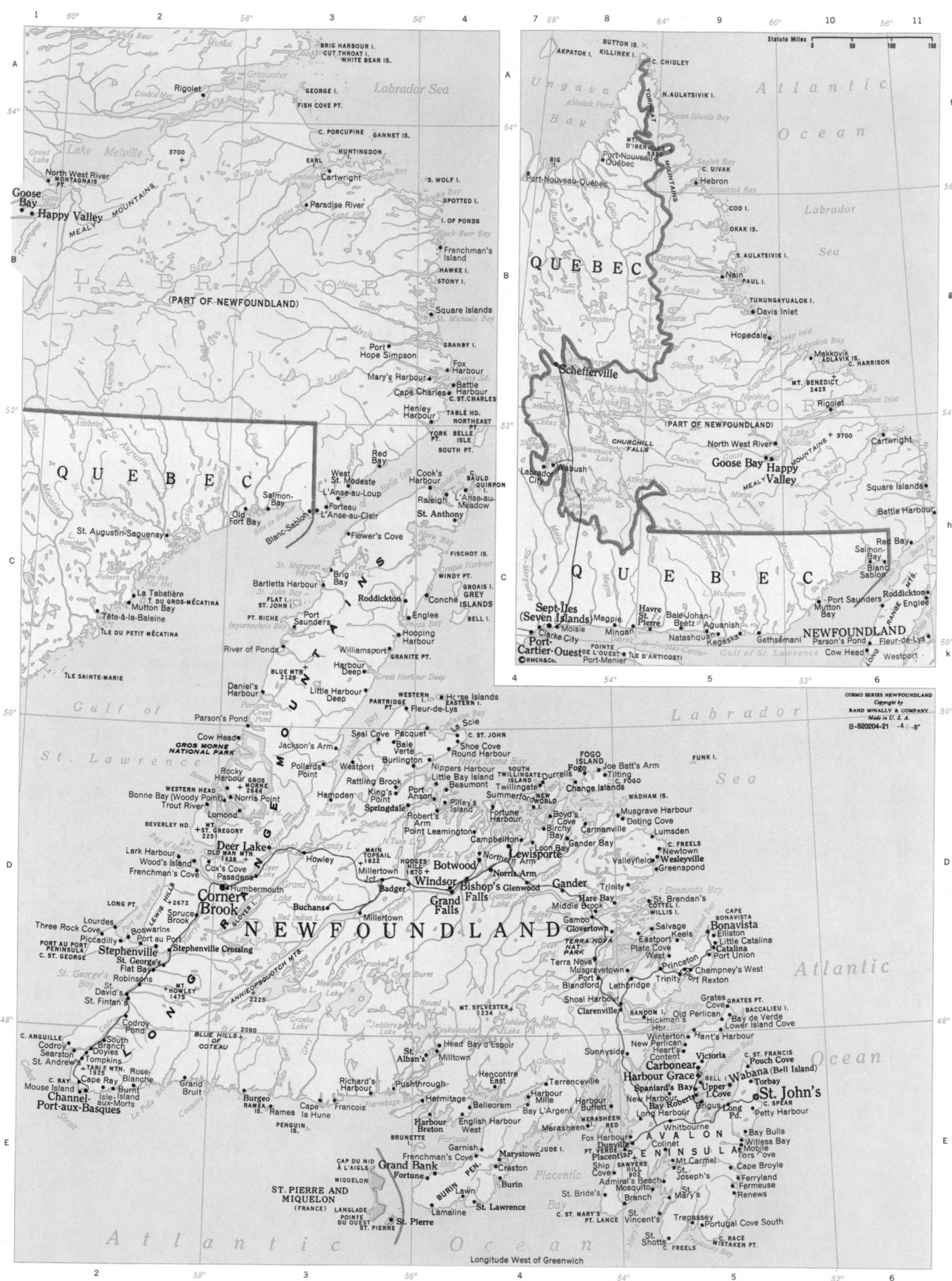

COSMO SERIES NEWFOUNDLAND
Copyright by
RAND McNALLY & COMPANY
Made in U.S.A.
B-520204-21 -4 -8°

Statute Miles 5 0 5 10   20   30   40   50   60
Kilometers 5 0 5 10 20 30 40 50 60 70 80

Lambert Conformal Conic Projection

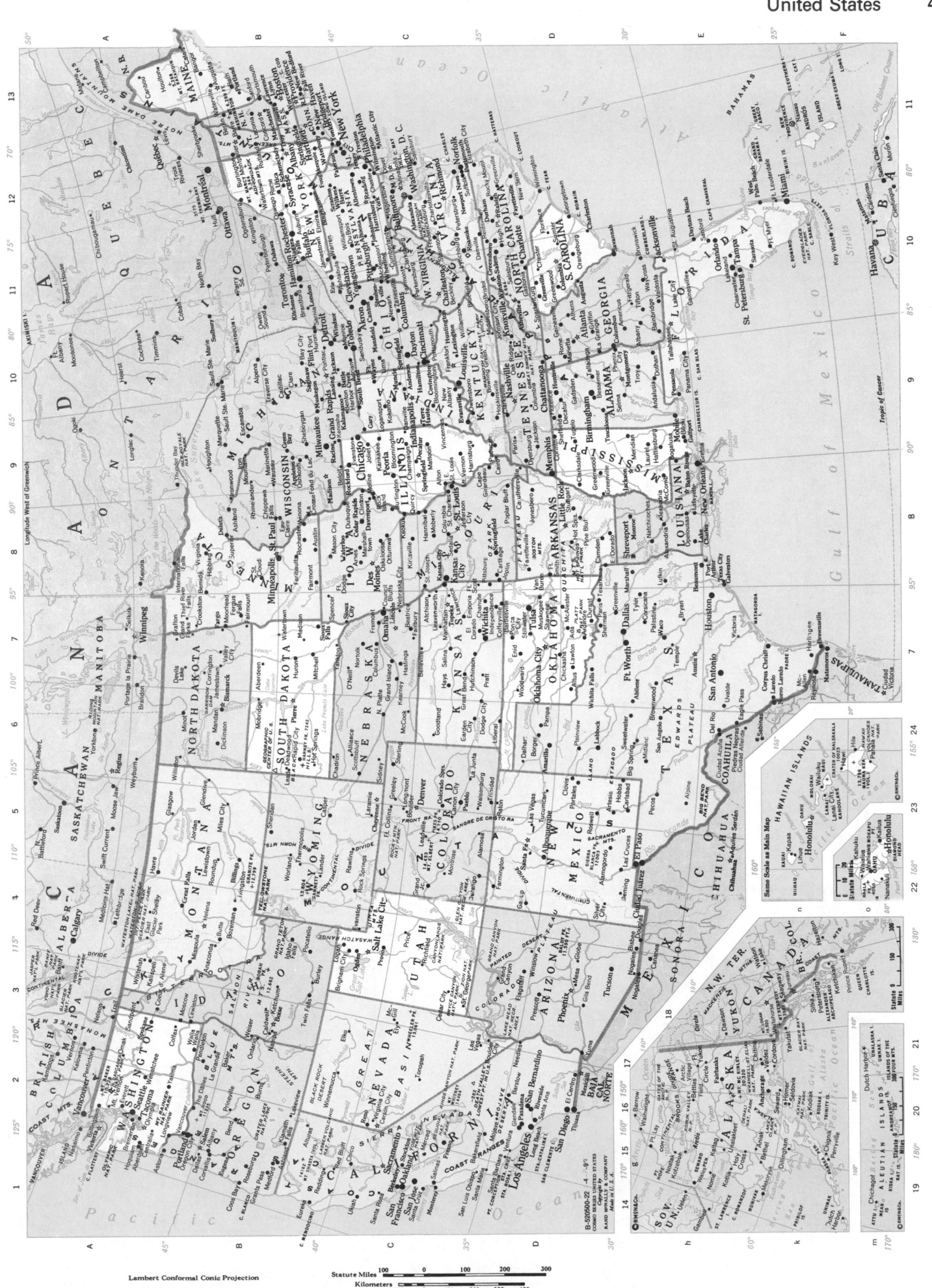

Lambert Conformal Conic Projection

Statute Miles
100   0   100   200   300

Kilometers
100   0   100   200   300   400

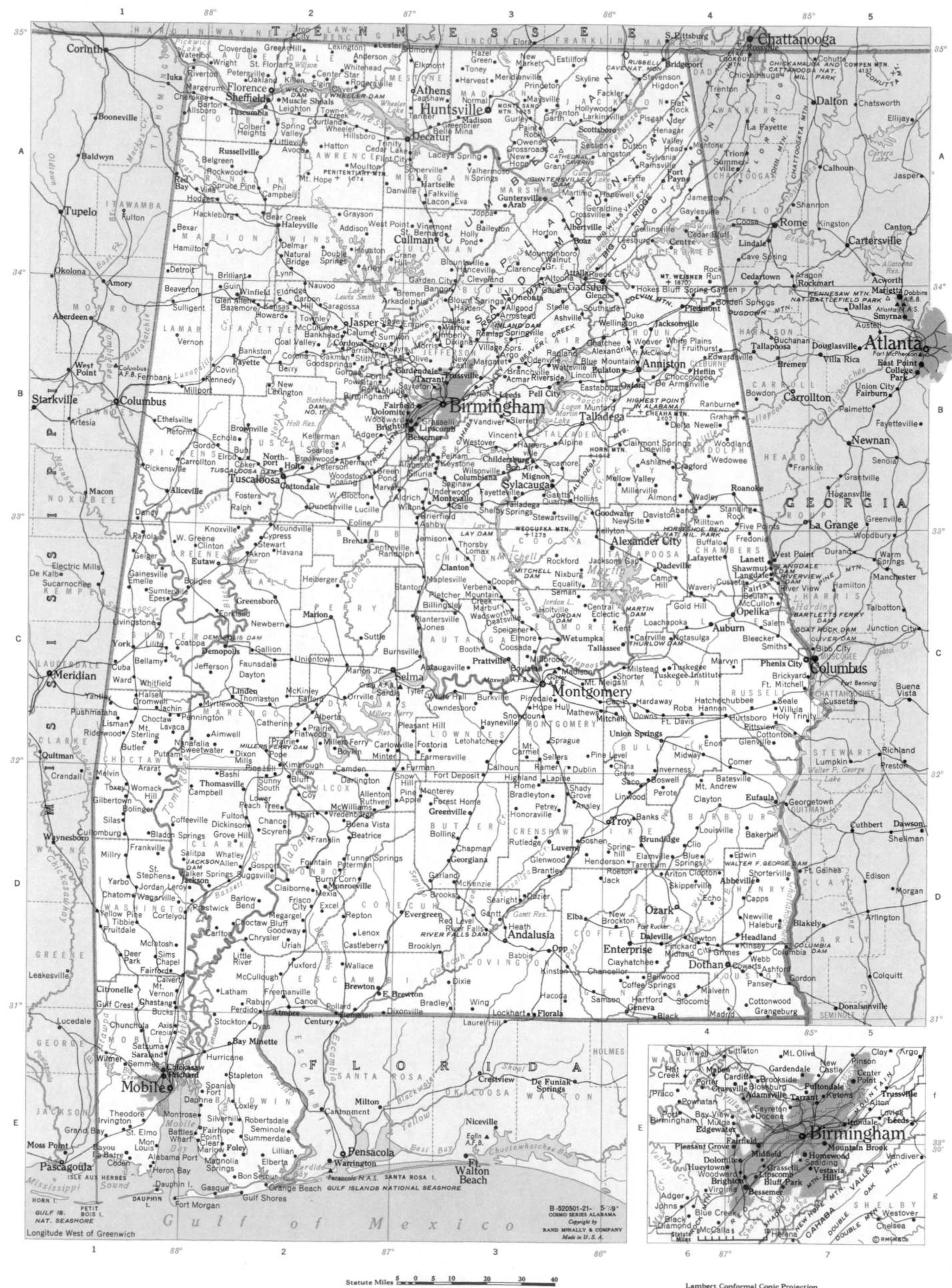

Statute Miles 5 0 5 10 20 30 40
Kilometers 5 0 15 25 35 45 55

Lambert Conformal Conic Projection

Longitude West of Greenwich

B-520501-21-5 7-9
COSMO SERIES ALABAMA
Copyright by
RAND McNALLY & COMPANY
Made in U.S.A.

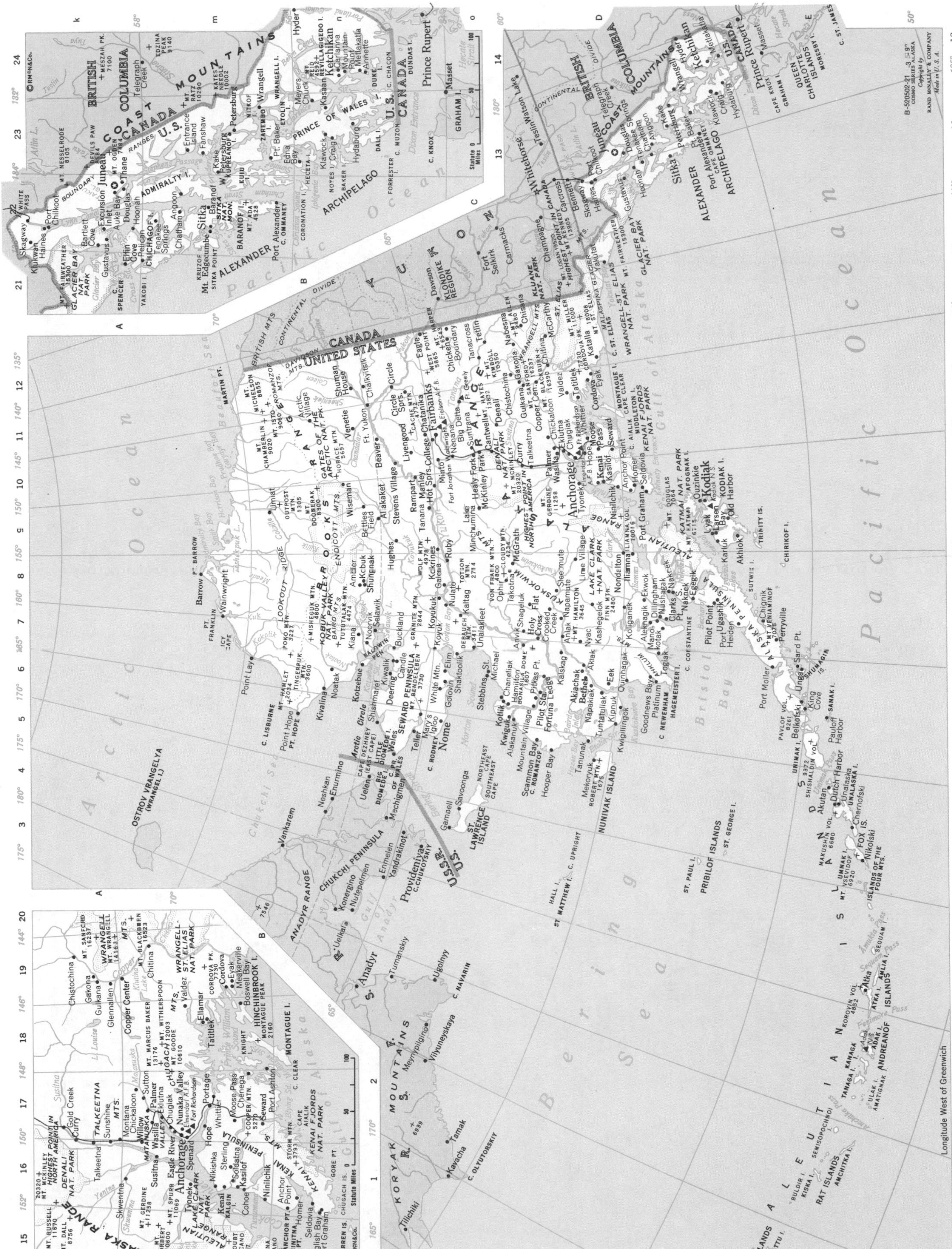

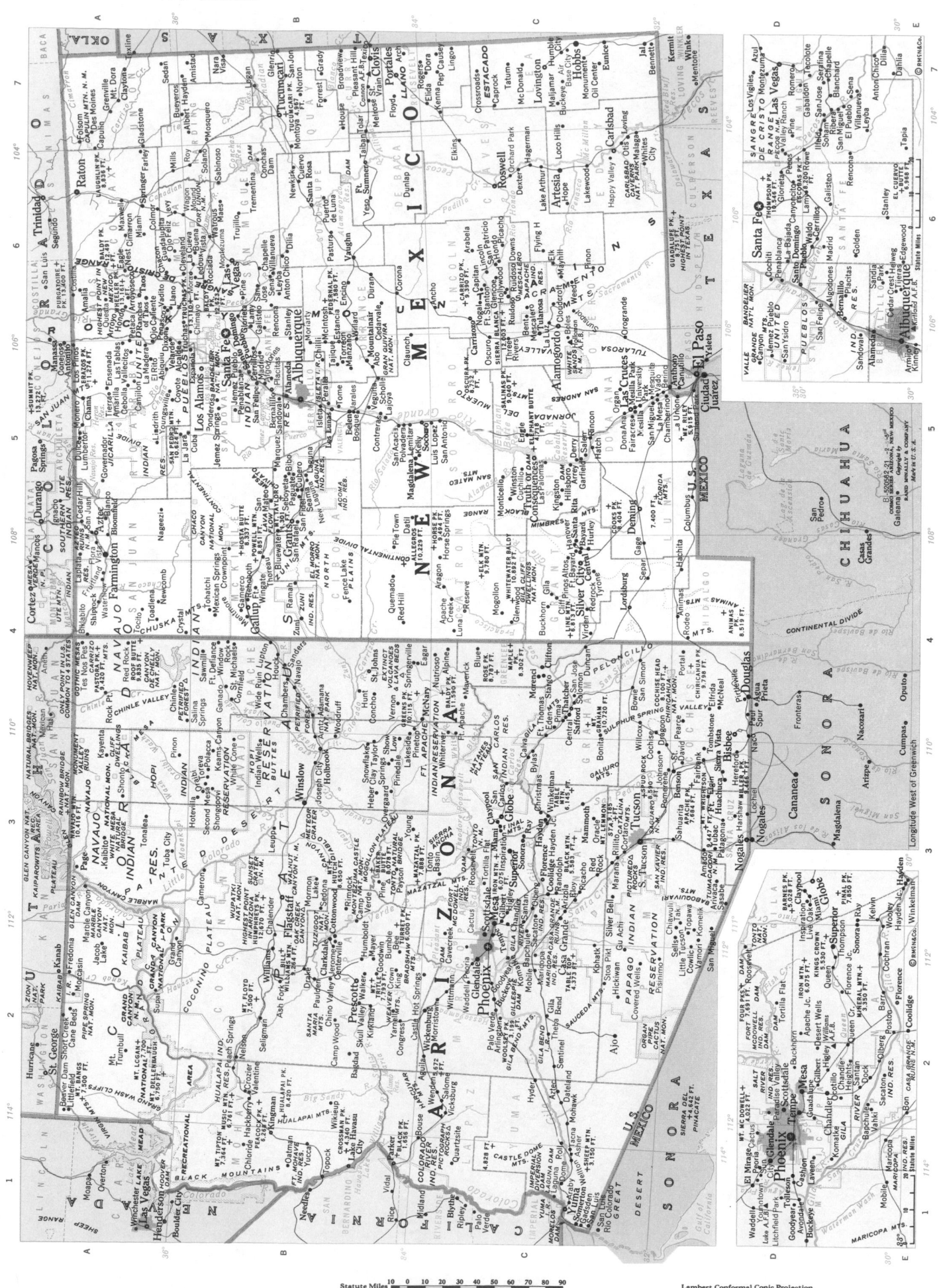

Statute Miles 10 0 10 20 30 40 50 60 70 80 90

Kilometers 10 0 10 20 30 40 50 60 70 80 90 100 120

Lambert Conformal Conic Projection

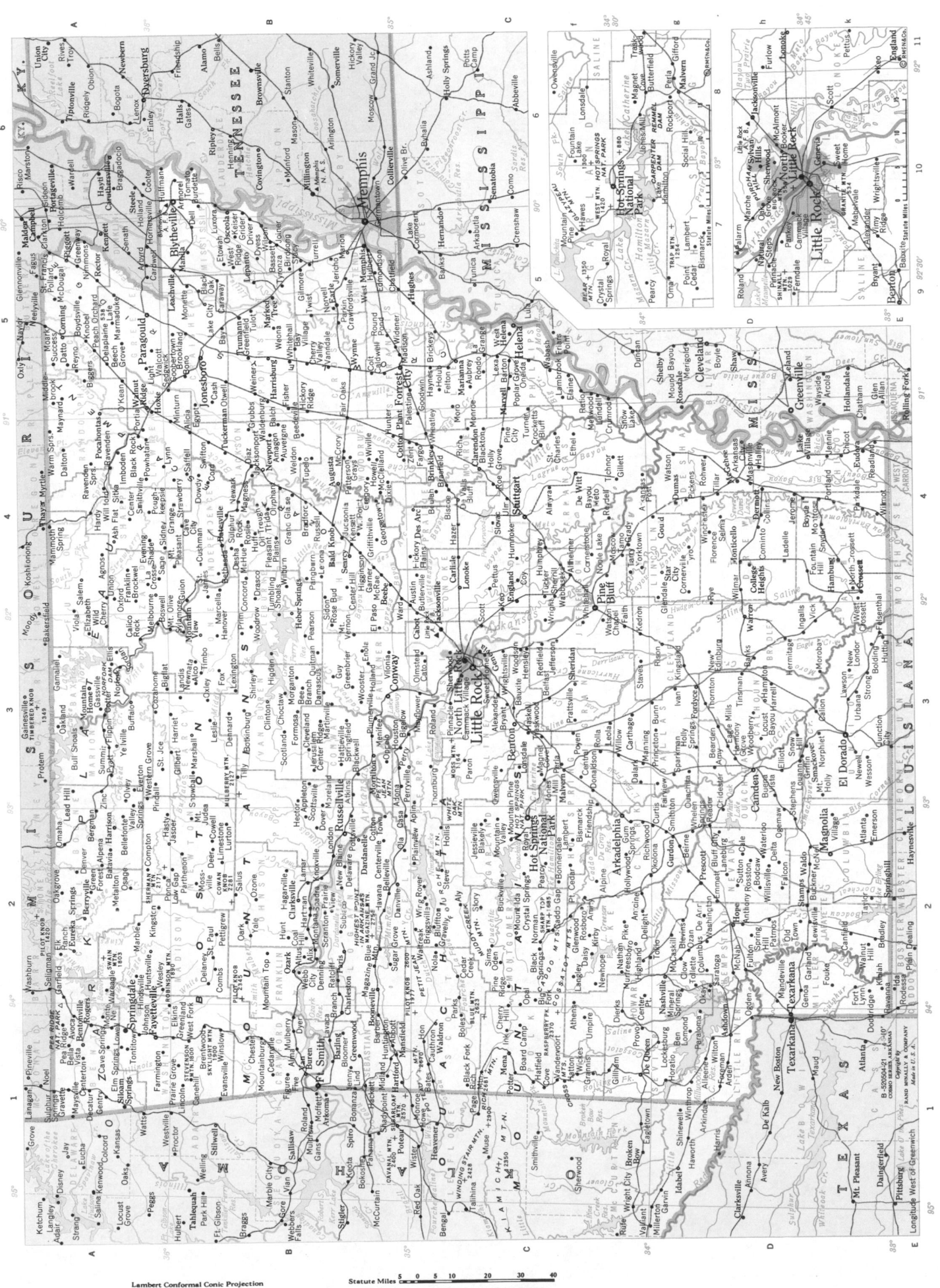

Statute Miles

Kilometers

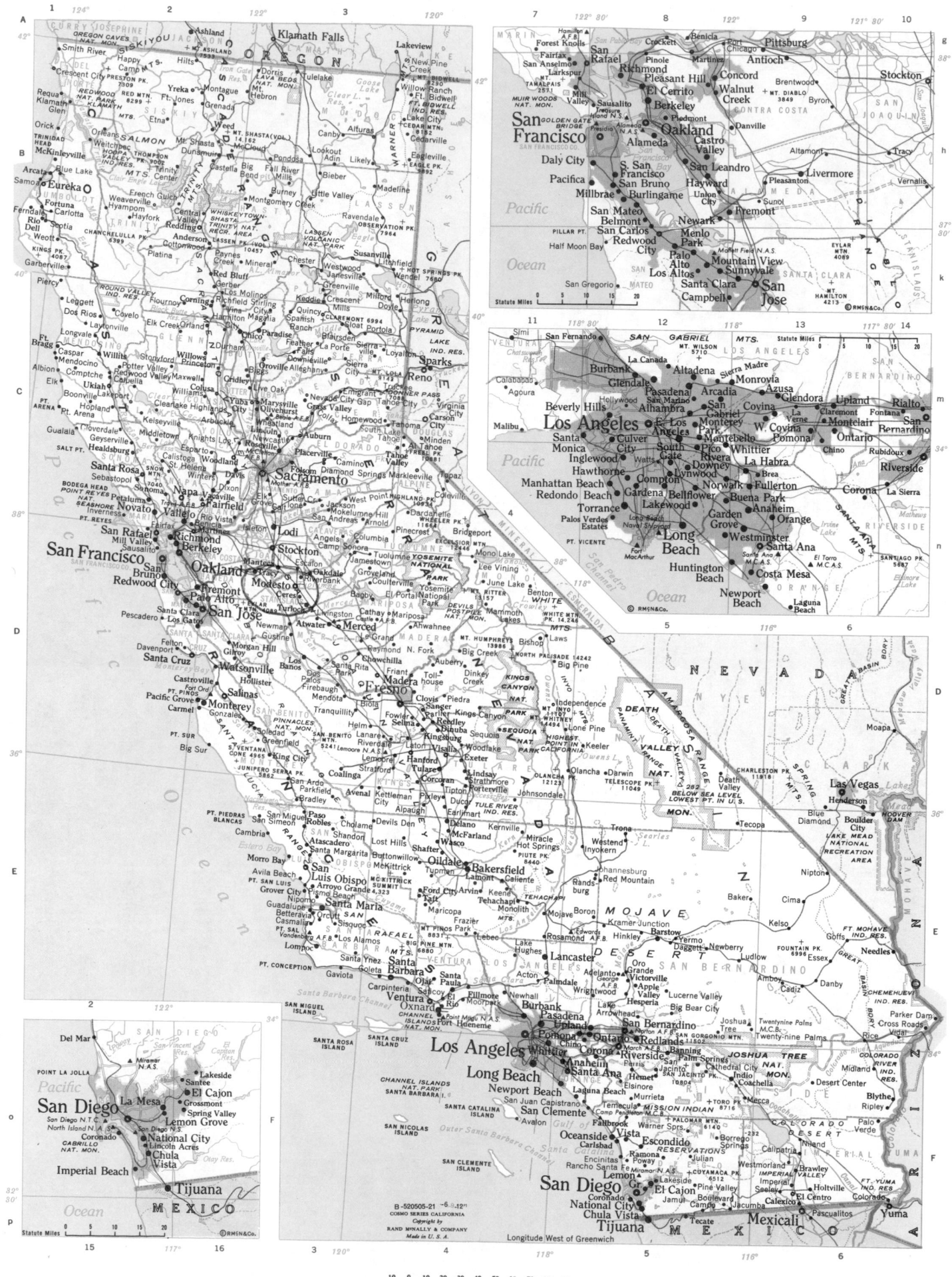

Statute Miles 10 0 10 20 30 40 50 60 70 80 90
Kilometers 10 0 10 20 40 60 80 100 120

Lambert Conformal Conic Projection

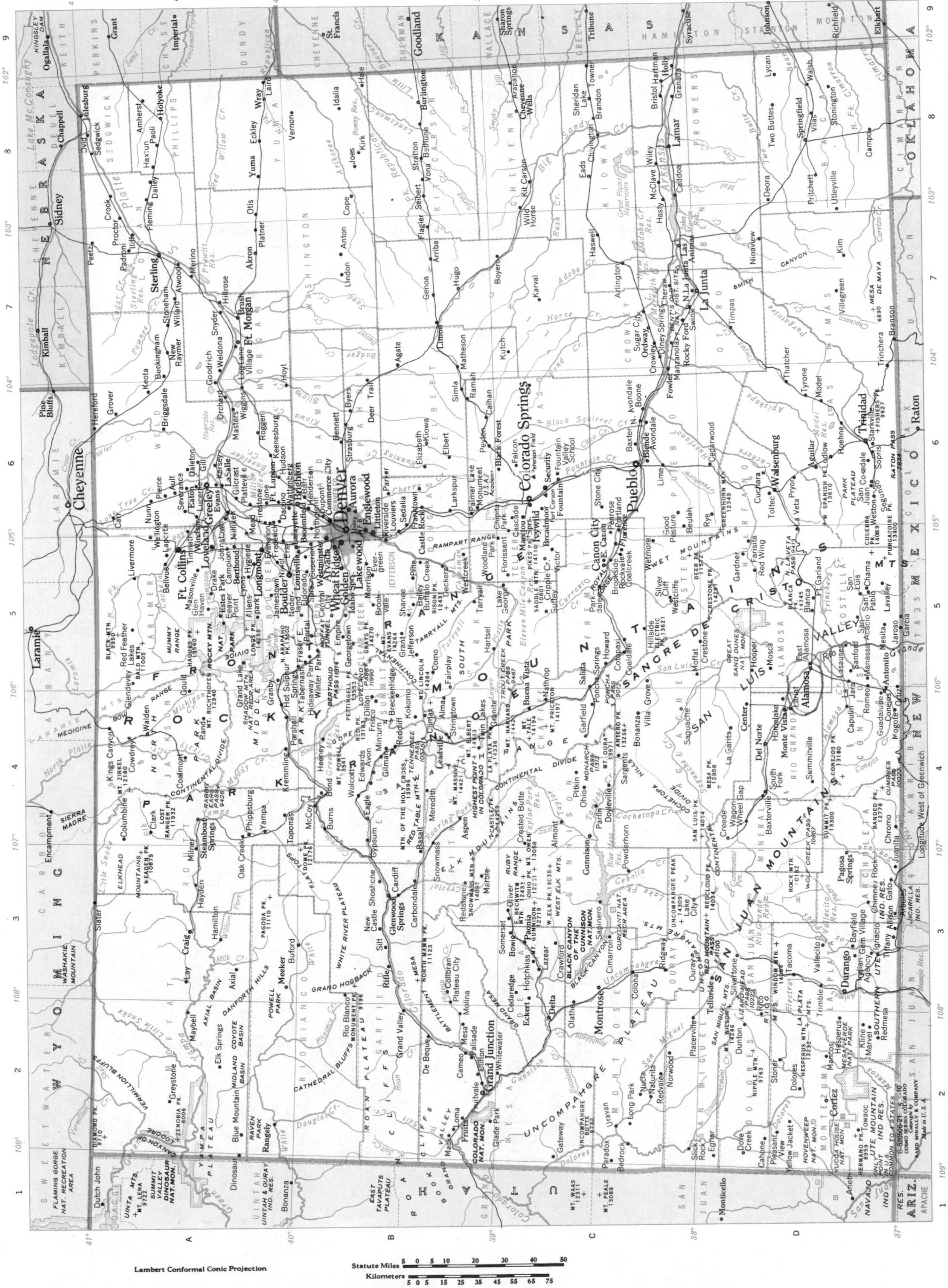

Lambert Conformal Conic Projection

Statute Miles
5 0 5 10 20 30 40 50

Kilometers
5 0 5 15 25 35 45 55 65 75

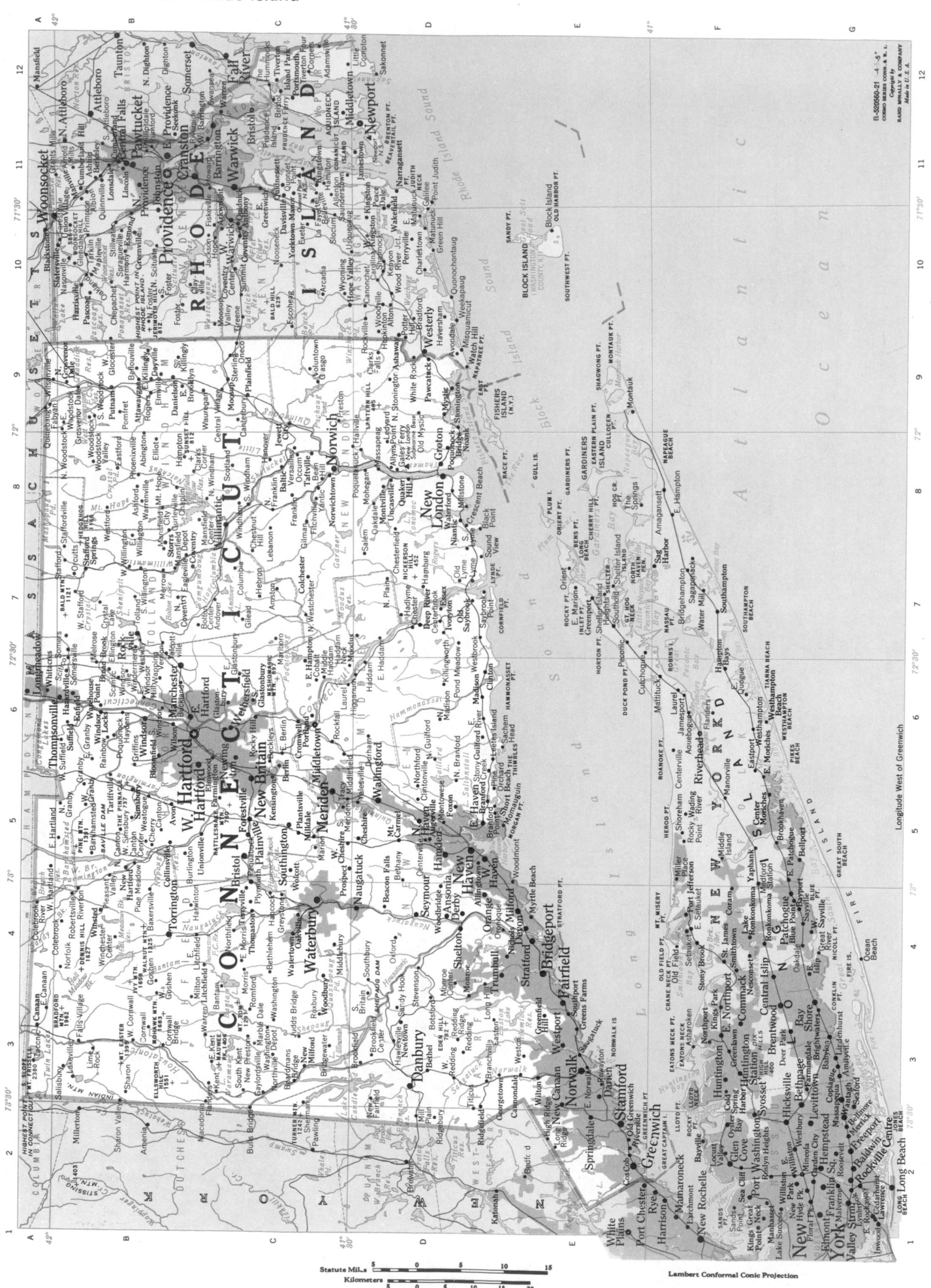

Statute Miles

Kilometers

Lambert Conformal Conic Projection

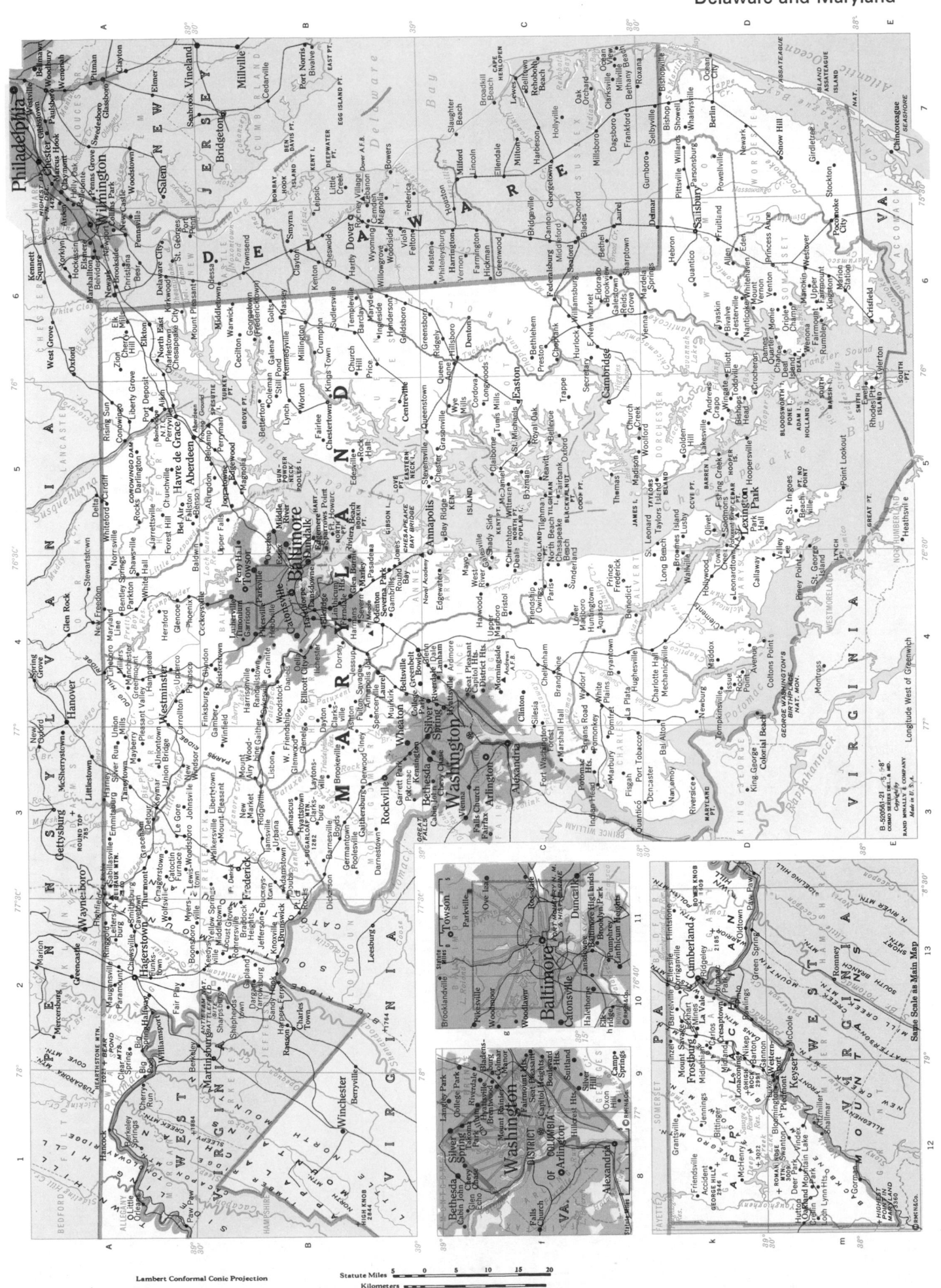

Lambert Conformal Conic Projection

Statute Miles

Kilometers

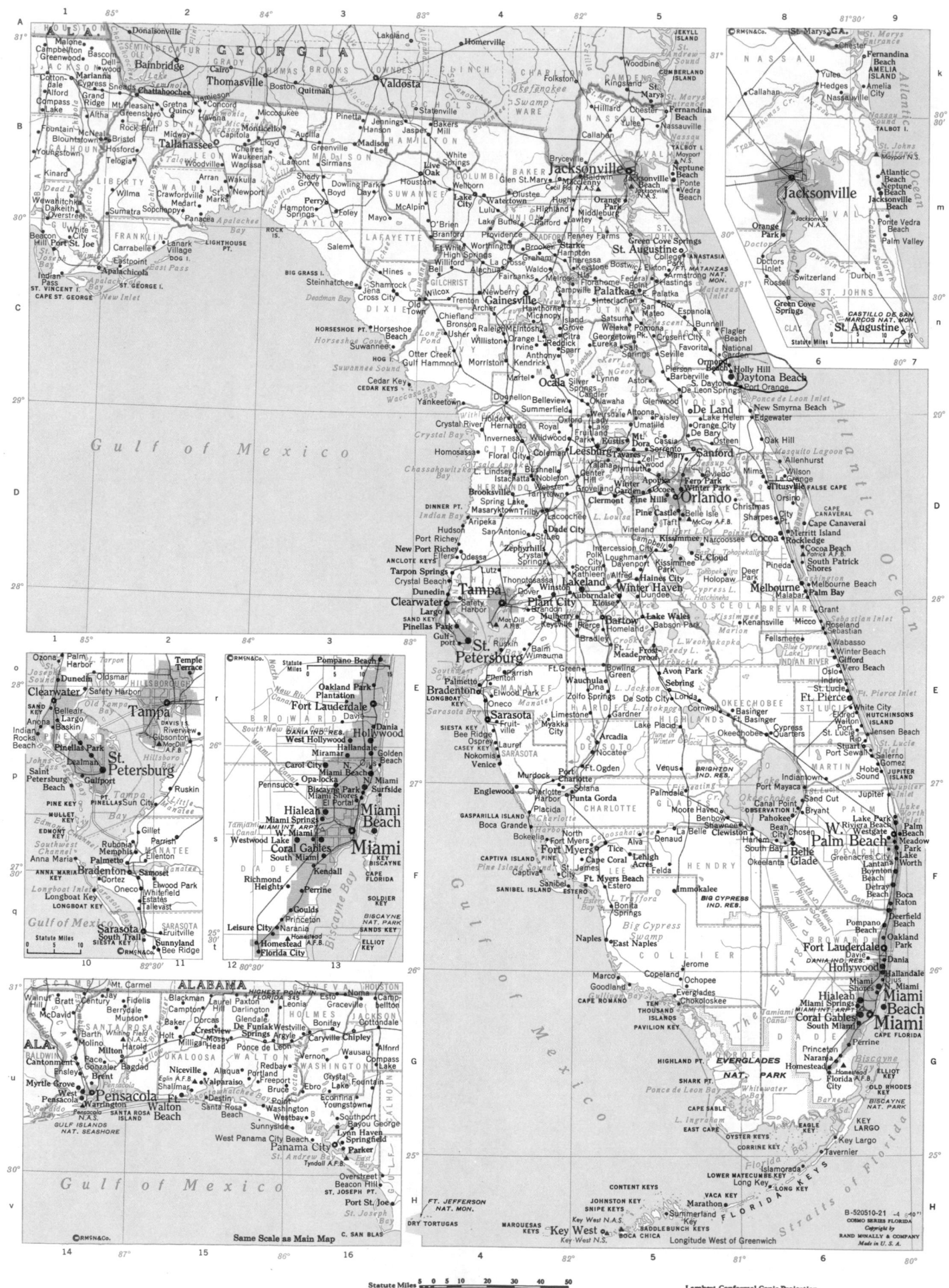

Statute Miles 5 0 5 10   20   30   40   50
Kilometers 5 0 5 15 25 35 45 65

Lambert Conformal Conic Projection

B-520510-21 -4
COSMO SERIES FLORIDA
Copyright by
RAND McNALLY & COMPANY
Made in U.S.A.

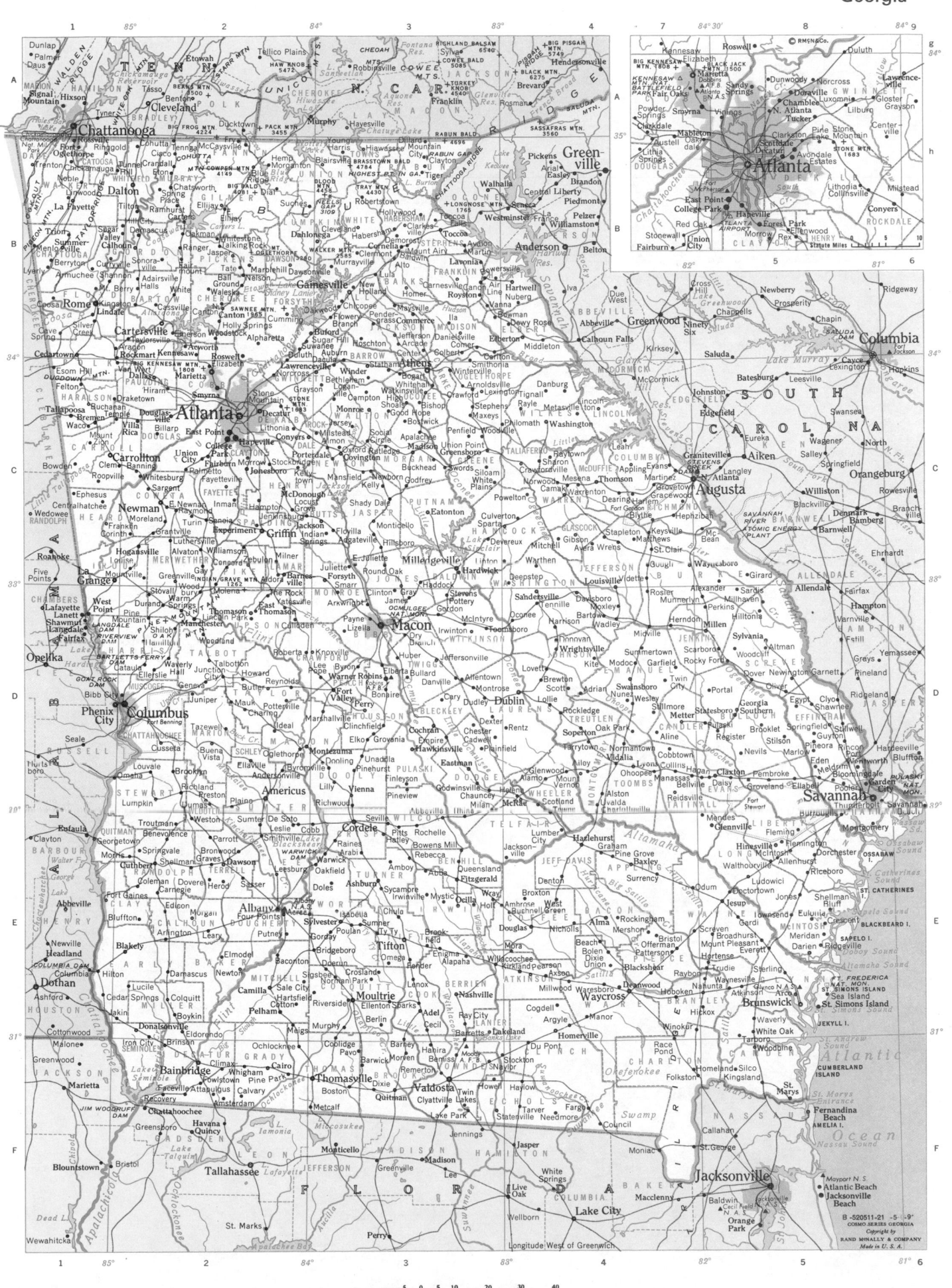

Lambert Conformal Conic Projection

Statute Miles
5 0 5 10 20 30 40

Kilometers
5 0 5 15 25 35 45 55

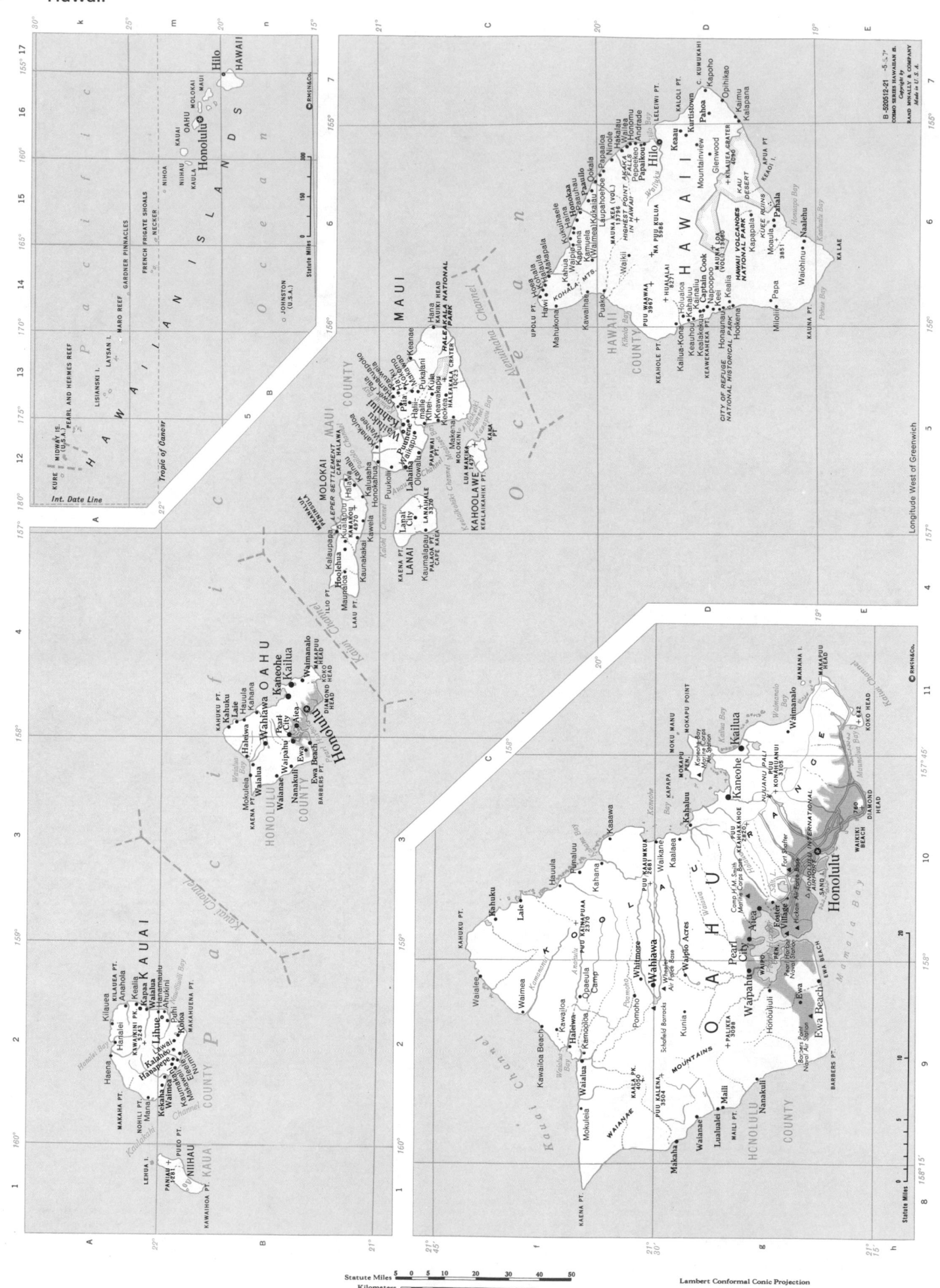

B-520512-21 -5-57*

COSMO SERIES HAWAIIAN &.
Copyright by
RAND McNALLY & COMPANY
Made in U.S.A.

Statute Miles

Kilometers

Lambert Conformal Conic Projection

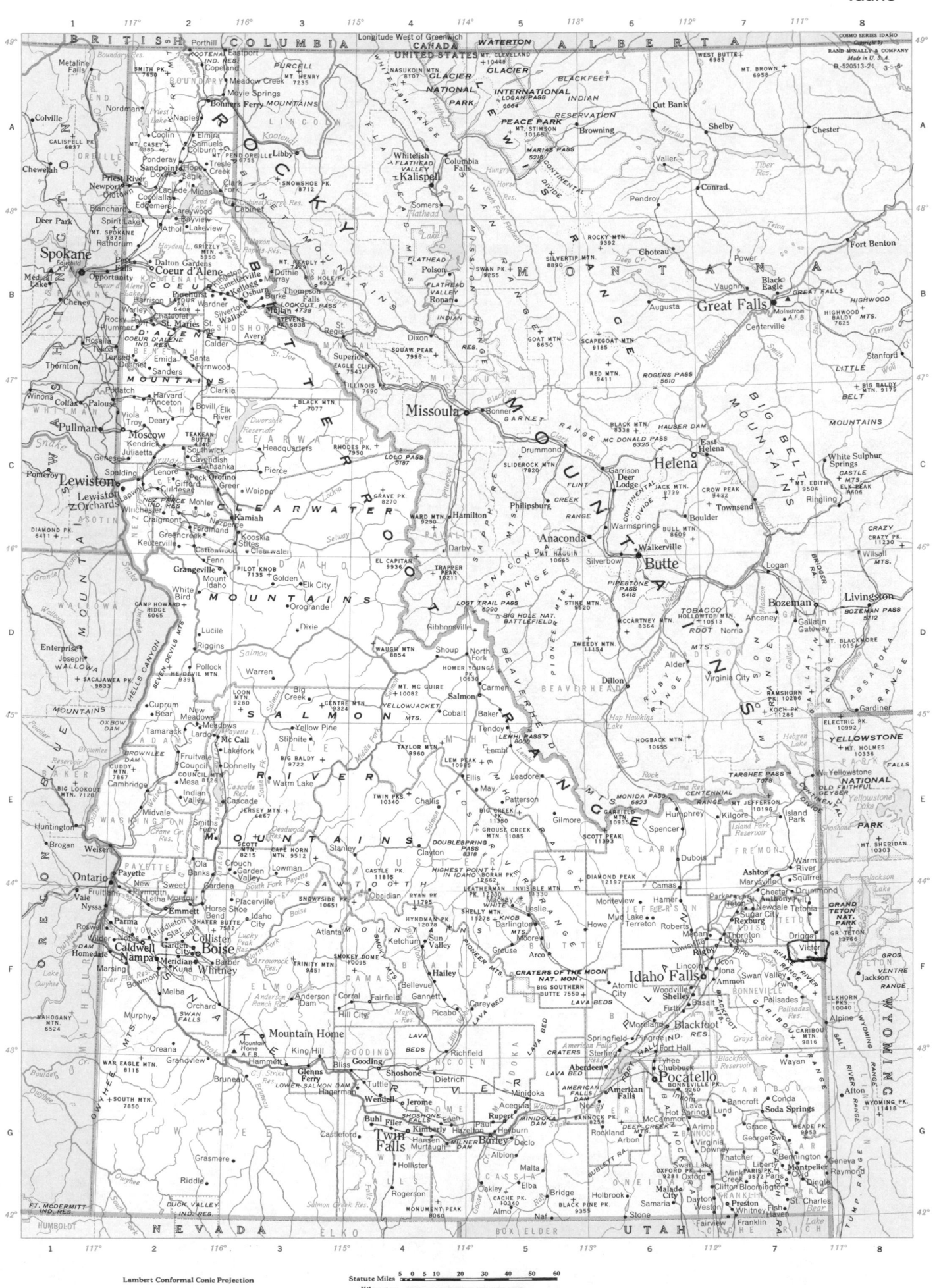

Lambert Conformal Conic Projection

Statute Miles

Kilometers

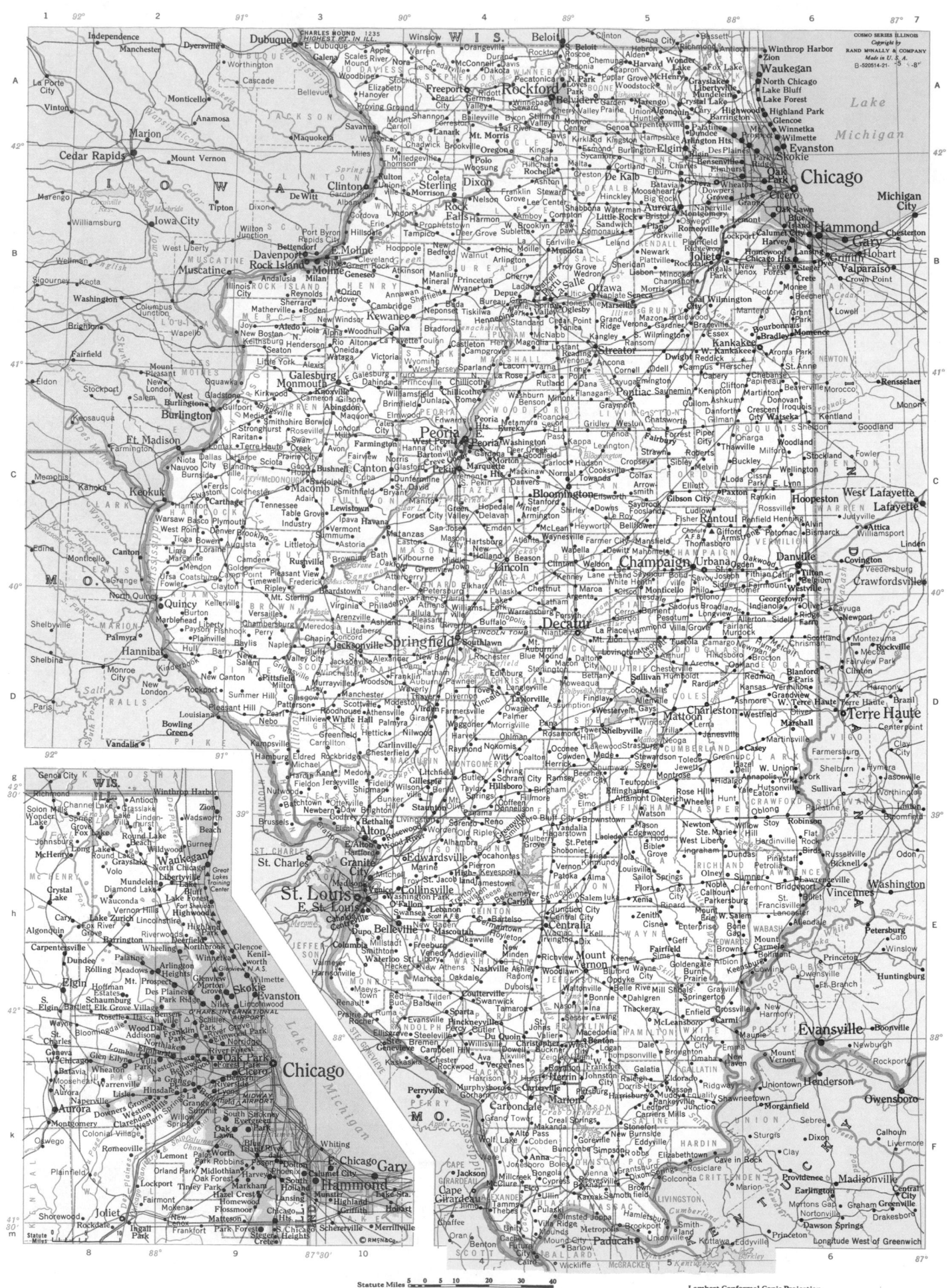

COSMO SERIES ILLINOIS
Copyright by
RAND McNALLY & COMPANY
Made in U.S.A.
B-520514-21

Statute Miles 5 0 10 20 30 40
Kilometers 5 0 15 25 35 45 55

Lambert Conformal Conic Projection

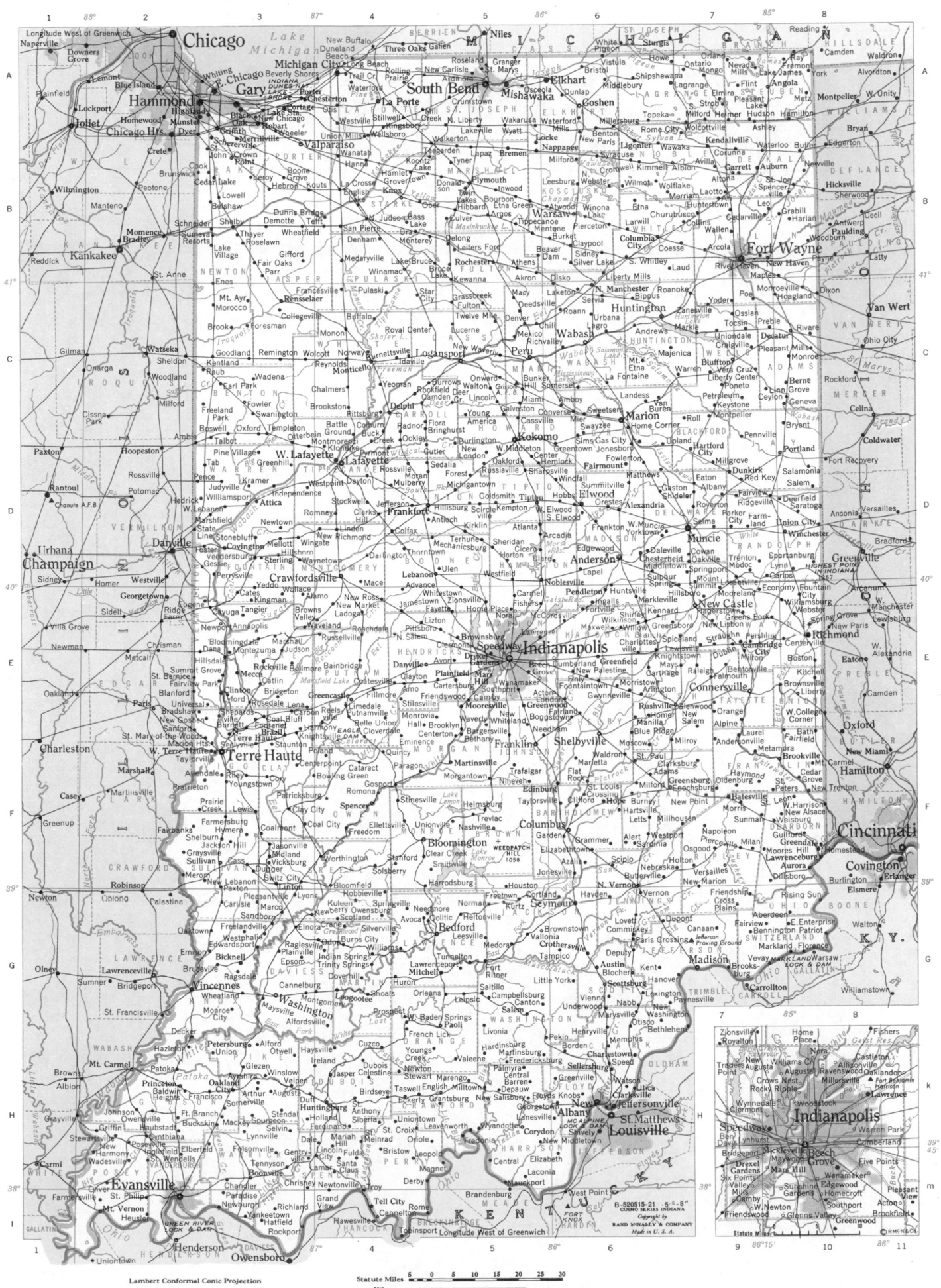

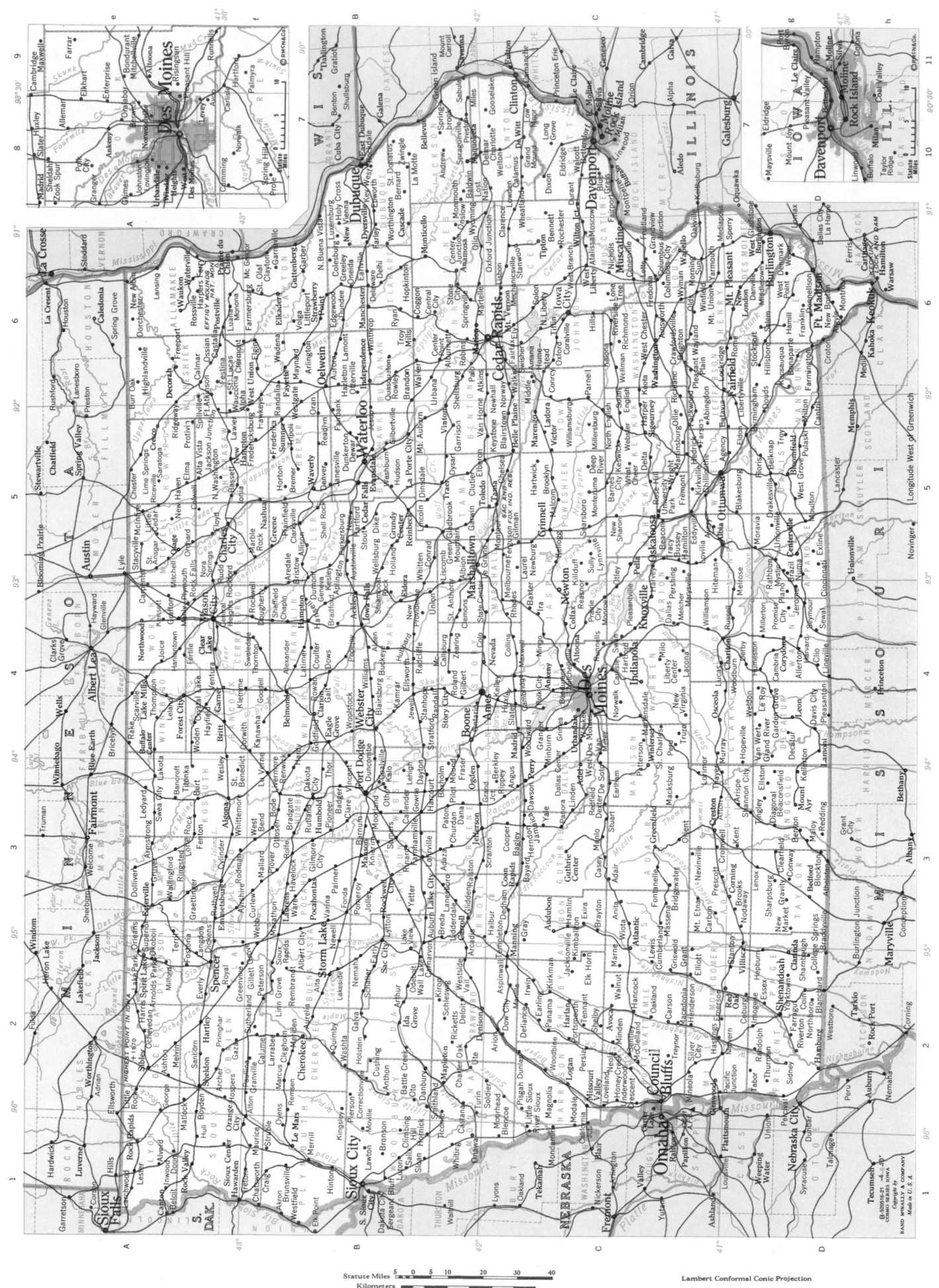

Statute Miles

Kilometers

Lambert Conformal Conic Projection

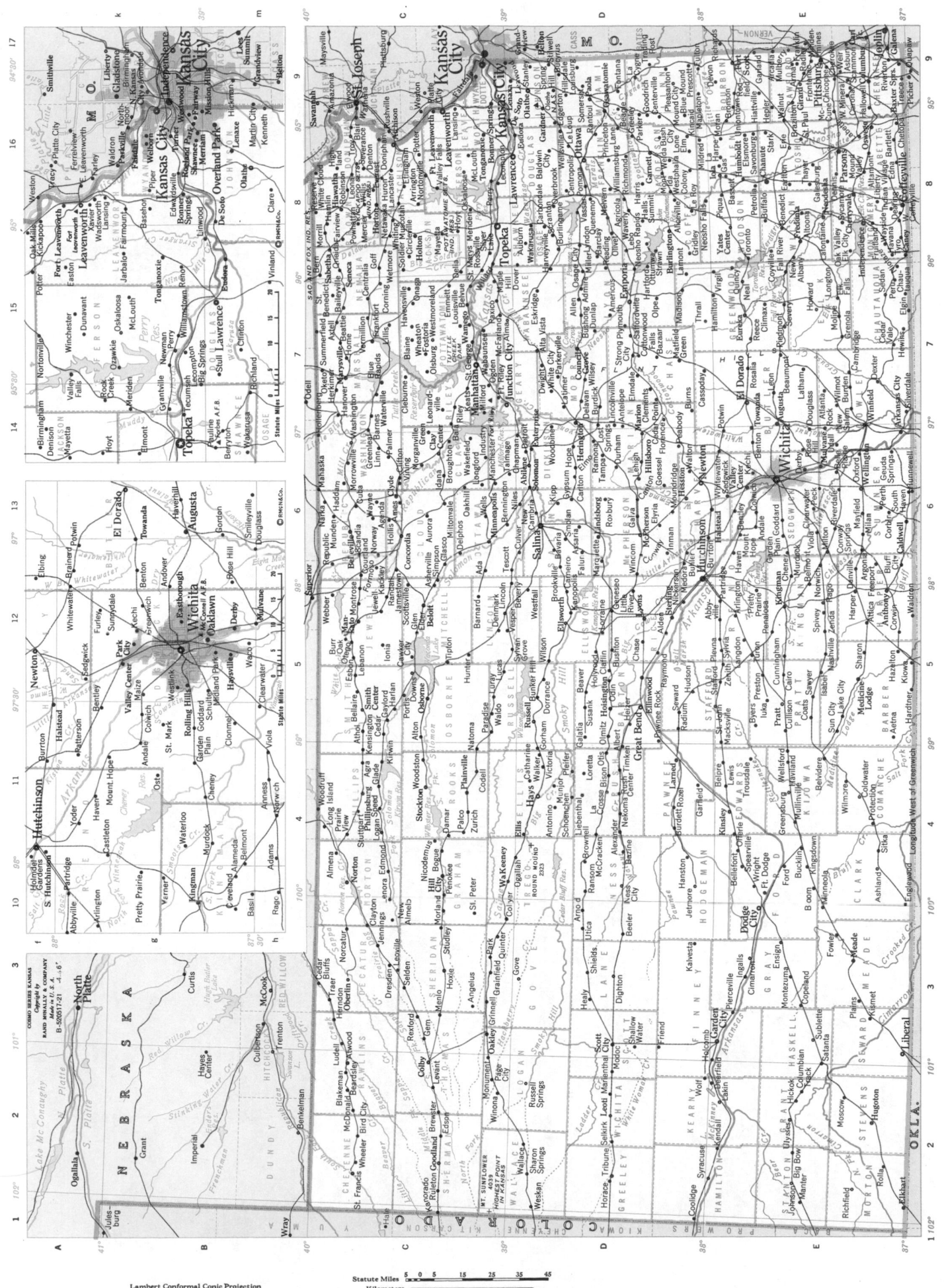

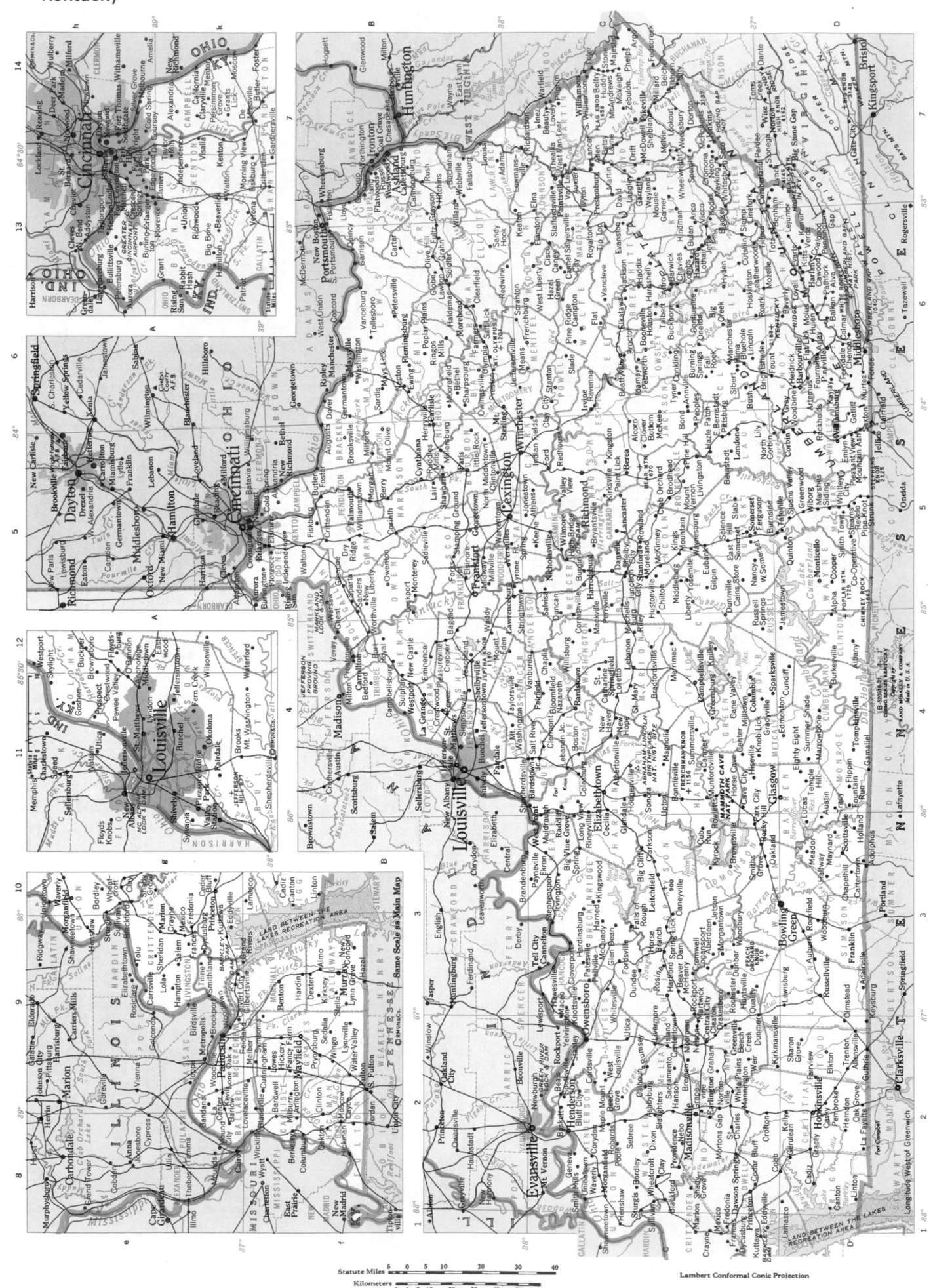

Statute Miles 5 0 5 10 20 30 40

Kilometers 5 0 5 10 20 30 40 50 60

Lambert Conformal Conic Projection

Lambert Conformal Conic Projection

Statute Miles 5 0 5 10 20 30 40

Kilometers 5 0 5 15 25 35 45 55

Longitude West of Greenwich

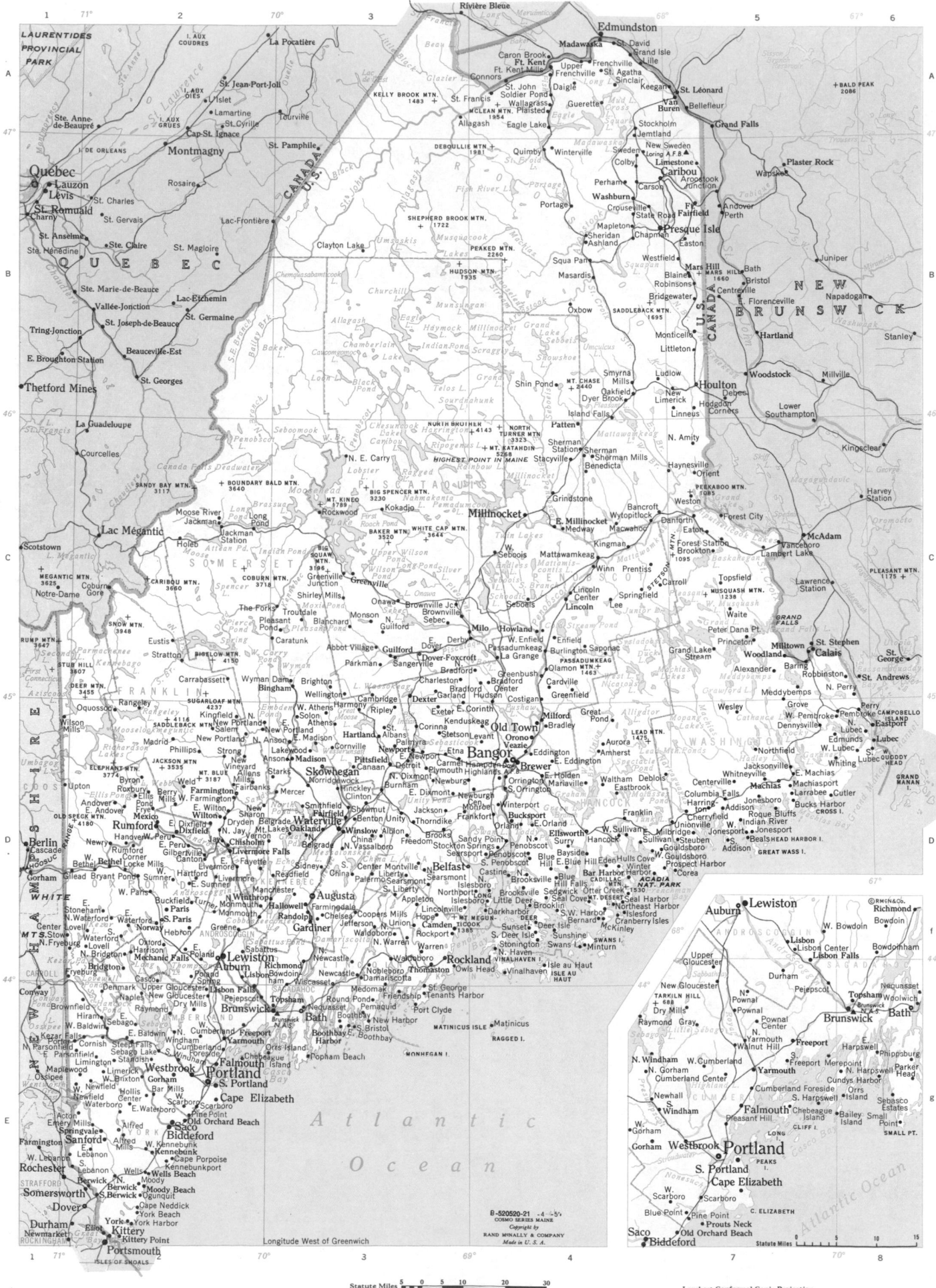

Statute Miles   5 0 5   10   20   30

Kilometers   5 0 5 10   20   30   40

Lambert Conformal Conic Projection

Longitude West of Greenwich

B-520520-21 -4 -5½
COSMO SERIES MAINE
Copyright by
RAND McNALLY & COMPANY
Made in U.S.A.

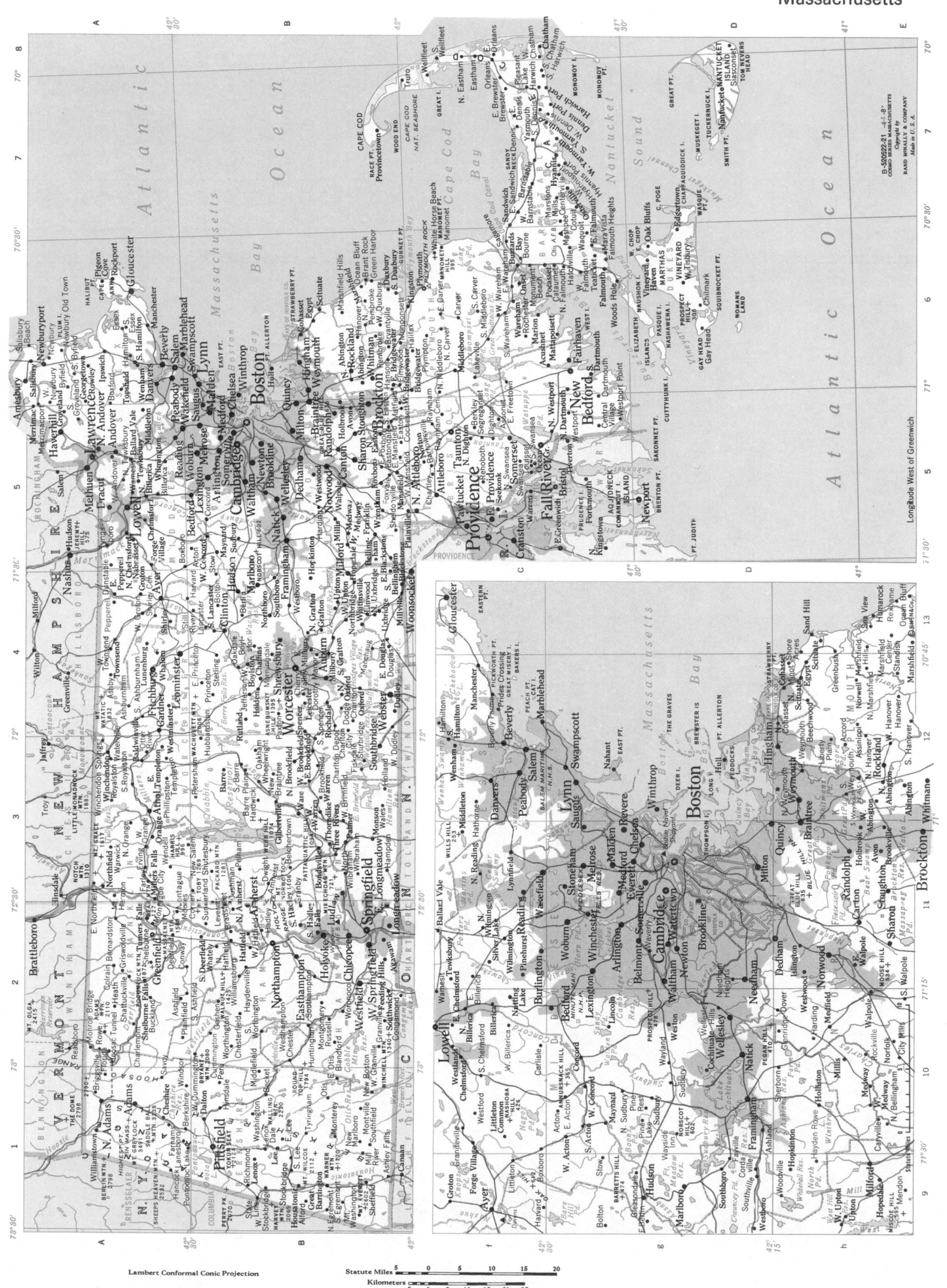

Lambert Conformal Conic Projection

Statute Miles

Kilometers

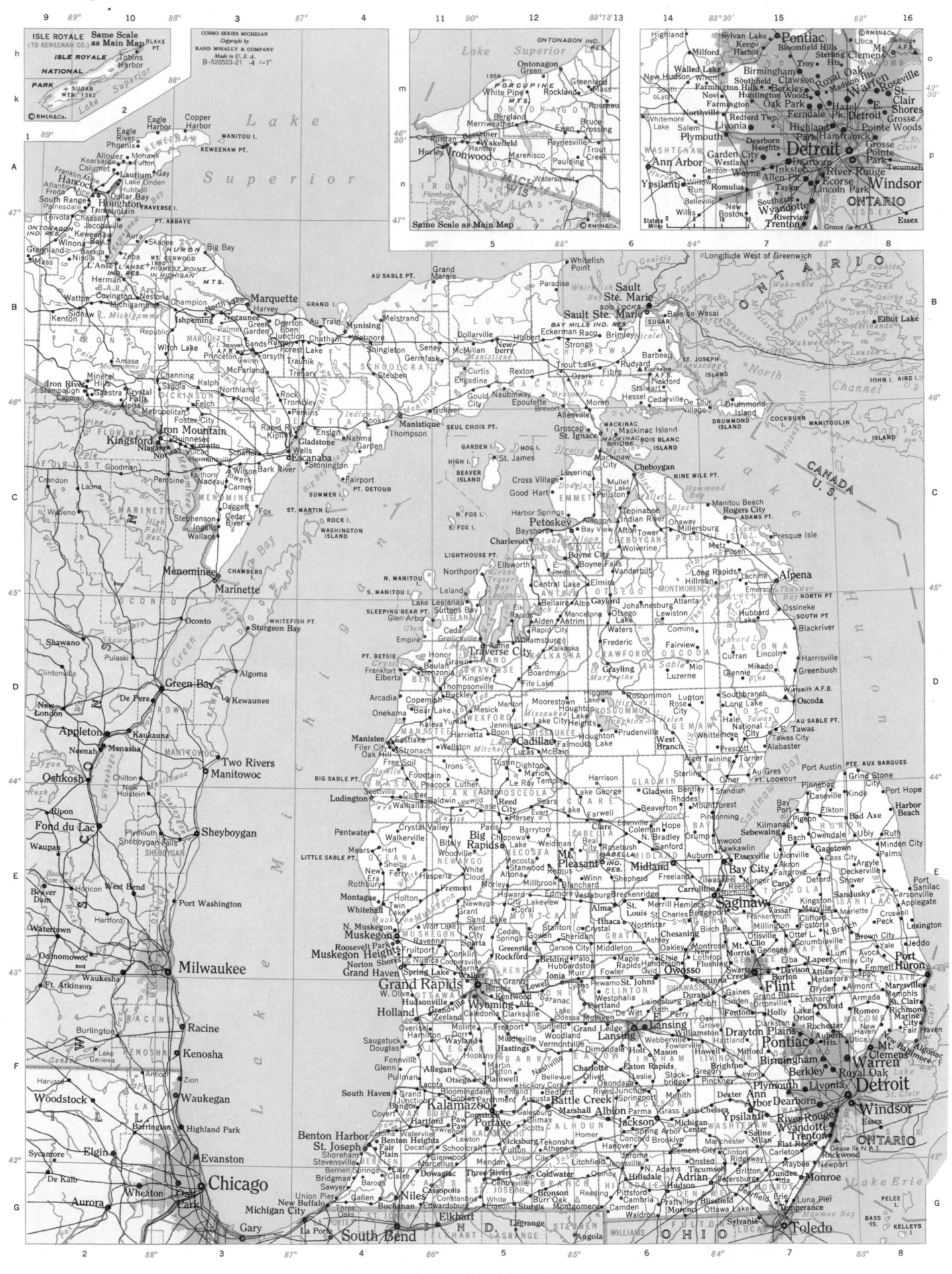

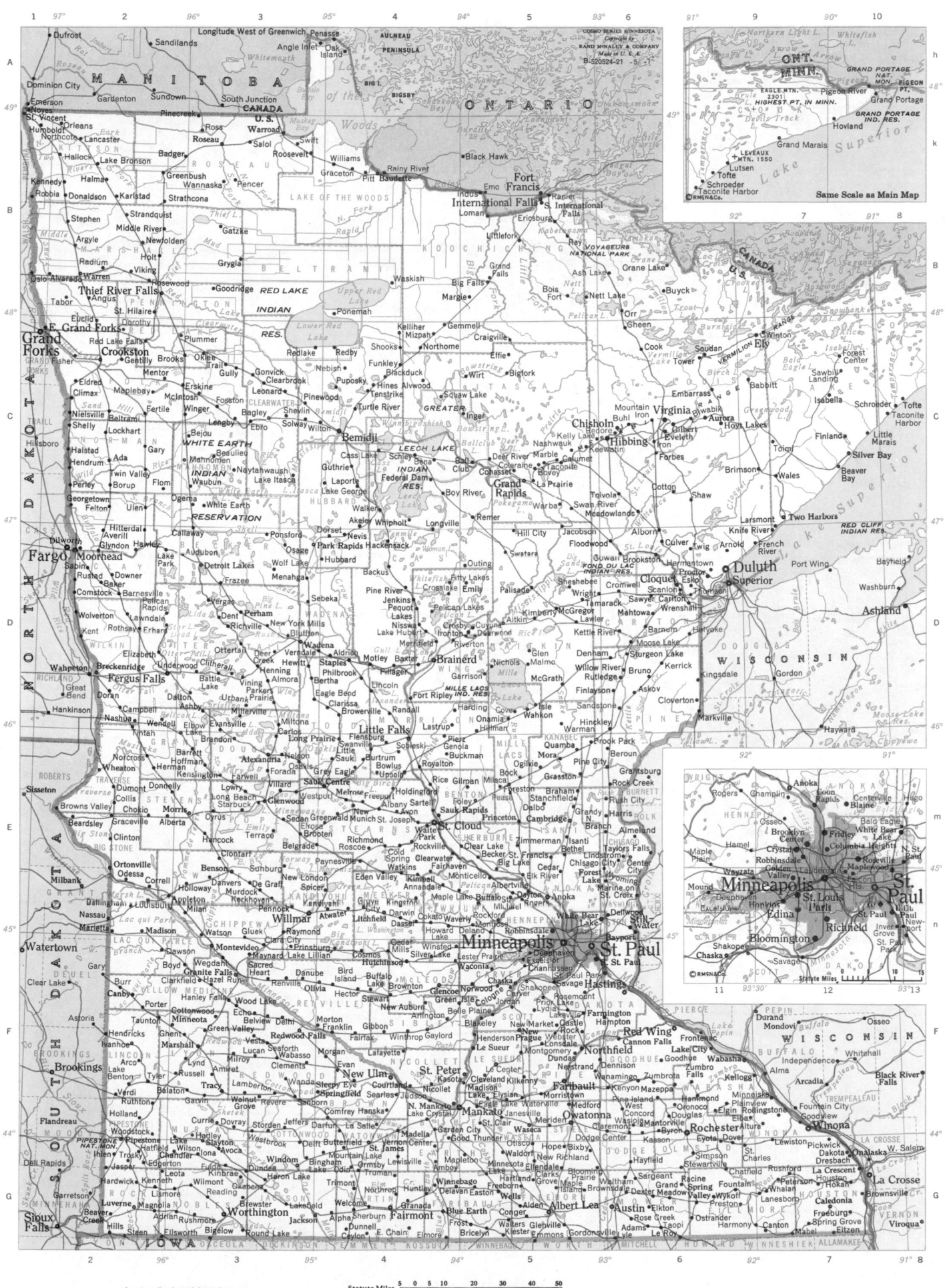

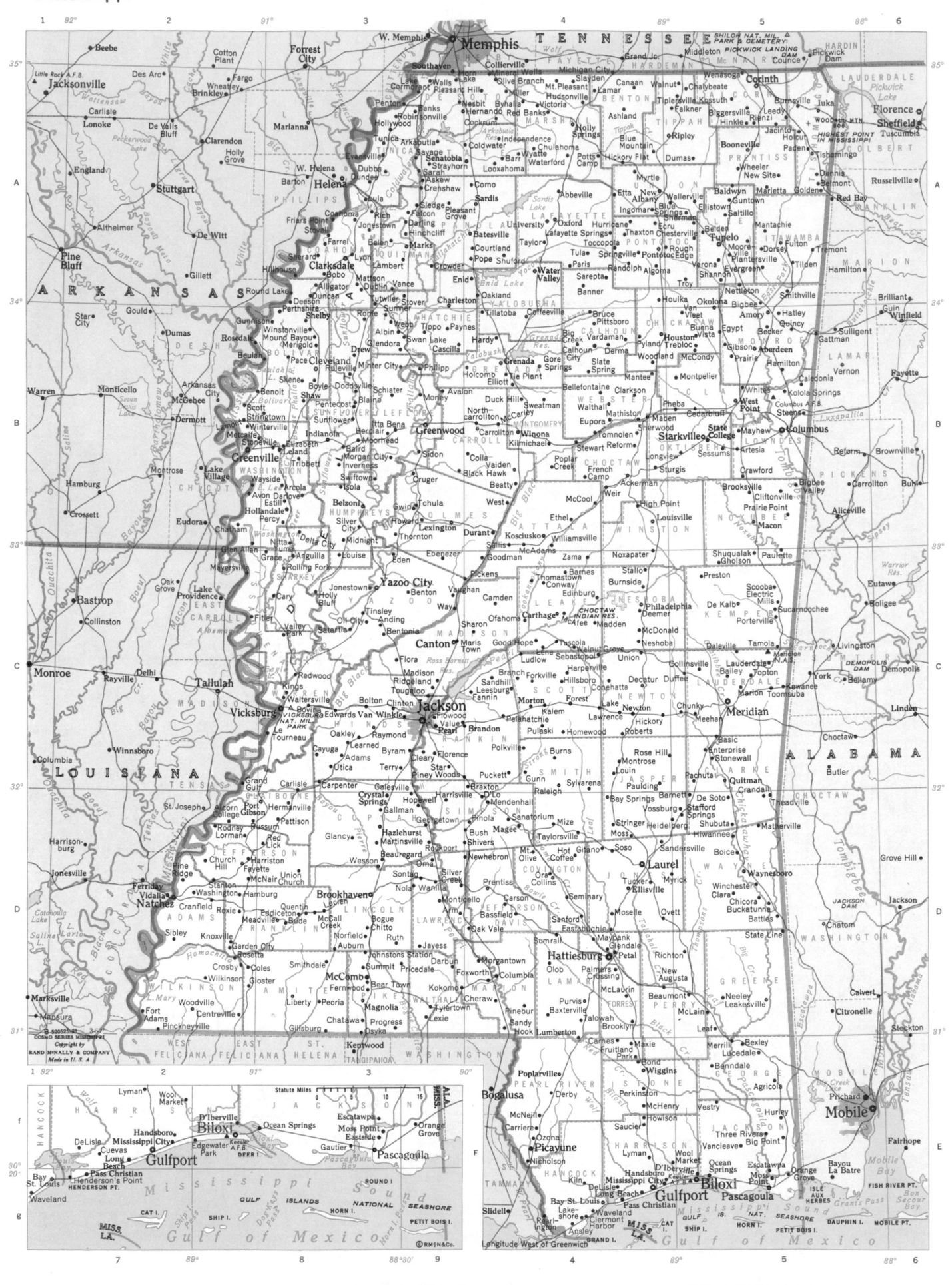

Statute Miles

Kilometers

Lambert Conformal Conic Projection

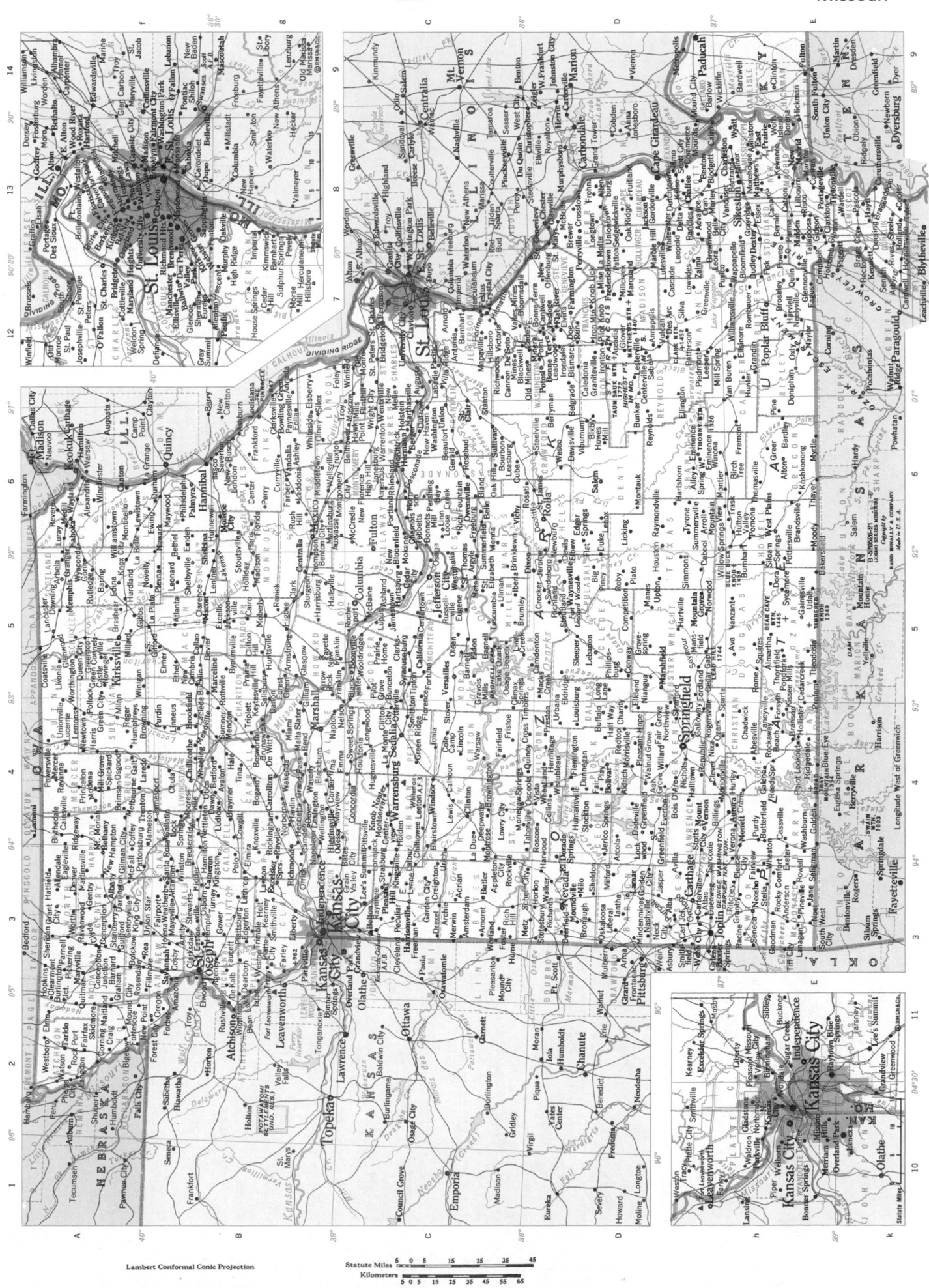

Statute Miles

Kilometers

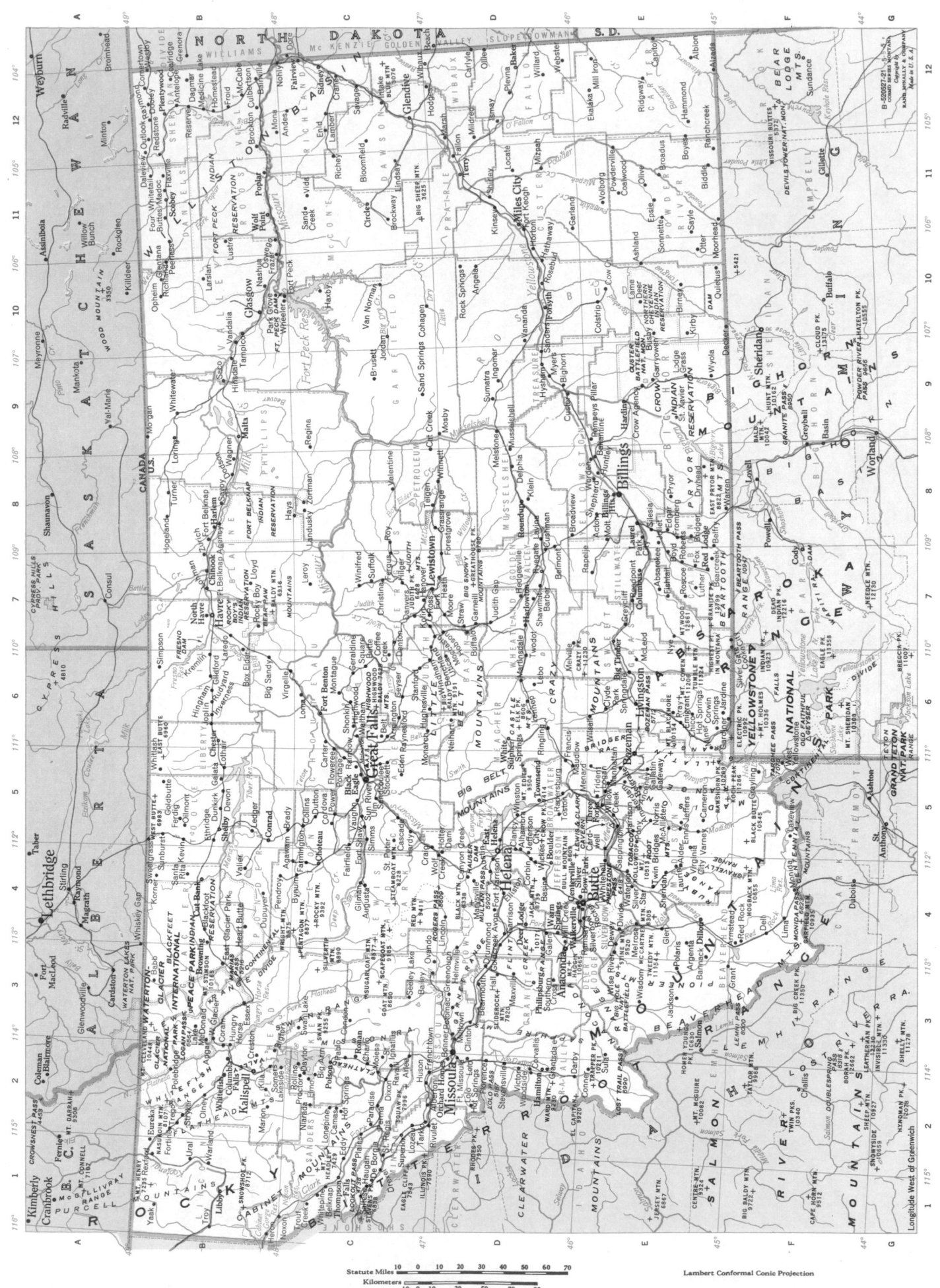

Statute Miles

Kilometers

Lambert Conformal Conic Projection

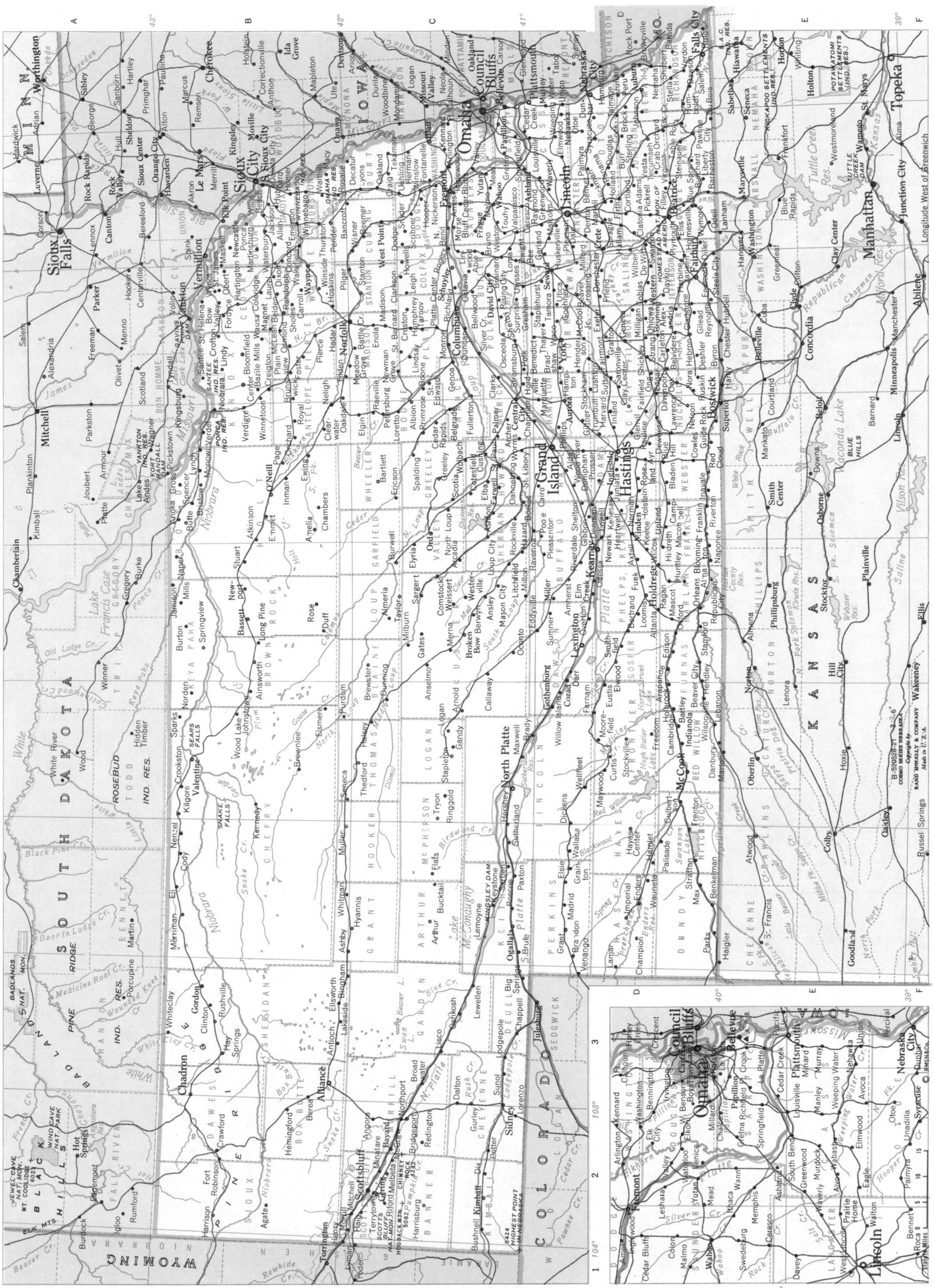

Lambert Conformal Conic Projection

Statute Miles
5 0 5 10 20 30 40 50 60
Kilometers
5 0 5 15 35 55 75 95

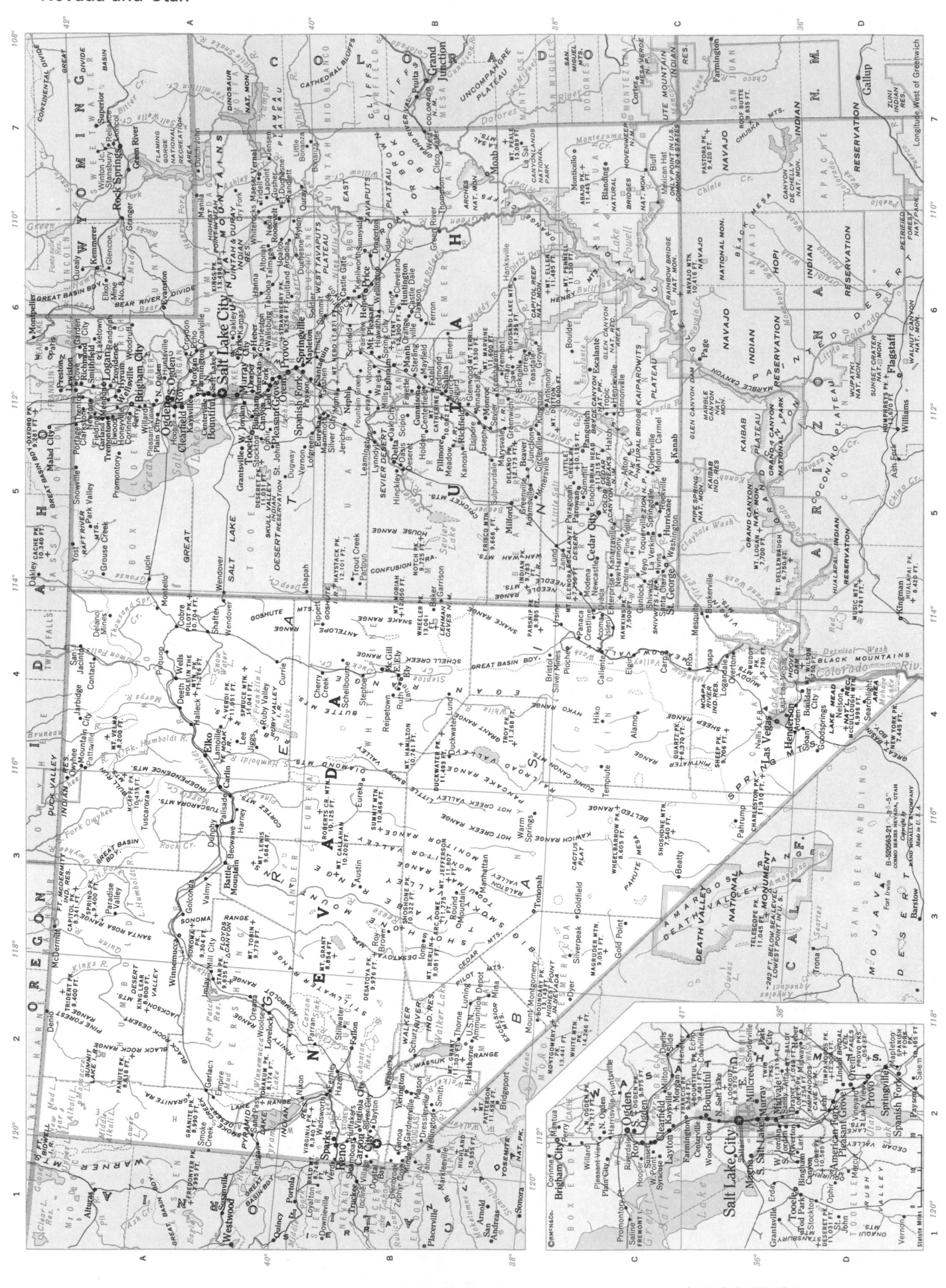

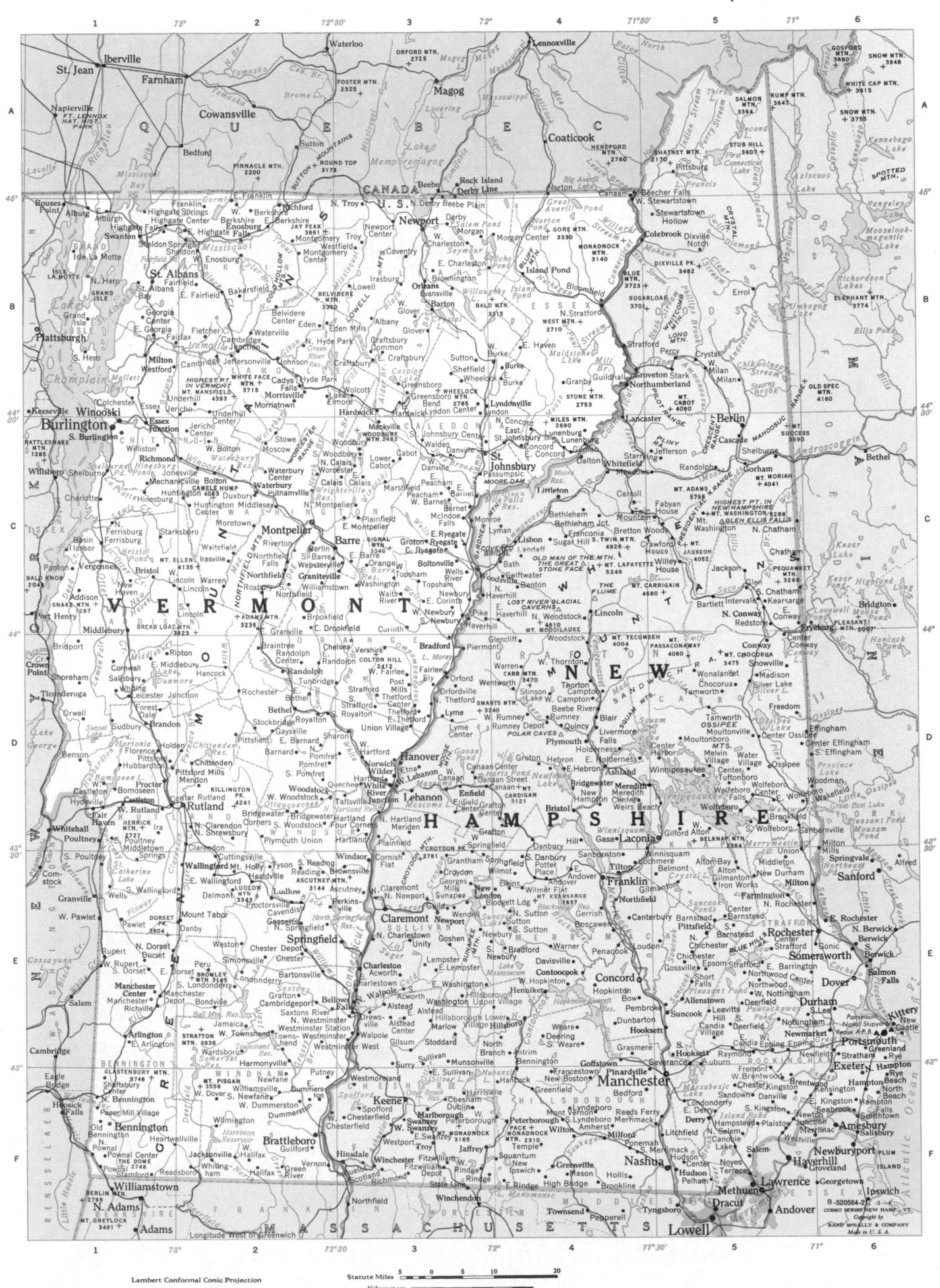

Statute Miles

Kilometers

B-520531-21 -5-1-11'
COSMO SERIES NEW JERSEY
Copyright by
RAND McNALLY & COMPANY
Made in U.S.A.

Longitude West of Greenwich

Lambert Conformal Conic Projection

©RM&N&Co.

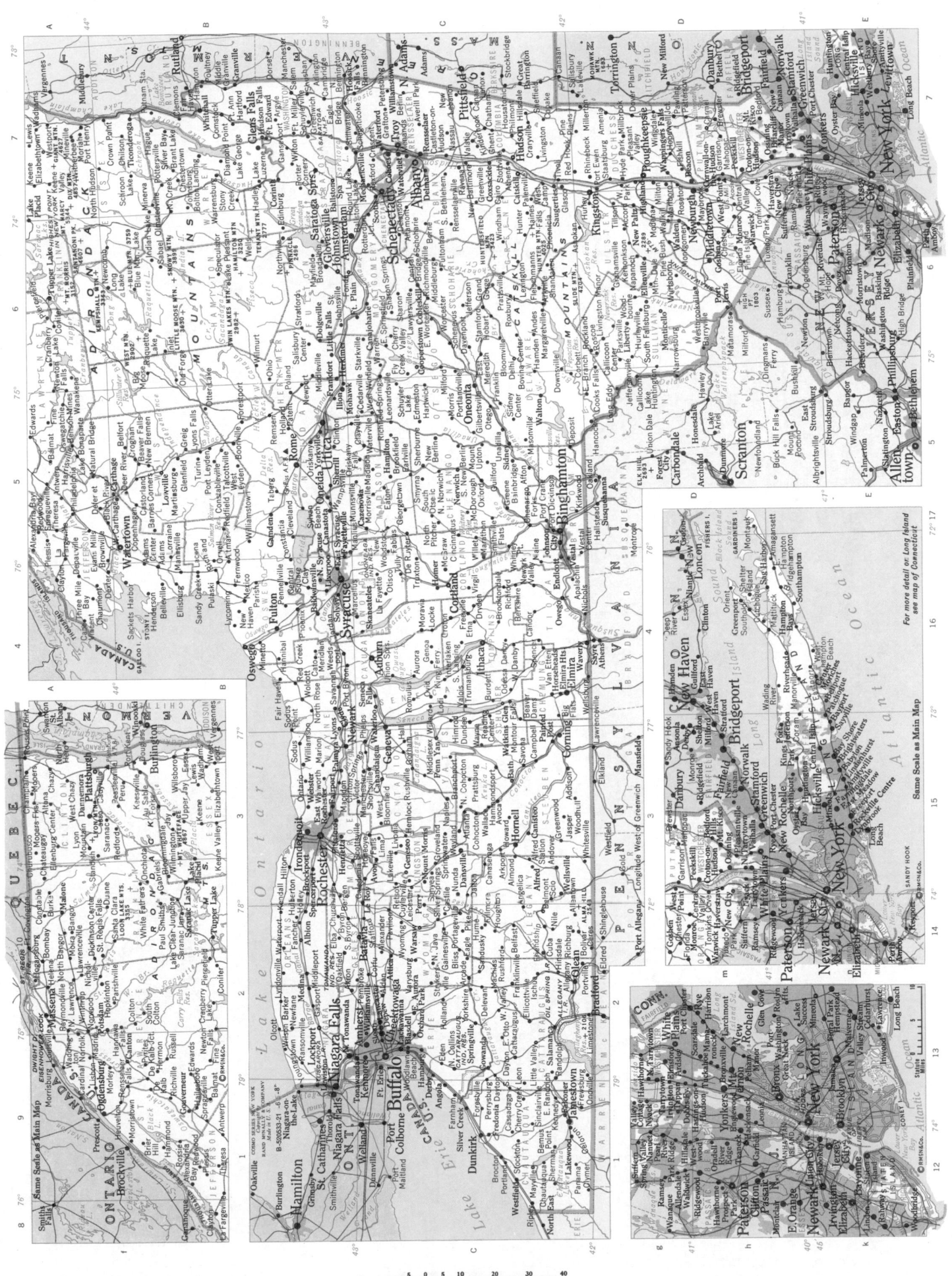

Lambert Conformal Conic Projection

Statute Miles

Kilometers

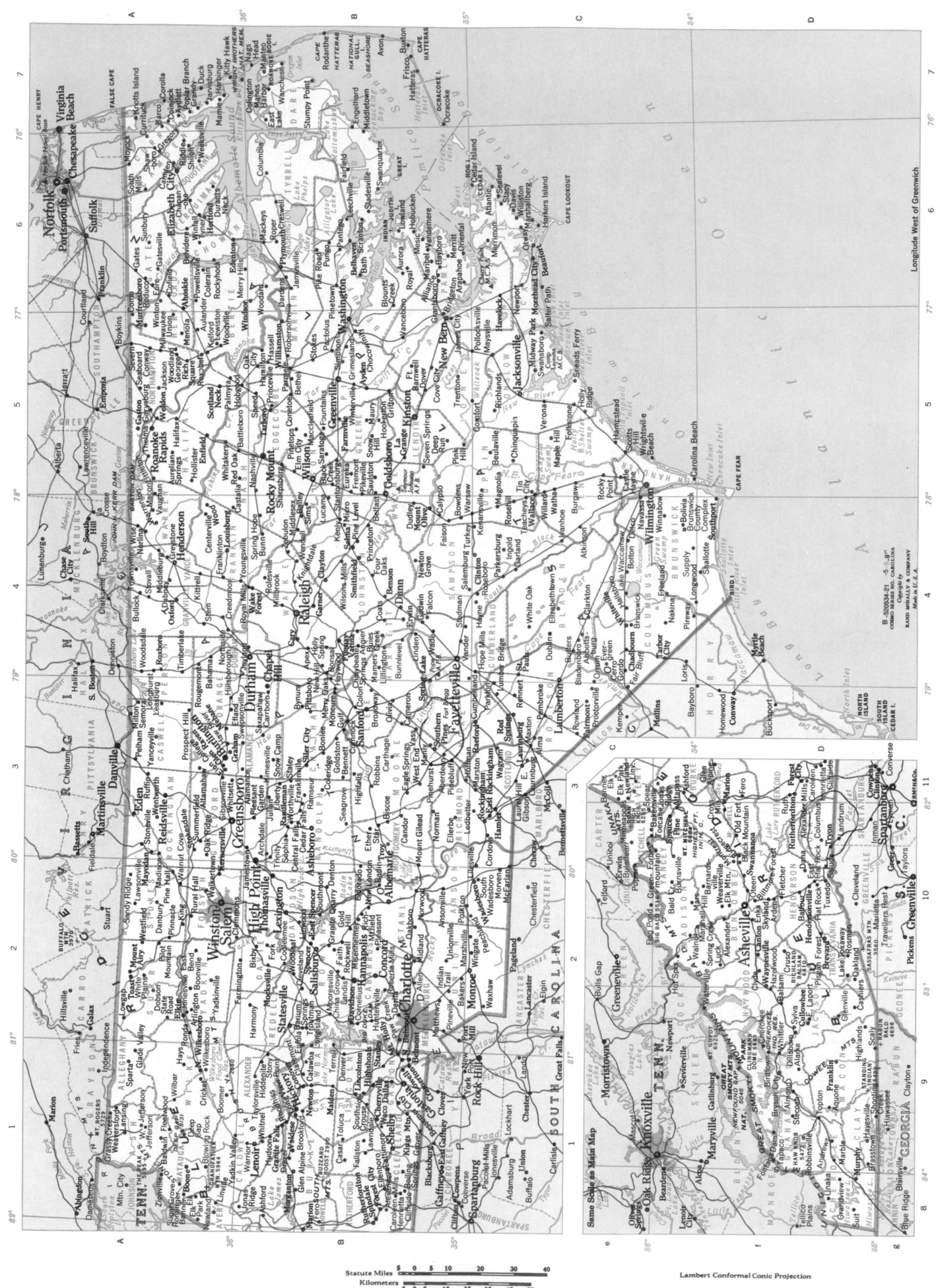

Statute Miles

Kilometers

Lambert Conformal Conic Projection

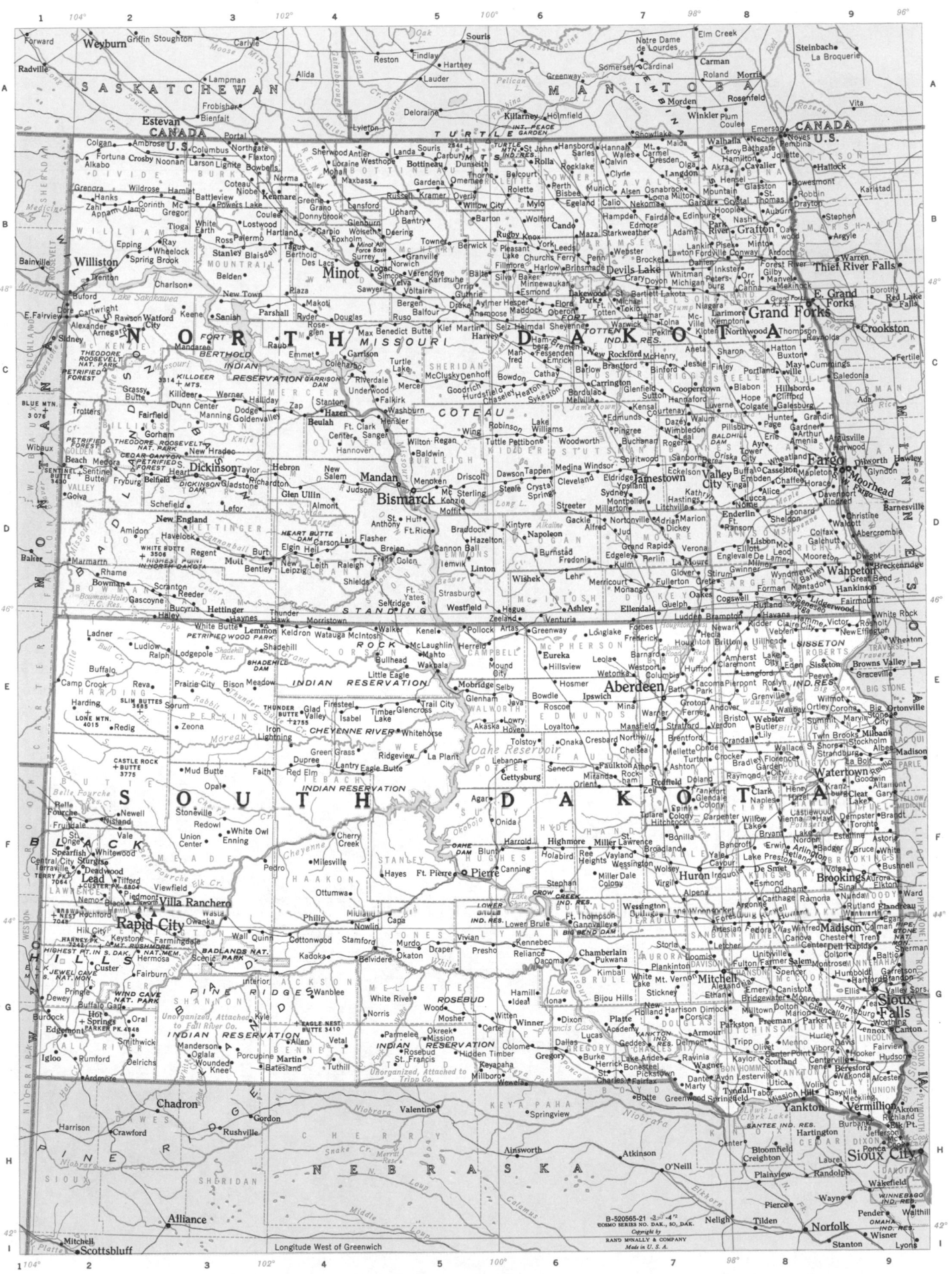

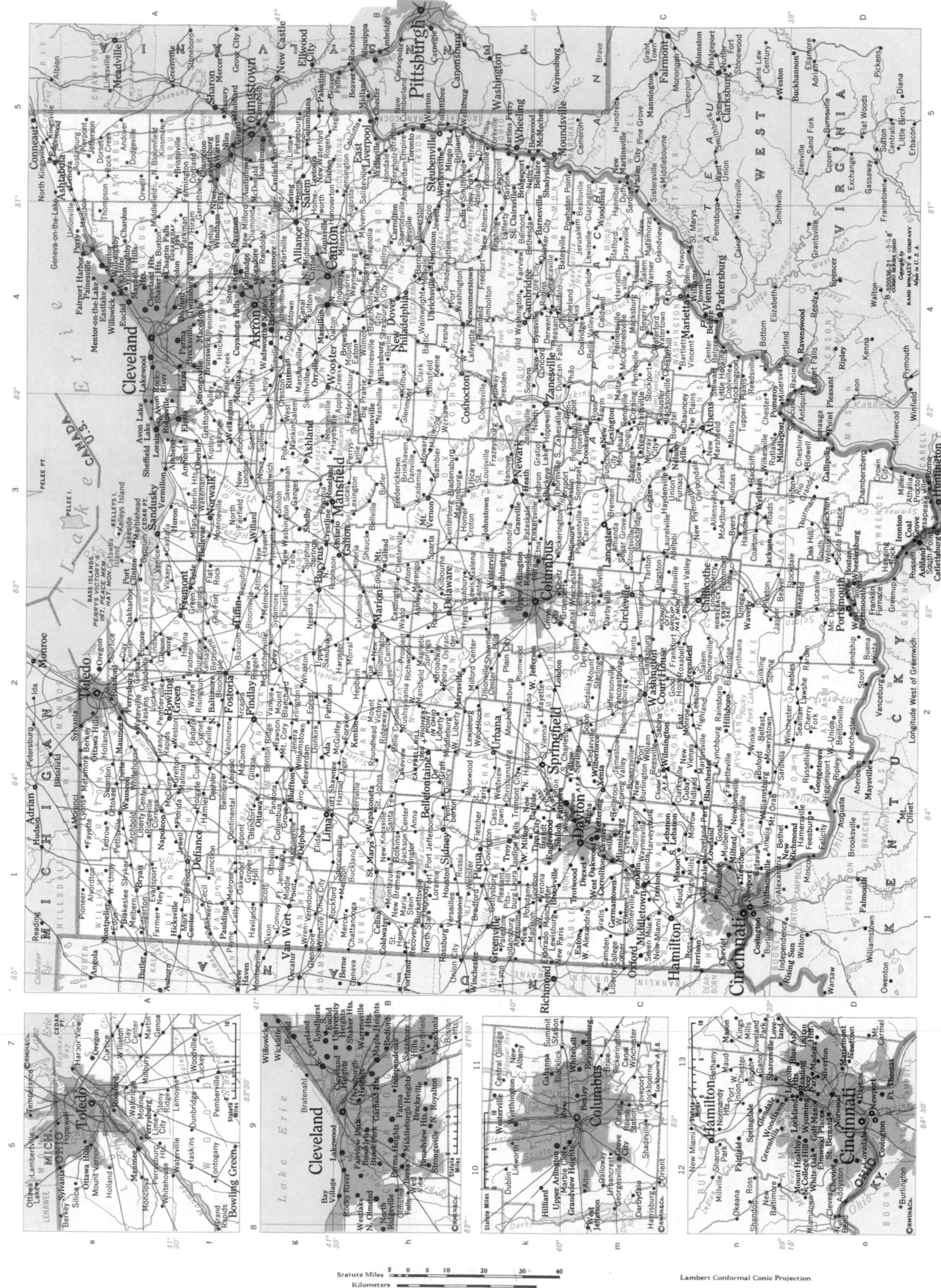

Statute Miles
5 0 5   10   20   30   40
Kilometers
5 0 5 15   25   35   45   55

Lambert Conformal Conic Projection

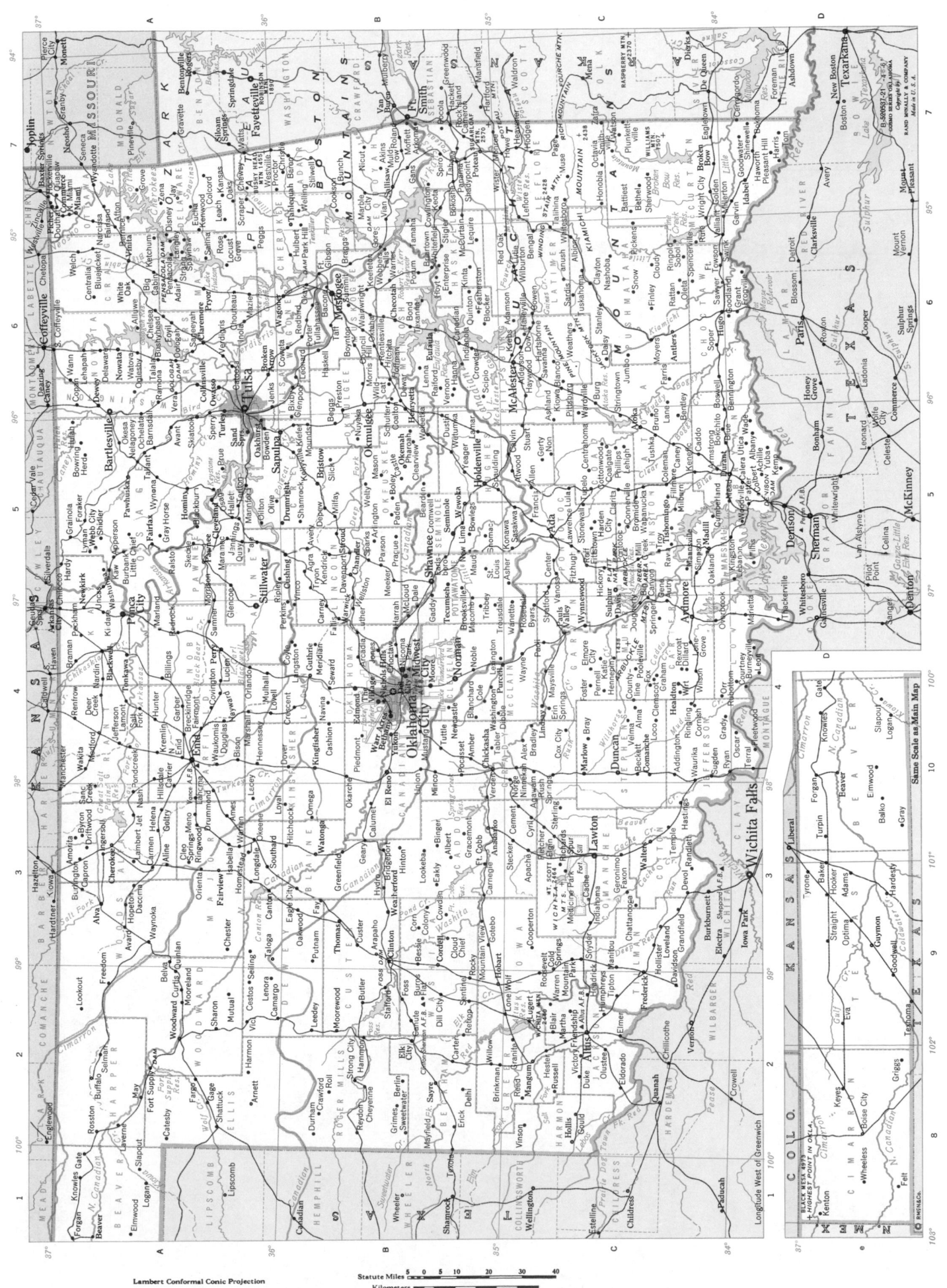

Lambert Conformal Conic Projection

Statute Miles 5 0 5 10   20   30   40

Kilometers 5 0 5 15 25 35 45 55

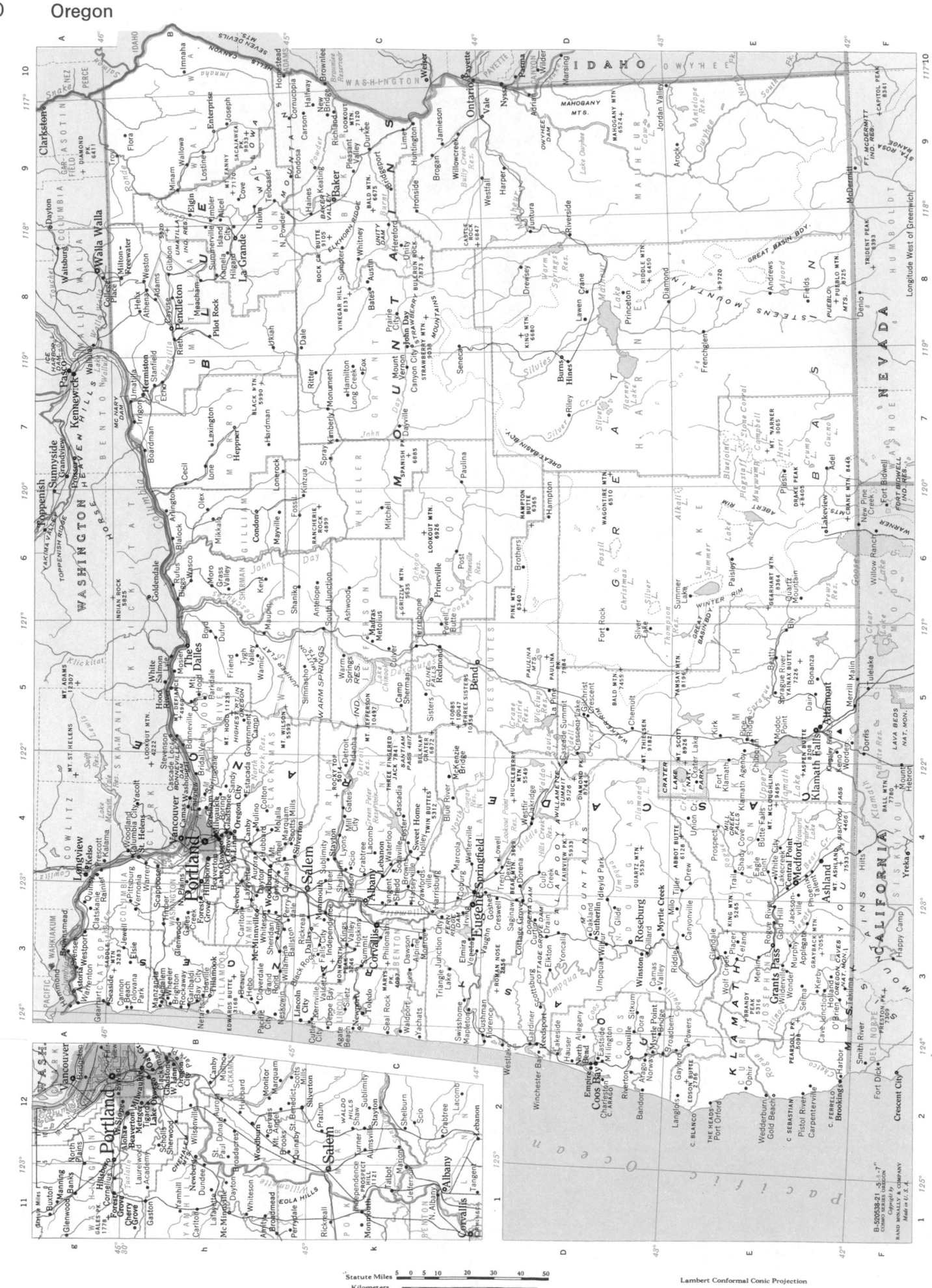

Statute Miles
Kilometers

Lambert Conformal Conic Projection

B-520538-21
RAND M?NALLY & COMPANY
Made in U.S.A.

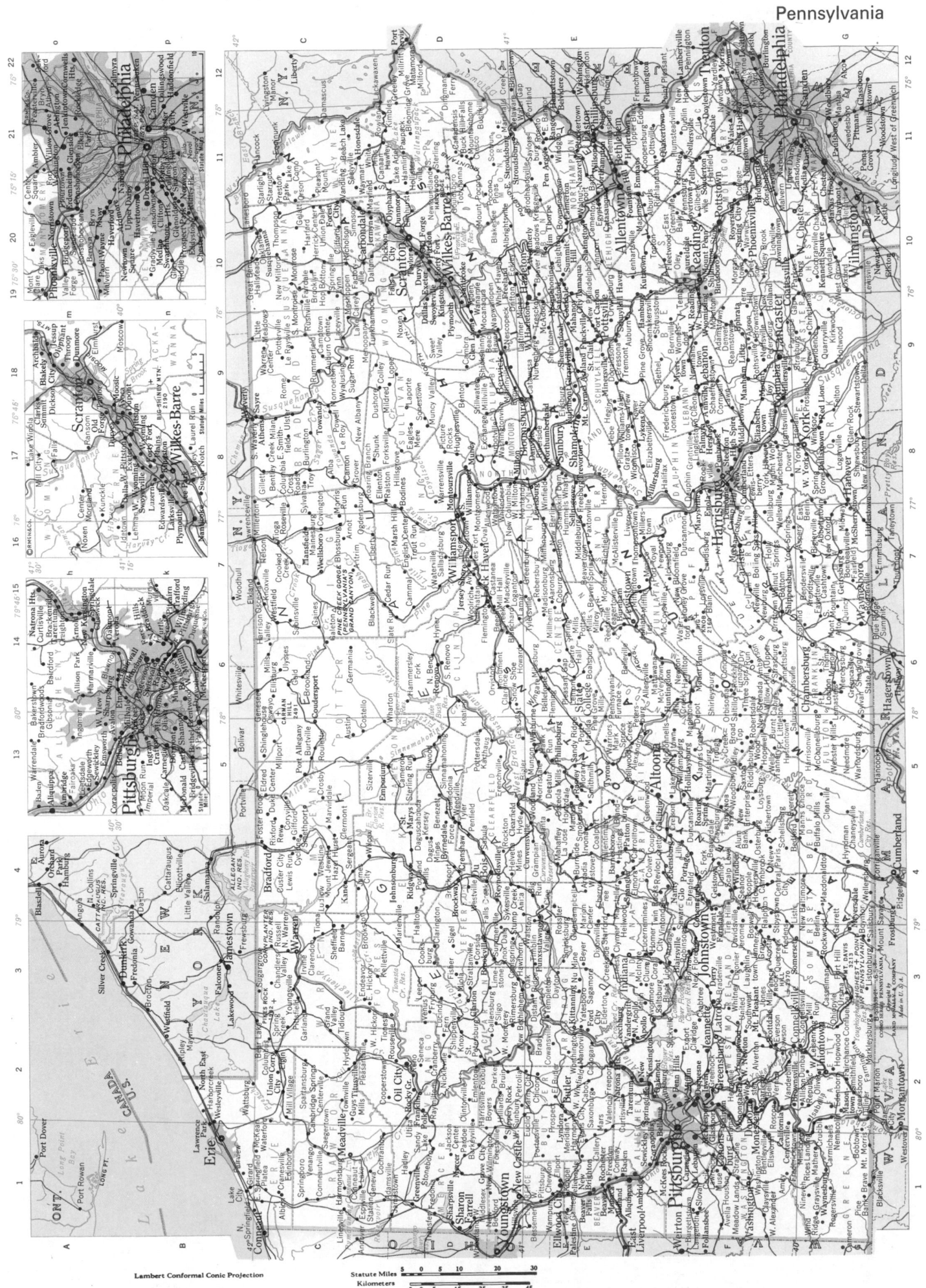

Lambert Conformal Conic Projection

Statute Miles
Kilometers

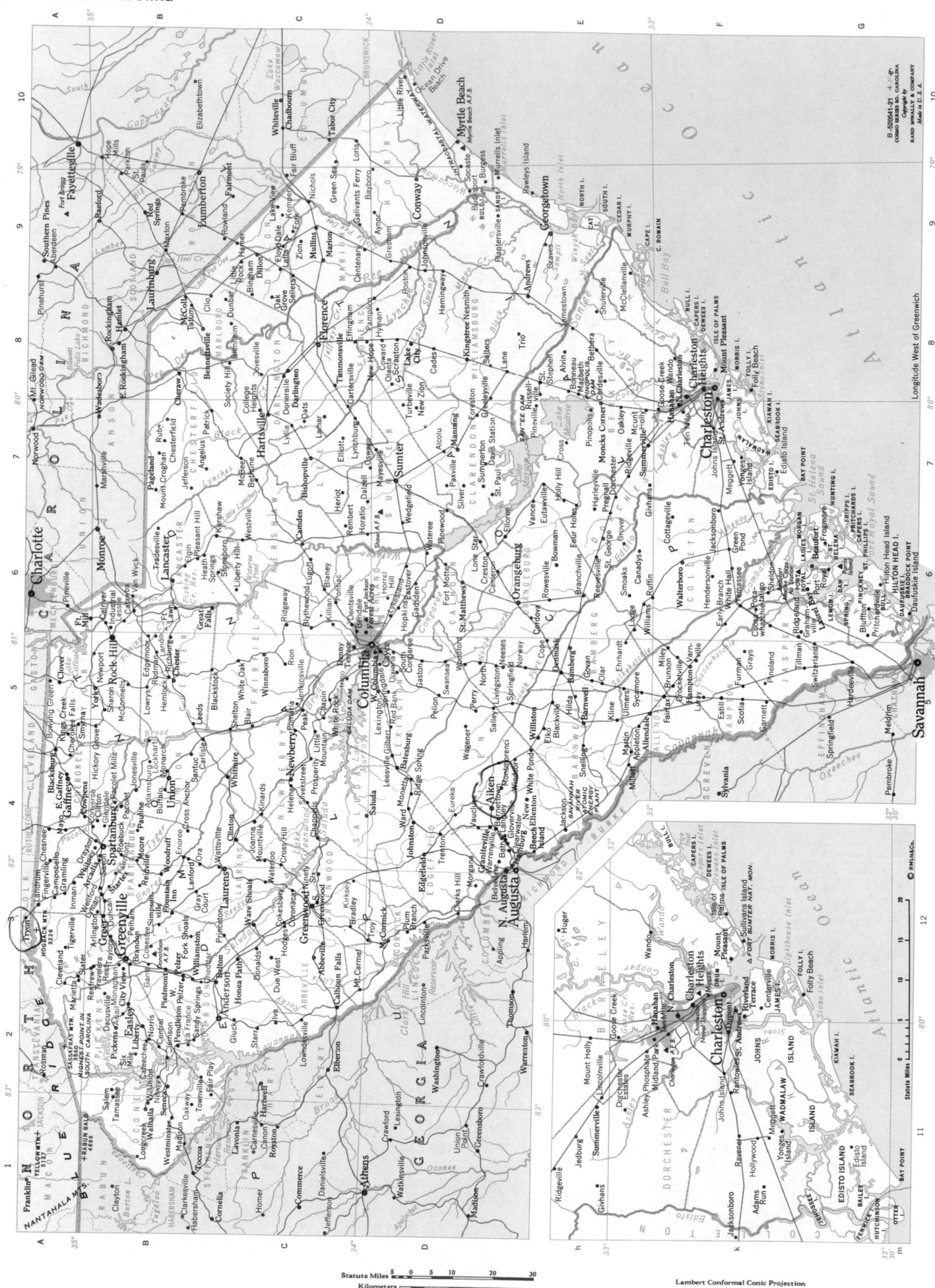

Statute Miles

Kilometers

Lambert Conformal Conic Projection

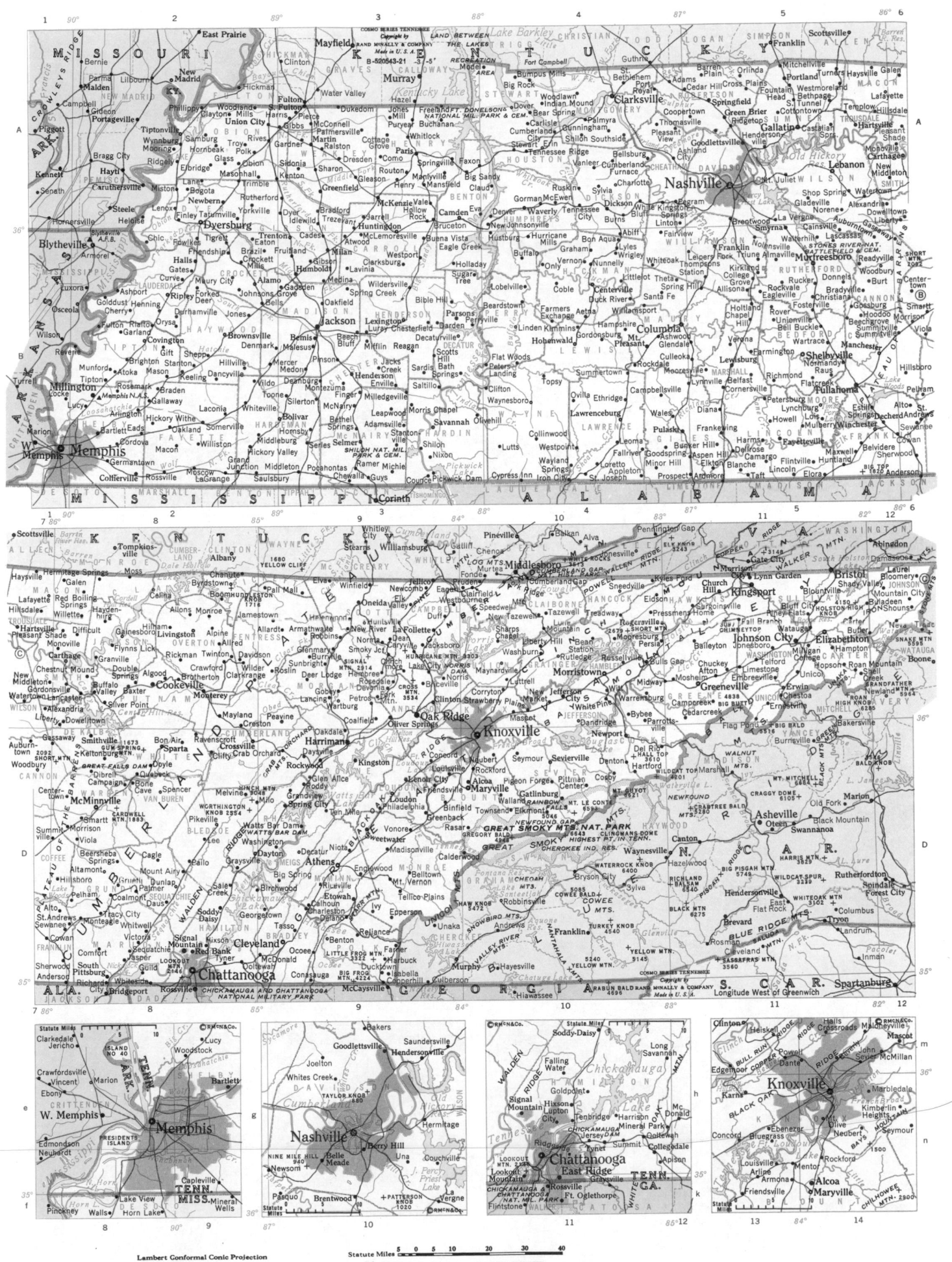

Lambert Conformal Conic Projection

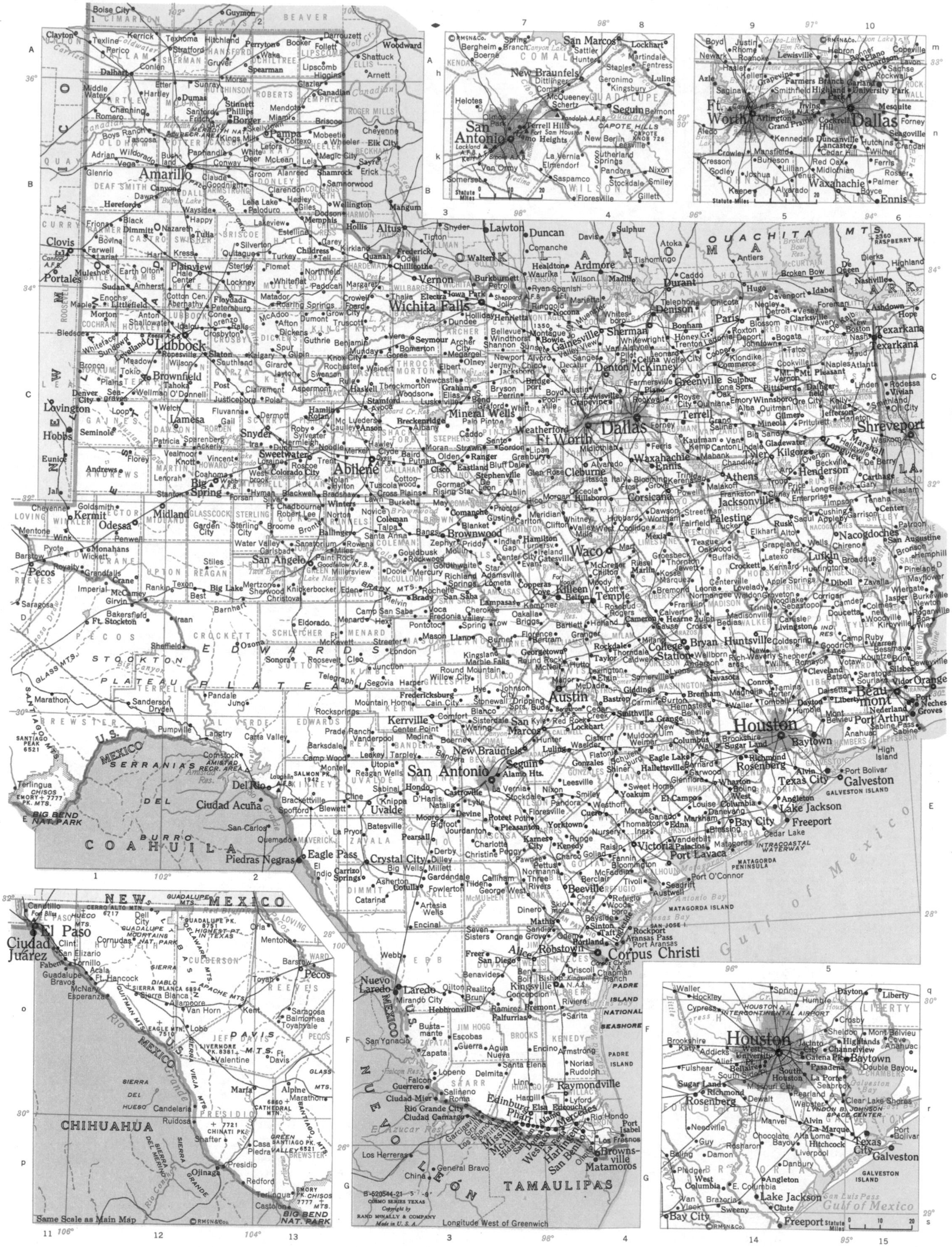

Statute Miles

Kilometers

Lambert Conformal Conic Projection

Same Scale as Main Map

Longitude West of Greenwich

B-520544-21
COSMO SERIES TEXAS
Copyright by
RAND McNALLY & COMPANY
Made in U.S.A.

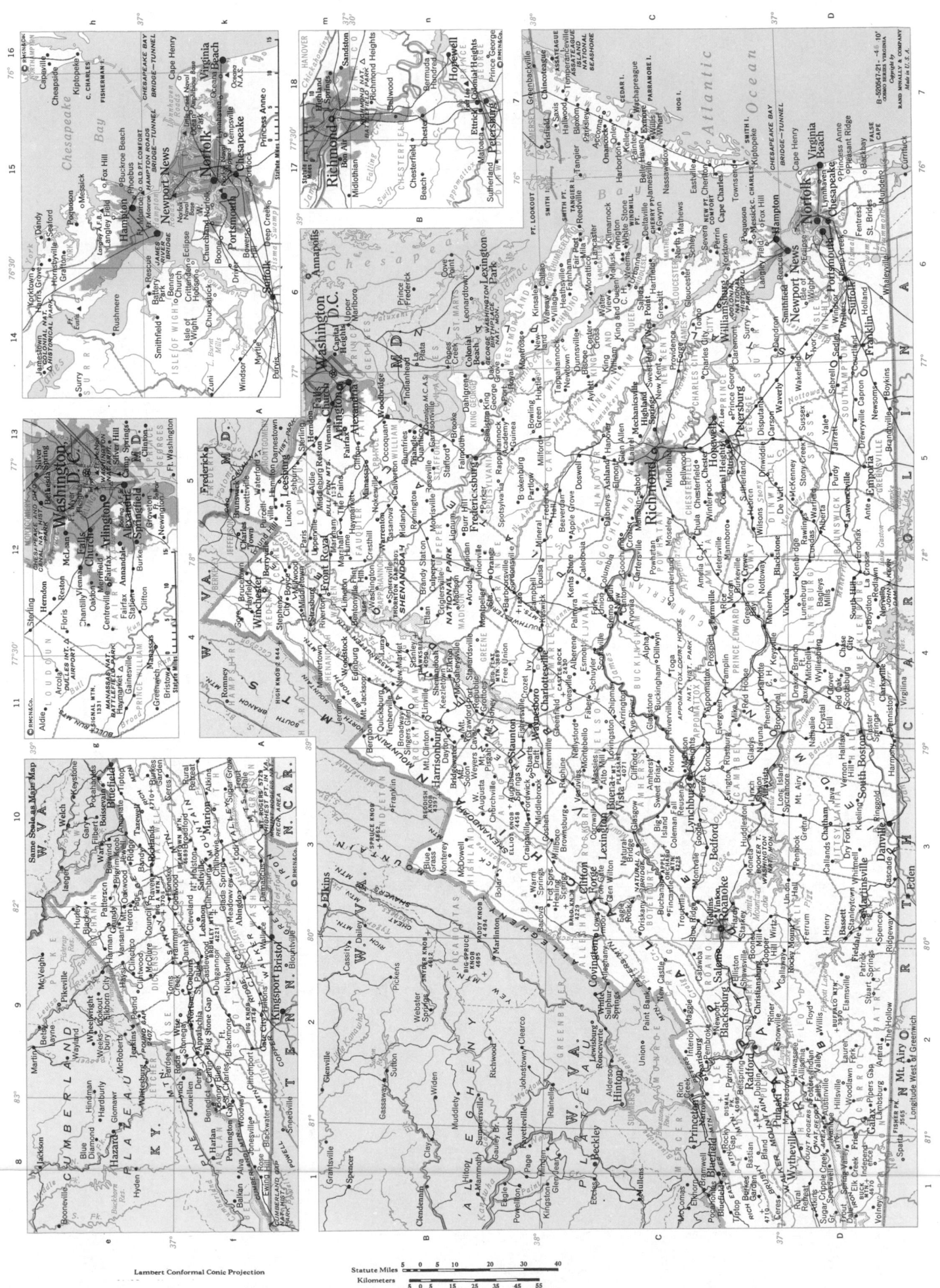

Statute Miles
Kilometers

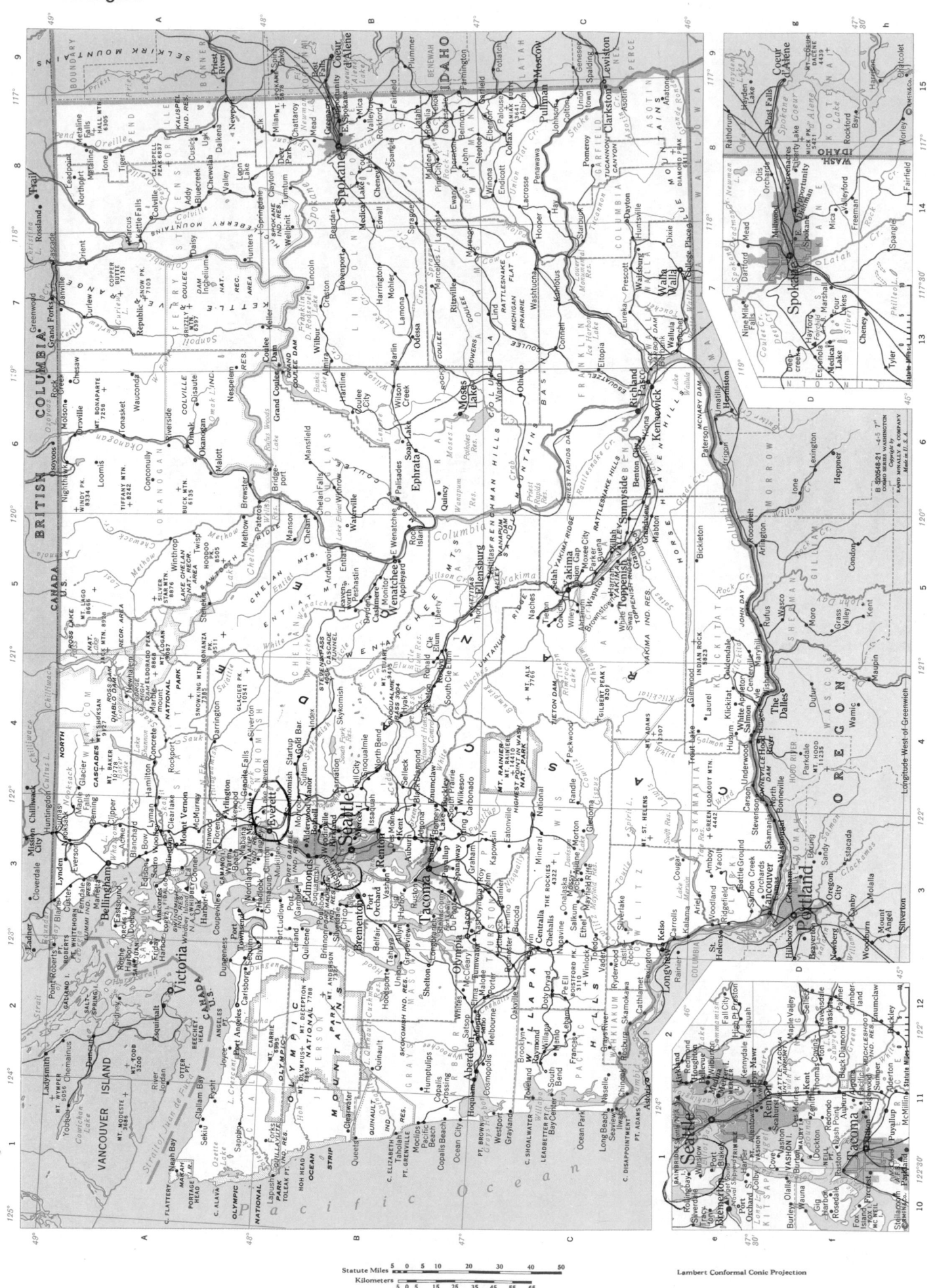

Statute Miles
Kilometers

Lambert Conformal Conic Projection

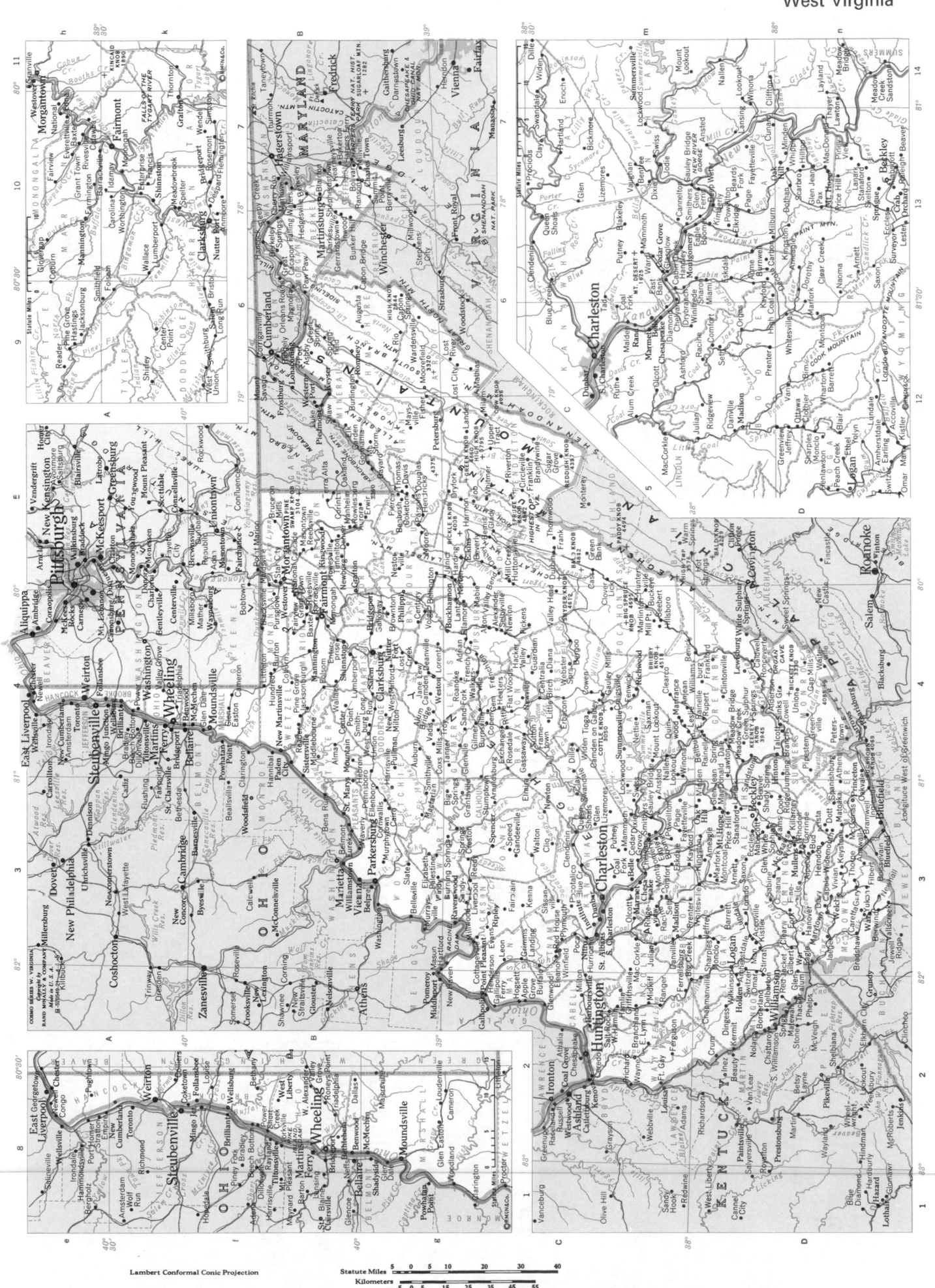

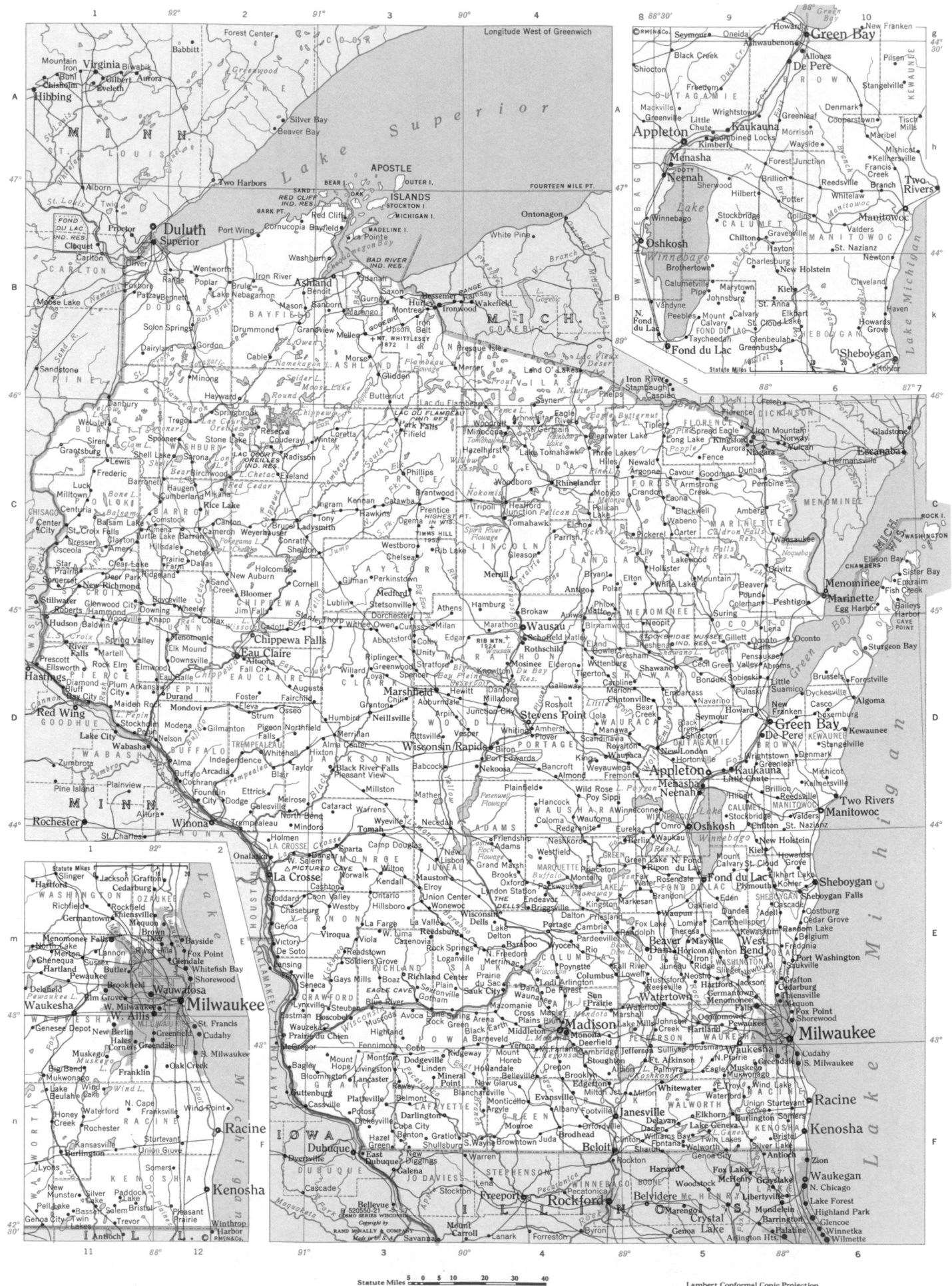

Longitude West of Greenwich

Lake Superior

APOSTLE ISLANDS

Lambert Conformal Conic Projection

Statute Miles

Kilometers

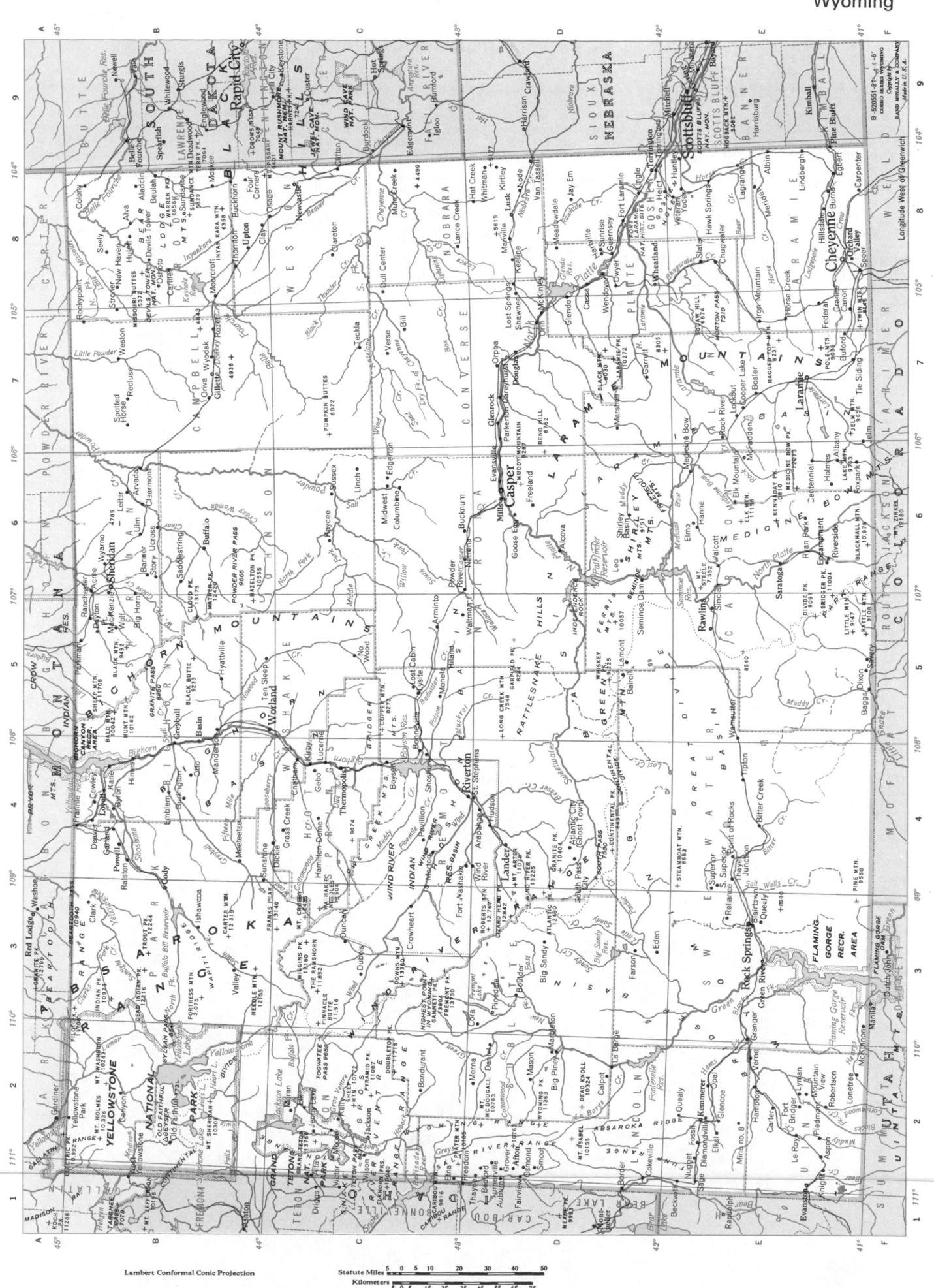

Lambert Conformal Conic Projection

Statute Miles 5 0 5 10   20   30   40   50

Kilometers
5 0 5 15 25 35 45 55 65 75

World Political Information Table

This table lists all countries and dependencies in the world, U.S. States, Canadian provinces, and other important regions and political subdivisions. Besides specifying the form of government for all political areas, the table classifies them into five groups according to their political status. Units labeled **A** are independent sovereign nations. Units labeled **B** are independent as regards internal affairs, but for purposes of foreign affairs they are under the protection of another country. Areas under military government are also labeled **B.** Units labeled **C** are colonies, overseas territories, dependencies, etc., of other countries. Together the **A, B,** and **C** areas comprise practically the entire inhabited area of the world. Units labeled **D** are States, provinces, Soviet Republics, or similar major administrative subdivisions of important countries. Units in the table with no letter designation are regions or other areas that do not constitute separate political units by themselves.

Country, Division, or Region English (Conventional)	Area* in sq. mi.	Estimated Population 1/1/84	Pop. per sq. mi.	Form of Government and Political Status	Capital: Largest City (unless same)	Predominant Language
Afars and Issas, *see* Djibouti	...	...	...	...	...	...
†Afghanistan	250,000	14,165,000	57	Socialist Republic A	Kābul	Dari, Pushtu
Africa	11,700,000	519,800,000	44	...	...; Cairo	...
Alabama	51,704	4,010,000	78	State (U.S.) D	Montgomery; Birmingham	English
Alaska	591,004	465,000	0.8	State (U.S.) D	Juneau; Anchorage	English, Indian, Eskimo
†Albania	11,100	2,600,000	234	Socialist Republic A	Tiranë	Albanian
Alberta	255,285	2,365,000	9.3	Province (Canada) D	Edmonton	English
†Algeria	919,595	21,290,000	23	Socialist Republic A	Algiers	Arabic, French, Berber
American Samoa	77	35,000	455	Unincorporated Territory (U.S.) C	Pago Pago	Samoan, English
Andaman and Nicobar Islands	3,202	205,000	64	Territory (India) D	Port Blair	Andaman, Nicobar Malay
Andorra	175	39,000	223	Co-Principality (Spanish and French protection) B	Andorra	Spanish, French
†Angola	481,353	7,735,000	16	Socialist Republic A	Luanda	Portuguese, native languages
Anguilla	35	7,000	200	Associated State (U.K.) B	The Valley; South Hill	English
Anhui	50,193	51,700,000	1,030	Province (China) D	Hefei, Huainan	Chinese
Antarctica	5,405,000	...(1)	...	...	...	...
†Antigua and Barbuda	170	80,000	471	Parliamentary State (Comm. of Nations) A	Saint John's	English
Arabian Peninsula	1,160,000	23,505,000	20	...	...; Riyadh	Arabic
†Argentina	1,068,301	28,955,000	27	Republic A	Buenos Aires	Spanish
Arizona	114,002	2,965,000	26	State (U.S.) D	Phoenix	English
Arkansas	53,191	2,315,000	44	State (U.S.) D	Little Rock	English
Armenian S.S.R.	11,506	3,200,000	278	Soviet Socialist Republic (U.S.S.R.) D	Yerevan	Armenian, Russian
Aruba	75	69,000	920	Division of Netherlands Antilles (Neth.) D	Oranjestad	Dutch, Spanish, English, Papiamento
Ascension	34	1,100	32	Dependency of St. Helena (U.K.) C	Georgetown	English
Asia	17,240,000	2,863,400,000	166	...	...; Tōkyō	...
†Australia	2,967,909	15,535,000	5.2	Parliamentary State (Federal) (Comm. of Nations) A	Canberra; Sydney	English
Australian Capital Territory	939	235,000	250	Territory (Australia) D	Canberra	English
†Austria	32,377	7,575,000	234	Federal Republic A	Vienna (Wien)	German
Azerbaidzhan S.S.R.	33,436	6,370,000	190	Soviet Socialist Republic (U.S.S.R.) D	Baku	Turkish, Russian, Armenian
Azores	868	240,000	276	Autonomous Region (Portugal) D	Ponta Delgada	Portguese
Baden-Württemberg	13,804	9,255,000	670	State (Federal Republic of Germany) D	Stuttgart	German
†Bahamas	5,382	225,000	42	Parliamentary State (Comm. of Nations) A	Nassau	English
†Bahrain	256	400,000	1,563	Constitutional Monarchy A	Manama	Arabic, English
Balearic Islands	1,936	695,000	359	Province of Spain (Baleares) D	Palma	Spanish
Baltic Republics	67,182	7,655,000	114	Part of U.S.S.R. (3 republics) ...	...; Riga	Lithuanian, Latvian, Estonian, Russian
†Bangladesh	55,598	95,600,000	1,719	Republic (Comm. of Nations) A	Dacca	Bangla, English
†Barbados	166	250,000	1,506	Parliamentary State (Comm. of Nations) A	Bridgetown	English
Bavaria (Bayern)	27,238	10,920,000	401	State (Federal Republic of Germany) D	Munich (München)	German
Beijing, *see* Peking	...	...	...	...	...	...
†Belgium	11,781	9,870,000	838	Constitutional Monarchy A	Brussels (Bruxelles)	French, Dutch (Flemish)
†Belize	8,866	155,000	17	Parliamentary State (Comm. of Nations) A	Belmopan; Belize City	English, Spanish, Indian languages
Benelux	28,672	24,655,000	860	Economic Union ...	...; Brussels (Bruxelles)	Dutch, French, Luxumbourgish
†Benin	43,484	3,655,000	84	Socialist Republic A	Porto-Novo; Cotonou	French, native languages
Berlin (West)	185	1,880,000	10,162	State (Federal Republic of Germany) D	Berlin (West)	German
Bermuda	21	68,000	3,238	Colony (U.K.) C	Hamilton	English
†Bhutan	18,147	1,400,000	77	Monarchy (Indian protection) B	Thimbu	Dzongkha, English, Nepalese dialects
Bioko	785	77,000	98	Province of Equatorial Guinea D	Malabo	Spanish, English
†Bolivia	424,164	6,160,000	15	Republic A	Sucre and La Paz; La Paz	Spanish, Quechua, Aymara
Bophuthatswana(6)	15,610	1,400,000	89	Bantu Homeland (South African protection) B	Mmabatho	Sesotho, Afrikaans
Borneo, Indonesian (Kalimantan)	208,287	7,185,000	34	Part of Indonesia (4 provinces) ...	...; Banjarmasin	Bahasa Indonesia
†Botswana	231,805	1,020,000	4.4	Republic (Comm. of Nations) A	Gaborone	Setswana, English
†Brazil	3,265,075	133,100,000	41	Federal Republic A	Brasília; São Paulo	Portuguese
Bremen	156	690,000	4,423	State (Federal Republic of Germany) D	Bremen	German
British Columbia	366,255	2,840,000	7.8	Province (Canada) D	Victoria; Vancouver	English
British Honduras, *see* Belize	...	...	...	...	...	...
British Indian Ocean Territory	23	...(1)	...	Colony (U.K.) C	...	...
British Solomon Islands, *see* Solomon Islands	...	...	...	...	...	...
Brunei	2,226	215,000	92	Constitutional Monarchy (Comm. of Nations) A	Bandar Seri Begawan	Malay, Chinese, English
†Bulgaria	42,823	9,370,000	219	Socialist Republic A	Sofia (Sofiya)	Bulgarian
†Burkina Faso (Upper Volta)	105,869	6,525,000	62	Provisional Military Government A	Ouagadougou	French, native languages
†Burma	261,228	37,505,000	144	Socialist Republic A	Rangoon	Burmese, ethnic languages
†Burundi	10,747	4,625,000	430	Republic A	Bujumbura	Kirundi, French, Swahili
†Byelorussian S.S.R.	80,155	9,925,000	124	Soviet Socialist Republic (U.S.S.R.) D	Minsk	Byelorussian, Polish, Russian
California	158,704	25,300,000	159	State (U.S.) D	Sacramento; Los Angeles	English
Cambodia, *see* Kampuchea	...	...	...	...	...	...
†Cameroon	183,569	9,125,000	50	Republic A	Yaoundé; Douala	English, French, native languages
†Canada	3,831,033	25,100,000	6.6	Parliamentary State (Federal) (Comm. of Nations) A	Ottawa; Toronto	English, French
Canary Islands (Islas Canarias)	2,808	1,470,000	524	...; Part of Spain (2 provinces) ...	...; Las Palmas de Gran Canaria	Spanish
†Cape Verde	1,557	310,000	199	Republic A	Praia	Portuguese, Crioulo
Cayman Islands	100	19,000	190	Colony (U.K.) C	Georgetown	English
Celebes	73,057	11,125,000	152	Part of Indonesia (4 provinces) ...	...; Ujung Pandang	Bahasa Indonesia, Malay-Polynesian languages
†Central African Republic	240,535	2,505,000	10	Republic A	Bangui	French, Sangho
Central America	202,000	24,920,000	123	...	...; Guatemala	Spanish, Indian languages
Central Asia, Soviet	493,090	27,390,000	56	Part of U.S.S.R. (4 republics) ...	...; Tashkent	Uzbek, Russian, Kirghiz, Turkoman, Tadzhik
Ceylon, *see* Sri Lanka	...	...	...	...	...	...
†Chad	495,755	4,785,000	9.7	Provisional Military Government A	Ndjamena	French, Arabic, native languages
Channel Islands	75	133,000	1,773	...	...; St. Helier	English, French
†Chile	292,135	11,740,000	40	Republic A	Santiago	Spanish
†China (excl. Taiwan)	3,630,747	1,046,530,000	288	Socialist Republic A	Peking (Beijing); Shanghai	Chinese dialects
China (Nationalist), *see* Taiwan	...	...	...	...	...	...
Christmas Island	52	3,200	62	External Territory (Australia) C	...; Flying Fish Cove	Chinese, Malay, English
Ciskei(6)	3,205	690,000	215	Bantu Homeland (South African protection) B	Bisho; Mdantsane	Xhosa, Afrikaans
Cocos (Keeling) Islands	5.4	500	92	External Territory (Australia) C	...	Malay, English
†Colombia	439,737	30,285,000	69	Republic A	Bogotá	Spanish
Colorado	104,094	3,130,000	30	State (U.S.) D	Denver	English

* Areas include inland water.
† Member of the United Nations (1983).
. . . None, or not applicable.
(1) No permanent population.
(6) Bophuthatswana, Ciskei, Transkei, and Venda are not recognized by the United Nations.

Country, Division, or Region English (Conventional)	Area* in sq. mi.	Estimated Population 1/1/84	Pop. per sq. mi.	Form of Government and Political Status	Capital: Largest City (unless same)	Predominant Language
Cook Islands	91	18,000	198	Self-governing Territory (New Zealand protection) B	Avarua	Malay-Polynesian languages, English
Corsica	3,352	235,000	70	Part of France (2 departments) ...	......; Ajaccio	French, Italian
†Costa Rica	19,730	2,395,000	121	Republic A	San José	Spanish
†Cuba	44,218	9,850,000	223	Socialist Republic A	Havana (La Habana)	Spanish
Curaçao	171	180,000	1,053	Division of Netherlands Antilles (Neth.) D	Willemstad	Dutch, Spanish, English, Papiamento
†Cyprus	3,572	665,000	186	Republic (Comm. of Nations) A	Nicosia	Greek, Turkish
†Czechoslovakia	49,378	15,415,000	312	Federal Socialist Republic A	Prague (Praha)	Czech, Slovak, Hungarian
Dahomey, *see* Benin	...	...	...	...	...	...
Delaware	2,045	615,000	301	State (U.S.) D	Dover; Wilmington	English
†Denmark	16,633	5,110,000	307	Constitutional Monarchy A	Copenhagen (København)	Danish
Denmark and Possessions	857,177	5,210,000	6.1	...	Copenhagen (København)	Danish, Faroese, Eskimo
District of Columbia	69	625,000	9,058	District (U.S.) D	Washington	English
†Djibouti	8,880	350,000	39	Republic A	Djibouti	Somali, French, Afar, Arabic
†Dominica	290	74,000	255	Republic (Comm. of Nations) A	Roseau	English, French
†Dominican Republic	18,704	5,975,000	319	Republic A	Santo Domingo	Spanish
†Ecuador	109,483	9,410,000	86	Republic A	Quito; Guayaquil	Spanish, Quechua
†Egypt	386,643	46,465,000	120	Socialist Republic A	Cairo (AlQāhirah)	Arabic, English, French
Ellice Islands, *see* Tuvalu	...	...	...	...	...	...
†El Salvador	8,124	5,140,000	633	Republic A	San Salvador	Spanish
England	50,362	46,465,000	923	Administrative division of U.K. D	London	English
†Equatorial Guinea	10,831	310,000	29	Republic A	Malabo	Spanish, English, native languages
Estonian S.S.R.	17,413	1,530,000	88	Soviet Socialist Republic (U.S.S.R.) D	Tallinn	Estonian, Russian
†Ethiopia	472,434	31,790,000	67	Provisional Military Government A	Addis Ababa	Amharic, Arabic, native languages
Eurasia	21,080,000	3,535,800,000	168	...	......; Tōkyō	...
Europe	3,840,000	672,400,000	175	...	......; London	...
Faeroe Islands	540	45,000	83	Part of Danish Realm B	Tórshavn	Danish, Faroese
Falkland Islands (Islas Malvinas) (excl. Dependencies)	4,700	2,000	0.4	Colony (U.K.)(3) C	Stanley	English
†Fiji	7,055	675,000	96	Parliamentary State (Comm. of Nations) A	Suva	English, Fijian, Hindustani
†Finland	130,558	4,860,000	37	Republic A	Helsinki	Finnish, Swedish
Florida	58,668	10,825,000	185	State (U.S.) D	Tallahassee; Miami	English
†France (excl. Overseas Depts.)	211,208	54,730,000	259	Republic A	Paris	French
France and Possessions	260,661	56,345,000	216	...	Paris	French
French Guiana	35,135	78,000	2.2	Overseas Department (France) D	Cayenne	French
French Polynesia	1,544	160,000	104	Overseas Territory (France) C	Papeete	Malay-Polynesian languages, French
French West Indies	1,112	615,000	553	...	......; Fort-de-France	French
Fujian	47,877	27,000,000	564	Province (China) D	Fuzhou	Chinese
†Gabon	103,347	940,000	9.1	Republic A	Libreville	French, native languages
Galapagos Islands (Archipiélago de Colón)	3,075	6,000	2.0	Province of Ecuador (Galápagos) D	Puerto Baquerizo Moreno	Spanish
†Gambia	4,361	660,000	161	Republic (Comm. of Nations) A	Banjul	English, native languages
Gansu	150,580	20,405,000	136	Province (China) D	Lanzhou	Chinese, Mongolian, Tibetan dialects
Georgia	58,914	5,790,000	98	State (U.S.) D	Atlanta	English
Georgian S.S.R.	26,911	5,195,000	193	Soviet Socialist Republic (U.S.S.R.) D	Tbilisi	Georgic, Armenian, Russian
†German Democratic Republic	41,768	16,725,000	400	Socialist Republic A	Berlin (East)	German
†Germany, Federal Republic of (incl. West Berlin)	96,016	61,480,000	640	Federal Republic A	Bonn; Essen	German
Germany (Entire)	137,784	78,205,000	568	...	......; Essen	German
†Ghana	92,100	14,670,000	160	Provisional Military Government (Comm. of Nations) A	Accra	English, native languages
Gibraltar	2.3	31,000	13,478	Colony (U.K.) C	Gibraltar	Spanish, English
Gilbert Islands, *see* Kiribati	...	...	...	...	...	...
Great Britain, *see* United Kingdom	...	...	...	...	...	...
†Greece	50,944	9,905,000	194	Republic A	Athens (Athínai)	Greek
Greenland	840,004	54,000	0.06	Part of Danish Realm B	Godthåb	Danish, Eskimo
†Grenada	133	105,000	789	Parliamentary State (Comm. of Nations) A	Saint George's	English
Guadeloupe (incl. Dependencies)	687	310,000	451	Overseas Department (France) D	Basse-Terre; Pointe-à-Pitre	French, Creole
Guam	209	117,000	560	Unincorporated Territory (U.S.) C	Agana	English, Chamorro
Guangdong	84,942	61,750,000	727	Province (China) D	Canton (Guangzhou)	Chinese, Miao-Yao
Guangxi Zhuangzu	89,190	37,990,000	426	Autonomous Region (China) D	Nanning	Chinese, Thai, Miao-Yao
†Guatemala	42,042	7,815,000	186	Republic A	Guatemala	Spanish, Indian languages
Guernsey (incl. Dependencies)	30	58,000	1,933	Bailiwick (U.K.) C	St. Peter Port	English, French
†Guinea	94,926	5,500,000	58	Republic A	Conakry	Native languages, French
†Guinea-Bissau	13,948	835,000	60	Republic A	Bissau	Native languages, Portuguese
Guizhou	67,182	29,825,000	444	Province (China) D	Guiyang	Chinese, Thai, Miao-Yao
†Guyana	83,000	835,000	10	Republic (Comm. of Nations) A	Georgetown	English
†Haiti	10,714	5,185,000	484	Republic A	Port-au-Prince	Creole, French
Hamburg	292	1,630,000	5,582	State (Federal Republic of Germany) D	Hamburg	German
Hawaii	6,473	1,020,000	158	State (U.S.) D	Honolulu	English, Japanese, Hawaiian
Hebei	73,359	55,150,000	752	Province (China) D	Shijiazhuang; Tangshan	Chinese
Heilongjiang	177,607	34,000,000	191	Province (China) D	Harbin	Chinese, Mongolian
Henan	64,093	77,440,000	1,208	Province (China) D	Zhengzhou	Chinese
Hesse (Hessen)	8,152	5,590,000	686	State (Federal Republic of Germany) D	Wiesbaden; Frankfurt am Main	German
Hispaniola	29,418	11,160,000	379	...	......; Santo Domingo	French, Spanish, Creole
Holland, *see* Netherlands	...	...	...	...	...	...
†Honduras	43,277	4,155,000	96	Republic A	Tegucigalpa	Spanish
Hong Kong	410	5,360,000	13,073	Colony (U.K.) C	Victoria; New Kowloon	Chinese, English
Hubei	69,498	49,815,000	717	Province (China) D	Wuhan	Chinese
Hunan	81,081	56,200,000	693	Province (China) D	Changsha	Chinese, Miao-Yao
†Hungary	35,921	10,685,000	297	Socialist Republic A	Budapest	Hungarian (Magyar)
†Iceland	39,769	235,000	5.9	Republic A	Reykjavík	Icelandic
Idaho	83,566	1,000,000	12	State (U.S.) D	Boise	English
Illinois	57,872	11,530,000	199	State (U.S.) D	Springfield; Chicago	English
†India (incl. part of Jammu and Kashmir)	1,237,061	738,240,000	597	Federal Republic (Comm. of Nations) A	New Delhi; Calcutta	Hindi, English, Bengali, Tegulu, Marathi, and other languages
Indiana	36,417	5,505,000	151	State (U.S.) D	Indianapolis	English
†Indonesia	741,101	157,560,000	213	Republic A	Jakarta	Bahasa Indonesia, Malay-Polynesian languages
Inner Mongolia (Nei Monggol)	424,772	20,200,000	48	Autonomous Region (China) D	Hohhot; Baotou	Mongolian
Iowa	56,275	2,920,000	52	State (U.S.) D	Des Moines	English
†Iran	636,296	43,335,000	68	Republic A	Tehrān	Farsi, Turkish, Kurdish, Arabic
†Iraq	167,925	14,530,000	87	Republic A	Baghdād	Arabic, Kurdish
†Ireland	27,136	3,555,000	131	Republic A	Dublin	English, Irish Gaelic
Isle Of Man	227	67,000	295	Self-governing Territory (U.K. protection) B	Douglas	English
†Israel	7,848	4,055,000	517	Republic A	Jerusalem (Yerushalayim); Tel Aviv-Yafo	Hebrew, Arabic, English
Israeli Occupied Areas	2,703	1,285,000	475	...	......; Gaza (Ghazzah)	Hebrew, Arabic, English
†Italy	116,319	56,685,000	487	Republic A	Rome; Milano	Italian
†Ivory Coast	123,847	8,980,000	73	Republic A	Abidjan and Yamoussoukro; Abidjan	French, native languages
†Jamaica	4,244	2,310,000	544	Parliamentary State (Comm. of Nations) A	Kingston	English
†Japan	145,834	119,680,000	821	Constitutional Monarchy A	Tōkyō	Japanese
Java (incl. Madura)	51,038	97,500,000	1,910	Part of Indonesia (5 provinces) ...	......; Jakarta	Bahasa Indonesia, Chinese, English
Jersey	45	75,000	1,667	Bailiwick (U.K.) C	St. Helier	English, French
Jiangsu	38,996	63,000,000	1,616	Province (China) D	Nanjing	Chinese
Jiangxi	62,162	34,640,000	557	Province (China) D	Nanchang	Chinese
Jilin	69,498	23,545,000	339	Province (China) D	Changchun	Chinese, Mongolian, Korean

* Areas include inland water.
† Member of the United Nations (1983).
. . .None, or not applicable.
(3) Claimed by Argentina.

Country, Division, or Region English (Conventional)	Area* in sq. mi.	Estimated Population 1/1/84	Pop. per sq. mi.	Form of Government and Political Status		Capital: Largest City (unless same)	Predominant Language
†Jordan	35,135	2,420,000	69	Constitutional Monarchy	A	'Ammān	Arabic, English
†Kampuchea	69,898	7,180,000	103	Socialist Republic	A	Phnom Penh	Khmer (Cambodian)
Kansas	82,282	2,415,000	29	State (U.S.)	D	Topeka; Wichita	English
Kashmir, Jammu and	86,024	9,335,000	109	In dispute (India and Pakistan)		......; Srīnagar and Jammu; Srīnagar	Urdu, Kashmiri, Dogri, Balti, Ladakhi, Punjabi
Kazakh S.S.R.	1,049,155	15,445,000	15	Soviet Socialist Republic (U.S.S.R.)	D	Alma-Ata	Turkish, Russian
Kentucky	40,414	3,740,000	93	State (U.S.)	D	Frankfort; Louisville	English
†Kenya	224,961	18,915,000	84	Republic (Comm. of Nations)	A	Nairobi	English, Swahili, native languages
Kerguelen Islands (Iles Kerguèlen)	2,700	92	0.03	Part of French Southern and Antarctic Territory (France)	C	......	French
Kirghiz S.S.R.	76,641	3,745,000	19	Soviet Socialist Republic (U.S.S.R.)	D	Frunze	Turkish, Farsi, Russian
†Kiribati	291	62,000	213	Republic (Comm. of Nations)	A	Bairiki	Gilbertese, English
Korea, North	46,540 (4)	19,400,000	417	Socialist Republic	A	Pyŏngyang	Korean
Korea, South	38,025 (4)	40,945,000	1,077	Republic	A	Seoul (Sŏul)	Korean
Korea (Entire)	85,052	60,345,000	710			......; Seoul (Sŏul)	Korean
†Kuwait	6,880	1,705,000	248	Constitutional Monarchy	A	Kuwait	Arabic, English
Labrador	112,826	30,000	0.3	Part of Newfoundland Province (Canada)		......; Labrador City	English, Eskimo
†Laos	91,429	4,035,000	44	Socialist Republic	A	Viangchan	Lao, French
Latin America	7,916,000	392,965,000	50			......; Mexico City (Ciudad de México)	Spanish, Portuguese
Latvian S.S.R.	24,595	2,600,000	106	Soviet Socialist Republic (U.S.S.R.)	D	Riga	Latvian, Russian
†Lebanon	4,015	2,960,000	737	Republic	A	Beirut (Bayrūt)	Arabic, French, English
†Lesotho	11,720	1,460,000	125	Monarchy (Comm. of Nations)	A	Maseru	Sesotho, English
Liaoning	57,915	37,260,000	643	Province (China)	D	Shenyang (Mukden)	Chinese, Mongolian
†Liberia	43,000	2,260,000	53	Provisional Military Government	A	Monrovia	Native languages, English
†Libya	679,362	3,415,000	5.0	Socialist Republic	A	Tripoli	Arabic
Liechtenstein	62	27,000	435	Constitutional Monarchy	A	Vaduz	German
Lithuanian S.S.R.	25,174	3,525,000	140	Soviet Socialist Republic (U.S.S.R.)	D	Vilnius	Lithuanian, Polish, Russian
Louisiana	47,750	4,505,000	94	State (U.S.)	D	Baton Rouge; New Orleans	English
Lower Saxony (Niedersachsen)	18,311	7,250,000	396	State (Federal Republic of Germany)	D	Hannover	German
†Luxembourg	999	365,000	365	Constitutional Monarchy	A	Luxembourg	Luxembourgish, French, German, English
Macao	6.0	370,000	61,667	Overseas Province (Portugal)	D	Macao	Chinese dialects
†Madagascar	226,658	9,620,000	42	Socialist Republic	A	Antananarivo	French, Malagasy
Madeira Islands (Arquipélago da Madeira)	307	240,000	782	Autonomous Region (Portugal)	D	Funchal	Portuguese
Maine	33,265	1,160,000	35	State (U.S.)	D	Augusta; Portland	English
Malagasy Republic, see Madagascar							
†Malawi	45,747	6,510,000	142	Republic (Comm. of Nations)	A	Lilongwe; Blantyre	Chichewa, English
Malaya	50,700	12,575,000	248	Part of Malaysia (11 States)		......; Kuala Lumpur	Bahasa Malaysia, English, Chinese, Tamil
†Malaysia	128,430	15,165,000	118	Federal Constitutional Monarchy (Comm. of Nations)	A	Kuala Lumpur	Bahasa Malaysia, English, Chinese, Tamil
†Maldives	115	160,000	1,391	Republic	A	Male	Divehi
†Mali	478,766	7,600,000	16	Republic	A	Bamako	French, Bambara
†Malta	122	365,000	2,992	Republic (Comm. of Nations)	A	Valletta	English, Maltese
Manitoba	251,000	1,055,000	4.2	Province (Canada)	D	Winnipeg	English
Maritime Provinces (excl. Newfoundland)	51,963	1,711,000	33	Part of Canada (3 provinces)		......; Halifax	English
Marshall Islands	70	33,000	471	Part of Trust Territory of the Pacific Islands (U.S. administration)	B	Majuro (island); Jarej-Uliga-Delap	Malay-Polynesian languages, English
Martinique	425	305,000	718	Overseas Department (France)	D	Fort-de-France	French, Creole
Maryland	10,461	4,325,000	413	State (U.S.)	D	Annapolis; Baltimore	English
Massachusetts	8,286	5,785,000	698	State (U.S.)	D	Boston	English
†Mauritania	397,955	1,805,000	4.5	Provisional Military Government	A	Nouakchott	Arabic, French
†Mauritius (incl. Dependencies)	790	1,000,000	1,266	Parliamentary State (Comm. of Nations)	A	Port Louis	French, Creole, English
Mayotte	144	57,000	396	Overseas Department (France)	D	Dzaoudzi	Swahili, French
†Mexico	761,604	75,750,000	99	Federal Republic	A	Mexico City (Ciudad de México)	Spanish
Michigan	97,107	9,195,000	95	State (U.S.)	D	Lansing; Detroit	English
Micronesia, Federated States of	271	78,000	288	Part of Trust Territory of the Pacific Islands (U.S. administration)	B	Kolonia	Malay-Polynesian languages, English
Middle America	1,056,000	130,665,000	124			......; Mexico City (Ciudad de México)	Spanish, English
Midway Islands	2.0	2,300	1,150	Unincorporated Territory (U.S.)	C	......	English
Minnesota	86,614	4,230,000	49	State (U.S.)	D	St. Paul; Minneapolis	English
Mississippi	47,691	2,630,000	55	State (U.S.)	D	Jackson	English
Missouri	69,697	5,035,000	72	State (U.S.)	D	Jefferson City; St. Louis	English
Moldavian S.S.R.	13,012	4,075,000	313	Soviet Socialist Republic (U.S.S.R.)	D	Kishinev	Moldavian, Russian, Ukrainian
Monaco	0.6	28,000	46,667	Constitutional Monarchy	A	Monaco	French, Italian, English, Monegasque
†Mongolia	604,250	1,845,000	3.1	Socialist Republic	A	Ulan Bator	Khalka Mongol
Montana	147,045	815,000	5.5	State (U.S.)	D	Helena; Billings	English
Montserrat	40	12,000	300	Colony (U.K.)	C	Plymouth	English
†Morocco (excl. Western Sahara)	172,414	23,045,000	134	Constitutional Monarchy	A	Rabat; Casablanca	Arabic, Berber, French
†Mozambique	302,329	13,360,000	44	Socialist Republic	A	Maputo	Portuguese, native languages
Muscat and Oman, see Oman							
Namibia (excl. Walvis Bay)	318,261	1,095,000	3.4	Under South African Administration(5)	C	Windhoek	Afrikkans, German, native languages
Nauru	8.2	8,200	1,000	Republic (Comm. of Nations)	A	Uaboe District;	Nauruan, English
Nebraska	77,350	1,610,000	21	State (U.S.)	D	Lincoln; Omaha	English
Nei Monggol, see Inner Mongolia							
†Nepal	56,135	15,960,000	284	Constitutional Monarchy	A	Kathmandu	Nepali, Tibeto-Burman languages
†Netherlands	15,892	14,420,000	907	Constitutional Monarchy	A	Amsterdam and The Hague; Amsterdam	Dutch
Netherlands Guiana, see Suriname							
Netherlands Antilles	383	275,000	718	Self-governing Territory (Netherlands protection)	B	Willemstad	Dutch, Spanish, English, Papiamento
Nevada	110,562	955,000	8.6	State (U.S.)	D	Carson City; Las Vegas	English
New Brunswick	28,354	715,000	25	Province (Canada)	D	Fredericton; Saint John	English, French
New Caledonia (incl. Dependencies)	7,358	148,000	20	Overseas Territory (France)	C	Nouméa	Malay-Polynesian languages, French
New England	66,674	12,580,000	189	Part of U.S. (6 states)		......; Boston	English
Newfoundland	156,185	580,000	3.7	Province (Canada)	D	St. John's	English
Newfoundland (excl. Labrador)	43,359	550,000	13	Part of Newfoundland Province, Canada		......; St. John's	English
New Hampshire	9,278	980,000	106	State (U.S.)	D	Concord; Manchester	English
New Hebrides, see Vanuatu							
New Jersey	7,787	7,555,000	970	State (U.S.)	D	Trenton; Newark	English
New Mexico	121,594	1,415,000	12	State (U.S.)	D	Santa Fe; Albuquerque	English, Spanish
New South Wales	309,433	5,435,000	18	State (Australia)	D	Sydney	English
New York	52,737	17,555,000	333	State (U.S.)	D	Albany; New York	English
†New Zealand	103,883	3,300,000	32	Parliamentary State (Comm. of Nations)	A	Wellington; Auckland	English, Maori
†Nicaragua	50,193	3,060,000	61	Republic	A	Managua	Spanish
†Niger	489,191	5,905,000	12	Provisional Military Government	A	Niamey	French, Hausa, native languages
†Nigeria	356,669	84,945,000	238	Federal Republic (Comm. of Nations)	A	Lagos	Hausa, Ibo, Yoruba, English
Ningxia Huizu	25,483	4,185,000	164	Autonomous Region (China)	D	Yinchuan	Chinese
Niue	102	3,000	29	Self-governing Territory (New Zealand)	B	Alofi	Malay-Polynesian languages, English

* Areas include inland water.
† Member of the United Nations (1983).
.... None, or not applicable.
(4) The 1,262 km² or 487 sq mi of the demilitarized zone are not included in either North or South Korea.
(5) In October 1966 the United Nations terminated the South African mandate over Namibia, a decision which South Africa did not accept.

Country, Division, or Region English (Conventional)	Area* in sq. mi.	Estimated Population 1/1/84	Pop. per sq. mi.	Form of Government and Political Status	Capital: Largest City (unless same)	Predominant Language
Norfolk Island.............	14	2,300	164	External Territory (Australia) C	Kingston	English
North America.............	9,410,000	391,100,000	42	....	......; New York	....
North Borneo, see Sabah......						
North Carolina.............	52,669	6,170,000	117	State (U.S.) .... D	Raleigh; Charlotte	English
North Dakota.............	70,702	675,000	9.5	State (U.S.) .... D	Bismarck; Fargo	English
Northern Ireland.............	5,452	1,560,000	286	Administrative division of United Kingdom .... D	Belfast	English
Northern Mariana Islands......	184	19,000	103	Part of Trust Territory of the Pacific Islands (U.S. administration) .... B	Saipan (island); Chalan Kanoa	Malay-Polynesian languages, English
Northern Territory, Austl.....	520,280	130,000	0.2	Territory (Australia) .... D	Darwin	English, Aboriginal languages
North Rhine-Westphalia (Nordrhein-Westfalen)........	13,153	16,980,000	1,291	State (Federal Republic of Germany) ... D	Düsseldorf; Essen	German
Northwest Territories.............	1,304,903	49,000	0.04	Territory (Canada) .... D	Yellowknife	English, Eskimo, Indian
†Norway (incl. Svalbard and Jan Mayen).............	149,158	4,140,000	28	Constitutional Monarchy .... A	Oslo	Norwegian (Riksmal and Landsmal)
Nova Scotia	21,425	870,000	41	Province (Canada) .... D	Halifax	English
Oceania (incl. Australia)........	3,290,000	24,000,000	7.3		......; Sydney	
Ohio.............	44,786	10,825,000	242	State (U.S.) .... D	Columbus; Cleveland	English
Oklahoma.............	69,957	3,250,000	46	State (U.S.) .... D	Oklahoma City	English
†Oman.............	82,030	990,000	12	Monarchy .... A	Muscat; Maṭrah	Arabic
Ontario.............	412,582	8,875,000	22	Province (Canada) .... D	Toronto	English
Oregon.............	97,076	2,715,000	28	State (U.S.) .... D	Salem; Portland	English
Orkney Islands.............	376	19,000	51	Part of Scotland, U.K. Orkney Island Area	Kirkwall	English
Pacific Islands, Trust Territory of the	717	143,000	199	U.N. Trusteeship (Administered by U.S.) .... B	Saipan (island); Jarej-Uliga-Delap	Malay-Polynesian languages, English
†Pakistan (incl. part of Jammu and Kashmir)	319,867	100,580,000	314	Federal Republic .... A	Islāmābād; Karāchi	Urdu, English, Punjabi, Sindhi
Palau.............	192	13,000	68	Part of Trust Territory of the Pacific Islands (U.S. administration) .... B	Koror	Malay-Polynesian languages, English
†Panama.............	29,762	2,200,000	74	Republic....................... A	Panamá	Spanish, English
†Papua New Guinea.............	178,703	3,155,000	18	Parliamentary State (Comm. of Nations) .. A	Port Moresby	Papuan and Negrito languages, English
†Paraguay.............	157,048	3,575,000	23	Republic....................... A	Asunción	Spanish, Guaraní
Peking (Beijing).............	6,487	9,735,000	1,501	Autonomous City (China) .... D	Peking (Beijing)	Chinese
Pennsylvania.............	46,047	11,885,000	258	State (U.S.) .... D	Harrisburg; Philadelphia	English
Persia, see Iran						
†Peru.............	496,224	19,555,000	39	Republic....................... A	Lima	Spanish, Quechua, Aymara
†Philippines.............	115,831	52,720,000	455	Republic....................... A	Manila	Pilipino, English, Spanish
Pitcairn (excl. Dependencies) ...	1.8	54	30	Colony (U.K.) C	Adamstown	English
†Poland.............	120,728	36,725,000	304	Socialist Republic .... A	Warsaw (Warszawa); Katowice	Polish
†Portugal.............	35,516	10,230,000	288	Republic....................... A	Lisbon (Lisboa)	Portuguese
Portuguese Guinea, see Guinea-Bissau						
Prairie Provinces.............	757,985	4,420,000	5.8	Part of Canada (3 provinces) .... D	......; Winnipeg	English
Prince Edward Island	2,184	126,000	58	Province (Canada) .... D	Charlottetown	English
Puerto Rico.............	3,515	3,365,000	957	Commonwealth (U.S. protection). .... B	San Juan	Spanish, English
†Qatar.............	4,247	270,000	64	Monarchy .... A	Doha	Arabic, English
Qinghai.............	277,993	4,185,000	15	Province (China) .... D	Xining	Tibetan dialects, Mongolian, Turkish, Chinese
Quebec.............	594,860	6,600,000	11	Province (Canada) .... D	Québec; Montréal	French, English
Queensland.............	667,000	2,470,000	5.2	State (Australia) .... D	Brisbane	English
Reunion.............	969	540,000	557	Overseas Department (France) .... D	Saint-Denis	French
Rhineland-Palatinate (Rheinland-Pfalz).............	7,663	3,625,000	473	State (Federal Republic of Germany) .... D	Mainz	German
Rhode Island.............	1,212	960,000	792	State (U.S.) .... D	Providence	English
Rhodesia, see Zimbabwe						
Rodrigues.............	42	34,000	810	Part of Mauritius	......; Port Mathurin	English, French
†Romania.............	91,699	23,025,000	251	Socialist Republic .... A	Bucharest (Bucureşti)	Romanian, Hungarian, German
Russian Soviet Federated Socialist Republic	6,592,846	142,705,000	22	Soviet Federated Socialist Republic (U.S.S.R.) .... D	Moscow (Moskva)	Russian, Finno-Ugric languages, Farsi, Turkish, Mongolian
†Rwanda.............	10,169	5,380,000	529	Republic....................... A	Kigali	French, Kinyarwanda
Saar (Saarland).............	992	1,055,000	1,064	State (Federal Republic of Germany) .... D	Saarbrücken	German
Sabah.............	29,388	1,130,000	38	State (Malaysia) .... D	Kota Kinabalu	Bahasa Malaysia, Chinese, English, native languages
St. Christopher-Nevis	104	45,000	433	Parliamentary State (Comm. of Nations) .... A	Basseterre	English
St. Helena (incl. Dependencies).............	162	6,000	37	Colony (U.K.) C	Jamestown	English
†St. Lucia.............	238	120,000	504	Parliamentary State (Comm. of Nations) .... A	Castries	English, French
St. Pierre and Miquelon	93	6,100	66	Overseas Department (France) .... D	Saint-Pierre	French
†St. Vincent and the Grenadines	150	136,000	360	Parliamentary State (Comm. of Nations) .... A	Kingstown	English
San Marino.............	24	22,000	917	Republic....................... A	San Marino	Italian
†Sao Tome and Principe	372	89,000	239	Republic....................... A	São Tomé	Portuguese, native languages
Sarawak.............	48,342	1,460,000	30	State (Malaysia) .... D	Kuching	Bahasa Malaysia, Chinese, English, native languages
Sardinia.............	9,301	1,590,000	171	Part of Italy (Sardegna Autonomous Region)....................... D	Cagliari	Italian
Saskatchewan.............	251,700	1,000,000	4.0	Province (Canada) .... D	Regina	English
†Saudi Arabia.............	830,000	10,220,000	12	Monarchy .... A	Riyadh	Arabic
Scandinavia (incl. Finland and Iceland).............	510,000	22,740,000	45		......; Copenhagen (København)	Swedish, Danish, Norwegian, Finnish, Icelandic
Schleswig-Holstein.............	6,070	2,605,000	429	State (Federal Republic of Germany) .... D	Kiel	German
Scotland.............	30,416	5,175,000	170	Administrative division of U.K. ...... D	Edinburgh	English, Scots Gaelic
†Senegal.............	75,955	6,190,000	81	Republic....................... A	Dakar	Wolof, French, native languages
†Seychelles.............	171	65,000	380	Republic (Comm. of Nations). .... A	Victoria	French, Creole, English
Shaanxi.............	76,062	30,140,000	396	Province (China) .... D	Xi'an	Chinese
Shandong.............	59,074	77,440,000	1,311	Province (China) .... D	Jinan; Qingdao	Chinese
Shanghai.............	2,239	12,455,000	5,563	Autonomous City (China) .... D	Shanghai	Chinese
Shanxi.............	61,004	26,380,000	432	Province (China) .... D	Taiyuan	Chinese
Shetland Islands.............	551	27,000	19	Part of Scotland, U.K. (Shetland Island Area)	Lerwick	English
Siam, see Thailand.............						
Sichuan.............	216,217	103,710,000	480	Province (China) .... D	Chengdu; Chongging	Chinese, Tibetan dialects, Miao-Yao
Sicily.............	9,926	4,880,000	492	Part of Italy (Sicilia Autonomous Region) .... D	Palermo	Italian
†Sierra Leone.............	27,925	3,825,000	137	Republic (Comm. of Nations)......... A	Freetown	English, Krio, native languages
†Singapore.............	224	2,540,000	11,339	Republic (Comm. of Nations)......... A	Singapore	Chinese, Malay, English, Tamil
†Solomon Islands.............	11,506	260,000	23	Parliamentary State (Comm. of Nations) .... A	Honiara	Malay-Polynesian languages, English
†Somalia.............	246,200	7,160,000	29	Socialist Republic .... A	Mogadishu (Muqdisho)	Somali, Arabic, English, Italian
†South Africa (incl. Walvis Bay).............	434,674	24,465,000	56	Republic....................... A	Pretoria and Cape Town; Johannesburg	English, Afrikaans, native languages
South America.............	6,860,000	262,300,000	38		......; São Paulo	
South Australia.............	380,070	1,370,000	3.6	State (Australia)................. D	Adelaide	English
South Carolina.............	31,116	3,280,000	105	State (U.S.) .... D	Columbia; Charleston	English
South Dakota.............	77,120	705,000	9.1	State (U.S.) .... D	Pierre; Sioux Falls	English
Southern Yemen, see Yemen, People's Democratic Republic of.............						

* Areas include inland water.
† Member of the United Nations (1983).
.... None, or not applicable.

World Political Information Table (continued)

Country, Division, or Region English (Conventional)	Area* in sq. mi.	Estimated Population 1/1/84	Pop. per sq. mi.	Form of Government and Political Status		Capital: Largest City (unless same)	Predominant Language
South Georgia (incl. Dependencies)	1,580	22	0.01	Dependency of Falkland Islands (U.K.)[3]	C		English, Norwegian
South West Africa, see Namibia							
Soviet Union, see Union of Soviet Socialist Republics	....	....	...	....			
†Spain	194,882	38,350,000	197	Constitutional Monarchy	A	Madrid	Spanish
Spanish North Africa (Sp.)[2]	12	136,000	11,333	Five Possessions (No Central Government)	C	......; Cueta	Spanish, Arabic, Berber
Spanish Sahara, see Western Sahara							
†Sri Lanka	24,962	15,510,000	621	Socialist Republic (Comm. of Nations)	A	Colombo	Sinhala, Tamil, English
†Sudan	967,500	20,500,000	21	Republic	A	Khartoum	Arabic, native languages, English
Sumatra	182,860	29,935,000	164	Part of Indonesia (7 provinces)		......; Medan	Bahasa Indonesia, English, Chinese
†Suriname	63,037	375,000	5.9	Republic	A	Paramaribo	Dutch, English, Sranang Tongo
Svalbard	23,958	4,200	0.2	Part of Norway		......; Longyearbyen	Norwegian, Russian
†Swaziland	6,704	615,000	92	Monarchy (Comm. of Nations)	A	Mbabane; Manzini	English, siSwati
†Sweden	173,780	8,350,000	48	Constitutional Monarchy	A	Stockholm	Swedish
Switzerland	15,943	6,470,000	406	Federal Republic	A	Bern; Zürich	German, French, Italian
†Syria	71,498	10,635,000	149	Socialist Republic	A	Damascus (Dimashq)	Arabic
Tadzhik S.S.R.	55,251	4,100,000	74	Soviet Socialist Republic (U.S.S.R.)	D	Dushanbe	Tadzhik, Turkish, Russian
Taiwan	13,900	18,870,000	1,358	Republic	A	Taipei	Chinese dialects
†Tanzania	364,900	20,005,000	55	Republic (Comm. of Nations)	A	Dar es Salaam	Swahili, English, native languages
Tasmania	26,383	435,000	16	State (Australia)	D	Hobart	English
Tennessee	42,143	4,765,000	113	State (U.S.)	D	Nashville; Memphis	English
Texas	266,805	15,565,000	58	State (U.S.)	D	Austin; Dallas	English, Spanish
†Thailand	198,115	51,230,000	259	Constitutional Monarchy	A	Bangkok (Krung Thep)	Thai
Tianjin	4,247	8,165,000	1,923	Autonomous City (China)	D	Tianjin (Tientsin)	Chinese, Mongolian
Tibet (Xizang)	471,044	2,095,000	4.4	Autonomous Region (China)	D	Lhasa	Tibetan dialects
†Togo	21,926	2,825,000	129	Republic	A	Lomé	Native languages, French
Tokelau	3.9	1,500	385	Island Territory (New Zealand)	C	......; Fakaofo	Malay-Polynesian languages, English
Tonga	270	104,000	385	Constitutional Monarchy (Comm. of Nations)	A	Nuku'alofa	Tongan, English
Transcaucasia	71,853	14,765,000	205	Part of U.S.S.R. (3 republics)		......; Baku	Russian, Armenian, Georgic, Turkish
Transkei[6]	15,831	2,495,000	158	Bantu Homeland (South African protection)	B	Umtata	Xhosa, Afrikaans
†Trinidad and Tobago	1,980	1,220,000	616	Republic (Comm. of Nations)	A	Port of Spain	English
Tristan da Cunha	40	300	7.5	Dependency of St. Helena (U.K.)	C	Edinburgh	English
Trucial States, see United Arab Emirates							
†Tunisia	63,170	6,905,000	109	Republic	A	Tunis	Arabic, French
†Turkey	300,948	47,715,000	159	Republic	A	Ankara; İstanbul	Turkish, Kurdish, Arabic
Turkey in Europe	9,175	4,495,000	490	Part of Turkey		......; İstanbul	Turkish
Turkmen S.S.R.	188,456	2,980,000	16	Soviet Socialist Republic (U.S.S.R.)	D	Ashkhabad	Turkish, Russian
Turks and Caicos Islands	166	8,000	48	Colony (U.K.)	C	Grand Turk	English
Tuvalu	10	7,800	780	Parliamentary State (Comm. of Nations)	A	Funafuti	English, Tuvaluan
†Uganda	91,134	14,140,000	155	Republic (Comm. of Nations)	A	Kampala	English, Swahili, Luganda, native languages
†Ukrainian S.S.R.	233,090	51,420,000	221	Soviet Socialist Republic (U.S.S.R)	D	Kiev	Ukrainian, Russian
†Union of Soviet Socialist Republics	8,600,383	273,380,000	32	Federal Socialist Republic	A	Moskow (Moskva)	Russian and other Slavic languages various Altaic and Indo-European languages
U.S.S.R. in Europe	1,920,789	177,360,000	92	Part of U.S.S.R.		......; Moskow (Moskva)	Russian and other Slavic languages
†United Arab Emirates	32,278	1,450,000	45	Federation of Monarchs	A	Abu Dhabi	Arabic, English, Farsi
United Arab Republic, see Egypt	....	....	...				......
†United Kingdom	94,249	56,010,000	594	Constitutional Monarchy (Comm. of Nations)	A	London	English, Gaelic
United Kingdom and Possessions	102,311	61,715,000	603			London	English
†United States	3,679,245	235,310,000	64	Federal Republic	A	Washington; New York	English
United States and Possessions	3,683,901	239,075,000	65			Washington; New York	English, Spanish
Upper Volta, see Burkina Faso							
†Uruguay	68,037	2,980,000	44	Republic	A	Montevideo	Spanish
Utah	84,902	1,640,000	19	State (U.S.)	D	Salt Lake City	English
Uzbek S.S.R.	172,742	16,565,000	96	Soviet Socialist Republic (U.S.S.R.)	D	Tashkent	Turkish, Sart, Russian
†Vanuatu	5,714	129,000	23	Republic (Comm. of Nations)	A	Port-Vila	Bislama, French, English
Vatican City	0.2	700	3,500	Ecclesiastical State	A	Vatican City	Italian, Latin
Venda[6]	2,774	390,000	141	Bantu Homeland (South African protection)	B	Thohoyandou; Makearela	Venda, Afrikaans
†Venezuela	352,144	15,325,000	44	Federal Republic	A	Caracas	Spanish
Vermont	9,614	530,000	55	State (U.S.)	D	Montpelier; Burlington	English
Victoria	87,884	4,100,000	47	State (Australia)	D	Melbourne	English
Vietnam	127,242	58,070,000	456	Socialist Republic	A	Hanoi; Ho Chi Minh City	Vietnamese
Virginia	40,763	5,615,000	138	State (U.S.)	D	Richmond; Norfolk	English
Virgin Islands (U.S.)	133	104,000	782	Unincorporated Territory (U.S.)	C	Charlotte Amalie	English, Spanish
Virgin Islands, British	59	13,000	220	Colony (U.K.)	C	Road Town	English
Wake Island	3.0	400	133	Unincorporated Territory (U.S.)	C		English
Wales	8,019	2,810,000	350	Administrative division of U.K.	D	Cardiff	English, Welsh
Wallis and Futuna	98	12,000	122	Overseas Territory (France)	C	Mata-Utu; Ono	French, Uvean, Futunan
Washington	68,139	4,290,000	63	State (U.S.)	D	Olympia; Seattle	English
Western Australia	975,920	1,360,000	1.4	State (Australia)	D	Perth	English
Western Sahara	102,703	150,000	1.5	Occupied by Morocco	C	El Aaiún	Arabic
†Western Samoa	1,097	160,000	146	Constitutional Monarchy (Comm. of Nations)	A	Apia	Samoan, English
West Indies	92,000	29,995,000	326			......; Havana	Spanish, English, French, Creole
West Virginia	24,236	1,985,000	82	State (U.S.)	D	Charleston; Huntington	English
White Russia, see Byelorussian S.S.R.							
Wisconsin	66,213	4,835,000	73	State (U.S.)	D	Madison; Milwaukee	English
Wyoming	97,808	535,000	5.5	State (U.S.)	D	Cheyenne	English
Xinjiang Uygur	635,910	13,710,000	22	Autonoumous Region (China)	D	Urumqi	Turkish, Mongolian, Tunguq
Xizang, see Tibet							
†Yemen	75,290	6,285,000	83	Republic	A	San'á'	Arabic
†Yemen, People's Democratic Republic of	128,560	2,185,000	17	Socialist Republic	A	Aden	Arabic
†Yugoslavia	98,766	22,915,000	232	Federal Socialist Republic	D	Belgrade (Beograd)	Serbo-Croatian, Slovene, Macedonian
Yukon Territory	186,300	25,000	0.1	Territory (Canada)	D	Whitehorse	English, Eskimo, Indian
Yunnan	147,105	33,910,000	231	Province (China)	D	Kunming	Chinese, Tibetan dialects, Khmer Miao-Yao
†Zaire	905,567	31,705,000	35	Republic	A	Kinshasa (Léopoldville)	French, English, Lingala, Swahili, Kikongo, Tshiluba
†Zambia	290,586	6,435,000	22	Republic (Comm. of Nations)	A	Lusaka	English, native languages
Zanzibar	950	540,000	568	Part of Tanzania	D	Zanzibar	Swahili, English, native languages
Zhejiang	38,996	40,500,000	1,039	Province (China)	D	Hangzhou	Chinese
†Zimbabwe	150,804	8,510,000	56	Republic (Comm. of Nations)	A	Harare (Salisbury)	English, native languages
World	57,740,000	4,733,000,000	82			......; Tōkyō	

* Areas include inland water.
† Member of the United Nations (1983).
... None, or not applicable.
[2] Comprises Ceuta, Melilla, and several small islands.
[6] Bophuthatswana, Ciskei, Transkei, and Venda are not recognized by the United Nations.

World Facts and Comparisons

MOVEMENTS OF THE EARTH

The earth makes one complete revolution around the sun every 365 days, 5 hours, 48 minutes, and 46 seconds.

The earth makes one complete rotation on its axis in 23 hours and 56 minutes.

The earth revolves in its orbit around the sun at a speed of 66,700 miles per hour.

The earth rotates on its axis at an equatorial speed of more than 1,000 miles per hour.

MEASUREMENTS OF THE EARTH

Estimated age of the earth, at least 3 billion years.
Equatorial diameter of the earth, 7,926.68 miles.
Polar diameter of the earth, 7,899.99 miles.
Mean diameter of the earth, 7,918.78 miles.
Equatorial circumference of the earth, 24,902.45 miles.
Polar circumference of the earth, 24,818.60 miles.

Difference between equatorial and polar circumference of the earth, 83.85 miles.
Weight of the earth, 6,600,000,000,000,000,000,000 tons, or 6,600 billion billion tons.
Total area of the earth, 196,940,400 square miles.
Total land area of the earth (including inland water and Antarctica), 57,740,000 square miles.

THE EARTH'S INHABITANTS

Total population of the earth is estimated to be 4,733,000,000 (January 1, 1984).
Estimated population density of the earth, 82 per square mile.

THE EARTH'S SURFACE

Highest point on the earth's surface, Mount Everest, China (Tibet)–Nepal, 29,028 feet.
Lowest point on the earth's land surface, shores of the Dead Sea, Israel-Jordan, 1,299 feet below sea level.

Greatest ocean depth, the Marianas Trench, south of Guam, Pacific Ocean, 36,198 feet.

EXTREMES OF TEMPERATURE AND RAINFALL OF THE EARTH

Highest temperature ever recorded, 136.4°F. at Al 'Azīzīyah, Libya, Africa, on September 13, 1922.
Lowest temperature ever recorded, −126.9°F. at Vostok, Antarctica, on August 24, 1960.
Highest mean annual temperature, 88°F. at Lugh Ferrandi, Somalia.
Lowest mean annual temperature, −67°F. at Vostok, Antarctica.
At Cilaos, Réunion Island, in the Indian Ocean, 74 inches of rainfall was reported in a 24-hour period, March 15-16, 1952. This is believed to be the world's record for a 24-hour rainfall.
An authenticated rainfall of 366 inches in 1 month—July, 1861—was reported at Cherrapunji, India. More than 131 inches fell in a period of 7 consecutive days in June, 1931. Average annual rainfall at Cherrapunji is 450 inches.

The Continents

CONTINENT	Area (sq. mi.)	Population Estimated Jan. 1, 1984	Population per sq. mi.	Mean Elevation (feet)	Highest Elevation (Feet)	Lowest Elevation (Feet)	Highest Recorded Temperature	Lowest Recorded Temperature
North America......	9,410,000	391,100,000	42	2,000	Mt. McKinley, United States (Alaska), 20,320	Death Valley, California, 282 below sea level	Death Valley, California 134°F.	Snag, Yukon, Canada, −81°F.
South America......	6,860,000	262,300,000	38	1,800	Mt. Aconcagua, Argentina, 22,831	Salinas Chicas, Argentina, 138 below sea level	Rivadavia, Argentina, 120°F.	Sarmiento, Argentina, −27.4°F.
Europe...........	3,840,000	672,400,000	175	980	Mt. Elbrus, Soviet Union, 18,510	Caspian Sea, Soviet Union—Iran, 92 below sea level	Sevilla (Seville), Spain, 122°F.	Ust-Shchugor, Soviet Union, −67°F.
Asia.............	17,240,000	2,863,400,000	166	3,000	Mt. Everest, China (Tibet)-Nepal, 29,028	Dead Sea, Israel-Jordan, 1,299 below sea level	Tirat Zvi, Israel, 129.2°F.	Oymyakon, Soviet Union, −89.9°F.
Africa...........	11,700,000	519,800,000	44	1,900	Mt. Kilimanjaro, Tanzania, 19,340	Lac Assal, Djibouti, 509 below sea level	Al 'Azīzīyah, Libya, 139.4°F.	Ifrane, Morocco, −11.2°F.
Oceania, incl. Australia.........	3,290,000	24,000,000	7	.....	Mt. Wilhelm, Papua New Guinea, 14,793	Lake Eyre, South Australia, 52 below sea level	Cloncurry, Queensland, Australia, 127.5°F.	Charlotte Pass, New South Wales, Australia, −8°F.
Australia........	2,967,909	15,535,000	5	1,000	Mt. Kosciusko, New South Wales, 7,310	Lake Eyre, South Australia, 52 below sea level	Cloncurry, Queensland, 127.5°F.	Charlotte Pass, New South Wales, −8°F.
Antarctica........	5,405,000	Uninhabited	...	6,000	Vinson Massif, 16,864	Unknown	Esperanza (Antarctic Peninsula), 58.3°F.	Vostok, −126.9°F.
World...........	57,740,000	4,733,000,000	82	.....	Mt. Everest, China (Tibet)-Nepal, 29,028	Dead Sea, Israel-Jordan, 1,299 below sea level	Al 'Azīzīyah, Libya, 136.4°F.	Vostok, −126.9°F.

Approximate Population of the World 1650-1984*

AREA	1650	1750	1800	1850	1900	1914	1920	1939	1950	1984
North America.................	5,000,000	5,000,000	13,000,000	39,000,000	106,000,000	141,000,000	147,000,000	186,000,000	219,000,000	391,100,000
South America.................	8,000,000	7,000,000	12,000,000	20,000,000	38,000,000	55,000,000	61,000,000	90,000,000	111,000,000	262,300,000
Europe.......................	100,000,000	140,000,000	190,000,000	265,000,000	400,000,000	470,000,000	453,000,000	526,000,000	530,000,000	672,400,000
Asia.........................	335,000,000	476,000,000	593,000,000	754,000,000	932,000,000	1,006,000,000	1,000,000,000	1,247,000,000	1,418,000,000	2,863,400,000
Africa.......................	100,000,000	95,000,000	90,000,000	95,000,000	118,000,000	130,000,000	140,000,000	170,000,000	199,000,000	519,800,000
Oceania, incl. Australia............	2,000,000	2,000,000	2,000,000	2,000,000	6,000,000	8,000,000	9,000,000	11,000,000	13,000,000	24,000,000
Australia............					4,000,000	5,000,000	6,000,000	7,000,000	8,000,000	15,535,000
World.......................	550,000,000	725,000,000	900,000,000	1,175,000,000	1,600,000,000	1,810,000,000	1,810,000,000	2,230,000,000	2,490,000,000	4,733,000,000

*Figures prior to 1984 are rounded to the nearest million.   Figures in italics represent very rough estimates.

Largest Countries of the World in Population

	Population 1/1/84			Population 1/1/84			Population 1/1/84
1 China (excl. Taiwan)..................	1,046,530,000	10 Nigeria............................	84,945,000	17 Philippines........................	52,720,000
2 India (incl. part of Jammu and Kashmir).....	738,240,000	11 Mexico............................	75,750,000	18 Thailand..........................	51,230,000
3 Soviet Union......................	273,380,000	12 Federal Republic of Germany (incl. West Berlin)...................	61,480,000	19 Turkey............................	47,715,000
4 United States.....................	235,310,000	13 Vietnam...........................	58,070,000	20 Egypt.............................	46,465,000
5 Indonesia........................	157,560,000	14 Italy..............................	56,685,000	21 Iran..............................	43,335,000
6 Brazil............................	133,100,000	15 United Kingdom....................	56,010,000	22 South Korea.......................	40,945,000
7 Japan............................	119,680,000	16 France............................	54,730,000	23 Spain.............................	38,350,000
8 Pakistan (incl. part of Jammu and Kashmir)..	100,580,000			24 Burma............................	37,505,000
9 Bangladesh.......................	95,600,000			25 Poland............................	36,725,000

Largest Countries of the World in Area

	Area (sq. mi.)			Area (sq. mi.)			Area (sq. mi.)
1 Soviet Union.....................	8,600,383	9 Sudan............................	967,500	18 Mongolia.........................	604,250
2 Canada..........................	3,831,033	10 Algeria...........................	919,595	19 Peru.............................	496,224
3 United States.....................	3,679,245	11 Zaire.............................	905,567	20 Chad.............................	495,755
4 China (excl. Taiwan)...............	3,630,747	12 Greenland........................	840,004	21 Niger............................	489,191
5 Brazil............................	3,265,075	13 Saudi Arabia......................	830,000	22 Angola...........................	481,353
6 Australia.........................	2,967,909	14 Mexico...........................	761,604	23 Mali.............................	478,766
7 India (incl. part of Jammu and Kashmir)........	1,237,061	15 Indonesia.........................	741,101	24 Ethiopia..........................	472,434
8 Argentina........................	1,068,301	16 Libya.............................	679,362	25 Colombia.........................	439,737
		17 Iran..............................	636,296		

Principal Mountains of the World

North America

	Height (Feet)
McKinley, △Alaska (△United States; △North America)	20,320
Logan, △Canada (△St. Elias Mts.)	19,520
Citlaltépetl (Orizaba), △Mexico	18,701
St. Elias, Alaska–Canada	18,008
Popocatépetl, Mexico	17,887
Foraker, Alaska	17,400
Ixtacihuatl, Mexico	17,343
Lucania, Yukon, Canada	17,147
Whitney, △California	14,494
Elbert, △Colorado (△Rocky Mts.)	14,433
Massive, Colorado	14,421
Harvard, Colorado	14,420
Rainier, △Washington (△Cascade Range)	14,410
Williamson, California	14,375
Blanca Pk., Colorado (△Sangre de Cristo Range)	14,345
Uncompahgre Pk., Colorado (△San Juan Mts.)	14,309
Grays Pk., Colorado (△Front Range)	14,270
Evans, Colorado	14,264
Longs Pk., Colorado	14,255
Wrangell, Alaska	14,163
Shasta, California	14,162
Pikes Peak, Colorado	14,110
Colima, Nevado de, Mexico	13,993
Tajumulco, △Guatemala (△Central America)	13,846
Gannett Pk., △Wyoming	13,804
Mauna Kea, △Hawaii (△Hawaii I.)	13,796
Grand Teton, Wyoming	13,766
Mauna Loa, Hawaii	13,680
Kings Pk., △Utah	13,528
Cloud Pk., Wyoming (△Big Horn Mts.)	13,175
Wheeler Pk., △New Mexico	13,161
Boundary Pk., △Nevada	13,143
Gunnbjörn, △Greenland	13,120
Waddington, Canada (△Coast Mts.)	13,104
Robson, Canada (△Canadian Rockies)	12,972
Granite Pk., △Montana	12,799
Borah Pk., △Idaho	12,662
Humphreys Pk., △Arizona	12,633
Chirripó Grande, △Costa Rica	12,533
Adams, Washington	12,307
San Gorgonio, California	11,502
Chiriquí, △Panama	11,411
Hood, △Oregon	11,239
Lassen Pk., California	10,457
Duarte, Pico, △Dominican Rep. (△West Indies)	10,417
Haleakala, Hawaii (△Maui)	10,023
Paricutin, Mexico	9,213
La Selle, Pic, △Haiti	8,773
Guadalupe Pk., △Texas	8,751
Olympus, Washington (△Olympic Mts.)	7,965
Monte Cristo, △El Salvador–Guatemala–Honduras	7,936
Blue Mountain Pk., △Jamaica	7,402
Harney Pk., △South Dakota (△Black Hills)	7,242
Mitchell, △North Carolina (△Appalachian Mts.)	6,684
Clingmans Dome, North Carolina–△Tennessee (△Great Smoky Mts.)	6,643
Turquino, Pico, △Cuba	6,542
Washington, △New Hampshire (△White Mts.)	6,288
Rogers, △Virginia	5,729
Marcy, △New York (△Adirondack Mts.)	5,344
Katahdin, △Maine	5,268
Kawaikini, Hawaii (△Kauai)	5,243
Spruce Knob, △West Virginia	4,862
Pelée, △Martinique	4,583
Mansfield, △Vermont (△Green Mts.)	4,393
Punta, Cerro de, △Puerto Rico	4,389
Black Mtn., △Kentucky	4,145
Kaala Pk., Hawaii (△Oahu)	4,050

South America

	Height (Feet)
Aconcagua, △Argentina (△Andes Mts.; △South America)	22,831
Ojos del Salado, Argentina–△Chile	22,590
Tupungato, Argentina–Chile	22,310
Pissis, Argentina	22,241
Mercedario, Argentina	22,211
Huascarán, △Peru	22,205
Llullaillaco, Argentina–Chile	22,057
Yerupaja, Peru	21,765
Incahuasi, Argentina–Chile	21,719
Sajama, Nevado, △Bolivia	21,391
Illimani, Bolivia	21,201
Chimborazo, △Ecuador	20,561
Cotopaxi, Ecuador	19,347
Misti, Peru	19,098
Cristóbal Colón, △Colombia	19,029
Huila, Colombia (△Cordillera Central)	18,865
Bolívar (La Columna), △Venezuela	16,411
Fitz Roy, Argentina	11,073
Neblina, Pico da, △Brazil	9,888

△*Highest mountain in state, country, range, or region named.*

Europe

	Height (Feet)
Elbrus, Soviet Union (△Caucasus Mts.; △Europe)	18,510
Dykh–Tau, Soviet Union	17,070
Shkhara, Soviet Union	16,594
Kazbek, Soviet Union	16,512
Blanc, Mont, △France–△Italy (△Alps)	15,771
Rosa, Monte (Dufourspitze) △Switzerland	15,200
Weisshorn, Switzerland	14,803
Matterhorn, Italy–Switzerland	14,685
Finsteraarhorn, Switzerland	14,026
Jungfrau, Switzerland	13,668
Grossglockner, △Austria	12,457
Teide, Pico de, △Spain (△Canary Is.)	12,162
Mulhacén, △Spain (continental)	11,424
Aneto, Pico de, Spain (△Pyrenees)	11,168
Etna, Italy (△Sicily)	11,122
Perdido (Perdu), Spain	11,007
Clapier, France–Italy (△Maritime Alps)	9,993
Zugspitze, Austria–△Germany, Fed. Rep. of	9,721
Coma Pedrosa, △Andorra	9,665
Musala, △Bulgaria	9,592
Corno, Italy (△Apennines)	9,560
Olympus, △Greece	9,550
Triglav, △Yugoslavia	9,393
Korab, △Albania–Yugoslavia	9,068
Cinto, France (△Corsica)	8,891
Gerlachovka, △Czechoslovakia (△Carpathian Mts.)	8,737
Moldoveanu, △Romania	8,343
Rysy, Czechoslovakia–△Poland	8,199
Glittertinden, △Norway (△Scandinavia)	8,110
Parnassós, Greece	8,061
Ídhi (Ida), Greece (△Crete)	8,058
Pico, △Portugal (△Azores Is.)	7,713
Hvannadalshnúkur, △Iceland	6,952
Kebnekaise, △Sweden	6,926
Estrela, △Portugal (continental)	6,539
Narodnaya, Soviet Union (△Ural Mts.)	6,217
Marmora, Punta la, Italy (△Sardinia)	6,017
Hekla, Iceland	4,747
Nevis, Ben, △United Kingdom (△Scotland)	4,406
Haltia, △Finland–Norway	4,357
Vesuvius, Italy	3,842
Snowdon, △Wales	3,560
Carrantuohill, △Ireland	3,414
Kékes, △Hungary	3,330
Scafell Pikes, △England	3,210

Asia

	Height (Feet)
Everest, △China (△Tibet)–△Nepal (△Himalayas; △Asia; △World)	29,028
K2 (Godwin Austen), China–△Pakistan (△Kashmir) (△Karakoram Range)	28,250
Känchenjunga, Nepal–△India	28,208
Makālu, China (Tibet)–Nepal	27,825
Dhaulāgiri, Nepal	26,810
Nānga Parbat, Pakistan (Kashmir)	26,650
Annapurna, Nepal	26,504
Gasherbrum, Pakistan (Kashmir)	26,453
Xixabangma Mtn. (Gosainthar), China (Tibet)	26,289
Nanda Devi, India	25,645
Rakaposhi, Pakistan (Kashmir)	25,550
Kamet, India	25,447
Namcha Barwa, China (Tibet)	25,446
Guerla Mandatashan, China (Tibet)	25,354
Muztag, China (△Kunlun Mts.)	25,338
Tirich Mir, Pakistan (△Hindu Kush)	25,230
Gongga Mtn. (Minya Konka), China	24,902
Muztagata, China	24,757
Kula Kangri, △Bhutan	24,784
Communism Pk., △Soviet Union (△Pamir–Alay Mts.)	24,590
Pobedy, Peak, China–Soviet Union (△Tian Shan)	24,406
Lenin Pk., Soviet Union	23,406
Api, Nepal	23,399
Khan–Tengri, Soviet Union	22,949
Kailas, China (Tibet)	22,028
Hkakabo Razi, △Burma–China	19,296
Demavend, △Iran	18,386
Ararat, △Turkey	16,804
Jaya Pk., △Indonesia (△New Guinea)	16,503
Klyuchevskaja Sopka, Soviet Union (△Kamchatka)	15,584
Trikora Pk., Indonesia	15,584
Belukha, Soviet Union	14,783
Tavan Bogd Uul, China–△Mongolia–Soviet Union (△Altai Mts.)	14,350
Kinabalu, △Malaysia (△Borneo)	13,432
Yu, △Taiwan (Formosa)	13,114
Türgen Mtn., Mongolia	13,051
Erciyeş, Turkey	12,848
Kerinci, Indonesia (△Sumatra)	12,467
Fuji, △Japan (△Honshu)	12,388
Nabī Shu'ayb, Jabal an, △Yemen (△Arabian Peninsula)	12,336
Rinjani, Indonesia (△Lombok)	12,224
Semeru, Indonesia (△Java)	12,060
Munku–Sardyk, Mongolia–Soviet Union (△Sayan Mts.)	11,453
Rantekombola, Indonesia (△Celebes)	11,335
Sawdā', Qurnat as, △Lebanon	10,115
Shām, Jabal ash, △Oman	9,957
Apo, △Philippines (△Mindanao)	9,692
Pulog, Philippines (△Luzon)	9,606
Bia, △Laos	9,252
Hermon, Lebanon–△Syria	9,232
Paektu, China–△Korea	9,003
Ānai Mudi, India	8,841
Inthanon, △Thailand	8,514
Pidurutalagala, △Sri Lanka	8,281
Mayon Vol., Philippines (Luzon)	7,943
Asahi, Japan (△Hokkaido)	7,513
Tahan, Malaysia (△Malaya)	7,174
Ólimbos, △Cyprus	6,401
Kuju, Japan (△Kyushu)	5,866
Meron, △Israel	3,963
Carmel, Israel	1,791

Africa

	Height (Feet)
Kilimanjaro (Kibo), △Tanzania (△Africa)	19,340
Kirinyaga (Kenya), △Kenya	17,058
Margherita Pk., △Zaire–△Uganda	16,763
Ras Dashen, △Ethiopia	15,158
Meru, Tanzania	14,978
Elgon, Kenya–Uganda	14,178
Toubkal, Jbel, △Morocco (△Atlas Mts.)	13,661
Cameroun, △Cameroon	13,354
Thabana Ntlenyana, △Lesotho	11,425
Koussi, Emi, △Chad (△Tibesti Mts.)	11,204
Injasuti, △South Africa	11,182
Neiges, Piton des, △Reunion	10,069
Santa Isabel, △Equatorial Guinea (△Bioko)	9,868
Tahat, △Algeria (△Ahaggar Mts.)	9,852
Maromokotro, △Madagascar	9,436
Pico, △Cape Verde	9,281
Kātrīnā, Jabal, △Egypt	8,668
São Tomé, Pico de, △Sao Tome	6,640

Oceania

	Height (Feet)
Wilhelm, △Papua New Guinea	14,793
Giluwe, Papua New Guinea	14,330
Bangeta, Papua New Guinea	13,520
Victoria, Papua New Guinea (△Owen Stanley Range)	13,240
Cook, △New Zealand (△South Island)	12,349
Ruapehu, New Zealand (△North Island)	9,175
Balbi, △Solomon Is. (△Bougainville)	9,000
Egmont, New Zealand	8,260
Sinewit, Papua New Guinea (△Bismarck Archipelago)	8,000
Orohena, △Fr. Polynesia (△Tahiti)	7,352
Kosciusko, △Australia (△New South Wales)	7,310
Silisili, Mauga, △Western Samoa	6,095
Panié, △New Caledonia	5,341
Ossa, Australia (△Tasmania)	5,305
Bartle Frere, Australia (△Queensland)	5,287
Humboldt, New Caledonia	5,282
Woodroffe, Australia (△South Australia)	4,723
Tomaniivi (Victoria), △Fiji (△Viti Levu)	4,341
Bruce, Australia (△Western Australia)	4,024

Antarctica

	Height (Feet)
Vinson Massif (△Antarctica)	16,864
Kirkpatrick	14,856
Markham	14,272
Jackson	13,747
Sidley	13,717
Wade	13,396

Great Oceans and Seas of the World

OCEANS AND SEAS

	Area (sq. mi.)	Greatest Depth (feet)
Pacific Ocean	63,800,000	35,810
Atlantic Ocean	31,800,000	28,232
Indian Ocean	28,900,000	23,376
Arctic Ocean	5,400,000	17,881
Arabian Sea	1,492,000	19,029

OCEANS AND SEAS

	Area (sq. mi.)	Greatest Depth (feet)
South China Sea	1,331,000	18,241
Caribbean Sea	1,063,000	25,197
Mediterranean Sea	967,000	16,470
Bering Sea	876,000	25,194
Bengal, Bay of	839,000	17,251

OCEANS AND SEAS

	Area (sq. mi.)	Greatest Depth (feet)
Okhotsk, Sea of	610,000	11,063
Norwegian Sea	597,000	13,189
Mexico, Gulf of	596,000	14,370
Hudson Bay	475,000	850
Greenland Sea	465,000	15,899

Principal Lakes of the World

LAKES

	Area (sq. mi.)
Caspian, Soviet Union–Iran (salt)	143,240
Superior, United States–Canada	31,700
Victoria, Kenya–Uganda–Tanzania	26,820
Aral, Soviet Union (salt)	24,909
Huron, United States–Canada	23,000
Michigan, United States	22,300
Tanganyika, Zaire–Tanzania–Burundi Zambia	12,350
Baikal, Soviet Union	12,160
Great Bear, Canada	12,028
Nyasa, Malawi–Tanzania–Mozambique	11,150
Great Slave, Canada	11,030
Erie, United States–Canada	9,910
Winnipeg, Canada	9,417
Ontario, United States–Canada	7,540

LAKES

	Area (sq. mi.)
Balkhash, Soviet Union	△7,115
Ladoga, Soviet Union	6,835
Chad, Chad–Nigeria–Cameroon	6,300
Onega, Soviet Union	3,720
Titicaca, Peru–Bolivia	3,200
Nicaragua, Nicaragua	3,150
Mai-Ndombe, Zaire	△3,100
Athabasca, Canada	3,064
Eyre, Australia (salt)	△2,970
Reindeer, Canada	2,568
Tonle Sap, Kampuchea	△2,500
Rudolf, Kenya–Ethiopia (salt)	2,473
Issyk-Kul, Soviet Union (salt)	2,355
Torrens, Australia (salt)	△2,230
Albert, Uganda–Zaire	2,160
Vänern, Sweden	2,156

LAKES

	Area (sq. mi.)
Winnipegosis, Canada	2,075
Bangweulu, Zambia	1,930
Nipigon, Canada	1,872
Nettilling, Canada	1,870
Gairdner, Australia (salt)	△1,840
Urmia, Iran (salt)	△1,815
Manitoba, Canada	1,800
Kyoga, Uganda	1,710
Khanka, China–Soviet Union	1,700
Lake of the Woods, United States–Canada	1,695
Great Salt, United States (salt)	1,680
Mweru, Zambia–Zaire	1,680
Peipus, Soviet Union	1,660
Qinghai, China (salt)	1,650
Van, Turkey (salt)	1,470

△Due to seasonal fluctuations in water level, areas of these lakes vary considerably.

Principal Rivers of the World

Length (miles)

	Length (miles)
Nile–Kangera, Africa	4,145
Yangtze (Chang), Asia	3,915
Amazon–Ucayali, South America	3,902
Mississippi–Missouri, North America	3,740
Yellow (Huang), Asia	3,395
Ob–Irtysh, Asia	3,362
Río de la Plata–Paraná, South America	2,920
Mekong, Asia	2,796
Paraná, South America	2,796
Amur, Asia	2,744
Lena, Asia	2,734
Mackenzie, North America	2,635
Congo, Africa	2,610
Niger, Africa	2,585
Yenisey, Asia	2,543
Mississippi, North America	2,348
Missouri, North America	2,315
Ob, Asia	2,287
Volga, Europe	2,194
Murray–Darling, Australia	2,169
Madeira–Mamoré, South America	1,988
Purús, South America	1,988
Yukon, North America	1,979
Indus, Asia	1,976
Rio Grande, North America	1,885
Syrdarya, Asia	1,859
Brahmaputra, Asia	1,802
São Francisco, South America	1,802
Danube, Europe	1,777
Salween, Asia	1,770
Euphrates, Asia	1,715
Orinoco, South America	1,700
Darling, Australia	1,690
Ganges, Asia	1,678
Saskatchewan, North America	1,660
Zambezi, Africa	1,653

	Length (miles)
Tocantins, South America	1,640
Amu Darya, Asia	1,616
Murray, Australia	1,609
Kolyma, Asia	1,600
Paraguay, South America	1,584
Pilcomayo, South America	1,550
Angara, Asia	1,549
Vilyuy, Asia	1,513
Ural, Asia	1,509
Arkansas, North America	1,450
Colorado, North America (U.S.–Mexico)	1,450
Irrawaddy, Asia	1,425
Aldan, Asia	1,392
Dnepr, Europe	1,368
Araguaia, South America	1,367
Kasai, Africa	1,338
Tarim, Asia	1,328
Negro, South America	1,305
Orange, Africa	1,300
Red, North America	1,270
Kama, Europe	1,263
Juruá, South America	1,250
Columbia, North America	1,243
Xingú, South America	1,230
Ucayali, South America	1,220
Peace, North America	1,195
Tigris, Asia	1,181
Don, Europe	1,162
Songhua, Asia	1,140
Pechora, Europe	1,124
Limpopo, Africa	1,100
Tobol, Asia	1,093
Snake, North America	1,038
Uruguay, South America	1,025
Churchill, North America	1,000
Marañón, South America	1,000
Ohio, North America	981
Magdalena, South America	950
Roosevelt (River of Doubt), South America	950

	Length (miles)
Godavari, Asia	930
Xiang, Asia	930
Oka, Europe	920
Canadian, North America	906
Dnestr, Europe	876
Brazos, North America	870
Salado, South America	870
Fraser, North America	850
Parnaíba, South America	850
Colorado, North America (Texas)	840
Rhine, Europe	820
Narbada, Asia	800
Athabasca, North America	765
Donets, Europe	735
Pecos, North America	735
Green, North America	730
Elbe, Europe	720
White, North America	720
Cumberland, North America	720
James, North America	710
Ottawa, North America	696
Gambia, Africa	680
Yellowstone, North America	671
Tennessee, North America	652
Gila, North America	630
Vistula (Wisła), Europe	630
Loire, Europe	625
Tagus (Tajo) (Tejo), Europe	625
North Platte, North America	618
Albany, North America	610
Tisza (Tisa), Europe	607
Back, North America	605
Ouachita, North America	605
Cimarron, North America	600
Sava, Europe	585
Nemunas (Niemen), Europe	582
Branco, South America	580
Oder, Europe	565

Principal Islands of the World

Area (sq. mi.)

	Area (sq. mi.)
Greenland, North America	840,004
New Guinea, Indonesia–Papua New Guinea	303,090
Borneo, Asia	258,855
Madagascar, Africa	226,658
Baffin, Canada	183,810
Sumatra, Indonesia	182,860
Great Britain, Europe	88,797
Honshū, Japan	87,805
Victoria, Canada	75,767
Ellesmere, Canada	83,896
Celebes, Indonesia	73,057
South Island, New Zealand	58,093
Java, Indonesia	51,038
North Island, New Zealand	44,297
Cuba, North America	44,218
Newfoundland, Canada	43,359
Luzon, Philippines	40,420
Iceland, Europe	39,769
Mindanao, Philippines	36,537
Ireland, Europe	32,588
Hokkaidō, Japan	30,144
Sakhalin, Soviet Union	29,498

	Area (sq. mi.)
Hispaniola, North America	29,418
Banks, Canada	27,038
Tasmania, Australia	26,383
Sri Lanka (Ceylon), Asia	24,962
Devon, Canada	21,331
Novaya Zemlya (N. part), Soviet Union	18,882
Tierra del Fuego, South America	18,600
Melville, Canada	16,274
Kyūshū, Japan	16,215
Southampton, Canada	15,913
West Spitsbergen, Norway	15,260
New Britain, Papua New Guinea	14,592
Taiwan (Formosa), Asia	13,885
Hainan, China	13,127
Timor, Indonesia	13,094
Prince of Wales, Canada	12,872
Vancouver, Canada	12,079
Sicily, Italy	9,926
Somerset, Canada	9,570
Sardinia, Italy	9,301
Shikoku, Japan	7,245
North East Land, Norway	6,350

	Area (sq. mi.)
Ceram, Indonesia	6,046
New Caledonia, Oceania	5,671
Flores, Indonesia	5,513
Samar, Philippines	5,124
Negros, Philippines	4,903
Palawan, Philippines	4,500
Panay, Philippines	4,448
Jamaica, North America	4,244
Hawaii, United States	4,021
Cape Breton, Canada	3,981
Bougainville, Papua New Guinea	3,880
Mindoro, Philippines	3,794
Kodiak, United States	3,670
Cyprus, Asia	3,572
Puerto Rico, North America	3,515
Corsica, France	3,352
Crete, Greece	3,217
New Ireland, Papua New Guinea	3,205
Leyte, Philippines	3,090
Wrangel, Soviet Union	2,819
Guadalcanal, Solomon Islands	2,500
Long Island, United States	1,401

Population of Foreign Cities and Towns, Countries and Important Political Divisions

This table includes every urban center of 50,000 or more population in the world (excluding the United States), as well as many other important or well-known cities and towns. The table also lists major political subdivisions (states, provinces, etc.) of the leading countries.

The population figures are all from recent censuses (designated C) or official estimates (designated E), except for a few cities for which only unofficial estimates are available (designated UE). The date of the census or estimate is specified for each country. Individual exceptions are dated in parentheses or with a dagger symbol (‡ or †).

For many cities, a second population figure is given accompanied by a star (★). The starred population refers to the city's entire metropolitan area, including suburbs. These metropolitan areas have been defined by Rand McNally & Company, following consistent rules to facilitate comparisons among the urban centers of various countries. Where a place is part of the metropolitan area of another city, that city's name is specified in parentheses preceded by (★). Some important places that are considered to be secondary central cities of their areas are designated by (★★) preceding the name of the metropolitan area's main city. A population marked with a triangle (▲) refers to an entire municipality, commune, or other district, which includes rural areas in addition to the urban center itself. The names of capital cities appear in CAPITALS; the largest city in each country is designated by the symbol (•).

AFGHANISTAN / Afghānestān

1973 E....18,294,000

Andkhvoy (1975 E)....46,000
Baghlān....29,000
Chārikār....19,000
Ghaznī....24,000
Herāt (1975 E)....157,000
Jalālābād (1975 E)....58,000
•KĀBUL (1975 E)....749,000
Kandahār (Qandahār) (1975 E)....209,000
Khānābād....18,000
Kholm....22,000
Mazār-e-Sharīf (1975 E)....97,000
Meymaneh (1975 E)....29,000
Pol-e-Khomrī....25,000
Qondūz....46,000
Sheberghān....17,000

ALBANIA / Shqipëri

1976 E....2,482,000

Berat (1975 E)....30,000
Durrës....61,000
Elbasan....50,700
Fier (1975 E)....28,000
Gjirokastër (1975 E)....22,000
Kavajë (1973 E)....19,900
Korçë....50,900
Lushnje (1975 E)....21,000
Shkodër....62,500
Stalin (Kuçovë) (1971 E)....14,300
•TIRANË....192,300
Vlorë (Valona)....58,400

ALGERIA / Algérie

1974 E....16,275,000

Aïn Beïda....40,011
Aïn Benian (★Algers) (1966 C)....17,653
Aïn M'Lila (1966 C) (44,662▲)....12,632
Aïn Sefra (26,234▲)....13,100
Aïn Taya (★Algiers) (1966 C)....22,542
Aïn Témouchent....47,977
•ALGIERS (ALGER) (★1,800,000)....1,503,720
Annaba (Bône)....313,174
Arzew (1966 C)....13,080
Barika (1966 C) (40,957▲)....13,689
Batna (115,138▲)....91,500
Béchar (Colomb-Béchar)....71,081
Bejaïa (Bougie) (103,996▲)....80,000
Béni Saf (1966 C) (23,368▲)....18,507
Biskra....84,971
Blida....158,947
Bordj Bou Arreridj (85,545▲)....66,400
Bordj Ménaïel (87,736▲)....38,700
Boufarik (109,234▲)....77,700
Bouguerra (1966 C) (21,401▲)....13,373
Bouira (50,007▲)....26,800
Bou Saâda....36,433
Chelghoum el Aïd (1966 C) (27,985▲)....15,031
Cherchell (40,308▲)....17,100
Collo (40,860▲)....14,100
Constantine....350,183
Dellys (31,729▲)....13,700
Djelfa (1966 C) (30,304▲)....25,472
Djidjelli (61,545▲)....43,500
Douéra....55,993
El Affroun (67,566▲)....47,500
El Arba (1966 C) (22,857▲)....14,415
El Asnam (Orléansville) (114,327▲)....80,500
El Bayadh (33,743▲)....21,200
El Eulma (54,406▲)....41,500
El Goléa (1966 C) (16,679▲)....13,708
El Meghaier (1966 C) (23,506▲)....11,324
El Oued (1966 C) (43,547▲)....11,429
Fouka (1966 C)....10,208
Frenda (23,349▲)....16,400
Ghardaïa (85,230▲)....55,200
Ghazaouet (29,592▲)....16,600
Guelma (1966 C)....39,817
Guerrara (1966 C) (14,173▲)....12,546
Hadjout (32,334▲)....27,100
Hamma Bouziane (1966 C) (21,040▲)....11,472
Hammam Bou Hadjar (1966 C) (14,637▲)....11,219
Khemis Miliana (63,370▲)....41,400
Khenchela (49,922▲)....40,900
Koléa (48,133▲)....35,900
Ksar el Boukhari (36,986▲)....18,400
Laghouat (60,249▲)....41,900
Lakhdaria (53,780▲)....30,800
Maghnia (44,777▲)....31,000
Mascara (82,468▲)....70,600
Mecheria....23,681
Médéa (102,336▲)....70,700
Mers el Kébir (1966 C) (20,193▲)....5,624
Mila (1966 C) (33,007▲)....12,733
Miliana (46,217▲)....27,200
Mohammadia (49,730▲)....30,000
Mostaganem....101,780
M'Sila (1966 C) (36,930▲)....19,883
Oran (Ouahran)....485,139
Ouargla (69,509▲)....26,200
Oued Zenati (81,036▲)....31,900
Relizane....65,918
Rouiba (★Algiers) (87,540▲)....20,300
Saïda (59,344▲)....51,800
Sétif....157,065
Sidi bel Abbès....151,148
Sig (41,725▲)....33,900
Skikda (Philippeville)....127,968
Souk Ahras (60,551▲)....48,800
Sour el Ghozlane (67,205▲)....32,100
Tébessa....58,008
Tiaret....63,039
Tighennif (1966 C) (25,839▲)....11,834
Tizi-Ouzou (223,702▲)....108,000
Tlemcen....115,054
Touggourt (65,935▲)....34,800

AMERICAN SAMOA

1970 C....27,159

•PAGO PAGO....2,451

ANDORRA

1971 C....20,550

•ANDORRA....2,000

ANGOLA

1970 C....5,673,046

Benguela....40,996
Cabinda....21,124
Huambo (Nova Lisboa)....61,885
Lobito....59,528
•LUANDA....475,328
Lubango (Sá da Bandeira)....31,674
Malanje....31,599

ANGUILLA

1974 C....6,519

•South Hill....774
THE VALLEY....760

ANTIGUA

1970 C....65,525

•ST. JOHNS....21,814

ARGENTINA

1970 C....23,364,431

Almirante Brown (★Buenos Aires)....245,017
Avellaneda (★Buenos Aires)....337,538
Azul....36,023
Bahía Blanca (1979 E)....253,000
Balcarce....26,461
Berazategui (★Buenos Aires)....127,740
Berisso (★La Plata)....58,833
Bolívar....18,643
Bragado....23,366
•BUENOS AIRES (1979 E) (★10,300,000)....2,978,000
Campana (★Buenos Aires)....33,919
Cañada de Gómez....20,611
Caseros (Tres de Febrero) (★Buenos Aires)....313,460
Catamarca (★64,410)....57,228
Chivilcoy....37,190
Cipolletti....23,768
Comodoro Rivadavia....72,906
Concepción del Uruguay....38,967
Concordia....72,136
Córdoba (1979 E) (★1,026,000)....985,000
Corrientes (1979 E)....186,000
Cruz del Eje....23,401
Curuzú-Cuatiá....20,636
Cutral-Có....19,404
Ensenada (★La Plata)....39,154
Esquel....13,771
Esteban Echeverría (★Buenos Aires)....111,150
Florencio Varela (★Buenos Aires)....98,446
Formosa....61,071
General Pico....21,897
General Roca....29,320
General San Martín (★Buenos Aires)....360,573
General Sarmiento (★Buenos Aires)....315,457
Godoy Cruz (★Mendoza)....112,481
Goya....39,367
Gualeguay....20,401
Gualeguaychú....40,661
Guaymallén (★Mendoza)....112,081
Junín....59,020
La Banda (★Santiago del Estero)....33,032
Lanús (★Buenos Aires)....449,824
La Plata (1979 E) (★557,000)....435,000
La Rioja....46,090
Las Heras (★Mendoza)....67,789
Lomas de Zamora (★Buenos Aires)....410,806
Luján (★Buenos Aires)....38,393
Maipú....34,839
Mar del Plata (1979 E)....417,000
Mendoza (1979 E) (★677,000)....125,000
Mercedes (*San Luis Prov.*)....40,052
Mercedes (*Buenos Aires Prov.*) (★Buenos Aires)....39,760
Merlo (★Buenos Aires)....188,868
Moreno (★Buenos Aires)....114,041
Morón (★Buenos Aires)....485,983
Necochea....39,868
Neuquén....43,070
Olavarría....52,453
Paraná....127,635
Pergamino....56,078
Pilar (★Buenos Aires)....34,372
Posadas....97,514
Presidencia Roque Sáenz Peña....38,620
Punta Alta....36,805
Quilmes (★Buenos Aires)....355,265
Rafaela....43,695
Reconquista....25,333
Resistencia (1979 E)....183,000
Río Cuarto....88,852
Río Gallegos....27,833
Rosario (1979 UE) (★975,000)....810,000
Salta (1979 E)....254,000
San Carlos de Bariloche....26,799
San Fernando (★Buenos Aires)....119,565
San Francisco (★48,896)....45,023
San Isidro (★Buenos Aires)....250,008
San Juan (1979 E) (★310,000)....115,000
San Justo (★Buenos Aires)....659,193
San Lorenzo (★Rosario)....56,487
San Luis....50,771
San Martín....24,300
San Miguel de Tucumán (1979 E) (★442,000)....375,000
San Nicolás de los Arroyos....64,730
San Rafael....58,237
San Salvador de Jujuy....82,637
Santa Fe (1979 E)....282,000
Santa Rosa....33,649
Santiago del Estero (★140,000)....105,127
Tandil....65,876
Tartagal....23,696
Tigre (★Buenos Aires)....152,335
Trelew....24,214
Tres Arroyos....37,991
Ushuaia....5,373
Venado Tuerto....35,677
Vicente López (★Buenos Aires)....285,178
Villa Krause (★San Juan)....47,794
Villa María....56,087
Zárate....54,772

AUSTRALIA

1979 E....14,423,500

Adelaide (★933,300)....13,400
Albury (★54,900)....36,600
Alice Springs (1976 C)....14,149
Ashfield (★Sydney)....42,850
Auburn (★Sydney)....48,400
Ballarat (★73,200)....38,400
Bankstown (★Sydney)....159,500
Bendigo (★59,600)....33,300
Blacktown (★Sydney)....179,350
Blue Mountains (★Sydney)....51,150
Botany (★Sydney)....36,150
Box Hill (★Melbourne)....49,200
Brighton (★Melbourne)....35,000
Brisbane (★1,014,700)....702,000
Brisbane Water (★Sydney) (1976 C)....54,819
Broadmeadows (★Melbourne)....112,300
Broken Hill....28,600
Brunswick (★Melbourne)....44,800
Bundaberg (★41,900)....32,500
Burnside (★Adelaide)....37,800
Cairns (★53,000)....36,000
Camberwell (★Melbourne)....88,700
Campbelltown (★Adelaide)....42,300
Campbelltown (★Sydney)....78,000
CANBERRA (★241,500)....221,000
Canning (★Perth)....48,350
Canterbury (★Sydney)....131,900
Caulfield (★Melbourne)....74,700
Coburg (★Melbourne)....57,100
Croydon (★Melbourne)....36,400
Dandenong (★Melbourne)....54,700
Darwin (1976 C) (★46,655)....39,193
Doncaster and Templestowe (★Melbourne)....89,100
Drummoyne (★Sydney)....32,700
Dubbo....22,850
Enfield (★Adelaide)....70,200
Essendon (★Melbourne)....50,300
Fairfield (★Sydney)....120,850
Footscray (★Melbourne)....51,700
Frankston (★Melbourne)....80,300
Fremantle (★Perth)....23,500
Geelong (★141,100)....15,200
Glenorchy (★Hobart) (1980 C)....42,400
Gosnells (★Perth)....46,850
Heidelberg (★Melbourne)....67,000
Hobart (1980 E) (★170,200)....49,020
Holroyd (★Sydney)....82,600
Hurstville (★Sydney)....66,950
Ipswich (★Brisbane)....71,200
Kalgoorlie (★19,300)....9,400
Keilor (★Melbourne)....76,800
Knox (★Melbourne)....83,100
Kogarah (★Sydney)....47,850
Ku-ring-gai (★Sydney)....103,100
Lake Macquarie (★Newcastle)....140,450
Launceston (1980 E) (★86,100)....32,300
Leichhardt (★Sydney)....62,550
Lismore....31,900
Liverpool (★Sydney)....95,950
Mackay (★44,800)....21,800
Maitland (★Newcastle)....38,950
Malvern (★Melbourne)....45,000
Manly (★Sydney)....36,350
Marion (★Adelaide)....69,700
Marrickville (★Sydney)....90,150
Melbourne (★2,739,700)....65,800
Melville (★Perth)....56,900
Mitcham (★Adelaide)....59,500
Moe....16,300
Moorabbin (★Melbourne)....102,900
Mount Gambier (★20,750)....18,950
Mount Isa....26,800
Newcastle (★379,800)....139,400
Northcote (★Melbourne)....53,000
North Sydney (★Sydney)....47,900
Nunawading (★Melbourne)....95,900
Oakleigh (★Melbourne)....55,400
Orange....30,650
Parramatta (★Sydney)....134,300
Penrith (★Sydney)....94,000
Perth (★883,600)....88,850
Port Adelaide (★Adelaide)....36,400
Port Augusta (★15,650)....14,400
Port Lincoln (★11,050)....10,250
Port Pirie (★14,900)....12,150
Prahran (★Melbourne)....47,900
Preston (★Melbourne)....87,900
Queanbeyan (★Canberra)....20,100
Randwick (★Sydney)....123,750
Redcliffe (★Brisbane)....41,200
Ringwood (★Melbourne)....37,900
Rockdale (★Sydney)....86,650
Rockhampton (★54,600)....53,900
Ryde (★Sydney)....91,900
St. Kilda (★Melbourne)....52,400
Salisbury (★Adelaide)....83,800
Sandringham (★Melbourne)....32,600
Shellharbour (★Wollongong)....41,650
Shepparton (★34,100)....23,200
South Perth (★Perth)....31,400
Southport (Gold Coast) (★128,000)....102,500
South Sydney (★Sydney)....32,100
Springvale (★Melbourne)....79,000
Stirling (★Perth)....169,350
Sunshine (★Melbourne)....94,600
•Sydney (★3,193,300)....49,750
Tamworth....32,650
Tea Tree Gully (★Adelaide)....63,300
Toowoomba....72,500
Townsville (★96,100)....84,900
Unley (★Adelaide)....35,700
Wagga Wagga....38,150
Waverley (★Melbourne)....121,500
Waverley (★Sydney)....64,050
West Torrens (★Adelaide)....46,100
Whyalla (★31,150)....31,000
Willoughby (★Sydney)....52,250
Wollongong (★223,950)....172,350
Woodville (★Adelaide)....76,600
Woollahra (★Sydney)....54,500

AUSTRIA / Österreich

1971 C....7,456,745

Bruck an der Mur (★50,000)....16,359
Dornbirn....33,810
Graz (1976 E) (★275,000)....250,900
Innsbruck (1976 E) (★150,000)....120,400
Kapfenberg (★★Bruck)....26,001
Klagenfurt (1973 L)....82,512
Leoben (★48,000)....35,153
Linz (1976 E) (★290,000)....208,000
Salzburg (1976 E) (★165,000)....139,000
Sankt Pölten (1973 L)....50,144
Steyr (★54,000)....40,578
Stockerau (★Vienna) (1976 L)....12,768
Ternitz (1978 L)....16,343
Traun (★Linz)....20,843
•VIENNA (WIEN) (1979 E) (★1,925,000)....1,572,300
Villach (1973 L)....50,993
Wels (★59,000)....47,279
Wiener Neustadt (★41,000)....34,774
Wolfsberg (1974 L)....29,002

BAHAMAS

1970 C....168,812

Freeport....15,286
•NASSAU (★101,503)....3,233

BAHRAIN / Al-Bahrayn

1971 C....216,078

Al-Muḥarraq (★Manama)....37,577
•MANAMA (★145,000)....89,112

BANGLADESH

1974 C....76,398,120

Barisāl....98,127
Bhairab Bazar....43,702
Bogra....47,154
Brāhmanbāria....62,407
Chāndpur....51,668
Chittagong (★1,200,000)....497,026
Chuadanga....36,381
Comilla....86,446
•DACCA (★2,750,000)....1,563,517
Dinājpur....61,866
Doublemooring (★Chittagong)....125,453
Farīdpur....46,232
Ghorāsāl....34,321
Gopālpur....39,066
Jamālpur....60,261
Jessore (★82,817)....76,168
Jhenida....34,020
Khulna....521,543
Kishorganj....35,605
Kurigram....30,129
Kushtia....36,199
Mādārīpur....32,488
Mymensingh (★182,153)....76,036
Naogaon....34,395
Nārāyanganj (★★Dacca)....201,450
Narsingdi....39,140
Nawābganj....46,059
Noākhāli....32,490
Pābna....62,254
Pānchlāish (★Chittagong)....127,839
Pārbatipur....10,604
Rājshāhi (Rampur Boalia) (★132,909)....96,645
Rangpur....72,829
Saidpur....90,132
Sātkhira....40,507
Sherpur....35,578
Sirājganj....74,457
Sitākunda (★Chittagong)....99,929
Sylhet....59,546
Tangail....51,863
Tongi (★Dacca)....67,420

BARBADOS

1970 C....238,141

•BRIDGETOWN (★115,000)....8,789

BELGIUM / Belgique / België

1980 E....9,855,110

Provinces

Antwerpen (Anvers)....1,573,647
Brabant....2,220,699
Hainaut (Henegouwen)....1,308,931
Liège (Luik)....1,005,947
Limburg (Limbourg)....710,715
Luxembourg (Luxemburg)....222,317
Namur (Namen)....404,481
Oost-Vlaanderen; Flandre Orientale (East Flanders)....1,330,134
West-Vlaanderen; Flandre Occidentale (West Flanders)....1,078,239

Cities

Aalst (Alost) (★Brussels)....79,340
Anderlecht (★Brussels)....95,969
Antwerp (Antwerpen) (★1,105,000)....194,073
Arlon (23,218▲)....17,400
Ath (Aat) (24,171▲)....14,400
Auderghem (★Brussels)....31,174
Bastogne (11,357▲)....6,700
Berchem (★Antwerp)....46,368
Berchem-Sainte-Agathe (Sint-Agatha-Berchem) (★Brussels)....18,792
Beveren (★Antwerp) (40,510▲)....20,300
Binche....33,743
Borgerhout (★Antwerp)....44,369
Braine-l'Alleud (★Brussels)....29,116
Brasschaat (★Antwerp)....31,663
Brugge (Bruges) (★217,000)....118,243
•BRUSSELS (BRUXELLES) (BRUSSEL) (★2,400,000)....143,957
Charleroi (★495 000)....221,911
Châtelet (★Charleroi)....38,753

C Census. E Official estimate. UE Unofficial estimate.
L Population within municipal limits of year specified. • Largest city in country.

★ Population or designation of metropolitan area, including suburbs (see headnote).
▲ Population of an entire municipality, commune, or district, including rural area.
‡† Year of information specified at start of country.

Dendermonde 40,856
Deurne (★Antwerp) 78,646
Edegem (★Antwerp) 23,422
Eeklo 19,541
Ekeren (★Antwerp) 30,347
Etterbeek (★Brussels) 46,650
Eupen 17,072
Evere (★Brussels) 29,772
Forest (Vorst) (★Brussels) 51,314
Ganshoren (★Brussels) 21,593
Geel (31,450▲) 17,300
Genk (★★Hasselt) 61,512
Gent (Ghent) (★470,000) 241,695
Geraardsbergen (Grammont) (30,447▲) 14,900
Halle (Hal) (★Brussels) 32,124
Hamme 22,938
Harelbeke (★Kortrijk) 25,213
Hasselt (★275,000) 64,439
Herentals 23,682
Herstal (★Liège) 39,190
Hoboken (★Antwerp) 34,640
Huy 18,038
Ieper (Ypres) (34,446▲) 21,000
Ixelles (★Brussels) 76,545
Izegem 26,237
Jette (★Brussels) 40,361
Knokke-Heist 28,757
Kortrijk (Courtrai) (★200,000) 76,424
La Louvière (★148,000) 76,892
Leuven (Louvain) (★167,000) 85,632
Liège (Luik) (★765,000) 220,183
Lier (★Antwerp) 31,319
Lokeren 33,126
Maasmechelen 33,262
Mechelen (Malines) (★120,000) 77,667
Menen 33,972
Merksem (★Antwerp) 41,202
Mol (29,474▲) 16,600
Molenbeek St.-Jean (Sint-Jans-Molenbeek) (★Brussels) 70,958
Mons (Bergen) (★250,000) 96,784
Mortsel (★Antwerp) 26,834
Mouscron (Moeskroen) (★Lille, France) 54,553
Namur (★143,000) 100,712
Nivelles (21,318▲) 16,300
Oostende (Ostende) (★120,000) 70,125
Oudenaarde (Audenarde) (27,308▲) 13,600
Roeselare (Roulers) 51,752
Ronse (Renaix) 24,463
Saint-Gilles (Sint-Gillis) (★Brussels) 47,932
Schaerbeek (Schaarbeek) (★Brussels) 109,005
Schoten (★Antwerp) 31,180
Seraing (★Liège) 65,371
Sint-Niklaas (St.-Nicolas) 68,080
Sint-Truiden (St.-Trond) (36,160▲) 17,000
Soignies (23,344▲) 11,600
Spa 9,766
Tienen (Tirlemont) 32,842
Tongeren (Tongres) (29,375▲) 18,400
Tournai (Doornik) (69,862▲) 46,700
Turnhout 37,652
Uccle (Ukkel) (★Brussels) 75,861
Verviers (★103,000) 56,209
Veurne (Furnes) (11,212▲) 7,500
Vilvoorde (★Brussels) 33,644
Waregem 32,088
Waterloo (★Brussels) 24,536
Watermael-Boitsfort (★Brussels) 24,965
Wilrijk (★Antwerp) 43,161
Woluwe-St.-Lambert (★Brussels) 46,823
Woluwe-St.-Pierre (★Brussels) 39,166
Zottegem (25,152▲) 13,000

BELIZE

1972 E 127,200

•Belize City 41,500
BELMOPAN (1971 E) 5,000
Corozal 5,000
Orange Walk 6,100
Punta Gorda 2,200
San Ignacio 4,600
Stann Creek 7,400

BENIN (DAHOMEY)

1975 E 3,112,000

•Cotonou 178,000
PORTO-NOVO 104,000

BERMUDA

1970 C 52,330

•HAMILTON (★13,757) 2,060
St. George 1,604

BHUTAN / Druk-Yul

1977 E 1,232,000

THIMBU 8,982

BOLIVIA

1976 C 4,647,816

Cobija 3,636
Cochabamba 205,002
•LA PAZ 654,713
Oruro 124,121
Potosí 77,334
Santa Cruz 256,946
SUCRE 62,207
Tarija 39,087
Trinidad 27,583

BOTSWANA

1971 C 574,094

Francistown 18,613
•GABORONE (GABERONES) 18,799
Kanye 10,664
Lobatse 11,936
Mahalapye 12,056
Mochudi 6,945
Molepolole 9,448
Serowe 15,723

BRAZIL / Brasil

1975 E 107,145,200

States

Acre 249,100
Alagoas 1,786,200
Amapá (Ter.) 142,100
Amazonas 1,089,700
Bahia 8,438,900
Ceará 5,111,600
Distrito Federal (Brasília) 763,000
Espírito Santo 1,725,100
Fernando de Noronha (Ter.) (1970 C) 1,239
Goiás 3,558,100
Maranhão 3,330,000
Mato Grosso (1978 L) 753,700
Mato Grosso do Sul (1978 L) 1,253,200
Minas Gerais 12,550,600
Pará 2,544,300
Paraíba 2,675,100
Paraná 8,449,200
Pernambuco ‡5,853,400
Piauí 1,988,200
Rio de Janeiro 10,400,200
Rio Grande do Norte 1,855,700
Rio Grande do Sul 7,457,600
Rondônia (Ter.) 141,300
Roraima (Ter.) 48,200
Santa Catarina 3,351,400
São Paulo 20,636,900
Sergipe 992,400

‡Includes 1975 estimated population for Fernando de Noronha

Cities (1970 C or †1975 E)

Alagoinhas 53,891
Alegrete 45,522
Alvorada 39,485
Americana 62,387
Anápolis 89,405
Andradina 43,465
Anil 37,719
Apucarana 41,800
Aracaju 179,512
Araçatuba 85,660
Araguari 48,702
Arapiraça 43,875
Arapongas 36,628
Araraquara 82,607
Araras 40,945
Araxá 31,498
Arcoverde 33,308
Assis 45,531
Bagé 57,036
Barbacena 57,766
Barra do Piraí 42,713
Barra Mansa (★★Volta Redonda) 75,006
Barretos 53,050
Bauru 120,178
Bayeux (★João Pessoa) 34,681
Belém (★660,000) 565,097
Belford Roxo (★Rio de Janeiro) 173,427
Belo Horizonte (★1,945,000) †1,557,464
Blumenau 85,942
Boa Vista (*Roraima Ter.*) 16,720
Boa Vista (*Santa Catarina State*) 33,503
Botucatu 42,252
Bragança Paulista 39,573
BRASÍLIA (1975 UE) (★750,000) 350,000
Brusque 32,427
Cabedelo (★João Pessoa) 12,811
Cachoeira do Sul 50,001
Cachoeiro de Itapemirim 58,968
Camarajibe (★Recife) 41,216
Campina Grande 163,206
Campinas 328,629
Campo Grande 130,792
Campos 153,310
Campos Elyseos (★Rio de Janeiro) 104,636
Canoas (★Porto Alegre) 148,798
Carapicuíba (★São Paulo) 54,907
Caruaru 101,006
Cascavel 33,809
Cataguases 32,515
Catanduva 48,446
Cavaleiro (★Recife) 58,811
Caxias 31,089
Caxias do Sul 107,487
Coelho da Rocha (★Rio de Janeiro) 100,781
Colatina 46,012
Conselheiro Lafaiete 44,894
Corumbá 48,607
Crato 36,836
Criciúma 50,430
Cruz Alta 43,568
Cruzeiro 42,366
Cubatão (★Santos) 37,255
Cuiabá 83,621
Curitiba (★680,000) 483,038
Curvelo 30,225
Diadema (★São Paulo) 68,552
Divinópolis 69,872
Duque de Caxias (★Rio de Janeiro) 256,582
Erechim 32,426
Feira de Santana 127,105
Florianópolis 115,665
Fortaleza (★1,175,000) †1,109,837
Franca 86,852
Garanhuns 49,579
Goiânia 362,152
Governador Valadares 125,174
Guaratinguetá 55,069
Guarujá (★Santos) 30,741
Guarulhos (★São Paulo) 221,639
Ijuí 31,879
Ilhéus 58,529
Imperatriz 34,709
Inhomirim (★Rio de Janeiro) 40,322
Ipatinga 35,808
Ipiíba (★Rio de Janeiro) 55,486
Itabira 40,143
Itabuna 89,928
Itajaí 54,135
Itajubá 42,485
Itapetinga 30,578
Itapetininga 42,331
Itaquari (★Vitória) 64,559
Itaúna 32,731
Itu 35,907
Ituiutaba 46,784
Jaboatão (★Recife) 52,537
Jacareí 48,684
Jaú 40,989
Jequié 62,341
João Monlevade 38,689
João Pessoa (★310,000) 197,398
Joinvile 77,760
Juàzeiro 36,273
Juàzeiro do Norte 79,796
Juiz de Fora 218,832
Jundiaí 145,785
Lajes 82,325
Lavras 35,489
Limeira 77,243
Limoeiro 30,726
Lins 38,080
Londrina 156,675
Lorena 39,653
Macapá 51,567
Maceió 242,860
Manaus 284,118
Marília 73,165
Maringá 51,620
Mauá (★São Paulo) 101,569
Mesquita (★Rio de Janeiro) 93,926
Mogi das Cruzes (★São Paulo) 90,330
Monjolo (★Rio de Janeiro) 46,793
Montes Claros 81,572
Mossoró 77,251
Muriaé 34,118
Muribeca dos Guararapes (★Recife) 74,963
Nanuque 34,714
Natal 250,787
Neves (★Rio de Janeiro) 112,912
Nilópolis (★Rio de Janeiro) 86,720
Niterói (★Rio de Janeiro) †376,033
Nova Friburgo 65,732
Nova Iguaçu (★Rio de Janeiro) 331,457
Nôvo Hamburgo (★Porto Alegre) 81,248
Olinda (★Recife) 187,553
Olinda (★Rio de Janeiro) 41,378
Osasco (★São Paulo) 283,303
Ourinhos 40,733
Paranaguá 51,510
Parnaíba 57,031
Parque Industrial (★Belo Horizonte) 80,572
Passo Fundo 69,135
Passos 39,184
Patos 39,850
Patos de Minas 42,215
Paulo Afonso 38,494
Pelotas 150,278
Petrolina 37,801
Petrópolis (★Rio de Janeiro) 116,080
Pinheirinho (★Curitiba) 50,302
Piracicaba 125,490
Poços de Caldas 51,844
Ponta Grossa 92,344
Porto Alegre (★1,760,000) †1,043,964
Porto Velho 41,146
Presidente Prudente 91,188
Queimados (★Rio de Janeiro) 62,560
Recife (★2,100,000) †1,249,821
Ribeirão Prêto 190,897
Rio Branco 34,531
Rio Claro 69,240
Rio de Janeiro (★8,235,000) †4,857,716
Rio Grande 98,863
Salvador (★1,270,000) †1,237,373
Santa Maria 120,667
Santana do Livramento 48,448
Santarém 51,123
Santo André (★São Paulo) 415,025
Santo Ângelo 36,020
Santos (★610,000) 341,317
São Bernardo do Campo (★São Paulo) 187,368
São Caetano do Sul (★São Paulo) 150,171
São Carlos 74,835
São Gonçalo (★Rio de Janeiro) 161,392
São João del Rei 45,019
São João de Meriti (★Rio de Janeiro) 163,934
São José do Rio Prêto 108,319
São José dos Campos 130,118
São Leopoldo (★Porto Alegre) 62,861
São Luís 167,529
São Mateus (★Rio de Janeiro) 38,393
•São Paulo (★9,900,000) †7,198,608
São Vicente (★Santos) 116,075
Sapucaia do Sul (★Porto Alegre) 41,154
Sete Lagoas 61,063
Sete Pontes (★Rio de Janeiro) 53,766
Sobral 51,864
Sorocaba 165,990
Taboão da Serra (★São Paulo) 40,959
Taubaté 98,933
Teófilo Otoni 64,568
Teresina 181,071
Teresópolis 53,462
Três Lagoas 40,157
Tubarão 51,121
Uberaba 108,576
Uberlândia 110,463
Uruguaiana 60,667
Varginha 36,447
Vicente de Carvalho (★Santos) 59,767
Vila Velha (Espírito Santo) (★Vitória) 43,177
Vitória (★345,000) 121,978
Vitória da Conquista 82,477
Vitória de Santo Antão 41,130
Volta Redonda (★205,000) 120,645

BRITISH VIRGIN ISLANDS
See Virgin Islands, British

BRUNEI

1971 C 136,256

•BANDAR SERI BEGAWAN (BRUNEI) (★37,000) 17,410
Seria 20,824

BULGARIA / Bâlgarija

1979 E 8,846,417

Asenovgrad (1969 E) 38,500
Blagoevgrad (Gorna Dzhumaya) 57,457
Burgas 165,994
Dimitrovgrad (1969 E) 44,200
Gabrovo 78,092
Gorna Oryakhovitsa (1969 E) 28,300
Karlovo (Levskigrad) (1969 E) 22,900
Karnobat (Polyanovgrad) (1969 E) 20,500
Kazanlŭk 56,483
Khaskovo 82,636
Kŭrdzhali 52,487
Kyustendil 52,118
Lom (1969 E) 29,100
Lovech (1969 E) 40,000
Mikhaylovgrad (1969 E) 34,200
Nova Zagora (1969 E) 21,000
Panagyurishte (1969 E) 21,800
Pazardzhik 71,933
Pernik (Dimitrovo) 91,428
Petrich (1969 E) 21,900
Pleven 122,916
Plovdiv 342,000
Razgrad (1969 E) 35,600
Ruse 170,594
Samokov (1969 E) 23,800
Sevlievo (1969 E) 21,900
Shumen (Kolarovgrad) 92,157
Silistra 53,085
Sliven 96,090
Smolyan (1969 E) 20,300
•SOFIA (SOFIYA) (★1,133,733) 1,047,920
Stanke Dimitrov (1969 E) 37,800
Stara Zagora 133,201
Svishtov (1969 E) 22,900
Tolbukhin (Dobrich) 94,132
Tŭrgovishte (Eski Dzhumaya) (1969 E) 31,100
Varna 286,382
Veliko Tŭrnovo (Tŭrnovo) 62,565
Vidin 58,213
Vratsa 64,697
Yambol 81,477

BURKINA FASO see Upper Volta

BURMA / Myanma

1977 E 31,512,000

Bassein 138,000
Henzada (1970 E) 85,000
Insein (★Rangoon) (1973 C) 143,625
Kanbe (★Rangoon) (1973 C) 253,600
Mandalay 458,000
Meiktila (1953 C) 25,180
Mergui (1953 C) 33,697
Monywa (1953 C) 26,172
Moulmein 188,000
Myaungmya (1953 C) 24,532
Myingyan (1970 E) 65,000
Pakokku (1953 C) [illegible]
Pegu 135,000
Prome (Pyè) (1970 E) 65,000
•RANGOON (★3,000,000) 2,276,000
Sittwe (Akyab) (1970 E) 82,000
Tavoy (1970 E) 53,000
Thaton (1953 C) 38,047
Thingangyun (★Rangoon) (1973 C) 141,210
Toungoo (1953 C) 31,589

BURUNDI

1976 E 3,864,000

•BUJUMBURA 157,000
Gitega (1970 E) 15,000
Muyinga (1970 E) 19,000

CAMBODIA
See Kampuchea

CAMEROON / Cameroun

1976 C 7,663,246

Bafoussam 62,239
Bamenda 48,111
•Douala 458,246
Foumban 33,944
Garoua 63,900
Kumba 44,175
Maroua 67,187
Ngaoundere 38,992
Nkongsamba 71,298
Victoria 27,016
YAOUNDÉ 313,706

CANADA

1976 C 22,992,604

CANADA/ALBERTA 1,838,037

Banff 3,410
Blairmore (★7,292) 2,321
Brooks 6,339
Calgary 469,917
Camrose 10,104
Cardston 3,043
Claresholm 3,276
Coaldale 3,654
Drayton Valley 4,303
Drumheller 6,154
Edmonton (★554,228) 461,361
Edson 4,038
Fort MacLeod 3,067
Fort McMurray 15,424
Fort Saskatchewan (★Edmonton) 8,304
Grand Cache 4,116
Grande Prairie 17,626
High River 3,598
Hinton 6,731
Jasper 3,404
Lacombe 3,888
Leduc 8,576
Lethbridge 46,752
Lloydminster (*Alta. and Sask.*) 10,311
Medicine Hat (★36,326) 32,811
Olds 3,658
Peace River 4,840
Pincher Creek 3,448
Ponoka 4,636
Redcliff (★Medicine Hat) 3,006
Red Deer 32,184
Rocky Mountain House 3,432
St. Albert (★Edmonton) 24,129
St. Paul 4,337
Sherwood Park (★Edmonton) 26,534
Slave Lake 3,561
Spruce Grove 6,907
Stettler 4,182
Taber 5,296
Vegreville 4,158
Wainwright 3,890
Westlock 3,721
Wetaskiwin 6,754
Whitecourt 3,878

CANADA/ BRITISH COLUMBIA 2,466,608

Burnaby (★Vancouver) 131,599
Campbell River 11,781
Castlegar 6,255
Chemainus 2,129
Chilliwack (★37,525) 8,634
Clear Brook 4,849
Comox (★Courtenay) 5,359
Courtenay (★19,012) 7,733
Cranbrook 13,510
Creston 3,552
Dawson Creek 10,528
Duncan (★20,410) 4,106
Esquimalt (★Victoria) 15,053
Fernie 4,608
Fort Nelson 2,916
Fort St. John 8,947
Kamloops 58,311
Kelowna 51,955
Kimberley 7,111
Kitimat 11,791
Ladysmith 4,004
Langley (★Vancouver) 10,123
MacKenzie 5,266
Merritt 5,680
Mission City 8,278
Nanaimo 40,336
Nelson 9,235
New Westminster (★Vancouver) 38,393
North Vancouver (★Vancouver) 31,934
Oak Bay (★Victoria) 17,658
Penticton 21,344
Port Alberni (★26,254) 19,585
Port Coquitlam (★Vancouver) 23,926
Port Moody (★Vancouver) 11,649
Powell River 13,694
Prince George 59,929
Prince Rupert 14,754
Quesnel 7,637
Richmond (★Vancouver) 80,034
Sidney (★Victoria) 6,732
Smithers 3,783
Summerland 6,724
Terrace (★15,000) 10,251
Trail (★15,649) 9,976
Vancouver (★1,166,348) 410,188
Vernon (★22,541) 17,546
Victoria (★218,250) 62,551
West Vancouver (★Vancouver) 37,144
White Rock (★Vancouver) 12,497
Williams Lake (★15,966) 6,199

CANADA/MANITOBA 1,021,506

Brandon 34,901
Churchill 1,699
Dauphin 9,109
Flin Flon (*Man. and Sask.*) (★10,306) 8,560
Morden 3,886
Neepawa 3,508
Portage-la-Prairie 12,555
Selkirk 9,862
Steinbach 5,979
Swan River 3,742
The Pas 6,602
Thompson 17,291
Winkler 3,749
Winnipeg (★578,217) 560,874

C Census. E Official estimate. UE Unofficial estimate.
L Population within municipal limits of year specified. • Largest city in country.

★ Population or designation of metropolitan area, including suburbs (see headnote).
▲ Population of an entire municipality, commune, or district, including rural area.
‡† Year of information specified at start of country.

CANADA/ NEW BRUNSWICK ... 677,250

Bathurst (★19,500)	16,301
Beresford (★Bathurst)	3,199
Campbellton (★11,144)	9,282
Caraquet (★5,678)	3,950
Chatham (★★Newcastle)	7,601
Dalhousie	5,640
Dieppe (★Moncton)	7,460
Edmundston (★15,851)	12,710
Fairvale (★Saint John)	3,258
Fredericton	45,248
Grand Falls	6,223
Minto	3,714
Moncton (★77,571)	55,934
Newcastle (★18,419)	6,423
Oromocto	10,276
Quispamsis (★Saint John)	4,968
Riverview (★Moncton)	14,177
Sackville	5,755
St. Basile (★Edmundston)	3,072
Saint John (★112,974)	85,956
St. Stephen	5,264
Shediac	4,216
Sussex	3,938
Woodstock	4,869

CANADA/ NEWFOUNDLAND ... 557,725

Bay Roberts (★5,640)	4,072
Bishop's Falls	4,504
Bonavista	4,299
Botwood	4,554
Carbonear (★11,326)	5,026
Channel-Port-aux-Basques	6,187
Conception Bay South (St. John's)	9,743
Corner Brook	25,198
Deer Lake	4,546
Gander	9,301
Grand Bank	3,802
Grand Falls (★15,078)	8,729
Happy Valley	8,075
Labrador City (★15,781)	12,012
Lewisporte	3,782
Marystown	5,915
Mount Pearl (★St. John's)	10,193
St. John's (★143,390)	86,576
Springdale	3,513
Stephenville	10,284
Wabana	4,824
Wabush (★Labrador City)	3,769
Windsor (★Grand Falls)	6,349

CANADA/ NORTHWEST TERRITORIES ... 42,609

Fort Smith	2,288
Frobisher Bay	2,320
Hay River	3,268
Inuvik	3,116
Pine Point	1,915
Yellowknife	8,256

CANADA/NOVA SCOTIA ... 828,571

Amherst	10,263
Antigonish	5,442
Bible Hill (★Truro)	4,266
Bridgewater	6,010
Dartmouth (★Halifax)	65,341
Glace Bay (★★Sydney)	21,836
Halifax (★267,991)	117,882
Kentville (★12,973)	5,056
Liverpool	3,336
Louisbourg	1,519
New Glasgow (★23,513)	10,672
New Waterford (★Sydney)	9,223
North Sydney (★★Sydney Mines)	8,319
Pictou	4,588
Port Hawkesbury	4,008
Sackville	14,590
Springhill	5,220
Stellarton (★New Glasgow)	5,366
Sydney (★88,614)	30,645
Sydney Mines (★35,455)	8,965
Truro (★27,551)	12,840
Westville (★New Glasgow)	4,251
Windsor	3,702
Yarmouth	7,801

CANADA/ONTARIO ... 8,264,465

Ajax (★Toronto)	20,774
Amherstburg	5,566
Amherstview	5,295
Ancaster (★Hamilton)	14,255
Arnprior (★10,662)	6,111
Atikokan	5,668
Aurora (★Toronto)	14,249
Aylmer West	5,125
Barrie (★49,228)	34,389
Belleville	35,311
Blackburn Hamlet (★Ottawa)	8,290
Bracebridge	8,428
Bradford	5,080
Brampton (★Toronto)	103,459
Brantford (★82,800)	66,950
Brockville (★26,883)	19,903
Burlington (★Hamilton)	104,314
Caledon (★Toronto)	22,434
Cambridge (Galt) (★★Kitchener)	72,383
Capreol	4,089
Carleton Place	5,256
Chatham	38,685
Cobourg (★20,256)	11,421
Cochrane	4,974
Collingwood	11,114
Collins Bay (★Kingston)	6,897
Cornwall	46,121
Deep River	5,565
Delhi	3,929
Dryden	6,799
Dundas (★Hamilton)	19,179
Dunnville	11,642
East York (★Toronto)	106,950
Elliot Lake	8,849
Elmira	7,034
Espanola	5,926
Essex (★Windsor)	5,577
Etobicoke (★Toronto)	297,109
Exeter	3,494
Fergus (★11,727)	6,001
Fort Erie	24,031
Fort Frances	9,325
Gananoque	5,103
Goderich	7,385
Gravenhurst	7,986
Grimsby (★Hamilton)	15,567
Guelph (★70,388)	67,538
Haileybury (★12,596)	4,939
Haldimand	16,375
Halton Hills	34,477
Hamilton (★529,371)	312,003
Hanover	5,691
Hawkesbury (★11,306)	9,789
Hearst	5,195
Huntsville	11,123
Ingersoll	8,198
Iroquois Falls	6,887
Kanata (★Ottawa)	6,304
Kapuskasing	12,676
Kenora (★12,519)	10,565
Kincardine	4,182
Kingston (★90,741)	56,032
Kingsville (★11,836)	4,692
Kirkland Lake	13,567
Kitchener (★272,158)	131,870
Lambeth (★London)	2,876
Leamington	11,169
Lincoln	14,460
Lindsay	13,062
Listowel	5,126
London (★270,383)	240,392
Manitouwadge Lake	3,507
Marathon	2,258
Markham (★Toronto)	56,206
Meaford	4,319
Midland (★26,239)	11,568
Milton	20,756
Mississauga (★Toronto)	250,017
Mount Forest	3,376
Nanticoke	19,489
Napanee	4,844
Newcastle	31,928
New Hamburg	3,628
New Liskeard (★Haileybury)	5,601
Newmarket (★Toronto)	24,795
Niagara Falls (★★St. Catharines)	69,423
Niagara-on-the-Lake (★St. Catharines)	12,485
Nickel Centre (★Sudbury)	13,157
North Bay (★53,961)	51,639
North York (★Toronto)	558,398
Oakville (★Toronto)	68,950
Onaping Falls	6,776
Orangeville	12,021
Orillia	24,412
Oshawa (★135,196)	107,023
OTTAWA (★693,288)	304,462
Owen Sound	19,525
Paris (★Brantford)	6,713
Parry Sound	5,501
Pelham (★St. Catharines)	10,071
Pembroke (★18,468)	14,927
Penetanguishene (★Midland)	5,460
Perth	5,675
Petawawa (★14,326)	5,815
Peterborough (★65,293)	59,683
Petrolia	4,393
Pickering (★Toronto)	27,879
Picton	4,629
Port Colborne (★St. Catharines)	20,536
Port Elgin (★9,481)	5,069
Port Hope	9,788
Prescott	4,975
Rayside-Balfour (★Sudbury)	16,035
Renfrew	8,617
Richmond Hill (★Toronto)	34,716
St. Catharines (★301,921)	123,351
St. Marys	4,843
St. Thomas	27,206
Sarnia (★81,342)	55,576
Sault Ste. Marie (★81,992)	81,048
Scarborough (★Toronto)	387,149
Simcoe	14,189
Smiths Falls (★13,327)	9,279
Stoney Creek (★Hamilton)	30,294
Stratford	25,657
Strathroy	7,769
Sturgeon Falls	6,400
Sudbury (★157,030)	97,604
Tecumseh (★Windsor)	5,326
Thorold (★St. Catharines)	14,944
Thunder Bay (★119,253)	111,476
Tilbury	4,248
Tillsonburg	9,404
Timmins	44,747
•Toronto (★2,803,101)	633,318
Trenton (★32,634)	15,465
Valley East (★Sudbury)	19,591
Vanier (Eastview) (★Ottawa)	19,812
Vaughan (Woodbridge) (★Toronto)	17,782
Walden (★Sudbury)	10,453
Walkerton	4,626
Wallaceburg	11,132
Waterloo (★Kitchener)	46,623
Wawa (Jamestown)	4,272
Welland (★★St. Catharines)	45,047
Whitchurch Stouffville (★Toronto)	12,884
Whitby (★Oshawa)	28,173
Windsor (★247,582)	196,526
Woodstock	26,779
York (★Toronto)	141,367

CANADA/PRINCE EDWARD ISLAND ... 118,229

Charlottetown (★24,837)	17,063
Kensington	1,150
Montague	1,827
Parkdale (★Charlottetown)	2,172
St. Eleanors (★Summerside)	2,495
Sherwood (★Charlottetown)	5,602
Souris	1,447
Summerside (★14,145)	8,592

CANADA/QUEBEC ... 6,234,445

Acton Vale	4,326
Alma	25,638
Amos	9,213
Amqui	3,949
Ancienne-Lorette (Notre-Dame-de-Lorette) (★Québec)	11,694
Anjou (★Montréal)	36,596
Arthabaska (★Victoriaville)	5,907
Asbestos (★14,395)	9,075
Aylmer East (★Ottawa)	25,714
Baie-Comeau (★26,635)	11,911
Baie-d'Urfé (★Montréal)	3,955
Baie-St. Paul	4,062
Beaconsfield (★Montréal)	20,417
Beauceville	4,276
Beauharnois (★Montréal)	7,665
Beauport (★Québec)	55,339
Beaupré (★7,490)	2,821
Bécancour	9,043
Beloeil (★Montréal)	15,913
Berthierville	4,249
Black Lake (★Thetford Mines)	4,051
Blainville (★Montréal)	12,517
Boisbriand (★Montréal)	10,132
Bois-des-Filion (★Montréal)	4,346
Boucherville (★Montréal)	25,530
Bromptonville	2,992
Brossard (★Montréal)	37,641
Brownsburg (★Lachute)	3,114
Buckingham	14,328
Cabano	3,193
Candiac (★Montréal)	7,166
Cap-aux-Meules (★6,847)	1,305
Cap-Chat	3,617
Cap-de-la-Madeleine (★Trois-Rivières)	32,126
Carignan (★Montréal)	3,585
Chambly (★Montréal)	11,815
Chandler	4,011
Chapais	3,147
Charlemagne (★Montréal)	4,025
Charlesbourg (★Québec)	63,147
Charny (★Québec)	6,461
Châteauguay (★Montréal)	36,329
Château-Richer (★Québec)	3,075
Chibougamau	10,536
Chicoutimi (★128,643)	57,737
Clermont	3,518
Coaticook	6,392
Côte-St.-Luc (★Montréal)	25,721
Cowansville	11,902
Deux-Montagnes (★Montréal)	8,957
Dolbeau (★13,924)	8,451
Dollard-des-Ormeaux (★Montréal)	36,837
Donnacona (★7,876)	5,800
Dorion-Vaudreuil (Dorion) (★Montréal)	5,843
Dorval (★Montréal)	19,131
Drummondville (★45,018)	29,286
Drummondville-Sud (★Drummondville)	9,420
East Angus	4,417
East Broughton Station (★2,562)	1,191
Farnham	6,476
Forestville (★4,358)	1,819
Gaspé	16,842
Gatineau (★Ottawa)	73,479
Granby (★41,462)	37,132
Grande-Rivière	4,390
Grand'Mere (★Shawinigan)	15,999
Greenfield Park (★Montréal)	18,430
Hampstead (★Montréal)	7,562
Hauterive (★Baie-Comeau)	14,724
Havre-St.-Pierre	3,208
Hébertville-Station (★3,621)	1,362
Hudson (★Montréal)	4,480
Hull (★Ottawa)	61,039
Iberville (★St.-Jean)	8,897
Île-Perrot (★Montréal)	5,272
Joliette (★30,116)	18,118
Jonquière (★★Chicoutimi)	60,691
Kirkland (★Montréal)	7,476
La Baie	20,116
Lac-Brome	4,117
Lachenaie (★Montréal)	7,118
Lachine (★Montréal)	41,503
Lachute (★15,042)	11,928
Lac-Mégantic	6,457
La Malbaie (★5,135)	4,069
La Pocatière	4,319
Laprairie (★Montréal)	9,173
La Salle (★Montréal)	76,713
La Sarre	4,978
L'Assomption (★Montréal)	4,832
La Tuque	12,067
Lauzon (★Québec)	12,663
Laval (Ville de Laval) (★Montréal)	246,243
LeMoyne (★Montréal)	7,202
Lévis (★Québec)	17,819
Longueuil (★Montréal)	122,429
Loretteville (★Québec)	14,767
Louiseville	3,993
Magog (★14,598)	13,290
Malartic	5,092
Maniwaki	5,969
Marieville (★Montréal)	4,853
Mascouche (★Montréal)	14,266
Matane	12,726
Mercier (Ste.-Philomène) (★Montréal)	4,957
Métabetchouan	3,016
Mirabel	13,486
Mistassini (★Dolbeau)	5,473
Mont-Joli	6,508
Mont-Laurier	8,565
Montmagny	12,326
Montréal (★2,802,485)	1,080,546
Montréal-Est (★Montréal)	4,372
Montréal-Nord (★Montréal)	97,250
Montréal-Ouest (★Montréal)	5,980
Mont-Royal (★Montréal)	20,514
Mont-St.-Hilaire (★Montréal)	7,688
Murdochville	3,704
Napierville	2,166
New Richmond	4,295
Nicolet	4,818
Noranda (★★Rouyn)	9,809
Notre-Dame-des-Prairies	5,714
Otterburn Park (★Montréal)	4,159
Outremont (★Montréal)	27,089
Percé	5,198
Pierrefonds (★Montréal)	35,402
Pierreville (★2,510)	1,311
Pincourt (★Montréal)	7,892
Plessisville	7,238
Pohénégamook	3,627
Pointe-aux-Trembles (★Montréal)	35,618
Pointe-Claire (★Montréal)	25,917
Pontiac	3,365
Pont-Rouge	3,342
Port-Cartier	8,139
Portneuf (★3,225)	1,320
Price	2,461
Princeville	3,852
Québec (★542,158)	177,082
Rawdon	2,808
Repentigny (★Montréal)	26,698
Richmond	4,021
Rimouski (★30,225)	27,897
Rivière-du-Loup	13,103
Roberval	8,543
Rock Island (★3,548)	1,230
Rosemère (★Montréal)	7,112
Rouyn (★27,487)	17,678
Roxboro (★Montréal)	7,106
Ste.-Adèle (★6,273)	4,186
Ste.-Agathe-des-Monts	5,435
St.-Ambroise-de-Chicoutimi	3,169
Ste.-Anne-de-Bellevue (★Montréal)	3,738
Ste.-Anne-des-Monts (★7,606)	5,945
St.-Antoine (★St.-Jérôme)	6,872
St.-Basile-le-Grand (★Montréal)	5,843
St.-Boniface-de-Shawinigan	2,680
St.-Bruno (★Montréal)	21,272
Ste.-Catherine (★Montréal)	5,036
St.-Césaire	2,701
St.-Constant (★Montréal)	7,659
St.-David-de-l'Auberivière (★Québec)	4,386
St.-Eustache (★Montréal)	21,248
St.-Félicien	4,985
St.-Ferdinand (Bernierville)	2,182
Ste.-Foy (★Québec)	71,237
Ste.-Geneviève (★Montréal)	2,869
St.-Georges-Ouest (★Ville-St.-Georges)	6,478
St.-Hubert (★Montréal)	49,706
St.-Hyacinthe (★40,202)	37,500
St.-Jacques	2,095
St.-Jean (★50,363)	34,363
St.-Jérôme (★36,489)	25,175
St.-Joseph-de-Beauce	3,213
St.-Joseph-de-Sorel (★Sorel)	2,811
St.-Jovite	3,595
Ste.-Julie (★Montréal)	8,666
St.-Lambert (★Montréal)	20,318
St.-Laurent (★Montréal)	64,404
St.-Léonard (★Montréal)	78,452
St.-Luc (★St.-Jean)	7,103
St.-Marc-des-Carrières	2,625
Ste.-Marie-de-Beauce	4,462
St.-Pamphile	3,450
St.-Paul-l'Ermite (★Montréal)	6,107
St.-Pierre (★Montréal)	6,039
St.-Raymond	3,742
St. Rémi	4,866
St.-Romuald-d'Etchemin (★Québec)	9,160
Ste.-Thérèse-de Blainville (★Montréal)	17,479
St.-Tite	3,128
Sayabec	1,818
Schefferville	3,429
Senneterre	4,289
Sept-Îles (Seven Islands)	30,617
Shawinigan (★55,414)	24,921
Shawinigan-Sud (★Shawinigan)	11,155
Sherbrooke (★104,505)	76,804
Sillery (★Québec)	13,580
Sorel (★37,029)	19,666
Témiscaming	2,165
Terrebonne (★Montréal)	11,204
Thetford Mines (★28,826)	20,784
Thurso	3,066
Tracy (★Sorel)	12,284
Trois-Pistoles	4,554
Trois-Rivières (★98,583)	52,518
Trois-Rivières-Ouest (★Trois-Rivières)	10,564
Val-Bélair (★Québec)	10,716
Val-d'Or (★21,378)	19,915
Valleyfield (Salaberry-de) (★35,920)	29,716
Vanier (Québec-Ouest) (★Québec)	10,683
Varennes (★Montréal)	6,469
Vaudreuil (★Montréal)	5,630
Verdun (★Montréal)	68,013
Victoriaville (★27,732)	21,825
Ville-St.-Georges (★15,083)	8,605
Warwick	2,865
Waterloo	4,746
Westmount (★Montréal)	22,153
Windsor	5,637

CANADA/ SASKATCHEWAN ... 921,323

Assiniboia	2,738
Battleford (★North Battleford)	2,569
Biggar	2,491
Canora	2,689
Esterhazy	2,894
Estevan	8,847
Hudson Bay	2,280
Humboldt	4,265
Kamsack	2,726
Kindersley	3,523
Lloydminster (*Sask. and Alta.*)	10,311
Maple Creek	2,330
Meadow Lake	3,662
Melfort	5,141
Melville	5,149
Moose Jaw (★34,829)	32,581
Nipawin	4,317
North Battleford (★16,124)	13,158
Prince Albert	28,631
Regina (★151,191)	149,593
Rosetown	2,551
Saskatoon	133,750
Shaunavon	2,183
Swift Current	14,264
Tisdale	3,026
Unity	2,244
Uranium City	1,765
Weyburn	8,892
Wynyard	2,045
Yorkton	14,119

CANADA/YUKON ... 21,836

Dawson	838
Elsa	456
Faro	1,544
Watson Lake	808
Whitehorse	13,311

CAPE VERDE / Cabo Verde

1970 C	**272,071**
•Mindelo	28,797
PRAIA	21,494

CAYMAN IS.

1970 C	**10,652**
•GEORGETOWN	3,975

CENTRAL AFRICAN REPUBLIC
République centrafricaine

1971 E	**1,637,000**
Bambari (1968 E)	35,300
•BANGUI	187,000
Bouar (1968 E)	24,600

CHAD / Tchad

1975 E	**4,030,000**
Abéché	32,000
Kélo	18,500
Koumra	18,800
Moundou	45,000
•NDJAMENA (FORT-LAMY)	224,000
Sarh (Fort-Archambault)	50,000

CHILE

1970 C	**8,880,889**
Angol	22,123
Antofagasta	138,821
Apoquindo (★Santiago)	90,722
Arica	87,726
Calama	45,863
Chillán	87,555
Concepción (★395,000)	175,853
Conchalí (★Santiago)	246,046
Copiapó	45,194
Coquimbo	50,405
Coronel	37,312
Curicó	41,262
Iquique	65,040
La Cisterna (★Santiago)	246,537
La Granja (★Santiago)	163,882
La Serena	61,897
Las Rejas (★Santiago)	44,681
Linares	37,913
Lo Prado Arriba (★Santiago)	112,548
Los Ángeles	49,175
Lota	48,166
Ñuñoa (★Santiago)	280,733
Osorno	68,815
Ovalle	31,756
Providencia (★Santiago)	85,678
Puente Alto (★Santiago)	61,077
Puerto Montt	62,726
Punta Arenas	61,813
Quillota	35,488
Quilpué (★Valparaíso)	40,163
Quinta Normal (★Santiago)	138,007
Rancagua	86,404
Renca (★Santiago)	68,440
San Antonio	46,744
San Bernardo (★Santiago)	100,225
San Fernando	27,997
San Miguel (★Santiago)	320,883
•SANTIAGO (★2,925,000)	517,473
Talca	94,449
Talcahuano (★★Concepción)	152,755
Temuco	110,335
Tocopilla	22,241
Tomé	29,597
Valdivia	82,362
Vallenar	26,800
Valparaíso (★530,000)	250,358
Victoria	16,509
Villa Alemana	29,605
Viña del Mar (★Valparaíso)	188,811

C Census. E Official estimate. UE Unofficial estimate.
L Population within municipal limits of specified year. • Largest city in country.

★ Population or designation of metropolitan area, including suburbs (see headnote).
▲ Population of an entire municipality, commune, or district, including rural area.
‡† Year of information specified at start of country.

CHINA / Zhongguo

1982 C	**1,008,175,288**

Provinces

Anhui	49,665,724
Beijing (Auton. City)	9,230,687
Fujian	25,873,259
Gansu	19,569,261
Guangdong	59,299,220
Guangxi Zhuang (Auton. Region)	36,420,960
Guizhou	28,552,997
Hebei	53,005,875
Heilongjiang	32,665,546
Henan	74,422,739
Hubei	47,804,150
Hunan	54,008,851
Jiangsu	60,521,114
Jiangxi	33,184,827
Jilin	22,560,053
Liaoning	35,721,693
Nei Monggol (Auton. Region)	19,274,279
Ningxia Huizu (Auton. Region)	3,895,578
Qinghai	3,895,706
Shaanxi	28,904,423
Shandong	74,419,054
Shanghai (Auton. City)	11,859,748
Shanxi	25,291,389
Sichuan	99,713,310
Tianjin (Auton. City)	7,764,141
Xinjiang Uygur (Auton. Region)	13,081,681
Xizang (Auton. Region)	1,892,393
Yunnan	32,553,817
Zhejiang	38,884,603

Cities (1982C, † 1981E or ‡ 1975UE)

Acheng	‡60,000
Anda	‡60,000
Anqing	‡135,000
Anshan (1,215,000▲)	1,028,000
Anshun	‡50,000
Anyang	‡175,000
Baicheng	‡125,000
Baiyin	‡50,000
Baoding (Paoting)	‡350,000
Baoji (Paoki)	‡250,000
Baotou (1,026,000▲)	†846,000
Baoying	‡50,000
Bei'an	‡80,000
Beihai	‡95,000
Beipiao	‡100,000
Bengbu (Pengpu)	‡400,000
Benxi (770,000▲)	†643,000
Boshan	‡100,000
Boxian	‡90,000
Butha Qi	‡55,000
Cangzhou	‡100,000
Canton (Guangzhou) (1,296,000▲)	827,000
Changchun (Hsinking) (1,606,000▲)	†1,309,000
Changde	‡125,000
Changsha (1,047,000▲)	†835,000
Changshu	‡95,000
Changzhi	‡100,000
Changzhou (Changchow)	‡300,000
Chao'an	‡95,000
Chaoyang (*Liaoning prov.*)	‡120,000
Chaoyang (*Guangdong prov.*)	‡60,000
Chengde	‡90,000
Chengdu (2,428,000▲)	†1,376,000
Chenghai	‡50,000
Chengxian	‡60,000
Chifeng	‡75,000
Chongqing (Chungking) (2,597,000▲)	†1,900,000
Dachangzhen	‡50,000
Dandong (Antung)	‡300,000
Datong (872,000▲)	†590,000
Deyang	‡50,000
Dezhou	‡70,000
Didao	‡50,000
Dongguan	‡55,000
Dongtai	‡50,000
Dukou	‡120,000
Dunhua	‡60,000
Duyun	‡75,000
Erenhot	‡60,000
Foshan	‡125,000
Fushun (Foochow) (1,193,000▲)	1,038,000
Fuxian	‡85,000
Fuxin (619,000▲)	†516,000
Fuyang	‡70,000
Fuzhou (1,130,000▲)	710,000
Fuzhou	‡55,000
Ganzhou	‡140,000
Gejiu	‡100,000
Guilin (Kweilin)	‡250,000
Guiyang (1,296,000▲)	†827,000
Haicheng	‡90,000
Haikou (Hoihow)	‡275,000
Hailar	‡85,000
Hami	‡50,000
Handan (895,000▲)	†656,000
Hangu	‡100,000
Hangzhou (1,192,000▲)	933,000
Hanzhong	‡90,000
Harbin (2,460,000▲)	†2,094,000
Hebi	‡100,000
Hechuan	‡60,000
Hefei (795,000▲)	†539,000
Hegang (Hokang)	‡250,000
Hengyang	‡350,000
Hepu	‡50,000
Hohhot (Kweisui)	‡450,000
Horqin Youyi Qianqi (Ulan Hot)	‡80,000
Huadian	‡55,000
Huaian	‡50,000
Huaide	‡75,000
Huaibei	‡75,000
Huainan (1,015,000▲)	†539,000
Huangshi	‡140,000
Huizhou	‡80,000
Hulan	‡75,000
Hunjiang	‡50,000
Jiamusi (Kiamusze)	‡300,000
Ji'an	‡110,000
Jiangmen	‡120,000
Jiaozuo (Tsiaotso)	‡275,000
Jiawang	‡50,000
Jiaxing	‡150,000
Jieyang	‡65,000
Jilin (Kirin) (1,049,000▲)	†815,000
Jinan (Tsinan) (1,338,000▲)	1,048,000
Jingdezhen (Kingtechen)	‡300,000
Jinhua	‡55,000
Jining	‡100,000
Jining (Tsining)	‡130,000
Jinshi	‡65,000
Jinxi	‡50,000
Jinxian	‡75,000
Jinzhou (Chinchow)	‡450,000
Jiujiang	‡100,000
Jixi (Chihsi) (773,000▲)	†606,000
Kaifeng	‡350,000
Kaiyuan	‡50,000
Karamay	‡60,000
Kashi	‡100,000
Kunming (1,399,000▲)	†997,000
Lanzhou (1,381,000▲)	†1,075,000
Leshan	‡70,000
Lhasa	‡80,000
Lianyungang	‡250,000
Liaoyang	‡250,000
Liaoyuan (Shwangliao)	‡250,000
Linfen	‡50,000
Linqing	‡65,000
Linxia	‡65,000
Liuzhou	‡300,000
Liyujiang	‡50,000
Lu'an	‡55,000
Lüda (Dairen) (1,425,000▲)	1,185,000
Luohe	‡60,000
Luoyang (951,000▲)	†563,000
Lüshun (Port Arthur)	‡40,000
Luzhou	‡175,000
Ma'anshan	‡60,000
Manzhouli	‡65,000
Maoming	‡100,000
Meixian	‡50,000
Mianyang	‡50,000
Minhang	‡60,000
Mudanjiang (Mutankiang)	‡350,000
Nancha	‡50,000
Nanchang (1,033,000▲)	†815,000
Nanchong	‡225,000
Nanjing (Nanking) (2,134,000▲)	1,740,000
Nanning (657,000▲)	†505,000
Nanping	‡50,000
Nantong	‡275,000
Nanyang	‡60,000
Neijiang	‡225,000
Ningbo	‡300,000
PEKING (BEIJING) (★6,100,000) (9,230,687▲)	5,597,972
Pingdingshan	‡85,000
Pingliang	‡80,000
Pingxiang	‡120,000
Qingdao (1,174,000▲)	1,031,000
Qingjiang	‡100,000
Qinhuangdao (Chinwangtao)	‡275,000
Qiqihar (1,193,000▲)	†899,000
Quanzhou	‡130,000
Quxian	‡50,000
Sanmenxia	‡60,000
Shache	‡50,000
•Shanghai (★9,000,000) (11,859,748▲)	6,320,872
Shangqiu	‡100,000
Shangrao	‡60,000
Shantou (Swatow)	‡325,000
Shaoguan	‡100,000
Shaoxing	‡150,000
Shaoyang	‡215,000
Shashi	‡120,000
Shenyang (Mukden) (4,003,000▲)	3,700,000
Shijiazhuang (1,066,000▲)	837,000
Shiquaigou	‡50,000
Shuangyashan	‡150,000
Siping	‡165,000
Songjiang	‡60,000
Suihua	‡70,000
Suining	‡60,000
Suxian	‡50,000
Suzhou (Soochow) (658,000▲)	†556,000
Tai'an	‡50,000
Taiyuan (1,775,000▲)	1,292,000
Taizhou	‡175,000
Tangshan (1,338,000▲)	895,000
Tao'an	‡75,000
Tianjin (Tientsin) (7,764,141▲)	4,300,000
Tianshui	‡85,000
Tieling	‡75,000
Tongchuan	‡75,000
Tonghua	‡175,000
Tongliao	‡60,000
Tongling	‡65,000
Tongxian	‡80,000
Tunxi	‡65,000
Ürümqi (942,000▲)	†880,000
Wanxian	‡120,000
Weifang	‡240,000
Wenzhou	‡260,000
Wuhan (Hankow) (3,157,000▲)	†2,662,000
Wuhu	‡325,000
Wuxi (Wusih) (781,000▲)	†618,000
Wuzhou	‡160,000
Xaimen (Amoy)	‡300,000
Xi'an (Sian) (2,197,000▲)	1,618,000
Xiangfan	‡110,000
Xiangtan (Siangtan)	‡325,000
Xianyang	‡85,000
Xinghua	‡85,000
Xingtai	‡115,000
Xinhui	‡50,000
Xining (Sining)	‡300,000
Xinwen	‡50,000
Xinxiang (Sinsiang)	‡250,000
Xinyang	‡100,000
Xuanhua	‡140,000
Xuchang	‡100,000
Xuguit Qi	‡50,000
Xuzhou (Süchow) (750,000▲)	†648,000
Ya'an	‡50,000
Yancheng	‡60,000
Yangjiang	‡60,000
Yangquan (Yangchüan)	‡275,000
Yangzhou	‡175,000
Yanji	‡90,000
Yantai	‡150,000
Yibin (Ipin)	‡250,000
Yichang	‡120,000
Yichun (Ichun) (788,000▲)	†736,000
Yidu	‡50,000
Yinchuan	‡125,000
Yingcheng	‡50,000
Yingkou	‡50,000
Yingkou (Yingkow)	‡175,000
Yining	‡90,000
Yiyang	‡110,000
Yuci	‡90,000
Yueyang	‡60,000
Yumen	‡90,000
Zaozhuang (1,238,000▲)	80,000
Zhangjiakou (Kalgan)	‡300,000
Zhangzhou	‡110,000
Zhanjiang	‡200,000
Zhaodong	‡65,000
Zhaoqing	‡75,000
Zhengzhou (1,381,000▲)	†859,000
Zhenjiang	‡225,000
Zhongshan	‡90,000
Zhoucun	‡50,000
Zhoukouzhen	‡90,000
Zhuzhou (Chuchow)	‡250,000
Zibo (Tzupo) (2,192,000▲)	†623,000
Zigong (Tzekung)	‡325,000
Zunyi (Tsunyi)	‡250,000

COLOMBIA

1973 C	**22,551,811**
Armenia (1979 E) (★205,000)	164,000
Barrancabermeja (1979 E)	115,000
Barranquilla (1979 E) (★950,000)	859,000
Bello (★Medellín)	121,204
•BOGOTÁ (1979 E) (★4,150,000)	4,067,000
Bucaramanga (1979 E) (★470,000)	402,000
Buenaventura (1979 E)	144,000
Buga (84,057▲)	71,016
Caicedonia	23,567
Calarcá (★Armenia) (49,936▲)	29,349
Caldas	27,394
Cali (1979 E) (★1,340,000)	1,293,000
Cartagena (1979 E)	388,000
Cartago (77,890▲)	69,154
Ciénaga (89,723▲)	42,540
Cúcuta (1979 UE)	355,000
Dos Quebradas (★Pereira)	37,837
Duitama (48,459▲)	36,551
Envigado (★Medellín)	69,921
Espinal	32,475
Facatativá	27,892
Florencia	31,817
Floridablanca (★Bucaramanga)	38,446
Fusagasugá	25,456
Girardot (★78,000)	61,829
Ibaqué (1979 E)	257,000
Ipiales	30,871
Itagüí (★Medellín)	96,972
La Dorada	30,962
Líbano (42,832▲)	19,132
Lorica (59,757▲)	18,251
Magangué (62,746▲)	34,396
Manizales (1979 UE)	252,000
Medellín (1979 E) (★2,025,000)	1,477,000
Montería (1979 E)	123,000
Neiva (1979 E)	145,000
Ocaña	38,352
Palmira (1979 E)	168,000
Pamplona	31,817
Pasto (1979 E)	171,000
Pereira (1979 UE)](★325,000)	260,000
Popayán (1977 E)	88,768
Pradera	15,732
Puerto Berrío	19,579
Quibdó (1977 E)	33,588
Ríohacha (1977 E)	35,000
Santa Marta (1979 UE)	155,000
Santa Rosa de Cabal (★Pereira) (42,717▲)	28,368
Sevilla	31,143
Sincelejo (1977 E)	86,569
Sogamoso (67,738▲)	48,891
Soledad (★Barranquilla)	64,469
Sonsón	15,990
Tuluá (1979 E)	113,000
Tumaco (87,448▲)	38,742
Tunja (1977 E)	64,551
Valledupar (1979 E)	164,000
Villavicencio (1979 E)	133,000

COMOROS / Comores

1974 E	**292,000**
•MORONI	12,000
Mutsamudu (1966 C)	7,652

CONGO (PEOPLE'S REPUBLIC OF THE CONGO)

1970 C	**1,089,300**
•BRAZZAVILLE	175,000
Jacob (1969 E)	18.000
Loubomo (1969 E)	15,000
Pointe-Noire	135,000

COOK IS.

1971 C	**21,227**
•AVARUA (1961 E)	4,000

COSTA RICA

1976 E	**1,993,800**
Alajuela	35,000
Cartago	23,100
Desamparados (★San José)	32,700
Guadalupe (★San José)	29,100
Heredia	24,200
Liberia (18,000▲)	11,600
Limón (43,800▲)	31,900
Puntarenas	29,000
•SAN JOSÉ (1978 E) (★519,400)	239,800
San Juan (★San José)	19,600
San Pedro (★San José)	25,100
San Vicente (★San José)	16,400

CUBA

1970 C	**8,553,400**
Amancio Rodríguez (37,900▲)	12,300
Artemisa	31,200
Banes (39,300▲)	27,100
Baracoa (35,600▲)	20,900
Bauta (★Havana) (25,400▲)	21,100
Bayamo (1976 E) (88,994▲)	68,900
Camagüey (1976 E)	230,891
Camajuaní (32,300▲)	15,900
Cárdenas	55,700
Chaparra (51,000▲)	8,400
Ciego de Avila (1976 E) (66,542▲)	57,700
Cienfuegos (1976 E) (92,210▲)	86,600
Colón (40,800▲)	26,000
Consolación del Sur (42,000▲)	15,100
Contramaestre (43,900▲)	22,900
Cruces (32,100▲)	19,100
Florida (37,500▲)	32,700
Fomento (33,600▲)	12,900
Guanabacoa (★Havana)	69,700
Guantánamo (1976 E)	155,217
Güines (45,300▲)	41,400
Guisa (44,100▲)	9,000
•HAVANA (LA HABANA) (1976 E) (★2,000,000)	1,961,674
Holguín (1976 E) (160,965▲)	129,800
Manzanillo (88,900▲)	77,900
Matanzas (1976 E)	99,003
Mayarí (34,000▲)	17,600
Mayarí Arriba (31,400▲)	2,300
Morón (31,100▲)	29,000
Niquero (36,500▲)	11,300
Nueva Gerona (1976 E) (28,342▲)	24,300
Nuevitas (21,500▲)	20,700
Palma Soriano (59,600▲)	41,200
Pinar del Rio (1976 E)	89,978
Placetas (48,400▲)	32,300
Sagua la Grande (41,900▲)	35,800
San Antonio de los Baños (30,000▲)	25,300
Sancti-Spíritus (1976 E) (67,569▲)	58,600
San Germán (30,200▲)	12,400
San José de las Lajas (33,600▲)	24,900
San Juan y Martínez (45,700▲)	11,100
San Luis (35,000▲)	17,400
Santa Clara (1976 E)	152,361
Santiago de Cuba (1976 E)	326,066
Santiago de las Vegas (★Havana)	29,300
Trinidad (37,000▲)	31,500
Vertientes (32,600▲)	14,000
Victoria de las Tunas (1976 E) (65,767▲)	54,400

CYPRUS / Kípros / Kıbrıs

1974 E	**639,000**
Ammókhostos (Famagusta)	39,400
Kirínia	3,900
Lárnax (Larnaca)	19,800
Lemesós (Limassol) (★80,600)	55,000
•NICOSIA (LEVKOSÍA) (★117,100)	51,000
Páfos	9,100

CZECHOSLOVAKIA / Československo

1979 E	**15,280,148**
Banská Bystrica	66,279
Beroun (★26,000)	18,149
Bratislava	374,860
Břeclav	24,258
Brno	372,793
České Budějovice (Budweis)	89,399
Cheb	31,030
Chomutov	49,960
Děčín	48,424
Frýdek-Místek (★Ostrava)	54,112
Gottwaldov (Zlín)	82,926
Havířov (★Ostrava)	93,832
Havlíčkův Brod	24,859
Hlohovec (★26,000)	16,815
Hodonín	25,504
Hradec Králové	93,165
Humenné	26,885
Jablonec [nad Nisou]	39,692
Jihlava	50,995
Karlovy Vary (Karlsbad)	61,212
Karviná (★★Ostrava)	80,017
Kladno (★86,000)	66,370
Kolín	31,169
Komárno	30,886
Košice	200,943
Krnov	26,393
Kroměříž	26,166
Levice	25,610
Liberec (★96,000)	85,119
Liptovský Mikuláš	23,795
Litvínov	23,572
Lučenec	26,300
Martin	56,294
Michalovce	28,012
Mladá Boleslav	43,876
Most	61,411
Náchod	19,812
Nitra	72,140
Nové Zámky	32,694
Nový Jičín	31,101
Olomouc	102,501
Opava	59,481
Orlová (★Ostrava)	30,938
Ostrava (★745,000)	325,473
Pardubice	93,042
Piešt'any	30,070
Pisek	28,067
Plzeň (Pilsen)	169,466
Poprad	36,428
Považská Bystrica	24,747
•PRAGUE (PRAHA) (★1,275,000)	1,193,345
Přerov	47,933
Prešov	69,453
Příbram	36,441
Prievidza	38,948
Prostějov	48,516
Ružomberok	26,803
Sokolov	27,338
Spišská Nová Ves	31,537
Šumperk	29,872
Tábor	31,005
Teplice	53,822
Třebíč	27,708
Trenčín	47,832
Třinec	34,226
Trnava	61,617
Trutnov	27,402
Uherské Hradiště	35,909
Ústí nad Labem (★103,000)	80,309
Valašské Meziříčí	24,485
Vsetín	29,023
Žilina	67,204
Znojmo	35,711
Zvolen	35,754

DENMARK / Danmark

1980 E	**5,122,065**
Åbenrå (21,172▲)	18,200
Albertslund (★Copenhagen)	30,425
Ålborg	153,948
Århus	244,839
Ballerup-Måløv (★Copenhagen)	48,938
Brøndby (★Copenhagen)	38,034
•COPENHAGEN (KØBENHAVN) (★1,470,000)	498,850
Esbjerg	79,310
Fredericia	45,820
Frederiksberg (★Copenhagen)	88,287
Frederikshavn	35,038
Gentofte (★Copenhagen)	67,300
Gladsakse (★Copenhagen)	64,954
Glostrup (★Copenhagen)	19,573
Haderslev (29,973▲)	23,100
Helsingør (Elsinore)	56,566
Herlev (★Copenhagen)	28,530
Herning (56,033▲)	47,900
Hillerød	33,686
Hjørring (34,456▲)	24,900
Høje Tåstrup (★Copenhagen)	43,292
Holbæk (29,578▲)	23,300
Holstebro (36,777▲)	29,900
Horsens	54,533
Hvidovre (★Copenhagen)	50,608
Køge (34,511▲)	30,300
Kolding	55,769
Lyngby (Kongens Lyngby)-Tårbæk (★Copenhagen)	52,013
Middelfart	17,996
Næstved (45,237▲)	39,800
Odense	168,528
Randers	62,486
Rødovre (★Copenhagen)	38,020
Roskilde	48,746
Silkeborg (46,774▲)	40,300
Søllerød (★Copenhagen)	31,920
Sønderborg	27,790
Svendborg (37,996▲)	33,200
Tårnby (★Copenhagen)	42,075
Vejle	49,471
Viborg (38,757▲)	32,600

DJIBOUTI

1971 E	**125,000**
•DJIBOUTI	40,000

DOMINICA

1970 C	**70,302**
•ROSEAU	10,157

DOMINICAN REPUBLIC / República Dominicana

1976 E	**4,835,207**
Baní	31,763
Barahona	53,912
Bonao	32,132
La Romana	49,498
La Vega	41,658
Mao (Valverde)	32,723
Moca	32,621
Puerto Plata	44,113
San Cristóbal	36,504
San Francisco de Macorís	60,821
San Juan [de la Maguana]	43,417
San Pedro de Macorís	66,022
Santiago [de los Caballeros]	219,846
•SANTO DOMINGO	979,608

C Census. E Official estimate. UE Unofficial estimate.
L Population within municipal limits of year specified. • Largest city in country.

★ Population or designation of metropolitan area, including suburbs (see headnote).
▲ Population of an entire municipality, commune, or district, including rural area.
‡† Year of information specified at start of country.

ECUADOR

1974 C 6,521,710

Ambato (1976 E) 80,000
Azogues 10,939
Babahoyo 28,345
Chone 23,647
Cuenca (1978 E) 128,788
Esmeraldas 60,132
Guaranda 11,387
•Guayaquil (1978 E) 1,022,010
Ibarra 41,057
Jipijapa 19,719
Latacunga 22,106
Loja 47,268
Machala 68,379
Manta 63,514
Milagro 53,058
Pasaje 20,822
Portoviejo 59,404
Quevedo 43,123
QUITO (1978 E) 742,858
Riobamba 58,029
Santo Domingo 30,487
Tulcán 24,443

EGYPT / Mişr

1966 C 30,083,419

Abnūb 31,195
Abū Kabīr 41,789
Abū Tīj 28,161
Akhmīm 44,829
Al-'Arīsh ††40,338
Al-Badārī 26,531
Alexandria (Al-Iskandarīyah) (1978 E) (★2,850,000) 2,409,000
Al-Fashn 27,746
Al-Fayyūm (1976 C) 167,081
Al-Ḥawāmidīyah (★Cairo) 36,227
Al-Ismā'īlīyah (Ismailia) (1976 C) (★185,000) 145,478
Al-Jīzah (Giza) (★Cairo) (1976 C) 1,246,713
Al Madīnah al Fikrīyah 21,504
Al-Maḥallah al Kubrā (1976 C) 292,853
Al-Manshāh 25,027
Al-Manşūrah (El Mansura) (1976 C) (★290,000) 257,866
Al-Manzilah 33,298
Al-Maṭarīyah 41,105
Al-Minyā (1976 C) 146,423
Al Qanāṭir al Khayrīyah 22,477
Al-Quşayr 5,525
Al-Qūşīyah 25,991
Al-Uqşur (Luxor) 77,578
Armant 38,308
Ashmūn 32,168
Ash Shuhadā' 21,947
As-Sallūm 2,483
As-Sinbillāwayn 40,686
Aswān (1976 C) 144,377
Asyūt (1976 C) 213,983
Aṭ Ṭalibīyah 20,438
Az-Zaqāzīq (1976 C) 202,637
Bahtīm (★Cairo) 32,510
Banhā 63,849
Banī Mazār 34,053
Banī Suwayf (1976 C) 118,148
Bibā 22,871
Bilbays 58,070
Bilqās Qism Awwal 41,067
Biyalā 33,008
Būsh 21,174
•CAIRO (AL QĀHIRAH) (1978 E) (★8,500,000) 5,278,000
Damanhūr (1976 C) 188,927
Dayrūt 27,646
Dishnā 21,857
Disūq 45,580
Dumyāt (Damietta) (1975 E) 113,200
Fāqūs 40,561
Fuwah 30,654
Giheina al Gharbiya 24,203
Ḥawsh 'Īsá 30,006
Idfū 27,326
Idkū 42,239
Isnā 27,383
Jirjā 44,150
Kafr ad-Dawwār (★Alexandria) (1976 C) 160,554
Kafr ash-Shaykh 51,544
Kafr az-Zayyāt 34,084
Kafr Salīm (★Alexandria) 40,381
Kawm Umbū 27,227
Maghāghah 33,211
Mallawī 59,938
Manfalūṭ 34,132
Minūf 48,256
Minyā al-Qamḥ 31,533
Mīt Ghamr (★82,000) 43,665
Nafīshah (★Al-Ismā'īlīyah) 29,483
Port Said (Bur Sa'īd) (1978 E) 271,000
Qalyūb 49,303
Qinā 68,536
Qūş 27,462
Rashīd (Rosetta) 36,711
Samālūt 37,861
Samannūd 29,749
Sāqiyat Makkī 22,967
Sawhāj (1976 C) 101,758
Shibīn al-Kawm (1976 C) 102,844
Shirbīn 25,089
Shubrā al-Khaymah (★Cairo) (1976 C) 393,700
Sīdī Sālim 21,096
Sinnūris 34,855
Suez (As Suways) (1978 E) 204,000
Ṭahṭā 38,915
Ṭalā 25,448
Ṭanṭā (1976 C) 284,636
Ṭimā 29,293
Warrāq al-'Arab (★Cairo) 31,263
Ziftá (★★Mīt Ghamr) 37,883

††31,733 per 1967 census taken by Israeli occupation authorities.

EL SALVADOR

1977 E 4,255,000

Ahuachapán (63,600▲) 18,100
Chalchuapa (51,200▲) 22,000
Delgado (★San Salvador) (77,100▲) 53,600
Mejicanos (★San Salvador) (85,000▲) 70,500
Nueva San Salvador (63,500▲) 44,000
San Miguel (144,900▲) 72,900
•SAN SALVADOR (★720,000) 397,100
Santa Ana (189,000▲) 112,800
San Vicente (56,900▲) 21,500
Sonsonate (61,000▲) 40,100
Soyapango (★San Salvador) (56,900▲) 32,700
Usulután (57,600▲) 25,100
Zacatecoluca (71,500▲) 20,200

EQUATORIAL GUINEA / Guinea Ecuatorial

1965 C 254,684

Bata (1960 C) (27,024▲) 4,000
•MALABO (SANTA ISABEL) (37,152▲) 17,500

ETHIOPIA / Yaitopya

1978 E 29,408,200

•ADDIS ABABA 1,125,340
Asmera 373,827
Bahir Dar 45,955
Dabra-Mārk'os 35,818
Debre Zeyt 43,654
Desē 65,571
Dirē Dawa 72,202
Gonder 67,790
Hārer 55,401
Jimā 56,278
Keren 33,368
Mak'alē 41,235
Mitsiwa 29,064
Nazreth (Adāmā) 61,468

FAEROE IS. / Føroyar

1977 E 41,575

•TÓRSHAVN 11,586

FALKLAND ISLANDS

1972 C 1,957

•STANLEY 1,081

FIJI

1976 C 588,068

Lautoka (★28,847) 22,672
•SUVA (★117,827) 63,628

FINLAND / Suomi

1978 E 4,758,088

Espoo (Esbo) (★Helsinki) 129,758
Hämeenlinna 41,303
•HELSINKI (HELSINGFORS) (★885,000) 484,879
Hyvinkää 37,104
Iisalmi 22,131
Imatra 36,593
Joensuu 43,940
Jyväskylä (★86,000) 62,937
Kajaani 33,662
Kotka 61,320
Kouvola (★53,000) 30,524
Kuopio 73,567
Kuusankoski (★★Kouvola) 22,649
Lahti (★109,000) 94,980
Lappeenranta 53,393
Mikkeli 27,919
Nokia (★Tampere) 23,612
Oulu (★112,000) 93,497
Pori 79,815
Rauma 30,429
Tampere (★241,000) 165,519
Turku (Åbo) (★221,000) 164,586
Vaasa (Vasa) 53,774
Vantaa (Vanda) (★Helsinki) 127,403
Varkaus 24,536

FRANCE

1980 E 53,589,000

Regions and Departments

ALSACE 1,560,000
Bas-Rhin 904,300
Haut-Rhin 655,700
AQUITAINE 2,576,700
Dordogne 365,800
Gironde 1,089,000
Landes 292,000
Lot-et-Garonne 287,800
Pyrénées-Atlantiques (Basses-Pyrénées) 542,100
AUVERGNE 1,319,500
Allier 365,400
Cantal 160,500
Haute-Loire 199,300
Puy-de-Dôme 594,300
BASSE-NORMANDIE 1,314,000
Calvados 579,100
Manche 444,600
Orne 290,300
BOURGOGNE 1,589,600
Côte-d'Or 474,100
Nièvre 239,500
Saône-et-Loire 569,000
Yonne 307,000
BRETAGNE 2,652,800
Côtes-du-Nord 531,700
Finistère 817,800
Ille-et-Vilaine 731,600
Morbihan 571,700
CENTRE 2,224,000
Cher 319,100
Eure-et-Loir 352,700
Indre 243,000
Indre-et-Loire 498,700
Loiret 521,900
Loir-et-Cher 288,600
CHAMPAGNE-ARDENNE 1,346,600
Ardennes 300,700
Aube 286,900
Haute-Marne 205,700
Marne 553,300
CORSE (CORSICA) 229,400
Corse-du-Sud 102,400
Haute-Corse 127,000
FRANCHE-COMTÉ 1,085,800
Belfort, Territoire de 132,000
Doubs 492,500
Haute-Saône 223,500
Jura 237,800
HAUTE-NORMANDIE 1,638,500
Eure 443,800
Seine-Maritime 1,194,700
ÎLE-DE-FRANCE 10,064,700
Essonne 1,087,600
Hauts-de-Seine 1,350,000
Paris 2,050,500
Seine-et-Marne 889,400
Seine-Saint-Denis 1,292,400
Val-de-Marne 1,226,000
Val-d'Oise 921,000
Yvelines 1,247,800
LANGUEDOC-ROUSSILLON 1,832,100
Aude 265,200
Gard 500,000
Hérault 685,500
Lozère 72,300
Pyrénées-Orientales 300,100
LIMOUSIN 733,500
Corrèze 238,600
Creuse 138,100
Haute-Vienne 356,800
LORRAINE 2,312,900
Meurthe-et-Moselle 716,500
Meuse 191,400
Moselle 1,007,200
Vosges 397,800
MIDI-PYRÉNÉES 2,272,100
Ariège 135,500
Aveyron 268,300
Gers 167,200
Haute-Garonne 816,600
Hautes-Pyrénées 222,200
Lot 148,300
Tarn 334,900
Tarn-et-Garonne 179,100
NORD-PAS-DE-CALAIS 3,920,300
Nord 2,521,300
Pas-de-Calais 1,399,000
PAYS DE LA LOIRE 2,860,800
Loire-Atlantique 977,700
Maine-et-Loire 652,700
Mayenne 264,700
Sarthe 499,500
Vendée 466,200
PICARDIE 1,714,600
Aisne 527,200
Oise 642,100
Somme 545,300
POITOU-CHARENTES 1,537,200
Charente 334,200
Charente-Maritime 499,800
Deux-Sèvres 338,000
Vienne 365,200
PROVENCE-ALPES-CÔTE D'AZUR 3,873,100
Alpes-de-Haute-Provence (Basses-Alpes) 115,800
Alpes-Maritimes 862,600
Bouches-du-Rhône 1,715,400
Hautes-Alpes 99,800
Var 667,300
Vaucluse 412,200
RHÔNE-ALPES 4,930,800
Ain 398,000
Ardèche 252,000
Drôme 366,700
Haute-Savoie 483,400
Isère 903,900
Loire 735,500
Rhône 1,478,900
Savoie 312,400

Cities (1975 C)

Aix-en-Provence 110,659
Aix-les-Bains 22,210
Ajaccio 50,726
Albi 46,162
Alençon 33,680
Alès (★67,513) 44,245
Alfortville (★Paris) 38,057
Amiens (★152,997) 131,476
Angers (★188,695) 137,587
Angoulême (★100,528) 47,221
Annecy (★103,543) 53,262
Antibes (★★Cannes) 55,960
Antony (★Paris) 57,540
Arcachon (★38,000) 13,892
Argenteuil (★Paris) 102,530
Arles (50,059▲) 37,340
Armentières (★58,000) 26,346
Arras (★79,783) 46,446
Asnières [-sur-Seine] (★Paris) 75,431
Athis-Mons (★Paris) 30,737
Aubervilliers (★Paris) 72,976
Aulnay-sous-Bois (★Paris) 78,137
Aurillac 30,863
Autun 21,556
Auxerre 38,342
Avignon (★162,562) 90,786
Avranches 10,136
Bagneux (★Paris) 40,674
Bagnolet (★Paris) 35,906
Barentin (★12,000) 10,773
Bar-le-Duc 19,288
Bastia (★56,984) 50,718
Bayeux 13,457
Bayonne (★121,474) 42,938
Beauvais 54,089
Belfort (★75,795) 54,615
Besançon (★126,349) 120,315
Béthune (★145,155) 26,982
Béziers (★88,619) 84,029
Biarritz (★★Bayonne) 27,595
Blois 49,778
Bobigny (★Paris) 43,125
Bois-Colombes (★Paris) 26,657
Bondy (★Paris) 48,333
Bordeaux (★612,456) 223,131
Boulogne-Billancourt (★Paris) 103,578
Boulogne-sur-Mer (★100,581) 48,440
Bourg-en-Bresse 42,181
Bourges (★86,041) 77,300
Brest (★190,812) 166,826
Briançon 9,489
Brive-la-Gaillarde 51,864
Bron (★Lyon) 44,563
Bruay-en-Artois (★116,340) 25,714
Caen (★181,390) 119,474
Cagnes [-sur-Mer] (★Nice) (29,538▲) 23,353
Cahors 20,311
Calais (★100,327) 78,820
Caluire-et-Cuire (★Lyon) 43,041
Cambrai (★51,357) 39,049
Cannes (★210,000) 70,527
Carcassonne 42,154
Carmaux (★23,000) 13,208
Castres 45,978
Châlons-sur-Marne (★63,407) 52,275
Chalon-sur-Saône (★72,407) 58,187
Chambéry (★88,081) 54,415
Chamonix-Mont-Blanc 6,285
Champigny-sur-Marne (★Paris) 80,291
Chantilly 10,552
Charleville-Mézières (★69,124) 60,176
Chartres (★72,246) 38,928
Châteauroux (★66,836) 53,429
Châtellerault (★66,836) 37,080
Châtenay-Malabry (★Paris) 30,497
Châtillon (★Paris) 26,574
Chatou (★Paris) 26,550
Chaumont 27,226
Chauny (★21,000) 14,405
Chelles (★Paris) 36,516
Cherbourg (★82,539) 32,536
Chinon 5,391
Choisy-le-Roi (★Paris) 38,705
Cholet 52,976
Clamart (★Paris) 52,952
Clermont-Ferrand (★253,244) 156,900
Clichy (★Paris) 47,764
Cognac 22,237
Colmar (★83,435) 64,771
Colombes (★Paris) 83,390
Compiègne (★57,210) 37,699
Concarneau (18,759▲) 15,096
Corbeil-Essonnes (★Paris) 38,859
Courbevoie (★Paris) 54,488
Coutances 8,349
Creil (★77,225) 32,509
Créteil (★Paris) 59,023
Dax (★27,000) 19,137
Deauville 5,664
Decazeville (★26,000) 10,231
Denain (★★Valenciennes) 26,204
Dieppe (★40,000) 25,822
Dijon (★208,432) 151,705
Dinard 9,234
Dives-sur-Mer (★11,500) 5,872
Dole 29,295
Douai (★210,508) 45,239
Douarnenez 19,096
Drancy (★Paris) 64,430
Dreux 33,101
Dunkerque (★186,314) 83,163
Elbeuf (★48,000) 19,116
Épernay 29,677
Épinal (★53,522) 39,525
Épinay-sur-Seine (★Paris) 46,578
Étaples (★22,000) 10,559
Eu (★21,000) 8,626
Évreux 47,412
Fécamp 21,910
Foix 9,599
Fontaine (★Grenoble) 25,036
Fontainebleau (★36,000) 16,778
Fontenay-sous-Bois (★Paris) 46,475
Forbach (★62,000) 25,244
Fougères 26,610
Fréjus (★50,000) 28,851
Gagny (★Paris) 36,772
Gap (28,233▲) 25,052
Garges-lès-Gonesse (★Paris) 37,927
Gennevilliers (★Paris) 50,290
Givors (★35,000) 21,968
Granville 13,330
Grasse (34,579▲) 24,442
Grenoble (★389,088) 166,037
Guebwiller (★25,566) 11,072
Guéret 14,855
Haguenau 25,147
Hayange (★75,000) 20,426
Hendaye 9,470
Hénin-Beaumont (Hénin-Liétard) (★★Lens) 26,359
Houilles (★Paris) 30,345
Hyères (★★Toulon) (36,123▲) 29,611
Issy-les-Moulineaux (★Paris) 47,561
Ivry-sur-Seine (★Paris) 62,856
Jœuf (★30,000) 10,649
La Baule-Escoublac (★St.-Nazaire) 15,006
La Ciotat (32,721▲) 29,319
La Courneuve (★Paris) 37,958
La Garenne-Colombes (★Paris) 24,038
La Grand' Combe (★17,500) 10,452
Lambersart (★Lille) 29,642
Laon 27,914
La Rochelle (★100,649) 75,367
La Roche-sur-Yon 44,713
La Seyne-sur-Mer (★Toulon) 51,155
Laval 51,544
Le Blanc-Mesnil (★Paris) 49,107
Le Creusot 33,366
Le Grand-Quevilly (★Rouen) 31,963
Le Havre (★264,422) 217,881
Le Mans (★192,057) 152,285
Lens (★328,741) 40,199
Le Perreux-sur-Marne (★Paris) 28,333
Le Puy-en-Velay (★41,000) 26,594
Les Sables-d'Olonne (★29,000) 17,463
Levallois-Perret (★Paris) 52,523
Le Vésinet (★Paris) 17,986
L'Hay-les-Roses (★Paris) 31,412
Libourne 21,651
Liévin (★Lens) 33,070
Lille (★1,015,000) 172,280
Limoges (★167,664) 143,689
Lisieux 25,521
Livry-Gargan (★Paris) 32,917
Loches 6,738
Lomme (★Lille) 29,255
Longwy (★83,000) 20,131
Lons-le-Saunier 20,942
Lorient (★105,797) 69,769
Lourdes 17,870
Lunéville 22,709
Lyon (★1,170,660) 456,716
Mâcon 39,344
Maisons-Alfort (★Paris) 54,146
Maisons-Laffitte (★Paris) 23,504
Malakoff (★Paris) 34,121
Mantes-la-Jolie 42,465
Marcq-en-Baroeul (★Lille) 36,126
Marignane (★Marseille) 26,477
Marseille (★1,070,912) 908,600
Martigues (38,373▲) 26,897
Massy (★Paris) 41,344
Maubeuge (★105,000) 35,399
Mazamet (★28,000) 14,440
Meaux 42,243
Melun (★77,272) 37,705
Mende 10,451
Menton (★34,000) 25,129
Mérignac (★Bordeaux) 50,652
Metz (★181,191) 111,869
Meudon (★Paris) 52,806
Millau 21,907
Montargis (★50,200) 18,380
Montauban (48,053▲) 35,940
Montbéliard (★132,343) 30,425
Montceau-les-Mines (★51,385) 28,177
Mont-de-Marsan 26,166
Montélimar 28,058
Montereau-faut-Yonne 21,568
Montigny-lès-Metz (★Metz) 24,519
Montluçon (★71,988) 56,468
Montmorency (★Paris) 20,860
Montpellier (★211,430) 191,354
Montreuil-sous-Bois (★Paris) 96,587
Montrouge (★Paris) 40,304
Morlaix (19,237▲) 17,256
Moulins (★42,000) 26,067
Moyeuvre-Grande (★77,000) 12,523
Mulhouse (★218,743) 117,013
Nancy (★280,569) 107,902
Nanterre (★Paris) 95,032
Nantes (★453,500) 256,693
Narbonne 39,342
Neuilly-sur-Seine (★Paris) 65,983
Nevers (★59,424) 45,480
Nice (★437,566) 344,481
Nîmes (★131,638) 127,933
Niort (★64,128) 62,267
Nogent-sur-Marne (★Paris) 25,634
Noisy-le-Grande (★Paris) 26,662
Noisy-le-Sec (★Paris) 37,734
Noyon 13,889
Orange (25,371▲) 20,779
Orléans (★209,234) 106,246
Orly (★Paris) 26,109
Oullins (★Lyon) 27,772
Oyonnax 23,007
Palaiseau (★Paris) 28,716
Pantin (★Paris) 42,739
Paray-le-Monial 11,545
•PARIS (1980 E) (★9,450,000) 2,050,500
Pau (★126,859) 83,498
Périgueux (★57,830) 35,120
Perpignan (★117,689) 106,426
Pessac (★Bordeaux) 51,360
Poissy (★Paris) 37,431
Poitiers (★98,554) 81,313
Pont-à-Mousson (★23,000) 14,830
Pontoise (★Paris) 27,240
Port-de-Bouc 21,424
Privas 10,808
Puteaux (★Paris) 35,514
Quimper 55,977
Reims (★197,021) 178,381
Rennes (★229,310) 198,305
Rezé (★Nantes) 35,730
Rive-de-Gier (★38,000) 17,706
Roanne (★83,561) 55,195
Rochefort 28,155
Rodez (★35,000) 25,550
Romainville (★Paris) 26,260
Romans-sur-Isère (★46,000) 33,030
Rosny-sous-Bois (★Paris) 35,784
Roubaix (★★Lille) 109,553
Rouen (★388,711) 114,927
Royan (★29,000) 18,062
Rueil-Malmaison (★Paris) 62,727
St.-Avold (★28,000) 17,955
St. Brieuc (★82,148) 52,559
St.-Chamond 40,250
St.-Cloud (★Paris) 28,139
St. Cyr-l'École (★Paris) 16,537
St.-Denis (★Paris) 96,132
St.-Dié 25,423
St.-Dizier 37,266
Saintes 26,891
St.-Étienne (★334,846) 220,070

C Census. E Official estimate. UE Unofficial estimate.
L Population within municipal limits of year specified. • Largest city in country.

★ Population or designation of metropolitan area, including suburbs (see headnote).
▲ Population of an entire municipality, commune, or district, including rural area.
‡† Year of information specified at start of country.

St.-Étienne-du-Rouvray (★Rouen)...37,242
St.-Germain-en-Laye (★Paris)...37,509
St.-Jean-de-Luz (★23,000)...11,854
St.-Lô...23,221
St.-Malo...45,030
St.-Martin-d'Hères (★Grenoble)...38,052
St.-Maur-des-Fossés (★Paris)...80,920
St.-Nazaire (★119,418)...69,251
St.-Omer (★27,000)...16,932
St.-Ouen (★Paris)...43,588
St.-Quentin (★75,056)...67,243
St.-Tropez...4,523
Salon-de-Provence...34,576
Sarcelles (★Paris)...55,007
Sarreguemines...25,729
Sartrouville (★Paris)...42,253
Saumur...32,515
Savigny-sur-Orge (★Paris)...34,607
Schiltigheim (★Strasbourg)...30,144
Sedan...23,995
Senlis...13,639
Sens...26,463
Sète...39,258
Sèvres (★Paris)...21,149
Soissons (★49,000)...30,009
Sotteville (★Rouen)...31,659
Stains (★Paris)...35,545
Strasbourg (★390,000)...253,384
Suresnes (★Paris)...37,537
Talence (★Bordeaux)...34,127
Tarbes (★78,645)...54,897
Thann (★28,187)...8,519
Thionville (★141,881)...43,020
Thonon-les-Bains...26,354
Toul (★23,000)...16,454
Toulon (★378,430)...181,801
Toulouse (★509,939)...373,796
Tourcoing (★★Lille)...102,239
Tours (★245,631)...140,686
Trouville-sur-Mer (★16,000)...6,618
Troyes (★126,611)...72,167
Tulle...20,100
Valence (★104,330)...68,460
Valenciennes (★350,599)...42,473
Vannes...40,359
Vanves (★Paris)...22,528
Vénissieux (★Lyon)...74,347
Verdun...23,621
Versailles (★Paris)...94,145
Vesoul...18,173
Vichy (★59,062)...32,117
Vienne...27,830
Vierzon...35,699
Villefranche (★Nice)...7,200
Villefranche-sur-Saône (★42,000)...30,341
Villejuif (★Paris)...55,606
Villemomble (★Paris)...28,727
Villeneuve-d'Ascq (★Lille)...36,769
Villeneuve-St.-Georges (★Paris)...31,664
Villeurbanne (★Lyon)...116,535
Vincennes (★Paris)...44,261
Viry-Châtillon (★Paris)...32,411
Vitry-le-François...19,372
Vitry-sur-Seine (★Paris)...87,316
Voiron (★31,000)...19,420
Wattrelos (★Lille)...45,440

FRENCH GUIANA / Guyane française

1974 C...55,125

•CAYENNE...30,461
St.-Laurent-du-Maroni...3,182

FRENCH POLYNESIA / Polynésie française

1977 C...137,382

•PAPEETE (★42,000)...23,453

GABON

1976 E...530,000

Lambaréné...24,000
•LIBREVILLE...251,000
Port-Gentil...85,000

GAMBIA

1978 E...569,000

•BANJUL (BATHURST) (★88,000)...45,600

GAZA STRIP

1967 C...356,261

•GAZA (GHAZZAH)...118,272
Jabālyah...43,604
Khān Yūnis...52,997
Rafaḩ...49,812

GERMAN DEMOCRATIC REPUBLIC (EAST GERMANY) / Deutsche Demokratische Republik

1978 E...16,751,375

Altenburg...54,281
Annaberg-Buchholz...25,584
Apolda...28,961
Arnstadt...29,820
Aschersleben...35,259
Aue...30,053
Bautzen...47,450
•BERLIN, EAST (OST-BERLIN) (★★Berlin)...1,128,983
Bernburg...43,221
Bitterfeld (★105,000)...24,644
Blankenburg...18,143
Borna...23,326
Brandenburg...94,505
Burg [bei Magdeburg]...28,805
Coswig (★Dresden)...26,250
Cottbus...107,623
Crimmitschau...27,208
Delitzsch...24,124
Dessau (★135,000)...101,322
Döbeln...27,549
Dresden (★640,000)...514,508
Eberswalde...50,994
Eilenburg...21,969
Eisenach...49,850
Eisenhüttenstadt...48,677
Eisleben...27,785
Erfurt...208,800
Falkensee (★Berlin)...24,442
Finsterwalde...23,335
Forst [Lausitz]...27,030
Frankfurt an der Oder...77,175
Freiberg...50,808
Freital (★Dresden)...46,626
Fürstenwalde [Spree]...33,570
Gera...121,251
Glauchau...29,690
Görlitz...81,963
Gotha...58,369
Greifswald...60,636
Greiz...36,606
Güstrow...36,794
Halberstadt...47,919
Halle (★485,000)...232,543
Halle-Neustadt (★Halle)...91,860
Heidenau (★Dresden)...20,644
Hennigsdorf bei Berlin (★Berlin)...26,899
Hettstedt...19,646
Hoyerswerda...70,133
Ilmenau...24,026
Jena...102,025
Karl-Marx-Stadt (Chemnitz) (★460,000)...313,850
Köthen [Anhalt]...34,651
Lauchhammer...25,710
Leipzig (★710,000)...563,980
Leuna (★Halle) (1977 E)...10,132
Limbach-Oberfrohna (★Karl-Marx-Stadt)...24,272
Lübbenau [Spreewald]...22,365
Luckenwalde...27,677
Ludwigsfelde...20,081
Magdeburg (★395,000)...283,109
Meissen...40,858
Merseburg (★★Halle)...51,684
Mühlhausen (Thomas-Müntzer-Stadt)...43,678
Naumburg [an der Saale]...34,675
Neubrandenburg...73,258
Neuruppin...25,258
Neustrelitz...27,342
Nordhausen...46,317
Oranienburg (★Berlin)...24,258
Parchim...22,998
Pirna...48,233
Plauen...79,190
Potsdam (★Berlin)...126,262
Prenzlau...22,283
Quedlinburg...29,179
Radebeul (★Dresden)...35,497
Rathenow...32,341
Reichenbach [Vogtland]...25,909
Riesa...51,411
Rostock...224,834
Rudolstadt...31,435
Saalfeld [Saale]...33,876
Salzwedel...22,732
Sangerhausen...33,494
Schneeberg...21,842
Schönebeck...44,485
Schwedt [Oder]...52,228
Schwerin...115,950
Senftenberg...31,447
Sömmerda...21,933
Sondershausen...23,148
Sonneberg...28,663
Spremberg...22,582
Stassfurt...26,404
Stendal...42,942
Stralsund...73,889
Strausberg (★Berlin)...22,930
Suhl...42,324
Torgau...21,627
Waren...23,322
Weimar...62,803
Weissenfels...40,958
Weisswasser...29,632
Werdau...21,028
Wernigerode...35,435
Wilhelm-Pieck-Stadt Guben...36,826
Wismar...57,055
Wittenberg [Lutherstadt]...53,211
Wittenberge...32,893
Wolfen (★★Bitterfeld)...34,284
Zeitz...44,135
Zittau...41,822
Zwickau (★170,000)...123,446

GERMANY, FEDERAL REPUBLIC OF (WEST GERMANY) / Bundesrepublik Deutschland

1979 E...61,439,342

States

BADEN-WÜRTTEMBERG...9,190,052
BAYERN (BAVARIA)...10,870,968
BERLIN (WEST)...1,902,250
BREMEN...695,115
HAMBURG...1,653,043
HESSEN (HESSE)...5,576,085
NIEDERSACHSEN (LOWER SAXONY)...7,234,000
NORDRHEIN-WESTFALEN (NORTH RHINE-WESTPHALIA)...17,017,075
RHEINLAND-PFALZ (RHINE-LAND-PALATINATE)...3,633,195
SAARLAND...1,068,555
SCHLESWIG-HOLSTEIN...2,599,004

Cities

Aachen (★540,000)...242,971
Aalen (★80,000)...62,854
Achern...20,442
Achim (★Bremen)...27,442
Ahaus...27,824
Ahlen...53,681
Ahrensburg (★Hamburg)...25,416
Albstadt...48,192
Alfeld (Leine)...23,447
Alsdorf (★Aachen)...46,328
Altena...24,729
Amberg...44,541
Andernach (★★Neuwied)...26,897
Ansbach...38,338
Arnsberg...78,282
Aschaffenburg (★145,000)...59,054
Augsburg (★390,000)...245,940
Aurich...34,344
Backnang...29,104
Baden-Baden...49,399
Bad Harzburg (★Goslar)...25,095
Bad Hersfeld...28,240
Bad Homburg (★Frankfurt)...50,909
Bad Honnef am Rhein (★Bonn)...20,877
Bad Kissingen...22,331
Bad Kreuznach...41,255
Bad Nauheim (★Frankfurt)...26,852
Bad Neuenahr-Ahrweiler...26,027
Bad Oeynhausen...44,126
Bad Oldesloe...20,009
Bad Reichenhall...17,919
Bad Salzuflen (★★Herford)...51,181
Bad Vilbel (★Frankfurt)...25,875
Baesweiler (★Aachen)...23,471
Balingen...29,638
Bamberg (★120,000)...71,993
Barsinghausen (★Hannover)...32,699
Bayreuth (★89,000)...70,210
Beckum...37,952
Bensheim...32,874
Berchtesgaden...8,276
Bergheim (Erft) (★Cologne)...53,205
Bergisch Gladbach (★Cologne)...101,007
Bergkamen (★Essen)...47,533
Berlin, West- (★3,775,000)...1,902,250
Biberach...28,122
Bielefeld (★525,000)...312,357
Bietigheim-Bissingen (★Stuttgart)...33,982
Bingen...23,837
Böblingen (★Stuttgart)...41,065
Bocholt...65,346
Bochum (★★Essen)...402,988
BONN (★555,000)...286,184
Borken...31,939
Bornheim (★Bonn)...33,819
Bottrop (★Essen)...114,510
Brake...17,511
Bramsche...23,762
Braunschweig (Brunswick) (★335,000)...261,669
Bremen (★800,000)...556,128
Bremerhaven (★190,000)...138,987
Bretten...22,615
Brilon...24,439
Bruchsal...37,232
Brühl (★Cologne)...43,012
Buchholz in der Nordheide (★Hamburg)...27,999
Bückeburg...20,626
Bünde...39,871
Burgdorf (★Hannover)...27,949
Butzbach...21,096
Buxtehude (★Hamburg)...31,162
Calw...22,881
Castrop-Rauxel (★Essen)...79,264
Celle...72,804
Cloppenburg...20,681
Coburg...45,906
Coesfeld...31,093
Cologne (Köln) (★1,815,000)...976,136
Crailsheim...24,636
Cuxhaven...58,891
Dachau (★Munich)...34,162
Darmstadt (★305,000)...138,661
Datteln (★Essen)...37,004
Deggendorf...30,455
Delmenhorst (★★Bremen)...72,140
Detmold...67,116
Dillingen (★Saarlouis)...20,722
Dinslaken (★Essen)...58,334
Dormagen (★Cologne)...55,826
Dorsten (★Essen)...68,862
Dortmund (★★Essen)...609,954
Duderstadt...22,886
Duisburg (★★Essen)...559,066
Dülmen...38,074
Düren (★110,000)...86,308
Düsseldorf (★1,225,000)...594,770
Einbeck...28,923
Elmshorn...41,628
Emden...51,607
Emmendingen...24,448
Emmerich...29,378
Emsdetten...30,900
Ennepetal (★Essen)...35,965
Erftstadt (★Cologne)...42,905
Erkelenz...35,579
Erkrath (★Düsseldorf)...42,637
Erlangen (★★Nürnberg)...100,760
Eschwege...24,097
Eschweiler (★★Aachen)...53,065
Espelkamp...23,124
•Essen (★5,125,000)...652,501
Esslingen (★Stuttgart)...91,733
Ettlingen (★Karlsruhe)...36,259
Euskirchen...44,593
Fellbach (★Stuttgart)...41,653
Filderstadt (★Stuttgart)...36,757
Flensburg (★103,000)...88,810
Forchheim...28,932
Frankenthal (★Mannheim)...43,511
Frankfurt am Main (★1,880,000)...628,203
Frechen (★Cologne)...43,161
Freiburg (★220,000)...174,121
Freising...34,252
Friedrichshafen...51,541
Fulda (★79,000)...57,114
Fürstenfeldbruck (★Munich)...31,354
Fürth (★★Nürnberg)...98,266
Gaggenau...28,611
Garbsen (★Hannover)...57,406
Garmisch-Partenkirchen...27,765
Geldern...25,730
Gelsenkirchen (★★Essen)...306,323
Georgsmarienhütte (★Osnabrück)...30,857
Gevelsberg (★Essen)...31,138
Giessen (★160,000)...76,485
Gifhorn...33,006
Gladbeck (★Essen)...80,434
Goch...28,634
Göppingen (★155,000)...53,034
Goslar (★84,000)...52,815
Göttingen...128,118
Greven...28,414
Grevenbroich (★Düsseldorf)...58,644
Gronau (★Enschede, Netherlands)...41,042
Gummersbach...48,344
Gütersloh (★★Bielefeld)...77,792
Hagen (★★Essen)...220,676
Haltern (★Essen)...30,783
Hamburg (★2,260,000)...1,653,043
Hameln (★72,000)...59,005
Hamm...171,595
Hanau [am Main] (★★Frankfurt)...86,144
Hannover (★1,005,000)...535,854
Hattingen (★Essen)...57,255
Heidelberg (★★Mannheim)...128,773
Heidenheim (★89,000)...48,470
Heilbronn (★230,000)...111,426
Heinsberg...36,343
Helmstedt...26,816
Hemer...32,891
Hennef (★Siegburg)...28,835
Heppenheim (★Mannheim)...23,908
Herford (★120,000)...62,977
Herne (★Essen)...183,065
Herten (★Essen)...69,400
Herzogenrath (★Aachen)...42,425
Hilden (★Düsseldorf)...52,708
Hildesheim (★139,000)...102,512
Hof...53,398
Hofheim am Taunus (★Frankfurt)...33,262
Homburg (★★Zweibrücken)...41,581
Höxter...32,457
Hückelhoven...34,919
Hürth (★Cologne)...50,654
Ibbenbüren...42,149
Idar-Oberstein...35,811
Ingolstadt (★135,000)...89,467
Iserlohn...94,478
Itzehoe...33,707
Jülich...30,495
Kaarst (★Düsseldorf)...37,595
Kaiserslautern (★138,000)...99,197
Kamen (★Essen)...43,278
Kamp-Lintfort (★Essen)...37,859
Karlsruhe (★485,000)...271,417
Kassel (★370,000)...196,224
Kaufbeuren...42,204
Kempen (★Essen)...30,101
Kempten...57,390
Kerpen (★Cologne)...53,932
Kiel (★335,000)...250,750
Kirchheim (★Stuttgart)...31,756
Kleve (Cleves)...44,036
Koblenz (★180,000)...113,795
Königswinter (★Bonn)...34,935
Konstanz...67,948
Krefeld (★★Essen)...222,750
Kreuztal (★Siegen)...30,295
Kulmbach...28,324
Laatzen (★Hannover)...33,919
Lage...32,044
Lahr...35,516
Lampertheim (★Mannheim)...31,307
Landau...36,502
Landshut...55,538
Langen (★Frankfurt)...29,198
Langenfeld (★Düsseldorf)...46,590
Langenhagen (★Hannover)...46,825
Leer...31,316
Lehrte (★Hannover)...38,271
Leichlingen (★Cologne)...24,616
Leinfelden-Echterdingen (★Stuttgart)...35,044
Lemgo...39,512
Leonberg (★Stuttgart)...37,848
Leverkusen (★Cologne)...161,453
Lingen...43,864
Lippstadt...61,692
Löhne...37,111
Lörrach (★Basel, Switzerland)...41,522
Lübeck (★265,000)...222,120
Lüdenscheid...74,561
Ludwigsburg (★Stuttgart)...81,049
Ludwigshafen (★★Mannheim)...160,479
Lüneburg...62,198
Lünen (★Essen)...85,685
Mainz (★★Wiesbaden)...186,200
Mannheim (★1,395,000)...303,247
Marburg an der Lahn...74,724
Marl (★Essen)...89,441
Meerbusch (★Düsseldorf)...49,794
Melle...40,757
Memmingen...37,885
Menden [Sauerland]...53,101
Meppen...28,062
Merzig...30,008
Meschede...31,352
Mettmann (★Düsseldorf)...36,724
Minden (★125,000)...77,989
Moers (★Essen)...100,110
Mönchengladbach (★410,000)...258,001
Monheim (★Düsseldorf)...39,932
Mülheim an der Ruhr (★Essen)...182,465
Münden...26,047
Munich (München) (★1,940,000)...1,299,693
Münster...267,478
Nettetal...37,366
Neuburg an der Donau...23,945
Neu Isenburg (★Frankfurt)...35,899
Neumarkt in der Oberpfalz...30,226
Neumünster...80,331
Neunkirchen (★135,000)...52,216
Neuss (★Düsseldorf)...149,333
Neustadt am Rübenberge (★Hannover)...37,941
Neustadt an der Weinstrasse...50,405
Neu-Ulm (★Ulm)...47,263
Neuwied (★150,000)...60,461
Niederkassel (★Cologne)...25,460
Nienburg...30,207
Nordenham (★★Bremerhaven)...30,320
Norderstedt (★Hamburg)...64,302
Nordhorn...48,580
Northeim...32,307
Nürnberg (★1,025,000)...484,184
Nürtingen (★Stuttgart)...35,046
Oberammergau...4,800
Oberhausen (★★Essen)...229,613
Oberursel (★Frankfurt)...39,477
Oelde...27,335
Oer-Erkenschwick (★Essen)...26,702
Offenbach (★Frankfurt)...111,310
Offenburg...50,471
Oldenburg...136,155
Osnabrück (★270,000)...158,150
Paderborn...109,218
Papenburg...27,420
Passau...50,323
Peine...47,559
Pforzheim (★220,000)...106,677
Pinneberg (★Hamburg)...36,823
Pirmasens...50,250
Pulheim (★Cologne)...43,501
Rastatt...36,942
Ratingen (★Düsseldorf)...89,039
Ravensburg (★74,000)...42,081
Recklinghausen (★Essen)...119,472
Regensburg (★200,000)...132,399
Remagen (★Bonn)...14,342
Remscheid (★★Wuppertal)...129,507
Rendsburg...32,860
Reutlingen (★155,000)...94,737
Rheda-Wiedenbrück (★Bielefeld)...37,723
Rheinbach (★Bonn)...21,609
Rheinberg (★Essen)...26,205
Rheine...71,525
Rodgau (★Frankfurt)...34,854
Rosenheim...51,485
Rottenburg am Neckar...31,468
Rottweil...23,732
Rüsselsheim (★★Wiesbaden)...62,606
Saarbrücken (★390,000)...194,452
Saarlouis (★115,000)...39,028
Salzgitter...113,427
Sankt Augustin (★Bonn)...47,288
Sankt Ingbert...41,896
Sankt Wendel...26,880
Schleswig...30,118
Schmallenberg...24,929
Schorndorf (★Stuttgart)...33,527
Schwabach (★Nürnberg)...34,693
Schwäbisch Gmünd...56,621
Schwäbisch Hall...31,548
Schweinfurt (★110,000)...53,035
Schwelm (★Wuppertal)...31,207
Schwerte (★Essen)...47,333
Seelze (★Hannover)...30,293
Seevetal (★Hamburg)...35,409
Selb...21,428
Siegburg (★160,000)...34,475
Siegen (★205,000)...112,740
Sindelfingen (★Stuttgart)...54,153
Singen...43,653
Soest...40,373
Solingen (★★Wuppertal)...166,654
Speyer...43,663
Springe...30,528
Stade...42,519
Steinfurt...32,090
Stolberg (★★Aachen)...57,552
Straubing...42,718
Stuttgart (★1,935,000)...581,989
Sundern (Sauerland)...25,400
Trier (★125,000)...00,700
Troisdorf (★★Siegburg)...57,733
Tübingen...72,167
Tuttlingen...31,555
Uelzen...36,536
Ulm (★210,000)...99,560
Unna (★Essen)...56,903
Velbert (★Essen)...93,302
Verden...24,275
Viernheim (★Mannheim)...29,645
Viersen (★★Mönchengladbach)...81,419
Villingen-Schwenningen...78,465
Voerde (★Essen)...31,442
Völklingen (★★Saarbrücken)...44,901
Waiblingen (★Stuttgart)...44,968
Warendorf...32,909
Warstein...28,413
Wedel (★Hamburg)...30,075
Weiden...44,319
Weinheim (★Mannheim)...41,498
Wermelskirchen (★Wuppertal)...34,730
Wesel...56,760
Wetzlar (★105,000)...52,138
Wiesbaden (★795,000)...273,267
Wilhelmshaven (★135,000)...99,426
Willich (★Essen)...38,916
Witten (★Essen)...106,185
Wolfenbüttel (★★Braunschweig)...50,218
Wolfsburg...126,942
Worms (★★Mannheim)...73,505
Wunstorf (★Hannover)...37,318
Wuppertal (★870,000)...394,605
Würselen (★Aachen)...34,802
Würzburg (★205,000)...127,370
Zweibrücken (★105,000)...35,074

C Census. E Official estimate. UE Unofficial estimate.
L Population within municipal limits of year specified. • Largest city in country.
★ Population or designation of metropolitan area, including suburbs (see headnote).
▲ Population of an entire municipality, commune, or district, including rural area.
‡† Year of information specified at start of country.

GHANA
1970 C 8,559,313
•ACCRA (*738,498) 633,880
Bawku 20,567
Bolgatanga 18,896
Cape Coast 71,594
Ho 24,199
Keta 14,446
Koforidua 46,235
Kumasi 345,117
Nkawkaw 23,219
Nsawam 25,518
Obuasi 31,005
Oda 20,957
Sekondi-Takoradi 160,868
Tamale 83,653
Tarkwa 14,702
Tema 60,767
Wa 21,374
Winneba 30,778
Yendi 22,072

GIBRALTAR
1979 E 29,760
•GIBRALTAR 29,760

GREECE / Ellás
1971 C 8,768,641
Agrinion (*41,794) 30,973
Aiyáleo (*Athens) 79,961
Aíyion (*23,756) 18,829
Akharnaí (Acharnae) 24,621
Alexandroúpolis 22,995
Amaliás 14,177
Amaroúsion (*Athens) 27,112
Ambelókipoi (*Thessaloníki) 24,892
Árgos 18,890
Árta 19,498
•ATHENS (ATHÍNAI) (*2,540,241) 867,023
Ayía Varvára (*Athens) 26,409
Áyioi Anáryiroi (*Athens) 26,094
Áyios Dhimítrios (*Athens) 40,968
Dháfni (*Athens) 26,608
Dráma 29,692
Édhessa 13,967
Elevsís (Eleusis) 18,535
Ermoúpolis (Síros) (*16,082) 13,502
Flórina (Phlorina) 11,164
Galátsion (*Athens) 27,240
Glifádha (*Athens) 23,449
Grevená 8,016
Ilioúpolis (*Athens) 49,215
Ioánnina (Yanina) 40,130
Iráklion (Candia) (*84,710) 77,506
Iráklion (*Athens) 24,302
Kaisarianí (*Athens) 26,833
Kalámai (*40,402) 39,133
Kalamákion (*Athens) 26,957
Kalamariá 36,978
Kallithéa (*Athens) 82,438
Kardhítsa 25,685
Kastoría 15,407
Kateríni (*30,512) 28,808
Kavála 46,234
Keratsínion (*Athens) 67,672
Kérkira (Corfu) 28,630
Khaïdhárion (*Athens) 34,673
Khálandrion (*Athens) 35,944
Khalkís (Chalcis) 36,300
Khaniá (Canea) (*53,026) 40,564
Khíos (Chios) (*30,021) 24,084
Kifisiá (*Athens) 20,082
Komotiní 28,896
Koridhallós (*Athens) 47,335
Kórinthos (Corinth) 20,773
Kozáni 23,240
Lamía 37,872
Lárisa 72,336
Levádhia (Lebadea) 15,445
Mégara 17,294
Néa Ionía (*Athens) 54,906
Néa Liósia (*Athens) 56,217
Néa Smírni (*Athens) 42,512
Níkaia (*Athens) 86,269
Palaión Fáliron (*Athens) 35,066
Pátrai (Patras) (*120,847) 111,607
Peristérion (*Athens) 118,413
Piraiévs (Piraeus) (**Athens) 187,362
Pírgos (Pyrgos) 20,599
Ródhos (Rhodes) 32,092
Salamís 18,256
Sérrai 39,897
Spárti (Sparta) (*13,432) 10,549
Thessaloníki (Salonika) (*557,360) 345,799
Thívai (Thebes) 15,971
Tríkkala 34,794
Trípolis (Tripolitza) 20,209
Véroia 29,528
Víron (*Athens) 44,021
Vólos (*88,096) 51,290
Xánthi 24,867
Zákinthos 9,339
Zografós (*Athens) 56,722

GREENLAND / Grønland
1977 E 49,719
Angmagssalik 1,023
Egedesminde 3,347
•GODTHÅB 8,545
Holsteinsborg 3,741
Julianehåb 2,670
Sukkertoppen 2,937
Thule 357

GRENADA
1976 E 109,609
•ST. GEORGE'S (*26,000) 10,000

GUADELOUPE
1974 C 324,530
BASSE-TERRE (*25,202) 15,457
Capesterre (18,143▲) 6,861
Les Abymes (*Pointe-à-Pitre) (53,605▲) 10,573
•Pointe-à-Pitre (*59,000) 23,889

GUAM
1980 C 105,816
•AGANA (*25,000) 881
Dededo 23,659

GUATEMALA
1973 C 5,211,929
Amatitlán 15,372
Antigua Guatemala 17,692
Chiquimula 16,181
Coatepeque 15,949
Escuintla 37,180
•GUATEMALA (*945,000) 717,322
Mazatenango 24,156
Puerto Barrios 19,696
Quezaltenango 45,977
Retalhuleu 20,222

GUERNSEY
1971 C 53,734
•ST. PETER PORT (*36,000) 16,303

GUINEA / Guinée
1967 E 3,702,000
•CONAKRY (1967 C) 197,267
Kankan 50,000
Kindia 45,000
Labé 26,000
Mamou 18,000
Nzérékoré 26,000
Siguiri 15,000

GUINEA-BISSAU
1970 C 487,448
•BISSAU 71,169

GUYANA
1976 E 783,000
•GEORGETOWN (*187,056) 72,049
New Amsterdam (1970 C) 17,782

HAITI / Haïti
1975 E 4,583,785
Cap-Haïtien 52,220
Gonaïves 33,837
Jérémie 19,227
Les Cayes 24,931
Pétionville (*Port-au-Prince) (1971 C) 35,257
•PORT-AU-PRINCE (1978 E) (*800,000) 745,700
Port-de-Paix 16,151
St.-Marc 19,354

HONDURAS
1977 E 2,998,700
Choluteca 29,300
Comayagua (1974 C) 15,941
El Progreso 32,800
La Ceiba 44,900
La Lima (1974 C) 14,631
Puerto Cortés 30,200
San Pedro Sula 172,900
•TEGUCIGALPA 316,800
Tela 22,700

HONG KONG
1976 C 4,402,990
Kowloon (**Victoria) 749,600
New Kowloon (*Victoria) 1,628,880
Tai Wan Tsun (Ngau Tau Kok) (*Victoria) (1961 C) 53,836
Tsun Wan (*Victoria) 455,270
•VICTORIA (HONG KONG) (*3,975,000) 1,026,870

HUNGARY / Magyarország
1980 C 10,710,000
Ajka 30,000
Baja 39,000
Békés (22,000▲) 17,900
Békéscsaba (66,000▲) 57,400
•BUDAPEST (*2,600,000) 2,060,000
Cegléd (40,000▲) 32,500
Csongrád (22,000▲) 19,100
Debrecen 195,000
Dunaújváros 60,000
Eger 60,000
Érd (*Budapest) 40,000
Esztergom 31,000
Gödöllő (*Budapest) 26,000
Gyöngyös 38,000
Győr 125,000
Gyula (34,000▲) 29,300
Hajdúböszörmény (32,000▲) 28,600
Hajdúszoboszló 24,000
Hatvan 24,000
Hódmezővásárhely (54,000▲) 45,100
Jászberény (31,000▲) 24,900
Kaposvár 73,000
Karcag 24,000
Kazincbarcika 37,000
Kecskemét (93,000▲) 74,200
Kiskunfélegyháza (36,000▲) 27,300
Kiskunhalas (31,000▲) 22,700
Komló 30,000
Makó 30,000
Miskolc 210,000
Mohács (21,000▲) 17,700
Mosonmagyaróvár 30,000
Nagykanizsa 48,000
Nagykőrös (27,000▲) 21,600
Nyíregyháza (107,000▲) 84,600
Orosháza (36,000▲) 31,500
Ózd 47,000
Pápa 32,000
Pécs 170,000
Salgótarján 49,000
Sopron 56,000
Szeged 175,000
Székesfehérvár 102,000
Szekszárd 34,000
Szentes (35,000▲) 30,600
Szolnok 77,000
Szombathely 82,000
Tata 24,000
Tatabánya 75,000
Törökszentmiklós (26,000▲) 22,500
Vác 34,000
Várpalota 28,000
Veszprém 55,000
Zalaegerszeg 55,000

ICELAND / Ísland
1979 E 226,724
Akureyri 13,137
Hafnarfjördur (*Reykjavík) 12,158
Keflavík 6,539
Kópavogur (*Reykjavík) 13,533
•REYKJAVÍK (*120,085) 83,536

INDIA / Bhārat
1976 E 609,264,000
(total excludes Sikkim, annexed in 1975)

States
Andaman and Nicobar Islands (Ter.) 128,000
Andhra Pradesh 47,944,000
Arunachal Pradesh (Ter.) 520,000
Assam 17,354,000
Bihār 61,790,000
Chandīgarh (Ter.) 285,000
Dādra and Nagar Haveli (Ter.) 83,000
Delhi (Ter.) 5,116,000
Goa, Damān and Diu (Ter.) 954,000
Gujarāt 30,269,000
Haryana 11,221,000
Himāchal Pradesh 3,657,000
Jammu and Kashmīr 5,120,000
Karnataka (Mysore) 32,448,000
Kerala 23,955,000
Lakshadweep (Ter.) 36,000
Madhya Pradesh 47,167,000
Mahārāshtra 56,341,000
Manipur (Ter.) 1,195,000
Meghalaya 1,125,000
Mizoram (pop. included with Assam)
Nāgāland 557,000
Orissa 24,391,000
Pondicherry (Ter.) 524,000
Punjab 14,954,000
Rājasthān 29,005,000
Sikkim (1971 E) 196,852
Tamil Nadu (Madras) 45,434,000
Tripura (Ter.) 1,731,000
Uttar Pradesh 96,172,000
West Bengal 49,788,000

Cities (1971 C)
Abohar 58,925
Achalpur (Ellichpur) (*66,451) 42,326
Adilābād 30,368
Ādoni 85,311
Agartala (*100,264) 59,625
Āgra (*634,622) 591,917
Āgra Cantonment (*Āgra) 37,074
Ahmadābād (*1,950,000) 1,585,544
Ahmadnagar (*148,405) 118,236
Aijal 31,740
Ajmer (*264,291) 262,851
Akola 168,438
Akot 41,534
Alandur (*Madras) 65,039
Alīgarh 252,314
Alīpur Duār (*54,454) 36,667
Allahābād (*513,036) 490,622
Alleppey 160,166
Almora (*20,881) 19,671
Alwar 100,378
Amalāpuram 30,518
Amalner 55,544
Ambāla (*186,126) 83,633
Ambāla Cantonment (*Ambāla) 102,493
Ambarnāth (*Bombay) 56,276
Ambāsamudram (*49,255) 27,709
Ambattur (*Madras) 45,586
Āmbūr 54,011
Amrāvati (Amraoti) (*221,277) 193,800
Amreli (*43,794) 39,520
Amritsar (*458,029) 407,628
Amroha 82,702
Anakapalle 57,273
Ānand 59,155
Anantapur 80,069
Arcot (*75,911) 30,230
Arkonam 43,347
Arni 38,664
Arrah 92,919
Aruppukkottai 62,223
Asansol (*925,000) 155,968
Ashoknagar-Kalyangarh (*Hābra) 41,916
Āttūr 41,569
Aurangābād (*165,253) 150,483
Avadi (*Madras) 77,413
Azamgarh 40,963
Badagara 53,938
Bāgalkot 51,746
Bahraich 73,931
Baidyabāti (*Calcutta) 54,130
Balasore 46,239
Ballarpur 34,268
Ballia 47,101
Balrāmpur 36,191
Bālurghāt 67,088
Bānda 50,575
Bangalore (*1,750,000) 1,540,741
Bangaon 50,538
Bānkura 79,129
Bansbāria (*Calcutta) 61,748
Bāpatla 41,947
Baranagar (*Calcutta) 136,842
Bārāsat (*Calcutta) 42,642
Baraut 31,264
Bareilly (*326,106) 296,248
Barmer 38,630
Barnāla 31,388
Baroda (Vadodara) (*467,487) 466,696
Barrackpore (*Calcutta) 96,889
Bārsi 62,374
Basīrhāt 63,816
Basti 49,635
Batāla (*76,488) 58,200
Beāwar 66,114
Begusarai (*44,084) 35,736
Behāla (South Suburban) (*Calcutta) 272,600
Belgaum (*213,872) 192,427
Bellampalle 30,290
Bellary 125,183
Berhampore (*West Bengal state*) (*78,909) 72,605
Berhampur (*Orissa state*) 117,662
Bettiah 51,018
Betūl 30,862
Bhadrakh 40,487
Bhadrāvati (*101,358) 40,203
Bhadreswar (*Calcutta) 45,586
Bhāgalpur 172,202
Bhandāra 39,423
Bharatpur (*69,902) 68,036
Bhatinda (*65,318) 53,684
Bhātpāra (*Calcutta) 204,750
Bhaunagar (*225,974) 225,358
Bhavāni (*56,696) 23,114
Bhilai (Bhilainagar) (*245,124) 157,173
Bhīlwāra 82,155
Bhīmavaram 63,762
Bhind (*45,794) 42,371
Bhiwandi (*Bombay) 79,576
Bhiwāni 73,086
Bhopāl (*384,859) 298,022
Bhubaneswar 105,491
Bhuj (*52,861) 52,177
Bhusāwal (*104,708) 96,800
Bīdar 50,670
Bihar 100,046
Bijāpur 103,931
Bijnor 43,290
Bīkaner (*208,894) 188,518
Bilāspur (*130,740) 98,410
Bīr (Bhir) 49,965
Bishnupur 38,135
Bodhan 37,589
Bodināyakkanūr 54,176
Bokāro Steel City (*107,159) 94,007
Bolāngīr 35,748
Bombay (*6,750,000) 5,970,575
Botād 32,179
Broach (Bharuch) (*92,251) 91,589
Budaun 72,204
Budge Budge (*Calcutta) 51,039
Bulandshahr 59,505
Bulsār (Valsad) (*54,966) 43,254
Būndi 34,279
Burdwān 143,318
Burhānpur (*105,335) 105,246
Buxar 31,691
•Calcutta (*9,100,000) 3,148,746
Calicut (Kozhikode) 333,979
Cambay 62,097
Cannanore (*59,912) 55,162
Chaibāsā 35,386
Chākdaha 46,345
Chakradharpur (*34,967) 22,709
Chālakudi 37,562
Chālisgaon 41,720
Champdāni (*Calcutta) 58,596
Chandannagar (Chandernagore) (*Calcutta) 75,238
Chandausi 53,393
Chandīgarh (*232,940) 218,743
Chandrapur 75,134
Changanācheri 48,545
Chāpra (*98,401) 83,101
Chhatarpur 32,271
Chhindwāra (*53,508) 53,492
Chidambaram (*57,658) 48,811
Chikmagalūr 41,639
Chilakalūrupet 41,543
Chingleput 38,419
Chīrāla 54,487
Chitradurga 50,254
Chittaranjan 40,736
Chittoor 63,035
Chopda 32,656
Churu (*53,185) 52,502
Cochin 439,066
Coimbatore (*750,000) 356,368
Cooch Behār (*62,664) 53,684
Coonoor (*70,813) 38,007
Cuddalore 101,335
Cuddapah 66,195
Cumbum 40,796
Cuttack (*205,759) 194,068
Dabhoi 37,892
Dabra (*21,430) 18,623
Dalhousie (*5,123) 4,296
Daltonganj 32,367
Damān 17,317
Damoh (*59,983) 59,489
Dānāpur (*Patna) 42,694
Darbhanga 132,059
Darjeeling 42,873
Datia 36,439
Dāvangere 121,110
Dehra Dūn (*203,464) 166,073
Dehri 46,037
Delhi (*4,500,000) 3,706,558
Delhi Cantonment (*Delhi) 57,339
Deoband 38,194
Deoghar (*45,060) 40,356
Deolāli (**Nāsik) 55,436
Deoria 38,161
Dewās (*51,866) 51,545
Dhānbād (*600,000) 79,838
Dhār 36,172
Dhārāpuram 34,500
Dharmapuri 40,086
Dholka 35,520
Dholpur 31,865
Dhorāji (*60,080) 59,773
Dhrāngadhra 40,791
Dhubri (*45,589) 36,503
Dhule 137,129
Dibrugarh 80,348
Digboi (*32,388) 16,538
Dindigul 128,429
Dohad (*51,406) 44,506
Dombivli (*Bombay) 51,108
Dum-Dum (*Calcutta) 31,363
Durg (**Bhilai) 67,892
Durgapur 206,638
Dwarka 17,801
Elūru (Ellore) 127,023
English Bāzār (*68,026) 61,335
Erode (*169,613) 105,111
Etah 33,514
Etāwah 85,894
Faizābād (*109,806) 102,835
Farīdābād New Township (*Delhi) 85,762
Farrukhābād (*110,835) 102,768
Fatehābād 22,630
Fatehpur 54,665
Fatehpur Sikri 13,561
Fāzilka 36,281
Firozābād 133,863
Firozpur (Ferozepore) (*97,709) 49,545
Gadag 95,426
Garden Reach (*Calcutta) 154,913
Garulia (*Calcutta) 44,271
Gauhāti (*200,377) 123,783
Gaya 179,884
Ghāziābād (*Delhi) 118,836
Ghāzīpur 45,635
Giridih 40,308
Godhra (*66,853) 66,403
Gonda 52,662
Gondal (*55,329) 54,928
Gondia 77,992
Gopichettipālaiyam 36,356
Gorakhpur 230,911
Govindpura (*Bhopāl) 53,922
Gūdalūr 32,843
Gudivāda 61,068
Gudiyāttam (*67,966) 63,007
Gūdūr 33,778
Gulbarga 145,588
Guna 40,006
Guntakal 66,320
Guntūr 269,991
Gurdāspur 32,064
Gurgaon 57,151
Gwalior (*406,140) 384,772
Hābra (*93,351) 51,435
Hājīpur 41,890
Haldwāni 52,205
Hālisahar (*Calcutta) 68,906
Hānsi 41,108
Hāpur 71,266
Hardoi 46,639
Hardwār (*79,277) 77,864
Harihar 33,888
Haripād 31,145
Hassan 51,325
Hāthras 74,349
Hazāribāgh 54,818
Hindupur 42,959
Hinganghāt 44,349
Hingoli 31,948
Hisār 89,437
Hooghly-Chinsura (*Calcutta) 105,241
Hoshiārpur 57,691
Hospet 65,196
Howrah (*Calcutta) 737,877
Hubli-Dhārwār 379,166
Hyderābād (*2,000,000) 1,607,396
Ichalkaranji 87,731
Imphāl 100,366
Indore (*560,936) 543,381
Itārsi (*46,866) 44,191
Jabalpur (*534,845) 426,224
Jabalpur Cantonment (*Jabalpur) 50,195
Jagādhri (*115,020) 35,094
Jagannāthnagar (*Rānchī) 55,663
Jagraon 32,999
Jagtiāl 30,900
Jaipur (*636,768) 615,258
Jālgaon 106,711
Jālna 91,099
Jalpaiguri 55,159
Jamālpur (**Monghyr) 61,731
Jammu (*164,207) 155,338
Jāmnagar (*227,640) 199,709
Jamshedpur (*456,146) 341,576
Jaora 37,235
Jaridih Bazar (*69,321) 33,084
Jaunpur 80,737
Jetpur (*41,943) 41,926

C Census. E Official estimate. UE Unofficial estimate.
L Population within municipal limits of year specified. • Largest city in country.
* Population or designation of metropolitan area, including suburbs (see headnote).
▲ Population of an entire municipality, commune, or district, including rural area.
‡† Year of information specified at start of country.

Jeypore 34,319
Jhānsi (*198,135) 173,292
Jharia (**Dhānbād) 45,236
Jīnd 38,161
Jodhpur 317,612
Jorhāt (*70,674) 30,247
Jullundur (*329,830) 296,106
Junāgadh (*95,900) 95,485
Kadaiyanallūr 50,295
Kadiri 33,810
Kairāna 32,353
Kaithal 45,199
Kākināda 164,200
Kālol (*Ahmadābād) 50,321
Kalyān (*Bombay) 99,547
Kamarhati (*Calcutta) 169,404
Kāmthi (*Nāgpur) 53,412
Kānchipuram (Conjeeveram) (*119,693) 110,657
Kānchrāpāra (*Calcutta) 78,768
Kānpur (*1,320,000) 1,154,388
Kānpur Cantonment (*Kānpur) 69,452
Kapadvanj 30,748
Kapūrthala 35,482
Karād 42,329
Kāraikkudi (*88,371) 55,449
Kāranja 31,150
Karimganj 31,618
Karīmnagar 48,918
Karnāl 92,784
Karūr 65,706
Kāsaragod 34,984
Kāsganj 46,467
Kāshīpur 33,457
Katihār (*80,121) 67,014
Kayankulam (Kayamkulam) 54,102
Kerkend (*Dhānbād) 51,314
Khadki (Kirkee) (*Pune) 65,497
Khāmgaon 53,692
Khammam 56,919
Khandwa (*85,403) 84,517
Khanna 34,182
Kharagpur (*161,257) 61,783
Khargone 41,316
Khurja 50,245
Kilikollūr 41,871
Kishanganj 36,893
Kishangarh 37,405
Kohima 21,545
Kolār 43,418
Kolār Gold Fields (*118,861) 76,112
Kolhāpur (*267,513) 259,050
Konnagar (*Calcutta) 34,424
Kota 212,991
Kot Kapūra (*34,116) 33,907
Kottagūdem 75,542
Kottayam 59,714
Kovilpatti 48,509
Krishnanagar 85,923
Kulti (**Asansol) 29,665
Kumbakonam (*119,655) 113,130
Kundla 37,957
Kurichi (*Coimbatore) 40,537
Kurnool 136,710
Lakhīmpur 43,752
Lalitpur 34,462
Lātūr 70,156
Leh 5,519
Lucknow (*840,000) 749,239
Lucknow Cantonment (*Lucknow) 39,338
Ludhiāna (*401,176) 397,850
Machilīpatnam (Bandar) 112,612
Madras (*3,200,000) 2,469,449
Madakulam (*Madurai) 46,317
Madanapalle 36,458
Madgaon (Margao) (*48,593) 41,655
Madhubani 32,919
Madurai (*725,000) 549,114
Mahbūbnagar 51,756
Mahuva 39,497
Mainpurī 43,849
Mālegaon 191,847
Māler Kotla (*48,859) 48,536
Malkāpur 35,476
Manappārai 32,092
Mandasor (*56,988) 52,347
Mandya 72,132
Mangalagiri 32,850
Mangalore (*215,122) 165,174
Mannārgudi 42,703
Mānsa 31,351
Mathura (*140,150) 132,028
Maunath Bhanjan 64,058
Māyūram 60,195
Meerut (*367,754) 270,993
Meerut Cantonment (*Meerut) 85,415
Mehsāna (Mahesāna) (*51,713) 51,598
Melappālaiyam (*Tirunelveli) 47,731
Mettupālaiyam 48,365
Mettūr 38,380
Mhow (*63,739) 59,037
Midnapore 71,326
Mira (**Sāngli) 77,606
Mirzāpur 105,939
Modinagar 43,470
Moga (*61,625) 55,270
Mokameh 38,164
Monghyr (*164,205) 102,474
Morādābād (*272,652) 258,590
Morena 44,901
Mormugão 44,065
Morvi 60,976
Motihāri (*40,352) 37,032
Muktsar 36,750
Murtazāpur 23,141
Murwāra (Katni) (*86,535) 54,864
Mussoorie 18,038
Muzaffarnagar 114,783
Muzaffarpur 126,379
Mysore 355,685
Nabadwip 94,204
Nābha 34,761
Nadiād 108,269
Nāgappattinam (*74,019) 68,026
Nāgaur 36,448
Nāgda 32,569
Nāgercoil 141,288
Nagīna 37,066
Nāgpur (*950,000) 866,076
Naihāti (*Calcutta) 82,080
Naini Tāl (*25,167) 23,986
Najībābād 42,586
Nalgonda 33,126
Nānded 126,538
Nandurbār 54,070
Nandyāl 63,193
Nangi (*Calcutta) 47,555
Narasapur 36,147
Narasaraopet 43,467
Nārnaul 31,875
Nāsik (*271,681) 176,091
Navsāri (*80,101) 72,979
Nawābganj 35,395
Neemuch (*49,748) 47,113
Nellikkuppam 37,638
Nellore 133,590
NEW DELHI (**Delhi) 301,801
Neyveli 58,285
Nipāni 35,116
Nizāmābād 115,640
North Barrackpore (*Calcutta) 76,335
North Dum-Dum (*Calcutta) 63,873
Nowgong 56,537
Ongole 53,330
Ootacamund 63,310
Orai 42,513
Outer Burnpur (*Asansol) 56,900
Pālakollu 36,196
Pālanpur 42,114
Pālayankottai (**Tirunelveli) 70,070
Pālghāt 95,788
Pāli 49,834
Pallavaram (*Madras) 51,374
Palni (*51,664) 49,575
Palwal 36,207
Panaji (Panjim) (Nova Goa) (*59,258) 34,953
Pānchur (*Calcutta) 59,021
Pandharpur 53,638
Pandu (*Gauhati) 38,876
Pānihāti (*Calcutta) 148,046
Pānīpat 87,981
Panruti 34,065
Paramagudi 48,880
Parbhani 61,570
Parli 31,078
Pātan 64,519
Pattukkottai 37,682
Pathānkot (*78,192) 76,355
Patiāla (*151,041) 148,686
Patna (*625,000) 473,001
Periyakulam 41,501
Petlād 39,535
Phagwāra (*55,012) 50,863
Pīlibhīt 68,273
Pimpri-Chinchwad (*Pune) 83,542
Pithāpuram 31,391
Pollāchi (*93,838) 68,655
Pondicherry (*153,325) 90,637
Ponnāni 35,723
Porbandar (*106,727) 96,881
Port Blair 26,218
Proddatūr 70,822
Pudukkottai 66,384
Pulgaon 33,382
Puliyangudi 38,742
Pune (Poona) (*1,175,000) 856,105
Pune Cantonment (*Pune) 77,774
Puri 72,674
Purnea (*71,311) 56,484
Purūlia 57,708
Quilon 124,208
Rabkavi Banhatti 37,509
Rāe-Bareli 38,765
Rāichūr 79,831
Raiganj 43,191
Raigarh (*48,049) 46,745
Raipur (*205,986) 174,518
Rājahmundry (*188,805) 165,912
Rājapālaiyam 86,952
Rājkot 300,612
Rāj-Nāndgaon (*55,827) 41,183
Rājpur (*Calcutta) 34,393
Rāmanāthapuram 36,122
Rāmpur 161,417
Rānāghāt 47,815
Rānchī (*255,551) 175,934
Rānībennur 40,749
Rānīganj (**Asansol) 40,104
Ratangarh 31,506
Ratlām (*119,247) 106,666
Ratnāgiri 37,551
Raurkela (*172,502) 125,426
Rewa 69,182
Rewāri 43,885
Rishīkesh 17,646
Rishra (*Calcutta) 63,486
Rohtak 124,755
Roorkee (*62,456) 47,561
Sāgar (*154,785) 118,574
Sahāranpur 225,396
Sāhibganj 35,640
Salem (*416,440) 308,716
Sāmalkot 34,607
Sambalpur (*105,085) 64,675
Sambhal 86,323
Sāngli (*201,597) 115,138
Sāntipur 61,166
Sardārshahr 37,703
Sāsarām 48,282
Sātāra 66,433
Satna (*62,162) 57,531
Secunderābād Cantonment (*Hyderābād) 94,416
Sehore 35,657
Seoni 38,396
Serampore (*Calcutta) 102,023
Shāhābād 33,408
Shāhjahānpur (*144,065) 135,604
Shāmli 36,959
Shikohābād 31,442
Shillong (*122,752) 87,659
Shimoga 102,709
Shivpuri (*50,858) 42,120
Sholāpur 398,361
Sidhpur (*41,334) 40,521
Sīkar 70,987
Silchar 52,596
Silīguri (*136,343) 97,484
Simla 55,368
Sindri (**Dhānbād) 46,385
Singānallūr (*Coimbatore) 112,206
Sirsa 48,808
Sītāpur 66,715
Sivakāsi (*60,753) 44,883
Siwān 33,162
Sonīpat 62,393
South Dum-Dum (*Calcutta) 174,342
Sri Gangānagar (Gangānagar) 90,042
Srīkākulam 45,179
Srīnagar (*423,253) 403,413
Srīrangam (*Tiruchchirāppalli) 51,069
Srīvilliputtūr 53,855
Sūjāngarh 39,073
Sultānpur 32,330
Surat (*493,001) 471,656
Surendranagar (*97,251) 66,667
Sūri 30,110
Tādepallegūdem 43,610
Tādpatri 31,618
Tāmbaram (*Madras) 58,805
Tandā 41,611
Tanuku 34,197
Tellicherry 68,759
Tenāli 102,937
Tenkāsi 42,627
Tezpur 39,870
Thāna (*Bombay) 170,675
Thanjāvūr (Tanjore) 140,547
Theni-Allinagaram 34,854
Tindivanam 45,058
Tinsukia 54,911
Tiruchchirāppalli (Trichinopoly) (*475,000) 307,400
Tiruchendūr (*55,636) 18,126
Tiruchengodu 36,990
Tirunelveli (*266,688) 108,498
Tirupati (*71,984) 65,843
Tiruppattūr 40,357
Tiruppur (*151,127) 113,302
Tiruvannāmalai 61,370
Tiruvottiyūr (*Madras) 82,853
Titāgarh (*Calcutta) 88,218
Tonk 55,866
Trichūr 76,241
Trivandrum 409,627
Tumkūr 70,476
Tuticorin (*181,913) 155,310
Udaipur 161,278
Udamalpet 39,311
Udgīr 30,647
Ujjain (*208,561) 203,278
Ulhāsnagar (*Bombay) 168,462
Upleta 35,326
Uttarpara-Kotrung (*Calcutta) 67,568
Valparai 95,175
Vāniyambādi (*67,686) 51,810
Vārānasi (Benares) (*606,271) 583,856
Vellore (*178,554) 139,082
Verāval (*75,520) 58,771
Vidisha 43,212
Vijayawāda (*344,607) 317,258
Vikramasingapuram 40,274
Villupuram 60,242
Viramgām 43,790
Virudunagar 61,902
Vishākhapatnam (*363,467) 352,504
Visnagar 34,863
Vizianagaram 86,608
Warangal 207,520
Wardha 69,037
Yādgīr 32,756
Yamunānagar (**Jagādhri) 72,594
Yavatmāl 64,830

INDONESIA

1979 E †144,911,000

Island Groups

BORNEO, INDONESIAN (KALIMANTAN) 6,406,000
CELEBES 10,605,000
JAVA AND MADURA 90,780,000
LESSER SUNDA ISLANDS †8,153,000
MOLUCCAS 2,481,000
SUMATRA 26,486,000

†Total excludes Timor Timur, annexed in 1976

Cities (‡1971 C or 1961 C)

Amahai 18,256
Ambon (Amboina) (1976 E) 91,000
Amuntai 27,383
Balikpapan ‡137,340
Banda Aceh (Kutaradja) ‡53,668
Bandung (*1,250,000) ‡1,201,730
Bangil 28,275
Bangkalan 25,514
Banjarmasin ‡281,673
Bantul 30,572
Banyuwangi ‡89,303
Baubau 21,060
Bekasi ‡45,694
Bengkulu ‡31,866
Binjai ‡59,882
Blitar ‡67,856
Blora ‡53,504
Bogor ‡195,882
Bojonegoro ‡52,597
Bondowoso 35,760
Brebes ‡44,456
Bukittinggi ‡63,132
Ciamis 35,189
Cianjur (Tjiandjur) 62,546
Cilacap (Tjilatjap) ‡82,043
Cimahi (Tjimahi) ‡72,367
Cirebon (Tjirebon) ‡178,529
Denpasar ‡88,142
Dili (1970 C) (65,451▲) 6,730
Ende 26,843
Garut ‡81,234
Gorontalo ‡82,328
Gresik ‡48,561
Indramayu 25,710
•JAKARTA (DJAKARTA) (1979 UE) (*6,500,000) 6,400,000
Jambi (Telanaipura) ‡158,559
Jayapura (Sukarnapura) (1976 E) 61,054
Jember ‡122,712
Jepara 18,921
Jombang ‡45,450
Kediri ‡178,865
Klaten 33,400
Kotabumi 37,496
Krawang ‡61,361
Kualakapuas 18,573
Kudus ‡87,767
Kuningan 21,542
Kupang ‡52,698
Lahat ‡41,030
Langsa ‡55,016
Lawang 35,852
Lhokseumawe 28,386
Lumajang ‡48,995
Madiun ‡136,147
Magelang ‡110,308
Magetan 26,818
Majalengka 14,361
Majene 24,259
Makale 32,578
Malang ‡422,428
Manado ‡169,684
Martapura ‡69,729
Medan ‡635,562
Mojokerto ‡60,013
Nganjuk 23,499
Ngawi 29,220
Padang ‡196,339
Padangpanjang ‡30,711
Padangsidempuan ‡49,090
Pakanbaru ‡145,030
Palangkaraya ‡27,132
Palembang ‡582,961
Palopo 29,724
Palu 16,977
Pamekasan ‡41,416
Pangkalpinang ‡74,733
Parepare ‡72,538
Pasuruan ‡75,266
Pati ‡46,037
Payakumbuh ‡63,388
Pekalongan ‡111,537
Pemalang ‡77,672
Pematangsiantar ‡129,232
Perabumulih 41,951
Pinrang 23,818
Ponorogo ‡67,711
Pontianak ‡217,555
Praya 26,729
Probolinggo ‡82,008
Purbolinggo 22,698
Purwakarta ‡49,703
Purwokerto ‡94,023
Purworejo ‡52,956
Raba 29,881
Rangkasbitung 30,822
Salatiga ‡69,831
Samarinda ‡137,521
Semarang ‡646,590
Serang ‡56,263
Sibolga ‡42,223
Sidoarjo ‡41,254
Singaraja ‡42,289
Singkawang 35,169
Situbondo ‡55,348
Solok ‡24,771
Sragen 25,685
Subang ‡42,437
Sukabumi ‡96,242
Sungaipenuh 36,766
Surabaya (*1,400,000) ‡1,332,249
Surakarta ‡414,285
Tangerang ‡50,893
Tanjungbalai ‡33,604
Tanjungkarang-Telukbetung ‡198,986
Tanjungpandan 29,412
Tanjungpinang 37,638
Tarutung 24,998
Tasikmalaya ‡100,004
Tebingtinggi ‡30,314
Tegal ‡105,752
Ternate 24,287
Tidore 26,160
Tual 38,403
Tuban 38,575
Tulungagung ‡68,899
Ujung Pandang (Makasar) ‡434,766
Watampone ‡54,720
Yogyakarta (Jogjakarta) ‡342,267

IRAN / Īrān

1976 C 33,591,875

Ābādān 296,081
Ahvāz 329,006
Āmol 68,782
Arāk 114,507
Ardabīl 147,404
Bābol 67,790
Bakhtarān 290,861
Bandar 'Abbās 89,103
Bandar-e Anzalī (Bandar-e Pahlavī) 55,978
Behbehān (1966 C) 39,874
Behshahr (1966 C) 26,032
Bīrjand (1966 C) 25,854
Bojnūrd (1966 C) 31,248
Borūjerd 100,103
Dezfūl 110,287
Emāmshahr (Shahrūd) (1966 C) 30,767
Eşfahān (Isfahan) 671,825
Gonbad-e Qābūs 59,868
Gorgān 88,348
Hamadān 155,846
Homāyunshahr (1966 C) 46,836
Jahrom (1966 C) 38,236
Karaj 138,774
Kāshān 84,545
Kāzerūn 51,309
Kermān 140,309
Khorramābād 104,928
Khorramshahr 146,709
Khvoy 70,040
Lāhījān (1966 C) 25,725
Lār (1966 C) 21,576
Mahābād (1966 C) 28,610
Malāyer (1966 C) 28,434
Marāgheh 60,820
Marand (1966 C) 23,818
Marv Dasht (1966 C) 25,498
Mashhad (Meshed) 670,180
Masjed Soleymān 77,161
Mīāneh (1966 C) 28,447
Najafābād 76,236
Neyshābūr 59,101
Orūmīyeh (Rezā'īyeh) 163,991
Qā'emshahr (Shāhī) 63,289
Qazvīn 138,527
Qom 246,831
Qūchān (1966 C) 29,133
Rasht 187,203
Sabzevār 69,174
Sanandaj 95,834
Sārī 70,936
Semnān (1966 C) 31,058
Shīrāz 416,408
Tabrīz 598,576
•TEHRĀN (*4,700,000) 4,496,159
Torbat-e Ḩeydarīyeh (1966 C) 30,106
Yazd 135,978
Zāhedān 92,628
Zanjān 99,967

IRAQ / Al-'Irāq

1970 E 9,465,800

Ad-Dīwānīyah 62,300
Al-'Amārah 80,100
Al-Başrah (Basra) 370,900
Al-Fallūjah (1965 C) 38,072
Al-Ḩillah (Hilla) 128,800
Al-Kūfah (1965 C) 30,862
Al-Mawşil (Mosul) 293,100
An-Najaf 179,200
An-Nāşirīyah 62,400
Ar-Ramādī (1965 C) 28,723
As-Samāwah (1965 C) 33,473
As-Sulaymānīyah 98,100
Az-Zubayr (1965 C) 41,408
•BAGHDĀD (*2,183,800) 1,300,000
Ba'qūbah (1965 C) 34,575
Irbīl 107,400
Karbalā' 107,500
Kirkūk 207,900
Kūt al-Imāra (Al-Kūt) (1965 C) 42,116
Sāmarrā (1965 C) 24,746
Tall 'Afar (1965 C) 36,837

IRELAND / Eire

1979 C 3,368,217

An Uaimh (Navan) (*7,000) 4,277
Arklow (Inbhear Mór) 8,446
Athlone (Áth Luain) (*12,500) 9,760
Ballina (Béal Átha an Fheadha) 6,941
Ballinasloe (Béal Átha na Sluagh) 6,461
Bray (Brí Chualann) (*Dublin) 21,672
Carlow (Ceatharlach) 11,404
Carrick-on-Suir (Carraig na Siúire) 5,510
Castlebar (Caisleán an Bharraigh) 6,482
Clonmel (Cluain Meala) 12,411
Cobh 6,670
Cork (Corcaigh) (*175,000) 138,267
Drogheda (Droichead Átha) 22,555
Droichead Nua (1971 C) 5,053
•DUBLIN (BAILE ÁTHA CLIATH) (*1,110,000) 544,586
Dundalk (Dún Dealgan) [illegible]
Dungarvan (Dún Garbháin) 6,578
Dún Laoghaire (*Dublin) 54,244
Ennis (Inis) (*12,000) 6,277
Enniscorthy (Inis Coirthe) 5,253
Galway (Gaillimh) 36,824
Kilkenny (Cill Choinnigh) (*14,800) 10,075
Killarney (Cill Áirne) 7,724
Limerick (Luimneach) (*80,000) 60,665
Mallow (Mala) 6,609
Monaghan (Muineachán) 6,173
Mullingar (Muileann Cearr) (1971 C) (*9,245) 6,790
Naas (Nás na Ríogh) (*Dublin) 7,740
Nenagh (Aonach Urmhumhan) 5,647
New Ross (Ros Mhic Treoin) 5,230
Portlaoise (1971 C) (*6,470) 3,902
Sligo (Sligeach) 16,836
Thurles (Durlas Éile) 7,436
Tipperary (Tiobrad Árann) 4,929
Tralee (Tráighlí) 15,011
Tuam (Tuaim) (1971 C) (*4,952) 3,808
Tullamore (Tulach Mhór) 7,720
Waterford (Port Láirge) (*42,000) 32,617
Wexford (Loch Garman) 11,848
Youghal (Eochaill) 5,739

ISLE OF MAN

1976 C 61,723

•DOUGLAS (*28,500) 20,262
Peel 3,338
Ramsey 5,458

C Census. E Official estimate. UE Unofficial estimate.
L Population within municipal limits of specified year. • Largest city in country.
* Population or designation of metropolitan area, including suburbs (see headnote).
▲ Population of an entire municipality, commune, or district, including rural area.
‡† Year of information specified at start of country.

ISRAEL / Yisra'el

1979 E....................†3,836,200
'Afula....19,700
'Akko (Acre) (★Haifa)....37,900
Ashdod....62,300
Ashqelon....52,000
Bat Yam (★Tel Aviv-Yafo)....130,100
Be'er Sheva' (Beersheba)....107,000
Bene Beraq (★Tel Aviv-Yafo)....89,600
Dimona....27,800
Elat (Elath)....18,900
Giv'atayim (★Tel Aviv-Yafo)....49,300
Hadera....37,800
Haifa (Hefa) (★415,000)....229,300
Herzliyya (★Tel Aviv-Yafo)....56,400
Holon (★Tel Aviv-Yafo)....128,400
JERUSALEM (YERUSHALAYIM) (AL-QUDS) *(includes Old City area occupied in 1967)* (★420,000)....398,200
Kefar Ata (★Haifa)....31,400
Kefar Sava (★Tel Aviv-Yafo)....38,100
Lod (Lydda)....39,400
Nahariyya....28,200
Nazerat (Nazareth) (★63,000)....40,400
Nazerat 'Illit (★Nazerat)....21,400
Nes Ziyyona....13,700
Netanya....95,900
Or Yehuda (★Tel Aviv-Yafo)....19,400
Petah Tiqwa (★Tel Aviv-Yafo)....117,000
Qiryat Bialik (★Haifa)....27,500
Qiryat Gat....24,300
Qiryat Motzkin (★Haifa)....23,200
Qiryat Ono (★Tel Aviv-Yafo)....22,500
Qiryat Shemona....15,800
Qiryat Yam (★Haifa)....28,400
Ra'ananna (★Tel Aviv-Yafo)....29,700
Ramat Gan (★Tel Aviv-Yafo)....120,400
Ramat HaSharon (★Tel Aviv-Yafo)....30,100
Ramla....40,600
Rehovot....63,700
Rishon le Ziyyon (★Tel Aviv-Yafo)....87,800
•Tel Aviv-Yafo (Tel Aviv-Jaffa) (★1,350,000)....336,300
Teverya (Tiberias)....28,300
Tirat Karmel (★Haifa)....15,500
Umm el Fahm....18,600
Zefat....15,500

ITALY / Italia

1979 E....................56,999,047

Regions and Provinces

ABRUZZI....1,239,738
  Chieti....372,791
  L'Aquila....302,480
  Pescara....291,592
  Teramo....272,875
APULIA, see PUGLIA
BASILICATA (LUCANIA)....618,703
  Matera....204,273
  Potenza....414,430
CALABRIA....2,078,264
  Catanzaro....748,166
  Cosenza....735,673
  Reggio di Calabria....594,425
CAMPANIA....5,457,838
  Avellino....440,712
  Benevento....294,438
  Caserta....753,207
  Napoli (Naples)....2,945,181
  Salerno....1,024,300
EMILIA-ROMAGNA....3,964,538
  Bologna....937,136
  Ferrara....385,503
  Forlì....598,672
  Modena....590,547
  Parma....399,560
  Piacenza....280,981
  Ravenna....361,634
  Reggio nell'Emilia....410,505
FRIULI-VENEZIA GIULIA....1,245,130
  Gorizia....146,600
  Pordenone....274,550
  Trieste....291,581
  Udine....532,399
LAZIO (LATIUM)....5,059,174
  Frosinone....464,439
  Latina....434,787
  Rieti....143,983
  Roma (Rome)....3,747,003
  Viterbo....268,962
LIGURIA....1,844,779
  Genova....1,065,846
  Imperia....229,936
  La Spezia....244,558
  Savona....304,439
LOMBARDIA (LOMBARDY)....8,941,704
  Bergamo....890,540
  Brescia....1,015,350
  Como....772,532
  Cremona....333,403
  Mantova....380,413
  Milano....4,065,584
  Pavia....519,369
  Sondrio....175,188
  Varese....789,325
MARCHE (MARCHES)....1,415,563
  Ancona....434,091
  Ascoli Piceno....354,667
  Macerata....292,728
  Pesaro e Urbino....334,077
MOLISE....334,091
  Campobasso....238,564
  Isernia....95,527
PIEMONTE (PIEDMONT)....4,531,141
  Alessandria....472,865
  Asti....217,982
  Cuneo....548,236
  Novara....509,830
  Torino (Turin)....2,380,674
  Vercelli....401,554
PUGLIA (APULIA)....3,917,029
  Bari....1,471,563
  Brindisi....400,092
  Foggia....692,245
  Lecce....778,830
  Taranto....574,299
SARDEGNA (SARDINIA)....1,601,586
  Cagliari....730,333
  Nuoro....278,267
  Oristano....157,151
  Sassari....435,835
SICILIA (SICILY)....4,999,032
  Agrigento....489,020
  Caltanissetta....295,817
  Catania....1,014,493
  Enna....204,114
  Messina....686,764
  Palermo....1,206,291
  Ragusa....276,312
  Siracusa....397,818
  Trapani....428,403
TOSCANA (TUSCANY)....3,600,233
  Arezzo....313,801
  Firenze....1,209,407
  Grosseto....223,661
  Livorno....346,395
  Lucca....388,576
  Massa-Carrara....205,535
  Pisa....388,560
  Pistoia....266,526
  Siena....257,772
TRENTINO-ALTO ADIGE....876,249
  Bolzano....432,073
  Trento....444,176
UMBRIA....808,351
  Perugia....579,311
  Terni....229,040
VALLE D'AOSTA....114,591
VENETO (VENETIA)....4,351,313
  Belluno....224,829
  Padova....813,289
  Rovigo....254,466
  Treviso....716,250
  Venezia (Venice)....844,391
  Verona....774,347
  Vicenza....723,741

Cities

Abano Terme....16,115
Acerra (★Naples) (37,629▲)....33,100
Acireale (49,813▲)....30,600
Adrano....34,190
Afragola (★Naples)....58,927
Agrigento....51,725
Alassio....13,943
Alba....31,309
Albano Laziale (★Rome) (27,889▲)....22,000
Alberobello....9,983
Alcamo....43,593
Alessandria....101,684
Alghero (37,892▲)....31,700
Altamura....49,878
Amalfi....6,446
Ancona....108,371
Andria....83,734
Anzio....27,223
Aosta....39,072
Arezzo....92,245
Ascoli Piceno....56,200
Assisi (24,910▲)....19,400
Asti....79,407
Augusta....38,181
Avellino....59,324
Aversa (★Naples)....51,837
Avezzano (34,353▲)....29,800
Avola....30,565
Bagheria....41,373
Barcellona Pozzo di Gotto (37,737▲)....26,000
Bari (★460,000)....387,266
Barletta....81,414
Bassano del Grappa....37,801
Battipaglia (40,604▲)....32,200
Belluno....37,003
Benevento (62,524▲)....52,800
Bergamo (★340,000)....125,544
Biella....55,857
Bisceglie....46,962
Bitonto....48,052
Bollate (★Milan)....43,115
Bologna (★550,000)....471,554
Bolzano (Bozen)....106,199
Bordighera (12,014▲)....9,600
Brescia....212,265
Bresso (★Milan)....34,245
Brindisi....89,241
Busto Arsizio (★Milan)....81,139
Cagliari (★305,000)....241,472
Caltagirone....38,525
Caltanissetta (61,461▲)....54,700
Camaiore (31,110▲)....22,700
Camerino (8,085▲)....3,400
Campobasso....47,316
Canicatti....32,603
Canosa di Puglia....30,781
Cantù....36,664
Capannori (43,972▲)....36,900
Capua....18,435
Carbonia....33,162
Carpi (59,824▲)....51,800
Carrara (★★Massa)....70,227
Casale Monferrato....42,711
Cascina....35,073
Caserta....67,257
Casoria (★Naples)....67,242
Cassino (32,181▲)....27,200
Castel Gandolfo (★Rome) (5,953▲)....3,400
Castellammare di Stabia (★Naples)....74,452
Castelvetrano....31,382
Catania (★515,000)....398,426
Catanzaro....93,845
Cattolica....15,811
Cava de' Tirreni (★Salerno) (51,611▲)....45,500
Cefalù (13,624▲)....11,600
Cerignola (51,349▲)....45,300
Cesano Maderno (★Milan)....32,637
Cesena (90,269▲)....68,100
Cesenatico (20,222▲)....15,900
Chiavari....30,508
Chieri (31,012▲)....26,400
Chieti....57,140
Chioggia (53,611▲)....38,200
Chivasso....27,064
Ciampino (★Rome)....30,561
Cinisello Balsamo (★Milan)....80,387
Cittadella (17,182▲)....7,000
Città di Castello (37,497▲)....28,600
Civitanova Marche (36,002▲)....31,500
Civitavecchia....48,342
Collegno (★Turin)....46,326
Cologno Monzese (★Milan)....51,855
Como (★160,000)....96,665
Conegliano (36,000▲)....29,500
Corato....41,623
Corsico (★Milan)....43,769
Cortina d'Ampezzo....8,326
Cosenza (★130,000)....102,338
Crema....34,742
Cremona....82,056
Crotone....57,009
Cuneo....55,784
Desio (★Milan)....33,051
Domodossola....20,704
Eboli....29,044
Empoli....45,725
Enna....29,370
Ercolano (Resina) (★Naples)....57,114
Erice....26,282
Este....18,283
Faenza (55,538▲)....40,100
Fano (53,273▲)....44,000
Fasano (36,420▲)....23,300
Favara....33,046
Fermo (35,186▲)....27,000
Ferrara (152,752▲)....125,200
Fiesole (★Florence)....14,760
Florence (Firenze) (★660,000)....462,690
Foggia....157,727
Foligno (52,580▲)....46,300
Forlì (110,523▲)....92,500
Francavilla Fontana....34,565
Frascati (★Rome)....19,587
Frattamaggiore (★Naples)....38,134
Frosinone....45,725
Gaeta....24,437
Gallarate (★Milan)....47,741
Gela....75,201
Genoa (Genova) (★855,000)....782,476
Giugliano in Campania (★Naples)....42,347
Gorizia....42,580
Gravina in Puglia....36,628
Grosseto (69,699▲)....61,600
Grottaglie....28,477
Grugliasco (★Turin)....34,202
Gubbio (32,164▲)....9,900
Guidonia Montecelio (★Rome)....48,821
Iesi (Jesi) (41,974▲)....35,600
Iglesias....29,561
Imola (60,234▲)....48,000
Imperia....42,159
Isernia (19,121▲)....14,500
Ivrea....28,650
L'Aquila....66,644
La Spezia (★192,000)....117,761
Latina (94,910▲)....83,200
Lecce....90,121
Lecco....52,806
Legnago....27,044
Legnano (★Milan)....49,600
Lentini....34,350
Licata....42,250
Limbiate (★Milan)....32,815
Lissone (★Milan)....30,482
Livorno (Leghorn)....176,757
Lodi....43,927
Loreto (10,851▲)....6,000
Lucca....91,256
Lucera (33,307▲)....28,500
Lugo (34,518▲)....20,300
Macerata (44,492▲)....37,700
Maddaloni (33,228▲)....26,100
Magenta....23,627
Manduria....30,488
Manfredonia (53,052▲)....45,800
Mantova....64,008
Marino (★Rome)....30,464
Marsala (86,051▲)....50,400
Martina France (44,340▲)....32,600
Massa (★145,000)....66,060
Matera....50,424
Mazara del Vallo....43,825
Merano (Meran)....34,460
Messina....271,660
•Milan (Milano) (★3,800,000)....1,677,109
Milazzo (30,710▲)....20,500
Modena....180,428
Modica (47,742▲)....31,400
Molfetta....66,699
Moncalieri (★Turin)....65,066
Monfalcone....31,053
Monopoli (44,017▲)....29,800
Monreale....25,416
Montecatini Terme....21,843
Montepulciano (14,255▲)....9,500
Monte Sant'Angelo....17,421
Monza (★Milan)....123,834
Naples (Napoli) (★2,740,000)....1,223,228
Nardò (30,916▲)....24,200
Nettuno (29,321▲)....25,300
Nicastro (Lamezia Terme) (62,069▲)....29,800
Nichelino (★Turin)....45,092
Nocera Inferiore (51,533▲)....43,300
Nola (29,282▲)....22,400
Novara....101,947
Novi Ligure....31,783
Nuoro....36,503
Oristano....29,769
Orvieto (23,414▲)....17,500
Otranto....4,748
Paderno Dugnano (★Milan)....38,885
Padova (★280,000)....242,216
Pagani....32,713
Palermo....693,949
Parma....176,945
Partinico....28,162
Paternò....48,992
Pavia....87,005
Perugia....139,871
Pesaro....90,705
Pescara....137,059
Piacenza....108,888
Pinerolo....36,589
Piombino....39,659
Pisa....103,772
Pistoia (94,344▲)....84,300
Poggibonsi....26,743
Pompei (★Naples) (22,526▲)....13,300
Pontedera....28,254
Pordenone....52,106
Portici (★Naples)....83,372
Portoferraio....11,212
Portofino....773
Potenza....64,513
Pozzuoli (★Naples) (70,429▲)....61,400
Prato (★201,000)....158,229
Ragusa (66,545▲)....55,200
Rapallo....29,809
Ravello (2,387▲)....1,400
Ravenna (139,392▲)....102,300
Reggio di Calabria....181,293
Reggio nell'Emilia....130,005
Rho (★Milan)....49,657
Riccione....31,688
Rieti (43,277▲)....38,700
Rimini....127,714
Riva [del Garda]....13,240
Rivoli (★Turin)....50,992
ROME (ROMA) (★3,195,000)....2,911,671
Rosignano Marittimo....29,402
Rovereto....33,082
Rovigo....52,588
Salerno (★240,000)....161,997
Salsomaggiore Terme....17,982
San Benedetto del Tronto....46,256
San Donà di Piave (32,058▲)....22,500
San Gimignano (7,521▲)....2,800
San Giorgio a Cremano (★Naples)....65,245
San Remo (63,423▲)....52,400
San Severo....54,914
Santa Maria Capua Vetere....32,529
Saronno....36,683
Sassari....119,597
Sassuolo....39,471
Savona (★120,000)....78,216
Scandicci (★Florence)....54,102
Schio....36,388
Sciacca (36,148▲)....32,300
Senigallia (40,567▲)....34,500
Seregno (★Milan)....37,717
Sesto Fiorentino (★Florence)....44,862
Sesto San Giovanni (★Milan)....98,151
Settimo Torinese (★Turin)....44,895
Siena....63,961
Siracusa....116,755
Sorrento (★42,900)....16,868
Spoleto (37,593▲)....32,200
Taranto....247,681
Teramo (51,768▲)....41,000
Termini Imerese....26,815
Terni....113,241
Tivoli (★Rome)....46,201
Todi (17,244▲)....3,900
Torre Annunziata (★Naples)....57,659
Torre del Greco (★Naples)....101,905
Trani....43,243
Trapani (72,036▲)....62,400
Trento....99,052
Treviso....89,121
Trieste....260,291
Turin (Torino) (★1,670,000)....1,160,686
Udine (★128,000)....102,973
Urbino (16,211▲)....13,000
Varese....91,100
Venice (Venezia) (★445,000)....355,865
Verbania....33,384
Vercelli....54,063
Verona....269,763
Viareggio....59,600
Vicenza....117,571
Vigevano....67,034
Villa San Giovanni (12,106▲)....9,000
Viterbo (58,529▲)....50,000
Vittoria....50,739
Vittorio Veneto....30,897
Voghera....42,781

IVORY COAST / Côte d'Ivoire

1978 E....................7,613,000
Abengourou (1975 C)....31,239
•ABIDJAN....1,100,000
Agboville (1975 C)....27,192
Bouaké....230,000
Daloa....70,000
Danane (1975 C)....19,872
Dimbokro (1975 C)....30,986
Divo (1975 C)....37,896
Gagnoa (1975 C)....42,362
Grand-Bassam (1975 C)....25,808
Korhogo (1975 C)....47,657
Man....55,000
Séguéla (1975 C)....12,587

JAMAICA

1978 E....................2,137,300
•KINGSTON....665,050
Mandeville (1970 C)....14,421
May Pen (1970 C)....26,074
Montego Bay (1970 C)....43,754
Ocho Rios (1970 C)....6,900
Port Antonio (1970 C)....10,538
Savanna-la-Mar (1970 C)....11,759
Spanish Town (1970 C)....40,731

JAPAN

1979 E....................116,133,000

Districts and Prefectures

CHUBU....19,844,000
  Aichi....6,176,000
  Fukui....792,000
  Gifu....1,945,000
  Ishikawa....1,110,000
  Nagano....2,071,000
  Niigata....2,437,000
  Shizuoka....3,420,000
  Toyama....1,098,000
  Yamanashi....795,000
CHUGOKU....7,557,000
  Hiroshima....2,723,000
  Okayama....1,865,000
  Shimane....782,000
  Tottori....599,000
  Yamaguchi....1,588,000
HOKKAIDŌ....5,532,000
  Hokkaidō....5,532,000
KANTŌ (KWANTŌ)....34,428,000
  Chiba....4,617,000
  Gumma....1,826,000
  Ibaraki....2,503,000
  Kanagawa....6,809,000
  Saitama....5,309,000
  Tochigi....1,768,000
  Tōkyō....11,596,000
KINKI....21,158,000
  Hyōgo....5,139,000
  Kyōto....2,515,000
  Mie....1,674,000
  Nara....1,190,000
  Ōsaka....8,487,000
  Shiga....1,063,000
  Wakayama....1,090,000
KYŪSHŪ....13,985,000
  Fukuoka....4,527,000
  Kagoshima....1,770,000
  Kumamoto....1,776,000
  Miyazaki....1,141,000
  Nagasaki....1,592,000
  Ōita....1,224,000
  Okinawa....1,096,000
  Saga....859,000
SHIKOKU....4,143,000
  Ehime....1,499,000
  Kagawa....995,000
  Kōchi....828,000
  Tokushima....821,000
TŌHOKU....9,486,000
  Akita....1,251,000
  Aomori....1,514,000
  Fukushima....2,015,000
  Iwate....1,411,000
  Miyagi....2,054,000
  Yamagata....1,241,000

Cities (1975 C or †1979 E)

Abashiri (43,825▲)....34,900
Abiko (★Tōkyō)....76,218
Ageo (★Tōkyō)....†163,985
Aioi....42,008
Aizu-wakamatsu....†113,175
Akashi (★Ōsaka) (1980 C)....254,873
Akishima (★Tōkyō)....83,864
Akita (1980 C)....284,830
Akō....49,583
Amagasaki (★Ōsaka) (1980 C)....523,657
Amagi (42,725▲)....25,700
Anan (60,439▲)....37,200
Anjō....†121,178
Aomori (1980 C)....287,609
Arao (★Ōmuta) (58,296▲)....47,300
Arida....34,865
Asahikawa (1980 C)....352,620
Asaka (★Tōkyō)....81,755
Ashibetsu (36,520▲)....29,100
Ashikaga....†165,024
Ashiya (★Ōsaka)....76,211
Atami....51,437
Atsugi (★Tōkyō)....†136,652
Ayabe (43,490▲)....29,000
Ayase (★Tōkyō)....50,365
Beppu....†137,477
Bibai (38,416▲)....29,200
Bisai....54,247
Chiba (★Tōkyō) (1980 C)....746,428
Chichibu....61,798
Chigasaki (★Tōkyō)....†168,849
Chikugo....39,520
Chikushino (★Fukuoka)....47,741
Chiryū (★Nagoya)....47,209
Chita (★Nagoya)....56,560
Chitose....61,031
Chōfu (★Tōkyō)....†179,631
Chōshi....90,374
Daitō (★Ōsaka)....†115,678
Ebetsu....77,624
Ebina (★Tōkyō)....59,783
Fuchū *(Hiroshima pref.)*....50,217
Fūchū (★Hiroshima) *(Hiroshima pref.)*....47,538
Fuchū (★Tōkyō)....†190,048
Fuji (1980 C) (★325,000)....205,752
Fujieda (101,216▲)....†72,000
Fujiidera (★Ōsaka)....59,515
Fujimi (★Tōkyō)....70,391
Fujinomiya (★★Fuji) (106,524▲)....†82,800
Fujioka (49,169▲)....30,000
Fujisawa (★Tōkyō) (1980 C)....300,181
Fuji-yoshida....51,976
Fukaya (75,748▲)....53,100
Fukuchiyama (60,003▲)....43,000
Fukui (1980 C)....240,264
Fukuoka (1980 C) (★1,575,000)....1,088,617
Fukuroi (42,581▲)....25,700
Fukushima (1980 C)....262,847
Fukuyama (1980 C)....346,031
Funabashi (★Tōkyō) (1980 C)....479,437
Furukawa (54,356▲)....31,100
Fussa (★Tōkyō)....46,457
Futtsu....56,653

C Census. E Official estimate. UE Unofficial estimate.
L Population within municipal limits of year specified. • Largest city in country.
★ Population or designation of metropolitan area, including suburbs (see headnote).
▲ Population of an entire municipality, commune, or district, including rural area.
‡† Year of information specified at start of country.

Gamagōri....85,282
Gifu (1980 C)....410,368
Ginowan....53,835
Gose (★Ōsaka)....37,554
Gotemba (62,722▲)....49,300
Gushikawa....42,133
Gyōda....66,069
Habikino (★Ōsaka)....†102,217
Hachinohe (1980 C)....238,208
Hachiōji (★Tōkyō) (1980 C)....387,162
Hadano (★Tōkyō)....†118,528
Hagi (52,724▲)....42,100
Hakodate (1980 C)....320,152
Hamada....50,316
Hamakita (67,180▲)....49,600
Hamamatsu (1980 C)....490,827
Hanamaki (65,826▲)....38,200
Handa....85,824
Hannō (★Tōkyō)....55,926
Haranomachi (43,483▲)....26,800
Hashima (52,570▲)....40,500
Hatogaya (★Tōkyō)....56,693
Hekinan....60,680
Higashihiroshima (★Hiroshima)....66,231
Higashikurume (★Tōkyō)....†106,566
Higashimatsuyama....57,684
Higashimurayama (★Tōkyō)....†119,684
Higashiōsaka (★Ōsaka) (1980 C)....521,635
Higashiyamato (★Tōkyō)....58,464
Hikari (★Tokuyama)....48,794
Hikone....85,066
Himeji (1980 C)....446,255
Himi (61,789▲)....38,600
Hino (★Tōkyō)....†142,982
Hirakata (★Ōsaka) (1980 C)....353,360
Hiratsuka (★Tōkyō) (1980 C)....214,299
Hirosaki (173,550▲)....†112,300
Hiroshima (1980 C) (★1,525,000)....899,394
Hisai....36,587
Hita (63,969▲)....47,300
Hitachi (1980 C)....204,612
Hōfu (109,762▲)....†86,100
Honjō....51,090
Hōya (★Tōkyō)....91,546
Hyūga (53,448▲)....40,600
Ibaraki (★Ōsaka) (1980 C)....234,059
Ichihara (★Tōkyō) (1980 C)....216,395
Ichikawa (★Tōkyō) (1980 C)....364,244
Ichinomiya (1980 C)....253,138
Ichinoseki (59,122▲)....36,000
Iida (77,112▲)....51,900
Iizuka (★103,000)....75,417
Ikeda (★Ōsaka)....†101,872
Ikoma (★Ōsaka)....48,848
Imabari....†123,928
Imaichi (46,760▲)....29,800
Imari (60,913▲)....36,600
Ina (54,468▲)....32,500
Inagi (★Tōkyō)....43,924
Inazawa (★Nagoya)....88,606
Innoshima....41,683
Inuyama (★Nagoya)....58,731
Iruma (★Tōkyō)....83,997
Isahaya (73,341▲)....49,400
Ise (Uji-yamada)....†105,624
Isehara (★Tōkyō)....61,616
Isesaki....†104,300
Ishinomaki....†119,758
Ishioka (43,679▲)....30,400
Itami (★Ōsaka)....†177,745
Itō....68,072
Itsukaichi (★Hiroshima)....64,885
Iwai....38,304
Iwaki (Taira) (1980 C) (342,076▲)....271,800
Iwakuni....†112,200
Iwakura (★Nagoya)....41,935
Iwamizawa (72,305▲)....56,800
Iwata....67,665
Iwatsuki (★Tōkyō) (83,825▲)....60,900
Iyo-mishima....38,409
Izumi (★Ōsaka)....†122,464
Izumi (*Kagoshima pref.*)....37,483
Izumi (★Sendai)....70,087
Izumi-ōtsu (★Ōsaka)....66,250
Izumi-sano (★Ōsaka)....86,139
Izumo (71,568▲)....47,700
Joetsu....†120,474
Jōyō (★Ōsaka)....58,923
Kadoma (★Ōsaka)....†142,167
Kaga (61,599▲)....47,400
Kagoshima (1980 C)....505,077
Kainan....53,250
Kaizuka (★Ōsaka)....79,506
Kakamigahara....†112,802
Kakegawa (61,731▲)....38,600
Kakogawa (★Ōsaka) (1980 C)....212,232
Kamagaya (★Tōkyō)....63,288
Kamaishi....68,981
Kamakura (★Tōkyō)....†173,331
Kameoka (58,184▲)....36,400
Kamifukuoka (★Tōkyō)....58,332
Kanazawa (1980 C)....417,681
Kanonji (44,131▲)....31,700
Kanoya (67,951▲)....38,500
Kanuma (81,799▲)....55,800
Karatsu....75,224
Kariya (★Nagoya)....†103,643
Karuizawa....13,951
Kasai (50,161▲)....30,600
Kasaoka (63,413▲)....42,700
Kashihara (★Ōsaka)....†105,691
Kashiwa (★Tōkyō) (1980 C)....239,199
Kashiwara (★Ōsaka)....63,586
Kashiwazaki (80,351▲)....53,500
Kasuga (★Fukuoka)....55,160
Kasugai (★Nagoya) (1980 C)....244,114
Kasukabe (★Tōkyō)....†151,083
Katano (★Ōsaka)....52,732
Katsuta....79,996
Kawachi-nagano (★Ōsaka)....66,936
Kawagoe (★Tōkyō)....259,317
Kawaguchi (★Tōkyō) (1980 C)....379,357
Kawanishi (★Ōsaka)....†128,861
Kawanoe....35,961
Kawasaki (★Tōkyō) (1980 C)....1,040,698
Kazo (45,183▲)....27,900
Kesennuma....66,616
Kimitsu....76,016
Kiryū....†132,950
Kisarazu....†108,065
Kishiwada (★Ōsaka)....†179,038
Kitaibaraki (44,332▲)....33,500
Kitakami (48,759▲)....28,200
Kitakyūshū (1980 C) (★1,515,000)....1,065,084
Kitami (91,519▲)....73,000
Kitamoto (★Tōkyō)....46,632
Kiyose (★Tōkyō)....60,574
Kobayashi....38,325
Kōbe (★★Ōsaka) (1980 C)....1,367,392
Kōchi (1980 C)....300,830
Kodaira (★Tōkyō)....†156,758
Kōfu....†197,803
Koga (★Tōkyō)....55,973
Koganei (★Tōkyō)....†103,487
Kokubunji (★Tōkyō)....88,159
Komae (★Tōkyō)....70,043
Komaki (★Nagoya)....†101,299
Komatsu....†103,606
Komatsushima (42,203▲)....32,300
Kōnan....90,426
Kōnosu (★Tōkyō)....51,632
Kōriyama (1980 C) (286,497▲)....195,700
Koshigaya (★Tōkyō) (1980 C)....223,243
Kudamatsu (★★Tokuyama)....55,825
Kuki (★Tōkyō)....45,797
Kumagaya....†134,347
Kumamoto (1980 C)....525,613
Kunitachi (★Tōkyō)....64,495
Kurashiki (1980 C)....403,785
Kurayoshi (50,785▲)....34,800
Kure (★★Hiroshima) (1980 C)....234,550
Kurume (1980 C)....216,974
Kusatsu (★Ōsaka)....64,873
Kushiro (1980 C)....214,694
Kuwana....83,440
Kyōto (★★Ōsaka) (1980 C)....1,472,993
Machida (★Tōkyō) (1980 C)....295,354
Maebashi (1980 C)....265,171
Maizuru (97,780▲)....82,600
Marugame....65,662
Masuda (50,734▲)....34,400
Matsubara (★Ōsaka)....†135,741
Matsudo (★Tōkyō) (1980 C)....400,870
Matsue....†134,190
Matsumoto....†190,780
Matsuyama (1980 C)....401,682
Matsuzaka (112,870▲)....†81,800
Mihara....83,679
Miki (★Ōsaka) (55,731▲)....41,200
Minamiashigara....36,928
Minō (★Ōsaka)....79,621
Mino-kamo....37,524
Misato (★Tōkyō)....79,355
Misawa (37,437▲)....28,600
Mishima (★★Numazu)....89,248
Mitaka (★Tōkyō)....†166,514
Mito (1980 C)....215,563
Mitsuke (40,954▲)....30,900
Miura....47,888
Miyako....61,912
Miyakonojō (127,528▲)....†82,200
Miyazaki (1980 C)....264,858
Mizusawa (52,266▲)....34,700
Mobara....64,942
Mōka (47,345▲)....20,700
Mombetsu (32,825▲)....28,000
Moriguchi (★Ōsaka)....†164,716
Morioka (1980 C)....229,123
Moriyama....41,439
Mukō (★Ōsaka)....45,886
Muroran (★220,000)....†162,731
Musashi-murayama (★Tōkyō)....50,842
Musashino (★Tōkyō)....†138,874
Mutsu....44,646
Nagahama....54,064
Nagano (1980 C) (324,360▲)....244,300
Nagaoka....†178,201
Nagaokakyo (★Ōsaka)....65,557
Nagareyama (★Tōkyō)....†103,864
Nagasaki (1980 C)....447,091
Nagoya (1980 C) (★3,700,000)....2,087,884
Naha (1980 C)....295,801
Nakama (★Kitakyūshū)....43,145
Nakatsu (59,111▲)....44,200
Nakatsugawa (51,183▲)....36,800
Nanao (49,493▲)....38,800
Nankoku (42,832▲)....25,500
Nara (★Ōsaka) (1980 C)....297,893
Narashino (★Tōkyō)....†120,257
Narita (50,915▲)....30,500
Naruto (61,959▲)....50,600
Natori (46,730▲)....29,700
Naze....46,335
Nemuro....45,817
Neyagawa (★Ōsaka) (1980 C)....255,864
Nichinan (52,171▲)....38,200
Niigata (1980 C)....457,783
Niihama....†133,178
Niitsu (58,970▲)....42,900
Niiza (★Tōkyō)....†119,991
Nikkō....26,279
Nishinomiya (★Ōsaka) (1980 C)....410,329
Nishio (82,524▲)....62,600
Nishiwaki....38,108
Nobeoka....†136,572
Noboribetsu (★Muroran)....50,885
Noda (★Tōkyō)....78,193
Nōgata....58,551
Noshiro (59,215▲)....43,600
Numata (45,255▲)....32,000
Numazu (1980 C) (★435,000)....203,699
Obihiro....†150,337
Ōbu (★Nagoya)....56,211
Ōda....37,449
Ōdate (71,828▲)....50,200
Odawara....†177,047
Ōfunato (39,632▲)....32,700
Ōgaki....†141,877
Ōita (1980 C)....360,484
Ojiya (44,375▲)....26,900
Ōkawa....50,395
Okaya....61,776
Okayama (1980 C)....545,737
Okazaki (1980 C)....262,370
Okegawa (★Tōkyō)....48,034
Okinawa....91,347
Ōme (★Tōkyō)....86,152
Ōmi-hachiman (★Ōsaka) (51,537▲)....34,100
Ōmiya (★Tōkyō) (1980 C)....354,082
Ōmura (60,919▲)....44,200
Ōmuta (★225,000)....†163,436
Ōno (*Fukui pref.*) (41,918▲)....25,800
Ōno (*Hyōgo pref.*)....40,576
Onojo (★Fukuoka)....52,169
Onoda (★Ube)....43,804
Onomichi....†102,190
Ōsaka (1980 C) (★15,200,000)....2,648,158
Ōta....†120,472
Ōtake....38,457
Otaru....†185,737
Ōtawara (42,332▲)....22,900
Ōtsu (★Ōsaka) (1980 C)....215,318
Ōtsuki....36,766
Oyama (125,565▲)....†81,000
Rumoi....36,882
Ryūgasaki (40,565▲)....25,000
Sabae (57,252▲)....45,700
Saga....†162,038
Sagamihara (★Tōkyō) (1980 C)....439,257
Saijō (52,615▲)....39,100
Saiki (52,863▲)....42,200
Sakado (★Tōkyō)....51,230
Sakai (★Ōsaka) (1980 C)....810,120
Sakaide....67,624
Sakaiminato....35,821
Sakata (101,454▲)....†73,900
Saku (56,143▲)....32,500
Sakura (★Tōkyō) (80,804▲)....61,500
Sakurai (54,314▲)....42,800
Sanda (★Ōsaka)....35,261
Sanjō....81,806
Sano....75,844
Sapporo (1980 C) (★1,450,000)....1,401,758
Sasebo (1980 C)....251,188
Sawara (48,670▲)....26,000
Sayama (★Tōkyō)....†121,433
Seki....53,881
Sendai (*Kagoshima pref.*) (61,788▲)....34,700
Sendai (*Miyagi pref.*) (1980 C) (★925,000)....664,799
Sennan (★Ōsaka)....40,741
Seto....†119,473
Settsu (★Ōsaka)....76,704
Shibata (74,025▲)....48,700
Shibukawa....47,071
Shijōnawate (★Ōsaka)....52,368
Shimabara (45,179▲)....34,000
Shimada....68,820
Shimizu (★★Shizuoka) (1980 C)....241,578
Shimminato (★Takaoka)....44,700
Shimodate (57,778▲)....36,000
Shimonoseki (★★Kitakyūshū) (1980 C)....268,964
Shingū....39,023
Shinjō (42,227▲)....28,100
Shiogama (★Sendai)....59,235
Shiojiri (47,421▲)....29,200
Shirakawa (42,685▲)....32,300
Shizuoka (1980 C) (★735,000)....458,342
Sōja....47,027
Sōka (★Tōkyō)....†186,759
Suita (★Ōsaka) (1980 C)....332,413
Sukagawa (54,922▲)....33,700
Sumoto (44,137▲)....35,700
Suwa....49,594
Suzaka....49,513
Suzuka (152,431▲)....†106,900
Tachikawa (★Tōkyō)....†142,793
Tagajō (★Sendai)....44,862
Tajimi....68,901
Takaishi (★Ōsaka)....66,824
Takamatsu (1980 C)....316,662
Takaoka (★220,000)....†174,334
Takarazuka (★Ōsaka)....†179,394
Takasago (★Ōsaka)....77,080
Takasaki (1980 C)....221,432
Takatsuki (★Ōsaka) (1980 C)....340,722
Takawa....61,464
Takayama....60,504
Takefu (65,012▲)....48,700
Takehara....36,273
Takikawa....50,090
Tama (★Tōkyō)....65,466
Tamana (42,837▲)....28,100
Tamano....78,516
Tanabe (66,999▲)....51,800
Tanashi (★Tōkyō)....67,433
Tatebayashi....66,410
Tateyama (56,139▲)....40,700
Tatsuno....39,646
Tendō (48,082▲)....27,900
Tenri (62,909▲)....45,200
Toba....29,346
Tochigi....83,189
Toda (★Tōkyō)....77,137
Tokai (★Nagoya)....95,457
Tōkamachi (50,211▲)....33,400
Toki....63,324
Tokoname....54,865
Tokorozawa (★Tōkyō) (1980 C)....236,477
Tokushima (1980 C)....249,343
Tokuyama (★255,000)....†111,347
•TŌKYŌ (1980 C) (★25,800,000)....8,349,209
Tomakomai....†146,088
Tomioka (46,821▲)....29,200
Tondabayashi (★Ōsaka)....91,393
Toride (★Tōkyō)....52,816
Tosu....50,733
Tottori....†128,789
Towada (54,365▲)....27,900
Toyama (1980 C)....305,054
Toyoake (★Nagoya)....45,837
Toyohashi (1980 C)....304,274
Toyokawa....†102,484
Toyonaka (★Ōsaka) (1980 C)....403,185
Toyooka (46,210▲)....33,000
Toyota (1980 C)....281,609
Tsu....†144,587
Tsubame....43,265
Tsuchiura....†110,912
Tsuruga....60,205
Tsuruoka (95,932▲)....74,600
Tsushima....58,241
Tsuyama (79,907▲)....56,500
Ube (★222,000)....†167,732
Ueda....†110,340
Ueno (59,716▲)....42,500
Uji (★Ōsaka)....†150,869
Uozu....48,419
Urawa (★Tōkyō) (1980 C)....358,180
Usa (50,677▲)....25,400
Usuki (39,163▲)....28,200
Utsunomiya (1980 C)....377,748
Uwajima....70,428
Wakayama (1980 C)....401,462
Wakkanai....55,464
Warabi (★Tōkyō)....76,311
Yachiyo (★Tōkyō)....†132,989
Yaizu....†103,544
Yamagata (1980 C)....236,984
Yamaguchi (111,725▲)....†80,800
Yamato (★Tōkyō)....†165,858
Yamato-kōriyama (★Ōsaka)....71,001
Yamato-takada (★Ōsaka)....58,637
Yame....38,843
Yao (★Ōsaka) (1980 C)....272,706
Yashio (★Tōkyō)....56,127
Yatsushiro (107,200▲)....†80,000
Yawata (★Ōsaka)....50,131
Yawatahama (45,259▲)....34,700
Yokkaichi (1980 C)....255,442
Yokohama (★★Tōkyō) (1980 C)....2,773,322
Yokosuka (★Tōkyō) (1980 C)....421,112
Yonago....†125,291
Yonezawa (91,974▲)....71,400
Yono (★Tōkyō)....71,044
Yūbari....50,131
Yukuhashi (53,750▲)....39,300
Zama (★Tōkyō)....80,562
Zushi (★Tōkyō)....56,298

JERSEY

1976 C....74,470

•ST. HELIER (★45,000)....26,343

JORDAN / Al-Urdunn

1979 E....2,152,273

Al-'Aqabah ('Aqaba)....26,986
Al-Karak....11,806
Al-Khalīl (Hebron) (††1971 E)....43,000
Al-Mafraq (1973 E)....15,500
•AMMĀN....648,587
Arīḥā (Jericho) (††1967 C)....6,829
Ar-Ramthā (1973 E)....19,000
As-Salt....32,866
Az-Zarqā'....215,687
Bayt Laḥm (Bethlehem) (††1971 E)....25,000
Irbid....112,864
Janīn (††1971 E)....20,000
Jerusalem (★Jerusalem, Israel) (††1976 E)....90,000
Ma'ān....11,308
Nābulus (††1971 E)....64,000

††Located in area occupied by Israel in 1967. See note under Israel.

KAMPUCHEA / Kâmpŭchéa Prâchéathīpâtéyy

1962 C....5,728,711

Battambang....38,780
Kompong Cham....28,532
•PHNUM PÉNH....393,995

KENYA

1979 C....15,322,000

Eldoret....50,000
Kisumu....150,000
Mombasa....342,000
•NAIROBI....835,000
Nakuru....93,000
Nyeri....36,000
Thika....41,000

KOREA, NORTH / Chosŏn Minjujuŭi In'min Konghwaguk

1967 E....12,700,000

Aoji (1944 C)....39,616
Ch'ŏngjin....265,000
Haeju....115,000
Hamhŭng (1944 C)....112,184
Hŭngnam (1944 C)....143,600
Kaesŏng....140,000
Kilchu (1944 C)....30,026
Kimch'aek (Sŏngjin)....265,000
Najin (1944 C)....34,338
Namp'o (Chinnamp'o)....130,000
Ongjin (1949 C)....32,965
Pukch'ŏng (1944 C)....30,709
•P'YONGYANG....840,000
Sariwŏn (1944 C)....42,957
Sinŭiju....165,000
Songnim (1944 C)....53,035
Tanch'ŏn (1944 C)....32,761
Wŏnsan....215,000

KOREA, SOUTH / Taehan-Min'guk

1978 E....37,019,000

Andong (101,494▲)....85,000
Anyang (★Seoul)....187,887
Bucheon (★Seoul)....163,341
Ch'angwŏn....70,707
Chech'ŏn (80,124▲)....55,400
Cheju (152,486▲)....83,100
Chinhae....108,730
Chinju....174,918
Ch'ŏnan (109,324▲)....76,800
Ch'ŏngju....223,016
Chŏngŭp (1975 C) (54,864▲)....37,600
Chŏnju....348,053
Ch'unch'ŏn....152,606
Ch'ungju (110,091▲)....76,500
Chungmu....71,511
Inch'ŏn (★★Seoul)....936,497
Iri (132,272▲)....109,800
Kangnŭng (102,153▲)....67,100
Kimch'ŏn (70,348▲)....53,200
Kumi....89,612
Kunsan....167,422
Kwangju....694,646
Kyŏngju (113,921▲)....68,100
Masan....391,874
Mokp'o....210,922
Namwŏn (55,043▲)....37,900
P'ohang (1975 C) (134,404▲)....110,000
Pusan....2,879,570
Pyŏngtaek....56,324
Samch'ŏnp'o (61,701▲)....37,100
Sangju (55,242▲)....29,500
Seongnam (★Seoul)....324,064
•SEOUL (SŎUL) (1979 E) (★10,775,000)....8,114,000
Sŏkch'o....71,737
Songjŏng (47,070▲)....29,900
Sunch'ŏn (114,588▲)....76,900
Suwŏn (★Seoul)....266,135
Taegu....1,487,098
Taejŏn....508,574
Ŭijŏngbu (★Seoul)....117,849
Ulsan (364,456▲)....247,000
Wŏnju....131,047
Yŏngju (1975 C) (70,793▲)....50,800
Yŏsu....151,337

KUWAIT / Al-Kuwayt

1975 C....994,837

Ahraq Khīṭān (★Kuwait)....59,443
Al-Farwānīyah (★Kuwait)....44,875
Al-Jahrah (★Kuwait)....52,302
As-Sālimīyah (★Kuwait)....113,943
Ḥawallī (★Kuwait)....130,565
•KUWAIT (Al-Kuwayt) (★780,000)....78,116

LAOS / Lao

1973 E....3,181,000

Louangphrabang....43,000
Pakxé....44,860
Savannakhet....50,691
Sayaboury....13,760
•VIANGCHAN (VIENTIANE)....174,229

LEBANON / Al-Lubnān

1970 E....2,126,355

Ba'labakk (Baalbek)....16,000
•BEIRUT (BAYRŪT) (★1,010,000)....474,870
Ṣaydā (Sidon)....34,000
Ṣūr (Tyre)....12,500
Ṭarābulus (Tripoli)....157,320
Zaḥlah....20,500

LESOTHO

1972 E....972,000

•MASERU....17,000

LIBERIA

1974 C....1,503,368

Buchanan....23,994
•MONROVIA....204,210

LIBYA / Lībiyā

1970 E....1,938,000

Ajdābiyah (1964 C)....15,400
Beida (1964 C)....12,800
Benghāzī (Bengasi)....170,000
Darnah (Derna) (1964 C)....21,400
Misrātah....44,000
•TRIPOLI (ṬARĀBULUS)....264,000
Ṭubruq (Tobruk) (1964 C)....15,900

LIECHTENSTEIN

1977 E....24,715

•VADUZ....4,704

LUXEMBOURG

1976 E....358,000

Bettembourg....7,100
Clervaux (1970 C)....1,428
Diekirch....5,500
Differdange (★Esch-sur-Alzette)....18,000
Dudelange....14,600
Echternach (1970 C)....3,792
Esch-sur-Alzette (★98,000)....27,600
Ettelbruck....6,100
•LUXEMBOURG (★110,000)....79,300
Pétange (★★Longwy, France)....12,100
Sanem (★Esch-sur-Alzette)....10,900
Wiltz (1970 C)....3,920

C Census. E Official estimate. UE Unofficial estimate.
L Population within municipal limits of year specified. • Largest city in country.
★ Population or designation of metropolitan area, including suburbs (see headnote).
▲ Population of an entire municipality, commune, or district, including rural area.
‡† Year of information specified at start of country.

MACAO

1970 C.......248,636
•MACAO (*248,636).......241,413

MADAGASCAR / Madagasikara

1977 E.......8,520,000
•ANTANANARIVO (TANANARIVE).......484,000
Antsirabe (85,000▲).......45,000
Diégo-Suarez (Antsirane).......43,000
Fianarantsoa.......73,000
Majunga.......71,000
Manakara (1972 E) (25,070▲).......23,225
Marovoay (1972 E).......20,780
Tamatave.......83,000
Tuléar.......49,000

MALAWI

1977 C.......5,561,821
•Blantyre.......229,000
LILONGWE.......102,924
Mzuzu.......16,000
Zomba.......16,000

MALAYSIA

1970 C.......10,319,324
Alor Setar (*85,748).......66,179
Ayer Itam (*Pinang).......25,640
Batu Pahat.......53,291
Bentong.......22,683
Bukit Mertajam.......26,631
Butterworth (**Pinang).......61,187
Chukai.......12,514
George Town (Pinang) (*450,000).......270,019
Ipoh (*257,309).......247,689
Johor Baharu (*Singapore).......136,229
Kajang.......21,950
Kampar.......26,591
Kangar.......8,758
Kelang.......113,607
Keluang.......43,272
Kota Baharu (*69,756).......55,052
Kota Kinabalu (Jesselton).......40,939
•KUALA LUMPUR (*750,000).......451,728
Kuala Terengganu (*59,494).......53,353
Kuantan.......43,358
Kuching.......63,535
Kulim.......18,505
Melaka (Malacca) (*99,782).......86,357
Miri.......35,702
Muar (Bandar Maharani).......61,218
Petaling Jaya (*Kuala Lumpur).......93,447
Sandakan.......42,413
Segamat.......17,796
Seremban (*90,062).......79,915
Sibu.......50,635
Sungai Petani.......35,959
Sungai Siput.......21,383
Taiping.......54,645
Tawau.......24,247
Telok Anson.......44,524

MALDIVES

1978 C.......143,046
•MALE.......29,555

MALI

1972 E.......5,257,000
•BAMAKO (1976 C).......404,022
Gao.......17,000
Kati (1971 E).......13,800
Kayes.......37,000
Kita (1971 E).......11,700
Koulikoro.......15,000
Koutiala.......16,000
Mopti.......43,000
Nioro du Sahel (1971 E).......13,200
San.......18,000
Ségou.......40,000
Sikasso.......29,000
Tombouctou (Timbuktu) (1971 E).......11,900

MALTA

1979 E.......346,970
Birkirkara (*Valletta).......16,832
Cospicua (*Valletta).......9,440
Gzira (*Valletta).......10,046
Hamrun (*Valletta).......13,875
Msida (*Valletta).......12,448
Paola (*Valletta).......11,974
Qormi (*Valletta).......15,784
Rabat.......11,823
Sliema (*Valletta).......20,095
•VALLETTA (*215,000).......14,042
Victoria (*Gozo I.*).......5,249
Zabbar (*Valletta).......10,366
Zejtun.......10,252

MARTINIQUE

1974 C.......324,832
•FORT-DE-FRANCE (*113,556).......98,807
Le Lamentin (23,145▲).......7,558
Saint-Pierre.......5,358
Schœlcher (*Fort-de-France) (14,749▲).......13,792

MAURITANIA / Mauritanie

1971 E.......1,190,000
Atar (1967 E).......8,500
Kaédi (1967 E).......10,000
Nouadhibou (1966 E).......11,000
•NOUAKCHOTT.......35,000

MAURITIUS

1978 E.......924,663
Beau Bassin (*Port Louis).......83,714
Curepipe (*Port Louis).......54,356
•PORT LOUIS (*405,000).......142,853
Quatre Bornes (*Port Louis).......53,835
Vacoas-Phoenix (*Port Louis).......51,793

MEXICO / México

1976 E.......62,329,000

States

Aguascalientes.......430,000
Baja California Norte.......1,253,000
Baja California Sur.......181,000
Campeche.......337,000
Chiapas.......1,933,000
Chihuahua.......2,000,000
Coahuila.......1,334,000
Colima.......317,000
Distrito Federal (Federal District).......8,906,000
Durango.......1,122,000
Guanajuato.......2,811,000
Guerrero.......2,013,000
Hidalgo.......1,409,000
Jalisco.......4,157,000
México.......6,245,000
Michoacán.......2,805,000
Morelos.......866,000
Nayarit.......699,000
Nuevo León.......2,344,000
Oaxaca.......2,337,000
Puebla.......3,055,000
Querétaro.......618,000
Quintana Roo.......131,000
San Luis Potosí.......1,527,000
Sinaloa.......1,714,000
Sonora.......1,414,000
Tabasco.......1,054,000
Tamaulipas.......1,901,000
Tlaxcala.......498,000
Veracruz.......4,917,000
Yucatán.......904,000
Zacatecas.......1,097,000

Cities (1970 C)

Acámbaro.......32,257
Acaponeta.......11,844
Acapulco [de Juárez] (1978 E).......421,100
Acayucan.......21,173
Actopan.......11,037
Agua Dulce.......21,060
Agua Prieta.......20,754
Aguascalientes (1978 E).......247,800
Alvarado.......15,792
Ameca.......21,018
Amecameca [de Juárez].......16,276
Apatzingán.......44,849
Apizaco.......21,189
Arandas.......18,934
Arriaga.......13,193
Atlixco.......41,967
Atotonilco el Alto.......16,271
Autlán de Navarro.......20,398
Caborca.......20,771
Campeche (1978 E).......103,600
Cananea.......17,518
Cárdenas.......15,643
Celaya (1978 E).......114,400
Cerro Azul.......20,259
Chihuahua (1978 E).......369,500
Chilpancingo [de los Bravos].......36,193
Cholula [de Rivadabia].......15,399
Ciudad Acuña.......30,276
Ciudad Camargo.......24,030
Ciudad Chetumal.......23,685
Ciudad del Carmen.......34,656
Ciudad de Valles.......47,587
Ciudad Guzmán.......48,166
Ciudad Hidalgo.......24,692
Ciudad Ixtepec.......14,025
Ciudad Jiménez.......18,095
Ciudad Juárez (**El Paso, Tex.) (1978 E).......597,100
Ciudad Lerdo (*Torreón).......19,803
Ciudad Madero (*Tampico) (1978 E).......135,100
Ciudad Mante.......51,247
Ciudad Melchor Múzquiz.......18,868
Ciudad Mendoza (*Orizaba).......18,696
Ciudad Obregón (1978 E).......173,000
Ciudad Serdán.......9,581
Ciudad Victoria (1978 E).......121,400
Coatepec.......21,542
Coatzacoalcos (1978 E).......120,100
Colima.......58,450
Comalcalco.......14,963
Comitán [de Domínguez].......21,249
Córdoba (1978 E).......116,100
Cortazar.......25,794
Cosamaloapan.......19,766
Cumauhtéoc.......26,598
Cuautla.......13,946
Cuernavaca (1978 E).......226,600
Culiacán (1978 E).......302,200
Delicias.......52,446
Dolores Hidalgo.......16,849
Durango (1978 E).......218,600
Ecatepec de Morelos (*Mexico City).......11,899
El Grullo.......10,538
Empalme.......24,927
Encarnación de Díaz.......10,474
Ensenada.......77,687
Escuinapa de Hidalgo.......16,442
Fresnillo [de González Echeverría].......44,475
Garza García (*Monterrey).......20,934
Gómez Palacio (**Torreón) (1978 E).......100,200
Guadalajara (1978 E) (*2,350,000).......1,813,100
Guadalupe (*Monterrey).......51,899
Guamúchil.......17,151
Guanajuato.......36,809
Guasave.......26,080
Guaymas.......57,492
Hermosillo (1978 E).......299,700
Hidalgo del Parral.......57,619
Huajuapan de León.......13,822
Huamantla.......15,565
Huatabampo.......18,506
Huauchinango.......16,826
Huixtla.......15,737
Iguala.......45,355
Irapuato (1978 E).......155,600
Izúcar de Matamoros.......21,164
Jacona de Plancarte.......22,724
Jalapa Enríquez (1978 E).......191,100
Jalostotitlán.......11,719
Jerez de García Salinas.......20,325
Juchitán [de Zaragoza].......30,218
La Barca.......18,055
Lagos de Moreno.......33,782
La Paz.......46,011
La Piedad [Cavadas].......34,963
Las Choapas.......20,166
Léon [de los Aldamas] (1978 E).......590,000
Linares.......24,456
Loma Bonita.......15,804
Los Mochis (1978 E).......111,800
Los Reyes.......19,452
Magdalena.......10,281
Manzanillo.......20,777
Martínez de la Torre.......17,203
Matamoros (**Brownsville, Tex.) (1978 E).......186,500
Matamoros de la Laguna.......15,125
Matehuala.......28,799
Matías Romero.......13,200
Mazatlán (1978 E).......177,700
Meoqui.......12,308
Mérida (1978 E).......263,200
Mesa de Tijuana (*San Diego, Calif.).......50,094
Mexicali (1978 E)(*355,000).......338,400
•MEXICO CITY (CIUDAD DE MÉXICO) (1978 E) (*14,400,000).......8,988,200
Minatitlán (1978 E).......112,600
Mineral del Monte.......8,887
Monclova (1978 E).......130,900
Montemorelos.......18,642
Monterrey (1978 E) (*1,925,000).......1,054,000
Morelia (1978 E).......239,400
Moroleón.......25,620
Motul de Felipe Carrillo Puerto.......12,949
Navojoa.......43,817
Netzahualcóyotl (*Mexico City).......580,438
Nogales (*Sonora*).......52,108
Nogales (*Veracruz*) (*Orizaba).......14,254
Nueva Rosita.......34,706
Nuevo Casas Grandes.......20,023
Nuevo Laredo (**Laredo, Tex.) (1978 E).......214,200
Oaxaca [de Juárez] (1978 E).......131,200
Ocotlán.......35,367
Ojinaga.......12,757
Orizaba (1978 E) (*265,000).......118,400
Pachuca [de Soto] (1978 E).......105,200
Pánuco.......14,277
Papantla [de Olarte].......26,773
Parras de la Fuente.......18,707
Pátzcuaro.......17,299
Pénjamo.......9,245
Piedras Negras.......41,033
Poza Rica de Hidalgo (1978 E).......188,900
Progreso.......17,518
Puebla [de Zaragoza] (1978 E).......678,000
Puerto Vallarta.......24,155
Puruándiro.......9,956
Querétaro (1978 E).......176,200
Reynosa (1978 E).......218,700
Río Bravo.......39,018
Rioverde.......16,804
Romita.......11,947
Rosario.......10,276
Sabinas.......20,538
Sabinas Hidalgo.......17,439
Sahuayo.......28,727
Salamanca.......61,039
Salina Cruz.......22,004
Saltillo (1978 E).......245,700
Salvatierra.......18,975
San Andrés Tuxtla.......24,267
San Cristóbal de las Casas.......25,700
San Francisco del Oro.......12,116
San Francisco del Rincón.......27,079
San Juan de los Lagos.......19,570
San Juan del Río.......15,422
San Juan Teotihuacán (*Mexico City).......2,238
San Luis de la Paz.......12,654
San Luis Potosí (1978 E).......315,200
San Luis Río Colorado.......49,990
San Martín Texmelucan.......23,355
San Miguel de Allende.......24,286
San Miguel el Alto.......7,909
San Nicolás de los Garzas (*Monterrey).......28,803
San Pedro de las Colonias.......26,882
Santa Ana Chiautempan.......12,327
Santa Bárbara.......16,978
Santa Cruz de Juventino Rosas.......15,859
Santa Inés Zacatelco.......14,117
Santa Rosalía.......7,356
Santiago Ixcuintla.......17,321
Sayula.......14,339
Silao.......31,825
Sombrerete.......11,077
Tala.......15,744
Tamazula de Gordiano.......13,521
Tamazunchale.......12,302
Tampico (1978 E) (*420,000).......240,000
Tangancícuaro [de Arista].......12,650
Tapachula.......60,620
Taxco de Alarcón.......27,089
Tecomán.......31,625
Tecuala.......12,461
Tehuacán.......47,497
Tehuantepec.......16,179
Teocaltiche.......13,745
Tepatitlán [de Morelos].......29,292
Tepic (1978 E).......133,400
Tequila.......11,839
Texcoco [de Mora] (*Mexico City).......18,044
Teziutlán.......23,948
Ticul.......14,341
Tierra Blanca.......22,727
Tijuana (**San Diego, Calif.) (1978 E).......535,000
Tizimín.......18,343
Tlalnepantla (*Mexico City).......45,575
Tlapacoyan.......13,172
Tlaquepaque (*Guadalajara).......59,760
Tlaxcala [de Xicohténcatl].......9,972
Toluca [de Lerdo] (1978 E).......222,900
Tonalá.......15,611
Torreón (1978 E) (*450,000).......268,700
Tulancingo.......35,799
Tuxpan (*Jalisco*).......14,693
Tuxpan (*Nayarit*).......20,322
Tuxpan de Rodríguez Cano (*Veracruz*).......33,901
Tuxtepec.......17,700
Tuxtla Gutiérrez (1978 E).......101,700
Umán.......8,371
Unión de Tula.......6,399
Uriangato.......14,626
Uruapan [del Progreso] (1978 E).......138,300
Valladolid.......14,663
Valle de Santiago.......16,517
Valle Hermoso.......19,278
Venustiano Carranza.......23,624
Veracruz [Llave] (1978 E) (*365,000).......295,300
Vicente Guerrero (*Tlaxcala*).......18,280
Vicente Guerrero (*Veracruz*) (*Orizaba).......11,688
Villa Frontera.......25,761
Villahermosa (1978 E).......165,500
Xicotepec de Juárez.......12,656
Yautepec.......13,952
Yurécuaro.......13,611
Yuriria.......10,085
Zaachila.......7,270
Zacapu.......31,989
Zacatecas.......50,251
Zacatepec.......16,839
Zacoalco de Torres.......11,343
Zamora de Hidalgo.......57,775
Zapopan (*Guadalajara).......18,512
Zapotiltic.......11,733
Zihuatanejo.......4,879
Zitácuaro.......36,911
Zumpango.......12,923

MONACO

1975 E.......25,000
•MONACO (*50,000).......25,000

MONGOLIA / Mongol Ard Uls

1969 C.......1,197,600
Cecerleg (Tsetserleg).......12,400
Choibalsan.......20,500
Darchan.......22,800
Jirgalanta (Chovd).......12,400
Süchbaatar.......10,000
•ULAN BATOR (URGA) (1970 E).......287,000

MONTSERRAT

1970 C.......11,458
•PLYMOUTH.......1,267

MOROCCO / Al-Magreb

1971 C.......15,379,259
Agadir.......61,192
Beni-Mellal.......53,826
Berkane.......39,015
Berrechid.......20,113
•Casablanca (Dar-el-Beida) (*1,575,000).......1,506,373
El-Jadida (Mazagan).......55,501
Essaouira (Mogador).......30,061
Fès (Fez).......325,327
Fkih Ben Salah.......26,918
Jerada.......30,633
Kenitra.......139,206
Khemisset.......21,811
Khenifra.......25,526
Khouribga.......73,667
Ksar-el-Kebir.......48,262
Ksar-es-Souk.......16,775
Larache.......45,710
Marrakech.......332,741
Meknès.......248,369
Mohammedia (Fedala).......70,392
Nador.......32,490
Ouarzazate.......11,142
Oued-Zem.......33,323
Ouezzane.......33,267
Oujda.......175,532
RABAT (*540,000).......367,620
Safi.......129,113
Salé (**Rabat).......155,557
Sefrou.......28,607
Settat.......42,325
Sidi Ifni.......13,650
Sidi Kacem.......26,831
Sidi Slimane.......20,398
Tanger (Tangier).......187,894
Taroudant.......22,272
Taza.......55,157
Tétouan.......139,105
Villa Alhucemas (Al Hoceima).......18,686
Youssoufia.......22,435

MOZAMBIQUE / Moçambique

1970 C.......8,168,933
Beira.......110,752
Inhambane.......24,090
João Belo.......63,494
•MAPUTO (LOURENÇO MARQUES).......341,922
Nampula.......120,188
Quelimane.......71,289
Tete.......51,453
Villa Cabral.......41,251

NAMIBIA

1970 C.......722,867
Gobabis.......4,428
Keetmanshoop.......10,297
Lüderitz.......6,642
Mariental.......4,629
Otjiwarongo.......8,018
Rehoboth.......5,363
Swakopmund.......5,681
Tsumeb.......12,338
•WINDHOEK.......61,260

NEPAL / Nepāl

1971 C.......11,555,983
Bhaktapur.......40,112
Birātnagar.......45,100
•KATHMANDU (*215,000).......150,402
Lalitpur (*Katmandu).......59,049
Nepālganj.......23,523

NETHERLANDS / Nederland

1980 E.......14,091,014
(includes 1,546 persons with no fixed residence in any province)

Provinces

Drenthe.......418,479
Dronten.......19,658
Friesland.......583,989
Gelderland.......1,694,416
Groningen.......553,709
Lelystad.......38,971
Limburg.......1,069,038
North Brabant (Noord-Brabant).......2,051,195
North Holland (Noord-Holland).......2,307,646
Overijssel.......1,018,208
Southern IJsselmeer Polders (Zuidelijke IJsselmeerpolders) (not part of any province).......6,872
South Holland (Zuid-Holland).......3,083,555
Utrecht.......895,464
Zeeland.......348,268

Cities

Aalsmeer.......20,486
Alkmaar (*107,000).......71,245
Almelo.......63,381
Alphen aan den Rijn.......51,780
Amersfoort (*128,678).......88,097
Amstelveen (*Amsterdam).......69,488
•AMSTERDAM (*1,810,000).......716,919
Apeldoorn.......138,164
Arnhem (*287,305).......127,846
Assen.......45,036
Bergen op Zoom.......43,715
Beverwijk (*Amsterdam).......35,980
Breda (*151,236).......117,259
Brunssum (*Heerlen).......26,281
Bussum (*Amsterdam).......35,316
Castricum (*Amsterdam).......22,783
De Bilt (*Utrecht).......32,397
Delft (*The Hague).......83,939
Delfzijl.......25,433
Den Helder.......61,761
Deventer.......64,561
Doetinchem (36,995▲).......27,800
Dordrecht (*195,792).......107,453
Edam-Volendam (*Amsterdam).......23,091
Ede (82,829▲).......43,500
Eindhoven (*369,352).......194,451
Emmen (89,763▲).......35,500
Enschede (*285,000).......143,042
Geldrop (*Eindhoven).......26,474
Geleen (*181,250).......35,371
Goes.......30,193
Gorinchem.......28,957
Gouda.......58,784
Groningen (*200,467).......161,322
Haarlem (*Amsterdam).......158,291
Haarlemmermeer (77,657▲).......10,600
Harderwijk.......30,174
Harlingen.......15,427
Heemstede (*Amsterdam).......26,729
Heerenveen (36,729▲).......20,400
Heerlen (*267,003).......71,102
Helmond.......58,490
Hengelo (**Enschede).......75,216
Hilversum (*Amsterdam).......92,964
Hoensbroek (*Heerlen).......22,748
Hoogeveen (43,645▲).......33,000
Hoorn.......39,300
IJmuiden (Velsen) (*Amsterdam).......61,202
Kampen.......30,353
Katwijk aan Zee.......38,163
Kerkrade (*Heerlen).......47,001
Leeuwarden.......84,518
Leiden (*173,386).......103,046
Lelystad (38,971▲).......9,900
Maassluis (*Rotterdam).......32,937
Maastricht (*145,346).......109,285
Meppel.......22,377
Middelburg.......38,077
Nijmegen (*217,951).......147,614
Oldenzaal.......28,134
Oss.......43,462

C Census. E Official estimate. UE Unofficial estimate.
L Population within municipal limits of year specified. • Largest city in country.

* Population or designation of metropolitan area, including suburbs (see headnote).
▲ Population of an entire municipality, commune, or district, including rural area.
‡† Year of information specified at start of country.

Papendrecht (★Dordrecht)......24,995
Purmerend (★Amsterdam)......32,565
Renkum (★Arnhem) (34,168▲)....12,600
Rheden (★Arnhem) (48,637▲)....10,100
Ridderkerk (★Rotterdam)........45,908
Rijswijk (★The Hague)..........52,605
Roermond......................37,539
Roosendaal....................54,838
Rotterdam (★1,085,000)........579,194
Schiedam (★Rotterdam)........74,895
's-Hertogenbosch (★183,583)....87,897
Sittard (★★Geleen)..............33,702
Sliedrecht......................22,504
Sneek..........................28,457
Soest (★Amersfoort)............40,581
Spijkenisse (★Rotterdam).......36,863
Tegelen (★Venlo)................18,079
Terneuzen (35,393▲)..............22,200
THE HAGUE ('s-GRAVENHAGE) (★775,000)....................456,886
Tiel............................28,919
Tilburg (★216,873)..............151,799
Utrecht (★481,875)..............237,037
Valkenswaard (★Eindhoven).....27,441
Veendam........................28,169
Veenendaal.....................39,210
Veldhoven (★Eindhoven).........33,382
Venlo (★86,000).................62,595
Vlaardingen (★Rotterdam)......79,531
Vlissingen (Flushing) (45,726▲)..26,200
Voorburg (★The Hague)........44,227
Vught (★'s-Hertogenbosch).....23,582
Waalwijk........................28,514
Wageningen.....................30,447
Wassenaar (★The Hague).......26,989
Weert (38,311▲)..................27,800
Winschoten.....................21,101
Woerden........................23,715
Zaanstad (Zaandam) (★Amsterdam)...............128,809
Zeist (★Utrecht)................61,532
Zoetermeer (★The Hague)......63,832
Zutphen........................31,767
Zwijndrecht (★★Dordrecht).....39,641
Zwolle..........................82,190

NETHERLANDS ANTILLES / Nederlandse Antillen

1960 C........................188,914

Kralendijk *(Bonaire)* (1953 E)......600
Oranjestad *(Aruba)* (1965 E).....14,700
•WILLEMSTAD *(Curaçao)* (★94,133).....................43,547

NEW CALEDONIA / Nouvelle-Calédonie

1976 C........................133,233

•NOUMEA (★70,600).............56,100

NEW HEBRIDES
see Vanuatu

NEW ZEALAND

1979 E........................3,144,700

•Auckland (★775,000)...........147,600
Birkenhead (★Auckland)........20,600
Blenheim........................17,450
Christchurch (★309,000)........171,300
Dunedin (★113,000)..............81,600
East Coast Bays (★Auckland)...24,500
Gisborne (★32,000)..............30,000
Hamilton (★97,400)..............90,900
Hastings (★★Napier)............35,500
Invercargill (★53,800)...........49,900
Lower Hutt (★Wellington).......65,100
Manukau (★Auckland)..........143,500
Masterton (★21,200).............19,650
Mount Albert (★Auckland)......28,300
Mount Eden (★Auckland)........19,500
Mount Roskill (★Auckland)......34,800
Mount Wellington (★Auckland)..20,500
Napier (★110,600)...............47,900
Nelson (★42,800)................33,100
New Plymouth (★44,700)........38,300
Palmerston North (★64,900).....58,800
Papakura (★Auckland)..........22,200
Papatoetoe (★Auckland)........23,100
Porirua (★Wellington)...........42,500
Rotorua (★47,400)...............37,700
Takapuna (★Auckland)..........63,700
Tauranga (★49,000)..............34,300
Timaru (★30,100)................29,500
Tokoroa.........................19,150
Upper Hutt (★Wellington).......31,300
Wainuiomata (★Wellington) (1978 E)........................19,650
Waitemata (★Auckland).........81,900
Wanganui (★39,800).............37,500
WELLINGTON (★349,900).......137,600
Whangarei (★39,600)............35,900

NICARAGUA

1978 E........................2,451,418

Bluefields......................18,252
Chinandega.....................44,435
Granada........................56,232
León...........................81,647
•MANAGUA.....................552,900
Masaya........................47,276
Matagalpa......................26,986
Rivas...........................16,222

NIGER

1977 E........................5,098,000

Maradi..........................45,900
•NIAMEY.......................225,300
Tahoua..........................31,300
Zinder..........................58,400

NIGERIA

1963 C.....................55,670,052

Aba (1975 E)..................177,000
Abeokuta (1975 E).............253,000
Ado-Ekiti (1975 E).............213,000
Afikpo..........................36,096
Agege..........................45,986
Akure..........................71,106
Awka...........................48,725
Bauchi.........................37,778
Benin City (1975 E)...........136,000
Bida...........................55,007
Calabar (1975 E)..............103,000
Deba...........................60,679
Ede (1975 E)..................182,000
Effon-Alaiye...................67,090
Ejigbo.........................46,410
Enugu (1975 E)................187,000
Epe............................44,268
Gombe.........................47,265
Gusau..........................69,231
Ibadan (1975 E)...............847,000
Ife (1975 E)....................176,000
Igboho.........................46,776
Ihiala..........................40,198
Ijebu-Igbo......................43,180
Ijebu-Ode.......................68,543
Ijero Ekiti......................41,935
Ikare...........................61,696
Ikerre (1975 E)................145,000
Ikire...........................54,022
Ikirun..........................79,516
Ikorodu.........................81 024
Ikot Ekpene.....................38,107
Ila (1975 E)....................155,000
Ilawe...........................80,833
Ilegboro........................44,543
Ilesha (1975 E)................224,000
Ilobu...........................87,223
Ilorin (1975 E).................282,000
Inisa...........................52,482
Ise Ekiti........................45,323
Iseyin (1971 E)................115,000
Iwo (1975 E)...................214,000
Jos.............................90,402
Kaduna (1975 E)...............202,000
Kano (1975 E).................399,000
Katsina (1971 E)...............109,000
Kishi...........................42,374
Kumo...........................64,878
Lafia............................53,667
•LAGOS (1975 E) (★1,450,000)..1,060,800
Maiduguri (1975 E).............189,000
Makurdi.........................53,967
Minna...........................59,988
Mushin (★Lagos) (1975 E)......197,000
Nguru...........................43,234
Offa............................86,425
Ogbomosho (1975 E)...........432,000
Oka............................62,761
Ondo...........................74,343
Onitsha (1975 E)..............220,000
Oshogbo (1975 E)..............282,000
Owo............................89,693
Oyo (1975 E)..................152,000
Port Harcourt (1975 E).........242,000
Sapele..........................61,007
Shagamu........................51,371
Shaki...........................76,290
Shomolu (★Lagos)..............64,731
Sokoto..........................89,817
Ugep...........................44,945
Warri...........................55,254
Zaria (1975 E)..................224,000

NORWAY / Norge

1979 E........................4,073,000

Ålesund.........................34,744
Arendal (1980 E) (★20,000).......11,400
Bergen (1980 E) (★238,000).....209,000
Bodø............................32,163
Drammen (1980 E) (★71,000).....49,700
Eigersund.......................11,694
Fredrikstad (1980 E) (★48,000).....28,000
Gjøvik..........................26,150
Grimstad........................13,588
Halden..........................26,810
Hamar...........................16,053
Hammerfest......................7,457
Harstad.........................21,579
Haugesund......................27,081
Horten..........................13,476
Kongsberg.......................20,385
Kongsvinger.....................17,018
Kristiansand.....................60,722
Kristiansund.....................18,412
Larvik (1980 E) (★16,500)..........8,300
Lillehammer.....................21,762
Mandal..........................11,847
Mo (1970 C).....................21,033
Molde...........................20,886
Moss............................25,407
Namsos..........................11,640
Narvik..........................19,202
Notodden........................12,973
•OSLO (1980 E) (★725,000).......454,819
Porsgrunn (★★Skien) (1980 E)...31,365
Ringerike.......................26,839
Sandefjord......................34,405
Sandnes (★Stavanger) (1980 E)..36,200
Sarpsborg (1980 E) (★37,500)....12,100
Skien (1980 E) (★78,815).........47,450
Stavanger (1980 E) (★128,000)....90,000
Steinkjer.......................20,526
Tønsberg (1980 E) (★35,000)......9,200
Tromsø..........................45,360
Trondheim......................134,683
Vadsø............................6,054

OMAN / 'Umān

1962 E........................565,000

•Maṭraḥ..........................14,000
MUSCAT (MASQAṬ)...............6,000

PACIFIC ISLANDS TRUST TERRITORY

1973 C........................114,773

Island Groups

Caroline Islands...............75,394
Mariana Islands (excl. Guam)...14,335
Marshall Islands...............25,044

PAKISTAN / Pākistān

1972 C.....................64,979,732

(excl. population in section of Jammu and Kashmir occupied by Pakistan)

Abbottābād (★47,122)...........27,963
Ahmadpur East..................43,312
Bahāwalnagar...................50,991
Bahāwalpur (★133,782).........115,660
Baldia (★Karāchi)...............79,529
Bannu (★43,795)................33,000
Bhakkar.........................34,638
Burewala.......................57,741
Campbellpore (★29,172).........21,633
Chakwāl........................29,143
Chārsadda......................45,555
Chiniot.........................70,108
Dādu...........................30,184
Dera Ghāzi Khān................72,343
Dera Ismāil Khān (★58,778).....57,296
Faisalabad (Lyallpur)..........823,343
Gujrānwāla (★360,478)..........323,880
Gujrāt.........................100,333
Gwādar.........................15,758
Hāfizābād.......................61,597
Hyderābād (★660,000)..........600,796
ISLĀMĀBĀD (★★Rāwalpindi)...77,000
Jacobābād.......................57,596
Jhang Maghiāna.................131,843
Jhelum (★70,157)...............63,676
Kamālia.........................50,934
Kāmoke.........................50,257
•Karāchi (1975 E) (★4,500,000)..2,800,000
Karāchi Cantonment (★Karāchi)..................133,176
Kasūr..........................102,531
Khānewāl.......................67,746
Khānpur........................49,235
Kohāt (★65,202)................48,096
Lahore (★2,200,000)..........2,022,577
Lahore Cantonment (★Lahore)..147,165
Landhi Korangi (★Karāchi).......551,236
Lārkāna........................71,893
Leiah..........................33,549
Mardān (★115,194).............105,167
Miānwāli.......................48,304
Mīrpur-Khās....................81,965
Multān (★538,949).............504,365
Nawābshāh.....................81,045
New Karāchi No. 1 (★Karāchi)..85,398
New Karāchi No. 2 (★Karāchi)..67,682
Nowshera (★55,916).............31,101
Okāra (★101,052)...............84,334
Orangi (★Karāchi)..............109,979
Peshāwar (★284,833)...........219,562
Quetta (★158,026).............137,659
Rahīmyār Khān (★85,699)........74,262
Rāwalpindi (★725,000)..........372,919
Rāwalpindi Cantonment (★Rāwalpindi)................241,890
Sāhiwāl (Montgomery)..........106,648
Sargodha (★200,460)...........166,391
Shekhūpura......................80,560
Shikārpur.......................70,924
Shujāābād.......................24,422
Siālkot (★203,650)..............183,685
Sibi............................19,989
Sukkur.........................158,781
Turbat..........................27,671
Wah Cantonment................107,510

PANAMA / Panamá

1970 C........................†1,472,280

†Includes former Canal Zone

Balboa (★Panamá)...............2,569
Balboa Heights (★Panamá)........232
Colón (1976 E) (★82,000)..........73,600
David...........................35,677
Gamboa..........................2,102
La Chorrera.....................25,873
•PANAMÁ (1978 E) (★645,000)...439,800
Puerto Armuelles...............12,015
San Miguelito (★Panamá) (1977 E)......................135,100
Santiago........................14,595

PAPUA NEW GUINEA

1977 E........................2,905,000

Lae.............................45,100
Madang..........................20,100
•PORT MORESBY.................106,600
Rabaul..........................13,400
Wewak..........................18,100

PARAGUAY

1972 C........................2,357,955

•ASUNCIÓN (1978 E) (★655,000).463,700
Caacupé.........................7,278
Concepción.....................19,392
Coronel Oviedo.................13,786
Encarnación....................23,343
Fernando de la Mora (★Asunción)..................36,834
Lambaré (★Asunción)...........31,656
Luque (★Asunción).............13,921
Paraguarí.......................5,036
Pedro Juan Caballero...........21,033
Pilar...........................12,506
Villa Hayes.....................4,749
Villarrica.......................17,687

PERU / Perú

1972 C.....................13,572,052

Arequipa (★304,653)............98,605
Ayacucho (★43,304)............34,593
Barranco (★Lima)...............46,449
Barrio Obrero Industrial (★Lima)......................238,402
Breña (★Lima)..................123,345
Cajamarca......................37,608
Callao (★★Lima)...............196,919
Cerro de Pasco (★47,178)......35,975
Chiclayo (★189,685)............148,932
Chimbote.......................159,045
Chorrillos (★Lima)..............87,021
Cuzco (★120,881)...............67,658
Huacho.........................36,697
Huancayo (★115,693)............64,777
Huánuco........................41,123
Ica.............................73,883
Iquitos.........................111,327
Jesús María (★Lima)............82,988
Juliaca.........................38,475
La Victoria (★Lima)...........265,157
•LIMA (★3,250,000)............340,339
Lince (★Lima)...................82,749
Magdalena del Mar (★Lima).....54,855
Miraflores (★Lima)..............93,926
Pisco...........................41,429
Piura (★126,702)................81,683
Pucallpa........................57,525
Pueblo Libre (★Lima)...........76,279
Puno............................41,166
Rímac (★Lima).................165,340
San Isidro (★Lima)..............61,682
Sullana.........................60,112
Surco (★Lima)...................70,949
Surquillo (★Lima)...............89,201
Tacna...........................55,752
Trujillo (★241,882).............127,535
Tumbes.........................32,972
Vitarte (★Lima).................54,417

PHILIPPINES / Pilipinas

1975 C.....................42,070,660

Angeles........................151,164
Antipolo (40,944▲)..............35,672
Bacolod........................223,392
Bacoor (★Manila)................62,225
Daguio..........................97,449
Baliuag.........................61,624
Batangas (125,363▲).............18,592
Biñan (★Manila).................67,444
Bocaue..........................40,577
Butuan (132,682▲)...............53,578
Cabanatuan (115,050▲)...........32,003
Cadiz (127,653▲)................26,581
Cagayan de Oro (165,220▲)......37,272
Calamba (97,432▲)...............33,321
Calapan (55,608▲)................13,982
Caloocan (★Manila).............397,201
Cavite (★160,000)................82,456
Cebu (★500,000)................413,025
Cotabato (67,097▲)...............49,134
Dagupan.........................90,092
Davao (484,678▲)...............214,849
General Santos (Dadiangas) (91,154▲)........................37,527
Gingoog (66,577▲)................16,590
Ilagan (70,075▲).................12,234
Iligan (118,778▲).................10,367
Iloilo...........................227,027
Iriga (75,885▲)...................13,938
Isabela (Basilan) (27,261▲)........7,204
Jolo............................37,623
Koronadal (62,764▲)..............15,066
La Carlota (40,984▲)..............20,251
Laoag (66,259▲)..................31,336
Lapu-Lapu.......................79,484
Las Piñas (★Manila).............81,610
Legazpi (88,378▲)................37,724
Lingayen (59,034▲)...............16,096
Lipa (106,094▲)..................18,330
Lucena..........................92,336
Maasin (54,737▲).................12,348
Makati (★Manila)...............334,448
Malabon (★Manila).............174,878
Malaybalay (65,198▲).............10,207
Malolos.........................83,491
Mandaluyong (★Manila).........182 267
Mandaue (★Cebu)................75,904
•MANILA (★5,500,000).........1,479,116
Marawi.........................63,332
Marikina (★Manila).............168,453
Mati (73,125▲)...................18,188
Mecauayan (★Manila)............60,225
Muntinglupa (★Manila)..........94,563
Naga...........................83,337
Navotas (★Manila)...............97,098
Olongapo......................147,109
Ormoc (89,466▲).................13,075
Ozamiz (71,559▲).................17,372
Pagadian (66,062▲)...............28,645
Parañaque (★Manila)...........158,974
Pasay (★Manila)................254,999
Pasig (★Manila)................209,915
Puerto Princesa (45,709▲)........18,480
Quezon City (★Manila).........956,864
Roxas (Capiz) (71,305▲)..........18,869
Sagay (95,421▲)..................32,417
San Carlos *(Negros Occidental Prov.)* (90,982▲)................23,950
San Carlos *(Pangasinan Prov.)* (90,882▲)......................12,003
San Fernando *(La Union Prov.)* (61,166▲)......................14,133
San Fernando *(Pampanga Prov.)*.98,382
San Juan del Monte (★Manila).122,492
San Pablo (116,607▲).............42,489
San Pedro.......................43,439
Santa Cruz......................52,672
Santa Rosa (★Manila)...........47,639
Tacloban (80,707▲)...............63,693
Tagbilaran......................37,335
Tagig (★Manila).................73,702
Valenzuela (★Manila)...........150,605
Zamboanga (265,023▲)...........53,678

POLAND / Polska

1979 E.....................35,414,000

Będzin (★Katowice).............75,000
Biała Podlaska..................38,100
Białystok......................218,700
Bielawa (Langenbielau) (★★Dzierżoniów)..............32,100
Bielsko-Biała...................160,300
Bolesławiec (Bunzlau)..........39,200
Brzeg (Brieg)...................35,300
Bydgoszcz......................343,800
Bytom (Beuthen) (★★Katowice)................231,600
Chełm..........................51,200
Chojnice........................31,100
Chorzów (★★Katowice).........149,900
Częstochowa...................232,400
Dąbrowa Górnicza (★Katowice)..................137,300
Dzierżoniów (Reichenbach) (★85,000)......................35,800
Elbląg (Elbing).................108,100
Ełk (Lyck)......................37,300
Gdańsk (Danzig) (★820,000)....449,200
Gdynia (★★Gdańsk)............232,500
Gliwice (Gleiwitz) (★★Katowice)................195,300
Głogów (Glogau).................49,200
Gniezno.........................61,100
Gorzów Wielkopolski (Landsberg)...................102,500
Grudziądz.......................88,700
Inowrocław......................65,100
Jarosław........................34,900
Jastrzębie Zdrój.................97,800
Jaworzno (★Katowice)..........88,200
Jelenia Góra (Hirschberg)......86,000
Kalisz..........................97,700
•Katowice (★2,590,000).........351,300
Kędzierzyn-Koźle (Heydebreck).68,700
Kielce.........................181,000
Knurów (★Katowice)............40,200
Kołobrzeg (Kolberg).............37,500
Konin...........................65,300
Koszalin (Köslin)................90,000
Kraków (★780,000)..............706,100
Krosno..........................38,000
Kutno...........................40,500
Legionowo (★Warsaw)...........37,200
Legnica (Liegnitz)...............88,400
Leszno..........................47,500
Łódź (★1,025,000)..............830,800
Łomża...........................38,100
Lubin (Lüben)...................63,000
Lublin (★345,000)..............297,600
Mielec..........................41,300
Mysłowice (★Katowice)..........78,100
Nowa Sól (Neusalz)..............38,000
Nowy Sącz.......................62,600
Nysa (Neisse)....................40,700
Olsztyn (Allenstein)............130,400
Opole (Oppeln).................114,000
Ostrowiec Świętokrzyski........62,300
Ostrów Wielkopolski.............61,400
Oświęcim........................44,200
Otwock (★Warsaw)...............47,400
Pabianice (★Łódź)...............69,800
Piekary Śląskie (★Katowice).....63,500
Piła (Schneidemühl).............57,200
Piotrków Trybunalski............70,900
Płock...........................99,800
Poznań (★610,000)..............545,600
Pruszków (★Warsaw).............49,000
Przemyśl........................60,100
Pszczyna........................34,800
Puławy..........................44,800
Racibórz (Ratibor)...............52,900
Radom..........................187,600
Radomsko.......................39,900
Ruda Śląska (★Katowice)......156,800
Rybnik.........................118,200
Rzeszów........................116,900
Siedlce.........................52,500
Siemianowice Śląskie (★Katowice)..................77,200
Skarżysko-Kamienna............43,100
Słupsk (Stolp)...................84,200
Sopot (Zoppot) (★Gdańsk)........51,800
Sosnowiec (★★Katowice).......241,700
Stalowa Wola....................52,200
Starachowice....................48,400
Stargard Szczeciński.............57,200
Starogard Gdański...............43,300
Suwałki.........................38,500
Świdnica (Schweidnitz)..........55,700
Świętochłowice (★Katowice).....57,700
Świnoujście (Swinemünde).......46,000
Szczecin (Stettin) (★425,000)...388,000
Szczecinek (Neustettin)..........35,200
Tarnobrzeg......................35,200
Tarnów.........................102,800
Tarnowskie Góry (★Katowice)...65,900
Tczew...........................52,300
Tomaszów Mazowiecki...........62,800
Toruń...........................170,100
Tychy (★Katowice)..............160,700
Wałbrzych (Waldenburg) (★195,000).....................132,900
Wałcz (Deutsch Krone)..........22,000
WARSAW (WARSZAWA) (★2,080,000)................1,576,600
Wejherowo......................41,600
Włocławek......................104,400
Wodzisław Śląski...............104,500
Wołomin (★Warsaw).............30,600
Wrocław (Breslau)..............609,100
Zabrze (Hindenburg) (★★Katowice)................195,000
Zamość.........................45,700
Żary (Sorau)....................34,700
Zawiercie.......................61,600
Zduńska Wola...................38,200
Zgierz (★Łódź)...................52,100
Zgorzelec.......................32,800
Zielona Góra (Grünberg).........98,000
Żyrardów (★Warsaw).............36,700

C Census. E Official estimate. UE Unofficial estimate.
L Population within municipal limits of specified year. • Largest city in country.

★ Population or designation of metropolitan area, including suburbs (see headnote).
▲ Population of an entire municipality, commune, or district, including rural area.
‡† Year of information specified at start of country.

PORTUGAL

1970 C 8,568,703

Almada (*Lisbon) 38,714
Amadora (*Lisbon) 66,189
Angra do Heroísmo (*Azores Is.*) 14,328
Aveiro 20,651
Barreiro (*Lisbon) 53,200
Beja 15,909
Braga 49,693
Bragança 10,001
Coimbra 56,568
Covilhã 27,018
Évora 24,003
Faro 20,687
Funchal (*Madeira Is.*) 40,057
Guimarães 25,113
Horta (*Azores Is.*) 6,025
•LISBON (LISBOA) (1975 E) (*1,950,000) 829,900
Matosinhos (*Porto) 22,475
Montijo (*Lisbon) 25,949
Moscavide (*Lisbon) 21,647
Odivelas (*Lisbon) 25,978
Piedade (*Lisbon) 21,004
Ponta Delgada (*Azores Is.*) 21,262
Portimão 10,389
Porto (Oporto) (1975 E) (*1,150,000) 335,700
Póvoa de Varzim 17,555
Queluz (*Lisbon) 25,913
Santarem 18,069
Setúbal 50,730
Sintra (*Lisbon) (1960 C) 7,705
Vila do Conde 16,390
Vila Nova de Gaia (*Porto) 50,219
Viseu 16,036

PUERTO RICO

1980 C 3,187,570

Adjuntas (18,617▲) 5,184
Aguadilla (52,627▲) 20,879
Aibonito (22,230▲) 9,369
Arecibo (86,660▲) 48,586
Bayamón (*San Juan) 184,854
Cabo Rojo (33,909▲) 10,254
Caguas (*San Juan) (118,020▲) 87,218
Carolina (*San Juan) 147,100
Cataño (*San Juan) 26,318
Cayey (40,927▲) 23,315
Cidra (28,135▲) 6,065
Coamo (30,752▲) 12,834
Corozal (28,218▲) 5,891
Fajardo (32,011▲) 26,845
Guánica (18,784▲) 9,627
Guayama (40,137▲) 21,044
Guayanilla (21,012▲) 6,191
Guaynabo (*San Juan) 65,091
Humacao (45,916▲) 19,135
Isabela (37,451▲) 12,097
Juncos (25,433▲) 7,898
Manatí (36,480▲) 17,254
Mayagüez (*132,814) 82,703
Ponce (*252,420) 161,260
San Germán (32,941▲) 13,093
•SAN JUAN (*1,535,000) 422,701
San Lorenzo (32,333▲) 8,886
San Sebastian (35,877▲) 10,792
Trujillo Alto (*San Juan) (51,389▲) 41,097
Utuado (34,384▲) 11,049
Vega Alta (*San Juan) (28,225▲) 10,584
Vega Baja (*San Juan) (46,841▲) 18,020
Yabucoa (30,589▲) 6,782
Yauco (37,682▲) 14,598

QATAR / Qaṭar

1971 E 160,000

•DOHA (AD-DAWḤAH) 95,000

REUNION / Réunion

1974 C 476,675

Le Port (25,068▲) 21,621
•ST. DENIS (103,512▲) 80,802
St. Pierre (46,060▲) 22,022

RHODESIA see Zimbabwe

ROMANIA / România

1978 E 21,854,622

Aiud 25,929
Alba-Iulia 44,870
Alexandria 39,531
Arad 174,411
Bacău 135,841
Baia-Mare 107,945
Bîrlad 57,954
Bistriţa 48,959
Blaj 21,465
Bocşa 21,317
Borşa 25,427
Botoşani 68,325
Brăila 200,435
Braşov 268,226
•BUCHAREST (BUCUREŞTI) (*2,050,000) 1,858,418
Buzău 102,868
Călăraşi 50,601
Caracal 31,433
Caransebeş 28,437
Carei 24,473
Cîmpia Turzii 23,750
Cîmpina 33,554
Cîmpulung 33,329
Cluj 273,199
Codlea 23,691
Constanţa (*301,758) 267,612
Craiova 230,721
Cugir 27,892
Curtea de Argeş 26,081
Dej 33,350
Deva 65,009
Dorohoi 22,332
Drobeta-Turnu-Severin 80,200
Făgăraş 35,831
Feteşti 28,257
Focşani 60,038
Galaţi 252,592
Gheorghe Gheorghiu-Dej 43,282
Giurgiu 53,072
Hunedoara 81,963
Huşi 23,652
Iaşi 278,545
Lugoj 45,957
Lupeni 27,857
Mangalia 30,404
Medgidia 41,792
Mediaş 66,795
Miercurea Ciuc 33,884
Odorheiu Secuiesc 30,756
Olteniţa 25,185
Oradea 179,780
Petroşani (*74,000) 41,720
Piatra-Neamţ 83,168
Piteşti 133,081
Ploieşti (*270,000) 206,138
Rădăuţi 22,750
Reghin 31,035
Reşiţa 90,664
Rîmnicu-Sărat 29,246
Rîmnicu-Vîlcea 72,915
Roman 53,797
Roşiori de Vede 29,462
Săcele 31,615
Satu-Mare 107,852
Sebeş 26,881
Sfîntu Gheorghe 45,739
Sibiu 157,519
Sighetul Marmaţiei 39,095
Sighişoara 33,359
Slatina 50,683
Slobozia 33,701
Suceava 66,527
Tecuci 37,423
Timişoara 277,779
Tîrgovişte 67,024
Tîrgu-Jiu 67,694
Tîrgu-Mureş 136,679
Tîrnăveni 26,877
Tulcea 66,054
Turda 56,350
Turnu-Măgurele 33,404
Vaslui 42,718
Vulcan 29,216
Zalău 35,734
Zărneşti 24,317

RWANDA

1978 C 4,819,000

Butare 21,700
•KIGALI 117,700
Ruhengeri 16,000

ST. HELENA
(*excl. Dependencies*)

1976 C 5,147

•JAMESTOWN 1,516

ST. KITTS-NEVIS

1970 C 47,457

•BASSETERRE (*St. Kitts*) 13,055
Charlestown (*Nevis*) 1,880

SAINT LUCIA

1978 E 117,500

•CASTRIES 47,600

ST. PIERRE & MIQUELON / Saint-Pierre-et-Miquelon

1974 C 5,840

•ST.-PIERRE 5,232

ST. VINCENT

1970 C 89,129

•KINGSTOWN (*23,782) 17,258

SAN MARINO

1977 E 20,000

•SAN MARINO 4,628

SAO TOME & PRINCIPE / São Tomé e Príncipe

1970 C 73,631

•SÃO TOMÉ 17,380

SAUDI ARABIA / Al-'Arabīyah as-Sa'ūdīyah

1974 C 7,012,642

Abhā 30,150
Ad-Dammām 127,844
Al-Hufūf (Hofuf) 101,271
Al-Jawf (1961 UE) 20,000
Al-Khubar 48,817
Al-Madīnah (Medina) 198,186
Al-Mubarraz 54,325
Al-Qaṭīf (1961 UE) 30,000
At-Tā'if 204,857
Aẓ-Ẓahrān (Dhahran) (1974 UE) 25,000
Buraydah 69,940
Ḥā'il 40,502
Juddah (Jidda) 561,104
Khamīs Mushayṭ 49,581
Mecca (Makkah) 366,801
Najran 47,501
Qal'at Bīshah (1961 UE) 20,000
Qīzān 32,812
•RIYADH (AR-RIYĀḌ) 666,840
Tabūk 74,825
Yanbu' (1961 UE) 20,000

SENEGAL / Sénégal

1976 C 5,085,388

•DAKAR 798,792
Diourbel 51,000
Kaolack 106,899
Rufisque (*Dakar) (1973 E) 54,000
Saint-Louis 88,000
Thiès 117,333
Ziguinchor 73,000

SEYCHELLES

1971 C 52,437

•VICTORIA 13,622

SIERRA LEONE

1974 C 2,730,000

Bo 30,000
Bonthe (1963 C) 6,230
•FREETOWN (*335,000) 274,000
Kenema 15,000
Kissy (*Freetown) (1963 C) 13,143
Koidu (1963 C) 11,706
Lunsar (1963 C) 12,132
Makeni 12,000
Port Loko (1963 C) 5,809

SINGAPORE

1980 E 2,390,800

•SINGAPORE (*2,600,000) 2,390,800

SOLOMON ISLANDS

1976 C 196,823

•HONIARA 14,942

SOMALIA / Somaliya

1972 E 2,941,000

Afgoi (1964 C) 16,575
Berbera (1966 E) 14,000
Hargeisa (1966 E) 42,000
Kismayu (1968 C) 17,872
Marka (Merca) (1967 E) 17,700
•MOGADISHU (MOGADISCIO) 230,000

SOUTH AFRICA / Suid-Afrika

1970 C 21,794,328

Provinces

Cape (Kaap) 6,827,756
Natal 4,315,847
Orange Free State (Oranje-Vrystaat) 1,749,671
Transvaal 8,901,054

Cities

Alberton (*Johannesburg) 23,988
Alexandra (*Johannesburg) 57,040
Aliwal North 12,311
Beaufort West 17,862
Bellville (*Cape Town) 49,026
Benoni (*Johannesburg) 151,294
Bethal 17,337
Bethlehem 29,918
Bishop Levis (*Cape Town) 26,386
Bloemfontein (*182,329) 149,836
Boksburg (*Johannesburg) 106,126
Brakpan (*Johannesburg) 73,210
CAPE TOWN (KAAPSTAD) (*1,125,000) 697,514
Carletonville 93,096
Clermont (*Durban) 26,125
Cradock 20,822
De Aar 18,057
Dundee 17,162
Durban (*1,040,000) 736,852
East London (Oos-Londen) (*190,000) 119,727
Edendale (*Pietermaritzburg) 41,194
Edenvale (*Johannesburg) 25,126
Elsies River (*Cape Town) 64,539
Ermelo 19,036
Ga-Rankuwa 45,631
George 24,625
Germiston (**Johannesburg) 221,972
Goodwood (*Cape Town) 31,592
Graaff-Reinet 22,392
Grahamstown 41,302
Grassy Park (*Cape Town) 32,709
Hammarsdale 21,657
Harrismith 16,082
•Johannesburg (*2,550,000) 654,232
Kempton Park (*Johannesburg) 37,205
Kimberley 105,258
Klerksdorp (*175,000) 63,558
Kroonstad 51,988
Krugersdorp (*Johannesburg) 92,725
Ladysmith 28,920
Mabopane 22,559
Madadeni 32,398
Mafeking 6,515
Mariannhill (*Durban) 22,484
Mdantsane (*East London) 67,501
Middelburg 26,942
Mosselbaai 17,574
Nelspruit 25,092
Newcastle 14,407
Nigel 41,179
Odendaalsrus (*29,026) 15,603
Orkney (**Klerksdorp) 22,117
Oudtshoorn 26,907
Paarl 49,244
Parow (*Cape Town) 60,768
Parys 17,447
Pietermaritzburg (*160,855) 114,822
Pietersburg 27,174
Port Elizabeth (*475,869) 392,231
Potchefstroom 57,443
Potgietersrus 6,667
PRETORIA (*575,000) 545,450
Queenstown 39,304
Randburg (*Johannesburg) 46,011
Randfontein (*Johannesburg) 50,481
Roodepoort-Maraisburg (*Johannesburg) 115,366
Rustenburg 22,303
Sandton (*Johannesburg) 49,022
Sasolburg (*Vereeniging) 29,056
Soweto (*Johannesburg) 602,043
Springs (*Johannesburg) 142,812
Standerton 21,038
Stellenbosch 29,955
Stilfontein (*Klerksdorp) 70,661
Strand (*Cape Town) 24,503
Tembisa (*Johannesburg) 83,637
Uitenhage (**Port Elizabeth) 70,517
Umlazi (*Durban) 123,495
Umtata 25,216
Upington 28,632
Vanderbijlpark (**Vereeniging) 80,375
Vereeniging (*310,188) 172,549
Virginia 46,138
Welkom (*132,880) 67,472
Westonaria (*Johannesburg) 36,253
Witbank 37,456
Worcester 41,198
Zwelitsha 22,131

SOVIET UNION
See Union of Soviet Socialist Republics

SPAIN / España

1978 E 38,141,157

Regions and Provinces

ANDALUSIA (ANDALUCÍA) 6,560,445
Almería 418,471
Cádiz 1,016,340
Córdoba 751,833
Granada 780,848
Huelva 427,991
Jaén 677,756
Málaga 1,013,346
Sevilla 1,473,860
ARAGON (ARAGÓN) 1,204,244
Huesca 218,364
Teruel 157,454
Zaragoza 828,426
ASTURIAS 1,172,301
Oviedo 1,172,301
BALEARIC IS. (BALEARES) 642,702
Baleares 642,702
BASQUE PROVINCES (VASCONGADAS) 2,192,755
Álava 256,883
Guipúzcoa 714,690
Vizcaya 1,221,182
CANARY IS. (CANARIAS) 1,410,665
Las Palmas 704,389
Santa Cruz de Tenerife 706,276
CATALONIA (CATALUÑA) 6,071,953
Barcelona 4,724,063
Gerona 467,749
Lérida 358,430
Tarragona 521,711
ESTREMADURA (EXTREMADURA) 1,110,457
Badajoz 666,389
Cáceres 444,068
GALICIA 2,895,467
La Coruña 1,126,202
Lugo 418,770
Orense 447,980
Pontevedra 902,515
LEON (LEÓN) 1,156,113
León 549,709
Salamanca 368,833
Zamora 237,571
MURCIA 1,300,878
Albacete 343,868
Murcia 957,010
NAVARRE (NAVARRA) 511,699
Navarra 511,699
NEW CASTILE (CASTILLA LA NUEVA) 6,010,575
Ciudad Real 498,205
Cuenca 226,496
Guadalajara 143,520
Madrid 4,659,478
Toledo 482,876
OLD CASTILE (CASTILLA LA VIEJA) 2,261,956
Ávila 194,913
Burgos 368,302
Logroño 252,110
Palencia 192,102
Santander 515,109
Segovia 153,771
Soria 104,595
Valladolid 481,054
VALENCIA 3,638,947
Alicante 1,142,323
Castellón 430,845
Valencia 2,065,779

Cities (1975 C or ‡1978 E)

Aguilas (18,900▲) 16,900
Albacete ‡107,725
Alcalá [de Guadaira] (39,593▲) 33,500
Alcalá de Henares (*Madrid) ‡114,788
Alcalá la Real (20,184▲) 9,300
Alcantarilla 21,891
Alcázar de San Juan 26,930
Alcira 35,428
Alcobendas (*Madrid) ‡57,951
Alcorcón (*Madrid) ‡124,348
Alcoy ‡65,078
Algeciras ‡92,933
Algemesí 23,623
Algorta (66,306▲) ‡29,500
Alicante ‡235,868
Almadén 10,312
Almendralejo 22,074
Almería ‡136,720
Andújar (34,459▲) 28,400
Antequera (40,113▲) 27,500
Aranjuez 31,275
Arcos de la Frontera (24,867▲) 15,500
Arizgoiti (Basauri) (*Bilbao) (55,303▲) ‡46,800
Arrecife (*Canary Is.*) 25,201
Ávila ‡38,105
Avilés (*129,000) ‡90,458
Badajoz (112,573▲) ‡89,500
Badalona (*Barcelona) ‡216,041
Baracaldo (*Bilbao) ‡123,178
Barcelona (*3,975,000) ‡1,902,713
Baza (20,113▲) 14,400
Bilbao (*995,000) ‡452,921
Burgos ‡148,487
Burjasot (*Valencia) 30,739
Burriana 23,846
Cabra (20,140▲) 15,900
Cáceres ‡64,539
Cádiz (*230,000) ‡156,328
Camas (*Sevilla) 23,840
Carmona 21,548
Cartagena (165,557▲) ‡135,200
Castellón de la Plana ‡118,648
Chiclana [de la Frontera] 31,711
Cieza 28,228
Ciudad Real ‡48,871
Córdoba ‡276,255
Cornellá (*Barcelona) ‡95,933
Cuenca ‡39,064
Daimiel 16,986
Don Benito 26,117
Dos Hermanas 47,800
Écija (33,505▲) 25,400
Éibar 37,838
Elche (165,203▲) ‡136,400
Elda ‡53,558
El Ferrol del Caudillo (*126,000) ‡90,317
El Puerto de Santa María ‡52,350
Esplugas Llobregat (*Barcelona) 38,110
Figueras 28,102
Gandía (41,565▲) 32,600
Gavá (*Barcelona) 30,586
Gerona ‡85,522
Getafe (*Madrid) ‡128,523
Gijón ‡256,904
Granada ‡229,108
Granollers (*Barcelona) 36,366
Guadalajara ‡49,130
Guadix (19,234▲) 14,900
Guernica y Luno (17,271▲) 11,704
Hellín (22,327▲) 16,109
Hospitalet (*Barcelona) ‡294,280
Huelva ‡125,810
Huesca ‡38,986
Ibiza 20,552
Igualada 30,024
Irún ‡54,781
Jaén ‡91,198
Játiva 22,613
Jerez de la Frontera (183,534▲) ‡137,700
La Coruña ‡228,637
La Línea ‡57,940
Langreo (Sama de Langreo) (63,128▲) ‡10,600
La Orotava (*Canary Is.*) (30,190▲) 9,300
Las Palmas de Gran Canaria (*Canary Is.*) ‡357,158
Leganés (*Madrid) ‡151,353
Léon (*144,000) ‡122,827
Lérida (108,212▲) ‡86,100
Linares (56,356▲) ‡50,520
Logroño ‡104,928
Loja (22,001▲) 11,700
Lorca (65,806▲) 27,400
Lucena 29,373
Lugo (72,686▲) ‡60,900
•MADRID (*4,415,000) ‡3,367,438
Mahón 21,619
Málaga ‡467,637
Manacor 24,275
Manresa ‡68,213
Marbella (59,445▲) ‡35,200
Martos (21,375▲) 16,300
Mataró ‡98,589
Mérida 38,319
Mieres (62,826▲) ‡22,200
Miranda de Ebro 35,354
Mislata (*Valencia) 26,100
Morón de la Frontera (26,047▲) 22,700
Móstoles (*Madrid) ‡108,290
Motril (35,471▲) 28,100
Murcia (290,414▲) ‡190,600
Onteniente 26,297
Orense (89,485▲) ‡77,600
Orihuela (51,163▲) ‡20,000
Oviedo ‡181,556
Palencia ‡67,755
Palma [de Mallorca] ‡287,389
Pamplona ‡175,833

C Census. E Official estimate. UE Unofficial estimate.
L Population within municipal limits of year specified. • Largest city in country.

* Population or designation of metropolitan area, including suburbs (see headnote).
▲ Population of an entire municipality, commune, or district, including rural area.
‡† Year of information specified at start of country.

Peñarroya-Pueblonuevo 13,579
Plasencia 28,574
Ponferrada ‡53,400
Pontevedra (64,722▲) ‡33,500
Portugalete (★Bilbao) ‡57,053
Prat de Llobregat (★Barcelona) ‡57,330
Priego [de Córdoba] (20,560▲) 12,300
Puente-Genil (25,277▲) 21,900
Puerto de la Cruz *(Canary Is.)* (50,173▲) 37,100
Puertollano ‡52,722
Rentería (★San Sebastián) 46,329
Reus ‡84,986
Ronda (30,099▲) 22,100
Rota 25,702
Rubí (★Barcelona) 35,855
Sabadell (★Barcelona) ‡188,344
Sagunto ‡57,840
Salamanca ‡144,446
San Adrián de Besós (★Barcelona) 37,286
San Baudilio de Llobregat (★Barcelona) ‡67,321
San Cristóbal de la Laguna (Canary Is.) (114,183▲) ‡24,900
San Fernando (★★Cádiz) ‡69,123
Sanlúcar (43,867▲) 31,500
San Sebastián (★290,000) ‡176,023
Santa Coloma de Gramanet (★Barcelona) ‡143,568
Santa Cruz de Tenerife *(Canary Is.)* ‡186,949
Santander ‡176,363
Santiago de Compostela (83,841▲) ‡61,100
Santurce-Antiguo (★Bilboa) ‡55,159
Segovia ‡49,583
Sestao (★Bilbao) 41,399
Sevilla (Seville) (★740,000) ‡630,329
Soria ‡29,315
Sueca 22,522
Talavera de la Reina ‡60,964
Tarragona ‡109,969
Tarrasa (★Barcelona) ‡160,403
Telde *(Canary Is.)* (58,503▲) ‡17,300
Teruel ‡24,856
Toledo ‡56,414
Tomelloso 26,089
Torrejón de Ardoz (★Madrid) ‡63,500
Torrelavega (55,695▲) ‡25,900
Torrente (★Valencia) 46,686
Tortosa (47,246▲) 20,400
Úbeda 30,223
Valencia (★1,140,000) ‡750,994
Valladolid ‡315,486
Vall de Uxó 25,087
Vélez-Málaga (38,249▲) 18,700
Vich 27,615
Vigo ‡260,059
Villanueva y Geltrú 41,229
Vitoria ‡185,271
Zamora ‡55,822
Zaragoza (Saragossa) ‡563,375

SPANISH NORTH AFRICA / Plazas de Soberanía en el Norte de África

1978 E 120,719

•Ceuta 64,567
Melilla 56,152

SRI LANKA

1977 E 13,940,000

Anuradhapura 38,000
Badulla 38,000
Battaramulla (★Colombo) (1971 C) 43,057
Batticaloa 40,000
•COLOMBO (★1,540,000) 616,000
Dalugama (★Colombo) (1971 C) 41,200
Dehiwala-Mount Lavinia (★Colombo) 169,000
Galle 79,000
Jaffna 118,000
Kalutara 32,000
Kandy 103,000
Kegalla 14,000
Kotikawatta (★Colombo) (1971 C) 43,764
Kotte (★Colombo) 102,000
Kurunegala 28,000
Maharagama (★Colombo) (1971 C) 40,378
Matale 34,000
Matara 40,000
Moratuwa (★Colombo) 104,000
Negombo 63,000
Ratnapura 32,000
Trincomalee 46,000

SUDAN / As-Sūdān

1973 C 12,427,795

Al-Fāshir 51,932
Al-Junaynah 35,424
Al-Khurṭūm Baḥrī (Khartoum North (★Khartoum) 150,991
Al-Qaḍārif 66,465
Al-Ubayyiḍ (El Obeid) 90,060
'Aṭbarah 66,116
Būr-Sūdān (Port Sudan) 132,631
Jūbā 56,737
Kassalā 98,751
•KHARTOUM (AL-KHARṬŪM) (★790,000) 333,921
Kūstī 65,257
Malakāl 34,898
Nyala 59,852
Umm Durmān (Omdurman) (★★Khartoum) 299,401
Wad Madanī 106,776
Wāw 52,752

SURINAME

1971 C 384,900

•PARAMARIBO (★175,000) 102,300

SWAZILAND

1976 C 494,534

•Manzini (★26,000) 10,019
MBABANE 23,109

SWEDEN / Sverige

1979 E 8,303,010

Counties

Älvsborg 424,240
Blekinge 154,135
Gävleborg 293,959
Göteborg och Bohus 713,242
Gotland 55,261
Halland 229,211
Jämtland 134,653
Jönköping 302,475
Kalmar 241,448
Kopparberg 285,545
Kristianstad 278,917
Kronoberg 172,401
Malmöhus 743,133
Norrbotten 266,983
Örebro 274,223
Östergötland 392,390
Skaraborg 268,702
Södermanland 252,026
Stockholm 1,524,266
Uppsala 241,722
Värmland 284,615
Västerbotten 241,898
Västernorrland 267,895
Västmanland 259,670

Cities

Alingsås (29,109▲) 19,800
Angelholm (29,397▲) 16,700
Arvika (26,962▲) 13,600
Avesta (26,471▲) 18,600
Boden (28,770▲) 20,200
Bollnäs (27,683▲) 11,100
Borås 102,914
Borlänge 46,318
Enköping (32,286▲) 18,800
Eskilstuna 90,414
Eslöv (26,939▲) 14,000
Falkenberg (34,610▲) 14,800
Falun (50,079▲) 31,000
Gällivare (24,661▲) 8,500
Gävle 87,364
Göteborg (Gothenburg) (★665,000) 434,699
Halmstad (75,663▲) 50,400
Härnösand (27,616▲) 19,400
Hässleholm (48,751▲) 17,000
Helsingborg 101,370
Huddinge (★Stockholm) 66,038
Hudiksvall (37,336▲) 15,200
Järfälla (★Stockholm) 52,442
Jönköping 107,652
Kalmar (52,657▲) 32,200
Karlshamn (31,907▲) 17,400
Karlskoga 37,070
Karlskrona (60,270▲) 33,400
Karlstad 73,904
Katrineholm (32,308▲) 22,700
Kiruna 30,177
Koping (27,291▲) 19,700
Kristianstad (68,675▲) 31,300
Kristinehamn (27,166▲) 20,700
Kungsbacka (42,905▲) 13,400
Landskrona 37,027
Lidingö (★Stockholm) 37,390
Linköping 111,866
Ljungby (27,097▲) 13,400
Ludvika 31,976
Luleå 67,190
Lund 78,003
Malmö (★305,000) 235,111
Mariestad (24,377▲) 16,200
Mjölby (25,885▲) 12,700
Mölndal (★Göteborg) 47,692
Motala (41,945▲) 25,100
Nacka (★Stockholm) 56,825
Nässjö (31,891▲) 18,200
Norrköping 119,993
Norrtälje (40,400▲) 31,200
Nyköping (63,918▲) 31,000
Örebro 116,877
Örnsköldsvik (60,665▲) 29,600
Oskarshamn (28,021▲) 19,000
Östersund (55,440▲) 41,000
Piteå (38,146▲) 17,400
Ronneby (30,270▲) 12,000
Sandviken 43,139
Skellefteå (73,647▲) 29,800
Skövde (45,847▲) 30,200
Söderhamn (31,264▲) 14,200
Södertälje (★Stockholm) 79,396
Sollefteå (26,133▲) 8,900
Sollentuna (★Stockholm) 45,864
Solna (★Stockholm) 51,324
•STOCKHOLM (★1,384,310) 649,384
Sundyberg (★Stockholm) 25,676
Sundsvall (94,358▲) 52,500
Täby (★Stockholm) 46,142
Trelleborg (34,473▲) 22,300
Trollhättan 49,846
Uddevalla (46,139▲) 32,300
Umeå (79,930▲) 52,800
Uppsala 145,032
Vänersborg (34,613▲) 20,600
Varberg (43,829▲) 19,800
Värnamo (30,156▲) 15,700
Västerås 117,257
Västervik (41,303▲) 21,000
Växjö (63,763▲) 41,500
Vetlanda (28,714▲) 12,400
Visby (Gotland) (55,261▲) 20,200

SWITZERLAND / Schweiz / Suisse / Svizzera

1980 E 6,314,200

Aarau (★51,100) 15,900
Adliswil (★Zürich) 16,100
Allschwil (★Basel) 18,000
Altdorf 8,200
Appenzell 5,300
Arbon (★15,100) 11,500
Arosa (1970 C) 2,717
Baar (★Zug) 15,300
Baden (★67,300) 13,900
Basel (Bâle) (★575,000) 180,900
Bellinzona (★33,700) 17,200
BERN (BERNE) (★282,400) 141,300
Biel (Bienne) (★87,000) 56,800
Bolligen (★Bern) 32,500
Bülach 12,200
Burgdorf (★17,900) 14,900
Château d'Oex (1970 C) 3,203
Chiasso 8,900
Chur (Coire) 32,500
Davos 11,200
Delémont 11,600
Einsiedeln 9,700
Emmen (★Luzern) 22,800
Frauenfeld 18,600
Fribourg (Freiburg) (★51,800) 37,700
Genève (Geneva) (★425,000) 151,100
Glarus 5,800
Grenchen (★25,300) 16,800
Herisau 13,900
Illnau (★Zürich) 14,600
Interlaken (1970 C) 4,735
Köniz (★Bern) 34,400
Kreuzlingen 16,100
Kriens (★Luzern) 21,200
La Chaux-de-Fonds 38,100
Langenthal (★21,900) 13,400
Lausanne (★225,200) 128,800
Lauterbrunnen (1970 C) 3,431
Le Locle 12,600
Liestal (★Basel) 11,700
Locarno (★41,600) 15,100
Lugano (★69,100) 28,000
Luzern (Lucerne) (★156,400) 62,400
Martigny 11,100
Meiringen (1970 C) 3,759
Monthey 11,400
Montreux (★★Vevey) 20,200
Morges (★19,100) 13,300
Neuchâtel (Neuenburg) (★59,000) 34,900
Nyon 12,500
Olten (★47,200) 19,200
Opfikon (★Zürich) 11,200
Riehen (★Basel) 20,600
Rorschach (★23,000) 9,800
Sankt Gallen (St.-Gall) (★112,000) 73,800
Schaffhausen (Schaffhouse) (★51,300) 31,900
Schwyz 12,100
Sierre 14,200
Sion (Sitten) 23,400
Solothurn (Soleure) (★34,500) 15,600
Thun (Thoune) (★65,400) 37,000
Uster 23,000
Vernier (★Genève) 28,000
Vevey (★60,400) 15,700
Wädenswil 18,300
Wettingen (★Baden) 18,200
Wil (★21,500) 15,100
Winterthur (★106,800) 86,100
Wohlen (★15,700) 11,600
Yverdon (Iferten) 20,800
Zug (Zoug) (★52,200) 21,900
•Zürich (★780,000) 374,200

SYRIA / As-Sūrīyah

1978 E 8,401,100

Aleppo (Ḥalab) 878,000
Al-Ḥasakah 29,900
Al-Lādhiqīyah (Latakia) 204,000
Al-Qāmishlī (1970 C) 47,714
Ar-Raqqah 48,500
As-Suwaydā' 30,400
•DAMASCUS (DIMASHQ) (1979 E) (★1,550,000) 1,156,000
Dayr az-Zawr 99,100
Dūmā (★Damascus) (1970 C) 30,980
Ḥamāh 180,000
Ḥimṣ (Homs) 306,000
Idlib 52,600
Mukhayyam al-Yarmūk (★Damascus) (1970 C) 64,273

TAIWAN / T'aiwan

1977 E 16,813,127

Changhua (166,612▲) 129,000
Chiai 252,972
Chilung (Keelung) 345,392
Chungho (★T'aipei) 175,778
Chungli (Chunli) (180,689▲) 151,000
Chutung 52,000
Fengshan (Kaohsiunghsien) (★Kaohsiung) 177,982
Fengyüan (T'aichunghsien) (121,491▲) 94,000
Hsichih 51,000
Hsinchu 233,459
Hsinchuang (★T'aipei) 124,609
Hsintien (★T'aipei) 145,809
Hsinying (T'ainanhsien) 45,000
Hualien 101,010
Ilan (78,983▲) 66,000
Kangshan 58,000
Kaohsiung (★1,480,000) 1,172,977
Lotung 49,000
Lukang (Luchiang) 32,000
Makung (Penghuhsien) 23,000
Miaoli 66,000
Nant'ou 60,000
Panch'iao (T'aipeihsien) (★T'aipei) 314,848
Peikang 31,000
P'ingtung 182,114
Sanch'ung (★T'aipei) 292,909
Shulin (★T'aipei) 54,000
T'aichung 585,205
T'ainan 572,590
•T'AIPEI (★3,825,000) 2,196,237
T'aitung (111,647▲) 78,000
T'aoyüan 163,404
Touliu (Yünlin) 31,000
Yungho (★T'aipei) 162,731

TANZANIA

1978 C 17,557,000

Arusha 48,000
•DAR-ES-SALAAM 870,000
Dodoma (1970 E) 28,000
Iringa (1967 C) 21,746
Morogoro (1970 E) 30,000
Moshi 52,000
Mwanza 171,000
Tabora (1970 E) 23,000
Tanga 144,000
Ujiji (1967 C) 21,369
Zanzibar (1975 E) 80,000

THAILAND / Prathet Thai

1972 E 36,286,000

Ayutthaya 46,664
•BANGKOK (KRUNG THEP) (★3,375,000) 3,133,834
Ban Pong 22,036
Chachoengsao 27,071
Chiang Mai 93,353
Chon Buri 46,368
Hat Yai 57,255
Hua Hin 24,041
Khon Kaen 35,055
Lampang 42,007
Lop Buri 33,302
Nakhon Phanom 21,019
Nakhon Pathom 37,807
Nakhon Ratchasima 77,397
Nakhon Sawan 51,378
Nakhon Si Thammarat 50,761
Narathiwat 24,069
Nong Khai 24,680
Nonthaburi (★Bangkok) 25,654
Pattani 26,243
Phayao 22,217
Phet Buri 32,928
Phitsanulok 70,649
Phuket 38,493
Rat Buri 34,966
Samut Prakan (★Bangkok) 44,916
Samut Sakhon 39,982
Sara Buri 23,300
Songkhla 50,687
Suphan Buri 20,128
Surat Thani (Ban Don) 35,560
Surin 27,995
Trang 35,859
Ubon Ratchathani 52,171
Udon Thani 70,110
Warin Chamrap 25,850
Yala 39,983

TOGO

1977 E 2,348,000

•LOMÉ 229,400
Palimé 25,500
Sokodé 33,500

TONGA

1976 C 90,085

•NUKUALOFA 18,312

TRINIDAD & TOBAGO

1977 E 1,118,500

Arima (1970 C) 11,792
Débé (★Port of Spain) (1970 UE) 13,200
Point Fortin (1970 C) 7,738
•PORT OF SPAIN (★395,000) 42,950
Princess Town (1970 C) 7,784
San Fernando (★73,000) 36,650
San Juan (★Port of Spain) (1970 C) 30,802
Scarborough *(Tobago)* (1970 C) 1,724
Tunapuna (★Port of Spain) (1970 C) 11,984

TUNISIA / Tunisie

1975 C 5,588,209

Ariana (★Tunis) 47,833
Béja 39,226
Bizerte (Binzert) 62,856
Gabès 40,585
Gafsa 42,225
Hammam Lif (★Tunis) 35,634
Kairouan 54,546
Kasserine 22,594
La Goulette (★Tunis) 41,912
Le Bardo (★Tunis) 49,367
Menzel Bourguiba 42,111
Moknine 26,035
Monastir 26,759
Msaken 33,559
Nabeul 30,498
Sfax (★260,000) 171,297
Sousse 69,530
•TUNIS (★915,000) 550,404

TURKEY / Türkiye

1980 C 45,217,556

(Cities designated (E) are in Turkey in Europe)

Adana 568,513
Adapazarı 131,400
Adıyaman 55,030
Afyonkarahisar 73,832
Akhisar 60,061
Aksaray 65,306
Akşehir 40,418
Alaşehir 25,605
Alibeyköy (★İstanbul) (1975 C) 33,387
Amasya 48,010
ANKARA (★2,290,000) 2,203,729
Antakya (Antioch) 91,551
Antalya 176,446
Aydın 71,576
Bafra 50,167
Balıkesir 124,122
Bandırma 53,187
Batman 86,034
Bayburt 22,540
Bayrampaşa (E) (★İstanbul) (1975 C) 157,367
Bergama 34,386
Bolu 38,400
Bolvadin 30,733
Bornova (★İzmir) 54,965
Buca (★İzmir) (1975 C) 70,715
Burdur 44,750
Bursa 466,178
Çamdibi (★İzmir) (1975 C) 42,376
Çanakkale 39,943
Çankiri 35,040
Çarşamba 28,524
Ceyhan 57,097
Çorlu (E) 45,675
Çorum 76,020
Denizli 134,673
Diyarbakır 233,289
Düzce 37,659
Edirne (E) 71,927
Elâzığ 142,787
Ereğli *(Konya prov.)* 61,100
Ereğli *(Zonguldak prov.)* 50,096
Erzincan 73,335
Erzurum 190,121
Esenler (E) (★İstanbul) (1975 C) 49,379
Eskişehir 309,335
Gaziantep 371,000
Gebze (★İzmit) 58,212
Gelibolu (Gallipoli) (E) 14,554
Giresun 46,068
Gölcük 45,006
İnegöl 45,314
İskenderun (Alexandretta) 120,985
Isparta 91,544
•İstanbul (E) (★4,765,000) 2,853,539
İzmir (Smyrna) (★1,190,000) 753,749
İzmit (Kocaeli) 191,340
Kadirli 38,125
Kâğıthane (E) (★İstanbul) (1975 C) 164,448
Karabük 84,975
Karaköse (Ağrı) 41,103
Karaman 51,868
Kars 58,651
Kartal (★İstanbul) 67,627
Kastamonu 35,636
Kayseri 273,362
Keşan (E) 28,428
Kilis 58,686
Kırıkhan 47,688
Kırıkkale 175,235
Kırklareli (E) 36,183
Kırşehir 50,063
Konya 325,850
Kozan 42,410
Küçükçekmece (★İstanbul) (1975 C) 58,709
Kütahya 101,087
Lüleburgaz (E) 35,643
Malatya 184,390
Manisa 93,970
Maraş 177,919
Mardin 37,750
Mersin 215,300
Merzifon 32,031
Muğla 27,162
Muş 40,007
Mustafakemalpaşa 30,099
Nazilli 64,015
Nevşehir 37,106
Niğde 39,972
Nizip 39,267
Ödemiş 40,652
Ordu 52,080
Osmaniye 84,338
Polatlı 43,514
Reyhanli 30,843
Rize 41,740
Salihli 51,638
Samsun 198,266
Siirt 42,692
Silvan 44,412
Sinop 18,381
Sivas 173,831
Siverek 30,000
Söke 37,362
Tarsus 120,270
Tatvan 40,324
Tekirdağ (E) 51,327
Tire 32,242
Tokat 60,369
Trabzon 107,412
Turgutlu 55,575
Turhal 47,364
Urfa 148,434
Uşak 70,822
Uzunköprü (E) 27,706
Van 93,823
Viranşehir 41,934
Yozgat 36,220
Zile 30,066
Zonguldak (★195,000) 108,661

C Census. E Official estimate. UE Unofficial estimate.
L Population within municipal limits of year specified. • Largest city in country.

★ Population or designation of metropolitan area, including suburbs (see headnote).
▲ Population of an entire municipality, commune, or district, including rural area.
‡† Year of information specified at start of country.

TURKS & CAICOS IS.

1970 C ... 5,607
•GRAND TURK ... 2,287

UGANDA

1969 C ... 9,548,847

Arua ... 10,837
Bugembe ... 46,884
Entebbe ... 21,096
Fort Portal ... 7,949
Gulu ... 18,170
Jinja ... 52,509
Kabale ... 8,234
•KAMPALA ... 330,700
Lugazi ... 12,000
Masaka ... 12,987
Mbale ... 23,544
Soroti ... 12,398
Tororo ... 15,977

UNION OF SOVIET SOCIALIST REPUBLICS / Sojuz Sovetskich Socialističeskich Respublik

1980 E ... 264,486,000

UNION OF SOVIET SOCIALIST REPUBLICS IN EUROPE ... 172,022,000

Soviet Socialist Republics

Byelorussia (White Russia) ... 9,611,000
Estonia ... 1,474,000
Latvia ... 2,529,000
Lithuania ... 3,420,000
Moldavia ... 3,968,000
Russian Soviet Federated Socialist Republic (part) ... 101,067,000
Ukraine ... 49,953,000

Cities (1974 E, ‡1980 E)

Abdulino ... 25,000
Akhtubinsk ... 44,000
Akhtyrka ... 43,000
Alatyr ... 46,000
Aleksandriya ... ‡84,000
Aleksandrov ... ‡61,000
Aleksin ... ‡68,000
Almetyevsk ... ‡111,000
Alytus ... ‡57,000
Anapa ... 30,000
Antratsit (**Krasnyy Luch) ... ‡62,000
Apatity ... ‡64,000
Apsheronsk ... 33,000
Arkhangelsk ... ‡387,000
Armavir ... ‡163,000
Artemovsk ... ‡88,000
Arzamas ... ‡95,000
Astrakhan ... ‡465,000
Atkarsk ... 30,000
Avdeyevka (*Donetsk) ... 33,000
Azov ... ‡76,000
Bakhchisaray ... 20,000
Balakhna (*Gorkiy) ... 37,000
Balakleya ... 31,000
Balakovo ... ‡156,000
Balashikha (*Moscow) ... ‡119,000
Balashov ... ‡94,000
Baranovichi ... ‡135,000
Bataysk (*Rostov-na-Donu) ... ‡91,000
Belaya Kalitva ... 35,000
Belaya Tserkov ... ‡157,000
Belebey ... 39,000
Belgorod ... ‡248,000
Belgorod-Dnestrovskiy ... 37,000
Belorechensk ... 38,000
Beloretsk ... ‡72,000
Beltsy ... ‡128,000
Bendery ... ‡104,000
Berdichev ... ‡81,000
Berdyansk ... ‡124,000
Berezniki ... ‡186,000
Bezhetsk ... 30,000
Bobruysk ... ‡197,000
Bogoroditsk ... 32,000
Bogorodsk (*Gorkiy) ... 37,000
Bologoye ... 34,000
Bor (*Gorkiy) ... ‡63,000
Borislav ... 36,000
Borisoglebsk ... ‡67,000
Borispol' ... 36,000
Borisov ... ‡115,000
Borovichi ... ‡60,000
Boyarka (*Kiev) ... 31,000
Brest ... ‡186,000
Brezhnev ... ‡319,000
Brovary (*Kiev) ... ‡60,000
Bryanka (*Stakhanov) ... ‡63,000
Bryansk ... ‡401,000
Bugulma ... ‡81,000
Buguruslan ... ‡54,000
Buy ... 28,000
Buynaksk ... 42,000
Buzuluk ... ‡77,000
Chapayevsk ... ‡85,000
Chaykovskij ... ‡71,000
Cheboksary ... ‡323,000
Chekhov ... ‡53,000
Cherepovets ... ‡274,000
Cherkassy ... ‡234,000
Cherkessk ... ‡92,000
Chernigov ... ‡245,000
Chernovtsy ... ‡221,000
Chernyakhovsk (Insterburg) ... 34,000
Chervonograd ... ‡56,000
Chistopol ... ‡65,000
Chusovoy ... ‡57,000
Daugavpils ... ‡117,000
Debaltsevo ... 37,000
Derbent ... ‡71,000
Dimitrov (**Krasnoarmeysk) ... ‡59,000
Dimitrovgrad (Melekess) ... ‡108,000
Dmitrov ... ‡59,000
Dneprodzerzhinsk (**Dnepropetrovsk) ... ‡253,000
Dnepropetrovsk (*1,460,000) ... ‡1,083,000
Dobropolye ... 31,000
Dolgoprudnyy (*Moscow) ... ‡66,000
Domodedovo (*Moscow) ... 39,000
Donetsk *(Donetsk obl.)* (*2,075,000) ... ‡1,032,000
Donetsk *(Rostov obl.)* ... 42,000
Donskoy (*Novomoskovsk) ... 34,000
Drogobych ... ‡68,000
Druzhkovka (*Kramatorsk) ... ‡66,000
Dubna ... ‡56,000
Dzerzhinsk (*Gorkiy) ... ‡260,000
Dzerzhinsk (*Gorlovka) ... 46,000
Dzhankoy ... 46,000
Elektrostal ... ‡141,000
Elista ... ‡72,000
Engels (**Saratov) ... ‡165,000
Fastov ... ‡52,000
Feodosiya ... ‡78,000
Frolovo ... 38,000
Fryazino (*Moscow) ... 39,000
Furmanov ... 41,000
Galich ... 21,000
Gatchina (*Leningrad) ... ‡76,000
Gelendzhik ... 31,000
Georgiu-Dezh (Liski) ... ‡52,000
Georgiyevsk ... ‡55,000
Glazov ... ‡83,000
Glukhov ... 30,000
Gomel ... ‡393,000
Gorkiy (Gorki) (*1,900,000) ... ‡1,358,000
Gorlovka (*700,000) ... ‡337,000
Gorodets ... 35,000
Gremyachinsk ... 27,000
Grodno ... ‡202,000
Groznyy ... ‡377,000
Gryazi ... 42,000
Gubakha ... 32,000
Gubkin ... ‡65,000
Gudermes ... 34,000
Gukovo ... ‡69,000
Gusev ... 23,000
Gus-Khrustalnyy ... ‡72,000
Ilichevsk ... 43,000
Ingulets ... 35,000
Inta ... ‡51,000
Ishimbay ... ‡58,000
Ivano-Frankovsk ... ‡159,000
Ivanovo ... ‡466,000
Ivanteyevka (*Moscow) ... 41,000
Izberbash ... 20,000
Izmail ... ‡84,000
Izyum ... ‡61,000
Jelgava ... ‡69,000
Jurmala (*Rīga) ... ‡62,000
Kagul ... 31,000
Kakhovka ... 35,000
Kalinin ... ‡416,000
Kaliningrad (*Moscow) ... ‡135,000
Kaliningrad (Königsberg) ... ‡361,000
Kaluga ... ‡270,000
Kalush ... ‡61,000
Kamenets-Podolskiy ... ‡86,000
Kamenka ... 32,000
Kamensk-Shakhtinskiy ... ‡72,000
Kamyshin ... ‡112,000
Kanash ... 46,000
Kandalaksha ... 43,000
Kapsukas ... 33,000
Kashira ... 42,000
Kasimov ... 34,000
Kaspiysk ... 42,000
Kaunas ... ‡377,000
Kazan (*1,050,000) ... ‡1,002,000
Kerch ... ‡158,000
Kharkov (*1,750,000) ... ‡1,464,000
Khartsyzsk (*Donetsk) ... ‡59,000
Khasavyurt ... ‡67,000
Kherson ... ‡324,000
Khimki (*Moscow) ... ‡120,000
Khmelnitskiy ... ‡179,000
Kiev (Kiyev) (*2,430,000) ... ‡2,192,000
Kimovsk ... 44,000
Kimry ... ‡58,000
Kinel' ... 40,000
Kineshma ... ‡102,000
Kirishi ... 34,000
Kirov *(Kirov obl.)* ... ‡392,000
Kirov *(Kaluga obl.)* ... 30,000
Kirovo-Chepetsk ... ‡74,000
Kirovograd ... ‡242,000
Kirovsk *(Murmansk obl.)* ... 40,000
Kirovsk *(Voroshilovgrad obl.)* (*Stakhanov) ... 40,000
Kishinev ... ‡519,000
Kislovodsk ... ‡102,000
Kizel ... 42,000
Klaipėda (Memel) ... ‡178,000
Klimovsk (*Moscow) ... ‡55,000
Klin ... ‡92,000
Klintsy ... ‡69,000
Kobrin ... 28,000
Kohtla-Järve ... ‡73,000
Kolchugino ... 43,000
Kolomna ... ‡149,000
Kolomyya ... ‡53,000
Kolpino (*Leningrad) ... ‡118,000
Kommunarsk (*Stakhanov) ... ‡120,000
Komrat ... 24,000
Konakovo ... 33,000
Kondopoga ... 32,000
Konotop ... ‡84,000
Konstantinovka ... ‡113,000
Korosten ... ‡66,000
Kostroma ... ‡255,000
Kotel'nich ... 31,000
Kotlas ... ‡63,000
Kotovsk *(Odessa obl.)* ... 39,000
Kotovsk *(Tambov obl.)* ... 36,000
Kovel ... 40,000
Kovrov ... ‡144,000
Kramatorsk (*445,000) ... ‡180,000
Krasnoarmeysk (*155,000) ... ‡61,000
Krasnodar ... ‡572,000
Krasnodon ... 46,000
Krasnogorsk (*Moscow) ... ‡80,000
Krasnokamsk ... ‡56,000
Krasnyy Luch (*230,000) ... ‡107,000
Krasnyy Sulin ... 43,000
Kremenchug ... ‡212,000
Krichev ... 28,000
Krivoy Rog ... ‡657,000
Kronshtadt (*Leningrad) (1970 C) ... 39,477
Kropotkin ... ‡71,000
Krymsk (Krymskaya) ... 43,000
Kstovo (*Gorkiy) ... ‡60,000
Kudymkar (1975 E) ... 27,000
Kulebaki ... 46,000
Kumertau ... ‡54,000
Kungur ... ‡80,000
Kupyansk ... 34,000
Kurganinsk ... 38,000
Kursk ... ‡383,000
Kuybyshev (*1,440,000) ... ‡1,226,000
Kuznetsk ... ‡94,000
Labinsk ... ‡55,000
Leningrad (*5,360,000) ... ‡4,119,000
Leninogorsk ... ‡68,000
Lida ... ‡67,000
Liepāja ... ‡108,000
Lipetsk ... ‡405,000
Lisichansk (*365,000) ... ‡120,000
Livny ... 42,000
Lobnya (*Moscow) ... ‡53,000
Lomonosov (*Leningrad) ... 43,000
Lozovaya ... ‡55,000
Lubny ... ‡55,000
Luga ... 35,000
Lutsk ... ‡146,000
Lvov ... ‡676,000
Lysva ... ‡75,000
Lytkarino (*Moscow) ... 42,000
Lyubertsy (*Moscow) ... ‡162,000
Lyubotin ... 33,000
Lyudinovo ... 36,000
Makeyevka (**Donetsk) ... ‡439,000
Makhachkala ... ‡261,000
Marganets ... ‡51,000
Marks ... 22,000
Maykop ... ‡130,000
Mednogorsk ... 36,000
Melitopol ... ‡163,000
Michurinsk ... ‡102,000
Mikhaylovka ... ‡59,000
Millerovo ... 37,000
Mineralnyye Vody ... ‡68,000
Minsk (*1,330,000) ... ‡1,295,000
Mogilev ... ‡300,000
Molodechno ... ‡74,000
Monchegorsk ... ‡53,000
Morshansk (1977 E) ... 50,000
•MOSCOW (MOSKVA) (*11,950,000) ... ‡7,915,000
Mozdok ... 33,000
Mozhga ... 41,000
Mozyr ... ‡75,000
Mtsensk ... 34,000
Mukachevo ... ‡74,000
Murmansk ... ‡388,000
Murom ... ‡116,000
Mytishchi (*Moscow) ... ‡143,000
Nalchik ... ‡211,000
Naro-Fominsk ... ‡57,000
Narva ... ‡74,000
Neftekamsk ... ‡72,000
Nevinnomyssk ... ‡106,000
Nezhin ... ‡71,000
Nikolayev ... ‡449,000
Nikopol ... ‡149,000
Nizhnekamsk ... ‡139,000
Noginsk ... ‡120,000
Novaya Kakhovka ... ‡54,000
Novgorod ... ‡192,000
Novocheboksarsk ... ‡89,000
Novocherkassk ... ‡185,000
Novo-Ekonomicheskoye (**Krasnoarmeysk) (1970 C) ... 31,214
Novograd-Volynskiy ... 44,000
Novokuybyshevsk (*Kuybyshev) ... ‡110,000
Novomoskovsk *(Dnepropetrovsk obl.)* ... ‡70,000
Novomoskovsk *(Tula obl.)* (*370,000) ... ‡147,000
Novopolotsk ... ‡70,000
Novorossiysk ... ‡162,000
Novoshakhtinsk ... ‡105,000
Novo-Troitsk ... ‡97,000
Novovolynsk ... 44,000
Novozybkov ... 39,000
Nyandoma ... 23,000
Obninsk ... ‡76,000
Odessa (*1,120,000) ... ‡1,057,000
Odintsovo (*Moscow) ... ‡104,000
Oktyabr'sk ... 33,000
Oktyabr'skiy ... ‡91,000
Onega ... 25,000
Ordzhonikidze *(Severo-Osetinsk obl.)* ... ‡283,000
Ordzhonikidze *(Dnepropetrovsk obl.)* ... 39,000
Orekhovo-Zuyevo (*200,000) ... ‡133,000
Orel ... ‡309,000
Orenburg ... ‡471,000
Orsha ... ‡113,000
Orsk ... ‡252,000
Otradnyy ... 46,000
Panevėžys ... ‡104,000
Pärnu ... ‡51,000
Pavlograd ... ‡111,000
Pavlovo ... ‡69,000
Pavlovskiy Posad ... ‡71,000
Pechora ... ‡57,000
Penza ... ‡490,000
Pereslavl-Zalesskiy ... 33,000
Pereval'sk (*Stakhanov) ... 32,000
Perm (*1,075,000) ... ‡1,008,000
Pervomaysk (*Stakhanov) *(Voroshilovgrad obl.)* ... 46,000
Pervomaysk *(Nikolayev obl.)* ... ‡73,000
Petrodvorets (*Leningrad) ... ‡74,000
Petrovsk ... 34,000
Petrozavodsk ... ‡238,000
Pinsk ... ‡93,000
Podolsk (*Moscow) ... ‡203,000
Polotsk ... ‡72,000
Poltava ... ‡282,000
Priluki ... ‡66,000
Prokhladnyy ... 44,000
Pskov ... ‡177,000
Pugachev ... 35,000
Pushkin (*Leningrad) ... ‡89,000
Pushkino ... ‡71,000
Pyatigorsk ... ‡112,000
Ramenskoye (*Moscow) ... ‡79,000
Rasskazovo ... 40,000
Rechitsa ... ‡62,000
Reutov (*Moscow) ... ‡62,000
Rēzekne ... 34,000
Rīga (*920,000) ... ‡843,000
Rodniki ... 30,000
Romny ... ‡53,000
Roslavl ... ‡56,000
Rossosh' ... 38,000
Rostov ... 31,000
Rostov-na-Donu (*1,075,000) ... ‡946,000
Rovenki ... ‡62,000
Rovno ... ‡185,000
Rtishchevo ... 41,000
Rubezhnoye (**Lisichansk) ... ‡66,000
Ruzayevka ... 44,000
Ryazan ... ‡462,000
Rybinsk ... ‡241,000
Rybnitsa ... 39,000
Rzhev ... ‡69,000
Safonovo ... ‡53,000
Salavat ... ‡140,000
Salsk ... ‡58,000
Saransk ... ‡271,000
Sarapul ... ‡107,000
Saratov (*1,090,000) ... ‡864,000
Serdobsk ... 37,000
Serpukhov ... ‡141,000
Sevastopol ... ‡308,000
Severodonetsk (**Lisichansk) ... ‡115,000
Severodvinsk (Molotovsk) ... ‡203,000
Severomorsk ... ‡51,000
Shakhtersk (**Torez) ... ‡70,000
Shakhty ... ‡212,000
Shchekino ... ‡71,000
Shchelkovo (*Moscow) ... ‡101,000
Shebekino ... 36,000
Shepetovka ... 42,000
Shostka ... ‡82,000
Shumerlya ... 35,000
Shuya ... ‡72,000
Šiauliai ... ‡121,000
Sibay ... 40,000
Simferopol ... ‡307,000
Slantsy ... 42,000
Slavyansk (**Kramatorsk) ... ‡141,000
Slavyansk-na-Kubani ... ‡55,000
Slobodskoy ... 36,000
Slutsk ... 39,000
Smela ... ‡63,000
Smolensk ... ‡305,000
Snezhnoye (*Torez) ... ‡67,000
Sochi ... ‡291,000
Sokol ... 48,000
Soligorsk ... ‡68,000
Solikamsk ... ‡102,000
Solnechnogorsk (*Moscow) ... 37,000
Solntsevo (*Moscow) ... ‡62,000
Sovetsk ... 40,000
Stakhanov (Kadiyevka) (*590,000) ... ‡108,000
Staraya Russa ... 37,000
Staryy Oskol ... ‡123,000
Stavropol ... ‡265,000
Sterlitamak ... ‡224,000
Stryy ... ‡56,000
Stupino ... ‡71,000
Sumy ... ‡233,000
Suzdal (1959 C) ... 9,000
Sverdlovsk ... ‡75,000
Svetlogorsk ... ‡56,000
Svetlovodsk (Kremges) ... 41,000
Syktyvkar ... ‡175,000
Syzran ... ‡168,000
Taganrog ... ‡278,000
Tallinn ... ‡436,000
Tambov ... ‡270,000
Tartu ... ‡106,000
Ternopol ... ‡149,000
Teykovo ... 42,000
Tikhoretsk ... ‡64,000
Tikhvin ... ‡61,000
Timashevsk ... 31,000
Tiraspol ... 142,000
Tokmak ... 39,000
Tolyatti (Stavropol) ... ‡517,000
Torez (Chistyakovo) (*295,000) ... ‡87,000
Torzhok (1977 E) ... 50,000
Tuapse ... ‡61,000
Tula (*615,000) ... ‡518,000
Tuymazy ... 42,000
Ufa (*1,000,000) ... ‡986,000
Uglich ... 37,000
Ukhta ... ‡89,000
Ulyanovsk ... ‡473,000
Uman ... ‡80,000
Uryupinsk ... 39,000
Ustinov ... ‡562,000
Ust'-Labinsk ... 38,000
Uzhgorod ... ‡93,000
Uzlovaya (Novomoskovsk)** ... ‡65,000
Valuyki ... 30,000
Velikiye Luki ... ‡103,000
Velikiy Ustyug ... 38,000
Ventspils ... 44,000
Vichuga ... ‡52,000
Vidnoye ... 40,000
Vilnius ... ‡492,000
Vinnitsa ... ‡323,000
Vitebsk ... ‡303,000
Vladimir ... ‡301,000
Vogodonsk ... ‡109,000
Volgograd (Stalingrad) (*1,230,000) ... ‡939,000
Volkhov ... 48,000
Vologda ... ‡241,000
Volsk ... ‡65,000
Volzhsk ... ‡53,000
Volzhskiy (*Volgograd) ... ‡214,000
Vorkuta ... ‡101,000
Voronezh ... ‡796,000
Voroshilovgrad (Lugansk) ... ‡469,000
Voskresensk ... ‡77,000
Votkinsk ... ‡92,000
Voznesensk ... 39,000
Vyatskiye Polyany ... 35,000
Vyazma ... ‡52,000
Vyazniki ... 44,000
Vyborg ... ‡77,000
Vyksa ... ‡54,000
Vyshniy Volochek ... ‡71,000
Yalta ... ‡81,000
Yaroslavl ... ‡603,000
Yartsevo ... 39,000
Yasinovataya ... 39,000
Yefremov ... ‡53,000
Yegoryevsk ... ‡73,000
Yelabuga ... 35,000
Yelets ... ‡112,000
Yenakiyevo (**Gorlovka) ... ‡115,000
Yessentuki ... ‡79,000
Yevpatoriya ... ‡95,000
Yeysk ... ‡72,000
Yoshkar-Ola ... ‡207,000
Yuryev-Polskiy ... 23,000
Zagorsk ... ‡108,000
Zaporozhye ... ‡799,000
Zavolzh'ye ... 38,000
Zelenodolsk ... ‡85,000
Zelenograd (*Moscow) ... ‡132,000
Zelenokumsk ... 30,000
Zhdanov ... ‡507,000
Zheleznodorozhnyy (*Moscow) ... ‡78,000
Zheleznogorsk ... ‡67,000
Zheltyye Vody ... ‡53,000
Zhigulevsk (1977 E) ... 50,000
Zhitomir ... ‡250,000
Zhlobin ... 29,000
Zhmerinka ... 38,000
Zhukovskiy ... ‡92,000

UNION OF SOVIET SOCIALIST REPUBLICS IN ASIA ... 92,464,000

Soviet Socialist Republics

Armenia ... 3,074,000
Azerbaidzhan ... 6,112,000
Georgia ... 5,041,000
Kazakh S.S.R. ... 14,858,000
Kirghiz S.S.R. ... 3,588,000
Russian Soviet Federated Socialist Republic (part) ... 37,298,000
Tadzhik S.S.R. ... 3,901,000
Turkmen S.S.R. ... 2,827,000
Uzbek S.S.R. ... 15,765,000

Cities (1974 E, ‡1980 E)

Abakan ... ‡133,000
Abay ... 41,000
Abovyan (*Yerevan) ... 32,000
Achinsk ... ‡117,000
Akhaltsikhe ... 19,000
Aktyubinsk ... ‡197,000
Alapayevsk (1977 E) ... 52,000
Aldan ... 20,000
Aleysk ... 37,000
Ali-Bayramly ... 38,000
Alma-Ata (*970,000) ... ‡928,000
Almalyk ... ‡102,000
Andizhan ... ‡233,000
Angarsk ... ‡241,000
Angren ... ‡108,000
Anzhero-Sudzhensk ... ‡107,000
Aral'sk ... 39,000
Arkalyk (1975 E) ... 35,000
Arsenyev ... ‡61,000
Artem ... ‡69,000
Artemovskiy ... 38,000
Arys ... 28,000
Asbest ... ‡80,000
Asha ... 38,000
Ashkhabad ... ‡318,000
Asino ... 31,000
Atbasar ... 39,000
Ayaguz ... 40,000
Baku (*1,800,000) ... ‡1,030,000
Balkhash ... ‡78,000
Barabinsk ... 37,000
Barnaul (*600,000) ... ‡542,000
Batumi ... ‡124,000
Bayram-Ali ... 36,000
Bekabad (Begovat) ... ‡69,000
Belogorsk ... ‡64,000
Belovo ... ‡112,000
Berdsk (*Novosibirsk) ... ‡68,000
Berezovskiy (*Sverdlovsk) ... 39,000
Berezovskiy *(Kemerovo obl.)* ... 37,000
Birobidzhan ... ‡70,000
Biysk ... ‡213,000
Blagoveshchensk ... ‡175,000
Bratsk ... ‡219,000
Bukhara ... ‡188,000
Chardzhou ... ‡143,000
Chebarkul' ... 42,000
Chelkar ... 20,000
Chelyabinsk (*1,215,000) ... ‡1,042,000
Cheremkhovo ... ‡75,000
Chernogorsk ... ‡73,000
Chimkent ... ‡327,000
Chirchik (*Tashkent) ... ‡134,000
Chita ... ‡308,000
Chu ... 35,000
Chust ... 31,000
Dudinka (1975 E) ... 23,000
Dushanbe ... ‡501,000
Dzhalal-Abad ... ‡55,000
Dzhambul ... ‡270,000
Dzhetygara ... 39,000
Dzhezkazgan ... ‡92,000
Dzhizak ... ‡71,000
Echmiadzin (*Yerevan) ... 37,000
Ekibastuz ... ‡74,000

C Census. E Official estimate. UE Unofficial estimate.
L Population within municipal limits of year specified. • Largest city in country.
* Population or designation of metropolitan area, including suburbs (see headnote).
▲ Population of an entire municipality, commune, or district, including rural area.
‡† Year of information specified at start of country.

Fergana ‡177,000
Frunze ‡543,000
Gagra 22,000
Geokchay 30,000
Gori ‡57,000
Gorno-Altaysk (1975 E) 39,000
Gulistan (1975 E) 39,000
Guryev ‡134,000
Igarka 16,000
Irbit ‡52,000
Irkutsk ‡561,000
Ishim ‡62,000
Iskitim ‡60,000
Kachkanar 38,000
Kafan 31,000
Kagan 38,000
Kamen-na-Obi 40,000
Kamensk-Uralskiy ‡189,000
Kamyshlov 31,000
Kansk ‡100,000
Karaganda ‡577,000
Karpinsk 37,000
Karshi ‡113,000
Kartaly 44,000
Katta-Kurgan ‡54,000
Kemerovo ‡478,000
Kentau ‡52,000
Kerki (1967E) 18,000
Khabarovsk ‡538,000
Khanty-Mansiysk (1975 E) 26,000
Khiva 26,000
Khodzheyli 40,000
Kholmsk 43,000
Khorog (1975 E) 15,000
Kirovabad ‡237,000
Kirovakan ‡149,000
Kiselevsk (**Prokopyevsk) ‡122,000
Kokand ‡154,000
Kokchetav ‡106,000
Komsomolsk-na-Amure ‡269,000
Kopeysk (*Chelyabinsk) ‡146,000
Korkino ‡63,000
Korsakov 40,000
Krasnokamensk 54,000
Krasnotur'insk ‡61,000
Krasnoufimsk 40,000
Krasnouralsk 40,000
Krasnovodsk ‡53,000
Krasnoyarsk ‡807,000
Kuba 19,000
Kulyab ‡57,000
Kurgan ‡316,000
Kurgan-Tyube 39,000
Kushva 43,000
Kustanay ‡169,000
Kutaisi ‡197,000
Kuybyshev 44,000
Kyakhta 16,000
Kyshtym 39,000
Kyzyl ‡67,000
Kyzyl-Kiya 33,000
Kzyl-Orda ‡159,000
Leninabad ‡132,000
Leninakan ‡210,000
Leninogorsk ‡54,000
Leninsk 31,000
Leninsk-Kuznetskiy ‡133,000
Lenkoran 38,000
Lesozavodsk 38,000
Magadan ‡124,000
Magnitogorsk ‡410,000
Margelan ‡112,000
Mariinsk 40,000
Mary ‡76,000
Mezhdurechensk ‡93,000
Miass ‡152,000
Mingechaur ‡63,000
Minusinsk ‡61,000
Myski 38,000
Nakhichevan-na-Arakse (1975 E) 37,000
Nakhodka ‡136,000
Namangan ‡234,000
Naryn (1975 E) 26,000
Navoy ‡86,000
Nazarovo ‡55,000
Nazyvayevsk 15,000
Nebit-Dag ‡73,000
Nefteyugansk 51,000
Nev'yansk 31,000
Nikolayevsk-na-Amure 33,000
Nizhneudinsk 42,000
Nizhnevartovsk ‡122,000
Nizhniy Tagil ‡400,000
Norilsk ‡182,000
Novoaltaysk (*Barnaul) ‡50,000
Novokazalinsk (1970 C) 34,815
Novokuznetsk ‡545,000
Novosibirsk (*1,460,000) ‡1,328,000
Nukus ‡113,000
Omsk (*1,040,000) ‡1,028,000
Osh ‡173,000
Osinniki ‡60,000
Partizansk (Suchan) 49,000
Pavlodar ‡281,000
Pervouralsk ‡130,000
Petropavlovsk ‡209,000
Petropavlovsk-Kamchatskiy ‡219,000
Polevskoy ‡64,000
Poti (1977 E) 54,000
Prokopyevsk (*395,000) ‡266,000
Przhevalsk ‡52,000
Razdan 33,000
Revda ‡63,000
Rezh 34,000
Rubtsovsk ‡158,000
Rudnyy ‡111,000
Rustavi (*Tbilisi) ‡132,000
Rybachye 33,000
Samarkand ‡481,000
Saran ‡56,000
Satka 44,000
Semipalatinsk ‡286,000
Serov ‡101,000
Shadrinsk ‡82,000
Shakhtinsk ‡51,000
Shchuchinsk 46,000
Sheki (Nukha) 44,000
Shevchenko ‡116,000
Spassk-Dalniy ‡53,000
Sukhumi ‡116,000
Sumgait *Baku) ‡196,000
Surgut ‡121,000
Sverdlovsk (*1,450,000) ‡1,225,000
Svobodnyy ‡75,000
Taldy-Kurgan ‡91,000
Tashauz ‡87,000
Tashkent (*2,015,000) ‡1,816,000
Tavda 47,000
Tayshet 35,000
Tbilisi (*1,240,000) ‡1,080,000
Temirtau ‡215,000
Termez ‡58,000
Tobolsk ‡64,000
Tokmak ‡60,000
Tomsk ‡431,000
Troitsk ‡83,000
Tselinograd (Akmolinsk) ‡237,000
Tskhinvali (1975 E) 34,000
Tulun ‡52,000
Turkestan ‡69,000
Tyumen ‡369,000
Ulan-Ude ‡305,000
Uralsk ‡170,000
Ura-Tyube 36,000
Urgench ‡103,000
Usolye-Sibirskoye ‡104,000
Ussuriysk ‡148,000
Ust-Ilimsk ‡76,000
Ust-Kamenogorsk ‡280,000
Ust-Kut ‡51,000
Verkhniy Ufaley 38,000
Verkhnyaya Pyshma *Sverdlovsk) 40,000
Verkhnyaya Salda ‡55,000
Vladivostok ‡558,000
Yakutsk ‡155,000
Yangi-Yul ‡64,000
Yerevan (*1,155,000) ‡1,036,000
Yermak 40,000
Yurga ‡80,000
Yuzhno-Sakhalinsk ‡143,000
Zima (1977 E) 51,000
Zlatoust ‡199,000
Zugdidi 41,000
Zyryanovsk ‡52,000

UNITED ARAB EMIRATES / Ittiḥād al-Imārāt al-'Arabīyah

1968 C 180,200

ABU DHABI (ABŪ ẒABY) (1973 E) 50,000
'Ajmān 3,725
Al Fujayrah 760
Ash Shāriqah 19,200
•Dubai (Dubayy) (1970 E) 60,000
Ra's al Khaymah 5,300
Umm al Qaywayn 2,900

UNITED KINGDOM

1979 E 55,880,000

Political Divisions

ENGLAND 46,396,100
WALES 2,774,700
SCOTLAND 5,167,000
NORTHERN IRELAND 1,542,200

ENGLAND

Metropolitan Counties

Greater London 6,877,100
Greater Manchester 2,648,300
South York 1,301,300
Tyne & Wear 1,155,900
West Midlands 2,696,000
West York 2,064,100

Non-metropolitan Counties

Avon 924,200
Bedford 498,800
Berks 682,000
Buckingham 535,800
Cambridge 579,300
Cheshire 926,500
Cleveland 568,600
Cornwall & Isles of Scilly 419,300
Cumbria 469,900
Derby 898,300
Devon 952,100
Dorset 591,100
Durham 603,200
East Sussex 654,600
Essex 1,446,700
Gloucester 497,100
Hampshire 1,459,500
Hereford & Worcester 617,900
Hertford 952,000
Humberside 849,600
Isle of Wight 115,300
Kent 1,456,100
Lancashire 1,369,700
Leicester 836,300
Lincoln 533,800
Merseyside 1,531,600
Norfolk 686,300
Northampton 523,300
Northumberland 289,800
North York 663,200
Nottingham 974,100
Oxford 542,100
Shropshire 369,500
Somerset 415,500
Stafford 999,900
Suffolk 597,600
Surrey 993,700
Warwick 468,900
West Sussex 643,800
Wilts 516,400

***Cities* *(1979 E or ‡1973 E)**

Abingdon (*Oxford) ‡20,130
Accrington (Hyndburn) (**Blackburn) 79,400
Adur (*Brighton) 57,700
Aldershot (Rushmoor) (*London) 81,000
Aldridge-Brownhills (Walsall) *‡89,370*
Andover ‡27,620
Ashford ‡36,380
Ashton-under-Lyne (Tameside) (**Manchester) 218,500
Aycliffe (1971 C) 20,190
Aylesbury ‡41,420
Banbury ‡31,060
Barnsley 221,800
Barnstaple ‡17,820
Barrow-in-Furness 71,100
Basildon (*London) 148,200
Basingstoke ‡60,910
Bath 83,900
Batley (*Leeds) ‡41,630
Battle (1971 C) 4,987
Bebington (Wirral) *‡62,500*
Bedford ‡74,390
Bedworth (Nuneaton) *‡41,600*
Beeston & Stapleford (*Nottingham) ‡65,360
Benfleet (Castle Point) (*London) 84,400
Berkhamsted (*London) ‡15,920
Berwick-upon-Tweed ‡11,610
Bexhill-on-Sea ‡34,680
Birkenhead (Wirral) (*Liverpool) 342,300
Birmingham (*2,660,000) 1,033,900
Bishop Auckland ‡32,940
Bishop's Stortford (*London) ‡21,720
Blackburn (*221,900) 142,500
Blackpool (*275,000) 145,400
Bletchley ‡33,450
Blyth (Blyth Valley) 75,700
Blyth Valley see Blyth
Bodmin ‡10,430
Bognor Regis ‡34,620
Bolton (**Manchester) 260,100
Bootle (*Liverpool) ‡71,160
Boston ‡26,700
Bournemouth (*315,000) 144,200
Bracknell (*London) (1971 C) 33,953
Bradford (**Leeds) 461,600
Bradford-on-Avon ‡8,310
Braintree ‡26,300
Brentwood (*London) ‡58,690
Bridgwater ‡26,700
Bridlington ‡26,920
Brighouse (*Halifax) ‡35,320
Brighton (*425,000) 152,700
Bristol (*635,000) 408,000
Broadstairs and St. Peters ‡21,670
Bromsgrove (*Birmingham) ‡41,430
Broxbourne see Cheshunt
Burgess Hill (*London) ‡20,030
Burnham-on-Sea ‡12,690
Burnley (*160,000) 92,300
Burton-upon-Trent ‡49,480
Bury (**Manchester) 178,600
Bury St. Edmunds ‡26,800
Buxton ‡20,050
Camborne-Redruth ‡43,970
Cambridge 101,600
Cannock (Cannock Chase) (*Birmingham) 83,600
Cannock Chase see Cannock
Canterbury ‡34,510
Carlisle ‡70,930
Carlton (Gedling) (*Nottingham) 102,800
Castleford (*Leeds) ‡37,650
Castle Point see Benfleet
Caterham & Warlingham (*London) ‡35,840
Chatham (Medway) (*London) 147,400
Cheadle and Gatley (Stockport) *‡62,460*
Chelmsford (*London) ‡58,320
Cheltenham 85,000
Chertsey (Runnymede) (*London) 72,800
Chesham (*London) ‡20,830
Cheshunt (Broxbourne) (*London) 79,200
Chester ‡61,370
Chesterfield (*127,000) 96,300
Chester-le-Street (*Newcastle) ‡20,720
Chichester ‡20,940
Chigwell (*London) ‡54,220
Chippenham ‡18,550
Chorley (**Preston) ‡31,800
Christchurch (*Bournemouth) 38,600
Cirencester ‡14,500
Clacton-on-Sea ‡39,380
Cleethorpes (*Grimsby) ‡37,200
Clevedon ‡15,140
Coalville ‡28,740
Colchester ‡79,600
Consett (*Newcastle) ‡35,080
Corby 53,000
Coventry (*655,000) 339,300
Cowes ‡19,190
Crawley (*London) 71,800
Crewe ‡50,450
Crosby (*Liverpool) ‡56,750
Cuckfield (*London) ‡26,500
Darlington ‡85,120
Dartford (*London) ‡44,130
Dartmouth ‡6,720
Dawley ‡30,720
Deal ‡26,840
Derby (*270,000) 215,900
Dewsbury (**Leeds) ‡50,560
Doncaster (*160,000) ‡81,530
Dorchester ‡13,880
Dorking (*London) ‡22,410
Dover ‡34,160
Dronfield (*Sheffield) ‡20,000
Dudley (**Birmingham) 296,000
Dunstable (*Luton) ‡32,090
Durham ‡29,490
Eastbourne 73,100
East Grinstead (*London) ‡19,420
Eastleigh (*Southampton) ‡46,340
East Retford ‡18,260
Ellesmere Port (*Liverpool) ‡63,870
Elmbridge see Walton and Weybridge
Ely ‡10,630
Epsom and Ewell (*London) 70,500
Esher (Elmbridge) *‡63,970*
Eton (*London) ‡4,950
Evesham ‡14,090
Exeter 95,600
Exmouth ‡26,840
Falmouth ‡17,530
Fareham (*Portsmouth) 85,000
Farnham (*London) ‡33,140
Faversham ‡15,010
Felixstowe ‡19,460
Fleet (*London) ‡22,930
Fleetwood (**Blackpool) ‡30,070
Folkestone ‡45,610
Formby (*Liverpool) ‡24,850
Frimley & Camberley (*London) ‡47,390
Frome ‡13,780
Gainsborough ‡17,440
Gateshead (*Newcastle) 212,200
Gedling see Carlton
Gillingham (*London) 92,800
Glastonbury ‡6,580
Glossop (*Manchester) ‡24,820
Gloucester (*115,000) 91,300
Goole ‡17,920
Gosport (*Portsmouth) 79,400
Grantham ‡27,830
Gravesend (Gravesham) (*London) 95,900
Gravesham see Gravesend
Great Yarmouth ‡49,410
Grimsby (*145,000) 91,900
Guildford (*London) ‡58,470
Halesowen (Dudley) *‡54,120*
Halifax (*173,000) ‡88,580
Haltemprice (*Hull) ‡54,850
Halton see Widnes
Harlow (*London) 79,100
Harrogate ‡64,620
Hartlepool (**Middlesbrough) 95,100
Harwich ‡15,280
Hastings 74,200
Havant (*Portsmouth) 116,100
Haverhill ‡14,550
Heanor †24,590
Hemel Hempstead (*London) ‡71,150
Hemsworth ‡14,680
Henley-on-Thames ‡11,860
Hereford 46,800
Herne Bay ‡26,510
Hertford (*London) ‡20,760
Hertsmere (*London) 87,800
Hexham ‡9,820
High Wycombe ‡61,190
Hinckley (**Coventry) ‡49,310
Hitchin ‡29,190
Horsham (*London) ‡26,770
Hove (*Brighton) 87,800
Hucknall (*Nottingham) ‡27,110
Huddersfield (*209,000) ‡130,060
Huntingdon & Godmanchester ‡17,200
Huyton-with-Roby (Knowsley) (*Liverpool) 179,700
Hyndburn see Accrington
Hythe ‡12,210
Ilkeston (*Nottingham) ‡33,690
Ipswich 118,900
Keighley (Bradford) *‡56,040*
Kendal ‡22,440
Kenilworth (*Coventry) ‡19,730
Keswick ‡4,790
Kettering ‡44,480
Kidderminster ‡49,960
King's Lynn ‡29,990
Kingston-upon-Hull (Hull) (*350,000) 274,500
Kingswood (*Bristol) 82,100
Kirkby (Knowsley) *‡59,100*
Knowsley see Huyton-with-Roby
Lancaster (*100,000) ‡50,570
Leamington Spa (**Coventry) ‡44,060
Leatherhead (*London) ‡40,830
Leeds (*1,540,000) 724,300
Leek ‡19,460
Leicester (*480,000) 276,600
Leighton-Linslade ‡22,590
Letchworth ‡31,520
Lewes ‡14,170
Leyland (South Ribble) (*Preston) 96,100
Lichfield ‡23,690
Lincoln 71,900
Littlehampton ‡20,320
Liverpool (*1,535,000) 520,200
•LONDON (*11,050,000) 6,877,100
Longbenton (North Tyneside) *‡50,120*
Long Eaton (*Nottingham) ‡33,560
Loughborough ‡49,010
Lowestoft ‡53,260
Ludlow (1971 C) 7,466
Luton (*215,000) 160,300
Lymington ‡36,760
Lytham St. Annes (*Blackpool) ‡42,120
Macclesfield ‡45,420
Maidenhead (*London) ‡48,210
Maidstone ‡72,110
Malvern ‡30,420
Manchester (*2,800,000) 479,100
Mansfield (*198,000) ‡58,450
Margate ‡50,290
Market Harborough ‡15,230
Marlborough ‡6,370
Matlock ‡20,300
Medway see Chatham
Melton Mowbray ‡20,680
Middlesbrough (*580,000) 153,000
Middleton (Rochdale) *‡53,340*
Morecambe [& Heysham] (**Lancaster) ‡42,010
Morley (Leeds) *‡44,790*
Nelson (**Burnley) ‡31,220
Newark-upon-Trent ‡24,760
Newbury ‡24,850
Newcastle-under-Lyme (**Stoke-on-Trent) ‡75,940
Newcastle-upon-Tyne (*1,295,000) 287,300
Newmarket ‡13,370
Newport ‡22,430
Newton Abbot ‡19,940
Northampton 154,900
North Tyneside see Tynemouth
Northwich ‡17,710
Norwich (*220,000) 119,300
Nottingham (*645,000) 278,600
Nuneaton (**Coventry) 110,300
Oadby and Wigston (*Leicester) 52,300
Oakengates ‡17,340
Oakham ‡7,280
Oldham (**Manchester) 223,500
Ormskirk (*Liverpool) ‡28,860
Oxford (*240,000) 122,400
Penrith ‡11,400
Penzance ‡19,360
Peterborough ‡72,270
Peterlee (1971 C) 21,836
Plymouth (*295,000) 255,500
Poole (**Bournemouth) 115,500
Portsmouth (*490,000) 191,000
Preston (*245,000) 126,200
Queenborough-in-Sheppey ‡31,550
Ramsgate ‡40,090
Rawtenstall ‡20,950
Rayleigh (*London) ‡26,740
Reading (*200,000) 138,400
Redditch (*Birmingham) 64,300
Reigate and Banstead (*London) 114,000
Rickmansworth (*London) ‡29,030
Ripon ‡12,580
Rochdale (**Manchester) 209,000
*Rochester (Medway) (*London)* ‡56,030
Rotherham (**Sheffield) 248,800
Rugby ‡60,380
Runnymede see Chertsey
Rushden ‡21,840
Rushmoor see Aldershot
Ryde ‡23,170
Rye ‡4,530
Saint Albans (*London) 124,300
St. Austell [with Fowey] ‡32,710
St. Helens 188,700
Sale (Trafford) *‡59,060*
Salford (*Manchester) 252,600
Salisbury ‡35,460
Sandwell see Smethwick
Sandwich ‡4,420
Scarborough ‡43,300
Scunthorpe 67,200
Seaford ‡18,020
Seaham (*Newcastle) ‡22,470
Selby ‡11,590
Sevenoaks (*London) ‡18,160
Sheffield (*705,000) 544,200
Shrewsbury ‡56,120
Sittingbourne & Milton ‡32,830
Skelmersdale [& Holland] (*Manchester) ‡35,850
Slough (*London) 98,400
Smethwick (Sandwell) (*Birmingham) 306,900
Solihull (*Birmingham) 198,300
Southampton (*410,000) 207,800
Southend-on-Sea (*London) 154,700
Southport (**Liverpool) ‡86,030
South Ribble see Leyland
South Shields (South Tyneside) (**Newcastle) 162,600
South Tyneside see South Shields
Spenborough (*Leeds) ‡41,460
Spennymoor ‡19,050
Stafford ‡54,860
Staines (Spelthorne) (*London) 93,500
Stamford ‡14,980
Stanley (*Newcastle) ‡42,280
Stevenage 73,100
Stockport (*Manchester) 291,700
Stockton-on-Tees (**Middlesbrough) 171,800
Stoke-on-Trent (*445,000) 257,200
Stourbridge (Dudley) *‡56,530*
Stratford-on-Avon ‡20,080
Stretford (Trafford) (*Manchester) 224,000
Stroud ‡19,600
Sudbury ‡8,860
Sunderland (**Newcastle) 300,800
Sutton Coldfield (Birmingham) *‡83,630*
Sutton-in-Ashfield (**Mansfield) ‡40,330
Swadlincote ‡21,060
Swindon (Thamesdown) 143,800
Tameside see Ashton-under-Lyne
Tamworth 60,300
Taunton ‡37,570
Tewkesbury ‡9,210
Thamesdown see Swindon
Thetford ‡15,690
Thornton Cleveleys (*Blackpool) ‡27,090
Thurrock (*London) 127,100
Tiverton ‡16,190
Todmorden ‡14,540
Tonbridge (*London) ‡31,410
Torquay (Torbay) 108,700
Trafford see Stretford

(England continued)

C Census. E Official estimate. UE Unofficial estimate.
L Population within municipal limits of year specified. • Largest city in country.

* Population or designation of metropolitan area, including suburbs (see headnote).
▲ Population of an entire municipality, commune, or district, including rural area.
‡† Year of information specified at start of country.

* Italicized place names are now a part of the city shown in parentheses following the place name. These changes are part of the April 1974 reorganization of local administrative areas.

(England continued)

Trowbridge ... ‡20,120
Truro ... ‡15,690
Tunbridge Wells ... ‡44,800
Tynemouth (North Tyneside) (★Newcastle) ... 193,000
Ulverston ... ‡12,370
Wakefield (★★Leeds) ... ‡58,490
Wallasey (Wirral) ... *‡94,520*
Walsall (★★Birmingham) ... 263,400
Walton and Weybridge (Elmbridge) (★London) ... 110,000
Wansbeck ... 61,000
Warrington ... 168,200
Warwick (★★Coventry) ... ‡17,870
Watford (★London) ... 76,500
Wellingborough ... ‡39,570
Wells ... ‡8,960
Welwyn Garden City (★London) ... ‡39,900
West Bridgford (★Nottingham) ... ‡28,340
West Bromwich (Sandwell) ... *‡162,740*
Weston-super-Mare ... ‡51,960
Weymouth and Portland ... 57,700
Whitby ... ‡12,710
Whitehaven ... ‡26,260
Whitstable ... ‡26,980
Widnes (Halton) ... 120,700
Wigan (★★Manchester) ... 311,200
Wilmslow (★Manchester) ... ‡31,250
Winchester ... ‡31,070
Windermere ... ‡7,860
Windsor (New Windsor) (★London) ... ‡29,660
Winsford ... ‡26,920
Wirral see Birkenhead
Woking (★London) ... 80,500
Wokingham ... ‡22,390
Wolverhampton (★★Birmingham) ... 258,200
Worcester ... 75,000
Workington ... ‡28,260
Worksop ... ‡30,590
Worthing (★★Brighton) ... 90,600
Yeovil ... ‡26,180
York (★140,000) ... 100,900

WALES

Counties

Clwyd ... 385,100
Dyfed ... 325,600
Gwent ... 435,900
Gwynedd ... 226,300
Mid Glamorgan ... 537,500
Powys ... 107,100
South Glamorgan ... 390,600
West Glamorgan ... 366,600

Cities (1973 E)

Aberdare ... 38,030
Abertillery (★Newport) ... 20,550
Aberystwyth ... 10,900
Bangor ... 16,030
Barry (★Cardiff) ... 42,780
Brecon ... 6,460
Bridgend ... 14,690
Caernarfon ... 8,840
Caerphilly (★Cardiff) ... 42,190
•CARDIFF (1979 E) (★625,000) ... 282,000
Carmarthen ... 12,860
Colwyn Bay ... 25,370
Ebbw Vale ... 25,670
Flint ... 15,070
Islwyn (★Newport) (1979 E) ... 63,400
Llandudno ... 17,700
Llanelli ... 25,870
Merthyr Tydfil ... 53,680
Milford Haven ... 13,960
Monmouth ... 7,000
Neath (★★Swansea) ... 27,280
Newport (1979 E) (★310,000) ... 132,800
Pembroke ... 14,570
Pontypool (Torfaen) (★★Newport) (1979 E) ... 90,400
Pontypridd (★Cardiff) ... 34,180
Port Talbot (★132,000) ... 50,200
Prestatyn ... 15,480
Rhondda (★★Cardiff) (1979 E) ... 81,800
Rhyl ... 22,150
Swansea (1979 E) (★270,000) ... 186,900
Torfaen see Pontypool
Wrexham ... 39,530

SCOTLAND

Regions (1979 E)

Borders ... 99,938
Central ... 271,177
Dumfries and Galloway ... 142,547
Fife ... 340,170
Grampian ... 469,168
Highland ... 190,507
Lothian ... 750,728
Orkney (Island Area) ... 18,134
Shetland (Island Area) ... 22,111
Strathclyde ... 2,431,101
Tayside ... 401,661
Western Isles (Island Area) ... 29,758

Cities (‡1979 E or 1974 E)

Aberdeen ... ‡209,189
Airdrie (Monklands) (★Glasgow) ... *38,833*
Alloa ... 13,498
Arbroath ... 23,207
Ardrossan (★★Irvine) ... 11,166
Ayr (★97,000) ... 47,991
Bearsden and Milngavie (★Glasgow) ... ‡38,812
Clydebank (★Glasgow) ... ‡52,835
Cumbernauld (★Glasgow) ... ‡49,300
Dumbarton (★Glasgow) ... 25,440
Dumfries ... 29,431
Dundee ... ‡190,793
Dunfermline (★124,893) ... 53,418
East Kilbride (★Glasgow) ... ‡76,000
EDINBURGH (★635,000) ... ‡455,126
Elgin ... 17,589
Falkirk (★142,058) ... 36,589
Forfar ... 11,395
•Glasgow (★1,830,000) ... ‡794,316
Glenrothes (★★Kirkcaldy) ... ‡36,500
Grangemouth (★★Falkirk) ... 24,347
Hamilton (★Glasgow) ... ‡107,490
Hawick ... 16,378
Helensburgh (★Glasgow) ... 13,956
Inverclyde (Greenock) ... ‡102,598
Inverness ... 36,595
Irvine (★97,000) ... ‡57,900
Johnstone (★Glasgow) ... 23,603
Kilmarnock (★82,000) ... 50,318
Kirkcaldy (★148,028) ... 50,063
Kirkintilloch (★Glasgow) ... 26,845
Kirkwall ... 4,814
Lerwick ... 6,307
Livingston ... ‡35,900
Monklands (Coatbridge) ... ‡109,645
Montrose ... 10,112
Motherwell (★Glasgow) ... ‡150,857
Oban ... 6,410
Paisley (Renfrew) (★Glasgow) ... *94,025*
Perth ... 44,066
Peterhead ... 14,994
Port Glasgow (Inverclyde) ... *22,278*
Prestwick (★Ayr) ... 13,138
Renfrew (★★Glasgow) ... ‡214,534
St. Andrews ... 13,137
Stirling (★58,000) ... 29,818
Stranraer ... 10,170
Thurso ... 9,107
Wick ... 7,842

NORTHERN IRELAND

Cities (1971 C)

Armagh ... 13,606
•BELFAST (1978 E) (★710,000) ... 354,400
Castlereagh (★Belfast) (1978 E) ... 63,900
Enniskillen ... 9,679
Larne ... 18,482
Lisburn (★Belfast) ... 31,836
Londonderry (1973 E) (★87,000) ... 51,200
Lurgan (★59,000) ... 25,431
Newry ... 20,279
Newtownabbey (★Belfast) (1978 E) ... 75,000
North Down (Bangor) (★Belfast) (1978 E) ... 61,500
Omagh ... 14,594
Portadown (★★Lurgan) ... 22,207

UPPER VOLTA (BURKINA FASO)

1977 E ... 6,390,000

Bobo Dioulasso ... 120,000
Koudougou ... 38,000
•OUAGADOUGOU ... 180,000
Quahigouya ... 27,000

URUGUAY

1975 C ... 2,763,964

Artigas ... 29,256
Canelones (1963 C) ... 14,180
Colonia del Sacramento (1963 C) ... 12,839
Dolores (1963 C) ... 12,483
Durazno ... 25,811
Florida ... 25,030
Fray Bentos (1963 C) ... 20,755
La Paz (★Montevideo) (1963 C) ... 13,204
Las Piedras (★Montevideo) ... 53,983
Maldonado (1963 C) ... 15,361
Melo ... 38,260
Mercedes ... 34,667
Minas ... 35,433
•MONTEVIDEO (★1,350,000) ... 1,229 748
Paysandú ... 62,412
Rivera ... 49 013
Rocha (1963 C) ... 19,063
Salto ... 71,881
San Carlos (1963 C) ... 13,663
San José de Mayo ... 28,427
Santa Lucía (1963 C) ... 12,630
Tacuarembo ... 34,157
Treinta y Tres ... 25,757
Trinidad (1963 C) ... 15,460

VANUATU

1979 C ... 112,596

•VILA (★14,801) ... 10,158

VATICAN CITY / Città del Vaticano

1977 E ... 723

VENEZUELA

1971 C ... 10,721,522

Acarigua ... 56,743
Altagracia de Orituco ... 18,717
Anaco ... 29,003
Araure ... 22,466
Bachaquero ... 17,896
Barcelona ... 78,201
Barinas ... 56,329
Barquisimeto ... 330,815
Baruta (★Caracas) ... 121,066
Boconó ... 15,915
Cabimas ... 118,037
Cagua ... 29,601
Calabozo ... 38,360
Caraballeda (★Caracas) ... 20,725
•CARACAS (★2,475,000) ... 1,658,500
Caripito ... 19,053
Carora ... 36,115
Carúpano ... 50,935
Catia La Mar (★Caracas) ... 62,200
Chacao (★Caracas) ... 78,528
Chivacoa ... 19,210
Ciudad Bolívar ... 103,728
Ciudad Guayana (Santo Tomé de Guayana) ... 143,540
Ciudad Ojeda (Lagunillas) ... 83,083
Coro ... 68,701
Cumaná ... 119,751
El Tigre ... 49,801
El Tocuyo ... 19,351
El Vigía ... 20,970
Guacara ... 38,793
Guanare ... 34,148
Guarenas (★Caracas) ... 33,374
Guatire (★Caracas) ... 18,604
Güigüe ... 18,067
La Guaira (★Caracas) ... 20,344
La Victoria ... 40,731
Los Dos Caminos (★Caracas) ... 59,211
Los Teques (★Caracas) ... 63,106
Machiques ... 18,898
Maiquetía (★Caracas) ... 59,238
Maracaibo ... 651,574
Maracay ... 255,134
Mariara ... 24,284
Maturín ... 98,188
Mérida ... 74,214
Morón ... 19,451
Ocumare del Tuy ... 24,229
Palo Negro ... 19,173
Petare (★Caracas) ... 227,727
Porlamar ... 31,985
Pozuelos ... 44,011
Puerto Cabello ... 72,103
Puerto la Cruz ... 63,276
Punta Cardón ... 18,182
Punto Fijo ... 55,483
San Antonio del Táchira ... 20,342
San Carlos ... 21,029
San Carlos del Zulia ... 26,762
San Cristobal ... 151,717
San Felipe ... 42,905
San Fernando de Apure ... 38,960
San José de Guanipa ... 22,530
San Juan de Colón ... 16,615
San Juan de los Morros ... 38,265
San Mateo ... 17,389
Táriba ... 15,683
Trujillo ... 25,921
Tucupita ... 21,417
Turmero ... 43,832
Upata ... 22,793
Valencia ... 367,171
Valera ... 76,740
Valle de la Pascua ... 36,809
Villa de Cura ... 27,832
Villa del Rosario ... 17,491
Yaritagua ... 21,363
Zaraza ... 15,480

VIETNAM / Viet-nam Dan-chu Cong-hoa

1967 E ... 37,073,000

Bac-ninh (1960 C) ... 22,520
Ban-me-thuot ... 37,500
Bien-hoa ... 52,200
Cam-pha (1971 E) ... 90,000
Cam-ranh ... 46,600
Can-tho ... 61,100
Chau-phu (1971 E) ... 40,400
Da-lat (1971 E) ... 86,600
Da-nang (1971 E) ... 437,700
Gia-dinh (★Saigon) (1968 E) ... 151,100
Ha-dong (1960 C) ... 25,001
Hai-duong (1960 C) ... 24,752
Hai-phong (1971 E) (650,000▲) ... 400,000
HANOI (1971 E) ... 1,600,000
•Ho Chi Minh City (Than-pho Ho Chi Minh) (Saigon) (1971 E) (★2,750,000) ... 1,804,900
Hon-gai (1960 C) ... 35,412
Hue (1971 E) ... 199,900
Khanh-hung ... 40,300
Long-xuyen ... 45,800
My-tho ... 62,700
Nam-dinh (1960 C) ... 86,132
Nha-trang ... 59,600
Phan-rang ... 21,900
Phan-thiet ... 58,300
Phu-cuong (1971 E) ... 34,400
Phu-vinh (1971 E) ... 51,500
Pleiku ... 23,700
Quang-tri (1971 E) ... 16,900
Quan-long ... 33,500
Qui-nhon ... 50,000
Rach-gia ... 56,000
Sa-dec ... 34,800
Truc-giang ... 45,200
Vinh (1960 C) ... 43,954
Vinh-loi ... 41,700
Vinh-long (1971 E) ... 35,300
Vung-tau ... 54,200

VIRGIN ISLANDS, BRITISH

1970 C ... 10,484

•ROAD TOWN ... 2,183

VIRGIN ISLANDS OF THE U.S.

1970 C ... 62,468

•CHARLOTTE AMALIE ... 12,220
Christiansted ... 3,020

WALLIS AND FUTUNA
Wallis et Futuna

1976 C ... 9,192

MATA-UTU ... 558
•Ono ... 624

WESTERN SAHARA

1974 E ... 108,000

•EL AAIÚN (AIÚN) ... 20,000

WESTERN SAMOA

1976 C ... 151,983

•APIA ... 32,099

YEMEN / Al-Yaman

1979 E ... 5,785,000

Hodeida (Al Ḩudaydah) (1978 E) ... 106,080
Mocha (Al-Mukhā) (1975 C) ... 1,110
•ṢAN'Ā' ... 192,045
Ta'izz (1975 C) ... 81,000

YEMEN, PEOPLE'S DEMOCRATIC REPUBLIC OF / Al-Yaman ash-Sha'bīyah

1973 E ... 1,555,000

•ADEN (1977 E) ... 271,600
Al Mukallā (1970 E) ... 65,000
Madīnat ash Sha'b (Al-Ittiḩad) (1966 UE) ... 10,000

YUGOSLAVIA / Jugoslavija

1976 E ... 21,560,000

People's Republics

Bosnia-Hercegovina (Bosna i Hercegovina) ... 4,029,000
Croatia (Hrvatska) ... 4,530,000
Macedonia (Makedonija) ... 1,784,000
Montenegro (Crna Gora) ... 565,000
Serbia (Srbija) ... 8,860,000
Slovenia (Slovenija) ... 1,792,000

Cities (1971 C)

Banja Luka ... 89 866
Bečej ... 26,470
•BELGRADE (BEOGRAD) (★1,150,000) ... 770,140
Bihać ... 24,026
Bijeljina ... 24,722
Bitola ... 65,851
Bor ... 29,039
Brčko ... 25,422
Čačak ... 38,170
Celje ... 31,788
Cetinje ... 11,892
Djakovica ... 29,638
Dubrovnik ... 31,106
Karlovac ... 47,532
Kikinda ... 37,487
Kosovska Mitrovica ... 42,241
Kragujevac ... 71,180
Kraljevo ... 27,817
Kranj ... 27,209
Kruševac ... 29,469
Kumanovo ... 46,406
Leskovac ... 44,255
Ljubljana ... 173,662
Maribor ... 97,167
Mostar ... 47,606
Nikšić ... 28,547
Niš ... 127,178
Novi Pazar ... 29,072
Novi Sad ... 141,712
Ohrid ... 26,370
Osijek ... 93,912
Pančevo (★Belgrade) ... 54,269
Peć ... 42,113
Pirot ... 29,228
Požarevac ... 33,121
Prilep ... 48,242
Priština ... 69,524
Prizren ... 41,661
Pula ... 47,414
Rijeka ... 132,933
Šabac ... 42,307
Sarajevo ... 244,045
Šibenik ... 30,090
Sisak ... 38,421
Skopje ... 312,092
Slavonski Brod ... 38,762
Smederevo ... 40,289
Sombor ... 43,971
Split ... 151,875
Sremska Mitrovica ... 31,921
Štip ... 27,289
Subotica ... 88,787
Svetozarevo ... 27,542
Tetovo ... 35,792
Titograd ... 54,509
Titovo Užice ... 34,312
Titov Veles ... 36,026
Tuzla ... 53,825
Valjevo ... 26,367
Varaždin ... 34,270
Vinkovci ... 29,072
Vranje ... 25,685
Vršac ... 34,231
Vukovar ... 30,149
Zadar ... 43,187
Zagreb ... 566,084
Zaječar ... 27,677
Zenica ... 51,279
Zrenjanin ... 59 580

ZAIRE / Zaïre

1974 E ... 24,222,000

Bandundu (1970 C) ... 74,467
Boma (1970 E) ... 61,100
Bukavu ... 182 000
Gandajika (1970 E) ... 60,100
Goma (1970 E) ... 48,600
Isiro (1970 E) ... 49,300
Kabinda (1970 E) ... 60,500
Kalemie (Albertville) (1970 E) ... 62,300
Kamina (1970 E) ... 56,300
Kananga (Luluabourg) ... 601,000
Kikwit ... 150,000
•KINSHASA (LÉOPOLDVILLE) (1975 E) ... 2,202,000
Kisangani (Stanleyville) ... 311,000
Kolwezi (1970 E) ... 81,600
Likasi (Jadotville) (1970 C) ... 146,394
Lubumbashi (Élisabethville) ... 404,000
Matadi ... 144,000
Mbandaka (Coquilhatville) ... 134,000
Mbanza Ngungu (1970 E) ... 55,800
Mbuji-Mayi (Bakwanga) ... 337,000
Mwene-Ditu (1970 E) ... 71,100

ZAMBIA

1980 E ... 5,834,000

Chililabombwe (Bancroft) ... 77,000
Chingola ... 192,000
Kabwe (Broken Hill) ... 147,000
Kalulushi ... 60,000
Kitwe ... 341,000
Livingstone ... 80,000
Luanshya ... 164,000
•LUSAKA ... 641,000
Mufulira ... 187,000
Ndola ... 323,000

ZIMBABWE (RHODESIA)

1979 E ... 7,130,000

Bulawayo (★363,000) ... 85,700
Fort Victoria (★24,000) ... 11,300
Gatooma (★33,000) ... 4,700
Gwelo (★70,000) ... 22,500
•HARARE (SALISBURY) (★633,000) ... 118,500
Harari (★Salisbury) (1969 C) ... 58,007
Highfield (★Salisbury) (1969 C) ... 52,560
Que Que (★51,000) ... 17,700
Sinola (★27,000) ... 7,200
Umtali (★64,000) ... 20,800
Wankie (★33,000) ... 14,700

C Census. E Official estimate. UE Unofficial estimate.
L Population within municipal limits of year specified. • Largest city in country.
★ Population or designation of metropolitan area, including suburbs (see headnote).
▲ Population of an entire municipality, commune, or district, including rural area.
‡† Year of information specified at start of country.
* Italicized place names are now a part of the city shown in parentheses following the place name. These changes are part of the April 1974 reorganization of local administrative areas.

United States City and County Populations and ZIP Codes

The following alphabetical list shows populations for nearly 18,000 cities and counties and ZIP codes for cities. The state abbreviation following each name is that used by the United States Postal Service.

ZIP codes are listed for cities and towns after the state abbreviations. For each city with more than one ZIP code, the range of numbers assigned to the city is shown. For example, the ZIP code range for Chicago is 60601–99, and this indicates that the numbers between 60601 and 60699 are valid Chicago ZIP codes. ZIP code ranges are not listed for counties.

Populations for cities and towns appear as *italics* after the ZIP codes, and populations for counties appear after the state abbreviations. These populations are either 1980 census figures or, where census data are not available, estimates created by Rand McNally & Company. City populations are for central cities, not metropolitan areas. For New England, 1980 census populations are given for incorporated cities. Estimates are used for unincorporated places that are not treated separately by the census. "Town" (or "township") populations are not included unless the town is considered to be primarily urban and contains only one commonly used place-name.

Counties are identified by a square symbol (□).

Abbreviations for State Names

AK	Alaska
AL	Alaska
AR	Arkansas
AZ	Arizona
CA	California
CO	Colorado
CT	Connecticut
DC	District of Columbia
DE	Delaware
FL	Florida
GA	Georgia
HI	Hawaii
IA	Iowa
ID	Idaho
IL	Illinois
IN	Indiana
KS	Kansas
KY	Kentucky
LA	Louisiana
MA	Massachusetts
MD	Maryland
ME	Maine
MI	Michigan
MN	Minnesota
MO	Missouri
MS	Mississippi
MT	Montana
NC	North Carolina
ND	North Dakota
NE	Nebraska
NH	New Hampshire
NJ	New Jersey
NM	New Mexico
NV	Nevada
NY	New York
OH	Ohio
OK	Oklahoma
OR	Oregon
PA	Pennsylvania
RI	Rhode Island
SC	South Carolina
SD	South Dakota
TN	Tennessee
TX	Texas
UT	Utah
VA	Virginia
VT	Vermont
WA	Washington
WI	Wisconsin
WV	West Virginia
WY	Wyoming

A

Abbeville, AL 36310 • *3,155*
Abbeville, GA 31001 • *985*
Abbeville, LA 70510 • *12,391*
Abbeville, SC 29620 • *5,833*
Abbeville □, SC • *22,627*
Abbotsford, WI 54405 • *1,901*
Abbott Run Valley, RI 02864 • *1,300*
Abbottstown, PA 17301 • *689*
Aberdeen, ID 83210 • *1,528*
Aberdeen, MD 21001 • *11,533*
Aberdeen, MS 39730 • *7,184*
Aberdeen, NC 28315 • *1,945*
Aberdeen, OH 45101 • *1,566*
Aberdeen, SD 57401 • *25,851*
Aberdeen, WA 98520 • *18,739*
Abernathy, TX 79311 • *2,904*
Abilene, KS 67410 • *6,572*
Abilene, TX 79601–99 • *98,315*
Abingdon, IL 61410 • *4,210*
Abingdon, VA 24210 • *4,318*
Abington, MA 02351 • *13,517*
Abington, PA 19001 • *7,900*
Abita Springs, LA 70420 • *1,072*
Absarokee, MT 59001 • *750*
Absecon, NJ 08201 • *6,859*
Academia, OH 43050 • *1,447*
Acadia □, LA • *56,427*
Accomack □, VA • *31,268*
Ackerman, MS 39735 • *1,598*
Ackley, IA 50601 • *1,900*
Acton, CA 93510 • *900*
Acton, MA 01720 • *2,500*
Acushnet, MA 02743 • *6,400*
Acworth, GA 30101 • *3,648*
Ada, MN 56510 • *1,971*
Ada, OH 45810 • *5,669*
Ada, OK 74820 • *15,902*
Ada □, ID • *173,036*
Adair, IA 50002 • *883*
Adair □, IA • *9,509*
Adair □, KY • *15,233*
Adair □, MO • *24,870*
Adair □, OK • *18,575*
Adairsville, GA 30103 • *1,739*
Adairville, KY 42202 • *1,105*
Adams, MA 01220 • *10,381*
Adams, MN 55909 • *797*
Adams, NY 13605 • *1,701*
Adams, WI 53910 • *1,744*
Adams □, CO • *245,944*
Adams □, ID • *3,347*
Adams □, IL • *71,622*
Adams □, IN • *29,619*
Adams □, IA • *5,731*
Adams □, MS • *38,035*
Adams □, NE • *30,656*
Adams □, ND • *3,584*
Adams □, OH • *24,328*
Adams □, PA • *68,292*
Adams □, WA • *13,267*
Adams □, WI • *13,457*
Adams Center, NY 13606 • *800*
Adams City, CO 80022 • *2,200*
Adamston, NJ 08723 • *1,300*
Adamstown, PA 19501 • *1,119*
Adamsville, AL 35005 • *2,498*
Adamsville, TN 38310 • *1,453*
Addis, LA 70710 • *1,320*
Addison, AL 35540 • *746*
Addison, CT 06033 • *1,100*
Addison, IL 60101 • *29,826*
Addison, NY 14801 • *2,028*
Addison, TX 75001 • *5,553*
Addison □, VT • *29,406*
Addyston, OH 45001 • *1,195*
Adel, GA 31620 • *5,592*
Adel, IA 50003 • *2,846*
Adelanto, CA 92301 • *2,164*
Adena, OH 43901 • *1,062*
Adobe Acres, NM 87105 • *3,400*
Adrian, GA 31002 • *756*
Adrian, MI 49221 • *21,186*
Adrian, MN 56110 • *1,336*
Adrian, MO 64720 • *1,484*
Advance, MO 63730 • *1,054*
Affton, MO 63123 • *23,181*
Afton, IA 50830 • *985*
Afton, MN 55001 • *2,550*
Afton, NY 13730 • *982*
Afton, OK 74331 • *1,174*
Afton, WY 83110 • *1,481*
Agate Beach, OR 97365 • *700*
Agawam, MA 01001 • *10,300*
Agency, IA 52530 • *657*
Agua Fria, NM 87501 • *850*
Aguilar, CO 81020 • *624*
Ahoskie, NC 27910 • *4,887*
Ahwahnee, CA 93601 • *900*
Aiea, HI 96701 • *15,200*
Aiken, SC 29801 • *14,978*
Aiken □, SC • *105,625*
Ainsworth, NE 69210 • *2,256*
Air Park West, NE 68524 • *3,100*
Aitkin, MN 56431 • *1,770*
Aitkin □, MN • *13,404*
Ajo, AZ 85321 • *5,189*
Akron, AL 35441 • *604*
Akron, CO 80720 • *1,716*
Akron, IN 46910 • *1,045*
Akron, IA 51001 • *1,517*
Akron, NY 14001 • *2,971*
Akron, OH 44301–99 • *237,177*
Akron, PA 17501 • *3,471*
Alabaster, AL 35007 • *7,079*
Alachua, FL 32615 • *3,561*
Alachua □, FL • *151,348*
Alamance □, NC • *99,319*
Alameda, CA 94501 • *63,852*
Alameda, NM 87114 • *7,800*
Alameda □, CA • *1,105,379*
Alamo, GA 30411 • *993*
Alamo, TN 38001 • *2,615*
Alamo, TX 78516 • *5,831*
Alamogordo, NM 88310 • *24,024*
Alamo Heights, TX 78209 • *6,252*
Alamosa, CO 81101 • *6,830*
Alamosa □, CO • *11,799*
Alamosa East, CO 81101 • *1,175*
Alapaha, GA 31622 • *771*
Albany, CA 94706 • *15,130*
Albany, GA 31701–08 • *74,550*
Albany, IL 61230 • *1,014*
Albany, IN 47320 • *2,625*
Albany, KY 42602 • *2,083*
Albany, LA 70711 • *857*
Albany, MN 56307 • *1,569*
Albany, MO 64402 • *2,152*
Albany, NY 12201–99 • *101,727*
Albany, OH 45710 • *905*
Albany, OR 97321 • *26,678*
Albany, TX 76430 • *2,450*
Albany, WI 53502 • *1,051*
Albany □, NY • *285,909*
Albany □, WY • *29,062*
Albemarle, NC 28001 • *15,110*
Albemarle □, VA • *55,783*
Albert City, IA 50510 • *818*
Albert Lea, MN 56007 • *19,200*
Albertson, NY 11507 • *11,200*
Albertville, AL 35950 • *12,039*
Albia, IA 52531 • *4,184*
Albion, IL 62806 • *2,285*
Albion, IN 46701 • *1,637*
Albion, IA 50005 • *739*
Albion, MI 49224 • *11,059*
Albion, NE 68620 • *1,997*
Albion, NY 14411 • *4,897*
Albion, PA 16401 • *1,818*
Albion, RI 02802 • *1,200*
Albion, WA 99102 • *631*
Albuquerque, NM 87101–99 • *331,767*
Alburtis, PA 18011 • *1,428*
Alcalde, NM 87511 • *800*
Alcester, SD 57001 • *885*
Alcoa, TN 37701 • *6,870*
Alcona □, MI • *9,740*
Alcorn □, MS • *33,036*
Alda, NE 68810 • *601*
Alden, IA 50006 • *953*
Alden, MN 56009 • *687*
Alden, NY 14004 • *2,488*
Alden, PA 18634 • *800*
Alderson, WV 24910 • *1,375*
Aledo, IL 61231 • *3,881*
Aledo, TX 76008 • *1,027*
Alex, OK 73002 • *769*
Alexander □, IL • *12,264*
Alexander □, NC • *24,999*
Alexander City, AL 35010 • *13,807*
Alexander Mills, NC 28043 • *643*
Alexandria, IN 46001 • *6,028*
Alexandria, KY 41001 • *4,735*
Alexandria, LA 71301–03 • *51,565*
Alexandria, MN 56308 • *7,608*
Alexandria, TN 37012 • *689*
Alexandria, VA 22301–99 • *103,217*
Alexandria Bay, NY 13607 • *1,265*
Alexis, IL 61412 • *1,076*
Alfalfa □, OK • *7,077*
Alfred, NY 14802 • *4,907*
Alger, OH 45812 • *992*
Alger □, MI • *9,225*
Algoma, WI 54201 • *3,656*
Algona, IA 50511 • *6,289*
Algona, WA 98002 • *1,467*
Algonac, MI 48001 • *4,412*
Algonquin, IL 60102 • *5,834*
Algood, TN 38501 • *2,406*
Alhambra, CA 91801–99 • *64,615*
Alhambra, IL 62001 • *643*
Alice, TX 78332 • *20,961*
Aliceville, AL 35442 • *3,207*
Aliquippa, PA 15001 • *17,094*
Allamakee □, IA • *15,108*
Allardt, TN 38504 • *654*
Allegan, MI 49010 • *4,576*
Allegan □, MI • *81,555*
Allegany, NY 14706 • *2,078*
Allegany □, MD • *80,548*
Allegany □, NY • *51,742*
Alleghany □, NC • *9,587*
Alleghany □, VA • *14,333*
Allegheny □, PA • *1,450,085*
Allen, OK 74825 • *998*
Allen, TX 75002 • *8,314*
Allen □, IN • *294,335*
Allen □, KS • *1,564*
Allen □, KY • *14,128*
Allen □, LA • *21,390*
Allen □, OH • *112,241*
Allendale, IL 62410 • *613*
Allendale, NJ 07401 • *5,901*
Allendale, SC 29810 • *4,400*
Allendale □, SC • *10,700*
Allenhurst, GA 31301 • *606*
Allenhurst, NJ 07711 • *912*
Allen Park, MI 48101 • *34,196*
Allentown, NJ 08501 • *1,962*
Allentown, PA 18101–99 • *103,758*
Allerton, IA 50008 • *670*
Alliance, NE 69301 • *9,920*
Alliance, NC 28509 • *616*
Alliance, OH 44601 • *24,315*
Allison, IA 50602 • *1,132*
Allison, PA 15413 • *1,040*
Allison Park, PA 15101 • *5,600*
Allouez, WI 54301 • *13,753*
Alloway, NJ 08001 • *1,370*
Allyn, WA 98524 • *900*
Alma, AR 72921 • *2,755*
Alma, GA 31510 • *3,819*
Alma, KS 66401 • *925*
Alma, MI 48801 • *9,652*
Alma, NE 68920 • *1,369*
Alma, WI 54610 • *876*
Almont, MI 48003 • *1,857*
Aloha, OR 97007 • *10,000*
Alondra, CA 90249 • *12,096*
Alpaugh, CA 93201 • *900*
Alpena, MI 49707 • *12,214*
Alpena □, MI • *32,315*
Alpha, IL 61413 • *815*
Alpha, NJ 08865 • *2,644*
Alpharetta, GA 30201 • *3,128*
Alpine, NJ 07620 • *1,549*
Alpine, TX 79830 • *5,465*
Alpine, UT 84003 • *2,649*
Alpine □, CA • *1,097*
Alsip, IL 60658 • *17,134*
Alta, IA 51002 • *1,720*
Altadena, CA 91001 • *40,983*
Altamont, IL 62411 • *2,389*
Altamont, KS 67330 • *1,054*
Altamont, NY 12009 • *1,292*
Altamont, OR 97601 • *19,805*
Altamont, TN 37301 • *679*
Altamonte Springs, FL 32701 • *22,028*
Altavista, VA 24517 • *3,849*
Altheimer, AR 72004 • *1,231*
Alto, GA 30510 • *618*
Alto, TX 75925 • *1,203*
Alton, IL 62002 • *34,171*
Alton, IA 51003 • *986*
Alton, MO 65606 • *721*
Alton, NH 03809 • *900*
Altona, IL 61414 • *610*
Alton Bay, NH 03810 • *900*
Altoona, AL 35952 • *928*
Altoona, FL 32702 • *1,300*
Altoona, IA 50009 • *5,764*
Altoona, PA 16601–03 • *57,078*
Altoona, WI 54720 • *4,393*
Alturas, CA 96101 • *3,025*
Altus, OK 73521 • *23,101*
Alum Rock, CA 95127 • *17,471*
Alva, FL 33920 • *1,200*
Alva, OK 73717 • *6,416*
Alvarado, TX 76009 • *2,701*
Alvin, TX 77511 • *16,515*
Alvord, TX 76225 • *874*
Ama, LA 70031 • *875*
Amador □, CA • *19,314*
Amagansett, NY 11930 • *1,800*
Amanda, OH 43102 • *720*
Amarillo, TX 79101–99 • *149,230*
Ambler, PA 19002 • *6,628*
Amboy, IL 61310 • *2,377*
Amboy, MN 56010 • *606*
Ambridge, PA 15003 • *9,575*
Amelia, LA 70340 • *3,612*
Amelia, OH 45102 • *1,108*
Amelia □, VA • *8,405*
Amelia Court House, VA 23002 • *700*
Amenia, NY 12501 • *1,157*
American Falls, ID 83211 • *3,626*
American Fork, UT 84003 • *12,693*
Americus, GA 31709 • *16,120*
Americus, KS 66835 • *915*
Amery, WI 54001 • *2,404*
Ames, IA 50010 • *45,775*
Amesbury, MA 01913 • *13,971*
Amherst, MA 01002 • *26,300*
Amherst, NH 03031 • *750*
Amherst, NY 14226 • *66,100*
Amherst, OH 44001 • *10,638*
Amherst, TX 79312 • *971*
Amherst, VA 24521 • *1,135*
Amherst, WI 54406 • *701*
Amherst □, VA • *29,122*
Amherstdale, WV 25607 • *800*
Amite, LA 70422 • *4,301*
Amite □, MS • *13,369*
Amity, AR 71921 • *859*
Amity, OR 97101 • *1,092*
Amityville, NY 11701 • *9,076*
Ammon, ID 83401 • *4,669*
Amory, MS 38821 • *7,307*
Amsterdam, NY 12010 • *21,872*
Amsterdam, OH 43903 • *783*
Anacoco, LA 71403 • *820*
Anaconda, MT 59711 • *12,518*
Anacortes, WA 98221 • *9,013*
Anadarko, OK 73005 • *6,378*
Anaheim, CA 92801–99 • *219,494*
Anahola, HI 96703 • *915*
Anahuac, TX 77514 • *1,840*
Anamosa, IA 52205 • *4,958*
Anandale, LA 71301 • *2,000*
Anawalt, WV 24808 • *652*
Anchorage, AK 99501–40 • *174,431*
Anchorage, KY 40223 • *1,726*
Andalusia, AL 36420 • *10,415*
Andalusia, IL 61232 • *1,238*
Anderson, CA 96007 • *7,381*
Anderson, IN 46011–18 • *64,695*
Anderson, MO 64831 • *1,237*
Anderson, SC 29621–24 • *27,965*
Anderson □, KS • *8,749*
Anderson □, KY • *12,567*
Anderson □, SC • *133,235*
Anderson □, TN • *67,346*
Anderson □, TX • *38,381*
Andover, IL 61233 • *612*
Andover, KS 67002 • *2,801*
Andover, MA 01810 • *8,445*
Andover, MN 55303 • *9,387*
Andover, NY 14806 • *1,120*
Andover, OH 44003 • *1,205*
Andrew □, MO • *13,980*
Andrews, IN 46702 • *1,243*
Andrews, NC 28901 • *1,621*
Andrews, SC 29510 • *3,129*
Andrews, TX 79714 • *11,061*
Andrews □, TX • *13,323*
Androscoggin □, ME • *99,657*
Angelica, NY 14709 • *982*
Angelina □, TX • *64,172*
Angels Camp, CA 95222 • *2,302*
Angier, NC 27501 • *1,709*
Angleton, TX 77515 • *13,929*
Angola, IN 46703 • *5,486*
Angola, NY 14006 • *2,292*
Anguilla, MS 38721 • *950*
Anita, IA 50020 • *1,153*
Ankeny, IA 50021 • *15,429*
Anna, IL 62906 • *5,408*
Anna, OH 45302 • *1,038*
Annalee Heights, VA 22042 • *1,750*
Anna Maria, FL 33501 • *1,537*
Annandale, MN 55302 • *1,568*
Annandale, NJ 08801 • *1,040*
Annandale, VA 22003 • *35,300*
Annapolis, MD 21401–99 • *31,740*
Ann Arbor, MI 48103–09 • *107,966*
Annawan, IL 61234 • *908*
Anne Arundel □, MD • *370,775*
Anniston, AL 36201–05 • *29,523*
Annville, PA 17003 • *4,493*
Anoka, MN 55303 • *15,634*
Anoka □, MN • *195,998*
Ansley, NE 68814 • *644*
Anson, ME 04911 • *900*
Anson, TX 79501 • *2,831*
Anson □, NC • *25,649*
Ansonia, CT 06401 • *19,039*
Ansonia, OH 45303 • *1,267*
Ansonville, NC 28007 • *794*
Ansted, WV 25812 • *1,952*
Antelope □, NE • *8,675*
Anthon, IA 51004 • *687*
Anthony, FL 32617 • *1,200*
Anthony, KS 67003 • *2,661*
Anthony, NM 88021 • *3,285*
Anthony, RI 02816 • *4,500*
Antigo, WI 54409 • *8,653*
Antioch, CA 94509 • *42,683*
Antioch, IL 60002 • *4,419*
Antlers, OK 74523 • *2,989*
Anton, TX 79313 • *1,180*
Antonito, CO 81120 • *1,103*
Antrim, NH 03440 • *1,142*
Antrim □, MI • *16,194*
Antwerp, NY 13608 • *749*
Antwerp, OH 45813 • *1,765*
Apache, OK 73006 • *1,560*
Apache □, AZ • *52,108*
Apache Junction, AZ 85220 • *9,935*
Apalachicola, FL 32320 • *2,565*
Apalachin, NY 13732 • *1,233*
Apex, NC 27502 • *2,847*
Aplington, IA 50604 • *1,027*
Apollo, PA 15613 • *2,212*
Apopka, FL 32703 • *6,019*
Appalachia, VA 24216 • *2,418*
Appanoose □, IA • *15,511*

Apple Creek, OH 44606 • 741
Applegate, OR 97530 • 800
Appleton, MN 56208 • 1,842
Appleton, WI 54911–19 • 58,913
Appleton City, MO 64724 • 1,257
Apple Valley, CA 92307 • 14,305
Apple Valley, MN 55124 • 21,818
Applewood, CO 80401 • 7,200
Appleyard, WA 98801 • 1,500
Appling □, GA • 15,565
Appomattox, VA 24522 • 1,345
Appomattox □, VA • 11,971
Aptos, CA 95003 • 7,039
Aquebogue, NY 11931 • 1,300
Arab, AL 35016 • 5,967
Arabi, LA 70032 • 10,248
Aragon, GA 30104 • 855
Aransas □, TX • 14,260
Aransas Pass, TX 78336 • 7,173
Arapaho, OK 73620 • 851
Arapahoe, NE 68922 • 1,107
Arapahoe □, CO • 293,621
Arbuckle, CA 95912 • 1,306
Arbyrd, MO 63821 • 704
Arcade, CA 95821 • 37,600
Arcade, NY 14009 • 2,052
Arcadia, CA 91006 • 45,994
Arcadia, FL 33821 • 6,002
Arcadia, IN 46030 • 1,801
Arcadia, LA 71001 • 3,403
Arcadia, MO 63621 • 683
Arcadia, SC 29320 • 2,088
Arcadia, WI 54612 • 2,109
Arcanum, OH 45304 • 2,002
Arcata, CA 95521 • 12,850
Archbald, PA 18403 • 6,295
Archbold, OH 43502 • 3,318
Archdale, NC 27263 • 5,326
Archer, FL 32618 • 1,230
Archer □, TX • 7,266
Archer City, TX 76351 • 1,862
Archie, MO 64725 • 753
Archuleta □, CO • 3,664
Arco, ID 83213 • 1,241
Arcola, IL 61910 • 2,714
Arden, CA 95825 • 49,130
Arden Hills, MN 55112 • 8,012
Ardmore, AL 35739 • 1,096
Ardmore, IN 46628 • 3,400
Ardmore, MD 20706 • 900
Ardmore, OK 73401 • 23,689
Ardmore, PA 19003 • 13,600
Ardmore, TN 38449 • 835
Ardsley, NY 10502 • 4,183
Arenac □, MI • 14,706
Argenta, IL 62501 • 994
Argos, IN 46501 • 1,547
Argyle, MN 56713 • 741
Argyle, WI 53504 • 720
Ariton, AL 36311 • 844
Arizona Sunsites, AZ 85625 • 900
Arjay, KY 40902 • 650
Arkadelphia, AR 71923 • 10,005
Arkansas □, AR • 24,175
Arkansas City, AR 71630 • 668
Arkansas City, KS 67005 • 13,201
Arkoma, OK 74901 • 2,175
Arkport, NY 14807 • 811
Arkwright, RI 02816 • 1,500
Arlington, GA 31713 • 1,572
Arlington, KS 67514 • 631
Arlington, LA 70808 • 850
Arlington, MA 02174 • 48,219
Arlington, MN 55307 • 1,779
Arlington, NE 68002 • 1,117
Arlington, NC 28642 • 872
Arlington, NY 12603 • 11,203
Arlington, OH 45814 • 1,187
Arlington, SD 57212 • 991
Arlington, TN 38002 • 1,778
Arlington, TX 76010–19 • 160,113
Arlington, VT 05250 • 800
Arlington, VA 22201–99 • 152,700
Arlington, WA 98223 • 3,282
Arlington □, VA • 152,599
Arlington Heights, IL 60004–08 • 66,116
Arma, KS 66712 • 1,676
Armada, MI 48005 • 1,392
Armijo, NM 87105 • 18,900
Armonk, NY 10504 • 5,900
Armour, SD 57313 • 819
Armstrong, IA 50514 • 1,153
Armstrong □, PA • 77,768
Armstrong □, TX • 1,994
Arnaudville, LA 70512 • 1,679
Arnett, OK 73832 • 714
Arnold, CA 95223 • 2,385
Arnold, MN 55803 • 1,350
Arnold, MO 63010 • 19,141
Arnold, NE 69120 • 813
Arnold, PA 15068 • 6,853
Arnolds Park, IA 51331 • 1,051
Aroma Park, IL 60910 • 673
Aroostook □, ME • 91,331
Arp, TX 75750 • 939
Arrowhead Village, NJ 08723 • 3,100
Arroyo Grande, CA 93420 • 11,290
Artesia, CA 90701 • 14,301
Artesia, NM 88210 • 10,385
Arthur, IL 61911 • 2,122
Arthur □, NE • 513
Arundel Village, MD 21225 • 5,300
Arvada, CO 80001–05 • 84,576
Arvin, CA 93203 • 6,863
Arvonia, VA 23004 • 700
Asbury Park, NJ 07712 • 17,015
Ascension □, LA • 50,068
Ashaway, RI 02804 • 1,747
Ashburn, GA 31714 • 4,766
Ashburnham, MA 01430 • 1,150
Ashdown, AR 71822 • 4,218
Ashe □, NC • 22,325
Asheboro, NC 27203 • 15,252
Asher, OK 74826 • 659
Asherton, TX 78827 • 1,574
Asheville, NC 28801–99 • 53,583
Ashford, AL 36312 • 2,165
Ash Grove, MO 65604 • 1,157
Ashkum, IL 60911 • 735
Ashland, AL 36251 • 2,052
Ashland, CA 94541 • 13,893
Ashland, IL 62612 • 1,351
Ashland, KS 67831 • 1,096
Ashland, KY 41101 • 27,064
Ashland, ME 04732 • 800
Ashland, MA 01721 • 9,165
Ashland, MO 65010 • 1,021
Ashland, NE 68003 • 2,274
Ashland, NH 03217 • 1,479
Ashland, OH 44805 • 20,326
Ashland, OR 97520 • 14,943
Ashland, PA 17921 • 4,235
Ashland, VA 23005 • 4,640
Ashland, WI 54806 • 9,115
Ashland □, OH • 46,178
Ashland □, WI • 16,783
Ashland City, TN 37015 • 2,329
Ashley, IL 62808 • 658
Ashley, IN 46705 • 841
Ashley, ND 58413 • 1,192
Ashley, OH 43003 • 1,057
Ashley, PA 18706 • 3,512
Ashley □, AR • 26,538
Ashmore, IL 61912 • 883
Ashtabula, OH 44004 • 23,449
Ashtabula □, OH • 104,215
Ashton, ID 83420 • 1,219
Ashton, IL 61006 • 1,140
Ashton, MD 20861 • 1,010
Ashton, RI 02864 • 875
Ashville, AL 35953 • 1,489
Ashville, OH 43103 • 2,046
Ashwaubenon, WI 54304 • 14,486
Asotin, WA 99402 • 943
Asotin □, WA • 16,823
Aspen, CO 81611 • 3,678
Aspen Hill, MD 20906 • 9,800
Aspermont, TX 79502 • 1,357
Aspinwall, PA 15215 • 3,284
Assinippi, MA 02339 • 1,400
Assonet, MA 02702 • 900
Assumption, IL 62510 • 1,283
Assumption □, LA • 22,084
Aston, PA 19014 • 6,900
Astor, FL 32002 • 950
Astoria, IL 61501 • 1,370
Astoria, OR 97103 • 9,998
Atascadero, CA 93422 • 16,232
Atascosa □, TX • 25,055
Atchison, KS 66002 • 11,407
Atchison □, KS • 18,397
Atchison □, MO • 8,605
Atco, NJ 08004 • 2,100
Athena, OR 97813 • 965
Athens, AL 35611 • 14,558
Athens, GA 30601–13 • 42,549
Athens, IL 62613 • 1,371
Athens, MI 49011 • 960
Athens, NY 12015 • 1,738
Athens, OH 45701 • 19,743
Athens, PA 18810 • 3,622
Athens, TN 37303 • 12,080
Athens, TX 75751 • 10,197
Athens, WV 24712 • 1,147
Athens, WI 54411 • 988
Athens □, OH • 56,399
Atherton, CA 94025 • 7,797
Athol, MA 01331 • 10,634
Atkins, AR 72823 • 3,002
Atkinson, IL 61235 • 1,138
Atkinson, NE 68713 • 1,521
Atkinson, NH 03811 • 900
Atkinson □, GA • 6,141
Atlanta, GA 30301–99 • 425,022
Atlanta, IL 61723 • 1,807
Atlanta, IN 46031 • 657
Atlanta, MI 49709 • 650
Atlanta, NY 14808 • 750
Atlanta, TX 75551 • 6,272
Atlantic, IA 50022 • 7,789
Atlantic, NC 28511 • 900
Atlantic □, NJ • 194,119
Atlantic Beach, FL 32233 • 7,847
Atlantic City, NJ 08401–99 • 40,199
Atlantic Highlands, NJ 07716 • 4,950
Atmore, AL 36502 • 8,789
Atoka, OK 74525 • 3,409
Atoka, TN 38004 • 691
Atoka □, OK • 12,748
Attala □, MS • 19,865
Attalla, AL 35954 • 7,737
Attapulgus, GA 31715 • 623
Attica, IN 47918 • 3,841
Attica, KS 67009 • 730
Attica, NY 14011 • 2,659
Attica, OH 44807 • 865
Attleboro, MA 02703 • 34,196
Atwater, CA 95301 • 17,530
Atwater, MN 56209 • 1,128
Atwood, IL 61913 • 1,464
Atwood, KS 67730 • 1,665
Atwood, TN 38220 • 1,143
Auberry, CA 93602 • 1,100
Auburn, AL 36830 • 28,471
Auburn, CA 95603 • 7,540
Auburn, GA 30203 • 692
Auburn, IL 62615 • 3,616
Auburn, IN 46706 • 8,122
Auburn, KS 66402 • 890
Auburn, KY 42206 • 1,467
Auburn, ME 04210 • 23,128
Auburn, MA 01501 • 14,845
Auburn, MI 48611 • 1,921
Auburn, NE 68305 • 3,482
Auburn, NY 13021 • 32,548
Auburn, PA 17922 • 999
Auburn, WA 98002–03 • 26,417
Auburndale, FL 33823 • 6,501
Auburndale, WI 54412 • 641
Auburn Heights, MI 48057 • 4,000
Audrain □, MO • 26,458
Audubon, IA 50025 • 2,841
Audubon, NJ 08106 • 9,533
Audubon □, IA • 8,559
Auglaize □, OH • 42,554
Au Gres, MI 48703 • 768
Augusta, AR 72006 • 3,496
Augusta, GA 30901–99 • 47,532
Augusta, IL 62311 • 764
Augusta, KS 67010 • 6,968
Augusta, KY 41002 • 1,455
Augusta, ME 04330 • 21,819
Augusta, MI 49012 • 913
Augusta, WI 54722 • 1,560
Augusta □, VA • 53,732
Aulander, NC 27805 • 1,214
Ault, CO 80610 • 1,056
Aumsville, OR 97325 • 1,432
Aurelia, IA 51005 • 1,143
Aurora, CO 80010–17 • 158,588
Aurora, IL 60504–07 • 81,293
Aurora, IN 47001 • 3,816
Aurora, MN 55705 • 2,670
Aurora, MO 65605 • 6,437
Aurora, NE 68818 • 3,717
Aurora, NC 27806 • 698
Aurora, NY 13026 • 926
Aurora, OH 44202 • 8,177
Aurora, UT 84620 • 874
Aurora □, SD • 3,628
Au Sable, MI 48750 • 1,240
Au Sable Forks, NY 12912 • 2,100
Austell, GA 30001 • 3,939
Austin, IN 47102 • 4,857
Austin, MN 55912 • 23,020
Austin, PA 16720 • 740
Austin, TX 78701–99 • 345,496
Austin □, TX • 17,726
Austintown, OH 44512 • 33,636
Austinville, VA 24312 • 800
Autauga □, AL • 32,259
Autaugaville, AL 36003 • 843
Auxier, KY 41602 • 900
Auxvasse, MO 65231 • 858
Ava, IL 62907 • 811
Ava, MO 65608 • 2,761
Avalon, CA 90704 • 2,022
Avalon, NJ 08202 • 2,162
Avalon, PA 15202 • 6,240
Avella, PA 15312 • 1,109
Avenal, CA 93204 • 4,137
Avenel, MD 20783 • 5,600
Avenel, NJ 07001 • 11,500
Averill Park, NY 12018 • 1,500
Avery □, NC • 14,409
Avilla, IN 46710 • 1,272
Avis, PA 17721 • 1,718
Aviston, IL 62216 • 846
Avoca, IA 51521 • 1,650
Avoca, NY 14809 • 1,144
Avoca, PA 18641 • 3,536
Avocado Heights, CA 91746 • 11,721
Avon, CT 06001 • 1,434
Avon, IL 61415 • 1,019
Avon, MA 02322 • 5,026
Avon, MN 56310 • 804
Avon, NY 14414 • 3,006
Avon, OH 44011 • 7,241
Avon by the Sea, NJ 07717 • 2,337
Avondale, AZ 85323 • 8,168
Avondale, CO 81022 • 800
Avondale, LA 70094 • 6,699
Avondale, MO 64117 • 612
Avondale, OH 45404 • 5,000
Avondale, PA 19311 • 891
Avondale Estates, GA 30002 • 1,313
Avon Lake, OH 44012 • 13,222
Avonmore, PA 15618 • 1,234
Avon Park, FL 33825 • 8,026
Avoyelles □, LA • 41,393
Axtell, NE 68924 • 602
Ayden, NC 28513 • 4,361
Ayer, MA 01432–33 • 6,993
Aynor, SC 29511 • 643
Azalea Park, FL 32807 • 8,304
Azle, TX 76020 • 5,822
Aztec, NM 87410 • 5,512
Azusa, CA 91702 • 29,380

B

Babbitt, MN 55706 • 2,435
Babbitt, NV 89416 • 1,800
Babson Park, FL 33827 • 950
Babylon, NY 11702–04 • 12,388
Baca □, CO • 5,419
Bacon □, GA • 9,379
Baconton, GA 31716 • 763
Bad Axe, MI 48413 • 3,184
Baden, PA 15005 • 5,318
Badger, IA 50516 • 653
Badin, NC 28009 • 1,514
Bagdad, AZ 86321 • 2,331
Bagdad, FL 32530 • 1,479
Bagley, MN 56621 • 1,321
Bailey, NC 27807 • 685
Bailey □, TX • 8,168
Bailey Island, ME 04003 • 650
Baileys Crossroads, VA 22041 • 4,600
Bainbridge, GA 31717 • 10,553
Bainbridge, IN 46105 • 644
Bainbridge, NY 13733 • 1,603
Bainbridge, OH 45612 • 1,042
Baird, TX 79504 • 1,696
Bairdford, PA 15006 • 950
Baker, CA 92309 • 650
Baker, LA 70714 • 12,865
Baker, MT 59313 • 2,354
Baker, OR 97814 • 9,471
Baker □, FL • 15,289
Baker □, GA • 3,808
Baker □, OR • 16,134
Bakersfield, CA 93301–99 • 105,735
Bakerstown, PA 15007 • 1,000
Bala-Cynwyd, PA 19004 • 8,600
Balaton, MN 56115 • 752
Balch Springs, TX 75180 • 13,746
Bald Knob, AR 72010 • 2,756
Baldwin, FL 32234 • 1,526
Baldwin, GA 30511 • 1,080
Baldwin, LA 70514 • 2,644
Baldwin, MI 49304 • 674
Baldwin, NY 11510 • 35,100
Baldwin, PA 15234 • 24,712
Baldwin, SC 29706 • 700
Baldwin, WI 54002 • 1,620
Baldwin □, AL • 78,556
Baldwin □, GA • 34,686
Baldwin City, KS 66006 • 2,829
Baldwin Park, CA 91706 • 50,554
Baldwinsville, NY 13027 • 6,446
Baldwinville, MA 01436 • 1,709
Baldwyn, MS 38824 • 3,427
Balfour, NC 28706 • 1,772
Ball, LA 71405 • 3,405
Ballard □, KY • 8,798
Ballardvale, MA 01810 • 1,300
Ball Ground, GA 30107 • 640
Ballinger, TX 76821 • 4,207
Ballston Spa, NY 12020 • 4,711
Ballwin, MO 63011 • 12,656
Bally, PA 19503 • 1,051
Balmville, NY 12550 • 3,214
Balsam Lake, WI 54810 • 749
Baltic, CT 06330 • 1,500
Baltic, SD 57003 • 679
Baltimore, MD 21201–99 • 786,775
Baltimore, OH 43105 • 2,689
Baltimore □, MD • 655,615
Baltimore Highlands, MD 21227 • 6,750
Bamberg, SC 29003 • 3,672
Bamberg □, SC • 18,118
Bancroft, IA 50517 • 1,082
Bancroft, MI 48414 • 618
Bandera, TX 78003 • 947
Bandera □, TX • 7,084
Bandon, OR 97411 • 2,311
Bangor, ME 04401 • 31,643
Bangor, MI 49013 • 2,001
Bangor, PA 18013 • 5,006
Bangor, WI 54614 • 1,012
Bangor Township, MI 48706 • 17,494
Bangs, TX 76823 • 1,716
Banks □, GA • 8,702
Banner □, NE • 918
Banner Elk, NC 28604 • 1,087
Banning, CA 92220 • 14,020
Bannock □, ID • 65,421
Bantam, CT 06750 • 860
Baraboo, WI 53913 • 8,081
Baraga, MI 49908 • 1,055
Baraga □, MI • 8,484
Barataria, LA 70036 • 1,123
Barber □, KS • 6,548
Barberton, OH 44203 • 29,751
Barbour □, AL • 24,756
Barbour □, WV • 16,639
Barboursville, WV 25504 • 2,871
Barbourville, KY 40906 • 3,333
Bardstown, KY 40004 • 6,155
Bardwell, KY 42023 • 988
Bargersville, IN 46106 • 1,647
Bar Harbor, ME 04609 • 2,685
Barker Heights, NC 28739 • 1,267
Barling, AR 72923 • 3,761
Barlow, KY 42024 • 746
Bar Mills, ME 04004 • 825
Barnegat, NJ 08005 • 1,012
Barnegat Light, NJ 08006 • 619
Barnes □, ND • 13,960
Barnesboro, PA 15714 • 2,741
Barnesville, GA 30204 • 4,887
Barnesville, MN 56514 • 2,207
Barnesville, OH 43713 • 4,633
Barnhart, MO 63012 • 800
Barnsdall, OK 74002 • 1,501
Barnstable, MA 02630 • 2,033
Barnstable □, MA • 147,925
Barnwell, SC 29812 • 5,572
Barnwell □, SC • 19,868
Baroda, MI 49101 • 627
Barrackville, WV 26559 • 1,815
Barre, MA 01005 • 1,136
Barre, VT 05641 • 9,824
Barren □, KY • 34,009
Barrett, WV 25013 • 800
Barrington, IL 60010 • 9,029
Barrington, NJ 08007 • 7,418
Barrington, RI 02806 • 16,174
Barron, WI 54812 • 2,595
Barron □, WI • 38,730
Barron Lake, MI 49120 • 1,600
Barrow, AK 99723 • 2,207
Barrow □, GA • 21,354
Barry, IL 62312 • 1,487
Barry □, MI • 45,781
Barry □, MO • 24,408
Barstow, CA 92311 • 17,690
Barstow, TX 79719 • 637
Bartholomew □, IN • 65,088
Bartlesville, OK 74003–06 • 34,568
Bartlett, IL 60103 • 13,254
Bartlett, NH 03812 • 700
Bartlett, TN 38134 • 17,170
Bartlett, TX 76511 • 1,567
Barton, MD 21521 • 617
Barton, OH 43905 • 1,039
Barton, VT 05822 • 1,062
Barton □, KS • 31,343
Barton □, MO • 11,292
Bartonville, IL 61607 • 6,137
Bartow, FL 33830 • 14,780
Bartow □, GA • 40,760
Barview, OR 97420 • 1,462
Basehor, KS 66007 • 1,483
Basile, LA 70515 • 2,635
Basin, WY 82410 • 1,349
Baskin, FL 33540 • 800
Basking Ridge, NJ 07920 • 4,800
Bassett, NE 68714 • 1,009
Bassett, VA 24055 • 2,950
Bass Lake, IN 46534 • 1,500
Bastrop, LA 71220 • 15,527
Bastrop, TX 78602 • 3,789
Bastrop □, TX • 24,726
Batavia, IL 60510 • 12,574
Batavia, NY 14020 • 16,703
Batavia, OH 45103 • 1,896
Bates □, MO • 15,873
Batesburg, SC 29006 • 4,023
Batesville, AR 72501 • 8,263
Batesville, IN 47006 • 4,152
Batesville, MS 38606 • 4,692
Batesville, TX 78829 • 800
Bath, ME 04530 • 10,246
Bath, NY 14810 • 6,042
Bath, PA 18014 • 1,953
Bath, SC 29816 • 2,242
Bath □, KY • 10,025
Bath □, VA • 5,860
Baton Rouge, LA 70801–99 • 219,419
Batson, TX 77519 • 650
Battleboro, NC 27809 • 632
Battle Creek, IA 51006 • 919
Battle Creek, MI 49014–17 • 56,339
Battle Creek, NE 68715 • 948
Battle Ground, IN 47920 • 812
Battle Ground, WA 98604 • 2,774
Battle Lake, MN 56515 • 708
Battle Mountain, NV 89820 • 2,755
Baudette, MN 56623 • 1,170
Bawcomville, LA 71291 • 2,500
Baxley, GA 31513 • 3,586
Baxter, IA 50028 • 951
Baxter, MN 56401 • 2,625
Baxter, TN 38544 • 1,411
Baxter □, AR • 27,409
Baxter Springs, KS 66713 • 4,730
Bay, AR 72411 • 1,605
Bay □, FL • 97,740
Bay □, MI • 119,881
Bayard, IA 50029 • 637
Bayard, NE 69334 • 1,435
Bayard, NM 88023 • 3,036
Bayberry, NY 13088 • 5,900
Bayboro, NC 28515 • 759
Bay City, MI 48706–08 • 41,593
Bay City, OR 97107 • 986
Bay City, TX 77414 • 17,837
Bayfield, CO 81122 • 724
Bayfield, WI 54814 • 778
Bayfield □, WI • 13,822
Bay Head, NJ 08742 • 1,340
Baylor □, TX • 4,919
Bay Minette, AL 36507 • 7,455
Bayonne, NJ 07002 • 65,047
Bayou George, FL 32401 • 1,500
Bayou Goula, LA 70716 • 800
Bayou La Batre, AL 36509 • 2,005
Bay Port, MI 48720 • 800
Bayport, MN 55003 • 2,932
Bayport, NY 11705 • 8,900
Bay Ridge, MD 21403 • 1,989
Bay Saint Louis, MS 39520 • 7,891
Bay Shore, NY 11706 • 31,200
Bayshore Gardens, FL 33507 • 14,945
Bayside, WI 53217 • 4,724
Bay Springs, MS 39422 • 1,884
Baytown, TX 77520–22 • 56,923
Bayview, AL 35005 • 830
Bay View, MI 49770 • 1,000
Bay Village, OH 44140 • 17,846
Bayville, NJ 08721 • 900

Bayville, NY 11709 • *7,034*
Beach, IL 60085 • *4,650*
Beach, ND 58621 • *1,381*
Beach City, OH 44608 • *1,083*
Beach Haven, NJ 08008 • *1,714*
Beachwood, NJ 08722 • *7,687*
Beachwood, OH 44122 • *9,983*
Beacon, NY 12508 • *12,937*
Beacon Falls, CT 06403 • *1,500*
Beadle □, SD • *19,195*
Beallsville, OH 43716 • *601*
Bear, DE 19701 • *950*
Bearden, AR 71720 • *1,191*
Beardstown, IL 62618 • *6,338*
Bear Lake □, ID • *6,931*
Bear Town, MS 39648 • *1,277*
Beatrice, NE 68310 • *12,891*
Beatty, NV 89003 • *900*
Beattyville, KY 41311 • *1,068*
Beaufort, NC 28516 • *3,826*
Beaufort, SC 29902 • *8,634*
Beaufort □, NC • *40,355*
Beaufort □, SC • *65,364*
Beaumont, CA 92223 • *6,818*
Beaumont, MS 39423 • *1,112*
Beaumont, TX 77701–99 • *118,102*
Beauregard □, LA • *29,692*
Beaver, OK 73932 • *1,939*
Beaver, PA 15009 • *5,441*
Beaver, UT 84713 • *1,792*
Beaver, WV 25813 • *1,400*
Beaver □, OK • *6,806*
Beaver □, PA • *204,441*
Beaver □, UT • *4,378*
Beaver City, NE 68926 • *775*
Beavercreek, OH 45385 • *31,589*
Beaverdale, PA 15921 • *1,579*
Beaver Dam, KY 42320 • *3,185*
Beaver Dam, WI 53916 • *14,149*
Beaver Falls, PA 15010 • *12,525*
Beaverhead □, MT • *8,186*
Beaver Meadows, PA 18216 • *1,078*
Beaver Springs, PA 17812 • *725*
Beaverton, MI 48612 • *1,025*
Beaverton, OR 97005–07 • *30,582*
Beavertown, PA 17813 • *853*
Beckemeyer, IL 62219 • *1,119*
Becker, MN 55308 • *601*
Becker □, MN • *29,336*
Beckham □, OK • *19,243*
Beckley, WV 25001 • *20,492*
Beckville, TX 75631 • *945*
Bedford, IN 47421 • *14,410*
Bedford, IA 50833 • *1,692*
Bedford, KY 40006 • *835*
Bedford, MA 01730 • *13,067*
Bedford, NH 03102 • *1,300*
Bedford, OH 44146 • *15,056*
Bedford, PA 15522 • *3,326*
Bedford, TX 76021–22 • *20,821*
Bedford, VA 24523 • *5,991*
Bedford □, PA • *46,784*
Bedford □, TN • *27,916*
Bedford □, VA • *34,927*
Bedford Heights, OH 44146 • *13,214*
Bedford Hills, NY 10507 • *3,200*
Bee □, TX • *26,030*
Beebe, AR 72012 • *3,599*
Beech Creek, PA 16822 • *760*
Beecher, IL 60401 • *2,024*
Beecher, MI 48505 • *17,178*
Beech Grove, IN 46107 • *13,196*
Beech Island, SC 29841 • *1,300*
Beemer, NE 68716 • *853*
Bee Ridge, FL 33578 • *3,313*
Beersheba Springs, TN 37305 • *643*
Beeville, TX 78102 • *14,574*
Beggs, OK 74421 • *1,428*
Bel Air, MD 21014 • *7,814*
Bel Aire, KS 67220 • *2,650*
Bel Aire Estates, CT 06355 • *900*
Belcamp, MD 21017 • *650*
Belchertown, MA 01007 • *2,531*
Belcourt, ND 58316 • *1,803*
Belding, MI 48809 • *5,634*
Belen, NM 87002 • *5,617*
Belfast, ME 04915 • *6,243*
Belfast, NC 27530 • *950*
Belfast, NY 14711 • *900*
Belfield, ND 58622 • *1,274*
Belford, NJ 07718 • *6,000*
Belfry, KY 41514 • *900*
Belgium, WI 53004 • *892*
Belgrade, MN 56312 • *805*
Belgrade, MT 59714 • *2,336*
Belhaven, NC 27810 • *2,430*
Belington, WV 26250 • *2,038*
Belknap □, NH • *42,884*
Bell, CA 90201 • *25,450*
Bell □, KY • *34,330*
Bell □, TX • *157,820*
Bellair, FL 32073 • *5,200*
Bellaire, MI 49615 • *1,063*
Bellaire, OH 43906 • *8,241*
Bellaire, TX 77401 • *14,950*
Bellamy, AL 36901 • *750*
Bella Vista, AR 72712 • *2,589*
Bellbrook, OH 45305 • *5,174*
Belle, MO 65013 • *1,233*
Belle, WV 25015 • *1,621*
Belleair, FL 33516 • *5,200*
Belle Center, OH 43310 • *930*
Belle Chasse, LA 70037 • *5,412*
Bellefontaine, OH 43311 • *11,888*
Bellefontaine Neighbors, MO 63137 • *12,082*

Bellefonte, DE 19809 • *1,279*
Bellefonte, PA 16823 • *6,300*
Belle Fourche, SD 57717 • *4,692*
Belle Glade, FL 33430 • *16,535*
Belle Isle, FL 32809 • *2,848*
Belle Meade, TN 37205 • *3,182*
Belle Plaine, IA 52208 • *2,903*
Belle Plaine, KS 67013 • *1,706*
Belle Plaine, MN 56011 • *2,754*
Belle Rose, LA 70341 • *700*
Belle Vernon, PA 15012 • *1,489*
Belleview, FL 32620 • *1,913*
Belle View, VA 22307 • *3,500*
Belleville, IL 62220–25 • *41,580*
Belleville, KS 66935 • *2,805*
Belleville, MI 48111 • *3,366*
Belleville, NJ 07109 • *35,367*
Belleville, PA 17004 • *1,817*
Belleville, WI 53508 • *1,302*
Bellevue, ID 83313 • *1,016*
Bellevue, IA 52031 • *2,450*
Bellevue, KY 41073 • *7,678*
Bellevue, MI 49021 • *1,289*
Bellevue, NE 68005 • *21,813*
Bellevue, OH 44811 • *8,187*
Bellevue, PA 15202 • *10,128*
Bellevue, WA 98004–09 • *73,903*
Bellflower, CA 90706 • *53,441*
Bell Gardens, CA 90201 • *34,117*
Bellingham, MA 02019 • *14,300*
Bellingham, WA 98225–27 • *45,794*
Bellmawr, NJ 08031 • *13,721*
Bellmead, TX 76705 • *7,569*
Bellmore, NY 11710 • *18,431*
Bellows Falls, VT 05101 • *3,456*
Bellport, NY 11713 • *2,809*
Bells, TN 38006 • *1,571*
Bellville, OH 44813 • *1,714*
Bellville, TX 77418 • *2,860*
Bellwood, IL 60104 • *19,811*
Bellwood, PA 16617 • *2,114*
Belmar, NJ 07719 • *6,771*
Belmond, IA 50421 • *2,505*
Belmont, CA 94002 • *24,505*
Belmont, MA 02178 • *26,100*
Belmont, MS 38827 • *1,420*
Belmont, NH 03220 • *900*
Belmont, NC 28012 • *4,607*
Belmont, NY 14813 • *1,024*
Belmont, OH 43718 • *714*
Belmont, WV 26134 • *887*
Belmont, WI 53510 • *826*
Belmont □, OH • *82,569*
Bel-Nor, MO 63133 • *2,047*
Beloit, KS 67420 • *4,367*
Beloit, OH 44609 • *1,093*
Beloit, WI 53511 • *35,207*
Beloit North, WI 53511 • *5,912*
Belpre, OH 45714 • *7,193*
Belt, MT 59412 • *825*
Belton, MO 64012 • *12,708*
Belton, SC 29627 • *5,312*
Belton, TX 76513 • *10,660*
Beltrami □, MN • *30,982*
Beltsville, MD 20705 • *12,760*
Belvedere, SC 29841 • *6,859*
Belvedere Park, GA 30032 • *17,766*
Belvidere, DE 19804 • *1,100*
Belvidere, IL 61008 • *15,176*
Belvidere, NJ 07823 • *2,475*
Belzoni, MS 39038 • *2,982*
Bement, IL 61813 • *1,770*
Bemidji, MN 56601 • *10,949*
Bemis, TN 38314 • *1,883*
Benavides, TX 78341 • *1,978*
Benbrook, TX 76126 • *13,579*
Bend, OR 97701–09 • *17,263*
Benedict, MD 20612 • *700*
Benewah □, ID • *8,292*
Benham, KY 40807 • *936*
Ben Hill □, GA • *16,000*
Benicia, CA 94510 • *15,376*
Benkelman, NE 69021 • *1,235*
Benld, IL 62009 • *1,638*
Bennett, CO 80102 • *942*
Bennett □, SD • *3,044*
Bennettsville, SC 29512 • *8,774*
Bennington, NE 68007 • *631*
Bennington, VT 05201 • *9,349*
Bennington □, VT • *33,345*
Bennion, UT 84107 • *950*
Bensenville, IL 60106 • *16,124*
Bensley, VA 23234 • *3,300*
Benson, AZ 85602 • *4,190*
Benson, MN 56215 • *3,656*
Benson, NC 27504 • *2,792*
Benson □, ND • *7,944*
Bent □, CO • *5,945*
Bentleyville, PA 15314 • *2,525*
Benton, AR 72015 • *17,717*
Benton, IL 62812 • *7,778*
Benton, KS 67017 • *609*
Benton, KY 42025 • *3,700*
Benton, LA 71006 • *1,864*
Benton, MO 63736 • *674*
Benton, PA 17814 • *981*
Benton, TN 37307 • *1,115*
Benton, WI 53803 • *983*
Benton □, AR • *78,115*
Benton □, IN • *10,218*
Benton □, IA • *23,649*
Benton □, MN • *25,187*
Benton □, MS • *8,153*
Benton □, MO • *12,183*
Benton □, OR • *68,211*
Benton □, TN • *14,901*

Benton □, WA • *109,444*
Benton City, WA 99320 • *1,980*
Benton Harbor, MI 49022 • *14,707*
Benton Heights, MI 49022 • *6,787*
Bentonville, AR 72712 • *8,756*
Benwood, WV 26031 • *1,994*
Benzie □, MI • *11,205*
Berea, KY 40403 • *8,226*
Berea, OH 44017 • *19,567*
Berea, SC 29611 • *7,500*
Beresford, SD 57004 • *1,865*
Bergen, NY 14416 • *976*
Bergen □, NJ • *845,385*
Bergenfield, NJ 07621 • *25,568*
Bergholz, OH 43908 • *914*
Bergland, MI 49910 • *700*
Berkeley, CA 94701–99 • *103,328*
Berkeley, IL 60162 • *5,467*
Berkeley, MO 63134 • *15,922*
Berkeley, RI 02864 • *930*
Berkeley □, SC • *94,727*
Berkeley □, WV • *46,775*
Berkeley Heights, NJ 07922 • *12,549*
Berkeley Springs, WV 25411 • *789*
Berkley, MI 48072 • *18,637*
Berks □, PA • *312,509*
Berkshire □, MA • *145,110*
Berlin, CT 06037 • *2,000*
Berlin, MD 21811 • *2,162*
Berlin, NH 03570 • *13,084*
Berlin, NJ 08009 • *5,786*
Berlin, NY 12022 • *850*
Berlin, OH 44610 • *800*
Berlin, PA 15530 • *1,999*
Berlin, WI 54923 • *5,478*
Berlin Heights, OH 44814 • *756*
Bernalillo, NM 87004 • *3,012*
Bernalillo □, NM • *419,700*
Bernardston, MA 01337 • *700*
Bernardsville, NJ 07924 • *6,715*
Berne, IN 46711 • *3,300*
Bernice, LA 71222 • *1,956*
Bernie, MO 63822 • *1,975*
Bernville, PA 19506 • *798*
Berrien □, GA • *13,525*
Berrien □, MI • *171,276*
Berrien Springs, MI 49103 • *2,042*
Berry, AL 35546 • *916*
Berry Hill, TN 37204 • *1,113*
Berryville, AR 72616 • *2,966*
Berryville, VA 22611 • *1,752*
Berthoud, CO 80513 • *2,362*
Bertie □, NC • *21,024*
Bertram, TX 78605 • *824*
Bertrand, MI 49120 • *5,000*
Bertrand, MO 63823 • *688*
Bertrand, NE 68927 • *775*
Berwick, LA 70342 • *4,466*
Berwick, ME 03901 • *2,378*
Berwick, PA 18603 • *11,850*
Berwyn, IL 60402 • *46,849*
Berwyn, PA 19312 • *9,300*
Bessemer, AL 35020–23 • *31,729*
Bessemer, MI 49911 • *2,553*
Bessemer, PA 16112 • *1,293*
Bessemer City, NC 28016 • *4,787*
Bethalto, IL 62010 • *8,630*
Bethany, CT 06525 • *890*
Bethany, IL 61914 • *1,550*
Bethany, MO 64424 • *3,095*
Bethany, OK 73008 • *22,130*
Bethany, WV 26032 • *1,336*
Bethel, AK 99559 • *3,576*
Bethel, CT 06801 • *8,755*
Bethel, ME 04217 • *1,225*
Bethel, NC 27812 • *1,825*
Bethel, OH 45106 • *2,231*
Bethel, VT 05032 • *1,016*
Bethel Acres, OK 74801 • *747*
Bethel Park, PA 15102 • *34,755*
Bethel Springs, TN 38315 • *873*
Bethesda, MD 20814–17 • *63,022*
Bethesda, OH 43719 • *1,429*
Bethlehem, CT 06751 • *1,762*
Bethlehem, NH 03574 • *700*
Bethlehem, PA 18015–18 • *70,419*
Bethpage, NY 11714 • *29,900*
Betsy Layne, KY 41605 • *900*
Bettendorf, IA 52722 • *27,381*
Bettsville, OH 44815 • *752*
Beulah, ND 58523 • *2,908*
Beulaville, NC 28518 • *1,060*
Beverly, MA 01915 • *37,655*
Beverly, NJ 08010 • *2,919*
Beverly, OH 45715 • *1,471*
Beverly Hills, CA 90210–13 • *32,367*
Beverly Hills, MI 48009 • *11,598*
Beverly Shores, IN 46301 • *864*
Bexar □, TX • *988,798*
Bexley, OH 43209 • *13,405*
Bibb □, AL • *15,723*
Bibb □, GA • *150,256*
Bibb City, GA 31904 • *667*
Bicknell, IN 47512 • *4,713*
Biddeford, ME 04005 • *19,638*
Bienville □, LA • *16,387*
Big Bear City, CA 92314 • *3,500*
Big Bend, WI 53103 • *1,345*
Big Creek, CA 93605 • *700*
Big Flats, NY 14814 • *2,500*
Bigfork, MT 59911 • *1,080*
Biggs, CA 95917 • *1,413*
Big Horn □, MT • *11,096*
Big Horn □, WY • *11,896*
Big Lake, MN 55309 • *2,210*
Big Lake, TX 76932 • *3,404*

Biglerville, PA 17307 • *991*
Big Pine, CA 93513 • *1,510*
Bigpoint, MS 39567 • *900*
Big Rapids, MI 49307 • *14,361*
Big Run, PA 15715 • *822*
Big Sandy, MT 59520 • *835*
Big Sandy, TN 38221 • *650*
Big Sandy, TX 75755 • *1,258*
Big Spring, TX 79720 • *24,804*
Big Stone □, MN • *7,716*
Big Stone City, SD 57216 • *672*
Big Stone Gap, VA 24219 • *4,748*
Big Timber, MT 59011 • *1,690*
Big Wells, TX 78830 • *939*
Billerica, MA 01821 • *6,400*
Billings, MO 65610 • *911*
Billings, MT 59101–99 • *66,842*
Billings, OK 74630 • *632*
Billings □, ND • *1,138*
Billings Heights, MT 59105 • *8,480*
Biloxi, MS 39530–34 • *49,311*
Biltmore Forest, NC 28803 • *1,499*
Bingen, WA 98605 • *644*
Binger, OK 73009 • *791*
Bingham, ME 04920 • *1,074*
Bingham □, ID • *36,489*
Binghamton, NY 13901–99 • *55,860*
Biola, CA 93606 • *800*
Birch Run, MI 48415 • *1,196*
Birch Tree, MO 65438 • *622*
Birchwood City, MD 20745 • *8,000*
Birchwood Park, DE 19711 • *1,500*
Bird Island, MN 55310 • *1,372*
Birdsboro, PA 19508 • *3,481*
Birmingham, AL 35201–99 • *286,799*
Birmingham, MI 48008–12 • *21,689*
Birnamwood, WI 54414 • *688*
Biron, WI 54494 • *698*
Bisbee, AZ 85603 • *7,154*
Biscayne Gardens, FL 33168 • *13,000*
Biscayne Park, FL 33161 • *3,088*
Biscoe, NC 27209 • *1,334*
Bishop, CA 93514 • *3,333*
Bishop, TX 78343 • *3,706*
Bishopville, SC 29010 • *3,429*
Bismarck, IL 61814 • *750*
Bismarck, MO 63624 • *1,625*
Bismarck, ND 58501 • *44,485*
Biwabik, MN 55708 • *1,428*
Bixby, OK 74008 • *6,969*
Black Creek, WI 54106 • *1,097*
Black Diamond, WA 98010 • *1,170*
Blackduck, MN 56630 • *653*
Black Eagle, MT 59414 • *1,100*
Black Earth, WI 53515 • *1,145*
Blackfoot, ID 83221 • *10,065*
Blackford □, IN • *15,570*
Black Forest, CO 80908 • *3,372*
Black Hawk, SD 57718 • *1,608*
Black Hawk □, IA • *137,961*
Black Jack, MO 63031 • *5,293*
Black Lick, PA 15716 • *1,074*
Blacklick Estates, OH 43227 • *11,223*
Black Mountain, NC 28711 • *4,083*
Black Oak, IN 46406 • *10,000*
Black River, NY 13612 • *1,384*
Black River Falls, WI 54615 • *3,434*
Black Rock, AR 72415 • *848*
Blacksburg, SC 29702 • *1,873*
Blacksburg, VA 24060 • *30,638*
Blackshear, GA 31516 • *3,222*
Blackstone, MA 01504 • *5,100*
Blackstone, VA 23824 • *3,624*
Blackville, SC 29817 • *2,840*
Blackwell, OK 74631 • *8,400*
Blackwood, NJ 08012 • *5,219*
Bladen □, NC • *30,491*
Bladenboro, NC 28320 • *1,428*
Bladensburg, MD 20710 • *7,691*
Blades, DE 19973 • *664*
Blaine, ME 04734 • *620*
Blaine, MN 55433 • *28,558*
Blaine, TN 37709 • *1,147*
Blaine, WA 98230 • *2,363*
Blaine □, ID • *9,841*
Blaine □, MT • *6,999*
Blaine □, NE • *867*
Blaine □, OK • *13,443*
Blair, NE 68008 • *6,418*
Blair, OK 73526 • *1,092*
Blair, WI 54616 • *1,142*
Blair □, PA • *136,621*
Blairstown, IA 52209 • *695*
Blairsville, PA 15717 • *4,166*
Blakely, GA 31723 • *5,880*
Blakely, PA 18447 • *7,438*
Blanchard, LA 71009 • *1,128*
Blanchard, OK 73010 • *1,688*
Blanchard, PA 16826 • *750*
Blanchardville, WI 53516 • *803*
Blanchester, OH 45107 • *3,202*
Blanco, TX 78606 • *1,179*
Blanco □, TX • *4,681*
Bland, MO 65014 • *662*
Bland □, VA • *6,349*
Blandburg, PA 16619 • *775*
Blandford, MA 01008 • *800*
Blanding, UT 84511 • *3,118*
Blandinsville, IL 61420 • *886*
Blanford, IN 47831 • *700*
Blasdell, NY 14219 • *3,288*
Blauvelt, NY 10913 • *5,426*
Blawnox, PA 15238 • *1,653*
Bleckley □, GA • *10,767*

Bledsoe □, TN • *9,478*
Blende, CO 81006 • *1,500*
Blennerhassett, WV 26101 • *2,200*
Blessing, TX 77419 • *950*
Blissfield, MI 49228 • *3,107*
Block Island, RI 02807 • *620*
Bloomdale, OH 44817 • *744*
Bloomer, WI 54724 • *3,342*
Bloomfield, CT 06002 • *7,400*
Bloomfield, IN 47424 • *2,705*
Bloomfield, IA 52537 • *2,849*
Bloomfield, KY 40008 • *954*
Bloomfield, MO 63825 • *1,795*
Bloomfield, NE 68718 • *1,393*
Bloomfield, NJ 07003 • *47,792*
Bloomfield, NM 87413 • *4,881*
Bloomfield Hills, MI 48013 • *3,985*
Bloomingburg, OH 43106 • *869*
Bloomingdale, GA 31302 • *1,855*
Bloomingdale, IL 60108 • *12,659*
Bloomingdale, NJ 07403 • *7,867*
Bloomingdale, NY 12913 • *608*
Bloomingdale, TN 37660 • *9,000*
Blooming Grove, TX 76626 • *823*
Blooming Prairie, MN 55917 • *1,969*
Bloomington, CA 92316 • *6,674*
Bloomington, IL 61701 • *44,189*
Bloomington, IN 47401 • *52,044*
Bloomington, MN 55420 • *81,831*
Bloomington, TX 77951 • *1,750*
Bloomington, WI 53804 • *743*
Bloomsburg, PA 17815 • *11,717*
Bloomsbury, NJ 08804 • *864*
Bloomville, OH 44818 • *1,019*
Blossburg, PA 16912 • *1,757*
Blossom, TX 75416 • *1,487*
Blount □, AL • *36,459*
Blount □, TN • *77,770*
Blountstown, FL 32424 • *2,632*
Blountsville, AL 35031 • *1,509*
Blountville, TN 37617 • *2,554*
Blowing Rock, NC 28605 • *1,337*
Blue Ash, OH 45242 • *9,506*
Blue Earth, MN 56013 • *4,132*
Blue Earth □, MN • *52,314*
Bluefield, VA 24605 • *5,946*
Bluefield, WV 24701 • *16,060*
Blue Grass, IA 52726 • *1,377*
Blue Hill, ME 04614 • *700*
Blue Hill, NE 68930 • *883*
Blue Hills, CT 06002 • *6,600*
Blue Island, IL 60406 • *21,855*
Blue Lake, CA 95525 • *1,201*
Blue Mound, IL 62513 • *1,338*
Blue Mountain, MS 38610 • *867*
Blue Rapids, KS 66411 • *1,280*
Blue Ridge, GA 30513 • *1,376*
Blue Ridge, VA 24064 • *1,200*
Blue Ridge Summit, PA 17214 • *800*
Blue Springs, MO 64015 • *25,927*
Bluewell, WV 24701 • *1,000*
Bluff City, TN 37618 • *1,121*
Bluffdale, UT 84065 • *1,300*
Bluff Park, AL 35226 • *12,000*
Bluffs, IL 62621 • *821*
Bluffton, IN 46714 • *8,705*
Bluffton, OH 45817 • *3,310*
Bluford, IL 62814 • *728*
Bly, OR 97622 • *750*
Blythe, CA 92225 • *6,805*
Blytheville, AR 72315 • *23,844*
Boalsburg, PA 16827 • *950*
Boardman, OH 44512 • *39,161*
Boardman, OR 97818 • *1,261*
Boaz, AL 35957 • *7,151*
Bobtown, PA 15315 • *1,055*
Boca Grande, FL 33921 • *1,200*
Boca Raton, FL 33431–34 • *49,505*
Boerne, TX 78006 • *3,229*
Bogalusa, LA 70427 • *16,976*
Bogart, GA 30622 • *819*
Bogata, TX 75417 • *1,508*
Boger City, NC 28092 • *2,252*
Bogota, NJ 07603 • *8,344*
Bohemia, NY 11716 • *9,800*
Boiling Springs, NC 28017 • *2,381*
Boiling Springs, PA 17007 • *1,521*
Boise, ID 83701–99 • *102,160*
Boise □, ID • *2,999*
Boise City, OK 73933 • *1,761*
Boissevain, VA 24606 • *900*
Bokchito, OK 74726 • *628*
Bokeelia, FL 33922 • *900*
Boling, TX 77420 • *1,000*
Bolingbrook, IL 60439 • *37,261*
Bolivar, MO 65613 • *5,919*
Bolivar, NY 14715 • *1,345*
Bolivar, OH 44612 • *989*
Bolivar, PA 15923 • *706*
Bolivar, TN 38008 • *6,597*
Bolivar, WV 25425 • *672*
Bolivar □, MS • *45,965*
Bollinger □, MO • *10,301*
Bolton, MS 39041 • *664*
Bolton Landing, NY 12814 • *1,500*
Bon Air, VA 23235 • *13,000*
Bonaire, GA 31005 • *800*
Bond □, IL • *16,224*
Bondsville, MA 01009 • *1,906*
Bonduel, WI 54107 • *1,160*
Bondurant, IA 50035 • *1,283*
Bonham, TX 75418 • *7,338*
Bon Homme □, SD • *8,059*
Bonifay, FL 32425 • *2,534*
Bonita Springs, FL 33923 • *3,400*
Bonneauville, PA 17325 • *920*

Bonner ☐, ID • 24,163
Bonners Ferry, ID 83805 • 1,906
Bonner Springs, KS 66012 • 6,266
Bonne Terre, MO 63628 • 3,797
Bonneville ☐, ID • 65,980
Bonney Lake, WA 98390 • 5,328
Bonnie Doone, NC 28303 • 5,950
Bono, AR 72416 • 967
Booker, TX 79005 • 1,219
Boomer, WV 25031 • 1,100
Boone, IA 50036 • 12,602
Boone, NC 28607 • 10,191
Boone ☐, AR • 26,067
Boone ☐, IL • 28,630
Boone ☐, IN • 36,446
Boone ☐, IA • 26,184
Boone ☐, KY • 45,842
Boone ☐, MO • 100,376
Boone ☐, NE • 7,391
Boone ☐, WV • 30,447
Booneville, AR 72927 • 3,718
Booneville, MS 38829 • 6,199
Boonsboro, MD 21713 • 1,908
Boonton, NJ 07005 • 8,620
Boonville, CA 95415 • 1,000
Boonville, IN 47601 • 6,300
Boonville, MO 65233 • 6,959
Boonville, NC 27011 • 1,028
Boonville, NY 13309 • 2,344
Boothbay Harbor, ME 04538 • 2,207
Boothwyn, PA 19061 • 7,100
Borden ☐, TX • 859
Bordentown, NJ 08505 • 4,441
Borger, TX 79007 • 15,837
Boron, CA 93516 • 2,040
Borrego Springs, CA 92004 • 1,405
Boscobel, WI 53805 • 2,662
Bosque ☐, TX • 13,401
Bossert Estates, NJ 08505 • 2,800
Bossier ☐, LA • 80,721
Bossier City, LA 71111-13 • 50,817
Boston, GA 31626 • 1,424
Boston, MA 02101-99 • 562,994
Boston Heights, OH 44236 • 781
Boswell, IN 47921 • 810
Boswell, OK 74727 • 702
Boswell, PA 15531 • 1,480
Botetourt ☐, VA • 23,270
Bothell, WA 98011-12 • 7,943
Botkins, OH 45306 • 1,372
Bottineau, ND 58318 • 2,829
Bottineau ☐, ND • 9,239
Boulder, CO 80301-99 • 76,685
Boulder, MT 59632 • 1,441
Boulder ☐, CO • 189,625
Boulder City, NV 89005 • 9,590
Boulder Hill, IL 60538 • 9,333
Boulevard Heights, MD 20743 • 1,700
Boundary ☐, ID • 7,289
Bound Brook, NJ 08805 • 9,710
Bountiful, UT 84010 • 32,877
Bourbon, IN 46504 • 1,522
Bourbon, MO 65441 • 1,259
Bourbon ☐, KS • 15,969
Bourbon ☐, KY • 19,405
Bourbonnais, IL 60914 • 13,280
Bourg, LA 70343 • 2,073
Bourne, MA 02532 • 800
Boutte, LA 70039 • 1,200
Bovey, MN 55709 • 813
Bovina, TX 79009 • 1,499
Bowdle, SD 57428 • 644
Bowdon, GA 30108 • 1,743
Bowie, MD 20715-16 • 33,695
Bowie, TX 76230 • 5,610
Bowie ☐, TX • 75,301
Bowling Green, FL 33834 • 2,310
Bowling Green, KY 42101 • 40,450
Bowling Green, MO 63334 • 3,022
Bowling Green, OH 43402 • 25,728
Bowling Green, SC 29703 • 850
Bowling Green, VA 22427 • 665
Bowman, GA 30624 • 890
Bowman, ND 58623 • 2,071
Bowman, SC 29018 • 1,137
Bowman ☐, ND • 4,229
Bowmanstown, PA 18030 • 1,078
Bow Mar, CO 80120 • 930
Box Butte ☐, NE • 13,696
Box Elder, SD 57719 • 3,186
Box Elder ☐, UT • 33,222
Boxford, MA 01921 • 1,841
Boyce, LA 71409 • 1,198
Boyceville, WI 54725 • 862
Boyd, TX 76023 • 889
Boyd, WI 54726 • 660
Boyd ☐, KY • 55,513
Boyd ☐, NE • 3,331
Boyden, IA 51234 • 708
Boyertown, PA 19512 • 3,979
Boykins, VA 23827 • 791
Boyle, MS 38730 • 888
Boyle ☐, KY • 25,066
Boylston, MA 01505 • 950
Boyne City, MI 49712 • 3,348
Boynton Beach, FL 33435-37 • 35,624
Boys Ranch, TX 79010 • 650
Boys Town, NE 68010 • 622
Bozeman, MT 59715 • 21,645
Braceville, IL 60407 • 721
Bracken ☐, KY • 7,738
Brackenridge, PA 15014 • 4,297
Brackettville, TX 78832 • 1,676
Braddock, PA 15104 • 5,634

Braddock Heights, MD 21714 • 4,223
Bradenton, FL 33505-08 • 30,170
Bradenville, PA 15620 • 1,200
Bradford, AR 72020 • 950
Bradford, IL 61421 • 924
Bradford, OH 45308 • 2,166
Bradford, PA 16701 • 11,211
Bradford, RI 02808 • 1,354
Bradford, TN 38316 • 1,146
Bradford, VT 05033 • 831
Bradford ☐, FL • 20,023
Bradford ☐, PA • 62,919
Bradfordwoods, PA 15015 • 1,264
Bradley, AR 71826 • 790
Bradley, FL 33835 • 1,108
Bradley, IL 60915 • 11,008
Bradley, ME 04411 • 625
Bradley, WV 25818 • 1,200
Bradley ☐, AR • 13,803
Bradley ☐, TN • 67,547
Bradley Beach, NJ 07720 • 4,772
Bradner, OH 43406 • 1,175
Bradshaw, MD 21021 • 800
Bradshaw, WV 24817 • 628
Brady, TX 76825 • 5,969
Braham, MN 55006 • 1,015
Braidwood, IL 60408 • 3,429
Brainerd, MN 56401 • 11,489
Braintree, MA 02184 • 36,337
Bramwell, WV 24715 • 989
Branch ☐, MI • 40,188
Branchville, SC 29432 • 1,769
Brandenburg, KY 40108 • 1,831
Brandon, FL 33511 • 29,100
Brandon, MS 39042 • 9,626
Brandon, SC 29611 • 2,170
Brandon, SD 57005 • 2,589
Brandon, VT 05733 • 1,925
Brandon, WI 53919 • 862
Brandywine, MD 20613 • 1,319
Branford, CT 06405 • 5,438
Branford, FL 32008 • 622
Branford Hills, CT 06405 • 2,200
Branford Point, CT 06405 • 700
Branson, MO 65616 • 2,550
Brant Lake, NY 12815 • 700
Brantley, AL 36009 • 1,151
Brantley ☐, GA • 8,701
Brant Rock, MA 02020 • 1,500
Bratenahl, OH 44108 • 1,485
Brattleboro, VT 05301 • 8,596
Brawley, CA 92227 • 14,946
Braxton ☐, WV • 13,894
Braymer, MO 64624 • 986
Brazil, IN 47834 • 7,852
Brazoria, TX 77422 • 3,025
Brazoria ☐, TX • 169,587
Brazos ☐, TX • 93,588
Brea, CA 92621 • 27,913
Breathitt ☐, KY • 17,004
Breaux Bridge, LA 70517 • 5,922
Breckenridge, CO 80424 • 818
Breckenridge, MI 48615 • 1,495
Breckenridge, MN 56520 • 3,909
Breckenridge, TX 76024 • 6,921
Breckenridge Hills, MO 63114 • 5,666
Breckinridge ☐, KY • 16,861
Brecksville, OH 44141 • 10,132
Breese, IL 62230 • 3,516
Bremen, GA 30110 • 3,966
Bremen, IN 46506 • 3,565
Bremen, OH 43107 • 1,432
Bremer ☐, IA • 24,820
Bremerton, WA 98310-15 • 36,208
Bremond, TX 76629 • 1,025
Brenham, TX 77833 • 10,966
Brent, AL 35034 • 2,862
Brent, FL 32503 • 4,100
Brenton, WV 24818 • 800
Brentwood, CA 94513 • 4,434
Brentwood, MD 20722 • 2,988
Brentwood, MO 63144 • 8,209
Brentwood, NY 11717 • 48,800
Brentwood, OH 45231 • 5,508
Brentwood, PA 15227 • 11,861
Brentwood, SC 29405 • 2,000
Brentwood, TN 37027 • 9,431
Breton Woods, NJ 08723 • 1,300
Brevard, NC 28712 • 5,323
Brevard ☐, FL • 272,959
Brewer, ME 04412 • 9,017
Brewster, MA 02631 • 1,744
Brewster, NY 10509 • 1,650
Brewster, OH 44613 • 2,321
Brewster, WA 98812 • 1,337
Brewster ☐, TX • 7,573
Brewton, AL 36426 • 6,680
Briarcliff, PA 19036 • 9,300
Briarcliff Manor, NY 10510 • 7,115
Briceville, TN 37710 • 800
Brick, NJ 08723-24 • 3,200
Bridge City, LA 70094 • 2,500
Bridgehampton, NY 11932 • 950
Bridgeport, AL 35740 • 2,974
Bridgeport, CA 93517 • 900
Bridgeport, CT 06601-99 • 142,546
Bridgeport, IL 62417 • 2,281
Bridgeport, MI 48722 • 3,500
Bridgeport, NE 69336 • 1,668
Bridgeport, NJ 08014 • 900
Bridgeport, OH 43912 • 2,642
Bridgeport, PA 19405 • 4,843
Bridgeport, TX 76026 • 3,737
Bridgeport, WA 98813 • 1,174

Bridgeport, WV 26330 • 6,604
Bridger, MT 59014 • 724
Bridgeton, MO 63044 • 18,445
Bridgeton, NJ 08302 • 18,795
Bridgetown, OH 45211 • 11,460
Bridgeview, IL 60455 • 14,155
Bridgeville, DE 19933 • 1,238
Bridgeville, PA 15017 • 6,154
Bridgewater, MA 02324 • 6,781
Bridgewater, NJ 08807 • 5,800
Bridgewater, SD 57319 • 653
Bridgewater, VA 22812 • 3,289
Bridgman, MI 49106 • 2,235
Bridgton, ME 04009 • 1,639
Brielle, NJ 08730 • 4,068
Brigantine, NJ 08203 • 8,318
Brigham City, UT 84302 • 15,596
Brighton, AL 35020 • 5,308
Brighton, CO 80601 • 12,773
Brighton, IL 62012 • 2,364
Brighton, IA 52540 • 804
Brighton, MI 48116 • 4,268
Brighton, NY 14610 • 35,776
Brighton, TN 38011 • 976
Brilliant, AL 35548 • 871
Brilliant, OH 43913 • 1,751
Brillion, WI 54110 • 2,907
Brimfield, IL 61517 • 890
Brinkley, AR 72021 • 4,909
Briscoe ☐, TX • 2,579
Bristol, CT 06010 • 57,370
Bristol, FL 32321 • 1,044
Bristol, IN 46507 • 1,203
Bristol, NH 03222 • 1,258
Bristol, PA 19007 • 10,867
Bristol, RI 02809 • 20,128
Bristol, TN 37620 • 23,986
Bristol, VT 05443 • 1,793
Bristol, VA 24201 • 19,042
Bristol ☐, MA • 474,641
Bristol ☐, RI • 46,942
Bristow, OK 74010 • 4,702
Britt, IA 50423 • 2,185
Britton, MI 49229 • 693
Britton, SD 57430 • 1,590
Broadalbin, NY 12025 • 1,415
Broad Brook, CT 06016 • 1,548
Broadmoor, CO 80906 • 1,900
Broadus, MT 59317 • 712
Broadview, IL 60153 • 8,618
Broadview Heights, OH 44141 • 10,920
Broadview Park, FL 33314 • 6,022
Broadwater ☐, MT • 3,267
Broadway, NC 27505 • 908
Broadway, VA 22815 • 1,234
Brockport, NY 14420 • 9,776
Brockton, MA 02401-99 • 95,172
Brockway, PA 15824 • 2,376
Brocton, NY 14716 • 1,416
Broderick, CA 95605 • 9,900
Brodhead, KY 40409 • 686
Brodhead, WI 53520 • 3,153
Broken Arrow, OK 74012-14 • 35,761
Broken Bow, NE 68822 • 3,979
Broken Bow, OK 74728 • 3,965
Bronson, FL 32621 • 853
Bronson, MI 49028 • 2,271
Bronte, TX 76933 • 983
Bronx ☐, NY • 1,168,972
Bronxville, NY 10708 • 6,267
Brook, IN 47922 • 926
Brooke ☐, WV • 31,117
Brookfield, CT 06804 • 1,000
Brookfield, IL 60513 • 19,395
Brookfield, MA 01506 • 1,037
Brookfield, MO 64628 • 5,555
Brookfield, VA 22021 • 2,500
Brookfield, WI 53005 • 34,035
Brookfield Center, CT 06805 • 900
Brookhaven, MS 39601 • 10,800
Brookhaven, PA 19015 • 7,912
Brookhaven, WV 26505 • 1,200
Brookings, OR 97415 • 3,384
Brookings, SD 57006 • 14,951
Brookings ☐, SD • 24,332
Brookland, AR 72417 • 840
Brooklawn, NJ 08030 • 2,133
Brooklet, GA 30415 • 1,035
Brookline, MA 02146 • 55,062
Brooklyn, CT 06234 • 900
Brooklyn, IN 46111 • 889
Brooklyn, IA 52211 • 1,509
Brooklyn, MI 49230 • 1,110
Brooklyn, MS 39425 • 800
Brooklyn, OH 44144 • 12,342
Brooklyn, SC 29720 • 1,800
Brooklyn, WI 53521 • 627
Brooklyn Center, MN 55429 • 31,230
Brooklyn Park, MD 21225 • 11,508
Brooklyn Park, MN 55443 • 43,332
Brookneal, VA 24528 • 1,454
Brook Park, OH 44142 • 26,195
Brookport, IL 62910 • 1,128
Brookridge, CO 80120 • 1,200
Brooks, KY 40109 • 1,344
Brooks ☐, GA • 15,255
Brooks ☐, TX • 8,428
Brookshire, TX 77423 • 2,175
Brookside, AL 35036 • 1,409
Brookside, DE 19713 • 15,255
Brookston, IN 47923 • 1,701
Brooksville, FL 33512 • 5,582
Brooksville, KY 41004 • 680
Brooksville, MS 39739 • 1,038

Brookville, IN 47012 • 2,874
Brookville, MA 02343 • 950
Brookville, NY 11545 • 3,290
Brookville, OH 45309 • 4,322
Brookville, PA 15825 • 4,568
Brookwood, NJ 08527 • 4,000
Broomall, PA 19008 • 23,642
Broome ☐, NY • 213,648
Broomfield, CO 80020 • 20,730
Brooten, MN 56316 • 647
Broussard, LA 70518 • 2,923
Broward ☐, FL • 1,018,200
Browardale, FL 33311 • 7,571
Browerville, MN 56438 • 693
Brown ☐, IL • 5,411
Brown ☐, IN • 12,377
Brown ☐, KS • 11,955
Brown ☐, MN • 28,645
Brown ☐, NE • 4,377
Brown ☐, OH • 31,920
Brown ☐, SD • 36,962
Brown ☐, TX • 33,057
Brown ☐, WI • 175,280
Brown City, MI 48416 • 1,163
Brown Deer, WI 53209 • 12,921
Brownfield, TX 79316 • 10,387
Brownfields, LA 70811 • 1,800
Browning, MT 59417 • 1,226
Brownsburg, IN 46112 • 6,242
Brownsdale, MN 55918 • 691
Browns Mills, NJ 08015 • 10,568
Brownstown, IL 62418 • 708
Brownstown, IN 47220 • 2,704
Brownstown, PA 15906 • 800
Browns Valley, MN 56219 • 887
Brownsville, FL 33142 • 18,058
Brownsville, KY 42210 • 674
Brownsville, LA 71291 • 3,000
Brownsville, OH 07327 • 1,261
Brownsville, PA 15417 • 4,043
Brownsville, TN 38012 • 9,307
Brownsville, TX 78520-26 • 84,997
Brownton, MN 55312 • 697
Brownville, NY 13615 • 1,099
Brownville Junction, ME 04415 • 775
Brownwood, TX 76801 • 19,396
Broxton, GA 31519 • 1,117
Broyhill Park, VA 22042 • 3,600
Bruce, MS 38915 • 2,208
Bruce, WI 54819 • 905
Bruce ☐, SD • 5,245
Bruceton, TN 38317 • 1,579
Bruceville, IN 47516 • 646
Brule ☐, SD • 5,245
Brundidge, AL 36010 • 3,213
Brunswick, GA 31520 • 17,605
Brunswick, ME 04011 • 10,990
Brunswick, MD 21716 • 4,572
Brunswick, MO 65236 • 1,272
Brunswick, OH 44212 • 28,104
Brunswick ☐, NC • 35,777
Brunswick ☐, VA • 15,632
Brush, CO 80723 • 4,082
Brusly, LA 70719 • 1,762
Bryan, OH 43506 • 7,879
Bryan, TX 77801-06 • 44,337
Bryan ☐, GA • 10,175
Bryan ☐, OK • 30,535
Bryans Road, MD 20616 • 3,739
Bryant, AR 72022 • 2,682
Bryantville, MA 02327 • 1,500
Bryn Mawr, PA 19010 • 9,500
Bryn Mawr, WA 98178 • 2,100
Bryson City, NC 28713 • 1,556
Buchanan, GA 30113 • 1,019
Buchanan, MI 49107 • 5,142
Buchanan, VA 24066 • 1,205
Buchanan ☐, IA • 22,900
Buchanan ☐, MO • 87,888
Buchanan ☐, VA • 37,989
Buckatunna, MS 39322 • 700
Buckeye, AZ 85326 • 3,434
Buckeye Lake, OH 43008 • 2,521
Buckhannon, WV 26201 • 6,820
Buckhorn, AZ 85205 • 4,000
Buckingham ☐, VA • 11,751
Buckley, IL 60918 • 604
Buckley, WA 98321 • 3,143
Bucklin, KS 67834 • 786
Bucklin, MO 64631 • 713
Bucknell Manor, VA 22307 • 2,350
Buckner, MO 64016 • 2,848
Bucks ☐, PA • 479,211
Bucksport, ME 04416 • 2,853
Bucksport, SC 29527 • 1,125
Bucyrus, OH 44820 • 13,433
Buda, IL 61314 • 668
Bude, MS 39630 • 1,092
Buechel, KY 40218 • 6,912
Buena, NJ 08310 • 3,642
Buena, WA 98921 • 800
Buena Park, CA 90620-24 • 64,165
Buena Vista, CO 81211 • 2,075
Buena Vista, FL 33589 • 3,000
Buena Vista, GA 31803 • 1,544
Buena Vista, VA 24416 • 6,717
Buena Vista ☐, IA • 20,774

Buffalo, WY 82834 • 3,799
Buffalo ☐, NE • 34,797
Buffalo ☐, SD • 1,795
Buffalo ☐, WI • 14,309
Buffalo Center, IA 50424 • 1,233
Buffalo Grove, IL 60089 • 22,230
Buffalo Lake, MN 55314 • 782
Buford, GA 30518 • 6,578
Buhl, ID 83316 • 3,629
Buhl, MN 55713 • 1,284
Buhler, KS 67522 • 1,188
Buies Creek, NC 27506 • 1,939
Bullhead City, AZ 86430 • 5,000
Bullitt ☐, KY • 43,346
Bulloch ☐, GA • 35,785
Bullock ☐, AL • 10,596
Bullock Creek, MI 48640 • 900
Bulls Gap, TN 37711 • 821
Bull Shoals, AR 72619 • 1,312
Buna, TX 77612 • 1,900
Bunche Park, FL 33054 • 4,000
Buncombe ☐, NC • 160,934
Bunker, MO 63629 • 673
Bunker Hill, IL 62014 • 1,700
Bunker Hill, IN 46914 • 984
Bunker Hill, OR 97420 • 1,555
Bunker Hill, WV 25309 • 800
Bunkie, LA 71322 • 5,364
Bunnell, FL 32010 • 1,816
Buras, LA 70041 • 2,600
Burbank, CA 91501-99 • 84,625
Burbank, IL 60459 • 28,462
Burbank, WA 99323 • 900
Bureau ☐, IL • 39,114
Burgaw, NC 28425 • 1,738
Burgettstown, PA 15021 • 1,867
Burgin, KY 40310 • 1,008
Burien, WA 98166 • 14,250
Burkburnett, TX 76354 • 10,668
Burke, SD 57523 • 859
Burke, VA 22015 • 1,500
Burke ☐, GA • 19,349
Burke ☐, NC • 72,504
Burke ☐, ND • 3,822
Burke City, MO 63135 • 2,600
Burkesville, KY 42717 • 2,051
Burkeville, VA 23922 • 606
Burleigh ☐, ND • 54,811
Burleson, TX 76028 • 11,734
Burleson ☐, TX • 12,313
Burley, ID 83318 • 8,761
Burlingame, CA 94010 • 26,173
Burlingame, KS 66413 • 1,239
Burlington, CO 80807 • 3,107
Burlington, IN 46915 • 680
Burlington, IA 52601 • 29,529
Burlington, MA 01803 • 23,486
Burlington, NJ 08016 • 10,246
Burlington, NC 27215 • 37,266
Burlington, ND 58722 • 762
Burlington, VT 05401 • 37,712
Burlington, WA 98233 • 3,894
Burlington, WI 53105 • 8,385
Burlington ☐, NJ • 362,542
Burlington Beach, IN 46383 • 900
Burlington Junction, MO 64428 • 657
Burnet, TX 78611 • 3,410
Burnet ☐, TX • 17,803
Burnett ☐, WI • 12,340
Burney, CA 96013 • 3,187
Burnham, PA 17009 • 2,457
Burns, OR 97720 • 3,579
Burns, TN 37029 • 777
Burns Flat, OK 73624 • 2,431
Burnside, KY 42519 • 775
Burnsville, MN 55337 • 35,674
Burnsville, MS 38833 • 889
Burnsville, NC 28714 • 1,452
Burnt Hills, NY 12027 • 2,000
Burr Oak, MI 49030 • 853
Burrton, KS 67020 • 976
Burt, IA 50522 • 689
Burt ☐, NE • 8,813
Burton, MI 48509 • 29,976
Burton, OH 44021 • 1,401
Burwell, NE 68823 • 1,383
Bushnell, FL 33513 • 983
Bushnell, IL 61422 • 3,811
Butler, AL 36904 • 1,882
Butler, GA 31006 • 1,959
Butler, IN 46721 • 2,509
Butler, KY 41006 • 663
Butler, MO 64730 • 4,107
Butler, NJ 07405 • 7,616
Butler, OH 44822 • 991
Butler, PA 16001 • 17,026
Butler, WI 53007 • 2,059
Butler ☐, AL • 21,680
Butler ☐, IA • 17,668
Butler ☐, KS • 44,782
Butler ☐, KY • 11,064
Butler ☐, MO • 37,693
Butler ☐, NE • 9,330
Butler ☐, OH • 258,787
Butler ☐, PA • 147,912
Butner, NC 27509 • 4,240
Butte, MT 59701 • 37,205
Butte ☐, CA • 143,851
Butte ☐, ID • 3,342
Butte ☐, SD • 8,372
Butterfield, MN 56120 • 634
Buttonwillow, CA 93206 • 1,350
Butts ☐, GA • 13,665
Buxton, NC 27920 • 700

Buzzards Bay, MA 02532 • 3,375
Byers, CO 80103 • 1,100
Byesville, OH 43723 • 2,572
Byfield, MA 01922 • 950
Byhalia, MS 38611 • 757
Bylas, AZ 85530 • 1,175
Byng, OK 74820 • 833
Byrdstown, TN 38549 • 884
Byron, CA 94514 • 900
Byron, GA 31008 • 1,661
Byron, IL 61010 • 2,035
Byron, MN 55920 • 1,715
Byron, WY 82412 • 633

C

Cabarrus ☐, NC • 85,895
Cabell ☐, WV • 106,835
Cabin Creek, WV 25035 • 900
Cabin John, MD 20818 • 1,500
Cabool, MO 65689 • 2,090
Cabot, AR 72023 • 4,806
Cache, OK 73527 • 1,661
Cache ☐, UT • 57,176
Caddo, OK 74729 • 923
Caddo ☐, LA • 252,358
Caddo ☐, OK • 30,905
Cadillac, MI 49601 • 10,199
Cadiz, KY 42211 • 1,661
Cadiz, OH 43907 • 4,058
Cadott, WI 54727 • 1,247
Cahaba Heights, AL 35243 • 3,800
Cahokia, IL 62206 • 18,904
Cairnbrook, PA 15924 • 800
Cairo, GA 31728 • 8,777
Cairo, IL 62914 • 5,931
Cairo, NE 68824 • 737
Cairo, NY 12413 • 725
Calabasas, CA 91302 • 900
Calais, ME 04619 • 4,262
Calaveras ☐, CA • 20,710
Calavo Gardens, CA 92041 • 6,100
Calcasieu ☐, LA • 167,223
Calcutta, OH 43920 • 1,121
Caldwell, ID 83605 • 17,699
Caldwell, KS 67022 • 1,401
Caldwell, NJ 07006 • 7,624
Caldwell, OH 43724 • 1,935
Caldwell, TX 77836 • 2,953
Caldwell ☐, KY • 13,473
Caldwell ☐, LA • 10,761
Caldwell ☐, MO • 8,660
Caldwell ☐, NC • 67,746
Caldwell ☐, TX • 23,637
Caledonia, MI 49316 • 722
Caledonia, MN 55921 • 2,691
Caledonia, NY 14423 • 2,188
Caledonia, OH 43314 • 759
Caledonia ☐, VT • 25,808
Calera, AL 35040 • 2,035
Calera, OK 74730 • 1,390
Calexico, CA 92231 • 14,412
Calhoun, GA 30701 • 5,563
Calhoun, KY 42327 • 1,080
Calhoun ☐, AL • 119,761
Calhoun ☐, AR • 6,079
Calhoun ☐, FL • 9,294
Calhoun ☐, GA • 5,717
Calhoun ☐, IL • 5,867
Calhoun ☐, IA • 13,542
Calhoun ☐, MI • 141,557
Calhoun ☐, MS • 15,664
Calhoun ☐, SC • 12,206
Calhoun ☐, TX • 19,574
Calhoun ☐, WV • 8,250
Calhoun City, MS 38916 • 2,033
Calhoun Falls, SC 29628 • 2,491
Calico Rock, AR 72519 • 1,046
Caliente, NV 89008 • 982
Califon, NJ 07830 • 1,023
California, MO 65018 • 3,381
California, PA 15419 • 5,703
Calion, AR 71724 • 638
Calipatria, CA 92233 • 2,636
Calistoga, CA 94515 • 3,879
Callahan, FL 32011 • 869
Callahan, KS 67209 • 900
Callahan ☐, TX • 10,992
Callaway, FL 32401 • 7,154
Callaway ☐, MO • 32,252
Calloway ☐, KY • 30,031
Calmar, IA 52132 • 1,053
Calumet, MI 49913 • 1,013
Calumet ☐, WI • 30,867
Calumet City, IL 60409 • 39,697
Calumet Park, IL 60643 • 8,788
Calvert, TX 77837 • 1,732
Calvert ☐, MD • 34,638
Calvert City, KY 42029 • 2,388
Calverton, MD 20705 • 7,649
Calverton Park, MO 63136 • 1,717
Calwa, CA 93725 • 6,640
Calypso, NC 28325 • 689
Camanche, IA 52730 • 4,725
Camarillo, CA 93010 • 37,797
Camas, WA 98607 • 5,681
Camas ☐, ID • 818
Cambria, CA 93428 • 3,061
Cambria, WI 53923 • 680
Cambria ☐, PA • 183,263
Cambrian Park, CA 95124 • 4,000
Cambridge, IL 61238 • 2,217
Cambridge, IA 50046 • 732
Cambridge, MD 21613 • 11,703
Cambridge, MA 02138 • 95,322
Cambridge, MN 55008 • 3,287
Cambridge, NE 69022 • 1,206
Cambridge, NY 12816 • 1,820
Cambridge, OH 43725 • 13,573
Cambridge, WI 53523 • 844
Cambridge City, IN 47327 • 2,407
Cambridge Springs, PA 16403 • 2,102
Camden, AL 36726 • 2,406
Camden, AR 71701 • 15,356
Camden, DE 19934 • 1,757
Camden, IN 46917 • 618
Camden, ME 04843 • 3,743
Camden, NJ 08101-99 • 84,910
Camden, NY 13316 • 2,667
Camden, OH 45311 • 1,971
Camden, SC 29020 • 7,462
Camden, TN 38320 • 3,279
Camden ☐, GA • 13,371
Camden ☐, MO • 20,017
Camden ☐, NJ • 471,650
Camden ☐, NC • 5,829
Camdenton, MO 65020 • 2,303
Cameron, LA 70631 • 1,736
Cameron, MO 64429 • 4,519
Cameron, TX 76520 • 5,721
Cameron, WV 26033 • 1,474
Cameron, WI 54822 • 1,115
Cameron ☐, LA • 9,336
Cameron ☐, PA • 6,674
Cameron ☐, TX • 209,727
Camilla, GA 31730 • 5,414
Camino, CA 95709 • 900
Cammack Village, AR 72207 • 920
Camp ☐, TX • 9,275
Campbell, CA 95008 • 26,910
Campbell, FL 32741 • 2,941
Campbell, MO 63933 • 2,134
Campbell, OH 44405 • 11,619
Campbell ☐, KY • 83,317
Campbell ☐, SD • 2,243
Campbell ☐, TN • 34,923
Campbell ☐, VA • 45,424
Campbell ☐, WY • 24,367
Campbellsburg, IN 47108 • 695
Campbellsburg, KY 40011 • 714
Campbellsport, WI 53010 • 1,740
Campbellsville, KY 42718 • 8,715
Camp Hill, AL 36850 • 1,628
Camp Hill, PA 17011 • 8,422
Camp Point, IL 62320 • 1,285
Camp Springs, MD 20748 • 2,500
Campti, LA 71411 • 1,069
Camp Verde, AZ 86322 • 1,125
Camp Wood, TX 78833 • 728
Canaan, CT 06018 • 1,160
Canadensis, PA 18325 • 800
Canadian, TX 79014 • 3,491
Canadian ☐, OK • 56,452
Canajoharie, NY 13317 • 2,412
Canal Fulton, OH 44614 • 3,481
Canal Point, FL 33438 • 950
Canal Winchester, OH 43110 • 2,749
Canandaigua, NY 14424 • 10,419
Canaseraga, NY 14822 • 700
Canastota, NY 13032 • 4,773
Canby, MN 56220 • 2,143
Canby, OR 97013 • 7,659
Candler ☐, GA • 7,518
Candlewood Isle, CT 06812 • 750
Candlewood Shores, CT 06804 • 1,950
Cando, ND 58324 • 1,496
Candor, NC 27229 • 868
Candor, NY 13743 • 917
Caney, KS 67333 • 2,284
Caneyville, KY 42721 • 642
Canfield, OH 44406 • 5,535
Canisteo, NY 14823 • 2,679
Canistota, SD 57012 • 626
Cannelton, IN 47520 • 2,373
Cannelton, WV 25036 • 750
Cannon ☐, TN • 10,234
Cannon Beach, OR 97110 • 1,187
Cannondale, CT 06897 • 1,300
Cannon Falls, MN 55009 • 2,653
Canon, GA 30520 • 704
Canon City, CO 81212 • 13,037
Canonsburg, PA 15317 • 10,459
Canton, CT 06019 • 1,680
Canton, GA 30114 • 3,601
Canton, IL 61520 • 14,626
Canton, KS 67428 • 926
Canton, MA 02021 • 18,182
Canton, MI 48187 • 5,000
Canton, MS 39046 • 11,116
Canton, MO 63435 • 2,435
Canton, NC 28716 • 4,631
Canton, NY 13617 • 7,055
Canton, OH 44701-99 • 93,077
Canton, OK 73724 • 854
Canton, PA 17724 • 1,959
Canton, SD 57013 • 2,886
Canton, TX 75103 • 2,845
Cantonment, FL 32533 • 3,200
Canute, OK 73626 • 676
Canutillo, TX 79835 • 2,000
Canyon, TX 79015 • 10,724
Canyon ☐, ID • 83,756
Canyon City, OR 97820 • 639
Canyon Lake, TX 78130 • 6,000
Canyonville, OR 97417 • 1,288
Capac, MI 48014 • 1,377
Cape Canaveral, FL 32920 • 5,733
Cape Charles, VA 23310 • 1,512
Cape Coral, FL 33904 • 32,103
Cape Elizabeth, ME 04107 • 7,838
Cape Girardeau, MO 63701 • 34,361
Cape Girardeau ☐, MO • 58,837
Cape May, NJ 08204 • 4,853
Cape May ☐, NJ • 82,266
Cape May Court House, NJ 08210 • 3,597
Cape Vincent, NY 13618 • 785
Capitan, NM 88316 • 762
Capitola, CA 95010 • 9,095
Capitol Heights, IA 50317 • 815
Capitol Heights, MD 20743 • 3,271
Capron, IL 61012 • 678
Captain Cook, HI 96704 • 2,008
Captiva, FL 33924 • 1,200
Caraway, AR 72419 • 1,165
Carbon ☐, MT • 8,099
Carbon ☐, PA • 53,285
Carbon ☐, UT • 22,179
Carbon ☐, WY • 21,896
Carbondale, CO 81623 • 2,084
Carbondale, IL 62901 • 26,414
Carbondale, KS 66414 • 1,518
Carbondale, PA 18407 • 11,255
Carbon Hill, AL 35549 • 2,452
Cardiff-By-The-Sea, CA 92007 • 10,054
Cardington, OH 43315 • 1,665
Cardwell, MO 63829 • 831
Carencro, LA 70520 • 3,712
Caretta, WV 24821 • 950
Carey, OH 43316 • 3,674
Caribou, ME 04736 • 9,916
Caribou ☐, ID • 8,695
Carle Place, NY 11514 • 6,300
Carleton, MI 48117 • 2,786
Carlin, NV 89822 • 1,232
Carlinville, IL 62626 • 5,439
Carlisle, AR 72024 • 2,567
Carlisle, IN 47838 • 717
Carlisle, IA 50047 • 3,073
Carlisle, KY 40311 • 1,757
Carlisle, OH 45005 • 4,276
Carlisle, PA 17013 • 18,314
Carlisle ☐, KY • 5,487
Carl Junction, MO 64834 • 3,937
Carlsbad, CA 92008 • 35,490
Carlsbad, NM 88220 • 25,496
Carlstadt, NJ 07072 • 6,166
Carlton, MN 55718 • 862
Carlton, OR 97111 • 1,302
Carlton ☐, MN • 29,936
Carlyle, IL 62231 • 3,388
Carmel, CA 93923 • 4,707
Carmel, IN 46032 • 18,272
Carmel, NY 10512 • 3,395
Carmi, IL 62821 • 6,264
Carmichael, CA 95608 • 43,108
Carmichaels, PA 15320 • 630
Carnation, WA 98014 • 913
Carnegie, OK 73015 • 2,016
Carnegie, PA 15106 • 10,099
Carney, OK 74832 • 622
Carneys Point, NJ 08069 • 7,574
Carnot, PA 15108 • 5,400
Caro, MI 48723 • 4,317
Carol City, FL 33055 • 47,349
Caroleen, NC 28019 • 1,000
Carolina, WV 26563 • 650
Carolina Beach, NC 28428 • 2,000
Caroline ☐, MD • 23,143
Caroline ☐, VA • 17,904
Carol Stream, IL 60188 • 15,472
Carpentersville, IL 60110 • 23,272
Carpinteria, CA 93013 • 10,835
Carrabelle, FL 32322 • 1,304
Carrboro, NC 27510 • 7,336
Carrier Mills, IL 62917 • 2,268
Carrington, ND 58421 • 2,641
Carrizo Springs, TX 78834 • 6,886
Carrizozo, NM 88301 • 1,222
Carroll, IA 51401 • 9,705
Carroll, OH 43112 • 641
Carroll ☐, AR • 16,203
Carroll ☐, GA • 50,040
Carroll ☐, IL • 18,779
Carroll ☐, IN • 19,722
Carroll ☐, IA • 22,951
Carroll ☐, KY • 9,270
Carroll ☐, MD • 96,356
Carroll ☐, MS • 9,776
Carroll ☐, MO • 12,131
Carroll ☐, NH • 27,931
Carroll ☐, OH • 25,598
Carroll ☐, TN • 28,285
Carroll ☐, VA • 27,270
Carrollton, AL 35447 • 1,104
Carrollton, GA 30117 • 14,078
Carrollton, IL 62016 • 2,816
Carrollton, KY 41008 • 3,967
Carrollton, MI 48724 • 7,482
Carrollton, MO 64633 • 4,700
Carrollton, OH 44615 • 3,065
Carrollton, TX 75006-08 • 40,595
Carrolltown, PA 15722 • 1,395
Carrville, AL 36023 • 820
Carson, CA 90745 • 81,221
Carson, IA 51525 • 716
Carson, WA 98610 • 950
Carson ☐, TX • 6,672
Carson City, MI 48811 • 1,229
Carson City, NV 89701 • 32,022
Carsonville, MI 48419 • 622
Carter ☐, KY • 25,060
Carter ☐, MO • 5,428
Carter ☐, MT • 1,799
Carter ☐, OK • 43,610
Carter ☐, TN • 50,205
Carteret, NJ 07008 • 20,598
Carteret ☐, NC • 41,092
Carter Lake, IA 51510 • 3,438
Cartersville, GA 30120 • 9,247
Carterville, IL 62918 • 3,445
Carterville, MO 64835 • 1,973
Carthage, IL 62321 • 2,978
Carthage, IN 46115 • 886
Carthage, MS 39051 • 3,453
Carthage, MO 64836 • 11,104
Carthage, NC 28327 • 925
Carthage, NY 13619 • 3,643
Carthage, TN 37030 • 2,672
Carthage, TX 75633 • 6,447
Caruthersville, MO 63830 • 7,958
Carver, MA 02330 • 650
Carver, MN 55315 • 642
Carver ☐, MN • 37,046
Carver Ranch Estates, FL 33023 • 5,600
Carville, LA 70721 • 1,037
Cary, IL 60013 • 6,640
Cary, NC 27511 • 21,763
Caryville, FL 32427 • 633
Caryville, TN 37714 • 2,039
Casa Grande, AZ 85222 • 14,971
Casas Adobes, AZ 85704 • 5,300
Cascade, ID 83611 • 945
Cascade, IA 52033 • 1,912
Cascade, MT 59421 • 773
Cascade, WI 53011 • 615
Cascade ☐, MT • 80,696
Cascade Locks, OR 97014 • 838
Caseville, MI 48725 • 851
Casey, IL 62420 • 3,026
Casey ☐, KY • 14,818
Cashion, AZ 85329 • 3,014
Cashmere, WA 98815 • 2,240
Cashton, WI 54619 • 827
Casper, WY 82601-15 • 51,016
Caspian, MI 49915 • 1,038
Cass ☐, IL • 15,084
Cass ☐, IN • 40,936
Cass ☐, IA • 16,932
Cass ☐, MI • 49,499
Cass ☐, MN • 21,050
Cass ☐, MO • 51,029
Cass ☐, NE • 20,297
Cass ☐, ND • 88,247
Cass ☐, TX • 29,430
Cassadaga, NY 14718 • 821
Cass City, MI 48726 • 2,258
Casselberry, FL 32707-08 • 15,247
Casselton, ND 58012 • 1,661
Cassia ☐, ID • 19,427
Cass Lake, MN 56633 • 1,001
Cassopolis, MI 49031 • 1,933
Cassville, MO 65625 • 2,091
Cassville, WI 53806 • 1,270
Castalia, OH 44824 • 973
Castanea, PA 17726 • 1,204
Castile, NY 14427 • 1,135
Castleberry, AL 36432 • 847
Castle Dale, UT 84513 • 1,910
Castle Hayne, NC 28429 • 1,087
Castle Hills, DE 19720 • 1,950
Castle Park, CA 92011 • 6,300
Castle Point, MO 63136 • 6,500
Castle Rock, CO 80104 • 3,921
Castle Rock, WA 98611 • 2,162
Castle Shannon, PA 15234 • 10,164
Castleton on Hudson, NY 12033 • 1,627
Castro ☐, TX • 10,556
Castro Valley, CA 94546 • 44,011
Castroville, CA 95012 • 4,396
Castroville, TX 78009 • 1,821
Caswell ☐, NC • 20,705
Catahoula ☐, LA • 12,287
Catalina Foothills, AZ 85718 • 1,500
Catasauqua, PA 18032 • 6,711
Cataumet, MA 02534 • 800
Catawba ☐, NC • 105,208
Catawissa, PA 17820 • 1,568
Cathedral City, CA 92234 • 4,130
Cathlamet, WA 98612 • 635
Catlettsburg, KY 41129 • 3,005
Catlin, IL 61817 • 2,226
Catonsville, MD 21228 • 33,208
Catoosa, OK 74015 • 1,561
Catoosa ☐, GA • 36,991
Catron ☐, NM • 2,720
Catskill, NY 12414 • 4,718
Cattaraugus, NY 14719 • 1,200
Cattaraugus ☐, NY • 85,697
Cavalier, ND 58220 • 1,505
Cavalier ☐, ND • 7,636
Cave City, AR 72521 • 1,634
Cave City, KY 42127 • 2,098
Cave Creek, AZ 85331 • 1,589
Cave Junction, OR 97523 • 1,023
Cave Spring, GA 30124 • 883
Cave Spring, VA 24018 • 6,300
Cavetown, MD 21720 • 1,533
Cawker City, KS 67430 • 640
Cawood, KY 40815 • 800
Cayce, SC 29033 • 11,701
Cayuga, IN 47928 • 1,258
Cayuga ☐, NY • 79,894
Cayuga Heights, NY 14850 • 3,170
Cazenovia, NY 13035 • 2,599
Cecil, PA 15321 • 900
Cecil ☐, MD • 60,430
Cedar ☐, IA • 18,635
Cedar ☐, MO • 11,894
Cedar ☐, NE • 11,375
Cedar Bluff, AL 35959 • 1,129
Cedar Bluff, TN 37722 • 1,200
Cedar Bluffs, NE 68015 • 632
Cedarburg, WI 53012 • 9,005
Cedar City, UT 84720 • 10,972
Cedar Crest, NM 87008 • 900
Cedaredge, CO 81413 • 1,184
Cedar Falls, IA 50613 • 36,322
Cedar Grove, NJ 07009 • 12,600
Cedar Grove, WV 25039 • 1,479
Cedar Grove, WI 53013 • 1,420
Cedar Hill, MO 63016 • 1,512
Cedar Hill, TX 75104 • 6,849
Cedar Hills, OR 97225 • 8,000
Cedarhurst, NY 11516 • 6,162
Cedar Key, FL 32625 • 700
Cedar Knolls, NJ 07927 • 3,000
Cedar Lake, IN 46303 • 8,754
Cedar Rapids, IA 52401-99 • 110,243
Cedar Springs, MI 49319 • 2,615
Cedartown, GA 30125 • 8,619
Cedar Vale, KS 67024 • 848
Cedarville, CA 96104 • 950
Cedarville, IL 61013 • 766
Cedarville, NJ 08311 • 990
Cedarville, OH 45314 • 2,799
Celina, OH 45822 • 9,137
Celina, TN 38551 • 1,580
Celina, TX 75009 • 1,520
Celoron, NY 14720 • 1,405
Cement, OK 73017 • 884
Cementon, PA 18052 • 1,200
Center, CO 81125 • 1,630
Center, MO 63436 • 669
Center, ND 58530 • 900
Center, TX 75935 • 5,827
Centerbrook, CT 06409 • 900
Centerburg, OH 43011 • 1,275
Centereach, NY 11720 • 34,600
Centerfield, UT 84622 • 653
Center Hill, FL 34254 • 751
Center Line, MI 48015 • 9,293
Center Moriches, NY 11934 • 4,000
Center Point, AL 35215 • 23,317
Center Point, IA 52213 • 1,591
Centerville, IN 47330 • 2,284
Centerville, IA 52544 • 6,558
Centerville, MA 02632 • 3,640
Centerville, OH 45459 • 18,886
Centerville, PA 15417 • 4,207
Centerville, SD 57014 • 892
Centerville, TN 37033 • 2,824
Centerville, TX 75833 • 799
Centerville, UT 84014 • 8,069
Central, NM 88026 • 1,968
Central, SC 29630 • 1,914
Central City, IL 62801 • 1,505
Central City, IA 52214 • 1,067
Central City, KY 42330 • 5,214
Central City, NE 68826 • 3,083
Central City, PA 15926 • 1,496
Central Falls, RI 02863 • 16,995
Central Heights, AZ 85501 • 1,500
Centralia, IL 62801 • 15,126
Centralia, MO 65240 • 3,537
Centralia, WA 98531 • 11,555
Central Islip, NY 11722 • 26,000
Central Lake, MI 49622 • 895
Central Park, WA 98520 • 2,900
Central Point, OR 97502 • 6,357
Central Square, NY 13036 • 1,418
Central Valley, CA 96019 • 3,424
Central Valley, NY 10917 • 1,200
Central Village, CT 06332 • 1,200
Centre, AL 35960 • 2,351
Centre ☐, PA • 112,760
Centre City, NJ 08051 • 2,500
Centre Hall, PA 16828 • 1,233
Centreville, AL 35042 • 2,504
Centreville, IL 62207 • 9,747
Centreville, MD 21617 • 2,018
Centreville, MI 49032 • 1,202
Centreville, MS 39631 • 1,844
Centreville, VA 22020 • 950
Centuria, WI 54824 • 711
Century, FL 32535 • 1,805
Ceredo, WV 25507 • 2,255
Ceres, CA 95307 • 13,281
Ceresco, NE 68017 • 836
Cerritos, CA 90701 • 53,020
Cerro Gordo, IL 61818 • 1,553
Cerro Gordo ☐, IA • 48,458
Chadbourn, NC 28431 • 1,975
Chadron, NE 69337 • 5,933
Chadwick, IL 61014 • 631
Chadwicks, NY 13319 • 1,500
Chaffee, MO 63740 • 3,241
Chaffee ☐, CO • 13,227
Chaffin, MA 01520 • 3,700
Chagrin Falls, OH 44022 • 4,335
Chalfonte, DE 19810 • 2,200
Challis, ID 83226 • 758
Chalmette, LA 70043 • 33,847
Chama, NM 87520 • 1,090
Chamberlain, SD 57325 • 2,258
Chambers ☐, AL • 39,191
Chambers ☐, TX • 18,538
Chambersburg, PA 17201 • 16,174
Chamblee, GA 30341 • 7,137
Champaign, IL 61820-21 • 58,133
Champaign ☐, IL • 168,392
Champaign ☐, OH • 33,649
Champion, OH 44481 • 5,270
Champlain, NY 12919 • 1,410

Champlin, MN 55316 • 9,006
Chandler, AZ 85224 • 29,673
Chandler, IN 47610 • 3,043
Chandler, OK 74834 • 2,926
Chandler, TX 75758 • 1,308
Chandler Heights, AZ 85227 • 750
Chandlerville, IL 62627 • 842
Chanhassen, MN 55317 • 6,359
Channahon, IL 60410 • 3,734
Channel Lake, IL 60002 • 1,613
Channelview, TX 77530 • 16,000
Chantilly, VA 22021 • 950
Chanute, KS 66720 • 10,506
Chapel Hill, NC 27514 • 32,421
Chapel Hill, TN 37034 • 861
Chapel Square, VA 22003 • 2,000
Chapin, IL 62628 • 648
Chapman, KS 67431 • 1,255
Chapmanville, WV 25508 • 1,164
Chappaqua, NY 10514 • 5,100
Chappell, NE 69129 • 1,095
Chardon, OH 44024 • 4,434
Charenton, LA 70523 • 950
Chariton, IA 50049 • 4,987
Chariton □, MO • 10,489
Charleroi, PA 15022 • 5,717
Charles □, MD • 72,751
Charles City, IA 50616 • 8,778
Charles City □, VA • 6,692
Charles Mix □, SD • 9,680
Charleston, AR 72933 • 1,748
Charleston, IL 61920 • 19,355
Charleston, MS 38921 • 2,878
Charleston, MO 63834 • 5,230
Charleston, OR 97420 • 700
Charleston, SC 29401–25 • 69,510
Charleston, TN 37310 • 756
Charleston, WV 25301–99 • 63,968
Charleston □, SC • 276,974
Charlestown, IN 47111 • 5,596
Charlestown, MD 21914 • 720
Charlestown, NH 03603 • 1,294
Charlestown, RI 02813 • 1,200
Charles Town, WV 25414 • 2,857
Charlevoix, MI 49720 • 3,296
Charlevoix □, MI • 19,907
Charlotte, MI 48813 • 8,251
Charlotte, NC 28201–99 • 314,447
Charlotte, TN 37036 • 788
Charlotte, TX 78011 • 1,443
Charlotte □, FL • 58,460
Charlotte □, VA • 12,266
Charlotte Hall, MD 20622 • 1,000
Charlotte Harbor, FL 33950 • 2,084
Charlottesville, VA 22901–10 • 39,916
Charlton □, GA • 7,343
Charlton City, MA 01508 • 1,100
Charmco, WV 25958 • 800
Charter Oak, IA 51439 • 615
Chase, KS 67524 • 753
Chase, MD 21027 • 700
Chase □, KS • 3,309
Chase □, NE • 4,758
Chase City, VA 23924 • 2,749
Chaska, MN 55318 • 8,346
Chassell, MI 49916 • 700
Chateaugay, NY 12920 • 869
Chatfield, MN 55923 • 2,055
Chatham, IL 62629 • 5,597
Chatham, LA 71226 • 714
Chatham, MA 02633 • 1,922
Chatham, NJ 07928 • 8,537
Chatham, NY 12037 • 2,001
Chatham, VA 24531 • 1,390
Chatham □, GA • 202,226
Chatham □, NC • 33,415
Chatom, AL 36518 • 1,122
Chatsworth, GA 30705 • 2,493
Chatsworth, IL 60921 • 1,187
Chattahoochee, FL 32324 • 5,332
Chattahoochee □, GA • 21,732
Chattanooga, TN 37401–99 • 169,558
Chattaroy, WV 25667 • 1,200
Chattooga □, GA • 21,856
Chaumont, NY 13622 • 620
Chauncey, OH 45719 • 1,050
Chautauqua □, KS • 5,016
Chautauqua □, NY • 146,925
Chauvin, LA 70344 • 3,338
Chaves □, NM • 51,103
Chazy, NY 12921 • 800
Cheatham □, TN • 21,616
Chebanse, IL 60922 • 1,191
Cheboygan, MI 49721 • 5,106
Cheboygan □, MI • 20,649
Checotah, OK 74426 • 3,454
Cheektowaga, NY 14225 • 100,400
Chehalis, WA 98532 • 6,100
Chelan, WA 98816 • 2,802
Chelan □, WA • 45,061
Chelmsford, MA 01824 • 31,174
Chelsea, MA 02150 • 25,431
Chelsea, MI 48118 • 3,816
Chelsea, OK 74016 • 1,754
Chelsea Estates, DE 19720 • 1,500
Cheltenham, PA 19012 • 7,700
Chelyan, WV 25035 • 800
Chemung □, NY • 97,656
Chenango □, NY • 49,344
Chenango Bridge, NY 13745 • 2,600
Cheney, KS 67025 • 1,404
Cheney, WA 99004 • 7,630
Cheneyville, LA 71325 • 865
Chenoa, IL 61726 • 1,847
Chenoweth, OR 97058 • 2,820
Chepachet, RI 02814 • 900
Cheraw, SC 29520 • 5,654
Cheriton, VA 23316 • 695
Cherokee, AL 35616 • 1,589
Cherokee, IA 51012 • 7,004
Cherokee, KS 66724 • 775
Cherokee, OK 73728 • 2,105
Cherokee □, AL • 18,760
Cherokee □, GA • 51,699
Cherokee □, IA • 16,238
Cherokee □, KS • 22,304
Cherokee □, NC • 18,933
Cherokee □, OK • 30,684
Cherokee □, SC • 40,983
Cherokee □, TX • 38,127
Cherokee Village, AR 72525 • 3,200
Cherry □, NE • 6,758
Cherry Creek, NY 14723 • 677
Cherry Hill, NJ 08002–03 • 68,785
Cherry Hills Village, CO 80110 • 5,127
Cherryvale, KS 67335 • 2,769
Cherry Valley, AR 72324 • 729
Cherry Valley, IL 61016 • 946
Cherry Valley, MA 01611 • 1,400
Cherry Valley, NY 13320 • 684
Cherryville, NC 28021 • 4,844
Chesaning, MI 48616 • 2,656
Chesapeake, OH 45619 • 1,370
Chesapeake, VA 23320–25 • 114,486
Chesapeake, WV 25315 • 2,364
Chesapeake Beach, MD 20732 • 1,408
Chesapeake City, MD 21915 • 899
Cheshire, CT 06410 • 5,722
Cheshire, MA 01225 • 1,100
Cheshire □, NH • 62,116
Chesilhurst, NJ 08089 • 1,590
Chesnee, SC 29323 • 1,069
Chester, CA 96020 • 1,756
Chester, CT 06412 • 1,388
Chester, IL 62233 • 8,401
Chester, MA 01011 • 750
Chester, MT 59522 • 963
Chester, NJ 07930 • 1,433
Chester, NY 10918 • 1,910
Chester, PA 19013–16 • 45,794
Chester, SC 29706 • 6,820
Chester, VA 23831 • 7,000
Chester, WV 26034 • 3,297
Chester □, PA • 316,660
Chester □, SC • 30,148
Chester □, TN • 12,727
Chesterfield, IN 46017 • 2,701
Chesterfield, SC 29709 • 1,432
Chesterfield □, SC • 38,161
Chesterfield □, VA • 141,372
Chesterton, IN 46304 • 8,531
Chestertown, MD 21620 • 3,300
Chestertown, NY 12817 • 750
Chester Township, PA 19013 • 5,687
Chestnut Hill Estates, DE 19713 • 2,000
Cheswick, PA 15024 • 2,336
Chetek, WI 54728 • 1,931
Chetopa, KS 67336 • 1,751
Cheverly, MD 20785 • 5,751
Cheviot, OH 45211 • 9,888
Chevy Chase, MD 20815 • 12,232
Chewelah, WA 99109 • 1,888
Cheyenne, OK 73628 • 1,207
Cheyenne, WY 82001–09 • 47,283
Cheyenne □, CO • 2,153
Cheyenne □, KS • 3,678
Cheyenne □, NE • 10,057
Cheyenne Canon, CO 80907 • 1,100
Cheyenne Wells, CO 80810 • 950
Chicago, IL 60601–99 • 3,005,072
Chicago Heights, IL 60411 • 37,026
Chicago Ridge, IL 60415 • 13,473
Chickamauga, GA 30707 • 2,232
Chickasaw, AL 36611 • 7,402
Chickasaw □, IA • 15,437
Chickasaw □, MS • 17,853
Chickasha, OK 73018 • 15,828
Chico, CA 95926 • 26,603
Chico, TX 76030 • 890
Chico, WA 98310 • 750
Chicopee, GA 30501 • 900
Chicopee, MA 01013–22 • 55,112
Chicora, PA 16025 • 1,192
Chicot □, AR • 17,793
Chiefland, FL 32626 • 1,986
Childersburg, AL 35044 • 5,084
Childress, TX 79201 • 5,817
Childress □, TX • 6,950
Chilhowie, VA 24319 • 1,269
Chili Center, NY 14624 • 5,300
Chillicothe, IL 61523 • 6,176
Chillicothe, MO 64601 • 9,089
Chillicothe, OH 45601 • 23,420
Chillicothe, TX 79225 • 1,052
Chillum, MD 20783 • 14,900
Chiloquin, OR 97624 • 778
Chilton, WI 53014 • 2,965
Chilton □, AL • 30,612
Chimayo, NM 87522 • 1,993
China Grove, NC 28023 • 2,081
Chincoteague, VA 23336 • 1,607
Chinle, AZ 86503 • 2,815
Chino, CA 91710 • 40,165
Chinook, MT 59523 • 1,660
Chinook, WA 98614 • 650
Chino Valley, AZ 86323 • 2,858
Chipley, FL 32428 • 3,330
Chippewa □, MI • 29,029
Chippewa □, MN • 14,941
Chippewa □, WI • 52,127
Chippewa Falls, WI 54729 • 12,270
Chisago □, MN • 25,717
Chisago City, MN 55013 • 1,634
Chisholm, ME 04239 • 1,796
Chisholm, MN 55719 • 5,930
Chittenango, NY 13037 • 4,290
Chittenden □, VT • 115,534
Chocowinity, NC 27817 • 644
Choctaw, OK 73020 • 7,520
Choctaw □, AL • 16,839
Choctaw □, MS • 8,996
Choctaw □, OK • 17,203
Choteau, MT 59422 • 1,798
Choudrant, LA 71227 • 809
Chouteau, OK 74337 • 1,559
Chouteau □, MT • 6,092
Chowan □, NC • 12,558
Chowchilla, CA 93610 • 5,122
Chrisman, IL 61924 • 1,413
Christian □, IL • 36,446
Christian □, KY • 66,878
Christian □, MO • 22,402
Christiana, PA 17509 • 1,183
Christiansburg, VA 24073 • 10,345
Christmas, FL 32709 • 1,200
Christopher, IL 62822 • 3,086
Christoval, TX 76935 • 700
Chubbuck, ID 83202 • 7,052
Chula Vista, CA 92010–12 • 83,927
Church Hill, TN 37642 • 4,110
Churchill, OH 44505 • 7,700
Churchill □, NV • 13,917
Church Point, LA 70525 • 4,599
Churchton, MD 20733 • 800
Churchville, NY 14428 • 1,399
Churubusco, IN 46723 • 1,638
Cibecue, AZ 85911 • 950
Cibola □, NM • 30,102
Cicero, IL 60650 • 61,232
Cicero, IN 46034 • 2,557
Cimarron, KS 67835 • 1,491
Cimarron, NM 87714 • 888
Cimarron □, OK • 3,648
Cincinnati, OH 45201–99 • 385,457
Cinnaminson, NJ 08077 • 16,072
Circle, MT 59215 • 931
Circle Pines, MN 55014 • 3,321
Circleville, OH 43113 • 11,700
Cisco, TX 76437 • 4,517
Cisne, IL 62823 • 705
Cissna Park, IL 60924 • 825
Citra, FL 32627 • 1,500
Citronelle, AL 36522 • 2,841
Citrus □, FL • 54,703
Citrus Heights, CA 95610 • 85,911
City of Commerce, CA 90040 • 10,509
City View, SC 29611 • 1,662
Clackamas, OR 97015 • 3,250
Clackamas □, OR • 241,911
Claflin, KS 67525 • 764
Claiborne, LA 71291 • 2,000
Claiborne □, LA • 17,095
Claiborne □, MS • 12,279
Claiborne □, TN • 24,595
Clair-Mel City, FL 33619 • 7,000
Clairton, PA 15025 • 12,188
Clallam □, WA • 51,648
Clanton, AL 35045 • 5,832
Clara City, MN 56222 • 1,574
Clare, MI 48617 • 3,300
Clare □, MI • 23,822
Claremont, CA 91711 • 30,950
Claremont, NH 03743 • 14,557
Claremont, NC 28610 • 880
Claremore, OK 74017 • 12,085
Clarence, IA 52216 • 1,001
Clarence, LA 71414 • 612
Clarence, MO 63437 • 1,147
Clarendon, AR 72029 • 2,361
Clarendon, PA 16313 • 776
Clarendon, TX 79226 • 2,220
Clarendon □, SC • 27,464
Clarendon Hills, IL 60514 • 6,870
Clarinda, IA 51632 • 5,458
Clarion, IA 50525 • 3,060
Clarion, PA 16214 • 6,198
Clarion □, PA • 43,362
Clarissa, MN 56440 • 663
Clark, NJ 07066 • 16,699
Clark, SD 57225 • 1,351
Clark □, AR • 23,326
Clark □, ID • 798
Clark □, IL • 16,913
Clark □, IN • 88,838
Clark □, KS • 2,599
Clark □, KY • 28,322
Clark □, MO • 8,493
Clark □, NV • 463,087
Clark □, OH • 150,236
Clark □, SD • 4,894
Clark □, WA • 192,227
Clark □, WI • 32,910
Clarkdale, AZ 86324 • 1,512
Clarke □, AL • 27,702
Clarke □, GA • 74,498
Clarke □, IA • 8,612
Clarke □, MS • 16,945
Clarke □, VA • 9,965
Clarkesville, GA 30523 • 1,348
Clarkfield, MN 56223 • 1,171
Clarks, LA 71415 • 931
Clarksboro, NJ 08020 • 800
Clarksburg, WV 26301 • 22,371
Clarksdale, MS 38614 • 21,137
Clarks Grove, MN 56016 • 620
Clarks Hill, IN 47930 • 653
Clarkson, KY 42726 • 666
Clarkson, NE 68629 • 817
Clarks Summit, PA 18411 • 5,272
Clarkston, GA 30021 • 4,539
Clarkston, MI 48016 • 968
Clarkston, WA 99403 • 6,903
Clarksville, AR 72830 • 5,237
Clarksville, IN 47130 • 15,164
Clarksville, IA 50619 • 1,424
Clarksville, TN 37040–43 • 54,777
Clarksville, TX 75426 • 4,917
Clarksville, VA 23927 • 1,468
Clarkton, MO 63837 • 1,228
Clarkton, NC 28433 • 664
Clatskanie, OR 97016 • 1,648
Clatsop □, OR • 32,489
Claude, TX 79019 • 1,112
Clawson, MI 48017 • 15,103
Claxton, GA 30417 • 2,694
Clay, KY 42404 • 1,356
Clay, WV 25043 • 940
Clay □, AL • 13,703
Clay □, AR • 20,616
Clay □, FL • 67,052
Clay □, GA • 3,553
Clay □, IL • 15,283
Clay □, IN • 24,862
Clay □, IA • 19,576
Clay □, KS • 9,802
Clay □, KY • 22,752
Clay □, MN • 49,327
Clay □, MS • 21,082
Clay □, MO • 136,488
Clay □, NE • 8,106
Clay □, NC • 6,619
Clay □, SD • 13,689
Clay □, TN • 7,676
Clay □, TX • 9,582
Clay □, WV • 11,265
Clay Center, KS 67432 • 4,948
Clay Center, NE 68933 • 962
Clay City, IL 62824 • 1,038
Clay City, IN 47841 • 883
Clay City, KY 40312 • 1,276
Claymont, DE 19702 • 10,022
Claypool, AZ 85532 • 2,362
Claysburg, PA 16625 • 1,516
Claysville, PA 15323 • 1,029
Clayton, AL 36016 • 1,589
Clayton, DE 19938 • 1,216
Clayton, GA 30525 • 1,838
Clayton, IL 62324 • 889
Clayton, IN 46118 • 703
Clayton, LA 71326 • 1,204
Clayton, MO 63105 • 14,273
Clayton, NJ 08312 • 6,013
Clayton, NM 88415 • 2,968
Clayton, NC 27520 • 4,091
Clayton, NY 13624 • 1,816
Clayton, OK 74536 • 833
Clayton □, GA • 150,357
Clayton □, IA • 21,098
Clear Creek □, CO • 7,308
Clearfield, KY 40313 • 1,250
Clearfield, PA 16830 • 7,580
Clearfield, UT 84015 • 17,982
Clearfield □, PA • 83,578
Clearlake, CA 95422 • 13,300
Clear Lake, IA 50428 • 7,458
Clear Lake, SD 57226 • 1,310
Clearlake, WA 98235 • 900
Clear Lake, WI 54005 • 899
Clear Lake City, TX 77062 • 8,700
Clear Lake Shores, TX 77565 • 755
Clearwater, FL 33515–20 • 85,528
Clearwater, KS 67026 • 1,684
Clearwater, SC 29822 • 3,967
Clearwater □, ID • 10,390
Clearwater □, MN • 8,761
Cleburne, TX 76031 • 19,218
Cleburne □, AL • 12,595
Cleburne □, AR • 16,909
Cle Elum, WA 98922 • 1,773
Cleland Heights, DE 19805 • 1,500
Clementon, NJ 08021 • 5,764
Clemmons, NC 27012 • 7,401
Clemson, SC 29631 • 8,118
Clendenin, WV 25045 • 1,373
Cleona, PA 17042 • 2,003
Clermont, FL 32711 • 5,461
Clermont, IA 52135 • 602
Clermont □, OH • 128,483
Cleveland, GA 30528 • 1,578
Cleveland, MN 56017 • 699
Cleveland, MS 38732 • 14,524
Cleveland, NY 13042 • 855
Cleveland, OH 44101–99 • 573,822
Cleveland, OK 74020 • 2,972
Cleveland, TN 37311–12 • 26,415
Cleveland, TX 77327 • 5,977
Cleveland, WI 53015 • 1,270
Cleveland □, AR • 7,868
Cleveland □, NC • 83,435
Cleveland □, OK • 133,173
Cleveland Heights, OH 44118 • 56,438
Cleves, OH 45002 • 2,094
Clewiston, FL 33440 • 5,219
Cliffside Park, NJ 07010 • 21,464
Cliffwood Beach, NJ 07735 • 6,300
Clifton, AZ 85533 • 4,245
Clifton, CO 81520 • 5,223
Clifton, IL 60927 • 1,390
Clifton, KS 66937 • 695
Clifton, NJ 07011–15 • 74,388
Clifton, SC 29324 • 800
Clifton, TN 38425 • 773
Clifton, TX 76634 • 3,063
Clifton Forge, VA 24422 • 5,046
Clifton Heights, PA 19018 • 7,320
Clifton Knolls, NY 12065 • 4,000
Clifton Springs, NY 14432 • 2,039
Climax, MI 49034 • 619
Clinch □, GA • 6,660
Clinchco, VA 24226 • 1,000
Clint, TX 79836 • 1,314
Clinton, AR 72031 • 1,284
Clinton, CT 06413 • 11,195
Clinton, IL 61727 • 8,014
Clinton, IN 47842 • 5,267
Clinton, IA 52732 • 32,828
Clinton, KY 42031 • 1,720
Clinton, LA 70722 • 1,919
Clinton, ME 04927 • 1,305
Clinton, MD 20735 • 16,438
Clinton, MA 01510 • 12,771
Clinton, MI 49236 • 2,342
Clinton, MN 56225 • 622
Clinton, MS 39056 • 14,660
Clinton, MO 64735 • 8,366
Clinton, NJ 08809 • 1,910
Clinton, NC 28328 • 7,552
Clinton, NY 13323 • 2,107
Clinton, OK 73601 • 8,796
Clinton, SC 29325 • 8,596
Clinton, TN 37716 • 5,245
Clinton, UT 84015 • 5,777
Clinton, WA 98236 • 2,000
Clinton, WI 53525 • 1,751
Clinton □, IL • 32,617
Clinton □, IN • 31,545
Clinton □, IA • 57,122
Clinton □, KY • 9,321
Clinton □, MI • 55,893
Clinton □, MO • 15,916
Clinton □, NY • 80,750
Clinton □, OH • 34,603
Clinton □, PA • 38,971
Clinton Township, MI 48043 • 72,400
Clintonville, WI 54929 • 4,567
Clintwood, VA 24228 • 1,369
Clio, AL 36017 • 1,224
Clio, MI 48420 • 2,669
Clio, SC 29525 • 1,031
Clive, IA 50053 • 6,064
Cloquet, MN 55720 • 11,142
Closter, NJ 07624 • 8,164
Cloud □, KS • 12,494
Clover, SC 29710 • 3,451
Cloverdale, CA 95425 • 3,989
Cloverdale, IN 46120 • 1,357
Cloverdale, VA 24077 • 850
Cloverleaf, TX 77015 • 11,800
Cloverport, KY 40111 • 1,585
Clovis, CA 93612 • 33,021
Clovis, NM 88101 • 31,194
Clute, TX 77531 • 9,577
Clyde, KS 66938 • 909
Clyde, NC 28721 • 1,008
Clyde, NY 14433 • 2,491
Clyde, OH 43410 • 5,489
Clyde, TX 79510 • 2,562
Clymer, PA 15728 • 1,761
Coachella, CA 92236 • 9,129
Coahoma, TX 79511 • 1,069
Coahoma □, MS • 36,918
Coal □, OK • 6,041
Coal City, IL 60416 • 3,028
Coaldale, PA 18218 • 2,762
Coal Fork, WV 25306 • 900
Coalgate, OK 74538 • 2,001
Coal Grove, OH 45638 • 2,602
Coal Hill, AR 72832 • 859
Coalinga, CA 93210 • 6,593
Coalmont, TN 37313 • 625
Coalport, PA 16627 • 739
Coalton, OH 45621 • 639
Coalville, UT 84017 • 1,031
Coalwood, WV 24824 • 1,100
Coatesville, PA 19320 • 10,698
Coats, NC 27521 • 1,385
Cobb □, GA • 297,718
Cobden, IL 62920 • 1,210
Cobleskill, NY 12043 • 5,272
Coburg, OR 97401 • 699
Cochise □, AZ • 85,686
Cochituate, MA 01778 • 6,126
Cochran, GA 31014 • 5,121
Cochran □, TX • 4,825
Cochranton, PA 16314 • 1,240
Cocke □, TN • 28,792
Cockeysville, MD 21030 • 17,013
Cockrell Hill, TX 75211 • 3,262
Cocoa, FL 32922–27 • 16,096
Cocoa Beach, FL 32931 • 10,926
Cocoa West, FL 32922 • 6,432
Coconino □, AZ • 75,008
Coconut Creek, FL 33060 • 6,288
Codington □, SD • 20,885
Cody, WY 82414 • 6,790
Coeburn, VA 24230 • 2,625
Coeur d'Alene, ID 83814 • 20,054
Coffee □, AL • 38,533
Coffee □, GA • 26,894
Coffee □, TN • 38,311

Coffeen, IL 62017 • *842*
Coffeeville, MS 38922 • *1,129*
Coffey □, KS • *9,370*
Coffeyville, KS 67337 • *15,185*
Coggon, IA 52218 • *639*
Cohasset, MA 02025 • *5,300*
Cohocton, NY 14826 • *902*
Cohoes, NY 12047 • *18,144*
Cokato, MN 55321 • *2,056*
Coke □, TX • *3,196*
Colbert, OK 74733 • *1,122*
Colbert □, AL • *54,519*
Colby, KS 67701 • *5,544*
Colby, WI 54421 • *1,496*
Colchester, CT 06415 • *3,190*
Colchester, IL 62326 • *1,729*
Cold Spring, KY 41076 • *2,117*
Cold Spring, MN 56320 • *2,294*
Cold Spring, NJ 08204 • *850*
Cold Spring Harbor, NY 11724 • *5,490*
Coldwater, KS 67029 • *989*
Coldwater, MI 49036 • *9,461*
Coldwater, MS 38618 • *1,505*
Coldwater, OH 45828 • *4,220*
Cole □, MO • *56,663*
Colebrook, NH 03576 • *1,131*
Cole Camp, MO 65325 • *1,022*
Coleman, FL 34255 • *1,022*
Coleman, MI 48618 • *1,429*
Coleman, TX 76834 • *5,960*
Coleman, WI 54112 • *852*
Coleman □, TX • *10,439*
Coleraine, MN 55722 • *1,116*
Coleridge, NE 68727 • *673*
Coles □, IL • *52,260*
Colfax, CA 95713 • *981*
Colfax, IL 61728 • *920*
Colfax, IN 46035 • *823*
Colfax, IA 50054 • *2,234*
Colfax, LA 71417 • *1,680*
Colfax, WA 99111 • *2,780*
Colfax, WI 54730 • *1,149*
Colfax □, NE • *9,890*
Colfax □, NM • *13,667*
College, AK 99701 • *800*
Collegedale, TN 37315 • *1,500*
College Park, GA 30337 • *24,632*
College Park, MD 20740 • *23,614*
College Place, WA 99324 • *5,771*
College Station, AR 72053 • *4,000*
College Station, TX 77840 • *37,272*
Collegeville, IN 47978 • *1,059*
Collegeville, PA 19426 • *3,406*
Colleton □, SC • *31,776*
Colleyville, TX 76034 • *6,700*
Collier □, FL • *85,971*
Collierville, TN 38017 • *7,839*
Collin □, TX • *144,576*
Collingdale, PA 19023 • *9,539*
Collingswood, NJ 08108 • *15,838*
Collingsworth □, TX • *4,648*
Collins, GA 30421 • *639*
Collins, MS 39428 • *2,131*
Collins Park, DE 19720 • *2,850*
Collinsville, AL 35961 • *1,383*
Collinsville, CT 06022 • *2,555*
Collinsville, IL 62234 • *19,613*
Collinsville, OK 74021 • *3,556*
Collinsville, VA 24078 • *7,400*
Collinwood, TN 38450 • *1,064*
Colmar Manor, MD 20722 • *1,286*
Colo, IA 50056 • *808*
Coloma, MI 49038 • *1,833*
Colon, MI 49040 • *1,190*
Colonia, NJ 07067 • *20,900*
Colonial Beach, VA 22443 • *2,474*
Colonial Heights, TN 37663 • *6,744*
Colonial Heights, VA 23834 • *16,509*
Colonial Park, PA 17109 • *10,000*
Colonie, NY 12212 • *8,869*
Colorado □, TX • *18,823*
Colorado City, CO 81019 • *950*
Colorado City, TX 79512 • *5,405*
Colorado Springs, CO 80901–99 • *214,821*
Colquitt, GA 31737 • *2,065*
Colquitt □, GA • *35,376*
Colstrip, MT 59323 • *1,476*
Colter Bay, WY 83001 • *2,000*
Colton, CA 92324 • *15,201*
Colton, SD 57018 • *757*
Columbia, AL 36319 • *881*
Columbia, CA 95310 • *950*
Columbia, IL 62236 • *4,269*
Columbia, KY 42728 • *3,710*
Columbia, LA 71418 • *687*
Columbia, MD 21045–46 • *52,518*
Columbia, MS 39429 • *7,733*
Columbia, MO 65201–18 • *62,061*
Columbia, NC 27925 • *758*
Columbia, PA 17512 • *10,466*
Columbia, SC 29201–99 • *100,385*
Columbia, TN 38401 • *26,571*
Columbia □, AR • *26,644*
Columbia □, FL • *35,399*
Columbia □, GA • *40,118*
Columbia □, NY • *59,487*
Columbia □, OR • *35,646*
Columbia □, PA • *61,967*
Columbia □, WA • *4,057*
Columbia □, WI • *43,222*
Columbia City, IN 46725 • *5,091*
Columbia City, OR 97018 • *678*
Columbia Falls, MT 59912 • *3,112*
Columbia Heights, MN 55421 • *20,029*
Columbiana, AL 35051 • *2,655*
Columbiana, OH 44408 • *4,987*
Columbiana □, OH • *113,572*
Columbiaville, MI 48421 • *953*
Columbus, GA 31901–99 • *169,441*
Columbus, IN 47201–03 • *30,614*
Columbus, KS 66725 • *3,426*
Columbus, MS 39701–04 • *27,383*
Columbus, MT 59019 • *1,439*
Columbus, NE 68601 • *17,328*
Columbus, NJ 08022 • *700*
Columbus, NC 28722 • *727*
Columbus, OH 43201–99 • *565,032*
Columbus, TX 78934 • *3,923*
Columbus, WI 53925 • *4,049*
Columbus □, NC • *51,037*
Columbus Grove, OH 45830 • *2,313*
Columbus Junction, IA 52738 • *1,429*
Colusa, CA 95932 • *4,075*
Colusa □, CA • *12,791*
Colver, PA 15927 • *1,175*
Colville, WA 99114 • *4,510*
Colwich, KS 67030 • *935*
Comal □, TX • *36,446*
Comanche, OK 73529 • *1,937*
Comanche, TX 76442 • *4,075*
Comanche □, KS • *2,554*
Comanche □, OK • *112,456*
Comanche □, TX • *12,617*
Combined Locks, WI 54113 • *2,573*
Combs, KY 41729 • *700*
Comer, GA 30629 • *930*
Comfort, TX 78013 • *950*
Commack, NY 11725 • *24,300*
Commerce, GA 30529 • *4,092*
Commerce, OK 74339 • *2,556*
Commerce, TX 75428 • *8,136*
Commerce City, CO 80022 • *16,234*
Common Fence Point, RI 02871 • *850*
Como, MS 38619 • *1,378*
Compton, CA 90220–24 • *81,286*
Comstock, MI 49041 • *5,310*
Concho □, TX • *2,915*
Concord, CA 94518–24 • *103,255*
Concord, MA 01742 • *6,400*
Concord, MI 49237 • *900*
Concord, MO 63851 • *20,896*
Concord, NH 03301–06 • *30,400*
Concord, NC 28025 • *16,942*
Concordia, KS 66901 • *6,847*
Concordia, MO 64020 • *2,129*
Concordia □, LA • *22,981*
Condon, OR 97823 • *783*
Conecuh □, AL • *15,884*
Conejos □, CO • *7,794*
Conemaugh, PA 15909 • *2,128*
Confluence, PA 15424 • *968*
Congers, NY 10920 • *5,000*
Conklin, NY 13748 • *1,900*
Conneaut, OH 44030 • *13,835*
Conneaut Lake, PA 16316 • *767*
Conneautville, PA 16406 • *971*
Connell, WA 99326 • *1,981*
Connellsville, PA 15425 • *10,319*
Connersville, IN 47331 • *17,023*
Conover, NC 28613 • *4,245*
Conrad, IA 50621 • *1,133*
Conrad, MT 59425 • *3,074*
Conroe, TX 77301–05 • *18,034*
Conshohocken, PA 19428 • *8,475*
Constantia, NY 13044 • *900*
Constantine, MI 49042 • *1,680*
Continental, OH 45831 • *1,179*
Contoocook, NH 03229 • *1,499*
Contra Costa □, CA • *656,380*
Converse, IN 46919 • *1,279*
Converse, SC 29329 • *1,173*
Converse □, WY • *14,069*
Convoy, OH 45832 • *1,140*
Conway, AR 72032 • *20,375*
Conway, FL 32809 • *10,000*
Conway, MO 65632 • *601*
Conway, NH 03818 • *1,781*
Conway, NC 27820 • *678*
Conway, PA 15027 • *2,747*
Conway, SC 29526 • *10,240*
Conway □, AR • *19,505*
Conway Springs, KS 67031 • *1,313*
Conyers, GA 30207–08 • *6,567*
Cook, MN 55723 • *800*
Cook □, GA • *13,490*
Cook □, IL • *5,253,655*
Cook □, MN • *4,092*
Cooke □, TX • *27,656*
Cookeville, TN 38501 • *20,535*
Cooleemee, NC 27014 • *1,448*
Coolidge, AZ 85228 • *6,851*
Coolidge, GA 31738 • *736*
Coolidge, TX 76635 • *810*
Coolville, OH 45723 • *649*
Coon Rapids, IA 50058 • *1,448*
Coon Rapids, MN 55433 • *35,826*
Coon Valley, WI 54623 • *758*
Cooper, TX 75432 • *2,338*
Cooper □, MO • *14,643*
Cooper City, FL 33328 • *10,140*
Cooper Road, LA 71107 • *10,000*
Coopersburg, PA 18036 • *2,595*
Cooperstown, ND 58425 • *1,308*
Cooperstown, NY 13326 • *2,342*
Cooperstown, PA 16317 • *644*
Coopersville, MI 49404 • *2,889*
Coos □, NH • *35,147*
Coos □, OR • *64,047*
Coosa □, AL • *11,377*
Coosada, AL 36020 • *980*
Coos Bay, OR 97420 • *14,424*
Copake, NY 12516 • *700*
Copalis Beach, WA 98535 • *800*
Copan, OK 74022 • *960*
Copeland, FL 33926 • *700*
Copenhagen, NY 13626 • *656*
Copiague, NY 11726 • *21,000*
Copiah □, MS • *26,503*
Coplay, PA 18037 • *3,130*
Copperas Cove, TX 76522 • *19,469*
Copperton, UT 84006 • *850*
Coquille, OR 97423 • *4,481*
Coral, PA 15731 • *700*
Coral Gables, FL 33134 • *43,241*
Coralville, IA 52241 • *7,687*
Coram, NY 11727 • *5,400*
Coraopolis, PA 15108 • *7,308*
Corbin, KY 40701 • *8,075*
Corcoran, CA 93212 • *6,454*
Corcoran, MN 55340 • *4,252*
Cordaville, MA 01772 • *1,384*
Cordele, GA 31015 • *11,184*
Cordell, OK 73632 • *3,301*
Cordova, AL 35550 • *3,123*
Cordova, AK 99574 • *1,879*
Cordova, IL 61242 • *697*
Cordova, NC 28330 • *1,200*
Corfu, NY 14036 • *689*
Corinna, ME 04928 • *950*
Corinth, MS 38834 • *13,839*
Corinth, NY 12822 • *2,702*
Cornelia, GA 30531 • *3,203*
Cornelius, NC 28031 • *1,460*
Cornelius, OR 97113 • *4,462*
Cornell, IL 61319 • *603*
Cornell, WI 54732 • *1,583*
Cornersville, TN 37047 • *722*
Corning, AR 72422 • *3,650*
Corning, CA 96021 • *4,745*
Corning, IA 50841 • *1,939*
Corning, NY 14830 • *12,953*
Corning, OH 43730 • *789*
Cornville, AZ 86325 • *800*
Cornwall, PA 17016 • *2,653*
Cornwall On Hudson, NY 12520 • *3,164*
Cornwells Heights, PA 19020 • *8,700*
Corona, CA 91720 • *37,791*
Coronado, CA 92118 • *18,790*
Corpus Christi, TX 78401–99 • *231,999*
Correctionville, IA 51016 • *935*
Corrigan, TX 75939 • *1,770*
Corriganville, MD 21524 • *1,020*
Corry, PA 16407 • *7,149*
Corsica, SD 57328 • *644*
Corsicana, TX 75110 • *21,712*
Corson □, SD • *5,196*
Corte Madera, CA 94925 • *8,074*
Cortez, CO 81321 • *7,095*
Cortez, FL 33522 • *1,450*
Cortland, IL 60112 • *1,019*
Cortland, NY 13045 • *20,138*
Cortland, OH 44410 • *5,011*
Cortland □, NY • *48,820*
Corunna, MI 48817 • *3,206*
Corvallis, OR 97330–33 • *40,960*
Corydon, IN 47112 • *2,724*
Corydon, IA 50060 • *1,818*
Corydon, KY 42406 • *874*
Coryell □, TX • *56,767*
Coshocton, OH 43812 • *13,405*
Coshocton □, OH • *36,024*
Cosmopolis, WA 98537 • *1,575*
Costa Mesa, CA 92626–27 • *82,562*
Costilla □, CO • *3,071*
Cottage Grove, MN 55016 • *18,994*
Cottage Grove, OR 97424 • *7,148*
Cotter, AR 72626 • *920*
Cottle □, TX • *2,047*
Cotton □, OK • *7,338*
Cottondale, AL 35453 • *2,300*
Cottondale, FL 32431 • *1,056*
Cotton Plant, AR 72036 • *1,323*
Cottonport, LA 71327 • *1,911*
Cotton Valley, LA 71018 • *1,445*
Cottonwood, AL 36320 • *1,352*
Cottonwood, AZ 86326 • *4,550*
Cottonwood, CA 96022 • *1,553*
Cottonwood, ID 83522 • *941*
Cottonwood, MN 56229 • *924*
Cottonwood, UT 84121 • *11,554*
Cottonwood □, MN • *14,854*
Cottonwood Falls, KS 66845 • *954*
Cottonwood Heights, UT 84121 • *18,000*
Cotuit, MA 02635 • *1,300*
Cotulla, TX 78014 • *3,912*
Coudersport, PA 16915 • *2,791*
Coulee Dam, WA 99116 • *1,412*
Coulterville, IL 62237 • *1,118*
Council, ID 83612 • *917*
Council Bluffs, IA 51501 • *56,449*
Council Grove, KS 66846 • *2,381*
Country Club Hills, IL 60477 • *14,676*
Country Homes, WA 99218 • *3,850*
Countryside, IL 60525 • *6,538*
Coupeville, WA 98239 • *1,006*
Courtland, VA 23837 • *976*
Coushatta, LA 71019 • *2,084*
Covedale, OH 45238 • *6,530*
Covelo, CA 95428 • *1,448*
Coventry, CT 06238 • *3,769*
Coventry, DE 19720 • *830*
Coventry, RI 02816 • *8,000*
Covina, CA 91722–24 • *33,751*
Covington, GA 30209 • *10,586*
Covington, IN 47932 • *2,883*
Covington, KY 41011–19 • *49,563*
Covington, LA 70433 • *7,892*
Covington, OH 45318 • *2,610*
Covington, OK 73730 • *715*
Covington, TN 38019 • *6,065*
Covington, VA 24426 • *9,063*
Covington □, AL • *36,850*
Covington □, MS • *15,927*
Cowan, TN 37318 • *1,790*
Cowden, IL 62422 • *623*
Cowen, WV 26206 • *723*
Coweta, OK 74429 • *4,554*
Coweta □, GA • *39,268*
Cowley □, KS • *36,824*
Cowlitz □, WA • *79,548*
Cowpens, SC 29330 • *2,023*
Coxsackie, NY 12051 • *2,786*
Cozad, NE 69130 • *4,453*
Crab Orchard, KY 40419 • *843*
Crab Orchard, TN 37723 • *1,065*
Crab Orchard, WV 25827 • *1,900*
Crabtree, PA 15624 • *1,021*
Crafton, PA 15205 • *7,623*
Craig, CO 81625 • *8,133*
Craig □, OK • *15,014*
Craig □, VA • *3,948*
Craighead □, AR • *63,239*
Craigmont, ID 83523 • *617*
Craigsville, VA 24430 • *845*
Craigsville, WV 26205 • *900*
Cramerton, NC 28032 • *1,869*
Cranbury, NJ 08512 • *1,255*
Crandall, TX 75114 • *831*
Crandon, WI 54520 • *1,969*
Crane, AZ 85364 • *2,400*
Crane, MO 65633 • *1,185*
Crane, TX 79731 • *3,622*
Crane □, TX • *4,600*
Cranesville, PA 16410 • *703*
Cranford, NJ 07016 • *24,573*
Cranston, RI 02910 • *71,992*
Craven □, NC • *71,043*
Crawford, NE 69339 • *1,315*
Crawford □, AR • *36,892*
Crawford □, GA • *7,684*
Crawford □, IL • *20,818*
Crawford □, IN • *9,820*
Crawford □, IA • *18,935*
Crawford □, KS • *37,916*
Crawford □, MI • *9,465*
Crawford □, MO • *18,300*
Crawford □, OH • *50,075*
Crawford □, PA • *88,869*
Crawford □, WI • *16,556*
Crawfordsville, AR 72327 • *685*
Crawfordsville, IN 47933 • *13,325*
Crawfordville, FL 32327 • *1,110*
Creal Springs, IL 62922 • *845*
Creede, CO 81130 • *610*
Creedmoor, NC 27522 • *1,641*
Creek □, OK • *59,016*
Creighton, NE 68729 • *1,341*
Creighton, PA 15030 • *1,658*
Crenshaw, MS 38621 • *1,019*
Crenshaw □, AL • *14,110*
Creola, AL 36525 • *1,652*
Cresaptown, MD 21502 • *4,645*
Crescent, OK 73028 • *1,651*
Crescent, OR 97733 • *700*
Crescent City, CA 95531 • *3,075*
Crescent City, FL 32012 • *1,722*
Crescent City, IL 60928 • *641*
Crescent Springs, KY 41016 • *1,951*
Cresco, IA 52136 • *3,860*
Cresskill, NJ 07626 • *7,609*
Cresson, PA 16630 • *2,184*
Cressona, PA 17929 • *1,810*
Crested Butte, CO 81224 • *959*
Cresthaven, FL 33064 • *2,400*
Crest Hill, IL 60435 • *9,252*
Crestline, OH 44827 • *5,406*
Creston, IA 50801 • *8,429*
Creston, OH 44217 • *1,828*
Crestview, FL 32536 • *7,617*
Crestview, HI 96797 • *1,000*
Crestwood, IL 60445 • *10,852*
Crestwood, MO 63126 • *12,815*
Crestwood Village, NJ 08759 • *7,965*
Creswell, OR 97426 • *1,770*
Crete, IL 60417 • *5,417*
Crete, NE 68333 • *4,872*
Creve Coeur, IL 61611 • *6,851*
Creve Coeur, MO 63141 • *11,757*
Crewe, VA 23930 • *2,325*
Cricket, NC 28659 • *2,307*
Cridersville, OH 45806 • *1,843*
Cripple Creek, CO 80813 • *655*
Crisfield, MD 21817 • *2,924*
Crisp □, GA • *19,489*
Crittenden □, AR • *49,499*
Crittenden □, KY • *9,207*
Crivitz, WI 54114 • *1,041*
Crocker, MO 65452 • *979*
Crockett, CA 94525 • *2,900*
Crockett, TX 75835 • *7,405*
Crockett □, TN • *14,941*
Crockett □, TX • *4,608*
Crofton, KY 42217 • *823*
Crofton, MD 21114 • *12,009*
Crofton, NE 68730 • *948*
Croghan, NY 13327 • *703*
Cromona, KY 41810 • *700*
Cromwell, CT 06416 • *10,100*
Crook □, OR • *13,091*
Crook □, WY • *5,308*
Crookston, MN 56716 • *8,628*
Crooksville, OH 43731 • *2,766*
Crosby, MN 56441 • *2,218*
Crosby, ND 58730 • *1,469*
Crosby, TX 77532 • *1,450*
Crosby □, TX • *8,859*
Crosbyton, TX 79322 • *2,289*
Cross □, AR • *20,434*
Cross City, FL 32628 • *2,154*
Crossett, AR 71635 • *6,706*
Cross Hill, SC 29332 • *604*
Crosslake, MN 56442 • *1,064*
Cross Lanes, WV 25313 • *3,500*
Cross Mill, NC 28752 • *1,200*
Cross Plains, TN 37049 • *655*
Cross Plains, TX 76443 • *1,240*
Cross Plains, WI 53528 • *2,156*
Crossville, AL 35962 • *1,222*
Crossville, IL 62827 • *944*
Crossville, TN 38555 • *6,394*
Croswell, MI 48422 • *2,073*
Crothersville, IN 47229 • *1,747*
Croton-on-Hudson, NY 10520 • *6,889*
Crouse, NC 28033 • *900*
Crow Agency, MT 59022 • *750*
Crowder, MS 38622 • *789*
Crowell, TX 79227 • *1,509*
Crowley, LA 70526 • *16,036*
Crowley, TX 76036 • *5,852*
Crowley □, CO • *2,988*
Crown Point, IN 46307 • *16,455*
Crown Point, LA 70072 • *1,016*
Crown Point, NE 68122 • *700*
Crownpoint, NM 87313 • *1,134*
Crown Point, NY 12928 • *900*
Crow Wing □, MN • *41,722*
Croydon, PA 19020 • *10,000*
Crozet, VA 22932 • *1,433*
Crucible, PA 15325 • *800*
Crystal, MN 55428 • *25,543*
Crystal Bay, NV 89402 • *1,200*
Crystal Beach, FL 34256 • *1,450*
Crystal City, MO 63019 • *3,618*
Crystal City, TX 78839 • *8,334*
Crystal Falls, MI 49920 • *1,965*
Crystal Lake, FL 33803 • *6,827*
Crystal Lake, IL 60014 • *18,590*
Crystal Lawns, IL 60435 • *2,800*
Crystal Manor, IL 60014 • *750*
Crystal River, FL 32629 • *2,778*
Crystal Springs, FL 34257 • *800*
Crystal Springs, MS 39059 • *4,902*
Cuba, IL 61427 • *1,648*
Cuba, MO 65453 • *2,120*
Cuba, NM 87013 • *609*
Cuba, NY 14727 • *1,739*
Cuba City, WI 53807 • *2,129*
Cucamonga, CA 91730 • *55,250*
Cudahy, CA 90201 • *17,984*
Cudahy, WI 53110 • *19,547*
Cuero, TX 77954 • *7,124*
Culberson □, TX • *3,315*
Culbertson, MT 59218 • *887*
Culbertson, NE 69024 • *767*
Cullen, LA 71021 • *1,869*
Cullman, AL 35055 • *13,084*
Cullman □, AL • *61,642*
Culloden, WV 25510 • *1,500*
Cullom, IL 60929 • *608*
Cullowhee, NC 28723 • *2,000*
Culpeper, VA 22701 • *6,621*
Culpeper □, VA • *22,620*
Culver, IN 46511 • *1,601*
Culver City, CA 90230–32 • *38,139*
Cumberland, KY 40823 • *3,712*
Cumberland, MD 21502 • *25,933*
Cumberland, NC 28331 • *900*
Cumberland, WI 54829 • *1,983*
Cumberland □, IL • *11,062*
Cumberland □, KY • *7,289*
Cumberland □, ME • *215,789*
Cumberland □, NJ • *132,866*
Cumberland □, NC • *247,160*
Cumberland □, PA • *178,541*
Cumberland □, TN • *28,676*
Cumberland □, VA • *7,881*
Cumberland Center, ME 04021 • *2,015*
Cumberland Foreside, ME 04110 • *1,000*
Cumberland Hill, RI 02864 • *5,421*
Cuming □, NE • *11,664*
Cumming, GA 30130 • *2,094*
Cupertino, CA 95014 • *34,265*
Currituck □, NC • *11,089*
Curry □, NM • *42,019*
Curry □, OR • *16,992*
Curtice, OH 43412 • *800*
Curtis, NE 69025 • *1,014*
Curtisville, PA 15032 • *1,337*
Curwensville, PA 16833 • *3,116*
Cushing, OK 74023 • *7,720*
Cusseta, GA 31805 • *1,218*
Custer, SD 57730 • *1,830*
Custer □, CO • *1,528*
Custer □, ID • *3,385*
Custer □, MT • *13,109*
Custer □, NE • *13,877*

Custer □, OK • 25,995
Custer □, SD • 6,000
Cut Bank, MT 59427 • 3,688
Cutchogue, NY 11935 • 1,000
Cuthbert, GA 31740 • 4,340
Cutler Ridge, FL 33157 • 20,886
Cutlerville, MI 49508 • 8,256
Cut Off, LA 70345 • 5,049
Cuyahoga □, OH • 1,498,400
Cuyahoga Falls, OH 44221-24 • 43,890
Cygnet, OH 43413 • 646
Cynthiana, IN 47612 • 874
Cynthiana, KY 41031 • 5,881
Cypress, CA 90630 • 40,391
Cypress, TX 77429 • 700
Cypress Quarters, FL 33472 • 1,479
Cyril, OK 73029 • 1,220

D

Dacono, CO 80514 • 2,321
Dacula, GA 30211 • 1,577
Dade □, FL • 1,625,781
Dade □, GA • 12,318
Dade □, MO • 7,383
Dade City, FL 33525 • 4,923
Dadeville, AL 36853 • 3,263
Daggett, CA 92327 • 650
Daggett □, UT • 769
Dahlonega, GA 30533 • 2,844
Daingerfield, TX 75638 • 3,030
Daisetta, TX 77533 • 1,177
Dakota □, MN • 194,279
Dakota □, NE • 16,573
Dakota City, IA 50529 • 1,072
Dakota City, NE 68731 • 1,440
Dale, IN 47523 • 1,693
Dale □, AL • 47,821
Dale City, VA 22193 • 23,000
Daleville, AL 36322 • 4,250
Daleville, IN 47334 • 2,000
Dalhart, TX 79022 • 6,854
Dallam □, TX • 6,531
Dallas, GA 30132 • 2,508
Dallas, NC 28034 • 3,340
Dallas, OR 97338 • 8,530
Dallas, PA 18612 • 2,679
Dallas, TX 75201-99 • 904,078
Dallas □, AL • 53,981
Dallas □, AR • 10,515
Dallas □, IA • 29,513
Dallas □, MO • 12,096
Dallas □, TX • 1,556,390
Dallas Center, IA 50063 • 1,360
Dallas City, IL 62330 • 1,408
Dallastown, PA 17313 • 3,949
Dalton, GA 30720 • 20,939
Dalton, MA 01226 • 6,797
Dalton, OH 44618 • 1,357
Dalton, PA 18414 • 1,383
Dalton Gardens, ID 83814 • 1,795
Daly City, CA 94014-17 • 78,519
Dalzell, IL 61320 • 824
Damariscotta, ME 04543 • 950
Damascus, MD 20872 • 4,129
Damascus, VA 24236 • 1,330
Damon, TX 77430 • 700
Dana, IN 47847 • 803
Danbury, CT 06810-17 • 60,470
Danbury, TX 77534 • 1,357
Dandridge, TN 37725 • 1,383
Dane □, WI • 323,545
Dania, FL 33004 • 11,811
Daniels □, MT • 2,835
Danielson, CT 06239 • 4,553
Dannemora, NY 12929 • 3,770
Dansville, NY 14437 • 4,979
Dante, VA 24237 • 1,200
Danvers, IL 61732 • 921
Danvers, MA 01923 • 24,100
Danville, AR 72833 • 1,698
Danville, CA 94526 • 26,000
Danville, IL 61832-33 • 38,985
Danville, IN 46122 • 4,220
Danville, IA 52623 • 994
Danville, KY 40422 • 12,942
Danville, OH 43014 • 1,127
Danville, PA 17821 • 5,239
Danville, VA 24541-43 • 45,642
Danville, WV 25053 • 727
Daphne, AL 36526 • 3,406
Darby, PA 19023 • 11,513
Darbydale, OH 43123 • 825
Dardanelle, AR 72834 • 3,621
Dare □, NC • 13,377
Darien, CT 06820 • 18,892
Darien, GA 31305 • 1,731
Darien, IL 60559 • 14,536
Darien, WI 53114 • 1,152
Darke □, OH • 55,096
Darley Woods, DE 19810 • 1,400
Darlington, IN 47940 • 811
Darlington, SC 29532 • 7,989
Darlington, WI 53530 • 2,300
Darlington □, SC • 62,717
Darrington, WA 98241 • 1,064
Dassel, MN 55325 • 1,066
Dauphin, PA 17018 • 901
Dauphin □, PA • 232,317
Davenport, FL 33837 • 1,509
Davenport, IA 52801-99 • 103,264
Davenport, OK 74026 • 974
Davenport, WA 99122 • 1,559
David City, NE 68632 • 2,514
Davidson, NC 28036 • 3,241
Davidson □, NC • 113,162
Davidson □, TN • 477,811
Davidsville, PA 15928 • 900
Davie, FL 33329 • 20,877
Davie □, NC • 24,599
Daviess □, IN • 27,836
Daviess □, KY • 85,949
Daviess □, MO • 8,905
Davis, CA 95616 • 36,640
Davis, OK 73030 • 2,782
Davis, WV 26260 • 979
Davis □, IA • 9,104
Davis □, UT • 146,540
Davison, MI 48423 • 6,087
Davison □, SD • 17,820
Davy, WV 24828 • 882
Dawes □, NE • 9,609
Dawson, GA 31742 • 5,699
Dawson, MN 56232 • 1,901
Dawson, PA 15428 • 661
Dawson, TX 76639 • 747
Dawson □, GA • 4,774
Dawson □, MT • 11,805
Dawson □, NE • 22,304
Dawson □, TX • 16,184
Dawson Springs, KY 42408 • 3,275
Day □, SD • 8,133
Dayton, IN 47941 • 781
Dayton, IA 50530 • 941
Dayton, KY 41074 • 6,979
Dayton, MD 21036 • 700
Dayton, MN 55327 • 4,070
Dayton, NJ 08810 • 900
Dayton, OH 45401-99 • 193,444
Dayton, OR 97114 • 1,409
Dayton, PA 16222 • 648
Dayton, TN 37321 • 5,913
Dayton, TX 77535 • 4,908
Dayton, VA 22821 • 1,017
Dayton, WA 99328 • 2,565
Dayton, WY 82836 • 701
Daytona Beach, FL 32014-23 • 54,176
Dayville, CT 06241 • 1,100
Deadwood, SD 57732 • 2,035
Deaf Smith □, TX • 21,165
Deal, NJ 07723 • 1,952
Deale, MD 20751 • 3,008
Dearborn, MI 48120-26 • 90,660
Dearborn □, IN • 34,291
Dearborn Heights, MI 48127 • 67,706
De Baca □, NM • 2,454
De Bary, FL 32713 • 4,980
Debolt, NE 68152 • 800
Decatur, AL 35601-03 • 42,002
Decatur, AR 72722 • 1,013
Decatur, GA 30030-38 • 18,404
Decatur, IL 62521-26 • 94,081
Decatur, IN 46733 • 8,649
Decatur, MI 49045 • 1,915
Decatur, MS 39327 • 1,148
Decatur, NE 68020 • 723
Decatur, TN 37322 • 1,069
Decatur, TX 76234 • 4,104
Decatur □, GA • 25,495
Decatur □, IN • 23,841
Decatur □, IA • 9,794
Decatur □, KS • 4,509
Decatur □, TN • 10,857
Decaturville, TN 38329 • 1,004
Decherd, TN 37324 • 2,233
Deckerville, MI 48427 • 887
Decorah, IA 52101 • 7,991
Dedham, MA 02026 • 25,298
Deep River, CT 06417 • 2,495
Deepwater, NJ 08023 • 650
Deer Creek, IL 61733 • 688
Deerfield, IL 60015 • 17,430
Deerfield, MI 49238 • 957
Deerfield, WI 53531 • 1,466
Deerfield Beach, FL 33441 • 39,193
Deer Lodge, MT 59722 • 4,023
Deer Lodge □, MT • 12,518
Deer Park, NY 11729 • 33,400
Deer Park, OH 45236 • 6,745
Deer Park, TX 77536 • 22,648
Deer Park, WA 99006 • 2,140
Deer River, MN 56636 • 907
Defiance, OH 43512 • 16,810
Defiance □, OH • 39,987
De Forest, WI 53532 • 3,367
De Funiak Springs, FL 32433 • 5,563
De Graff, OH 43318 • 1,358
De Kalb, IL 60115 • 33,099
De Kalb, MS 39328 • 1,159
De Kalb, TX 75559 • 2,217
De Kalb □, AL • 53,658
De Kalb □, GA • 483,024
De Kalb □, IL • 74,624
De Kalb □, IN • 33,606
De Kalb □, MO • 8,222
De Kalb □, TN • 13,589
Delafield, WI 53018 • 4,083
Del Aire, CA 90250 • 3,900
Delanco, NJ 08075 • 3,730
De Land, FL 32720-24 • 15,354
Delano, CA 93215 • 16,491
Delano, MN 55328 • 2,480
Delavan, IL 61734 • 1,973
Delavan, WI 53115 • 5,684
Delavan Lake, WI 53115 • 2,124
Delaware, OH 43015 • 18,780
Delaware □, IN • 128,587
Delaware □, IA • 18,933
Delaware □, NY • 46,824
Delaware □, OH • 53,840
Delaware □, OK • 23,946
Delaware □, PA • 555,007
Delaware City, DE 19706 • 1,858
Delbarton, WV 25670 • 981
Delcambre, LA 70528 • 2,216
Del City, OK 73115 • 28,523
De Leon, TX 76444 • 2,478
De Leon Springs, FL 32028 • 1,669
Delevan, NY 14042 • 1,113
Delhi, LA 71232 • 3,290
Delhi, NY 13753 • 3,374
Delhi Hills, OH 45238 • 7,650
Dell Rapids, SD 57022 • 2,389
Dellslow, WV 26531 • 700
Dellwood, MO 63136 • 6,200
Del Mar, CA 92014 • 5,017
Delmar, DE 19940 • 948
Delmar, IA 52037 • 633
Delmar, MD 21875 • 1,232
Delmar, NY 12054 • 8,900
Del Norte, CO 81132 • 1,709
Del Norte □, CA • 18,217
Del Park Manor, DE 19808 • 1,700
Delphi, IN 46923 • 3,042
Delphos, OH 45833 • 7,314
Delran, NJ 08075 • 10,065
Delray Beach, FL 33444-47 • 34,325
Del Rio, TX 78840 • 30,034
Delta, CO 81416 • 3,931
Delta, OH 43515 • 2,831
Delta, PA 17314 • 692
Delta, UT 84624 • 1,930
Delta □, CO • 21,225
Delta □, MI • 38,947
Delta □, TX • 4,839
Delta Junction, AK 99737 • 945
Deltona, FL 32725 • 4,868
Demarest, NJ 07627 • 4,963
Deming, NM 88030 • 9,964
Demopolis, AL 36732 • 7,678
Demorest, GA 30535 • 1,130
Demotte, IN 46310 • 2,559
Denham Springs, LA 70726 • 8,563
Denison, IA 51442 • 6,675
Denison, TX 75020 • 23,884
Denmark, SC 29042 • 4,434
Denmark, WI 54208 • 1,475
Dennis, MA 02638 • 900
Dennison, OH 44621 • 3,398
Dennis Port, MA 02639 • 2,570
Denny Terrace, SC 29203 • 1,885
Dent □, MO • 14,517
Denton, MD 21629 • 1,927
Denton, NC 27239 • 949
Denton, TX 76201-06 • 48,063
Denton □, TX • 143,126
Dentsville, SC 29204 • 5,000
Denver, CO 80201-99 • 492,365
Denver, IA 50622 • 1,647
Denver, PA 17517 • 2,018
Denver □, CO • 492,365
Denver City, TX 79323 • 4,704
Denville, NJ 07834 • 14,045
De Pere, WI 54115 • 14,892
Depew, NY 14043 • 19,819
Depew, OK 74028 • 682
Depoe Bay, OR 97341 • 723
Deport, TX 75435 • 724
Deposit, NY 13754 • 1,897
Depue, IL 61322 • 1,873
De Queen, AR 71832 • 4,594
De Quincy, LA 70633 • 3,966
Derby, CT 06418 • 12,346
Derby, KS 67037 • 9,786
Derby, NY 14047 • 1,200
Derby Line, VT 05830 • 874
De Ridder, LA 70634 • 11,057
Derma, MS 38839 • 793
Dermott, AR 71638 • 4,731
Derry, NH 03038 • 12,248
Derry, PA 15627 • 3,072
Des Allemands, LA 70030 • 2,920
Des Arc, AR 72040 • 2,001
Deschutes □, OR • 62,142
Desert Hot Springs, CA 92240 • 5,941
Desha, AR 72527 • 750
Desha □, AR • 19,760
Deshler, NE 68340 • 997
Deshler, OH 43516 • 1,870
Desloge, MO 63601 • 2,934
De Smet, SD 57231 • 1,237
Des Moines, IA 50301-99 • 191,003
Des Moines, WA 98188 • 7,378
Des Moines □, IA • 46,203
De Soto, IL 62924 • 1,589
De Soto, IA 50069 • 1,035
De Soto, KS 66018 • 2,061
De Soto, MO 63020 • 5,993
De Soto, TX 75115 • 15,538
De Soto □, FL • 19,039
De Soto □, LA • 25,727
De Soto □, MS • 53,930
Despard, WV 26301 • 1,200
Des Peres, MO 63131 • 8,254
Des Plaines, IL 60016-18 • 53,568
Destin, FL 32541 • 3,672
Destrehan, LA 70047 • 2,382
Detroit, MI 48201-99 • 1,203,339
Detroit, TX 75436 • 805
Detroit Lakes, MN 56501 • 7,106
Deuel □, NE • 2,462
Deuel □, SD • 5,289
De Valls Bluff, AR 72041 • 738
Devils Lake, ND 58301 • 7,442
Devine, TX 78016 • 3,756
Devola, OH 45750 • 2,708
Devon, PA 19333 • 6,700
Devonshire, DE 19810 • 1,800
Dewar, OK 74431 • 1,048
Dewey, OK 74029 • 3,545
Dewey □, OK • 5,922
Dewey □, SD • 5,366
Dewey Beach, DE 19971 • 1,500
Deweyville, TX 77614 • 950
De Witt, AR 72042 • 3,928
De Witt, IA 52742 • 4,512
De Witt, MI 48820 • 3,165
De Witt, NE 68341 • 642
De Witt, NY 13214 • 10,032
De Witt □, IL • 18,108
De Witt □, TX • 18,903
Dexter, IA 50070 • 678
Dexter, ME 04930 • 3,118
Dexter, MI 48130 • 1,524
Dexter, MO 63841 • 7,043
Dexter, NM 88230 • 882
Dexter, NY 13634 • 1,053
Diamond Bar, CA 91765 • 28,045
Diamond Hill, RI 02864 • 1,150
Diamond Lake, IL 60060 • 1,503
Diamond Springs, CA 95619 • 2,287
Diamondville, WY 83116 • 1,000
Diaz, AR 72043 • 1,192
D'Iberville, MS 39532 • 9,000
Diboll, TX 75941 • 5,227
Dickens □, TX • 3,539
Dickenson □, VA • 19,806
Dickey □, ND • 7,207
Dickeyville, WI 53808 • 1,156
Dickinson, ND 58601 • 15,924
Dickinson, TX 77539 • 7,505
Dickinson □, IA • 15,629
Dickinson □, KS • 20,175
Dickinson □, MI • 25,341
Dickson, OK 73401 • 996
Dickson, TN 37055 • 7,040
Dickson □, TN • 30,037
Dickson City, PA 18519 • 6,699
Dierks, AR 71833 • 1,249
Dieterich, IL 62424 • 633
Dighton, KS 67839 • 1,390
Dighton, MA 02715 • 900
Dike, IA 50624 • 987
Dillard, OR 97432 • 1,000
Dill City, OK 73641 • 649
Dilley, TX 78017 • 2,579
Dillingham, AK 99576 • 914
Dillon, MT 59725 • 3,976
Dillon, SC 29536 • 7,060
Dillon □, SC • 31,083
Dillonvale, OH 43917 • 912
Dillsboro, IN 47018 • 1,038
Dillsburg, PA 17019 • 1,733
Dillwyn, VA 23936 • 637
Dilworth, MN 56529 • 2,585
Dimmit □, TX • 11,367
Dimmitt, TX 79027 • 5,019
Dimondale, MI 48821 • 1,008
Dinuba, CA 93618 • 9,907
Dinwiddie □, VA • 22,602
Dishman, WA 99213 • 9,900
District Heights-Forestville, MD 20747 • 6,799
Divernon, IL 62530 • 1,081
Divide □, ND • 3,494
Dix, IL 62830 • 3,198
Dixfield, ME 04224 • 1,725
Dix Hills, NY 11746 • 10,500
Dixie □, FL • 7,751
Dixon, CA 95620 • 7,541
Dixon, IL 61021 • 15,701
Dixon, MO 65459 • 1,402
Dixon □, NE • 7,137
Dixonville, PA 15734 • 900
Dobbs Ferry, NY 10522 • 10,053
Dobson, NC 27017 • 1,222
Docena, AL 35060 • 1,140
Dock Junction, GA 31520 • 6,189
Doddridge □, WV • 7,433
Dodge, NE 68633 • 815
Dodge □, GA • 16,955
Dodge □, MN • 14,773
Dodge □, NE • 35,847
Dodge □, WI • 75,064
Dodge Center, MN 55927 • 1,816
Dodge City, KS 67801 • 18,001
Dodgeville, WI 53533 • 3,458
Doerun, GA 31744 • 1,062
Doe Run, MO 63637 • 900
Dolgeville, NY 13329 • 2,602
Dollar Bay, MI 49922 • 900
Dolomite, AL 35061 • 2,400
Dolores, CO 81323 • 802
Dolores □, CO • 1,658
Dolton, IL 60419 • 24,766
Dona Ana □, NM • 96,340
Donaldsonville, LA 70346 • 7,901
Donalsonville, GA 31745 • 3,320
Doneraile, SC 29532 • 1,276
Dongola, IL 62926 • 886
Doniphan, MO 63935 • 1,921
Doniphan, NE 68832 • 696
Doniphan □, KS • 9,268
Donley □, TX • 4,075
Donna, TX 78537 • 9,952
Donnellson, IA 52625 • 972
Donora, PA 15033 • 7,524
Doolittle, MO 65401 • 701
Dooly □, GA • 10,826
Door □, WI • 25,029
Dora, AL 35062 • 2,327
Doraville, GA 30340 • 7,414
Dorchester, NE 68343 • 611
Dorchester, WI 54425 • 613
Dorchester □, MD • 30,623
Dorchester □, SC • 58,761
Dormont, PA 15216 • 11,275
Dorothy Pond, MA 01527 • 1,900
Dorris, CA 96023 • 836
Dorsey, MD 21227 • 1,186
Dothan, AL 36301-03 • 48,750
Double Springs, AL 35553 • 1,057
Dougherty □, GA • 100,718
Douglas, AZ 85607 • 13,058
Douglas, GA 31533 • 10,980
Douglas, MI 49406 • 948
Douglas, WY 82633 • 6,030
Douglas □, CO • 25,153
Douglas □, GA • 54,573
Douglas □, IL • 19,774
Douglas □, KS • 67,640
Douglas □, MN • 27,839
Douglas □, MO • 11,594
Douglas □, NE • 397,038
Douglas □, NV • 19,421
Douglas □, OR • 93,748
Douglas □, SD • 4,181
Douglas □, WA • 22,144
Douglas □, WI • 44,421
Douglass, KS 67039 • 1,450
Douglasville, GA 30133-35 • 7,641
Dousman, WI 53118 • 1,153
Dove Creek, CO 81324 • 826
Dover, AR 72837 • 948
Dover, DE 19901 • 23,507
Dover, FL 33527 • 2,354
Dover, MA 02030 • 2,051
Dover, NH 03820 • 22,377
Dover, NJ 07801 • 14,681
Dover, OH 44622 • 11,782
Dover, PA 17315 • 1,910
Dover, TN 37058 • 1,197
Dover-Foxcroft, ME 04426 • 2,974
Dover Plains, NY 12522 • 800
Dowagiac, MI 49047 • 6,307
Dow City, IA 51528 • 616
Downers Grove, IL 60515-17 • 42,572
Downey, CA 90240-42 • 82,602
Downey, ID 83234 • 645
Downieville, CA 95936 • 950
Downingtown, PA 19335 • 7,650
Downs, KS 67437 • 1,324
Downsville, NY 13755 • 950
Dows, IA 50071 • 771
Doyle, CA 96109 • 900
Doylestown, OH 44230 • 2,493
Doylestown, PA 18901 • 8,717
Doyline, LA 71023 • 801
Dracut, MA 01826 • 21,249
Drain, OR 97435 • 1,148
Drakesboro, KY 42337 • 798
Drakes Branch, VA 23937 • 617
Draper, UT 84020 • 5,521
Drayton, ND 58225 • 1,082
Drayton, SC 29333 • 1,443
Drayton Plains, MI 48020 • 18,000
Dreamland Villa, AZ 85205 • 3,200
Dresden, OH 43821 • 1,646
Dresden, TN 38225 • 2,256
Dresser, WI 54009 • 670
Drew, MS 38737 • 2,528
Drew □, AR • 17,910
Drexel, MO 64742 • 908
Drexel, NC 28619 • 1,392
Drexel, OH 45427 • 2,250
Drexel Hill, PA 19026 • 29,600
Driggs, ID 83422 • 727
Dripping Springs, TX 78620 • 606
Driscoll, TX 78351 • 648
Drumright, OK 74030 • 3,162
Drybranch, WV 25061 • 700
Dryden, MI 48428 • 650
Dryden, NY 13053 • 1,761
Dry Ridge, KY 41035 • 1,250
Duarte, CA 91010 • 16,766
Dubach, LA 71235 • 1,161
Dublin, CA 94568 • 19,000
Dublin, GA 31021 • 16,083
Dublin, IN 47335 • 979
Dublin, OH 43017 • 3,855
Dublin, PA 18917 • 1,565
Dublin, TX 76446 • 2,723
Dublin, VA 24084 • 2,368
Du Bois, PA 15801 • 9,290
Dubois, WY 82513 • 1,067
Dubois □, IN • 34,238
Duboistown, PA 17701 • 1,218
Dubuque, IA 52001 • 62,321
Dubuque □, IA • 93,745
Duchesne, UT 84021 • 1,677
Duchesne □, UT • 12,565
Duck Hill, MS 38925 • 706
Dudley, MA 01570 • 3,700
Duenweg, MO 64841 • 703
Due West, SC 29639 • 1,366
Dugger, IN 47848 • 1,118
Duke Center, PA 16729 • 900
Dukes □, MA • 8,942
Dulce, NM 87528 • 1,648
Duluth, GA 30136 • 2,956
Duluth, MN 55801-99 • 92,811
Dumas, AR 71639 • 6,091
Dumas, TX 79029 • 12,194
Dumfries, VA 22026 • 3,214

Dumont, IA 50625 • 815
Dumont, NJ 07628 • 18,334
Dunaire, GA 30032 • 5,400
Dunbar, PA 15431 • 1,369
Dunbar, WV 25064 • 9,285
Duncan, AZ 85534 • 603
Duncan, OK 73533 • 22,517
Duncan, SC 29334 • 1,259
Duncan Falls, OH 43734 • 1,200
Duncannon, PA 17020 • 1,645
Duncansville, PA 16635 • 1,355
Duncanville, TX 75116 • 27,781
Dundalk, MD 21222 • 71,293
Dundee, FL 33838 • 2,227
Dundee, IL 60118 • 3,551
Dundee, MI 48131 • 2,575
Dundee, NY 14837 • 1,556
Dundee, OR 97115 • 1,223
Dundy □, NE • 2,861
Dunedin, FL 33528 • 30,203
Dunellen, NJ 08812 • 6,593
Dunkerton, IA 50626 • 718
Dunkirk, IN 47336 • 3,180
Dunkirk, NY 14048 • 15,310
Dunkirk, OH 45836 • 954
Dunklin □, MO • 36,324
Dunlap, IL 61525 • 824
Dunlap, IN 46514 • 2,500
Dunlap, IA 51529 • 1,374
Dunlap, TN 37327 • 3,681
Dunleith, DE 19801 • 2,700
Dunlo, PA 15930 • 950
Dunmore, PA 18512 • 16,781
Dunn, NC 28334 • 8,962
Dunn □, ND • 4,627
Dunn □, WI • 34,314
Dunnellon, FL 32630 • 1,427
Dunn Loring Woods, VA 22180 • 2,800
Dunseith, ND 58329 • 625
Dunsmuir, CA 96025 • 2,253
Dunstable, MA 01827 • 900
Dunwoody, GA 30338 • 5,100
Du Page □, IL • 658,829
Duplin □, NC • 40,952
Dupont, CO 80024 • 2,000
Dupont, PA 18641 • 3,460
Dupont City, WV 25015 • 900
Dupont Manor, DE 19901 • 1,059
Duquesne, PA 15110 • 10,094
Du Quoin, IL 62832 • 6,594
Durand, IL 61024 • 1,073
Durand, MI 48429 • 4,241
Durand, WI 54736 • 2,047
Durango, CO 81301 • 11,649
Durant, IA 52747 • 1,583
Durant, MS 39063 • 2,889
Durant, OK 74701 • 11,972
Durham, CA 95938 • 950
Durham, CT 06422 • 2,641
Durham, NH 03824 • 8,448
Durham, NC 27701–99 • 100,538
Durham □, NC • 152,785
Duryea, PA 18642 • 5,415
Dushore, PA 18614 • 692
Duson, LA 70529 • 1,253
Dutchess □, NY • 245,055
Duval □, FL • 571,003
Duval □, TX • 12,517
Duxbury, MA 02332 • 1,685
Dwight, IL 60420 • 4,146
Dyer, AR 72935 • 608
Dyer, IN 46311 • 9,555
Dyer, TN 38330 • 2,419
Dyer □, TN • 34,663
Dyersburg, TN 38024 • 15,856
Dyersville, IA 52040 • 3,825
Dysart, IA 52224 • 1,355

E

Eads, CO 81036 • 878
Eagan, MN 55121 • 20,700
Eagar, AZ 85925 • 2,791
Eagle, CO 81631 • 950
Eagle, ID 83616 • 2,620
Eagle, NE 68347 • 832
Eagle, WI 53119 • 1,008
Eagle □, CO • 13,320
Eagle Grove, IA 50533 • 4,324
Eagle Lake, MN 56024 • 1,470
Eagle Lake, TX 77434 • 3,921
Eagle Lake, WI 53139 • 1,000
Eagle Pass, TX 78852 • 21,407
Eagle Point, OR 97524 • 2,764
Eagle River, WI 54521 • 1,326
Earle, AR 72331 • 3,517
Earlham, IA 50072 • 1,140
Earlimart, CA 93219 • 4,578
Earlington, KY 42410 • 2,011
Earlville, IL 60518 • 1,382
Earlville, IA 52041 • 844
Earlville, NY 13332 • 985
Early, IA 50535 • 670
Early □, GA • 13,158
Earth, TX 79031 • 1,512
Easley, SC 29640 • 14,264
East Acton, MA 01720 • 1,200
East Alton, IL 62024 • 7,096
East Aurora, NY 14052 • 6,803
East Bangor, PA 18013 • 955
East Bank, WV 25067 • 1,155
East Barre, VT 05649 • 900
East Baton Rouge □, LA • 366,191
East Bend, NC 27018 • 602
East Berlin, CT 06023 • 900
East Berlin, PA 17316 • 1,054
East Bernard, TX 77435 • 1,700
East Bernstadt, KY 40729 • 700
East Bethel, MN 55005 • 6,626
East Billerica, MA 01821 • 2,900
Eastborough, KS 67206 • 854
East Brady, PA 16028 • 1,153
East Brewster, MA 02631 • 700
East Brewton, AL 36426 • 3,012
East Bridgewater, MA 02333 • 3,300
East Brookfield, MA 01515 • 1,443
East Brooklyn, CT 06239 • 1,251
East Brunswick, NJ 08816 • 37,711
East Butler, PA 16029 • 799
East Canaan, CT 06024 • 800
East Carbon, UT 84520 • 1,942
East Carroll □, LA • 11,772
East Chelmsford, MA 01824 • 2,900
Eastchester, NY 10709 • 22,600
East Chicago, IN 46312 • 39,786
East Chicago Heights, IL 60411 • 5,347
East Cleveland, OH 44112 • 36,957
East Dennis, MA 02641 • 800
East Detroit, MI 48021 • 38,280
East Douglas, MA 01516 • 1,683
East Dubuque, IL 61025 • 2,194
East Falmouth, MA 02536 • 5,181
East Feliciana □, LA • 19,015
East Flat Rock, NC 28726 • 3,365
East Fultonham, OH 43735 • 650
East Gaffney, SC 29340 • 4,092
East Galesburg, IL 61430 • 928
Eastgate, WA 98004 • 5,300
East Glenville, NY 12302 • 11,800
East Grand Forks, MN 56721 • 8,537
East Grand Rapids, MI 49506 • 10,914
East Greenville, PA 18041 • 2,456
East Greenwich, RI 02818 • 10,211
East Half Hollow Hills, NY 11746 • 9,691
Eastham, MA 02642 • 1,100
East Hampden, ME 04401 • 950
East Hampstead, NH 03826 • 900
East Hampton, CT 06424 • 2,152
Easthampton, MA 01027 • 15,580
East Hampton, NY 11937 • 1,886
East Hanover, NJ 07936 • 9,319
East Hartford, CT 06108 • 52,563
East Haven, CT 06512 • 25,028
East Helena, MT 59635 • 1,647
East Hills, NY 11576 • 7,160
East Islip, NY 11730 • 13,700
East Jordan, MI 49727 • 2,185
Eastlake, OH 44094 • 22,104
Eastland, TX 76448 • 3,747
Eastland □, TX • 19,480
East Lansing, MI 48823 • 51,392
East Las Vegas, NV 89112 • 6,449
East Liverpool, OH 43920 • 16,687
East Longmeadow, MA 01028 • 12,905
East Los Angeles, CA 90022 • 110,017
East Lyme, CT 06333 • 700
Eastman, GA 31023 • 5,330
East Marion, NY 11939 • 900
East Meadow, NY 11554 • 47,300
East Millbury, MA 01527 • 1,000
East Millinocket, ME 04430 • 2,361
East Moline, IL 61244 • 20,907
East Naples, FL 33940 • 9,000
East Newark, NJ 07029 • 1,923
East Newnan, GA 30263 • 1,499
East Norriton, PA 19401 • 12,711
East Northport, NY 11731 • 22,200
East Olympia, WA 98540 • 700
Easton, MD 21601 • 7,536
Easton, PA 18042 • 26,027
Eastondale, MA 02375 • 900
East Orange, NJ 07017–19 • 77,690
East Orleans, MA 02643 • 1,200
Eastover, SC 29044 • 899
East Palatka, FL 32031 • 1,613
East Palestine, OH 44413 • 5,306
East Palo Alto, CA 94303 • 18,191
East Patchogue, NY 11772 • 8,300
East Pea Ridge, WV 25705 • 1,900
East Peoria, IL 61611 • 22,385
East Pepperell, MA 01463 • 2,212
East Petersburg, PA 17520 • 3,600
East Pittsburgh, PA 15112 • 2,493
Eastpoint, FL 32328 • 1,246
East Point, GA 30344 • 37,486
Eastport, ME 04631 • 1,982
Eastport, NY 11941 • 1,308
East Prairie, MO 63845 • 3,713
East Providence, RI 02914 • 50,980
East Quogue, NY 11942 • 1,200
East Randolph, NY 14730 • 655
East Ridge, TN 37412 • 21,236
East River, CT 06443 • 1,800
East Rochester, NY 14445 • 7,596
East Rockaway, NY 11518 • 10,917
East Rockingham, NC 28379 • 5,190
East Rutherford, NJ 07073 • 7,849
East Saint Louis, IL 62201–08 • 55,200
Eastside, OR 97420 • 1,601
Eastsound, WA 98245 • 900
East Sparta, OH 44626 • 868
East Spencer, NC 28039 • 2,150
East Stroudsburg, PA 18301 • 8,039
East Sudbury, MA 01776 • 1,500
East Tawas, MI 48730 • 2,584
East Templeton, MA 01438 • 980
East Troy, WI 53120 • 2,385
East Tustin, CA 92705 • 10,000
East Vestal, NY 13902 • 5,300
East View, WV 26301 • 1,618
East Walpole, MA 02032 • 4,900
East Wareham, MA 02538 • 1,000
East Washington, PA 15301 • 2,241
East Wenatchee, WA 98801 • 1,640
East Windsor, NJ 08520 • 15,000
Eastwood, MI 49001 • 7,186
Eastwood Hills, UT 84106 • 1,200
Eaton, CO 80615 • 1,932
Eaton, IN 47338 • 1,804
Eaton, OH 45320 • 6,839
Eaton □, MI • 88,337
Eaton Rapids, MI 48827 • 4,510
Eatonton, GA 31024 • 4,833
Eatontown, NJ 07724 • 12,703
Eatonville, WA 98328 • 998
Eau Claire, WI 54701–03 • 51,509
Eau Claire □, WI • 78,805
Ebensburg, PA 15931 • 4,096
Eccles, WV 25836 • 1,100
Echo, OR 97826 • 624
Echols □, GA • 2,297
Eckhart Mines, MD 21528 • 1,333
Eckman, WV 24829 • 700
Eclectic, AL 36024 • 1,124
Economy, PA 15005 • 9,538
Ecorse, MI 48229 • 14,447
Ecru, MS 38841 • 687
Ector □, TX • 115,374
Edcouch, TX 78538 • 3,092
Eddy □, NM • 47,855
Eddy □, ND • 3,554
Eddystone, PA 19013 • 2,555
Eddyville, IA 52553 • 1,116
Eddyville, KY 42038 • 1,949
Eden, NC 27288 • 15,672
Eden, NY 14057 • 3,000
Eden, TX 76837 • 1,294
Eden Prairie, MN 55344 • 16,263
Edenton, NC 27932 • 5,357
Eden Valley, MN 55329 • 763
Edgar, NE 68935 • 705
Edgar, WI 54426 • 1,194
Edgar □, IL • 21,725
Edgard, LA 70049 • 680
Edgartown, MA 02539 • 1,138
Edgecombe □, NC • 55,988
Edgefield, SC 29824 • 2,713
Edgefield □, SC • 17,528
Edgeley, ND 58433 • 843
Edgemere, MD 21222 • 7,800
Edgemont, SD 57735 • 1,468
Edgemoor, DE 19802 • 7,397
Edgerton, KS 66021 • 1,214
Edgerton, MN 56128 • 1,123
Edgerton, OH 43517 • 1,813
Edgerton, WI 53534 • 4,335
Edgewater, AL 35224 • 1,400
Edgewater, CO 80214 • 4,766
Edgewater, FL 32032 • 6,726
Edgewater, MD 21037 • 800
Edgewater, NJ 07020 • 4,628
Edgewater Park, NJ 08010 • 9,273
Edgewood, IN 46011 • 2,215
Edgewood, IA 52042 • 900
Edgewood, KY 41017 • 7,230
Edgewood, MD 21040 • 19,455
Edgewood, OH 44004 • 3,099
Edgewood, PA 15218 • 4,382
Edgewood, WA 98371 • 1,800
Edgeworth, PA 15143 • 1,738
Edina, MN 55424 • 46,073
Edina, MO 63537 • 1,520
Edinboro, PA 16412 • 6,324
Edinburg, IL 62531 • 1,231
Edinburg, TX 78539 • 24,075
Edinburg, VA 22824 • 752
Edinburgh, IN 46124 • 4,856
Edison, GA 31746 • 1,128
Edison, NJ 08817–20 • 70,193
Edmond, OK 73034 • 34,637
Edmonds, WA 98020 • 27,679
Edmondson Heights, MD 21207 • 5,000
Edmonson □, KY • 9,962
Edmonton, KY 42129 • 1,401
Edmore, MI 48829 • 1,176
Edmunds □, SD • 5,159
Edna, TX 77957 • 5,650
Edon, OH 43518 • 947
Edwards, MS 39066 • 1,515
Edwards □, IL • 7,961
Edwards □, KS • 4,271
Edwards □, TX • 2,033
Edwardsburg, MI 49112 • 1,135
Edwardsville, IL 62025 • 12,480
Edwardsville, KS 66113 • 3,364
Edwardsville, PA 18704 • 5,729
Effingham, IL 62401 • 11,270
Effingham, KS 66023 • 634
Effingham □, GA • 18,327
Effingham □, IL • 30,944
Egg Harbor City, NJ 08215 • 4,618
Egypt, MA 02066 • 1,100
Ehrenberg, AZ 85334 • 900
Ekalaka, MT 59324 • 620
Elaine, AR 72333 • 991
Elba, AL 36323 • 4,355
Elba, NY 14058 • 750
Elberfeld, IN 47613 • 640
Elbert □, CO • 6,850
Elbert □, GA • 18,758
Elberton, GA 30635 • 5,686
Elbow Lake, MN 56531 • 1,358
Elburn, IL 60119 • 1,224
El Cajon, CA 92020–22 • 73,892
El Campo, TX 77437 • 10,462
El Centro, CA 92243 • 23,996
El Cerrito, CA 94530 • 22,731
Eldon, IA 52554 • 1,255
Eldon, MO 65026 • 4,342
Eldora, IA 50627 • 3,063
El Dorado, AR 71730 • 25,270
Eldorado, GA 31794 • 1,000
Eldorado, IL 62930 • 5,198
El Dorado, KS 67042 • 10,510
Eldorado, OK 73537 • 688
Eldorado, TX 76936 • 2,061
El Dorado □, CA • 85,812
El Dorado Springs, MO 64744 • 3,868
Eldred, PA 16731 • 965
Eldridge, IA 52748 • 3,279
Eleanor, WV 25070 • 1,282
Electra, TX 76360 • 3,755
El Encanto Heights, CA 93117 • 7,700
Elgin, IL 60120 • 63,981
Elgin, IA 52141 • 702
Elgin, MN 55932 • 667
Elgin, NE 68636 • 807
Elgin, ND 58533 • 930
Elgin, OK 73538 • 1,003
Elgin, OR 97827 • 1,701
Elgin, SC 29720 • 900
Elgin, TX 78621 • 4,535
Elida, OH 45807 • 1,349
Eliot, ME 03903 • 2,450
Elizabeth, CO 80107 • 789
Elizabeth, GA 30060 • 1,700
Elizabeth, IL 61028 • 772
Elizabeth, NJ 07201–99 • 106,201
Elizabeth, WV 26143 • 856
Elizabeth City, NC 27909 • 13,784
Elizabethton, TN 37643 • 12,431
Elizabethtown, IN 47232 • 603
Elizabethtown, KY 42701 • 15,380
Elizabethtown, NC 28337 • 3,551
Elizabethtown, NY 12932 • 650
Elizabethtown, PA 17022 • 8,233
Elizabethville, PA 17023 • 1,531
El Jebel, CO 81628 • 900
Elk □, KS • 3,918
Elk □, PA • 38,338
Elkader, IA 52043 • 1,688
Elk City, ID 83525 • 670
Elk City, OK 73644 • 9,579
Elk Grove, CA 95624 • 10,059
Elk Grove Village, IL 60007 • 28,907
Elkhart, IN 46514–17 • 41,305
Elkhart, KS 67950 • 2,243
Elkhart, TX 75839 • 1,317
Elkhart □, IN • 137,330
Elkhart Lake, WI 53020 • 1,054
Elk Horn, IA 51531 • 746
Elkhorn, NE 68022 • 1,344
Elkhorn, WV 24831 • 700
Elkhorn, WI 53121 • 4,605
Elkhorn City, KY 41522 • 1,446
Elkin, NC 28621 • 2,858
Elkins, WV 26241 • 8,536
Elkins Park, PA 19117 • 14,000
Elkland, PA 16920 • 1,974
Elk Mound, WI 54739 • 737
Elko, NV 89801 • 8,758
Elko □, NV • 17,269
Elk Point, SD 57025 • 1,661
Elk Rapids, MI 49629 • 1,504
Elkridge, MD 21227 • 2,100
Elk River, MN 55330 • 6,785
Elkton, KY 42220 • 1,815
Elkton, MD 21921 • 6,468
Elkton, MI 48731 • 953
Elkton, SD 57026 • 632
Elkton, VA 22827 • 1,520
Elkview, WV 25071 • 1,406
Elkville, IL 62932 • 973
Ellaville, GA 31806 • 1,684
Ellendale, ND 58436 • 1,967
Ellensburg, WA 98926 • 11,752
Ellenton, FL 33532 • 1,561
Ellenville, NY 12428 • 4,405
Ellerbe, NC 28338 • 1,415
Ellerslie, MD 21529 • 1,150
Ellettsville, IN 47429 • 3,328
Ellicott City, MD 21043 • 4,000
Ellicottville, NY 14731 • 713
Ellijay, GA 30540 • 1,507
Ellington, CT 06029 • 1,000
Ellington, MO 63638 • 1,215
Ellinwood, KS 67526 • 2,508
Elliott, MS 38926 • 1,200
Elliott □, KY • 6,908
Ellis, KS 67637 • 2,062
Ellis □, KS • 26,098
Ellis □, OK • 5,596
Ellis □, TX • 59,743
Elliston, VA 24087 • 750
Ellisville, MS 39437 • 4,652
Ellisville, MO 63011 • 6,233
Elloree, SC 29047 • 909
Ellport, PA 16117 • 1,290
Ellsworth, KS 67439 • 2,465
Ellsworth, ME 04605 • 5,179
Ellsworth, MN 56129 • 629
Ellsworth, PA 15331 • 1,228
Ellsworth, WI 54011 • 2,143
Ellsworth □, KS • 6,640
Ellwood City, PA 16117 • 9,998
Elma, IA 50628 • 714
Elma, WA 98541 • 2,720
Elm City, NC 27822 • 1,561
Elm Creek, NE 68836 • 862
Elmer, NJ 08318 • 1,569
Elm Grove, WI 53122 • 6,735
Elmhurst, IL 60126 • 44,276
Elmhurst, PA 18416 • 953
Elmira, NY 14901–99 • 35,327
El Mirage, AZ 85335 • 4,307
Elmira Heights, NY 14903 • 4,279
Elmont, NY 11003 • 30,000
El Monte, CA 91731–35 • 79,494
Elmora, PA 15737 • 950
Elmore, MN 56027 • 882
Elmore, OH 43416 • 1,271
Elmore □, AL • 43,390
Elmore □, ID • 21,565
Elm Springs, AR 72728 • 781
Elmwood, IL 61529 • 2,117
Elmwood, MA 02337 • 750
Elmwood, WI 54740 • 885
Elmwood Park, IL 60635 • 24,016
Elmwood Park, NJ 07407 • 18,377
Elmwood Place, OH 45216 • 2,840
Elnora, IN 47529 • 756
Eloise, FL 33880 • 1,408
Elon College, NC 27244 • 2,873
Eloy, AZ 85231 • 6,240
El Paso, IL 61738 • 2,676
El Paso, TX 79901–99 • 425,259
El Paso □, CO • 309,424
El Paso □, TX • 479,899
El Portal, CA 95318 • 850
El Portal, FL 33138 • 2,055
El Prado, NM 87529 • 700
Elrama, PA 15038 • 800
El Reno, OK 73036 • 15,486
El Rio, CA 93030 • 5,674
Elroy, WI 53929 • 1,504
Elsa, TX 78543 • 5,061
Elsah, IL 62028 • 990
Elsberry, MO 63343 • 1,272
El Segundo, CA 90245 • 13,752
Elsie, MI 48831 • 1,022
Elsinore, UT 84724 • 612
Elsmere, DE 19805 • 6,493
Elsmere, KY 41018 • 7,203
Elsmere, NY 12054 • 5,500
El Sobrante, CA 94803 • 10,505
Elton, LA 70532 • 1,450
El Toro, CA 92630 • 38,153
Elvins, MO 63601 • 1,548
Elwood, IN 46036 • 10,867
Elwood, KS 66024 • 1,275
Elwood, NE 68937 • 716
Elwood, NJ 08217 • 900
Elwood, NY 11731 • 15,400
Ely, MN 55731 • 4,820
Ely, NV 89301 • 4,882
Elyria, OH 44035–39 • 57,538
Elysburg, PA 17824 • 1,337
Emanuel □, GA • 20,795
Emerson, GA 30137 • 1,110
Emerson, NE 68733 • 874
Emerson, NJ 07630 • 7,793
Emery □, UT • 11,451
Eminence, KY 40019 • 2,260
Eminence, MO 65466 • 614
Emlenton, PA 16373 • 807
Emmaus, PA 18049 • 11,001
Emmet □, IA • 13,336
Emmet □, MI • 22,992
Emmetsburg, IA 50536 • 4,621
Emmett, ID 83617 • 4,605
Emmitsburg, MD 21727 • 1,552
Emmons □, ND • 5,877
Emory, TX 75440 • 813
Empire, LA 70050 • 630
Emporia, KS 66801 • 25,287
Emporia, VA 23847 • 4,840
Emporium, PA 15834 • 2,837
Emsworth, PA 15202 • 3,074
Encampment, WY 82325 • 611
Encinal, TX 78019 • 704
Encinitas, CA 92024 • 10,796
Enderlin, ND 58027 • 1,151
Endicott, NY 13760 • 14,457
Endwell, NY 13760 • 15,999
Enfield, CT 06082 • 8,151
Enfield, IL 62835 • 890
Enfield, NH 03748 • 1,581
Enfield, NC 27823 • 2,995
England, AR 72046 • 3,081
Engleside, VA 22309 • 21,400
Englewood, CO 80110–12 • 30,021
Englewood, FL 33533 • 10,242
Englewood, NJ 07631–32 • 23,701
Englewood, OH 45322 • 11,329
Englewood, TN 37329 • 1,840
Englewood Cliffs, NJ 07632 • 5,698
English, IN 47118 • 633
Englishtown, NJ 07726 • 976
Enid, OK 73701 • 50,363
Enka, NC 28728 • 5,567
Ennis, MT 59729 • 660
Ennis, TX 75119 • 12,110
Enoch, UT 84720 • 678
Enola, PA 17025 • 3,600
Enon, OH 45323 • 2,597
Enoree, SC 29335 • 1,107
Enosburg Falls, VT 05450 • 1,207
Ensley, FL 32504 • 2,200
Enterprise, AL 36330 • 18,033

Enterprise, KS 67441 • 839
Enterprise, MS 39330 • 607
Enterprise, OR 97828 • 2,003
Enterprise, UT 84725 • 905
Enterprise, WV 26568 • 950
Enumclaw, WA 98022 • 5,427
Ephraim, UT 84627 • 2,810
Ephrata, PA 17522 • 11,095
Ephrata, WA 98823 • 5,359
Epping, NH 03042 • 1,384
Epps, LA 71237 • 672
Epworth, IA 52045 • 1,380
Equality, IL 62934 • 831
Erath, LA 70533 • 2,133
Erath □, TX • 22,560
Erdenheim, PA 19118 • 3,300
Erial, NJ 08081 • 900
Erick, OK 73645 • 1,375
Erie, CO 80516 • 1,254
Erie, IL 61250 • 1,725
Erie, KS 66733 • 1,415
Erie, MI 48133 • 700
Erie, PA 16501-99 • 119,123
Erie □, NY • 1,015,472
Erie □, OH • 79,655
Erie □, PA • 279,780
Erin, TN 37061 • 1,614
Erlanger, KY 41018 • 14,433
Erma, NJ 08204 • 1,200
Errol Heights, OR 97266 • 7,800
Erwin, NC 28339 • 2,828
Erwin, TN 37650 • 4,739
Escalante, UT 84726 • 652
Escalon, CA 95320 • 3,127
Escambia □, AL • 38,440
Escambia □, FL • 233,794
Escanaba, MI 49829 • 14,355
Escatawpa, MS 39552 • 5,367
Escondido, CA 92025-27 • 64,355
Eskridge, KS 66423 • 603
Esmeralda □, NV • 777
Esmond, RI 02917 • 3,500
Espanola, NM 87532 • 6,803
Esparto, CA 95627 • 1,303
Espy, PA 17815 • 1,652
Essex, CT 06426 • 2,501
Essex, IA 51638 • 1,001
Essex, MD 21221 • 39,614
Essex, MA 01929 • 1,490
Essex, VT 05451 • 800
Essex □, MA • 633,632
Essex □, NJ • 851,116
Essex □, NY • 36,176
Essex □, VT • 6,313
Essex □, VA • 8,864
Essex Fells, NJ 07021 • 2,363
Essex Junction, VT 05452 • 7,033
Essexville, MI 48732 • 4,378
Estacada, OR 97023 • 1,419
Estancia, NM 87016 • 830
Estelline, SD 57234 • 719
Estell Manor, NJ 08319 • 848
Estero, FL 33928 • 950
Estes Park, CO 80517 • 2,703
Estherville, IA 51334 • 7,518
Estherwood, LA 70534 • 691
Estill, SC 29918 • 2,308
Estill □, KY • 14,495
Estill Springs, TN 37330 • 1,324
Etna, CA 96027 • 754
Etna, PA 15223 • 4,534
Etowah, TN 37331 • 3,758
Etowah □, AL • 103,057
Ettrick, VA 23803 • 4,000
Euclid, OH 44117 • 59,999
Eudora, AR 71640 • 3,840
Eudora, KS 66025 • 2,934
Eufaula, AL 36027 • 12,097
Eufaula, OK 74432 • 3,159
Eugene, OR 97401-05 • 105,624
Eulaton, AL 36201 • 1,869
Euless, TX 76039-40 • 24,002
Eunice, LA 70535 • 12,479
Eunice, NM 88231 • 2,970
Eupora, MS 39744 • 2,048
Eureka, CA 95501 • 24,153
Eureka, IL 61530 • 4,306
Eureka, KS 67045 • 3,425
Eureka, MO 63025 • 3,862
Eureka, MT 59917 • 1,119
Eureka, SC 29706 • 1,627
Eureka, SD 57437 • 1,360
Eureka, UT 84628 • 670
Eureka □, NV • 1,547
Eureka Springs, AR 72632 • 1,989
Eustis, FL 32726 • 9,453
Eutaw, AL 35462 • 2,444
Eutawville, SC 29048 • 615
Evangeline □, LA • 33,343
Evans, CO 80620 • 5,063
Evans, GA 30809 • 800
Evans □, GA • 8,428
Evans City, PA 16033 • 2,299
Evansdale, IA 50707 • 4,798
Evans Mills, NY 13637 • 651
Evanston, IL 60201-99 • 73,706
Evanston, WY 82930 • 6,421
Evansville, IL 62242 • 863
Evansville, IN 47701-99 • 130,496
Evansville, WI 53536 • 2,835
Evansville, WY 82636 • 2,335
Evart, MI 49631 • 1,945
Evarts, KY 40828 • 1,234
Eveleth, MN 55734 • 5,042
Everett, PA 15537 • 1,828

Everett, WA 98201-07 • 54,413
Evergreen, AL 36401 • 4,171
Evergreen, CO 80439 • 6,376
Evergreen Park, IL 60642 • 22,260
Everly, IA 51338 • 796
Everman, TX 76140 • 5,387
Everson, PA 15631 • 1,032
Everson, WA 98247 • 898
Ewa, HI 96706 • 2,637
Ewa Beach, HI 96706-07 • 14,369
Ewing Township, NJ 08618 • 34,842
Excelsior Springs, MO 64024 • 10,424
Exeter, CA 93221 • 5,606
Exeter, NE 68351 • 807
Exeter, NH 03833 • 8,947
Exeter, PA 18643 • 5,493
Exira, IA 50076 • 978
Exmore, VA 23350 • 1,300
Experiment, GA 30212 • 3,000
Export, PA 15632 • 1,143
Eyota, MN 55934 • 1,244

F
Fabens, TX 79838 • 3,500
Factoryville, PA 18419 • 924
Fairbank, IA 50629 • 980
Fairbanks, AK 99701 • 22,645
Fair Bluff, NC 28439 • 1,095
Fairborn, OH 45324 • 29,702
Fairburn, GA 30213 • 3,466
Fairbury, IL 61739 • 3,544
Fairbury, NE 68352 • 5,265
Fairchance, PA 15436 • 2,106
Fairdale, KY 40118 • 7,315
Fairfax, AL 36854 • 3,776
Fairfax, CA 94930 • 7,391
Fairfax, DE 19803 • 2,850
Fairfax, IA 52228 • 683
Fairfax, MN 55332 • 1,405
Fairfax, MO 64446 • 835
Fairfax, OK 74637 • 1,949
Fairfax, SC 29827 • 2,154
Fairfax, VA 22030-39 • 19,390
Fairfax □, VA • 596,901
Fairfield, AL 35064 • 13,242
Fairfield, CA 94533 • 58,099
Fairfield, CT 06430 • 54,849
Fairfield, IL 62837 • 5,439
Fairfield, IA 52556 • 9,428
Fairfield, ME 04937 • 3,169
Fairfield, MT 59436 • 650
Fairfield, NJ 07006 • 7,987
Fairfield, OH 45014 • 30,777
Fairfield, TX 75840 • 3,505
Fairfield □, CT • 807,143
Fairfield □, OH • 93,678
Fairfield □, SC • 20,700
Fairfield Bay, AR 72088 • 1,000
Fairgrove, MI 48733 • 691
Fair Grove, MO 65648 • 863
Fair Grove, NC 27360 • 1,500
Fairhaven, MA 02719 • 15,759
Fair Haven, MI 48023 • 900
Fair Haven, NJ 07701 • 5,679
Fair Haven, NY 13064 • 976
Fair Haven, VT 05743 • 2,819
Fairhope, AL 36532 • 7,286
Fairland, IN 46126 • 900
Fairland, OK 74343 • 1,073
Fair Lawn, NJ 07410 • 32,229
Fairlawn, OH 44313 • 6,100
Fairlawn, VA 24141 • 2,000
Fairlea, WV 24902 • 1,200
Fairless Hills, PA 19030 • 12,500
Fairmont, IL 60441 • 2,600
Fairmont, MN 56031 • 11,506
Fairmont, NE 68354 • 767
Fairmont, NC 28340 • 2,658
Fairmont, WV 26554 • 23,863
Fairmount, GA 30139 • 842
Fairmount, IL 61841 • 851
Fairmount, IN 46928 • 3,286
Fairmount, NY 13219 • 8,700
Fairmount Heights, MD 20743 • 1,616
Fair Oaks, CA 95628 • 20,235
Fair Oaks, CA 30060 • 8,486
Fairoaks, PA 15003 • 1,854
Fair Plain, MI 49022 • 8,289
Fairport, NY 14450 • 5,970
Fairport Harbor, OH 44077 • 3,357
Fairton, NJ 08320 • 1,107
Fairview, MT 59221 • 1,366
Fairview, NJ 07022 • 10,519
Fairview, NY 12601 • 8,517
Fairview, OK 73737 • 3,370
Fairview, OR 97024 • 1,749
Fairview, PA 16415 • 1,855
Fairview, TN 37062 • 3,648
Fairview, UT 84629 • 916
Fairview, WV 26570 • 759
Fairview Heights, IL 62208 • 12,414
Fairview Park, NY 47842 • 1,545
Fairview Park, OH 44126 • 19,311
Fairview Shores, FL 32804 • 6,100
Fairway, KS 66205 • 4,619
Faison, NC 28341 • 636
Falconer, NY 14733 • 2,778
Falcon Heights, MN 55113 • 5,291
Falcon Heights, OR 97601 • 1,389
Falfurrias, TX 78355 • 6,103
Falkville, AL 35622 • 1,310
Fall Branch, TN 37656 • 1,340
Fallbrook, CA 92028 • 14,041

Fall City, WA 98024 • 1,600
Fall Creek, WI 54742 • 1,148
Fall Mountain Lake, CT 06786 • 730
Fallon, NV 89406 • 4,262
Fallon □, MT • 3,763
Fall River, MA 02720-26 • 92,574
Fall River, WI 53932 • 850
Fall River □, SD • 8,439
Fall River Mills, CA 96028 • 900
Falls □, TX • 17,946
Falls Church, VA 22040-48 • 9,515
Falls City, NE 68355 • 5,374
Falls City, OR 97344 • 804
Falls Creek, PA 15840 • 1,208
Fallston, MD 21047 • 5,572
Fallston, NC 28042 • 614
Falmouth, KY 41040 • 2,482
Falmouth, ME 04105 • 6,853
Falmouth, MA 02540-41 • 4,200
Falmouth, VA 22403 • 970
Fannin □, GA • 14,748
Fannin □, TX • 24,285
Fanwood, NJ 07023 • 7,767
Fargo, ND 58102-99 • 61,383
Far Hills, NJ 07931 • 677
Faribault, MN 55021 • 16,241
Faribault □, MN • 19,714
Farley, IA 52046 • 1,287
Farmer City, IL 61842 • 2,252
Farmers Branch, TX 75234 • 24,863
Farmersburg, IN 47850 • 1,240
Farmersville, CA 93223 • 5,544
Farmersville, IL 62533 • 686
Farmersville, TX 75031 • 2,360
Farmerville, LA 71241 • 3,768
Farmingdale, ME 04345 • 2,014
Farmingdale, NJ 07727 • 1,348
Farmingdale, NY 11735 • 7,946
Farmington, AR 72730 • 1,283
Farmington, CT 06032 • 2,000
Farmington, IL 61531 • 3,118
Farmington, IA 52626 • 869
Farmington, ME 04938 • 3,583
Farmington, MI 48024 • 11,022
Farmington, MN 55024 • 4,370
Farmington, MO 63640 • 8,270
Farmington, NH 03835 • 3,284
Farmington, NM 87401 • 31,222
Farmington, UT 84025 • 4,691
Farmington Hills, MI 48018 • 58,056
Farmingville, NY 11738 • 5,700
Farmland, IN 47340 • 1,560
Farmville, NC 27828 • 4,707
Farmville, VA 23901 • 6,067
Farragut, IA 51639 • 603
Farrell, PA 16121 • 8,645
Farwell, MI 48622 • 804
Farwell, TX 79325 • 1,354
Faulk □, SD • 3,327
Faulkland Heights, DE 19808 • 1,650
Faulkner □, AR • 46,192
Faulkton, SD 57438 • 981
Fauquier □, VA • 35,889
Fayette, AL 35555 • 5,287
Fayette, IA 52142 • 1,515
Fayette, MS 39069 • 2,033
Fayette, MO 65248 • 2,983
Fayette, OH 43521 • 1,222
Fayette □, AL • 18,809
Fayette □, GA • 29,043
Fayette □, IL • 22,167
Fayette □, IN • 28,272
Fayette □, IA • 25,488
Fayette □, KY • 204,165
Fayette □, OH • 27,467
Fayette □, PA • 159,417
Fayette □, TN • 25,305
Fayette □, TX • 18,832
Fayette □, WV • 57,863
Fayetteville, AR 72701-03 • 36,608
Fayetteville, GA 30214 • 2,715
Fayetteville, NC 28301-08 • 59,507
Fayetteville, PA 17222 • 2,449
Fayetteville, TN 37334 • 7,559
Fayetteville, WV 25840 • 2,366
Fayville, MA 01745 • 1,000
Feasterville, PA 19047 • 6,900
Federal Heights, CO 80221 • 7,846
Federalsburg, MD 21632 • 1,952
Federal Way, WA 98003 • 17,850
Feeding Hills, MA 01030 • 8,500
Felicity, OH 45120 • 929
Fellowship, NJ 08057 • 1,900
Fellsmere, FL 32948 • 1,161
Felton, CA 95018 • 4,000
Fennimore, WI 53809 • 2,212
Fennville, MI 49408 • 934
Fenton, MI 48430 • 8,098
Fentress □, TN • 14,826
Ferdinand, IN 47532 • 2,192
Fergus □, MT • 13,076
Fergus Falls, MN 56537 • 12,519
Ferguson, KY 42533 • 1,027
Ferguson, MO 63135 • 24,740
Fernandina Beach, FL 32034 • 7,224
Fern Creek, KY 40291 • 16,866
Ferndale, CA 95536 • 1,367
Ferndale, MD 21061 • 2,600
Ferndale, MI 48220 • 26,227
Ferndale, PA 15905 • 2,204
Ferndale, WA 98248 • 3,855
Fernley, NV 89408 • 1,200
Fernwood, ID 83830 • 680
Ferriday, LA 71334 • 4,472
Ferris, TX 75125 • 2,228
Ferron, UT 84523 • 1,718

Ferry □, WA • 5,811
Ferry Farms, VA 22401 • 1,300
Fertile, MN 56540 • 869
Fessenden, ND 58438 • 761
Festus, MO 63028 • 7,574
Fieldale, VA 24089 • 1,400
Field Crest Estates, CT 06355 • 1,200
Fig Garden, CA 93704 • 9,000
Filer, ID 83328 • 1,645
Fillmore, CA 93015 • 9,602
Fillmore, UT 84631 • 2,083
Fillmore □, MN • 21,930
Fillmore □, NE • 7,920
Findlay, IL 62534 • 868
Findlay, OH 45840 • 35,594
Finley, ND 58230 • 718
Finley, TN 38030 • 1,014
Finney □, KS • 23,825
Fircrest, WA 98466 • 5,477
Firebaugh, CA 93622 • 3,740
Firestone, CO 80520 • 1,204
Fisher, IL 61843 • 1,572
Fisher □, TX • 5,891
Fishers, IN 46038 • 2,008
Fishersville, VA 22939 • 700
Fishing Creek, MD 21634 • 650
Fishkill, NY 12524 • 1,555
Fiskdale, MA 01518 • 1,859
Fitchburg, MA 01420 • 39,580
Fitzgerald, GA 31750 • 10,187
Five Points, NM 87105 • 5,500
Flagler □, FL • 10,913
Flagler Beach, FL 32036 • 2,208
Flagtown, NJ 08821 • 800
Flanagan, IL 61740 • 978
Flanders, NJ 07836 • 6,000
Flandreau, SD 57028 • 2,114
Flathead □, MT • 51,966
Flat Lick, KY 40935 • 700
Flatonia, TX 78941 • 1,070
Flat River, MO 63601 • 4,443
Flat Rock, MI 48134 • 6,853
Flat Rock, NC 28731 • 1,200
Flatwoods, KY 41139 • 8,354
Fleetwood, PA 19522 • 3,422
Fleming □, KY • 12,323
Fleming-Neon, KY 41816 • 1,195
Flemingsburg, KY 41041 • 2,835
Flemington, NJ 08822 • 4,132
Flemington, PA 17745 • 1,416
Fletcher, NC 28732 • 700
Fletcher, OK 73541 • 1,074
Flint, MI 48501-99 • 159,611
Flint City, AL 35601 • 673
Flippin, AR 72634 • 1,072
Flomaton, AL 36441 • 1,882
Floodwood, MN 55736 • 648
Flora, IL 62839 • 5,379
Flora, IN 46929 • 2,303
Flora, MS 39071 • 1,507
Florala, AL 36442 • 2,165
Floral City, FL 32636 • 1,181
Floral Park, NY 11001-05 • 16,805
Florence, AL 35630-33 • 37,029
Florence, AZ 85232 • 3,391
Florence, CA 90001 • 38,000
Florence, CO 81226 • 2,987
Florence, KS 66851 • 729
Florence, KY 41042 • 15,586
Florence, MS 39073 • 1,111
Florence, NJ 08518 • 5,000
Florence, OR 97439 • 4,411
Florence, SC 29501-03 • 29,176
Florence, TX 76527 • 764
Florence □, SC • 110,163
Florence □, WI • 4,172
Floresville, TX 78114 • 4,381
Florham Park, NJ 07932 • 9,359
Florida, NY 10921 • 1,947
Florida City, FL 33034 • 6,174
Florien, LA 71429 • 964
Florin, CA 95828 • 16,523
Florissant, MO 63031-34 • 55,372
Flossmoor, IL 60422 • 8,423
Flourtown, PA 19031 • 5,200
Flower Hill, NY 11050 • 4,558
Flowery Branch, GA 30542 • 755
Flowood, MS 39208 • 943
Floyd □, GA • 79,800
Floyd □, IN • 61,205
Floyd □, IA • 19,597
Floyd □, KY • 48,764
Floyd □, TX • 9,834
Floyd □, VA • 11,563
Floydada, TX 79235 • 4,193
Flushing, MI 48433 • 8,624
Flushing, OH 43977 • 1,266
Fluvanna □, VA • 10,244
Foard □, TX • 2,158
Folcroft, PA 19032 • 8,231
Foley, AL 36535 • 4,003
Foley, MN 56329 • 1,606
Folkston, GA 31537 • 2,243
Follansbee, WV 26037 • 3,994
Folly Beach, SC 29439 • 1,478
Folsom, CA 95630 • 11,003
Folsom, NJ 08037 • 1,892
Folsom, PA 19033 • 7,600
Fonda, IA 50540 • 863
Fonda, NY 12068 • 1,006
Fond du Lac, WI 54935 • 35,863
Fond du Lac □, WI • 88,964
Fontana, CA 92335 • 37,107
Fontana, WI 53125 • 1,764
Fontanelle, IA 50846 • 805

Foothill Farms, CA 95841 • 13,700
Footville, WI 53537 • 794
Ford □, IL • 15,265
Ford □, KS • 24,315
Ford City, CA 93268 • 3,392
Ford City, PA 16226 • 3,923
Fordoche, LA 70732 • 676
Fords, NJ 08863 • 12,600
Fords Prairie, WA 98531 • 2,000
Fordyce, AR 71742 • 5,175
Foreman, AR 71836 • 1,377
Forest, MS 39074 • 5,229
Forest, OH 45843 • 1,633
Forest □, PA • 5,072
Forest □, WI • 9,044
Forest Acres, SC 29206 • 6,071
Forest City, IA 50436 • 4,270
Forest City, NC 28043 • 7,688
Forest City, PA 18421 • 1,924
Forest Grove, OR 97116 • 11,499
Forest Hill, TX 76119 • 11,684
Forest Hills, PA 15221 • 8,198
Forest Knolls, CA 94933 • 2,000
Forest Lake, MN 55025 • 4,596
Forest Park, GA 30050 • 18,782
Forest Park, IL 60130 • 15,177
Forest Park, LA 71291 • 1,500
Forest Park, OH 45240 • 18,675
Forestville, MD 20747 • 16,401
Forgan, OK 73938 • 611
Forge Village, MA 01886 • 1,400
Forked River, NJ 08731 • 1,422
Forks, WA 98331 • 3,060
Forman, ND 58032 • 629
Forney, TX 75126 • 2,483
Forrest, IL 61741 • 1,246
Forrest □, MS • 66,018
Forrest City, AR 72335 • 13,803
Forreston, IL 61030 • 1,384
Forsyth, GA 31029 • 4,624
Forsyth, IL 62535 • 1,072
Forsyth, MO 65653 • 1,010
Forsyth, MT 59327 • 2,553
Forsyth □, GA • 27,958
Forsyth □, NC • 243,683
Fort Ashby, WV 26719 • 1,200
Fort Atkinson, WI 53538 • 9,785
Fort Bend □, TX • 130,846
Fort Benton, MT 59442 • 1,693
Fort Bragg, CA 95437 • 5,019
Fort Branch, IN 47648 • 2,504
Fort Calhoun, NE 68023 • 641
Fort Cobb, OK 73038 • 760
Fort Collins, CO 80521-26 • 65,092
Fort Covington, NY 12937 • 1,200
Fort Davis, TX 79734 • 850
Fort Defiance, AZ 86504 • 3,431
Fort Deposit, AL 36032 • 1,519
Fort Dodge, IA 50501 • 29,423
Fort Edward, NY 12828 • 3,561
Fort Fairfield, ME 04742 • 2,282
Fort Gaines, GA 31751 • 1,260
Fort Gay, WV 25514 • 886
Fort Gibson, OK 74434 • 2,477
Fort Hall, ID 83203 • 900
Fort Howard, MD 21052 • 1,050
Fort Kent, ME 04743 • 2,375
Fort Lauderdale, FL 33301-99 • 153,279
Fort Lee, NJ 07024 • 32,449
Fort Loramie, OH 45845 • 977
Fort Loudon, PA 17224 • 900
Fort Lupton, CO 80621 • 4,251
Fort Madison, IA 52627 • 13,520
Fort McKinley, OH 45426 • 11,536
Fort Meade, FL 33841 • 5,546
Fort Mill, SC 29715 • 4,162
Fort Mitchell, KY 41017 • 7,297
Fort Morgan, CO 80701 • 8,768
Fort Myers, FL 33901-14 • 36,638
Fort Myers Beach, FL 33931 • 5,753
Fort Ogden, FL 33842 • 900
Fort Oglethorpe, GA 30742 • 5,443
Fort Payne, AL 35967 • 11,485
Fort Pierce, FL 33450-54 • 33,802
Fort Pierre, SD 57532 • 1,789
Fort Plain, NY 13339 • 2,555
Fort Recovery, OH 45846 • 1,370
Fort Scott, KS 66701 • 8,893
Fort Shawnee, OH 45806 • 4,541
Fort Smith, AR 72901-16 • 71,626
Fort Stockton, TX 79735 • 8,688
Fort Sumner, NM 88119 • 1,421
Fort Thomas, KY 41075 • 16,012
Fort Totten, ND 58335 • 750
Fort Towson, OK 74735 • 789
Fortuna, CA 95540 • 7,591
Fort Valley, GA 31030 • 9,000
Fortville, IN 46040 • 2,787
Fort Walton Beach, FL 32548 • 20,829
Fort Washington, PA 19034 • 4,500
Fort Washington Forest, MD 20744 • 1,800
Fort Wayne, IN 46801-99 • 172,028
Fort Wingate, NM 87316 • 900
Fort Worth, TX 76101-99 • 385,164
Fort Wright, KY 41011 • 4,481
Fort Yates, ND 58538 • 771
Forty Fort, PA 18704 • 5,590
Fort Yukon, AK 99740 • 619
Fosston, MN 56542 • 1,599
Foster □, ND • 4,611
Foster Brook, PA 16701 • 950
Foster City, CA 94404 • 23,287

Foster Village, HI 96818 • 3,700
Fostoria, OH 44830 • 15,743
Fouke, AR 71837 • 614
Fountain, CO 80817 • 8,324
Fountain ☐, IN • 19,033
Fountain City, IN 47341 • 839
Fountain City, WI 54629 • 963
Fountain Hill, PA 18015 • 4,805
Fountain Inn, SC 29644 • 4,226
Fountain Place, LA 70811 • 9,200
Fountain Valley, CA 92708 • 55,080
Four Corners, OR 97301 • 11,331
Four Oaks, NC 27524 • 1,049
Fowler, CA 93625 • 2,496
Fowler, CO 81039 • 1,227
Fowler, IN 47944 • 2,319
Fowler, MI 48835 • 1,021
Fowlerville, MI 48836 • 2,289
Foxboro, MA 02035 • 5,697
Fox Chapel, PA 15238 • 5,049
Fox Lake, IL 60020 • 6,831
Fox Lake, WI 53933 • 1,373
Fox Point, WI 53217 • 7,649
Fox River Grove, IL 60021 • 2,515
Foxworth, MS 39483 • 1,000
Frackville, PA 17931 • 5,308
Framingham, MA 01701 • 65,113
Francesville, IN 47946 • 944
Francisco, IN 47649 • 612
Frankenmuth, MI 48734 • 3,753
Frankford, DE 19945 • 828
Frankfort, IL 60423 • 4,357
Frankfort, IN 46041 • 15,168
Frankfort, KS 66427 • 1,038
Frankfort, KY 40601 • 25,973
Frankfort, MI 49635 • 1,603
Frankfort, NY 13340 • 2,995
Frankfort, OH 45628 • 1,008
Franklin, GA 30217 • 711
Franklin, IL 62638 • 645
Franklin, IN 46131 • 11,563
Franklin, LA 70538 • 9,584
Franklin, MA 02038 • 18,217
Franklin, NE 68939 • 1,167
Franklin, NH 03235 • 7,901
Franklin, NJ 07416 • 4,486
Franklin, OH 45005 • 10,711
Franklin, PA 16323 • 8,146
Franklin, TN 37064 • 12,407
Franklin, TX 77856 • 1,349
Franklin, VA 23851 • 7,308
Franklin, WV 26807 • 780
Franklin, WI 53132 • 16,871
Franklin ☐, AL • 28,350
Franklin ☐, AR • 14,705
Franklin ☐, FL • 7,661
Franklin ☐, GA • 15,185
Franklin ☐, ID • 8,895
Franklin ☐, IL • 43,201
Franklin ☐, IN • 19,612
Franklin ☐, IA • 13,036
Franklin ☐, KS • 22,062
Franklin ☐, KY • 41,830
Franklin ☐, LA • 24,141
Franklin ☐, ME • 27,447
Franklin ☐, MA • 64,317
Franklin ☐, MS • 8,208
Franklin ☐, MO • 71,233
Franklin ☐, NE • 4,377
Franklin ☐, NC • 30,055
Franklin ☐, NY • 44,929
Franklin ☐, OH • 869,126
Franklin ☐, PA • 113,629
Franklin ☐, TN • 31,983
Franklin ☐, TX • 6,893
Franklin ☐, VT • 34,788
Franklin ☐, VA • 35,740
Franklin ☐, WA • 35,025
Franklin Grove, IL 61031 • 965
Franklin Lakes, NJ 07417 • 8,769
Franklin Park, IL 60131 • 17,507
Franklin Park, PA 15143 • 6,135
Franklin Square, NY 11010 • 32,800
Franklinton, LA 70438 • 4,119
Franklinton, NC 27525 • 1,394
Franklinville, NJ 08322 • 900
Franklinville, NC 27248 • 607
Franklinville, NY 14737 • 1,887
Frankston, TX 75763 • 1,255
Frankton, IN 46044 • 2,080
Fraser, MI 48026 • 14,560
Frazee, MN 56544 • 1,284
Frazeysburg, OH 43822 • 1,025
Frazier Park, CA 93225 • 1,444
Frederic, WI 54837 • 1,039
Frederica, DE 19946 • 864
Frederick, CO 80530 • 855
Frederick, MD 21701 • 28,086
Frederick, OK 73542 • 6,153
Frederick ☐, MD • 114,792
Frederick ☐, VA • 34,150
Fredericksburg, IA 50630 • 1,075
Fredericksburg, PA 17026 • 750
Fredericksburg, TX 78624 • 6,412
Fredericksburg, VA 22401-05
• 15,322
Fredericktown, MO 63645 • 4,036
Fredericktown, OH 43019 • 2,299
Frederickson, WA 15333 • 1,067
Fredonia, AZ 86022 • 1,040
Fredonia, KS 66736 • 3,047
Fredonia, NY 14063 • 11,126
Fredonia, PA 16124 • 712
Fredonia, WI 53021 • 1,437

Freeborn ☐, MN • 36,329
Freeburg, IL 62243 • 2,989
Freeburg, PA 17827 • 643
Freedom, CA 95019 • 6,416
Freedom, PA 15042 • 2,272
Freehold, NJ 07728 • 10,020
Freeland, MI 48623 • 1,364
Freeland, PA 18224 • 4,285
Freelandville, IN 47535 • 680
Freeman, SD 57029 • 1,462
Freemansburg, PA 18017 • 1,879
Freeport, FL 32439 • 669
Freeport, IL 61032 • 26,266
Freeport, ME 04032 • 1,906
Freeport, NY 11520 • 38,272
Freeport, PA 16229 • 2,381
Freeport, TX 77541 • 13,444
Freer, TX 78357 • 3,213
Freestone ☐, TX • 14,830
Fremont, CA 94536-39 • 131,945
Fremont, IN 46737 • 1,180
Fremont, IA 52561 • 730
Fremont, MI 49412 • 3,672
Fremont, NE 68025 • 23,979
Fremont, NC 27830 • 1,736
Fremont, OH 43420 • 17,834
Fremont ☐, CO • 28,676
Fremont ☐, ID • 10,813
Fremont ☐, IA • 9,401
Fremont ☐, WY • 38,992
French Island, WI 54601 • 3,000
French Lick, IN 47432 • 2,265
French Settlement, LA 70733 • 761
Frenchtown, NJ 08825 • 1,573
Frenchville, ME 04745 • 615
Fresno, CA 93701-99 • 217,289
Fresno ☐, CA • 514,229
Frewsburg, NY 14738 • 2,000
Friars Point, MS 38631 • 1,400
Friday Harbor, WA 98250 • 1,200
Fridley, MN 55432 • 30,228
Friedens, PA 18080 • 900
Friend, NE 68359 • 1,079
Friendship, NY 14739 • 1,285
Friendship, TN 38034 • 763
Friendship, WI 53934 • 744
Friendsville, TN 37737 • 694
Friendswood, TX 77546 • 10,719
Fries, VA 24330 • 758
Frio ☐, TX • 13,785
Friona, TX 79035 • 3,809
Frisco, CO 80443 • 1,221
Frisco City, AL 36445 • 1,424
Fritch, TX 79036 • 2,299
Frontenac, KS 66762 • 2,586
Frontier ☐, NE • 3,647
Front Royal, VA 22630 • 11,126
Frostburg, MD 21532 • 7,715
Frostproof, FL 33843 • 2,995
Fruita, CO 81521 • 2,810
Fruit Heights, UT 84037 • 2,728
Fruitland, ID 83619 • 2,559
Fruitland, MD 21826 • 2,694
Fruitland, NM 87416 • 700
Fruitland Park, FL 32731 • 2,259
Fruitport, MI 49415 • 1,143
Fruitvale, WA 98902 • 3,490
Fruitville, FL 33582 • 3,070
Fryeburg, ME 04037 • 1,644
Fulda, MN 56131 • 1,308
Fullerton, CA 92631-35 • 102,034
Fullerton, NE 68638 • 1,506
Fulton, AL 36446 • 606
Fulton, IL 61252 • 3,936
Fulton, KY 42041 • 3,137
Fulton, MI 49052 • 750
Fulton, MS 38843 • 3,238
Fulton, MO 65251 • 11,046
Fulton, NY 13069 • 13,312
Fulton ☐, AR • 9,975
Fulton ☐, GA • 589,904
Fulton ☐, IL • 43,687
Fulton ☐, IN • 19,335
Fulton ☐, KY • 8,971
Fulton ☐, NY • 55,153
Fulton ☐, OH • 37,751
Fulton ☐, PA • 12,842
Fultondale, AL 35068 • 6,217
Funkstown, MD 21734 • 1,103
Fuquay-Varina, NC 27526 • 3,110
Furnas ☐, NE • 6,486
Fyffe, AL 35971 • 1,305

G

Gabbs, NV 89409 • 811
Gadsden, AL 35901-05 • 47,565
Gadsden, TN 38337 • 683
Gadsden ☐, FL • 41,565
Gaffney, SC 29340 • 13,453
Gage, OK 73843 • 667
Gage ☐, NE • 24,456
Gahanna, OH 43230 • 18,001
Gaines ☐, TX • 13,150
Gainesboro, TN 38562 • 1,119
Gainesville, FL 32601-14 • 81,371
Gainesville, GA 30501-06 • 15,280
Gainesville, MO 65655 • 707
Gainesville, TX 76240 • 14,081
Gaithersburg, MD 20877-79
• 26,424
Galatia, IL 62935 • 1,042
Galax, VA 24333 • 6,524
Galena, AK 99741 • 765
Galena, IL 61036 • 3,876
Galena, KS 66739 • 3,587

Galena Park, TX 77547 • 9,879
Galesburg, IL 61401 • 35,305
Galesburg, MI 49053 • 1,822
Gales Ferry, CT 06335 • 1,191
Galesville, WI 54630 • 1,239
Galeton, PA 16922 • 1,462
Galien, MI 49113 • 692
Galion, OH 44833 • 12,391
Gallatin, MO 64640 • 2,063
Gallatin, TN 37066 • 17,191
Gallaway, TN 38036 • 804
Gallia ☐, OH • 30,098
Galliano, LA 70354 • 5,159
Gallipolis, OH 45631 • 5,576
Gallitzin, PA 16641 • 2,315
Gallup, NM 87301 • 18,167
Galt, CA 95632 • 5,514
Galva, IL 61434 • 3,185
Galva, KS 67443 • 651
Galveston, IN 46932 • 1,822
Galveston, TX 77550-53 • 61,902
Galveston ☐, TX • 195,940
Gambier, OH 43022 • 2,056
Gambrills, MD 21054 • 650
Ganado, AZ 86505 • 1,200
Ganado, TX 77962 • 1,770
Gang Mills, NY 14870 • 1,258
Gantt, SC 29605 • 1,600
Gap, PA 17527 • 1,022
Garber, OK 73738 • 1,215
Garberville, CA 95440 • 1,200
Garden ☐, NE • 2,802
Garden City, AL 35070 • 655
Garden City, GA 31408 • 6,895
Garden City, ID 83704 • 4,571
Garden City, KS 67846 • 18,256
Garden City, MI 48135 • 35,640
Garden City, MO 64747 • 1,021
Garden City, NY 11530 • 22,927
Garden City Park, NY 11040 • 5,200
Gardendale, AL 35071 • 7,928
Garden Grove, CA 92640-45
• 123,307
Garden Home, OR 97223 • 5,500
Garden Plain, KS 67050 • 775
Gardiner, ME 04345 • 6,485
Gardner, IL 60424 • 1,322
Gardner, KS 66030 • 2,392
Gardner, MA 01440 • 17,900
Gardnerville, NV 89410 • 2,800
Garfield, NJ 07026 • 26,803
Garfield ☐, CO • 22,514
Garfield ☐, MT • 1,656
Garfield ☐, NE • 2,363
Garfield ☐, OK • 62,820
Garfield ☐, UT • 3,673
Garfield ☐, WA • 2,468
Garfield Heights, OH 44125 • 34,938
Garfield Park, DE 19720 • 1,000
Garibaldi, OR 97118 • 999
Garland, AR 71839 • 660
Garland, NC 28441 • 885
Garland, TX 75040-43 • 138,857
Garland, UT 84312 • 1,405
Garland ☐, AR • 70,531
Garnavillo, IA 52049 • 723
Garner, IA 50438 • 2,908
Garner, NC 27529 • 10,073
Garnett, KS 66032 • 3,310
Garrard ☐, KY • 10,853
Garretson, SD 57030 • 963
Garrett, IN 46738 • 4,751
Garrett ☐, MD • 26,498
Garrett Park, MD 20896 • 2,800
Garrettsville, OH 44231 • 1,769
Garrison, KY 41141 • 650
Garrison, MD 21055 • 750
Garrison, ND 58540 • 1,830
Garrison, NY 10524 • 650
Garrison, TX 75946 • 1,059
Garvin ☐, OK • 27,856
Garwin, IA 50632 • 626
Garwood, NJ 07027 • 4,752
Gary, IN 46401-99 • 151,953
Gary, WV 24836 • 2,233
Garysburg, NC 27831 • 1,434
Garyville, LA 70051 • 2,856
Garza ☐, TX • 5,336
Gas City, IN 46933 • 6,370
Gasconade ☐, MO • 13,181
Gasport, NY 14067 • 950
Gassaway, WV 26624 • 1,225
Gassville, AR 72635 • 859
Gaston, IN 47342 • 1,150
Gaston, NC 27832 • 883
Gaston, SC 29053 • 960
Gaston ☐, NC • 162,568
Gastonia, NC 28052-54 • 47,333
Gate City, VA 24251 • 2,494
Gates, NY 14624 • 29,756
Gates, TN 38037 • 729
Gates ☐, NC • 8,875
Gatesville, TX 76528 • 6,260
Gatlinburg, TN 37738 • 3,210
Gauley Bridge, WV 25085 • 1,177
Gautier, MS 39553 • 8,977
Gaylord, MI 49735 • 3,011
Gaylord, MN 55334 • 1,933
Gays Mills, WI 54631 • 627
Gearhart, OR 97138 • 967
Geary, OK 73040 • 1,700

Geary ☐, KS • 29,852
Geauga ☐, OH • 74,474
Geistown, PA 15904 • 3,304
Gem ☐, ID • 11,972
Genesee, ID 83832 • 791
Genesee, MI 48437 • 950
Genesee ☐, MI • 450,449
Genesee ☐, NY • 59,400
Geneseo, IL 61254 • 6,373
Geneseo, NY 14454 • 6,746
Geneva, AL 36340 • 4,866
Geneva, IL 60134 • 9,881
Geneva, IN 46740 • 1,430
Geneva, NE 68361 • 2,400
Geneva, NY 14456 • 15,133
Geneva, OH 44041 • 6,655
Geneva ☐, AL • 24,253
Geneva-on-the-Lake, OH 44041
• 1,634
Genoa, IL 60135 • 3,276
Genoa, NE 68640 • 1,090
Genoa, OH 43430 • 2,213
Genoa City, WI 53128 • 1,202
Genola, UT 84655 • 630
Gentry, AR 72734 • 1,468
Gentry ☐, MO • 7,887
George, IA 51237 • 1,241
George ☐, MS • 15,297
Georgetown, CA 95634 • 2,000
Georgetown, CO 80444 • 830
Georgetown, CT 06829 • 1,834
Georgetown, DE 19947 • 1,710
Georgetown, GA 31754 • 935
Georgetown, IL 61846 • 4,220
Georgetown, IN 47122 • 1,494
Georgetown, KY 40324 • 10,972
Georgetown, MA 01833 • 2,600
Georgetown, OH 45121 • 3,467
Georgetown, SC 29440 • 10,144
Georgetown, TX 78626 • 9,468
Georgetown ☐, SC • 42,461
George West, TX 78022 • 2,627
Georgiana, AL 36033 • 1,993
Gerald, MO 63037 • 921
Geraldine, AL 35974 • 911
Gerber, CA 96035 • 950
Gering, NE 69341 • 7,760
Germantown, IL 62245 • 1,191
Germantown, MD 20874 • 9,721
Germantown, OH 45327 • 5,015
Germantown, TN 38138 • 21,482
Germantown, WI 53022 • 10,729
Geronimo, OK 73543 • 726
Gervais, OR 97026 • 799
Gettysburg, PA 17325 • 7,194
Gettysburg, SD 57442 • 1,623
Geyserville, CA 95441 • 950
Giants Neck, CT 06357 • 1,150
Gibbon, MN 55335 • 787
Gibbon, NE 68840 • 1,531
Gibbstown, NJ 08027 • 5,676
Gibsland, LA 71028 • 1,354
Gibson, GA 30810 • 730
Gibson ☐, IN • 33,156
Gibson ☐, TN • 49,467
Gibsonburg, OH 43431 • 2,479
Gibson City, IL 60936 • 3,498
Gibsonia, PA 15044 • 2,065
Gibsonton, FL 33534 • 3,700
Gibsonville, NC 27249 • 2,865
Giddings, TX 78942 • 3,950
Gideon, MO 63848 • 1,240
Gifford, FL 32960 • 6,240
Gifford, IL 61847 • 848
Gig Harbor, WA 98335 • 2,429
Gila ☐, AZ • 37,080
Gila Bend, AZ 85337 • 1,585
Gilbert, AZ 85234 • 5,717
Gilbert, IA 50105 • 805
Gilbert, LA 71336 • 800
Gilbert, MN 55741 • 2,721
Gilbert, OR 97266 • 4,000
Gilbert, WV 25621 • 757
Gilbertsville, PA 19525 • 900
Gilbertville, IA 50634 • 740
Gilbertville, MA 01031 • 1,029
Gilchrist ☐, FL • 5,767
Gilcrest, CO 80623 • 1,025
Giles ☐, TN • 24,625
Giles ☐, VA • 17,810
Gillespie, IL 62033 • 3,740
Gillespie ☐, TX • 13,532
Gillett, AR 72055 • 927
Gillett, WI 54124 • 1,356
Gillette, WY 82716 • 12,134
Gilliam ☐, OR • 2,057
Gilman, IL 60938 • 1,913
Gilman, IA 50106 • 642
Gilmer, TX 75644 • 5,167
Gilmer ☐, GA • 11,110
Gilmer ☐, WV • 8,334
Gilmore City, IA 50541 • 626
Gilpin ☐, CO • 2,441
Gilroy, CA 95020 • 21,641
Girard, IL 62640 • 2,246
Girard, KS 66743 • 2,888
Girard, OH 44420 • 12,517
Girard, PA 16417 • 2,615
Girardville, PA 17935 • 2,268
Glacier ☐, MT • 10,628
Gladbrook, IA 50635 • 970
Glades ☐, FL • 5,992
Glade Spring, VA 24340 • 1,722
Gladewater, TX 75647 • 6,548
Gladstone, MI 49837 • 4,533
Gladstone, MO 64118 • 24,990

Gladstone, NJ 07934 • 2,038
Gladstone, OR 97027 • 9,500
Gladwin, MI 48624 • 2,479
Gladwin ☐, MI • 19,957
Glandorf, OH 45848 • 746
Glasco, KS 67445 • 710
Glasco, NY 12432 • 1,169
Glascock ☐, GA • 2,382
Glasford, IL 61533 • 1,201
Glasgow, KY 42141 • 12,958
Glasgow, MO 65254 • 1,336
Glasgow, MT 59230 • 4,455
Glasgow, VA 24555 • 1,259
Glasgow, WV 25086 • 1,031
Glasgow Village, MO 63137 • 7,200
Glassboro, NJ 08028 • 14,574
Glascock ☐, TX • 1,304
Glassport, PA 15045 • 6,242
Glastonbury, CT 06033 • 7,049
Gleason, TN 38229 • 1,335
Glen Allen, VA 23060 • 1,100
Glen Alpine, NC 28628 • 645
Glen Avon, CA 92509 • 8,444
Glen Burnie, MD 21061 • 30,000
Glen Carbon, IL 62034 • 5,197
Glencoe, AL 35905 • 4,648
Glencoe, IL 60022 • 9,200
Glencoe, MN 55336 • 4,396
Glen Cove, NY 11542 • 24,618
Glendale, AZ 85301-11 • 97,172
Glendale, CA 91201-99 • 139,060
Glendale, CO 80222 • 2,496
Glendale, MS 39401 • 1,329
Glendale, MO 63122 • 6,035
Glendale, OH 45246 • 2,368
Glendale, OR 97442 • 712
Glendale, SC 29346 • 1,049
Glen Dale, WV 26038 • 1,875
Glendale, WI 53209 • 13,882
Glendale Heights, IL 60139 • 23,163
Glendale Heights, WV 26038 • 700
Glendive, MT 59330 • 5,978
Glendola, NJ 07719 • 2,300
Glendora, CA 91740 • 38,500
Glendora, NJ 08029 • 5,632
Glen Ellyn, IL 60137 • 23,717
Glen Gardner, NJ 08826 • 834
Glenham, NY 12527 • 2,720
Glen Head, NY 11545 • 6,800
Glen Lyon, PA 18617 • 2,430
Glenmora, LA 71433 • 1,479
Glenn ☐, CA • 21,350
Glenns Ferry, ID 83623 • 1,374
Glennville, GA 30427 • 4,144
Glenolden, PA 19036 • 7,633
Glenpool, OK 74033 • 2,706
Glen Raven, NC 27215 • 2,755
Glen Ridge, NJ 07028 • 7,855
Glen Rock, NJ 07452 • 11,497
Glen Rock, PA 17327 • 1,662
Glenrock, WY 82637 • 2,736
Glen Rose, TX 76043 • 2,075
Glens Falls, NY 12801 • 15,897
Glenshaw, PA 15116 • 14,000
Glenside, PA 19038 • 17,400
Glen Ullin, ND 58631 • 1,125
Glenview, IL 60025 • 32,060
Glenville, MN 56036 • 851
Glenville, WV 26351 • 2,155
Glenwood, AR 71943 • 1,402
Glenwood, FL 32722 • 950
Glenwood, GA 30428 • 824
Glenwood, IL 60425 • 10,538
Glenwood, IA 51534 • 5,280
Glenwood, MN 56334 • 2,523
Glenwood, VA 24541 • 1,000
Glenwood City, WI 54013 • 950
Glenwood Farms, VA 23223 • 3,200
Glenwood Springs, CO 81601
• 4,637
Glidden, IA 51443 • 1,076
Glide, OR 97443 • 900
Globe, AZ 85501 • 6,886
Gloster, MS 39638 • 1,726
Gloucester, MA 01930 • 27,768
Gloucester, VA 23061 • 900
Gloucester ☐, NJ • 199,917
Gloucester ☐, VA • 20,107
Gloucester City, NJ 08030 • 13,121
Gloucester Point, VA 23062 • 850
Glouster, OH 45732 • 2,211
Gloversville, NY 12078 • 17,836
Glouverville, SC 29828 • 2,619
Gluck, SC 29621 • 650
Glyndon, MD 21071 • 1,100
Glyndon, MN 56547 • 882
Glynn ☐, GA • 54,981
Gnadenhutten, OH 44629 • 1,320
Gobles, MI 49055 • 816
Goddard, KS 67052 • 1,427
Godfrey, IL 62035 • 2,600
Godley, TX 76044 • 614
Goffstown, NH 03045 • 2,500
Gogebic ☐, MI • 19,686
Golconda, IL 62938 • 960
Gold Bar, WA 98251 • 794
Gold Beach, OR 97444 • 1,515
Golden, CO 80401-19 • 12,237
Golden Beach, FL 33160 • 612
Golden City, MO 64748 • 900
Goldendale, WA 98620 • 3,575
Golden Meadow, LA 70357 • 2,282
Golden Valley, MN 55427 • 22,775
Golden Valley ☐, MT • 1,026
Golden Valley ☐, ND • 2,391
Goldfield, IA 50542 • 789

Gold Hill, OR 97525 • 904
Goldsboro, NC 27530 • 31,871
Goldsby, OK 73093 • 603
Goldthwaite, TX 76844 • 1,783
Goleta, CA 93117 • 28,100
Golf Manor, OH 45237 • 4,317
Goliad, TX 77963 • 1,990
Goliad □, TX • 5,193
Gonzales, CA 93926 • 2,891
Gonzales, LA 70737 • 7,287
Gonzales, TX 78629 • 7,152
Gonzales □, TX • 16,949
Gonzalez, FL 32560 • 6,084
Goochland □, VA • 11,761
Goodhue, MN 55027 • 657
Goodhue □, MN • 38,749
Gooding, ID 83330 • 2,949
Gooding □, ID • 11,874
Goodland, FL 33933 • 1,000
Goodland, IN 47948 • 1,200
Goodland, KS 67735 • 5,708
Goodlettsville, TN 37072 • 8,327
Goodman, MS 39079 • 1,285
Goodman, MO 64843 • 1,030
Good Pine, LA 71342 • 900
Goodview, MN 55987 • 2,567
Goodwater, AL 35072 • 1,895
Goodwell, OK 73939 • 1,186
Goodyear, AZ 85323 • 2,747
Goose Creek, SC 29445 • 17,811
Gordo, AL 35466 • 2,112
Gordon, GA 31031 • 2,768
Gordon, NE 69343 • 2,167
Gordon □, GA • 30,070
Gordonsville, TN 38563 • 893
Gordonsville, VA 22942 • 1,421
Goreville, IL 62939 • 978
Gorham, ME 04038 • 4,052
Gorham, NH 03581 • 2,180
Gorham, NY 14461 • 800
Gorman, TX 76454 • 1,258
Goshen, IN 46526 • 19,665
Goshen, NY 10924 • 4,874
Goshen, OH 45122 • 1,400
Goshen □, WY • 12,040
Gosnell, AR 72319 • 3,215
Gosper □, NE • 2,140
Gosport, IN 47433 • 729
Gothenburg, NE 69138 • 3,479
Gould, AR 71643 • 1,671
Goulds, FL 33170 • 7,078
Gouverneur, NY 13642 • 4,285
Gove □, KS • 3,726
Gowanda, NY 14070 • 2,713
Gower, MO 64454 • 1,276
Gowrie, IA 50543 • 1,089
Grabill, IN 46741 • 658
Grace, ID 83241 • 1,216
Graceville, FL 32440 • 2,918
Graceville, MN 56240 • 780
Grady □, GA • 19,845
Grady □, OK • 39,490
Graettinger, IA 51342 • 923
Grafton, IL 62037 • 1,024
Grafton, MA 01519 • 2,000
Grafton, ND 58237 • 5,293
Grafton, OH 44044 • 2,231
Grafton, VA 23692 • 900
Grafton, WV 26354 • 6,845
Grafton, WI 53024 • 8,381
Grafton □, NH • 65,806
Graham, CA 90002 • 10,600
Graham, NC 27253 • 8,674
Graham, TX 76046 • 9,170
Graham □, AZ • 22,862
Graham □, KS • 3,995
Graham □, NC • 7,217
Grainger □, TN • 16,751
Grain Valley, MO 64029 • 1,327
Grambling, LA 71245 • 4,226
Gramercy, LA 70052 • 3,211
Granbury, TX 76048 • 3,332
Granby, CO 80446 • 963
Granby, CT 06035 • 1,192
Granby, MA 01033 • 1,302
Granby, MO 64844 • 1,908
Grand □, CO • 7,475
Grand □, UT • 8,241
Grand Bay, AL 36541 • 3,185
Grand Blanc, MI 48439 • 6,848
Grand Caillou, LA 70360 • 1,400
Grand Canyon, AZ 86023 • 1,348
Grand Coteau, LA 70541 • 1,165
Grand Coulee, WA 99133 • 1,180
Grandfalls, TX 79742 • 635
Grandfield, OK 73546 • 1,445
Grand Forks, ND 58201 • 43,765
Grand Forks □, ND • 66,100
Grand Gorge, NY 12434 • 800
Grand Haven, MI 49417 • 11,763
Grand Island, NE 68801 • 33,180
Grand Isle, LA 70358 • 1,982
Grand Isle □, VT • 4,613
Grand Junction, CO 81501-05 • 27,956
Grand Junction, IA 50107 • 970
Grand Ledge, MI 48837 • 6,920
Grand Marais, MN 55604 • 1,289
Grand Meadow, MN 55936 • 965
Grand Mound, IA 52751 • 674
Grand Prairie, TX 75050-52 • 71,462
Grand Rapids, MI 49501-99 • 181,843
Grand Rapids, MN 55744 • 7,934
Grand Rapids, OH 43522 • 962
Grand Ridge, IL 61325 • 684

Grand Saline, TX 75140 • 2,709
Grand Terrace, CA 92324 • 8,498
Grand Tower, IL 62942 • 748
Grand Traverse □, MI • 54,899
Grandview, IN 47615 • 670
Grandview, MO 64030 • 24,502
Grandview, WA 98930 • 5,615
Grandview Heights, OH 43212 • 7,420
Grandville, MI 49418 • 12,412
Granger, IA 50109 • 619
Granger, TX 76530 • 1,236
Granger, WA 98932 • 1,812
Grangeville, ID 83530 • 3,666
Granite, OK 73547 • 1,617
Granite, UT 84070 • 650
Granite □, MT • 2,040
Granite City, IL 62040 • 36,815
Granite Falls, MN 56241 • 3,451
Granite Falls, NC 28630 • 2,580
Granite Falls, WA 98252 • 911
Granite Park, UT 84106 • 5,554
Granite Quarry, NC 28072 • 1,294
Graniteville, MA 01886 • 1,000
Graniteville, SC 29829 • 1,158
Graniteville, VT 05654 • 1,800
Grant, AL 35747 • 632
Grant, FL 32949 • 900
Grant, MI 49327 • 683
Grant, NE 69140 • 1,270
Grant □, AR • 13,008
Grant □, IN • 80,934
Grant □, KS • 6,977
Grant □, KY • 13,308
Grant □, LA • 16,703
Grant □, MN • 7,171
Grant □, NE • 877
Grant □, NM • 26,204
Grant □, ND • 4,274
Grant □, OK • 6,518
Grant □, OR • 8,210
Grant □, SD • 9,013
Grant □, WA • 48,522
Grant □, WV • 10,210
Grant □, WI • 51,736
Grant City, MO 64456 • 1,068
Grant Park, IL 60940 • 1,038
Grants, NM 87020 • 11,439
Grantsburg, WI 54840 • 1,153
Grants Pass, OR 97526-27 • 15,032
Grantsville, UT 84029 • 4,419
Grantsville, WV 26147 • 788
Grant Town, WV 26574 • 987
Grantville, GA 30220 • 1,110
Granville, IL 61326 • 1,537
Granville, NY 12832 • 2,696
Granville, OH 43023 • 3,851
Granville, WV 26534 • 992
Granville □, NC • 34,043
Grapeland, TX 75844 • 1,634
Grapevine, KY 42431 • 900
Grapevine, TX 76051 • 11,801
Grasonville, MD 21638 • 1,910
Grasselli, AL 35211 • 2,400
Grassflat, PA 16839 • 750
Grass Lake, IL 60002 • 2,191
Grass Lake, MI 49240 • 962
Grass Valley, CA 95945-49 • 6,697
Gratiot □, MI • 40,448
Gratis, OH 45330 • 809
Gratz, PA 17030 • 678
Graves □, KY • 34,049
Gravette, AR 72736 • 1,218
Gray, GA 31032 • 2,145
Gray, KY 40734 • 750
Gray, LA 70359 • 4,000
Gray, ME 04039 • 900
Gray □, KS • 5,138
Gray □, TX • 26,386
Gray Court, SC 29645 • 988
Grayling, MI 49738 • 1,792
Graylyn Crest, DE 19810 • 5,000
Grays Harbor □, WA • 66,314
Grayslake, IL 60030 • 5,260
Grayson, KY 41143 • 3,423
Grayson □, KY • 20,854
Grayson □, TX • 89,796
Grayson □, VA • 16,579
Graysville, AL 35073 • 2,642
Graysville, TN 37338 • 1,380
Grayville, IL 62844 • 2,313
Great Barrington, MA 01230 • 3,150
Great Bend, KS 67530 • 16,608
Great Bend, PA 18821 • 740
Great Falls, MT 59401-06 • 56,725
Great Falls, SC 29055 • 2,601
Great Neck, NY 11020-24 • 5,604
Great Neck Estates, NY 11021 • 2,936
Greece, NY 14616 • 63,700
Greeley, CO 80631-39 • 53,006
Greeley □, KS • 1,845
Greeley □, NE • 3,462
Green, OR 97470 • 3,897
Green □, KY • 11,043
Green □, WI • 30,012
Green Acres, DE 19803 • 1,200
Greenacres, WA 99016 • 3,650
Greenacres City, FL 33463 • 8,843
Green Bay, WI 54301-99 • 87,899
Greenbelt, MD 20770 • 17,332
Greenbriar, VA 22033 • 6,000
Greenbrier, AR 72058 • 1,423
Green Brier, TN 37073 • 3,180
Greenbrier □, WV • 37,665
Green Brook, NJ 08812 • 4,500

Greenbush, MN 56726 • 817
Greencastle, IN 46135 • 8,403
Greencastle, PA 17225 • 3,679
Green City, MO 63545 • 719
Green Cove Springs, FL 32043 • 4,154
Greendale, IN 47025 • 3,795
Greendale, WI 53129 • 16,928
Greene, IA 50636 • 1,332
Greene, NY 13778 • 1,747
Greene □, AL • 11,021
Greene □, AR • 30,744
Greene □, GA • 11,391
Greene □, IL • 16,661
Greene □, IN • 30,416
Greene □, IA • 12,119
Greene □, MS • 9,827
Greene □, MO • 185,302
Greene □, NC • 16,117
Greene □, NY • 40,861
Greene □, OH • 129,769
Greene □, PA • 40,476
Greene □, TN • 54,422
Greene □, VA • 7,625
Greeneville, TN 37743 • 14,097
Greenfield, CA 93927 • 4,181
Greenfield, IL 62044 • 1,090
Greenfield, IN 46140 • 11,299
Greenfield, IA 50849 • 2,243
Greenfield, MA 01301 • 14,198
Greenfield, MO 65661 • 1,394
Greenfield, OH 45123 • 5,150
Greenfield, TN 38230 • 2,109
Greenfield, WI 53220 • 31,467
Greenfield Plaza, IA 50315 • 2,100
Green Forest, AR 72638 • 1,609
Green Harbor, MA 02041 • 2,002
Greenhills, OH 45218 • 4,927
Green Island, NY 12183 • 2,696
Groon Lako, WI 54941 • 1,208
Green Lake □, WI • 18,370
Greenland, AR 72737 • 622
Greenlawn, NY 11740 • 8,600
Greenlee □, AZ • 11,406
Green Manorville, CT 06082 • 3,250
Green Mountain Falls, CO 80819 • 607
Greenock, PA 15047 • 2,800
Greenport, NY 11944 • 2,273
Green River, UT 84525 • 1,048
Green River, WY 82935 • 12,807
Green Rock, IL 61241 • 3,324
Greensboro, AL 36744 • 3,248
Greensboro, GA 30642 • 2,985
Greensboro, MD 21639 • 1,253
Greensboro, NC 27401-99 • 155,642
Greensburg, IN 47240 • 9,254
Greensburg, KS 67054 • 1,885
Greensburg, KY 42743 • 2,377
Greensburg, LA 70441 • 662
Greensburg, PA 15601 • 17,558
Green Springs, OH 44836 • 1,568
Greensville □, VA • 10,903
Greentown, IN 46936 • 2,265
Green Tree, PA 15220 • 5,722
Greenup, IL 62428 • 1,655
Greenup, KY 41144 • 1,386
Greenup □, KY • 39,132
Green Valley, AZ 85614 • 7,999
Green Valley, IL 61534 • 768
Greenview, IL 62642 • 830
Greenville, AL 36037 • 7,807
Greenville, CA 95947 • 1,537
Greenville, FL 32331 • 1,096
Greenville, GA 30222 • 1,213
Greenville, IL 62246 • 5,271
Greenville, KY 42345 • 4,631
Greenville, ME 04441 • 1,640
Greenville, MI 48838 • 8,019
Greenville, MS 38701-03 • 40,613
Greenville, NH 03048 • 1,447
Greenville, NC 27834 • 35,740
Greenville, NY 10583 • 5,500
Greenville, OH 45331 • 12,999
Greenville, PA 16125 • 7,730
Greenville, RI 02828 • 7,576
Greenville, SC 29601-16 • 58,242
Greenville, TX 75401 • 22,161
Greenville □, SC • 287,913
Greenwich, CT 06830 • 59,578
Greenwich, NY 12834 • 1,955
Greenwich, OH 44837 • 1,458
Greenwood, AR 72936 • 3,317
Greenwood, IN 46142 • 19,327
Greenwood, LA 71033 • 1,043
Greenwood, MS 38930 • 20,115
Greenwood, MO 64034 • 1,315
Greenwood, PA 16601 • 1,700
Greenwood, SC 29646 • 21,613
Greonwood, WI 54437 • 1,124
Greenwood □, KS • 8,764
Greenwood □, SC • 57,847
Greenwood Lake, NY 10925 • 2,809
Greenwood Village, CO 80110 • 5,729
Greer, SC 29651 • 10,525
Greer □, OK • 7,028
Gregg □, TX • 99,495
Gregory, SD 57533 • 1,503
Gregory □, SD • 6,015
Greilickville, MI 49684 • 1,000
Grenada, MS 38901 • 12,641
Grenada □, MS • 21,043
Gresham, OR 97030 • 33,005
Gresham Park, GA 30316 • 6,232
Gretna, FL 32332 • 1,448

Gretna, LA 70053 • 20,615
Gretna, NE 68028 • 1,609
Gretna, VA 24557 • 1,255
Greybull, WY 82426 • 2,277
Gridley, CA 95948 • 3,982
Gridley, IL 61744 • 1,246
Griffin, GA 30223 • 20,728
Griffith, IN 46319 • 17,026
Grifton, NC 28530 • 2,179
Griggs □, ND • 3,714
Griggsville, IL 62340 • 1,301
Grimes, IA 50111 • 1,973
Grimes □, TX • 13,580
Grindall Creek, VA 23234 • 1,900
Grinnell, IA 50112 • 8,868
Griswold, IA 51535 • 1,176
Groesbeck, OH 45239 • 9,594
Groesbeck, TX 76642 • 3,373
Groom, TX 79039 • 736
Grosse Ile, MI 48138 • 9,320
Grosse Pointe, MI 48236 • 5,901
Grosse Pointe Park, MI 48236 • 13,639
Grosse Pointe Woods, MI 48236 • 18,886
Grosse Tete, LA 70740 • 749
Grossmont, CA 92041 • 2,600
Grosvenor Dale, CT 06246 • 700
Groton, CT 06340 • 10,086
Groton, MA 01450 • 1,264
Groton, NY 13073 • 2,313
Groton, SD 57445 • 1,230
Groton Long Point, CT 06340 • 800
Grottoes, VA 24441 • 1,369
Grove, OK 74344 • 3,378
Grove City, FL 33533 • 2,587
Grove City, OH 43123 • 16,816
Grove City, PA 16127 • 8,162
Grove Hill, AL 36451 • 1,912
Groveland, FL 32736 • 1,992
Groveland, MA 01834 • 4,300
Groveport, OH 43125 • 3,286
Grover City, CA 93433 • 8,827
Groves, TX 77619 • 17,090
Groveton, NH 03582 • 1,389
Groveton, TX 75845 • 1,262
Groveton, VA 22306 • 6,800
Groveton Gardens, VA 22303 • 2,800
Grovetown, GA 30813 • 3,384
Groveville, NJ 08620 • 1,200
Gruetli-Laager, TN 37339 • 2,000
Grulla, TX 78548 • 1,442
Grundy, VA 24614 • 1,699
Grundy □, IL • 30,582
Grundy □, IA • 14,366
Grundy □, MO • 11,959
Grundy □, TN • 13,787
Grundy Center, IA 50638 • 2,880
Gruver, TX 79040 • 1,216
Guadalupe, AZ 85283 • 4,506
Guadalupe, CA 93434 • 3,629
Guadalupe □, NM • 4,496
Guadalupe □, TX • 46,708
Gualala, CA 95445 • 700
Guernsey, WY 82214 • 1,512
Guernsey □, OH • 42,024
Gueydan, LA 70542 • 1,695
Guilford, CT 06437 • 2,555
Guilford, ME 04443 • 1,235
Guilford □, NC • 317,154
Guin, AL 35563 • 2,418
Gulf □, FL • 10,658
Gulf Breeze, FL 32561 • 5,478
Gulf Gate Estates, FL 33581 • 9,428
Gulfport, FL 33737 • 11,180
Gulfport, MS 39501-03 • 39,676
Gulf Shores, AL 36542 • 1,349
Gunnison, CO 81230 • 5,785
Gunnison, MS 38746 • 708
Gunnison, UT 84634 • 1,255
Gunnison □, CO • 10,689
Guntersville, AL 35976 • 7,041
Gurdon, AR 71743 • 2,707
Gurley, AL 35748 • 735
Gurnee, IL 60031 • 7,179
Gustine, CA 95322 • 3,142
Guthrie, KY 42234 • 1,361
Guthrie, OK 73044 • 10,312
Guthrie, WV 25312 • 800
Guthrie □, IA • 11,983
Guthrie Center, IA 50115 • 1,713
Guttenberg, IA 52052 • 2,428
Guttenberg, NJ 07093 • 7,340
Guymon, OK 73942 • 8,492
Guyton, GA 31312 • 749
Gwinhurst, DE 19809 • 1,400
Gwinn, MI 49841 • 1,408
Gwinner, ND 58040 • 725
Gwinnett □, GA • 166,903
Gypsum, CO 81637 • 743

H

Haakon □, SD • 2,794
Habersham □, GA • 25,020
Hacienda Heights, CA 91745 • 49,422
Hackberry, LA 70645 • 800
Hackensack, NJ 07601-08 • 36,039
Hackettstown, NJ 07840 • 8,850
Hackleburg, AL 35564 • 883
Haddock, GA 31033 • 700
Haddonfield, NJ 08033 • 12,337
Haddon Heights, NJ 08035 • 8,361
Hadley, MA 01035 • 890

Hadlock, WA 98339 • 950
Hagan, GA 30429 • 880
Hagerman, ID 83332 • 602
Hagerman, NM 88232 • 936
Hagerstown, IN 47346 • 1,950
Hagerstown, MD 21740 • 34,132
Hahira, GA 31632 • 1,534
Hahnville, LA 70057 • 2,947
Haiku, HI 96708 • 619
Hailey, ID 83333 • 2,109
Haileyville, OK 74546 • 832
Haines, AK 99827 • 993
Haines City, FL 33844 • 10,799
Haines Falls, NY 12436 • 700
Hainesport, NJ 08036 • 900
Halawa Heights, HI 96701 • 7,000
Hale □, AL • 15,604
Hale □, TX • 37,592
Hale Center, TX 79041 • 2,297
Haledon, NJ 07508 • 6,607
Haleiwa, HI 96712 • 2,412
Hales Corners, WI 53130 • 7,110
Halethorpe, MD 21227 • 20,163
Haleyville, AL 35565 • 5,306
Half Hollow Hills, NY 11746 • 12,800
Half Moon Bay, CA 94019 • 7,282
Halfway, MD 21740 • 8,659
Halifax, MA 02338 • 900
Halifax, PA 17032 • 909
Halifax, VA 24558 • 772
Halifax □, NC • 55,286
Halifax □, VA • 30,599
Haliimaile, HI 96768 • 741
Hall □, GA • 75,649
Hall □, NE • 47,690
Hall □, TX • 5,594
Hallandale, FL 33009 • 36,517
Hallettsville, TX 77964 • 2,865
Hallie, WI 54729 • 1,223
Hallock, MN 56728 • 1,405
Halloway, ME 04347 • 2,502
Halls, TN 38040 • 2,444
Halls Crossroads, TN 37918 • 1,600
Hallstead, PA 18822 • 1,280
Hallsville, MO 65255 • 624
Hallsville, TX 75650 • 1,556
Halsey, OR 97348 • 693
Halstad, MN 56548 • 690
Halstead, KS 67056 • 1,994
Haltom City, TX 76117 • 29,014
Hamblen □, TN • 49,300
Hamburg, AR 71646 • 3,394
Hamburg, IA 51640 • 1,597
Hamburg, NJ 07419 • 1,832
Hamburg, NY 14075 • 10,442
Hamburg, PA 19526 • 4,011
Hamden, CT 06514 • 51,071
Hamden, OH 45634 • 1,010
Hamel, MN 55340 • 2,623
Hamersville, OH 45130 • 688
Hamilton, AL 35570 • 5,093
Hamilton, IL 62341 • 3,509
Hamilton, MA 01936 • 1,000
Hamilton, MI 49419 • 900
Hamilton, MO 64644 • 1,582
Hamilton, MT 59840 • 2,661
Hamilton, NC 27840 • 638
Hamilton, NY 13346 • 3,725
Hamilton, OH 45011-26 • 63,189
Hamilton, TX 76531 • 3,189
Hamilton □, FL • 8,761
Hamilton □, IL • 9,172
Hamilton □, IN • 82,027
Hamilton □, IA • 17,862
Hamilton □, KS • 2,514
Hamilton □, NE • 9,301
Hamilton □, NY • 5,283
Hamilton □, OH • 873,224
Hamilton □, TN • 287,740
Hamilton □, TX • 8,297
Hamilton City, CA 95951 • 800
Hamilton Square, NJ 08690 • 10,000
Ham Lake, MN 55303 • 7,832
Hamler, OH 43524 • 625
Hamlet, IN 46532 • 738
Hamlet, NC 28345 • 4,720
Hamlin, TX 79520 • 3,248
Hamlin, WV 25523 • 1,219
Hamlin □, SD • 5,261
Hammon, OK 73650 • 866
Hammond, IN 46320-27 • 93,714
Hammond, LA 70401-03 • 15,043
Hammond, WI 54015 • 991
Hammondsport, NY 14840 • 1,065
Hammonton, NJ 08037 • 12,298
Hampden, ME 04444 • 2,300
Hampden, MA 01036 • 700
Hampden □, MA • 443,018
Hampden Highlands, ME 04444 • 1,540
Hampshire, IL 60140 • 1,735
Hampshire □, MA • 138,813
Hampshire □, WV • 14,867
Hampstead, MD 21074 • 1,293
Hampstead, NC 28443 • 700
Hampton, AR 71744 • 1,627
Hampton, GA 30228 • 2,059
Hampton, IA 50441 • 4,630
Hampton, NH 03842 • 6,779
Hampton, NJ 08827 • 1,614
Hampton, SC 29924 • 3,143
Hampton, TN 37658 • 2,236
Hampton, VA 23660-70 • 122,617
Hampton □, SC • 18,159
Hampton Bays, NY 11946 • 3,550
Hampton Beach, NH 03842 • 900

Hamtramck, MI 48212 • 21,300	Harrisburg, PA 17101-99 • 53,264	Hawley, PA 18428 • 1,181	Hennessey, OK 73742 • 2,287	Hildale, UT 86021 • 1,009
Hana, HI 96713 • 643	Harrison, AR 72601 • 9,567	Hawley, TX 79525 • 679	Henniker, NH 03242 • 1,538	Hill □, MT • 17,985
Hanahan, SC 29410 • 13,224	Harrison, MI 48625 • 1,700	Haworth, NJ 07641 • 3,509	Henning, MN 56551 • 832	Hill □, TX • 25,024
Hanamaulu, HI 96715 • 3,227	Harrison, NJ 07029 • 12,242	Haw River, NC 27258 • 1,858	Henning, TN 38041 • 638	Hill City, KS 67642 • 2,028
Hanapepe, HI 96716 • 1,417	Harrison, NY 10528 • 23,046	Hawthorne, CA 90250 • 56,447	Henrico □, VA • 180,735	Hillcrest, IL 61068 • 818
Hanceville, AL 35077 • 2,220	Harrison, OH 45030 • 5,855	Hawthorne, FL 32640 • 1,303	Henrietta, NC 28076 • 1,412	Hillcrest, NY 10977 • 5,357
Hancock, MD 21750 • 1,887	Harrison, TN 37341 • 6,206	Hawthorne, NV 89415 • 3,741	Henrietta, NY 14467 • 1,200	Hillcrest Center, CA 93306 • 30,000
Hancock, MI 49930 • 5,122	Harrison □, IN • 27,276	Hawthorne, NJ 07506 • 18,200	Henrietta, TX 76365 • 3,149	Hilliard, FL 32046 • 1,869
Hancock, MN 56244 • 877	Harrison □, IA • 16,348	Hawthorne, NY 10532 • 4,900	Henry, IL 61537 • 2,740	Hilliard, OH 43026 • 8,008
Hancock, NY 13783 • 1,526	Harrison □, KY • 15,166	Haxtun, CO 80731 • 1,014	Henry □, AL • 15,302	Hillsboro, IL 62049 • 4,408
Hancock □, GA • 9,466	Harrison □, MS • 157,665	Hayden, AZ 85235 • 1,205	Henry □, GA • 36,309	Hillsboro, KS 67063 • 2,717
Hancock □, IL • 23,877	Harrison □, MO • 9,890	Hayden, CO 81639 • 1,720	Henry □, IL • 57,968	Hillsboro, MO 63050 • 1,508
Hancock □, IN • 43,939	Harrison □, OH • 18,152	Hayden, ID 83835 • 2,586	Henry □, IN • 53,336	Hillsboro, NH 03244 • 1,797
Hancock □, KY • 7,742	Harrison □, TX • 52,265	Haydenville, MA 01039 • 900	Henry □, IA • 18,890	Hillsboro, ND 58045 • 1,600
Hancock □, ME • 41,781	Harrison □, WV • 77,710	Hayes, LA 70646 • 830	Henry □, KY • 12,740	Hillsboro, OH 45133 • 6,356
Hancock □, MS • 24,537	Harrisonburg, LA 71340 • 610	Hayes □, NE • 1,356	Henry □, MO • 19,672	Hillsboro, OR 97123-24 • 27,664
Hancock □, OH • 64,581	Harrisonburg, VA 22801 • 19,671	Hayesville, OR 97303 • 9,213	Henry □, OH • 28,383	Hillsboro, TX 76645 • 7,397
Hancock □, TN • 6,887	Harrisonville, MO 64701 • 6,372	Hayfield, MN 55940 • 1,243	Henry □, TN • 28,656	Hillsboro, WI 54634 • 1,263
Hancock □, WV • 41,053	Harristown, IL 62537 • 1,456	Hayfield, VA 22310 • 2,200	Henry □, VA • 57,654	Hillsborough, CA 94010 • 10,372
Hand □, SD • 4,948	Harrisville, NY 13648 • 937	Hayfork, CA 96041 • 1,788	Henryetta, OK 74437 • 6,432	Hillsborough, NC 27278 • 3,019
Handley, WV 25102 • 633	Harrisville, PA 16038 • 1,033	Haynesville, LA 71038 • 3,454	Henryville, IN 47126 • 1,132	Hillsborough □, FL • 646,960
Hanford, CA 93230 • 20,958	Harrisville, RI 02830 • 1,224	Hays, KS 67601 • 16,301	Hephzibah, GA 30815 • 1,452	Hillsborough □, NH • 276,608
Hankinson, ND 58041 • 1,158	Harrisville, UT 84404 • 1,371	Hays, NC 28635 • 900	Heppner, OR 97836 • 1,498	Hillsdale, IL 61257 • 731
Hanna, WY 82327 • 2,288	Harrisville, WV 26362 • 1,673	Hays □, TX • 40,594	Herculaneum, MO 63048 • 2,293	Hillsdale, MI 49242 • 7,432
Hanna City, IL 61536 • 1,361	Harrodsburg, KY 40330 • 7,265	Hay Springs, NE 69347 • 794	Hercules, CA 94547 • 5,963	Hillsdale, NJ 07642 • 10,495
Hannibal, MO 63401 • 18,811	Hart, MI 49420 • 1,888	Haysville, KS 67060 • 8,006	Hereford, TX 79045 • 15,853	Hillsdale □, MI • 42,071
Hannibal, NY 13074 • 680	Hart, TX 79043 • 1,008	Hayti, MO 63851 • 3,964	Herington, KS 67449 • 2,930	Hillside, IL 60162 • 8,279
Hannibal, OH 43931 • 650	Hart □, GA • 18,585	Hayti Heights, MO 63851 • 1,023	Heritage Village, CT 06488 • 5,200	Hillside, NJ 07205 • 21,440
Hanover, IL 61041 • 1,069	Hart □, KY • 15,402	Hayward, CA 94540-46 • 94,342	Herkimer, NY 13350 • 8,383	Hillside Heights, DE 19711 • 800
Hanover, IN 47243 • 4,054	Hartford, AL 36344 • 2,647	Hayward, WI 54843 • 1,698	Herkimer □, NY • 66,714	Hillsville, PA 16132 • 915
Hanover, KS 66945 • 802	Hartford, AR 72938 • 613	Hayward Addition, SD 57106 • 725	Hermann, MO 65041 • 2,695	Hillsville, VA 24343 • 2,123
Hanover, MA 02339 • 2,500	Hartford, CT 06101-99 • 136,392	Haywood □, NC • 46,495	Hermansville, MI 49847 • 700	Hillview, KY 40229 • 5,196
Hanover, MN 55341 • 647	Hartford, IL 62048 • 1,887	Haywood □, TN • 20,318	Hermantown, MN 55811 • 6,759	Hilo, HI 96720 • 35,269
Hanover, NH 03755 • 6,861	Hartford, IA 50118 • 761	Hazard, KY 41701 • 5,371	Herminie, PA 15637 • 1,100	Hilton, NY 14468 • 4,151
Hanover Township, NJ • 11,846	Hartford, KY 42347 • 2,512	Hazardville, CT 06082 • 5,436	Hermiston, OR 97838 • 9,408	Hilton Head Island, SC 29928 • 11,344
Hanover, OH 43055 • 926	Hartford, MI 49057 • 2,493	Hazel Crest, IL 60429 • 13,973	Hermitage, PA 16148 • 16,365	Hima, KY 40951 • 700
Hanover, PA 17331 • 14,890	Hartford, SD 57033 • 1,207	Hazel Dell, WA 98665 • 6,000	Hermosa Beach, CA 90254 • 18,070	Hinckley, IL 60520 • 1,447
Hanover □, VA • 50,398	Hartford, WI 53027 • 7,046	Hazel Green, AL 35750 • 1,503	Hernando, FL 32642 • 1,653	Hinckley, MN 55037 • 963
Hanover Center, MA 02339 • 1,000	Hartford □, CT • 851,783	Hazel Green, WI 53811 • 1,282	Hernando, MS 38632 • 2,969	Hindman, KY 41822 • 876
Hanover Park, IL 60103 • 28,850	Hartford City, IN 47348 • 7,622	Hazel Park, MI 48030 • 20,914	Hernando □, FL • 44,469	Hinds □, MS • 250,998
Hansen, ID 83334 • 1,078	Hartington, NE 68739 • 1,730	Hazelwood, MO 63042-45 • 12,935	Herndon, VA 22070-71 • 11,449	Hines, OR 97738 • 1,632
Hansford □, TX • 6,209	Hartland, ME 04943 • 1,041	Hazelwood, NC 28738 • 1,811	Heron Lake, MN 56137 • 783	Hinesville, GA 31313 • 11,309
Hanson, MA 02341 • 2,120	Hartland, WI 53029 • 5,559	Hazen, AR 72064 • 1,636	Herrin, IL 62948 • 10,708	Hingham, MA 02043 • 12,800
Hanson □, SD • 3,415	Hartley, IA 51346 • 1,700	Hazen, ND 58545 • 2,365	Herscher, IL 60941 • 1,214	Hinkley, CA 92347 • 700
Hapeville, GA 30354 • 6,166	Hartley □, TX • 3,987	Hazlehurst, GA 31539 • 4,249	Hershey, NE 69143 • 633	Hinsdale, IL 60521 • 16,726
Happy, TX 79042 • 674	Hartsdale, NY 10530 • 12,226	Hazlehurst, MS 39083 • 4,437	Hershey, PA 17033 • 9,000	Hinsdale, MA 01235 • 950
Happy Camp, CA 96039 • 1,110	Hartselle, AL 35640 • 8,858	Hazlet, NJ 07730 • 28,013	Hertford, NC 27944 • 1,941	Hinsdale, NH 03451 • 1,546
Happy Valley, NM 88220 • 630	Hartshorne, OK 74547 • 2,380	Hazleton, IA 50641 • 877	Hertford □, NC • 23,368	Hinsdale □, CO • 408
Happy Valley, OR 97236 • 1,499	Hartsville, SC 29550 • 7,631	Hazleton, PA 18201 • 27,318	Hesperia, CA 92345 • 13,540	Hinton, IA 51024 • 669
Harahan, LA 70123 • 11,384	Hartsville, TN 37074 • 2,674	Headland, AL 36345 • 3,327	Hesperia, MI 49421 • 876	Hinton, OK 73047 • 1,432
Haralson □, GA • 18,422	Hartville, OH 44632 • 1,772	Healdsburg, CA 95448 • 7,217	Hessmer, LA 71341 • 743	Hinton, WV 25951 • 4,622
Harbor, OR 97415 • 2,856	Hartwell, GA 30643 • 4,855	Healdton, OK 73438 • 3,769	Hesston, KS 67062 • 3,013	Hiram, GA 30141 • 1,030
Harbor Beach, MI 48441 • 2,000	Harvard, IL 60033 • 5,126	Heard □, GA • 6,520	Hettinger, ND 58639 • 1,739	Hiram, OH 44234 • 1,360
Harborcreek, PA 16421 • 800	Harvard, MA 01451 • 900	Hearne, TX 77859 • 5,418	Hettinger □, ND • 4,275	Hitchcock, TX 77563 • 6,655
Harbor Springs, MI 49740 • 1,567	Harvard, NE 68944 • 1,217	Heath, OH 43056 • 6,969	Heuvelton, NY 13654 • 777	Hitchcock □, NE • 4,079
Hardee □, FL • 19,379	Harvey, IL 60426 • 35,810	Heath Springs, SC 29058 • 979	Hewitt, TX 76643 • 5,247	Hitchcock Lake, CT 06716 • 1,600
Hardeeville, SC 29927 • 1,250	Harvey, LA 70058 • 15,000	Hebbronville, TX 78361 • 4,079	Hewlett, NY 11557 • 6,880	Hitchins, KY 41146 • 700
Hardeman □, TN • 23,873	Harvey, MI 49855 • 1,341	Heber City, UT 84032 • 4,362	Heyburn, ID 83336 • 2,889	Hoagland, IN 46745 • 650
Hardeman □, TX • 6,368	Harvey, ND 58341 • 2,527	Hebor Springs, AR 72543 • 4,589	Heyworth, IL 61745 • 1,598	Hobart, IN 46342 • 22,987
Hardin, IL 62047 • 1,107	Harvey □, KS • 30,531	Hebron, IL 60034 • 786	Hialeah, FL 33010-16 • 145,254	Hobart, OK 73651 • 4,735
Hardin, MO 64035 • 688	Harwich, MA 02645 • 1,000	Hebron, IN 46341 • 2,696	Hiawatha, IA 52233 • 4,825	Hobbs, NM 88240 • 29,153
Hardin, MT 59034 • 3,300	Harwich Port, MA 02646 • 1,900	Hebron, MD 21830 • 714	Hiawatha, KS 66434 • 3,702	Hobe Sound, FL 33455 • 6,822
Hardin □, IL • 5,383	Harwinton, CT 06791 • 3,293	Hebron, NE 68370 • 1,906	Hibbing, MN 55746 • 21,193	Hoboken, NJ 07030 • 42,460
Hardin □, IA • 21,776	Harwood, MA 01460 • 900	Hebron, ND 58638 • 1,078	Hickman, KY 42050 • 2,894	Hockessin, DE 19707 • 950
Hardin □, KY • 88,917	Harwood Heights, IL 60656 • 8,228	Hebron, OH 43025 • 2,035	Hickman, NE 68372 • 687	Hocking □, OH • 24,304
Hardin □, OH • 32,719	Hasbrouck Heights, NJ 07604 • 12,166	Hector, MN 55342 • 1,252	Hickman □, KY • 6,065	Hockley, TX • 23,230
Hardin □, TN • 22,280	Haskell, AR 72015 • 1,074	Hedges, FL 32097 • 900	Hickman □, TN • 15,151	Hodge, LA 71247 • 708
Hardin □, TX • 40,721	Haskell, OK 74436 • 1,953	Hedrick, IA 52563 • 847	Hickory, MS 39332 • 670	Hodgeman □, KS • 2,269
Harding, MA 02052 • 950	Haskell, TX 79521 • 3,782	Heflin, AL 36264 • 3,014	Hickory, NC 28601 • 20,757	Hodgenville, KY 42748 • 2,531
Harding □, NM • 1,090	Haskell □, KS • 3,814	Hegins, PA 17938 • 900	Hickory □, MO • 6,367	Hoffman, MN 56339 • 631
Harding □, SD • 1,700	Haskell □, OK • 11,010	Heidelberg, MS 39439 • 1,098	Hickory Hills, IL 60457 • 13,778	Hoffman Estates, IL 60195 • 37,272
Hardinsburg, KY 40143 • 2,211	Haskell □, TX • 7,725	Heilwood, PA 15745 • 700	Hicksville, NY 11801-99 • 43,245	Hogansville, GA 30230 • 3,362
Hardwick, GA 31034 • 6,000	Haslett, MI 48840 • 7,025	Helena, AL 35080 • 2,130	Hicksville, OH 43526 • 3,929	Hohenwald, TN 38462 • 3,922
Hardwick, VT 05843 • 1,476	Hastings, FL 32045 • 636	Helena, AR 72342 • 9,598	Hico, TX 76457 • 1,375	Ho-Ho-Kus, NJ 07423 • 4,129
Hardy, AR 72542 • 643	Hastings, MI 49058 • 6,418	Helena, GA 31037 • 1,390	Hico, WV 25854 • 700	Hoisington, KS 67544 • 3,678
Hardy □, WV • 10,030	Hastings, MN 55033 • 12,827	Helena, MT 59601 • 23,938	Hidalgo, TX 78557 • 2,288	Hokah, MN 55941 • 686
Harford, MD • 145,930	Hastings, NE 68901 • 23,045	Helena, OK 73741 • 710	Hidalgo □, NM • 6,049	Hoke □, NC • 20,383
Hargill, TX 78549 • 800	Hastings, PA 16646 • 1,574	Hellam, PA 17406 • 1,428	Hidalgo □, TX • 283,323	Hokes Bluff, AL 35903 • 3,216
Harker Heights, TX 76543 • 7,345	Hastings-On-Hudson, NY 10706 • 8,573	Hellertown, PA 18055 • 6,025	Hiddenite, NC 28636 • 800	Holbrook, AZ 86025 • 5,785
Harkers Island, NC 28531 • 1,901	Hatboro, PA 19040 • 7,579	Helmetta, NJ 08828 • 955	Higbee, MO 65257 • 817	Holbrook, MA 02343 • 11,140
Harlan, IN 46743 • 1,000	Hatch, NM 87937 • 1,028	Helotes, TX 78023 • 1,409	Higganum, CT 06441 • 1,660	Holbrook, NY 11741 • 12,800
Harlan, IA 51537 • 5,357	Hatfield, MA 01038 • 1,251	Helper, UT 84526 • 2,724	Higgins, TX 79046 • 702	Holcomb, KS 67851 • 816
Harlan, KY 40831 • 3,024	Hatfield, PA 19440 • 2,533	Hemet, CA 92343-44 • 22,454	Higginsville, MO 64037 • 4,595	Holcomb, MO 63852 • 632
Harlan □, KY • 41,889	Hatteras, NC 27943 • 700	Hemingford, NE 69348 • 1,023	High Bridge, NJ 08829 • 3,435	Holden, MA 01520 • 3,900
Harlan □, NE • 4,292	Hattiesburg, MS 39401-02 • 40,829	Hemingway, SC 29554 • 600	Highland, CA 92346 • 10,400	Holden, MO 64040 • 2,195
Harlem, FL 33440 • 2,669	Hatton, ND 58240 • 787	Hemlock, MI 48626 • 1,362	Highland, IL 62249 • 7,122	Holden, WV 25625 • 1,600
Harlem, GA 30814 • 1,485	Haubstadt, IN 47639 • 1,389	Hemphill, TX 75948 • 1,353	Highland, IN 46322 • 25,935	Holden Heights, FL 32805 • 8,000
Harlem, MT 59526 • 1,023	Haughton, LA 71037 • 1,510	Hemphill □, TX • 5,304	Highland, KS 66035 • 954	Holdenville, OK 74848 • 5,469
Harleyville, SC 29448 • 606	Hauppauge, NY 11788 • 14,200	Hempstead, NY 11550-54 • 40,404	Highland, MI 48031 • 1,000	Holdingford, MN 56340 • 635
Harlingen, TX 78550-52 • 43,543	Hauser, OR 97459 • 630	Hempstead, TX 77445 • 3,456	Highland, NY 12528 • 2,184	Holdrege, NE 68949 • 5,624
Harlowton, MT 59036 • 1,181	Hauula, HI 96717 • 2,997	Hempstead □, AR • 23,635	Highland, WI 53543 • 860	Holgate, OH 43527 • 1,315
Harmon □, OK • 4,519	Havana, FL 32333 • 2,782	Henagar, AL 35978 • 1,188	Highland □, OH • 33,477	Holiday, FL 33590 • 15,400
Harmony, IN 47853 • 613	Havana, IL 62644 • 4,277	Henderson, KY 42420 • 24,834	Highland □, VA • 2,937	Holladay, UT 84117 • 22,189
Harmony, MN 55939 • 1,133	Havelock, NC 28532 • 17,718	Henderson, LA 70517 • 1,560	Highland Falls, NY 10928 • 4,187	Holland, IN 47541 • 683
Harmony, PA 16037 • 1,334	Haven, KS 67543 • 1,125	Henderson, MN 56044 • 739	Highland Heights, OH 44124 • 5,739	Holland, MI 49423 • 26,281
Harmony, RI 02829 • 800	Haverford Township, PA 19041 • 5,800	Henderson, NE 68371 • 1,072	Highland Lakes, NJ 07422 • 2,888	Holland, NY 14080 • 1,000
Harmony Hills, DE 19711 • 1,350	Haverhill, MA 01830 • 46,865	Henderson, NV 89015 • 24,363	Highland Park, IL 60035 • 30,611	Holland, OH 43528 • 1,048
Harnett □, NC • 59,570	Haverstraw, NY 10927 • 8,800	Henderson, NC 27536 • 13,522	Highland Park, MI 48203 • 27,909	Holland, TX 76534 • 863
Harney □, OR • 8,314	Havertown, PA 19083 • 36,000	Henderson, TN 38340 • 4,449	Highland Park, NJ 08904 • 13,396	Hollandale, MS 38748 • 4,336
Harper, KS 67058 • 1,823	Haviland, KS 67059 • 770	Henderson, TX 75652 • 11,473	Highland Park, TX 75205 • 8,909	Holley, NY 14470 • 1,882
Harper □, KS • 7,778	Havre, MT 59501 • 10,891	Henderson, WV 25106 • 604	Highlands, NJ 07732 • 5,187	Holliday, TX 76366 • 1,349
Harper □, OK • 4,715	Havre de Grace, MD 21078 • 8,763	Henderson □, IL • 9,114	Highlands, NC 28741 • 653	Hollidaysburg, PA 16648 • 5,892
Harpersville, AL 35078 • 934	Havre North, MT 59501 • 1,073	Henderson □, KY • 40,849	Highlands, TX 77562 • 4,450	Hollins, VA 24019 • 11,000
Harper Woods, MI 48225 • 16,361	Hawaii □, HI • 92,053	Henderson □, NC • 58,580	Highlands □, FL • 47,526	Hollis, OK 73550 • 2,958
Harrah, OK 73045 • 2,897	Hawaiian Gardens, CA 90716 • 10,548	Henderson □, TN • 21,390	Highland Springs, VA 23075 • 7,500	Hollister, CA 95023 • 11,488
Harriman, TN 37748 • 8,303	Hawarden, IA 51023 • 2,722	Henderson □, TX • 42,606	Highmore, SD 57345 • 1,055	Hollister, MO 65672 • 1,439
Harrington, DE 19952 • 2,405	Hawesville, KY 42348 • 1,036	Henderson's Point, MS 39571 • 1,114	High Point, NC 27260-64 • 63,808	Holliston, MA 01746 • 12,622
Harrington Park, NJ 07640 • 4,532	Hawi, HI 96719 • 795	Hendersonville, NC 28739 • 6,862	High Ridge, MO 63049 • 900	Holloway Terrace, DE 19720 • 1,000
Harris, MN 55032 • 678	Hawkins, TN • 43,751	Hendersonville, TN 37075 • 26,561	High Rolls Mountain Park, NM 88325 • 650	Hollow Rock, TN 38342 • 955
Harris, RI 02816 • 1,000	Hawkinsville, GA 31036 • 4,372	Hendricks, MN 56136 • 737	High Spire, PA 17034 • 2,959	Hollsopple, PA 15935 • 900
Harris □, GA • 15,464	Hawk Run, PA 16840 • 750	Hendricks □, IN • 69,804	High Springs, FL 32643 • 2,491	Holly, CO 81047 • 969
Harris □, TX • 2,409,547	Hawley, MN 56549 • 1,634	Hendry □, FL • 18,599	Hightstown, NJ 08520 • 4,581	Holly, MI 48442 • 4,874
Harrisburg, AR 72432 • 1,921		Henlawson, WV 25624 • 950	Highview, KY 40228 • 13,286	Holly Grove, AR 72069 • 754
Harrisburg, IL 62946 • 10,410		Hennepin, IL 61327 • 716	Highwood, IL 60040 • 5,452	
Harrisburg, OR 97446 • 1,881		Hennepin □, MN • 941,411	Hilbert, WI 54129 • 1,176	

Holly Hill, FL 32017 • 9,953
Holly Hill, SC 29059 • 1,785
Holly Springs, GA 30142 • 687
Holly Springs, MS 38635 • 7,285
Holly Springs, NC 27540 • 688
Hollywood, AL 35752 • 1,110
Hollywood, FL 33020-29 • 121,323
Hollywood, SC 29449 • 729
Holmdel, NJ 07733 • 800
Holmen, WI 54636 • 2,411
Holmes, FL • 14,723
Holmes □, MS • 22,970
Holmes □, OH • 29,416
Holstein, IA 51025 • 1,477
Holt, AL 35404 • 4,300
Holt, FL 32564 • 780
Holt, MI 48842 • 10,097
Holt □, MO • 6,882
Holt □, NE • 13,552
Holton, KS 66436 • 3,132
Holtville, CA 92250 • 4,399
Holualoa, HI 96725 • 1,243
Holyoke, CO 80734 • 2,092
Holyoke, MA 01040 • 44,678
Homecroft, IN 46227 • 831
Homedale, ID 83628 • 2,078
Home Gardens, CA 91720 • 5,783
Homeland, GA 31537 • 683
Home Place, IN 46240 • 2,000
Homer, AK 99603 • 2,209
Homer, GA 30547 • 734
Homer, IL 61849 • 1,279
Homer, LA 71040 • 4,307
Homer, MI 49245 • 1,791
Homer, NY 13077 • 3,635
Homer City, PA 15748 • 2,248
Homerville, GA 31634 • 3,112
Homestead, FL 33030-35 • 20,668
Homestead, PA 15120 • 5,092
Hometown, IL 60456 • 5,324
Homewood, AL 35209 • 21,412
Homewood, IL 60430 • 19,724
Homewood, OH 45015 • 2,550
Hominy, OK 74035 • 3,130
Homosassa, FL 32646 • 1,426
Honaker, VA 24260 • 1,475
Hondo, TX 78861 • 6,057
Honea Path, SC 29654 • 4,114
Honeoye Falls, NY 14472 • 2,410
Honesdale, PA 18431 • 5,128
Honey Brook, PA 19344 • 1,164
Honey Grove, TX 75446 • 1,973
Honeypot Glen, CT 06410 • 900
Honeyville, UT 84314 • 915
Honokaa, HI 96727 • 1,936
Honolulu, HI 96801-99 • 365,048
Honolulu □, HI • 762,565
Hood □, TX • 17,714
Hood River, OR 97031 • 4,329
Hood River □, OR • 15,835
Hoodsport, WA 98548 • 900
Hooker, OK 73945 • 1,788
Hooker □, NE • 990
Hooksett, NH 03106 • 1,868
Hoonah, AK 99829 • 680
Hooper, NE 68031 • 932
Hooper Bay, AK 99604 • 627
Hoopeston, IL 60942 • 6,411
Hoosick Falls, NY 12090 • 3,609
Hoover, AL 35216 • 19,792
Hooverson Heights, WV 26037 • 1,500
Hooversville, PA 15936 • 863
Hopatcong, NJ 07843 • 15,531
Hope, AR 71801 • 10,290
Hope, IN 47246 • 2,185
Hopedale, IL 61747 • 913
Hopedale, MA 01747 • 3,905
Hopedale, OH 43976 • 857
Hopelawn, NJ 08861 • 12,600
Hope Mills, NC 28348 • 5,412
Hope Valley, RI 02832 • 1,414
Hopewell, NJ 08525 • 2,001
Hopewell, VA 23860 • 23,397
Hopewell Junction, NY 12533 • 2,055
Hopkins, MN 55343-45 • 15,336
Hopkins, MO 64461 • 634
Hopkins, SC 29061 • 1,600
Hopkins □, KY • 46,174
Hopkins □, TX • 25,247
Hopkinsville, KY 42240 • 27,318
Hopkinton, IA 52237 • 774
Hopkinton, MA 01748 • 2,542
Hopland, CA 95449 • 900
Hopwood, PA 15445 • 2,190
Hoquiam, WA 98550 • 9,719
Horatio, AR 71842 • 989
Horicon, WI 53032 • 3,584
Horine, MO 63070 • 850
Hornell, NY 14843 • 10,234
Hornersville, MO 63855 • 704
Horn Lake, MS 38637 • 4,326
Horry □, SC • 101,419
Horse Cave, KY 42749 • 2,045
Horseheads, NY 14845 • 7,348
Horseshoe Bend, ID 83629 • 700
Horsham, PA 19044 • 6,000
Horton, KS 66439 • 2,130
Hortonville, WI 54944 • 2,016
Hosford, FL 32334 • 700
Hospers, IA 51238 • 655
Hotchkiss, CO 81419 • 849
Hotevilla, AZ 86030 • 700
Hot Spring □, AR • 26,819
Hot Springs, MT 59845 • 601

Hot Springs
  → Truth or Consequences, NM • 5,219
Hot Springs, NC 28743 • 678
Hot Springs, SD 57747 • 4,742
Hot Springs □, WY • 5,710
Hot Springs National Park, AR 71901-13 • 35,781
Houghton, MI 49931 • 7,512
Houghton, NY 14744 • 1,620
Houghton □, MI • 37,872
Houghton Lake, MI 48629 • 1,500
Houghton Lake Heights, MI 48630 • 2,449
Houlka, MS 38850 • 710
Houlton, ME 04730 • 5,730
Houma, LA 70360-64 • 32,602
Housatonic, MA 01236 • 1,314
Houston, MN 55943 • 1,057
Houston, MS 38851 • 3,747
Houston, MO 65483 • 2,157
Houston, PA 15342 • 1,568
Houston, TX 77001-99 • 1,595,138
Houston □, AL • 74,632
Houston □, GA • 77,605
Houston □, MN • 18,382
Houston □, TN • 6,871
Houston □, TX • 22,299
Houtzdale, PA 16651 • 1,222
Hoven, SD 57450 • 615
Howard, KS 67349 • 965
Howard, PA 16841 • 838
Howard, SD 57349 • 1,169
Howard, WI 54303 • 8,240
Howard □, AR • 13,459
Howard □, IN • 86,896
Howard □, IA • 11,114
Howard □, MD • 118,572
Howard □, MO • 10,008
Howard □, NE • 6,773
Howard □, TX • 33,142
Howard City, MI 49329 • 1,118
Howard Lake, MN 55349 • 1,240
Howards Grove-Millersville, WI 53081 • 1,838
Howell, MI 48843 • 6,976
Howell □, MO • 28,807
Howells, NE 68641 • 677
Howland, ME 04448 • 1,602
Hoxie, AR 72433 • 2,961
Hoxie, KS 67740 • 1,462
Hoyt Lakes, MN 55750 • 3,186
Huachuca City, AZ 85616 • 1,661
Hubbard, IA 50122 • 852
Hubbard, OH 44425 • 9,245
Hubbard, OR 97032 • 1,640
Hubbard, TX 76648 • 1,676
Hubbard □, MN • 14,098
Hubbell, MI 49934 • 1,278
Huber Heights, OH 45424 • 35,480
Huber South, OH 45439 • 4,800
Huckleberry Hill, CT 06001 • 700
Hudson, CO 80642 • 698
Hudson, FL 33567 • 5,799
Hudson, IL 61748 • 929
Hudson, IA 50643 • 2,247
Hudson, MA 01749 • 9,714
Hudson, MI 49247 • 2,545
Hudson, NH 03051 • 6,248
Hudson, NC 28638 • 2,888
Hudson, NY 12534 • 7,986
Hudson, OH 44236 • 4,615
Hudson, WI 54016 • 5,434
Hudson □, NJ • 556,972
Hudson Falls, NY 12839 • 7,419
Hudson Lake, IN 46552 • 1,347
Hudsonville, MI 49426 • 4,844
Hudspeth □, TX • 2,728
Huerfano □, CO • 6,440
Hueytown, AL 35023 • 13,478
Hughes, AR 72348 • 1,919
Hughes □, OK • 14,338
Hughes □, SD • 14,220
Hughesville, MD 20637 • 1,208
Hughesville, PA 17737 • 2,174
Hugo, CO 80821 • 776
Hugo, MN 55038 • 3,771
Hugo, OK 74743 • 7,172
Hugoton, KS 67951 • 3,165
Huguley, AL 36854 • 2,947
Hulbert, OK 74441 • 633
Hull, IA 51239 • 1,714
Hull, MA 02045 • 9,714
Humansville, MO 65674 • 907
Humble, TX 77338-39 • 6,729
Humboldt, IA 50548 • 4,794
Humboldt, KS 66748 • 2,230
Humboldt, NE 68376 • 1,176
Humboldt, TN 38343 • 10,209
Humboldt □, CA • 108,514
Humboldt □, IA • 12,246
Humboldt □, NV • 9,434
Humeston, IA 50123 • 671
Hummels Wharf, PA 17831 • 750
Humphrey, AR 72073 • 872
Humphrey, NE 68642 • 799
Humphreys □, MS • 13,931
Humphreys □, TN • 15,957
Hungry Horse, MT 59919 • 900
Hunt □, TX • 55,248
Hunterdon □, NJ • 87,361
Huntertown, IN 46748 • 1,265
Huntingburg, IN 47542 • 5,376
Huntingdon, PA 16652 • 7,042
Huntingdon, TN 38344 • 3,962
Huntingdon □, PA • 42,253

Huntingdon Valley, PA 19006 • 10,400
Huntington, AR 72940 • 662
Huntington, IN 46750 • 16,202
Huntington, MA 01050 • 950
Huntington, NJ 08865 • 700
Huntington, NY 11743 • 12,601
Huntington, TX 75949 • 1,672
Huntington, UT 84528 • 2,316
Huntington, WV 25701-99 • 63,684
Huntington □, IN • 35,596
Huntington Bay, NY 11743 • 1,783
Huntington Beach, CA 92646-49 • 170,505
Huntington Park, CA 90255 • 46,223
Huntington Station, NY 11746 • 30,300
Huntington Woods, MI 48070 • 6,937
Huntland, TN 37345 • 983
Huntley, IL 60142 • 1,646
Huntsville, AL 35801-99 • 142,513
Huntsville, AR 72740 • 1,394
Huntsville, MO 65259 • 1,657
Huntsville, TX 77340 • 23,936
Hurley, NM 88043 • 1,616
Hurley, NY 12443 • 4,081
Hurley, WI 54534 • 2,015
Hurlock, MD 21643 • 1,690
Huron, OH 44839 • 7,123
Huron, SD 57350 • 13,000
Huron □, MI • 36,459
Huron □, OH • 54,608
Hurricane, UT 84737 • 2,361
Hurricane, WV 25526 • 3,751
Hurst, IL 62949 • 938
Hurst, TX 76053-54 • 31,420
Hurt, VA 24563 • 1,481
Hurtsboro, AL 36860 • 752
Hustisford, WI 53034 • 874
Hutchins, TX 75141 • 2,837
Hutchinson, KS 67501-05 • 40,284
Hutchinson, MN 55350 • 9,244
Hutchinson □, SD • 9,350
Hutchinson □, TX • 26,304
Hutsonville, IL 62433 • 705
Huttig, AR 71747 • 976
Hutto, TX 78634 • 659
Huxley, IA 50124 • 1,884
Hyannis, MA 02601 • 8,000
Hyannis Port, MA 02647 • 1,150
Hyattsville, MD 20780-88 • 12,709
Hybla Valley, VA 22306 • 4,350
Hyde, IN 46843 • 1,791
Hyde □, NC • 5,873
Hyde □, SD • 2,069
Hyde Park, NY 12538 • 2,805
Hyde Park, UT 84318 • 1,495
Hydetown, PA 16328 • 760
Hydro, OK 73048 • 938
Hymera, IN 47855 • 1,054
Hyndman, PA 15545 • 1,106
Hyrum, UT 84319 • 3,952

I

Iaeger, WV 24844 • 833
Iberia, MO 65486 • 852
Iberia □, LA • 63,752
Iberville □, LA • 32,159
Ida, MI 48140 • 1,000
Ida □, IA • 8,908
Ida Grove, IA 51445 • 2,285
Idaho □, ID • 14,769
Idaho Falls, ID 83401-15 • 39,590
Idaho Springs, CO 80452 • 2,077
Idalou, TX 79329 • 2,348
Idaville, IN 47950 • 625
Ideal, GA 31041 • 619
Ider, AL 35981 • 698
Ignacio, CO 81137 • 667
Ilion, NY 13357 • 9,450
Illiopolis, IL 62539 • 1,118
Illmo, MO 63780 • 1,368
Ilwaco, WA 98624 • 604
Imboden, AR 72434 • 661
Imlay City, MI 48444 • 2,495
Immokalee, FL 33934 • 11,038
Imperial, CA 92251 • 3,451
Imperial, MO 63052 • 950
Imperial, NE 69033 • 1,941
Imperial, PA 15126 • 2,385
Imperial, TX 79743 • 750
Imperial □, CA • 92,110
Imperial Beach, CA 92032 • 22,689
Incline Village, NV 89450 • 4,500
Independence, CA 93526 • 1,000
Independence, IA 50644 • 6,392
Independence, KS 67301 • 10,598
Independence, KY 41051 • 7,998
Independence, LA 70443 • 1,684
Independence, MO 64050-58 • 111,806
Independence, OH 44131 • 6,607
Independence, OR 97351 • 4,024
Independence, VA 24348 • 1,112
Independence, WI 54747 • 1,180
Independence □, AR • 30,147
Indiana, PA 15701 • 16,051
Indiana □, PA • 92,281
Indianapolis, IN 46201-99 • 700,807
Indian Harbour Beach, FL 32937 • 5,967
Indian Head, MD 20640 • 1,492
Indian Heights, IN 46901 • 4,277
Indian Hills, CO 80454 • 900

Indian Mound Beach, MA 02532 • 800
Indian Neck, CT 06405 • 2,200
Indianola, IA 50125 • 10,843
Indianola, MS 38751 • 8,221
Indianola, NE 69034 • 856
Indian Ridge Estates, AZ 85715 • 2,300
Indian River □, FL • 59,896
Indian Rocks Beach, FL 33535 • 3,717
Indian Springs, NV 89018 • 900
Indiantown, FL 33456 • 3,383
Indian Trail, NC 28079 • 811
Indio, CA 92201 • 21,611
Inez, TX 77968 • 900
Ingalls, IN 46048 • 909
Ingalls Park, IL 60431 • 3,500
Ingham □, MI • 275,520
Ingleside, TX 78362 • 5,436
Inglewood, CA 90301-99 • 94,245
Ingram, PA 15205 • 4,346
Inkom, ID 83245 • 830
Inkster, MI 48141 • 35,190
Inman, KS 67546 • 947
Inman, SC 29349 • 1,554
Inniswold, LA 70809 • 1,800
Inola, OK 74036 • 1,550
Institute, WV 25112 • 1,500
Intercession City, FL 33848 • 950
Interlachen, FL 32048 • 848
Interlaken, NY 14847 • 685
International Falls, MN 56649 • 5,611
Inver Grove Heights, MN 55075 • 17,171
Inverness, CA 94937 • 1,400
Inverness, FL 32650 • 4,095
Inverness, MS 38753 • 1,034
Inwood, FL 33880 • 6,668
Inwood, IA 51240 • 755
Inwood, NY 11696 • 8,200
Inwood, WV 25428 • 800
Inyo □, CA • 17,895
Inyokern, CA 93527 • 900
Iola, KS 66749 • 6,938
Iola, WI 54945 • 957
Iona, ID 83427 • 1,072
Ione, CA 95640 • 2,207
Ionia, MI 48846 • 5,920
Ionia □, MI • 51,815
Iosco □, MI • 28,349
Iota, LA 70543 • 1,326
Iowa, LA 70647 • 2,437
Iowa □, IA • 15,429
Iowa □, WI • 19,802
Iowa City, IA 52240 • 50,508
Iowa Falls, IA 50126 • 6,174
Iowa Park, TX 76367 • 6,184
Ipava, IL 61441 • 661
Ipswich, MA 01938 • 4,548
Ipswich, SD 57451 • 1,153
Iraan, TX 79744 • 1,358
Iredell □, NC • 82,538
Irion □, TX • 1,386
Irmo, SC 29063 • 3,957
Iron □, MI • 13,635
Iron □, MO • 11,084
Iron □, UT • 17,349
Iron □, WI • 6,730
Irondale, AL 35210 • 6,510
Irondequoit, NY 14617 • 57,648
Iron Gate, VA 24448 • 620
Ironia, NJ 07845 • 900
Iron Mountain, MI 49801 • 8,341
Iron Ridge, WI 53035 • 766
Iron River, MI 49935 • 2,426
Iron River, WI 54847 • 650
Ironton, MO 63650 • 1,743
Ironton, OH 45638 • 14,290
Ironwood, MI 49938 • 7,741
Iroquois □, IL • 32,976
Irrigon, OR 97844 • 700
Irvine, CA 92714 • 62,134
Irvine, KY 40336 • 2,889
Irving, IL 62051 • 612
Irving, TX 75060-63 • 109,943
Irvington, IL 62848 • 789
Irvington, KY 40146 • 1,409
Irvington, NJ 07111 • 61,493
Irvington, NY 10533 • 5,774
Irvona, PA 16656 • 644
Irwin, PA 15642 • 4,995
Irwin □, GA • 8,988
Irwinton, GA 31042 • 841
Isabella, PA 15447 • 700
Isabella □, MI • 54,110
Isanti, MN 55040 • 858
Isanti □, MN • 23,600
Iselin, NJ 08830 • 16,500
Ishpeming, MI 49849 • 7,538
Islamorada, FL 33036 • 1,441
Island □, WA • 44,048
Island Falls, ME 04747 • 650
Island Heights, NJ 08732 • 1,575
Island Park, NY 11558 • 4,847
Island Park, RI 02871 • 1,000
Island Pond, VT 05846 • 1,216
Isla Vista, CA 93117 • 16,700
Isle of Palms, SC 29451 • 3,421
Isle of Wight □, VA • 21,603
Isleta, NM 87022 • 1,246
Isleton, CA 95641 • 914
Islington, MA 02090 • 5,100
Islip, NY 11751 • 12,100
Islip Terrace, NY 11752 • 5,200

Isola, MS 38754 • 834
Issaquah, WA 98027 • 5,536
Issaquena □, MS • 2,513
Italy, TX 76651 • 1,306
Itasca, IL 60143 • 7,129
Itasca, TX 76055 • 1,600
Itasca □, MN • 43,069
Itawamba □, MS • 20,518
Ithaca, MI 48847 • 2,950
Ithaca, NY 14850 • 28,732
Itta Bena, MS 38941 • 2,904
Iuka, MS 38852 • 2,846
Iva, SC 29655 • 1,369
Ivanhoe, MN 56142 • 761
Ivoryton, CT 06442 • 950
Ivywild, CO 80906 • 4,000
Izard □, AR • 10,768

J

Jacinto City, TX 77029 • 8,953
Jack □, TX • 7,408
Jackman, ME 04945 • 800
Jacksboro, TN 37757 • 1,722
Jacksboro, TX 76056 • 4,000
Jackson, AL 36545 • 6,073
Jackson, CA 95642 • 2,331
Jackson, GA 30233 • 4,133
Jackson, KY 41339 • 2,651
Jackson, LA 70748 • 3,133
Jackson, MI 49201-04 • 39,739
Jackson, MN 56143 • 3,797
Jackson, MS 39201-99 • 202,895
Jackson, MO 63755 • 7,827
Jackson, NC 27845 • 720
Jackson, OH 45640 • 6,675
Jackson, SC 29831 • 1,771
Jackson, TN 38301-05 • 49,131
Jackson, WI 53037 • 1,813
Jackson, WY 83001 • 4,511
Jackson □, AL • 51,407
Jackson □, AR • 21,646
Jackson □, CO • 1,863
Jackson □, FL • 39,154
Jackson □, GA • 25,343
Jackson □, IL • 61,649
Jackson □, IN • 36,523
Jackson □, IA • 22,503
Jackson □, KS • 11,644
Jackson □, KY • 11,996
Jackson □, LA • 17,321
Jackson □, MI • 151,495
Jackson □, MN • 13,690
Jackson □, MS • 118,015
Jackson □, MO • 629,266
Jackson □, NC • 25,811
Jackson □, OH • 30,592
Jackson □, OK • 30,356
Jackson □, OR • 132,456
Jackson □, SD • 3,437
Jackson □, TN • 9,398
Jackson □, TX • 13,352
Jackson □, WV • 25,794
Jackson □, WI • 16,831
Jackson Center, OH 45334 • 1,310
Jacksonville, AL 36265 • 9,735
Jacksonville, AR 72076 • 27,589
Jacksonville, FL 32201-99 • 540,920
Jacksonville, IL 62650 • 20,284
Jacksonville, NC 28540 • 18,237
Jacksonville, OH 45740 • 651
Jacksonville, OR 97530 • 2,030
Jacksonville, TX 75766 • 12,264
Jacksonville Beach, FL 32250 • 15,462
Jaffrey, NH 03452 • 2,684
Jal, NM 88252 • 2,675
Jamesburg, NJ 08831 • 4,114
James City, NC 28560 • 700
James City □, VA • 22,763
James Island, SC 29412 • 24,124
Jamesport, MO 64648 • 651
Jamestown, NY 45327 • 2,206
Jamestown, IN 46147 • 924
Jamestown, KY 42629 • 1,441
Jamestown, NC 27282 • 2,148
Jamestown, ND 58401 • 16,280
Jamestown, VA 14701 • 35,775
Jamestown, OH 45335 • 1,702
Jamestown, PA 16134 • 854
Jamestown, RI 02835 • 4,040
Jamestown, TN 38556 • 2,364
Jamesville, NC 27846 • 604
Jamul, CA 92035 • 1,826
Janesville, CA 96114 • 1,200
Janesville, IA 50647 • 840
Janesville, MN 56048 • 1,897
Janesville, WI 53545-47 • 51,071
Jarratt, VA 23867 • 614
Jarrettsville, MD 21084 • 1,485
Jasmine Estates, FL 33568 • 3,500
Jasonville, IN 47438 • 2,497
Jasper, AL 35501 • 11,894
Jasper, FL 32052 • 2,093
Jasper, GA 30143 • 1,556
Jasper, IN 47546 • 9,097
Jasper, MN 56144 • 731
Jasper, MO 64755 • 1,012
Jasper, TN 37347 • 2,633
Jasper, TX 75951 • 6,959
Jasper □, GA • 7,553
Jasper □, IL • 11,318
Jasper □, IN • 26,138
Jasper □, IA • 36,425
Jasper □, MS • 17,265
Jasper □, MO • 86,958

Jasper □, SC • 14,504
Jasper □, TX • 30,781
Jay, FL 32565 • 633
Jay, OK 74346 • 2,100
Jay □, IN • 23,239
Jayton, TX 79528 • 638
Jeanerette, LA 70544 • 6,511
Jeannette, PA 15644 • 13,106
Jeff Davis □, GA • 11,473
Jeff Davis □, TX • 1,647
Jefferson, GA 30549 • 1,820
Jefferson, IA 50129 • 4,854
Jefferson, LA 70121 • 15,550
Jefferson, MA 01522 • 800
Jefferson, NC 28640 • 1,086
Jefferson, OH 44047 • 2,952
Jefferson, OR 97352 • 1,702
Jefferson, PA 15025 • 8,643
Jefferson, SC 29718 • 651
Jefferson, TX 75657 • 2,643
Jefferson, WI 53549 • 5,647
Jefferson □, AL • 671,324
Jefferson □, AR • 90,718
Jefferson □, CO • 371,753
Jefferson □, FL • 10,703
Jefferson □, GA • 18,403
Jefferson □, ID • 15,304
Jefferson □, IL • 36,558
Jefferson □, IN • 30,419
Jefferson □, IA • 16,316
Jefferson □, KS • 15,207
Jefferson □, KY • 684,565
Jefferson □, LA • 454,592
Jefferson □, MS • 9,181
Jefferson □, MO • 146,183
Jefferson □, MT • 7,029
Jefferson □, NE • 9,817
Jefferson □, NY • 88,151
Jefferson □, OH • 91,564
Jefferson □, OK • 8,183
Jefferson □, OR • 11,599
Jefferson □, PA • 48,303
Jefferson □, TN • 31,284
Jefferson □, TX • 250,938
Jefferson □, WA • 15,965
Jefferson □, WV • 30,302
Jefferson □, WI • 66,152
Jefferson City, MO 65101 • 33,619
Jefferson City, TN 37760 • 5,612
Jefferson Davis □, LA • 32,168
Jefferson Davis □, MS • 13,846
Jefferson Farms, DE 19720 • 2,400
Jefferson Manor, VA 22303 • 2,550
Jefferson Village, VA 22042 • 2,800
Jeffersontown, KY 40299 • 15,795
Jeffersonville, GA 31044 • 1,473
Jeffersonville, IN 47130 • 21,220
Jeffersonville, KY 40337 • 1,528
Jeffersonville, OH 43128 • 1,252
Jeffrey, WV 25114 • 900
Jellico, TN 37762 • 2,798
Jemez Pueblo, NM 87024 • 1,503
Jemison, AL 35085 • 1,828
Jena, LA 71342 • 4,375
Jenison, MI 49428 • 16,330
Jenkins, KY 41537 • 3,271
Jenkins □, GA • 8,841
Jenkintown, PA 19046 • 4,942
Jenks, OK 74037 • 5,876
Jenners, PA 15546 • 800
Jennings, FL 32053 • 749
Jennings, LA 70546 • 12,401
Jennings, MO 63136 • 17,026
Jennings □, IN • 22,854
Jennings Lodge, OR 97222 • 3,000
Jensen Beach, FL 33458 • 6,639
Jerauld □, SD • 2,929
Jericho, NY 11753 • 14,200
Jericho, VT 05465 • 1,340
Jermyn, PA 18433 • 2,411
Jerome, FL 33926 • 675
Jerome, ID 83338 • 6,891
Jerome, PA 15937 • 1,158
Jerome □, ID • 14,840
Jersey □, IL • 20,538
Jersey City, NJ 07301–99 • 223,532
Jersey Shore, PA 17740 • 4,631
Jerseyville, IL 62052 • 7,506
Jessamine □, KY • 26,065
Jessup, MD 20794 • 4,288
Jessup, PA 18434 • 4,974
Jesup, GA 31545 • 9,418
Jesup, IA 50648 • 2,343
Jetmore, KS 67854 • 862
Jewell, IA 50130 • 1,145
Jewell □, KS • 5,241
Jewett, OH 43986 • 972
Jewett City, CT 06351 • 3,294
Jim Hogg □, TX • 5,168
Jim Thorpe, PA 18229 • 5,263
Jim Wells □, TX • 36,498
Joanna, SC 29351 • 1,839
Jo Daviess □, IL • 23,520
Johnsburg, IL 60050 • 900
Johnson, KS 67855 • 1,244
Johnson, VT 05656 • 1,393
Johnson □, AR • 17,423
Johnson □, GA • 8,660
Johnson □, IL • 9,624
Johnson □, IN • 77,240
Johnson □, IA • 81,717
Johnson □, KS • 270,269
Johnson □, KY • 24,432
Johnson □, MO • 39,059
Johnson □, NE • 5,285

Johnson □, TN • 13,745
Johnson □, TX • 67,649
Johnson □, WY • 6,700
Johnsonburg, PA 15845 • 3,938
Johnson City, NY 13790 • 17,126
Johnson City, TN 37601–04 • 39,753
Johnson City, TX 78636 • 872
Johnson Creek, WI 53038 • 1,136
Johnsonville, SC 29555 • 1,421
Johnston, IA 50131 • 2,617
Johnston, RI 02919 • 24,907
Johnston, SC 29832 • 2,624
Johnston □, NC • 70,599
Johnston □, OK • 10,356
Johnston City, IL 62951 • 3,873
Johnstown, CO 80534 • 1,535
Johnstown, NY 12095 • 9,360
Johnstown, OH 43031 • 3,143
Johnstown, PA 15901–15 • 35,496
Joiner, AR 72350 • 725
Joliet, IL 60431–36 • 77,956
Jones □, GA • 16,579
Jones □, IA • 20,401
Jones □, MS • 61,912
Jones □, NC • 9,705
Jones □, SD • 1,463
Jones □, TX • 17,268
Jonesboro, AR 72401 • 31,530
Jonesboro, GA 30236 • 4,132
Jonesboro, IL 62952 • 1,842
Jonesboro, IN 46938 • 2,279
Jonesboro, LA 71251 • 5,061
Jonesboro, TN 37659 • 2,829
Jonesburg, MO 63351 • 614
Jones Creek, TX 77541 • 2,634
Jonesport, ME 04649 • 1,050
Jonestown, MS 38639 • 1,231
Jonestown, PA 17038 • 814
Jonesville, LA 71343 • 2,828
Jonesville, MI 49250 • 2,172
Jonesville, NC 28642 • 1,752
Jonesville, SC 29353 • 1,201
Jonesville, VA 24263 • 874
Joplin, MO 64801 • 39,023
Joppa, MD 21085 • 11,348
Jordan, MN 55352 • 2,663
Jordan, NY 13080 • 1,371
Joseph, OR 97846 • 999
Joseph City, AZ 86032 • 900
Josephine □, OR • 58,855
Joshua, TX 76058 • 1,470
Joshua Tree, CA 92252 • 2,083
Jourdanton, TX 78026 • 2,743
Joyce, LA 71440 • 900
Juab □, UT • 5,530
Judith Basin □, MT • 2,646
Judsonia, AR 72081 • 2,025
Julesburg, CO 80737 • 1,528
Julian, CA 92036 • 1,320
Julian, WV 25529 • 700
Junction, TX 76849 • 2,593
Junction City, AR 71749 • 813
Junction City, KS 66441 • 19,305
Junction City, KY 40440 • 2,045
Junction City, LA 71749 • 727
Junction City, OH 43748 • 754
Junction City, OR 97448 • 3,320
Juneau, AK 99801 • 19,528
Juneau, WI 53039 • 2,045
Juneau □, WI • 21,039
June Lake, CA 93529 • 900
Juniata, NE 68955 • 703
Juniata □, PA • 19,188
Juniata Terrace, PA 17044 • 631
Jupiter, FL 33458 • 9,868
Justice, IL 60458 • 10,552
Justin, TX 76247 • 920

K

Kaaawa, HI 96730 • 959
Kadoka, SD 57543 • 832
Kahaluu, HI 96744 • 2,025
Kahoka, MO 63445 • 2,101
Kahuku, HI 96731 • 935
Kahului, HI 96732 • 12,978
Kailua, HI 96734 • 35,812
Kailua Kona, HI 96740 • 4,751
Kalaheo, HI 96741 • 2,500
Kalama, WA 98625 • 1,216
Kalamazoo, MI 49001–09 • 79,722
Kalamazoo □, MI • 212,378
Kalawao □, HI • 144
Kalispell, MT 59901 • 10,648
Kalkaska, MI 49646 • 1,654
Kalkaska □, MI • 10,952
Kalona, IA 52247 • 1,862
Kamas, UT 84036 • 1,064
Kamiah, ID 83536 • 1,478
Kamuela (Waimea), HI 96743 • 1,179
Kanab, UT 84741 • 2,148
Kanabec □, MN • 12,161
Kanawha, IA 50447 • 756
Kanawha □, WV • 231,414
Kandiyohi □, MN • 36,763
Kane, PA 16735 • 4,916
Kane □, IL • 278,405
Kane □, UT • 4,024
Kaneohe, HI 96744 • 29,919
Kankakee, IL 60901 • 30,141
Kankakee □, IL • 102,926
Kannapolis, NC 28081 • 34,564
Kanopolis, KS 67454 • 729
Kansas, IL 61933 • 791

Kansas City, KS 66101–99 • 161,148
Kansas City, MO 64101–99 • 448,159
Kapaa, HI 96746 • 4,467
Kaplan, LA 70548 • 5,016
Karlstad, MN 56732 • 934
Karnak, IL 62956 • 646
Karnes □, TX • 13,593
Karnes City, TX 78118 • 3,296
Karns, TN 37921 • 1,173
Kasota, MN 56050 • 739
Kasson, MN 55944 • 2,827
Kathleen, FL 33849 • 1,866
Katy, TX 77449–50 • 5,660
Kauai □, HI • 39,082
Kaufman, TX 75142 • 4,658
Kaufman □, TX • 39,029
Kaukauna, WI 54130 • 11,310
Kaumakani, HI 96747 • 888
Kaunakakai, HI 96748 • 2,231
Kay □, OK • 49,852
Kayenta, AZ 86033 • 3,343
Kaysville, UT 84037 • 9,811
Keaau, HI 96749 • 775
Kealakekua, HI 96750 • 1,033
Kealia, HI 96751 • 700
Keansburg, NJ 07734 • 10,613
Kearney, MO 64060 • 1,433
Kearney, NE 68847 • 21,158
Kearney □, NE • 7,053
Kearns, UT 84118 • 21,353
Kearny, AZ 85237 • 2,646
Kearny, NJ 07032 • 35,735
Kearny □, KS • 3,435
Keego Harbor, MI 48033 • 3,083
Keene, NH 03431 • 21,449
Keene, TX 76059 • 3,013
Keeseville, NY 12944 • 2,025
Keewatin, MN 55753 • 1,443
Keiser, AR 72351 • 962
Keith □, NE • 9,364
Keithsburg, IL 61442 • 936
Keizer, OR 97303 • 18,592
Kekaha, HI 96752 • 3,260
Keller, TX 76248 • 4,156
Kellogg, ID 83837 • 3,417
Kellogg, IA 50135 • 654
Kelly Lake, MN 55754 • 900
Kellyville, OK 74039 • 960
Kelseyville, CA 95451 • 1,567
Kelso, WA 98626 • 11,129
Kemmerer, WY 83101 • 3,273
Kemp, TX 75143 • 1,035
Kemper □, MS • 10,148
Kenai, AK 99611 • 4,324
Kenansville, FL 32739 • 700
Kenansville, NC 28349 • 931
Kenbridge, VA 23944 • 1,352
Kendall, FL 33156 • 61,000
Kendall □, IL • 37,202
Kendall □, TX • 10,635
Kendall Park, NJ 08824 • 7,419
Kendallville, IN 46755 • 7,299
Kenedy, TX 78119 • 4,356
Kenedy □, TX • 543
Kenesaw, NE 68956 • 854
Kenilworth, IL 60043 • 2,708
Kenilworth, NJ 07033 • 8,221
Kenly, NC 27542 • 1,433
Kenmare, ND 58746 • 1,456
Kenmawr, PA 15136 • 5,100
Kenmore, NY 14217 • 18,474
Kenmore, WA 98028 • 7,900
Kennebec, ME • 109,889
Kennebunk, ME 04043 • 3,294
Kennebunkport, ME 04046 • 1,685
Kennedale, TX 76060 • 2,594
Kennedy, AL 35574 • 604
Kennedy Heights, LA 70094 • 2,000
Kenner, LA 70062–65 • 66,382
Kennesaw, GA 30144 • 5,095
Kennett, MO 63857 • 10,145
Kennett Square, PA 19348 • 4,715
Kennewick, WA 99336–37 • 34,397
Kennydale, WA 98055 • 1,000
Keno, OR 97627 • 900
Kenosha, WI 53140–42 • 77,685
Kenosha □, WI • 123,137
Kenova, WV 25530 • 4,454
Ken Rock, IL 61109 • 5,945
Kensett, AR 72082 • 1,751
Kensington, CA 94707 • 5,342
Kensington, CT 06037 • 7,502
Kensington, KS 66951 • 681
Kensington, MD 20895 • 1,822
Kent, OH 44240 • 26,164
Kent, WA 98031–32 • 23,152
Kent □, DE • 98,219
Kent □, MD • 16,695
Kent □, MI • 444,506
Kent □, RI • 154,163
Kent □, TX • 1,145
Kent City, MI 49330 • 860
Kentland, IN 47951 • 1,936
Kenton, OH 43326 • 8,605
Kenton, TN 38233 • 1,551
Kenton □, KY • 137,058
Kentwood, LA 70444 • 2,667
Kentwood, MI 49508 • 30,438
Kenvil, NJ 07847 • 3,000
Kenvir, KY 40847 • 950
Kenwood, MD 45236 • 9,928
Kenyon, MN 55946 • 1,529
Keokea, HI 96790 • 900
Keokuk, IA 52632 • 13,536
Keokuk □, IA • 12,921

Keosauqua, IA 52565 • 1,003
Keota, IA 52248 • 1,034
Keota, OK 74941 • 661
Kerens, TX 75144 • 1,582
Kerhonkson, NY 12446 • 1,243
Kerkhoven, MN 56252 • 761
Kermit, TX 79745 • 8,015
Kermit, WV 25674 • 705
Kern □, CA • 403,089
Kernersville, NC 27284 • 6,802
Kernville, CA 93238 • 1,660
Kerr □, TX • 28,780
Kerrville, TX 78028 • 15,276
Kersey, CO 80644 • 913
Kershaw, SC 29067 • 1,993
Kershaw □, SC • 39,015
Ketchikan, AK 99901 • 7,198
Ketchum, ID 83340 • 2,200
Kettering, OH 45429 • 61,186
Kettle Falls, WA 99141 • 1,087
Kettleman City, CA 93239 • 1,051
Kewanee, IL 61443 • 14,508
Kewanna, IN 46939 • 711
Kewaskum, WI 53040 • 2,381
Kewaunee, WI 54216 • 2,801
Kewaunee □, WI • 19,539
Keweenaw □, MI • 1,963
Keya Paha □, NE • 1,301
Key Largo, FL 33037 • 7,447
Keyport, NJ 07735 • 7,413
Keyser, WV 26726 • 6,569
Keystone, IA 52249 • 618
Keystone, WV 24852 • 902
Keystone Heights, FL 32656 • 1,056
Keysville, VA 23947 • 704
Keytesville, MO 65261 • 689
Key West, FL 33040 • 24,382
Kezar Falls, ME 04047 • 900
Kidder □, ND • 3,833
Kiefer, OK 74041 • 912
Kiel, WI 53042 • 3,083
Kiester, MN 56051 • 670
Kihei, HI 96753 • 5,644
Kilauea, HI 96754 • 895
Kilgore, TX 75662 • 11,006
Killbuck, OH 44637 • 937
Killdeer, ND 58640 • 790
Killeen, TX 76541–46 • 46,296
Killen, AL 35645 • 747
Killian, LA 70462 • 611
Kilmarnock, VA 22482 • 945
Kilmichael, MS 39747 • 906
Kiln, MS 39556 • 950
Kimball, MN 55353 • 651
Kimball, NE 69145 • 3,120
Kimball, SD 57355 • 752
Kimball, WV 24853 • 871
Kimball □, NE • 4,882
Kimberly, AL 35091 • 1,043
Kimberly, ID 83341 • 2,307
Kimberly, WV 25118 • 800
Kimberly, WI 54136 • 5,881
Kimble □, TX • 4,063
Kincaid, IL 62540 • 1,591
Kincaid, WV 25119 • 700
Kinder, LA 70648 • 2,603
Kinderhook, NY 12106 • 1,377
King, NC 27021 • 5,000
King, WI 54946 • 750
King □, TX • 425
King □, WA • 1,269,749
King and Queen □, VA • 5,968
King City, CA 93930 • 5,495
King City, MO 64463 • 1,063
Kingfield, ME 04947 • 700
Kingfisher, OK 73750 • 4,245
Kingfisher □, OK • 14,187
King George □, VA • 10,543
Kingman, AZ 86401 • 9,257
Kingman, KS 67068 • 3,563
Kingman □, KS • 8,960
King of Prussia, PA 19406 • 18,200
Kings, MS 39180 • 1,165
Kings □, CA • 73,738
Kings □, NY • 2,230,936
Kingsburg, CA 93631 • 5,115
Kingsbury □, SD • 6,679
Kingsford, MI 49801 • 5,290
Kingsland, GA 31548 • 2,008
Kingsland, TX 78639 • 1,600
Kingsley, IA 51028 • 1,209
Kingsley, MI 49649 • 664
Kings Mountain, NC 28086 • 9,080
Kings Park, VA 22151 • 4,450
Kings Park West, VA 22030 • 5,000
Kings Point, NY 11024 • 5,234
Kingsport, TN 37660–65 • 32,027
Kingston, GA 30145 • 733
Kingston, ID 83839 • 1,000
Kingston, IL 60145 • 618
Kingston, MA 02364 • 4,405
Kingston, NH 03848 • 900
Kingston, NJ 08528 • 900
Kingston, NY 12401 • 24,481
Kingston, OH 45644 • 1,208
Kingston, OK 73439 • 1,171
Kingston, PA 18704 • 15,681
Kingston, RI 02881 • 5,419
Kingston, TN 37763 • 4,441
Kingston Springs, TN 37082 • 1,017
Kingstree, SC 29556 • 4,147
Kingstown, MD 21620 • 1,192
Kingsville, MD 21087 • 2,824
Kingsville, OH 44048 • 1,243
Kingsville, TX 78363 • 28,808
King William □, VA • 9,334

Kingwood, WV 26537 • 2,877
Kinloch, MO 63140 • 4,455
Kinmundy, IL 62854 • 945
Kinnelon, NJ 07405 • 7,770
Kinney □, TX • 2,279
Kinsey, AL 36301 • 1,239
Kinsley, KS 67547 • 2,074
Kinsman, OH 44428 • 800
Kinston, AL 36453 • 604
Kinston, NC 28501 • 25,234
Kiowa, KS 67070 • 1,409
Kiowa, OK 74553 • 866
Kiowa □, CO • 1,936
Kiowa □, KS • 4,046
Kiowa □, OK • 12,711
Kirby, TX 78280 • 6,435
Kirbyville, TX 75956 • 1,972
Kirkersville, OH 43033 • 626
Kirkland, IL 60146 • 1,155
Kirkland, WA 98033–34 • 18,779
Kirklin, IN 46050 • 662
Kirksville, MO 63501 • 17,167
Kirkville, IL 61447 • 1,008
Kirkwood, MO 63122 • 27,987
Kirtland, NM 87417 • 2,358
Kirtland, OH 44094 • 5,969
Kissimmee, FL 32741–43 • 15,487
Kistler, WV 25628 • 750
Kit Carson □, CO • 7,599
Kitsap □, WA • 147,152
Kittanning, PA 16201 • 5,432
Kittery, ME 03904 • 5,465
Kittery Point, ME 03905 • 1,260
Kittitas, WA 98934 • 782
Kittitas □, WA • 24,877
Kittson □, MN • 6,672
Klamath, CA 95548 • 850
Klamath □, OR • 59,117
Klamath Falls, OR 97601–03 • 16,661
Kleberg □, TX • 33,358
Klein, TX 77379 • 9,000
Klemme, IA 50449 • 620
Klickitat, WA 98628 • 700
Klickitat □, WA • 15,822
Knightdale, NC 27545 • 985
Knights Landing, CA 95645 • 1,000
Knightstown, IN 46148 • 2,325
Knightsville, IN 47857 • 763
Knob Noster, MO 65336 • 2,040
Knollwood, WV 25302 • 700
Knott □, KY • 17,940
Knox, IN 46534 • 3,674
Knox, PA 16232 • 1,364
Knox □, IL • 61,607
Knox □, IN • 41,838
Knox □, KY • 30,239
Knox □, ME • 32,941
Knox □, MO • 5,508
Knox □, NE • 11,457
Knox □, OH • 46,304
Knox □, TN • 319,694
Knox □, TX • 5,329
Knox City, TX 79529 • 1,546
Knoxville, IL 61448 • 3,432
Knoxville, IA 50138 • 8,143
Knoxville, PA 16928 • 650
Knoxville, TN 37901–99 • 175,045
Kodiak, AK 99615 • 4,756
Kohler, WI 53044 • 1,817
Kokomo, IN 46901–02 • 47,808
Koloa, HI 96756 • 1,457
Konawa, OK 74849 • 1,711
Koochiching □, MN • 17,571
Koontz Lake, IN 46574 • 1,436
Kooskia, ID 83539 • 784
Kootenai □, ID • 59,770
Koppel, PA 16136 • 1,146
Kosciusko, MS 39090 • 7,415
Kosciusko □, IN • 59,555
Kossuth □, IA • 21,891
Kotzebue, AK 99752 • 2,054
Kountze, TX 77625 • 2,716
Kouts, IN 46347 • 1,619
Krebs, OK 74554 • 1,754
Kremmling, CO 80459 • 1,290
Kress, TX 79052 • 783
Krotz Springs, LA 70750 • 1,374
Kula, HI 96790 • 1,300
Kulpmont, PA 17834 • 3,675
Kuna, ID 83634 • 1,767
Kurtistown, HI 96760 • 1,200
Kutztown, PA 19530 • 4,040
Kyle, TX 78640 • 2,093

L

Labadieville, LA 70372 • 2,138
La Belle, FL 33935 • 2,287
La Belle, MO 63447 • 845
Labette □, KS • 25,682
La Canada Flintridge, CA 91011 • 20,153
Lac du Flambeau, WI 54538 • 900
La Center, KY 42056 • 1,044
Lacey, WA 98503 • 13,940
Lackawanna, NY 14218 • 22,701
Lackawanna □, PA • 227,908
Laclede □, MO • 24,323
Lacombe, LA 70445 • 5,146
Lacon, IL 61540 • 2,135
Laconia, NH 03246 • 15,575
La Conner, WA 98257 • 633
Lacoochee, FL 34261 • 1,720
Lac Qui Parle □, MN • 10,592
La Crescent, MN 55947 • 3,674

La Crescenta, CA 91214 • 12,500
La Crosse, IN 46348 • 713
La Crosse, KS 67548 • 1,618
La Crosse, VA 23950 • 734
La Crosse, WI 54601-03 • 48,347
La Crosse □, WI • 91,056
La Cygne, KS 66040 • 1,025
Ladd, IL 61329 • 1,337
Laddonia, MO 63352 • 726
Ladera Heights, CA 90045 • 6,647
Ladoga, IN 47954 • 1,151
Ladonia, TX 75449 • 761
Ladson, SC 29456 • 13,246
Lady Lake, FL 32659 • 1,193
Ladysmith, WI 54848 • 3,826
La Farge, WI 54639 • 746
Lafayette, AL 36862 • 3,647
Lafayette, CA 94549 • 20,879
Lafayette, CO 80026 • 8,985
Lafayette, GA 30728 • 6,517
Lafayette, IN 47901-07 • 43,011
Lafayette, LA 70501-09 • 81,961
Lafayette, NC 28304 • 4,100
Lafayette, OR 97127 • 1,215
La Fayette, RI 02852 • 680
Lafayette, TN 37083 • 3,808
Lafayette □, AR • 10,213
Lafayette □, FL • 4,035
Lafayette □, LA • 150,017
Lafayette □, MS • 31,030
Lafayette □, MO • 29,925
Lafayette □, WI • 17,412
Lafayette Hill, PA 19444 • 6,600
Lafayette Southwest, LA 70501 • 5,500
La Feria, TX 78559 • 3,495
Lafitte, LA 70067 • 1,312
La Follette, TN 37766 • 8,198
La Fontaine, IN 46940 • 946
Lafourche □, LA • 82,483
La France, SC 29656 • 800
Lagonda, LA 70380 • 5,805
La Grande, OR 97850 • 11,354
La Grange, GA 30240 • 24,204
La Grange, IL 60525 • 15,445
Lagrange, IN 46761 • 2,164
La Grange, KY 40031 • 2,971
La Grange, MO 63448 • 1,217
La Grange, NC 28551 • 3,147
Lagrange, OH 44050 • 1,258
La Grange, TX 78945 • 3,768
Lagrange □, IN • 25,550
La Grange Highlands, IL 60525 • 7,100
La Grange Park, IL 60525 • 13,359
Laguna, NM 87026 • 800
Laguna Beach, CA 92651-53 • 17,901
Laguna Hills, CA 92653 • 16,400
La Habra, CA 90631 • 45,232
Lahaina, HI 96761 • 6,095
La Harpe, IL 61450 • 1,471
La Harpe, KS 66751 • 687
Laie, HI 96762 • 4,643
Laingsburg, MI 48848 • 1,145
La Jara, CO 81140 • 858
La Junta, CO 81050 • 8,338
Lake □, CA • 36,366
Lake □, CO • 8,830
Lake □, FL • 104,870
Lake □, IL • 440,372
Lake □, IN • 522,965
Lake □, MI • 7,711
Lake □, MN • 13,043
Lake □, MT • 19,056
Lake □, OH • 212,801
Lake □, OR • 7,532
Lake □, SD • 10,724
Lake □, TN • 7,455
Lake Alfred, FL 33850 • 3,134
Lake Andes, SD 57356 • 1,029
Lake Arrowhead, CA 92352 • 2,500
Lake Arthur, LA 70549 • 3,615
Lake Barcroft, VA 22041 • 2,250
Lake Benton, MN 56149 • 869
Lake Bluff, IL 60044 • 4,434
Lake Butler, FL 32054 • 1,830
Lake Charles, LA 70601-11 • 75,226
Lake City, AR 72437 • 1,842
Lake City, FL 32055 • 9,257
Lake City, IA 51449 • 2,006
Lake City, MI 49651 • 843
Lake City, MN 55041 • 4,505
Lake City, PA 16423 • 2,384
Lake City, SC 29560 • 6,731
Lake City, TN 37769 • 2,335
Lake Crystal, MN 56055 • 2,078
Lake Delta, NY 13440 • 2,400
Lake Delton, WI 53940 • 1,158
Lake Elmo, MN 55042 • 5,296
Lake Elsinore, CA 92330 • 5,982
Lake Erie Beach, NY 14006 • 3,500
Lakefield, MN 56150 • 1,845
Lake Forest, FL 33023 • 5,400
Lake Forest, IL 60045 • 15,245
Lake Geneva, WI 53147 • 5,612
Lake George, NY 12845 • 1,047
Lake Grove, NY 11755 • 9,692
Lake Hamilton, AR 71913 • 1,054
Lake Havasu City, AZ 86403 • 15,909
Lake Helen, FL 32744 • 2,047
Lake Hiawatha, NJ 07034 • 14,000
Lake Hughes, CA 93532 • 800
Lakehurst, NJ 08733 • 2,908
Lake in the Hills, IL 60102 • 5,651

Lake Jackson, TX 77566 • 19,102
Lake Katrine, NY 12449 • 1,092
Lakeland, FL 33801-07 • 50,455
Lakeland, GA 31635 • 2,647
Lake Linden, MI 49945 • 1,181
Lake Luzerne, NY 12846 • 1,000
Lake Magdalene, FL 33612 • 13,331
Lake Mary, FL 32746 • 2,853
Lake Mills, IA 50450 • 2,281
Lake Mills, WI 53551 • 3,670
Lakemont, PA 16602 • 1,500
Lakemore, OH 44250 • 2,744
Lake Nebagamon, WI 54849 • 780
Lake Odessa, MI 48849 • 2,171
Lake Of The Woods □, MN • 3,764
Lake Orion, MI 48035 • 2,907
Lake Oswego, OR 97034 • 22,527
Lake Park, FL 33403 • 6,909
Lake Park, IA 51347 • 1,123
Lake Park, MN 56554 • 716
Lake Placid, FL 33852 • 963
Lake Placid, NY 12946 • 2,490
Lakeport, CA 95453 • 3,675
Lake Preston, SD 57249 • 789
Lake Providence, LA 71254 • 6,361
Lake Ridge, VA 22191 • 6,500
Lake Ronkonkoma, NY 11779 • 9,600
Lake Shore, MD 21122 • 2,100
Lakeshore, MS 39558 • 800
Lakeside, AZ 85929 • 1,333
Lakeside, CA 92040 • 23,921
Lakeside, CT 06488 • 900
Lakeside, OH 43440 • 950
Lakeside, OR 97449 • 1,453
Lakeside, VA 23228 • 29,400
Lakeside Park, KY 41017 • 3,038
Lake Station, IN 46405 • 14,294
Lake Station, OK 74127 • 800
Lake Stevens, WA 98258 • 1,660
Lake Telemark, NJ 07866 • 1,216
Lakeview, GA 30741 • 5,403
Lake View, IA 51450 • 1,291
Lakeview, MI 48850 • 1,139
Lake View, NY 14085 • 4,600
Lakeview, OH 43331 • 1,089
Lakeview, OR 97630 • 2,770
Lake View, SC 29563 • 939
Lake Villa, IL 60046 • 1,462
Lake Village, AR 71653 • 3,088
Lake Village, IN 46349 • 650
Lakeville, CT 06039 • 1,200
Lakeville, IN 46536 • 629
Lakeville, MA 02346 • 1,948
Lakeville, MN 55044 • 14,790
Lakeville, NY 14480 • 950
Lake Waccamaw, NC 28450 • 1,133
Lake Wales, FL 33853 • 8,466
Lake Wissota, WI 54729 • 1,419
Lakewood, CA 90712-16 • 74,654
Lakewood, CO 80215 • 113,808
Lakewood, IA 50211 • 900
Lakewood, NJ 08701 • 22,863
Lakewood, NY 14750 • 3,941
Lakewood, OH 44107 • 61,963
Lakewood Center, WA 98499 • 51,300
Lake Worth, FL 33460-67 • 27,048
Lake Zurich, IL 60047 • 8,225
Lakin, KS 67860 • 1,823
Lakota, ND 58344 • 963
La Luz, NM 88337 • 1,194
Lamar, AR 72846 • 708
Lamar, CO 81052 • 7,713
Lamar, MO 64759 • 4,053
Lamar, PA 16848 • 650
Lamar, SC 29069 • 1,333
Lamar □, AL • 16,453
Lamar □, GA • 12,215
Lamar □, MS • 23,821
Lamar □, TX • 42,156
La Marque, TX 77568 • 15,372
Lamb □, TX • 18,669
Lambert, MS 38643 • 1,624
Lamberton, MN 56152 • 1,032
Lambertville, MI 48144 • 6,341
Lambertville, NJ 08530 • 4,044
La Mesa, CA 92041 • 50,308
La Mesa, NM 88044 • 900
Lamesa, TX 79331 • 11,790
La Mirada, CA 90638 • 40,986
La Moille, IL 61330 • 734
Lamoille □, VT • 16,767
Lamoni, IA 50140 • 2,705
Lamont, CA 93241 • 9,616
La Monte, MO 65337 • 1,054
La Moure, ND 58458 • 1,077
La Moure □, ND • 6,473
Lampasas, TX 76550 • 6,165
Lampasas □, TX • 12,005
Lanai City, HI 96763 • 2,092
Lanark, IL 61046 • 1,483
Lanark Village, FL 32323 • 650
Lancaster, CA 93534-39 • 48,027
Lancaster, KY 40444 • 3,365
Lancaster, MA 01523 • 900
Lancaster, MO 63548 • 855
Lancaster, NH 03584 • 2,134
Lancaster, NY 14086 • 13,056
Lancaster, OH 43130 • 34,953
Lancaster, PA 17601-99 • 54,725
Lancaster, SC 29720 • 9,703
Lancaster, TX 75146 • 14,807
Lancaster, WI 53813 • 4,076
Lancaster □, NE • 192,884
Lancaster □, PA • 362,346

Lancaster □, SC • 53,361
Lancaster □, VA • 10,129
Lander, WY 82520 • 7,867
Lander □, NV • 4,076
Landis, NC 28088 • 2,092
Lando, SC 29724 • 850
Landrum, SC 29356 • 2,141
Lane □, KS • 2,472
Lane □, OR • 275,226
Lanesboro, MA 01237 • 950
Lanesboro, MN 55949 • 923
Lanett, AL 36863 • 6,897
Langdale, AL 36854 • 2,034
Langdon, ND 58249 • 2,335
Langeloth, PA 15054 • 950
Langhorne, PA 19047 • 1,697
Langlade □, WI • 19,978
Langley, SC 29834 • 1,714
Langley, WA 98260 • 650
Langley Park, MD 20787 • 11,100
Lanham, MD 20706 • 7,300
Lanier □, GA • 5,654
Lannon, WI 53046 • 987
Lanoka Harbor, NJ 08734 • 700
Lansdale, PA 19446 • 16,526
Lansdowne, MD 21227 • 10,000
Lansdowne, PA 19050 • 11,891
L'Anse, MI 49946 • 2,500
Lansford, PA 18232 • 4,466
Lansing, IL 60438 • 29,039
Lansing, IA 52151 • 1,181
Lansing, KS 66043 • 5,307
Lansing, MI 48901-99 • 130,414
Lantana, FL 33462 • 8,048
Laona, WI 54541 • 700
La Palma, CA 90623 • 15,399
Lapaz, IN 46537 • 651
La Paz □, AZ • 12,557
Lapeer, MI 48446 • 6,198
Lapeer □, MI • 70,038
Lapel, IN 46051 • 1,881
La Pine, OR 97739 • 900
La Place, LA 70068 • 16,112
La Plata, MD 20646 • 2,484
La Plata, MO 63549 • 1,423
La Plata □, CO • 27,195
Laporte, CO 80535 • 900
La Porte, IN 46350 • 21,796
La Porte, TX 77571 • 16,836
La Porte □, IN • 108,632
La Porte City, IA 50651 • 2,324
La Pryor, TX 78872 • 1,000
La Puente, CA 91744-49 • 30,882
Lapwai, ID 83540 • 1,043
Laramie, WY 82070 • 24,410
Laramie □, WY • 68,649
Larchmont, NY 10538 • 6,308
Larchmont North, NY 10538 • 11,500
Larchwood, IA 51241 • 701
Laredo, TX 78040-44 • 91,449
Largo, FL 33540-43 • 58,977
Larimer □, CO • 149,184
Larimore, ND 58251 • 1,524
Larkspur, CA 94939 • 11,064
Larksville, PA 18704 • 4,410
Larned, KS 67550 • 4,811
Larose, LA 70373 • 5,234
La Rue, OH 43332 • 861
Larue □, KY • 11,922
La Salle, CO 80645 • 1,929
La Salle, IL 61301 • 10,347
La Salle □, IL • 112,033
La Salle □, LA • 17,004
La Salle □, TX • 5,514
Las Animas, CO 81054 • 2,818
Las Animas □, CO • 14,897
Las Cruces, NM 88001-08 • 45,086
Lassen □, CA • 21,661
Las Vegas, NV 89101-99 • 164,674
Las Vegas, NM 87701 • 14,322
Latah □, ID • 28,749
Latham, NY 12110 • 8,000
Lathrop, MO 64465 • 1,732
Latimer □, OK • 9,840
Laton, CA 93242 • 1,100
Latrobe, PA 15650 • 10,799
Latta, SC 29565 • 1,804
Lattimer Mines, PA 18234 • 650
Lauderdale, MS 39335 • 750
Lauderdale □, AL • 80,546
Lauderdale □, MS • 77,285
Lauderdale □, TN • 24,555
Lauderdale Lakes, FL 33313 • 25,426
Lauderhill, FL 33313 • 37,271
Laughlintown, PA 15655 • 750
Laurel, DE 19956 • 3,052
Laurel, FL 33545 • 1,500
Laurel, IN 47024 • 819
Laurel, MD 20707-08 • 12,103
Laurel, MS 39440 • 21,897
Laurel, MT 59044 • 5,481
Laurel, NE 68745 • 1,031
Laurel, VA 23060 • 1,500
Laurel □, KY • 38,982
Laurel Bay, SC 29902 • 5,238
Laureldale, PA 19605 • 4,047
Laurel Hill, FL 32567 • 610
Laurel Hill, NC 28351 • 2,314
Laurel Run, PA 18702 • 725
Laurence Harbor, NJ 08879 • 5,000
Laurens, IA 50554 • 1,606
Laurens, SC 29360 • 10,587
Laurens □, GA • 36,990
Laurens □, SC • 52,214

Laurinburg, NC 28352 • 11,480
Laurium, MI 49913 • 2,678
Lavaca, AR 72941 • 1,092
Lavaca □, TX • 19,004
La Vale, MD 21502 • 5,500
Lavallette, NJ 08735 • 2,072
La Vergne, TN 37086 • 5,495
La Verkin, UT 84745 • 1,174
La Verne, CA 91750 • 23,508
Laverne, OK 73848 • 1,563
La Vernia, TX 78121 • 632
La Veta, CO 81055 • 611
La Vista, GA 30329 • 5,200
La Vista, NE 68128 • 9,588
Lavonia, GA 30553 • 2,024
Lawai, HI 96765 • 950
Lawndale, CA 90260 • 23,460
Lawnside, NJ 08045 • 3,042
Lawrence, IN 46226 • 25,591
Lawrence, KS 66044-46 • 52,738
Lawrence, MA 01840-45 • 63,175
Lawrence, MI 49064 • 903
Lawrence, NY 11559 • 6,175
Lawrence, PA 15055 • 970
Lawrence □, AL • 30,170
Lawrence □, AR • 18,447
Lawrence □, IL • 17,807
Lawrence □, IN • 42,472
Lawrence □, KY • 14,121
Lawrence □, MS • 12,518
Lawrence □, MO • 28,973
Lawrence □, OH • 63,849
Lawrence □, PA • 107,150
Lawrence □, SD • 18,339
Lawrence □, TN • 34,110
Lawrenceburg, IN 47025 • 4,403
Lawrenceburg, KY 40342 • 5,167
Lawrenceburg, TN 38464 • 10,184
Lawrence Park, PA 16511 • 4,584
Lawrenceville, GA 30245 • 8,928
Lawrenceville, IL 62439 • 5,652
Lawrenceville, NJ 08648 • 1,800
Lawrenceville, VA 23868 • 1,484
Lawson, MO 64062 • 1,688
Lawsonia, MD 21817 • 1,687
Lawtell, LA 70550 • 1,014
Lawtey, FL 32058 • 692
Lawton, MI 49065 • 1,558
Lawton, OK 73501-05 • 80,054
Layton, UT 84041 • 26,393
Laytonville, CA 95454 • 1,096
Lea □, NM • 55,993
Leachville, AR 72438 • 1,882
Lead, SD 57754 • 4,330
Leadville, CO 80461 • 3,879
Leadwood, MO 63653 • 1,371
Leaf River, IL 61047 • 637
League City, TX 77573 • 16,578
Leake □, MS • 18,790
Leakesville, MS 39451 • 1,120
Lealman, FL 33714 • 19,875
Leary, GA 31762 • 783
Leavenworth, KS 66048 • 33,656
Leavenworth, WA 98826 • 1,522
Leavenworth □, KS • 54,809
Leavittsburg, OH 44430 • 2,220
Leawood, KS 66206 • 13,360
Lebanon, IL 62254 • 3,245
Lebanon, IN 46052 • 11,456
Lebanon, KY 40033 • 6,590
Lebanon, MO 65536 • 9,507
Lebanon, NH 03766 • 11,134
Lebanon, NJ 08833 • 820
Lebanon, OH 45036 • 9,636
Lebanon, OR 97355 • 10,413
Lebanon, PA 17042 • 25,711
Lebanon, TN 37087 • 11,872
Lebanon, VA 24266 • 3,206
Lebanon □, PA • 108,582
Lebanon Junction, KY 40150 • 1,581
Lebec, CA 93243 • 900
Lebo, KS 66856 • 966
Le Center, MN 56057 • 1,967
Le Claire, IA 52753 • 2,899
Lecompte, LA 71346 • 1,661
Ledgewood, NJ 07852 • 1,100
Lee, MA 01238 • 2,140
Lee □, AL • 76,283
Lee □, AR • 15,539
Lee □, FL • 205,266
Lee □, GA • 11,684
Lee □, IL • 36,328
Lee □, IA • 43,106
Lee □, KY • 7,754
Lee □, MS • 57,061
Lee □, NC • 36,718
Lee □, SC • 18,929
Lee □, TX • 10,952
Lee □, VA • 25,956
Leechburg, PA 15656 • 2,682
Leedom Estates, DE 19720 • 1,300
Leeds, AL 35094 • 8,638
Leeds, ND 58346 • 678
Leelanau □, MI • 14,007
Lee Park, PA 18702 • 3,900
Leesburg, FL 32748-49 • 13,191
Leesburg, GA 31763 • 1,301
Leesburg, IN 46538 • 629
Leesburg, NJ 08327 • 700
Leesburg, OH 45135 • 1,019
Leesburg, VA 22075 • 8,357
Lees Summit, MO 64063 • 28,741
Leesville, LA 71446 • 9,054
Leesville, SC 29070 • 2,296
Leeton, MO 64761 • 604
Leetonia, OH 44431 • 2,121

Leetsdale, PA 15056 • 1,604
Lee Vining, CA 93541 • 900
Leflore □, MS • 41,525
Le Flore □, OK • 40,698
Lefors, TX 79054 • 829
Leggett, CA 95455 • 700
Le Grand, CA 95333 • 1,500
Le Grand, IA 50142 • 921
Lehi, UT 84043 • 6,848
Lehigh, IA 50557 • 654
Lehigh □, PA • 272,349
Lehigh Acres, FL 33936 • 9,604
Lehighton, PA 18235 • 5,826
Leicester, MA 01524 • 3,400
Leighton, AL 35646 • 1,218
Leipsic, OH 45856 • 2,171
Leisure City, FL 33033 • 17,905
Leitchfield, KY 42754 • 4,533
Leland, IL 60531 • 775
Leland, MS 38756 • 6,667
Le Mars, IA 51031 • 8,276
Lemay, MO 63125 • 35,424
Lemhi □, ID • 7,460
Lemmon, SD 57638 • 1,871
Lemmon Valley, NV 89501 • 2,000
Lemon Grove, CA 92045 • 20,780
Lemont, IL 60439 • 5,640
Lemont, PA 16851 • 2,613
Lemoore, CA 93245 • 8,832
Lena, IL 61048 • 2,295
Lenawee □, MI • 89,948
Lenexa, KS 66215 • 18,639
Lennox, CA 90304 • 18,445
Lennox, SD 57039 • 1,827
Lenoir, NC 28645 • 13,748
Lenoir □, NC • 59,819
Lenoir City, TN 37771 • 5,446
Lenox, GA 31637 • 965
Lenox, IA 50851 • 1,338
Lenox, MA 01240 • 2,668
Leo, IN 46765 • 800
Leola, SD 57456 • 645
Leominster, MA 01453 • 34,508
Leon, IA 50144 • 2,094
Leon, KS 67074 • 667
Leon □, FL • 148,655
Leon □, TX • 9,594
Leonard, TX 75452 • 1,421
Leonardo, NJ 07737 • 3,600
Leonardtown, MD 20650 • 1,448
Leonia, NJ 07605 • 8,027
Leon Valley, TX 78268 • 9,088
Leonville, LA 70551 • 1,143
Leoti, KS 67861 • 1,869
Lepanto, AR 72354 • 1,964
Le Roy, IL 61752 • 2,870
Le Roy, KS 66857 • 701
Le Roy, MN 55951 • 930
Le Roy, NY 14482 • 4,900
Leslie, MI 49251 • 2,110
Leslie, SC 29730 • 1,102
Leslie □, KY • 14,882
Lester, WV 25865 • 626
Lester Prairie, MN 55354 • 1,229
Le Sueur, MN 56058 • 3,763
Le Sueur □, MN • 23,434
Letcher □, KY • 30,687
Leto, FL 33614 • 9,003
Leucadia, CA 92024 • 9,478
Levelland, TX 79336-38 • 13,809
Levittown, NY 11756 • 65,400
Levittown, PA 19053-59 • 17,420
Levy □, FL • 19,870
Lewes, DE 19958 • 2,197
Lewis □, ID • 4,118
Lewis □, KY • 14,545
Lewis □, MO • 10,901
Lewis □, NY • 25,035
Lewis □, TN • 9,700
Lewis □, WA • 56,025
Lewis □, WV • 18,813
Lewis And Clark □, MT • 43,039
Lewisburg, KY 42256 • 972
Lewisburg, OH 45338 • 1,450
Lewisburg, PA 17837 • 5,407
Lewisburg, TN 37091 • 8,760
Lewisburg, WV 24901 • 3,065
Lewisport, KY 42351 • 1,832
Lewis Run, PA 16738 • 677
Lewiston, ID 83501 • 27,986
Lewiston, ME 04240 • 40,481
Lewiston, MN 55952 • 1,226
Lewiston, NY 14092 • 3,326
Lewiston, UT 84320 • 1,438
Lewiston Woodville, NC 27849 • 671
Lewistown, IL 61542 • 2,758
Lewistown, MT 59457 • 7,104
Lewistown, PA 17044 • 9,830
Lewisville, AR 71845 • 1,476
Lewisville, TX 75067 • 24,273
Lexington, AL 35648 • 884
Lexington, IL 61753 • 1,806
Lexington, KY 40501-99 • 204,165
Lexington, MA 02173 • 29,479
Lexington, MI 48450 • 765
Lexington, MS 39095 • 2,628
Lexington, MO 64067 • 5,063
Lexington, NE 68850 • 7,040
Lexington, NC 27292 • 15,711
Lexington, OH 44904 • 3,823
Lexington, OK 73051 • 1,731
Lexington, SC 29072 • 2,131
Lexington, TN 38351 • 5,934
Lexington, TX 78947 • 1,065
Lexington, VA 24450 • 7,292
Lexington □, SC • 140,353

Lexington Park, MD 20653 • 10,361
Libby, MT 59923 • 2,748
Liberal, KS 67901 • 14,911
Liberal, MO 64762 • 701
Liberty, IN 47353 • 1,844
Liberty, KY 42539 • 2,206
Liberty, MS 39645 • 669
Liberty, MO 64068 • 16,251
Liberty, NC 27298 • 1,997
Liberty, NY 12754 • 4,293
Liberty, SC 29657 • 3,167
Liberty, TX 77575 • 7,945
Liberty ☐, FL • 4,260
Liberty ☐, GA • 37,583
Liberty ☐, MT • 2,329
Liberty ☐, TX • 47,088
Liberty Acres, CA 90250 • 4,600
Liberty Center, OH 43532 • 1,111
Liberty Corner, NJ 07938 • 800
Liberty Lake, WA 99019 • 900
Libertyville, IL 60048 • 16,520
Libuse, LA 71348 • 700
Licking, MO 65542 • 1,272
Licking ☐, OH • 120,981
Lidgerwood, ND 58053 • 971
Liftwood, DE 19803 • 800
Lighthouse Point, FL 33064 • 11,488
Ligonier, IN 46767 • 3,134
Ligonier, PA 15658 • 1,917
Lihue, HI 96766 • 4,000
Lilbourn, MO 63862 • 1,463
Lilburn, GA 30247 • 3,765
Lillington, NC 27546 • 1,948
Lilly, PA 15938 • 1,462
Lilly Grove, WV 24740 • 1,700
Lima, NY 14485 • 2,025
Lima, OH 45801–09 • 47,381
Limestone, ME 04750 • 1,334
Limestone ☐, AL • 46,005
Limestone ☐, TX • 20,224
Limon, CO 80828 • 1,805
Lincoln, AL 35096 • 2,081
Lincoln, AR 72744 • 1,422
Lincoln, CA 95648 • 4,132
Lincoln, ID 83401 • 700
Lincoln, IL 62656 • 16,327
Lincoln, KS 67455 • 1,599
Lincoln, ME 04457 • 3,524
Lincoln, MA 01773 • 3,300
Lincoln, MO 65338 • 819
Lincoln, NE 68501–99 • 171,932
Lincoln ☐, AR • 13,369
Lincoln ☐, CO • 4,663
Lincoln ☐, GA • 6,716
Lincoln ☐, ID • 3,436
Lincoln ☐, KS • 4,145
Lincoln ☐, KY • 19,053
Lincoln ☐, LA • 39,763
Lincoln ☐, ME • 25,691
Lincoln ☐, MN • 8,207
Lincoln ☐, MS • 30,174
Lincoln ☐, MO • 22,193
Lincoln ☐, MT • 17,752
Lincoln ☐, NE • 36,455
Lincoln ☐, NV • 3,732
Lincoln ☐, NM • 10,997
Lincoln ☐, NC • 42,372
Lincoln ☐, OK • 26,601
Lincoln ☐, OR • 35,264
Lincoln ☐, SD • 13,942
Lincoln ☐, TN • 26,483
Lincoln ☐, WA • 9,604
Lincoln ☐, WV • 23,675
Lincoln ☐, WI • 26,555
Lincoln ☐, WY • 12,177
Lincoln Acres, CA 92047 • 1,800
Lincoln City, OR 97367 • 5,469
Lincoln Heights, OH 45215 • 5,259
Lincoln Park, CO 81212 • 3,426
Lincoln Park, GA 30286 • 1,755
Lincoln Park, MI 48146 • 45,105
Lincoln Park, NJ 07035 • 8,806
Lincolnshire, IL 60069 • 4,151
Lincolnton, GA 30817 • 1,106
Lincolnton, NC 28092 • 4,879
Lincoln Village, CA 95207 • 6,476
Lincoln Village, OH 43228 • 10,548
Lincolnville, SC 29483 • 808
Lincolnwood, IL 60645 • 11,921
Lincroft, NJ 07738 • 4,102
Linda, CA 95901 • 10,225
Lindale, GA 30147 • 2,958
Lindale, TX 75771 • 2,180
Linden, AL 36748 • 2,773
Linden, IN 47955 • 700
Linden, MI 48451 • 2,174
Linden, NJ 07036 • 37,836
Linden, TN 37096 • 1,087
Linden, TX 75563 • 2,443
Lindenhurst, IL 60046 • 6,220
Lindenhurst, NY 11757 • 26,919
Lindenwold, NJ 08021 • 18,196
Lindon, UT 84062 • 2,796
Lindsay, CA 93247 • 6,924
Lindsay, OK 73052 • 3,454
Lindsborg, KS 67456 • 3,155
Lindstrom, MN 55045 • 1,972
Linesville, PA 16424 • 1,198
Lineville, AL 36266 • 2,257
Linglestown, PA 17112 • 3,000
Linn, MO 65051 • 1,211
Linn ☐, IA • 169,775
Linn ☐, KS • 8,234
Linn ☐, MO • 15,495
Linn ☐, OR • 89,495
Lino Lakes, MN 55014 • 4,966

Linthicum Heights, MD 21090 • 7,457
Linton, IN 47441 • 6,315
Linton, ND 58552 • 1,561
Linwood, MA 01525 • 1,100
Linwood, NJ 08221 • 6,144
Linworth, OH 43085 • 650
Lipscomb, AL 35020 • 3,741
Lipscomb ☐, TX • 3,766
Lisbon, IA 52253 • 1,458
Lisbon, ME 04250 • 1,200
Lisbon, NH 03585 • 1,151
Lisbon, ND 58054 • 2,283
Lisbon, OH 44432 • 3,159
Lisbon Center, ME 04251 • 625
Lisbon Falls, ME 04252 • 4,370
Lisle, IL 60532 • 13,625
Lisman, AL 36912 • 638
Litchfield, CT 06759 • 1,489
Litchfield, IL 62056 • 7,204
Litchfield, MI 49252 • 1,353
Litchfield, MN 55355 • 5,904
Litchfield ☐, CT • 156,769
Litchfield Park, AZ 85340 • 3,657
Lithia Springs, GA 30057 • 9,145
Lithonia, GA 30058 • 2,637
Lititz, PA 17543 • 7,590
Little Canada, MN 55110 • 7,102
Little Chute, WI 54140 • 7,907
Little Falls, MN 56345 • 7,232
Little Falls, NJ 07424 • 11,496
Little Falls, NY 13365 • 6,156
Little Ferry, NJ 07643 • 9,399
Littlefield, TX 79339 • 7,409
Littlefork, MN 56653 • 918
Little Hocking, OH 45742 • 800
Little Lake, MI 49833 • 900
Little River ☐, AR • 13,952
Little Rock, AR 72201–99 • 158,461
Little Silver, NJ 07739 • 5,548
Little Valley, NY 14755 • 1,203
Littlestown, PA 17340 • 2,870
Littleton, CO 80120–27 • 28,631
Littleton, MA 01460 • 3,109
Littleton, NH 03561 • 4,480
Littleton, NC 27850 • 820
Live Oak, CA 95953 • 3,103
Live Oak, FL 32060 • 6,732
Live Oak, TX 78233 • 8,183
Live Oak ☐, TX • 9,000
Live Oak Manor, LA 70094 • 1,500
Livermore, CA 94550 • 48,349
Livermore, KY 42352 • 1,672
Livermore Falls, ME 04254 • 2,441
Liverpool, PA 17045 • 809
Liverpool, TX 77577 • 602
Livingston, AL 35470 • 3,187
Livingston, CA 95334 • 5,326
Livingston, IL 62058 • 949
Livingston, LA 70754 • 1,260
Livingston, MT 59047 • 6,994
Livingston, NJ 07039 • 28,040
Livingston, TN 38570 • 3,372
Livingston, TX 77351 • 4,928
Livingston, WI 53554 • 642
Livingston ☐, IL • 41,381
Livingston ☐, KY • 9,219
Livingston ☐, LA • 58,806
Livingston ☐, MI • 100,289
Livingston ☐, MO • 15,739
Livingston ☐, NY • 57,006
Livingston Manor, NY 12758 • 1,522
Livonia, LA 70755 • 980
Livonia, MI 48150–54 • 104,814
Livonia, NY 14487 • 1,238
Llangollen Estates, DE 19720 • 870
Llano, TX 78643 • 3,071
Llano ☐, TX • 10,144
Lloyd Harbor, NY 11743 • 3,405
Loami, IL 62661 • 770
Lobelville, TN 37097 • 993
Loch Lomond, VA 22110 • 2,300
Lockesburg, AR 71846 • 616
Lockhart, FL 32810 • 10,571
Lockhart, TX 78644 • 7,953
Lock Haven, PA 17745 • 9,617
Lockland, OH 45215 • 4,292
Lockney, TX 79241 • 2,334
Lockport, IL 60441 • 9,170
Lockport, LA 70374 • 2,424
Lockport, NY 14094 • 24,844
Lockwood, MO 65682 • 971
Lockwood, MT 59101 • 1,600
Locust, NC 28097 • 1,590
Locust, NJ 07760 • 700
Locust Grove, GA 30248 • 1,479
Locust Grove, NY 11791 • 11,648
Locust Grove, OK 74352 • 1,179
Lodge Grass, MT 59050 • 771
Lodi, CA 95240 • 35,221
Lodi, NJ 07644 • 23,956
Lodi, OH 44254 • 2,942
Lodi, WI 53555 • 1,959
Logan, IA 51546 • 1,540
Logan, KS 67646 • 720
Logan, NM 88426 • 735
Logan, OH 43138 • 6,557
Logan, UT 84321 • 26,844
Logan, WV 25601 • 3,029
Logan ☐, AR • 20,144
Logan ☐, CO • 19,800
Logan ☐, IL • 31,802
Logan ☐, KS • 3,478
Logan ☐, KY • 24,138
Logan ☐, NE • 983

Logan ☐, ND • 3,493
Logan ☐, OH • 39,155
Logan ☐, OK • 26,881
Logan ☐, WV • 50,679
Logansport, IN 46947 • 17,731
Logansport, LA 71049 • 1,565
Loganville, GA 30249 • 1,841
Loganville, PA 17342 • 1,020
Log Lane Village, CO 80701 • 709
Lolo, MT 59847 • 2,418
Loma Linda, CA 92354 • 10,694
Lomax, IL 61454 • 601
Lombard, IL 60148 • 36,897
Lometa, TX 76853 • 666
Lomira, WI 53048 • 1,446
Lomita, CA 90717 • 18,807
Lompoc, CA 93436 • 26,267
Lonaconing, MD 21539 • 1,420
London, AR 72847 • 859
London, KY 40741 • 4,002
London, OH 43140 • 6,958
Londonderry, NH 03053 • 950
Londontowne, MD 21037 • 3,500
Lone Grove, OK 73443 • 3,369
Lone Pine, CA 93545 • 1,684
Lone Tree, IA 52755 • 1,014
Lone Wolf, OK 73655 • 613
Long ☐, GA • 4,524
Long Bar Harbor, MD 21009 • 700
Long Beach, CA 90801–99 • 361,334
Long Beach, IN 46360 • 2,262
Long Beach, MD 20685 • 900
Long Beach, MS 39560 • 7,967
Long Beach, NY 11561 • 34,073
Long Beach, WA 98631 • 1,199
Longboat Key, FL 33548 • 4,843
Long Branch, NJ 07740 • 29,819
Longbranch, WA 98351 • 900
Long Lake, IL 60041 • 2,201
Longmeadow, MA 01106 • 16,301
Longmont, CO 80501 • 42,942
Longport, NJ 08403 • 1,249
Long Prairie, MN 56347 • 2,859
Long Valley, NJ 07853 • 1,682
Long View, KY 42701 • 650
Long View, NC 28601 • 3,587
Longview, TX 75601–08 • 62,762
Longview, WA 98632 • 31,052
Longwood, FL 32750 • 10,029
Lonoke, AR 72086 • 4,120
Lonoke ☐, AR • 34,518
Lonsdale, MN 55046 • 1,160
Lonsdale, RI 02865 • 800
Loogootee, IN 47553 • 3,100
Lookout Mountain, TN 37350 • 1,886
Loon Lake, WA 99148 • 650
Lorain, OH 44052–55 • 75,416
Lorain ☐, OH • 274,909
Loraine, TX 79532 • 929
Lordsburg, NM 88045 • 3,195
Loreauville, LA 70552 • 860
Lorenzo, TX 79343 • 1,394
Loretto, KY 40037 • 954
Loretto, PA 15940 • 1,395
Loretto, TN 38469 • 1,612
Lorida, FL 33857 • 620
Loris, SC 29569 • 2,193
Lorman, MS 39096 • 650
Los Alamitos, CA 90720 • 11,529
Los Alamos, CA 93440 • 950
Los Alamos, NM 87544 • 11,039
Los Altos, CA 94022 • 25,769
Los Altos Hills, CA 94022 • 7,421
Los Angeles, CA 90001–99 • 2,966,850
Los Angeles ☐, CA • 7,477,503
Los Banos, CA 93635 • 10,341
Los Fresnos, TX 78566 • 2,173
Los Gatos, CA 95030 • 26,906
Los Lunas, NM 87031 • 3,525
Los Molinos, CA 96055 • 1,241
Los Nietos, CA 90606 • 7,100
Los Padillas, NM 87105 • 2,500
Los Ranchos de Albuquerque, NM 87107 • 2,702
Lost Creek, WV 26385 • 604
Lost Hills, CA 93249 • 800
Lott, TX 76656 • 865
Loudon, TN 37774 • 3,943
Loudon ☐, TN • 28,553
Loudonville, NY 12211 • 9,000
Loudonville, OH 44842 • 2,945
Loudoun ☐, VA • 57,427
Loughman, FL 33858 • 800
Louisa, KY 41230 • 1,832
Louisa, VA 23093 • 932
Louisa ☐, IA • 12,055
Louisa ☐, VA • 17,825
Louisburg, KS 66053 • 1,744
Louisburg, NC 27549 • 3,238
Louise, TX 77455 • 900
Louisiana, MO 63353 • 4,261
Louisville, AL 36048 • 791
Louisville, CO 80027 • 5,593
Louisville, GA 30434 • 2,823
Louisville, IL 62858 • 1,166
Louisville, KY 40201–99 • 298,840
Louisville, MS 39339 • 7,323
Louisville, NE 68037 • 1,022
Louisville, OH 44641 • 7,996
Loup ☐, NE • 859
Loup City, NE 68853 • 1,368
Love ☐, OK • 7,469

Loveland, CO 80537 • 30,244
Loveland, OH 45140 • 9,106
Loveland Park, OH 45140 • 1,653
Lovell, WY 82431 • 2,447
Lovelock, NV 89419 • 1,680
Lovely, KY 41231 • 700
Loves Park, IL 61111 • 13,192
Lovettsville, VA 22080 • 613
Lovilia, IA 50150 • 637
Loving, NM 88256 • 1,355
Loving ☐, TX • 91
Lovington, IL 61937 • 1,313
Lovington, IA 50322 • 850
Lovington, NM 88260 • 9,727
Lowden, IA 52255 • 717
Lowell, AR 72745 • 1,078
Lowell, IN 46356 • 5,827
Lowell, MA 01850–54 • 92,418
Lowell, MI 49331 • 3,707
Lowell, NC 28098 • 2,917
Lowell, OH 45744 • 729
Lowell, OR 97452 • 661
Lowellville, OH 44436 • 1,558
Lower Burrell, PA 15068 • 13,200
Lower Paia, HI 96779 • 1,500
Lowmoor, VA 24457 • 700
Lowndes ☐, AL • 13,253
Lowndes ☐, GA • 67,972
Lowndes ☐, MS • 57,304
Lowry City, MO 64763 • 676
Lowville, NY 13367 • 3,364
Loxley, AL 36551 • 804
Loyal, WI 54446 • 1,252
Loyalton, CA 96118 • 1,030
Loyall, KY 40854 • 1,210
Lubbock, TX 79401–99 • 173,979
Lubbock ☐, TX • 211,651
Lubec, ME 04652 • 990
Lucama, NC 27851 • 1,070
Lucas, IA 50842 • 753
Lucas ☐, IA • 10,313
Lucas ☐, OH • 471,741
Lucasville, OH 45648 • 3,349
Luce ☐, MI • 6,659
Lucedale, MS 39452 • 2,429
Lucerne, CA 95458 • 1,767
Lucernemines, PA 15754 • 1,380
Lucerne Valley, CA 92356 • 1,300
Luck, WI 54853 • 997
Luckey, OH 43443 • 895
Ludington, MI 49431 • 8,037
Ludlow, KY 41016 • 4,959
Ludlow, MA 01056 • 18,150
Ludlow, PA 16333 • 800
Ludlow, VT 05149 • 1,352
Ludowici, GA 31316 • 1,286
Lufkin, TX 75901 • 28,562
Lugoff, SC 29078 • 2,976
Lukachukai, AZ 86507 • 1,049
Lula, GA 30554 • 857
Luling, LA 70070 • 4,006
Luling, TX 78648 • 5,039
Lumber City, GA 31549 • 1,426
Lumberport, WV 26386 • 939
Lumberton, MS 39455 • 2,217
Lumberton, NJ 08048 • 700
Lumberton, NC 28358 • 18,241
Lumpkin, GA 31815 • 1,335
Lumpkin ☐, GA • 10,762
Luna ☐, NM • 15,585
Luna Pier, MI 48157 • 1,443
Lunenburg, MA 01462 • 1,789
Lunenburg ☐, VA • 12,124
Luray, VA 22835 • 3,584
Lusk, WY 82225 • 1,650
Lutcher, LA 70071 • 4,730
Lutesville, MO 63762 • 865
Luther, OK 73054 • 1,159
Lutherville-Timonium, MD 21093 • 17,854
Luttrell, TN 37779 • 962
Lutz, FL 33549 • 5,555
Luverne, AL 36049 • 2,639
Luverne, MN 56156 • 4,568
Luxemburg, WI 54217 • 1,040
Luxora, AR 72358 • 1,739
Luzerne, PA 18709 • 3,703
Luzerne ☐, PA • 343,079
Lycoming ☐, PA • 118,416
Lyford, TX 78569 • 1,618
Lykens, PA 17048 • 2,181
Lyle, WA 98635 • 700
Lyman, SC 29365 • 1,067
Lyman, WY 82937 • 2,284
Lyman ☐, SD • 3,864
Lynch, KY 40855 • 1,614
Lynchburg, OH 45142 • 1,205
Lynchburg, TN 37352 • 668
Lynchburg, VA 24501–15 • 66,743
Lynden, WA 98264 • 4,022
Lyndhurst, NJ 07071 • 20,326
Lyndhurst, OH 44124 • 18,092
Lyndon, IL 61261 • 777
Lyndon, KS 66451 • 1,132
Lyndon, KY 40222 • 1,553
Lyndonville, NY 14098 • 916
Lyndonville, VT 05851 • 1,401
Lyndora, PA 16045 • 1,900
Lynn, IN 47355 • 1,250
Lynn, MA 01901–10 • 78,471
Lynn ☐, TX • 8,605
Lynne Acres, MD 21207 • 7,700
Lynnfield, MA 01940 • 11,267
Lynn Garden, TN 37665 • 7,213
Lynn Haven, FL 32444 • 6,239
Lynnwood, WA 98036–37 • 22,641

Lynwood, CA 90262 • 48,548
Lyon ☐, IA • 12,896
Lyon ☐, KS • 35,108
Lyon ☐, KY • 6,490
Lyon ☐, MN • 25,207
Lyon ☐, NV • 13,594
Lyon Mountain, NY 12952 • 950
Lyons, CO 80540 • 1,137
Lyons, GA 30436 • 4,203
Lyons, IL 60534 • 9,925
Lyons, IN 47443 • 782
Lyons, KS 67554 • 4,134
Lyons, MI 48851 • 708
Lyons, NE 68038 • 1,214
Lyons, NY 14489 • 4,160
Lyons, OR 97358 • 877
Lyons Falls, NY 13368 • 755
Lytle, TX 78052 • 1,920

M

Mabank, TX 75147 • 1,443
Mabel, MN 55954 • 861
Maben, MS 39750 • 855
Mableton, GA 30059 • 20,200
Mabscott, WV 25871 • 1,668
Mabton, WA 98935 • 1,248
McAdoo, PA 18237 • 2,942
McAlester, OK 74501 • 17,255
McAlisterville, PA 17049 • 650
McAllen, TX 78501–04 • 66,281
McAlmont, AR 72117 • 1,600
McAlpine, MD 21043 • 2,500
McArthur, OH 45651 • 1,912
McBee, SC 29101 • 774
McCall, ID 83638 • 2,188
McCamey, TX 79752 • 2,436
McCammon, ID 83250 • 770
McCandless, PA 15237 • 26,250
McCaysville, GA 30555 • 1,219
McClain ☐, OK • 20,291
McCleary, WA 98557 • 1,419
MacClenny, FL 32063 • 3,851
McCloud, CA 96057 • 1,656
McClure, IL 62957 • 700
McClure, OH 43534 • 694
McClure, PA 17841 • 1,024
McClusky, ND 58463 • 658
McColl, SC 29570 • 2,524
McComas, WV 24735 • 800
McComb, MS 39648 • 12,331
McComb, OH 45858 • 1,608
McCone ☐, MT • 2,702
McConnellsburg, PA 17233 • 1,178
McConnelsville, OH 43756 • 2,018
McCook, NE 69001 • 8,404
McCook ☐, SD • 6,444
McCormick, SC 29835 • 1,725
McCormick ☐, SC • 7,797
McCracken ☐, KY • 61,310
McCreary ☐, KY • 15,634
McCrory, AR 72101 • 1,942
McCulloch ☐, TX • 8,735
McCurtain ☐, OK • 36,151
McDonald, MO • 14,917
McDonough, GA 30253 • 2,778
McDonough ☐, IL • 37,467
McDowell, NC • 35,135
McDowell, WV • 49,899
McDuffie ☐, GA • 18,546
Macedon, NY 14502 • 1,400
Macedonia, OH 44056 • 6,571
McEwen, TN 37101 • 1,352
McFarland, CA 93250 • 5,151
McFarland, WI 53558 • 3,783
McGehee, AR 71654 • 5,671
McGill, NV 89318 • 1,419
McGraw, NY 13101 • 1,188
McGregor, IA 52157 • 945
McGregor, TX 76657 • 4,513
McGuffey, OH 45859 • 646
McHenry, IL 60050 • 11,949
McHenry ☐, IL • 147,897
McHenry ☐, ND • 7,858
Machias, ME 04654 • 1,277
Machias, NY 14101 • 700
McIntosh, MN 56556 • 681
McIntosh ☐, GA • 8,046
McIntosh ☐, ND • 4,800
McIntosh ☐, OK • 15,562
McKean ☐, PA • 50,635
McKee, KY 40447 • 759
McKeesport, PA 15130–35 • 31,012
McKees Rocks, PA 15136 • 8,742
McKenzie, AL 36456 • 605
McKenzie, TN 38201 • 5,405
McKenzie ☐, ND • 7,132
Mackinac ☐, MI • 10,178
Mackinaw, IL 61755 • 1,354
Mackinaw City, MI 49701 • 820
McKinley ☐, NM • 56,536
McKinleyville, CA 95521 • 7,772
McKinney, TX 75069 • 16,256
McLain, MS 39456 • 688
McLaughlin, SD 57642 • 754
McLean, IL 61754 • 836
McLean, TX 79057 • 1,160
McLean, VA 22101–03 • 22,000
McLean ☐, IL • 119,149
McLean ☐, KY • 10,090
McLean ☐, ND • 12,383
McLeansboro, IL 62859 • 2,960
McLennan ☐, TX • 170,755
McLeod ☐, MN • 29,657
McLoud, OK 74851 • 4,061
McLouth, KS 66054 • 700

McMechen, WV 26040 • 2,402
McMinn □, TN • 41,878
McMinnville, OR 97128 • 14,080
McMinnville, TN 37110 • 10,683
McMullen □, TX • 789
McNairy □, TN • 22,525
McNary, AZ 85930 • 1,320
McNeil, AR 71752 • 725
McNulty, OR 97051 • 1,805
Macomb, IL 61455 • 19,863
Macomb □, MI • 694,600
Macon, GA 31201-99 • 116,896
Macon, IL 62544 • 1,300
Macon, MS 39341 • 2,396
Macon, MO 63552 • 5,680
Macon □, AL • 26,829
Macon □, GA • 14,003
Macon □, IL • 131,375
Macon □, MO • 16,313
Macon □, NC • 20,178
Macon □, TN • 15,700
Macoupin □, IL • 49,384
McPherson, KS 67460 • 11,753
McPherson □, KS • 26,855
McPherson □, NE • 593
McPherson □, SD • 4,027
McQueeney, TX 78123 • 950
McRae, AR 72102 • 641
McRae, GA 31055 • 3,409
McRoberts, KY 41835 • 1,106
McSherrystown, PA 17344 • 2,764
Macungie, PA 18062 • 1,899
McVeigh, KY 41546 • 800
McVille, ND 58254 • 626
Madawaska, ME 04756 • 4,165
Maddock, ND 58348 • 677
Madeira, OH 45243 • 9,341
Madelia, MN 56062 • 2,130
Madera, CA 93637-39 • 21,732
Madera, PA 16661 • 900
Madera □, CA • 63,116
Madill, OK 73446 • 3,173
Madison, AL 35758 • 4,057
Madison, AR 72359 • 1,238
Madison, CT 06443 • 2,069
Madison, FL 32340 • 3,487
Madison, GA 30650 • 2,954
Madison, IL 62060 • 5,915
Madison, IN 47250 • 12,472
Madison, KS 66860 • 1,099
Madison, ME 04950 • 2,788
Madison, MN 56256 • 2,212
Madison, MS 39110 • 2,241
Madison, MO 65263 • 656
Madison, NE 68748 • 1,950
Madison, NJ 07940 • 15,357
Madison, NC 27025 • 2,806
Madison, OH 44057 • 2,291
Madison, SD 57042 • 6,210
Madison, WV 25130 • 3,228
Madison, WI 53701-99 • 170,616
Madison □, AL • 196,966
Madison □, AR • 11,373
Madison □, FL • 14,894
Madison □, GA • 17,747
Madison □, ID • 19,480
Madison □, IL • 247,661
Madison □, IN • 139,336
Madison □, IA • 12,597
Madison □, KY • 53,352
Madison □, LA • 15,975
Madison □, MS • 41,613
Madison □, MO • 10,725
Madison □, MT • 5,448
Madison □, NE • 31,382
Madison □, NC • 16,827
Madison □, NY • 65,150
Madison □, OH • 33,004
Madison □, TN • 74,546
Madison □, TX • 10,649
Madison □, VA • 10,232
Madison Heights, MI 48071 • 35,375
Madison Heights, VA 24572 • 3,500
Madisonville, KY 42431 • 16,979
Madisonville, LA 70447 • 799
Madisonville, TN 37354 • 2,884
Madisonville, TX 77864 • 3,660
Madras, OR 97741 • 2,235
Madrid, IA 50156 • 2,281
Madrid, NY 13660 • 800
Maeser, UT 84078 • 2,216
Magalia, CA 95954 • 950
Magazine, AR 72943 • 799
Magdalena, NM 87825 • 1,022
Magee, MS 39111 • 3,497
Magna, UT 84044 • 13,138
Magnolia, AR 71753 • 11,909
Magnolia, MS 39652 • 2,461
Magnolia, NJ 08049 • 4,881
Magnolia, OH 44643 • 986
Magnolia, TX 77355 • 867
Magoffin □, KY • 13,515
Mahanoy City, PA 17948 • 6,167
Mahaska □, IA • 22,867
Mahnomen, MN 56557 • 1,283
Mahnomen □, MN • 5,535
Mahomet, IL 61853 • 1,986
Mahoning □, OH • 289,487
Mahopac, NY 10541 • 5,265
Mahwah, NJ 07430 • 7,500
Maiden, NC 28650 • 2,574
Maili, HI 96792 • 5,026
Maine, NY 13802 • 700
Maitland, FL 32751 • 8,763
Maize, KS 67101 • 1,294
Major □, OK • 8,772
Makaha, HI 96792 • 7,905
Makakilo City, HI 96706 • 7,691
Makawao, HI 96768 • 1,066
Makaweli, HI 96769 • 700
Malabar, FL 32950 • 1,118
Malad City, ID 83252 • 1,915
Malaga, NJ 08328 • 950
Malakoff, TX 75148 • 2,082
Malden, MA 02148 • 53,386
Malden, MO 63863 • 6,096
Malden, WV 25306 • 950
Malheur □, OR • 26,896
Malibu, CA 90265 • 10,000
Malone, FL 32445 • 897
Malone, NY 12953 • 7,668
Malta, IL 60150 • 995
Malta, MT 59538 • 2,367
Malta, OH 43758 • 956
Malvern, AR 72104 • 10,163
Malvern, IA 51551 • 1,244
Malvern, OH 44644 • 1,032
Malvern, PA 19355 • 2,999
Malverne, NY 11565 • 9,262
Mamaroneck, NY 10543 • 17,616
Mammoth, AZ 85618 • 1,906
Mammoth, WV 25132 • 750
Mammoth Lakes, CA 93546 • 3,000
Mammoth Spring, AR 72554 • 1,158
Mamou, LA 70554 • 3,194
Man, WV 25635 • 1,333
Manahawkin, NJ 08050 • 1,467
Manasquan, NJ 08736 • 5,354
Manassa, CO 81141 • 945
Manassas, VA 22110-11 • 15,438
Manassas Park, VA 22111 • 6,524
Manatee □, FL • 148,442
Manawa, WI 54949 • 1,205
Mancelona, MI 49659 • 1,432
Manchaug, MA 01526 • 1,000
Manchester, CT 06040 • 49,761
Manchester, GA 31816 • 4,796
Manchester, IA 52057 • 4,942
Manchester, KY 40962 • 1,838
Manchester, MD 21102 • 1,830
Manchester, MA 01944 • 5,424
Manchester, MI 48158 • 1,686
Manchester, MO 63011 • 6,191
Manchester, NH 03101-99 • 90,936
Manchester, NY 14504 • 1,698
Manchester, OH 45144 • 2,313
Manchester, PA 17345 • 2,027
Manchester, TN 37355 • 7,250
Manchester Center, VT 05255 • 1,719
Mancos, CO 81328 • 870
Mandan, ND 58554 • 15,513
Mandeville, AR 75501 • 700
Mandeville, LA 70448 • 6,076
Mangham, LA 71259 • 867
Mangum, OK 73554 • 3,833
Manhasset, NY 11030 • 8,530
Manhattan, KS 66502 • 32,644
Manhattan, MT 59741 • 988
Manhattan Beach, CA 90266 • 31,542
Manheim, PA 17545 • 5,015
Manila, AR 72442 • 2,553
Manilla, IA 51454 • 1,020
Manistee, MI 49660 • 7,566
Manistee □, MI • 23,019
Manistique, MI 49854 • 3,962
Manito, IL 61546 • 1,869
Manitou Beach, MI 49779 • 4,500
Manitou Springs, CO 80829 • 4,475
Manitowoc, WI 54220 • 32,547
Manitowoc □, WI • 82,918
Mankato, KS 66956 • 1,205
Mankato, MN 56001 • 28,651
Manlius, NY 13104 • 5,241
Manly, IA 50456 • 1,496
Mannford, OK 74044 • 1,610
Manning, IA 51455 • 1,609
Manning, SC 29102 • 4,746
Mannington, WV 26582 • 3,036
Manomet, MA 02345 • 950
Manor, TX 78653 • 1,044
Manorhaven, NY 11050 • 5,384
Mansfield, AR 72944 • 1,000
Mansfield, IL 61854 • 921
Mansfield, LA 71052 • 6,485
Mansfield, MA 02048 • 6,786
Mansfield, MO 65704 • 1,423
Mansfield, OH 44901-99 • 53,927
Mansfield, PA 16933 • 3,322
Mansfield, TX 76063 • 8,102
Mansfield Center, CT 06250 • 1,043
Manson, IA 50563 • 1,924
Mansura, LA 71350 • 2,074
Mantachie, MS 38855 • 732
Manteca, CA 95336 • 24,925
Manteno, IL 60950 • 3,155
Manteo, NC 27954 • 902
Manti, UT 84642 • 2,080
Manton, MI 49663 • 1,212
Mantorville, MN 55955 • 705
Mantua, NJ 08051 • 1,900
Mantua, OH 44255 • 1,041
Mantua Hills, VA 22030 • 1,550
Manvel, TX 77578 • 3,549
Manville, NJ 08835 • 11,278
Manville, RI 02838 • 3,100
Many, LA 71449 • 3,988
Many Farms, AZ 86538 • 1,364
Maple Bluff, WI 53704 • 1,351
Maple Grove, MN 55369 • 20,525
Maple Heights, OH 44137 • 29,735
Maple Lake, MN 55358 • 1,132
Maple Plain, MN 55359 • 1,421
Maple Rapids, MI 48853 • 683
Maple Shade, NJ 08052 • 20,525
Maplesville, AL 36750 • 754
Mapleton, IA 51034 • 1,495
Mapleton, MN 56065 • 1,516
Mapleton, OR 97453 • 900
Mapleton, UT 84663 • 2,726
Maple Valley, WA 98038 • 900
Mapleville, RI 02839 • 900
Maplewood, MN 55109 • 26,990
Maplewood, MO 63143 • 10,960
Maplewood, NJ 07040 • 22,950
Maquoketa, IA 52060 • 6,313
Marana, AZ 85653 • 1,674
Marathon, FL 33050 • 7,508
Marathon, NY 13803 • 1,046
Marathon, TX 79842 • 750
Marathon, WI 54448 • 1,552
Marathon □, WI • 111,270
Marble, MN 55764 • 757
Marble, NC 28905 • 700
Marble Cliff, OH 43212 • 630
Marble Falls, TX 78654 • 3,252
Marblehead, MA 01945 • 20,126
Marblehead, OH 43440 • 679
Marble Hill, MO 63764 • 601
Marbury, MD 20658 • 1,189
Marceline, MO 64658 • 2,938
Marcellus, MI 49067 • 1,134
Marco, FL 33937 • 4,679
Marcus, IA 51035 • 1,206
Marcus Hook, PA 19061 • 2,638
Marengo, IL 60152 • 4,361
Marengo, IN 47140 • 892
Marengo, IA 52301 • 2,308
Marengo □, AL • 25,047
Marfa, TX 79843 • 2,466
Margaret, AL 35112 • 757
Margaretville, NY 12455 • 755
Margate, FL 33063 • 35,900
Margate, MD 21061 • 4,800
Margate City, NJ 08402 • 9,179
Marianna, AR 72360 • 6,220
Marianna, FL 32446 • 7,006
Maricopa, AZ 85239 • 900
Maricopa, CA 93252 • 946
Maricopa □, AZ • 1,509,262
Mariemont, OH 45227 • 3,295
Marienville, PA 16239 • 900
Maries □, MO • 7,551
Marietta, GA 30060-69 • 30,829
Marietta, OH 45750 • 16,467
Marietta, OK 73448 • 2,494
Marietta, SC 29661 • 900
Marin □, CA • 222,592
Marina, CA 93933 • 20,647
Marina del Rey, CA 90292 • 8,065
Marine, IL 62061 • 957
Marine City, MI 48039 • 4,414
Marinette, WI 54143 • 11,965
Marinette □, WI • 39,314
Maringouin, LA 70757 • 1,291
Marion, AL 36756 • 4,467
Marion, AR 72364 • 2,996
Marion, CT 06444 • 800
Marion, IL 62959 • 14,031
Marion, IN 46952-53 • 35,874
Marion, IA 52302 • 19,474
Marion, KS 66861 • 1,951
Marion, KY 42064 • 3,392
Marion, LA 71260 • 989
Marion, MA 02738 • 1,438
Marion, MI 49665 • 816
Marion, MS 39342 • 771
Marion, NC 28752 • 3,684
Marion, NY 14505 • 950
Marion, OH 43302 • 37,040
Marion, PA 17235 • 900
Marion, SC 29571 • 7,700
Marion, SD 57043 • 830
Marion, VA 24354 • 7,029
Marion, WI 54950 • 1,348
Marion □, AL • 30,041
Marion □, AR • 11,334
Marion □, FL • 122,488
Marion □, GA • 5,297
Marion □, IL • 43,523
Marion □, IN • 765,233
Marion □, IA • 29,669
Marion □, KS • 13,522
Marion □, KY • 17,910
Marion □, MS • 25,708
Marion □, MO • 28,638
Marion □, OH • 67,974
Marion □, OR • 204,692
Marion □, SC • 34,179
Marion □, TN • 24,416
Marion □, TX • 10,360
Marion □, WV • 65,789
Marionville, MO 65705 • 1,920
Mariposa, CA 95338 • 1,150
Mariposa □, CA • 11,108
Marissa, IL 62257 • 2,568
Marked Tree, AR 72365 • 3,201
Markesan, WI 53946 • 1,446
Markham, IL 60426 • 15,172
Markham, TX 77456 • 1,100
Markle, IN 46770 • 975
Marks, MS 38646 • 2,260
Marksville, LA 71351 • 5,113
Marlboro, NJ 07746 • 5,700
Marlboro, NY 12542 • 1,580
Marlboro, VA 23224 • 950
Marlboro □, SC • 31,634
Marlborough, CT 06447 • 1,039
Marlborough, MA 01752 • 30,617
Marlborough, NH 03455 • 1,231
Marlene Village, OR 97005 • 1,500
Marlette, MI 48453 • 1,761
Marley, MD 21061 • 4,800
Marlin, TX 76661 • 7,099
Marlinton, WV 24954 • 1,352
Marlow, OK 73055 • 5,017
Marlowe, WV 25419 • 700
Marlton, NJ 08053 • 9,411
Marmaduke, AR 72443 • 1,168
Marmet, WV 25315 • 2,196
Maroa, IL 61756 • 1,760
Marquette, KS 67464 • 639
Marquette, MI 49855 • 23,288
Marquette □, MI • 74,101
Marquette □, WI • 11,672
Marquette Heights, IL 61554 • 3,386
Marrero, LA 70072 • 36,548
Marrtown, WV 26101 • 900
Mars, PA 16046 • 1,803
Marseilles, IL 61341 • 4,766
Marshall, AR 72650 • 1,595
Marshall, IL 62441 • 3,655
Marshall, MI 49068 • 7,201
Marshall, MN 56258 • 11,161
Marshall, MO 65340 • 12,781
Marshall, NC 28753 • 809
Marshall, TX 75670 • 24,921
Marshall, WI 53559 • 2,363
Marshall □, AL • 65,622
Marshall □, IL • 14,479
Marshall □, IN • 39,155
Marshall □, IA • 41,652
Marshall □, KS • 12,787
Marshall □, KY • 25,637
Marshall □, MN • 13,027
Marshall □, MS • 29,296
Marshall □, OK • 10,550
Marshall □, SD • 5,404
Marshall □, TN • 19,698
Marshall □, WV • 41,608
Marshallton, DE 19808 • 3,950
Marshalltown, IA 50158 • 26,938
Marshallville, GA 31057 • 1,540
Marshallville, OH 44645 • 788
Marshfield, MA 02050 • 4,421
Marshfield, MO 65706 • 3,871
Marshfield, WI 54449 • 18,290
Marshfield Hills, MA 02051 • 2,308
Mars Hill, ME 04758 • 1,500
Mars Hill, NC 28754 • 2,126
Marshville, NC 28103 • 2,011
Marsing, ID 83639 • 786
Marston, MO 63866 • 742
Mart, TX 76664 • 2,324
Martin, KY 41649 • 827
Martin, SD 57551 • 1,018
Martin, TN 38237 • 8,898
Martin □, FL • 64,014
Martin □, IN • 11,001
Martin □, KY • 13,925
Martin □, MN • 24,687
Martin □, NC • 25,948
Martin □, TX • 4,684
Martinez, CA 94553 • 22,582
Martinez, GA 30907 • 16,472
Martinsburg, PA 16662 • 2,231
Martinsburg, WV 25401 • 13,063
Martins Ferry, OH 43935 • 9,331
Martinsville, IL 62442 • 1,298
Martinsville, IN 46151 • 11,311
Martinsville, VA 24112 • 18,149
Marvell, AR 72366 • 1,724
Maryland City, MD 20707 • 6,250
Maryland Heights, MO 63043 • 5,676
Marysville, CA 95901 • 9,898
Marysville, KS 66508 • 3,670
Marysville, MI 48040 • 7,345
Marysville, OH 43040 • 7,414
Marysville, PA 17053 • 2,452
Marysville, WA 98270 • 5,080
Maryville, KY 40229 • 6,000
Maryville, MO 64468 • 9,558
Maryville, TN 37801 • 17,480
Masaryktown, FL 33512 • 800
Mascot, TN 37806 • 2,203
Mascoutah, IL 62258 • 4,962
Mason, MI 48854 • 6,019
Mason, OH 45040 • 8,692
Mason, TX 76856 • 2,153
Mason, WV 25260 • 1,432
Mason □, IL • 19,492
Mason □, KY • 17,765
Mason □, MI • 26,365
Mason □, TX • 3,683
Mason □, WA • 31,104
Mason □, WV • 27,045
Mason City, IL 62664 • 2,719
Mason City, IA 50401 • 30,144
Masontown, PA 15461 • 4,909
Masontown, WV 26542 • 1,052
Massac □, IL • 14,990
Massapequa, NY 11758 • 27,500
Massapequa Park, NY 11762 • 19,779
Massena, NY 13662 • 12,851
Massillon, OH 44646 • 30,557
Mastic, NY 11950 • 5,200
Mastic Beach, NY 11951 • 5,200
Masury, OH 44438 • 1,836
Matador, TX 79244 • 1,052
Matagorda, TX 77457 • 850
Matagorda □, TX • 37,828
Matamoras, PA 18336 • 2,111
Matawan, NJ 07747 • 8,837
Matewan, WV 25678 • 822
Matfield, MA 02379 • 700
Mather, PA 15346 • 860
Matherville, IL 61263 • 793
Mathews, LA 70375 • 900
Mathews, VA 23109 • 650
Mathews □, VA • 7,995
Mathis, TX 78368 • 5,667
Mathiston, MS 39752 • 632
Matoaca, VA 23803 • 2,000
Matoaka, WV 24736 • 613
Mattapoisett, MA 02739 • 3,159
Mattawamkeag, ME 04459 • 750
Matteson, IL 60443 • 10,223
Matthews, IN 46957 • 745
Matthews, NC 28105 • 1,648
Mattituck, NY 11952 • 1,200
Mattoon, IL 61938 • 19,055
Mattydale, NY 13211 • 8,292
Maud, OK 74854 • 1,444
Maugansville, MD 21767 • 1,707
Maui □, HI • 70,847
Mauldin, SC 29662 • 8,143
Maumee, OH 43537 • 15,747
Maunaloa, HI 96770 • 633
Maunawili, HI 96734 • 2,200
Maury □, TN • 51,095
Maury City, TN 38050 • 989
Mauston, WI 53948 • 3,284
Maverick □, TX • 31,398
Maxton, NC 28364 • 2,711
Maxwell, CA 95955 • 800
Maxwell, IA 50161 • 783
Maxwell Acres, WV 26041 • 1,000
Maybeury, WV 24861 • 700
Mayer, AZ 86333 • 950
Mayes □, OK • 32,201
Mayesville, SC 29104 • 663
Mayfield, KY 42066 • 10,705
Mayfield, NY 12117 • 944
Mayfield, PA 18433 • 1,812
Mayfield Heights, OH 44124 • 21,550
Mayflower, AR 72106 • 1,381
Maynard, MA 01754 • 9,590
Maynardville, TN 37807 • 924
Mayo, FL 32066 • 891
Mayo, MD 21106 • 1,500
Mayo, SC 29368 • 900
Mayodan, NC 27027 • 2,627
May Park, OR 97850 • 1,466
Mays Landing, NJ 08330 • 2,054
Maysville, GA 30558 • 619
Maysville, KY 41056 • 7,983
Maysville, MO 64469 • 1,187
Maysville, NC 28555 • 877
Maysville, OK 73057 • 1,396
Mayville, MI 48744 • 958
Mayville, ND 58257 • 2,255
Mayville, NY 14757 • 1,626
Mayville, WI 53050 • 4,333
Maywood, CA 90270 • 21,810
Maywood, IL 60153 • 27,998
Maywood, NJ 07607 • 9,895
Maywood Park, OR 97220 • 1,083
Mazeppa, MN 55956 • 680
Mazomanie, WI 53560 • 1,248
Mazon, IL 60444 • 828
Mead, WA 99021 • 1,400
Meade, KS 67864 • 1,777
Meade □, KS • 4,788
Meade □, KY • 22,854
Meade □, SD • 20,717
Meadow Lands, PA 15347 • 1,200
Meadowood, DE 19711 • 2,260
Meadville, PA 16335 • 15,544
Meagher □, MT • 2,154
Mebane, NC 27302 • 2,782
Mecca, CA 92254 • 1,698
Mechanic Falls, ME 04256 • 2,616
Mechanicsburg, OH 43044 • 1,792
Mechanicsburg, PA 17055 • 9,487
Mechanicsville, IA 52306 • 1,166
Mechanicsville, VA 23111 • 9,000
Mechanicville, NY 12118 • 5,500
Mecklenburg □, NC • 404,270
Mecklenburg □, VA • 29,444
Mecosta □, MI • 36,961
Medaryville, IN 47957 • 731
Medfield, MA 02052 • 6,108
Medford, MA 02155 • 58,076
Medford, MN 55049 • 775
Medford, NJ 08055 • 1,448
Medford, NY 11763 • 5,000
Medford, OK 73759 • 1,419
Medford, OR 97501-04 • 39,603
Medford, WI 54451 • 4,035
Medford Lakes, NJ 08055 • 4,958
Media, PA 19063-65 • 6,119
Mediapolis, IA 52637 • 1,685
Medical Lake, WA 99022 • 3,600
Medicine Bow, WY 82329 • 953
Medicine Lodge, KS 67104 • 2,384
Medina, NY 14103 • 6,392
Medina, OH 44256 • 15,268
Medina, TN 38355 • 687
Medina, WA 98039 • 3,220
Medina □, OH • 113,150
Medina □, TX • 23,164
Medora, IN 47260 • 853
Medway, MA 02053 • 4,300
Meeker, CO 81641 • 2,356
Meeker, OK 74855 • 1,032
Meeker □, MN • 20,594

Mehlville, MO 63129 • *22,900*
Meigs, GA 31765 • *1,231*
Meigs □, OH • *23,641*
Meigs □, TN • *7,431*
Meiners Oaks, CA 93023 • *5,600*
Melbourne, AR 72556 • *1,619*
Melbourne, FL 32901–19 • *46,536*
Melbourne, IA 50162 • *732*
Melbourne, KY 41059 • *628*
Melbourne Beach, FL 32951 • *2,713*
Melcher, IA 50163 • *953*
Mellen, WI 54546 • *1,046*
Mellette □, SD • *2,249*
Melrose, FL 32666 • *1,700*
Melrose, MA 02176 • *30,055*
Melrose, MN 56352 • *2,409*
Melrose, NM 88124 • *649*
Melrose Park, FL 33312 • *5,725*
Melrose Park, IL 60160–65 • *20,735*
Melville, LA 71353 • *1,764*
Melville, NY 11747 • *10,250*
Melvin, KY 41650 • *700*
Melvindale, MI 48122 • *12,322*
Memphis, FL 33561 • *5,501*
Memphis, MI 48041 • *1,171*
Memphis, MO 63555 • *2,105*
Memphis, TN 38101–99 • *646,174*
Memphis, TX 79245 • *3,352*
Mena, AR 71953 • *5,154*
Menahga, MN 56464 • *980*
Menan, ID 83434 • *605*
Menands, NY 12204 • *4,012*
Menard, TX 76859 • *1,697*
Menard □, IL • *11,700*
Menard □, TX • *2,346*
Menasha, WI 54952 • *14,728*
Mendenhall, MS 39114 • *2,533*
Mendham, NJ 07945 • *4,899*
Mendocino, CA 95460 • *1,008*
Mendocino □, CA • *66,738*
Mendon, IL 62351 • *979*
Mendon, MA 01756 • *900*
Mendon, MI 49072 • *951*
Mendon, OH 45862 • *749*
Mendon, UT 84325 • *663*
Mendota, CA 93640 • *5,038*
Mendota, IL 61342 • *7,134*
Mendota Heights, MN 55118 • *7,288*
Menifee □, KY • *5,117*
Menlo, GA 30731 • *611*
Menlo Park, CA 94025 • *26,369*
Menno, SD 57045 • *793*
Menominee, MI 49858 • *10,099*
Menominee □, MI • *26,201*
Menominee □, WI • *3,373*
Menomonee Falls, WI 53051 • *27,845*
Menomonie, WI 54751 • *12,769*
Mentone, IN 46539 • *973*
Mentor, OH 44060 • *42,065*
Mentor-on-the-Lake, OH 44060 • *7,919*
Mequon, WI 53092 • *16,193*
Meraux, LA 70075 • *4,100*
Merced, CA 95340 • *36,499*
Merced □, CA • *134,558*
Mercedes, TX 78570 • *11,851*
Mercer, PA 16137 • *2,532*
Mercer, WI 54547 • *1,250*
Mercer □, IL • *19,286*
Mercer □, KY • *19,011*
Mercer □, MO • *4,685*
Mercer □, NJ • *307,863*
Mercer □, ND • *9,404*
Mercer □, OH • *38,334*
Mercer □, PA • *128,299*
Mercer □, WV • *73,942*
Mercer Island, WA 98040 • *21,522*
Mercersburg, PA 17236 • *1,617*
Mercerville, NJ 08619 • *15,500*
Merchantville, NJ 08109 • *3,972*
Meredith, NH 03253 • *1,202*
Meredosia, IL 62665 • *1,272*
Meriden, CT 06450 • *57,118*
Meriden, KS 66512 • *707*
Meridian, ID 83642 • *6,658*
Meridian, MS 39301–05 • *46,577*
Meridian, PA 16001 • *2,400*
Meridian, TX 76665 • *1,330*
Meridian Hills, IN 46260 • *1,801*
Meridianville, AL 35759 • *1,403*
Merion Station, PA 19066 • *7,400*
Meriwether □, GA • *21,229*
Merkel, TX 79536 • *2,493*
Mermentau, LA 70556 • *771*
Merriam, KS 66203 • *10,794*
Merrick, NY 11566 • *26,400*
Merrick □, NE • *8,945*
Merrifield, VA 22116 • *2,100*
Merrill, IA 51038 • *737*
Merrill, MI 48637 • *851*
Merrill, OR 97633 • *809*
Merrill, WI 54452 • *9,578*
Merrillville, IN 46410 • *27,677*
Merrimac, MA 01860 • *2,300*
Merrimack, NH 03054 • *1,200*
Merrimack □, NH • *98,302*
Merritt Island, FL 32952–54 • *30,708*
Mer Rouge, LA 71261 • *802*
Merryville, LA 70653 • *1,286*
Merton, WI 53056 • *1,045*
Mertzon, TX 76941 • *687*
Mesa, AZ 85201–08 • *152,453*
Mesa □, CO • *81,530*
Mescalero, NM 88340 • *1,259*
Mesilla, NM 88046 • *2,029*
Mesquite, NV 89024 • *700*
Mesquite, TX 75149–50 • *67,053*
Metairie, LA 70001–11 • *164,160*
Metamora, IL 61548 • *2,482*
Metcalfe, MS 38760 • *952*
Metcalfe □, KY • *9,484*
Methuen, MA 01844 • *36,701*
Metlakatla, AK 99926 • *1,056*
Metropolis, IL 62960 • *7,171*
Metter, GA 30439 • *3,531*
Metuchen, NJ 08840 • *13,762*
Metzger, OR 97223 • *5,544*
Mexia, TX 76667 • *7,094*
Mexico, IN 46958 • *850*
Mexico, ME 04257 • *3,207*
Mexico, MO 65265 • *12,276*
Mexico, NY 13114 • *1,621*
Meyersdale, PA 15552 • *2,581*
Miami, AZ 85539 • *2,716*
Miami, FL 33101–99 • *346,865*
Miami, OK 74354 • *14,237*
Miami, TX 79059 • *813*
Miami □, IN • *39,820*
Miami □, KS • *21,618*
Miami □, OH • *90,381*
Miami Beach, FL 33139 • *96,298*
Miamisburg, OH 45342 • *15,304*
Miami Shores, FL 33153 • *9,244*
Miami Springs, FL 33166 • *12,350*
Miamitown, OH 45041 • *650*
Micanopy, FL 32667 • *737*
Micco, FL 32958 • *3,585*
Michigan Center, MI 49254 • *5,244*
Michigan City, IN 46360 • *36,850*
Middleboro, MA 02346 • *7,012*
Middlebourne, WV 26149 • *941*
Middleburg, FL 32068 • *2,500*
Middleburg, NY 12122 • *1,358*
Middleburg, PA 17842 • *1,357*
Middleburg, VA 22117 • *619*
Middleburgh, NY 12122 • *1,358*
Middleburg Heights, OH 44130 • *16,218*
Middlebury, CT 06762 • *3,900*
Middlebury, IN 46540 • *1,665*
Middlebury, VT 05753 • *5,591*
Middlefield, OH 44062 • *1,997*
Middle Point, OH 45863 • *709*
Middleport, NY 14105 • *1,995*
Middleport, OH 45760 • *2,971*
Middle River, MD 21220 • *26,756*
Middlesboro, KY 40965 • *12,251*
Middlesex, NJ 08846 • *13,480*
Middlesex, NC 27557 • *837*
Middlesex □, CT • *129,017*
Middlesex □, MA • *1,367,034*
Middlesex □, NJ • *595,893*
Middlesex □, VA • *7,719*
Middleton, ID 83644 • *1,901*
Middleton, MA 01949 • *4,135*
Middleton, WI 53562 • *11,848*
Middletown, CA 95461 • *2,000*
Middletown, CT 06457 • *39,040*
Middletown, DE 19709 • *2,946*
Middletown, IN 47356 • *2,978*
Middletown, MD 21769 • *1,748*
Middletown, NJ 07718 • *61,615*
Middletown, NY 10940 • *21,454*
Middletown, OH 45042–43 • *43,719*
Middletown, PA 17057 • *10,122*
Middletown, RI 02840 • *3,350*
Middletown, VA 22645 • *841*
Middleville, MI 49333 • *1,797*
Middleville, NY 13406 • *647*
Midfield, AL 35228 • *6,203*
Midland, MD 21542 • *601*
Midland, MI 48640 • *37,250*
Midland, PA 15059 • *4,310*
Midland, TX 79701–11 • *70,525*
Midland □, MI • *73,578*
Midland □, TX • *82,636*
Midland City, AL 36350 • *1,903*
Midland Park, KS 67216 • *1,350*
Midland Park, NJ 07432 • *7,381*
Midland Park, SC 29405 • *1,300*
Midlothian, IL 60445 • *14,274*
Midlothian, TX 76065 • *3,219*
Midlothian, VA 23113 • *1,000*
Midvale, OH 44653 • *654*
Midvale, UT 84047 • *10,146*
Midville, GA 30441 • *670*
Midway, KY 40347 • *1,445*
Midway, OR 97233 • *19,000*
Midway, PA 15060 • *1,187*
Midway, UT 84049 • *1,194*
Midwest, WY 82643 • *638*
Midwest City, OK 73110 • *49,559*
Mifflin, PA 17058 • *648*
Mifflin □, PA • *46,908*
Mifflinburg, PA 17844 • *3,151*
Mifflintown, PA 17059 • *783*
Mifflinville, PA 18631 • *1,074*
Milaca, MN 56353 • *2,104*
Milam □, TX • *22,732*
Milan, GA 31060 • *1,115*
Milan, IL 61264 • *6,264*
Milan, IN 47031 • *1,566*
Milan, MI 48160 • *4,182*
Milan, MO 63556 • *1,947*
Milan, NM 87021 • *3,747*
Milan, OH 44846 • *1,569*
Milan, TN 38358 • *8,083*
Milbank, SD 57252 • *4,120*
Mildred, PA 18632 • *800*
Miles, TX 76861 • *720*
Milesburg, PA 16853 • *1,309*
Miles City, MT 59301 • *9,602*
Milford, CT 06460 • *49,101*
Milford, DE 19963 • *5,366*
Milford, IL 60953 • *1,716*
Milford, IN 46542 • *1,153*
Milford, IA 51351 • *2,076*
Milford, ME 04461 • *1,688*
Milford, MA 01757 • *23,390*
Milford, MI 48042 • *5,041*
Milford, NE 68405 • *2,108*
Milford, NH 03055 • *6,289*
Milford, NJ 08848 • *1,368*
Milford, OH 45150 • *5,232*
Milford, PA 18337 • *1,143*
Milford, UT 84751 • *1,293*
Milford Center, OH 43045 • *764*
Mililani Town, HI 96789 • *20,351*
Millard □, UT • *8,970*
Millbrae, CA 94030 • *20,058*
Millbrook, AL 36054 • *3,101*
Millbrook, NY 12545 • *1,343*
Millburn, NJ 07041 • *19,543*
Millbury, MA 01527 • *5,700*
Millbury, OH 43447 • *955*
Mill City, OR 97360 • *1,565*
Millcreek, UT 84109 • *24,150*
Mill Creek, WV 26280 • *801*
Millcreek Township, PA 16505 • *44,303*
Milldale, CT 06467 • *1,100*
Milledgeville, GA 31061 • *12,176*
Milledgeville, IL 61051 • *1,209*
Mille Lacs □, MN • *18,430*
Millen, GA 30442 • *3,988*
Miller, SD 57362 • *1,931*
Miller □, AR • *37,766*
Miller □, GA • *7,038*
Miller □, MO • *18,532*
Millersburg, IN 46543 • *809*
Millersburg, KY 40348 • *987*
Millersburg, OH 44654 • *3,247*
Millersburg, PA 17061 • *2,770*
Millers Falls, MA 01349 • *1,101*
Millersport, OH 43046 • *844*
Millersville, PA 17551 • *7,668*
Millerton, NY 12546 • *1,013*
Mill Grove, MO 64673 • *850*
Mill Hall, PA 17751 • *1,744*
Millheim, PA 16854 • *800*
Milligan College, TN 37682 • *1,200*
Milliken, CO 80543 • *1,506*
Millington, MI 48746 • *1,237*
Millington, TN 38053 • *20,236*
Millinocket, ME 04462 • *7,567*
Millis, MA 02054 • *3,777*
Millport, AL 35576 • *1,287*
Millry, AL 36558 • *956*
Mills, WY 82644 • *2,139*
Mills □, IA • *13,406*
Mills □, TX • *4,477*
Millsboro, DE 19966 • *1,233*
Millsboro, PA 15348 • *900*
Millstadt, IL 62260 • *2,736*
Milltown, IN 47145 • *1,006*
Milltown, NJ 08850 • *7,136*
Milltown, WI 54858 • *732*
Millvale, PA 15209 • *4,772*
Mill Valley, CA 94941 • *12,967*
Millville, MA 01529 • *1,764*
Millville, NJ 08332 • *24,815*
Millville, OH 45013 • *809*
Millville, PA 17846 • *975*
Millville, UT 84326 • *848*
Millwood, WA 99212 • *1,717*
Milnor, ND 58060 • *716*
Milo, IA 50166 • *778*
Milo, ME 04463 • *2,255*
Milpitas, CA 95035 • *37,820*
Milroy, IN 46156 • *900*
Milroy, PA 17063 • *1,575*
Milstead, GA 30207 • *1,157*
Milton, DE 19968 • *1,359*
Milton, FL 32570 • *7,206*
Milton, IN 47357 • *729*
Milton, KY 40045 • *718*
Milton, MA 02186 • *25,860*
Milton, NH 03851 • *1,000*
Milton, PA 17847 • *6,730*
Milton, VT 05468 • *1,411*
Milton, WA 98354 • *3,162*
Milton, WV 25541 • *2,178*
Milton, WI 53563 • *4,092*
Milton-Freewater, OR 97862 • *5,086*
Milwaukee, WI 53201–99 • *636,236*
Milwaukee □, WI • *964,988*
Milwaukie, OR 97222 • *17,931*
Mimosa Park, LA 70070 • *3,737*
Mims, FL 32754 • *7,583*
Minatare, NE 69356 • *969*
Minco, OK 73059 • *1,489*
Minden, LA 71055 • *15,084*
Minden, NE 68959 • *2,939*
Minden, NV 89423 • *1,300*
Minden, WV 25879 • *800*
Mine Hill, NJ 07801 • *3,250*
Mineola, NY 11501 • *20,757*
Mineola, TX 75773 • *4,346*
Miner, MO 63801 • *1,182*
Miner □, SD • *3,739*
Mineral □, CO • *804*
Mineral □, MT • *3,675*
Mineral □, NV • *6,217*
Mineral □, WV • *27,234*
Mineral City, OH 44656 • *884*
Mineral Point, WI 53565 • *2,259*
Mineral Springs, AR 71851 • *936*
Mineral Wells, TX 76067 • *14,468*
Minersville, PA 17954 • *5,635*
Minerva, OH 44657 • *4,549*
Minetto, NY 13115 • *900*
Mineville, NY 12956 • *1,000*
Mingo □, WV • *37,336*
Mingo Junction, OH 43938 • *4,834*
Minidoka □, ID • *19,718*
Minier, IL 61759 • *1,261*
Minneapolis, KS 67467 • *2,075*
Minneapolis, MN 55401–99 • *370,951*
Minnehaha □, SD • *109,435*
Minneola, KS 67865 • *712*
Minneota, MN 56264 • *1,470*
Minnesota Lake, MN 56068 • *744*
Minnetonka, MN 55345 • *38,683*
Minocqua, WI 54548 • *900*
Minonk, IL 61760 • *2,039*
Minooka, IL 60447 • *1,565*
Minot, MA 02055 • *800*
Minot, ND 58701 • *32,843*
Minquadale, DE 19720 • *1,700*
Minster, OH 45865 • *2,557*
Mint Hill, NC 28212 • *7,915*
Minturn, CO 81645 • *1,060*
Mio, MI 48647 • *1,500*
Mira Loma, CA 91752 • *8,707*
Miramar, FL 33023 • *32,813*
Misenheimer, NC 28109 • *1,250*
Mishawaka, IN 46544–45 • *40,201*
Mishicot, WI 54228 • *1,503*
Missaukee □, MI • *10,009*
Mission, KS 66222 • *8,643*
Mission, SD 57555 • *748*
Mission, TX 78572 • *22,653*
Mission Hills, KS 66205 • *3,904*
Mission Viejo, CA 92691 • *50,666*
Mississippi □, AR • *59,517*
Mississippi □, MO • *15,726*
Mississippi State, MS 39762 • *4,595*
Missoula, MT 59801–12 • *33,388*
Missoula □, MT • *76,016*
Missouri City, TX 77459 • *24,533*
Missouri Valley, IA 51555 • *3,107*
Mitchell, IL 62040 • *1,500*
Mitchell, IN 47446 • *4,641*
Mitchell, NE 69357 • *1,956*
Mitchell, SD 57301 • *13,916*
Mitchell □, GA • *21,114*
Mitchell □, IA • *12,329*
Mitchell □, KS • *8,117*
Mitchell □, NC • *14,428*
Mitchell □, TX • *9,088*
Mitchellville, IA 50169 • *1,530*
Moab, UT 84532 • *5,333*
Moberly, MO 65270 • *13,418*
Mobile, AL 36601–99 • *200,452*
Mobile □, AL • *364,980*
Mobridge, SD 57601 • *4,174*
Mocanaqua, PA 18655 • *990*
Mocksville, NC 27028 • *2,637*
Moclips, WA 98562 • *700*
Modesto, CA 95350–56 • *106,602*
Modoc □, CA • *8,610*
Moenkopi, AZ 86045 • *900*
Moffat □, CO • *13,133*
Mogadore, OH 44260 • *4,190*
Mohall, ND 58761 • *1,049*
Mohave □, AZ • *55,865*
Mohave Valley, AZ 86440 • *750*
Mohawk, MI 49950 • *950*
Mohawk, NY 13407 • *2,956*
Mohnton, PA 19540 • *2,156*
Mojave, CA 93501 • *2,886*
Mokelumne Hill, CA 95245 • *950*
Mokena, IL 60448 • *4,578*
Molalla, OR 97038 • *2,992*
Moline, IL 61265 • *46,278*
Moline, MI 49335 • *800*
Molino, FL 32577 • *1,456*
Momence, IL 60954 • *3,297*
Monaca, PA 15061 • *7,661*
Monahans, TX 79756 • *8,397*
Monarch Mills, SC 29379 • *2,353*
Moncks Corner, SC 29461 • *3,699*
Mondovi, WI 54755 • *2,545*
Monee, IL 60449 • *993*
Monessen, PA 15062 • *11,928*
Monett, MO 65708 • *6,148*
Monette, AR 72447 • *1,165*
Monfort Heights, OH 45239 • *9,745*
Moniteau □, MO • *12,068*
Monmouth, IL 61462 • *10,706*
Monmouth, OR 97361 • *5,594*
Monmouth □, NJ • *503,173*
Monmouth Beach, NJ 07750 • *3,318*
Monmouth Junction, NJ 08852 • *2,579*
Mono □, CA • *8,577*
Monon, IN 47959 • *1,540*
Monona, IA 52159 • *1,530*
Monona, WI 53716 • *8,809*
Monona □, IA • *11,692*
Monongah, WV 26554 • *1,132*
Monongahela, PA 15063 • *5,950*
Monongalia □, WV • *75,024*
Monroe, CT 06468 • *760*
Monroe, GA 30655 • *8,854*
Monroe, IN 46772 • *739*
Monroe, IA 50170 • *1,875*
Monroe, LA 71201–12 • *57,597*
Monroe, MI 48161 • *23,531*
Monroe, NC 28110 • *12,639*
Monroe, NY 10950 • *5,996*
Monroe, OH 45050 • *4,256*
Monroe, UT 84754 • *1,476*
Monroe, WA 98272 • *2,869*
Monroe, WI 53566 • *10,027*
Monroe □, AL • *22,651*
Monroe □, AR • *14,052*
Monroe □, FL • *63,188*
Monroe □, GA • *14,610*
Monroe □, IL • *20,117*
Monroe □, IN • *98,785*
Monroe □, IA • *9,209*
Monroe □, KY • *12,353*
Monroe □, MI • *134,659*
Monroe □, MS • *36,404*
Monroe □, MO • *9,716*
Monroe □, NY • *702,238*
Monroe □, OH • *17,382*
Monroe □, PA • *69,409*
Monroe □, TN • *28,700*
Monroe □, WV • *12,873*
Monroe □, WI • *35,074*
Monroe Center, CT 06468 • *6,950*
Monroe City, MO 63456 • *2,557*
Monroe Park, DE 19807 • *1,250*
Monroeton, PA 18832 • *677*
Monroeville, AL 36460 • *5,674*
Monroeville, IN 46773 • *1,372*
Monroeville, OH 44847 • *1,329*
Monroeville, PA 15146 • *30,977*
Monrovia, CA 91016 • *30,531*
Monsey, NY 10952 • *7,400*
Monson, MA 01057 • *2,167*
Montague, CA 96064 • *1,285*
Montague, MA 01351 • *900*
Montague, MI 49437 • *2,332*
Montague □, TX • *17,410*
Mont Alto, PA 17237 • *1,592*
Montandon, PA 17850 • *650*
Montauk, NY 11954 • *1,300*
Mont Belvieu, TX 77580 • *1,730*
Montcalm □, MI • *47,555*
Montclair, CA 91763 • *22,628*
Montclair, NJ 07042–44 • *38,321*
Mont Clare, PA 19453 • *1,274*
Monteagle, TN 37356 • *1,126*
Montebello, CA 90640 • *52,929*
Montecito, CA 93108 • *9,300*
Montegut, LA 70377 • *800*
Montello, WI 53949 • *1,273*
Monterey, CA 93940 • *27,558*
Monterey, TN 38574 • *2,610*
Monterey □, CA • *290,444*
Monterey Park, CA 91754 • *54,338*
Montesano, WA 98563 • *3,247*
Montevallo, AL 35115 • *3,965*
Montevideo, MN 56265 • *5,845*
Monte Vista, CO 81144 • *3,902*
Montezuma, GA 31063 • *4,830*
Montezuma, IN 47862 • *1,352*
Montezuma, IA 50171 • *1,485*
Montezuma, KS 67867 • *730*
Montezuma □, CO • *16,510*
Montfort, WI 53569 • *616*
Montgomery, AL 36101–99 • *177,857*
Montgomery, IL 60538 • *3,369*
Montgomery, LA 71454 • *843*
Montgomery, MN 56069 • *2,349*
Montgomery, NY 12549 • *2,316*
Montgomery, OH 45242 • *10,088*
Montgomery, PA 17752 • *1,653*
Montgomery, WV 25136 • *3,104*
Montgomery □, AL • *197,038*
Montgomery □, AR • *7,771*
Montgomery □, GA • *7,011*
Montgomery □, IL • *31,686*
Montgomery □, IN • *35,501*
Montgomery □, IA • *13,413*
Montgomery □, KS • *42,281*
Montgomery □, KY • *20,046*
Montgomery □, MD • *579,053*
Montgomery □, MS • *13,366*
Montgomery □, MO • *11,537*
Montgomery □, NC • *22,469*
Montgomery □, NY • *53,439*
Montgomery □, OH • *571,697*
Montgomery □, PA • *643,621*
Montgomery □, TN • *83,342*
Montgomery □, TX • *128,487*
Montgomery □, VA • *63,516*
Montgomery City, MO 63361 • *2,101*
Montgomery Creek, CA 96065 • *800*
Montgomery Village, MD 20879 • *16,600*
Monticello, AR 71655 • *8,259*
Monticello, FL 32344 • *2,994*
Monticello, GA 31064 • *2,382*
Monticello, IL 61856 • *4,753*
Monticello, IN 47960 • *5,162*
Monticello, IA 52310 • *3,641*
Monticello, KY 42633 • *5,677*
Monticello, MN 55362 • *2,830*
Monticello, MS 39654 • *1,834*
Monticello, NY 12701 • *6,306*
Monticello, UT 84535 • *1,929*
Monticello, WI 53570 • *1,021*
Montmorenci, SC 29839 • *900*
Montmorency □, MI • *7,492*
Montour □, PA • *16,675*
Montour Falls, NY 14865 • *1,791*
Montoursville, PA 17754 • *5,403*
Montpelier, ID 83254 • *3,107*
Montpelier, IN 47359 • *1,995*
Montpelier, OH 43543 • *4,431*
Montpelier, VT 05602 • *8,241*
Montreal, WI 54550 • *887*
Montreat, NC 28757 • *741*

Montrose, AL 36559 • 1,200
Montrose, AR 71658 • 641
Montrose, CO 81401 • 8,722
Montrose, IA 52639 • 1,038
Montrose, MI 48457 • 1,706
Montrose, PA 18801 • 1,980
Montrose, VA 23231 • 2,200
Montrose □, CO • 24,352
Montvale, NJ 07645 • 7,318
Montville, CT 06353 • 1,711
Montville, NJ 07045 • 2,700
Monument, CO 80132 • 690
Monument Beach, MA 02553 • 1,500
Monument Heights, VA 23226 • 3,100
Moodus, CT 06469 • 1,179
Moody, TX 76557 • 1,385
Moody □, SD • 6,692
Moody Beach, ME 04054 • 3,000
Moonachie, NJ 07074 • 2,706
Moorcroft, WY 82721 • 1,014
Moore, OK 73160 • 35,063
Moore □, NC • 50,505
Moore □, TN • 4,510
Moore □, TX • 16,575
Moorefield, WV 26836 • 2,257
Moore Haven, FL 33471 • 1,250
Mooreland, OK 73852 • 1,383
Moorestown, NJ 08057 • 15,596
Mooresville, IN 46158 • 5,349
Mooresville, NC 28115 • 8,575
Moorhead, MN 56560 • 29,998
Moorhead, MS 38761 • 2,358
Mooringsport, LA 71060 • 911
Moose Lake, MN 55767 • 1,408
Moosic, PA 18507 • 6,068
Moosup, CT 06354 • 3,308
Mora, MN 55051 • 2,890
Mora, NM 87732 • 900
Mora □, NM • 4,205
Moraga, CA 94556 • 15,014
Moraine, OH 45439 • 5,325
Moran, KS 66755 • 643
Moravia, IA 52571 • 706
Moravia, NY 13118 • 1,582
Moreauville, LA 71355 • 853
Morehead, KY 40351 • 7,789
Morehead City, NC 28557 • 4,359
Morehouse, MO 63868 • 1,220
Morehouse □, LA • 34,803
Morenci, AZ 85540 • 1,200
Morenci, MI 49256 • 2,110
Morgan, MN 56266 • 975
Morgan, UT 84050 • 1,896
Morgan □, AL • 90,231
Morgan □, CO • 22,513
Morgan □, GA • 11,572
Morgan □, IL • 37,502
Morgan □, IN • 51,999
Morgan □, KY • 12,103
Morgan □, MO • 13,807
Morgan □, OH • 14,241
Morgan □, TN • 16,604
Morgan □, UT • 4,917
Morgan □, WV • 10,711
Morgan City, LA 70380 • 16,114
Morganfield, KY 42437 • 3,781
Morgan Hill, CA 95037 • 17,060
Morganton, NC 28655 • 13,763
Morgantown, IN 46160 • 897
Morgantown, KY 42261 • 2,000
Morgantown, MS 39120 • 3,445
Morgantown, PA 19543 • 800
Morgantown, WV 26505 • 27,605
Morganville, NJ 07751 • 900
Morganza, LA 70759 • 846
Moriarty, NM 87035 • 1,276
Morley, MO 63767 • 745
Morningdale, MA 01530 • 1,150
Morning Sun, IA 52640 • 959
Morocco, IN 47963 • 1,348
Moroni, UT 84646 • 1,086
Morrill, NE 69358 • 1,097
Morrill □, NE • 6,085
Morrilton, AR 72110 • 7,355
Morris, AL 35116 • 623
Morris, IL 60450 • 8,833
Morris, MN 56267 • 5,367
Morris, NY 13808 • 681
Morris, OK 74445 • 1,288
Morris □, KS • 6,419
Morris □, NJ • 407,630
Morris □, TX • 14,629
Morrison, IL 61270 • 4,605
Morrison, OK 73061 • 671
Morrison □, MN • 29,311
Morrison City, TN 37660 • 2,032
Morrisonville, IL 62546 • 1,208
Morrisonville, NY 12962 • 1,500
Morris Plains, NJ 07950 • 5,305
Morristown, IN 46161 • 989
Morristown, MN 55052 • 639
Morristown, NJ 07960 • 16,614
Morristown, TN 37814 • 19,683
Morrisville, NY 13408 • 2,707
Morrisville, PA 19067 • 9,845
Morrisville, VT 05661 • 2,074
Morro Bay, CA 93442 • 9,064
Morrow, GA 30260 • 3,791
Morrow, OH 45152 • 1,254
Morrow □, OH • 26,480
Morrow □, OR • 7,519
Morse, LA 70559 • 835
Morton, IL 61550 • 14,178

Morton, MS 39117 • 3,303
Morton, TX 79346 • 2,674
Morton, WA 98356 • 1,264
Morton □, KS • 3,454
Morton □, ND • 25,177
Morton Grove, IL 60053 • 23,747
Mortons Gap, KY 42440 • 1,201
Morven, NC 28119 • 765
Moscow, ID 83843 • 16,513
Moscow, PA 18444 • 1,536
Moses Lake, WA 98837 • 10,629
Mosheim, TN 37818 • 1,539
Mosinee, WI 54455 • 3,015
Moss Bluff, LA 70611 • 7,004
Moss Point, MS 39563 • 18,998
Motley □, TX • 1,950
Mott, ND 58646 • 1,315
Moulton, AL 35650 • 3,197
Moulton, IA 52572 • 762
Moultrie, GA 31768 • 15,708
Moultrie □, IL • 14,546
Mound, MN 55364 • 9,280
Mound Bayou, MS 38762 • 2,917
Mound City, IL 62963 • 1,102
Mound City, KS 66056 • 755
Mound City, MO 64470 • 1,447
Moundridge, KS 67107 • 1,453
Mounds, IL 62964 • 1,669
Mounds, OK 74047 • 1,086
Mounds View, MN 55432 • 12,593
Moundsville, WV 26041 • 12,419
Moundville, AL 35474 • 1,310
Mountainair, NM 87036 • 1,170
Mountainaire, AZ 86001 • 700
Mountain Brook, AL 35223 • 19,718
Mountain City, GA 30562 • 701
Mountain City, TN 37683 • 2,125
Mountain Dale, NY 12763 • 1,200
Mountain Grove, MO 65711 • 3,974
Mountain Home, AR 72653 • 8,066
Mountain Home, ID 83647 • 7,540
Mountain Iron, MN 55768 • 4,134
Mountain Lake, MN 56159 • 2,277
Mountain Lake Park, MD 21550 • 1,597
Mountain Lakes, NJ 07046 • 4,153
Mountain Pine, AR 71956 • 1,068
Mountainside, NJ 07092 • 7,118
Mountain View, AR 72560 • 2,147
Mountain View, CA 94040-43 • 58,655
Mountain View, CO 80521 • 1,693
Mountain View, MO 65548 • 1,664
Mountain View, NM 87105 • 1,900
Mountain View, OK 73062 • 1,189
Mountain View, WY 82601 • 1,500
Mountain View, WY 82939 • 628
Mount Airy, GA 30563 • 670
Mount Airy, MD 21771 • 2,450
Mount Airy, NC 27030 • 6,862
Mount Angel, OR 97362 • 2,876
Mount Arlington, NJ 07856 • 4,251
Mount Ayr, IA 50854 • 1,938
Mount Carmel, IL 62863 • 8,908
Mount Carmel, OH 45244 • 900
Mount Carmel, PA 17851 • 8,190
Mount Carroll, IL 61053 • 1,936
Mount Clare, WV 26408 • 900
Mount Clemens, MI 48043-46 • 18,806
Mount Dora, FL 32757 • 5,883
Mount Ephraim, NJ 08059 • 4,863
Mount Freedom, NJ 07970 • 1,621
Mount Gay, WV 25637 • 1,650
Mount Gilead, NC 27306 • 1,423
Mount Gilead, OH 43338 • 2,911
Mount Healthy, OH 45231 • 7,562
Mount Holly, NJ 08060 • 10,818
Mount Holly, NC 28120 • 4,530
Mount Holly Springs, PA 17065 • 2,068
Mount Hope, KS 67108 • 791
Mount Hope, WV 25880 • 1,849
Mount Horeb, WI 53572 • 3,251
Mount Ida, AR 71957 • 1,023
Mount Jackson, VA 22842 • 1,419
Mount Jewett, PA 16740 • 1,053
Mount Joy, PA 17552 • 5,680
Mount Juliet, TN 37122 • 2,879
Mount Kisco, NY 10549 • 8,025
Mountlake Terrace, WA 98043 • 16,534
Mount Lebanon, PA 15228 • 34,414
Mount Morris, IL 61054 • 2,989
Mount Morris, MI 48458 • 3,246
Mount Morris, NY 14510 • 3,039
Mount Olive, AL 35117 • 1,900
Mount Olive, IL 62069 • 2,357
Mount Olive, MS 39119 • 993
Mount Olive, NC 28365 • 4,876
Mount Orab, OH 45154 • 1,573
Mount Penn, PA 19606 • 3,025
Mount Pleasant, IA 52641 • 7,322
Mount Pleasant, MI 48858 • 23,746
Mount Pleasant, NC 28124 • 1,210
Mount Pleasant, PA 15666 • 5,354
Mount Pleasant, SC 29464 • 14,209
Mount Pleasant, TN 38474 • 3,375
Mount Pleasant, TX 75455 • 11,003
Mount Pleasant, UT 84647 • 2,049
Mount Pocono, PA 18344 • 1,237
Mount Prospect, IL 60056 • 52,634
Mount Pulaski, IL 62548 • 1,783
Mount Rainier, MD 20712 • 7,361
Mount Savage, MD 21545 • 1,640

Mount Shasta, CA 96067 • 2,837
Mount Sterling, IL 62353 • 2,186
Mount Sterling, KY 40353 • 5,820
Mount Sterling, OH 43143 • 1,623
Mount Union, PA 17066 • 3,101
Mount Vernon, AL 36560 • 1,038
Mount Vernon, GA 30445 • 1,737
Mount Vernon, IL 62864 • 17,193
Mount Vernon, IN 47620 • 7,656
Mount Vernon, IA 52314 • 3,325
Mount Vernon, KY 40456 • 2,334
Mount Vernon, MO 65712 • 3,341
Mount Vernon, NY 10550-59 • 66,713
Mount Vernon, OH 43050 • 14,323
Mount Vernon, TX 75457 • 2,025
Mount Vernon, WA 98273 • 13,009
Mount Victory, OH 43340 • 667
Mount Washington, KY 40047 • 3,997
Mount Wolf, PA 17347 • 1,517
Mount Zion, IL 62549 • 4,563
Moville, IA 51039 • 1,273
Moweaqua, IL 62550 • 1,922
Mower □, MN • 40,390
Moxee City, WA 98936 • 687
Moyock, NC 27958 • 700
Muenster, TX 76252 • 1,408
Muhlenberg □, KY • 32,238
Muir, MI 48860 • 658
Mukilteo, WA 98275 • 1,426
Mukwonago, WI 53149 • 4,014
Mulberry, AR 72947 • 1,444
Mulberry, FL 33860 • 2,932
Mulberry, IN 46058 • 1,225
Mulberry, KS 66756 • 647
Mulberry, NC 28659 • 1,210
Mulberry, OH 45150 • 800
Mulberry Grove, IL 62262 • 707
Muldraugh, KY 40155 • 1,752
Muldrow, OK 74948 • 2,538
Muleshoe, TX 79347 • 4,842
Mullan, ID 83846 • 1,269
Mullen, NE 69152 • 720
Mullens, WV 25882 • 2,919
Mullica Hill, NJ 08062 • 1,050
Mullins, SC 29574 • 6,068
Multnomah □, OR • 562,640
Mulvane, KS 67110 • 4,254
Muncie, IN 47302-06 • 77,216
Muncy, PA 17756 • 2,700
Munday, TX 76371 • 1,738
Mundelein, IL 60060 • 17,053
Munford, TN 38058 • 2,336
Munfordville, KY 42765 • 1,783
Munhall, PA 15120 • 14,535
Munising, MI 49862 • 3,083
Munster, IN 46321 • 20,671
Murdo, SD 57559 • 723
Murfreesboro, AR 71958 • 1,883
Murfreesboro, NC 27855 • 3,007
Murfreesboro, TN 37130 • 32,845
Murphy, MO 63026 • 8,121
Murphy, NC 28906 • 2,070
Murphys, CA 95247 • 950
Murphysboro, IL 62966 • 9,866
Murray, IA 50174 • 703
Murray, KY 42071 • 14,248
Murray, UT 84107 • 25,750
Murray □, GA • 19,685
Murray □, MN • 11,507
Murray □, OK • 12,147
Murrayville, IL 62668 • 712
Murrells Inlet, SC 29576 • 950
Murrysville, PA 17601 • 16,036
Muscatine, IA 52761 • 23,467
Muscatine □, IA • 40,436
Muscle Shoals, AL 35662 • 8,911
Muscoda, WI 53573 • 1,331
Muscogee □, GA • 170,108
Muscoy, CA 92405 • 6,188
Muse, PA 15350 • 1,233
Muskego, WI 53150 • 15,277
Muskegon, MI 49440-45 • 40,823
Muskegon □, MI • 157,589
Muskegon Heights, MI 49444 • 14,611
Muskingum □, OH • 83,340
Muskogee, OK 74401-03 • 40,011
Muskogee □, OK • 66,939
Musselshell □, MT • 4,428
Mustang, OK 73064 • 7,496
Myerstown, PA 17067 • 3,131
Myrtle Beach, SC 29577-79 • 18,446
Myrtle Creek, OR 97457 • 3,365
Myrtle Grove, FL 32506 • 14,238
Myrtle Point, OR 97458 • 2,859
Mystic, CT 06355 • 2,333
Mystic, IA 52574 • 665

N

Naalehu, HI 96772 • 1,168
Nabnasset, MA 01886 • 4,800
Naches, WA 98937 • 644
Naco, AZ 85620 • 800
Nacogdoches, TX 75961 • 27,149
Nacogdoches □, TX • 46,786
Nags Head, NC 27959 • 1,020
Nahant, MA 01908 • 3,947
Nahunta, GA 31553 • 951
Nampa, ID 83651 • 25,112
Nanakuli, HI 96792 • 8,185
Nance □, NE • 4,740
Nanticoke, PA 18634 • 13,044

Nantucket, MA 02554 • 3,229
Nantucket □, MA • 5,087
Nanty Glo, PA 15943 • 3,936
Nanuet, NY 10954 • 8,300
Napa, CA 94558-59 • 50,879
Napa □, CA • 99,199
Napanoch, NY 12458 • 800
Napavine, WA 98565 • 611
Naperville, IL 60540 • 42,601
Naples, FL 33940-42 • 17,581
Naples, NY 14512 • 1,225
Naples, TX 75568 • 1,908
Napoleon, ND 58561 • 1,103
Napoleon, OH 43545 • 8,614
Napoleonville, LA 70390 • 829
Nappanee, IN 46550 • 4,694
Naranja, FL 33032 • 5,000
Narberth, PA 19072 • 4,496
Narragansett, RI 02882 • 3,342
Narrows, VA 24124 • 2,516
Narrowsburg, NY 12764 • 700
Naselle, WA 98638 • 900
Nash, TX 75569 • 2,022
Nash □, NC • 67,153
Nashua, IA 50658 • 1,846
Nashua, NH 03060-63 • 67,865
Nashville, AR 71852 • 4,554
Nashville, GA 31639 • 4,831
Nashville, IL 62263 • 3,186
Nashville, IN 47448 • 705
Nashville, MI 49073 • 1,628
Nashville, NC 27856 • 3,033
Nashville, TN 37201-99 • 455,651
Nashwauk, MN 55769 • 1,419
Nassau, NY 12123 • 1,285
Nassau □, FL • 32,894
Nassau □, NY • 1,321,582
Nassau Shores, NY 11758 • 5,500
Nassawadox, VA 23413 • 630
Natalbany, LA 70451 • 700
Natalia, TX 78059 • 1,264
Natchez, MS 39120 • 22,015
Natchitoches, LA 71457 • 16,664
Natchitoches □, LA • 36,863
Natick, MA 01760 • 29,461
National City, CA 92050 • 48,772
National Park, NJ 08063 • 3,552
Natrona □, WY • 61,856
Natrona Heights, PA 15065 • 13,252
Natural Bridge, NY 13665 • 650
Naturita, CO 81422 • 819
Naugatuck, CT 06770 • 26,456
Nautilus Park, CT 06340 • 6,500
Nauvoo, IL 62354 • 1,133
Navajo □, AZ • 67,629
Navarre, OH 44662 • 1,343
Navarro □, TX • 35,323
Navasota, TX 77868 • 5,971
Navesink, NJ 07752 • 1,500
Naylor, MO 63953 • 602
Nazareth, KY 40048 • 700
Nazareth, PA 18064 • 5,443
Neah Bay, WA 98357 • 1,000
Nebraska City, NE 68410 • 7,127
Necedah, WI 54646 • 773
Nederland, CO 80466 • 1,212
Nederland, TX 77627 • 16,855
Nedrow, NY 13120 • 3,000
Needham, MA 02192 • 27,901
Needles, CA 92363 • 4,120
Needville, TX 77461 • 1,417
Neenah, WI 54956 • 22,432
Neffs, OH 43940 • 1,106
Neffsville, PA 17601 • 1,300
Negaunee, MI 49866 • 5,189
Negley, OH 44441 • 900
Neillsville, WI 54456 • 2,780
Nekoosa, WI 54457 • 2,519
Neligh, NE 68756 • 1,893
Nelson, NE 68961 • 733
Nelson □, KY • 27,584
Nelson □, ND • 5,233
Nelson □, VA • 12,204
Nelsonville, OH 45764 • 4,567
Nemacolin, PA 15351 • 1,273
Nemaha □, KS • 11,221
Nemaha □, NE • 8,367
Neodesha, KS 66757 • 3,414
Neoga, IL 62447 • 1,736
Neola, IA 51559 • 839
Neopit, WI 54150 • 1,122
Neosho, MO 64850 • 9,493
Neosho □, KS • 18,967
Nephi, UT 84648 • 3,285
Neptune, NJ 07753 • 28,366
Neptune Beach, FL 32233 • 5,248
Neptune City, NJ 07753 • 5,276
Nesconset, NY 11767 • 8,300
Nescopeck, PA 18635 • 1,768
Neshoba □, MS • 23,789
Nesquehoning, PA 18240 • 3,346
Ness □, KS • 4,498
Ness City, KS 67560 • 1,769
Netcong, NJ 07857 • 3,557
Nettleton, MS 38858 • 1,911
Nevada, IA 50201 • 5,912
Nevada, MO 64772 • 9,044
Nevada, OH 44849 • 945
Nevada □, AR • 11,097
Nevada □, CA • 51,645
Nevada City, CA 95959 • 2,431
New Albany, IN 47150 • 37,103
New Albany, MS 38652 • 7,072
New Albin, IA 52160 • 609
Newark, AR 72562 • 1,128
Newark, CA 94560 • 32,126

Newark, DE 19711-13 • 25,247
Newark, IL 60541 • 798
Newark, NJ 07101-99 • 329,248
Newark, NY 14513 • 10,017
Newark, OH 43055 • 41,200
Newark Valley, NY 13811 • 1,190
New Athens, IL 62264 • 1,937
Newaygo, MI 49337 • 1,271
Newaygo □, MI • 34,917
New Baden, IL 62265 • 2,476
New Baltimore, MI 48047 • 5,439
New Baltimore, NY 12124 • 700
New Bedford, MA 02740-48 • 98,478
New Bedford, PA 16140 • 900
Newberg, OR 97132 • 10,394
New Berlin, IL 62670 • 834
New Berlin, NY 13411 • 1,392
New Berlin, PA 17855 • 783
New Berlin, WI 53151 • 30,529
New Bern, NC 28560 • 14,557
Newbern, TN 38059 • 2,794
Newberry, FL 32669 • 1,826
Newberry, MI 49868 • 2,120
Newberry, SC 29108 • 9,866
Newberry □, SC • 31,242
Newberry Springs, CA 92365 • 900
New Bethlehem, PA 16242 • 1,441
New Bloomfield, PA 17068 • 1,109
New Boston, IL 61272 • 731
New Boston, MI 48164 • 1,200
New Boston, OH 45662 • 3,188
New Boston, TX 75570 • 4,628
New Braunfels, TX 78130 • 22,402
New Bremen, OH 45869 • 2,393
New Brighton, MN 55112 • 23,269
New Brighton, PA 15066 • 7,364
New Britain, CT 06050-53 • 73,840
New Brockton, AL 36351 • 1,392
New Brunswick, NJ 08901-99 • 41,442
New Buffalo, MI 49117 • 2,821
Newburg, MO 65550 • 743
Newburg, WI 53060 • 783
Newburgh, IN 47630 • 2,906
Newburgh, NY 12550 • 23,438
Newburgh Heights, OH 44105 • 2,678
Newbury, MA 01950 • 900
Newburyport, MA 01950 • 15,900
New Canaan, CT 06840 • 17,931
New Carlisle, IN 46552 • 1,439
New Carlisle, OH 45344 • 6,498
New Carrollton, MD 20784 • 12,632
New Cassel, NY 11590 • 8,817
New Castle, IN 47362 • 20,056
New Castle, DE 19720 • 4,907
New Castle, KY 40050 • 832
New Castle, NH 03854 • 975
Newcastle, OK 73065 • 3,076
New Castle, PA 16101-08 • 33,621
Newcastle, TX 76372 • 688
Newcastle, WY 82701 • 3,596
New Castle □, DE • 398,115
New City, NY 10956 • 30,800
Newcomb, NY 12852 • 900
Newcomerstown, OH 43832 • 3,986
New Concord, OH 43762 • 1,860
New Cumberland, PA 17070 • 8,051
New Cumberland, WV 26047 • 1,752
New Egypt, NJ 08533 • 2,111
Newell, IA 50568 • 913
Newell, SD 57760 • 638
Newell, WV 26050 • 1,900
New Ellenton, SC 29809 • 2,628
Newellton, LA 71357 • 1,726
New England, ND 58647 • 825
New Fairfield, CT 06812 • 2,150
Newfane, NY 14108 • 2,700
Newfield, NJ 08344 • 1,563
Newfields, NH 03856 • 700
New Florence, MO 63363 • 731
New Florence, PA 15944 • 855
Newfoundland, NJ 07435 • 900
New Franklin, MO 65274 • 1,228
New Freedom, PA 17349 • 2,205
New Glarus, WI 53574 • 1,763
Newhall, CA 91321 • 12,029
Newhall, IA 52315 • 899
New Hampton, IA 50659 • 3,940
New Hanover □, NC • 103,471
New Harmony, IN 47631 • 945
New Hartford, CT 06057 • 1,310
New Hartford, IA 50660 • 764
New Haven, CT 06501-99 • 126,109
New Haven, IN 46774 • 6,714
New Haven, KY 40051 • 926
New Haven, MI 48048 • 1,871
New Haven, MO 63068 • 1,581
New Haven, WV 25265 • 1,723
New Haven □, CT • 761,337
New Holland, GA 30501 • 800
New Holland, OH 43145 • 783
New Holland, PA 17557 • 4,147
New Holstein, WI 53061 • 3,412
New Hope, AL 35760 • 1,546
New Hope, MN 55428 • 23,087
New Hope, PA 18938 • 1,473
New Hudson, MI 48165 • 800
New Hyde Park, NY 11040 • 9,801
New Iberia, LA 70560 • 32,766
Newington, CT 06111 • 28,841
New Johnsonville, TN 37134 • 1,824
New Kensington, PA 15068 • 17,660
New Kent □, VA • 8,781

Newkirk, OK 74647 • 2,413
New Knoxville, OH 45871 • 760
Newland, NC 28657 • 722
New Lebanon, NY 12125 • 800
New Lenox, IL 60451 • 5,792
New Lexington, OH 43764 • 5,179
New Lisbon, WI 53950 • 1,390
Newllano, LA 71461 • 2,213
New London, CT 06320 • 28,842
New London, IA 52645 • 2,043
New London, MN 56273 • 812
New London, MO 63459 • 1,161
New London, NH 03257 • 1,335
New London, OH 44851 • 2,449
New London, WI 54961 • 6,210
New London □, CT • 238,409
New Lothrop, MI 48460 • 646
New Madison, OH 45346 • 1,008
New Madrid, MO 63869 • 3,204
New Madrid □, MO • 22,945
Newman, CA 95360 • 2,785
Newman, IL 61942 • 1,079
Newman Grove, NE 68758 • 930
Newmanstown, PA 17073 • 1,532
New Market, IN 47965 • 608
Newmarket, NH 03857 • 3,749
New Market, TN 37820 • 1,216
New Market, VA 22844 • 1,118
New Martinsville, WV 26155 • 7,109
New Matamoras, OH 45767 • 1,172
New Miami, OH 45011 • 2,980
New Milford, CT 06776 • 5,186
New Milford, NJ 07646 • 16,876
New Milford, PA 18834 • 1,040
Newnan, GA 30263–65 • 11,449
New Orleans, LA 70101–99 • 557,927
New Oxford, PA 17350 • 1,921
New Palestine, IN 46163 • 749
New Paltz, NY 12561 • 4,938
New Paris, IN 46553 • 1,062
New Paris, OH 45347 • 1,709
New Philadelphia, OH 44663 • 16,883
New Philadelphia, PA 17959 • 1,341
New Plymouth, ID 83655 • 1,186
Newport, AR 72112 • 8,339
Newport, DE 19804 • 1,167
Newport, IN 47966 • 704
Newport, KY 41071–76 • 21,587
Newport, ME 04953 • 1,740
Newport, MI 48166 • 900
Newport, MN 55055 • 3,323
Newport, NH 03773 • 4,388
Newport, NC 28570 • 1,883
Newport, NY 13416 • 746
Newport, OH 45768 • 950
Newport, OR 97365 • 7,519
Newport, PA 17074 • 1,600
Newport, RI 02840 • 29,259
Newport, TN 37821 • 7,580
Newport, VT 05855 • 4,756
Newport, WA 99156 • 1,665
Newport □, RI • 81,383
Newport Beach, CA 92660–63 • 62,556
Newport Hills, WA 98006 • 6,000
Newport News, VA 23601–07 • 144,903
New Port Richey, FL 33552–53 • 11,196
New Prague, MN 56071 • 2,952
New Preston, CT 06777 • 1,209
New Providence, NJ 07974 • 12,426
New Richland, MN 56072 • 1,263
New Richmond, OH 45157 • 2,769
New Richmond, WI 54017 • 4,306
New Roads, LA 70760 • 3,924
New Rochelle, NY 10801–99 • 70,794
New Rockford, ND 58356 • 1,791
New Salem, ND 58563 • 1,081
New Sarpy, LA 70078 • 2,249
New Sharon, IA 50207 • 1,225
New Smyrna Beach, FL 32069 • 13,557
New Straitsville, OH 43766 • 937
New Tazwell, TN 37825 • 1,677
Newton, AL 36352 • 1,540
Newton, GA 31770 • 711
Newton, IL 62448 • 3,186
Newton, IA 50208 • 15,292
Newton, KS 67114 • 16,332
Newton, MA 02158 • 83,622
Newton, MS 39345 • 3,708
Newton, NJ 07860 • 7,748
Newton, NC 28658 • 7,624
Newton, TX 75966 • 1,620
Newton, UT 84327 • 623
Newton □, AR • 7,756
Newton □, GA • 34,489
Newton □, IN • 14,844
Newton □, MS • 19,944
Newton □, MO • 40,555
Newton □, TX • 13,254
Newton Falls, OH 44444 • 4,960
Newtown, CT 06470 • 2,022
New Town, ND 58763 • 1,335
Newtown, OH 45244 • 1,817
Newtown Square, PA 19073 • 11,775
New Ulm, MN 56073 • 13,755
New Vienna, OH 45159 • 1,133
Newville, AL 36353 • 814
Newville, PA 17241 • 1,370
New Washington, OH 44854 • 1,213

New Washoe City, NV 89701 • 2,543
New Waterford, OH 44445 • 1,314
New Waverly, TX 77358 • 824
New Whiteland, IN 46184 • 4,502
New Wilmington, PA 16142 • 2,774
New Windsor, IL 61465 • 863
New Windsor, MD 21776 • 799
New Windsor, NY 12550 • 8,803
New York, NY 10001–99 • 7,071,639
New York □, NY • 1,428,285
New York Mills, MN 56567 • 972
Nez Perce □, ID • 33,220
Niagara, WI 54151 • 2,079
Niagara □, NY • 227,354
Niagara Falls, NY 14301–99 • 71,384
Niantic, CT 06357 • 3,151
Nibley, UT 84321 • 1,036
Niceville, FL 32578 • 8,543
Nicholas □, KY • 7,157
Nicholas □, WV • 28,126
Nicholasville, KY 40356 • 10,319
Nicholls, GA 31554 • 1,114
Nichols, NY 13812 • 613
Nichols, SC 29581 • 606
Nichols Hills, OK 73116 • 4,171
Nicholson, PA 18446 • 945
Nickerson, KS 67561 • 1,292
Nicollet, MN 56074 • 709
Nicollet □, MN • 26,929
Nicoma Park, OK 73066 • 2,588
Nikishka, AK 99635 • 1,109
Niland, CA 92257 • 1,042
Niles, IL 60648 • 30,363
Niles, MI 49120 • 13,115
Niles, OH 44446 • 23,088
Ninety Six, SC 29666 • 2,249
Niobrara □, WY • 2,924
Niota, TN 37826 • 765
Nipomo, CA 93444 • 5,247
Niskayuna, NY 12309 • 17,471
Nisswa, MN 56468 • 1,407
Nitro, WV 25143 • 8,074
Nixa, MO 65714 • 2,662
Nixon, TX 78140 • 2,008
Noank, CT 06340 • 1,406
Noble, IL 62868 • 832
Noble, OK 73068 • 3,497
Noble □, IN • 35,443
Noble □, OH • 11,310
Noble □, OK • 11,573
Nobles □, MN • 21,040
Noblesville, IN 46060 • 12,056
Nocatee, FL 33864 • 1,300
Nocona, TX 76255 • 2,992
Nodaway □, MO • 21,996
Noel, MO 64854 • 1,161
Nogales, AZ 85621 • 15,683
Nokomis, FL 33555 • 3,108
Nokomis, IL 62075 • 2,656
Nolan □, TX • 17,359
Nome, AK 99762 • 2,301
Nora Springs, IA 50458 • 1,572
Norborne, MO 64668 • 931
Norco, CA 91760 • 21,126
Norco, LA 70079 • 4,416
Norcross, GA 30071 • 3,317
Norfolk, CT 06058 • 1,500
Norfolk, NE 68701 • 19,449
Norfolk, NY 13667 • 1,379
Norfolk, VA 23501–99 • 266,979
Norfolk □, MA • 606,587
Norland, FL 33169 • 19,471
Norlina, NC 27563 • 901
Norma, NJ 08347 • 800
Normal, AL 35762 • 5,000
Normal, IL 61761 • 35,672
Norman, OK 73069–71 • 68,020
Norman □, MN • 9,379
Normandy, MO 63121 • 5,174
Normangee, TX 77871 • 636
Norman Park, GA 31771 • 757
Norphlet, AR 71759 • 756
Norridge, IL 60656 • 16,483
Norridgewock, ME 04957 • 1,318
Norris, SC 29667 • 903
Norris, TN 37828 • 1,374
Norris City, IL 62869 • 1,515
Norristown, PA 19401–09 • 34,684
North, SC 29112 • 1,304
North Abington, MA 02351 • 4,700
North Acton, MA 01720 • 900
North Adams, MA 01247 • 18,063
North Albany, OR 97321 • 4,499
North Amherst, MA 01059 • 5,616
North Amityville, NY 11701 • 11,936
Northampton, MA 01060 • 29,286
Northampton, PA 18067 • 8,240
Northampton □, NC • 22,584
Northampton □, PA • 225,418
Northampton □, VA • 14,625
North Andover, MA 01845 • 20,129
North Andrews Gardens, FL 33308 • 8,967
North Apollo, PA 15673 • 1,487
North Arlington, NJ 07032 • 16,587
North Atlanta, GA 30319 • 22,800
North Attleboro, MA 02760–63 • 21,095
North Augusta, SC 29841 • 13,593
North Aurora, IL 60542 • 5,205
North Babylon, NY 11703 • 23,000
North Baltimore, OH 45872 • 3,127
North Beach, MD 20714 • 1,504
North Bellmore, NY 11710 • 23,600
North Belmont, NC 28012 • 5,000
North Bend, NE 68649 • 1,368

North Bend, OR 97459 • 9,779
North Bend, PA 17760 • 700
North Bend, WA 98045 • 1,701
North Bennington, VT 05257 • 1,635
North Bergen, NJ 07047 • 47,019
North Berwick, ME 03906 • 1,436
North Billerica, MA 01862 • 6,700
Northborough, MA 01532 • 5,670
North Braddock, PA 15104 • 8,711
North Branch, MI 48461 • 896
North Branch, MN 55056 • 1,597
North Branch, NH 03440 • 800
North Branch, NJ 08876 • 2,500
North Branford, CT 06471 • 5,200
Northbridge, MA 01534 • 3,321
Northbrook, IL 60062 • 30,778
Northbrook, OH 45231 • 8,357
North Brookfield, MA 01535 • 2,677
North Brunswick, NJ 08902 • 22,220
North Caldwell, NJ 07006 • 5,832
North Canton, OH 44720 • 14,228
North Cape May, NJ 08204 • 4,029
North Carrollton, MS 38947 • 859
North Carver, MA 02355 • 700
North Charleston, SC 29406 • 62,534
North Chicago, IL 60064 • 38,774
North City, WA 98155 • 6,200
North Cohasset, MA 02025 • 900
North College Hill, OH 45239 • 11,114
North Collins, NY 14111 • 1,496
North Conway, NH 03860 • 2,184
North Corbin, KY 40701 • 1,000
North Creek, NY 12853 • 950
North Crossett, AR 71635 • 3,513
North Dartmouth, MA 02747 • 6,000
North Decatur, GA 30033 • 11,830
North Dighton, MA 02764 • 1,174
North Druid Hills, GA 30033 • 8,700
North Eagle Butte, SD 57625 • 1,354
North East, MD 21901 • 1,469
North East, PA 16428 • 4,568
North Eastham, MA 02651 • 1,318
Northeast Henrietta, NY 14534 • 12,000
North Easton, MA 02356 • 6,100
North English, IA 52316 • 990
North Enid, OK 73701 • 992
North Fair Oaks, CA 94025 • 10,294
North Falmouth, MA 02556 • 1,800
Northfield, IL 60093 • 5,807
Northfield, MA 01360 • 1,182
Northfield, MN 55057 • 12,562
Northfield, NH 03276 • 1,340
Northfield, NJ 08225 • 7,795
Northfield, OH 44067 • 3,913
Northfield, VT 05663 • 2,033
North Fond du Lac, WI 54935 • 3,844
Northford, CT 06472 • 2,800
North Fork, CA 93643 • 950
North Fort Myers, FL 33903 • 17,200
North Freedom, WI 53951 • 616
Northglenn, CO 80233 • 29,847
North Grafton, MA 01536 • 3,400
North Great River, NY 11722 • 12,400
North Grosvenordale, CT 06255 • 1,856
North Gulfport, MS 39501 • 6,660
North Haledon, NJ 07508 • 8,177
North Hampton, NH 03862 • 1,000
North Hanover, MA 02339 • 900
North Haven, CT 06473 • 22,080
North Highlands, CA 95660 • 37,825
North Hudson, WI 54016 • 2,218
North Industry, OH 44707 • 3,250
North Judson, IN 46366 • 1,653
North Kansas City, MO 64116 • 4,507
North Kingstown, RI 02852 • 3,100
North Kingsville, OH 44068 • 2,939
North La Junta, CO 81050 • 1,076
Northlake, IL 60164 • 12,166
North Las Vegas, NV 89030 • 42,739
North Lauderdale, FL 33068 • 18,653
North Lewisburg, OH 43060 • 1,072
North Liberty, IN 46554 • 1,211
North Liberty, IA 52317 • 2,046
North Lima, OH 44452 • 900
North Lindenhurst, NY 11757 • 11,400
North Little Rock, AR 72114–19 • 64,288
North Logan, UT 84321 • 2,258
North Manchester, IN 46962 • 5,998
North Mankato, MN 56001 • 9,145
North Massapequa, NY 11758 • 23,100
North Merrick, NY 11566 • 13,650
North Merrydale, LA 70812 • 3,500
North Miami, FL 33161 • 36,553
North Miami Beach, FL 33162 • 36,481
North Middletown, KY 40357 • 637
North Muskegon, MI 49445 • 4,024
North Myrtle Beach, SC 29582 • 3,960
North Naples, FL 33940 • 7,950
North New Hyde Park, NY 11040 • 16,100

North Oaks, CA 91350 • 5,800
North Ogden, UT 84404 • 9,309
North Olmsted, OH 44070 • 36,486
North Omaha, NE 68112 • 1,100
North Oxford, MA 01537 • 1,550
North Palm Beach, FL 33408 • 11,344
North Park, IL 61111 • 15,806
North Patchogue, NY 11772 • 8,000
North Pembroke, MA 02358 • 2,215
North Plainfield, NJ 07060 • 19,108
North Plains, OR 97133 • 715
North Platte, NE 69101 • 24,509
Northport, AL 35476 • 14,291
North Port, FL 33596 • 6,205
Northport, MI 49670 • 611
Northport, NY 11768 • 7,651
North Prairie, WI 53153 • 938
North Providence, RI 02911 • 18,220
North Reading, MA 01864 • 11,455
North Richland Hills, TX 76118 • 30,592
Northridge, OH 45502 • 5,559
North Ridgeville, OH 44039 • 21,522
North Riverside, IL 60546 • 6,764
North Rose, NY 14516 • 700
North Royalton, OH 44133 • 17,671
North Salt Lake, UT 84054 • 5,548
North Scituate, MA 02060 • 4,100
North Sioux City, SD 57049 • 1,992
North Springfield, VT 05150 • 750
North Springfield, VA 22151 • 8,631
North Star, DE 19711 • 650
North St. Paul, MN 55109 • 11,921
North Stratford, NH 03590 • 650
North Sudbury, MA 01776 • 1,700
North Swansea, MA 02777 • 950
North Swanzey, NH 03431 • 950
North Syracuse, NY 13212 • 7,970
North Tarrytown, NY 10591 • 7,994
North Terre Haute, IN 47805 • 1,500
North Tewksbury, MA 01876 • 1,400
North Tonawanda, NY 14120 • 35,760
North Troy, VT 05859 • 717
North Truro, MA 02652 • 700
North Tunica, MS 38676 • 1,026
Northumberland, PA 17857 • 3,636
Northumberland □, PA • 100,381
Northumberland □, VA • 9,828
North Uxbridge, MA 01538 • 1,400
Northvale, NJ 07647 • 5,046
North Valley Stream, NY 11580 • 14,881
North Vassalboro, ME 04962 • 850
North Vernon, IN 47265 • 5,768
North Versailles, PA 15137 • 13,294
Northville, MI 48167 • 5,698
Northville, NY 12134 • 1,304
North Wales, PA 19454 • 3,391
North Walpole, NH 03609 • 950
North Wantagh, NY 11793 • 15,117
North Warren, PA 16365 • 1,360
North Webster, IN 46555 • 709
North Wildwood, NJ 08260 • 4,714
North Wilkesboro, NC 28659 • 3,260
North Wilmington, MA 01887 • 4,200
North Windham, CT 06256 • 750
North Windham, ME 04062 • 5,492
Northwood, IA 50459 • 2,193
Northwood, ND 58267 • 1,240
Northwood, OH 43619 • 5,495
Northwoods, MO 63121 • 5,831
North York, PA 17404 • 1,755
Norton, KS 67654 • 3,400
Norton, MA 02766 • 2,035
Norton, OH 44203 • 12,242
Norton, VA 24273 • 4,757
Norton □, KS • 6,689
Norton Shores, MI 49441 • 22,025
Nortonville, KS 66060 • 692
Nortonville, KY 42442 • 1,336
Norwalk, CA 90650 • 85,286
Norwalk, CT 06850–57 • 77,767
Norwalk, IA 50211 • 2,676
Norwalk, OH 44857 • 14,358
Norway, IA 52318 • 633
Norway, ME 04268 • 2,653
Norway, MI 49870 • 2,919
Norwell, MA 02061 • 800
Norwich, CT 06360 • 38,074
Norwich, NY 13815 • 8,082
Norwich, VT 05055 • 1,000
Norwood, MA 02062 • 29,711
Norwood, MN 55368 • 1,219
Norwood, NJ 07648 • 4,413
Norwood, NC 28128 • 1,818
Norwood, NY 13668 • 1,902
Norwood, OH 45212 • 26,342
Norwood, PA 19074 • 6,647
Norwoodville, IA 50317 • 1,400
Notasulga, AL 36866 • 876
Nottoway □, VA • 14,666
Novato, CA 94947 • 43,916
Novi, MI 48050 • 22,525
Novinger, MO 63559 • 626
Nowata, OK 74048 • 4,270
Nowata □, OK • 11,486
Noxen, PA 18636 • 800
Noxubee □, MS • 13,212
Nuckolls □, NE • 6,726
Nucla, CO 81424 • 1,027
Nueces □, TX • 268,215
Nunda, NY 14517 • 1,169
Nuremberg, PA 18241 • 800
Nutley, NJ 07110 • 28,998

Nutter Fort, WV 26301 • 2,078
Nutting Lake, MA 01865 • 2,400
Nyack, NY 10960 • 6,428
Nye □, NV • 9,048
Nyssa, OR 97913 • 2,862

O

Oak Bluffs, MA 02557 • 1,984
Oak Brook, IL 60521 • 6,641
Oak Creek, CO 80467 • 929
Oak Creek, WI 53154 • 16,932
Oakdale, CA 95361 • 8,474
Oakdale, GA 30080 • 800
Oakdale, LA 71463 • 7,155
Oakdale, MN 55119 • 12,123
Oakdale, NY 11769 • 7,800
Oakdale, PA 15071 • 1,955
Oakes, ND 58474 • 2,112
Oakfield, NY 14125 • 1,791
Oakfield, WI 53065 • 990
Oak Forest, IL 60452 • 26,096
Oak Grove, KY 42262 • 2,088
Oak Grove, LA 71263 • 2,214
Oak Grove, OR 97267 • 11,640
Oak Harbor, OH 43449 • 2,678
Oak Harbor, WA 98277 • 12,271
Oak Hill, FL 32759 • 938
Oak Hill, MI 49660 • 1,000
Oak Hill, OH 45656 • 1,713
Oak Hill, WV 25901 • 7,120
Oakhurst, NJ 07755 • 4,600
Oakhurst, OK 74050 • 2,000
Oakland, CA 94601–99 • 339,337
Oakland, FL 32760 • 658
Oakland, IL 61943 • 1,035
Oakland, IA 51560 • 1,552
Oakland, ME 04963 • 3,387
Oakland, MD 21550 • 1,994
Oakland, NE 68045 • 1,393
Oakland, NJ 07436 • 13,443
Oakland, OR 97462 • 886
Oakland, PA 18847 • 734
Oakland □, MI • 1,011,793
Oakland City, IN 47660 • 3,301
Oakland Park, FL 33334 • 23,035
Oak Lawn, IL 60453–59 • 60,590
Oaklawn, KS 67216 • 4,200
Oakley, ID 83346 • 663
Oakley, KS 67748 • 2,343
Oaklyn, NJ 08107 • 4,223
Oakman, AL 35579 • 770
Oakmont, PA 15139 • 7,039
Oak Park, IL 60301–99 • 54,887
Oak Park, MI 48237 • 31,537
Oak Ridge, NC 27310 • 950
Oakridge, OR 97463 • 3,729
Oak Ridge, TN 37830 • 27,662
Oaks, PA 19456 • 700
Oakton, VA 22124 • 900
Oaktown, IN 47561 • 776
Oak Valley, NJ 08090 • 7,000
Oakville, CT 06779 • 8,737
Oakville, MO 63129 • 1,100
Oakwood, GA 30566 • 723
Oakwood, IL 61858 • 1,627
Oakwood, OH 45419 • 3,786
Oakwood, OH 45873 • 886
Oakwood, TX 75855 • 606
Oberlin, KS 67749 • 2,387
Oberlin, LA 70655 • 1,764
Oberlin, OH 44074 • 8,660
Obetz, OH 43207 • 3,095
Obion, TN 38240 • 1,282
Obion □, TN • 32,781
Oblong, IL 62449 • 1,840
O'Brien □, IA • 16,972
Ocala, FL 32670–78 • 37,170
Ocean, NJ 07755 • 23,570
Ocean □, NJ • 346,038
Oceana, WV 24870 • 2,143
Oceana □, MI • 22,002
Ocean Bluff, MA 02065 • 2,500
Ocean City, FL 32548 • 5,582
Ocean City, MD 21842 • 4,946
Ocean City, NJ 08226 • 13,949
Ocean Gate, NJ 08740 • 1,385
Ocean Grove, MA 02777 • 4,000
Ocean Grove, NJ 07756 • 4,200
Ocean Park, WA 98640 • 1,500
Ocean Port, NJ 07757 • 5,888
Oceanside, CA 92054–56 • 76,698
Oceanside, NY 11572 • 36,400
Ocean Springs, MS 39564 • 14,504
Ochiltree □, TX • 9,588
Ochlocknee, GA 31773 • 627
Ocilla, GA 31774 • 3,436
Ocoee, FL 32761 • 7,803
Oconee □, GA • 12,427
Oconee □, SC • 48,611
Oconomowoc, WI 53066 • 9,909
Oconto, WI 54153 • 4,505
Oconto □, WI • 28,947
Oconto Falls, WI 54154 • 2,500
Odebolt, IA 51458 • 1,299
Odell, IL 60460 • 1,083
Odem, TX 78370 • 2,363
Odenton, MD 21113 • 7,500
Odenville, AL 35120 • 724
Odessa, FL 33556 • 950
Odessa, MO 64076 • 3,088
Odessa, NY 14869 • 613
Odessa, TX 79760–68 • 90,027
Odessa, WA 99159 • 1,009
Odin, IL 62870 • 1,285
Odon, IN 47562 • 1,463

O'Donnell, TX 79351 • 1,200
Oelwein, IA 50662 • 7,564
O'Fallon, IL 62269 • 12,241
O'Fallon, MO 63366 • 8,677
Ogallala, NE 69153 • 5,638
Ogden, IL 61859 • 818
Ogden, IA 50212 • 1,953
Ogden, KS 66517 • 1,804
Ogden, UT 84401-99 • 64,407
Ogdensburg, NJ 07439 • 2,737
Ogdensburg, NY 13669 • 12,375
Ogemaw □, MI • 16,436
Ogle □, IL • 46,338
Oglesby, IL 61348 • 3,979
Oglethorpe, GA 31068 • 1,305
Oglethorpe □, GA • 8,929
Ogunquit, ME 03907 • 1,492
Ohatchee, AL 36271 • 860
Ohio □, IN • 5,114
Ohio □, KY • 21,765
Ohio □, WV • 61,389
Ohio City, OH 45874 • 881
Ohioville, PA 15059 • 4,217
Oil City, LA 71061 • 1,323
Oil City, PA 16301 • 13,881
Oildale, CA 93308 • 23,382
Oilton, OK 74052 • 1,244
Ojai, CA 93023 • 6,816
Okaloosa □, FL • 109,920
Okanogan, WA 98840 • 2,302
Okanogan □, WA • 30,639
Okarche, OK 73762 • 1,064
Okauchee, WI 53069 • 1,800
Okauchee Lake, WI 53058 • 1,400
Okawville, IL 62271 • 1,337
Okeechobee, FL 33472 • 4,225
Okeechobee □, FL • 20,264
Okeene, OK 73763 • 1,601
Okemah, OK 74859 • 3,381
Okemos, MI 48864 • 8,882
Okfuskee □, OK • 11,125
Oklahoma □, OK • 568,933
Oklahoma City, OK 73101-99 • 403,136
Oklawaha, FL 32679 • 1,200
Okmulgee, OK 74447 • 16,263
Okmulgee □, OK • 39,169
Okolona, KY 40219 • 20,039
Okolona, MS 38860 • 3,409
Oktibbeha □, MS • 36,018
Ola, AR 72853 • 1,121
Olanta, SC 29114 • 699
Olathe, CO 81425 • 1,262
Olathe, KS 66061-62 • 37,258
Olcott, NY 14126 • 1,650
Old Bethpage, NY 11804 • 7,160
Old Bridge, NJ 08857 • 12,500
Oldenburg, IN 47036 • 770
Old Forge, NY 13420 • 950
Old Forge, PA 18518 • 9,304
Old Fort, NC 28762 • 752
Oldham □, KY • 27,795
Oldham □, TX • 2,283
Oldham Village, MA 02359 • 900
Old Orchard Beach, ME 04064 • 6,291
Old Saybrook, CT 06475 • 1,857
Oldsmar, FL 33557 • 2,608
Old Tappan, NJ 07675 • 4,168
Old Town, ME 04468 • 8,422
Olean, NY 14760 • 18,207
Oley, PA 19547 • 700
Olin, IA 52320 • 735
Olive Branch, MS 38654 • 2,067
Olive Hill, KY 41164 • 2,539
Olivehurst, CA 95961 • 8,929
Oliver, PA 15472 • 1,500
Oliver □, ND • 2,495
Oliver Springs, TN 37840 • 3,659
Olivet, MI 49076 • 1,604
Olivette, MO 63132 • 7,985
Olivia, MN 56277 • 2,802
Olla, LA 71465 • 1,603
Olmito, TX 78575 • 1,500
Olmos Park, TX 78212 • 2,069
Olmsted □, MN • 92,006
Olmsted Falls, OH 44138 • 5,868
Olney, IL 62450 • 9,026
Olney, MD 20832 • 10,000
Olney, TX 76374 • 4,060
Olton, TX 79064 • 2,235
Olustee, OK 73560 • 721
Olympia, WA 98501-07 • 27,447
Olympia Heights, FL 33165 • 33,112
Olyphant, PA 18447 • 5,204
Omaha, NE 68101-99 • 313,911
Omak, WA 98841 • 4,007
Omar, WV 25638 • 950
Omega, GA 31775 • 996
Omro, WI 54963 • 2,763
Onaga, KS 66521 • 752
Onalaska, WI 54650 • 9,249
Onamia, MN 56359 • 691
Onancock, VA 23417 • 1,461
Onarga, IL 60955 • 1,269
Onawa, IA 51040 • 3,283
Onaway, MI 49765 • 1,084
Oneco, FL 34264 • 6,417
Oneida, IL 61467 • 765
Oneida, NY 13421 • 10,810
Oneida, OH 45042 • 1,650
Oneida, TN 37841 • 3,717
Oneida □, ID • 3,258
Oneida □, NY • 253,466
Oneida □, WI • 31,216
O'Neill, NE 68763 • 4,049
Oneonta, AL 35121 • 4,824
Oneonta, NY 13820 • 14,933
Onida, SD 57564 • 851
Onondaga □, NY • 463,920
Onset, MA 02558 • 1,493
Onslow □, NC • 112,784
Onsted, MI 49265 • 670
Ontario, CA 91761-62 • 88,820
Ontario, NY 14519 • 750
Ontario, OH 44862 • 4,123
Ontario, OR 97914 • 8,814
Ontario □, NY • 88,909
Ontonagon, MI 49953 • 2,182
Ontonagon □, MI • 9,861
Oolitic, IN 47451 • 1,495
Oologah, OK 74053 • 798
Ooltewah, TN 37363 • 900
Oostburg, WI 53070 • 1,647
Opal Cliffs, CA 95062 • 5,041
Opa-Locka, FL 33054-56 • 14,460
Opelika, AL 36801 • 21,896
Opelousas, LA 70570 • 18,903
Opp, AL 36467 • 7,204
Opportunity, WA 99214 • 17,600
Oquawka, IL 61469 • 1,533
Oracle, AZ 85623 • 2,484
Oradell, NJ 07649 • 8,658
Oran, MO 63771 • 1,266
Orange, CA 92667-69 • 91,450
Orange, CT 06477 • 13,237
Orange, MA 01364 • 3,942
Orange, NJ 07050-52 • 31,136
Orange, TX 77630 • 23,628
Orange, VA 22960 • 2,631
Orange □, CA • 1,932,709
Orange □, FL • 471,016
Orange □, IN • 18,677
Orange □, NC • 77,055
Orange □, NY • 259,603
Orange □, TX • 83,838
Orange □, VT • 22,739
Orange □, VA • 18,063
Orangeburg, SC 29115 • 14,933
Orangeburg □, SC • 82,276
Orange City, FL 32763 • 2,795
Orange City, IA 51041 • 4,588
Orange Grove, MS 39501 • 2,700
Orange Grove, TX 78372 • 1,212
Orange Lake, FL 32681 • 950
Orangevale, CA 95662 • 20,585
Orangeville, UT 84537 • 1,309
Orchard City, CO 81410 • 1,914
Orchard Homes, MT 59801 • 4,000
Orchard Mesa, CO 81501 • 4,876
Orchard Park, NY 14127 • 3,671
Orchards, WA 98662 • 3,950
Orchard Valley, WY 82001 • 800
Orcutt, CA 93455 • 1,500
Ord, NE 68862 • 2,658
Ordway, CO 81063 • 1,135
Oreana, IL 62554 • 999
Ore City, TX 75683 • 1,050
Oregon, IL 61061 • 3,559
Oregon, MO 64473 • 901
Oregon, OH 43616 • 18,675
Oregon, WI 53575 • 3,876
Oregon □, MO • 10,238
Oregon City, OR 97045 • 14,673
Oreland, PA 19075 • 9,000
Orem, UT 84057-59 • 52,399
Orfordville, WI 53576 • 1,143
Orient, NY 11957 • 800
Orinda, CA 94563 • 16,825
Orion, IL 61273 • 2,013
Oriskany, NY 13424 • 1,680
Oriskany Falls, NY 13425 • 802
Orland, CA 95963 • 4,031
Orlando, FL 32801-99 • 128,291
Orland Park, IL 60462 • 23,045
Orleans, CA 95556 • 900
Orleans, IN 47452 • 2,161
Orleans, MA 02653 • 1,811
Orleans, VT 05860 • 983
Orleans □, LA • 557,927
Orleans □, NY • 38,496
Orleans □, VT • 23,440
Ormond Beach, FL 32074 • 21,378
Ormond By The Sea, FL 32074 • 7,665
Orofino, ID 83544 • 3,711
Oro Grande, CA 92368 • 900
Orono, ME 04473 • 10,578
Orono, MN 55323 • 6,845
Oroville, CA 95965 • 8,683
Oroville, WA 98844 • 1,483
Orrick, MO 64077 • 922
Orrville, OH 44667 • 7,511
Orting, WA 98360 • 1,787
Ortonville, MI 48462 • 1,190
Ortonville, MN 56278 • 2,550
Orwell, OH 44076 • 1,067
Orwigsburg, PA 17961 • 2,700
Osage, IA 50461 • 3,718
Osage □, KS • 15,319
Osage □, MO • 12,014
Osage □, OK • 39,327
Osage Beach, MO 65065 • 1,992
Osage City, KS 66523 • 2,667
Osakis, MN 56360 • 1,355
Osawatomie, KS 66064 • 4,459
Osborne, KS 67473 • 2,120
Osborne □, KS • 5,959
Osbornsville, NJ 08723 • 800
Osburn, ID 83849 • 2,220
Osceola, AR 72370 • 8,881
Osceola, IN 46561 • 1,990
Osceola, IA 50213 • 3,750
Osceola, MO 64776 • 841
Osceola, NE 68651 • 975
Osceola, WI 54020 • 1,581
Osceola □, FL • 49,287
Osceola □, IA • 8,371
Osceola □, MI • 18,928
Osceola Mills, PA 16666 • 1,466
Oscoda, MI 48750 • 2,431
Oscoda □, MI • 6,858
Osgood, IN 47037 • 1,554
Oshkosh, NE 69154 • 1,057
Oshkosh, WI 54901-04 • 50,016
Oskaloosa, IA 52577 • 10,989
Oskaloosa, KS 66066 • 1,092
Osmond, NE 68765 • 871
Osprey, FL 33559 • 1,660
Osseo, MN 55369 • 2,974
Osseo, WI 54758 • 1,474
Ossian, IN 46777 • 1,945
Ossian, IA 52161 • 829
Ossining, NY 10562 • 20,196
Osteen, FL 32764 • 900
Osterville, MA 02655 • 1,799
Oswego, IL 60543 • 3,021
Oswego, KS 67356 • 2,218
Oswego, NY 13126 • 19,793
Oswego □, NY • 113,901
Otay, CA 92010 • 6,400
Oteen, NC 28805 • 2,200
Otego, NY 13825 • 1,089
Otero □, CO • 22,567
Otero □, NM • 44,665
Othello, WA 99344 • 4,454
Otho, IA 50569 • 692
Otis Orchards, WA 99027 • 1,000
Otisville, MI 48463 • 682
Otoe □, NE • 15,183
Otsego, MI 49078 • 3,802
Otsego □, MI • 14,993
Otsego □, NY • 59,075
Ottawa, IL 61350 • 18,166
Ottawa, KS 66067 • 11,016
Ottawa, OH 45875 • 3,874
Ottawa □, KS • 5,971
Ottawa □, MI • 157,174
Ottawa □, OH • 40,076
Ottawa □, OK • 32,870
Ottawa Hills, OH 43606 • 4,065
Otterbein, IN 47970 • 1,118
Otter Tail □, MN • 51,937
Ottoville, OH 45876 • 833
Ottumwa, IA 52501 • 27,381
Ouachita □, AR • 30,541
Ouachita □, LA • 139,241
Ouray, CO 81427 • 684
Ouray □, CO • 1,925
Outagamie □, WI • 128,730
Overbrook, KS 66524 • 930
Overland, MO 63114 • 19,620
Overland Park, KS 66204 • 81,784
Overlea, MD 21206 • 6,200
Overton, NE 68863 • 633
Overton, NV 89040 • 1,111
Overton, TX 75684 • 2,430
Overton □, TN • 17,575
Ovid, MI 48866 • 1,712
Ovid, NY 14521 • 666
Owasso, OK 74055 • 6,149
Owatonna, MN 55060 • 18,632
Owego, NY 13827 • 4,364
Owen, WI 54460 • 998
Owen □, IN • 15,841
Owen □, KY • 8,924
Owensboro, KY 42301 • 54,450
Owens Cross Roads, AL 35763 • 804
Owensville, IN 47665 • 1,261
Owensville, MO 65066 • 2,241
Owensville, OH 45160 • 858
Owenton, KY 40359 • 1,341
Owings Mills, MD 21117 • 9,526
Owingsville, KY 40360 • 1,419
Owosso, MI 48867 • 16,455
Owsley □, KY • 5,709
Owyhee, NV 89832 • 700
Owyhee □, ID • 8,272
Oxford, AL 36203 • 8,939
Oxford, CT 06483 • 900
Oxford, GA 30267 • 1,750
Oxford, IN 47971 • 1,327
Oxford, IA 52322 • 676
Oxford, KS 67119 • 1,125
Oxford, ME 04270 • 625
Oxford, MD 21654 • 754
Oxford, MA 01540 • 6,369
Oxford, MI 48051 • 2,746
Oxford, MS 38655 • 9,882
Oxford, NE 68967 • 1,109
Oxford, NJ 07863 • 1,587
Oxford, NC 27565 • 7,603
Oxford, NY 13830 • 1,765
Oxford, OH 45056 • 17,655
Oxford, PA 19363 • 3,633
Oxford □, ME • 48,968
Oxnard, CA 93030-39 • 108,195
Oxon Hill, MD 20745 • 8,100
Oyster Bay, NY 11771 • 7,200
Ozark, AL 36360 • 13,188
Ozark, AR 72949 • 3,597
Ozark, MO 65721 • 2,980
Ozark □, MO • 7,961
Ozaukee □, WI • 66,981
Ozona, FL 34265 • 1,200
Ozona, TX 76943 • 2,864

P

Paauilo, HI 96776 • 755
96776 • 755
Pace, FL 32570 • 5,006
Pacific, MO 63069 • 4,410
Pacific, WA 98047 • 2,261
Pacific □, WA • 17,237
Pacifica, CA 94044 • 36,866
Pacific Beach, WA 98571 • 1,000
Pacific City, OR 97135 • 1,500
Pacific Grove, CA 93950 • 15,755
Pacific Palisades, HI 96782 • 9,500
Packwood, WA 98361 • 1,150
Pacolet, SC 29372 • 1,556
Pacolet Mills, SC 29373 • 1,051
Paddock Lake, WI 53168 • 2,207
Paden City, WV 26159 • 3,671
Paducah, KY 42001 • 29,315
Paducah, TX 79248 • 2,216
Page, AZ 86040 • 4,907
Page □, IA • 19,063
Page □, VA • 19,401
Pageland, SC 29728 • 2,720
Page Manor, OH 45431 • 9,300
Pagosa Springs, CO 81147 • 1,331
Pahala, HI 96777 • 1,619
Pahoa, HI 96778 • 923
Pahokee, FL 33476 • 6,346
Pahrump, NV 89041 • 1,000
Paia, HI 96779 • 1,000
Paincourtville, LA 70391 • 2,004
Painesdale, MI 49955 • 650
Painesville, OH 44077 • 16,391
Painted Post, NY 14870 • 2,196
Paintsville, KY 41240 • 3,815
Pajarito, NM 87105 • 2,000
Palacios, TX 77465 • 4,667
Palatine, IL 60067 • 32,166
Palatka, FL 32077 • 10,175
Palestine, AR 72372 • 976
Palestine, IL 62451 • 1,718
Palestine, TX 75801 • 15,948
Palisade, CO 81526 • 1,551
Palisades Park, NJ 07650 • 13,732
Palm Bay, FL 32905 • 18,560
Palm Beach, FL 33480 • 9,729
Palm Beach □, FL • 576,863
Palm Beach Gardens, FL 33410 • 6,102
Palmdale, CA 93550 • 12,277
Palm Desert, CA 92260 • 11,801
Palmer, AK 99645 • 2,141
Palmer, MA 01069 • 3,854
Palmer, MI 49871 • 900
Palmer, MS 39401 • 2,765
Palmer, TN 37365 • 1,027
Palmer, TX 75152 • 1,187
Palmer Lake, CO 80133 • 1,130
Palmer Park, MD 20785 • 7,986
Palmerton, PA 18071 • 5,455
Palmetto, FL 33561 • 8,637
Palmetto, GA 30268 • 2,086
Palm Harbor, FL 33563 • 5,215
Palm Springs, CA 92262-64 • 32,366
Palm Springs, FL 33460 • 8,166
Palmyra, IL 62674 • 864
Palmyra, IN 47164 • 692
Palmyra, MO 63461 • 3,469
Palmyra, NJ 08065 • 7,085
Palmyra, NY 14522 • 3,729
Palmyra, PA 17078 • 7,228
Palmyra, WI 53156 • 1,515
Palo Alto, CA 94301-99 • 55,225
Palo Alto □, IA • 12,721
Palo Pinto □, TX • 24,062
Palos Heights, IL 60463 • 11,096
Palos Hills, IL 60465 • 16,654
Palos Park, IL 60464 • 3,150
Palos Verdes Estates, CA 90274 • 14,376
Palouse, WA 99161 • 1,005
Pamlico □, NC • 10,398
Pampa, TX 79065 • 21,396
Pamplico, SC 29583 • 1,213
Pana, IL 62557 • 6,040
Panacea, FL 32346 • 950
Panama, IL 62077 • 637
Panama, OK 74951 • 1,425
Panama City, FL 32401-10 • 33,346
Panama City Beach, FL 32407 • 2,148
Pandora, OH 45877 • 977
Pangburn, AR 72121 • 673
Panguitch, UT 84759 • 1,343
Panhandle, TX 79068 • 2,226
Panola □, MS • 28,164
Panola □, TX • 20,724
Panora, IA 50216 • 1,211
Panthersville, GA 30032 • 11,366
Paola, KS 66071 • 4,557
Paoli, IN 47454 • 3,637
Paoli, PA 19301 • 6,100
Paonia, CO 81428 • 1,425
Papaikou, HI 96781 • 1,567
Papillion, NE 68046 • 6,399
Paradis, LA 70080 • 800
Paradise, CA 95969 • 22,571
Paradise, NV 89109 • 45,000
Paradise, PA 17963 • 900
Paradise Hills, NM 87114 • 5,096
Paradise Valley, AZ 85253 • 11,085
Paradise Valley, WY 82601 • 2,300
Paragould, AR 72450 • 15,248
Paramount, CA 90723 • 36,407
Paramount, MD 21740 • 1,878
Paramus, NJ 07652 • 26,474
Parchment, MI 49004 • 1,817
Pardeeville, WI 53954 • 1,594
Paris, AR 72855 • 3,991
Paris, ID 83261 • 707
Paris, IL 61944 • 9,885
Paris, KY 40361 • 7,935
Paris, MO 65275 • 1,598
Paris, TN 38242 • 10,728
Paris, TX 75460 • 25,498
Park □, CO • 5,333
Park □, MT • 12,869
Park □, WY • 21,639
Park City, KS 67219 • 3,778
Park City, KY 42160 • 614
Park City, UT 84060 • 2,823
Parke □, IN • 16,372
Parker, AZ 85344 • 2,542
Parker, FL 32401 • 4,298
Parker, PA 16049 • 808
Parker, SD 57053 • 999
Parker □, TX • 44,609
Parker City, IN 47368 • 1,414
Parkersburg, IA 50665 • 1,968
Parkersburg, WV 26101-05 • 39,967
Parkers Prairie, MN 56361 • 917
Parkesburg, PA 19365 • 2,578
Park Falls, WI 54552 • 3,192
Park Forest, IL 60466 • 26,222
Park Forest South, IL 60466 • 6,245
Park Hills, KY 41015 • 3,500
Parkin, AR 72373 • 2,035
Parkland, WA 98444 • 22,300
Park Layne, OH 45431 • 5,372
Park Rapids, MN 56470 • 2,976
Park Ridge, IL 60068 • 38,704
Park Ridge, NJ 07656 • 8,515
Park River, ND 58270 • 1,844
Parkrose, OR 97230 • 21,103
Parksley, VA 23421 • 979
Parkston, SD 57366 • 1,545
Parkville, MD 21234 • 35,159
Parkville, MO 64152 • 1,997
Parkwater, WA 99211 • 4,850
Parkway, CA 95823 • 12,000
Parkwood, NC 27707 • 3,420
Parlier, CA 93648 • 2,902
Parma, ID 83660 • 1,820
Parma, MI 49269 • 873
Parma, MO 63870 • 1,081
Parma, OH 44129 • 92,548
Parma Heights, OH 44130 • 23,112
Parmer □, TX • 11,038
Parowan, UT 84761 • 1,836
Parrish, AL 35580 • 1,583
Parrish, FL 33564 • 950
Parshall, ND 58770 • 1,059
Parsippany, NJ 07054 • 8,000
Parsons, KS 67357 • 12,898
Parsons, TN 38363 • 2,422
Parsons, WV 26287 • 1,937
Pasadena, CA 91101-99 • 118,072
Pasadena, MD 21122 • 3,900
Pasadena, TX 77501-07 • 112,560
Pascagoula, MS 39567 • 29,318
Pasco, WA 99301 • 18,425
Pasco □, FL • 193,661
Pascoag, RI 02859 • 3,807
Paso Robles, CA 93446 • 9,163
Pasquotank □, NC • 28,462
Passaic, NJ 07055 • 52,463
Passaic □, NJ • 447,585
Pass Christian, MS 39571 • 5,014
Patagonia, AZ 85624 • 980
Pataskala, OH 43062 • 2,284
Patchogue, NY 11772 • 11,291
Paterson, NJ 07501-99 • 137,970
Patoka, IL 62875 • 662
Patoka, IN 47666 • 832
Patrick □, VA • 17,647
Patten, ME 04765 • 1,057
Patterson, GA 31557 • 763
Patterson, LA 70392 • 4,693
Patterson, NY 12563 • 950
Patton, PA 16668 • 2,441
Paul, ID 83347 • 940
Paulding, OH 45879 • 2,754
Paulding □, GA • 26,110
Paulding □, OH • 21,302
Paulina, LA 70763 • 980
Paullina, IA 51046 • 1,224
Paulsboro, NJ 08066 • 6,944
Pauls Valley, OK 73075 • 5,664
Pavo, GA 31778 • 830
Pawcatuck, CT 06379 • 5,216
Paw Creek, NC 28130 • 1,700
Pawhuska, OK 74056 • 4,771
Pawleys Island, SC 29585 • 2,200
Pawling, NY 12564 • 1,996
Pawnee, IL 62558 • 2,577
Pawnee, OK 74058 • 1,688
Pawnee □, KS • 8,065
Pawnee □, NE • 3,937
Pawnee □, OK • 15,310
Pawnee City, NE 68420 • 1,156
Pawpaw, IL 61353 • 839
Paw Paw, MI 49079 • 3,211
Paw Paw, WV 25434 • 644
Pawtucket, RI 02860-65 • 71,204
Paxton, FL 32538 • 659
Paxton, IL 60957 • 4,258
Paxton, MA 01612 • 1,800
Payette, ID 83661 • 5,448
Payette □, ID • 15,825
Payne, OH 45880 • 1,399

Payne □, OK • 62,435
Paynesville, MN 56362 • 2,140
Payson, AZ 85541 • 5,068
Payson, IL 62360 • 1,065
Payson, UT 84651 • 8,246
Peabody, KS 66866 • 1,474
Peabody, MA 01960 • 45,976
Peace Dale, RI 02883 • 3,100
Peach □, GA • 19,151
Peach Orchard, GA 30906 • 14,000
Peachtree City, GA 30269 • 6,429
Pea Ridge, AR 72751 • 1,488
Pearisburg, VA 24134 • 2,128
Pearl, MS 39208 • 18,580
Pearland, TX 77581 • 13,248
Pearl City, HI 96782 • 33,000
Pearl City, IL 61062 • 661
Pearl River, LA 70452 • 1,693
Pearl River, NY 10965 • 17,146
Pearl River □, MS • 33,795
Pearsall, TX 78061 • 7,383
Pearson, GA 31642 • 1,827
Pecatonica, IL 61063 • 1,732
Peck, MI 48466 • 606
Pecos, NM 87552 • 885
Pecos, TX 79772 • 12,855
Pecos □, TX • 14,618
Peculiar, MO 64078 • 1,571
Pedricktown, NJ 08067 • 900
Peebles, OH 45660 • 1,790
Peekskill, NY 10566 • 18,236
Pe Ell, WA 98572 • 617
Pegram, TN 37143 • 1,081
Pekin, IL 61554 • 33,967
Pekin, IN 47165 • 1,125
Pelahatchie, MS 39145 • 1,445
Pelham, AL 35124 • 6,759
Pelham, GA 31779 • 4,306
Pelham, NY 10803 • 6,848
Pelham Manor, NY 10803 • 6,130
Pelican Rapids, MN 56572 • 1,867
Pella, IA 50219 • 8,349
Pell City, AL 35125 • 6,616
Pell Lake, WI 53157 • 1,400
Pemberton, NJ 08068 • 1,198
Pemberville, OH 43450 • 1,321
Pembina, ND 58271 • 673
Pembina □, ND • 10,399
Pembroke, GA 31321 • 1,400
Pembroke, KY 42266 • 636
Pembroke, MA 02359 • 1,800
Pembroke, NC 28372 • 2,698
Pembroke, VA 24136 • 1,302
Pembroke Pines, FL 33024 • 35,776
Pemiscot □, MO • 24,987
Pen Argyl, PA 18072 • 3,388
Penbrook, PA 17103 • 3,006
Pender, NE 68047 • 1,318
Pender □, NC • 22,262
Pendleton, IN 46064 • 2,130
Pendleton, OR 97801 • 14,521
Pendleton, SC 29670 • 3,154
Pendleton □, KY • 10,989
Pendleton □, WV • 7,910
Pendley Hills, GA 30032 • 5,800
Pend Oreille □, WA • 8,580
Penfield, NY 14526 • 9,600
Peninsula, OH 44264 • 604
Penn Acres, DE 19720 • 1,950
Penney Farms, FL 32079 • 630
Penn Hills, PA 15235 • 57,632
Pennington, NJ 08534 • 2,109
Pennington □, MN • 15,258
Pennington □, SD • 70,361
Pennington Gap, VA 24277 • 1,716
Pennsauken, NJ 08110 • 33,775
Pennsboro, WV 26415 • 1,652
Pennsburg, PA 18073 • 2,339
Penns Grove, NJ 08069 • 5,760
Pennsville, NJ 08070 • 12,467
Penn Valley, PA 19072 • 6,100
Pennville, IN 47369 • 805
Penn Yan, NY 14527 • 5,248
Penobscot □, ME • 137,015
Pensacola, FL 32501-23 • 57,619
Pentwater, MI 49449 • 1,165
Peoria, AZ 85345 • 12,307
Peoria, IL 61601-99 • 124,160
Peoria □, IL • 200,466
Peoria Heights, IL 61613 • 7,453
Peotone, IL 60468 • 2,832
Pepeekeo, HI 96783 • 1,800
Pepin, WI 54759 • 890
Pepin □, WI • 7,477
Pepperell, MA 01463 • 2,076
Pepper Pike, OH 44124 • 6,177
Pequabuck, CT 06781 • 1,400
Pequannock, NJ 07440 • 13,776
Pequot Lakes, MN 56472 • 681
Percy, IL 62272 • 1,053
Perdido, AL 36562 • 1,100
Perham, MN 56573 • 2,086
Perkasie, PA 18944 • 5,241
Perkins, OK 74059 • 1,762
Perkins □, NE • 3,637
Perkins □, SD • 4,700
Perkinston, MS 39573 • 650
Perl-Mack, CO 80221 • 6,002
Perquimans □, NC • 9,486
Perrine, FL 33157 • 16,129
Perris, CA 92370 • 6,827
Perry, FL 32347 • 8,254
Perry, GA 31069 • 9,453
Perry, IA 50220 • 7,053
Perry, KS 66073 • 907

Perry, MI 48872 • 2,051
Perry, MO 63462 • 836
Perry, NY 14530 • 4,198
Perry, OH 44081 • 961
Perry, OK 73077 • 5,796
Perry, UT 84302 • 1,084
Perry □, AL • 15,012
Perry □, AR • 7,266
Perry □, IL • 21,714
Perry □, IN • 19,346
Perry □, KY • 33,763
Perry □, MS • 9,864
Perry □, MO • 16,784
Perry □, OH • 31,032
Perry □, PA • 35,718
Perry □, TN • 6,111
Perry Hall, MD 21128 • 13,455
Perry Heights, OH 44646 • 9,206
Perryman, MD 21130 • 1,819
Perrysburg, OH 43551 • 10,215
Perrysburg Heights, OH 43551 • 650
Perrysville, OH 44864 • 836
Perryville, AR 72126 • 1,058
Perryville, KY 40468 • 841
Perryville, MD 21903 • 2,018
Perryville, MO 63775 • 7,343
Pershing □, NV • 3,408
Person □, NC • 29,164
Perth Amboy, NJ 08861-63 • 38,951
Peru, IL 61354 • 10,886
Peru, IN 46970 • 13,764
Peru, NE 68421 • 998
Peru, NY 12972 • 1,300
Peshastin, WA 98847 • 900
Peshtigo, WI 54157 • 2,807
Pesotum, IL 61863 • 651
Petal, MS 39465 • 8,476
Petaluma, CA 94952 • 33,834
Peterborough, NH 03458 • 2,100
Petersburg, AK 99833 • 2,821
Petersburg, IL 62675 • 2,419
Petersburg, IN 47567 • 2,987
Petersburg, MI 49270 • 1,222
Petersburg, OH 44454 • 950
Petersburg, TN 37144 • 681
Petersburg, TX 79250 • 1,633
Petersburg, VA 23803-05 • 41,055
Petersburg, WV 26847 • 2,084
Peterstown, WV 24963 • 648
Petersville, AL 35633 • 2,000
Petoskey, MI 49770 • 6,097
Petroleum □, MT • 655
Petrolia, TX 76377 • 755
Petros, TN 37845 • 1,286
Pettis □, MO • 36,378
Pevely, MO 63070 • 2,732
Pewaukee, WI 53072 • 4,637
Pewee Valley, KY 40056 • 982
Pharr, TX 78577 • 21,381
Phelps, KY 41553 • 1,120
Phelps, NY 14532 • 2,004
Phelps, WI 54554 • 700
Phelps □, MO • 33,633
Phelps □, NE • 9,769
Phenix City, AL 36867 • 26,928
Philadelphia, MS 39350 • 6,434
Philadelphia, NY 13673 • 855
Philadelphia, PA 19101-99 • 1,688,210
Philadelphia □, PA • 1,688,210
Phil Campbell, AL 35581 • 1,549
Philip, SD 57567 • 1,088
Philippi, WV 26416 • 3,194
Philipsburg, MT 59858 • 1,138
Philipsburg, PA 16866 • 3,533
Phillips, ME 04966 • 700
Phillips, TX 79007 • 3,000
Phillips, WI 54555 • 1,522
Phillips □, AR • 34,772
Phillips □, CO • 4,542
Phillips □, KS • 7,406
Phillips □, MT • 5,367
Phillipsburg, KS 67661 • 3,229
Phillipsburg, NJ 08865 • 16,647
Philmont, NY 12565 • 1,539
Philo, IL 61864 • 973
Philo, OH 43771 • 799
Philomath, OR 97370 • 2,673
Phoenicia, NY 12464 • 700
Phoenix, AZ 85001-99 • 789,704
Phoenix, IL 60426 • 2,850
Phoenix, NY 13135 • 2,357
Phoenix, OR 97535 • 2,309
Phoenixville, PA 19460 • 14,165
Piatt □, IL • 16,581
Picayune, MS 39466 • 10,361
Picher, OK 74360 • 2,180
Pickaway □, OH • 43,662
Pickens, MS 39146 • 1,386
Pickens, SC 29671 • 3,199
Pickens □, AL • 21,481
Pickens □, GA • 11,652
Pickens □, SC • 79,292
Pickerington, OH 43147 • 3,917
Pickett □, TN • 4,358
Pico Rivera, CA 90660 • 53,387
Picture Rocks, PA 17762 • 615
Piedmont, AL 36272 • 5,544
Piedmont, CA 94611 • 10,498
Piedmont, MO 63957 • 2,359
Piedmont, OK 73078 • 2,016
Piedmont, SC 29673 • 2,992
Piedmont, WV 26750 • 1,491
Pierce, CO 80650 • 878

Pierce, ID 83546 • 1,060
Pierce, NE 68767 • 1,535
Pierce □, GA • 11,897
Pierce □, NE • 8,481
Pierce □, ND • 6,166
Pierce □, WA • 485,667
Pierce □, WI • 31,149
Pierce City, MO 65723 • 1,391
Pierceton, IN 46562 • 1,086
Pierre, SD 57501 • 11,973
Pierre Part, LA 70339 • 3,153
Pierson, FL 32080 • 1,085
Pierz, MN 56364 • 1,018
Pigeon, MI 48755 • 1,247
Pigeon Cove, MA 01966 • 1,700
Pigeon Forge, TN 37863 • 1,822
Piggott, AR 72454 • 3,762
Pike □, AL • 28,050
Pike □, AR • 10,373
Pike □, GA • 8,937
Pike □, IL • 18,896
Pike □, IN • 13,465
Pike □, KY • 81,123
Pike □, MS • 36,173
Pike □, MO • 17,568
Pike □, OH • 22,802
Pike □, PA • 18,271
Pike Lake, MN 55811 • 1,004
Pikesville, MD 21208 • 20,000
Piketon, OH 45661 • 1,726
Pikeville, KY 41501 • 4,756
Pikeville, NC 27863 • 662
Pikeville, TN 37367 • 2,085
Pilgrim Gardens, PA 19026 • 8,400
Pilot Grove, MO 65276 • 745
Pilot Knob, MO 63663 • 722
Pilot Mountain, NC 27041 • 1,090
Pilot Point, TX 76258 • 2,211
Pilot Rock, OR 97868 • 1,630
Pima, AZ 85543 • 1,599
Pima □, AZ • 531,443
Pimmit Hills, VA 22043 • 7,200
Pinal □, AZ • 90,918
Pinardville, NH 03045 • 4,500
Pinckard, AL 36371 • 771
Pinckney, MI 48169 • 1,390
Pinckneyville, IL 62274 • 3,319
Pinconning, MI 48650 • 1,430
Pine □, MN • 19,871
Pine Bluff, AR 71601-13 • 56,636
Pinebluff, NC 28373 • 935
Pine Bluffs, WY 82082 • 1,077
Pine Bridge, CT 06403 • 870
Pine Bush, NY 12566 • 1,200
Pine Castle, FL 32809 • 9,992
Pine City, MN 55063 • 2,489
Pinedale, WY 82941 • 1,066
Pine Grove, PA 17963 • 2,244
Pine Grove Mills, PA 16868 • 900
Pine Hill, NJ 08021 • 8,684
Pine Hills, FL 32808 • 26,000
Pinehurst, MA 01866 • 6,588
Pinehurst, NJ 08201 • 1,500
Pinehurst, NC 28374 • 3,421
Pine Island, MN 55963 • 1,986
Pine Island, NY 10969 • 950
Pine Knot, KY 42635 • 1,389
Pine Lake, GA 30072 • 901
Pine Lake, MA 01776 • 800
Pine Lawn, MO 63120 • 6,662
Pine Level, NC 27568 • 953
Pinellas □, FL • 728,531
Pinellas Park, FL 33565 • 32,811
Pine Mountain, GA 31822 • 984
Pine Orchard, CT 06405 • 1,500
Pine Plains, NY 12567 • 950
Pine Point, ME 04074 • 700
Pine Prairie, LA 70576 • 734
Pine Rest, MA 01776 • 900
Pine Ridge, SD 57770 • 3,059
Pine River, MN 56474 • 881
Pinetop, AZ 85935 • 1,527
Pinetops, NC 27864 • 1,465
Pine Valley, CA 92062 • 950
Pineville, KY 40977 • 2,599
Pineville, LA 71360 • 12,034
Pineville, NC 28134 • 1,525
Pineville, WV 24874 • 1,140
Pinewald, NJ 08721 • 900
Pinewood, FL 33168 • 7,900
Pinewood, SC 29125 • 689
Piney Point, MD 20674 • 900
Piney View, WV 25906 • 800
Pink Hill, NC 28572 • 644
Pinole, CA 94564 • 14,253
Pinson, AL 35126 • 1,600
Pioche, NV 89043 • 760
Pioneer, OH 43554 • 1,133
Piper, KS 66109 • 730
Piper City, IL 60959 • 905
Pipestone, MN 56164 • 4,887
Pipestone □, MN • 11,690
Piqua, OH 45356 • 20,480
Pirtleville, AZ 85626 • 1,423
Piscataquis □, ME • 17,634
Piscataway, NJ 08854 • 42,223
Pisgah, AL 35765 • 699
Pisgah, OH 45069 • 1,000
Pisgah Forest, NC 28768 • 1,899
Pismo Beach, CA 93449 • 5,364
Pitcairn, PA 15140 • 4,175
Pitkin, LA 70656 • 750
Pitkin □, CO • 10,338
Pitman, NJ 08071 • 9,744
Pitt □, NC • 90,146
Pittsboro, IN 46167 • 891

Pittsboro, NC 27312 • 1,332
Pittsburg, CA 94565 • 33,034
Pittsburg, IL 62974 • 605
Pittsburg, KS 66762 • 18,770
Pittsburg, KY 40755 • 620
Pittsburg, TX 75686 • 4,245
Pittsburg □, OK • 40,524
Pittsburgh, PA 15201-99 • 423,959
Pittsfield, IL 62363 • 4,170
Pittsfield, ME 04967 • 3,117
Pittsfield, MA 01201 • 51,974
Pittsfield, NH 03263 • 1,584
Pittsford, VT 05763 • 666
Pittston, PA 18640-44 • 9,930
Pittsville, WI 54466 • 810
Pittsylvania □, VA • 66,147
Piute □, UT • 1,329
Pixley, CA 93256 • 2,488
Placentia, CA 92670 • 35,041
Placer □, CA • 117,247
Placerville, CA 95667 • 6,739
Placida, FL 33946 • 700
Plain, WI 53577 • 676
Plain City, OH 43064 • 2,102
Plain City, UT 84404 • 2,379
Plain Dealing, LA 71064 • 1,213
Plainfield, CT 06374 • 2,799
Plainfield, IL 60544 • 3,767
Plainfield, IN 46168 • 9,191
Plainfield, NJ 07060-63 • 45,555
Plainfield, WI 54966 • 813
Plainfield Heights, MI 49505 • 5,000
Plains, GA 31780 • 651
Plains, KS 67869 • 1,044
Plains, MT 59859 • 1,116
Plains, PA 18705 • 6,606
Plains, TX 79355 • 1,457
Plainsboro, NJ 08536 • 800
Plainview, AR 72857 • 752
Plainview, MN 55964 • 2,416
Plainview, NE 68769 • 1,483
Plainview, NY 11803 • 32,300
Plainview, TX 79072 • 22,187
Plainville, CT 06062 • 16,401
Plainville, KS 67663 • 2,458
Plainville, MA 02762 • 4,953
Plainwell, MI 49080 • 3,751
Plaistow, NH 03865 • 1,800
Plankinton, SD 57368 • 644
Plano, IL 60545 • 4,875
Plano, TX 75074-75 • 72,331
Plantation, FL 33317 • 48,653
Plant City, FL 33566 • 17,064
Plantersville, AL 36758 • 650
Plantersville, MS 38862 • 920
Plantsite, AZ 85540 • 1,500
Plantsville, CT 06479 • 5,700
Plaquemine, LA 70764 • 7,521
Plaquemines □, LA • 26,049
Platte, SD 57369 • 1,334
Platte □, MO • 46,341
Platte □, NE • 28,852
Platte □, WY • 11,975
Platte City, MO 64079 • 2,114
Platteville, CO 80651 • 1,662
Platteville, WI 53818 • 9,580
Plattsburg, MO 64477 • 2,095
Plattsburgh, NY 12901 • 21,057
Plattsmouth, NE 68048 • 6,295
Pleasant Gap, PA 16823 • 1,773
Pleasant Garden, NC 27313 • 1,991
Pleasant Grove, AL 35127 • 7,102
Pleasant Grove, CA 94523 • 25,124
Pleasant Grove, UT 84062 • 10,833
Pleasant Hill, IL 62366 • 1,112
Pleasant Hill, IA 50301 • 3,493
Pleasant Hill, LA 71065 • 776
Pleasant Hill, MO 64080 • 3,301
Pleasant Hill, OH 45359 • 1,051
Pleasant Hills, PA 15236 • 9,374
Pleasanton, CA 94566 • 35,160
Pleasanton, KS 66075 • 1,303
Pleasanton, TX 78064 • 6,346
Pleasant Plains, IL 62677 • 688
Pleasants □, WV • 8,236
Pleasant Valley, IA 52767 • 750
Pleasant Valley, MO 64068 • 1,545
Pleasant Valley, NY 12569 • 1,372
Pleasant Valley, OH 45601 • 650
Pleasant View, CO 80401 • 4,500
Pleasant View, UT 84404 • 3,983
Pleasant View, WI 54615 • 700
Pleasantville, IA 50225 • 1,531
Pleasantville, NJ 08232 • 13,435
Pleasantville, NY 10570 • 6,749
Pleasantville, OH 43148 • 780
Pleasantville, PA 16341 • 1,099
Pleasure Beach, CT 06385 • 1,356
Pleasure Ridge Park, KY 40258 • 27,332
Pleasureville, KY 40057 • 837
Plentywood, MT 59254 • 2,476
Plover, WI 54467 • 5,310
Plum, PA 15239 • 25,390
Plumas □, CA • 17,340
Plumerville, AR 72127 • 785
Plummer, ID 83851 • 634
Plymouth, CT 06782 • 1,000
Plymouth, FL 32768 • 2,700
Plymouth, IN 46367 • 649
Plymouth, IN 46563 • 7,693
Plymouth, MA 02360 • 7,232
Plymouth, MN 55441 • 31,615
Plymouth, NH 03264 • 3,628
Plymouth, NC 27962 • 4,571

Plymouth, OH 44865 • 1,939
Plymouth, PA 18651 • 7,605
Plymouth, WI 53073 • 6,027
Plymouth □, IA • 24,743
Plymouth □, MA • 405,437
Plymouth Meeting, PA 19462 • 6,000
Plymouth Valley, PA 19401 • 8,200
Poca, WV 25159 • 1,142
Pocahontas, AR 72455 • 5,995
Pocahontas, IL 62275 • 866
Pocahontas, IA 50574 • 2,352
Pocahontas, VA 24635 • 708
Pocahontas □, IA • 11,369
Pocahontas □, WV • 9,919
Pocasset, MA 02559 • 2,000
Pocatalico, WV 25320 • 900
Pocatello, ID 83201-09 • 46,340
Pocola, OK 74902 • 3,268
Pocomoke City, MD 21851 • 3,558
Poinsett □, AR • 27,032
Point Clear, AL 36564 • 1,812
Pointe Coupee □, LA • 24,045
Point Independence, MA 02532 • 700
Point Lookout, MO 65726 • 900
Point Marion, PA 15474 • 1,642
Point Pleasant, NJ 08742 • 17,747
Point Pleasant, WV 25550 • 5,682
Point Pleasant Beach, NJ 08742 • 5,415
Point Roberts, WA 98281 • 750
Poipu, HI 96756 • 685
Pojoaque Valley, NM 87501 • 900
Polk, PA 16342 • 1,884
Polk □, AR • 17,007
Polk □, FL • 321,652
Polk □, GA • 32,386
Polk □, IA • 303,170
Polk □, MN • 34,844
Polk □, MO • 18,822
Polk □, NE • 6,320
Polk □, NC • 12,984
Polk □, OR • 45,203
Polk □, TN • 13,602
Polk □, TX • 24,407
Polk □, WI • 32,351
Polk City, IA 50226 • 1,658
Polkton, NC 28135 • 762
Polo, IL 61064 • 2,643
Polson, MT 59860 • 2,798
Pomeroy, IA 50575 • 895
Pomeroy, OH 45769 • 2,728
Pomeroy, WA 99347 • 1,716
Pomona, CA 91766-69 • 92,742
Pomona, KS 66076 • 868
Pomona, NJ 08240 • 2,358
Pomona Park, FL 32081 • 791
Pompano Beach, FL 33060-69 • 52,618
Pompano Beach Highlands, FL 33064 • 9,000
Pompton Lakes, NJ 07442 • 10,660
Ponca, NE 68770 • 1,057
Ponca City, OK 74601-04 • 26,238
Ponchatoula, LA 70454 • 5,469
Pond Creek, OK 73766 • 949
Pondera □, MT • 6,731
Ponte Vedra Beach, FL 32082 • 1,700
Pontiac, IL 61764 • 11,227
Pontiac, MI 48053-59 • 76,715
Pontotoc, MS 38863 • 4,723
Pontotoc □, MS • 20,918
Pontotoc □, OK • 32,598
Pooler, GA 31322 • 2,543
Poolesville, MD 20837 • 3,428
Pope □, AR • 39,021
Pope □, IL • 4,404
Pope □, MN • 11,657
Poplar, MT 59255 • 995
Poplar Bluff, MO 63901 • 17,139
Poplar Grove, IL 61065 • 818
Poplarville, MS 39470 • 2,562
Poquonock, CT 06064 • 900
Poquonock Bridge, CT 06340 • 2,549
Poquoson, VA 23662 • 8,726
Portage, IN 46368 • 27,409
Portage, MI 49081 • 38,157
Portage, PA 15946 • 3,510
Portage, WI 53901 • 7,896
Portage □, OH • 135,856
Portage □, WI • 57,420
Portage Lakes, OH 44319 • 11,310
Portageville, MO 63873 • 3,470
Portal, GA 30450 • 694
Portales, NM 88130 • 9,940
Port Allegany, PA 16743 • 2,593
Port Allen, LA 70767 • 6,114
Port Angeles, WA 98362 • 17,311
Port Aransas, TX 78373 • 1,968
Port Arthur, TX 77640-43 • 61,251
Port Austin, MI 48467 • 839
Port Barre, LA 70577 • 2,625
Port Bolivar, TX 77650 • 1,600
Port Byron, IL 61275 • 1,289
Port Byron, NY 13140 • 1,400
Port Carbon, PA 17965 • 2,576
Port Charlotte, FL 33952 • 25,770
Port Chester, NY 10573 • 23,565
Port Clinton, OH 43452 • 7,223
Port Deposit, MD 21904 • 664
Port Dickinson, NY 13901 • 1,974
Port Edwards, WI 54469 • 2,077
Porter, IN 46304 • 2,988
Porter, OK 74454 • 642

Porter, TX 77365 • 5,000
Porter □, IN • 119,816
Porterdale, GA 30270 • 1,451
Porterville, CA 93257 • 19,707
Port Ewen, NY 12466 • 2,600
Port Gibson, MS 39150 • 2,371
Port Henry, NY 12974 • 1,450
Port Hueneme, CA 93041 • 17,803
Port Huron, MI 48060 • 33,981
Port Isabel, TX 78578 • 3,769
Port Jefferson, NY 11777 • 6,731
Port Jefferson Station, NY 11776 • 7,500
Port Jervis, NY 12771 • 8,699
Portland, AR 71663 • 701
Portland, CT 06480 • 8,383
Portland, IN 47371 • 7,074
Portland, ME 04101–99 • 61,572
Portland, MI 48875 • 3,963
Portland, ND 58274 • 627
Portland, OR 97201–99 • 366,383
Portland, TN 37148 • 4,030
Portland, TX 78374 • 12,023
Port Lavaca, TX 77979 • 10,911
Port Leyden, NY 13433 • 740
Port Matilda, PA 16870 • 647
Port Monmouth, NJ 07758 • 3,600
Port Neches, TX 77651 • 13,944
Port Norris, NJ 08349 • 1,730
Port O'Connor, TX 77982 • 1,500
Portola, CA 96122 • 1,885
Port Orange, FL 32019 • 18,756
Port Orchard, WA 98366 • 4,787
Port Orford, OR 97465 • 1,061
Port Reading, NJ 07064 • 4,300
Port Republic, NJ 08241 • 837
Port Richey, FL 33568 • 2,165
Port Royal, PA 17082 • 835
Port Royal, SC 29935 • 2,977
Port Saint Joe, FL 32456 • 4,027
Port Saint Lucie, FL 33450 • 14,690
Port Salerno, FL 33492 • 4,511
Portsmouth, NH 03801 • 26,254
Portsmouth, OH 45662 • 25,943
Portsmouth, RI 02871 • 4,300
Portsmouth, VA 23701–99 • 104,577
Port Sulphur, LA 70083 • 3,318
Port Townsend, WA 98368 • 6,067
Portville, NY 14770 • 1,136
Port Vue, PA 15133 • 5,316
Port Washington, NY 11050 • 15,923
Port Washington, OH 43837 • 622
Port Washington, WI 53074 • 8,612
Port Wentworth, GA 31407 • 3,947
Porum, OK 74455 • 668
Posen, IL 60469 • 4,642
Posey □, IN • 26,414
Poseyville, IN 47633 • 1,247
Post, TX 79356 • 3,961
Post Falls, ID 83854 • 5,736
Postville, IA 52162 • 1,475
Poteau, OK 74953 • 7,089
Poteet, TX 78065 • 3,086
Poth, TX 78147 • 1,461
Potlatch, ID 83855 • 819
Potomac, IL 61865 • 874
Potomac, MD 20854 • 22,800
Potomac Heights, MD 20640 • 2,456
Potomac Park, MD 21502 • 1,250
Potosi, MO 63664 • 2,528
Potosi, WI 53820 • 736
Potsdam, NY 13676 • 10,635
Pottawatomie □, KS • 14,782
Pottawatomie □, OK • 55,239
Pottawattamie □, IA • 86,561
Potter □, PA • 17,726
Potter □, SD • 3,674
Potter □, TX • 98,637
Potter Valley, CA 95469 • 1,500
Pottstown, PA 19464 • 22,729
Pottsville, PA 17901 • 18,195
Poughkeepsie, NY 12601–99 • 29,757
Poulan, GA 31781 • 818
Poulsbo, WA 98370 • 3,453
Poultney, VT 05764 • 1,554
Pound, VA 24279 • 1,086
Poway, CA 92064 • 33,300
Powder River □, MT • 2,520
Powder Springs, GA 30073 • 3,381
Powell, WY 82435 • 5,310
Powell □, KY • 11,101
Powell □, MT • 6,958
Powellhurst, OR 97236 • 9,000
Powellton, WV 25161 • 1,200
Power □, ID • 6,844
Powers, OR 97466 • 819
Poweshiek □, IA • 19,306
Powhatan □, VA • 13,062
Powhatan Point, OH 43942 • 2,181
Poynette, WI 53955 • 1,447
Prague, OK 74864 • 2,208
Prairie □, AR • 10,140
Prairie □, MT • 1,836
Prairie City, IA 50228 • 1,278
Prairie City, OR 97869 • 1,106
Prairie du Chien, WI 53821 • 5,859
Prairie Du Rocher, IL 62277 • 701
Prairie du Sac, WI 53578 • 2,145
Prairie Grove, AR 72753 • 1,708
Prairie View, TX 77446 • 3,993
Prairie Village, KS 66208 • 24,657
Pratt, KS 67124 • 6,885
Pratt, WV 25162 • 821
Pratt □, KS • 10,275
Prattsburg, NY 14873 • 750
Prattville, AL 36067 • 18,647
Preble □, OH • 38,223
Premont, TX 78375 • 2,984
Prentice, WI 54556 • 605
Prentiss, MS 39474 • 1,465
Prentiss □, MS • 24,025
Prescott, AZ 86301 • 20,055
Prescott, AR 71857 • 4,103
Prescott, WI 54021 • 2,654
Presho, SD 57568 • 760
Presidio, TX 79845 • 1,100
Presidio □, TX • 5,188
Presque Isle, ME 04769 • 11,172
Presque Isle □, MI • 14,267
Preston, ID 83263 • 3,759
Preston, IA 52069 • 1,120
Preston, MN 55965 • 1,478
Preston □, WV • 30,460
Prestonsburg, KY 41653 • 4,011
Pretty Prairie, KS 67570 • 655
Price, TX 75687 • 650
Price, UT 84501 • 9,086
Price □, WI • 15,788
Prichard, AL 36610 • 39,541
Priest River, ID 83856 • 1,639
Primghar, IA 51245 • 1,050
Prince Edward □, VA • 16,456
Prince Frederick, MD 20678 • 1,805
Prince George □, VA • 25,733
Prince Georges □, MD • 665,071
Princes Lakes, IN 46164 • 937
Princess Anne, MD 21853 • 1,499
Princeton, FL 33032 • 5,300
Princeton, IL 61356 • 7,342
Princeton, IN 47670 • 8,976
Princeton, IA 52768 • 965
Princeton, KY 42445 • 7,073
Princeton, ME 04668 • 800
Princeton, MN 55371 • 3,146
Princeton, MO 64673 • 1,264
Princeton, NJ 08540 • 12,035
Princeton, NC 27569 • 1,034
Princeton, WV 24740 • 7,493
Princeton, WI 54968 • 1,479
Princeton Junction, NJ 08550 • 2,419
Princeville, IL 61559 • 1,712
Princeville, NC 27886 • 1,508
Prince William □, VA • 144,703
Prineville, OR 97754 • 5,276
Prior Lake, MN 55372 • 7,284
Proctor, MN 55810 • 3,180
Proctor, VT 05765 • 1,998
Proctorville, OH 45669 • 975
Prophetstown, IL 61277 • 2,141
Prospect, CT 06712 • 6,807
Prospect, KY 40059 • 1,981
Prospect, OH 43342 • 1,159
Prospect, OR 97536 • 1,200
Prospect, PA 16052 • 1,016
Prospect Heights, IL 60070 • 11,808
Prospect Park, NJ 07508 • 5,142
Prospect Park, PA 19076 • 6,593
Prosperity, SC 29127 • 803
Prosperity, WV 25909 • 1,000
Prosser, WA 99350 • 3,896
Protection, KS 67127 • 684
Provencal, LA 71468 • 695
Providence, KY 42450 • 4,434
Providence, RI 02901–99 • 156,804
Providence, UT 84332 • 2,675
Providence □, RI • 571,349
Provincetown, MA 02657 • 3,536
Provo, UT 84601–04 • 74,108
Prowers □, CO • 13,070
Prudenville, MI 48651 • 1,000
Pryor, OK 74361 • 8,483
Pueblo, CO 81001–19 • 101,686
Pueblo □, CO • 125,972
Puhi, HI 96766 • 991
Pukalani, HI 96788 • 3,950
Pulaski, NY 13142 • 2,415
Pulaski, TN 38478 • 7,184
Pulaski, VA 24301 • 10,106
Pulaski, WI 54162 • 1,875
Pulaski □, AR • 340,613
Pulaski □, GA • 8,950
Pulaski □, IL • 8,840
Pulaski □, IN • 13,258
Pulaski □, KY • 45,803
Pulaski □, MO • 42,011
Pulaski □, VA • 35,229
Pullman, WA 99163 • 23,579
Pumphrey, MD 21227 • 3,300
Punta Gorda, FL 33950–55 • 6,797
Punxsutawney, PA 15767 • 7,479
Purcell, OK 73080 • 4,638
Purcellville, VA 22132 • 1,567
Purdy, MO 65734 • 928
Purvis, MS 39475 • 2,256
Puryear, TN 38251 • 624
Pushmataha □, OK • 11,773
Putnam, CT 06260 • 6,855
Putnam □, FL • 50,549
Putnam □, GA • 10,295
Putnam □, IL • 6,085
Putnam □, IN • 29,163
Putnam □, MO • 6,092
Putnam □, NY • 77,193
Putnam □, OH • 32,991
Putnam □, TN • 47,690
Putnam □, WV • 38,181
Putney, GA 31782 • 650
Putney, VT 05346 • 1,100
Puxico, MO 63960 • 833
Puyallup, WA 98371–73 • 18,251

Q

Quail Oaks, VA 23234 • 1,700
Quaker City, OH 43773 • 698
Quaker Hill, CT 06375 • 2,052
Quakertown, PA 18951 • 8,867
Quanah, TX 79252 • 3,890
Quantico, VA 22134 • 621
Quapaw, OK 74363 • 1,097
Quarryville, PA 17566 • 1,558
Quay □, NM • 10,577
Queen Annes □, MD • 25,508
Queen City, MO 63561 • 783
Queen City, TX 75572 • 1,748
Queen Creek, AZ 85242 • 900
Queens □, NY • 1,891,325
Questa, NM 87556 • 1,202
Quidnessett, RI 02852 • 3,300
Quidnick, RI 02816 • 2,300
Quilcene, WA 98376 • 950
Quincy, CA 95971 • 2,700
Quincy, FL 32351 • 8,591
Quincy, IL 62301 • 42,554
Quincy, MA 02169 • 84,743
Quincy, MI 49082 • 1,569
Quincy, OH 43343 • 633
Quincy, WA 98848 • 3,525
Quinebaug, CT 06262 • 1,088
Quinlan, TX 75474 • 1,002
Quinnesec, MI 49876 • 900
Quinter, KS 67752 • 951
Quinton, OK 74561 • 1,228
Quitaque, TX 79255 • 696
Quitman, GA 31643 • 5,188
Quitman, MS 39355 • 2,632
Quitman, TX 75783 • 1,893
Quitman □, GA • 2,357
Quitman □, MS • 12,636
Quonochontaug, RI 02808 • 1,000

R

Rabun □, GA • 10,466
Raceland, KY 41169 • 1,970
Raceland, LA 70394 • 6,302
Racine, OH 45771 • 908
Racine, WV 25165 • 650
Racine, WI 53401–99 • 85,725
Racine □, WI • 173,132
Radcliff, KY 40160 • 14,519
Radford, VA 24141 • 13,225
Raeford, NC 28376 • 3,630
Ragland, AL 35131 • 1,860
Rahway, NJ 07065–67 • 26,723
Rainbow City, AL 35901 • 6,299
Rainelle, WV 25962 • 1,983
Rainier, OR 97048 • 1,655
Rainier, WA 98576 • 891
Rains □, TX • 4,839
Rainsville, AL 35986 • 3,907
Raleigh, MS 39153 • 998
Raleigh, NC 27601–99 • 150,255
Raleigh, WV 25911 • 900
Raleigh □, WV • 86,821
Raleigh Hills, OR 97225 • 6,500
Ralls, TX 79357 • 2,422
Ralls □, MO • 8,984
Ralston, NE 68127 • 5,143
Rambleton Acres, DE 19720 • 1,500
Ramblewood, NJ 08054 • 6,475
Ramona, CA 92065 • 8,173
Ramsay, MI 49959 • 1,068
Ramseur, NC 27316 • 1,162
Ramsey, IL 62080 • 1,058
Ramsey, MN 55303 • 10,093
Ramsey, NJ 07446 • 12,899
Ramsey □, MN • 459,784
Ramsey □, ND • 13,048
Ranchester, WY 82839 • 655
Rancho Cordova, CA 95670 • 42,881
Rancho Mirage, CA 92270 • 6,281
Rancho Palos Verdes, CA 90274 • 36,577
Rancho Rinconado, CA 95014 • 5,100
Rancho Santa Fe, CA 92067 • 4,014
Ranchos de Taos, NM 87557 • 1,411
Rancocas Woods, NJ 08060 • 1,400
Rand, WV 25306 • 2,500
Randall □, TX • 75,062
Randallstown, MD 21133 • 20,500
Randleman, NC 27317 • 2,156
Randolph, ME 04345 • 1,834
Randolph, MA 02368 • 22,218
Randolph, NE 68771 • 1,106
Randolph, NY 14772 • 1,398
Randolph, OH 44265 • 800
Randolph, UT 84064 • 659
Randolph, VT 05060 • 2,217
Randolph, WI 53956 • 1,691
Randolph □, AL • 20,075
Randolph □, AR • 16,834
Randolph □, GA • 9,599
Randolph □, IL • 35,652
Randolph □, IN • 29,997
Randolph □, MO • 25,460
Randolph □, NC • 91,728
Randolph □, WV • 28,734
Random Lake, WI 53075 • 1,287
Rangeley, ME 04970 • 700
Rangely, CO 81648 • 2,113
Ranger, TX 76470 • 3,142
Rankin, IL 60960 • 727
Rankin, PA 15104 • 2,892
Rankin, TX 79778 • 1,216
Rankin □, MS • 69,427
Ransom □, ND • 6,698
Ransomville, NY 14131 • 1,500
Ranson, WV 25438 • 2,471
Rantoul, IL 61866 • 20,161
Raoul, GA 30510 • 1,400
Rapid City, SD 57701–08 • 46,492
Rapides □, LA • 135,282
Rapid River, MI 49878 • 700
Rapids City, IL 61278 • 1,058
Rappahannock □, VA • 6,093
Raritan, NJ 08869 • 6,128
Rathdrum, ID 83858 • 1,369
Raton, NM 87740 • 8,225
Ravalli □, MT • 22,493
Raven, VA 24639 • 1,880
Ravena, NY 12143 • 3,091
Ravenel, SC 29470 • 1,655
Ravenna, KY 40472 • 793
Ravenna, MI 49451 • 951
Ravenna, NE 68869 • 1,296
Ravenna, OH 44266 • 11,987
Ravenswood, WV 26164 • 4,126
Rawlins, WY 82301 • 11,547
Rawlins □, KS • 4,105
Ray, ND 58849 • 766
Ray □, MO • 21,378
Ray City, GA 31645 • 658
Raymond, IL 62560 • 957
Raymond, MN 56282 • 723
Raymond, MS 39154 • 1,967
Raymond, NH 03077 • 1,192
Raymond, WA 98577 • 2,991
Raymondville, TX 78580 • 9,493
Raymore, MO 64083 • 3,154
Rayne, LA 70578 • 9,066
Raynham, MA 02767 • 2,124
Raynham Center, MA 02768 • 3,776
Raytown, MO 64133 • 31,759
Rayville, LA 71269 • 4,610
Reader, WV 26167 • 700
Reading, MA 01867 • 22,678
Reading, MI 49274 • 1,203
Reading, OH 45215 • 12,843
Reading, PA 19601–99 • 78,686
Readlyn, IA 50668 • 858
Reagan □, TX • 4,135
Real □, TX • 2,469
Reamstown, PA 17567 • 1,050
Rector, AR 72461 • 2,336
Red Bank, NJ 07701 • 12,031
Red Bank, TN 37415 • 13,299
Red Bay, AL 35582 • 3,232
Redbird, OH 44057 • 1,600
Red Bluff, CA 96080 • 9,490
Red Boiling Springs, TN 37150 • 1,173
Red Bud, IL 62278 • 2,850
Red Cloud, NE 68970 • 1,300
Red Creek, NY 13143 • 645
Reddick, FL 32686 • 657
Redding, CA 96001–03 • 41,995
Redding, CT 06875 • 950
Redfield, AR 72132 • 745
Redfield, IA 50233 • 959
Redfield, SD 57469 • 3,027
Redford, MI 48239 • 58,441
Redgranite, WI 54970 • 976
Red Hook, NY 12571 • 1,692
Red Jacket, WV 25692 • 1,000
Redkey, IN 47373 • 1,537
Red Lake □, MN • 5,471
Red Lake Falls, MN 56750 • 1,732
Redlands, CA 92373–74 • 43,619
Red Lion, PA 17356 • 5,824
Red Lodge, MT 59068 • 1,896
Redmond, OR 97756 • 6,452
Redmond, UT 84652 • 619
Redmond, WA 98052–53 • 23,318
Red Oak, GA 30272 • 1,200
Red Oak, IA 51566 • 6,810
Red Oak, OK 74563 • 676
Red Oak, TX 75154 • 1,882
Red Oaks, LA 70815 • 2,000
Redondo Beach, CA 90277–78 • 57,102
Red River □, LA • 10,433
Red River □, TX • 16,101
Red Springs, NC 28377 • 3,607
Red Willow □, NE • 12,615
Red Wing, MN 55066 • 13,736
Redwood, UT 84119 • 2,000
Redwood □, MN • 19,341
Redwood City, CA 94061–65 • 54,951
Redwood Falls, MN 56283 • 5,210
Redwood Valley, CA 95470 • 1,300
Reece City, AL 35954 • 718
Reed City, MI 49677 • 2,221
Reedley, CA 93654 • 11,071
Reedsburg, WI 53959 • 5,038
Reedsport, OR 97467 • 4,984
Reedsville, PA 17084 • 950
Reedsville, WI 54230 • 1,134
Reedurban, OH 44710 • 6,650
Reese, MI 48757 • 1,645
Reeseville, WI 53579 • 649
Reeves □, TX • 15,801
Reform, AL 35481 • 2,245
Refugio, TX 78377 • 3,898
Refugio □, TX • 9,289
Rehoboth Beach, DE 19971 • 1,730
Reidland, KY 42001 • 3,730
Reidsville, GA 30453 • 2,296
Reidsville, NC 27320 • 12,492
Reinbeck, IA 50669 • 1,808
Reisterstown, MD 21136 • 19,385
Remington, IN 47977 • 1,268
Remsen, IA 51050 • 1,592
Remsen, NY 13438 • 621
Reno, NV 89501–99 • 100,756
Reno, OH 45773 • 850
Reno □, KS • 64,983
Renovo, PA 17764 • 1,812
Rensselaer, IN 47978 • 4,944
Rensselaer, NY 12144 • 9,047
Rensselaer □, NY • 151,966
Renton, WA 98055–57 • 30,612
Renville, MN 56284 • 1,493
Renville □, MN • 20,401
Renville □, ND • 3,608
Republic, MI 49879 • 1,000
Republic, MO 65738 • 4,485
Republic, OH 44867 • 656
Republic, PA 15475 • 1,500
Republic, WA 99166 • 1,018
Republic □, KS • 7,569
Reserve, LA 70084 • 7,288
Reston, VA 22090 • 32,000
Revere, MA 02151 • 42,423
Revloc, PA 15948 • 800
Rex, GA 30273 • 700
Rexburg, ID 83440 • 11,559
Reynolds, GA 31076 • 1,298
Reynolds, IL 61279 • 701
Reynolds, IN 47980 • 632
Reynolds □, MO • 7,230
Reynoldsburg, OH 43068 • 20,661
Reynoldsville, PA 15851 • 3,016
Rhea □, TN • 24,235
Rhinebeck, NY 12572 • 2,542
Rhinelander, WI 54501 • 7,873
Rhodhiss, NC 28667 • 727
Rialto, CA 92376 • 37,474
Rib Lake, WI 54470 • 945
Rice □, KS • 11,900
Rice □, MN • 46,087
Rice Lake, WI 54868 • 7,691
Riceville, IA 50466 • 919
Rich □, UT • 2,100
Richardson, TX 75080–85 • 72,496
Richardson □, NE • 11,315
Richardton, ND 58652 • 699
Rich Creek, VA 24147 • 746
Richfield, MN 55423 • 37,851
Richfield, UT 84701 • 5,482
Richfield Springs, NY 13439 • 1,561
Richford, VT 05476 • 1,471
Rich Hill, MO 64779 • 1,471
Richland, GA 31825 • 1,802
Richland, MO 65556 • 1,922
Richland, NJ 08350 • 800
Richland, WA 99352 • 33,578
Richland □, IL • 17,587
Richland □, LA • 22,187
Richland □, MT • 12,243
Richland □, ND • 19,207
Richland □, OH • 131,205
Richland □, SC • 269,735
Richland □, WI • 17,476
Richland Center, WI 53581 • 4,997
Richlands, NC 28574 • 825
Richlands, VA 24641 • 5,796
Richlandtown, PA 18955 • 1,180
Richmond, CA 94801–99 • 74,676
Richmond, IL 60071 • 1,068
Richmond, IN 47374 • 41,349
Richmond, KY 40475 • 21,705
Richmond, ME 04357 • 1,578
Richmond, MI 48062 • 3,536
Richmond, MN 56368 • 867
Richmond, MO 64085 • 5,499
Richmond, TX 77469 • 9,692
Richmond, UT 84333 • 1,705
Richmond, VT 05477 • 865
Richmond, VA 23201–99 • 219,214
Richmond □, GA • 181,629
Richmond □, NC • 45,481
Richmond □, NY • 352,121
Richmond □, VA • 6,952
Richmond Beach, WA 98160 • 8,000
Richmond Dale, OH 45673 • 650
Richmond Heights, FL 33156 • 8,577
Richmond Heights, MO 63117 • 11,516
Richmond Heights, OH 44143 • 10,095
Richmond Highlands, WA 98133 • 20,300
Richmond Hill, GA 31324 • 1,177
Richmondville, NY 12149 • 792
Rich Square, NC 27869 • 1,057
Richton, MS 39476 • 1,205
Richton Park, IL 60471 • 9,403
Richwood, OH 43344 • 2,181
Richwood, WV 26261 • 3,568
Riddle, OR 97469 • 1,265
Ridgecrest, CA 93555 • 15,929
Ridgecrest, WA 98155 • 7,000
Ridge Farm, IL 61870 • 1,096
Ridgefield, CT 06877 • 6,066
Ridgefield, NJ 07657 • 10,294
Ridgefield, WA 98642 • 1,062
Ridgefield Park, NJ 07660 • 12,738
Ridgeland, MS 39157 • 5,461
Ridgeland, SC 29936 • 1,143
Ridgeley, WV 26753 • 994
Ridgely, MD 21660 • 933
Ridgely, TN 38080 • 1,932
Ridgemont, NY 14626 • 8,500

Ridge Spring, SC 29129 • *969*
Ridgetop, TN 37152 • *1,225*
Ridgeville, IN 47380 • *933*
Ridgeville, SC 29472 • *603*
Ridgeway, VA 24148 • *858*
Ridgewood, NJ 07450–52 • *25,208*
Ridgway, IL 62979 • *1,245*
Ridgway, PA 15853 • *5,604*
Ridley Park, PA 19078 • *7,889*
Riesel, TX 76682 • *691*
Rifle, CO 81650 • *3,215*
Rigby, ID 83442 • *2,624*
Riley, KS 66531 • *779*
Riley □, KS • *63,505*
Rimersburg, PA 16248 • *1,096*
Rincon, GA 31326 • *1,988*
Ringgold, GA 30736 • *1,882*
Ringgold, LA 71068 • *1,655*
Ringgold □, IA • *6,112*
Ringling, OK 73456 • *1,561*
Ringoes, NJ 08551 • *650*
Ringwood, NJ 07456 • *12,625*
Rio, FL 33457 • *1,205*
Rio, WI 53960 • *785*
Rio Arriba □, NM • *29,282*
Rio Blanco □, CO • *6,255*
Rio Dell, CA 95562 • *2,687*
Rio Grande, NJ 08242 • *2,016*
Rio Grande, OH 45674 • *864*
Rio Grande □, CO • *10,511*
Rio Grande City, TX 78582 • *7,000*
Rio Hondo, TX 78583 • *1,673*
Rio Linda, CA 95673 • *7,359*
Rio Rancho, NM 87124 • *12,000*
Rio Vista, CA 94571 • *3,142*
Ripley, MS 38663 • *4,271*
Ripley, NY 14775 • *1,000*
Ripley, OH 45167 • *2,174*
Ripley, TN 38063 • *6,366*
Ripley, WV 25271 • *3,464*
Ripley □, IN • *24,398*
Ripley □, MO • *12,458*
Ripon, WI 54971 • *7,111*
Rising Star, TX 76471 • *1,204*
Rising Sun, IN 47040 • *2,478*
Rising Sun, MD 21911 • *1,160*
Risingsun, OH 43457 • *698*
Rison, AR 71665 • *1,325*
Ritchie □, WV • *11,442*
Rittman, OH 44270 • *6,063*
Ritzville, WA 99169 • *1,800*
Riverbank, CA 95367 • *5,695*
Riverdale, CA 93656 • *1,866*
Riverdale, GA 30274 • *7,121*
Riverdale, IL 60627 • *13,233*
Riverdale, MD 20737 • *4,748*
Riverdale, NJ 07457 • *2,530*
Riverdale, UT 84401 • *6,031*
River Edge, NJ 07661 • *11,111*
River Falls, AL 36476 • *669*
River Falls, WI 54022 • *9,019*
River Forest, IL 60305 • *12,392*
River Grove, IL 60171 • *10,368*
Riverhaven, IN 46802 • *700*
Riverhead, NY 11901 • *7,400*
River Heights, UT 84321 • *1,211*
River Hills, WI 53217 • *1,642*
River Oaks, TX 76114 • *6,890*
River Pines, MA 01821 • *3,700*
River Ridge, LA 70123 • *17,146*
River Road, OR 97404 • *10,370*
River Rouge, MI 48218 • *12,912*
Riverside, AL 35135 • *849*
Riverside, CA 92501–99 • *170,591*
Riverside, IL 60546 • *9,236*
Riverside, IA 52327 • *826*
Riverside, NJ 08075 • *7,941*
Riverside, PA 17868 • *2,266*
Riverside □, CA • *663,199*
Riverton, IL 62561 • *2,783*
Riverton, NJ 08077 • *3,068*
Riverton, UT 84065 • *7,293*
Riverton, WY 82501 • *9,247*
Riverton Heights, WA 98188 • *33,500*
River Vale, NJ 07675 • *9,489*
River View, AL 36854 • *1,314*
Riverview, FL 33569 • *3,200*
Riverview, MI 48192 • *14,569*
Rivesville, WV 26588 • *1,327*
Riviera, AZ 86442 • *4,500*
Riviera Beach, FL 33404 • *26,489*
Riviera Beach, MD 21122 • *5,600*
Riviera Beach, NJ 08723 • *2,000*
Roachdale, IN 46172 • *958*
Roane □, TN • *48,425*
Roane □, WV • *15,952*
Roan Mountain, TN 37687 • *1,108*
Roanoke, AL 36274 • *5,896*
Roanoke, IL 61561 • *2,001*
Roanoke, IN 46783 • *891*
Roanoke, TX 76262 • *910*
Roanoke, VA 24001–50 • *100,220*
Roanoke □, VA • *72,945*
Roanoke Rapids, NC 27870 • *14,702*
Roaring Spring, PA 16673 • *2,962*
Robbins, IL 60472 • *8,853*
Robbins, NC 27325 • *1,256*
Robbinsdale, MN 55422 • *14,422*
Robbinsville, NC 28771 • *1,370*
Robersonville, NC 27871 • *1,981*
Roberta, GA 31078 • *859*
Robert Lee, TX 76945 • *1,202*
Roberts, WI 54023 • *833*
Roberts □, SD • *10,911*
Roberts □, TX • *1,187*
Robertsdale, AL 36567 • *2,306*
Robertson □, KY • *2,265*
Robertson □, TN • *37,021*
Robertson □, TX • *14,653*
Robeson □, NC • *101,610*
Robins, IA 52328 • *726*
Robinson, IL 62454 • *7,285*
Robinson, PA 15949 • *660*
Robinson, TX 76706 • *6,074*
Robstown, TX 78380 • *12,100*
Roby, TX 79543 • *814*
Rochdale, MA 01542 • *1,105*
Rochelle, GA 31079 • *1,626*
Rochelle, IL 61068 • *8,982*
Rochelle Park, NJ 07662 • *5,603*
Rochester, IL 62563 • *2,488*
Rochester, IN 46975 • *5,050*
Rochester, MI 48063–64 • *7,203*
Rochester, MN 55901–04 • *57,890*
Rochester, NH 03867 • *21,560*
Rochester, NY 14601–99 • *241,741*
Rochester, PA 15074 • *4,759*
Rochester, WA 98579 • *900*
Rochester, WI 53167 • *746*
Rock □, MN • *10,703*
Rock □, NE • *2,383*
Rock □, WI • *139,420*
Rockaway, NJ 07866 • *6,852*
Rockaway, OR 97136 • *906*
Rockbridge □, VA • *17,911*
Rockcastle □, KY • *13,973*
Rock Creek, MN 55067 • *890*
Rock Creek, OH 44084 • *652*
Rockdale, IL 60436 • *1,913*
Rockdale, MD 21207 • *4,200*
Rockdale, TX 76567 • *5,611*
Rockdale □, GA • *36,747*
Rock Falls, IL 61071 • *10,633*
Rockford, IL 61101–99 • *139,712*
Rockford, IA 50468 • *1,012*
Rockford, MI 49341 • *3,324*
Rockford, MN 55373 • *2,408*
Rockford, OH 45882 • *1,245*
Rock Hall, MD 21661 • *1,511*
Rock Hill, MO 63124 • *5,702*
Rock Hill, SC 29730 • *35,344*
Rockingham, NC 28379 • *8,300*
Rockingham □, NH • *190,345*
Rockingham □, NC • *83,426*
Rockingham □, VA • *57,038*
Rock Island, IL 61201 • *46,928*
Rock Island □, IL • *165,968*
Rockland, ME 04841 • *7,919*
Rockland, MA 02370 • *15,695*
Rockland □, NY • *259,530*
Rockledge, FL 32955 • *11,877*
Rocklin, CA 95677 • *7,344*
Rockmart, GA 30153 • *3,645*
Rockport, IN 47635 • *2,590*
Rockport, ME 04856 • *1,000*
Rockport, MA 01966 • *4,600*
Rock Port, MO 64482 • *1,511*
Rockport, TX 78382 • *3,686*
Rock Rapids, IA 51246 • *2,693*
Rocksprings, TX 78880 • *1,317*
Rock Springs, WY 82901 • *19,458*
Rockton, IL 61072 • *2,313*
Rock Valley, IA 51247 • *2,706*
Rockville, IN 47872 • *2,785*
Rockville, MD 20850–58 • *43,811*
Rockville Centre, NY 11570 • *25,412*
Rockwall, TX 75087 • *5,939*
Rockwall □, TX • *14,528*
Rockwell, IA 50469 • *1,039*
Rockwell, NC 28138 • *1,339*
Rockwell City, IA 50579 • *2,276*
Rockwell Park, NC 28213 • *2,600*
Rockwood, MI 48173 • *3,346*
Rockwood, OR 97233 • *11,000*
Rockwood, PA 15557 • *1,058*
Rockwood, TN 37854 • *5,767*
Rocky Creek, FL 33615 • *7,800*
Rocky Ford, CO 81067 • *4,804*
Rocky Hill, CT 06067 • *14,559*
Rocky Hill, NJ 08553 • *717*
Rocky Mount, NC 27801 • *41,283*
Rocky Mount, VA 24151 • *4,198*
Rocky Ripple, IN 46208 • *778*
Rocky River, OH 44116 • *21,084*
Rodeo, CA 94572 • *8,286*
Roderfield, WV 24881 • *1,100*
Rodney Village, DE 19901 • *1,100*
Roebling, NJ 08554 • *3,600*
Roebuck, SC 29376 • *1,088*
Roeland Park, KS 66203 • *7,962*
Roessleville, NY 12205 • *5,476*
Roff, OK 74865 • *729*
Roger Mills □, OK • *4,799*
Rogers, AR 72756 • *17,429*
Rogers, MN 55374 • *652*
Rogers, TX 76569 • *1,242*
Rogers □, OK • *46,436*
Rogers City, MI 49779 • *3,923*
Rogersville, AL 35652 • *1,224*
Rogersville, MO 65742 • *741*
Rogersville, TN 37857 • *4,368*
Rogue River, OR 97537 • *1,308*
Rohnert Park, CA 94928 • *22,965*
Roland, IA 50236 • *1,005*
Roland, OK 74954 • *1,472*
Rolette, ND 58366 • *667*
Rolette □, ND • *12,177*
Rolfe, IA 50581 • *796*
Rolla, MO 65401 • *13,303*
Rolla, ND 58367 • *1,538*
Rollingbay, WA 98061 • *700*
Rolling Fork, MS 39159 • *2,590*
Rolling Hills Estates, CA 90274 • *7,701*
Rolling Meadows, IL 60008 • *20,167*
Rollinsford, NH 03869 • *1,173*
Roma, TX 78584 • *3,384*
Rome, GA 30161 • *29,654*
Rome, IL 61562 • *2,744*
Rome, NY 13440 • *43,826*
Rome City, IN 46784 • *1,319*
Romeo, MI 48065 • *3,509*
Romeoville, IL 60441 • *15,519*
Romney, WV 26757 • *2,094*
Romulus, MI 48174 • *24,857*
Ronan, MT 59864 • *1,530*
Ronceverte, WV 24970 • *2,312*
Ronkonkoma, NY 11779 • *20,200*
Roodhouse, IL 62082 • *2,364*
Rooks □, KS • *7,006*
Roosevelt, NJ 08555 • *835*
Roosevelt, NY 11575 • *15,000*
Roosevelt, UT 84066 • *3,842*
Roosevelt □, MT • *10,467*
Roosevelt □, NM • *15,695*
Roosevelt Park, MI 49441 • *4,015*
Rootstown, OH 44272 • *650*
Roper, NC 27970 • *795*
Rosamond, CA 93560 • *2,869*
Roscoe, IL 61073 • *1,388*
Roscoe, PA 15477 • *1,123*
Roscoe, TX 79545 • *1,628*
Roscommon, MI 48653 • *834*
Roscommon □, MI • *16,374*
Roseau, MN 56751 • *2,272*
Roseau □, MN • *12,574*
Roseboro, NC 28382 • *1,227*
Rosebud, TX 76570 • *2,076*
Rosebud □, MT • *9,899*
Roseburg, OR 97470 • *16,644*
Rose City, MI 48654 • *661*
Rosedale, IN 47874 • *744*
Rosedale, MD 21237 • *19,956*
Rosedale, MS 38769 • *2,793*
Rose Hill, KS 67133 • *1,557*
Rose Hill, NC 28458 • *1,508*
Rose Hill, VA 24281 • *800*
Roseland, CA 95407 • *7,915*
Roseland, FL 32957 • *1,607*
Roseland, IN 46635 • *832*
Roseland, LA 70456 • *1,346*
Roseland, NJ 07068 • *5,330*
Roseland, OH 44906 • *3,000*
Roselle, IL 60172 • *16,948*
Roselle, NJ 07203 • *20,641*
Roselle Park, NJ 07204 • *13,377*
Rosemead, CA 91770 • *42,604*
Rosemount, MN 55068 • *5,083*
Rosenberg, TX 77471 • *17,995*
Rosendale, WI 54974 • *725*
Rosenhayn, NJ 08352 • *750*
Rosepine, LA 70659 • *953*
Roseto, PA 18013 • *1,484*
Roseville, CA 95678 • *24,347*
Roseville, IL 61473 • *1,254*
Roseville, MI 48066 • *54,311*
Roseville, MN 55113 • *35,820*
Roseville, OH 43777 • *1,915*
Rosewood Heights, IL 62024 • *5,085*
Rosiclare, IL 62982 • *1,441*
Roslyn, PA 19001 • *13,400*
Roslyn, WA 98941 • *938*
Roslyn Heights, NY 11577 • *7,270*
Ross, OH 45061 • *2,767*
Ross □, OH • *65,004*
Rossford, OH 43460 • *5,978*
Rossiter, PA 15772 • *750*
Rossmoor, CA 90720 • *10,457*
Rossville, GA 30741 • *3,851*
Rossville, IL 60963 • *1,363*
Rossville, IN 46065 • *1,148*
Rossville, KS 66533 • *1,045*
Roswell, GA 30075–77 • *23,337*
Roswell, NM 88201 • *39,676*
Rotan, TX 79546 • *2,284*
Rothschild, WI 54474 • *3,338*
Rothsville, PA 17543 • *1,318*
Rotterdam, NY 12303 • *24,800*
Roulette, PA 16746 • *1,100*
Round Lake, IL 60073 • *2,644*
Round Lake, NY 12151 • *791*
Round Lake Beach, IL 60073 • *12,921*
Round Rock, TX 78664 • *12,740*
Roundup, MT 59072 • *2,119*
Rouses Point, NY 12979 • *2,266*
Rouseville, PA 16344 • *734*
Routt □, CO • *13,404*
Rouzerville, PA 17250 • *1,371*
Rowan □, KY • *19,049*
Rowan □, NC • *99,186*
Rowland, NC 28383 • *1,841*
Rowland Heights, CA 91748 • *28,252*
Rowlesburg, WV 26425 • *966*
Rowlett, TX 75088 • *7,522*
Rowley, MA 01969 • *1,321*
Roxboro, NC 27573 • *7,532*
Roxbury, NY 12474 • *700*
Roxton, TX 75477 • *735*
Roy, UT 84067 • *19,694*
Royal Center, IN 46978 • *908*
Royal Oak, MI 48067–73 • *70,893*
Royal Pines, NC 28704 • *2,041*
Royalton, IL 62983 • *1,320*
Royalton, MN 56373 • *660*
Royersford, PA 19468 • *4,243*
Royerton, IN 47302 • *650*
Royse City, TX 75089 • *1,566*
Royston, GA 30662 • *2,404*
Rubidoux, CA 92509 • *13,200*
Rudyard, MI 49780 • *900*
Rugby, ND 58368 • *3,335*
Ruidoso, NM 88345 • *4,260*
Ruidoso Downs, NM 88346 • *949*
Rule, TX 79547 • *1,015*
Ruleville, MS 38771 • *3,332*
Rumford, ME 04276 • *6,256*
Rumson, NJ 07760 • *7,623*
Runge, TX 78151 • *1,244*
Runnels □, TX • *11,872*
Runnemede, NJ 08078 • *9,461*
Rupert, ID 83350 • *5,476*
Rupert, WV 25984 • *1,276*
Rural Hall, NC 27045 • *1,336*
Rural Retreat, VA 24368 • *1,083*
Rush □, IN • *19,604*
Rush □, KS • *4,516*
Rush City, MN 55069 • *1,198*
Rushford, MN 55971 • *1,478*
Rush Springs, OK 73082 • *1,451*
Rushsylvania, OH 43347 • *610*
Rushville, IL 62681 • *3,348*
Rushville, IN 46173 • *6,113*
Rushville, NE 69360 • *1,217*
Rusk, TX 75785 • *4,681*
Rusk □, TX • *41,382*
Rusk □, WI • *15,589*
Ruskin, FL 33570 • *5,117*
Russell, KS 67665 • *5,427*
Russell, KY 41169 • *3,824*
Russell, MA 01071 • *650*
Russell, PA 16345 • *800*
Russell □, AL • *47,356*
Russell □, KS • *8,868*
Russell □, KY • *13,708*
Russell □, VA • *31,761*
Russell Springs, KY 42642 • *1,831*
Russellville, AL 35653 • *8,195*
Russellville, AR 72801 • *14,031*
Russellville, KY 42276 • *7,520*
Russellville, MO 65074 • *667*
Russellville, OR 97216 • *6,500*
Russellville, TN 37860 • *1,069*
Russiaville, IN 46979 • *973*
Ruston, LA 71270 • *20,585*
Ruston, WA 98407 • *612*
Ruth, NV 89319 • *735*
Rutherford, NJ 07070–75 • *19,068*
Rutherford, TN 38369 • *1,378*
Rutherford □, NC • *53,787*
Rutherford □, TN • *84,058*
Rutherfordton, NC 28139 • *3,434*
Ruthven, IA 51358 • *769*
Rutland, MA 01543 • *2,312*
Rutland, OH 45775 • *635*
Rutland, VT 05701 • *18,436*
Rutland □, VT • *58,347*
Rutledge, GA 30663 • *694*
Rutledge, TN 37861 • *1,058*
Ryan, OK 73565 • *1,083*
Rye, NH 03870 • *800*
Rye, NY 10580 • *15,083*

S

Sabattus, ME 04280 • *1,234*
Sabetha, KS 66534 • *2,286*
Sabina, OH 45169 • *2,799*
Sabinal, TX 78881 • *1,827*
Sabine □, LA • *25,280*
Sabine □, TX • *8,702*
Sabine Pass, TX 77655 • *900*
Sabula, IA 52070 • *824*
Sac □, IA • *14,118*
Sacaton, AZ 85247 • *1,951*
Sac City, IA 50583 • *3,000*
Sachse, TX 75040 • *1,640*
Sackets Harbor, NY 13685 • *1,017*
Saco, ME 04072 • *12,921*
Sacramento, CA 95801–99 • *275,741*
Sacramento □, CA • *700,001*
Sacred Heart, MN 56285 • *666*
Saddle Brook, NJ 07662 • *14,084*
Saddle River, NJ 07458 • *2,763*
Saegertown, PA 16433 • *942*
Safety Harbor, FL 33572 • *6,461*
Safford, AZ 85546 • *7,010*
Sagadahoc □, ME • *28,795*
Sagamore, MA 02561 • *1,152*
Sagamore, PA 16250 • *850*
Sagamore Beach, MA 02562 • *800*
Sagamore Hills, OH 44067 • *4,700*
Sag Harbor, NY 11963 • *2,581*
Saginaw, MI 48601–08 • *77,508*
Saginaw, TX 76179 • *5,736*
Saginaw □, MI • *228,059*
Saguache, CO 81149 • *656*
Saguache □, CO • *3,935*
Saint Albans, VT 05478 • *7,308*
Saint Albans, WV 25177 • *12,402*
Saint Andrews, SC 29407 • *9,908*
Saint Andrews, SC 29210 • *20,245*
Saint Ann, MO 63074 • *15,523*
Saint Anne, IL 60964 • *1,421*
Saint Ansgar, IA 50472 • *1,100*
Saint Anthony, ID 83445 • *3,212*
Saint Augustine, FL 32084–86 • *11,985*
Saint Bernard, LA 70085 • *720*
Saint Bernard, OH 45217 • *5,396*
Saint Bernard □, LA • *64,097*
Saint Bernice, IN 47875 • *900*
Saint Charles, IL 60174 • *17,492*
Saint Charles, MI 48655 • *2,276*
Saint Charles, MN 55972 • *2,184*
Saint Charles, MO 63301–03 • *37,379*
Saint Charles □, LA • *37,259*
Saint Charles □, MO • *144,107*
Saint Clair, MI 48079 • *4,780*
Saint Clair, MN 56080 • *655*
Saint Clair, MO 63077 • *3,485*
Saint Clair, PA 17970 • *4,037*
Saint Clair □, AL • *41,205*
Saint Clair □, IL • *267,531*
Saint Clair □, MI • *138,802*
Saint Clair □, MO • *8,622*
Saint Clair Shores, MI 48080–82 • *76,210*
Saint Clairsville, OH 43950 • *5,452*
Saint Cloud, FL 32769 • *7,840*
Saint Cloud, MN 56301 • *42,566*
Saint Croix □, WI • *43,262*
Saint Croix Falls, WI 54024 • *1,497*
Saint David, AZ 85630 • *950*
Saint David, IL 61563 • *786*
Saint Edward, NE 68660 • *891*
Saint Elmo, IL 62458 • *1,611*
Saint Francis, KS 67756 • *1,610*
Saint Francis, MN 55070 • *1,184*
Saint Francis, SD 57572 • *766*
Saint Francis, WI 53207 • *10,042*
Saint Francis □, AR • *30,858*
Saint Francisville, IL 62460 • *1,040*
Saint Francisville, LA 70775 • *1,471*
Saint Francois □, MO • *42,600*
Sainte Genevieve, MO 63670 • *4,481*
Sainte Genevieve □, MO • *15,180*
Saint George, SC 29477 • *2,134*
Saint George, UT 84770 • *11,350*
Saint Helena, CA 94574 • *4,898*
Saint Helena □, LA • *9,827*
Saint Helens, OR 97051 • *7,064*
Saint Henry, OH 45883 • *1,596*
Saint Ignace, MI 49781 • *2,632*
Saint Ignatius, MT 59865 • *877*
Saint Jacob, IL 62281 • *792*
Saint James, MN 56081 • *4,346*
Saint James, MO 65559 • *3,328*
Saint James, NY 11780 • *11,000*
Saint James □, LA • *21,495*
Saint James City, FL 33956 • *1,298*
Saint Jo, TX 76265 • *1,071*
Saint John, IN 46373 • *3,974*
Saint John, KS 67576 • *1,501*
Saint Johns, AZ 85936 • *3,368*
Saint Johns, MI 48879 • *7,376*
Saint Johns, MO 63114 • *7,854*
Saint Johns □, FL • *51,303*
Saint Johnsbury, VT 05819 • *7,150*
Saint Johnsville, NY 13452 • *1,974*
Saint John the Baptist □, LA • *31,924*
Saint Joseph, IL 61873 • *1,900*
Saint Joseph, LA 71366 • *1,687*
Saint Joseph, MI 49085 • *9,622*
Saint Joseph, MN 56374 • *2,994*
Saint Joseph, MO 64501–08 • *76,691*
Saint Joseph, TN 38481 • *897*
Saint Joseph □, IN • *241,617*
Saint Joseph □, MI • *56,083*
Saint Landry □, LA • *84,128*
Saint Lawrence □, NY • *114,254*
Saint Leo, FL 33574 • *917*
Saint Louis, MI 48880 • *4,107*
Saint Louis, MO 63101–99 • *453,085*
Saint Louis □, MN • *222,229*
Saint Louis □, MO • *973,896*
Saint Louis Park, MN 55426 • *42,931*
Saint Lucie □, FL • *87,182*
Saint Maries, ID 83861 • *2,794*
Saint Martin □, LA • *40,214*
Saint Martinville, LA 70582 • *7,965*
Saint Mary □, LA • *64,253*
Saint Mary of the Woods, IN 47876 • *650*
Saint Marys, GA 31558 • *3,596*
Saint Marys, IN 46556 • *1,700*
Saint Marys, KS 66536 • *1,598*
Saint Marys, OH 45885 • *8,414*
Saint Marys, PA 15857 • *6,417*
Saint Marys, WV 26170 • *2,219*
Saint Marys □, MD • *59,895*
Saint Marys City, MD 20686 • *900*
Saint Matthews, KY 40207 • *13,519*
Saint Matthews, SC 29135 • *2,496*
Saint Michael, MN 55376 • *1,519*
Saint Michaels, MD 21663 • *1,301*
Saint Nazianz, WI 54232 • *738*
Saint Paris, OH 43072 • *1,742*
Saint Paul, IN 47272 • *976*
Saint Paul, KS 66771 • *746*
Saint Paul, MN 55101–99 • *270,230*
Saint Paul, MO 63366 • *607*
Saint Paul, NE 68873 • *2,094*
Saint Paul, VA 24283 • *973*
Saint Paul Park, MN 55071 • *4,864*
Saint Pauls, NC 28384 • *1,639*
Saint Peter, MN 56082 • *9,056*
Saint Peters, MO 63376 • *15,700*
Saint Petersburg, FL 33701–99 • *238,647*
Saint Petersburg Beach, FL 33736 • *9,354*
Saint Regis Falls, NY 12980 • *950*
Saint Rose, LA 70087 • *2,800*

Saint Simons Island, GA 31522 • 6,566
Saint Stephen, SC 29479 • 1,850
Saint Tammany □, LA • 110,869
Saint Thomas, PA 17252 • 700
Salamanca, NY 14779 • 6,890
Sale Creek, TN 37373 • 900
Salem, AR 72576 • 1,424
Salem, IL 62881 • 7,813
Salem, IN 47167 • 5,290
Salem, KY 42078 • 833
Salem, MA 01970 • 38,220
Salem, MO 65560 • 4,454
Salem, NH 03079 • 11,500
Salem, NJ 08079 • 6,959
Salem, NY 12865 • 959
Salem, OH 44460 • 12,869
Salem, OR 97301–14 • 89,233
Salem, SD 57058 • 1,486
Salem, UT 84653 • 2,233
Salem, VA 24153 • 23,958
Salem, WV 26426 • 2,706
Salem, WI 53168 • 1,000
Salem □, NJ • 64,676
Salemburg, NC 28385 • 742
Salida, CO 81201 • 4,870
Salina, KS 67401 • 41,843
Salina, OK 74365 • 1,115
Salina, UT 84654 • 1,992
Salinas, CA 93901–15 • 80,479
Saline, MI 48176 • 6,483
Saline □, AR • 53,161
Saline □, IL • 28,448
Saline □, KS • 48,905
Saline □, MO • 24,919
Saline □, NE • 13,131
Salineville, OH 43945 • 1,629
Salisbury, CT 06068 • 900
Salisbury, MD 21801 • 16,429
Salisbury, MA 01950 • 3,265
Salisbury, MO 65281 • 1,975
Salisbury, NC 28144 • 22,677
Salisbury, PA 15558 • 817
Sallisaw, OK 74955 • 6,403
Salmon, ID 83467 • 3,308
Salmon Creek, WA 98665 • 1,950
Saltillo, MS 38866 • 1,271
Salt Lake □, UT • 619,066
Salt Lake City, UT 84101–99 • 163,697
Salt Rock, WV 25559 • 900
Saltsburg, PA 15681 • 964
Salt Springs, FL 32627 • 1,500
Saltville, VA 24370 • 2,376
Saluda, NC 28773 • 607
Saluda, SC 29138 • 2,752
Saluda □, SC • 16,150
Salyer, CA 95563 • 950
Salyersville, KY 41465 • 1,352
Samoa, CA 95564 • 850
Samoset, FL 33508 • 5,747
Sampson □, NC • 49,687
Samson, AL 36477 • 2,402
Samtown, LA 71301 • 4,125
Samuels, ID 83862 • 650
San Andreas, CA 95249 • 1,564
San Angelo, TX 76901–09 • 73,240
San Anselmo, CA 94960 • 12,067
San Antonio, TX 78201–99 • 786,023
Sanatorium, MS 39112 • 700
San Augustine, TX 75972 • 2,930
San Augustine □, TX • 8,785
San Benito, TX 78586 • 17,988
San Benito □, CA • 25,005
San Bernardino, CA 92401–99 • 118,794
San Bernardino □, CA • 895,016
Sanborn, IA 51248 • 1,398
Sanborn □, SD • 3,213
Sanbornville, NH 03872 • 800
San Bruno, CA 94066 • 35,417
San Carlos, AZ 85550 • 2,668
San Carlos, CA 94070 • 24,710
San Clemente, CA 92672 • 27,325
Sanders □, MT • 8,675
Sanderson, TX 79848 • 1,300
Sandersville, GA 31082 • 6,137
Sandersville, MS 39477 • 800
Sand Hill, MA 02066 • 1,750
San Diego, CA 92101–99 • 875,538
San Diego, TX 78384 • 5,225
San Diego □, CA • 1,861,846
San Dimas, CA 91773 • 24,014
Sandoval, IL 62882 • 1,734
Sandoval □, NM • 34,799
Sand Point, AK 99661 • 625
Sandpoint, ID 83864 • 4,460
Sand Springs, OK 74063 • 13,121
Sandston, VA 23150 • 4,500
Sandstone, MN 55072 • 1,594
Sandusky, MI 48471 • 2,071
Sandusky, OH 44870 • 31,360
Sandusky □, OH • 63,267
Sandwich, IL 60548 • 5,244
Sandwich, MA 02563 • 1,784
Sandy, OR 97055 • 2,905
Sandy, UT 84070 • 52,210
Sandy Creek, NY 13145 • 765
Sandy Hook, CT 06482 • 950
Sandy Hook, KY 41171 • 627
Sandy Lake, PA 16145 • 779
Sandy Springs, GA 30328 • 20,300
Sandy Springs, SC 29677 • 1,100
San Elizario, TX 79849 • 1,100
San Felipe Pueblo, NM 87001 • 1,465
San Fernando, CA 91340–46 • 17,731
Sanford, CO 81151 • 687
Sanford, FL 32771 • 23,176
Sanford, ME 04073 • 10,268
Sanford, MI 48657 • 864
Sanford, NC 27330 • 14,773
San Francisco, CA 94101–99 • 678,974
San Francisco □, CA • 678,974
San Gabriel, CA 91775–78 • 30,072
Sangamon □, IL • 176,070
Sanger, CA 93657 • 12,542
Sanger, TX 76266 • 2,574
Sanibel, FL 33957 • 3,363
Sanilac □, MI • 40,789
San Isidro, TX 78588 • 700
San Jacinto, CA 92383 • 7,098
San Jacinto □, TX • 11,434
San Joaquin □, CA • 347,342
San Jose, CA 95101–99 • 629,546
San Jose, IL 62682 • 784
San Juan, TX 78589 • 7,608
San Juan □, CO • 833
San Juan □, NM • 81,433
San Juan □, UT • 12,253
San Juan □, WA • 7,838
San Juan Capistrano, CA 92675 • 18,959
San Leandro, CA 94577–79 • 63,952
San Lorenzo, CA 94580 • 20,545
San Luis, CO 81152 • 842
San Luis Obispo, CA 93401 • 34,252
San Luis Obispo □, CA • 155,435
San Manuel, AZ 85631 • 5,443
San Marcos, CA 92069 • 17,479
San Marcos, TX 78666 • 23,420
San Marino, CA 91108 • 13,307
San Mateo, CA 94401–99 • 77,640
San Mateo, FL 32088 • 950
San Mateo □, CA • 587,329
San Miguel, CA 93451 • 800
San Miguel □, CO • 3,192
San Miguel □, NM • 22,751
San Pablo, CA 94806 • 19,750
San Patricio □, TX • 58,013
Sanpete □, UT • 14,620
San Rafael, CA 94901–15 • 44,700
San Remo, NY 11754 • 8,700
San Saba, TX 76877 • 2,847
San Saba □, TX • 6,204
Santa Ana, CA 92701–99 • 204,023
Santa Anna, TX 76878 • 1,535
Santa Barbara, CA 93101–99 • 74,414
Santa Barbara □, CA • 298,694
Santa Clara, CA 95050–55 • 87,700
Santa Clara, OR 97401 • 11,288
Santa Clara, UT 84765 • 1,091
Santa Clara □, CA • 1,295,071
Santa Cruz, CA 95060–66 • 41,483
Santa Cruz □, AZ • 20,459
Santa Cruz □, CA • 188,141
Santa Fe, NM 87501–09 • 48,953
Santa Fe, TX 77510 • 6,172
Santa Fe □, NM • 75,360
Santa Fe Springs, CA 90670 • 14,520
Santa Margarita, CA 93453 • 1,200
Santa Maria, CA 93454–56 • 39,685
Santa Monica, CA 90401–99 • 88,314
Santa Paula, CA 93060 • 20,552
Santaquin, UT 84655 • 2,175
Santa Rosa, CA 95401–07 • 83,320
Santa Rosa, NM 88435 • 2,469
Santa Rosa □, FL • 55,988
Santa Rosa Beach, FL 32459 • 950
Santa Ynez, CA 93460 • 3,335
Santee, CA 92071 • 40,313
Santo Domingo Pueblo, NM 87052 • 2,082
San Ygnacio, TX 78067 • 900
Sappington, MO 63126 • 11,388
Sapulpa, OK 74066 • 15,853
Saraland, AL 36571 • 9,833
Saranac, MI 48881 • 1,421
Saranac Lake, NY 12983 • 5,578
Sarasota, FL 33577–83 • 48,868
Sarasota □, FL • 202,251
Saratoga, CA 95070 • 29,261
Saratoga, TX 77585 • 1,000
Saratoga, WY 82331 • 2,410
Saratoga □, NY • 153,759
Saratoga Springs, NY 12866 • 23,906
Sarcoxie, MO 64862 • 1,381
Sardinia, OH 45171 • 826
Sardis, GA 30456 • 1,180
Sardis, MS 38666 • 2,278
Sarepta, LA 71071 • 831
Sargent, GA 30275 • 700
Sargent, NE 68874 • 828
Sargent □, ND • 5,512
Sarpy □, NE • 86,015
Sartell, MN 56377 • 3,427
Satanta, KS 67870 • 1,117
Satellite Beach, FL 32937 • 9,163
Satsuma, AL 36572 • 3,822
Satsuma, FL 32089 • 950
Saugatuck, MI 49453 • 1,079
Saugerties, NY 12477 • 3,882
Saugus, CA 91350 • 16,283
Saugus, MA 01906 • 24,746
Sauk □, WI • 43,469
Sauk Centre, MN 56378 • 3,709
Sauk City, WI 53583 • 2,703
Sauk Rapids, MN 56379 • 5,793
Sauk Village, IL 60411 • 10,906
Saukville, WI 53080 • 3,494
Saunders □, NE • 18,716
Sausalito, CA 94965 • 7,338
Savage, MD 20763 • 2,928
Savanna, IL 61074 • 4,529
Savanna, OK 74565 • 828
Savannah, GA 31401–99 • 141,390
Savannah, MO 64485 • 4,184
Savannah, NY 13146 • 640
Savannah, TN 38372 • 6,992
Savona, NY 14879 • 932
Savoy, IL 61874 • 2,126
Sawyer □, WI • 12,843
Saxon, SC • 1,200
Saxonburg, PA 16056 • 1,336
Saxton, PA 16678 • 814
Saybrook, IL 61770 • 882
Saybrook Manor, CT 06475 • 1,140
Saydel, IA 50313 • 4,200
Saylesville, RI 02865 • 3,200
Saylorville, IA 50313 • 780
Sayre, OK 73662 • 3,177
Sayre, PA 18840 • 6,951
Sayreville, NJ 08872 • 29,969
Sayville, NY 11782 • 15,300
Scalp Level, PA 15963 • 1,186
Scanlon, MN 55720 • 1,050
Scappoose, OR 97056 • 3,213
Scarborough, ME 04074 • 2,280
Scarsdale, NY 10583 • 17,650
Schaefferstown, PA 17088 • 800
Schaghticoke, NY 12154 • 677
Schaller, IA 51053 • 832
Schaumburg, IL 60194 • 53,305
Schenectady, NY 12301–99 • 67,972
Schenectady □, NY • 149,946
Schenevus, NY 12155 • 625
Schererville, IN 46375 • 13,209
Schertz, TX 78154 • 7,262
Schiller Park, IL 60176 • 11,458
Schleicher □, TX • 2,820
Schleswig, IA 51461 • 868
Schley □, GA • 3,433
Schofield, WI 54476 • 2,226
Schoharie, NY 12157 • 1,016
Schoharie □, NY • 29,710
Schoolcraft, MI 49087 • 1,359
Schoolcraft □, MI • 8,575
Schram City, IL 62049 • 708
Schroon Lake, NY 12870 • 1,000
Schulenburg, TX 78956 • 2,469
Schuyler, NE 68661 • 4,151
Schuyler □, IL • 8,365
Schuyler □, MO • 4,979
Schuyler □, NY • 17,686
Schuylerville, NY 12871 • 1,256
Schuylkill □, PA • 160,630
Schuylkill Haven, PA 17972 • 5,977
Science Hill, KY 42553 • 655
Scio, OH 43988 • 1,003
Scioto □, OH • 84,545
Scituate, MA 02066 • 5,351
Scobey, MT 59263 • 1,382
Scotch Plains, NJ 07076 • 20,774
Scotia, CA 95565 • 1,200
Scotia, NY 12302 • 7,280
Scotland, SD 57059 • 1,022
Scotland □, MO • 5,415
Scotland □, NC • 32,273
Scotland Neck, NC 27874 • 2,834
Scotlandville, LA 70807 • 15,113
Scott, LA 70583 • 2,239
Scott □, AR • 9,685
Scott □, IL • 6,142
Scott □, IN • 20,422
Scott □, IA • 160,022
Scott □, KS • 5,782
Scott □, KY • 21,813
Scott □, MN • 43,784
Scott □, MS • 24,556
Scott □, MO • 39,647
Scott □, TN • 19,259
Scott □, VA • 25,068
Scott City, KS 67871 • 4,154
Scott City, MO 63780 • 4,630
Scottdale, GA 30079 • 8,777
Scottdale, PA 15683 • 5,833
Scottsbluff, NE 69361 • 14,156
Scotts Bluff □, NE • 38,344
Scottsboro, AL 35768 • 14,758
Scottsburg, IN 47170 • 5,068
Scottsdale, AZ 85251–71 • 88,622
Scotts Hill, TN 38374 • 668
Scotts Valley, CA 95066 • 6,891
Scottsville, KY 42164 • 4,278
Scottsville, NY 14546 • 1,789
Scott Township, PA 15106 • 20,413
Scottville, MI 49454 • 1,241
Scranton, IA 51462 • 748
Scranton, KS 66537 • 664
Scranton, PA 18501–99 • 88,117
Scranton, SC 29591 • 861
Screven, GA 31560 • 872
Screven □, GA • 14,043
Scribner, NE 68057 • 1,011
Scurry □, TX • 18,192
Seaboard, NC 27876 • 687
Sea Bright, NJ 07760 • 1,812
Seabrook, MD 20706 • 7,100
Seabrook, NH 03874 • 700
Seabrook, NJ 08302 • 1,411
Seabrook, TX 77586 • 4,670
Sea Cliff, NY 11579 • 5,364
Seadrift, TX 77983 • 1,277
Seaford, DE 19973 • 5,256
Seaford, NY 11783 • 17,150
Seaford, VA 23696 • 1,700
Sea Girt, NJ 08750 • 2,650
Seagoville, TX 75159 • 7,304
Seagraves, TX 79359 • 2,596
Sea Isle City, NJ 08243 • 2,644
Seal Beach, CA 90740 • 25,975
Seal Rock, OR 97376 • 800
Sealy, TX 77474 • 3,875
Seaman, OH 45679 • 1,039
Searcy, AR 72143 • 13,612
Searcy □, AR • 8,847
Searsport, ME 04974 • 1,348
Seaside, CA 93955 • 36,567
Seaside, OR 97138 • 5,193
Seaside Heights, NJ 08751 • 1,802
Seaside Park, NJ 08752 • 1,795
Seat Pleasant, MD 20743 • 5,217
Seattle, WA 98101–99 • 493,846
Sebastian, FL 32958 • 2,831
Sebastian □, AR • 95,172
Sebastopol, CA 95472 • 5,595
Sebeka, MN 56477 • 774
Sebewaing, MI 48759 • 2,046
Sebree, KY 42455 • 1,516
Sebring, FL 33870 • 8,736
Sebring, OH 44672 • 5,078
Secaucus, NJ 07094 • 13,719
Section, AL 35771 • 821
Security, CO 80911 • 11,000
Sedalia, MO 65301 • 20,927
Sedan, KS 67361 • 1,579
Sedgwick, KS 67135 • 1,471
Sedgwick □, CO • 3,266
Sedgwick □, KS • 367,088
Sedona, AZ 86336 • 5,368
Sedro Woolley, WA 98284 • 6,110
Seekonk, MA 02771 • 12,269
Seeley, CA 92273 • 1,058
Seeley Lake, MT 59868 • 800
Seelyville, IN 47878 • 1,374
Seguin, TX 78155 • 17,854
Seiling, OK 73663 • 1,103
Selah, WA 98942 • 4,500
Selby, SD 57472 • 884
Selbyville, DE 19975 • 1,251
Selden, NY 11784 • 24,100
Seligman, AZ 86337 • 950
Selinsgrove, PA 17870 • 5,227
Sellersburg, IN 47172 • 3,211
Sellersville, PA 18960 • 3,143
Sells, AZ 85634 • 1,864
Selma, AL 36701 • 26,684
Selma, CA 93662 • 10,942
Selma, IN 47383 • 1,056
Selma, NC 27576 • 4,762
Selmer, TN 38375 • 3,979
Seminole, OK 74868 • 8,590
Seminole, TX 79360 • 6,080
Seminole □, FL • 179,752
Seminole □, GA • 9,057
Seminole □, OK • 27,473
Seminole Park, FL 33540 • 8,000
Semmes, AL 36575 • 1,200
Senath, MO 63876 • 1,728
Senatobia, MS 38668 • 5,013
Seneca, IL 61360 • 2,098
Seneca, KS 66538 • 2,389
Seneca, MO 64865 • 1,853
Seneca, PA 16346 • 980
Seneca, SC 29678 • 7,436
Seneca □, NY • 33,733
Seneca □, OH • 61,901
Seneca Falls, NY 13148 • 7,466
Senoia, GA 30276 • 900
Sentinel, OK 73664 • 1,016
Sequatchie □, TN • 8,605
Sequim, WA 98382 • 3,013
Sequoyah □, OK • 30,749
Sergeant Bluff, IA 51054 • 2,416
Sesser, IL 62884 • 2,238
Seth, WV 25181 • 650
Seven Hills, OH 44131 • 13,650
Seven Mile, OH 45062 • 841
Severn, MD 21144 • 20,147
Severna Park, MD 21146 • 21,253
Sevier □, AR • 14,060
Sevier □, TN • 41,418
Sevier □, UT • 14,727
Sevierville, TN 37862 • 4,556
Seville, FL 32090 • 800
Seville, OH 44273 • 1,568
Sewanee, TN 37375 • 2,218
Seward, AK 99664 • 1,843
Seward, NE 68434 • 5,713
Seward, PA 15954 • 675
Seward □, KS • 17,071
Seward □, NE • 15,789
Sewaren, NJ 07077 • 2,300
Sewell, NJ 08080 • 1,900
Sewickley, PA 15143 • 4,778
Seymour, CT 06483 • 13,434
Seymour, IN 47274 • 15,050
Seymour, IA 52590 • 1,036
Seymour, MO 65746 • 1,535
Seymour, TX 76380 • 3,657
Seymour, WI 54165 • 2,530
Seymourville, LA 70764 • 2,891
Shabbona, IL 60550 • 851
Shackelford □, TX • 3,915
Shady Cove, OR 97539 • 1,097
Shady Side, MD 20764 • 2,877
Shadyside, OH 43947 • 4,315
Shady Spring, WV 25918 • 1,000
Shafter, CA 93263 • 7,010
Shaftsbury, VT 05262 • 700
Shaker Heights, OH 44122 • 32,487
Shakopee, MN 55379 • 9,941
Shallotte, NC 28459 • 680
Shallowater, TX 79363 • 1,932
Shamokin, PA 17872 • 10,357
Shamokin Dam, PA 17876 • 1,622
Shamrock, TX 79079 • 2,834
Shandon, CA 93461 • 800
Shannon, GA 30172 • 2,040
Shannon, IL 61078 • 938
Shannon, MS 38868 • 680
Shannon □, MO • 7,885
Shannon □, SD • 11,323
Shannontown, SC 29150 • 7,900
Sharkey □, MS • 7,964
Sharon, CT 06069 • 900
Sharon, MA 02067 • 13,601
Sharon, PA 16146 • 19,057
Sharon, TN 38255 • 1,134
Sharon, WI 53585 • 1,280
Sharon Hill, PA 19079 • 6,221
Sharon Springs, KS 67758 • 982
Sharonville, OH 45241 • 10,108
Sharp □, AR • 14,607
Sharpes, FL 32959 • 1,250
Sharpley, DE 19803 • 1,700
Sharpsburg, MD 21782 • 721
Sharpsburg, NC 27878 • 997
Sharpsburg, PA 15215 • 4,351
Sharpsville, IN 46068 • 617
Sharpsville, PA 16150 • 5,375
Sharptown, MD 21861 • 654
Shasta □, CA • 115,715
Shattuck, OK 73858 • 1,759
Shaw, MS 38773 • 2,461
Shawano, WI 54166 • 7,013
Shawano □, WI • 35,928
Shawmut, AL 36854 • 2,284
Shawnee, KS 66203 • 29,653
Shawnee, OH 43782 • 924
Shawnee, OK 74801 • 26,506
Shawnee □, KS • 154,916
Shawneetown, IL 62984 • 1,841
Sheboygan, WI 53081 • 48,085
Sheboygan □, WI • 100,935
Sheboygan Falls, WI 53085 • 5,253
Sheffield, AL 35660–62 • 11,903
Sheffield, IL 61361 • 1,130
Sheffield, IA 50475 • 1,224
Sheffield, MA 01257 • 1,100
Sheffield, PA 16347 • 1,564
Sheffield Lake, OH 44054 • 10,484
Shelbina, MO 63468 • 2,169
Shelburn, IN 47879 • 1,259
Shelburne Falls, MA 01370 • 2,046
Shelby, IN 46377 • 700
Shelby, IA 51570 • 665
Shelby, MI 49455 • 1,624
Shelby, MS 38774 • 2,540
Shelby, MT 59474 • 3,142
Shelby, NE 68662 • 724
Shelby, NC 28150 • 15,310
Shelby, OH 44875 • 9,646
Shelby □, AL • 66,298
Shelby □, IL • 23,923
Shelby □, IN • 39,887
Shelby □, IA • 15,043
Shelby □, KY • 23,328
Shelby □, MO • 7,826
Shelby □, OH • 43,089
Shelby □, TN • 777,113
Shelby □, TX • 23,084
Shelby City, KY 40422 • 700
Shelbyville, IL 62565 • 5,259
Shelbyville, IN 46176 • 14,989
Shelbyville, KY 40065 • 5,329
Shelbyville, MO 63469 • 645
Shelbyville, TN 37160 • 13,530
Sheldon, IL 60966 • 1,215
Sheldon, IA 51201 • 5,003
Sheldon, TX 77028 • 2,800
Shelley, ID 83274 • 3,300
Shell Lake, WI 54871 • 1,135
Shellman, GA 31786 • 1,254
Shell Rock, IA 50670 • 1,478
Shellsburg, IA 52332 • 771
Shelter Island, NY 11964 • 1,000
Shelton, CT 06484 • 31,314
Shelton, NE 68876 • 1,046
Shelton, WA 98584 • 7,629
Shenandoah, IA 51601 • 6,274
Shenandoah, PA 17976 • 7,589
Shenandoah, VA 22849 • 1,861
Shenandoah □, VA • 27,559
Shepherd, MI 48883 • 1,534
Shepherd, TX 77371 • 1,674
Shepherdstown, WV 25443 • 1,791
Shepherdsville, KY 40165 • 4,454
Sheppton, PA 18248 • 650
Sherborn, MA 01770 • 950
Sherburn, MN 56171 • 1,275
Sherburne, NY 13460 • 1,561
Sherburne □, MN • 29,908
Sheridan, AR 72150 • 3,042
Sheridan, CO 80110 • 5,377
Sheridan, IL 60551 • 719
Sheridan, IN 46069 • 2,200
Sheridan, MI 48884 • 664
Sheridan, MT 59749 • 646
Sheridan, OR 97378 • 2,249
Sheridan, WY 82801 • 15,146
Sheridan □, KS • 3,544

Sheridan □, MT • *5,414*
Sheridan □, NE • *7,544*
Sheridan □, ND • *2,819*
Sheridan □, WY • *25,048*
Sherman, NY 14781 • *775*
Sherman, TX 75090 • *30,413*
Sherman □, KS • *7,759*
Sherman □, NE • *4,226*
Sherman □, OR • *2,172*
Sherman □, TX • *3,174*
Sherrard, IL 61281 • *811*
Sherrelwood, CO 80221 • *11,450*
Sherrill, NY 13461 • *2,830*
Sherwood, AR 72116 • *10,406*
Sherwood, OH 43556 • *915*
Sherwood, OR 97140 • *2,386*
Sherwood Manor, CT 06082 • *6,303*
Sherwood Park, DE 19808 • *2,300*
Shiawassee □, MI • *71,140*
Shickshinny, PA 18655 • *1,192*
Shidler, OK 74652 • *708*
Shillington, PA 19607 • *5,601*
Shiloh, NJ 08353 • *604*
Shiloh, OH 44878 • *857*
Shiner, TX 77984 • *2,213*
Shinglehouse, PA 16748 • *1,310*
Shinnston, WV 26431 • *3,059*
Shiocton, WI 54170 • *805*
Ship Bottom, NJ 08008 • *1,427*
Shippensburg, PA 17257 • *5,261*
Shiprock, NM 87420 • *7,237*
Shirley, IN 47384 • *919*
Shirley, MA 01464 • *1,630*
Shirley, NY 11967 • *8,200*
Shively, KY 40216 • *16,819*
Shoals, IN 47581 • *967*
Shoemakersville, PA 19555 • *1,391*
Shore Acres, MA 02066 • *1,200*
Shore Acres, NJ 08723 • *1,300*
Shoreham, MI 49085 • *742*
Shoreview, MN 55112 • *17,300*
Shorewood, IL 60435 • *4,714*
Shorewood, MN 55331 • *4,646*
Shorewood, WI 53211 • *14,327*
Shorewood Hills, WI 53705 • *1,837*
Short Beach, CT 06405 • *1,200*
Shortsville, NY 14548 • *1,669*
Shoshone, ID 83352 • *1,242*
Shoshone □, ID • *19,226*
Shoshoni, WY 82649 • *879*
Show Low, AZ 85901 • *4,290*
Shreve, OH 44676 • *1,608*
Shreveport, LA 71101–10 • *205,820*
Shrewsbury, MA 01545 • *22,674*
Shrewsbury, MO 63119 • *5,077*
Shrewsbury, NJ 07701 • *2,962*
Shrewsbury, PA 17361 • *2,688*
Shubuta, MS 39360 • *626*
Shullsburg, WI 53586 • *1,484*
Sibley, IA 51249 • *3,051*
Sibley, LA 71073 • *1,211*
Sibley □, MN • *15,448*
Sicily Island, LA 71368 • *691*
Sicklerville, NJ 08081 • *850*
Sidell, IL 61876 • *625*
Sidney, IL 61877 • *886*
Sidney, IA 51652 • *1,308*
Sidney, MT 59270 • *5,726*
Sidney, NE 69162 • *6,010*
Sidney, NY 13838 • *4,861*
Sidney, OH 45365 • *17,657*
Siegle, LA 71291 • *1,400*
Sierra □, CA • *3,073*
Sierra □, NM • *8,454*
Sierra Blanca, TX 79851 • *900*
Sierra City, CA 96125 • *800*
Sierra Madre, CA 91024 • *10,837*
Sierra Vista, AZ 85635 • *24,937*
Signal Hill, CA 90806 • *5,734*
Signal Mountain, TN 37377 • *5,818*
Sigourney, IA 52591 • *2,330*
Sikeston, MO 63801 • *17,431*
Siler City, NC 27344 • *4,446*
Siletz, OR 97380 • *1,001*
Siloam Springs, AR 72761 • *7,940*
Silsbee, TX 77656 • *7,684*
Silt, CO 81652 • *923*
Silver Bay, MN 55614 • *2,917*
Silver Bow □, MT • *38,092*
Silver City, NM 88061 • *9,887*
Silver Creek, NY 14136 • *3,088*
Silverdale, WA 98383 • *1,500*
Silver Grove, KY 41085 • *1,260*
Silverhill, AL 36576 • *624*
Silver Hill, MD 20746 • *2,400*
Silver Lake, KS 66539 • *1,350*
Silver Lake, MA 01887 • *3,400*
Silver Lake, MN 55381 • *698*
Silver Lake, WI 53170 • *1,598*
Silver Spring, MD 20901–99
 • *64,100*
Silver Springs, FL 32688 • *1,082*
Silver Springs, NY 14550 • *801*
Silverton, CO 81433 • *794*
Silverton, ID 83867 • *750*
Silverton, NJ 08753 • *7,236*
Silverton, OH 45236 • *6,172*
Silverton, OR 97381 • *5,168*
Silverton, TX 79257 • *918*
Silview, DE 19804 • *1,650*
Silvis, IL 61282 • *7,130*
Simi Valley, CA 93065 • *77,500*
Simmesport, LA 71369 • *2,293*
Simpson, PA 18407 • *2,200*
Simpson □, KY • *14,673*
Simpson □, MS • *23,441*
Simpsonville, KY 40067 • *642*
Simpsonville, SC 29681 • *9,037*
Simsbury, CT 06070 • *5,488*
Sinclairville, NY 14782 • *772*
Sinton, TX 78387 • *6,044*
Sioux □, IA • *30,813*
Sioux □, NE • *1,845*
Sioux □, ND • *3,620*
Sioux Center, IA 51250 • *4,588*
Sioux City, IA 51101–11 • *82,003*
Sioux Falls, SD 57101–99 • *81,343*
Sioux Rapids, IA 50585 • *897*
Sipsey, AL 35584 • *678*
Siren, WI 54872 • *896*
Siskiyou □, CA • *39,732*
Sisseton, SD 57262 • *2,789*
Sisters, OR 97759 • *696*
Sistersville, WV 26175 • *2,367*
Sitka, AK 99835 • *7,803*
Skagit □, WA • *64,138*
Skagway, AK 99840 • *768*
Skamania □, WA • *7,919*
Skaneateles, NY 13152 • *2,789*
Skellytown, TX 79080 • *899*
Skiatook, OK 74070 • *3,596*
Skidmore, TX 78389 • *800*
Skokie, IL 60076–77 • *60,278*
Skowhegan, ME 04976 • *6,517*
Skyland, NC 28776 • *2,200*
Skyway, CO 80906 • *3,600*
Skyway, WA 98178 • *12,500*
Slackwood, NJ 08638 • *8,100*
Slater, IA 50244 • *1,312*
Slater, MO 65349 • *2,492*
Slater, SC 29683 • *1,000*
Slatersville, RI 02876 • *2,000*
Slatington, PA 18080 • *4,277*
Slaton, TX 79364 • *6,804*
Slaughter, LA 70777 • *729*
Slayton, MN 56172 • *2,420*
Sledge, MS 38670 • *699*
Sleepy Eye, MN 56085 • *3,581*
Slickville, PA 15684 • *1,066*
Slidell, LA 70458–61 • *26,718*
Sligo, PA 16255 • *798*
Slinger, WI 53086 • *1,612*
Slippery Rock, PA 16057 • *3,047*
Sloan, IA 51055 • *978*
Sloan, NY 14225 • *4,529*
Sloatsburg, NY 10974 • *3,154*
Slocomb, AL 36375 • *2,153*
Slope □, ND • *1,157*
Slovan, PA 15078 • *900*
Smackover, AR 71762 • *2,453*
Smelterville, ID 83868 • *776*
Smethport, PA 16749 • *1,797*
Smith □, KS • *5,947*
Smith □, MS • *15,077*
Smith □, TN • *14,935*
Smith □, TX • *128,366*
Smith Center, KS 66967 • *2,240*
Smithers, WV 25186 • *1,482*
Smithfield, NC 27577 • *7,288*
Smithfield, OH 43948 • *1,308*
Smithfield, PA 15478 • *1,084*
Smithfield, UT 84335 • *4,993*
Smithfield, VA 23430 • *3,718*
Smith River, CA 95567 • *1,000*
Smiths, AL 36877 • *900*
Smithsburg, MD 21783 • *833*
Smiths Grove, KY 42171 • *767*
Smithton, IL 62285 • *1,447*
Smithtown, NY 11787 • *23,000*
Smithville, GA 31787 • *867*
Smithville, MS 38870 • *866*
Smithville, MO 64089 • *1,873*
Smithville, OH 44677 • *1,467*
Smithville, TN 37166 • *3,839*
Smithville, TX 78957 • *3,470*
Smyrna, DE 19977 • *4,750*
Smyrna, GA 30080 • *20,312*
Smyrna, TN 37167 • *8,839*
Smyth □, VA • *33,366*
Sneads, FL 32460 • *1,690*
Sneedville, TN 37869 • *1,110*
Snellville, GA 30278 • *8,514*
Snohomish, WA 98290 • *5,294*
Snohomish □, WA • *337,720*
Snoqualmie, WA 98065 • *1,370*
Snowflake, AZ 85937 • *3,510*
Snow Hill, MD 21863 • *2,192*
Snow Hill, NC 28580 • *1,374*
Snow Shoe, PA 16874 • *852*
Snyder, OK 73566 • *1,848*
Snyder, TX 79549 • *12,705*
Snyder □, PA • *33,584*
Soap Lake, WA 98851 • *1,196*
Socastee, SC 29577 • *1,082*
Social Circle, GA 30279 • *2,591*
Society Hill, SC 29593 • *848*
Socorro, NM 87801 • *7,173*
Socorro □, NM • *12,566*
Soda Springs, ID 83276 • *4,051*
Soddy-Daisy, TN 37379 • *8,388*
Sodus, NY 14551 • *1,790*
Sodus Point, NY 14555 • *1,334*
Solana, FL 33950 • *1,408*
Solana Beach, CA 92075 • *13,047*
Solano □, CA • *235,203*
Soldiers Grove, WI 54655 • *622*
Soldotna, AK 99669 • *2,320*
Soledad, CA 93960 • *5,928*
Solomon, KS 67480 • *1,018*
Solon, IA 52333 • *969*
Solon, OH 44139 • *14,341*
Solvay, NY 13209 • *7,140*
Somerdale, NJ 08083 • *5,900*
Somers, CT 06071 • *1,643*
Somers, MT 59932 • *800*
Somerset, KY 42501 • *10,649*
Somerset, MA 02725 • *18,813*
Somerset, NJ 08873 • *21,731*
Somerset, OH 43783 • *1,432*
Somerset, PA 15501 • *6,474*
Somerset, TX 78069 • *1,102*
Somerset, WI 54025 • *860*
Somerset □, ME • *45,046*
Somerset □, MD • *19,188*
Somerset □, NJ • *203,129*
Somerset □, PA • *81,243*
Somers Point, NJ 08244 • *10,330*
Somersville, CT 06072 • *750*
Somersworth, NH 03878 • *10,350*
Somerton, AZ 85350 • *5,761*
Somervell □, TX • *4,154*
Somerville, MA 02143 • *77,372*
Somerville, NJ 08876 • *11,973*
Somerville, TN 38068 • *2,264*
Somerville, TX 77879 • *1,814*
Somonauk, IL 60552 • *1,344*
Sonoma, CA 95476 • *6,054*
Sonoma □, CA • *299,681*
Sonora, CA 95370 • *3,247*
Sonora, TX 76950 • *3,856*
Soperton, GA 30457 • *2,981*
Sophia, WV 25921 • *1,216*
Soquel, CA 95073 • *6,212*
Sorento, IL 62086 • *677*
Sorrento, FL 32776 • *950*
Sorrento, LA 70778 • *1,197*
Soudan, MN 55782 • *950*
Souderton, PA 18964 • *6,657*
Sound Beach, NY 11789 • *5,400*
Sourlake, TX 77659 • *1,807*
South Acton, MA 01720 • *4,600*
South Amboy, NJ 08879 • *8,322*
South Amherst, MA 01002 • *4,861*
South Amherst, OH 44001 • *1,848*
Southampton, NY 11968 • *4,000*
Southampton, PA 18966 • *9,500*
Southampton □, VA • *18,731*
South Ashburnham, MA 01466
 • *1,123*
Southaven, MS 38671 • *16,071*
South Barre, VT 05670 • *1,301*
South Bay, FL 33493 • *3,886*
South Belmar, NJ 07719 • *1,566*
South Beloit, IL 61080 • *4,088*
South Bend, IN 46601–99 • *109,727*
South Bend, WA 98586 • *1,686*
South Berwick, ME 03908 • *2,120*
South Bloomfield, OH 43103 • *934*
Southborough, MA 01772 • *1,600*
South Boston, VA 24592 • *7,093*
South Bound Brook, NJ 08880
 • *4,331*
Southbridge, MA 01550 • *16,665*
South Broadway, WA 98902 • *3,620*
South Burlington, VT 05401 • *10,679*
Southbury, CT 06488 • *900*
South Charleston, OH 45368 • *1,682*
South Charleston, WV 25303
 • *15,968*
South Chatham, MA 02659 • *950*
South Chicago Heights, IL 60411
 • *3,932*
South Coffeyville, OK 74072 • *873*
South Congaree, SC 29169 • *2,113*
South Connellsville, PA 15425
 • *2,296*
South Corning, NY 14830 • *1,195*
South Dartmouth, MA 02748 • *7,000*
South Dayton, NY 14138 • *661*
South Daytona, FL 32021 • *11,252*
South Decatur, GA 30037 • *28,100*
South Deerfield, MA 01373 • *1,926*
South Dennis, MA 02660 • *1,500*
South Dos Palos, CA 93665 • *850*
South Duxbury, MA 02332 • *2,985*
South Easton, MA 02375 • *1,400*
South Elgin, IL 60177 • *5,970*
South El Monte, CA 91733 • *16,623*
Southern Pines, NC 28387 • *8,620*
South Euclid, OH 44121 • *25,713*
South Fallsburg, NY 12779 • *1,590*
South Farmingdale, NY 11735
 • *20,500*
Southfield, MI 48034 • *75,568*
South Fork, PA 15956 • *1,401*
South Fulton, TN 38257 • *2,735*
South Gastonia, NC 28052 • *2,000*
South Gate, CA 90280 • *66,784*
Southgate, KY 41071 • *2,833*
Southgate, MI 48195 • *32,058*
South Glastonbury, CT 06073
 • *1,600*
Southglenn, CO 80122 • *3,800*
South Glens Falls, NY 12801 • *3,714*
South Grafton, MA 01560 • *3,000*
South Hackensack, NJ 07606
 • *2,229*
South Hadley, MA 01075 • *8,900*
South Hadley Falls, MA 01075
 • *5,600*
South Hamilton, MA 01982 • *2,900*
South Hanover, MA 02339 • *950*
South Harwich, MA 02661 • *900*
South Haven, IN 46383 • *6,679*
South Haven, MI 49090 • *5,943*
South Hill, VA 23970 • *4,347*
South Hingham, MA 02043 • *5,200*
South Holland, IL 60473 • *24,977*
South Hooksett, NH 03106 • *1,200*
South Houston, TX 77587 • *13,293*
South Huntington, NY 11746 • *9,115*
South Hutchinson, KS 67505 • *2,226*
Southington, CT 06489 • *17,400*
South International Falls, MN 56679
 • *2,806*
South Jacksonville, IL 62650 • *3,382*
South Jordan, UT 84065 • *7,492*
South Kenosha, WI 53140 • *875*
South Lake Tahoe, CA 95705
 • *20,681*
South Lancaster, MA 01561 • *2,329*
South Laramie, WY 82070 • *1,500*
South Laurel, MD 20707 • *8,500*
South Lebanon, OH 45065 • *2,700*
South Lyon, MI 48178 • *5,214*
South Mansfield, LA 71052 • *1,463*
South Medford, OR 97501 • *2,898*
South Miami, FL 33143 • *10,944*
South Miami Heights, FL 33157
 • *18,000*
South Mills, NC 27976 • *800*
South Milwaukee, WI 53172
 • *21,069*
South Modesto, CA 95350 • *12,492*
Southmont, NC 27351 • *700*
South Nyack, NY 10960 • *3,602*
South Ogden, UT 84403 • *11,366*
Southold, NY 11971 • *2,030*
South Orange, NJ 07079 • *15,864*
South Paris, ME 04281 • *2,128*
South Pasadena, CA 91030 • *22,681*
South Patrick Shores, FL 32937
 • *9,816*
South Pekin, IL 61564 • *1,243*
South Pittsburg, TN 37380 • *3,636*
South Plainfield, NJ 07080 • *20,521*
Southport, FL 32409 • *1,992*
Southport, IN 46217 • *2,266*
Southport, NC 28461 • *2,824*
Southport, NY 14904 • *8,700*
South Portland, ME 04106 • *22,712*
South Range, MI 49963 • *861*
South Renovo, PA 17764 • *663*
South River, NJ 08882 • *14,361*
South Royalton, VT 05068 • *700*
South Salt Lake, UT 84115 • *9,884*
South San Francisco, CA 94080
 • *49,393*
South San Gabriel, CA 91770
 • *5,421*
Southside, AL 35901 • *5,141*
Southside Place, TX 77005 • *1,366*
South Sioux City, NE 68776 • *9,339*
South Stony Brook, NY 11790
 • *15,329*
South St. Paul, MN 55075 • *21,235*
South Streator, IL 61364 • *2,334*
South Swansea, MA 02777 • *1,700*
South Toms River, NJ 08757 • *3,954*
South Tucson, AZ 85725 • *6,554*
South Valley Stream, NY 11581
 • *6,600*
South Venice, FL 33595 • *8,075*
South Walpole, MA 02071 • *1,600*
South Waverly, PA 14892 • *1,176*
South Webster, OH 45682 • *886*
Southwest, PA 15685 • *700*
South Westbury, NY 11590 • *10,700*
Southwest Harbor, ME 04679
 • *1,052*
South Whitley, IN 46787 • *1,575*
South Whittier, CA 90605 • *43,815*
Southwick, MA 01077 • *1,400*
South Williamson, KY 41503 • *1,016*
South Williamsport, PA 17701
 • *6,581*
South Wilmington, IL 60474 • *747*
South Windham, CT 06266 • *1,399*
South Windham, ME 04082 • *1,366*
South Windsor, CT 06074 • *10,200*
Southwood, CO 80120 • *2,600*
Southwood Acres, CT 06082 • *9,779*
South Woodstock, CT 06267 • *1,319*
South Yarmouth, MA 02664 • *7,525*
South Zanesville, OH 43701 • *1,739*
Spalding, NE 68665 • *645*
Spalding □, GA • *47,899*
Spanaway, WA 98387 • *5,940*
Spangler, PA 15775 • *2,399*
Spanish Fork, UT 84660 • *9,825*
Spanish Fort, AL 36527 • *3,415*
Spanish Lake, MO 63138 • *20,632*
Sparkman, AR 71763 • *622*
Sparks, GA 31647 • *1,353*
Sparks, NV 89431–33 • *40,780*
Sparks, OK 74869 • *772*
Sparland, IL 61565 • *624*
Sparr, FL 32690 • *1,100*
Sparta, GA 31087 • *1,745*
Sparta, IL 62286 • *4,957*
Sparta, MI 49345 • *3,373*
Sparta, MO 65753 • *743*
Sparta, NJ 07871 • *8,498*
Sparta, NC 28675 • *1,687*
Sparta, TN 38583 • *4,864*
Sparta, WI 54656 • *6,934*
Spartanburg, SC 29301–18 • *43,826*
Spartanburg □, SC • *201,861*
Spavinaw, OK 74366 • *623*
Spearfish, SD 57783 • *5,251*
Spearman, TX 79081 • *3,413*
Spearville, KS 67876 • *693*
Speed, IN 47172 • *650*
Speedway, IN 46224 • *12,641*
Spencer, IN 47460 • *2,732*
Spencer, IA 51301 • *11,726*
Spencer, MA 01562 • *6,350*
Spencer, NC 28159 • *2,938*
Spencer, NY 14883 • *863*
Spencer, OH 44275 • *764*
Spencer, TN 38585 • *1,126*
Spencer, WV 25276 • *2,799*
Spencer, WI 54479 • *1,754*
Spencer □, IN • *19,361*
Spencer □, KY • *5,929*
Spencerport, NY 14559 • *3,424*
Spencerville, MD 20868 • *1,100*
Spencerville, OH 45887 • *2,184*
Sperry, OK 74073 • *1,276*
Spiceland, IN 47385 • *940*
Spicer, MN 56288 • *909*
Spindale, NC 28160 • *4,246*
Spink □, SD • *9,201*
Spirit Lake, ID 83869 • *834*
Spirit Lake, IA 51360 • *3,976*
Spiro, OK 74959 • *2,221*
Spokane, WA 99201–99 • *171,300*
Spokane □, WA • *341,835*
Spooner, WI 54801 • *2,365*
Spotswood, NJ 08884 • *7,840*
Spotsylvania □, VA • *34,435*
Sprague, WV 25926 • *900*
Spring, TX 77373 • *3,000*
Springboro, OH 45066 • *4,962*
Spring City, PA 19475 • *3,389*
Spring City, TN 37381 • *1,951*
Spring City, UT 84662 • *671*
Springdale, AR 72764 • *23,458*
Springdale, OH 45246 • *10,111*
Springdale, PA 15144 • *4,418*
Springdale, SC 29169 • *2,985*
Springer, NM 87747 • *1,657*
Springer, OK 73458 • *679*
Springerville, AZ 85938 • *1,452*
Springfield, CO 81073 • *1,657*
Springfield, FL 32401 • *7,220*
Springfield, GA 31329 • *1,075*
Springfield, IL 62701–99 • *100,054*
Springfield, KY 40069 • *3,179*
Springfield, MA 01101–99 • *152,319*
Springfield, MI 49015 • *5,917*
Springfield, MN 56087 • *2,303*
Springfield, MO 65801–99 • *133,116*
Springfield, NE 68059 • *782*
Springfield, NJ 07081 • *13,955*
Springfield, OH 45501–99 • *72,563*
Springfield, OR 97477–78 • *41,621*
Springfield, PA 19064 • *25,326*
Springfield, SC 29146 • *604*
Springfield, SD 57062 • *1,377*
Springfield, TN 37172 • *10,814*
Springfield, VT 05156 • *5,603*
Springfield, VA 22150–61 • *12,500*
Spring Glen, UT 84526 • *800*
Spring Green, WI 53588 • *1,265*
Spring Grove, MN 55974 • *1,275*
Spring Grove, PA 17362 • *1,832*
Spring Hill, FL 33526 • *6,468*
Spring Hill, KS 66083 • *2,005*
Springhill, LA 71075 • *6,516*
Spring Hill, TN 37174 • *989*
Spring Hope, NC 27882 • *1,254*
Spring Lake, MI 49456 • *2,731*
Spring Lake, NJ 07762 • *4,215*
Spring Lake, NC 28390 • *6,273*
Spring Lake Heights, NJ 07762
 • *5,424*
Springport, MI 49284 • *675*
Springvale, ME 04083 • *2,940*
Spring Valley, CA 92077–78
 • *40,191*
Spring Valley, IL 61362 • *5,822*
Spring Valley, MN 55975 • *2,616*
Spring Valley, NY 10977 • *20,537*
Spring Valley, WI 54767 • *982*
Springville, AL 35146 • *1,476*
Springville, IA 52336 • *1,165*
Springville, NY 14141 • *4,285*
Springville, UT 84663 • *12,101*
Spruce Pine, NC 28777 • *2,282*
Spur, TX 79370 • *1,690*
Squire, WV 24884 • *900*
Staatsburg, NY 12580 • *950*
Stafford, KS 67578 • *1,425*
Stafford, VA 22554 • *650*
Stafford □, KS • *5,694*
Stafford □, VA • *40,470*
Stafford Springs, CT 06076 • *3,392*
Staffordsville, KY 41256 • *700*
Stambaugh, MI 49964 • *1,442*
Stamford, CT 06901–99 • *102,453*
Stamford, NY 12167 • *1,240*
Stamford, TX 79553 • *4,542*
Stamps, AR 71860 • *2,859*
Stanaford, WV 25927 • *1,000*
Stanberry, MO 64489 • *1,387*
Standish, MI 48658 • *1,264*
Stanfield, AZ 85272 • *900*
Stanfield, OR 97875 • *1,568*
Stanford, CA 94305 • *11,045*
Stanford, IL 61774 • *720*
Stanford, KY 40484 • *2,764*
Stanhope, NJ 07874 • *3,638*
Stanislaus □, CA • *265,900*
Stanley, NC 28164 • *2,341*
Stanley, ND 58784 • *1,631*
Stanley, VA 22851 • *1,204*
Stanley, WI 54768 • *2,095*
Stanley □, SD • *2,533*
Stanleytown, VA 24168 • *650*

Stanleyville, NC 27045 • 5,039
Stanly ☐, NC • 48,517
Stanton, CA 90680 • 23,723
Stanton, IA 51573 • 747
Stanton, KY 40380 • 2,691
Stanton, MI 48888 • 1,315
Stanton, NE 68779 • 1,603
Stanton, ND 58571 • 623
Stanton, TX 79782 • 2,314
Stanton ☐, KS • 2,339
Stanton ☐, NE • 6,549
Stantonsburg, NC 27883 • 920
Stanwood, IA 52337 • 705
Stanwood, WA 98292 • 1,646
Staples, MN 56479 • 2,887
Stapleton, AL 36578 • 900
Star, NC 27356 • 816
Starbuck, MN 56381 • 1,224
Star City, AR 71667 • 2,066
Star City, WV 26505 • 1,464
Stargo, AZ 85540 • 1,038
Stark ☐, IL • 7,389
Stark ☐, ND • 23,697
Stark ☐, OH • 378,823
Starke, FL 32091 • 5,306
Starke ☐, IN • 21,997
Starks, LA 70661 • 780
Starkville, MS 39759 • 15,169
Starr ☐, TX • 27,266
Startex, SC 29377 • 1,006
State Center, IA 50247 • 1,292
State College, PA 16801–05 • 36,130
Stateline, NV 89449 • 1,500
State Line, PA 17263 • 700
Statenville, GA 31648 • 650
State Road, NC 28676 • 800
Statesboro, GA 30458 • 14,866
Statesville, NC 28677 • 18,622
Statham, GA 30666 • 1,101
Staunton, IL 62088 • 4,744
Staunton, IN 47881 • 607
Staunton, VA 24401 • 21,857
Stayton, OR 97383 • 4,396
Steamboat Springs, CO 80487 • 5,098
Stearns, KY 42647 • 1,557
Stearns ☐, MN • 108,161
Steele, AL 35987 • 795
Steele, MO 63877 • 2,419
Steele, ND 58482 • 796
Steele ☐, MN • 30,328
Steele ☐, ND • 3,106
Steeleville, IL 62288 • 2,240
Steelton, PA 17113 • 6,484
Steelville, MO 65565 • 1,470
Steger, IL 60475 • 9,269
Steilacoom, WA 98388 • 4,886
Steinhatchee, FL 32359 • 800
Stephen, MN 56757 • 898
Stephens, AR 71764 • 1,366
Stephens ☐, GA • 21,763
Stephens ☐, OK • 43,419
Stephens ☐, TX • 9,926
Stephens City, VA 22655 • 1,179
Stephenson, MI 49887 • 967
Stephenson ☐, IL • 49,536
Stephenville, TX 76401 • 11,881
Sterling, AK 99672 • 919
Sterling, CO 80751 • 11,385
Sterling, IL 61081 • 16,281
Sterling, KS 67579 • 2,312
Sterling, MA 01564 • 1,200
Sterling, OK 73567 • 702
Sterling, VA 22170 • 12,000
Sterling ☐, TX • 1,206
Sterling City, TX 76951 • 915
Sterling Heights, MI 48077 • 108,999
Sterlington, LA 71280 • 1,400
Steuben, IN • 24,694
Steuben ☐, NY • 99,217
Steubenville, OH 43952 • 26,400
Stevens ☐, KS • 4,736
Stevens ☐, MN • 11,322
Stevens ☐, WA • 28,979
Stevenson, AL 35772 • 2,568
Stevenson, WA 98648 • 1,172
Stevens Point, WI 54481 • 22,970
Stevensville, MI 49127 • 1,268
Stevensville, MT 59870 • 1,207
Stewardson, IL 62463 • 745
Stewart, MN 55385 • 616
Stewart ☐, GA • 5,896
Stewart ☐, TN • 8,665
Stewartstown, PA 17363 • 1,072
Stewartsville, MO 64490 • 832
Stewartsville, NJ 08886 • 900
Stewartville, MN 55976 • 3,925
Stickney, IL 60402 • 5,893
Stigler, OK 74462 • 2,630
Stillman Valley, IL 61084 • 961
Stillwater, MN 55082 • 12,290
Stillwater, NY 12170 • 1,572
Stillwater, OK 74074–78 • 38,268
Stillwater ☐, MT • 5,598
Stilwell, OK 74960 • 2,369
74960 • 2,369
Stinnett, TX 79083 • 2,222
Stirling, NJ 07980 • 2,000
Stockbridge, GA 30281 • 2,103
Stockbridge, MA 01262 • 1,109
Stockbridge, MI 49285 • 1,213
Stockdale, TX 78160 • 1,265
Stockertown, PA 18083 • 661
Stockton, CA 95201–12 • 149,779
Stockton, IL 61085 • 1,872

Stockton, KS 67669 • 1,825
Stockton, MO 65785 • 1,432
Stockton, NJ 08559 • 643
Stoddard, WI 54658 • 762
Stoddard ☐, MO • 29,009
Stokes ☐, NC • 33,086
Stokesdale, NC 27357 • 1,070
Stollings, WV 25646 • 900
Stone ☐, AR • 9,022
Stone ☐, MS • 9,716
Stone ☐, MO • 15,587
Stoneboro, PA 16153 • 1,177
Stoneham, MA 02180 • 21,424
Stone Harbor, NJ 08247 • 1,187
Stone Mountain, GA 30086–88 • 4,867
Stoneville, NC 27048 • 1,054
Stonewall, LA 71078 • 1,175
Stonewall, MS 39363 • 1,345
Stonewall, OK 74871 • 672
Stonewall ☐, TX • 2,406
Stonewood, WV 26301 • 2,058
Stonington, CT 06378 • 1,228
Stonington, IL 62567 • 1,184
Stonington, ME 04681 • 700
Stony Brook, NY 11790 • 6,600
Stony Creek, CT 06405 • 700
Stony Point, NC 28678 • 1,150
Stony Point, NY 10980 • 8,270
Storey ☐, NV • 1,503
Storm Lake, IA 50588 • 8,814
Storrs, CT 06268 • 11,394
Story, WY 82842 • 700
Story ☐, IA • 72,326
Story City, IA 50248 • 2,762
Stottville, NY 12172 • 1,300
Stoughton, MA 02072 • 26,710
Stoughton, WI 53589 • 7,589
Stover, MO 65078 • 1,041
Stow, MA 01775 • 1,100
Stow, OH 44224 • 25,303
Stowe, PA 19464 • 4,038
Stowe Township, PA 15136 • 10,119
Strabane, PA 15363 • 1,900
Strafford, MO 65757 • 1,121
Strafford ☐, NH • 85,408
Strasburg, CO 80136 • 1,105
Strasburg, ND 58573 • 623
Strasburg, OH 44680 • 2,091
Strasburg, PA 17579 • 1,999
Strasburg, VA 22657 • 2,311
Stratford, CA 93266 • 850
Stratford, CT 06497 • 50,541
Stratford, IA 50249 • 806
Stratford, NJ 08084 • 8,005
Stratford, OK 74872 • 1,459
Stratford, TX 79084 • 1,917
Stratford, WI 54484 • 1,385
Stratford Landing, VA 22308 • 2,650
Strathmore, CA 93267 • 1,221
Strathmore, NJ 07747 • 7,674
Stratton, CO 80836 • 705
Stratton Meadows, CO 80906 • 6,223
Strawberry Point, IA 52076 • 1,463
Strawn, TX 76475 • 694
Streamwood, IL 60103 • 23,456
Streator, IL 61364 • 14,795
Streetsboro, OH 44241 • 9,055
Stringtown, OK 74569 • 1,047
Stromsburg, NE 68666 • 1,290
Strong, AR 71765 • 785
Strong, ME 04983 • 700
Strong City, KS 66869 • 675
Stronghurst, IL 61480 • 865
Strongsville, OH 44136 • 28,577
Stroud, OK 74079 • 3,148
Stroudsburg, PA 18360 • 5,148
Strum, WI 54770 • 944
Struthers, OH 44471 • 13,624
Stryker, OH 43557 • 1,423
Stuart, FL 33494–97 • 9,467
Stuart, IA 50250 • 1,650
Stuart, NE 68780 • 641
Stuart, VA 24171 • 1,131
Stuarts Draft, VA 24477 • 950
Sturbridge, MA 01566 • 1,891
Sturgeon, MO 65284 • 901
Sturgeon Bay, WI 54235 • 8,847
Sturgis, KY 42459 • 2,293
Sturgis, MI 49091 • 9,468
Sturgis, SD 57785 • 5,184
Sturtevant, WI 53177 • 4,130
Stutsman ☐, ND • 24,154
Stuttgart, AR 72160 • 10,941
Subiaco, AR 72865 • 744
Sublette, KS 67877 • 1,293
Sublette ☐, WY • 4,548
Sublimity, OR 97385 • 1,077
Succasunna, NJ 07876 • 9,000
Sudan, TX 79371 • 1,091
Sudbury, MA 01776 • 2,200
Sudbury Center, MA 01776 • 2,900
Suffern, NY 10901 • 10,794
Suffield, CT 06078 • 1,122
Suffolk, VA 23434–38 • 47,621
Suffolk ☐, MA • 650,142
Suffolk ☐, NY • 1,284,231
Sugar City, ID 83448 • 1,022
Sugar Creek, MO 64054 • 4,305
Sugarcreek, PA 16323 • 5,954
Sugargrove, PA 16350 • 630
Sugar Hill, GA 30518 • 2,473
Sugar Land, TX 77478–79 • 8,826
Sugarland Run, VA 22170 • 4,500
Sugar Loaf, VA 24018 • 6,000

Sugar Notch, PA 18706 • 1,191
Suisun City, CA 94585 • 11,087
Suitland, MD 20746 • 24,800
Sulligent, AL 35586 • 2,130
Sullivan, IL 61951 • 4,526
Sullivan, IN 47882 • 4,774
Sullivan, MO 63080 • 5,461
Sullivan ☐, IN • 21,107
Sullivan ☐, MO • 7,434
Sullivan ☐, NH • 36,063
Sullivan ☐, NY • 65,155
Sullivan ☐, PA • 6,349
Sullivan ☐, TN • 143,968
Sullivans Island, SC 29482 • 1,867
Sully, IA 50251 • 828
Sully ☐, SD • 1,990
Sulphur, LA 70663 • 19,709
Sulphur, OK 73086 • 5,516
Sulphur Springs, TX 75482 • 12,804
Sultan, WA 98294 • 1,578
Sumas, WA 98295 • 712
Sumiton, AL 35148 • 2,815
Summerfield, NC 27358 • 1,680
Summers ☐, WV • 15,875
Summersville, WV 26651 • 2,972
Summerton, SC 29148 • 1,173
Summerville, GA 30747 • 4,878
Summerville, PA 15864 • 830
Summerville, SC 29483 • 6,706
Summit, IL 60501 • 10,110
Summit, MS 39666 • 1,753
Summit, NJ 07901 • 21,071
Summit, TN 37363 • 1,500
Summit ☐, CO • 8,848
Summit ☐, OH • 524,472
Summit ☐, UT • 10,198
Summit Hill, PA 18250 • 3,418
Summitville, IN 46070 • 1,085
Sumner, IL 62466 • 1,238
Sumner, IA 50674 • 2,335
Sumner, WA 98390 • 4,936
Sumner ☐, KS • 24,928
Sumner ☐, TN • 85,790
Sumrall, MS 39482 • 1,197
Sumter, SC 29150–52 • 24,890
Sumter ☐, AL • 16,908
Sumter ☐, FL • 24,272
Sumter ☐, GA • 29,360
Sumter ☐, SC • 88,243
Sunapee, NH 03782 • 900
Sunbury, OH 43074 • 2,101
Sunbury, PA 17801 • 12,292
Sun City, AZ 85351 • 40,505
Sun City, CA 92381 • 6,500
Sun City, FL 34268 • 700
Suncook, NH 03275 • 4,698
Sundance, WY 82729 • 1,087
Sundown, TX 79372 • 1,511
Sunflower, MS 38778 • 1,027
Sunflower ☐, MS • 34,844
Sunland Park, NM 88063 • 3,377
Sunman, IN 47041 • 924
Sunnyland, FL 33583 • 650
Sunnymead, CA 92388 • 11,554
Sunnyside, UT 84539 • 611
Sunnyside, WA 98944 • 9,225
Sunnyvale, CA 94086–88 • 106,618
Sunol, CA 94586 • 750
Sun Prairie, WI 53590 • 12,931
Sunray, TX 79086 • 1,952
Sunrise, FL 33313 • 39,681
Sunrise Manor, NV 89110 • 44,155
Sunset, LA 70584 • 2,300
Sunset, UT 84015 • 5,733
Sunset Beach, HI 96712 • 800
Sunset Park, KS 67217 • 1,050
Sun Valley, NV 89433 • 8,822
Superior, AZ 85273 • 4,600
Superior, MT 59872 • 1,054
Superior, NE 68978 • 2,502
Superior, WI 54880 • 29,571
Suquamish, WA 98392 • 1,500
Surf City, NJ 08008 • 1,571
Surfside, FL 33154 • 3,763
Surfside Beach, SC 29577 • 2,522
Surgoinsville, TN 37873 • 1,536
Surprise, AZ 85345 • 3,723
Surrey, ND 58785 • 999
Surry ☐, NC • 59,449
Surry ☐, VA • 6,046
Susanville, CA 96130 • 6,520
Susquehanna, PA 18847 • 1,994
Susquehanna ☐, PA • 37,876
Sussex, NJ 07461 • 2,418
Sussex, WI 53089 • 3,482
Sussex ☐, DE • 97,983
Sussex ☐, NJ • 116,119
Sussex ☐, VA • 10,874
Sutherland, IA 51058 • 897
Sutherland, NE 69165 • 1,238
Sutherlin, OR 97479 • 4,560
Sutter ☐, CA • 52,246
Sutter Creek, CA 95685 • 1,705
Sutton, NE 68979 • 1,416
Sutton, WV 26601 • 1,192
Sutton ☐, TX • 5,130
Sutton Park, NJ 07836 • 2,500
Suwanee, GA 30174 • 1,026
Suwannee ☐, FL • 22,287
Svensen, OR 97103 • 650
Swain ☐, NC • 10,283
Swainsboro, GA 30401 • 7,602
Swampscott, MA 01907 • 13,837
Swannanoa, NC 28778 • 5,586
Swansboro, NC 28584 • 976
Swansea, IL 62221 • 5,347

Swansea, MA 02777 • 750
Swansea, SC 29160 • 888
Swanton, OH 43558 • 3,424
Swanton, VT 05488 • 2,520
Swanwyck Estates, DE 19720 • 1,700
Swanzey Center, NH 03431 • 700
Swarthmore, PA 19081 • 5,950
Swartz Creek, MI 48473 • 5,013
Swayzee, IN 46986 • 1,127
Swea City, IA 50590 • 813
Swedesboro, NJ 08085 • 2,031
Sweeny, TX 77480 • 3,538
Sweet Briar, VA 24595 • 900
Sweet Grass ☐, MT • 3,216
Sweet Home, AR 72164 • 1,100
Sweet Home, OR 97386 • 6,921
Sweetser, IN 46987 • 944
Sweet Springs, MO 65351 • 1,694
Sweetwater, TN 37874 • 4,725
Sweetwater, TX 79556 • 12,242
Sweetwater ☐, WY • 41,723
Sweetwater Creek, FL 33614 • 18,000
Swepsonville, NC 27359 • 900
Swift ☐, MN • 12,920
Swifton, AR 72471 • 859
Swink, CO 81077 • 668
Swisher, IA 52338 • 654
Swisher ☐, TX • 9,723
Swissvale, PA 15218 • 11,345
Switzer, WV 25647 • 1,000
Switzerland, FL 32043 • 2,400
Switzerland ☐, IN • 7,153
Swoyerville, PA 18704 • 5,795
Sycamore, AL 35149 • 900
Sycamore, IL 60178 • 9,219
Sycamore, OH 44882 • 1,059
Sykesville, MD 21784 • 1,712
Sykesville, PA 15865 • 1,537
Sylacauga, AL 35150 • 12,708
Sylva, NC 28779 • 1,699
Sylvan Beach, NY 13157 • 1,243
Sylvan Hills, AR 72116 • 2,900
Sylvania, AL 35988 • 1,156
Sylvania, GA 30467 • 3,352
Sylvania, OH 43560 • 15,527
Sylvan Lake, MI 48053 • 1,949
Sylvester, GA 31791 • 5,860
Syosset, NY 11791 • 10,200
Syracuse, IN 46567 • 2,579
Syracuse, KS 67878 • 1,654
Syracuse, NE 68446 • 1,638
Syracuse, NY 13201–99 • 170,105
Syracuse, OH 45779 • 946
Syracuse, UT 84041 • 3,702

T

Tabor, IA 51653 • 1,088
Tabor City, NC 28463 • 2,710
Tacoma, WA 98401–99 • 158,501
Taft, CA 93268 • 5,316
Taft, TX 78390 • 3,686
Tahlequah, OK 74464 • 9,708
Tahoe City, CA 95730 • 1,300
Tahoka, TX 79373 • 3,262
Taholah, WA 98587 • 800
Takoma Park, MD 20912 • 16,231
Talbot ☐, GA • 6,536
Talbot ☐, MD • 25,604
Talbotton, GA 31827 • 1,140
Talco, TX 75487 • 751
Talent, OR 97540 • 2,577
Taliaferro ☐, GA • 2,032
Talihina, OK 74571 • 1,387
Talladega, AL 35160 • 19,128
Talladega ☐, AL • 73,826
Tallahassee, FL 32301–17 • 81,548
Tallahatchie ☐, MS • 17,157
Tallapoosa, GA 30176 • 2,647
Tallapoosa ☐, AL • 38,676
Tallassee, AL 36078 • 4,763
Talleyville, DE 19803 • 6,880
Tallmadge, OH 44278 • 15,269
Tallula, IL 62688 • 681
Tallulah, LA 71282 • 11,634
Tama, IA 52339 • 2,968
Tama ☐, IA • 19,533
Tamaqua, PA 18252 • 8,843
Tamarac, FL 33321 • 29,376
Tamaroa, IL 62888 • 885
Tamina, TX 77302 • 900
Tamms, IL 62988 • 826
Tampa, FL 33601–99 • 271,523
Tampico, IL 61283 • 966
Taney ☐, MO • 20,467
Taneytown, MD 21787 • 2,618
Tangier, VA 23440 • 771
Tangipahoa ☐, LA • 80,698
Tannersville, NY 12485 • 685
Taos, MO 65101 • 759
Taos, NM 87571 • 3,369
Taos ☐, NM • 19,456
Taos Pueblo, NM 87571 • 1,030
Tappahannock, VA 22560 • 1,821
Tappan, NY 10983 • 6,100
Tara Hills, CA 94564 • 6,000
Tarboro, NC 27886 • 8,634
Tarentum, PA 15084 • 6,419
Tariffville, CT 06081 • 1,324
Tarkio, MO 64491 • 2,375
Tarpey, CA 93727 • 4,000
Tarpon Springs, FL 33589–90 • 13,251
Tarrant ☐, TX • 860,880

Tarrant City, AL 35217 • 8,148
Tarrytown, NY 10591 • 10,648
Tate, GA 30177 • 900
Tate ☐, MS • 20,119
Tateville, KY 42558 • 725
Tatnall ☐, GA • 18,134
Tatum, NM 88267 • 896
Taunton, MA 02780 • 45,001
Tavares, FL 32778 • 4,103
Tavernier, FL 33070 • 1,834
Tawas City, MI 48763 • 1,967
Taylor, AZ 85939 • 1,915
Taylor, AR 71861 • 657
Taylor, MI 48180 • 77,568
Taylor, PA 18517 • 7,246
Taylor, TX 76574 • 10,619
Taylor ☐, FL • 16,532
Taylor ☐, GA • 7,902
Taylor ☐, IA • 8,353
Taylor ☐, KY • 21,178
Taylor ☐, TX • 110,932
Taylor ☐, WV • 16,584
Taylor ☐, WI • 18,817
Taylor Mill, KY 41015 • 4,509
Taylors, SC 29687 • 12,100
Taylors Falls, MN 55084 • 623
Taylor Springs, IL 62089 • 671
Taylorsville, IN 47280 • 1,247
Taylorsville, KY 40071 • 801
Taylorsville, MS 39168 • 1,387
Taylorsville, NC 28681 • 1,103
Taylorsville, UT 84107 • 17,448
Taylorville, IL 62568 • 11,386
Tazewell, TN 37879 • 2,090
Tazewell, VA 24651 • 4,468
Tazewell ☐, IL • 132,078
Tazewell ☐, VA • 50,511
Tchula, MS 39169 • 1,931
Tea, SD 57004 • 729
Teague, TX 75860 • 3,390
Teaneck, NJ 07666 • 39,007
Teaticket, MA 02536 • 2,000
Tecumseh, MI 49286 • 7,320
Tecumseh, NE 68450 • 1,926
Tecumseh, OK 74873 • 5,123
Tehachapi, CA 93561 • 4,126
Tehama, CA • 38,888
Tekamah, NE 68061 • 1,886
Tekoa, WA 99033 • 854
Tekonsha, MI 49092 • 755
Telfair ☐, GA • 11,445
Telford, PA 18969 • 3,507
Tell City, IN 47586 • 8,704
Teller ☐, CO • 8,034
Tellico Plains, TN 37385 • 698
Telluride, CO 81435 • 1,047
Temecula, CA 92390 • 1,783
Tempe, AZ 85281–89 • 106,743
Temperance, MI 48182 • 3,500
Temple, GA 30179 • 1,520
Temple, OK 73568 • 1,339
Temple, PA 19560 • 1,486
Temple, TX 76501–08 • 42,354
Temple City, CA 91780 • 28,972
Temple Terrace, FL 33617 • 11,097
Templeton, MA 01468 • 900
Templeton, PA 16259 • 700
Tenafly, NJ 07670 • 13,552
Tenaha, TX 75974 • 1,005
Tenino, WA 98589 • 1,280
Tennessee Ridge, TN 37178 • 1,325
Tennille, GA 31089 • 1,709
Tensas ☐, LA • 8,525
Terra Alta, WV 26764 • 1,946
Terral, OK 73569 • 604
Terrebonne, OR 97760 • 900
Terrebonne ☐, LA • 94,393
Terre Haute, IN 47801–12 • 61,125
Terre Hill, PA 17581 • 1,217
Terrell, TX 75160 • 13,269
Terrell ☐, GA • 12,017
Terrell ☐, TX • 1,595
Terrell Hills, TX 78209 • 4,644
Terry, MS 39170 • 655
Terry, MT 59349 • 929
Terry ☐, TX • 14,581
Terrytown, NE 69341 • 727
Terryville, CT 06786 • 5,234
Terryville, NY 11776 • 5,900
Tesuque, NM 87574 • 1,014
Teton ☐, ID • 2,897
Teton ☐, MT • 6,491
Teton ☐, WY • 9,355
Teutopolis, IL 62467 • 1,414
Tewksbury, MA 01876 • 11,500
Texarkana, AR 75502 • 21,459
Texarkana, TX 75501–07 • 31,271
Texas ☐, MO • 21,070
Texas ☐, OK • 17,727
Texas City, TX 77590–91 • 41,403
Texhoma, OK 73949 • 785
Texico, NM 88135 • 958
Thatcher, AZ 85552 • 3,374
Thayer, IL 62689 • 759
Thayer, MO 65791 • 2,211
Thayer ☐, NE • 7,582
The Colony, TX 75056 • 11,586
The Dalles, OR 97058 • 10,820
Theodore, AL 36582 • 6,392
The Plains, OH 45780 • 2,044
Theresa, NY 13691 • 827
Theresa, WI 53091 • 766
Thermopolis, WY 82443 • 3,852
The Village, OK 73120 • 11,049
Thibodaux, LA 70301–02 • 15,810
Thief River Falls, MN 56701 • 9,105

Thiensville, WI 53092 • 3,341
Thomas, OK 73669 • 1,515
Thomas, WV 26292 • 747
Thomas □, GA • 38,098
Thomas □, KS • 8,451
Thomas □, NE • 973
Thomasboro, IL 61878 • 1,242
Thomaston, AL 36783 • 679
Thomaston, CT 06787 • 3,500
Thomaston, GA 30286 • 9,682
Thomaston, ME 04861 • 2,348
Thomasville, AL 36784 • 4,387
Thomasville, GA 31792 • 18,463
Thomasville, NC 27360 • 14,144
Thompson, IA 50478 • 668
Thompson, ND 58278 • 785
Thompson Falls, MT 59873 • 1,478
Thompsonville, IL 62890 • 610
Thomson, GA 30824 • 7,001
Thomson, IL 61285 • 911
Thonotosassa, FL 33592 • 1,500
Thoreau, NM 87323 • 1,099
Thorndale, TX 76577 • 1,300
Thorndike, MA 01079 • 1,000
Thornton, AR 71766 • 711
Thornton, CO 80229 • 40,343
Thorntonville, TX 79756 • 717
Thorntown, IN 46071 • 1,468
Thornville, OH 43076 • 838
Thornwood, NY 10594 • 5,400
Thorofare, NJ 08086 • 1,400
Thorp, WI 54771 • 1,635
Thorsby, AL 35171 • 1,422
Thousand Oaks, CA 91359-63 • 77,072
Three Bridges, NJ 08887 • 650
Three Forks, MT 59752 • 1,247
Three Oaks, MI 49128 • 1,774
Three Rivers, MA 01080 • 3,322
Three Rivers, MI 49093 • 7,015
Three Rivers, TX 78071 • 2,133
Throckmorton, TX 76083 • 1,174
Throckmorton □, TX • 2,053
Throop, PA 18512 • 4,166
Thunderbolt, GA 31404 • 2,165
Thurmont, MD 21788 • 2,934
Thurston □, NE • 7,186
Thurston □, WA • 124,264
Tiburon, CA 94920 • 6,685
Tice, FL 33905 • 6,645
Ticonderoga, NY 12883 • 2,898
Tidioute, PA 16351 • 844
Tierra Amarilla, NM 87575 • 800
Tiffin, OH 44883 • 19,549
Tift □, GA • 32,862
Tifton, GA 31794 • 13,749
Tigard, OR 97223 • 14,286
Tigerton, WI 54486 • 865
Tignall, GA 30668 • 733
Tilden, IL 62292 • 1,025
Tilden, NE 68781 • 1,012
Tilghman, MD 21671 • 900
Tillamook, OR 97141 • 3,981
Tillamook □, OR • 21,164
Tillman □, OK • 12,398
Tillmans Corner, AL 36619 • 5,000
Tillson, NY 12486 • 1,300
Tilton, IL 61833 • 2,405
Tilton, NH 03276 • 1,230
Tiltonsville, OH 43963 • 1,750
Timber Lake, SD 57656 • 660
Timberlake, VA 24502 • 2,700
Timberville, VA 22853 • 1,510
Timmonsville, SC 29161 • 2,112
Timpson, TX 75975 • 1,164
Tinley Park, IL 60477 • 26,171
Tinton Falls, NJ 07724 • 7,740
Tioga, LA 71477 • 1,200
Tioga, ND 58852 • 1,597
Tioga □, NY • 49,812
Tioga □, PA • 40,973
Tionesta, PA 16353 • 659
Tippah □, MS • 18,739
Tipp City, OH 45371 • 5,595
Tippecanoe □, IN • 121,702
Tipton, CA 93272 • 1,185
Tipton, IN 46072 • 5,004
Tipton, IA 52772 • 3,055
Tipton, MO 65081 • 2,155
Tipton, OK 73570 • 1,475
Tipton □, IN • 16,819
Tipton □, TN • 32,930
Tiptonville, TN 38079 • 2,438
Tire Hill, PA 15959 • 750
Tishomingo, OK 73460 • 3,212
Tishomingo □, MS • 18,434
Tiskilwa, IL 61368 • 990
Titonka, IA 50480 • 607
Titus □, TX • 21,442
Titusville, FL 32780-83 • 31,910
Titusville, NJ 08560 • 900
Titusville, PA 16354 • 6,884
Tiverton, RI 02878 • 7,653
Tivoli, NY 12583 • 711
Toano, VA 23168 • 750
Toast, NC 27049 • 2,339
Tobyhanna, PA 18466 • 700
Toccoa, GA 30577 • 9,104
Todd □, KY • 11,874
Todd □, MN • 24,991
Todd □, SD • 7,328
Todd Estates, DE 19713 • 2,050
Tohatchi, NM 87325 • 1,011
Toledo, IL 62468 • 1,284
Toledo, IA 52342 • 2,445
Toledo, OH 43601-99 • 354,635
Toledo, OR 97391 • 3,151
Toledo, WA 98591 • 637
Tolland □, CT • 114,823
Tollesboro, KY 41189 • 808
Tolleson, AZ 85353 • 4,433
Tolono, IL 61880 • 2,434
Toluca, IL 61369 • 1,471
Tomah, WI 54660 • 7,204
Tomahawk, WI 54487 • 3,527
Tomball, TX 77375 • 3,996
Tombstone, AZ 85638 • 1,632
Tom Green □, TX • 84,784
Tomkins Cove, NY 10986 • 700
Tompkins □, NY • 87,085
Tompkinsville, KY 42167 • 4,366
Toms River, NJ 08753-59 • 7,465
Tonasket, WA 98855 • 985
Tonawanda, NY 14150 • 18,693
Tonganoxie, KS 66086 • 1,864
Tonica, IL 61370 • 695
Tonkawa, OK 74653 • 3,524
Tonopah, NV 89049 • 1,952
Tontitown, AR 72770 • 615
Tooele, UT 84074 • 14,335
Tooele □, UT • 26,033
Toole □, MT • 5,559
Toombs □, GA • 22,592
Toomsboro, GA 31090 • 673
Topeka, IN 46571 • 876
Topeka, KS 66601-99 • 115,266
Toppenish, WA 98948 • 6,517
Topsfield, MA 01983 • 2,647
Topsham, ME 04086 • 4,657
Topton, PA 19562 • 1,818
Toronto, OH 43964 • 6,934
Torrance, CA 90501-99 • 129,881
Torrance □, NM • 7,491
Torrington, CT 06790 • 30,987
Torrington, WY 82240 • 5,441
Totowa, NJ 07512 • 11,448
Touisset, MA 02777 • 1,300
Toulon, IL 61483 • 1,390
Towaco, NJ 07082 • 1,400
Towanda, IL 61776 • 630
Towanda, KS 67144 • 1,332
Towanda, PA 18848 • 3,526
Tower, MN 55790 • 640
Tower City, PA 17980 • 1,667
Tower Hill, IL 62571 • 715
Town and Country, WA 99210 • 7,100
Town Creek, AL 35672 • 1,201
Town Creek Manor, MD 20653 • 900
Towner, ND 58788 • 867
Towner □, ND • 4,052
Town of Tonawanda, NY 14223 • 78,100
Towns □, GA • 5,638
Townsend, MA 01469 • 1,266
Townsend, MT 59644 • 1,587
Towson, MD 21204 • 51,083
Tracy, CA 95376 • 18,428
Tracy, MN 56175 • 2,478
Tracy City, TN 37387 • 1,356
Tracyton, WA 98393 • 1,600
Traer, IA 50675 • 1,703
Trafford, PA 15085 • 3,662
Trail Creek, IN 46360 • 2,581
Traill □, ND • 9,624
Tranquillity, CA 93668 • 950
Transylvania □, NC • 23,417
Trappe, MD 21673 • 739
Travelers Rest, SC 29690 • 3,017
Traverse □, MN • 5,542
Traverse City, MI 49684 • 15,516
Travis □, TX • 419,573
Treasure □, MT • 981
Treasure Island, FL 33740 • 6,316
Trego □, KS • 4,165
Tremont, IL 61568 • 2,096
Tremont, PA 17981 • 1,796
Tremonton, UT 84337 • 3,464
Trempealeau, WI 54661 • 956
Trempealeau □, WI • 26,158
Trenton, FL 32693 • 1,131
Trenton, GA 30752 • 1,636
Trenton, IL 62293 • 2,504
Trenton, MI 48183 • 22,762
Trenton, MO 64683 • 6,811
Trenton, NE 69044 • 796
Trenton, NJ 08601-99 • 92,124
Trenton, OH 45067 • 6,401
Trenton, TN 38382 • 4,601
Trenton, TX 75490 • 691
Tresckow, PA 18254 • 1,146
Treutlen □, GA • 6,087
Trevorton, PA 17881 • 2,196
Trevose, PA 19047 • 7,000
Treynor, IA 51575 • 981
Trezevant, TN 38258 • 921
Triadelphia, WV 26059 • 1,461
Triangle, VA 22172 • 3,050
Tribune, KS 67879 • 955
Tri City, OR 97457 • 3,439
Trigg □, KY • 9,384
Tri Lakes, IN 46725 • 1,356
Trilby, FL 34271 • 950
Trimble, TN 38259 • 722
Trimble □, KY • 6,253
Trimont, MN 56176 • 805
Trinidad, CO 81082 • 9,663
Trinidad, TX 75163 • 1,130
Trinity, AL 35673 • 1,328
Trinity, TX 75862 • 2,620
Trinity □, CA • 11,858
Trinity □, TX • 9,450
Trinity Center, CA 96091 • 650
Trion, GA 30753 • 1,732
Tripoli, IA 50676 • 1,280
Tripp, SD 57376 • 804
Tripp □, SD • 7,268
Triumph, LA 70041 • 1,600
Trona, CA 93562 • 1,400
Trotwood, OH 45426 • 7,802
Troup, TX 75789 • 1,911
Troup □, GA • 50,003
Trousdale □, TN • 6,137
Troutdale, OR 97060 • 5,908
Troutman, NC 28166 • 1,360
Troy, AL 36081 • 12,945
Troy, ID 83871 • 820
Troy, IL 62294 • 3,772
Troy, KS 66087 • 1,240
Troy, MI 48084 • 67,102
Troy, MO 63379 • 2,624
Troy, MT 59935 • 1,088
Troy, NH 03465 • 1,318
Troy, NC 27371 • 2,702
Troy, NY 12180-83 • 56,638
Troy, OH 45373 • 19,086
Troy, PA 16947 • 1,381
Troy, SC 29848 • 705
Troy, TN 38260 • 1,093
Truckee, CA 95734 • 2,389
Truman, MN 56088 • 1,392
Trumann, AR 72472 • 6,405
Trumansburg, NY 14886 • 1,722
Trumbull, CT 06611 • 32,989
Trumbull □, OH • 241,863
Trussville, AL 35173 • 3,507
Truth or Consequences (Hot Springs), NM 87901 • 5,219
Tryon, NC 28782 • 1,796
Tualatin, OR 97062 • 7,483
Tuba City, AZ 86045 • 5,041
Tuckahoe, NJ 08250 • 650
Tuckahoe, NY 10707 • 6,076
Tucker, GA 30084 • 18,200
Tucker □, WV • 8,675
Tuckerman, AR 72473 • 2,078
Tuckerton, NJ 08087 • 2,472
Tucson, AZ 85701-99 • 330,537
Tucumcari, NM 88401 • 6,765
Tukwila, WA 98188 • 3,578
Tulare, CA 93274 • 22,526
Tulare □, CA • 245,738
Tularosa, NM 88352 • 2,536
Tulelake, CA 96134 • 783
Tulia, TX 79088 • 5,033
Tullahoma, TN 37388 • 15,800
Tullos, LA 71479 • 776
Tully, NY 13159 • 1,049
Tulsa, OK 74101-99 • 360,919
Tulsa □, OK • 470,593
Tumwater, WA 98502 • 6,705
Tunica, MS 38676 • 1,361
Tunica □, MS • 9,652
Tunkhannock, PA 18657 • 2,144
Tunnel Hill, GA 30755 • 936
Tuolumne, CA 95379 • 1,708
Tuolumne □, CA • 33,928
Tupelo, MS 38801 • 23,905
Tupper Lake, NY 12986 • 4,478
Turbotville, PA 17772 • 675
Turkey, TX 79261 • 644
Turley, OK 74156 • 6,336
Turlock, CA 95380 • 26,287
Turner, OR 97392 • 1,116
Turner □, GA • 9,510
Turner □, SD • 9,255
Turners Falls, MA 01376 • 4,711
Turrell, AR 72384 • 1,041
Turtle Creek, PA 15145 • 6,959
Turtle Lake, ND 58575 • 802
Turtle Lake, WI 54889 • 762
Tuscaloosa, AL 35401-06 • 75,211
Tuscaloosa □, AL • 137,541
Tuscarawas □, OH • 84,614
Tuscola, IL 61953 • 3,839
Tuscola, TX 79562 • 660
Tuscola □, MI • 56,961
Tuscumbia, AL 35674 • 9,137
Tuskegee, AL 36083 • 13,327
Tustin, CA 92680 • 32,317
Tuttle, OK 73089 • 3,051
Tutwiler, MS 38963 • 1,174
Tuxedo, NC 28784 • 950
Tuxedo Park, DE 19804 • 1,700
Twentynine Palms, CA 92277 • 7,465
Twiggs □, GA • 9,354
Twin City, GA 30471 • 1,402
Twin Falls, ID 83301 • 26,209
Twin Falls □, ID • 52,927
Twin Knolls, AZ 85207 • 4,700
Twin Lakes, GA 31636 • 800
Twin Lakes, WI 53181 • 3,474
Twin Rivers, NJ 08520 • 7,742
Twin Rocks, PA 15960 • 700
Twinsburg, OH 44087 • 7,632
Twin Valley, MN 56584 • 907
Twisp, WA 98856 • 911
Two Harbors, MN 55616 • 4,039
Two Rivers, WI 54241 • 13,354
Tybee Island, GA 31328 • 2,240
Tyler, MN 56178 • 1,353
Tyler, TX 75701-12 • 70,508
Tyler □, TX • 16,223
Tyler □, WV • 11,320
Tyler Heights, WV 25312 • 3,200
Tylertown, MS 39667 • 1,976
Tyndall, SD 57066 • 1,253
Tyrone, NM 88065 • 950
Tyrone, OK 73951 • 928
Tyrone, PA 16686 • 6,346
Tyronza, AR 72386 • 777
Tyrrell □, NC • 3,975
Ty Ty, GA 31795 • 618

U

Ubly, MI 48475 • 862
Ucon, ID 83454 • 833
Udall, KS 67146 • 891
Uhrichsville, OH 44683 • 6,130
Uinta □, WY • 13,021
Uintah □, UT • 20,506
Ukiah, CA 95482 • 12,035
Uleta, FL 33164 • 10,000
Ulster □, NY • 158,158
Ulysses, KS 67880 • 4,653
Ulysses, PA 16948 • 654
Umatilla, FL 32784 • 1,872
Umatilla, OR 97882 • 3,199
Umatilla □, OR • 58,861
Unadilla, GA 31091 • 1,566
Unadilla, NY 13849 • 1,367
Unalakleet, AK 99684 • 623
Uncasville, CT 06382 • 1,597
Underwood, AL 35630 • 750
Underwood, ND 58576 • 1,329
Unicoi □, TN • 16,362
Union, IL 60180 • 622
Union, KY 41091 • 601
Union, MS 39365 • 1,931
Union, MO 63084 • 5,506
Union, NJ 07083 • 50,184
Union, OH 45322 • 5,219
Union, OR 97883 • 2,062
Union, SC 29379 • 10,523
Union, UT 84047 • 3,100
Union, WV 24983 • 743
Union □, AR • 48,573
Union □, FL • 10,166
Union □, GA • 9,390
Union □, IL • 17,765
Union □, IN • 6,860
Union □, IA • 13,858
Union □, KY • 17,821
Union □, LA • 21,167
Union □, MS • 21,741
Union □, NJ • 504,094
Union □, NM • 4,725
Union □, NC • 70,380
Union □, OH • 29,536
Union □, OR • 23,921
Union □, PA • 32,870
Union □, SC • 30,764
Union □, SD • 10,938
Union □, TN • 11,707
Union Beach, NJ 07735 • 6,354
Union Bridge, MD 21791 • 927
Union City, CA 94587 • 39,406
Union City, GA 30291 • 4,780
Union City, IN 47390 • 3,908
Union City, MI 49094 • 1,667
Union City, NJ 07087 • 55,593
Union City, OH 45390 • 1,716
Union City, PA 16438 • 3,623
Union City, TN 38261 • 10,436
Uniondale, NY 11553 • 24,500
Union Gap, WA 98903 • 3,184
Union Grove, WI 53182 • 3,517
Union Lake, MI 48085 • 12,000
Union Pier, MI 49129 • 1,039
Union Point, GA 30669 • 1,750
Union Springs, AL 36089 • 4,431
Union Springs, NY 13160 • 1,201
Uniontown, AL 36786 • 2,112
Uniontown, KY 42461 • 1,169
Uniontown, OH 44685 • 1,450
Uniontown, PA 15401 • 14,510
Union Village, RI 02895 • 2,400
Unionville, CT 06085 • 4,900
Unionville, MO 63565 • 2,178
United, PA 15689 • 950
Universal City, TX 78148 • 10,720
University City, MO 63130 • 42,738
University Gardens, NY 11020 • 5,400
University Heights, IA 52240 • 1,069
University Heights, OH 44118 • 15,401
University Park, IA 52595 • 645
University Park, NM 88003 • 4,383
University Park, TX 75205 • 22,254
University Place, WA 98465 • 13,620
Upland, CA 91786 • 47,647
Upland, IN 46989 • 3,335
Upper Arlington, OH 43221 • 35,648
Upper Darby, PA 19082-84 • 50,200
Upper Greenwood Lake, NJ 07421 • 2,734
Upper Marlboro, MD 20772 • 828
Upper Saddle River, NJ 07458 • 7,958
Upper Saint Clair, PA 15241 • 19,023
Upper Sandusky, OH 43351 • 5,967
Upshur □, TX • 28,595
Upshur □, WV • 23,427
Upson □, GA • 25,998
Upton, KY 42784 • 731
Upton, MA 01568 • 1,500
Upton, WY 82730 • 1,193
Upton □, TX • 4,619
Urania, LA 71480 • 849
Uravan, CO 81436 • 800
Urbana, IL 61801 • 35,978
Urbana, OH 43078 • 10,762
Urbancrest, OH 43123 • 880
Urbandale, IA 50322 • 17,869
Utah □, UT • 218,106
Utica, IL 61373 • 1,067
Utica, IN 47130 • 644
Utica, MI 48077-78 • 5,282
Utica, MS 39175 • 865
Utica, NE 68456 • 689
Utica, NY 13501-99 • 75,632
Utica, OH 43080 • 2,238
Uvalda, GA 30473 • 646
Uvalde, TX 78801 • 14,178
Uvalde □, TX • 22,441
Uxbridge, MA 01569 • 3,500

V

Vacaville, CA 95688 • 43,367
Vacherie, LA 70090 • 2,169
Vadnais Heights, MN 55110 • 5,111
Vaiden, MS 39176 • 924
Vail, CO 81657 • 2,261
Vail Homes, NJ 07724 • 900
Valatie, NY 12184 • 1,492
Valders, WI 54245 • 984
Valdese, NC 28690 • 3,364
Valdez, AK 99686 • 3,079
Valdosta, GA 31601-05 • 37,596
Vale, OR 97918 • 1,558
Valencia, AZ 85326 • 1,300
Valencia □, NM • 31,013
Valencia Heights, SC 29205 • 5,328
Valentine, NE 69201 • 2,829
Valhalla, NY 10595 • 6,600
Valier, IL 62891 • 729
Valier, MT 59486 • 640
Valinda, CA 91744 • 18,700
Vallejo, CA 94590-92 • 80,303
Valley, NE 68064 • 1,716
Valley □, ID • 5,604
Valley □, MT • 10,250
Valley □, NE • 5,633
Valley Center, KS 67147 • 3,300
Valley City, ND 58072 • 7,774
Valley Cottage, NY 10989 • 6,007
Valley Falls, KS 66088 • 1,189
Valley Falls, RI 02864 • 10,892
Valley Forge, PA 19481 • 950
Valley Head, AL 35989 • 609
Valley Mills, TX 76689 • 1,236
Valley Park, MO 63088 • 3,232
Valley Springs, SD 57068 • 801
Valley Station, KY 40272 • 20,000
Valley Stream, NY 11580-83 • 35,769
Valley View, PA 17983 • 1,585
Valliant, OK 74764 • 927
Vallscreek, WV 24890 • 900
Valmeyer, IL 62295 • 898
Valparaiso, FL 32580 • 6,142
Valparaiso, IN 46383 • 22,247
Val Verda, UT 84010 • 6,422
Val Verde □, TX • 35,910
Van, TX 75790 • 1,881
Van Alstyne, TX 75095 • 1,860
Van Buren, AR 72956 • 12,020
Van Buren, IN 46991 • 935
Van Buren, ME 04785 • 3,282
Van Buren, MO 63965 • 850
Van Buren □, AR • 13,357
Van Buren □, IA • 8,626
Van Buren □, MI • 66,814
Van Buren □, TN • 4,728
Vance □, NC • 36,748
Vanceboro, NC 28586 • 833
Vanceburg, KY 41179 • 1,939
Vancleave, MS 39564 • 1,330
Vancouver, WA 98660-68 • 42,834
Vandalia, IL 62471 • 5,338
Vandalia, MO 63382 • 3,170
Vandalia, OH 45377 • 13,161
Vander, NC 28301 • 1,671
Vanderbilt, PA 15486 • 689
Vanderbilt, TX 77991 • 750
Vanderburgh □, IN • 167,515
Vandercook Lake, MI 49203 • 4,975
Vandergrift, PA 15690 • 6,823
Van Horn, TX 79855 • 2,772
Van Horne, IA 52346 • 682
Van Lear, KY 41265 • 2,035
Van Meter, IA 50261 • 747
Van Vleck, TX 77482 • 1,300
Van Wert, OH 45891 • 11,035
Van Wert □, OH • 30,458
Van Zandt □, TX • 31,426
Vardaman, MS 38878 • 1,009
Varina, VA 23231 • 2,000
Varnville, SC 29944 • 1,948
Vass, NC 28394 • 828
Vassar, MI 48768 • 2,727
Vaughn, MT 59487 • 2,270
Vaughn, NM 88353 • 737
Veachland, KY • 700
Veazie, ME 04401 • 1,610
Veedersburg, IN 47987 • 2,261
Vega, TX 79092 • 900
Velda Rose Estates, AZ 85201 • 2,250
Velma, OK 73091 • 831
Velva, ND 58790 • 1,101
Venango □, PA • 64,444
Veneta, OR 97487 • 2,449
Venice, FL 33595-96 • 12,153

Venice, IL 62090 • 3,480
Ventnor City, NJ 08406 • 11,704
Ventura (San Buenaventura), CA 93001-09 • 74,393
Ventura, IA 50482 • 614
Ventura □, CA • 529,174
Verda, KY 40828 • 1,132
Verden, OK 73092 • 625
Verdi, NV 89439 • 800
Verdigre, NE 68783 • 617
Verdunville, WV 25649 • 950
Vergennes, VT 05491 • 2,273
Vermilion, OH 44089 • 11,012
Vermilion □, IL • 95,222
Vermilion □, LA • 48,458
Vermillion, SD 57069 • 10,136
Vermillion □, IN • 18,229
Vermont, IL 61484 • 885
Vermontville, MI 49096 • 832
Vernal, UT 84078 • 6,600
Vernon, AL 35592 • 2,609
Vernon, CT 06066 • 27,974
Vernon, FL 32462 • 885
Vernon, TX 76384 • 12,695
Vernon □, LA • 53,475
Vernon □, MO • 19,806
Vernon □, WI • 25,642
Vernon Hills, IL 60061 • 9,827
Vernonia, OR 97064 • 1,785
Vero Beach, FL 32960-64 • 16,176
Verona, MS 38879 • 2,497
Verona, NJ 07044 • 14,166
Verona, PA 15147 • 3,179
Verona, WI 53593 • 3,336
Versailles, IN 47042 • 1,560
Versailles, KY 40383 • 6,427
Versailles, MO 65084 • 2,406
Versailles, OH 45380 • 2,384
Vestal, NY 13850 • 6,000
Vestal Center, NY 13850 • 900
Vestavia Hills, AL 35216 • 15,722
Vevay, IN 47043 • 1,343
Vian, OK 74962 • 1,521
Viborg, SD 57070 • 812
Viburnum, MO 65566 • 836
Vici, OK 73859 • 845
Vicksburg, MI 49097 • 2,224
Vicksburg, MS 39180 • 25,434
Victor, IA 52347 • 1,046
Victor, NY 14564 • 2,370
Victoria, KS 67671 • 1,328
Victoria, MS 38679 • 950
Victoria, TX 77901-04 • 50,695
Victoria, VA 23974 • 2,004
Victoria □, TX • 68,807
Victorville, CA 92392 • 14,220
Vidalia, GA 30474 • 10,393
Vidalia, LA 71373 • 5,936
Vidor, TX 77662 • 11,834
Vidor, TX 77662 • 12,117
Vienna, GA 31092 • 2,886
Vienna, IL 62995 • 1,420
Vienna, VA 22180 • 15,469
Vienna, WV 26105 • 11,618
View Park, CA 90043 • 5,900
Vigo □, IN • 112,385
Vilas □, WI • 16,535
Villa Grove, IL 61956 • 2,707
Villanova, PA 19085 • 6,600
Villa Park, CA 92667 • 7,137
Villa Park, IL 60181 • 23,185
Villa Rica, GA 30180 • 3,420
Villas, NJ 08251 • 5,909
Ville Platte, LA 70586 • 9,201
Villisca, IA 50864 • 1,434
Vilonia, AR 72173 • 736
Vinalhaven, ME 04863 • 900
Vincennes, IN 47591 • 20,857
Vincent, AL 35178 • 1,652
Vincentown, NJ 08088 • 800
Vine Grove, KY 40175 • 3,583
Vineland, NJ 08360 • 53,753
Vinemont, AL 35179 • 615
Vineyard Haven, MA 02568 • 1,704
Vinita, OK 74301 • 6,740
Vinton, IA 52349 • 5,040
Vinton, LA 70668 • 3,631
Vinton, VA 24179 • 8,027
Vinton □, OH • 11,584
Vintondale, PA 15961 • 697
Viola, IL 61486 • 1,144
Viola, WI 54664 • 696
Violet, LA 70092 • 6,000
Virden, IL 62690 • 3,899
Virginia, AL 35020 • 700
Virginia, IL 62691 • 1,825
Virginia, MN 55792 • 11,056
Virginia Beach, VA 23450-65 • 262,199
Viroqua, WI 54665 • 3,716
Visalia, CA 93277-79 • 49,729
Vista, CA 92083-84 • 35,834
Vivian, LA 71082 • 4,146
Volcano, HI 96785 • 900
Volga, SD 57071 • 1,221
Volusia □, FL • 258,762

W

Wabash, IN 46992 • 12,985
Wabash □, IL • 13,713
Wabash □, IN • 36,640
Wabasha, MN 55981 • 2,372
Wabasha □, MN • 19,335
Wabasso, FL 32970 • 2,157
Wabasso, MN 56293 • 745
Wabaunsee □, KS • 6,867
Wabeno, WI 54566 • 700
Waco, TX 76701-99 • 101,261
Waconia, MN 55387 • 2,638
Waddington, NY 13694 • 980
Wadena, MN 56482 • 4,699
Wadena □, MN • 14,192
Wadesboro, NC 28170 • 4,206
Wading River, NY 11792 • 2,500
Wadley, GA 30477 • 2,438
Wadsworth, IL 60083 • 1,104
Wadsworth, OH 44281 • 15,166
Waelder, TX 78959 • 942
Wagener, SC 29164 • 903
Wagner, SD 57380 • 1,453
Wagoner, OK 74467 • 6,191
Wagoner □, OK • 41,801
Wagram, NC 28396 • 617
Wahiawa, HI 96786 • 16,911
Wahkiakum □, WA • 3,832
Wahoo, NE 68066 • 3,555
Wahpeton, ND 58075 • 9,064
Waialua, HI 96791 • 4,051
Waianae, HI 96792 • 5,000
Waikapu, HI 96793 • 698
Wailua, HI 96746 • 1,587
Wailuku, HI 96793 • 10,260
Waimanalo, HI 96795 • 3,562
Waimea, HI 96796 • 1,569
Waipahu, HI 96797 • 29,139
Waipio Acres, HI 96786 • 4,091
Waite Park, MN 56387 • 3,496
Waitsburg, WA 99361 • 1,035
Wakarusa, IN 46573 • 1,281
Wake □, NC • 301,327
Wa Keeney, KS 67672 • 2,388
Wakefield, KS 67487 • 803
Wakefield, MA 01880 • 24,895
Wakefield, MI 49968 • 2,591
Wakefield, NE 68784 • 1,125
Wakefield, RI 02879-83 • 3,400
Wakefield, VA 23888 • 1,355
Wake Forest, NC 27587 • 3,780
Wakeman, OH 44889 • 906
Wakulla □, FL • 10,887
Walbridge, OH 43465 • 2,900
Walcott, IA 52773 • 1,425
Walden, CO 80480 • 947
Walden, NY 12586 • 5,659
Waldo, AR 71770 • 1,685
Waldo, FL 32694 • 993
Waldo □, ME • 28,414
Waldoboro, ME 04572 • 1,195
Waldorf, MD 20601 • 9,782
Waldport, OR 97394 • 1,274
Waldron, AR 72958 • 2,642
Waldron, IN 46182 • 800
Waldwick, NJ 07463 • 10,802
Walhalla, ND 58282 • 1,429
Walhalla, SC 29691 • 3,977
Walker, IA 52352 • 733
Walker, LA 70785 • 2,957
Walker, MI 49504 • 15,088
Walker, MN 56484 • 970
Walker □, AL • 68,660
Walker □, GA • 56,470
Walker □, TX • 41,789
Walkersville, MD 21793 • 2,212
Walkerton, IN 46574 • 2,051
Walkertown, NC 27051 • 2,100
Walkerville, MT 59701 • 887
Wall, SD 57790 • 770
Wallace, ID 83873 • 1,736
Wallace, NC 28466 • 2,903
Wallace, WV 26448 • 900
Wallace □, KS • 2,045
Walla Walla, WA 99362 • 25,618
Walla Walla □, WA • 47,435
Walled Lake, MI 48088 • 4,748
Wallen, IN 46806 • 1,200
Waller, TX 77484 • 1,241
Waller □, TX • 19,798
Wallingford, CT 06492 • 37,274
Wallingford, VT 05773 • 1,141
Wallington, NJ 07057 • 10,741
Wallis, TX 77485 • 1,138
Wallkill, NY 12589 • 1,849
Wall Lake, IA 51466 • 892
Wallowa, OR 97885 • 847
Wallowa □, OR • 7,273
Walnut, CA 91789 • 12,478
Walnut, IL 61376 • 1,513
Walnut, IA 51577 • 897
Walnut Cove, NC 27052 • 1,147
Walnut Creek, CA 94595-98 • 53,643
Walnut Grove, MN 56180 • 753
Walnut Park, CA 90255 • 11,811
Walnutport, PA 18088 • 2,007
Walnut Ridge, AR 72476 • 4,152
Walpole, MA 02081 • 5,274
Walpole, NH 03608 • 700
Walsenburg, CO 81089 • 3,945
Walsh, CO 81090 • 884
Walsh □, ND • 15,371
Walterboro, SC 29488 • 6,209
Walters, OK 73572 • 2,778
Walthall □, MS • 13,761
Waltham, MA 02154 • 58,200
Walthill, NE 68067 • 847
Walthourville, GA 31333 • 905
Walton, IN 46994 • 1,202
Walton, KY 41094 • 1,651
Walton, NY 13856 • 3,329
Walton □, FL • 21,300
Walton □, GA • 31,211
Walworth, WI 53184 • 1,607
Walworth □, SD • 7,011
Walworth □, WI • 71,507
Wamac, IL 62801 • 1,665
Wamego, KS 66547 • 3,159
Wamesit, MA 01876 • 2,700
Wampum, PA 16157 • 851
Wamsutter, WY 82336 • 681
Wanamingo, MN 55983 • 717
Wanaque, NJ 07465 • 10,025
Wanatah, IN 46390 • 879
Wanchese, NC 27981 • 1,105
Wando Woods, SC 29405 • 5,253
Wantagh, NY 11793 • 22,300
Wapakoneta, OH 45895 • 8,402
Wapato, WA 98951 • 3,307
Wapella, IL 61777 • 768
Wapello, IA 52653 • 2,011
Wapello □, IA • 40,241
Wappingers Falls, NY 12590 • 5,110
War, WV 24892 • 2,158
Ward, AR 72176 • 981
Ward □, ND • 58,392
Ward □, TX • 13,976
Warden, WA 98857 • 1,479
Ware, MA 01082 • 6,806
Ware □, GA • 37,180
Wareham, MA 02571 • 2,473
Warehouse Point, CT 06088 • 1,850
Ware Shoals, SC 29692 • 2,370
Waretown, NJ 08758 • 1,175
Warminster, PA 18974 • 35,543
Warner, NH 03278 • 700
Warner, OK 74469 • 1,310
Warner Robins, GA 31093 • 39,893
Warr Acres, OK 73132 • 9,940
Warren, AR 71671 • 7,646
Warren, IL 61087 • 1,595
Warren, IN 46792 • 1,254
Warren, MA 01083 • 1,548
Warren, MI 48089-93 • 161,134
Warren, MN 56762 • 2,105
Warren, OH 44481-86 • 56,629
Warren, OR 97053 • 800
Warren, PA 16365 • 12,146
Warren, RI 02885 • 10,640
Warren □, GA • 6,583
Warren □, IL • 21,943
Warren □, IN • 8,976
Warren □, IA • 34,878
Warren □, KY • 71,828
Warren □, MS • 51,627
Warren □, MO • 14,900
Warren □, NJ • 84,429
Warren □, NC • 16,232
Warren □, NY • 54,854
Warren □, OH • 99,276
Warren □, PA • 47,449
Warren □, TN • 32,653
Warren □, VA • 21,200
Warrendale, PA 15086 • 800
Warren Park, IN 46219 • 1,803
Warrensburg, IL 62573 • 1,372
Warrensburg, MO 64093 • 13,807
Warrensburg, NY 12885 • 2,743
Warrensville Heights, OH 44122 • 16,565
Warrenton, GA 30828 • 2,172
Warrenton, MO 63383 • 3,219
Warrenton, NC 27589 • 908
Warrenton, OR 97146 • 2,493
Warrenton, VA 22186 • 3,907
Warrenville, IL 60555 • 7,519
Warrenville, SC 29851 • 1,029
Warrick □, IN • 41,474
Warrington, FL 32507 • 15,792
Warrior, AL 35180 • 3,260
Warroad, MN 56763 • 1,216
Warsaw, IL 62379 • 1,842
Warsaw, IN 46580 • 10,647
Warsaw, KY 41095 • 1,328
Warsaw, MO 65355 • 1,494
Warsaw, NC 28398 • 2,910
Warsaw, NY 14569 • 3,619
Warsaw, OH 43844 • 765
Warsaw, VA 22572 • 771
Wartburg, TN 37887 • 761
Warwick, NY 10990 • 4,320
Warwick, RI 02886-89 • 87,123
Wasatch □, UT • 8,523
Wasco, CA 93280 • 9,613
Wasco □, OR • 21,732
Waseca, MN 56093 • 8,219
Waseca □, MN • 18,448
Washakie □, WY • 9,496
Washburn, IL 61570 • 1,206
Washburn, IA 50706 • 1,400
Washburn, ME 04786 • 1,221
Washburn, ND 58577 • 1,767
Washburn, WI 54891 • 2,080
Washburn □, WI • 13,174
Washington, DC 20001-99 • 638,432
Washington, GA 30673 • 4,662
Washington, IL 61571 • 10,364
Washington, IN 47501 • 11,325
Washington, IA 52353 • 6,584
Washington, KS 66968 • 1,488
Washington, KY 41096 • 624
Washington, LA 70589 • 1,266
Washington, MS 39190 • 900
Washington, MO 63090 • 9,251
Washington, NJ 07882 • 6,429
Washington, NC 27889 • 8,418
Washington, PA 15301 • 18,363
Washington, UT 84780 • 3,092
Washington □, AL • 16,821
Washington □, AR • 100,494
Washington □, CO • 5,304
Washington □, FL • 14,509
Washington □, GA • 18,842
Washington □, ID • 8,803
Washington □, IL • 15,472
Washington □, IN • 21,932
Washington □, IA • 20,141
Washington □, KS • 8,543
Washington □, KY • 10,764
Washington □, LA • 44,207
Washington □, ME • 34,963
Washington □, MD • 113,086
Washington □, MN • 113,571
Washington □, MS • 72,344
Washington □, MO • 17,983
Washington □, NE • 15,508
Washington □, NC • 14,801
Washington □, NY • 54,795
Washington □, OH • 64,266
Washington □, OK • 48,113
Washington □, OR • 245,860
Washington □, PA • 217,074
Washington □, RI • 93,317
Washington □, TN • 88,755
Washington □, TX • 21,998
Washington □, UT • 26,065
Washington □, VT • 52,393
Washington □, VA • 46,487
Washington □, WI • 84,848
Washington Court House, OH 43160 • 12,682
Washington Park, IL 62204 • 8,223
Washington Terrace, UT 84403 • 8,212
Washington Township, NJ 07675 • 9,550
Washita □, OK • 13,798
Washoe □, NV • 193,623
Washougal, WA 98671 • 3,834
Washtenaw □, MI • 264,748
Wasilla, AK 99687 • 1,559
Waskom, TX 75692 • 1,821
Wataga, IL 61488 • 996
Watauga, TX 76148 • 10,284
Watauga □, NC • 31,666
Watchung, NJ 07060 • 5,290
Waterbury, CT 06701-49 • 103,266
Waterbury, VT 05676 • 1,892
Waterford, CT 06385 • 2,736
Waterford, MI 48095 • 64,250
Waterford, NY 12188 • 2,405
Waterford, PA 16441 • 1,568
Waterford, WI 53185 • 2,051
Waterloo, IL 62298 • 4,646
Waterloo, IN 46793 • 1,951
Waterloo, IA 50701-99 • 75,985
Waterloo, NY 13165 • 5,303
Waterloo, WI 53594 • 2,393
Waterman, IL 60556 • 943
Waterproof, LA 71375 • 1,339
Watersmeet, MI 49969 • 700
Watertown, CT 06795 • 6,000
Watertown, MA 02172 • 34,384
Watertown, NY 13601 • 27,861
Watertown, SD 57201 • 15,649
Watertown, TN 37184 • 1,300
Watertown, WI 53094 • 18,113
Water Valley, MS 38965 • 4,147
Waterville, KS 66548 • 694
Waterville, ME 04901 • 17,779
Waterville, MN 56096 • 1,717
Waterville, NY 13480 • 1,672
Waterville, OH 43566 • 3,884
Waterville, WA 98858 • 908
Watervliet, MI 49098 • 1,867
Watervliet, NY 12189 • 11,354
Watford City, ND 58854 • 2,119
Wathena, KS 66090 • 1,418
Watkins, MN 55389 • 757
Watkins Glen, NY 14891 • 2,440
Watkinsville, GA 30677 • 1,240
Watonga, OK 73772 • 4,139
Watonwan □, MN • 12,361
Watseka, IL 60970 • 5,543
Watson Chapel, AR 71601 • 900
Watsontown, PA 17777 • 2,366
Watsonville, CA 95076 • 23,663
Wattsville, SC 29360 • 1,324
Waubay, SD 57273 • 675
Wauchula, FL 33873 • 2,986
Wauconda, IL 60084 • 5,688
Waukee, IA 50263 • 2,227
Waukegan, IL 60085-87 • 67,653
Waukesha, WI 53186-88 • 50,365
Waukesha □, WI • 280,080
Waukomis, OK 73773 • 1,551
Waukon, IA 52172 • 3,983
Waunakee, WI 53597 • 3,866
Wauneta, NE 69045 • 746
Waupaca, WI 54981 • 4,472
Waupaca □, WI • 42,831
Waupun, WI 53963 • 8,132
Wauregan, CT 06387 • 900
Waurika, OK 73573 • 2,258
Wausa, NE 68786 • 647
Wausau, WI 54401 • 32,426
Wausaukee, WI 54177 • 648
Wauseon, OH 43567 • 6,173
Waushara □, WI • 18,526
Wautoma, WI 54982 • 1,629
Wauwatosa, WI 53213 • 51,308
Waveland, MS 39576 • 4,186
Waverly, IL 62692 • 1,537
Waverly, IA 50677 • 8,444
Waverly, KS 66871 • 671
Waverly, MO 64096 • 941
Waverly, NE 68462 • 1,726
Waverly, NY 14892 • 4,738
Waverly, OH 45690 • 4,603
Waverly, TN 37185 • 4,405
Waverly, VA 23890 • 2,284
Waverly Hall, GA 31831 • 913
Waxahachie, TX 75165 • 14,624
Waxhaw, NC 28173 • 1,208
Waycross, GA 31501 • 19,371
Wayland, IA 52654 • 720
Wayland, KY 41666 • 601
Wayland, MA 01778 • 5,500
Wayland, MI 49348 • 2,023
Wayland, NY 14572 • 1,846
Waylyn, SC 29405 • 2,400
Waymart, PA 18472 • 1,248
Wayne, MI 48184 • 21,159
Wayne, NE 68787 • 5,240
Wayne, NJ 07470 • 46,474
Wayne, OH 43466 • 894
Wayne, OK 73095 • 621
Wayne, PA 19087 • 8,900
Wayne, WV 25570 • 1,495
Wayne □, GA • 20,750
Wayne □, IL • 18,059
Wayne □, IN • 76,058
Wayne □, IA • 8,199
Wayne □, KY • 17,022
Wayne □, MI • 2,337,891
Wayne □, MS • 19,135
Wayne □, MO • 11,277
Wayne □, NE • 9,858
Wayne □, NC • 97,054
Wayne □, NY • 84,581
Wayne □, OH • 97,408
Wayne □, PA • 35,237
Wayne □, TN • 13,946
Wayne □, UT • 1,911
Wayne □, WV • 46,021
Wayne City, IL 62895 • 1,132
Waynesboro, GA 30830 • 5,760
Waynesboro, MS 39367 • 5,349
Waynesboro, PA 17268 • 9,726
Waynesboro, TN 38485 • 2,109
Waynesboro, VA 22980 • 15,329
Waynesburg, OH 44688 • 1,160
Waynesburg, PA 15370 • 4,482
Waynesville, MO 65583 • 2,879
Waynesville, NC 28786 • 6,765
Waynesville, OH 45068 • 1,796
Waynetown, IN 47990 • 915
Waynewood, VA 22308 • 4,500
Waynoka, OK 73860 • 1,377
Wayzata, MN 55391 • 3,621
Weakley □, TN • 32,896
Weatherford, OK 73096 • 9,640
Weatherford, TX 76086 • 12,049
Weatherly, PA 18255 • 2,891
Weatogue, CT 06089 • 2,249
Weaver, AL 36277 • 2,765
Weaverville, CA 96093 • 2,787
Weaverville, NC 28787 • 1,495
Webb, MS 38966 • 782
Webb □, TX • 99,258
Webb City, MO 64870 • 7,309
Webberville, MI 48892 • 1,535
Weber □, UT • 144,616
Weber City, VA 24251 • 1,543
Webster, FL 33597 • 856
Webster, MA 01570 • 14,480
Webster, NY 14580 • 5,499
Webster, PA 15087 • 800
Webster, SD 57274 • 2,417
Webster, TX 77598 • 2,405
Webster, WI 54893 • 610
Webster □, GA • 2,341
Webster □, IA • 45,953
Webster □, KY • 14,832
Webster □, LA • 43,631
Webster □, MS • 10,300
Webster □, MO • 20,414
Webster □, NE • 4,858
Webster □, WV • 12,245
Webster City, IA 50595 • 8,572
Webster Groves, MO 63119 • 23,097
Webster Springs, WV 26288 • 939
Wedgewood, MO 63031 • 5,700
Wedowee, AL 36278 • 908
Weed, CA 96094 • 2,879
Weed Heights, NV 89447 • 650
Weedsport, NY 13166 • 1,952
Weehawken, NJ 07087 • 13,168
Weeksbury, KY 41667 • 700
Weeping Water, NE 68463 • 1,109
Weimar, TX 78962 • 2,128
Weiner, AR 72479 • 750
Weippe, ID 83553 • 828
Weir, KS 66781 • 705
Weirsdale, FL 32695 • 1,500
Weirton, WV 26062 • 25,371
Weiser, ID 83672 • 4,771
Welch, OK 74369 • 697
Welch, WV 24801 • 3,885
Welcome, MN 56181 • 855
Welcome, SC 29611 • 6,922
Weld □, CO • 123,438
Weldon, NC 27890 • 1,844
Weleetka, OK 74880 • 1,195
Wellesley, MA 02181 • 27,209
Wellfleet, MA 02667 • 950
Wellford, SC 29385 • 2,143
Wellington, CO 80549 • 1,215
Wellington, KS 67152 • 8,212
Wellington, MO 64097 • 780
Wellington, OH 44090 • 4,146

Wellington, TX 79095 • 3,043
Wellington, UT 84542 • 1,406
Wellman, IA 52356 • 1,125
Wells, ME 04090 • 850
Wells, MI 49894 • 1,100
Wells, MN 56097 • 2,777
Wells, NV 89835 • 1,218
Wells, TX 75976 • 926
Wells □, IN • 25,401
Wells □, ND • 6,979
Wellsboro, PA 16901 • 3,805
Wellsburg, IA 50680 • 761
Wellsburg, NY 14894 • 647
Wellsburg, WV 26070 • 3,963
Wellston, OH 45692 • 6,016
Wellston, OK 74881 • 802
Wellsville, KS 66092 • 1,612
Wellsville, MO 63384 • 1,546
Wellsville, NY 14895 • 5,769
Wellsville, OH 43968 • 5,095
Wellsville, UT 84339 • 1,952
Wellton, AZ 85356 • 911
Welsh, LA 70591 • 3,515
Wenatchee, WA 98801 • 17,257
Wendell, ID 83355 • 1,974
Wendell, NC 27591 • 2,222
Wendover, UT 84083 • 1,099
Wenham, MA 01984 • 3,897
Wenona, IL 61377 • 1,025
Wenonah, NJ 08090 • 2,303
Wentzville, MO 63385 • 3,193
Wequetequock, CT 02891 • 800
Weslaco, TX 78596 • 19,331
Wesleyville, PA 16510 • 3,998
Wessington Springs, SD 57382 • 1,203
Wesson, MS 39191 • 1,313
West, TX 76691 • 2,485
West Abington, MA 02351 • 2,000
West Acton, MA 01720 • 5,800
West Alexandria, OH 45381 • 1,313
West Allis, WI 53214 • 63,982
West Amityville, NY 11758 • 6,470
West Andover, MA 01810 • 3,700
West Athens, CA 90247 • 8,531
West Babylon, NY 11704 • 32,500
West Baden Springs, IN 47469 • 796
West Barrington, RI 02806 • 3,700
West Baton Rouge □, LA • 19,086
West Bay Shore, NY 11706 • 8,900
West Bend, IA 50597 • 941
West Bend, WI 53095 • 21,484
West Berlin, NJ 08091 • 3,300
West Billerica, MA 01862 • 2,000
West Blocton, AL 35184 • 1,147
Westborough, MA 01581 • 13,619
West Bountiful, UT 84087 • 3,556
West Boylston, MA 01583 • 3,500
West Branch, IA 52358 • 1,867
West Branch, MI 48661 • 1,785
West Bridgewater, MA 02379 • 2,100
Westbrook, CT 06498 • 2,035
Westbrook, ME 04092 • 14,976
Westbrook, MN 56183 • 978
West Brookfield, MA 01585 • 1,423
West Burlington, IA 52655 • 3,371
Westbury, NY 11590 • 13,871
Westby, WI 54667 • 1,797
West Caldwell, NJ 07006 • 11,407
West Cape May, NJ 08204 • 1,091
West Carroll □, LA • 12,922
West Carrollton, OH 45449 • 13,148
West Carson, CA 90502 • 17,997
West Carthage, NY 13619 • 1,824
West Chatham, MA 02669 • 1,398
West Chazy, NY 12992 • 700
Westchester, FL 33144 • 20,000
Westchester, IL 60153 • 17,730
West Chester, PA 19380-82 • 17,435
Westchester □, NY • 866,599
West Chicago, IL 60185 • 12,550
West City, IL 62812 • 886
West College Corner, IN 45003 • 614
West Columbia, SC 29169 • 10,409
West Columbia, TX 77486 • 4,109
West Concord, MA 01742 • 5,331
West Concord, MN 55985 • 762
West Concord, NC 28025 • 3,200
West Covina, CA 91790-93 • 80,291
West Crossett, AR 71635 • 1,466
West Cumberland, ME 04021 • 800
West Dennis, MA 02670 • 2,030
West Des Moines, IA 50265 • 21,894
West Elmira, NY 14905 • 5,901
West End, NC 27376 • 900
Westerly, RI 02891 • 14,093
Western Hills, CO 80221 • 6,000
Westernport, MD 21562 • 2,706
Western Springs, IL 60558 • 12,876
Westerville, OH 43081 • 23,414
West Fairview, PA 17025 • 1,426
West Falmouth, MA 02574 • 1,200
West Fargo, ND 58078 • 10,099
West Feliciana □, LA • 12,186
Westfield, IL 62474 • 733
Westfield, IN 46074 • 2,783
Westfield, MA 01085 • 36,465
Westfield, NJ 07090-92 • 30,447
Westfield, NY 14787 • 3,446
Westfield, PA 16950 • 1,268
Westfield, WI 53964 • 1,033
Westfield Center, OH 44251 • 791
Westford, MA 01886 • 1,000
West Fork, AR 72774 • 1,526
West Frankfort, IL 62896 • 9,437
Westgate, FL 33401 • 2,100
West Groton, MA 01472 • 950
West Grove, PA 19390 • 1,820
Westham, VA 23229 • 3,600
West Hamlin, WV 25571 • 643
West Hanover, MA 02339 • 1,600
West Hartford, CT 06107 • 61,306
West Haven, CT 06516 • 53,184
West Haven, OR 97225 • 3,400
West Haverstraw, NY 10993 • 9,181
West Hazleton, PA 18201 • 4,871
West Helena, AR 72390 • 11,367
West Hempstead, NY 11552 • 26,500
West Hollywood, CA 90069 • 35,703
Westhope, ND 58793 • 741
West Huntington, NY 11743 • 6,170
West Hyannisport, MA 02672 • 1,200
West Islip, NY 11795 • 29,533
West Jefferson, NC 28694 • 822
West Jefferson, OH 43162 • 4,448
West Jordan, UT 84084 • 27,192
West Kingston, RI 02892 • 700
West Lafayette, IN 47906 • 21,247
West Lafayette, OH 43845 • 2,225
Westlake, LA 70669 • 5,246
Westlake, OH 44145 • 19,483
Westland, MI 48185 • 84,603
West Laramie, WY 82070 • 2,000
West Lawn, PA 19609 • 1,686
West Lebanon, IN 47991 • 946
West Leisenring, PA 15489 • 700
West Liberty, IA 52776 • 2,723
West Liberty, KY 41472 • 1,381
West Liberty, OH 43357 • 1,653
West Liberty, WV 26074 • 744
West Linn, OR 97068 • 12,956
West Long Branch, NJ 07764 • 7,380
West Mansfield, OH 43358 • 716
West Marion, NC 28752 • 1,596
West Medway, MA 02053 • 2,269
West Melbourne, FL 32901 • 5,078
West Memphis, AR 72301 • 28,138
Westmere, NY 12203 • 5,500
West Miami, FL 33174 • 6,076
West Middlesex, PA 16159 • 1,064
West Mifflin, PA 15122 • 26,552
West Milford, NJ 07480 • 1,600
West Milton, OH 45383 • 4,119
West Milton, PA 17886 • 775
West Milwaukee, WI 53214 • 3,535
Westminster, CA 92683 • 71,133
Westminster, CO 80030 • 50,211
Westminster, MD 21157 • 8,808
Westminster, MA 01473 • 950
Westminster, SC 29693 • 3,114
West Modesto, CA 95351 • 6,135
West Monroe, LA 71291 • 14,993
Westmont, CA 90044 • 27,916
Westmont, IL 60559 • 16,718
Westmont, NJ 08108 • 5,700
Westmont, PA 15905 • 6,113
Westmoreland, TN 37186 • 1,754
Westmoreland □, PA • 392,294
Westmoreland □, VA • 14,041
Westmorland, CA 92281 • 1,590
West Mystic, CT 06388 • 3,364
West Newbury, MA 01985 • 950
West Newton, PA 15089 • 3,387
West New York, NJ 07093 • 39,194
West Norriton, PA 19401 • 14,034
Weston, CT 06883 • 1,200
Weston, MA 02193 • 11,169
Weston, MO 64098 • 1,440
Weston, OH 43569 • 1,708
Weston, OR 97886 • 719
Weston, WV 26452 • 6,250
Weston, WI 54476 • 3,400
Weston □, WY • 7,106
West Orange, NJ 07052 • 39,400
Westover, WV 26505 • 4,884
West Palm Beach, FL 33401-18 • 63,305
West Park, NY 12493 • 700
West Paterson, NJ 07424 • 11,293
West Pelzer, SC 29669 • 944
West Pensacola, FL 32505 • 24,571
West Peoria, IL 61604 • 5,219
Westphalia, MI 48894 • 896
West Pittsburg, CA 94565 • 6,000
West Pittsburg, PA 16160 • 950
West Pittston, PA 18643 • 5,980
West Plains, MO 65775 • 7,741
West Point, CA 95255 • 1,500
West Point, GA 31833 • 4,294
West Point, IA 52656 • 1,133
West Point, KY 40177 • 1,339
West Point, MS 39773 • 8,811
West Point, NE 68788 • 3,609
West Point, NY 10996 • 8,000
West Point, UT 84015 • 2,170
West Point, VA 23181 • 2,726
Westport, CT 06880 • 25,290
Westport, IN 47283 • 1,450
47283 • 1,450
Westport, MA 02790 • 1,850
Westport, NY 12993 • 613
Westport, WA 98595 • 1,954
West Portsmouth, OH 45662 • 4,095
West Puente Valley, CA 91744 • 20,445
West Reading, PA 19611 • 4,507
West Rutland, VT 05777 • 2,351
West Sacramento, CA 95691 • 10,875
West Saint Paul, MN 55118 • 18,527
West Salem, IL 62476 • 1,145
West Salem, OH 44287 • 1,357
West Salem, WI 54669 • 3,276
West Sayville, NY 11796 • 5,000
West Scarborough, ME 04074 • 700
West Seneca, NY 14224 • 51,210
West Simsbury, CT 06092 • 2,140
West Slope, OR 97225 • 5,364
West Springfield, MA 01089 • 27,042
West Springfield, VA 22152 • 16,000
West Stockbridge, MA 01266 • 800
West Swanzey, NH 03469 • 1,022
West Terre Haute, IN 47885 • 2,806
West Townsend, MA 01474 • 700
West Union, IA 52175 • 2,783
West Union, OH 45693 • 2,791
West Union, WV 26456 • 1,090
West Unity, OH 43570 • 1,639
West University Place, TX 77005 • 12,010
West Upton, MA 01587 • 1,000
Westvale, NY 13219 • 7,300
West Valley City, UT 84120 • 72,511
West Van Lear, KY 41268 • 900
West View, PA 15229 • 7,648
Westville, IL 61883 • 3,573
Westville, IN 46391 • 2,887
Westville, NH 03865 • 700
Westville, NJ 08093 • 4,786
Westville, OK 74965 • 1,049
West Wareham, MA 02576 • 1,837
West Warren, MA 01092 • 1,200
West Warwick, RI 02893 • 27,026
West Webster, NY 14580 • 10,600
Westwego, LA 70094 • 12,663
West Whittier, CA 90606 • 13,800
West Winfield, NY 13491 • 979
Westwood, CA 96137 • 2,081
Westwood, KS 66205 • 1,783
Westwood, KY 41101 • 5,973
Westwood, MA 02090 • 6,500
Westwood, MI 49007 • 8,519
Westwood, NJ 07675 • 10,714
Westwood Lakes, FL 33165 • 11,478
West Wyoming, PA 18644 • 3,288
West Yarmouth, MA 02673 • 3,882
West Yellowstone, MT 59758 • 735
West York, PA 17404 • 4,526
Wethersfield, CT 06109 • 26,013
Wetumka, OK 74883 • 1,726
Wetumpka, AL 36092 • 4,341
Wetzel □, WV • 21,874
Wewahitchka, FL 32465 • 1,742
Wewoka, OK 74884 • 5,480
Wexford □, MI • 25,102
Weyauwega, WI 54983 • 1,549
Weymouth, MA 02188 • 55,601
Whalom, MA 01420 • 1,400
Wharton, NJ 07885 • 5,485
Wharton, TX 77488 • 9,033
Wharton □, TX • 40,242
What Cheer, IA 50268 • 803
Whatcom □, WA • 106,701
Wheatfield, IN 46392 • 755
Wheatland, CA 95692 • 1,474
Wheatland, IA 52777 • 840
Wheatland, PA 16161 • 1,132
Wheatland, WY 82201 • 5,816
Wheatland □, MT • 2,359
Wheaton, IL 60187-89 • 43,043
Wheaton, MD 20902 • 48,600
Wheaton, MN 56296 • 1,969
Wheat Ridge, CO 80033 • 30,293
Wheeler, TX 79096 • 1,584
Wheeler □, GA • 5,155
Wheeler □, NE • 1,060
Wheeler □, OR • 1,513
Wheeler □, TX • 7,137
Wheelersburg, OH 45694 • 4,796
Wheeling, IL 60090 • 23,266
Wheeling, WV 26003 • 43,070
Wheelwright, KY 41669 • 865
Whitacres, CT 06082 • 2,500
Whitakers, NC 27891 • 924
White □, AR • 50,835
White □, GA • 10,120
White □, IL • 17,864
White □, IN • 23,867
White □, TN • 19,567
White Bear Lake, MN 55110 • 22,538
White Bluff, TN 37187 • 2,055
White Castle, LA 70788 • 2,160
White Center, WA 98126 • 19,700
White City, FL 32465 • 725
White City, OR 97503 • 5,445
White City, UT 84070 • 1,180
White Cloud, MI 49349 • 1,101
White Deer, TX 79097 • 1,210
Whitefield, NH 03598 • 1,005
Whitefish, MT 59937 • 3,703
Whitefish Bay, WI 53217 • 14,930
White Hall, AR 71602 • 2,214
White Hall, IL 62092 • 2,935
Whitehall, MI 49461 • 2,856
Whitehall, MT 59759 • 1,030
Whitehall, NY 12887 • 3,241
Whitehall, OH 43213 • 21,299
Whitehall, PA 15227 • 15,143
Whitehall, WI 54773 • 1,530
White Haven, PA 18661 • 1,921
White Horse, NJ 08610 • 10,098
White Horse Beach, MA 02381 • 800
Whitehouse, OH 43571 • 2,137
White House, TN 37188 • 2,225
White House Station, NJ 08889 • 1,019
White Island Shores, MA 02538 • 950
Whitelaw, WI 54247 • 649
White Meadow Lake, NJ 07866 • 8,429
White Oak, OH 45239 • 4,900
White Oak, PA 15131 • 9,480
White Pigeon, MI 49099 • 1,478
White Pine, MI 49971 • 1,400
White Pine, TN 37890 • 1,900
White Pine □, NV • 8,167
White Plains, KY 42464 • 859
White Plains, MD 20695 • 5,167
White Plains, NY 10601-99 • 46,999
Whiteriver, AZ 85941 • 1,400
White River Junction, VT 05001 • 2,582
White Salmon, WA 98672 • 1,853
Whitesboro, NJ 08252 • 900
Whitesboro, NY 13492 • 4,460
Whitesboro, TX 76273 • 3,197
Whitesburg, GA 30185 • 775
Whitesburg, KY 41858 • 1,525
White Settlement, TX 76108 • 13,508
Whiteside □, IL • 65,970
White Springs, FL 32096 • 781
White Sulphur Springs, MT 59645 • 1,302
White Sulphur Springs, WV 24986 • 3,371
Whitesville, KY 42378 • 788
Whitesville, WV 25209 • 689
Whiteville, NC 28472 • 5,565
Whiteville, TN 38075 • 1,270
Whitewater, KS 67154 • 751
Whitewater, WI 53190 • 11,520
Whitewood, SD 57793 • 821
Whitewright, TX 75491 • 1,760
Whitfield □, GA • 65,789
Whitfield Estates, FL 33580 • 3,000
Whiting, IN 46394 • 5,630
Whiting, IA 51063 • 734
Whiting, NJ 08759 • 700
Whiting, WI 54481 • 2,050
Whitinsville, MA 01588 • 5,379
Whitley □, IN • 26,215
Whitley □, KY • 33,396
Whitley City, KY 42653 • 1,683
Whitman, MA 02382 • 13,534
Whitman, WV 25652 • 950
Whitman □, WA • 40,103
Whitman Square, NJ 08012 • 2,600
Whitmire, SC 29178 • 2,038
Whitmore Lake, MI 48189 • 2,920
Whitmore Village, HI 96786 • 2,318
Whitney, SC 29303 • 1,800
Whitney, TX 76692 • 1,631
Whitney Point, NY 13862 • 1,093
Whittemore, IA 50598 • 647
Whittier, CA 90601-12 • 69,717
Whitwell, TN 37397 • 1,783
Wibaux, MT 59353 • 782
Wibaux □, MT • 1,476
Wichita, KS 67201-99 • 279,835
Wichita □, KS • 3,041
Wichita □, TX • 121,082
Wichita Falls, TX 76301-11 • 94,201
Wickenburg, AZ 85358 • 3,535
Wickett, TX 79788 • 689
Wickliffe, KY 42087 • 1,034
Wickliffe, OH 44515 • 8,800
Wicomico □, MD • 64,540
Wiconisco, PA 17097 • 1,236
Widefield, CO 80911 • 7,500
Wiggins, MS 39577 • 3,205
Wilbarger □, TX • 15,931
Wilber, NE 68465 • 1,624
Wilberforce, OH 45384 • 2,512
Wilbraham, MA 01095 • 3,379
Wilbur, WA 99185 • 1,122
Wilburton, OK 74578 • 2,996
Wilcox, PA 15870 • 900
Wilcox □, AL • 14,755
Wilcox □, GA • 7,682
Wilder, ID 83676 • 1,260
Wilder, VT 05088 • 1,461
Wild Rose, WI 54984 • 741
Wildwood, FL 32785 • 2,665
Wildwood, NJ 08260 • 4,913
Wildwood Crest, NJ 08260 • 4,149
Wilkes □, GA • 10,951
Wilkes □, NC • 58,657
Wilkes-Barre, PA 18701-99 • 51,551
Wilkesboro, NC 28697 • 2,335
Wilkin □, MN • 8,454
Wilkinsburg, PA 15221 • 23,669
Wilkinson, WV 25653 • 700
Wilkinson □, GA • 10,368
Wilkinson □, MS • 10,021
Will □, IL • 324,460
Willacoochee, GA 31650 • 1,166
Willacy □, TX • 17,495
Willamina, OR 97396 • 1,749
Willard, MO 65781 • 1,799
Willard, NY 14588 • 700
Willard, OH 44890 • 5,720
Willard, UT 84340 • 1,241
Willcox, AZ 85643 • 3,243
Williams, AZ 86046 • 2,266
Williams, CA 95987 • 1,655
Williams □, ND • 22,237
Williams □, OH • 36,369
Williams Bay, WI 53191 • 1,763
Williamsburg, IA 52361 • 2,033
Williamsburg, KY 40769 • 5,560
Williamsburg, MA 01096 • 950
Williamsburg, OH 45176 • 1,952
Williamsburg, PA 16693 • 1,400
Williamsburg, VA 23185 • 9,870
Williamsburg □, SC • 38,226
Williamson, NY 14589 • 1,991
Williamson, WV 25661 • 5,219
Williamson □, IL • 56,538
Williamson □, TN • 58,108
Williamson □, TX • 76,507
Williamsport, IN 47993 • 1,747
Williamsport, MD 21795 • 2,153
Williamsport, OH 43164 • 792
Williamsport, PA 17701 • 33,401
Williamston, MI 48895 • 2,981
Williamston, NC 27892 • 6,159
Williamston, SC 29697 • 4,310
Williamstown, KY 41097 • 2,502
Williamstown, MA 01267 • 4,798
Williamstown, NJ 08094 • 5,768
Williamstown, PA 17098 • 1,664
Williamstown, VT 05679 • 650
Williamstown, WV 26187 • 3,095
Williamsville, IL 62693 • 996
Williamsville, NY 14221 • 6,017
Willimantic, CT 06226 • 14,652
Willingboro, NJ 08046 • 39,912
Willis, TX 77378 • 1,674
Williston, FL 32696 • 2,240
Williston, ND 58801 • 13,336
Williston, SC 29853 • 3,173
Williston Park, NY 11596 • 8,216
Willisville, IL 62997 • 628
Willits, CA 95490 • 4,008
Willmar, MN 56201 • 15,895
Willoughby, OH 44094 • 19,329
Willoughby Hills, OH 44092 • 8,612
Willow Brook, CA 90222 • 30,845
Willow Grove, PA 19090 • 21,300
Willowick, OH 44094 • 17,834
Willow Run, DE 19805 • 1,950
Willow Run, MI 48197 • 6,400
Willows, CA 95988 • 4,777
Willow Springs, IL 60480 • 4,147
Willow Springs, MO 65793 • 2,215
Willsboro, NY 12996 • 950
Willston, VA 22044 • 2,500
Wilmar, AR 71675 • 747
Wilmer, TX 75172 • 2,367
Wilmerding, PA 15148 • 2,421
Wilmette, IL 60091 • 28,229
Wilmington, DE 19801-99 • 70,195
Wilmington, IL 60481 • 4,424
Wilmington, MA 01887 • 17,471
Wilmington, NC 28401-06 • 44,000
Wilmington, OH 45177 • 10,431
Wilmington Manor, DE 19720 • 2,000
Wilmington Manor Gardens, DE 19720 • 1,600
Wilmore, KY 40390 • 3,787
Wilmot, AR 71676 • 1,227
Wilson, AR 72395 • 1,115
Wilson, KS 67490 • 978
Wilson, LA 70789 • 656
Wilson, NC 27893 • 34,424
Wilson, NY 14172 • 1,259
Wilson, OK 73463 • 1,585
Wilson, PA 18042 • 7,564
Wilson □, KS • 12,128
Wilson □, NC • 63,132
Wilson □, TN • 56,064
Wilson □, TX • 16,756
Wilsonville, AL 35186 • 914
Wilsonville, IL 62093 • 608
Wilsonville, OR 97070 • 2,920
Wilton, AL 35187 • 642
Wilton, CT 06897 • 6,500
Wilton, IA 52778 • 2,502
Wilton, ME 04294 • 2,262
Wilton, NH 03086 • 1,310
Wilton, ND 58579 • 950
Wilton Manors, FL 33334 • 12,742
Wimauma, FL 33598 • 1,477
Winamac, IN 46996 • 2,370
Winburne, PA 16879 • 650
Winchendon, MA 01475 • 4,030
Winchester, IL 62694 • 1,716
Winchester, IN 47394 • 5,659
Winchester, KY 40391 • 15,216
Winchester, MA 01890 • 20,701
Winchester, NV 89101 • 19,728
Winchester, NH 03470 • 1,732
Winchester, OH 45697 • 1,080
Winchester, TN 37398 • 5,821
Winchester, VA 22601 • 20,217
Winchester Bay, OR 97467 • 900
Windber, PA 15963 • 5,585
Windcrest, TX 78239 • 5,332
Winder, GA 30680 • 6,705
Windfall, IN 46076 • 911
Windgap, PA 18091 • 2,651
Windham, CT 06280 • 700
Windham, OH 44288 • 3,721
Windham □, CT • 92,312
Windham □, VT • 36,933

Wind Lake, WI 53185 • 2,400
Windom, MN 56101 • 4,666
Window Rock, AZ 86515 • 2,230
Wind Point, WI 53402 • 1,695
Windsor, CO 80550 • 4,277
Windsor, CT 06095 • 17,517
Windsor, IL 61957 • 1,228
Windsor, MO 65360 • 3,058
Windsor, NC 27983 • 2,126
Windsor, PA 17366 • 1,205
Windsor, VT 05089 • 4,084
Windsor, VA 23487 • 985
Windsor □, VT • 51,030
Windsor Forest, GA 31406 • 7,288
Windsor Heights, IA 50311 • 5,474
Windsor Hills, CA 90052 • 6,200
Windsor Locks, CT 06096 • 12,190
Windy Hill, SC 29501 • 1,605
Windy Hills, DE 19711 • 1,300
Winfall, NC 27985 • 634
Winfield, AL 35594 • 3,781
Winfield, IA 52659 • 1,042
Winfield, KS 67156 • 10,736
Winfield, NJ 07036 • 1,785
Wingate, NC 28174 • 2,615
Wingo, KY 42088 • 606
Winifrede, WV 25214 • 800
Wink, TX 79789 • 1,182
Winkelman, AZ 85292 • 1,060
Winkler □, TX • 9,944
Winlock, WA 98596 • 1,052
Winn □, LA • 17,253
Winnebago, IL 61088 • 1,644
Winnebago, MN 56098 • 1,869
Winnebago, NE 68071 • 902
Winnebago □, IL • 250,884
Winnebago □, IA • 13,010
Winnebago □, WI • 131,772
Winneconne, WI 54986 • 1,935
Winnemucca, NV 89445 • 4,140
Winner, SD 57580 • 3,472
Winneshiek □, IA • 21,876
Winnetka, IL 60093 • 12,772
Winnfield, LA 71483 • 7,311
Winnsboro, LA 71295 • 5,921
Winnsboro, SC 29180 • 2,919
Winnsboro, TX 75494 • 3,458
Winnsboro Mills, SC 29180 • 1,890
Winona, MN 55987 • 25,075
Winona, MS 38967 • 6,177
Winona, MO 65588 • 1,050
Winona □, MN • 46,256
Winona Lake, IN 46590 • 2,827
Winooski, VT 05404 • 6,318
Winslow, AZ 86047 • 7,921
Winslow, IN 47598 • 1,017
Winslow, ME 04901 • 5,903
Winslow, WA 98110 • 2,196
Winsted, CT 06098 • 8,092
Winsted, MN 55395 • 1,522
Winston, FL 33803 • 5,500
Winston, OR 97496 • 3,359
Winston □, AL • 21,953
Winston □, MS • 19,474
Winston-Salem, NC 27101-99 • 131,885
Winter Beach, FL 32971 • 700
Winter Garden, FL 32787 • 6,789
Winter Harbor, ME 04693 • 900
Winter Haven, FL 33880-88 • 21,119
Winter Park, FL 32789-93 • 22,339
Winter Park, NC 28401 • 4,504
Winterport, ME 04496 • 1,126
Winters, CA 95694 • 2,652
Winters, TX 79567 • 3,061
Winterset, IA 50273 • 4,021
Winter Springs, FL 32708 • 10,475

Wintersville, OH 43952 • 4,724
Winterville, GA 30683 • 621
Winterville, NC 28590 • 2,052
Winthrop, IA 50682 • 767
Winthrop, ME 04364 • 3,264
Winthrop, MA 02152 • 19,294
Winthrop, MN 55396 • 1,376
Winthrop Harbor, IL 60096 • 5,431
Winton, NC 27986 • 825
Wirt □, WV • 4,922
Wiscasset, ME 04578 • 1,350
Wisconsin Dells, WI 53965 • 2,521
Wisconsin Rapids, WI 54494 • 17,995
Wise, VA 24293 • 3,894
Wise □, TX • 26,575
Wise □, VA • 43,863
Wishek, ND 58495 • 1,345
Wishram, WA 98673 • 675
Wisner, LA 71378 • 1,424
Wisner, NE 68791 • 1,335
Withamsville, OH 45245 • 3,650
Witherbee, NY 12998 • 1,000
Witt, IL 62094 • 1,205
Wittenberg, WI 54499 • 997
Wittmann, AZ 85361 • 700
Wixom, MI 48096 • 6,705
Woburn, MA 01801 • 36,626
Wolcott, CT 06716 • 5,500
Wolcott, IN 47995 • 923
Wolcott, NY 14590 • 1,496
Wolcottville, IN 46795 • 890
Wolfe □, KY • 6,698
Wolfeboro, NH 03894 • 1,800
Wolfe City, TX 75496 • 1,594
Wolf Lake, MI 49442 • 3,876
Wolf Point, MT 59201 • 3,074
Womelsdorf, PA 19567 • 1,827
Wonder Lake, IL 60097 • 752
Wonewoc, WI 53968 • 842
Wood □, OH • 107,372
Wood □, TX • 24,697
Wood □, WV • 93,648
Wood □, WI • 72,799
Woodbine, GA 31569 • 910
Woodbine, IA 51579 • 1,463
Woodbine, NJ 08270 • 2,809
Woodbourne, NY 12788 • 1,155
Woodbridge, CT 06525 • 7,600
Woodbridge, NJ 07095 • 16,400
Woodbridge, VA 22191-99 • 35,000
Woodburn, IN 46797 • 1,002
Woodburn, OR 97071 • 11,196
Woodbury, CT 06798 • 1,290
Woodbury, GA 30293 • 1,738
Woodbury, MN 55119 • 10,297
Woodbury, NJ 08096 • 10,353
Woodbury, TN 37190 • 2,160
Woodbury □, IA • 100,884
Woodcliff Lake, NJ 07675 • 5,644
Wood Dale, IL 60191 • 11,251
Woodfield, SC 29206 • 9,588
Woodford □, IL • 33,320
Woodford □, KY • 17,778
Woodhaven, MI 48183 • 10,902
Woodhull, IL 61490 • 901
Woodlake, CA 93286 • 4,343
Woodland, CA 95695 • 30,235
Woodland, GA 31836 • 664
Woodland, ME 04694 • 1,363
Woodland, NC 27897 • 861
Woodland, WA 98674 • 2,341
Woodland Acres, CO 81069 • 800
Woodland Park, CO 80863 • 2,634
Woodlawn, KY 42001 • 1,200
Woodlawn, MD 21207 • 8,000
Woodlawn, OH 45215 • 2,715

Woodlyn, PA 19094 • 6,000
Woodlynne, NJ 08107 • 2,578
Woodmere, NY 11598 • 19,700
Woodmont, CT 06460 • 1,797
Woodmoor, MD 21207 • 7,600
Woodridge, IL 60517 • 22,561
Wood-Ridge, NJ 07075 • 7,929
Wood River, IL 62095 • 12,446
Wood River, NE 68883 • 1,334
Woodruff, SC 29388 • 5,171
Woodruff, WI 54568 • 900
Woodruff □, AR • 11,222
Woods □, OK • 10,923
Woodsboro, TX 78393 • 1,974
Woods Cross, UT 84087 • 4,263
Woodsfield, OH 43793 • 3,145
Woods Hole, MA 02543 • 1,080
Woodside, CA 94062 • 5,291
Woodson □, KS • 4,600
Woodstock, GA 30188 • 2,699
Woodstock, IL 60098 • 11,725
Woodstock, MD 21163 • 700
Woodstock, NY 12498 • 1,073
Woodstock, VT 05091 • 1,178
Woodstock, VA 22664 • 2,627
Woodstown, NJ 08098 • 3,250
Woodsville, NH 03785 • 1,195
Woodville, FL 32362 • 1,768
Woodville, MS 39669 • 1,512
Woodville, OH 43469 • 2,050
Woodville, TX 75979 • 2,821
Woodville, WI 54028 • 725
Woodward, IA 50276 • 1,212
Woodward, OK 73801 • 13,610
Woodward □, OK • 21,172
Woodway, TX 76710 • 7,091
Woolmarket, MS 39532 • 670
Woolrich, PA 17779 • 700
Woonsocket, RI 02895 • 45,914
Woonsocket, SD 57385 • 799
Wooster, OH 44691 • 19,289
Worcester, MA 01601-99 • 161,799
Worcester, NY 12197 • 950
Worcester □, MD • 30,889
Worcester □, MA • 646,352
Worden, IL 62097 • 953
Worland, WY 82401 • 6,391
Worth, IL 60482 • 11,592
Worth □, GA • 18,064
Worth □, IA • 9,075
Worth □, MO • 3,008
Wortham, TX 76693 • 1,187
Worthington, IN 47471 • 1,574
Worthington, KY 41183 • 1,948
Worthington, MN 56187 • 10,243
Worthington, OH 43085 • 15,016
Worthington, PA 16262 • 760
Wrangell, AK 99929 • 2,184
Wray, CO 80758 • 2,131
Wrens, GA 30833 • 2,415
Wrentham, MA 02093 • 1,400
Wright □, IA • 16,319
Wright □, MN • 58,681
Wright □, MO • 16,188
Wright City, MO 63390 • 1,179
Wright City, OK 74766 • 1,168
Wrightstown, NJ 08562 • 3,031
Wrightstown, WI 54180 • 1,169
Wrightsville, AR 72183 • 1,100
Wrightsville, GA 31096 • 2,526
Wrightsville, PA 17368 • 2,365
Wrightsville Beach, NC 28480 • 2,910
Wrightwood, CA 92397 • 2,511
Wurtsboro, NY 12790 • 1,128
Wyalusing, PA 18853 • 716
Wyandanch, NY 11798 • 17,900

Wyandot □, OH • 22,651
Wyandotte, MI 48192 • 34,006
Wyandotte □, KS • 172,335
Wyanet, IL 61379 • 1,069
Wyckoff, NJ 07481 • 15,500
Wymore, NE 68466 • 1,841
Wyncote, PA 19095 • 5,300
Wyndmoor, PA 19118 • 5,800
Wynne, AR 72396 • 7,805
Wynnewood, OK 73098 • 2,615
Wynnewood, PA 19096 • 7,700
Wynona, OK 74084 • 780
Wyoming, DE 19934 • 960
Wyoming, IL 61491 • 1,614
Wyoming, IA 52362 • 702
Wyoming, MI 49509 • 59,616
Wyoming, MN 55092 • 1,559
Wyoming, OH 45215 • 8,282
Wyoming, PA 18644 • 3,655
Wyoming □, NY • 39,895
Wyoming □, PA • 26,433
Wyoming □, WV • 35,993
Wyomissing, PA 19610 • 6,551
Wythe □, VA • 25,522
Wytheville, VA 24382 • 7,135

X

Xenia, OH 45385 • 24,653

Y

Yadkin □, NC • 28,439
Yadkinville, NC 27055 • 2,216
Yakima, WA 98901-09 • 49,826
Yakima □, WA • 172,508
Yalaha, FL 32797 • 950
Yale, MI 48097 • 1,814
Yale, OK 74085 • 1,652
Yalobusha □, MS • 13,139
Yamhill, OR 97148 • 690
Yamhill □, OR • 55,332
Yancey, NC • 14,934
Yanceyville, NC 27379 • 1,511
Yankton, SD 57078 • 12,011
Yankton □, SD • 18,952
Yardley, PA 19067 • 2,533
Yardville, NJ 08620 • 8,400
Yarmouth, ME 04096 • 2,421
Yarmouth, MA 02675 • 900
Yarmouth Port, MA 02675 • 2,490
Yarnell, AZ 85362 • 950
Yates □, NY • 21,459
Yatesboro, PA 16263 • 700
Yates Center, KS 66783 • 1,998
Yates City, IL 61572 • 860
Yavapai □, AZ • 68,145
Yazoo □, MS • 27,349
Yazoo City, MS 39194 • 12,092
Yeadon, PA 19050 • 11,727
Yeagertown, PA 17099 • 1,363
Yell □, AR • 17,026
Yellow Medicine □, MN • 13,653
Yellow Springs, OH 45387 • 4,077
Yellowstone □, MT • 108,035
Yellowstone National Park □, MT • 275
Yellville, AR 72687 • 1,044
Yelm, WA 98597 • 1,294
Yemassee, SC 29945 • 789
Yerington, NV 89447 • 2,021
Yermo, CA 92398 • 1,092
Yoakum, TX 77995 • 6,148
Yoakum □, TX • 8,299
Yolo □, CA • 113,374

Yoncalla, OR 97499 • 805
Yonkers, NY 10701-99 • 195,351
Yorba Linda, CA 92686 • 28,254
York, AL 36925 • 3,392
York, ME 03909 • 3,130
York, NE 68467 • 7,723
York, PA 17401-99 • 44,619
York, SC 29745 • 6,412
York □, ME • 139,666
York □, NE • 14,798
York □, PA • 312,963
York □, SC • 106,720
York □, VA • 35,463
York Beach, ME 03910 • 860
York Harbor, ME 03911 • 1,400
York Haven, PA 17370 • 746
Yorkshire, NY 14173 • 850
Yorktown, IN 47396 • 3,945
Yorktown, NY 10598 • 5,400
Yorktown, TX 78164 • 2,498
Yorktown Heights, NY 10598 • 5,900
Yorktown Manor, RI 02852 • 1,300
Yorkville, IL 60560 • 3,422
Yorkville, NY 13495 • 3,115
Yorkville, OH 43971 • 1,447
Yosemite National Park, CA 95389 • 1,073
Young □, TX • 19,083
Young Harris, GA 30582 • 687
Youngstown, NY 14174 • 2,191
Youngstown, OH 44501-99 • 115,436
Youngsville, LA 70592 • 1,053
Youngsville, PA 16371 • 2,006
Youngtown, AZ 85363 • 2,254
Youngwood, PA 15697 • 3,749
Ypsilanti, MI 48197 • 24,031
Yreka, CA 96097 • 5,916
Yuba □, CA • 49,733
Yuba City, CA 95991 • 18,736
Yucaipa, CA 92399 • 20,000
Yukon, OK 73099 • 17,112
Yulee, FL 32097 • 3,168
Yuma, AZ 85364-69 • 42,481
Yuma, CO 80759 • 2,824
Yuma □, AZ • 78,054
Yuma □, CO • 9,682
Yutan, NE 68073 • 631

Z

Zachary, LA 70791 • 7,297
Zanesville, OH 43701 • 28,655
Zapata, TX 78076 • 2,500
Zapata □, TX • 6,628
Zavala □, TX • 11,666
Zavalla, TX 75980 • 762
Zearing, IA 50278 • 630
Zebulon, GA 30295 • 995
Zebulon, NC 27597 • 2,055
Zeeland, MI 49464 • 4,764
Zeigler, IL 62999 • 1,858
Zelienople, PA 16063 • 3,502
Zephyr Cove, NV 89448 • 1,300
Zephyrhills, FL 34248-49 • 5,742
Ziebach □, SD • 2,308
Zillah, WA 98953 • 1,599
Zilwaukee, MI 48604 • 2,201
Zimmerman, MN 55398 • 1,074
Zion, IL 60099 • 17,861
Zionsville, IN 46077 • 3,948
Zolfo Springs, FL 33890 • 1,495
Zumbrota, MN 55992 • 2,129
Zuni, NM 87327 • 5,551
Zwolle, LA 71486 • 2,602

Geographical Facts about the United States

ELEVATION

The highest elevation in the United States is Mount McKinley, Alaska, 20,320 feet.

The lowest elevation in the United States is in Death Valley, California, 282 feet below sea level.

The average elevation of the United States is 2,500 feet.

EXTREMITIES

Direction	Location	Latitude	Longitude
North	Point Barrow, Alaska	71°23'N.	156°29'W.
South	Ka Lae (point) Hawaii	18°56'N.	155°41'W.
East	West Quoddy Head, Maine	44°49'N.	66°57'W.
West	Cape Wrangell, Alaska	52°55'N.	172°27'E.

The two places in the United States separated by the greatest distance are Kure Island, Hawaii, and Mangrove Point, Florida. These points are 5,848 miles apart.

LENGTH OF BOUNDARIES

The total length of the Canadian boundary of the United States is 5,525 miles.

The total length of the Mexican boundary of the United States is 1,933 miles.

The total length of the Atlantic coastline of the United States is 2,069 miles.

The total length of the Pacific and Arctic coastline of the United States is 8,683 miles.

The total length of the Gulf of Mexico coastline of the United States is 1,631 miles.

The total length of all coastlines and land boundaries of the United States is 19,841 miles.

The total length of the tidal shoreline and land boundaries of the United States is 96,091 miles.

GEOGRAPHIC CENTERS

The geographic center of the United States (including Alaska and Hawaii) is in Butte County, South Dakota at 44°58'N., 103°46'W.

The geographic center of North America is in North Dakota, a few miles west of Devils Lake, at 48°10'N., 100°10'W.

EXTREMES OF TEMPERATURE

The highest temperature ever recorded in the United States was 134°F., at Greenland Ranch, Death Valley, California, on July 10, 1913.

The lowest temperature ever recorded in the United States was —76°F., at Tanana, Alaska, in January, 1886.

PRECIPITATION

The average annual precipitation for the United States is approximately 29 inches.

Hawaii is the wettest state, with an average annual rainfall of 82.48 inches. Nevada, with an average annual rainfall of 8.81 inches, is the driest state.

The greatest local average annual rainfall in the United States is at Mt. Waialeale, Kauai, Hawaii, 460 inches.

Greatest 24-hour rainfall in the United States, 23.22 inches at New Smyrna, Florida, October 10–11, 1924.

Extreme minimum rainfall records in the United States include a total fall of only 3.93 inches at Bagdad, California, for a period of 5 years, 1909–13, and an annual average of 1.78 inches at Death Valley, California.

Heavy snowfall records include 76 inches at Silver Lake, Colorado, in 1 day; 42 inches at Angola, New York, in 2 days; 87 inches at Giant Forest, California, in 3 days; and 108 inches at Tahoe, California, in 4 days.

Greatest seasonal snowfall, 1,000.3 inches, more than 83 feet, at Paradise Ranger Station, Washington, during the winter of 1955–56.

Historical Facts about the United States

TERRITORIAL ACQUISITIONS

Accession	Date	Area (sq. mi.)	Cost in Dollars
Original territory of the Thirteen States	1790	888,685	
Purchase of Louisiana Territory, from France	1803	827,192	$11,250,000.00
By treaty with Spain: Florida	1819	58,560	$ 5,000,000.00
Other areas	1819	13,443	
Annexation of Texas	1845	390,144	
Oregon Territory, by treaty with Great Britain	1846	285,580	
Mexican Cession	1848	529,017	$15,000,000.00
Gadsden Purchase, from Mexico	1853	29,640	$10,000,000.00
Purchase of Alaska, from Russia	1867	586,412	7,200,000.00
Annexation of Hawaiian Islands	1898	6,450	
Puerto Rico, by treaty with Spain	1899	3,435	
Guam, by treaty with Spain	1899	212	
American Samoa, by treaty with Great Britain and Germany	1900	76	
Virgin Islands, by purchase from Denmark	1917	133	$25,000,000.00
Total		3,618,979	$73,450,000.00

Note: The Philippines, ceded by Spain in 1898 for $20,000,000.00, were a territorial possession of the United States from 1898 to 1946. On July 4, 1946 they became the independent republic of the Philippines.

Note. The Canal Zone, ceded by Panama in 1903 for $10,000,000.00, was a territory of the United States from 1903 to 1979. As a result of treaties signed in 1977, sovereignty over the Canal Zone reverted to Panama in 1979.

WESTWARD MOVEMENT OF CENTER OF POPULATION

Year	U.S. Population Total at Census	Approximate Location
1790	3,929,214	23 miles east of Baltimore, Md.
1800	5,308,483	18 miles west of Baltimore, Md.
1810	7,239,881	40 miles northwest of Washington, D.C.
1820	9,638,453	16 miles east of Moorefield, W. Va.
1830	12,866,020	19 miles southwest of Moorefield, W. Va.
1840	17,069,453	16 miles south of Clarksburg, W. Va.
1850	23,191,876	23 miles southeast of Parkersburg, W. Va.
1860	31,443,321	20 miles southeast of Chillicothe, Ohio
1870	39,818,449	48 miles northeast of Cincinnati, Ohio
1880	50,155,783	8 miles southwest of Cincinnati, Ohio
1890	62,947,714	20 miles east of Columbus, Ind.
1900	75,994,575	6 miles southeast of Columbus, Ind.
1910	91,972,266	Bloomington, Ind.
1920	105,710,620	8 miles southeast of Spencer, Ind.
1930	122,775,046	3 miles northeast of Linton, Ind.
1940	131,669,275	2 miles southeast of Carlisle, Ind.
1950	150,697,361	8 miles northwest of Olney, Ill.
1960	179,323,175	6 miles northwest of Centralia, Ill.
1970	204,816,296	5 miles southeast of Mascoutah, Ill.
1980	226,504,825	Near DeSoto, Mo.

State Areas and Populations

STATE	Land Area square miles	Water Area* square miles	Total Area* square miles	Area Rank land area	1980 Resident Population	1980 Population per square mile	1970 Population	1960 Population	1950 Population	Population Rank 1980	Population Rank 1970	Population Rank 1960
Alabama	50,766	938	51,704	28	3,893,978	77	3,444,165	3,266,740	3,061,743	22	21	19
Alaska	570,833	20,171	591,004	1	401,851	0.7	302,173	226,167	128,643	50	50	50
Arizona	113,510	492	114,002	6	2,718,425	24	1,772,482	1,302,161	749,587	29	33	35
Arkansas	52,082	1,109	53,191	27	2,286,419	44	1,923,295	1,786,272	1,909,511	33	32	31
California	156,297	2,407	158,704	3	23,667,837	151	19,953,134	15,717,204	10,586,223	1	1	2
Colorado	103,598	490	104,004	8	2,889,735	28	2,207,259	1,753,947	1,325,089	28	30	33
Connecticut	4,872	147	5,019	48	3,107,576	638	3,032,217	2,535,234	2,007,280	25	24	25
Delaware	1,933	112	2,045	49	594,317	307	548,104	446,292	318,085	47	46	46
District of Columbia	63	6	69	..	638,432	10,134	756,510	763,956	802,178	..	..	..
Florida	54,157	4,511	58,668	26	9,746,421	180	6,789,443	4,951,560	2,771,305	7	9	10
Georgia	58,060	854	58,914	21	5,463,087	94	4,589,575	3,943,116	3,444,578	13	15	16
Hawaii	6,427	46	6,473	47	964,691	150	769,913	632,772	499,794	39	40	43
Idaho	82,413	1,153	83,566	11	944,038	11	713,008	667,191	588,637	41	42	42
Illinois	55,646	2,226	57,872	24	11,427,414	205	11,113,976	10,081,158	8,712,176	5	5	4
Indiana	35,936	481	36,417	38	5,490,260	153	5,193,669	4,662,498	3,934,224	12	11	11
Iowa	55,965	310	56,275	23	2,913,808	52	2,825,041	2,757,537	2,621,073	27	25	24
Kansas	81,783	499	82,282	13	2,364,236	29	2,249,071	2,178,611	1,905,299	32	28	28
Kentucky	39,674	740	40,414	37	3,660,257	92	3,219,311	3,038,156	2,944,806	23	23	22
Louisiana	44,520	3,230	47,750	33	4,206,098	94	3,643,180	3,257,022	2,683,516	19	20	20
Maine	30,995	2,270	33,265	39	1,125,030	36	993,663	969,265	913,774	38	38	36
Maryland	9,838	623	10,461	42	4,216,941	429	3,922,399	3,100,689	2,343,001	18	18	21
Massachusetts	7,826	460	8,286	45	5,737,081	733	5,689,170	5,148,578	4,690,514	11	10	9
Michigan	56,959	40,148	97,107	22	9,262,070	163	8,875,083	7,823,194	6,371,766	8	7	7
Minnesota	79,548	7,066	86,614	14	4,075,970	51	3,805,069	3,413,864	2,982,483	21	19	18
Mississippi	47,234	457	47,691	31	2,520,631	53	2,216,912	2,178,141	2,178,914	31	29	29
Missouri	68,945	752	69,697	18	4,916,759	71	4,677,399	4,319,813	3,954,653	15	13	13
Montana	145,388	1,657	147,045	4	786,690	5.4	694,409	674,767	591,024	44	43	41
Nebraska	76,639	711	77,350	15	1,569,825	20	1,483,791	1,411,330	1,325,510	35	35	34
Nevada	109,895	667	110,562	7	800,493	7.3	488,738	285,278	160,083	43	47	49
New Hampshire	8,992	286	9,278	44	920,610	102	737,681	606,921	533,242	42	41	45
New Jersey	7,468	319	7,787	46	7,365,011	986	7,168,164	6,066,782	4,835,329	9	8	8
New Mexico	121,336	258	121,594	5	1,303,445	11	1,016,000	951,023	681,187	37	37	37
New York	47,379	5,358	52,737	30	17,558,072	371	18,241,266	16,782,304	14,830,192	2	2	1
North Carolina	48,843	3,826	52,669	29	5,881,385	120	5,082,059	4,556,155	4,061,929	10	12	12
North Dakota	69,299	1,403	70,702	17	652,717	9.4	617,761	632,446	619,636	46	45	44
Ohio	41,004	3,782	44,786	35	10,797,624	263	10,652,017	9,706,397	7,946,627	6	6	5
Oklahoma	68,656	1,301	69,957	19	3,025,495	44	2,559,253	2,328,284	2,233,351	26	27	27
Oregon	96,187	889	97,076	10	2,633,149	27	2,091,385	1,768,687	1,521,341	30	31	32
Pennsylvania	44,892	1,155	46,047	32	11,864,751	264	11,793,909	11,319,366	10,498,012	4	3	3
Rhode Island	1,054	158	1,212	50	947,154	899	949,723	859,488	791,896	40	39	39
South Carolina	30,207	909	31,116	40	3,122,814	103	2,590,516	2,382,594	2,117,027	24	26	26
South Dakota	75,956	1,164	77,120	16	690,768	9.1	666,257	680,514	652,740	45	44	40
Tennessee	41,154	989	42,143	34	4,591,120	112	3,924,164	3,567,089	3,291,718	17	17	17
Texas	262,015	4,790	266,805	2	14,227,574	54	11,196,730	9,579,677	7,711,194	3	4	6
Utah	82,076	2,826	84,902	12	1,461,037	18	1,059,273	890,627	688,862	36	36	38
Vermont	9,273	341	9,614	43	511,456	55	444,732	389,881	377,747	48	48	47
Virginia	39,700	1,063	40,763	36	5,346,797	135	4,648,494	3,966,949	3,318,680	14	14	14
Washington	66,512	1,627	68,139	20	4,132,204	62	3,409,169	2,853,214	2,378,963	20	22	23
West Virginia	24,124	112	24,236	41	1,950,258	81	1,744,237	1,860,421	2,005,552	34	34	30
Wisconsin	54,424	11,789	66,213	25	4,705,642	86	4,417,933	3,951,777	3,434,575	16	16	15
Wyoming	96,988	820	97,808	9	469,557	4.8	332,416	330,066	290,529	49	49	48
United States	3,539,341	139,904	3,679,245		226,549,010	64	203,235,298	179,323,175	151,325,798	..	..	..

*Includes the United States area of the Great Lakes.

U.S. State General Information

STATE	CAPITAL	LARGEST CITY	ENTERED UNION AS STATE — Date of Entry	Rank of Entry	Greatest N-S Measurement (miles)	Greatest E-W Measurement (miles)	HIGHEST POINT — Location	Altitude (feet)	STATE FLOWER	STATE BIRD	STATE NICKNAME
Alabama	Montgomery	Birmingham	Dec. 14, 1819	22	330	200	Cheaha Mountain	2,407	Camellia	Yellowhammer	Yellowhammer
Alaska	Juneau	Anchorage	Jan. 3, 1959	49	1,332	2,250	Mt. McKinley	20,320	Forget-me-not	Willow Ptarmigan	Last Frontier
Arizona	Phoenix	Phoenix	Feb. 14, 1912	48	390	335	Humphreys Peak	12,633	Saguaro Cactus	Cactus Wren	Grand Canyon
Arkansas	Little Rock	Little Rock	June 15, 1836	25	240	275	Magazine Mtn.	2,753	Apple Blossom	Mockingbird	Land of Opportunity
California	Sacramento	Los Angeles	Sept. 9, 1850	31	800	375	Mt. Whitney	14,494	Golden Poppy	California Valley Quail	Golden
Colorado	Denver	Denver	Aug. 1, 1876	38	270	380	Mt. Elbert	14,433	Rocky Mountain Columbine	Lark Bunting	Centennial
Connecticut*	Hartford	Hartford	Jan. 9, 1788	5	75	90	S. slope of Mt. Frissell	2,380	Mountain Laurel	Robin	Constitution
Delaware*	Dover	Wilmington	Dec. 7, 1787	1	95	35	Ebright Road, New Castle Co.	442	Peach Blossom	Blue Hen Chicken	First
District of Columbia	Washington	Washington	March 3, 1791		15	15	Tenleytown	410	American Beauty Rose	Wood Thrush	....
Florida	Tallahassee	Jacksonville	March 3, 1845	27	460	400	N. boundary, Walton Co.	345	Orange Blossom	Mockingbird	Sunshine
Georgia*	Atlanta	Atlanta	Jan. 2, 1788	4	315	250	Brasstown Bald (mtn.)	4,784	Cherokee Rose	Brown Thrasher	Peach
Hawaii	Honolulu	Honolulu	Aug. 21, 1959	50	...	1,600	Mauna Kea	13,796	Red Hibiscus	Nene (Hawaiian Goose)	Aloha
Idaho	Boise	Boise	July 3, 1890	43	480	305	Borah Peak	12,662	Syringa	Mountain Bluebird	Gem
Illinois	Springfield	Chicago	Dec. 3, 1818	21	380	205	Charles Mound	1,235	Violet	Cardinal	Prairie
Indiana	Indianapolis	Indianapolis	Dec. 11, 1816	19	265	160	Near Spartanburg	1,257	Peony	Cardinal	Hoosier
Iowa	Des Moines	Des Moines	Dec. 28, 1846	29	205	310	N. W. corner Osceola Co.	1,670	Wild Rose	Eastern Goldfinch	Hawkeye
Kansas	Topeka	Wichita	Jan. 29, 1861	34	205	410	Mt. Sunflower	4,039	Sunflower	Western Meadowlark	Sunflower
Kentucky	Frankfort	Louisville	June 1, 1792	15	175	350	Black Mountain	4,145	Goldenrod	Kentucky Cardinal	Bluegrass
Louisiana	Baton Rouge	New Orleans	April 30, 1812	18	275	300	Driskill Mountain	535	Magnolia	Pelican	Pelican
Maine	Augusta	Portland	March 15, 1820	23	310	210	Mt. Katahdin	5,268	White Pine	Chickadee	Pine Tree
Maryland*	Annapolis	Baltimore	April 28, 1788	7	120	200	Backbone Mountain	3,360	Black-eyed Susan	Baltimore Oriole	Old Free
Massachusetts*	Boston	Boston	Feb. 6, 1788	6	110	190	Mt. Greylock	3,491	Mayflower	Chickadee	Old Bay
Michigan	Lansing	Detroit	Jan. 26, 1837	26	400	310	Mt. Curwood	1,980	Apple Blossom	Robin	Wolverine
Minnesota	St. Paul	Minneapolis	May 11, 1858	32	400	350	Eagle Mtn.	2,301	Showy Lady's-slipper	Loon	Gopher
Mississippi	Jackson	Jackson	Dec. 10, 1817	20	340	180	Woodall Mountain	806	Magnolia	Mockingbird	Magnolia
Missouri	Jefferson City	St. Louis	Aug. 10, 1821	24	280	300	Taum Sauk Mountain	1,772	Hawthorne	Bluebird	Show Me
Montana	Helena	Billings	Nov. 8, 1889	41	315	570	Granite Peak	12,799	Bitterroot	Western Meadowlark	Big Sky
Nebraska	Lincoln	Omaha	March 1, 1867	37	210	415	S.W. corner Kimball Co.	5,426	Goldenrod	Western Meadowlark	Cornhusker
Nevada	Carson City	Las Vegas	Oct. 31, 1864	36	485	315	Boundary Peak	13,143	Shrub Sagebrush	Mountain Bluebird	Silver
New Hampshire*	Concord	Manchester	June 21, 1788	9	185	90	Mt. Washington	6,288	Purple Lilac	Purple Finch	Granite
New Jersey*	Trenton	Newark	Dec. 18, 1787	3	166	70	High Point	1,803	Purple Violet	Eastern Goldfinch	Garden
New Mexico	Santa Fe	Albuquerque	Jan. 6, 1912	47	390	350	Wheeler Peak	13,161	Yucca	Roadrunner	Land of Enchantment
New York*	Albany	New York	July 26, 1788	11	310	330	Mt. Marcy	5,344	Rose	Bluebird	Empire
North Carolina*	Raleigh	Charlotte	Nov. 21, 1789	12	200	520	Mt. Mitchell	6,684	Dogwood	Cardinal	Tar Heel
North Dakota	Bismarck	Fargo	Nov. 2, 1889	39	210	360	White Butte	3,506	Wild Prairie Rose	Western Meadowlark	Flickertail
Ohio	Columbus	Cleveland	March 1, 1803	17	230	205	Campbell Hill	1,550	Scarlet Carnation	Cardinal	Buckeye
Oklahoma	Oklahoma City	Oklahoma City	Nov. 16, 1907	46	210	460	Black Mesa	4,973	Mistletoe	Scissor-tailed Flycatcher	Sooner
Oregon	Salem	Portland	Feb. 14, 1859	33	290	375	Mt. Hood	11,239	Oregon Grape	Western Meadowlark	Beaver
Pennsylvania*	Harrisburg	Philadelphia	Dec. 12, 1787	2	180	310	Mt. Davis	3,213	Mountain Laurel	Ruffed Grouse	Keystone
Rhode Island*	Providence	Providence	May 29, 1790	13	50	35	Jerimoth Hill	812	Violet	Rhode Island Red	Little Rhody
South Carolina*	Columbia	Columbia	May 23, 1788	8	215	285	Sassafras Mountain	3,560	Carolina Jessamine	Carolina Wren	Palmetto
South Dakota	Pierre	Sioux Falls	Nov. 2, 1889	40	240	360	Harney Peak	7,242	Pasque	Ringnecked Pheasant	Coyote
Tennessee	Nashville	Memphis	June 1, 1796	16	120	430	Clingmans Dome	6,643	Iris	Mockingbird	Volunteer
Texas	Austin	Houston	Dec. 29, 1845	28	710	760	Guadalupe Peak	8,751	Bluebonnet	Mockingbird	Lone Star
Utah	Salt Lake City	Salt Lake City	Jan. 4, 1896	45	345	275	Kings Peak	13,528	Sego Lily	Seagull	Beehive
Vermont	Montpelier	Burlington	March 4, 1791	14	155	90	Mt. Mansfield	4,393	Red Clover	Hermit Thrush	Green Mountain
Virginia*	Richmond	Norfolk	June 25, 1788	10	205	425	Mt. Rogers	5,729	Flowering Dogwood	Cardinal	Old Dominion
Washington	Olympia	Seattle	Nov. 11, 1889	42	230	340	Mt. Rainier	14,410	Rhododendron	Willow Goldfinch	Evergreen
West Virginia	Charleston	Huntington	June 20, 1863	35	200	225	Spruce Knob	4,862	Rhododendron	Cardinal	Mountain
Wisconsin	Madison	Milwaukee	May 29, 1848	30	300	290	Timms Hill	1,952	Violet	Robin	Badger
Wyoming	Cheyenne	Cheyenne	July 10, 1890	44	275	365	Gannett Peak	13,804	Indian Paint Brush	Meadowlark	Equality
United States	Washington, D.C.	New York	....	..	275	...	Mt. McKinley, Alaska	20,320	....	Bald Eagle	....

*One of the Thirteen Original States.

Abbreviations

admin	administered
Afg	Afghanistan
Afr	Africa
Ala	Alabama
Alb	Albania
Alg	Algeria
Alsk	Alaska
Alta	Alberta
Am	American
Am. Sam	American Samoa
And	Andorra
Ang	Angola
Ant	Antarctica
Arc	Arctic
arch	archipelago
Arg	Argentina
Ariz	Arizona
Ark	Arkansas
Atl. O	Atlantic Ocean
Aus	Austria
Austl	Australia, Australian
auton	autonomous
Az. Is	Azores Islands
Ba	Bahamas
Barb	Barbados
B. C.	British Columbia
Bel	Belgium, Belgian
Bhu	Bhutan
Bis. Arch	Bismarck Archipelago
Bngl	Bangladesh
Bol	Bolivia
Bots	Botswana
Br	British
Braz	Brazil
Bru	Brunei
Bul	Bulgaria
Bur	Burma
Calif	California
Cam	Cameroon
Can	Canada
Can. Is	Canary Islands
Cen. Afr. Rep	Central African Republic
Cen. Am	Central America
co	county
Col	Colombia
Colo	Colorado
Con	Congo
Conn	Connecticut
cont	continent
C. R.	Costa Rica
C. V.	Cape Verde
Cyp	Cyprus
Czech	Czechoslovakia
D.C.	District of Columbia
Del	Delaware
Den	Denmark
dep	dependency, dependencies
dept	department
dist	district
div	division
Dji	Djibouti
Dom. Rep	Dominican Republic
Ec	Ecuador
Eg	Egypt
Eng	England
Equat. Gui	Equatorial Guinea
Eth	Ethiopia
Eur	Europe
Falk. Is	Falkland Islands
Fed	Federation
Fin	Finland
Fla	Florida
Fr	France, French
Fr. Gu	French Guiana
Ga	Georgia
Gam	Gambia
Ger., Fed. Rep. of	Federal Republic of Germany
Ger. Dem. Rep	German Democratic Republic
Gib	Gibraltar
Grc	Greece
Grnld	Greenland
Guad	Guadeloupe
Guat	Guatemala
Guy	Guyana
Hai	Haiti
Haw	Hawaii
Hond	Honduras
Hung	Hungary
I	Island
I.C	Ivory Coast
Ice	Iceland
Ill	Illinois
incl	includes, including
Ind	Indiana
Indian res	Indian reservation
Indon	Indonesia
I. of Man	Isle of Man
Ire	Ireland
is	islands
isl	island
Isr	Israel
It	Italy
Jam	Jamaica
Jap	Japan
Kam	Kampuchea
Kans	Kansas
Ken	Kenya
Kor	Korea
Kuw	Kuwait
Ky	Kentucky
La	Louisiana
Leb	Lebanon
Le. Is	Leeward Islands
Leso	Lesotho
Lib	Liberia
Liech	Liechtenstein
Lux	Luxembourg
Mad	Madagascar
Mad. Is	Madeira Islands
Mala	Malaysia
Man	Manitoba
Mart	Martinique
Mass	Massachusetts
Maur	Mauritania
Md	Maryland
Medit	Mediterranean
Mex	Mexico
Mich	Michigan
Minn	Minnesota
Miss	Mississippi
Mo	Missouri
Mong	Mongolia
Mont	Montana
Mor	Morocco
Moz	Mozambique
mtn	mount, mountain
mts	mountains
mun	municipality
N.A.	North America
nat. mon	national monument
nat. park	national park
N.B	New Brunswick
N.C	North Carolina
N. Cal	New Caledonia
N. Dak	North Dakota
Nebr	Nebraska
Nep	Nepal
Neth	Netherlands
Nev	Nevada
Newf	Newfoundland
N.H	New Hampshire
Nic	Nicaragua
Nig	Nigeria
N. Ire	Northern Ireland
N.J	New Jersey
N. Mex	New Mexico
Nor	Norway, Norwegian
N.S	Nova Scotia
N.W. Ter	Northwest Territories
N.Y	New York
N.Z	New Zealand
occ	occupied area
Okla	Oklahoma
Om	Oman
Ont	Ontario
Oreg	Oregon
Pa	Pennsylvania
Pac. O	Pacific Ocean
Pak	Pakistan
Pan	Panama
Pap. N. Gui	Papua New Guinea
Par	Paraguay
par	parish
P.D.R. of Yem	Yemen, People's Democratic Republic of
P.E.I	Prince Edward Island
pen	peninsula
Phil	Philippines
Pol	Poland
pol. dist	political district
pop	population
Port	Portugal, Portuguese
poss	possession
P.R	Puerto Rico
pref	prefecture
prot	protectorate
prov	province, provincial
pt	point
Que	Quebec
reg	region
rep	republic
res	reservation, reservoir
R.I	Rhode Island
riv	river
Rom	Romania
S. A	South America
S. Afr	South Africa
Sal	El Salvador
Sask	Saskatchewan
Sau. Ar	Saudi Arabia
S.C	South Carolina
Scot	Scotland
S. Dak	South Dakota
Sen	Senegal
S.L	Sierra Leone
Sol. Is	Solomon Islands
Som	Somalia
Sov. Un	Soviet Union
Sp	Spain, Spanish
St., Ste	Saint, Sainte
Sud	Sudan
Sur	Suriname
Swaz	Swaziland
Swe	Sweden
Switz	Switzerland
Syr	Syria
Tan	Tanzania
Tenn	Tennessee
ter	territories, territory
Tex	Texas
Thai	Thailand
Trin	Trinidad & Tobago
trust	trusteeship
Tun	Tunisia
Tur	Turkey
U.A.E	United Arab Emirates
Ug	Uganda
U.K	United Kingdom
Ur	Uruguay
U.S	United States
Va	Virginia
Ven	Venezuela
Viet	Vietnam
Vir. Is	Virgin Islands
vol	volcano
Vt	Vermont
Wash	Washington
W.I	West Indies
Win. Is	Windward Islands
Wis	Wisconsin
W. Sah	Western Sahara
W. Sam	Western Samoa
W. Va	West Virginia
Wyo	Wyoming
Yugo	Yugoslavia
Zimb	Zimbabwe

Index

This universal index includes in a single alphabetical list all important names that appear on the reference maps. Each place name is followed by its location, the map index key, and the page number of the map.

State locations are given for all places in the United States. Province and country locations are given for all places in Canada. All other place name entries show only country locations.

The index reference key, always a letter and figure combination, and the map page number are the last items in each entry. Because some places are shown on both a main map and an inset map, more than one index key may be given for a single map page number. Reference also may be made to more than a single map. In each case, however, the index key *letter and figure* precede the map page number to which reference is made. A lowercase key letter indicates reference to an inset map which has been keyed separately.

Each major and minor political division is followed both by a descriptive term (co., dist., region, prov.; dept.; state, etc.) indicating political status, and by the name of the country in which it is located. United States counties are listed with state locations; all

other divisions are given with country references.

The more important physical names that are shown on the maps are listed in the index. Each entry is followed by a descriptive term (bay, hill, range, riv., mtn., isl., etc.), to indicate its nature.

Country locations are given for all names except features entirely within a state of the United States or a province of Canada, in which case this division is given.

Some names included in the index were omitted from the maps because of scale size or lack of space. These entries are identified by an asterisk (*), and reference is given to the approximate location on the map.

A long name may appear on the map in a shortened form, with the full name given in the index. The part of the name not on the map then appears in italics, thus: St. Gabriel-*de-Brandon*.

The system of alphabetizing used in the index is standard. When more than one name with the same spelling is shown, place names are listed *first* and political divisions *second*.

A

Aachen, Ger., Fed. Rep. of	C3	6
Aalen, Ger., Fed. Rep. of	D5	6
Aalst, Bel.	B6	5
Äänekoski, Fin.	F11	11
Aarau, Switz.	E4	6
Aargau, canton, Switz.	*E3	6
Aba, China	E5	17
Aba, Nig.	G6	22
Ābādān, Iran	B7	23
Abaetetuba, Braz.	*D6	27
Abakan, Sov. Un.	D12	13
Abancay, Peru	D3	31
Abashiri, Jap.	D12	18
Abbeville, Ala.	D4	46
Abbeville, Fr.	B4	5
Abbeville, La.	E3	63
Abbeville, S.C.	C3	82
Abbeville, co., S.C.	C2	82
Abbiategrasso, It.	C2	9
Abbotsford, B.C., Can.	f13	37
Abbotsford, Wis.	D3	88
Åbenrå, co., Den.	*J3	11
Abeokuta, Nig.	G5	22
Aberdare, Wales	E5	4
Aberdeen, Idaho	G6	57
Aberdeen, Md.	A5	53
Aberdeen, Miss.	B5	68
Aberdeen, N.C.	B3	76
Aberdeen, Scot.	B5	4
Aberdeen, S. Dak.	E7	77
Aberdeen, Wash.	C2	86
Aberdeen, co., Scot.	*B5	4
Abergavenny, Wales	E5	4
Abernathy, Tex.	C2	84
Aberystwyth, Wales	D4	4
Abidjan, I.C.	G4	22
Abilene, Kans.	D6	61
Abilene, Tex.	C3	84
Abingdon, Ill.	C3	58
Abingdon, Va.	f10	85
Abingdon, Mass.	B6, h12	65
Abington, Pa.	o12	81
Abitibi, co., Que., Can.	*h12	42
Åbo, see Turku, Fin.		
Abomey, Benin	G5	22
Abony, Hung.	B5	10
Abra, prov., Phil.	*B6	19
Abruzzi, reg., It.	C4	9
Abruzzi e Molise, pol. dist., It.	C4	9
Absecon, N.J.	E3	74
Abu Dhabi (Abū Ẓaby)	E5	15
Abū Kamāl, Syr.	E13	14
Aby, Swe.	u34	11
Acadia, par., La.	D3	63
Acámbaro, Mex.	C4, m13	34
Acaponeta, Mex.	C4	34
Acapulco de Juárez, Mex.	D5	34
Acarigua, Ven.	B4	32
Acatlán de Osorio, Mex.	D5, m14	34
Acayucan, Mex.	D6	34
Accomack, co., Va.	C7	85
Accoville, W. Va.	D3, n12	87
Accra, Ghana	G4	22
Achinsk, Sov. Un.	D12	13
Acireale, It.	F5	9
Ackerman, Miss.	B4	68
Ackley, Iowa	B4	60
Acmetonia, Pa.	*E1	81
Aconcagua, prov., Chile	A2	28

Aconcagua, peak, Arg.	A3	28
Acqui, It.	B2	9
Acre, state, Braz.	C3	31
Acre, riv., Braz.	D4	31
Acton, Ont., Can.	D4	41
Acton Vale, Que., Can.	D5	42
Açu, Braz.	*D7	27
Acushent, Mass.	C6	65
Acworth, Ga.	B2	55
Ada, Minn.	C2	67
Ada, Ohio	B2	78
Ada, Okla.	C5	79
Ada, Yugo.	C5	10
Ada, co., Idaho	F2	57
Adair, co., Iowa	C3	60
Adair, co., Ky.	C4	62
Adair, co., Mo.	A5	69
Adair, co., Okla.	B7	79
Adairsville, Ga.	B2	55
Adam, mtn., Wash.	C4	86
Adamantina, Braz.	C2	30
Adams, Mass.	A1	65
Adams, Minn.	G6	67
Adams, N.Y.	B4	75
Adams, Wis.	E4	88
Adams, co., Colo.	B6	51
Adams, co., Idaho	E2	57
Adams, co., Ill.	D2	58
Adams, co., Ind.	C8	59
Adams, co., Iowa	C3	60
Adams, co., Miss.	D2	68
Adams, co., Nebr.	D7	71
Adams, co., N. Dak.	D7	77
Adams, co., Ohio	D2	78
Adams, co., Pa.	G7	81
Adams, co., Wash.	B7	86
Adams, co., Wis.	D4	88
Adams, mtn., Mass.	A2	65
Adams, mtn, Wash.	C4	86
Adams Center, N.Y.	B5	75
Adamston, N.J.	C4	74
Adamstown, Pa.	F9	81
Adamsville, Ala.	f7	46
Adamsville, Tenn.	B3	83
Adana, Tur.	D10	14
Adapazari, Tur.	B8	14
Ad Dāmir, Sud.	E4	23
Addis Ababa, Eth.	G5	23
Addison, Ill.	k9	58
Addison, co., Vt.	C1	73
Ad Dīwānīyah, Iraq	C3	15
Ad Duwaym, Sud.	F4	23
Addyston, Ohio	o12	78
Adel, Ga.	E3	55
Adel, Iowa	C3	60
Adelaide, Austl.	F6	25
Adelphi, Md.	*C4	53
Aden, P.D.R. of Yem.	G4	15
Adena, Ohio	B5	78
Adigrat, Eth.	F5	23
Adirondack, mts., N.Y.	A6, f10	75
Adi Ugri, Eth.	F5	23
Adiyaman, Tur.	C12	14
Adjuntas, P.R.	*G11	35
Admiralty, is., Pap. N. Gui.	h12	25
Ado-Ekiti, Nig.	*E6	22
Adrano, It.	F5	9
Adria, It.	B4	9
Adrian, Mich.	G6	66

Adrian, Minn.	G3	67
Adrian, Mo.	C3	69
Adrianople, see Edirne, Tur.		
Adwā, Eth.	F5	23
Afars & Issas, see Djibouti, country, Fr.		
Affton, Mo.	C7	69
Afghanistan, country, Asia	B4	20
Africa, cont.		21
Afton, Iowa	C3	60
Afton, N.Y.	C5	75
Afton, Okla.	A7	79
Afton, Wyo.	D2	89
'Afula, Isr.	B3	15
Afyon, Tur.	C8	14
Agadèz, Niger	E6	22
Agadir, Mor.	B3	22
Agana, Guam	*F6	2
Agartala, India	D9	20
Agate Beach, Oreg.	C2	80
Agawam, Mass.	B2	65
Agboville, I.C.	G4	22
Agde, Fr.	F5	5
Agematsu, Jap.	n16	18
Agen, Fr.	E4	5
Agira, It.	F5	9
Agnone, It.	D5	9
Āgra, India	C6	20
Agrícola Oriental, Mex.	*D5	34
Agrigento, It.	F4	9
Agrínion, Grc.	C3	14
Aguada, P.R.	*G11	35
Aguadas, Col.	B2	32
Aguadilla, P.R.	G11	35
Aguascalientes, Mex.	C4, m12	34
Aguascalientes, state, Mex.	C4, k12	34
Aguilar, Colo.	D6	51
Aguita, Mex.	*B4	34
Agusan prov., Phil.	*D7	19
Ahlen, Ger., Fed. Rep. of	C3	6
Ahmadabad, India	D5	20
Ahmadnagar, India	E5	20
Ahmadpur East, Pak.	C5	20
Ahoskie, N.C.	A6	76
Ahrweiler, Ger., Fed. Rep. of	C3	6
Ahuachapan, Sal.	E7	34
Ahualulco de Mercado, Mex.	m12	34
Ahvāz, Iran	B7	23
Ahvenanmaa (Åland), prov. Fin.	G8	11
Aibonito, P.R.	*G11	35
Aichi, pref., Jap.	*I8	18
Aiea, Haw.	B4, g10	56
Aihui, China	A10	17
Aikawa, Jap.	G9	18
Aiken, S.C.	D4	82
Aiken, co., S.C.	D4	82
Aiken West, S.C.	*D4	82
Aimorés, Braz.	B4	30
Aïn, dept., Fr.	*D6	5
Aïn Sefna, Alg.	B4	22
Ainsworth, Nebr.	B6	71
Aire-sur-la-Lys, Fr.	B5	5
Aisén, prov., Chile	D2	28
Aitkin, Minn.	D5	67
Aitkin, co., Minn.	D5	67
Aitolía kai Akarnanía	*C3	14
Aitolikón, Grc.	C3	24
Aiud, Rom.	B6	10
Aix-en-Provence, Fr.	F6	5

Aix-la-Chapelle, see Aachen, Ger., Fed. Rep. of		
Aix-les-Bains, Fr.	E6	5
Aiyina, Grc.	D4	14
Aiyion, Grc.	C4	14
Aizu-wakamatsu, Jap.	H9	18
Ajaccio, Fr.	D2	9
Ajax, Ont. Can.	D6	41
Ajmer, India	C5	20
Ajo, Ariz.	C2	48
Akashi, Jap.	I7	18
Akcaabat, Tur.	B12	14
Akershus, co., Nor.	*H4	11
Aketi, Zaire	H2	23
Akhaía (Achaea), prov., Grc.	*C3	14
Akharnaí, Grc.	g11	14
Akhisar, Tur.	C6	14
Akhtyrka, Sov. Un.	F10	12
Aki, Jap.	J6	18
Akita, Jap.	G10	18
Akita, pref., Jap.	*G1	18
Akkeshi, Jap.	E12	18
'Akko (Acre), Isr.	B3, g5	15
Akola, India	D6	20
Akron, Colo.	A7	51
Akron, Ind.	B5	59
Akron, Iowa	B1	60
Akron, N.Y.	B2	75
Akron, Ohio	A4	78
Akron, Pa.	F9	81
Aksaray, Tur.	C10	14
Akşehir, Tur.	C8	14
Aksenovo-Zilovskove, Sov. Un.	D14	13
Aktyubinsk, Sov. Un.	D8	13
Akureyri, Ice.	n23	11
Alabama, state, U.S.		46
Alabaster, Ala.	B3	46
Alachua, Fla.	C4	54
Alachua, co., Fla.	*C4	54
Alagôa Grande, Braz.	*D7	27
Alagôas, state, Braz.	*D7	27
Alagoinhas, Braz.	*E7	27
Alajuela, C.R.	E8	34
Al 'Alamayn (El Alamein), Eg.	G7	14
Alamance, co. N.C.	B3	76
Alameda, Calif.	h8	50
Alameda, N. Mex.	B5, D5	48
Alameda, co. Calif.	D3	50
Alamo, Calif.	*D3	50
Alamo, Tenn.	B2	83
Alamo, Tex.	F3	84
Alamogordo, N. Mex.	C6	48
Alamo Heights, Tex.	E3, k7	84
Alamosa, Colo.	D5	51
Alamosa, co., Colo.	D5	51
Alanya, Tur.	D9	14
Alaşehir, Tur.	C7	14
Alaska, State, U.S.		47
Alassio, It.	C2	9
Alatyr, Sov. Un.	D16	12
Alava prov., Sp.	*A4	8
Alba, It.	B2	9
Albacete, Sp.	C5	8
Alba Iulia, Rom.	B6	10
Albania, country, Eur.	B2	10
Albano Laziale, It.	D4, h9	9
Albany, Ga.	E2	55
Albany, Ind.	D7	59
Albany, Ky.	D4	62

Albany, Minn. E4 67
Albany, Mo. A3 69
Albany, N.Y. C7 75
Albany, Oreg. C3, k11 80
Albany, Tex. C3 84
Albany, Wis. F4 88
Albany, co., N.Y. C6 75
Albany, co., Wyo. E6 89
Albany, riv., Ont. o18 41
Al Batrūn, Leb. f5 15
Albay, prov., Phil. *C6 19
Albemarle, N.C. B2 76
Albemarle, co., Va. C4 85
Albenga, It. B2 9
Albert, Fr. B5 5
Albert, co., N.B., Can. D5 43
Albert, Lake, Ug., Zaire H4 23
Alberta, prov., Can. 38
Alberta, mtn., Alta., Can. C2 38
Albert Edward, mtn., Pap. N. Gui. . k12 25
Albert Lea, Minn. G5 67
Albertson, N.Y. *G2 52
Albertville, Ala. A3 46
Albertville, Fr. E7 5
Albi, Fr. F5 5
Albia, Iowa C5 60
Albion, Ill. E5 58
Albion, Ind. B7 59
Albion, Mich. F6 66
Albion, Nebr. C7 71
Albion, N.Y. B2 75
Albion, R.I. B11 52
Ålborg, Den. I3 11
Albuñol, Sp. D4 8
Albuquerque, N. Mex. B5, D5 48
Alburquerque, Sp. C2 8
Alburtis, Pa. F10 81
Albury-Wodonga, Austl. G8 25
Alcalá de Guadaira, Sp. D3 8
Alcalá de Henares, Sp. B4, p18 8
Alcalá de los Gazules, Sp. D3 8
Alcamo, It. F4 9
Alcanar, Sp. B6 8
Alcañiz, Sp. B5 8
Alcalá de Henares, Sp. B4, p18 8
Alcalá de los Gazules, Sp. D3 8
Alcamo, It. F4 9
Alcanar, Sp. B6 8
Alcañiz, Sp. B5 8
Alcaraz, Sp. C4 8
Alcaudete, Sp. D3 8
Alcázar de San Juan, Sp. C4 8
Alcazarquivir, see Ksar el Kebir, Mor.
Alcoy, Sp. C5 8
Alcoy, Nevado, mtn., Peru *D2 31
Aldan, Pa. *G11 81
Aldan, Sov. Un. D15 13
Aldan, riv., Sov. Un. C16 13
Alden, Iowa B4 60
Alden, N.Y. C2 75
Alden, Pa. D9 81
Aldershot, Eng. E6 4
Alderson, W. Va. D4 87
Alderwood Manor, Wash. B3 86
Aledo, Ill. B3 58
Alegre, Braz. C4 30
Alegrete, Braz. D1 31
Aleksandriya, Sov. Un. G9 12
Aleksandrov, Sov. Un. C12 12
Aleksandrovsk -Sakhalinskiy,
  Sov. Un. D17 13
Aleksandrów, Pol. B5 7
Aleksinac, Yugo. D5 10
Alençon, Fr. C4 5
Aleppo (Halab), Syr. D11 14
Alert Bay, B.C., Can. D4 37
Alès, Fr. E6 5
Alessandria, It. B2 9
Alesund, Nor. F2 11
Alexander, co., Ill. F4 58
Alexander, co., N.C. B1 76
Alexander City, Ala. C4 46
Alexander Mills, N.C. B1, f11 76
Alexandria, Ont., Can. B10 41
Alexandria (Al Iskandariyah), Eg. .. G7 14
Alexandria, Ind. D6 59
Alexandria, Ky. B5, k14 62
Alexandria, La. C3 63
Alexandria, Minn. E3 67
Alexandria, Rom. D7 10
Alexandria
  (Independent City), Va B5, g12 85
Alexandria Bay, N.Y. A5, f9 75
Alexandria Southwest, La. *C3 63
Alexandroúpolis, Grc. B5 14
Alexis, Ill. B3 58
Aleysk, Sov. Un. D11 13
Alfalfa, co., Okla. A3 79
Al Fallūjah, Iraq F14 14
Alfaro, Sp. A5 8
Al Fayyūm, Eg. H8 14
Alfenas, Braz. C3, k9 30
Alfortville, Fr. g10 5

Alfred, Ont., Can., ... B10 41
Alfred, N.Y. C3 75
Algarve, prov., Port. D1 8
Algarve, reg., Port. *D2 8
Algeciras, Sp. D3 8
Algemesí, Sp. C5 8
Alger, Ohio B2 78
Alger, co., Mich. B4 66
Algeria, country, Afr. C3 22
Alghero, It. D2 9
Al Ghurdaqah, Eg. C4 23
Algiers (El Djazair), Alg. A5 22
Algoma, dist., Ont., Can. A2 41
Algoma, Wis. D6 88
Algona, Iowa A3 60
Algona, Wash. B3, f11 86
Algonac, Mich. F8 66
Algonquin, Ill. A5, h8 58
Al Hadīthah, Iraq E14 14
Alhama, Sp. D5 8
Alhambra, Calif. m12 50
Alhaurín el Grande, Sp. D3 8
Al Hillah, Iraq F15 14
Al Hufhūf (Hofhof), Sau. Ar. D4 15
Al Husayhişah, Sud. F4 23
Alicante, Sp. C5 8
Alice, Tex. F3 84
Alice, Southwest, Tex. *F3 84
Aliceville, Kans. D8 61
Alīgarh, India C6 20
Alingsås, Swe. I5 11
Aliquippa, Pa. E1, h13 81
Al Iskandariyah, see Alexandria, Eg.
Al Isma 'īlīyah, Eg. G9 14
Alistrái, Grc. B4 14
Aliwal North, S. Afr. G5 24
Al Jawf (Jauf), Sau. Ar. D2 15
Al Jīzah (Giza), Eg. H8 14
Al Junaynah, Sud. F2 23
Aljustrel, Port. D1 8
Al Kāzimiyah, Iraq F14 14
Al Khābūkrah, Om. D2 20
Al Khalīl (Hebron), Jordan ... C3, h5 15
Al Kharijah, Eg. C4 23
Alkmaar, Neth. A6 5
Al Kūfah, Iraq F15 14
Al Lādhiqiyah, see Latakia, Syr.
Allahābād, India C7 20
Allamakee, co., Iowa A6 60
Allanmyo, Bur. E10 20
Allariz, Sp. A2 8
Allaykha, Sov. Un. B17 13
Allegan, Mich. F5 66
Allegan, co., Mich. F4 66
Allegany, N.Y. C2 75
Allegany, co., Md. A1 53
Allegany, co., N.Y. C2 75
Allegany, co., N.C. A1 76
Allegany, co., Va. C3 85
Allegheny, co., Pa. E1 81
Allegheny, mts., U.S. C10 45
Allegheny, riv., Pa. E2 81
Allen, Okla. C5 79
Allen, co., Ind. B7 59
Allen, co., Kans. E8 61
Allen, co., Ky. D3 62
Allen, co., Ohio B1 78
Allen, par., La. D3 63
Allendale, N.J. A4 74
Allendale, S.C. E5 82
Allendale, co., S.C. F5 82
Allen Park, Mich. p15 66
Allenport, Pa. F1 81
Allenstein, see Olsztyn, Pol.
Allentown, N.J. C3 74
Allentown, Pa. E11 81
Alleppey, India G6 20
Aller (Cabañaquinta), Sp. A3 8
Alliance, Nebr. B3 71
Alliance, Ohio B4 78
Allier, dept., Fr. D5 5
Allinge, Den. A3 7
Allison, Iowa B5 60
Allison, Pa. G2 81
Allison Park, Pa. h14 81
Allison, Ont., Can. C5 41
Al Līth, Sau. Ar. D6 23
Alloa, Scot. B5 4
Allouez, Wis. h9 88
Al Luhayyah, Yemen F3 15
Alma, Ark. B1 49
Alma, Ga. E4 55
Alma, Kans. C7 61
Alma, Mich. E6 66
Alma, Nebr. D6 71
Alma, Wis. D2 88
Alma-Ata, Sov. Un. E10 13
Almada, Por. f9 8
Almadén, Sp. C3 8
Al Madīnah, see Medina, Sau. Ar.
Almagro, Sp. C4 8
Al Mahallah al Kubrā, Eg. G8 14

Almansa, Sp. C5 8
Al Manşūra, Eg. G8 14
Al Marj, Libya B2 23
Al Mawşil, see Mosul, Iraq
Almeirim, Port. C1 8
Almelo, Neth. A7 5
Almendralejo, Sp. C2 8
Almería, Sp. D4 8
Al Minyā, Eg. C4 23
Almiros, Grc. C4 14
Almodóvar, Sp. C3 8
Almogía, Sp. D3 8
Almon, Ga. C3 55
Almonesson, N.J. D2 74
Almont, Mich. F7 66
Almonte, Ont., Can. B8 41
Almora, Minn. *D3 67
Almoradí, Sp. C5 8
Al Mukallā, P.D.R. of Yem. G4 15
Al Mukhā, Yemen G3 15
Almuñécar, Sp. D4 8
Alnwick, Eng. C6 4
Aloha, Oreg. h12 80
Alor Setar, Mala. D2 19
Alorton (Fireworks), Ill. *E3 58
Alosno, Sp. D2 8
Alpaugh, Calif. E4 50
Alpena, Mich. C7 66
Alpena, co., Mich. C7 66
Alpes-Maritimes, dept., Fr. *F7 5
Alpha, Mich. B2 74
Alpharetta, Ga. B2 55
Alpiarça, Port. C1 8
Alpine, Calif. *F5 50
Alpine, N.J. h9 74
Alpine, Tex. o13 84
Alpine, co., Calif. C4 50
Alpoca, W. Va. D3 87
Al Qadarif, Sud. F5 23
Al Qāhirah, see Cairo, Eg.
Al Qantarah, Eg. G9 14
Al Qatīf, Sau. Ar. D4 15
Al Qunaytirah, see Kuneitra, Syr.
Alsfeld, Ger., Fed. Rep of. C4 6
Alsip, Ill. B6 58
Alta, Iowa B2 60
Altadena, Calif. m12 50
Alta Gracia, Arg. A4 28
Alta Loma, Tex. r14 84
Altamont, Ill. D5 58
Altamont, N.Y. C6 75
Altamont, Oreg. E5 80
Altamonte Springs, Fla. *D5 54
Altamura, It. D6 9
Altavista, Va. C3 85
Altay, China B2 17
Altdorf, Switz. E4 6
Altenburg, Mo. D8 69
Altheimer, Ark. C4 49
Alto, Tex. D5 84
Alto Alentejo, prov., Port. *C2 8
Alton, Ill. E3 58
Alton, Iowa B1 60
Altona, Man., Can. E3 40
Altoona, Ala. A3 46
Altoona, Iowa C4 60
Altoona, Pa. F5 81
Altoona, Wis. D2 88
Alto Paraná, dept., Par. D4 29
Alturas, Calif. B3 50
Altus, Okla. C2 79
Alula, Šom. F8 23
Al Uqşur (Luxor), Eg. C4 23
Alva, Ky. D6 62
Alva, Okla. A3 79
Alvarado, Tex. C4, n9 84
Alvin, Tex. E5, r4 84
Älvsborg, so., Swe. *H5 11
Alwar, India C6 20
Alx, mtn., Wash. C4 86
Alytus, Sov. Un. A8 7
Amador, co., Calif. C3 50
Amagansett, N.Y. n16 75
Amagasaki, Jap. o14 18
Amāl, Swe. H5 11
Amalias, Grc. D3 14
Amambay, dept., Par. D4 29
Amantea, It. E6 9
Amapá, Braz. C5 27
Amarillo, Tex. B2 84
Amaroúsion, Gr. g11 14
Amasya (Amasia), Tur. *B10 14
Amazonas, comisaría, Col. D3 32
Amazonas, dept., Peru B2 31
Amazonas, state, Braz. C3 31
Amazonas, (Amazon) riv.,
  Braz., Peru D5 27
Amazon, see Amazonas, riv., Braz., Peru
Ambāla, India B6 20
Ambarchik, Sov. Un. C19 13
Ambato, Ec. B2 31
Amberg, Ger. Fed. Rep. of D5 6

Ambérieu -en Bugey, Fr. E5 6
Amberley, Ohio *C1 78
Ambikapur, India D7 20
Ambler, Pa. F11, o21 81
Amboise, Fr. D4 5
Ambon (Amboina), Indon. F7 19
Amboy, Ill. B4 58
Ambridge, Pa. E1, h13 81
Ambridge Heights, Pa. *E1 81
Amderma, Sov. Un. C9 13
Ameca, Mex. C4, m11 34
Amecameca de Juárez, Mex. n14 34
Amelia, La. E4, k9 63
Amelia, Ohio C1 78
Amelia, co., Va. C4 85
Amelia Court House, Va. C5 85
Amenia, N. Dak. D8 77
Amenia, N.Y. D7 75
American Falls, Idaho G6 57
American Fork, Utah A6, D2 72
American Samoa,
  U.S. dep., Oceania *G9 2
Americus, Ga. D2 55
Amersfoort, Neth. A6 5
Amery, Wis. C1 88
Ames, Iowa B4 60
Amesbury, Mass. A6 65
Amfissa, Grc. C4 14
Amga, Sov. Un. C16 13
Amherst, N.S., Can. D5 43
Amherst, Mass. B2 65
Amherst, (Eggertsville), N.Y. *C2 75
Amherst, Ohio A3 78
Amherst, Tex. B1 84
Amherst, Va. C3 85
Amherst, co., Va. C3 85
Amherstburg, Ont., Can. E1 41
Amherstdale, W. Va. D3, n12 87
Amiens, Fr. C5 5
Amite, La. D5 63
Amite, co., Miss. D3 68
Amityville, N.Y. E7, n15 75
'Ammān, Jordan C3, h5 15
Ammon, Idaho F7 57
Amory, Miss. B5 68
Amos, Que., Can. o20 41
Amoy, see Xiamen, China
Amparo, Braz. C3, m8 30
Amqui, Que., Can. *k13 42
Amravati, India D6 20
Amritsar, India B5 20
Amsterdam, Neth. A6 5
Amsterdam, N.Y. C6 75
Amsterdam, Ohio B5 78
Amstetten, Aus. D7 6
Amu Darya, riv., Sov. Un. Fl9 13
Amur, riv., China, Sov. Un. E16 13
'Ānah, Iraq C3 15
Anaconda, Mont. D4 70
Anacortes, Wash. A3 86
Anadarko, Okla. B3 79
Anadyr, Sov. Un. C20 13
Anaheim, Calif. F5, n13 50
Anahuac, Tex. E5, r15 84
Anakapallel, India E7 20
Analalava, Mad. C9 24
Anamosa, Iowa B6 60
Anandale, Lal. *C3 63
Anantapur, India F6 20
Anantnag, India B6 20
Ananyev, Sov. Un. H7 12
Anápolis, Braz. B3 30
Anatuyá, Arg. E3 29
Anawalt, W. Va. D3 87
Ancash, dept., Peru C2 31
Anchorage, Alsk. C10, g17 47
Anchorage, Ky. g11 62
Ancienne Lorette, Que., Can. ... C6, n17 42
Ancon, C.Z. B2 32
Ancona, It. C4 9
Anda, China C2 18
Andalusia, Ala. D3 46
Andalusia reg., Sp. D3 8
Andaman and Nicobar Islands,
  ter., India F9, G9 20
Anderlecht, Bel. B6 5
Andernach, Ger., Fed. Rep of C3 6
Anderson, Calif. B2 50
Anderson, Ind. D6 59
Anderson Mo. E3 69
Anderson, S.C. B2 82
Anderson, co., Kans. D8 61
Anderson, co., Ky. C4 62
Anderson, co., S.C. B2 82
Anderson, co., Tenn. C9 83
Anderson, co., Tex. D5 84
Anderson, mtn., Wash. B2 86
Andes, Col. B2 32
Andhra Pradesh, state, India E6 20
Andizhan, Sov. Un. E10 13
Andkhui, Afg. A4 20
Andoany, Mad. C9 24
Andong, Kor. H4 18

Andorra, And. ... A6 8
Andorra, country, Eur. ... A6 8
Andover, Mass. ... A5 65
Andover, N.B., Can. ... C2 43
Andover, N.Y. ... C3 75
Andover, Ohio ... A5 78
Andraitx, Sp. ... C7 8
Andrew, co., Mo. ... B3 69
Andrew Jackson, mtn., Ant. ... K16 2
Andrews, Ind. ... C6 59
Andrews, N.C. ... f9 76
Andrews, S.C. ... El8 82
Andrews, Tex. ... C1 84
Andrews, co., Tex. ... C1 84
Andreyevka, Sov. Un. ... G11 12
Andria, It. ... D6 9
Androscoggin, co., Maine ... D2 64
Andropov (Rybinsk), Sov. Un. ... B12 12
Andros, isl., Ba. ... B4 35
Andrychów, Pol. ... h10 7
Andújar, Sp. ... C3 8
Aneto, mtn., Sp. ... A6 8
Angara, riv., Sov. Un. ... D13 13
Angarsk, Sov. Un. ... *D13 13
Angelholm, Swe. ... I5 11
Angelica, N.Y. ... C2 75
Angelina, co., Tex. ... D5 84
Angels Camp, Calif. ... C3 50
Angermunde, Ger. Dem. Rep. ... B7 6
Angers, Fr. ... D3 5
Angier, N.C. ... B4 76
Anglesey, is., Wales ... D4 4
Anglet, Fr. ... F3 5
Angleton, Tex. ... E5, r14 84
Ango, Zaire ... H3 23
Angol, Chile ... B2 28
Angola, Ind. ... A8 59
Angola, N.Y. ... C1 75
Angola, country, Afr. ... C3 24
Angoulême, Fr. ... E4 5
Angra do Heroismo, Port. ... k10 22
Angra dos Reis, Braz. ... C4, h5 30
Anguang, China ... D1 18
Angus, co., Scot. ... *B5 4
Anhui, prov., China ... E8 17
Anina, Rom. ... C5 10
Anita, Iowa ... C3 60
Anita, Pa. ... D4 81
Aniva (Rutaka), Sov. Un. ... C11 18
Anjo, Jap. ... o16 18
Anjou, Que., Can. ... p19 42
Anjou, former prov. Fr. ... D3 5
Anju, Kor. ... G2 18
Ankang, China ... E6 17
Ankara, Tur. ... C9 14
Ankeny, Iowa ... C4, e8 60
Anklam, Ger. Dem. Rep. ... B6 6
An Najaf, Iraq ... C3 15
Annaba (Bône), Alg. ... A6 22
Annalee Heights, Va. ... *B5 85
Annam, reg., Viet. ... *B3 19
Annandale, Minn. ... E4 67
Annandale, Va. ... g12 85
Annapolis, Md. ... C5 53
Annapolis Royal, N.S. ... E4 43
Annapurna 1, peak, Nep. ... C7 20
Ann Arbor, Mich. ... F7, p14 66
An Nasiriya, Iraq ... C4 15
Anne Arundel co., Md. ... B4 53
Annecy, Fr. ... E7 5
Annemasse, Fr. ... D7 5
Anniston, Ala. ... B4 46
Annonay, Fr. ... E6 5
An Nuhūd, Sud. ... F3 23
Annville, Pa. ... F8 81
Anoka, Minn. ... E5, m12 67
Anoka, co., Minn. ... E5 67
Ansbach, Ger., Fed. Rep. of ... D5 6
Anserma, Col. ... B2 32
Anshan, China ... C9 17
Anshun, China ... F6 17
Anson, Maine ... D3 64
Anson, Tex. ... C3 84
Anson, co., N.C. ... B2 76
Ansong, Kor. ... H3 18
Ansonia, Conn. ... D4 52
Ansonia, Ohio ... B1 78
Ansted, W.Va. ... C3, m13 87
Anta, Peru ... D3 31
Antakay (Antioch), Tur. ... D11 14
Antalaha, Mad. ... C10 24
Antalya (Adalia), Tur. ... D8 14
Antananarive, Mad. ... D9 24
Antarctic, pen., Ant. ... K16 2
Antelope, co., Nebr. ... B7 71
Antequera, Sp. ... D3 8
Anthon, Iowa ... B2 60
Anthony, Kans. ... E5 61
Anthony, N. Mex. ... D5 48
Anthony, R.I. ... C10 52
Antibes, Fr. ... F7 5
Antigo, Wis. ... C4 88
Antigonish, N.S., Can. ... D8 43

Antigonish, co., N.S., Can. ... D8 43
Antigua and Barbuda, country, N.A. ... H14 35
Antigua, Guatemala, Guat. ... E6 34
Antilla, Cuba ... D6 35
Antioch, Calif. ... h9 50
Antioch, Ill. ... A5, h8 58
Antioquia, Col. ... B2 32
Antioquia, dept. Col. ... B2 32
Antique, prov., Phil. ... *C6 19
Antlers, Okla. ... C6 79
Antofagasta, Chile ... D1 29
Antofagasta, prov., Chile ... D1 29
Anton, Tex. ... C1 84
Antonina, Braz. ... D3 30
António Enes, Moz. ... D7 24
Antonito, Colo. ... D5 51
Antony, Fr. ... g10 5
Antratsit, Sov. Un. ... g22 12
Antrim, co., Mich. ... C5 66
Antrim, co. N. Ire. ... *C3 4
Antsirabe, Mad. ... D9 24
Antsiranana, Mad. ... C9 24
Antwerp, N.Y. ... A5, f9 75
Antwerp, Ohio ... A1 78
Antwerp (Antwerpen), Bel. ... B6 5
Antwerpen, prov., Bel. ... *B6 5
Anuadhapura, Sri Lanka ... G7 20
Anyang, China ... D7 17
Anzhero-Sudzhensk, Sov. Un. ... D11 13
Anzio, It. ... D4, k7 9
Anzoátequi, state, Ven. ... B5 32
Aomori, Jap. ... F10 18
Aomori, pref., Jap. ... *F10 18
Aosta, It ... B1 9
Apache, Okla. ... C3 79
Apache co., Ariz. ... B4 48
Apache mts., Tex. ... o12 84
Apache Junction, Ariz. ... D2 48
Apalachicola, Fla. ... C2 54
Apalachin, N.Y. ... C4 75
Apam, Mex. ... n14 34
Aparri, Phil. ... B6 19
Apatin, Yugo. ... C4 10
Apeldoorn, Neth. ... A6 5
Apex, N.C. ... B4 76
Apia, W. Sam. ... G9 2
Apizaco, Mex. ... n14 34
Aplao, Peru ... E3 31
Apington, Iowa ... B5 60
Apo, vol., Phil. ... D7 19
Apolda, Ger. Dem. Rep. ... C5 6
Apollo, Pa. ... E2 8
Apopka, Fla. ... D5 54
Appalachia, Va. ... f9 85
Appalachian, mts., U.S. ... F12 33
Appanoose, co., Iowa ... D5 60
Appenzell, canton, Switz. ... *B7 6
Apple Orchard, mtn., Va. ... C3 85
Appleton, Minn. ... E2 67
Appleton, Wis. ... D5, h9 88
Appleton City, Mo. ... C3 69
Appleyard, Wash. ... B5 86
Appling, co., Ga. ... E4 55
Appomattox, Va. ... C4 85
Appomattox, co., Va. ... C4 85
Aprelsk, Sov. Un. ... D14 13
Apt, Fr. ... F6 5
Apulia, reg., It. ... D6 9
Apure, riv., Ven. ... B4 32
Apurímac, riv., Peru ... D3 31
Aquidauana, Braz. ... C1 30
Arab, Ala. ... A3 46
Arabi, La. ... k11 62
Arabia, see Saudi Arabia, Asia
Aracaju, Braz. ... E7 27
Aracati, Braz. ... D7 27
Arçatuba, Braz. ... C2 30
Arad, Rom. ... B5 10
Aragon, Ga. ... B1 55
Aragua, state, Ven. ... A4 32
Araguaia, riv., Braz. ... D6 27
Araguari, Braz. ... *E5 27
Arai, Jap. ... o16 18
Arāk (Sultanabad), Iran ... B7 23
Aral, sea, Sov. Un. ... E8 13
Aranda de Duero, Sp. ... B4 8
Arandas, Mex. ... m12 34
Aranjuez, Sp. ... B4 8
Aranos, S.W. Afr. ... B2 24
Aransas, co., Tex. ... E4 84
Aransas Pass, Tex. ... F4 84
Aranyaprathet, Thai. ... C2 19
Arapahoe, Nebr. ... D7 71
Arapahoe, co., Colo. ... B6 51
Arapkir, Tur. ... C12 14
Araraquara, Braz. ... C3 30
Araras, Braz. ... C3, m8 30
Ararat, Austl. ... G7, n14 25
Ararat, see Buyuk Agri Dagï, mtn., Tur.
Arauca, Col. ... B3 32
Arauca, intendencia, Col. ... B3 32
Arauco, prov., Chile ... B2 28
Araxá, Braz. ... B3 30

Arboga, Swe. ... t33 11
Arborg, Man., Can. ... D3 40
Arbor Terrace, Mo. ... *C7 69
Arbroath, Scot. ... B5 4
Arbuckle, Calif. ... C2 50
Arachon, Fr. ... E3 5
Arcade, N.Y. ... C2 75
Arcadia, Calif. ... m12 50
Arcadia, Fla. ... E5 54
Arcadia, Ind. ... D5 59
Arcadia, La. ... B3 63
Arcadia, S.C. ... B3 82
Arcadia, Wis. ... D2 88
Arcanum, Ohio ... C1 78
Arcata, Calif. ... B1 50
Archangel, see
  Arkhangelsk, Sov. Un.
Archbald, Pa. ... m18 81
Archbold, Ohio ... A1 78
Archdale, N.C. ... B3 76
Archer, co., Tex. ... C3 84
Archer City, Tex. ... C3 84
Archidona, Sp. ... D3 8
Archuleta, co., Colo. ... D3 51
Arcila, Mor. ... E2 8
Arco, Ga. ... E5 55
Arco, Idaho ... F5 57
Arcola, Ill. ... D5 58
Arcoverde, Braz. ... *D6 27
Arctic, Ocean. ... A6 2
Arcueil, Fr. ... g10 5
Ardabil (Ardebil), Iran ... B4 15
Ardatov, Sov. Un. ... D16 12
Ardèche, dept., Fr. ... *E6 5
Arden (Ardentown), Del. ... A7 53
Arden Hills, Minn. ... *E7 67
Ardennes, dept., Fr. ... *C6 5
Ardmore, Okla. ... C4 79
Ardmore, Pa. ... g20 81
Ardrossan, Scot. ... C4 4
Ardsley, N.Y. ... g13 75
Arecibo, P.R. ... g11 35
Areia Branca, Braz. ... *D7 27
Arenac, co., Mich. ... D7 66
Arendal, Nor. ... H3 11
Arequipa, Peru ... E3 31
Arequipa, dept., Peru ... E3 31
Arezzo, It. ... C3 9
Argenta, Ill. ... D5 58
Argenta, It. ... B3 8
Argentan, Fr. ... C4 5
Argenteuil, Fr. ... C5, g10 5
Argenteuil, co. Que. ... D3 42
Argentina, country, S.A. ... G4 27
Argenton-sur-Creuse, Fr. ... D4 5
Argolis, prov., Grc. ... *D4 14
Argos, Grc. ... D4 14
Argos, Ind. ... B5 59
Argostólion, Grc. ... C3 14
Argylll, co., Scot. ... *B4 4
Århus, Den. ... I4 11
Århus, co., Den. ... *I4 11
Ariail, S.C. ... B2 82
Ariano Irpino, It. ... D5 9
Arica, Chile ... *C1 29
Ariège, dept., Fr. ... *F4 5
Arîhã (Jericho), Jordan ... C3 15
Ario de Rosales, Mex. ... D4, n13 34
Aripo, El Cerro del, mtn.,
  Trin. ... K14 34
Arizona, state, U.S. ... 48
Arjay, Ky. ... D6 62
Arjona, Col ... A2 32
Arjona, Sp. ... D3 8
Arkadelphia, Ark. ... C2 49
Arkansas, state, U.S. ... 49
Arkansas, co., Ark. ... C4 49
Arkansas, riv., U.S. ... C8 45
Arkansas City, Ark. ... D4 49
Arkansas City, Kans. ... E6 61
Arkhangelsk, Sov. Un. ... C7 13
Arkoma, Okla. ... B7 79
Arkonam, India ... F6 20
Arkport, N.Y. ... C3 75
Arkwright, R.I. ... C10 52
Arkwright, S.C. ... *B4 82
Arles, Fr. ... F6 5
Arlington, Ga. ... E2 55
Arlington, Mass. ... B5, g11 65
Arlington, Minn. ... F4 67
Arlington, N.Y. ... *D7 75
Arlington, Ohio ... B2 78
Arlington, S.C. ... B3 82
Arlington, S. Dak. ... F8 77
Arlington, Tex. ... n9 84
Arlington, Vt. ... E1 73
Arlington, Va. ... B5, g12 85
Arlington, Wash. ... A3 86
Arlington, co., Va. ... B5, g12 85
Arlington Heights, Ill. ... A5, a9 58
Arlington Heights, Ohio ... *C1 78
Arlon, Bel. ... C6 5

Arma, Kans. ... E9 61
Armada, Mich. ... F8 66
Armagh, N. Ire. ... C3 4
Armagh, Que., Can. ... C7 42
Armagh, co., N. Ire. ... *C3 4
Armavir, Sov. Un. ... I13 12
Armenia, Col. ... C2 32
Armenia (S.S.R.), rep.
  Sov. Un. ... A4 15
Armentières, Fr. ... B5 5
Armero, Col. ... C3 32
Armidale, Austl. ... F9 25
Armijo, N. Mex. ... E5 48
Armona, Calif. ... *D4 50
Armonk, N.Y. ... *D7 75
Armour, S. Dak. ... G7 77
Armstrong, B.C., Can. ... D8 37
Armstrong, Iowa ... A3 60
Armstrong, co., Pa. ... E3 81
Armstrong, co., Tex. ... B2 84
Arnaudville, La. ... D4 63
Arnedo, Sp. ... A4 8
Arnhem, Neth. ... B6 5
Arnissa, Grc. ... E5 10
Arnold, Mo. ... C7 69
Arnold, Nebr. ... C5 71
Arnold, Pa. ... h14 81
Arnolds Park, Iowa ... A2 60
Arnouville -les-Gonesse, Fr. ... g10 5
Arnprior, Ont., Can. ... B8 41
Arnsberg, Ger., Fed. Rep. of ... C4 6
Arnstadt, Ger. Dem. Rep. ... C5 6
Aroostook, co., Maine ... B4 64
Arp, Tex. ... C5 84
Arrah, India ... C7 20
Ar Ramādī, Iraq ... F14 14
Ar Raqqah, Syr ... E12 14
Arras, Fr. ... B5 5
Arrecife, Sp. ... m15 8
Arrecifes, Arg. ... g6 28
Arroyo, P.R. ... *G11 35
Arroyo Grande, Calif. ... E3 50
Árta, Grc. ... C3 14
Arta, prov., Grc. ... *C3 14
Artem, Sov. Un. ... E16 13
Artemisa, Cuba ... C2 35
Artemovsk, Sov. Un. ... G12, o21 13
Arter, mtn., Wyo. ... D4 89
Artesia, Calif. ... *F4 50
Artesia, N. Mex. ... *C6 48
Arthabaska, Que., Can. ... C6 42
Arthabaska, co., Que., Can ... C5 42
Arthur, Ill. ... D5 58
Arthur, co., Nebr. ... C4 71
Artigas, Ur. ... E1 30
Artigas, dept., Ur. ... *E1 30
Artois, former prov., Fr. ... B5 5
Arunachal Pradesh, ter., India ... C9 20
Arusha, Tan. ... I5 23
Arvada, Colo. ... B5 51
Arvida, Que., Can. ... A6 42
Arvidsjaur, Swe. ... E8 11
Arvika, Swe ... H5 11
Arvin, Calif. ... E4 50
Arzamas, Sov. Un. ... D14 12
Arzúa, Sp. ... A1 8
As, Czech. ... C2 7
Asahi-Dake, mtn., Jap. ... E11 18
Asahikawa, Jap. ... E11 18
Asan, Guam ... *F6 2
Asansol, India ... D8 20
Asbest, Sov. Un. ... D9 13
Asbestos, Que., Can. ... D6 42
Asbury Park, N.J. ... C4 74
Ascension, par., La. ... D5 63
Ascension Isl. Br. dep., Atl. O. ... G20 2
Aschaffenburg, Ger., Fed.
  Rep. of ... D4 6
Aschersleben, Ger. Dem. Rep. ... C5 6
Ascoli Piceno, It. ... C4 9
Asenovgrad, Bul. ... E7 10
Ashaway, R.I. ... D9 52
Ashburn, Ga. ... E3 55
Ashburnham, Mass. ... A4 65
Ashburton, N.Z. ... O13 26
Ashby, Ala. ... B3 46
Ashcroft, B.C., Can. ... D7 37
Ashdown, Ark. ... D1 49
Ashe, co., N.C. ... A1 76
Asheboro, N.C. ... B3 76
Asheboro South, N.C. ... *B3 76
Asheboro West, N.C. ... *B3 76
Asherton, Tex. ... E3 84
Asheville, N.C. ... f10 76
Ashford, Ala. ... D4 46
Ash Grove, Mo. ... D4 69
Ashikaga, Jap. ... H9, m18 18
Ashio, Jap. ... H9 18
Ashkhabad, Sov. Un. ... F8 13
Ashland, Ala. ... B4 46
Ashland, Ill. ... D3 58
Ashland, Kans. ... E4 61
Ashland, Ky. ... B7 62

Entry	Ref	Pg
Ashland, Maine,	B4	64
Ashland, Mass.	g10	65
Ashland, Nebr.	C9, g12	71
Ashland, N.H.	D4	73
Ashland, Ohio	B3	78
Ashland, Oreg.	E4	80
Ashland, Pa.	E9	81
Ashland, Va.	C5	85
Ashland, Wis.	B3	88
Ashland, co., Ohio	B3	78
Ashland, co., Wis.	B3	88
Ashland, mtn. Oreg.	E4	80
Ashland City, Tenn.	A4	83
Ashley, N. Dak.	D6	77
Ashley, Ohio	B3	78
Ashley, Pa.	n17	81
Ashley, co., Ark.	D4	49
Ashmūn, Eg.	*G8	14
Ashqelon, Isr.	C2	15
Ash Shāmīyah, Iraq	*G15	14
Ash Shatt, Eg.	H9	14
Ash Shihr, P.D.R. of Yem.	C6	15
Ashtabula, Ohio	A5	78
Ashtabula, co., Ohio	A5	78
Ashton, Idaho	E7	57
Ashton, Ill.	B4	58
Ashton, R.I.	B11	52
Ashville, Ala.	B3	46
Ashville, Ohio	C3	78
Ashwaubenon, Wis.	g9	88
Asia, cont.	F9	16
Asir, reg., Sau. Ar.	E6	23
Asmara, Eth.	E5	23
Asnières -sur Seine, Fr.	g10	5
Asotin, co., Wash.	C8	86
Aspe, Sp.	C5	8
Aspen, Colo.	B4	51
Aspermont, Tex.	C2	84
Aspinwall, Pa.	k14	81
As Salṭ, Jordan	B3, g5	15
Assam, state, India	C9	20
Assateague, isl. Va.	C7	85
Assen, Neth.	A7	5
Assens, co. Den.	*J3	11
Assiniboia, Sask. Can.	H3	39
Assiniboine, mtn., Alta.	D3	38
Assini, I.C.	G4	22
Assis, Braz.	C2	30
Assisi, It.	C4	9
As Sulaymānīyah, Iraq	B3	15
Assumption, Ill.	D4	58
Assumption, par., La.	E4	63
As Suwaydā, Syr	F11	15
Asti, It.	B2	9
Aston, Pa.	*G11	81
Astorga, Sp.	A2	8
Astoria, Ill.	C3	58
Astoria, Oreg.	A3	80
Astrakhan, Sov. Un.	E7	13
Asturias, reg., Sp.	A2	8
Asunción, Par.	E4	29
Aswan, Eg.	D4	23
Asyut, Eg.	C4	23
Atacama, prov., Chile	E1	29
Atami, Jap.	n18	18
Atascadero, Calif.	E3	50
Atascosa, co., Tex.	E3	84
'Atbarah, Sud	E4	23
Atbasar, Sov. Un.	D9	13
Atchison, Kans.	C8	61
Atchison, co., Kans.	C8	61
Atchison, co. Mo.	A2	69
Atco, N.J.	D3	74
Athabasca, Alta., Can.	B4, g8	38
Athabasca, lake, Alta., Can.	m6	39
Athabasca, riv., Can.	E11	36
Athena, Oreg.	E8	80
Athens, Ala.	A3	46
Athens, Ont., Can.	C9	41
Athens, Ga.	C3	55
Athens (Athínai), Grc.	C4	14
Athens, Ill.	C4	58
Athens, Mich.	F5	66
Athens, N.Y.	C7	75
Athens, Ohio	C3	78
Athens, Pa.	C9	81
Athens, Tenn.	D9	83
Athens, Tex.	C5	84
Athens, W. Va.	D3	87
Athens, co., Ohio	C3	78
Atherton, Austl.	C8	25
Atherton, Calif.	*D2	60
Athis-Mons, Fr.	h10	5
Athleague, Ire.	D3	4
Athok, Bur.	E10	20
Athol, Mass.	A3	65
Athol, co., Mass.	A3	65
Atibaia, Braz.	m8	30
Atikokan, Ont., Can.	E8	41
Atkarsk, Sov. Un.	F15	12
Atkins, Ark.	B3	49
Atkinson, Ill.	B3	58
Atkinson, Nebr.	B7	71
Atkinson, co., Ga.	E4	55
Atlanta, Ga.	C2, h8	55
Atlanta, Ill.	C4	58
Atlanta, Tex.	C5	84
Atlantic, Iowa	C2	60
Atlantic, N.C.	C6	76
Atlantic, co., N.J.	E3	74
Atlantic, ocean	D17	2
Atlantic peak, Wyo.	D3	89
Atlantic Beach, N.Y.	n15	75
Atlantic City, N.J.	E4	74
Atlantic Highlands, N.J.	C4	74
Atlántico, dept., Col.	A2	32
Atlas, Pa.	*D8	81
Atlixco, Mex.	n14	34
Atmore, Ala.	D2	46
Atna, peak, B.C., Can.	C3	37
Atoka, Okla.	C5	79
Atoka, co., Okla.	C5	79
Atotonilco el Alto, Mex.	m12	34
Atrisco, N. Mex.	*B5	48
Atsugi, Jap.	n18	18
Aṭ Ṭafīlah, Jordan	D3, h5	15
Aṭ Ṭā'if, Sau. Ar.	E3	15
Attala, co., Miss.	B4	68
Attalia, Ala.	A3	46
Aṭ Ṭayyibah, Jordan	C3	15
Attica, Ind.	D3	59
Attica, Kans.	E5	61
Attica, N.Y.	C2	75
Attica, Ohio	A3	78
Attika (Attica), prov., Grc.	*C4	14
Attleboro, Mass.	C5	65
Atvidaberg, Swe.	H6	11
Atwater, Calif.	D3	50
Atwater, Minn.	E4	67
Atwood, Ill.	D5	58
Atwood, Kans.	C2	61
Atzcapotzalco (Azcapotzalco), Mex.	h9, n14	34
Atzmon, mtn., Isr.	A3	15
Aubagne, Fr.	F3	5
Aube, dept., Fr.	*C6	5
Aubervilliers, Fr.	g10	5
Aubin, Fr.	E5	5
Auburn, Ala.	C4	46
Auburn, Ill.	D4	58
Auburn, Ind.	B7	59
Auburn, Kans.	D8	61
Auburn, Ky.	D3	62
Auburn, Maine	D2, f7	64
Auburn, Mass.	B4	65
Auburn, Mich.	E6	66
Auburn, Nebr.	D10	71
Auburn, N.Y.	C4	75
Auburn, Pa.	E9	81
Auburn, Wash.	B3, f11	86
Auburndale, Fla.	D5	54
Auburn Heights, Mich.	F7	66
Aubusson, Fr.	E5	5
Auch, Fr.	F4	5
Aude, dept. Fr.	*C6	5
Audincourt, Fr.	D7	5
Audrain, co., Mo.	B6	69
Audubon, Iowa	C3	60
Audubon, N.J.	D2	74
Audubon, co., Iowa	C3	60
Audubon Park, N.J.	*C3	74
Aue, Ger. Dem. Rep.	C6	6
Auglaize, co., Ohio	B1	78
Augsburg, Ger., Fed. Rep. of	D5	6
Augusta, Ark.	B4	49
Augusta, Ga.	C5	55
Augusta, Ill.	C3	58
Augusta, It.	F6	9
Augusta, Kans.	E6, g13	61
Augusta, Ky.	B5	62
Augusta, Maine	D3	64
Augusta, Mich.	F5	66
Augusta, Wis.	D2	88
Augusta co., Va.	B3	85
Augustów, Pol.	B7	7
Augustus, mtn., Austl.	D2	25
Aulander, N.C.	A5	76
Aulnay-sous-Bois, Fr.	g11	5
Auray, Fr.	D2	5
Aurelia, Iowa	B2	60
Aurich, Ger., Fed. Rep. of	B3	6
Aurillac, Fr.	E5	5
Aurora, Ont.,Can.	D5	42
Aurora, Colo.	B6	51
Aurora, Ill.	B5, k8	58
Aurora, Ind.	F8	59
Aurora, Minn.	C6	67
Aurora, Mo.	E4	69
Aurora, Nebr.	D7	71
Aurora, Ohio	A4	78
Aurora co., S. Dak.	G7	77
Au Sable Forks, N.Y.	f11	75
Aust-Agder, co., Nor	*H3	11
Austell, Ga.	h7	55
Austin, Ind.	G6	59
Austin, Minn.	C6	67
Austin, Tex.	D4	84
Austin, co., Tex.	E4	84
Austintown, Ohio	A5	78
Australia, country, Oceania		25
Australian Capital Territory, Aust.	*G8	25
Austria, country, Eur.	E6	6
Autauga, co., Ala.	C3	46
Autlán de Navarro	D4, n11	34
Autun, Fr.	D6	5
Auvergne, former prov., Fr.	E5	5
Auxerre, Fr.	D5	5
Auxier, Ky.	C7	62
Ava, Mo.	E5	69
Avalon, Calif.	F4	50
Avalon, Pa.	h13	81
Avanos, Tur.	C10	14
Avaré, Braz.	C3	30
Aveiro, Port.	B1	8
Avella, Pa.	F1	81
Avellaneda, Arg.	A5, g7	28
Avellino, It	D5	9
Avenal, Calif.	E3	50
Avenel, N.J.	k7	74
Aversa, It.	D5	9
Avery, co., N.C.	e11	76
Avesta, Swe.	G7	11
Aveyron, dept., Fr.	*E5	5
Avezzano, It.	C4	9
Avigliano, It.	D5	9
Avignon, Fr.	F6	5
Ávila, Sp.	B3	8
Avilés, Sp.	A3	8
Avilla, Ind.	B7	59
Avis, Pa.	D7	81
Avoca, Ala.	A2	46
Avoca, Iowa	C2	60
Avoca, N.Y.	C3	75
Avoca, Pa.	m18	81
Avola, It.	F5	9
Avon, Conn	B5	52
Avon, Ill.	C3	58
Avon, Mass.	B5, a11	65
Avon, N.Y.	C3	75
Avon, Ohio	A3	78
Avon, Pa.	*F9	81
Avon by the Sea, N.J.	C4	74
Avondale, Ariz.	D1	48
Avondale, Pa.	G10	81
Avondale Estates, Ga.	h8	55
Avon Lake, Ohio	A3	78
Avonmore, Pa.	E3	81
Avon Park, Fla.	E5	54
Avoyelles, par., La.	C3	63
Avranches, Fr.	D3	5
Axim, Ghana	H4	22
Axis, Ala.	E1	46
Ay, Fr.	C5	5
Ayabe, Jap.	n14	18
Ayacucho, Arg.	B5	28
Ayacucho, Peru	D3	31
Ayacucho, dept., Peru	D3	31
Ayaguz, Sov. Un.	E11	13
Ayamonte, Sp.	D2	8
Ayan, Sov. Un.	D16	13
Ayaviri, Peru	D3	31
Ayden, N.C.	B5	76
Aydin, Tur.	D6	14
Ayer, Mass.	A4, f9	65
Ayion Oros (Mount Athos) prov., Grc.	*B5	14
Áyios Dhimítrios, Grc.	*C4	14
Aylesbury, Eng.	E6	4
Aylesford, N.S., Can.	D5	43
Aylmer East, Que., Can.	D2	42
Aylmer West, Ont., Can.	E4	41
Ayora, Sp.	C5	8
Ayr, Scot	C4	4
Ayr, co., Scot.	*C4	4
Aytos, Bul.	D8	10
Ayutthaya, Thai.	C2	19
Ayvalik, Tur.	C6	14
Azalea Park, Fla.	*D5	54
Azemmour, Mor.	B3	22
Azerbaidzhan (S.S.R.)	*E7	16
Azle, Tex.	n9	84
Azogues, Ec.	B2	31
Azores Islands, reg., Port.	C3	21
Azov, Sov. Un.	H12	12
Azrou, Mor.	B3	22
Aztec, N. Mex.	A4	48
Azua, Dom. Rep.	E8	35
Azuay, prov., Ec.	B2	31
Azul, Arg.	B5	28
Azuza, Calif.	m13	50
Az Zaqāzīq, Eg.	B4	23
Az Zarqā', Jor.	B4	15

B

Entry	Ref	Pg
Babaeski, Tur.	E8	10
Babahoyo, Ec.	B2	31
Babayevo, Sov. Un.	B11	12
Babbitt, Minn.	C7	67
Babbitt, Nev.	*B2	72
Bābol, Iran	A8	23
Babson Park, Fla.	E5	54
Babyak, Bul.	E6	10
Babylon, N.Y.	n15	75
Baca, co.,Colo.	D8	51
Bacalar, Mex.	D7	34
Bacău, Rom.	B8	10
Baccarat, Fr.	C7	5
Back, riv., Can.	C12	36
Bac Kan, Viet.	*G5	17
Backa Palanka, Yugo.	C4	10
Backa Topola, Yugo.	C4	10
Bac Lieu, Viet.	*D3	19
Bacliff, Tex.	*E5	84
Bac Ninh, Viet.	G6	17
Bacolod, Phil.	C6	19
Bacon, co., Ga.	E4	55
Bacsalmas, Hung.	B4	10
Bács-Kiskun, co., Hung.	*B4	10
Badajoz, Sp.	C2	8
Badalona, Sp.	B7	8
Bad Axe, Mich.	E8	66
Baddeck, N.S., Can.	C9	43
Bad Doberan, Ger. Dem Rep.	A5	6
Baden, Aus.	D8	6
Baden, Ont., Can.	D4	41
Baden, Pa.	E1	81
Baden, Switz.	E4	6
Baden, reg., Ger., Fed. Rep. of	D4	6
Baden-Baden, Ger., Fed. Rep. of	D4	6
Baden-Württemberg, state, Ger., Fed. Rep. of	*D4	6

Bad Freienwalde, Ger.
Dem. Rep. B7   6
Badger, Newf., Can. D3   44
Bad Hersfeld, Ger., Fed.
Rep. of............................C4   6
Badin, N.C. B2   76
Bad Ischl, Aus. E6   6
Bad Kissingen, Ger., Fed.
Rep. of............................C5   6
Bad Kreuznack, Ger., Fed.
Rep. of............................D3   6
Bad Langensalza, Ger.
Dem. Rep. C5   6
Bad Oldesloe, Ger., Fed.
Rep. of............................B5   6
Bad Reichenhall, Ger., Fed.
Rep. of............................E6   6
Bad Salzuflen, Ger., Fed.
Rep. of............................B4   6
Bad Tölz, Ger., Fed.
Rep. of............................E5   6
Badulla, Sri Lanka G7   20
Baffin, isl., Can. B19 36
Bafra, Tur. B10 14
Bagdad, Ariz. B2   48
Bagdad, Fla. u14 54
Bagé, Braz. E2   30
Baghdād, Iraq C3   15
Bagheria, It. E4   9
Baghlan, Afg. A4   20
Bagley, Minn. C3   67
Bagnara Calabra, It. E5   9
Bagnères-de-Bigorre, Fr. F4   5
Bagnolet, Fr. g10   5
Bagnols sur-Cèze, Fr. E6   5
Bagot, co., Que., Can. D5   42
Bahamas, country, N.A. B11 35
Bahawalpur, Pak. C5   20
Bahia, see Salvador, Braz.
Bahia, state, Braz A4   30
Bahia Blanca, Arg. B4   28
Bahia de Caráquiz, Ec. B1   31
Bahrain (Bahrein), country, Asia......C8   23
Baia-Mare, Rom. B6   10
Baicheng, China....................B9   17
Baie-Comeau, Que.. Can. k13 42
Baie-St. Paul, Que, Can. B7   42
Baie Verte, Newf., Can. D3   44
Baikal, lake, Sov. Un. D13 13
Baile Atha Cliath, see
Dublin, Ire.
Bailén, Sp. C4   8
Bailesti, Rom. C6   10
Bailey, co., Tex. B1   84
Bailundo, Ang. C3   24
Bainbridge, Ga.....................F2   55
Bainbridge, N.Y. C5   75
Bainbridge, Ohio C2   78
Baird, Tex. C3   84
Baixo Alentejo, prov., Port. *C2   8
Baja, Hung. B4   10
Baja, California, state, Mex. A1   34
Baja California Sur, ter., Mex. *C2   34
Baker, La. *D4   63
Baker, Mont. D12 70
Baker, Oreg. C9   80
Baker, co., Fla. B4   54
Baker, co., Ga. E2   55
Baker, co., Oreg. C9   80
Bakersfield, Calif. E4   50
Bakerton, see Elmora, Pa.
Bakhtarān, Iran B7   23
Baku, Sov. Un. E7   13
Ba'labakk, Leb. g6   15
Bala-Cynwyd, Pa. *F11 81
Balaguer, Sp. B6   8
Balakleya, Sov. Un.,...............G11 12
Balanda, Sov. Un. F15 12
Balanga, Phil *C6   19
Balashov, Sov. Un. F14 12
Balasore, India D8   20
Balassagyarmat, Hung. A4   10
Balboa, Pan. *B2   32
Balcarce, Arg. B5   28
Balch, Ark. B4   49
Balcones Heights, Tex. *E3   84
Bald Eagle, Minn. E7   67
Bald Knob, Ark. B4   49
Baldwin, La. E4   63
Baldwin, Mich. E5   66
Baldwin, N.Y. G2   52
Baldwin, N.Y. *k14 81
Baldwin, Wis. D1   88
Baldwin co., Ala. E2   46
Baldwin co., Ga. C3   55
Baldwin City, Kans. D8   61
Baldwin Park, Calif. *F4   50
Baldwinsville, N.Y. B4   75
Baldwinville, Mass. A3   65
Baldwyn, Miss. A5   68
Balearic, is., Sp. C6   8
Baler, Phil. B6   19
Balfour, N.C. f10   76

Balikesir, Tur. C6   14
Balikpapan, Indon. F5   19
Balkh, Afg. A4   20
Balkhash, Sov. Un. E10 13
Balkhash, lake, Sov. Un. E10 13
Balki, Sov. Un. H10 12
Ballarat, Austl. G7, n14 25
Ballard, co., Ky. e8   62
Ballard Vale, Mass. A5, f11 65
Ballina, Austl. E9   25
Ballina, Ire. C2   4
Ballinasloe, Ire. D2   4
Ballinger, Tex. D3   84
Ballston Lake, N.Y. C7   75
Ballston Spa, N.Y. B7   75
Ballville, Ohio *A2   78
Ballwin, Mo. g12 69
Bally, Pa. F10 81
Ballymena, N. Ire. C3   4
Balm, Fla. E4   54
Balmazújváros, Hung. B5   10
Balmville, N.Y. *D6   75
Bals, Rom. C7   10
Baltā, Sov. Un. H7   12
Baltic, Conn. C8   52
Baltic, sea, Eur. I8   11
Baltimore, Ohio C3   78
Baltimore, co., Md. B4   53
Baltimore (Independent City),
Md. B4, g11 53
Baluchistan, reg., Iran, Pak. C4   20
Bamako, Mali F3   22
Bamberg, Ger., Fed. Rep. of D5   6
Bamberg, S.C. E5   82
Bamberg, co., S.C. E5   82
Banat, reg. Rom. C5   10
Banbridge, N. Ire. C3   4
Banbury, Eng. D6   4
Bancroft, Ont., Can. B7   41
Bancroft, Iowa A3   6
Banda, India C7   20
Banda Aceh, Indon. k11 19
Bandar 'Abbās, Iran *D6   15
Bandar-e Anzalī, Iran B7   23
Bandar Seri Begawan,
(Brunei), Bru......................E4   19
Bande, Sp. A2   8
Bandeira, peak, Braz. C4   30
Bandera, Tex. E3   84
Bandera co., Tex. E3   84
Bandirma, Tur. B6   14
Bandon, Oreg. D2   80
Bandung, Indon. G3   19
Banes, Cuba D6   35
Banff, Alta., Can. D3, g7 38
Banff, co., Scot. *B5   4
Bangalore, India F6   20
Banggai, Indon. F6   19
Bangkok (Krung Thep), Thai. C2   19
Bangladesh, country, Asia D9   20
Bangor, Maine D4   64
Bangor, Mich. F4   66
Bangor, N. Ire. C4   4
Bangor, Pa. E11 81
Bangor, Wales D4   4
Bangor, Wis. E3   88
Bangs, Tex. D3   84
Bangued, Phil B6   19
Bangui, Cen. Afr. Rep. H1   23
Bangweulu, lake, Zambia C6   24
Banhã, Eg. G8   14
Baní, Dom. Rep. E8   35
Bani Suwayf, Eg. C4   23
Banja Luka, Yugo. C3   10
Banjarmasin, Indon. F4   19
Banjul, Gam. F1   22
Banks, co., Ga. B3   55
Banks isl., Can. B9   36
Bankura, India D8   20
Banner, co., Nebr. C2   71
Bannertown, N.C. *A2   76
Bannock, co., Idaho G6   57
Bannu, Pak. B5   20
Bañolas, Sp. A7   8
Bandska Bystrica, Czech. D5   7
Banska Stiavnica, Czech. D5   7
Bansko, Bul. E6   10
Bantam, Conn. C4   52
Banyuwangi, Indon. G4   19
Baoding, China D8   17
Baoji, China E6   17
Baotou, China C7   17
Ba'qūbah, Iraq C3   15
Bar, Sov. Un. B6   12
Barabinsk, Sov. Un. D10 13
Baraboo, Wis. E4   88
Baracaldo, Sp. A4   8
Baracoa, Cuba D6   35
Baradero, Arg. F7   28
Baraga, Mich. B2   66
Baraga, co., Mich. B2   66
Barahona, Dom. Rep. E8   35
Baramula, India B5   20

Baranovichi, Sov. Un. E3   12
Baraanya, co., Hung. *B4   10
Barataria, La. E5, k11 63
Barbacena, Braz. C4, g6 30
Barbar, Sud. E4   23
Barbados, country, N.A. J15 35
Barbastro, Sp. A6   8
Barbate, Sp. D3   8
Barber, co., Kans E5   61
Barberton, Ohio A4   78
Barberton, S. Afr. F6   24
Barbour, co., Ala D4   46
Barbour, co., W. Va. B4   87
Barbourville, W. Va. C2   87
Barbourville, Ky. D6   62
Barbuda, isl., Antigua and Barbuda..H14 35
Barcarrota, Sp. C2   8
Barcellona Pozzo di Gotto, It. E5   9
Barcelona, Sp. B7   8
Barcelona, Ven. A5   32
Barcelos, Port. B1   8
Bardejov, Czech. D6   7
Bardstown, Ky. C4   62
Bardwell, Ky. f8   62
Bareilly, India C6   2
Baresville, Pa. *G8   81
Barguzin, Sov. Un. D13 13
Bar Harbor, Maine D4   64
Bari, It. D6   9
Barinas, state, Ven. B3   32
Baripāda, India D8   20
Bariri, Braz. C3, m7 30
Barisāl, Bngl. D9   20
Barking, Eng. k13   4
Barkol, China C3   17
Bar-le-Duc, Fr. C6   5
Barletta, It. D6   9
Barling, Ark. B1   49
Barmer, India C5   20
Barnaul, Sov. Un. D11 13
Barnegat, N.J. D4   74
Barnes, co., N. Dak. C7   77
Barnesboro, Pa. E4   81
Barnesville, Ga. C2   55
Barnesville, Minn. D2   67
Barnesville, Ohio C4   78
Barnhill, Ohio B4   78
Barnsboro, N.J. D2   74
Barnsdall, Okla. A5   79
Barnsley, Eng. *D6   4
Barnstable, Mass. C7   65
Barnstable, co., Mass. C7   65
Barnstaple, Eng. E4   4
Barnwell, S.C. E5   82
Barnwell co., S.C. E4   82
Baroda, India D5   20
Barquisimeto, Ven. A4   32
Barra, Braz. *E5   27
Barraba, Austl. E8   26
Barrackville, W. Va. B4, h10 87
Barra do Piraí, Braz. C4, h6 30
Barra Mansa, Braz. C4, h6 30
Barrancabermeja, Col. B3   32
Barranquilla, Col. A3   32
Barre, Mass. B3   65
Barre, Vt. C3   73
Barreiras, Braz. *E5   27
Barreiro, Port. C1, f9   8
Barreiros, Braz. *D7   27
Barren, co., Ky. D4   62
Barretos, Braz. C3   30
Barrett, Tex. *E5   84
Barrhead, Alta., Can. B3   38
Barrie, Ont., Can. C5   41
Barrigada, Guam *F6   2
Barrington, Ill. A5, h8 58
Barrington, N.J. *D2   74
Barrington, R.I. C11 52
Barrington Hills, Ill. *A5   58
Barron, Wis. C2   88
Barron, co., Wis. C2   88
Barrow, Alsk. A8   47
Barrow, co., Ga. B3   55
Barrow-in Furness, Eng. C5   4
Barruelo de Santullán, Sp. A3   8
Barry, Ill. D2   58
Barry, co., Mich. F5   66
Barry, co., Mo. E4   69
Barrys Bay, Ont., Can. B7   41
Bārsi, India E6   20
Barstow, Calif. E5   50
Barth, Fla. u14 54
Barth, Ger. Dem. Rep. A6   6
Bartholomew, co., Ind. F6   59
Bartin, Tur. B9   14
Bartle Frere, mtn., Austl. C8   25
Bartlesville, Okla. A6   79
Bartlett, Ill. h8   58
Bartlett, Tex. D4   84
Barton, Ohio B5   78
Barton, Vt. *B3   73
Barton, co., Kans. D5   61

Barton, co. Mo. D3   69
Bartonville, Ill. C4   58
Bartow, Fla. E5   54
Bartow, co., Ga. B2   55
Barvas, Scot. A3   4
Barvenkovo, Sov. Un. G11 12
Basel, Switz. E3   6
Basel-Land, sub canton, Switz. *E3   6
Basel-Stadt, sub canton, Switz. *E3   6
Basildon, Eng. *E7   4
Basile, La. D3   63
Basilicata, pol. dist., It. *D5   9
Basin, Wyo. B4   89
Basingstoke, Eng. E6   4
Baskin, Fla. P10 54
Basking Ridge, N.J. B3   74
Basque Provinces, reg., Sp. A4   8
Basra, Iraq B7   23
Bas-Rhin, dept. Fr. *C7   5
Bassac, Laos C3   19
Bassano, Alta., Can. D4   38
Bassano del Grappa, It. B3   9
Bassein, Bur. E9   20
Basses-Alpes, dept., Fr. *E7   5
Basses-Pyrénées, dept. Fr. *F3   5
Basse-Terre, Guad. I14 35
Basseterre, St. Christopher-
Nevis-Anguilla H13 35
Bassett, Nebr. B6   71
Bassett, Va. D3   85
Bastia, Fr. C2   9
Bastogne, Bel. B6   5
Bastrop. La. B4   63
Bastrop, co., Tex. D4   84
Basutoland, see Lesotho,
county, Afr.
Bata, Equat., Gui. H6   22
Bataan, prov., Phil. *C6   19
Batāla, India B6   20
Batanes, prov., Phil. *A6   19
Batangas, Phil. p13 19
Batangas, prov., Phil. *C6   19
Bátaszék, Hung. B4   10
Batatais, Braz. C3   30
Batavia, Ill. B5, k8 58
Batavia, N.Y. C2   75
Batavia, Ohio C1   78
Batavia, see Jakarta, Indon.
Bataysk, Sov. Un. H12 12
Bates, co., Mo. C3   69
Batesburg, S.C. D4   82
Batesville, Ark. B4   49
Batesville, Ind. F7   57
Batesville, Miss. A4   68
Bath, Eng. E5   4
Bath, Maine E3, g8 64
Bath, N.Y. C3   75
Bath, Pa. E11 81
Bath, S.C. D4   82
Bath, co., Ky. B6   62
Bath, co., Va. B3   85
Bathurst, Austl. F8   25
Bathurst, N.B., Can. B4   43
Bathurst, see Banjul, Gam.
Batna, Alg. H6   22
Baton Rouge, La. D4, h9 63
Batouri, Cam H7   22
Battambang, Kam. C2   19
Batticaloa, Sri Lanka G7   20
Battle Creek, Mich. F5   66
Battleford, Sask., Can. E1   39
Battle Ground, Ind. C4   59
Battle Ground, Wash. D3   86
Battonya, Hung. B5   10
Batumi, Sov. Un. E7   13
Batu Pahat (Bandar
Penggaram), Mala. *E2   19
Baturité, Braz. D7   27
Bat Yam, Isr. *B2   15
Bauchi, Nig. F6   22
Baudette, Minn. B4   67
Bauru, Braz. C3   30
Bautzen, Ger. Dem. Rep. C7   6
Bauxite, Ark. C3, k9 49
Bavaria, reg., Ger.,
Fed. Rep. of D5   6
Bavispe, Mex. A3   34
Bawcomville, La. *B3   63
Baxley, Ga. E4   55
Baxter, Minn. D4   67
Baxter, co., Ark. A3   49
Baxter Estates, N.Y. *E7   75
Baxter Springs, Kans. E9   61
Bay, co., Fla. B1, u16 54
Bay, co., Mich. E6   66
Bayamo, Cuba D5   35
Bayamón, P.R. G1   35
Bayan, China C3   18
Bayanovka, Sov. Un. C8   13
Bayard, Nebr. C2   71
Bayard, N. Mex. C4   48
Baybay, Phil. *C6   19

Bayburt, Tur. B13 14
Bay City, Mich. E7 66
Bay City, Oreg. B3 80
Bay City, Tex. E5, s14 84
Bay de Verde, Newf. D5 44
Bayern, state, Ger. Fed. Rep. of ... *D5 6
Bayeux, Fr. C3 5
Bayfield, Wis. B3 88
Bayfield, co., Wis. B2 88
Bay Harbor Island, Fla. *F3 54
Bay Head, N.J. C4 74
Bayindir, Tur. *C6 14
Baylor, co., Tex. C3 84
Bay Minette, Ala. E2 46
Bayombong, Phil. *B6 19
Bayonne, Fr. F3 5
Bayonne, N.J. B4, k8 74
Bayou Cane, La. *E5 63
Bayou LaBatre, Ala. E1 46
Bay Park, N.Y. *E7 75
Bayport, N.Y. n15 75
Bayport, Min. E6 67
Bayreuth, Ger.
    Fed. Rep. of D5 6
Bay Roberts, Newf., Can. E5 44
Bay St. Louis, Miss. E4, g7 68
Bay Shore, N.Y. E7, n15 75
Bayshore Gardens, Fla. *E4 54
Bayside, Wis. m12 88
Bay Springs, Miss. D4 68
Bayt Lahm, see Bethlehem, Jordan
Baytown, Tex. E5, r15 84
Bay View, Ala. f7 46
Bayview, Calif. *B1 50
Bayview, Mass. A6 65
Bay Village, Ohio h9 78
Bayville, N.Y. F2 52
Baztán, Sp. A5 8
Beach, N. Dak. D2 77
Beach City, Ohio B4 78
Beach Haven, New Jersey D4 74
Beachville, Ont., Can. D4 41
Beachwood, N.J. *D4 74
Beachwood, Ohio A4 78
Beacon, N.Y. D7 75
Beacon Falls, Conn. D4 52
Beacon Hill, Wash. *C3 86
Beaconsfield, Que., Can. D8 42
Beadle, co., S.Dak. F7 77
Bearden, Ark. D3 49
Beardstown, Ill. C3 58
Bear Lake, co.,Idaho G7 57
Bear River,N.S., Can. E4 43
Bear Town, Miss. D3 68
Beas de Segura, Sp. C4 8
Beatrice, Nebr. D9 71
Beattyville, Ky. C6 62
Beaucaire, Fr. F6 5
Beauce, co., Que., Can. C7 42
Beauceville Est., Que., Can. *C7 42
Beauceville Quest, Que., Can. *C7 42
Beaufort, N.C. C6 76
Beaufort, S.C. G6 82
Beaufort, co., N.C. B5 76
Beaufort, co., S.C. G6 82
Beaufort West, S. Afr. G4 24
Beauharnois, Que., Can. D4, q19 42
Beauharnois, co., Que., Can. D3 42
Beaumont, Calif. *F5 50
Beaumont, Tex. D5 84
Beaumont Place, Tex. *E5 84
Beaune, Fr. D6 5
Beauport, Que., Can. C6, n17 42
Beaupré, Que., Can. B7 42
Beauregard, par., La. D2 63
Beaurepaire, Que., Can. D8 42
Beauséjour, Man., Can. D3 40
Beauvais, Fr. C5 5
Beaver, Okla. A1, e10 79
Beaver, Pa. E1 81
Beaver, Utah B5 72
Beaver, co., Okla. A1 79
Beaver, co., Pa. E1 81
Beaver, co., Utah B5 72
Beaver Bank, N.S., Can. E6 43
Beaver City, Nebr. D6 71
Beaverdale, Pa. F4 81
Beaver Dam, Ky. C3 62
Beaver Dam, Wis. E5 88
Beaver Falls, Pa. E1 81
Beaver (Glen Hedrick),
    W. Va. D3, n13 87
Beaverhead, co., Mont. E3 70
Beaverlodge, Alta., Can. B1 38
Beaver Meadows, Pa. E10 81
Beaverton, Ont., Can. C5 42
Beaverton, Mich. E6 66
Beaverton, Oreg. B4, h12 80
Beāwar, India C5 20
Bebedouro, Braz. C3 30
Bečej, Yugo. C5 10
Béchar, Alg. B4 22
Bechuanaland, see Botswana,
    country, Afr.

Becker, co., Minn. D3 67
Beckham, co., Okla. B2 79
Beckley, W. Va. D3, n13 87
Bédarieux, Fr. F5 5
Bedford, N.S., Can. E6 43
Bedford, Eng. D6 4
Bedford, Ind. G5 59
Bedford, Iowa D3 60
Bedford, Mass. B5, g10 65
Bedford, Ohio A4, h9 78
Bedford, Pa. F4 81
Bedford, Tex. *C4 84
Bedford, Va. C3 85
Bedford, co., Eng. *D6 4
Bedford, co., Pa. G4 81
Bedford, co. Tenn. B5 83
Bedford, co., Va. C3 85
Bedford Heights, Ohio *A4 78
Bedford Hills, N.Y. m15 75
Bedlington, Eng. C6 4
Bedminster, N.J. B3 74
Bedzin, Pol. g10 7
Bee, co., Tex E4 84
Beebe, Ark. B4 49
Beebe, Que., Can. D5 42
Beecher, Ill. B6 58
Beech Grove, Ind. E5, m10 59
Beenleigh, Austl. C9 26
Bee Ridge, Fla. E4, q11 54
Be'er Sheva' (Beersheba),
    Isr. C2, h5 15
Beeskow, Ger. Dem. Rep. B7 6
Beeton, Ont., Can. C5 41
Beeville, Tex. E4 84
Bègles, Fr. E3 5
Beida, Libya B2 23
Bei'an, China B10 17
Beihai, China G6 17
Beijing, see Peking, China
Beira, Moz. D6 24
Belra, reg. Port. B2 8
Beira Alta, prov., Port. *B2 8
Beira Baixa, prov., Port. *C2 8
Beira Litoral, prov., Port. *B1 8
Beirut (Bayrūt), Leb. g5 15
Beja, Port. C2 8
Béja, Tun. A6 22
Bejaïa (Bougie), Alg. A5 22
Bejeda (Ras Dashan), mtn., Eth. .. F5 23
Békés, Hung. B5 10
Békés, co., Hung. *B5 10
Békéscaba, Hung. B5 10
Bela, India C7 20
Bela Crkva, Yugo. C5 10
Bel Air, Md. A5 53
Belalcázar, Sp. C3 8
Bela Vista, Braz. C1 30
Belaya Tserkov, Sov. Un. G8 12
Belchertown, Mass. B3 65
Belding, Mich. E5 66
Belém, Braz. D6 27
Belen,N. Mex. B5 48
Belén, Par. D4 29
Belev, Sov. Un. E11 12
Belfair, Wash. B3 86
Belfast, Maine D3 64
Belfast, N.Y. C2 75
Belfast, Pa. B4 76
Belfast, N. Ire. C4 4
Belfield, N. Dak. D3 77
Belfort, N.J. C4 74
Belfort, Fr. D7 5
Belfort, dept., Fr. *D7 5
Belfry, Ky. C7 62
Belgaum, India E5 20
Belgium, country, Eur. B6 5
Belgorod, Sov. Un. F11 12
Belgorod-Dnestrovskiy, Sov. Un. .. H8 12
Belgrade, Mont. E5 70
Belgrade (Beograd), Yugo. C5 10
Belhaven, N.C. B6 76
Belington, W. Va. B5 87
Belize, country, N.A. D7 34
Belize City, Belize D7 34
Belknap, co., N.H. D5 73
Bell, Calif. *F4 50
Bell, co., Ky. D6 62
Bell, co., Tex. D4 84
Bell Acres, Pa. *E1 81
Bellaire, Ohio C5 78
Bellaire, Tex. r14 84
Bellary, India E6 20
Bella Unión, Ur. E1 30
Bella Vista, Arg. E2 29
Bella Vista, Arg. E4 29
Bella Vista, Par. D4 29
Bellbrook, Ohio C1 78
Belle, Mo. C6 69
Belle, W. Va. C6 87
Belleair, Fla. p10 54
Belle Center, Ohio B2 78
Bellechasse, co., Que., Can. C7 42
Bellefontaine, Ohio B2 78

Bellefontaine Neighbors, Mo. *C7 69
Bellefonte, Del. A7 53
Bellfonte, Pa. E6 81
Belle Fourche, S. Dak. F2 77
Belle Glade, Fla. F6 54
Belle Isle, Fla. D5 54
Bellemead, Md. *C4 53
Belle Plaine, Iowa C5 60
Belle Plaine, Kans. E6 61
Belle Plaine, Minn. F5 67
Belle River, Ont., Can. *E2 41
Belle Rose, La. D4, h9 63
Bellerose, N.Y. *E7 75
Belleterre, Que., Can. *o20 41
Belle Vernon, Pa. F2 81
Belleview, Fla. C4 54
Belleville, Ont., Can. C7 41
Belleville, Ill. E4 58
Belleville, Kans. C6 61
Belleville, Mich. p15 66
Belleville, N.J. B4, h8 74
Belleville, Pa. E6 81
Belleville, Wis. F4 88
Bellevue, Ill. *C4 58
Bellevue, Iowa B7 60
Bellevue, Ky. h13 62
Bellevue, Mich. F5 66
Bellevue, Nebr. C10, g3 71
Bellevue, Ohio A3 78
Bellevue, Wash. e11 86
Belley, Fr. E6 5
Bellflower, Calif. n12 50
Bell Gardens, Calif. *F4 50
Bellingham, Mass. B5, h10 65
Bellingham, Wash. A3 86
Bellinzona, Switz. E4 6
Bellmawr, N.J. D2 74
Bellmead, Tex. *D4 84
Bellmore, N.Y. G2 52
Bello, Col. B2 32
Bellows Falls, Vt. E3 73
Bellport, N.Y. G5 52
Dells, Tenn. C2 83
Belluno, It. A4 9
Bell Ville, Arg. A4 28
Bellville, Ohio B3 78
Bellville, Tex. E4 84
Bellwood, Ill. k9 58
Bellwood, Pa. E5 81
Belmar, N.J. C4 74
Bélmez, Sp. C3 8
Belmond, Iowa B4 60
Belmont, Calif. h8 50
Belmont, Mass. g11 65
Belmont, Miss. A5 68
Belmont, N.Y. C2 75
Belmont, N.C. B1 76
Belmont, co., Ohio C4 78
Belmonte, Braz. *E7 27
Belmopan, Belize D7 34
Bel-Nor, Mo. f13 69
Beloeil, Que., Can. D4 42
Belo Horizonte, Braz. B4 30
Beloit, Kans. C5 61
Beloit, Ohio B5 78
Beloit, Wis. F4 88
Beloit West, Wis. *F4 88
Belomorsk, Sov. Un. C6 13
Belopolye, Sov. Un. F10 12
Beloretsk, Sov. Un. D8 13
Belovo, Sov. Un. *D11 13
Belpre, Ohio C4 78
Bel-Ridge, Mo. *C7 69
Belton, Mo. C3 69
Belton, S.C. B3 82
Belton, Tex. D4 84
Beltrami, co., Minn. B3 67
Beltsville, Md. B4 53
Beltsy, Sov. Un. H6 12
Belukha, mtn., Sov. Un. E11 13
Belvedere, Calif. *C2 50
Belvedere, Va. *B5 85
Belvedere Marittimo, It. E5 9
Belvidere, Del. A6 53
Belvidere, Ill. A5 58
Belvidere, N.J. B2 74
Belzoni, Miss. B3 68
Bement, Ill. D5 58
Bemidji, Minn. C4 67
Bemis, Tenn. B3 83
Benalla, Austl. G7 25
Benares, see Varanasi, India
Benavente, Sp. A3 8
Ben Avon, Pa. *E1 81
Benbrook, Tex. *C4 84
Bend, Oreg. C5 80
Bendale, S.C. C6 82
Bendery, Sov. Un. H7 12
Bendigo, Austl. G7 25
Bene Beraq, Isr. B2 15
Benešov, Czech. D3, o18 7
Benevento, It. D5 9

Benewah, Idaho B2 57
Benewah, co., Idaho B2 57
Bengal, reg., Bngl., India D8 20
Bengasi (Banghāzī), Libya B2 23
Bengbu, China E8 17
Bengkulu, Indon. F2 19
Benguela, Ang. C2 24
Benguela, dist., Ang. C3 24
Benham, Ky. D7 62
Ben Hill, co., Ga. D3 55
Benicarló, Sp. B6 8
Benicia, Calif. C2, g8 50
Benin, country, Afr. G5 22
Benin City, Nig. G6 22
Benisa, Sp. C6 8
Benkelman, Nebr. D4 71
Benld, Ill. D4 58
Ben Lomond, Calif. *D2 50
Bennett, co., S. Dak. G4 77
Bennettsville, S.C. B8 82
Bennettsville Southwest, S.C. *B8 82
Ben Nevis, mtn., Scot. B4 4
Bennington, Vt. F1 73
Bennington, co., Vt. E1 73
Bensenville, Ill. B6, k9 58
Bensheim, Ger., Fed. Rep of D4 6
Benson, Ariz. D3 48
Benson, Minn. E3 67
Benson, N.C. B4 76
Benson, co., N. Dak. B6 77
Bent, co., Colo. D7 51
Bentleyville, Pa. F1 81
Benton, Ark. C3, k9 49
Benton, Ill. E5 58
Benton, Ky. f9 62
Benton, La. B2 63
Benton, Pa. D9 81
Benton, Tenn. D9 83
Benton, Wis. F3 88
Benton, co., Ark. A1 29
Benton, co., Ind. C3 59
Benton, co., Iowa B5 60
Benton, co.,Minn. E4 67
Benton, co., Miss. A4 00
Benton, co., Mo. C4 69
Benton, co., Oreg. C3 80
Benton, co., Tenn. A3 83
Benton, co.,Wash. C6 86
Benton City, Wash. C6 86
Benton Harbor, Mich. F4 66
Benton Heights, Mich. F4 66
Bentonville, Ark. A1 49
Benwood, W. Va. A4, f8 87
Benxi, China C9 17
Benzie, co., Mich. D4 66
Beograd, see Belgrade, Yugo.
Beppu, Jap. J5 18
Berat, Alb. *B2 14
Berat, pref., Alb. *B2 14
Berbera, Som. F7 23
Berchtesgaden, Ger., Fed. Rep. of E6 6
Berck, Fr. B4 5
Berdichev, Sov. Un. G7 12
Berdyansk, Sov. Un. H11 12
Berea, Ky. C5 62
Berea, Ohio A4, h9 78
Beregovo, Sov. Un. G4 12
Beresford, S. Dak. G9 77
Berettyóujfalu, Hung. B5 12
Berezhany, Sov. Un. G5 12
Berezna, Sov. Un. F8 12
Berezniki, Sov. Un. D8 13
Berg, Nor. q27 11
Berga, Sp. A6 8
Bergama, Tur. *C6 14
Bergamo, It. B2 9
Bergen, Ger. Dem. Rep. A6 6
Bergen, N.Y. B3 75
Bergen, Nor. G1 11
Bergen, see Mons, Bel.
Bergen, co., N.J. A4 74
Bergen, co., Nor. *G1 11
Bergenfield, N.J. B5, h8 74
Bergen op Zoom, Neth. B6 5
Bergerac, Fr. E4 5
Bergholz, Ohio B5 78
Bergisch Gladback, Ger.
    Fed. Rep. of C3 6
Berhampore, India D8 20
Berhampur, India E7 20
Bering, sea, Alsk., Sov. Un. D21 16
Berislav, Sov. Un. H9 12
Berja, Sp. D4 8
Berkeley, Calif. D2 50
Berkeley, Ill. *B6 58
Berkeley, Mo. f13 69
Berkeley, R.I. B11 52
Berkeley, co., S.C. E7 82
Berkeley, co., W. Va. B6 87
Berkeley Heights, N.J. B4 74
Berkeley Springs (Bath), W. Va. ... B6 87
Berkley, Mich. F7, o15 66
Berkovitsa, Bul. D6 10

Berks, co., Pa.	F9	81
Berkshire, Md.	*C4	53
Berkshire, co., Eng.	*E6	4
Berksire, co., Mass.	B1	65
Berlin, Md.	D7	53
Berlin, N.H.	C5	73
Berlin, N.J.	D3	74
Berlin, N.Y.	C7	75
Berlin, Pa.	G4	81
Berlin, Wis.	E5	88
Berlin, East, Ger., Dem. Rep.	B6	6
Berlin, West, Ger., Fed. Rep. of	B6	6
Berlin, West, state, Ger., Fed. Rep. of	*B6	6
Bermeo, Sp.	A4	8
Bermuda, Br. dep.,N.A.	p20	35
Bern, Switz.	E3	6
Bern, canton, Switz.	*E3	6
Bernalillo, N. Mex.	B5, D6	48
Bernalillo, co., N. Mex.	B5	48
Bernardsville, N.J.	B3	74
Bernau, Ger. Dem. Rep.	B6	6
Bernay, Fr.	C4	5
Bernberg, Ger. Dem. Rep.	C5	6
Berndorf, Aus.	E8	6
Berne, Ind.	C8	59
Bernice, La.	B3	63
Bernie, Mo.	E8	69
Bernville, Pa.	F9	81
Beroun, Czech	D3, o17	7
Berri, Austl.	F7	25
Berrien, co., Ga.	E3	55
Berrien, co., Mich.	F4	66
Berrien Springs, Mich.	G4	66
Berry, former prov., Fr.	D4	5
Berry Hill, Tenn.	g10	83
Berryville, Ark.	A2	49
Berryville, Va.	A5	85
Bershad, Sov. Un.	G7	12
Berthier, co., Que., Can.	C3	42
Bethierville, Que., Can.	C4	42
Berthoud, Colo.	A5	51
Bertie, co., N.C.	A5	76
Bertram, Tex.	D4	84
Bertrand, Mich.	*G4	66
Berwick, N.S., Can.	D5	43
Berwick, La.	E4	63
Berwick, Maine	E2	64
Berwick, Pa.	D9	81
Berwick, co., Scot	*C5	4
Berwick-upon-Tweed, Eng.	C6	4
Berwind, W. Va.	D3	87
Berwyn, Ill.	k9	58
Berwyn, Pa.	o20	81
Berwyn Heights, Md.	*B4	53
Besa, Indon.	E7	19
Besancon, Fr.	D7	5
Besni, Tur.	D11	14
Bessèges, Fr.	D5	5
Bessemer, Ala.	B3, g7	46
Bessemer, Mich.	n11	66
Bessemer, Pa.	E1	81
Bessemer City, N.C.	B1	76
Bethalto, Ill.	*E3	58
Bethany, Conn.	D5	52
Bethany, Ill.	D5	58
Bethany, Mo.	A3	69
Bethany, Okla.	B4	79
Bethany, W. Va.	f8	87
Bethayres-Huntingdon Valley, Pa.	*F11	81
Bethel, Alsk.	C7	47
Bethel, Conn.	D3	52
Bethel, Maine	D2	64
Bethel, N.C.	B6	76
Bethel, Ohio	D1	78
Bethel (Bethel, Park) Pa.	k13	81
Bethesda, Md.	C3, f8	53
Bethesda, Ohio	B4	78
Bethlehem (Bayt Lahm), Jordon	C3, h5	15
Bethlehem, Pa.	E11	81
Bethlehem, S. Afr.	F5	24
Bethlehem, W. Va.	f8	87
Bethpage, N.Y.	G3	52
Béthune, Fr.	B5	5
Bettendorf, Iowa	C7, g11	60
Betül, India	D6	20
Beulah, N. Dak	C4	77
Beulaville, N.C.	C5	76
Beverley, Eng	D6	4
Beverly, Mass.	A6, f12	65
Beverly, N.J.	C3	74
Beverly, Ohio	C4	78
Beverly Gardens, Ohio	*C1	78
Beverly Hills, Calif.	m12	50
Beverly Hills, Mich.	*F7	66
Beverwijk, Neth.	A6	5
Bexar, co., Tex.	E3	84
Bexhill-on-Sea, Eng.	E7	4
Bexley, Ohio	m11	78
Beypazari, Tur.	*B8	14
Bezerros, Braz.	*D7	27
Bezhetsk, Sov. Un.	C11	12
Bezhitsa, Sov. Un.	E10	12
Béziers, Fr.	F5	5
Bezons, Fr.	g9	5
Bhadgaon, Nep.	C8	20
Bhagalpur, India	C8	20
Bhakkar, Pak.	B5	20
Bhamo, Bur.	D10	20
Bharatpur, India	C6	20
Bhatpara, India	D8	20
Bhaunagar, India	D5	20
Bhind, India	C6	20
Bhopal, India	D6	20
Bhor, India	E5	20
Bhuj, India	D4	20
Bhutan, country, Asia	C9	20
Biala Podlaska, Pol.	B7	7
Bialogard, Pol.	A4	7
Bialystok, Pol.	B7	7
Bianco, It.	E6	9
Biarritz, Fr.	F3	5
Bibai, Jap.	E10	18
Bibb, co., Ala.	C2	46
Bibb, co., Ga.	D3	55
Bibb City, Ga.	D2	55
Biberach, Ger., Fed. Rep. of	D4	6
Bic, Que., Can.	A9	42
Bicknell, Ind.	G3	59
Bicske, Hung.	B4	10
Bida, Nig.	G6	22
Bidar, India	E6	20
Biddeford, Maine	E2, g7	64
Bideford, Eng.	E4	4
Biel, Switz.	E3	6
Bielawa, Pol.	C4	7
Bielefeld, Ger., Fed. Rep. of	B4	6
Biella, It.	B2	9
Bielsko-Biala, Pol.	D5, h10	7
Bielsk Podlaski, Pol.	B7	7
Bienfait, Sask.,Can.	H4	39
Beinville, par., La.	B2	63
Biga, Tur.	*B7	14
Big Bear City, Calif.	E5	50
Big Bear Lake, Calif.	*E5	50
Big Beaver, Pa.	*E1	81
Big Flats, N.Y.	C4	75
Biggar, Sask., Can.	E1	39
Biggs, Calif.	C3	50
Big Horn, co., Mont.	E9	70
Big Horn, co., Wyo.	B4	89
Big Lake, Tex.	D2	84
Biglerville, Pa.	G7	81
Big Pine, Calif.	D4	50
Big Rapids, Mich.	E5	66
Big River, Sask., Can.	D2	39
Big Run, Pa.	E4	81
Big Sandy, Mont.	B6	70
Big Spring, Tex.	C2	84
Big Stone, co., Minn.	E2	67
Big Stone Gap, Va.	f9	85
Big Timber, Mont.	E7	70
Big Wells, Tex.	E3	84
Bihac, Yugo.	C2	10
Bihar, India	C8	20
Bihar, state, India	D8	20
Bijapur, India	E6	20
Bijeljina, Yugo.	C4	10
Bikaner, India	C5	20
Bikin, Sov. Un.	C7	18
Bilaspur, India	D7	20
Bilbao, Sp.	A4	8
Bileca, Yugo.	D4	10
Bilin, Bur.	E10	20
Billerica, Mass.	A5, f10	65
Billings, Mont.	E8	70
Billings, co., N. Dak.	C2	77
Billings Heights, Mont.	E8	70
Biloela, Austl.	B8	26
Biloxi, Miss.	E5, f8	68
Bilqas Qism Awwal, Eg.	*G8	14
Biltmore Forest, N.C.	f10	76
Binalbagan, Phil	*C6	19
Bindura, Zimb.	D6	24
Bingen, Ger., Fed. Rep. of	D3	6
Bingham, Maine	C3	64
Bingham, co., Idaho	F6	57
Bingham Canyon, Utah	A5, D2	72
Binghamton, N.Y.	C5	75
Binjai, Indon.	m11	19
Bintulu, Mala.	E4	19
Binxian, China	D3	18
Bio-Bío, prov., Chile	B2	28
Bioko, isl., Equat. Gui.	H6	22
Birakan, Sov. Un.	B54	18
Bi'r Ar Rummanah, Eg.	G9	14
Birch Run, Mich.	E7	66
Bird Island, Minn.	F4	67
Birdsboro, Pa.	F10	81
Birecik, Tur.	D11	14
Bir Hasnnah, well, Eg.	*G8	14
Birkenhead, Eng.	D5	4
Birlad, Rom.	B8	10
Birmingham, Ala.	B3, f7	46
Birmingham, Eng.	D6	4
Birmingham, Mich.	F7, o15	66
Birobidzhan, Sov. Un.	E16	12
Birtle, Man., Can.	D1	40
Bisbee, Ariz.	D4	48
Biscayne Park, Fla.	s13	54
Bisceglie, It.	D6	9
Biscoe, N.C.	B3	76
Bishop, Calif.	D4	50
Bishop, Tex.	F4	84
Bishop's Falls, Newf., Can.	D4	44
Bishop's Stortford, Eng.	E7	4
Bishopville, S.C.	C7	82
Biskra, Alg.	B6	22
Bismarck, Mo.	D7	69
Bismarck, N. Dak.	D5	77
Bissau, Guinea-Bissau,	F1	22
Bissett, Man., Can.	D4	40
Bistrita, Rom.	B7	10
Bitlis, Tur.	C14	14
Bitola, Yugo.	E5	10
Bitonto, It.	D6	9
Bitterfeld, Ger. Dem. Rep.	*C6	6
Biwabik, Minn.	C6	67
Bixby, Okla.	B6	79
Biysk, Sov. Un.	D11	12
Bizerte, Tun.	A6	22
Bjelovar, Yugo.	C3	10
Black, mtn., Ky.	D7	62
Black, sea, Eur.	G14	3
Blackburn, Eng.	D5	4
Black Diamond, Alta.	D3	38
Black Diamond, Wash.	B4, f11	86
Black Eagle, Mont.	C5	70
Blackford, co., Ind.	D7	59
Black Forest, Colo.	C6	51
Black Hawk, co., Iowa	B5	60
Black Lake, Que., Can.	C6	42
Black Mountain, N.C.	f10	76
Black Oak, Ind.	*A3	59
Black Point, Calif.	*C2	50
Blackpool, Eng.	D5	4
Black River, N.Y.	A5	75
Black River Falls, Wis.	D3	88
Blacksburg, S.C.	A4	82
Blacksburg, Va.	C2	85
Blackshear, Ga.	E4	55
Blackstone, Mass.	B4	65
Blackstone, Va.	C5	85
Blackville, S.C.	E5	82
Blackwell. Okla.	A4	79
Blackwood, N.J.	*D2	74
Bladen, co., N.C.	C4	76
Bladenboro, N.C.	C4	76
Bladensburg, Md.	f9	53
Blagoevgrad (Gorna-Dzhumaya), Braz.	D6	10
Blagoveshchensk, Sov. Un.	D15	13
Blain, Fr.	D3	5
Blaine, Minn.	m12	67
Blaine, Wash.	A3	86
Blaine, co., Idaho	F4	57
Blaine, co., Mont.	B7	70
Blaine, co., Nebr.	C5	71
Blaine, Okla.	B3	79
Blair, Nebr.	C9	71
Blair, Okla.	C2	79
Blair, Wis.	D2	88
Blair, co., Pa.	E5	81
Blairgowrie & Rattray, Scot.	B5	4
Blairmore, Alta., Can.	E3	38
Blairsville, Pa.	F3	81
Blaj, Rom.	B7	10
Blakely, Ga.	E2	55
Blanc, mtn., Fr.	E7	5
Blanca, pk., Colo.	D5	51
Blanchard, Okla.	B4	79
Blanchester, Ohio	C2	78
Blanco, co., Tex.	D3	84
Bland, co., Va.	C1	85
Blanding, Utah	C7	72
Blandinsville, Ill.	C3	58
Blankenburg, Ger. Dem. Rep.	C5	6
Blantyre, Malawi	D6	24
Blasdell, N.Y.	C2	75
Blato, Yugo.	D3	10
Blauvelt, N.Y.	*D6	75
Bleckley, co., Ga.	D3	55
Bled-Grad, Yugo.	B10	10
Bledsoe, co., Tenn.	D8	83
Blekinge, co., Swe.	*I6	11
Blenheim, Ont., Can.	E2	41
Blenheim, N.Z.	N14	26
Blind River, Ont., Can.	A2	41
Blissfield, Mich.	G7	66
Blitar, Indon.	*G4	19
Bloemfontein, S. Afr.	F5	24
Blois, Fr.	D4	5
Blonie, Pol.	m13	7
Bloomer, Wis.	F7, C2	88
Bloomfield, Ont., Can.	D7	41
Bloomfield, Conn.	B6	52
Bloomfield, Ind.	F4	59
Bloomfield, Iowa	D5	60
Bloomfield, Ky.	C4	62
Bloomfield, Mo.	E8	69
Bloomfield, Nebr.	B2	71
Bloomfield, N.J.	h8	74
Bloomfield, N. Mex.	A5	48
Bloomfield Hills, Mich.	o15	66
Bloomfield Village, Mich.	*F7	66
Bloomingdale, Ga.	D5	55
Bloomingdale, Ill.	*B5	58
Bloomingdale, N.J.	A4	74
Blooming Prairie, Minn.	G5	67
Bloomington, Calif.	*F5	50
Bloomington, Ill.	C4	58
Bloomington, Ind.	F4	59
Bloomington, Minn.	n12	67
Bloomington, Tex.	E4	84
Bloomsburg, Pa.	E9	81
Bloomsbury, N.J.	B2	74
Bloomville, Ohio	A2	78
Blossburg, Pa.	C7	81
Blossom Hill, Pa.	*G9	81
Blount, co., Ala.	B3	46
Blount, co., Tenn.	D10	83
Blountstown, Fla.	B1	54
Bludenz, Aus.	E4	6
Blue Ash, Ohio	o13	78
Blue Bell, Pa.	*F11	81
Blue Earth, Minn.	G4	67
Blue Earth, co., Minn.	F4	67
Bluefield, Va.	e10	85
Bluefield, W. Va.	D3	87
Bluefields, Nic.	E8	34
Blue Hills, Conn.	*B6	52
Blue Island, Ill.	B6, k9	58
Blue Lake, Calif.	B2	50
Blue Mound, Ill.	D4	58
Blue Mountain, pk., Jam.	F5	35
Blue Point, N.Y.	G4	52
Blue Rapids, Kans.	C7	61
Blue Ridge, Ga.	B2	55
Blue Ridge, Va.	C3	85
Blue Ridge, mts., U.S.	C10	45
Blue Springs, Mo.	h11	69
Bluff City, Tenn.	C11	69
Bluff Park, Ala.	g7	46
Bluffton, Ind.	C7	59
Bluffton, Ohio	B2	78
Blumenau, Braz.	D3	30
Blyth, Eng.	C6	4
Blyth, Calif.	F6	50
Blytheville, Ark.	B6	49
Boac, Phil.	C6	19
Boalsburg, Pa.	E6	81
Boardman, Ohio	A5	78
Boaz, Ala.	A3	46
Bobbili, India	E7	20
Bobcaygeon, Ont., Can.	C6	41
Bobigny, Fr.	g10	5
Bobo Dioulasso, Burkina Faso.	F4	22
Bobtinets, Sov. Un.	G9	12
Bobrka, Sov. Un.	G5	12
Bobruysk, Sov. Un.	E7	12
Bobtown, Pa.	G2	81
Bobures, Ven.	B3	32
Boca Raton, Fla.	F6	54
Bochnia, Pol.	D6	7
Bochum, Ger., Fed. Rep. of	C3	6
Bodaybo, Sov. Un.	D14	13
Boden, Swe	E9	11
Bodmin, Eng.	E4	4
Bodö, Nor.	D6	11
Boerne, Tex.	E3, h7	84
Bogalusa, La.	D6	63
Bogata, Tex.	C5	84
Boger City,N.C.	B1	76
Bogo, Phil.	C6	19
Bogodukhov, Sov. Un.	F10	12
Bogor (Buitenzorg). Indon.	G3	19
Bogoroditsk, Sov. Un.	E12	12
Bogorodsk, Sov. Un.	C14	12
Bogotá, Col.	C3	32
Bogota, N.J.	h8	74
Bogra, Bngl.	D8	20
Boguslav, Sov. Un.	G8	12
Bohain -en-Vermandois, Fr.	C5	5
Bohemia, N.Y.	n15	75
Bohemia (Cechy), reg., Czech.	D3	7
Bohol, prov., Phil.	D6	19
Boiling Springs, N.C.	B1	76
Boiling Springs, Pa.	F7	81
Boischâtel, Que., Can.	C6, n17	42
Bois-Colombes, Fr.	G10	5
Bois-des-Filion, Que., Can.	p19	42
Boise, Idaho	F2	57
Boise, co., Idaho	F3	57
Boise City, Okla.	e8	79
Boissevain, Man., Can.	E1	40
Boissevain, Va.	e10	85
Bolbec, Fr.	C4	5

Name	Grid	Pg
Bolgrad, Sov. Un.	I7	12
Boling, Tex.	E5, r14	84
Boli, China	B11	17
Bolivar, Arg.	B4	28
Bolivar, Mo.	D4	69
Bolivar, N.Y.	C2	75
Bolivar, Ohio	B4	78
Bolivar, Tenn.	B3	83
Bolivar, co., Miss.	B3	68
Bolivar, dept., Col.	B2	32
Bolivar, prov., Ec.	B2	31
Bolivar, state, Ven.	B4	32
Bolivar, (La Columna), pk., Ven.	B3	32
Bolivia, country, S.A.	C2	29
Bolkhov, Sov. Un.	E11	12
Bollinger, co., Mo.	D7	69
Bollnäs, Swe.	G7	11
Bollullos, Sp.	D2	8
Bologna, It.	B3	9
Bologoye, Sov. Un.	C10	12
Bolshaya Lepetikha, Sov. Un.	H9	12
Bolshaya Viska, Sov. Un.	G8	12
Bolshoy Tokmak, Sov. Un.	H10	12
Bolton, Ont., Can.	D5	41
Bolton, Eng.	D5	4
Bolton Landing, N.Y.	B7	75
Bolu, Tur.	B8	14
Bolvadin, Tur.	C8	14
Bolzano, It.	A3	9
Boma, Zaire	B2	24
Bombay, India	E5	20
Bom Conselho, Braz.	*D7	27
Bom Despacho, Braz.	B3	30
Bon Air, Pa.	*G11	81
Bon Air, Va.	m17	85
Bonaventure, Que., Can.	*k13	42
Bonaventure, co., Que., Can.	A3	43
Bonavista, Newf., Can.	D5	44
Bond, co., Ill	E4	58
Bondy, Fr.	G10	5
Bone, see Annaba, Alg.		
Bonham, Tex.	C4	84
Bon Homme, co., S. Dak.	G8	77
Bonifay, Fla.	G3	54
Bonin, is., Jap.	E6	2
Bonita, Calif.	*E5	50
Bonita Springs, Fla.	F5	54
Bonn, Ger., Fed. Rep. of	C3	6
Bonner, co., Idaho	A2	57
Bonners Ferry, Idaho	A2	57
Bonner Springs, Kans.	C9, k16	61
Bonne Terre, Mo.	D7	69
Bonneville, co., Idaho	F7	57
Bonnyville, Alta., Can.	B5	38
Bonorva, It.	D2	9
Bonoua, I.C.	*E4	22
Bonthain, Indon.	G5	19
Bontoc, Phil.	*B6	19
Boomer, W. Va.	C3, m13	87
Boone, Iowa	B4	60
Boone, N.C.	A1	76
Boone, co., Ark.	A2	49
Boone, co., Ill.	A5	58
Boone, co., Ind.	D4	59
Boone, co., Iowa	B4	60
Boone, co., Ky.	B5	62
Boone, co., Mo.	B5	69
Boone, co., Nebr.	C7	71
Boone, co., W. Va.	C3	87
Booneville, Ark	B2	49
Booneville, Miss.	A5	68
Boonsboro, Md.	A2	53
Boon Terrace, Pa.	*F1	81
Boonton, N.J.	B4	74
Boonville, Calif.	C2	50
Boonville, Ind.	H3	59
Boonville, Mo.	C5	69
Boonville, N.Y.	B5	75
Boothbay Harbor, Maine	E3	64
Boothwyn, Pa.	*G11	81
Boppard, Ger., Fed. Rep. of	C3	6
Boquerón, dept., Par.	D3	29
Borah, pk., Idaho	E3	57
Borås, Swe.	I5	11
Bordeaux, Fr.	E3	5
Borden, co., Tex.	C2	84
Borden Springs, Ala.	B4	46
Bordentown, N.J.	C3	74
Bordighera, It.	C1	9
Borgå, Fin.	G11	11
Borger, Tex.	B2	84
Borgomanero, It.	B2	9
Borgo Val di Taro, It.	B2	9
Borislav, Sov. Un.	G7	12
Borisoglebsk, Sov. Un.	F13	12
Borisov, Sov. Un.	D7	12
Borispol, Sov. Un.	F8	12
Borja, Sp.	B5	8
Borkou, reg., Chad.	E1	23
Borlänge, Swe.	G6	11
Borneo (Kalimantan), isl., Asia	E4	19
Bornholm, co., Den.	*A3	7
Bornos, Sp.	D3	8
Boromlya, Sov. Un.	F10	12
Borovan, Bul.	D6	10
Borovichi, Sov. Un.	B9	12
Borovskoye, Sov. Un.	q21	12
Borsod-Abauj-Zemplen, co., Hung.	*A5	10
Bort-les-Orgues, Fr.	E5	5
Borüjerd, Iran	C4	15
Borzna, Sov. Un.	F9	12
Bosa, It.	D2	9
Bosanska Gradiska, Yugo.	C3	10
Bosanska Kostajnica, Yugo.	C3	10
Bosanski Novi, Yugo.	C3	10
Boscobel, Wis.	E3	88
Boshan, China	D8	17
Boskovice, Czech.	D4	7
Bosnia, reg., Yugo.	C3	10
Bosnia-Hercegovian, rep., Yugo	*C3	10
Bosque, co., Tex.	D4	84
Bossier, par. La.	B2	63
Bossier City, La.	B2	63
Boston, Eng.	D6	4
Boston,Ga.	F3	55
Boston, Mass.	B5, g11	65
Boston, Pa.	*E1	65
Boswell, Ind.	C3	59
Botetourt, co., Va.	C3	85
Bothwell, Ont., Can.	E3	41
Botkins, Ohio	B1	78
Botosani, Rom.	E8	10
Botswana, country, Afr.	E4	24
Bottineau, N. Dak.	A5	77
Bottineau, co.,N. Dak.	B5	77
Botucatu, Braz.	C3, m7	30
Botwood, Newf., Can.	D4	44
Bouaké, I.C.	G3	22
Boucherville, Que., Can.	D4, p20	42
Bouches-du-Rhône, dept., Fr.	*F6	5
Bougie, see Bejaïa, Alg.		
Boulder, Colo.	A5	51
Boulder, Mont.	D4	70
Boulder, co., Colo.	A5	51
Boulder City, Nev.	D4	72
Boulder Creek, Calif.	*D2	50
Boulogne-Billancourt, Fr.	C5	5
Boulogne-sur-Mer, Fr.	B4	5
Boundary, co., Idaho	A2	57
Boundary, pk., Nev.	C2	72
Bound Brook, N.J.	B3	74
Bountiful, Utah	A6, C2	72
Bourbon, Ind.	B5	59
Bourbon, co., Kans.	E9	61
Bourbon, co., Ky.	B5	62
Bourbonnais, Ill.	B6	58
Bourbonnais, former prov., Fr.	D5	5
Bourg, La.	E5	63
Bourg-de-Péage, Fr.	E6	5
Bourg -de-Bresse, Fr.	D6	5
Bourges, Fr.	D5	5
Bourg-la-Reine, Fr.	g10	5
Bourgoin -Jallieu, Fr.	E6	5
Bournemouth, Eng.	E6	4
Bovey, Minn.	C5	67
Bovina, Tex.	B1	84
Bowdon, Ga.	C1	55
Bowie, Md.	B4	53
Bowie, Tex.	C4	84
Bowie, co., Tex.	C5	84
Bow Island, Alta., Can.	E5	38
Bowling Green, Fla.	E5	54
Bowling Green, Ky.	D3	62
Bowling Green, Mo.	B6	69
Bowling Green, Ohio	A2, f6	78
Bowling Green, S.C.	A5	82
Bowman, N. Dak.	D2	77
Bowman, S.C.	E6	82
Bowman, co., N. Dak.	D2	77
Bowmanstown, Pa.	E10	81
Bowmanville, Ont. Can.	D6	41
Bowral, Austl.	G8	26
Box Butte, co., Nebr.	B2	71
Box Elder, co., Utah	A5	72
Boxian, China	E8	17
Boxtel, Neth.	B6	5
Boyacá, dept., Col.	B3	32
Boyce, La.	C3	63
Boyd, co., Ky.	B7	62
Boyd, co., Nebr.	B7	71
Boyertown, Pa.	F10	81
Boyes Hot Springs, Calif.	*C2	50
Boyle, co., Ky.	C5	62
Boylston, Ala.	C3	46
Boyne City, Mich.	*C5	66
Boynton Beach, Fla.	F6	54
Boys Town, Nebr.	g12	71
Bozeman, Mont.	E5	70
Bozüyük, Tur.	C8	14
Bra., It.	B1	9
Brabant, prov., Bel.	*B6	5
Bracciano, It.	g8	9
Bracebridge, Ont., Can.	B5	41
Bracken, co., Ky.	B5	62
Brackenridge, Pa.	h15	81
Brackettville, Tex.	E2	84
Brad, Sov. Un.	B6	10
Bradbury Heights, Md.	*C3	53
Braddock, Pa.	k14	81
Braddock Heights, Md.	B2	53
Braddock Hills, Pa.	*E1	81
Bradenton, Fla.	E4, q10	54
Bradenton Beach, Fla.	*E4	54
Bradenville, Pa.	F3	81
Bradford, Ont., Can.	C5	41
Bradford, Eng.	D6	4
Bradford, Ill.	B4	58
Bradford, Ohio	B1	78
Bradford, Pa.	C4	81
Bradford, R. I.	D10	52
Bradford, co., Fla.	C4	54
Bradford, co., Pa.	C8	81
Bradfordwoods, Pa.	h13	81
Bradley, Fla.	E5	54
Bradley, Ill.	B6	58
Bradley, co., Ark.	D3	49
Bradley, co., Tenn.	D9	83
Bradley Beach, N.J.	C4	74
Bradley Gardens, N.J.	*B3	74
Bradner, Ohio	A2	78
Bradshaw, W. Va.	D3	87
Brady, Tex.	D3	84
Braga, Port.	B1	8
Bragado, Arg.	B4, g6	28
Bragança, Braz.	*D6	27
Bragança, Port.	B2	8
Bragança, Páulista, Braz.	C3, m8	30
Brahmaputra, riv., Asia	C9	10
Braidwood, Ill.	B5	58
Bràila, Rom.	C8	10
Brainerd, Minn.	D4	67
Braintree, Mass.	B5, h11	65
Brampton, Ont., Can.	D5, m14	41
Bramwell, W. Va.	D3	87
Branch, co., Mich.	G5	66
Branchville, N.J.	A3	74
Branchville, S.C.	E6	82
Branco, riv., Braz.	C5	32
Brandenburg, Ger. Dem. Rep.	B6	6
Brandenburg, Ky.	B3	62
Brandenburg, former state, Ger. Dem. Rep.	B6	6
Brandenburg, reg., Ger. Dem. Rep.	B6	6
Brandon, Man., Can.	E2, h7	40
Brandon, Fla.	E4	54
Brandon, Miss.	C4	68
Brandon, S.C.	B3	82
Brandon, Vt.	D1	73
Brandys nad Ladem, Czech.	n18	7
Branford, Conn.	D5	2
Branson, Mo.	E4	69
Brant, co., Ont., Can.	D4	41
Brantford, Ont., Can.	D4	41
Brant Lake, N.Y.	B7	75
Brantley, Ala.	D3	46
Brantley, co., Ga.	E4	55
Bras-d'or, N.S., Can.	C9	43
Brasília, Braz.	B3	30
Brasilia (Federal District), Braz.	B3	30
Brasov, Rom	C7	10
Bratenahl, Ohio	g9	78
Bratislava, Czech.	D4	7
Bratsk, Sov. Un.	*D13	13
Bratslav, Sov. Un.	G7	12
Brattleboro, Vt.	F2	73
Braunau am Inn, Aus.	D6	6
Braunschweig, Ger. Fed. Rep. of	B5	6
Brawley, Calif.	F6	50
Braxton, co., W. Va.	C4	87
Bray, Ire.	D3	4
Braymer, Mo.	B4	69
Brazil, Ind.	E3	59
Brazil, country, S.A.	C3	30
Brazoria, Tex.	r14	84
Brazoria, co., Tex.	E5	84
Brazos, co., Tex.	D4	84
Brazzaville, Con.	A3	24
Brčko, Yugo.	C4	10
Brea. Calif.	n13	50
Breathitt, co., Ky.	C6	62
Breaux Bridge, La.	D4	63
Brechin, Scot.	B5	4
Breckenridge, Mich.,	E6	66
Breckenridge, Minn.	D2	67
Breckenridge, Tex.	*C3	84
Breckenridge Hills, Mo.	*C7	69
Breckenridge, co.,Ky.	C3	62
Brecknock, co., Wales	*E5	4
Brecksville, Ohio	A4, h9	78
Břeclav, Czech.	D4	7
Brecon, Wales	E5	4
Bregenz, Aus.	E4	6
Bregovo, Bul	C6	10
Bremen, Ga.	C1	55
Bremen, Ger., Fed. Rep. of	B4	6
Bremen, Ind.	B5	59
Bremen, Ohio	C3	78
Bremen, state, Ger., Fed. Rep of,	*B4	6
Bremer, co., Iowa	B5	60
Bremerhaven, Ger., Fed. Rep. of	B4	6
Bremerton, Wash.	B3, e10	86
Bremerton East (Enetai), Wash.	*B3	86
Bremond, Tex.	D4	84
Breham, Tex.	D4	84
Brent, Ala.	C2	46
Brent, Fla.	u14	54
Brenton, W. Va.	D3	87
Brentwood, Calif.	h9	50
Brentwood, Md.	F9	53
Brentwood, Mo.	f13	69
Brentwood, N.Y.	F4	52
Brentwood, Pa.	k14	81
Brescia, It.	B3	9
Breslau, see Wroclaw, Pol.		
Bressanone, It.	A3	9
Bressler, Pa.	*F8	81
Bressuire, Fr.	D3	5
Brest, Fr.	C1	4
Brest, Sov. Un.	E4	12
Brenton Woods, N.J.	C4	74
Brevard, co., Fla.	E6	54
Brevard, N.C.	f10	76
Brewer, Maine	D4	64
Brestwer, N.Y.	D7, m15	75
Brewster, Ohio	B4	78
Brewster, Wash.	A6	86
Brewster, co.,Tex.	p13	84
Brewton, Ala.	D2	46
Brezno nad Hronom, Czech.	D5	7
Briançon, Fr.	E7	5
Briarcliff, Pa.	*G11	81
Briarcliff Manor, N.Y.	D7	75
Briceville, Tenn.	C9	83
Bridge City, Tex.	*D6	84
Bridgehampton, N.Y.	n16	75
Bridgeport, Ala.	A4	46
Bridgeport, Ont., Can.	*D4	41
Bridgeport, Conn.	E4	52
Bridgeport, Ill.	E6	58
Bridgeport, Mich.	E7	66
Bridgeport, Nebr.	C2	71
Bridgeport, Ohio	B5	78
Bridgeport, Pa.	F11, o20	81
Bridgeport, Tex.	C4	84
Bridgeport, Wash.	B6	86
Bridgeport, W. Va.	B4, k10	87
Bridgeton, Mo.	C7, f13	69
Bridgeton, N.J.	E2	74
Bridgetown, Barb.	J15	35
Bridgetown, N.S., Can.	E4	43
Bridgetown, Ohio	*C1	78
Bridgeview, Ill	*B6	58
Bridgeville, Del.	C6	53
Bridgeville, Pa.	k13	81
Bridgewater, N.S., Can.	E5	43
Bridgewater, Mass.	C6	65
Bridgewater, Va.	B4	85
Bridgman, Mich.	G4	66
Bridgton, Maine	D2	64
Bridgwater, Eng.	E5	4
Bridlington, Eng.	C6	4
Brielle, N.J.	C4	74
Brigantine, N.J.	E4	74
Bringham City, Utah	A4, C2	72
Brighton, Ala.	B3, g7	46
Brighton, Colo.	B6	51
Brighton, Eng.	E6	4
Brighton, Ill.	D3	58
Brighton, Mich.	F7	66
Brighton, N.Y.	*B3	75
Brightwaters, N.Y.	n15	75
Brignoles, Fr.	F7	5
Brilliant, Ohio	B5	78
Brillion, Wis.	D5, h9	88
Brindisi, It.	D6	9
Brinkley, Ark.	C4	49
Brioude, Fr.	E5	5
Brisbane, Austl.	E9	25
Brisbane, Calif.	*D2	50
Bricoe, co., Tex.	B2	84
Bristol, Conn.	C5	52
Bristol, Eng.	A6	4
Bristol, Ind.	a6	59
Bristol, N.H.	D4	73
Bristol, Pa.	F12	81
Bristol, R.I.	C11	52
Bristol, Tenn.	C11	83
Bristol, Vt.	C1	73
Bristol (Independent City), Va.	f9	85
Bristol, co., Mass.	C5	65
Bristol, co., R.I.	C11	52
Bristow, Okla.	B5	79
Brittania Beach, B.C., Can.	E6	37
British Columbia, prov., Can.		37
British Guiana, see Guyana, country, S.A.		

British Honduras, see
  Belize, Br. dep., N.A.
British Indian Ocean
  Territory, ter., Ind. O. *B9 24
British North Borneo, see
  Sabah, reg., Mala.
Britt, Iowa............................ A4 60
Brittany (Bretagne),
  former Prov., Fr. C2   5
Britton, S. Dak E8 77
Brive -la-Gaillarde, Fr. E4   5
Brno, Czech.......................... D4   7
Broach, India........................ D5 20
Broadalbin, N.Y. B6 75
Broad Brook, Conn. B6 52
Broadmoor, Colo.. .... C6 51
Broadview, Sask., Can. G4 39
Broadview, Ill. *B6 58
Broadview, Ind. *F4 59
Broadview Heights, Ohio B2 78
Broadwater, co., Mont. D5 70
Brockport, N.Y. *B3 75
Brockton, Mass. B5, h11 65
Brockville, Ont., Can. C9 41
Brockway, Pa. D4 81
Brocton, Ill D6 58
Brod, Yugo. C4 10
Broderick, Calif. *C3 50
Brodhead, Wis. F4 88
Brodnica, Pol. B5   7
Brody, Sov. Un. F5 12
Broken Arrow, Okla. A6 79
Broken Bow, Nebr. C6 71
Broken Bow, Okla. C7 79
Broken Hill, Austl. F7 25
Broken Hill, Zambia C5 24
Brome, co., Que., Can. D5 42
Bromptonville, Que., Can. D6 42
Bronson, Mich. G5 66
Bronte, Tex. D2 84
Bronx, bourough and co., N.Y. E7 75
Bronxville, N.Y. h13 75
Brook, Ind. C3 59
Brooke, co., W. Va. A4 87
Brookfield, Ill. k9 58
Brookfield, Mass. B3 65
Brookfield, Mo. B4 69
Brookfield, Wis...................... m11 88
Brookhaven, Miss. D3 68
Brookhaven, Pa. *G11 81
Brookings, Oreg. E2 80
Brookings, S. Dak. F9 77
Brookings, co., S. Dak. F9 77
Brroklands, Man., Can. *E3 40
Brooklands, Mich. *F7 66
Brooklawn, N.J. D2 74
Brookline, Mass. B5, g11 65
Brooklyn, Conn. B9 52
Brooklyn, Ind. E5 59
Brooklyn, Iowa C5 60
Brooklyn, Mich. F6 66
Brooklyn, Ohio h9 78
Brooklyn (Lovejoy), Ill. g13 69
Brooklyn, borough, N.Y. k13 75
Brooklyn Center, Minn. E6 67
Brooklyn Park, Minn. *E6 67
Brookneal, Va....................... C4 85
Brook Park, Ohio h9 78
Brookport, Ill. F5 58
Brooks, Alta., Can. D5 38
Brooks, co., Ga. F3 55
Brooks, co., Tex. F3 84
Brookshire, Tex. E5, r14 84
Brookside, Ala. f7 46
Brookside, Del. A6 53
Brookside, N.J. B3 74
Brookston, Ind. C4 59
Brooksville, Fla. D4 54
Brookville, Ind. F7 59
Brookville, Mass. h11 65
Brookville, N.Y. *G2 52
Brookville, Ohio C1 78
Brookville, Pa. D3 81
Brookmall, Pa. *G11 81
Broome, co., N.Y. C5 75
Broomfield, Colo. B5 51
Broughton, Pa. *E1 81
Broussard, La. D4 63
Broward, co., Fla. F6 54
Brown, co., Ill. D3 58
Brown, co., Ind. F5 59
Brown co., Kans. C8 61
Brown, co., Minn. F4 67
Brown, co., Nebr. B6 71
Brown, co., Ohio D2 78

Brown, co., S. Dak. E7 77
Brown, co., Tex. D3 84
Brown, co., Wis. D6 88
Brown City, Mich. E8 66
Brown Deer, Wis. m12 88
Brownfield, Tex. C1 84
Browning, Mont. B3 70
Brownlee Park, Mich. *F5 66
Brownsburg, Que., Can. D3 42
Brownsburg, Ind. E5 59
Browns Mills, N.J. D3 74
Brownstown, Ind. G5 59
Brownstown, Pa. *E4 81
Browns Valley, Minn. E2 67
Brownsville, La. *B3 63
Brownsville, Oreg. C4 80
Brownsville, Pa. F2 81
Brownsville, Tenn. B2 83
Brownsville, Tex. G4 84
Brownville, Ala. B2 46
Brownville, N.Y. A5 75
Brownville Junction, Maine. C3 64
Brownwood, Tex. D3 84
Broxton, Ga. E4 55
Brozas, Sp. C2   8
Bruay en-Artios, Fr. B5   5
Bruce, mtn., Austl. D2 25
Bruce, Miss. B4 68
Bruceton, Tenn. A3 83
Bruchsal, Ger., Fed. Rep. of D4   6
Bruck ander Leitha, Aus. D8   6
Bruck an der Mur, Aus. E7   6
Brugge (Bruges), Bel. B5   5
Brule, co., S. Dak. G6 77
Brumath, Fr......................... C7   5
Brundidge, Ala...................... D4 46
Brunei, see Bandar Seri
  Begawan, Bru.
Brunei, country, Asia E4 19
Brunswick, Ga. E5 55
Brunswick, Maine E3, g8 64
Brunswick, Md. B23 53
Brunswick, Mo. B4 69
Brunswick, Ohio A4 78
Brunswick, co., N.C. C4 76
Brunswick, co., Va. D5 85
Brush, Colo. A7 51
Brusly, La. D4, h9 63
Brusque, Braz. D3 30
Brussels (Bruxelles), Bel. B6   5
Brussels, Ont., Can. D3 41
Bruxelles, see Brussels, Bel.
Bryan, Ohio A1 78
Bryan, Tex. D4 84
Bryan, co., Ga. D5 55
Bryan, co., Okla. D5 79
Bryansk, Sov. Un. E10 12
Bryant, Fla. F6 54
Bryantville, Mass. B6 65
Bryn Athyn, Pa...................... o21 81
Bryn Mawr, Pa. o20 81
Bryn Mawr, Wash. D2 86
Bryson City, N.C. f9 76
Bryte, Calif. *C3 50
Brzeg, Pol. C4   7
Brzeziny, Pol. C5   7
Bsa, It. B1   9
Bucaramanga, Col. B3 32
Buchanan, Mich. G4 66
Buchanan, N.Y. *D7 75
Buchanan, Va. C3 85
Buchanan, co., Iowa B6 60
Buchanan, co., Mo. B3 69
Buchanan, co., Va. e9 85
Buchans, Newf., Can. D3 44
Bucharest (Bucuresti), Rom. C8 10
Buchloe, Ger., Fed. Rep. of D5   6
Buckeye, Ariz. C2, D1 48
Buckeye Lake, Ohio C3 78
Buckhannon, W. Va. C4 87
Buckhaven & Methil, Scot. B5   4
Buckhorn, Ariz. D2 48
Buckie, Scot. B5   4
Buckingham, Que.,Can. D2 42
Buckingham, co., Eng. *C6   4
Buckingham, co., Va. C4 85
Buckley, Wash. B3, f11 86
Bucknell Manor, Va. *B5 85
Buckner, Mo. *B3 69
Bucks, co., Pa. F11 81
Bucksport, Maine D4 64
Bucksport, S.C. D9 82
Bucovina, reg., Rom. B7 10
Bucovina, reg., Sov. Un. B7 10
Bucuresti, see Bucharest, Rom.

Bucyrus, Ohio B3 78
Budapest, Hung. B4 10
Budd Lake, N.J. B3 74
Bude, Eng. E4   4
Bude, Miss.......................... D3 68
Budrio, It. B3   9
Buechel, Ky. B4, g11 62
Buena, N.J. D3 74
Buena Park, Calif. n13 50
Buenaventura, Col. C2 32
Buena Vista, Colo. C4 51
Buena Vista, Ga. D2 55
Buena Vista (Independent City),
  Va.............................. C3 85
Buena Vista, co., Iowa B2 60
Buenos Aires, Arg. A5, g7 28
Buenos Aires, prov. B4, g7 28
Buffalo, Iowa C7, h10 60
Buffalo, Minn. E5 67
Buffalo, Mo. D4 69
Buffalo, N.Y. C2 75
Buffalo, Ohio C4 78
Buffalo, Okla. A2 79
Buffalo, S.C. B4 82
Buffalo, Tex. D4 84
Buffalo, Wyo. B6 89
Buffalo, co., Nebr. D6 71
Buffalo, co., S. Dak. F6 77
Buffalo, co., Wis. D2 88
Buffalo Center, Iowa A4 60
Buffalo Grove, Ill. *A6 58
Bufford, Ga. B3 55
Buga, Col. C2 32
Bugojno, Yugo. C3 10
Buhi, Idaho G4 57
Buhl, Minn. C6 67
Buhler, Kans. D6 61
Buhusi, Rom. B8 10
Bujalance, Sp. D3   8
Bujumbura, Burundi I3 23
Bukama, Zaire B5 24
Bukavu, Zaire I3 23
Bukhara, Sov. Un. F9 13
Bukidnon, prov., Phil. *D6 19
Bukittinggi, Indon. F2 19
Bukoba, Tan. I4 23
Bulacan, prov., Phil. *C6 19
Bulan, Ky. C6 62
Bulan, Phil. *C6 19
Bulawayo, Zimb. E5 24
Bulgaria, country, Eur. D7 10
Bullas, Sp. C5   8
Bullitt, co., Ky. C4 62
Bulloch, co., Ga. D5 55
Bullock, co., Ala. C4 46
Bulun, Sov. Un. B15 13
Bunbury, Austl. F2 25
Buncombe, co., N.C. f10 76
Bundaberg, Austl. D9 25
Bunia, Zaire H4 23
Bunker Hill, Ill. D4 58
Bunker Hill, Ind. C5 59
Bunker Hill, Oreg. *D2 80
Bunker Hill, Tex. *E5 84
Bunkie, La. D3 63
Bunnell, Fla. C5 54
Bunny Run, Mich. *F7 66
Buo Ha, Viet. *G5 17
Burao, Som. G7 23
Buras, La. E6 63
Buraydah, Sau. Ar. D3 15
Burbank, Calif. E4, m12 50
Burbank, Ill. k9 58
Burdur, Tur. D8 14
Burdwan, India D8 20
Bureau, co., Ill. B4 58
Bureya, Sov.Un. B14 18
Burgas, Bul. D8 10
Burgas, pol. div., Bul. *D8 10
Burgaw, N.C. C5 76
Burgdorf, Switz. E3   6
Burgeo, Newf., Can. E3 44
Burgettstown, Pa. F1 81
Burgos, Sp. A4   8
Burgos, prov., Sp. *A4   8
Burgundy (Burgogne)
  former prov., Fr. D6   5
Burhanpur, India D6 20
Burin, Newf., Can. E4 44
Buriram, Thai. *C2 19
Burkburnett, Tex. B3 84
Burke, co., Ga. C4 55
Burke, co., N.C. B2 76
Burke, co., N. Dak. *B3 77
Burke City, Mo...................... f13 69
Burkina Faso, country, Afr. F4 22

Burks Falls, Ont., Can. B5 41
Burleigh, co., N. Dak. D5 77
Burleson, Tex. n9 84
Burleson, co., Tex. D4 84
Burlingame, Calif. h8 50
Burlingame, Kans. D8 61
Burlington, Ont., Can. D5 41
Burlington, Colo. B8 51
Burlington, Iowa D6 60
Burlington, Kans. D8 61
Burlington, Mass. f11 65
Burlington, N.J. C3 74
Burlington, N.C. A3 76
Burlington, Vt. C1 73
Burlington, Wash. A3 86
Burlington, Wis. F5, n11 88
Burlington, co., N.J. D3 74
Burma, country, Asia D10 20
Burnet, Tex. D3 84
Burnet, co., Tex. D3 84
Burnett, co., Wis. C1 88
Burney, Calif. B3 50
Burnham, Ill. *B6 58
Burnham, Pa. E6 81
Burnie, Austl. o15 25
Burnley, Eng. D5   4
Burns, Oreg. D7 80
Burns Flat, Okla. B2 79
Burns Lake, B.C., Can. B5 37
Burnsville, N.C. f10 76
Burnwell, Ala. f6 46
Burr Oak, Mich. G5 66
Bursa, Tur. B7 14
Burt, co., Nebr. C9 71
Burton, Mich. F7 66
Burton, Ohio A4 78
Burton-on-Trent, Eng. D6   4
Burundi, country, Afr. I3 23
Busehr, Iran G8 16
Buskerud, co., Nor. *H4 11
Busko, Pol. C6   7
Bussum, Neth. A6   5
Busto Arsizio, It. B2   9
Buta, Zaire H2 23
Bute, co., Scot. *C4   4
Butha Qi, China B9 17
Butler, Ala. C1 46
Butler, Ga. D2 55
Butler, Ind. B8 59
Butler, Mo. C3 69
Butler, N.J. B4 74
Butler, Ohio B3 78
Butler, Pa. E2 81
Butler, Wis. m11 88
Butler, co., Ala. D3 46
Butler, co., Iowa B5 60
Butler, co., Kans. E7 61
Butler, co., Ky. C3 62
Butler, co., Mo. F7 69
Butler, co., Nebr. C8 71
Butler, co., Ohio C1 78
Butler, co., Pa. E2 81
Butner, N.C. *A4 76
Butte, Mont. D4 70
Butte, co., Calif. C3 50
Butte, co., Idaho F5 57
Butte, co., S. Dak. F2 77
Butterworth, Mala. D2 19
Buttonwillow, Calif. E4 50
Butts, co., Ga. C3 55
Butuan, Phil. D7 19
Buturlinovka, Sov. Un. F13 12
Bützow, Ger. Dem. Rep. B5   6
Buxtehude, Ger. Fed. Rep. of B4   6
Buxton, Guy. C5 27
Büyük Ağri Dağı (Mt. Ararat),
  mtn., Tur. C15 14
Buzău, Rom. C8 10
Buzet, Yugo. C1 10
Buzzards Bay, Mass. C6 65
Byala Slatina, Bul. D6 10
Bydgoszcz, Pol. B5   7
Byelorussia (S.S.R.), rep.,
  Sov. Un. E5 12
Byesville, Ohio C4 78
Byfield, Mass. A6 65
Bykovo, Sov. Un. G15 12
Byron, Ga. D3 55
Byron, Ill. A4 58
Bystrzyca, Pol. C4   7
Bytom, Pol. C5, g9 7
Bytosh, Sov. Un. E10 12

C

Caacupé Par. E4 29
Caaguazú dept., Par. D4 29
Caapucú, Par. E4 29
Caazapá, Par. E4 29
Caazapá, dept., Par. E4 29
Cabaceiras, Braz. *D4 27
Cabana, Peru C2 31
Cabanatuan, Phil. o13 19
Cabano, Que., Can. B9 42
Cabarrus, co., N.C. B2 76
Cabedelo, Braz. *D7 27
Cabell, co., W. Va. C2 87
Cabeza, del Buey, Sp. C3 8
Cabimas, Ven. A3 32
Cabinda, Ang. B2 24
Cabinda, dist., Ang. B2 24
Cabin John, Md. C3, f8 53
Cabo, Braz. *D7 27
Cabo Frio, Braz. C4 30
Cabool, Mo. D5 69
Caboolture, Austl. *E9 25
Caborca, Mex. A2 34
Cabo Rojo, P.R. *G11 35
Cabo San Lucas, Mex. C3 34
Cabot, Ark. C3 49
Cacak, Yugo. D5 10
Caçapava, Braz. C3 30
Cacequi, Braz. D2 30
Cáceres, Sp. C2 8
Cáceres, prov., Sp. C2 8
Cachan, Fr. G10 5
Cache, Okla. C3 79
Cache, co., Utah A6 72
Cache, peak, Idaho G5 57
Cache Bay, Ont., Can. A5 41
Cachi, Arg. *E2 29
Cachoeira, Braz. *E7 27
Cachoeira do Sul, Braz. E2 30
Cachoeiro do Itapemirim, Braz. C4 30
Cacouna, Que., Can. B8 42
Caddo, Okla. C5 79
Caddo, co., Okla. B3 79
Caddo, par., La. B2 63
Cadillac, Mich. D5 66
Cadillac, mtn., Maine D4 64
Cadiz, Ky. D2 62
Cadiz, Ohio B4 78
Cádiz, Sp. D2 8
Cádiz, prov., Sp. *D2 8
Cadott, Wis. D2 88
Cadyville, N.Y. f11 75
Caen, Fr. C3 5
Caernarvon, Wales D4 4
Caernarvon, co., Wales *D4 4
Cagayan, de Oro, Phil. D6 19
Cagayan, prov., Phil. *B6 19
Cagli, It. C4 9
Cagliari, It. E2 9
Cagnes-sur-Mer, Fr. F7 5
Caguas, P.R. G12 35
Cahaba Heights, Ala. *B3 46
Cahokia, Ill. E3 58
Cahors, Fr. E4 5
Caibarién, Cuba C4 35
Caicedonia, Col. C2 32
Caicó, Braz. *D7 27
Cailloma, Peru E3 31
Cairnbrook, Pa. F4 81
Cairns, Austl. C8 25
Cairo, Ga. F2 55
Cairo, Ill. F4 58
Cairo, Eg. B4 23
Caithness, co., Scot. *A5 4
Cajabamba, Peru C2 31
Cajacay, Peru D2 41
Cajamarca, Peru C2 31
Cajamarca, dept., Peru C2 31
Cajatambo, Peru D2 31
Cajázeiras, Braz. *D7 27
Cakovec, Yugo. B3 10
Calabar, Nig. H6 22
Calabria, pol. dist., It. *E5 9
Calabria, reg., It. E6 9
Calafat, Rom. D6 10
Calahorra, Sp. A5 8
Calais, Fr. B4 5
Calais, Maine C5 64
Calamar, Col. A3 32
Calamba, Phil. C6 19
Calañas, Sp. D2 8
Calapan, Phil C6 19
Cǎlǎrǎsi, Rom. C8 10
Calarcá, Col. C2 32
Calasparra, Sp. C5 8
Calauag, Phil. P14 19
Calaveras, co., Calif. C3 50
Calca, Peru D3 31

Calcasieu, par., La. D2 63
Calceta, Ec. B1 31
Calcutta, India D8 10
Calcutta, Ohio B5 78
Caldas, dept. Col. B2 32
Caldas da Rainha, Port. C1 8
Caldwell, Idaho F2 57
Caldwell, Kans. E6 61
Caldwell, N.J. B4 74
Caldwell, Ohio C4 78
Caldwell, Tex. D4 84
Caldwell, co., Ky. C2 62
Caldwell, co., Mo. B3 69
Caldwell, co., N.C. B1 76
Caldwell, co., Tex. E4 84
Caldwell, par., La. B3 63
Caledonia, Ont., Can. D5 41
Caledonia, Minn. G7 67
Caledonia, N.Y. C3 75
Caledonia, Ohio B3 78
Caledonia, co., Vt. C3 73
Calella, Sp. B7 8
Calera, Ala. B3 46
Calera, Chile A2 28
Calexico, Calif. F6 50
Calgary, Alta., Can. D3, g8 38
Calhoun, Ga. B2 55
Calhoun, co., Ala. B4 46
Calhoun, co., Ark. D3 49
Calhoun, co., Fla. B1 54
Calhoun, co., Ga. E2 55
Calhoun, co., Ill. D3 58
Calhoun, co., Iowa B4 60
Calhoun, co., Mich. F5 66
Calhoun, co., Miss. B4 68
Calhoun, co., S.C. D6 82
Calhoun, co., Tex. E4 84
Calhoun, co., W. Va. C3 87
Calhoun City, Miss. B4 68
Calhoun Falls, S.C. C2 82
Cali, Col. C2 32
Calico Rock, Ark. A3 49
Calicut, India F6 20
Caliente, Nev. C4 72
California, Mo. C5 69
California, Pa. F2 81
California, state, U.S. C2 50
Calipatria, Calif. F6 50
Calispell, peak, Wash. A8 86
Calistoga, Calif. C2 50
Callahan, co., Tex. C3 84
Callander, Ont., Can. A5 41
Callander, Scot. B4 4
Callao, Peru D2 31
Callao, prov., Peru D2 31
Callaway, co., Mo. C6 69
Callicoon, N.Y. D5 75
Calloway, co., Ky. f9 62
Calmar, Alta., Can. C4 38
Calmar, Iowa A6 60
Caloundra, Austl. C9 26
Caltagirone, It. F5 9
Caltanissetta, It. F5 9
Caluire -et-Cuire, Fr. E6 5
Calumet, Que., Can. D3 42
Calumet, Mich. A2 66
Calumet, Pa. *F2 81
Calumet, co., Wis. D5 88
Calumet City, Ill. B6, k9 58
Calumet Park, Ill. *B6 58
Calvados, dept., Fr. *C3 5
Calvert, Tex. D4 84
Calvert, co., Md. C4 53
Calvert City, Ky. e9 62
Calverton Park, Mo. A8 69
Calvillo, Mex. m12 34
Calwa, Calif. *D4 50
Camacho, Mex. C4 34
Camagüey, Cuba D5 35
Camagüey, prov., Cuba D5 35
Camaná, Peru E2 31
Camanche, Iowa C7 60
Camargo, see Ciudad
  Camargo, Mex.
Camarillo, Calif. *E4 50
Camarines Norte, prov., Phil. *C6 19
Camarines Sur, prov., Phil. *C6 19
Camas, Wash. D3 86
Camas, co., Idaho F4 57
Cambay, India *D5 20
Cambodia, see Kampuchea,
  country, Asia
Camborne -Redruth, Eng. E4 4
Cambrai, Fr. B5 5
Cambria, Calif. E3 50
Cambria, co., Pa. E4 81
Cambrian Park, Calif. *D3 50

Cambridge, Eng. D7 4
Cambridge, Ill. B3 58
Cambridge, Md. C5 53
Cambridge, Mass. B5, g11 65
Cambridge, Minn. E5 67
Cambridge, Nebr. D5 71
Cambridge, N.J. *C3 74
Cambridge, N.Y. B7 75
Cambridge, Ohio B4 78
Cambridge & Isle of Ely,
  co., Eng. *D7 4
Cambridge City, Ind. E7 59
Cambridge Springs, Pa. C1 81
Camden, Ala. D2 46
Camden, Ark. D3 49
Camden, Del. B6 53
Camden, Maine D3 64
Camden, N.J. D2 74
Camden, N.Y. B5 75
Camden, Ohio C1 78
Camden, S.C. C6 82
Camden, Tenn. A3 83
Camden, Tex. D5 84
Camden, co., Ga. F5 55
Camden, co., Mo. C5 69
Camden, co., N.J. D3 74
Camden, co., N.C. A6 76
Camdenton Mo. D5 69
Camerino, It. C4 9
Cameron, La. E2 63
Cameron, Mo. B3 69
Cameron, Tex. D4 84
Cameron, W. Va. B4, g8 87
Cameron, Wis. C2 88
Cameron, co., Pa. D5 81
Cameron, co., Tex. F4 84
Cameron, par., La. E2 63
Cameroon, country, Afr. G7 22
Cameroun, Mont, mtn., Cam. H6 22
Camiling, Phil. o13 19
Camilla, Ga. E2 55
Camillus, N.Y. *B4 75
Camino, Calif. C3 50
Cammack Village, Ark. C3, h10 49
Camocim, Braz. *D6 27
Camp, co., Tex. C5 84
Campagna di Roma, reg., It. h9 9
Campana, Arg. g7 28
Campanario, Sp. C3 8
Campania, pol. dist., It. *D5 9
Campania, reg., It. D5 9
Campbell, Calif. k8 50
Campbell, Mo. E7 69
Campbell, Ohio A5 78
Campbell, co., Ky. B5 62
Campbell, co., S. Dak. E5 77
Campbell, co., Tenn. C9 83
Campbell, co., Va. C3 85
Campbell, co., Wyo. B7 89
Campbell, hill, Ohio B2 78
Campbellford, Ont., Can. C7 41
Campbellpore, Pak. B5 20
Campbell River, B.C. D5 37
Campbells Bay, Que., Can. B8 41
Campbellsport, Wis. E5 88
Campbellsville, Ky. C4 62
Campbellton, N.B., Can. A3 43
Campbelltown, Pa. *F9 81
Campbeltown, Scot. C4 4
Campeche, Mex. D6 34
Camp Hill, Ala. C4 46
Camp Hill, Pa. F8 81
Campiglia Marittima, It. C3 9
Campina Grande, Braz. D7 27
Campinas, Braz. C3, m8 30
Campoalegre, Col. C2 32
Campobasso, It. D5 9
Campo Belo, Braz. C3 30
Campo de Criptana, Sp. C4 8
Campo Grande, Braz. C2 30
Campo Maior, Braz. *D6 27
Campo Maior, Port. C2 8
Campos, Braz. C4 30
Camp Point, Ill. C2 58
Camp Springs, Md. f9 53
Campti, La. C2 63
Campton Heights, Calif. *B1 50
Camrose, Alta., Can. C4 38
Canaan, Conn. A3 52
Canada, country, N.A. D10 33
Cañada de Gómez, Arg. A4 28
Canadensis, Pa. D11 81
Canadian, Tex. B2 84
Canadian, co., Okla. B3 79
Canadian, riv., U.S. C6 45
Canajoharie, N.Y. C6 75
Çanakkale, Tur. B6 14

Canal Fulton, Ohio B4 78
Canal Point, Fla. F6 54
Canal Winchester, Ohio C3, m11 78
Canandaigua, N.Y. C3 75
Cananea, Mex. A2 34
Cañar, prov., Ec. B2 31
Canary Islands, reg., Sp. C1 22
Cañas, C.R. *E7 75
Canastota, N.Y. B5 34
Canavieiras, Braz. *E7 27
Canberra, Austl. G8 25
Canby, Minn. F2 67
Canby, Oreg. B4, h12 80
Candeleda, Sp. B3 8
Candia, see Iraklion, Grc.
Candiac, Que., Can. q19 42
Candler, co., Ga. D4 75
Cando, N. Dak. B6 77
Candor, N.Y. C4 75
Canea, see Khaniá, Grc.
Canelones, Ur. E1 30
Canelones, dept. Ur. *E1 30
Cañete, Peru D2 31
Caney, Kans. E8 61
Canfield, Ohio A5 78
Cangallo, Peru D3 31
Cangas, Sp. A1 8
Cangzhou, China D8 17
Canicatti, It. F4 9
Caniles, Sp. D4 8
Canisteo, N.Y. C3 75
Çankiri (Changra), Tur. B9 14
Canmore, Alta, Can. D3 38
Cannelton, Ind. I4 59
Cannes, Fr. F7 5
Canning, N.S., Can. D5 43
Cannington, Ont., Can. C5 41
Cannon, co., Tenn. B5 83
Cannon Falls, Minn. F6 67
Canoas, Braz. *D2 30
Canoinhas, Braz. D2 30
Canon City, Colo C5 51
Canonsburg, Pa. F1 81
Canora, Sask., Can. F4 39
Canosa de Puglia, It. D6 9
Canso, N.S., Can. D8 43
Cantal, dept., Fr. *E5 5
Canterbury, Eng. E7 4
Can Tho, Viet. *C3 19
Cantilan, Phil. *D7 19
Canton, China G7 17
Canton, Ga. B2 55
Canton, Ill. C3 58
Canton, Mass. B5, h11 65
Canton, Miss. C3 68
Canton, Mo. A6 69
Canton, N.Y. F9 75
Canton, N.C. D3 76
Canton, Ohio B4 78
Canton, Okla. A3 79
Canton, Pa. C8 81
Canton, S. Dak. G9 77
Canton, Tex. C5 84
Cantonment, Fla. u14 54
Cantwell, Mo. D7 69
Canutillo, Tex. o11 84
Canyon, Tex. B2 84
Canyon, co., Idaho F2 57
Canyonville, Oreg. E3 80
Cao Bang, Viet. G6 17
Capac, Mich. F8 66
Cap Chat, Que., Can. G20 36
Cap-de-la-Madeleine, Que., Can. C5 42
Cape, prov., S. Afr. G4 24
Cape Breton, Can. G21 36
Cape Breton, co., N.S., Can. D9 43
Cape Canaveral, Fla. D6 54
Cape Charles, Va. C6 85
Cape Coast, Ghana G4 22
Cape Coral, Fla. *F5 54
Cape Elizabeth, Maine E2, g7 64
Cape Girardeau, Mo. D8 69
Cape Girardeau, co., Mo. D8 69
Cape Horn, mtn., Idaho E3 57
Capels, W. Va. D3 87
Cape May, N.J. F3 74
Cape May, co., N.J. E3 74
Cape May Court House, N.J. E3 74
Capesterre, Guad. H14 35
Cape Town (Kaapstad), S. Afr. G3 24
Cape Verde, country, Afr. 012 22
Cape Vincent, N.Y. A4 75
Cap-Haïtien, Hai. E7 35
Capiata, Par. *E4 29
Capistrano Beach, Calif. *F5 50
Capitan, N. Mex. C6 48
Capitola, Calif. *D2 50

Capitol Heights, Md. C4, f9 53
Capivarí, Braz. m8 30
Capiz, prov., Phil *C6 19
Capoompeta, mtn., Austl. E9 25
Cap-Pelé, N.B., Can. C5 43
Capreol, Ont., Can. p19 41
Cap-St. Ignace, Que., Can. B7 42
Captain Cook, Haw. D6 56
Capua, It. D5 9
Caquetá, intendencia, Col. C3 32
Carabobo, state, Ven. A4 32
Caracal, Rom. C7 10
Caracas, Ven. A4 32
Caraguatay, Par. E4 29
Carangola, Braz. C4 30
Caransebes, Rom. C6 10
Carapeguá, Par. E4 29
Caraquet, N.B., Can. B5 43
Caratinga, Braz. B4 20
Caravelí, Peru E3 31
Caraway, Ark. B5 49
Caraz, Peru C2 31
Carázinho, Braz. D2 30
Carballino, Sp. A1 8
Carballo, Sp. A1 8
Carberry, Man., Can. E2 40
Carbó, Mex. B2 34
Carbon, co., Mont. E7 70
Carbon, co. Pa. E10 81
Carbon, co., Utah B6 72
Carbon, co., Wyo. E5 89
Carbondale, Ill. F4 58
Carbondale, Pa. C10 81
Carbonear, Newf., Can. E5 44
Carbon Hill, Ala. B2 46
Carbonia, It. E2 9
Carcagente, Sp. C5 8
Carcar, Phil. *C6 19
Carcassonne, Fr. F5 5
Carchi, prov., Ec. A2 31
Cardale, Pa. *G2 81
Cárdenas, Cuba. C3 35
Cárdenas, Mex. D6 34
Cárdenas, Mex. m14 34
Cardiff, Wales E5 4
Cardiff-by-the-Sea, Calif. *F5 50
Cardigan, Wales D4 4
Cardigan, co., Wales *D4 4
Cardinal, Ont., Can. C9 41
Cardington, Ohio B3 78
Cardston, Alta., Can. E4 38
Cardwell, Mo. E7 69
Carei, Rom. B6 10
Carencro, La. D3 63
Carenero, Ven. A4 32
Caretta, W. Va. D3 87
Carey, Ohio B2 78
Carhuaz, Peru C2 31
Cariati, It. E6 9
Caribbean, sea, N.A. H13 33
Cariboo mts., B.C. C7 37
Caribou, Maine B5 64
Caribou, co., Idaho F6 57
Caribou, mtn., Idaho F7 57
Caribou, mtn., Maine C2 64
Carichic, Mex. B3 34
Carini, It. E4 9
Carinthia, reg., Aus. E6 6
Caripito, Ven. A5 32
Carle Place, N.Y. *G2 75
Carleton, Mich. F7 66
Carleton, co., N.B., Can. C2 43
Carleton, mtn., N.B., Can. B3 43
Carleton Place, Ont., Can. B8 41
Carletonville, S. Afr. *F5 24
Carlin, Nev. A3 72
Carlinville, Ill. D4 58
Carlisle, Ark. C4 49
Carlisle, Eng. C5 4
Carlisle, Iowa C4 60
Carlisle, Ky. B5 62
Carlisle, Pa. F7 81
Carlisle, co., Ky. f8 62
Carl Junction, Mo. D3 69
Carloforte, It. E2 9
Carlos Casares, Arg. B4 28
Carlow, Ire. D3 4
Carlow, co., Ire. *D3 4
Carlsbad, Calif. F5 50
Carlsbad, N. Mex. C6 48
Carlstadt, N.J. h8 74
Carlton, Oreg. B3, h11 80
Calrton, co., Minn. D6 67
Carlyle, Sask., Can. H4 39
Carlyle, Ill. E4 58
Carmagnola, It. B1 9
Carman, Man., Can. E2 40
Carman, hill, Pa. C6 81
Carmanville, Newf., Can. D4 44
Carmarthen, Wales E4 4
Carmarthen, co.,Wales *E4 4
Carmaux, Fr. E5 5
Carmel, Calif. D3 50

Carmel, Ind. E5 59
Carmel, N.Y. D7 75
Carmel, mtn., Isr. B3 15
Carmelo, Ur. E1 30
Carmel Valley, Calif. *D3 50
Carmel Woods, Calif. *D3 50
Carmen, Par. E4 29
Carmen de Patagones, Arg. C4 28
Carmi, Ill. E5 58
Carmichael, Calif. *C3 50
Carmichaels, Pa. G2 81
Carmona, Sp. D3 8
Carnarvon, Austl. D1 25
Carnduff, Sask., Can. H5 39
Carnegie,Okla. B3 79
Carnegie, Pa. F1, k13 81
Carneys Point, N.J. D2 74
Caro, Mich. E7 66
Carol City, Fla. s13 54
Caroleen, N.C. B1, f11 76
Carolina, P.R. *G11 35
Carolina Beach, N.C. C5 76
Caroline, co., Md. C6 53
Caroline, co., Va. C5 85
Caroline, arch., Pac. O. F6 2
Carora, Ven. A3 32
Carouge, Switz. E3 6
Carpentersville, Ill. A5, h8 58
Carpentras, Fr. E6 5
Carpi, It. B3 9
Carpinteria, Calif. E4 50
Carrabelle, Fla. C2 54
Carrantuohill, mtn., Ire. D1 4
Carrara, It. B3 9
Carrboro, N.C. B3 76
Carrickfergus, N. Ire. C4 4
Carrie, mtn., Wash. B2 86
Carriers Mills, Ill. F5 58
Carrington, N. Dak. C6 77
Carrizo, see El Carrizo, Mex.
Carrizo Springs, Tex. E3 84
Carrizozo, N. Mex. C6 48
Carroll, Iowa B3 60
Carroll, co., Ark. A2 49
Carroll, co., Ga. C1 55
Carroll, co., Ill. A4 58
Carroll, co., Ind. C4 59
Carroll, co., Iowa B3 60
Carroll, co., Ky. B4 62
Carroll, co., Md. A3 53
Carroll, co., Miss. B4 68
Carroll, co., Mo. B4 69
Carroll, co., N.H. D5 73
Carroll, co., Ohio B4 78
Carroll, co., Tenn. B3 83
Carroll, co., Va. D2 85
Carrollton, Ga. C1 55
Carrollton, Ill. D3 58
Carrollton, Ky. B4 62
Carrollton, Md. A4 53
Carrollton, Mich. E7 66
Carrollton, Mo. B4 69
Carrollton, Ohio B4 78
Carrollton, Tex. *C4 84
Carrolltown, Pa. E4 81
Carrot River, Sask., Can. D4 39
Carrville, Ala. C4 46
Çarşamba, Tur. B11 14
Carson, Calif. *n12 50
Carson, Iowa C10 71
Carson, co., Tex. B2 84
Carson City, Mich. E6 66
Carson City, Nev. B2 72
Carsonville, Mo. *C7 69
Cartagena, Col. A2 32
Cartagena, Sp. D5 8
Cartago, Col. C2 32
Cartago, C.R. F8 34
Cartago, prov., C.R. *I12 33
Cartaxo, Port. C1 8
Cartaya, Sp. D2 8
Carter, co., Ky. B6 62
Carter, co., Mo. E7 69
Carter, co., Mont. E12 70
Carter, co., Okla. C4 79
Carter, co., Tenn. C11 83
Carteret, N.J. B4, k8 74
Carteret, co., N.C. C6 76
Carter Lake, Iowa C2 60
Cartersville, Ga. B2 55
Carterville, Ill. F4 58
Carterville, Mo. D3 69
Carthage, Ill. C2 58
Carthage, Ind. E6 59
Carthage, Miss. C4 68
Carthage, Mo. D3 69
Carthage, N.Y. B5 75
Carthage, N.C. B3 76
Carthage, Tenn. C8 83
Carthage, Tex. C5 84
Caruaru, Braz. D7 27
Carúpano, Ven. A5 32
Caruthersville, Mo. E8 69

Carver, Minn. F5 67
Carver, co., Minn. F5 67
Carville, La. h9 63
Cary, Ill. A5, h8 58
Cary, N.C. B4 76
Caryville, Tenn. C9 83
Casablanca, Mor. B3 22
Casa Branca, Braz. C3, k8 30
Casa Grande, Ariz. C3 48
Casale Monferrato, It. B2 9
Casarano, It. D7 9
Casas Adobes, Ariz. *C3 48
Cascade, Idaho E2 57
Cascade, Iowa B6 60
Cascade, co., Mont. C5 70
Cascade, range, Can., U.S. B2 45
Cascais, Port. C1, f9 8
Caseros (Tres de Febrero), Arg. .. *A5 28
Caserta, It. D5 9
Casey, Ill. D6 58
Casey, co., Ky. C4 62
Casey, mtn., Idaho A2 57
Caseyville, Ill. *E3 58
Cashion, Ariz. D1 48
Cashmere, Wash. B5 86
Cashton, Wis. E3 88
Casilda, Arg. A4 28
Casino, Austl. D9 26
Čáslav, Czech. D3 7
Casma, Peru C2 31
Caspe, Sp. B5 8
Casper, Wyo. D6 89
Caspian, Mich. B2 66
Caspian, sea, Asia E7 13
Cassadaga, N.Y. C1 75
Cass, co., Ill. D3 58
Cass, co., Ind. C5 59
Cass, co., Iowa C3 60
Cass, co., Mich. G4 66
Cass, co., Minn. D4 67
Cass, co., Mo. C3 69
Cass, co., Nebr. D9 71
Cass, co., N. Dak. C8 77
Cass, co., Tex. C5 84
Cass, City, Mich. E7 66
Casselberry, Fla. *D5 54
Casselman, Ont., Can. B9 41
Casselton, N. Dak. D8 77
Cassia, co., Idaho G5 57
Cassino, It. D4 9
Cass Lake Minn. C4 67
Cassopolis, Mich. G4 66
Cassville, Mo. E4 69
Cassville, Wis. F3 88
Castalia, Ohio A3 78
Castanea, Pa. D7 81
Castaños, Mex. B4 34
Castellammare di Stabia, It. *D5 9
Castellón (Castellón
  de la Plana), prov., Sp. *C5 8
Castellón de la Plana, Sp. C5 8
Castelnaudary, Fr. F4 5
Castelo Branco, Port. C2 8
Castelvetrano, It. F4 9
Castile, N.Y. C2 75
Castilla, Peru C1 31
Castle, peak, Idaho E4 57
Castle Douglas, Scot. C5 4
Castlegar, B.C., Can. E9 37
Castle Hills, Tex. *E3 84
Castlemaine, Austl. H5 26
Castle Park, Calif. *F5 50
Castle Rock, Colo. B6 51
Castle Rock, Wash. C3 86
Castle Rock, mtn., Oreg. C8 80
Castle Rock, mtn., Va. C4 85
Castle Shannon, Pa. k13 81
Castleton-on-Hudson, N.Y. C7 75
Castor, Alta., Can. C5 38
Castres, Fr. F5 5
Castries, St. Lucia J14 35
Castro, Braz. C3 30
Castro, Sp. D3 8
Castro, co., Tex. B1 84
Castro Alves, Braz. *E7 27
Castropol, Sp. A2 8
Castro Valley, Calif. h8 50
Castrovillari, It. E6 9
Castroville, Calif. D3 50
Castroville, Tex. E3 84
Castrovirreyna, Peru D2 31
Castuera, Sp. C3 8
Caswell, co., N.C. A3 76
Catacaos, Peru C1 31
Catacocha, Ec. B2 31
Cataguases, Braz. C4, g6 30
Catahoula, par., La. C4 63
Cataingan, Phil. *C6 19
Catalao, Braz. B3 30
Çatalca, Tur. B7 14
Catalina, Newf., Can. D5 44
Catamarca, Arg. E2 29
Catamarca, prov., Arg. E2 29

Catanduva, Braz. C3 30
Catania, It. F5 9
Cataño, P.R. *G11 35
Catanzaro, It. E6 9
Catarman, Phil. C6 19
Catarroja, Sp. C5 8
Catasauqua, Pa. E11 81
Catawba, co., N.C. B1 76
Catawissa, Pa. E9 81
Catbalogan, Phil. C6 19
Cathedral, mtn., Tex. o13 84
Cathedral City, Calif. F5 50
Catlettsburg, Ky. B7 62
Catlin, Ill. C6 58
Catonsville, Md. B4, g10 53
Catoosa, co., Ga. B1 55
Catron, co., N. Mex. C4 48
Catskill, N.Y. *C7 75
Catskill, mts., N.Y. C6 75
Catt, mtn., B.C., Can. B3 37
Cattaraugus, N.Y. C2 75
Cattaraugus, co.,N.Y. C2 75
Cattolica, It. C4 9
Cauca, dept., Col. C2 32
Caucasia, Col. B2 32
Caudebec -lès-Elbeuf, Fr. C4 5
Caudete, Sp. C5 8
Caudry, Fr. B5 5
Caughnawaga, Que., Can. D4, q19 43
Cauquenes, Chile B2 28
Causapscal, Que., Can. *h14 42
Cautín, prov., Chile B2 28
Cavadas, Mex. m12 34
Cavaillon, Fr. F6 5
Cavalier, N. Dak. B8 77
Cavalier, co., N. Dak. B7 77
Cavan, co., Ire. *D3 4
Cavarzere, It. B4 9
Cave, It. h9 9
Cave City, Ky. C4 62
Cave Junction, Oreg. E3 80
Cave Spring, Ga. B1 55
Cavite, Phil. o13 19
Cavite, prov., Phil. *C6 19
Cawnpore, see Kanpur, India
Cawood, Ky. D6 62
Caxias, Braz. *D6 27
Caxias do Sul., Braz. D2 30
Caxito, Ang. B2 24
Cayambe, Ec. A2 31
Cayce, S.C. D5 82
Cayenne, Fr. Gu. C5 27
Cayey, P.R. G11 35
Cayman Islands, Br. dep.,N.A. .. F3 35
Cayuga, Ont., Can. E5 41
Cayuga, Ind. E3 59
Cayuga, co., N.Y. C4 75
Cayuga Heights, N.Y. *C4 75
Cazalla de la Sierra, Sp. D3 8
Cazenovia, N.Y. C5 75
Cazorla, Sp. D4 8
Ceará, state, Braz. *D7 27
Ceará Mirim, Braz. *D7 27
Cebu, Phil. C6 19
Cebu, prov., Phil. *C6 19
Cecil, Pa. F1 81
Cecil, co., Md. A6 53
Cecina, It. C3 9
Cedar, co., Iowa C6 60
Cedar, co., Mo. D4 69
Cedar, co., Nebr. B8 71
Cedar, mtn., Cal. B3 50
Cedar Bluff, Va. e10 85
Cedarburg, Wis. E5, m12 88
Cedar City, Utah C5 72
Cedar Falls, Iowa B5 60
Cedar Grove, N.J. *B4 74
Cedar Grove, W. Va. C3, m13 87
Cedar Grove, Wis. E6 88
Cedar Hammock, Fla. *E4 54
Cedar Heights, Md. *C4 53
Cedar Hill, Tex. n10 84
Cedar Hills, Oreg. *B4 80
Cedarhurst, N.Y. k13 75
Cedar Key, Fla. C3 54
Cedar Knolls, N.J. B4 74
Cedar Lake, Ind. B3 59
Cedar Rapids, Iowa C6 60
Cedar Springs, Mich. E5 66
Cedar Terrace, S.C. *D5 82
Cedartown, Ga. B1 55
Cedar Vale, Kans. E7 61
Cedarville, Calif. B3 50
Cedarville, N.J. E2 74
Cedarville, Ohio C2 78
Cedarwood Park, N.J. *C4 74
Ceduna, Austl. F5 25
Cefalù, It. E5 9
Cegléd, Hung. B4 10
Ceglie Messapico, It. D6 9
Čelákovice, Czech. n18 7
Celaya, Mex. m13 34
Celebes (Sulawesi), isl., Indon. .. F6 19

Celendín, Peru C2 31
Celina, Ohio B1 78
Celina, Tenn. C8 83
Celina, Tex. C4 84
Celje, Yugo. B2 10
Celle, Ger., Fed. Rep. of B5 6
Celoron, N.Y. C1 75
Cement, Okla. C3 79
Cementon, Pa. E10 81
Cenon, Fr. E3 5
Centennial, mts., Mont. F4 70
Center, Colo D4 51
Center, Tex. D5 84
Centerburg, Ohio B3 78
Centereach, N.Y. E3 75
Center Line, Mich. *F8 66
Center Moriches, N.Y. n16 75
Center Point, Ala. f7 46
Center Point, Iowa B6 60
Centerport, N.Y. *n15 75
Centerville, Ind. E8 59
Centerville, Iowa D5 60
Centerville, Mont. D4 70
Centerville, Ohio C1 78
Centerville, Pa. F2 81
Centerville, S. Dak. G9 77
Centerville, Tenn. B4 83
Centerville, Tex. D5 84
Centerville, Utah A6, C2 72
Central, N. Mex. C4 48
Central, S.C. B2 62
Central, mts., Dom. Rep. E8 35
Central African Republic,
    country, Afr. G2 23
Central America, reg., N.A. E6 34
Central Avenue Park, Ohio *A2 78
Central City, Ill. E4 58
Central City, Iowa B6 60
Central City, Ky. C2 62
Central City, Nebr. C7 71
Central City, Pa. F4 81
Central Falls, R.I. B11 52
Central Heights, Ariz. *C3 48
Central Heights, Iowa A4 60
Centralia, Ill. E4 58
Centralia, Mo. B5 69
Centralia, Pa. *D8 81
Centralia, Wash. C3 86
Central Islip, N.Y. E7, n15 75
Central Nyack, N.Y. *D7 75
Central Park, Ill. *C6 58
Central Park, Wash. *C2 86
Central Point, Oreg. E4 80
Central Square, N.Y. B4 75
Central Valley, Calif. B2 50
Central Valley, N.Y. D6, m14 75
Centre, Ala. A4 46
Centre, co., Pa. E6 81
Centre, mtn., Idaho D3 57
Centre, peak, B.C., Can. B4 37
Centre Hall, Pa. E6 81
Centreville, Ala. C2 46
Centreville, Ill. E3 58
Centreville, Md. B5 53
Centreville, Mich. G5 66
Centreville, Miss. D2 68
Century, Fla. u14 54
Ceram, isl., Indon. F7 19
Ceredo, W. Va. C2 87
Ceres, Calif. D3 50
Cereté, Col. B2 32
Cerignola, It. D5 9
Cernavoda, Rom. C9 10
Cerralvo, Mex. B5 34
Cerritos, Calif. *F4 50
Cerritos, Mex. C4 34
Cerro Alto, mtn., Tex. o12 84
Cerro Azul, Peru D2 31
Cerro de Pasco, Peru D2 31
Cerro Gordo, Ill. D5 58
Cerro Gordo, co., Iowa A4 60
Cerro Largo, dept., Ur. *E2 30
Cervantes, Sp. A2 8
Cerva del Rio Alhama, Sp. A2 8
Cesena, It. B4 9
Cesenatico, It. B4 9
Ceská Lipa, Czech. C3 7
Ceská Trebova, Czech. D4 7
Ceske Budejovice, Czech. D3 7
Cesky Brod, Czech. n8 7
Cesky Krumlov, Czech. D3 7
Cessnock, Austl. F9 25
Cetinje, Yugo. D4 10
Cetraro, It. E5 9
Ceuta, Sp. dep., Afr. A3 2
Ceylon, see Sri Lanka,
    country, Asia.
Chacabuco, Arg. A4, m9 28
Chachapoyas, Peru C2 31
Chaco, prov., Arg. E3 29
Chad, country, Afr. F1 23
Chad, lake, Cam., Nig. E7 22
Chadbourn, N.C. C4 76

Chadron, Nebr. B3 71
Chadwicks, N.Y. *B5 75
Chaffee, Mo. D8 69
Chaffee, co., Colo. C4 51
Chaffins, Mass. *B4 65
Chagrin Falls, Ohio A4 78
Chahar Burjak, Afg. B3 20
Chaibāsā, India D8 20
Chakradharpur, India D8 20
Chakwāl, Pak. B5 20
Chalchuapa, Sal. *E7 34
Chalfant, Pa. *E1 81
Chalhuanca, Peru D3 31
Chalk River, Ont., Can. A7 41
Chalkville, Ala. f7 46
Chalmette, La. E6, k11 63
Châlons-sur-Marne, Fr. C6 5
Chalon-sur-Saône, Fr. E6 5
Chama, N. Mex. A5 48
Chamalières, Fr. E5 5
Chaman, Pak. B4 20
Chamberlain, S. Dak. G6 77
Chamberlayne Heights, Va. *C5 85
Chambers, co., Ala. C4 46
Chambers, co., Tex. E5 84
Chambersburg, Pa. G6 81
Chambéry, Fr. E6 5
Chamblee, Ga. h8 55
Chambly, Que., Can. D4 42
Chambly, co., Que., Can. D4 42
Chambord, Que., Can. A5 42
Champaign, Ill. C5 58
Champaign, co., Ill. C5 58
Champaign, co., Ohio B2 78
Champigny-sur-Marne, Fr. g11 5
Champion, Ohio A5 78
Champlain, N.Y. f11 75
Champlain, co., Que., Can. B4 42
Champlin, Minn. m12 67
Champotán, Mex. D6 34
Chañaral, Chile F3 27
Chancay, Peru D2 31
Chanchelulla, peak, Calif. B2 50
Chanchiang (Tsamkkong), China G7 17
Chandīgarh, India B6 20
Chandīgarh, ter., India *B6 20
Chandler, Ariz. C3, D2 48
Chandler, Que., Can. K14 42
Chandler, Ind. H3 59
Chandler, Okla. B5 79
Chāndpur, Bngl. D9 20
Chandrapur, India E6 20
Changchun (Hsinking), China C10 17
Changde, China F7 17
Changhua, Taiwan *G9 17
Changjin, Kor. F3 18
Changsha, China F7 17
Changting, China F8 17
Changyon, Kor. G2 18
Changahi, China D7 17
Changzhou, China E8 17
Channel, is., Eur. F5 4
Channel Lake, Ill. H8 58
Channel-Port-aux-Basques,
    Newf., Can. E2 44
Channelview, Tex. r14 84
Chantada, Sp. A2 8
Chanthaburi, Thai. C2 19
Chantilly, Fr. C5 5
Chanute, Kans. E8 61
Chao'an, China G8 17
Chaoyang, China C9 17
Chapala, Mex. m12 34
Chaparral, Col. C2 32
Chapayevsk, Sov. Un. *D7 13
Chapel Hill, N.C. *B3 76
Chapleau, Ont., Can. p19 41
Chaplygin, Sov. Un. E12 12
Chapman, Ala. D3 46
Chapman, Kans. D7 61
Chapmanville, W. Va. D2 87
Chappaqua, N.Y. *D7 75
Chappell, Nebr. C3 71
Chapra, India C7 20
Charalá, Col. B2 32
Charcas, Mex. C4 34
Chardon, Ohio A4 78
Chardzhou, Sov. Un. F9 13
Charente, dept., Fr. *E4 5
Charente-Maritime, dept., Fr. *D3 5
Charenton-le-Pont, Fr. g10 5
Charikar, Afg. A4 20
Chariton, Iowa C4 60
Chariton, co., Mo. B4 69
Charlack, Mo. *C7 69
Charlemagne, Que., Can. D4, p19 42
Charleroi, Bel. B6 5
Charleroi, Pa. F2 81
Charleroix West, co., Que.,
    Can. B7 42
Charles, co., Md. C3 53
Charlesbourg, Que., Can. N17 42
Charles City, Iowa A5 60

Charles City, co., Va. C5 85
Charles Mix, co., S. Dak. G7 77
Charleston, Ark. B1 49
Charleston, Ill. D5 58
Charleston, Miss. A3 68
Charleston, Mo. E8 69
Charleston, S.C. F8, k12 82
Charleston, W. Va. C3, m12 87
Charleston, Utah C4 72
Charleston, co., S.C. F8 82
Charlestown, Ind. H6 59
Charlestown, N.H. E3 73
Charlestown, St Kitts-
    Nevis-Anguilla H13 35
Charles Town, W. Va. B7 87
Charleville, Austl. E8 25
Charlevoix, Mich. C5 66
Charlevoix, co., Mich. C5 66
Charlieu, Fr. D6 5
Charlotte, Mich. F6 66
Charlotte, N.C. B2 76
Charlotte, Tex. E3 84
Charlotte, co., N.B., Can. D3 43
Charlotte, co., Fla. F5 54
Charlotte, co., Va. D4 85
Charlotte Amalie, Vir. Is.
    (U.S.) G12 35
Charlotte Harbor, Fla. F4 54
Charlottesville
    (Independent City), Va. B4 85
Charlottetown, P.E.I., Can. C6 43
Charlton, City, Mass. B4 65
Charlton, co., Ga. F4 55
Charmco, W. Va. *D4 87
Charny, Que., Can. C6, o17 42
Charter Oak, Calif. *E4 50
Charters Towers, Austl. D8 25
Chartres, Fr. C4 5
Chascomús, Arg. B5 28
Chase, B.C., Can. D8 37
Chase, Kans. D5 61
Chase, co., Kans. D7 61
Chase, co., Nebr. D4 71
Chase City, Va D4 85
Chase, mtn., Maine B4 64
Chaska, Minn. F5, n11 67
Chasong, Kor. F3 18
Chasov Yar, Sov., Un. q20 12
Chataignier, La. D3 63
Châteaubriant, Fr. D3 5
Châteaudun, Fr. C4 5
Chateaugay, N.Y. f11 10
Château-Gontier, Fr. D3 5
Châteauguay, Que., Can. D4, q19 42
Châteauguay, co., Que.,
    Can. D4 42
Châteauguay Heights,
    Que., Can. q19 42
Château-Richer, Que., Can. C6 42
Châteauroux, Fr. D4 5
Château-Theirry, Fr. C5 5
Châtellerault, Fr. D4 5
Chatfield, Minn. G6 67
Chatham, N.B., Can. B4 43
Chatham, Ont., Can. E2 41
Chatham, Eng. *E7 4
Chatham, Ill. D4 58
Chatham, Mass. C8 65
Chatham, N.J. B4 74
Chatham, N.Y. C7 75
Chatham, Va. D3 85
Chatham, co., Ga. E5 55
Chatham, co., N.C. B3 76
Chatom, Ala. D1 46
Chatsworth, Ga. B2 55
Chatsworth, Ill. C5 58
Chattahoochee, Fla. B2 54
Chattahoochee, co., Ga. D2 55
Chattanooga, Tenn. D8, h11 83
Chattaroy, W. Va. D2 87
Chattooga, co., Ga. B1 55
Chatwood, Pa. *G10 81
Chau Doc, Viet. *C3 19
Chauk, Bur. D9 20
Chaumont, Fr. C6 5
Chauncey, Ohio C3 78
Chauny, Fr. C5 5
Chautauqua, co., Kans. E7 61
Chautauqua, co., N.Y. C1 75
Chauvin, La. E5 63
Chaves, Port. B2 8
Chaves, co., N. Mex. C6 48
Chavinda, Mex. m12 34
Chazy, N.Y. f11 75
Cheatham, co., Tenn. A4 83
Cheb, Czech. C2 7
Chebanse, Ill. C6 58
Cheboksary, Sov. Un. C16 12
Cheboygan, Mich. C6 66
Cheboygan, co., Mich. C6 66
Chechaouene, Mor. A3 22
Checotah, Okla. B6 79

Cheddar, S.C. B3 82
Cheektowaga, N.Y. C2 75
Chefoo, see Yantai, China
Chehalis, Wash. C3 86
Cheju, Kor. J3 18
Chekhov, Sov. Un. C10 13
Chelan, Wash. B5 86
Chelan, co., Wash. B4 86
Chelan, mts., Wash. A5 86
Chelkar, Sov. Un. E3 13
Chelm *Lubelski*, Pol. C7 7
Chelmno, Pol. B4 7
Chelmsford, Ont., Can. *A3 41
Chelmsford, Eng. E7 4
Chelmsford, Mass. A5, f10 65
Chelmza, Pol. B5 7
Chelsea, Mass. B5, g11 65
Chelsea, Mich. F6 66
Chelsea, Okla. A6 79
Cheltenham, Eng. E5 4
Cheltenham, Md. C4 53
Cheltenham, Pa. *F11 81
Chelyabinsk, Sov. Un. D9 13
Chemainus, B.C., Can. E6, g12 37
Chemnitz, see Karl-Marx-
    Stadt, Ger. Dem. Rep.
Chemung, co., N.Y. C4 75
Chenango, co., N.Y. C5 75
Chenango Bridge, N.Y. *C5 75
Cheney, Kans E6, g11 61
Cheney, Wash. B8, h13 86
Cheneyville, La. C3 63
Chengde, China C8 17
Chengdu, China E5 17
Chenghai, China G8 17
Chenoa, Ill. C5 58
Chenxian, China F7 17
Chepén, Peru C2 31
Chepstow, Wales E5 4
Cher, dept., Fr. *D5 5
Cheraw, S.C. B8 82
Cherbourg, Fr. C3 5
Cheremkhovo, Sov. Un. D13 13
Cherepovets, Sov. Un. B11 12
Cherkassy, Sov. Un. G9 12
Chernigov, Sov. Un. F8 12
Chernobay, Sov. Un. G9 12
Chernobyl, Sov. Un. F8 12
Chernovtsy, Sov. Un. G5 12
Chernyakhovsk, (Insterburg),
    Sov. Un. D3 12
Cherokee, Ala. A2 46
Cherokee, Iowa B2 60
Cherokee, Kans. E9 61
Cherokee, Okla. A3 79
Cherokee, co. Ala. A4 46
Cherokee, co., Ga. B2 55
Cherokee, co., Iowa B2 60
Cherokee, co., Kans. E9 61
Cherokee, co., N.C. f8 76
Cherokee, co., Okla. B6 79
Cherokee, co., S.C. A4 82
Cherokee, co., Tex. D5 84
Cherokee Forest, S.C. *B3 82
Cherokee Ranch, Pa. *F9 81
Cherry, co., Nebr. B4 71
Cherry Grove, Ohio *C1 78
Cherry Hill, N.J. D2 74
Cherry Hills Village, Colo. *B6 51
Cherryvale, Kans. E8 61
Cherry Valley, Ill. A5 58
Cherry Valley, Mass. B4 65
Cherryville, N.C. B1 76
Chesaning, Mich. E6 66
Chesapeake, Ohio D3 78
Chesapeake (Independent
    City), Va. D6, k15 85
Chesapeake, W. Va. C3 87
Chesapeake City, Md. A6 53
Chesham, Eng. k11 4
Cheshire, Conn. D5 52
Cheshire, Mass. A1 65
Cheshire, co., Eng. *D5 4
Cheshire, co., N.H. F3 73
Cheshunt, Eng. k12 4
Chesley, Ont., Can. C3 41
Chesnee, S.C. A4 82
Chester, Calif. B3 50
Chester, N.S., Can. E5 43
Chester, Conn. D7 52
Chester, Eng. D5 4
Chester, Ill. F4 58
Chester, Md. C5 53
Chester, Mass. B2 65
Chester, Mont. B6 70
Chester, N.J. B3 74
Chester, N.S., Can. E5 43
Chester, N.Y. D6, m14 75
Chester, Pa. G11, p20 81
Chester, S.C. B5 82
Chester, Vt. E3 73
Chester, Va. C5, n18 85
Chester, W. Va. A4, e8 87

Chester, co., Pa. G10 81
Chester, co., S.C. B5 82
Chester, co., Tenn. B3 83
Chesterfield, Eng. D6 4
Chesterfield, Ind. D6 59
Chesterfield, S.C. B7 82
Chesterfield, co., S.C. B7 82
Chesterfield, co., Va. C5 85
Chesterhill, Ohio C4 78
Chesterton, Ind. A3 59
Chestertown, Md. B5 53
Chesterville, Ont., Can. B9 41
Cheswick, Pa. h14 81
Chetek, Wis. .C2 88
Cheticamp, N.S., Can. C8 43
Chetopa, Kans. E8 61
Chetumal, see Ciudad
  Chetumal, Mex.
Chetwynd, B.C., Can. B7 37
Cheverly, Md. *C4 53
Cheviot, Ohio C1, o12 78
Chevy Chase, Md. C3, f8 53
Chevy Chase Heights, Pa. *E3 81
Chevy Chase Section
  Four, Md. *C3 53
Chevy Chase View, Md. *C3 53
Chewelah, Wash. A8 86
Chews (Chews Landing), N.J. *C4 74
Cheyenne, Okla. B2 79
Cheyenne, Wyo. E8 89
Cheyenne, co., Colo. C8 51
Cheyenne, co., Kans. C2 61
Cheyenne, co., Nebr. C2 71
Cheyenne Wells, Colo. C8 51
Chiai, Taiwan *G9 17
Chiang Khong, Thai. A2 19
Chiang Mai,Thai B1 19
Chiang Rai, Thai B1 19
Chiapa de Corzo, Mex. D6 34
Chiapas, state, Mex. D6 34
Chiari, It. B2 9
Chiautla de Tapia, Mex. n14 34
Chiavari, It. B2 9
Chiba, Jap. I10, n19 18
Chiba, pref., Jap. *I10 18
Chicago, Ill. B6, k9 58
Chicago Heights, Ill. B6, k9 58
Chicago Ridge, Ill. *B6 58
Chichester, Eng. E6 4
Chichibu, Jap. m18 18
Chickamauga, Ga. B1 55
Chickasaw, Ala. E1 46
Chickasaw, co., Iowa A5 60
Chickasaw, co.,Miss. B5 68
Chickasha, Okla. B4 79
Chiclana, Sp. D2 8
Chiclayo, Peru C2 31
Chico, Calif. .C3 50
Chico, Tex. C4 84
Chico, Wash. B3 86
Chicontepec, Mex. m14 34
Chicopee, Ga. B3 55
Chicopee, Mass. B2 65
Chicora, Pa. .E2 81
Chicot, co., Ark. D4 49
Chicoutimi, Que., Can. A6, k12 42
Chicoutimi, co., Que., Can. A6 42
Chico Vecino, Calif. *C3 50
Chiefland, Fla. C4 54
Chieri, It. B1 9
Chieti, It. C5 9
Chifeng, China C8 17
Chigasaki, Jap. *I9 18
Chigirin, Sov. Un. G9 12
Chignahuapan, Mex. n14 34
Chigwell, Eng. k13 4
Chihuahua, Mex. B3 34
Chihuahua, state, Mex. B3 34
Chii-san, mtn., Korea I3 18
Chikura, Jap. o18 18
Chilapa de Alvarez, Mex. D5, o14 34
Childersburg, Ala. B3 46
Chilca, Peru .D2 31
Childress, Tex. B2 84
Childress, co., Tex. B2 84
Chile, country, S.A. E2 29
Chilecito, Arg. E2 29
Chilhowie, Va. f10 85
Chillán, Chile B2 28
Chillicothe, Ill. C4 58
Chillicothe, Mo. B4 69
Chillicothe, Ohio C3 78
Chillicothe, Tex. B3 84
Chilliwack, B.C., Can. E7, f14 37
Chillum, Md. *C3 53
Chiloé, prov., Chile C2 28
Chiloquin, Oreg. E5 80
Chilpancingo de los
  Bravos, Mex. D5, o14 34
Chilton, Tex. .D4 84
Chilton, Wis. D5, h10 88
Chilton, co., Ala. C3 46
Chilung, Taiwan F9 17

Chimalhuacán, Mex. h10 34
Chimayo, N. Mex. B6 48
Chimbay, Sov. Un. E8 13
Chimborazo, prov., Ec. B2 31
Chimborazo, vol., Ec. B2 31
Chimbote, Peru C2 31
Chimkent, Sov. Un. E19 13
China, Mex. .B5 34
China, country, Asia E4 17
China Grove, N.C. B2 76
Chinandega, Nic. E7 34
Chinati, peak, Tex. p12 84
Chincha Alta, Peru D2 31
Chincheros, Peru D3 31
Chinchilla, Austl. E9 25
Chinchilla, Pa. *D10 81
Chincoteague, Va. C7 85
Chindo,Kor. .I3 18
Chingford, Eng. k13 4
Chingola, Zam. *C5 24
Chinhae, Kor. I4 18
Chiniot,Pak. .B5 20
Chinju, Kor. .I4 18
Chinnampo (Nampo), Kor. G2 18
Chino, Calif. F5, m13 50
Chinook, Mont. B7 70
Chinquapin, N.C. C5 76
Chinú, Col. B3 32
Chioggia, It. .B4 9
Chipley, Fla. .u16 54
Chipman, N.B., Can. C4 43
Chippewa, co., Mich. B6 66
Chippewa, co. Minn. E3 67
Chippewa, co., Wis. C2 88
Chippewa Falls, Wis. D2 88
Chiquimula, Guat. E7 34
Chiquinquira, Col. B3 32
Chiriqui Grande, Pan. B1 32
Chirpan, Bul. D7 10
Chisago, co., Minn. E6 67
Chisholm, Maine D2 64
Chisholm, Minn. C6 67
Chişineu-Criş, Rom. B5 10
Chisos, mts., Tex. p13 84
Chita, Sov. Un. D14 13
Chitradurga, India F6 20
Chitré, Pan. .B1 32
Chittagong, Bngl. D9 20
Chittenango, N.Y. *B5 75
Chittenden, co.,Vt. C1 73
Chittoor, India F6 20
Chiusi, It. C3 9
Chivasso, It. .B1 9
Chivay, Peru .E3 31
Chivilcoy,Arg. A4, g6 28
Chochiwŏn, Kor. H3 18
Chocó, dept., Col. C2 32
Chocontá, Col. B3 32
Choctaw, co., Ala. C1 46
Choctaw, co., Miss. B4 68
Choctaw, co., Okla. C6 79
Chodziez, Pol. B4 7
Choisy-le-Roi, Fr. g10 5
Choix, Mex. .B3 34
Chojna, Pol. .B3 7
Chojnice, Pol. B4 7
Chojnów, Pol. B3 7
Chokai-zan mtn., Jap. G10 18
Cholet, Fr. D3 5
Cholula de Rivadabia, Mex. n14 34
Choluteca, Hond. E7 34
Chomutov, Czech. C2 7
Chonan, Kor. H3 18
Chon Buri,Thai C2 19
Chone, Ec. B1 31
Chongjin, Kor. F4 18
Chongju, Kor. H3 18
Chongqing, China F6 17
Chonju, Kor. I3 18
Chorrilos, Peru D2 31
Chŏrwŏn, Kor. G3 18
Chorzów, Pol. g9 7
Chosen, Fla. F6 54
Chosen, see Korea, Asia
Choshi, Jap. I10, n19 18
Chosica, Peru D2 31
Chota, Peru .C2 31
Choteau, Mont. C4 70
Choum, Maur. D2 22
Chouteau, Okla. A6 79
Chouteau, co., Mont. C6 70
Chowan, co., N.C. A6 76
Chowchilla,Calif. D3 50
Chrisman, Ill. D6 58
Christchurch, N.Z. O14 26
Christian, co., Ill. D4 58
Christian, co., Ky. D2 62
Christian, co., Mo. E4 69
Christiana, Pa. G9 81
Christiansburg, Va. C2 85
Christiansted, Vir. Is. (U.S.) H12 35
Christmas Island, Austl.
  dep., Oceania G4 2

Christopher, Ill. F4 58
Chrudim, Czech. D3 7
Chrzanów, Pol. g10 7
Chubbuck, Idaho G6 57
Chubut, prov.,Arg. C3 28
Chugiak, Alsk. C10, g17 47
Chuguyev, Sov. Un. G11 12
Chuius, mtn., B.C., Can. B5 37
Chula Vista, Calif. F5, o15 50
Chuluchana, Peru B1 31
Chumikán, Sov. Un. D16 13
Chunchŏn, Kor. H3 18
Chungju, Kor H3 18
Chungking, see Chongqing, China
Chupaca, Peru D2 31
Chuquibamba, Peru E3 31
Chuquisaca, dept., Bol. D3 29
Chur, Switz. .E4 6
Church, mtn., B.C., Can. f14 37
Church Hill, Tenn. C11 83
Churchhill, Man., Can. f9 40
Churchill, Pa. *E1 81
Churchill, co., Nev. B2 72
Churchhill, riv., Man.,
  Sask.,Can. B2 39
Church Point, La. D3 63
Churchs Ferry, N. Dak. B6 77
Churchville, Pa. *F11 81
Churmuco, Mex. n13 34
Churubusco, Ind. B7 59
Chusovoy, Sov. Un. *D8 13
Cibola, co, N. Mex. B4 48
Cicero, Ill. B6, k9 58
Cicero, Ind D5 59
Ciechanów, Pol. B6 7
Ciego de Avila, Cuba D4 35
Ciénaga, Col. A3 32
Ciénaga de Oro, Col. B2 32
Cienfuegos, Cuba C3 35
Cieszyn, Pol. D5 7
Cihuatlán, Mex. n11 34
Cilacap, Indon. G3 19
Cimarron, Kans. E3 62
Cimarron, N. Mex. A6 48
Cimarron, co., Okla. e8 79
Cimarron, riv., U.S. C7 45
Cîmpina, Rom. C7 10
Cimpulung, Rom. C7 10
Cimpulung Moldovenesc, Rom. B7 10
Cincinnati, Ohio C1, o12 78
Cinnaminson, N.J. D3 74
Cinnaminson Township, N.J. *C2 74
Cintalapa de Figueroa, Mex. D6 34
Cinto, mtn., Fr. *C2 9
Circle, Mont. C11 70
Circle Pines, Minn. *E5 67
Circleville, Ohio C3 78
Cirebon, Indon. G3 19
Cirencester, Eng. E6 4
Cisco, Tex. C3 84
Cisneros, Col. B2 32
Cissna Park, Ill. C6 58
Cisterna di Latina, It. h9 9
Citac, mtn., Peru D2 31
Citlaltépet (Pico de
  Orizaba), vol., Mex. n15 34
Citronelle, Ala. D1 46
Citrus, co., Fla. D4 54
Citrus Heights, Calif. *C3 50
Cittadella, It. .B3 9
Città de Castello, It. C4 9
City View, S.C. B3 82
Ciudad Acuña, Mex. B4 34
Ciudad Allende, Mex. B4 34
Ciudad Altamirano, Mex. n13 34
Ciudad Bolívar, Ven. B5 32
Ciudad Camargo, Mex. B3 34
Ciudad Chetumal, Mex. D7 34
Ciudad del Carmen, Mex. D6 34
Ciudad del Maíz, Mex. C5 34
Ciudad de Naucalpan de
  Juárez, Mex. h9 34
Ciudad de Valles, Mex. C5, m14 34
Ciudad de Villaldama, Mex. B4 34
Ciudad Dr. Hernández
  Alvarez, Mex. *m13 34
Ciudad Guzmán, Mex. D4, n12 34
Ciudad Hidalgo, Mex. n13 34
Ciudad Ixtepec, Mex. D5 34
Ciudad Jiménez, Mex. B4 34
Ciudad Juárez, Mex. A3 34
Ciudad Lerdo, Mex. B4 34
Ciudad Madero, Mex. C5 34
Ciudad Mante, Mex. C5 34
Ciudad Melchor Múzquiz,
  Mex. B4 34
Ciudad Mendoza, Mex. n15 34
Ciudad Obregón, Mex. B3 34
Ciudad Ojeda, Ven. A3 32
Ciudad Real, Sp. C4 8
Ciudad Real, prov., Sp. *C4 8
Ciudad Serdán, Mex. n14 34
Ciudad Victoria, Mex. C5 34

Cividale de Friuli, It. A4 9
Civitanova Marche, It. C4 9
Civitavecchia, It. C3 9
Cizre, Tur. D14 14
Clackamas, Oreg. h12 80
Clackamas, co., Oreg. B4 80
Clackmannan, co., Scot *B5 4
Claflin, Kans. D5 61
Claiborne, co.,Miss. D3 68
Claiborne, co., Tenn. C10 83
Claiborne, par.,La. B2 63
Clairfield, Tenn. C10 83
Clairton, Pa. .F2 81
Clallam, co.,Wash. A1 86
Clamart, Fr. .g10 5
Clamecy, Fr. .D5 5
Clanton, Ala. C3 46
Clara City, Minn. F3 67
Clare, Austl. .F6 25
Clare, Mich. .E6 66
Clare, co., Ire. D2 4
Clare, co., Mich. E6 66
Claremont, Calif. m13 50
Claremont, N.H. E3 73
Claremont, mtn., Cal. C3 50
Claremore, Okla. A6 79
Clarence, Iowa C6 60
Clarence, Mo. B5 69
Clarence, N.Y. *C2 75
Clarendon, Ark. C4 49
Clarendon, Tex. B2 84
Clarendon, co., S.C. D7 82
Clarendon Hills, Ill. k9 58
Clarenville, Newf., Can. D4 44
Claresholm, Alta., Can. D4 38
Claridge, Pa. F2 81
Clarinda, Iowa D2 60
Clarion, Iowa B4 60
Clarion, Pa. .D3 81
Clarion, co.,Pa. D2 81
Clark, N.J. B4 74
Clark, S. Dak. F8 77
Clark, co., Ark. C2 49
Clark, co., Idaho E6 57
Clark, co., Ill. D6 88
Clark, co., Ind. H6 59
Clark, co., Kans. E4 61
Clark, co., Ky. C5 62
Clark, co., Mo. A6 69
Clark, co., Nev. C4 72
Clark, co., Ohio C2 78
Clark, co., S. Dak. F8 77
Clark, co., Wash. D3 86
Clark, co., Wis. D3 88
Clark, mtn.,Mo. D7 69
Clarkdale, Ariz. B2 48
Clarke, co., Ala. D2 46
Clarke, co., Ga. C3 55
Clarke, co., Iowa D4 60
Clarke, co., Miss. C5 68
Clarke, co., Va. A4 85
Clarks Harbour, N.S., Can. F4 43
Clarkfield, Minn. F3 67
Clark Mills, N.Y. *B5 75
Clarks, La. B3 63
Clarksburg, W. Va. B4, k10 87
Clarksdale, Miss. A3 68
Clarks Green, Pa. *D10 75
Clarks Harbour, N.S., Can. F4 43
Clarks Summit, Pa. m18 81
Clarkston, Ga. h8 55
Clarkston, Wash. C8 86
Clarksville, Ark. B2 49
Clarksville, Ind. H6 59
Clarksville, Iowa B5 60
Clarksville, Tenn. A4 83
Clarksville, Tex. C5 84
Clarksville, Va. D4 84
Clarkton, Mo. E8 69
Clatskanie, Oreg. A3 80
Clatsop, co., Oreg. A3 80
Claude, Tex. .B3 84
Clausthal-Zellerfeld, Ger.,
  Fed. Rep. of C5 6
Clawson, Mich. o15 66
Claxton, Ga. .D5 55
Clay, Ky. C2 62
Clay, co., Ala. B4 46
Clay, co., Ark. A5 49
Clay, co., Fla. B5 54
Clay, co., Ga. E2 55
Clay, co., Ill. .E5 58
Clay, co., Ind. F3 59
Clay, co., Iowa A2 60
Clay, co., Kans. C6 61
Clay, co., Ky. C6 62
Clay, co., Minn. D2 67
Clay, co., Miss. B5 68
Clay, co., Mo. B3 69
Clay, co., Nebr. D7 71
Clay, co., N.C. f9 76
Clay, co., S. Dak. H9 77
Clay, co., Tenn. C8 83

Clay, co., Tex. C3 84
Clay, co., W. Va. C3 87
Clay Center, Kans. C6 61
Clay City, Ill. E5 58
Clay City, Ind. F3 59
Claycomo Mo. *B3 69
Claymont, Del. A7 53
Claypool, Ariz. C3, D3 48
Claysburg, Pa. F5 81
Clayville, Pa. F1 81
Clayton, Ala. D4 46
Clayton, Del. B6 53
Clayton, Ga. B3 55
Clayton, Ill. C3 58
Clayton, La. C4 63
Clayton, Mo. C7, f13 69
Clayton, N.J. D2 74
Clayton, N. Mex. A7 48
Clayton, N.Y. A4, f8 75
Clayton, N.C. B4 76
Clayton, Okla. C6 79
Clayton, co., Ga. C2 55
Clayton, co., Iowa B6 60
Clear Brook, B.C., Can. f13 37
Clear Creek, co., Colo. B5 51
Clearfield, Pa. D5 81
Clearfield, Utah A5 72
Clearfield, co., Pa. D4 81
Clear Lake, Iowa A4 60
Clear Lake, S. Dak. F9 77
Clearlake Highlands, Calif. C2 50
Clear Lake Shores, Tex. r14 84
Clearwater, Fla. E4, p10 54
Clearwater, Kans. E6 61
Clearwater, S. C. E4 82
Clearwater, co., Idaho C3 57
Clearwater co., Minn. C3 67
Clearwater, mts., Idaho C2 57
Cleburne, Tex. C4, n9 84
Cleburne, co., Ala. B4 46
Cleburne, co., Ark. B3 49
Cle Elum, Wash. B5 86
Clementon, N.J. D3 74
Clemmons, N.C. A2 76
Clemson, S.C. B2 82
Clemson College, S.C. *B2 82
Clendenin, W. Va. C3, m13 87
Cleona, Pa. F9 81
Clermont, Austl. D8 25
Clermont, Que., Can. B7 42
Clermont, Fla. D5 54
Clermont, co., Ohio C1 78
Clermont-Ferrand, Fr. E5 5
Clermont-l'Hérault, Fr. F5 5
Cleveland, Miss. B3 68
Cleveland, Ohio A4, h9 78
Cleveland, Okla. A5 79
Cleveland, Tenn. D9 83
Cleveland, Tex. D5 84
Cleveland, co.,Ark. D3 49
Cleveland, co., N.C. B1 76
Cleveland, co., Okla. B4 79
Cleveland, mtn., Mont. B3 70
Cleveland Heights, Ohio A4, g9 78
Cleves, Ohio o12 78
Clewiston, Fla. F6 54
Clichy *-la-Garenne*, Fr. C5, g10 5
Cliffside, N.C. B1, f11 76
Cliffside Park, N.J. h9 74
Cliffwood, N.J. *C4 74
Cliffwood Beach, N.J. *C4 74
Clifton, Ariz. C4 48
Clifton, Ill. C6 58
Clifton, N.J. B4, h8 74
Clifton, S.C. B4 82
Clifton, Tex. D4 84
Clifton Forge (Independent City), Va. D3 85
Clifton Heights, Pa. p20 81
Clifton Springs, N.Y. C3 75
Climax, Colo. B4 51
Clinch, co., Ga. F4 55
Clinch, mtn., Va. f8 85
Clinchco, co., Va. e9 85
Clinchfield, N.C. *F10 76
Clingmans Dome, mtn., N. Car. f9 76
Clint, Tex. o11 84
Clinton, Ark. B3 49
Clinton, B.C., Can. D7 37
Clinton, Ont., Can. D3 41
Clinton, Conn. D6 52
Clinton, Ill. D5 58
Clinton, Ind. E3 59
Clinton, Iowa C7 60
Clinton, Ky. f9 62
Clinton, La. D4 63
Clinton, Maine D3 64
Clinton, Md. C4 53
Clinton, Mass. B4 65
Clinton, Mich. F7 66
Clinton, Miss. C3 68
Clinton, Mo. C4 69
Clinton, N.J. B3 74
Clinton, N.Y. B5 75
Clinton, N.C. C4 76
Clinton, Ohio *A4 78
Clinton, Okla. B3 79
Clinton, S.C. C4 82
Clinton, Tenn. C9, m13 83
Clinton, Utah B3 72
Clinton, Wash. B3 86
Clinton, Wis. F5 88
Clinton, co., Ill. E4 58
Clinton, co., Ind. D4 59
Clinton, co., Iowa C7 60
Clinton, co., Ky. D4 62
Clinton, co., Mich. F6 66
Clinton, co., Mo. B3 69
Clinton, co., N.Y. f11 75
Clinton, co., Ohio C2 78
Clinton, co., Pa. D6 81
Clintonville, Wis. D5 88
Clintwood, Va. e9 85
Clio, Ala. D4 46
Clio, Mich. E7 66
Clio, S.C. B8 82
Cloncurry, Austl. D7 25
Clonmel, Ire. D3 4
Cloquet, Minn. D6 67
Closter, N.J. B5, h9 74
Clothier, W. Va. n12 87
Cloud, co., Kans. C6 61
Cloud, peak, Wyo. A5 89
Clover, S.C. A5 82
Cloverdale, Calif. C2 50
Cloverdale, B.C., Can. f13 37
Cloverleaf, Tex. *E5 84
Cloverport, Ky. C3 62
Clovis, Calif. D4 50
Clovis, N. Mex. B7 48
Cluj-Napoca, Rom. B6 10
Clute, Tex. r14 84
Clyde, Kans. C6 61
Clyde, N.Y. B4 75
Clyde, Ohio A3 78
Clyde, Tex. C3 84
Clydeband, Scot. C4 4
Clyde Hill, Wash. *B3 86
Clymer, Pa. E3 81
Coachella, Calif. F5 50
Coahoma, Tex. C2 84
Coahoma, co., Miss. A3 68
Coahuila, state, Mex. B4 34
Coal, co., Okla. C5 79
Coal City, Ill. B5 58
Coalcomán *de* Matamoros, Mex. D4, n12 34
Coaldale, Alta., Can. E4 38
Coaldale, Pa. E10 81
Coal Fork, W. Va. C3, m12 87
Coalgate, Okla. C5 79
Coalgood, Ky. D6 62
Coal Grove, Ohio D3 78
Coal Hill, Ark. B2 49
Coalinga, Calif. D3 50
Coalport, Pa. E4 81
Coaltown, Pa. *E1 81
Coalville, Utah A6, C2 72
Coalwood, W. Va. *D3 87
Coast, mts., B.C. B3, m16 37
Coast, ranges, Cal. B2 50
Coamo, P.R. *G11 35
Coatbridge, Scot. C5 4
Coatepec, Mex. n15 34
Coatepeque, Guat. *E6 34
Cobalt, Ont. p19 41
Cobán, guat. d6 34
Cobden, Ont.,Can. B8 41
Cobden, Ill. F4 58
Cobequid, mts., N.S., Can. D5 43
Cobh, Ire. E2 4
Cobija, Bol. E4 27
Cobleskill, N.Y. C6 75
Cobourg, Ont., Can. D6 41
Coburg, Ger. Fed. Rep. of C5 6
Coburn, mtn., Maine C2 64
Cocentaina, Sp. C5 8
Cochabamba, Bol. C2 29
Cochabamba, dept., Bol. C2 29
Cochin, India G6 20
Cochin China, reg., Viet. *D3 19
Cochise, co., Ariz. D4 48
Cochituate, Mass. g10 65
Cochran, Ga. D3 55
Cochran, co., Tex. C1 84
Cochrane, Alta., Can. D3 38
Cochrane, Ont., Can. o19 41
Cochrane, dist., Ont. e9 41
Cochranton, Pa. C1 81
Cocke, co., Tenn. D10 83
Cockeysville, Md. B4 53
Cockrell Hill, Tex. n10 84
Cocoa, Fla. D6 54
Cocoa Beach, Fla. D6 54
Cocoa West, Fla. *D6 54
Coconino, co., Ariz. B2 48
Cocula, Mex. C4, m12 34
Codington, co.,S. Dak. F8 77
Codogno, It. B2 9
Cody,Wyo. B3 89
Coeburn, Va. f9 85
Coesfeld, Ger., Fed. Rep. of C3 6
Coeur d'Alene, Idaho B2 57
Coeur d'Alene, mts., Idaho B2 57
Coffee, co., Ala. D3 46
Coffee, co., Ga. E4 55
Coffee, co., Tenn. B5 83
Coffey, co., Kans. D8 61
Coffeyville, Kans. E8 61
Coffs Harbour, Austl. E9 26
Cognac, Fr. E3 5
Cohasset, Mass. B6, h12 65
Cohocton, N.Y. C3 75
Cohoes, N.Y. C7 75
Coimbatore, India F6 20
Coimbra, Port. B1 8
Coín, Sp. D3 8
Cojedes, state, Ven. B4 32
Cojutepeque, Sal. *E7 34
Cokato, Minn. E4 67
Coke, co., Tex. D2 84
Cokeburg, Pa. *F1 81
Colac, Austl. I4 26
Cobert, co., Ala. A2 46
Colborne, Ont., Can. C7 41
Colby, Kans. C2 61
Colby, Wis. D3 88
Colchagua, prov., Chile A2 28
Colchester, Conn. C7 52
Colchester, Eng. E7 4
Colchester, Ill. C3 58
Colchester, co., N.S., Can. D6 43
Cold Lake, Alta., Can. B5 38
Cold Spring, Ky. A5, h14 62
Cold Spring, Minn. E4 67
Cold Spring, N.Y. *D7 75
Cold Spring Harbor, N.Y. F3 52
Coldwater, Kans. E4 61
Coldwater, Mich. G5 66
Coldwater, Miss. A4 68
Coldwater, Ohio B1 78
Cole, co., Mo. C5 69
Colebrook, N.H. B5 73
Cole Camp, Mo. C4 69
Coleman, Alta., Can. F3 52
Coleman, Fla. D4 54
Coleman, Mich. E6 66
Coleman, Tex. D3 84
Coleman, co., Tex. D3 84
Coleraine, Minn. C5 67
Coleraine, N. Ire. C3 4
Coles, co, Ill. D5 58
Colfax, Calif. C3 50
Colfax, Ill. C5 58
Colfax, Iowa C4 60
Colfax, La. C3 63
Colfax, Wash. C8 86
Colfax, Wis. D1 88
Colfax, co., Nebr. C8 71
Colfax, co., N. Mex. A6 48
Colima, Mex. D4, n12 34
Colima, state, Mex. D4, n12 34
College, Alsk. C10 47
Collegedale, Tenn. h11 83
College Heights, S.C. C7 82
College Park, Ga. C2, h8 55
College Park, Md. f9 53
College Place, Wash. C7 86
College Station, Tex. D4 84
Collegeville, Ind. C3 59
Collegeville (P.O.), Minn. *E4 67
Collegeville, Pa. F11 81
Colleton, co, S.C. F6 82
Colleyville, Tex. *C4 84
Collie, Austl. F2 25
Collier, co., Fla. F5 54
Collierville, Tenn. B2 83
Collin, co., Tex. C4 84
Collingdale, Pa. p20 81
Collingswood, N.J. D2 74
Collingsworth, co., Tex. B2 84
Collingwood, Ont., Can. C4 41
Collins, Miss. D4 68
Collins Park, Del. *A6 53
Collinsville, Ala. A4 46
Collinsville, Conn. B5 52
Collinsville, Ill. E4 58
Collinsville, Okla. A6 79
Collinsville, Va. *D3 85
Collister, Idaho F2 57
Colmar, Fr. C7 5
Colmar Manor, Md. f9 53
Colmenar Viejo, Sp. B4, o17 8
Cologne (Köln), Ger., Fed. Rep. of C3 6
Coloma, Mich. F4 66
Colomb-Bechar, see Bechar, Alg.
Colombes, Fr. g10 5
Colombia, Col. C3 32
Colombia, country, S.A. C3 32
Colombo, Sri Lanka G6 20
Colón, Arg. A5 28
Colón, Cuba C3 35
Colon, Mich. G5 66
Colón, Pan. B2 32
Colón, Archipiélago de, (Galapagos Islands), is., Ec g5 31
Colonia, N.J. *k7 74
Colonia, dept., Ur. *E1 30
Colonia del Sacramento, Ur. E1 30
Colonia Gustavo A. Madero, Mex. h9 34
Colonial Beach, Va. B6 85
Colonial Heights, (Independent City), Va. C5, n18 85
Colonial Manor, N.J. *D2 74
Colonial Park, Pa. *F8 81
Colonia Suiza, Ur. g8 28
Colonie, N.Y. *C7 75
Colorado, co., Tex. E4 84
Colorado, state, U.S. 51
Colorado, riv., Mex., U.S. C5 45
Colorado, riv., Tex. D3 84
Colorado City, Tex. C2 84
Colorado Springs, Colo. C6 51
Colored Hill, W. Va. *D3 87
Colotlan, Mex. C4, k12 34
Colquitt, Ga. E2 55
Colquitt, co., Ga. E3 55
Colton, Calif. *E5 50
Columbia, Ill. E3 58
Columbia, Ky. C4 62
Columbia, La. B3 63
Columbia, Miss. D4 68
Columbia, Mo. C5 69
Columbia, N.C. B6 76
Columbia, Pa. F9 81
Columbia, S.C. C5 82
Columbia, Tenn. B4 83
Columbia, co., Ark. D2 49
Columbia, co., Fla. B4 54
Columbia, co., Ga. C4 55
Columbia, co., N.Y. C7 75
Columbia, co., Oreg. B3 80
Columbia, co., Pa. D8 81
Columbia, co., Wash. C7 86
Columbia, co., Wis. E4 88
Columbia, mtn., Alta, Can. C2 38
Columbia, riv., Can.,U.S. G9 36
Columbia City, Ind. B7 59
Columbia Falls, Mont. B2 70
Columbia Heights, Minn. m12 67
Columbia Heights, Wash. *C3 86
Columbiana, Ala. B3 46
Columbiana, Ohio B5 78
Columbiana, co., Ohio B5 78
Columbia Station, Ohio *A3 78
Columbiaville, Mich. E7 66
Columbus, Ga. D2 55
Columbus, Ind. F6 59
Columbus, Kans. E9 61
Columbus, Miss. B5 68
Columbus, Mont. E7 70
Columbus, Nebr. C8 71
Columbus, Ohio C3, m11 78
Columbus, Tex. E4 84
Columbus, Wis. E4 88
Columbus, co., Ga. D2 55
Columbus, co., N.C. C4 76
Columbus Grove, Ohio B1 78
Columbus Junction, Iowa C6 60
Colusa, Calif. C2 50
Colusa, co., Calif. C2 50
Colver, Pa. E4 81
Colville, Wash. A8 86
Colwood, B.C.,Can. h12 37
Colwyn, Pa. *G11 81
Comacchio, It. B4 9
Comal, co., Tex. E3 84
Comalapa, Guat. E6 34
Comalcalco, Mex. D6 34
Comanche, Okla. C4 79
Comanche, Tex. D3 84
Comanche, co., Kans. E4 61
Comanche, co., Okla. C3 79
Comanche, co., Tex. D3 84
Combined Locks, Wis. h9 88
Combs, Ky. C6 62
Comerio, P.R. *G11 35
Comfort, Tex. E3 84
Comilla, Pak. D9 20
Comiso, It. F5 9
Comitán *de Dominguez*, Mex. D6 34
Commack, N.Y. *n15 75
Commentry, Fr. D5 5
Commerce, Calif. *E4 50
Commerce, Ga. B3 55
Commerce, Mich. *F7 66
Commerce, Okla. A7 79
Commerce, Tex. C5 84

Commerce City, Colo. B6 51
Commercy, Fr. C6 5
Communism, peak, Sov. Un. F10 13
Como, Que., Can. q18 42
Como, Colo. e11 86
Como, It. B2 9
Comodoro Rivadavia, Arg. D3 28
Comoros, country, Afr. C8 24
Comox, B.C., Can. E5 37
Compiègne, Fr. C5 5
Compostela, Mex. m11 34
Compton, Calif. n12 50
Compton, co., Que., Can. D6 42
Comstock, Mich. F5 66
Comstock Park, Mich. *E5 66
Conakry, Guinea G2 22
Concarneau, Fr. D2 5
Concepción, Arg. E2 29
Concepción, Chile B2 28
Concepción, prov., Chile B2 28
Concepción, Par. D4 29
Concepción, dept., Par. D4 29
Concepción del Oro, Mex. C4 34
Concepción del Uruguay, Arg. A5 28
Concho, co., Tex. D3 84
Concord, Calif. D4 50
Concord, Mass. B5, g10 65
Concord, Mich. F6 66
Concord, N.H. E4 73
Concord, N.C. B2 76
Concordia, Arg. A5 28
Concordia, Col. B2 32
Concordia, Kans. C6 61
Concordia, Mo. C4 69
Concordia, par., La. C4 63
Concrete, Wash. A4 86
Condobolin, Austl. F8 25
Condon, Oreg. B6 80
Conecuh, co., Ala. D2 46
Conegliano, It. B4 9
Conejos, co., Colo. D4 51
Conemaugh, Pa. F4 81
Conflans-Ste. Honorine, Fr. g9 5
Confluence, Pa. G3 81
Congamond, Mass. B2 65
Congers, N.Y. *D7 75
Congo, country, Afr. I7 22
Congo, The (Republic of
 the Congo), see Zaire, country, Afr.
Congo (Zaire), riv., Afr. H2 21
Conil, Sp. D2 8
Coniston, Ont., Can. A4, p19 41
Conjeeveram, see
 Kanchipuram, India
Connacht, prov., Ire. *D2 4
Conneaut, Ohio A5 78
Conneautville, Pa. C1 81
Connecticut, state, U.S. 52
Connell, Wash. C7 86
Connellsville, Pa. F2 81
Connersville, Ind. E7 59
Conning Towers, Conn. *D8 52
Conover, N.C. B1 76
Conrad, Iowa B5 60
Conrad, Mont. B5 70
Conroe, Tex. D5 84
Conselheiro Lafaiete, Braz. C4 30
Conshohocken, Pa. F11, o20 81
Consolación del Sur, Cuba C2 35
Constanța, Rom. C9 10
Constantia, N.Y. B5 75
Constantina, Sp. D3 8
Constantine, Alg. A6 22
Constantine, Mich. G5 66
Constantinople, see Istanbul,
 Tur.
Continental, peak, Wyo. D4 89
Constitución, Chile B2 28
Consuegra, Sp. C4 8
Contamana, Peru C2 31
Continental, Ohio A1 78
Contra Costa, co., Calif. D2 50
Contratación, Col. B3 32
Contrecoeur, Que., Can. D4 42
Contreras, Mex. h9 34
Contumaza, Peru C2 31
Convent, La. D5, h10 63
Converse, Ind. C6 59
Converse, S.C. B4 82
Converse, co., Wyo. C7 89
Convoy, Ohio B1 78
Conway, Ark. B3 49
Conway, Fla. *D5 54
Conway, N.H. D5 73
Conway, Pa. E1 81
Conway, S.C. D9 82
Conway, co., Ark. B3 49
Conway Springs, Kans. E6 66
Conyers, Ga. C2, h8 55
Conyngham, Pa. *D9 81
Cooch Behar, India C8 20
Cook, co., Ga. E3 55
Cook, co., Ill. B6 58

Cook, co., Minn. C8 67
Cooke, co., Tex. C4 84
Cookeville, Tenn. C8 83
Cookshire, Que., Can. D6 42
Cookstown, Ont., Can. C5 41
Cooleemee, N.C. B2 76
Coolidge, Ariz. C3, E2 48
Coolidge, Tex. D4 84
Cool Ridge, W. Va. D3 87
Cool Valley, Mo. *C7 69
Cooma, Austl. G8 25
Coonabarabran, Austl. F8 25
Coonamble, Austl. F8 25
Coon Rapids, Iowa C3 60
Coon Rapids, Minn. m12 67
Cooper, Tex. C5 84
Cooper, co., Mo. C5 69
Coopersburg, Pa. E11 81
Cooperstown, N.Y. C6 75
Cooperstown, N. Dak. C7 77
Coopersville, Mich. E5 66
Coos, co., N.H. B5 73
Coos, co., Oreg. D2 80
Coosa, co., Ala. C3 46
Coos Bay, Oreg. D2 80
Cootamundra, Austl. G7 26
Copainalá, Mex. D6 34
Copenhagen (København), Den. J5 11
Copiague, N.Y. G3 52
Copiah, co., Miss. D3 68
Copiapó, Chile E1 29
Coplay, Pa. *E10 81
Copley, Ohio *A4 78
Copparo, It. B3 9
Copper, mtn., Wyo. C5 89
Copperas Cove, Tex. D4 84
Copper Cliff, Ont., Can. A3 41
Copperhill, Tenn. D9 83
Coquille, Oreg. D2 80
Coquimbo, Chile E1 29
Coquimbo, prov., Chile A2 28
Corabia, Rom. D7 10
Coracora, Peru E3 31
Coral Gables, Fla. G6, s13 54
Coralville, Iowa D6 60
Coram, N.Y. n15 75
Coraopolis, Pa. E1, h13 81
Corato, It. D6 9
Corbeil, Fr. C5 5
Corbin, Ky. D5 62
Corcoran, Calif. D4 50
Corcoran, Minn. *E5 67
Cordele, Ga. E3 55
Cordell, Okla. B3 79
Cordillera, dept., Par. D4 29
Córdoba, Arg. A4 28
Córdoba, Mex. n15 34
Córdoba, Sp. D3 8
Córdoba, prov., Sp. *D3 8
Córdoba, prov., Arg. A4 28
Cordova, Ala. B2 46
Cordova, Alsk. C10, g19 47
Cordova, N.C. C3 76
Córdova, Peru D2 31
Cori, It. h9 9
Corigliano, It. E6 9
Corinna, Maine D3 64
Corinne, W. Va. D3 87
Corinth, Miss. A5 68
Corinth, N.Y. B7 75
Corinth, see Korinthos, Grc.
Corinto, Braz. B4 30
Corinto, Nic. H12 33
Cork, Ire. E2 4
Cork, co., Ire. E3 4
Corleone, It. F4 9
Çorlu, Tur. B6 14
Cormeilles-en-Parisis, Fr. g9 5
Cornelia, Ga. B3 55
Cornelius, N.C. B2 76
Cornelius, Oreg. g11 80
Cornell, Wis. C2 88
Corner Brook, Newf., Can. D3 44
Corning, Ark. A5 49
Corning, Calif. C2 50
Corning, Iowa D3 60
Corning, N.Y. C3 75
Corning, Ohio C3 78
Corno, mtn., It. C4 9
Cornwall, Ont., Can. B10 41
Cornwall, N.Y. D6 75
Cornwall, Pa. F9 81
Cornwall, see Cornwall-on-
 the-Hudson, N.Y.
Cornwall, co., Eng. *E4 4
Cornwall-on-the-Hudson, N.Y. D6 75
Cornwells Heights, Pa. o22 81
Coro, Ven. A4 32
Corona, Calif. F5, n13 50
Coronado, Calif. F5, o15 50
Coronation, Alta., Can. C5 38
Coronel, Chile B2 28
Coronel Dorrego, Arg. B4 28

Coronel Oviedo, Par. E4 29
Coronel Pringles, Arg. B4 28
Coronel Suárez, Arg. B4 28
Coropuna, mtn., Peru E3 31
Corozal, Col. B2 32
Corpus Christi, Tex. F4 84
Corral de Almaguer, Sp. C4 8
Corrales, Col. B3 32
Corralillo, Cuba C3 35
Correctionville, Iowa B2 60
Corréze, dept., Fr. *E4 5
Corrientes, Arg. E4 29
Corrigan, Tex. D5 84
Corry, Pa. C2 81
Corse, dept., Fr. *C2 9
Corsica, isl., Eur. C2 9
Corsicana, Tex. C4 84
Corson, co., S. Dak. E4 77
Cortazar, Mex. C4, m13 34
Cortegana, Sp. D2 8
Corte Madera, Calif. *C2 50
Cortez, Colo. D1 51
Cortez, Fla. q10 54
Cortland, N.Y. C4 75
Cortland, Ohio A5 78
Cortland, co., N.Y. C4 75
Cortona, It. C3 9
Corumbá, Braz. B1 30
Çorum (Chorum), Tur. B10 14
Corunna, Ont., Can. E2 41
Corvallis, Oreg. C3, k11 80
Corunna, Mich. F6 66
Corydon, Ind. H5 59
Corydon, Iowa D4 60
Coryell, co., Tex. D4 84
Cosalá, Mex. C3 34
Cosamaloapan de Carpio, Mex. D5 34
Coscomatepec de Bravo, Mex. n15 34
Cosenza, It. E6 9
Cosmopolis, Wash. C2 86
Cosne -sur-Loire, Fr. D5 5
Costa Mesa, Calif. n13 50
Costa Rica, country, N.A. E8 34
Costilla, N. Mex. A6 48
Costilla, co., Colo. D5 51
Cotabato, Phil. D6 19
Cotabato, prov., Phil. *D6 19
Cotahuasi, Peru D2 31
Cotati, Calif. *C2 50
Côte-d'or, dept., Fr. *D6 5
Côtes-du-Nord, dept., Fr. *C2 5
Côtes-St. Luc, Que., Can. *D4 42
Cotija de la Paz, Mex. n12 34
Cotonou, Benin G5 22
Cotopaxi, prov., Ec. B2 31
Cotopaxi, vol., Ec. A2 31
Cottage City, Md. *C4 53
Cottage Grove, Oreg. D3 80
Cottage Grove, Wis. *E4 88
Cottage Hills, Ill. *E3 58
Cottbus, Ger. Dem. Rep. C7 6
Cotter, Ark. A3 49
Cottle, co., Tex. B2 84
Cotton, co., Okla. C3 79
Cottondale, Fla. B1, u16 54
Cotton Plant, Ark. B4 49
Cottonport, La. D3 63
Cotton Valley, La. B2 63
Cottonwood, Ala. D4 46
Cottonwood, Ariz. B3 48
Cottonwood, Calif. B2 50
Cottonwood, Idaho C2 57
Cottonwood, co., Minn. F3 67
Cottonwood Falls, Kans. D6 61
Cottonwood Heights, Utah D2 72
Cotuit, Mass. C7 65
Cotulla, Tex. E3 84
Coudekerque-Branche, Fr. B5 5
Coudersport, Pa. C5 81
Coulee City, Wash. B6 86
Coulee Dam, Wash. B7 86
Coulommiers, Fr. C5 5
Coulterville, Ill. D4 58
Council, Idaho E2 57
Council, mtn., Idaho E2 57
Council Bluffs, Iowa C2 60
Council Grove, Kans. D7 61
Country Club Hills, Ill. *B6 58
Country Club Hills, Mo. *C7 69
Country Homes, Wash. *B8 86
Coupar Angus, Scot. B5 4
Courbevoie, Fr. g10 5
Courtdale, Pa. *D9 81
Courtenay, B.C., Can. E5 37
Courtland, Calif. *C3 50
Courtland, Va. D5 85
Courtrai, see Kortrijk, Bel.
Coushatta, La. B2 63
Coutances, Fr. C3 5
Coutras, Fr. E3 5

Covedale, Ohio o12 78
Covelo, Calif. C2 50
Coventry, Conn. B7 52
Coventry, Eng. D6 4
Coventry, R.I. C10 52
Covilhã, Port. B2 8
Covina, Calif. m13 50
Covington, Ga. C3 55
Covington, Ind. D3 59
Covington, Ky. A5, h13 62
Covington, La. D5, h11 63
Covington, Ohio B1 78
Covington, Tenn. B2 83
Covington, (Independent City)
 Va. C3 85
Covington, co., Ala. D3 46
Covington, co., Miss. D4 68
Cowan, Tenn. B5 83
Cowansville, Que., Can. D5 42
Cowansville, Pa. E2 81
Cowen, mtn., Mont. E6 70
Cowes, Eng. E6 4
Coweta, Okla. B6 79
Coweta, co., Ga. C2 55
Cowley, co., Kans. E7 61
Cowlitz, co., Wash. C3 86
Cowpens, S.C. A4 82
Cowra, Austl. F7 26
Coxsackie, N.Y. C7 75
Coyame, Mex. B3 34
Coyoacán, Mex. H9, n14 34
Coyuca de Catalán, Mex. n13 34
Cozad, Nebr. D6 71
Cozumel, Mex. C7 34
Crab Orchard, W. Va. n13 87
Crabtree, Pa. F3 81
Crabtree Mills, Que., Can. D4 42
Cradock, S. Afr. G5 24
Crafton, Pa. k13 81
Craig, Colo. A3 51
Craig, co., Okla. A6 79
Craig, co., Va. C2 85
Craig Beach, Ohio *B5 78
Craighead, co., Ark. B5 49
Craigsville, Va. B3 85
Crailsheim, Ger., Fed. Rep of D5 6
Craiova, Rom. C6 10
Cramerton, N.C. B1 76
Cranberry Portage, Man., Can. B10 40
Cranbrook, B.C., Can. E10 37
Cranbury, N.J. C3 74
Crandon, Wis. C5 88
Crane, Mo. E4 39
Crane, Tex. D1 84
Crane, co., Tex. D1 84
Crane, mtn., Oreg. E6 80
Cranford, N.J. B4 74
Cranston, R.I. B11 52
Crateús, Braz. *D6 27
Crato, Braz. *D7 27
Craven, co., N.C. B5 76
Crawford, Nebr. B2 71
Crawford, co., Ark. B1 49
Crawford, co., Ga. D2 55
Crawford, co., Ill. D6 58
Crawford, co., Ind. H4 59
Crawford, co., Iowa B2 60
Crawford, co., Kans. E9 61
Crawford, co., Mich. D6 66
Crawford, co., Mo. D6 69
Crawford, co., Ohio B2 78
Crawford, co., Pa. C1 81
Crawford, co., Wis. E3 88
Crawfordsville, Ind. D4 59
Crawfordville, Ga. C4 55
Crazy, peak, Mont. D6 70
Creedmoor, N.C. A4 76
Creek, co., Okla. B5 79
Creemore, Ont., Can. C4 41
Creighton, Sask., Can. C5 39
Creighton, Nebr. B8 71
Creighton, Pa. h14 81
Creighton Mine, Ont., Can. A3, p19 41
Creil, Fr. C5 5
Crema, It. B2 9
Cremona, It. B3 9
Crenshaw, Miss. A3 68
Crenshaw, co., Ala. D3 46
Cresaptown, Md. k13 53
Crescent, Okla. B4 79
Crescent City, Calif. B1 50
Crescent City, Fla. C5 54
Crescent City Northwest, Calif. *B1 50
Crescent Springs, Ky. h13 62
Cresco, Iowa A5 60
Cresskill, N.J. h9 74
Cresson, Pa. F4 81
Cressona, Pa. E9 81
Crest, Fr. E6 4
Crest Hill, Ill. *B5 58
Crestline, Calif. *E5 50
Crestline, Ohio B3 78
Crestmont, Pa. *F11 81

Creston, B.C., Can.	E9 37	Cross Plains, Tex.	C3 84
Creston, Newf., Can.	E4 44	Cross Plains, Wis.	E4 88
Creston, Iowa	C3 60	Crossville, Ill.	E5 58
Creston, Ohio	B4 78	Crossville, Tenn.	D8 83
Crestview, Fla.	u15 54	Croswell, Mich.	E8 66
Crestwood, Ill.	*B6 58	Crothersville, Ind.	G6 59
Crestwood, Mo.	*C7 69	Crotone, It.	E6 9
Crete, Ill.	B6, m9 58	Croton-on-Hudson, N.Y.	D7, m15 75
Crete, Nebr.	D9 71	Crouse, N.C.	B1 76
Crete, isl., Grc.	E5 14	Crow, peak, Mont.	D5 70
Crete, sea, Grc.	E5 14	Crow Agency, Mont.	E9 70
Creuse, dept., Fr.	*D4 5	Crowell, Tex.	C3 84
Creutzwald, Fr.	C7 5	Crowley, La.	D3 63
Creve Coeur, Ill.	C4 58	Crowley, co., Colo.	C7 51
Creve Coeur, Mo.	*C7 69	Crown Point, Ind.	B3 59
Crevillente, Sp.	C5 8	Crown Point, N.Y.	B7 75
Crewe, Eng.	D5 4	Crow Wing, co., Minn.	D4 67
Crewe, Va.	C4 85	Croydon, Pa.	F12 81
Cricket, N.C.	A1 76	Crozet, Va.	B4 85
Cridersville, Ohio	B1 78	Cruces, Cuba	C3 35
Crieff, Scot.	B5 4	Crucible, Pa.	G1 81
Crimmitschau, Ger. Dem. Rep.	C6 6	Cruden Bay, Scot.	B6 4
Crisana, reg., Rom.	B6 10	Crum Lynne, Pa.	*E1 81
Crisfield, Md.	E6 53	Cruz Alta, Braz.	D2 10
Crisp, co., Ga.	E3 55	Cruz del Eje, Arg.	A4 28
Cristóbal Colón, mtn., Col.	A3 32	Cruzeiro, Braz.	C4 30
Crittenden, co., Ark.	B5 49	Crystal, Minn.	m12 67
Crittenden, co., Ky.	e9 62	Crystal Beach, Fla.	D4 54
Croatia, reg. Yugo.	*C2 10	Crystal City, Mo.	C7, g13 69
Croatia, rep., Yugo.	C2 10	Crystal City, Tex.	E3 84
Crocker, Mo.	D5 69	Crystal Falls, Mich.	B2 66
Crockett, Calif.	g8 50	Crystal Lake, Fla.	u16 54
Crockett, Tex.	D5 84	Crystal Lake, Ill.	A5, h8 58
Crockett, co., Tenn.	B2 83	Crystal Lakes, Ohio	C1 78
Crockett, co., Tex.	B2 84	Crystal River, Fla.	D4 54
Croghan, N.Y.	B5 75	Crystal Springs, Miss.	D3 68
Cromona, Ky.	C7 62	Csongrád, Hung.	B5 10
Cromwell, Conn.	C6 52	Csongrád, co., Hung.	*B5 10
Crook, co., Oreg.	C6 80	Csorna, Hung.	B3 10
Crook, co., Wyo.	B8 89	Cuajimalpa, Mex.	h9 34
Crookston, Minn.	C2 67	Cuauhtémoc, Mex.	B3 34
Crooksville, Ohio	C3 78	Cuautepec, Mex.	g9 34
Crosby, Minn.	D5 67	Cuautla, Mex.	n14 34
Crosby, Miss.	D2 68	Cuba, Ill.	C3 58
Crosby, N. Dak.	A2 77	Cuba, Mo.	C6 69
Crosby, Tex.	r14 84	Cuba, N.Y.	C2 75
Crosby, co., Tex.	C2 84	Cuba, country, N.A.	C3 35
Crosby, mtn., Wyo.	C3 89	Cuba City, Wis.	F3 88
Crosbyton, Tex.	C2 84	Cucamonga, Calif.	*E5 50
Cross, co., Ark.	B5 49	Cúcuta, Col.	B3 32
Cross City, Fla.	C3 54	Cudahy,Calif.	*F4 50
Crossett, Ark.	D4 49	Cudahy, Wis.	F6, n12 88
Cross Mill, N.C.	f10 76	Cuddalore, India	F6 20

Cuddapah, India	F6 20	Cunnamulla, Austl.	E8 25
Cuddy, Pa.	*B5 81	Cupertino, Calif.	*D2 50
Cuenca, Ec.	B2 31	Curaçao, isl.,Neth.	
Cuenca, Sp.	B4 8	Antilles	A4 32
Cuenca, prov. Sp.	*B4 8	Curacautín, Chile	B2 28
Cuencamé de Ceniceros, Mex.	C4 34	Curicó, Chile	B2 28
Cuernavaca, Mex.	D5, n14 34	Curicó, prov., Chile	A2 28
Cuero, Tex	E4 84	Curitiba, Braz.	D3 30
Cuetzalan, Mex.	m15 34	Currais Novos, Braz.	*D7 27
Cuevas, Sp.	D5 8	Currituck, co.,N.C.	A6 76
Cuiabá, Braz.	B1 30	Curry, co., N. Mex.	B7 48
Cuicatlán, Mex.	o15 34	Curry, co., Oreg.	E2 80
Culberson, co., Tex.	o12 84	Curtea-de-Arges, Rom.	C7 10
Culbertson, Mont.	B12 70	Curtici, Rom.	B5 10
Culbertson, Nebr.	D5 71	Curtis, Nebr.	D5 71
Culhuacán, Mex.	h9 34	Curtisville, Pa.	E1, h14 81
Culiacán, Mex.	C3 34	Curug, Yugo.	C5 10
Cúllar de Baza, Sp.	D4 8	Curuzú Cuatia, Arg.	E4 29
Cullen, La.	B2 63	Curvelo, Braz.	B4 30
Cullera, Sp.	C5 8	Curwensville, Pa.	E4 81
Cullman, Ala.	A3 46	Cushing, Okla.	B5 79
Cullman, co., Ala.	A3 46	Cusset, Fr.	D5 5
Culloden, W. Va.	*C2 87	Custer, S. Dak.	G2 77
Cullowhee, N.C.	f9 76	Custer, co., Colo.	C5 51
Culmore, Va.	*B5 85	Custer, co., Idaho	E4 57
Culpeper, Va.	B4 85	Custer, co., Mont.	D11 70
Culpeper, co., Va.	B5 85	Custer, co., Nebr.	C6 79
Culver, Ind.	B5 59	Custer, co., Okla.	B2 71
Culver City, Calif.	m12 50	Custer, co., S. Dak.	G2 77
Cumaná, Ven.	A5 32	Cut Bank, Mont.	B4 70
Cumberland, B.C., Can.	E5 37	Cutchogue, N.Y.	m16 75
Cumberland, Ind.	E6, k11 59	Cutervo, Peru	C2 31
Cumberland, Ky.	D7 62	Cuthbert, Ga.	E2 55
Cumberland, Md.	k13 53	Cutler, Calif.	*D4 50
Cumberland, Wis.	C2 88	Cutler Ridge, Fla.	*G6 54
Cumberland, co., N.S., Can.	D5 43	Cutack, India	D8 20
Cumberland, co., Eng.	*C5 4	Cutten, Calif.	*B1 50
Cumberland, co.,Ill.	D5 58	Cuxhaven, Ger., Fed. Rep. of	B4 6
Cumberland, co., Ky.	D4 62	Cuyahoga, co., Ohio	A4 78
Cumberland, co., Maine	E2 64	Cuyahoga Falls, Ohio	A4 78
Cumberland, co., N.J.	E2 74	Cuzco, Peru	D3 31
Cumberland, co., N.C.	C4 76	Cuzco, dept., Peru	D3 31
Cumberland, co., Pa.	F7 81	Cynthiana, Ky.	B5 62
Cumberland, co., Tenn.	D8 83	Cypress, Calif.	*F4 50
Cumberland, co., Va.	C4 85	Cypress Quarters, Fla.	E6 54
Cumberland, mtn., Ky., Tenn.	C9 83	Cyprus, country, Asia	E9 14
Cumberland, riv., U.S.	C10 45	Cyprus, isl., Asia	E9 14
Cuming, co., Nebr.	C9 71	Cyrenaica, prov., Libya	B2 23
Cumming, Ga.	B2 55	Cyril, Okla.	C3 79
Cumpas, Mex.	A3 34	Czechoslovakia, country, Eur.	D4 7
Cumra, Tur.	D9 14	Czersk, Pol.	B4 7
Cuneo, It.	B1 9	Częstochowa, Pol.	C5 7

D

Da'an, China	D2 18	Dahlonega, Ga.	B3 55
Dab, Pol., (part of Katowice)	g9 7	Dailey, W. Va.	C5 87
Dab, Pol., (part of Szczecin)	B3 7	Daimiel, Sp.	C4 8
Dabeiba, Col.	B2 32	Daingerfield, Tex.	C5 84
Dablice, Czech.	n18 7	Daio, Jap.	o15 18
Dąbrowa, Pol.	C6 7	Dairen, see Lüda, China	
Dąbrowa Gornicza, Pol.	C5, g10 7	Dairy Valley, Calif.	*F4 50
Dacca, Bngl.	D9 20	Daisetta, Tex.	D5 84
Dachau, Ger., Fed. Rep. of	D5 6	Daisytown, Pa.	*F1 81
Dade, co., Fla.	G6 54	Dajabon, Dom. Rep.	E8 35
Dade, co., Ga.	B1 55	Dakar, Sen.	F1 22
Dade, co., Mo.	D4 69	Dakota, co., Minn.	F5 67
Dade City, Fla.	D4 54	Dakota, co., Nebr.	B9 71
Dadeville, Ala.	C4 46	Dakota City, Nebr.	B9 71
Dadra and Nagar Haveli,		Da Lat, Viet.	C3 19
ter., India	*D5 20	D'Albertis Dome, mtn.,	
Dadu, Pak.	C4 20	Pap. N. Gui.	h11 25
Daet, Phil.	*C6 19	Dalby, Austl.	E9 25
Daggett, co., Utah	A7 72	Dale, Ind.	H4 59
Dagupan, Phil.	n13 19	Dale, Pa.	*E4 81
Dahlgren, Va.	B5 85	Dale, co., Ala.	D4 46

Daleville, Ind.	D6 59	Dalnyaya, Sov. Un.	D11 18
Dalhart, Tex.	A1 84	Dalrymple, mtn., Austl.	D8 25
Dalhousie, N.B., Can.	A3 43	Dalton, Ga.	B2 55
Dall, mtn., Alsk.	f15 47	Dalton, Mass.	B1 65
Dallam, co., Tex.	A1 84	Dalton, Ohio	B4 78
Dallas, Ga.	C2 55	Dalton, Pa.	C10 81
Dallas, N.C.	B1 76	Daltonganj, India	D7 20
Dallas, Oreg.	C3 80	Dalton Gardens, Idaho	B2 57
Dallas, Pa.	D10, m17 81	Daly City, Calif.	h8 50
Dallas, Tex.	C4, n10 84	Damān, India	D5 20
Dallas, co., Ala.	C2 46	Damanhūr, Eg.	G8 14
Dallas, co., Ark.	D3 49	Damariscotta, Maine	D3 64
Dallas, co., Iowa	C3 60	Damascus, Md.	B3 53
Dallas, co., Mo.	D4 69	Damascus, Va.	f10 85
Dallas, co., Tex.	C4 84	Damascus (Dimashq), Syr.	F11 14
Dallas Center, Iowa	C4 60	Da Nang, Viet.	B3 19
Dallas City, Ill.	C2 58	Dana Point, Calif.	*F5 50
Dallastown, Pa.	G8 81	Danbury, Conn.	D3 52
Dalmatia, reg., Yugo	D3 10	Dandong, China	C9 17
Dalmellington, Scot.	C4 4	Dane, co., Wis.	E4 88
Dalnerechensk, Sov. Un.	E16 13	Dania, Fla.	F6, r13 54

Daniels, co., Mont. B11   70
Danielson, Conn. B9   52
Dannemora, N.Y. f11   75
Dannevirke, N.Z. N16   26
Dans, mtn., Md. k13   53
Dansalan, Phil. *D6   19
Dansville, N.Y. C3   75
Dante, Som. F8   23
Dante, Va. f9   85
Danube, riv., Eur. F10   3
Danubyu, Bur. *E10   20
Danvers, Mass. A6, f12   65
Danville, Ark. B2   49
Danville, Calif. h9   50
Danville, Que., Can. D5   42
Danville, Ill. C6   58
Danville, Ind. E4   59
Danville, Ky. C5   62
Danville, Ohio B3   78
Danville, Pa. E8   81
Danville (Independent City), Va. D3   85
Danville East, Pa. *D8   81
Danzig see Gdánsk, Pol.
Daphne, Ala. E2   46
Dar'a, Syr. F11   14
Darabani, Rom. A8   10
Darasun, Sov. Un. D14   13
Darbhanga, India C8   20
Darby, Pa. G11, p20   81
Dardanelle, Ark. B2   49
Dare, co., N.C. B7   76
Darenbe, Tur. C11   14
Dar-es-Salaam, Tan. B7   24
Darien, Conn. E3   52
Darien, Wis. F5   88
Darjeeling, India C8   20
Dark Cove, Newf., Can. *D4   44
Darke, co., Ohio B1   78
Darling Rante, mts., Austl. F2   25
Darling, riv., Aust. E5   26
Darlington, Eng. C6   4
Darlington, S.C. C8   82
Darlington, Wis. F3   88
Darlington, Co., S.C. C7   82
Darlowo, Pol. A4   7
Darmstadt, Ger., Fed.
  Rep. of D4   6
Darnah (Derna), Libya B2   23
Darrah, mtn., Alta. E3   38
Darrington, Wash. A4   86
Darrow, La. h10   63
Dartmouth, N.S., Can. E6   43
Dartmouth, Eng. E5   4
Daruvar, Yugo C3   10
Darwin, Austl. B5   25
Dassel, Minn. E4   67
Datong, China D7   17
Daugavpils, Sov. Un. D6   12
Dauphin, Man., Can. D1, g7   40
Dauphin, co., Pa. F8   81
Dauphiné, former prov., Fr. E6   5
Davao, Phil. D7   19
Davao, prov., Phil. *D7   19
Davenport, Fla. D5   54
Davenport, Iowa C7, g10   60
Davenport, Okla. B5   79
Davenport, Wash. B7   86
David, Pan. B1   32
David City, Nebr. C8   71
Davidson, Sask., Can. F3   39
Davidson, N.C. B2   76
Davidson, co., N.C. B2   76
Davidson, co., Tenn. A5   83
Davie, Fla. F6, r13   54
Davie, co., N.C. B2   76
Daviess, co., Ind. G3   59
Daviess, co., Ky. C2   72
Daviess, co., Mo. B3   69
Davis, Calif. C3   50
Davis, Okla. C4   79
Davis, W. Va. B5   87
Davis, co., Iowa D4   60
Davis, co., Utah A5   72
Davis, mtn. Pa. G3   81
Davison, Mich. E7   66
Davison, co., S. Dak. G7   77
Davisville, R.I. C11   52
Davos, Switz. E4   6
Davy, W. Va. D3   87
Dawes, co., Nebr. B2   71
Dawson, Yukon, Can. D6   36
Dawson, Ga. E2   55
Dawson, Minn. F2   67
Dawson, Tex. D4   84
Dawson, co., Ga. B2   55
Dawson, co., Mont. C11   70
Dawson, co., Nebr. D6   71
Dawson, co., Tex. C1   84
Dawson, mtn., B.C., Can. D9   37
Dawson Creek, B.C., Can. B7, m8   37
Dawson Springs, Ky. C2   62
Dax, Fr. F3   5
Daxian, China E6   17

Day, co., S. Dak. E8   77
Dayrūt, Eg. C4   23
Dayton, Ky. h14   62
Dayton, Ohio C1   78
Dayton, Tenn. D8   83
Dayton, Tex. D5, q15   84
Dayton, Va. B4   85
Dayton, Wash. C8   86
Daytona Beach, Fla. C5   54
Daytona Beach Shores, Fla. *C6   54
Dayville, Conn. B9   52
De Aar, S. Afr. G4   24
Dead Indian, peak, Wyo. B3   89
Dead Knoll, mtn., Wyo. D2   89
Deadwood, S. Dak. F2   77
Deaf Smith, co., Tex. B1   84
Deal N.J. C4   74
Deale, Md. C4   53
Déan Funes, Arg. A4   28
Dearborn, Mich. F7, p15   66
Dearborn, co., Ind. F8   59
Dearborn Heights, Mich. p15   66
Death, valley, Calif. D5   50
Deauville, Fr. C4   5
De Baca, co., N. Mex. B6   48
Debaltsevo, Sov. Un. q21   12
Debar, Yugo. E5   10
De Bary, Fla. D5   54
Dębica, Pol. C6   7
Dębno, Pol. B3   7
Deboullie, mtn., Maine B4   64
Debrecen, Hung. B5   10
Decatur, Ala. A3   46
Decatur, Ga. C2, h8   55
Decatur, Ill. D5   58
Decatur, Ind. C8   59
Decatur, Mich. F5   66
Decatur, Miss. C4   68
Decatur, Tex. C4   84
Decatur, co., Ga. F2   55
Decatur, co., Ind. F6   59
Decatur, co., Iowa D5   60
Decatur, co., Kans. C3   61
Decatur, co., Tenn. B3   83
Decazeville, Fr. E5   5
Deccan, reg., India E6   20
Deception, mtn.,Wash. B2   86
Decherd, Tenn. B5   83
Děčin, Czech. C3   7
Decorah, Iowa A6   60
Dededo, Guam *F6   2
Dedham, Mass. B5, h11   65
Dedinovo, Sov. Un. n19   12
Dedu, China B3   18
Deephaven, Minn. F5, n11   67
Deep River, Ont., Can. A7   41
Deep River, Conn. D7   52
Deepwater, N.J. D2   74
Deer, mtn., Maine. C2   74
Deerfield, Ill. h9   58
Deerfield, Mass. G7   66
Deerfield Beach, Fla. F6   54
Deer Lake, Newf., Can. D3   44
Deer Lodge, Mont. D4   70
Deer Lodge, co., Mont. D3   70
Deer Park, N.Y. *F3   75
Deer Park, Wash. B8   86
Deer Park, Ohio o13   78
Deer Park, Tex. *E5   84
Deer River, Minn. C5   67
Defense Highway, Md. *C4   53
Defiance, Ohio A1   78
Defiance, co., Ohio A1   78
Defiance, mtn., Oreg. B5   80
De Forest, Wis. E4   88
De Funiak Springs, Fla. u15   54
Dège, China E4   17
Deggendorf, Ger., Fed.
  Rep. of D6   6
De Graff, Ohio B2   78
Dehiwaia-Mount Lavinia,
  Sri Lanka *G7   20
Dehra Dūn, India B6   20
Dej, Rom. B6   10
De Kalb, Ill. B5   58
De Kalb, Miss. C5   68
De Kalb, Tex. C5   84
De Kalb, co., Ala. A4   46
De Kalb, co., Ga. C2   55
De Kalb, co., Ill. B5   58
De Kalb, co., Ind. B7   59
De Kalb, co., Mo. B3   69
De Kalb, co., Tenn. D8   83
Delafield, Wis. *E5   88
Del Aire, Calif. *F4   50
Delanco, N.J. C3   74
De Land, Fla. C5   54
Delano, Calif. E4   50
Delano, Minn. E5   67
Delavan, Ill. C4   58
Delavan, Wis. F5   88
Delaware, Ohio B2   78
Delaware, co., Ind. D7   59

Delaware, co., Iowa B6   60
Delaware, co., N.Y. C5   75
Delaware, co., Ohio B2   78
Delaware, co., Okla. A7   79
Delaware, co., Pa. G11   81
Delaware, state, U.S. C11   45
Delaware, bay, Del. B7   53
Delaware City, Del. A6   53
Delbarton, W. Va. D2   87
Delcambre, La. E4   63
Del city, Okla. B4   79
Delemont, Switz. E3   6
De Leon, Tex. C3   84
De Leon Springs, Fla. C5   54
Delft, Neth. A6   5
Delfzijl, Neth. A7   5
Delhi, Calif. *D3   50
Delhi, Ont., Can. E4   41
Delhi, India C6   20
Delhi, ter., India *C6   20
Delhi, La. B4   63
Delhi, N.Y. C6   75
Delhi Hills, Ohio *C1   78
Delisle, Que., Can. A6   42
Delitzsch, Ger. Dem. Rep. C6   6
Dellenbaugh, mtn., Ariz. A2   48
Dell Rapids, S. Dak. G9   77
Dellwood, Mo. *C7   69
Del Mar, Calif. o15   50
Delmar, Del. D6   53
Delmar, Md. D6   53
Delmar, N.Y. C7   75
Delmenhorst, Ger., Fed.
  Rep. of B4   6
Delmont, Pa. *F2   81
Del Monte Park, Calif. *D3   50
Del Norte, Colo. D4   51
Del Norte, co., Calif. B2   50
Deloraine, Man., Can. E1   40
Delphi, Ind. C4   59
Delphos, Ohio B1   78
Delran, N.J. C3   74
Delray Beach, Fla. F6   54
Del Rey Oaks, Calif. *D3   50
Del Rio, Tex. E2   84
Delson, Que., Can. q19   42
Delta, Colo. C2   51
Delta, Ohio A2   78
Delta, Pa. G9   81
Delta, Utah B5   72
Delta, co., Colo. C3   51
Delta, co., Mich. G3   66
Delta, co., Tex. C5   84
Delta, peak, B.C., Can. A3   37
Delta Amacuro, ter., Ven. B5   32
Deltaville, Va. C6   85
Demarest, N.J. h9   74
Demavend, mtn.,Iran F8   16
Demidov, Sov.,Un. D8   12
Deming, N. Mex. C5   48
Demirci, Tur. C7   14
Demmin, Ger., Dem. Rep. B6   6
Demopolis, Ala. C2   46
Demorest, Ga. B3   55
Demotte, Ind. B3   59
Dempo, mtn., Indon. F2   19
Denain, Fr. B5   5
Denbigh, Wales D5   4
Denbigh, co., Wales *D5   4
Denham Springs, La. D5, h10   63
Den Helder, Neth. A6   5
Denia, Sp. C6   8
Deniliquin, Austl. G7   25
Denison, Iowa B2   60
Denison, Tex. C4   84
Denizli, Tur. D7   14
Denmark, S.C. E5   82
Denmark, Wis. D6, h10   88
Denmark, country, Eur. I3   11
Dennison, Ohio B4   78
Dennis Port, Mass. C7   65
Denny Terrace, S.C. C5   82
Denpasar, Indon. G5   19
Dent, co., Mo. D6   69
Denton, Ga. F4   55
Denton, Md. C6   53
Denton, N.C. B2   76
Denton, Tex. C4   84
Denton, co., Tex. C4   84
Dentsville, S.C. C6   82
Denver, Colo. B6   51
Denver, Iowa B5   60
Denver, Pa. F9   81
Denver, co., Colo. B6   51
Denver City, Tex. C1   84
Denville, N.J. B4   74
Departure Bay, B.C., Can. f12   37
De Pere, Wis. D5, h9   88
Depew, N.Y. C2   75
Deposit, N.Y. C5   75
Depue, Ill. B4   58
De Queen, Ark. C1   49
De Quincy, La. D2   63

Dera Ghazi Khan, Pak. B5   20
Dera Ismail Khan, Pak. B5   20
Derby, Austl. C3   25
Derby, Colo. *B6   51
Derby, Conn. D4   52
Derby, Eng. D6   4
Derby, Kans. E6   61
Derby, N.Y. C2   75
Derby, co., Eng. *D6   4
Derecske, Hung. B5   10
De Ridder, La. D2   63
Derita, N.C. B2   76
Dermott, Ark. D4   49
Derry, N.H. F5   73
Derry, Pa. F3   81
Derventa, Yugo. C3   10
Derzhavinskoye, Sov. Un. D9   16
Des Allemands, La. E5, k11   63
Des Arc., Ark. C4   49
Desbiens, Que., Can. A6   42
Deschaillons sur St. Laurent,
  Que, Can. *C5   42
Deschambault, Que.,Can. C6   42
Deschênes, Que., Can. D2   42
Deschutes, co., Oreg. D5   80
Dese, Eth. F5   23
Deseronto, Ont., Can. C7   41
Desert Hot Springs, Calif. *F5   50
Desha, co.,Ark. D4   49
Deshler, Nebr. D8   71
Deshler, Ohio A2   78
Desloge, Mo. D7   69
De Smet, S. Dak. F8   77
Des Moines, Iowa C4, e8   60
Des Moines, Wash. B3, f11   86
Des Moines, co., Iowa D6   60
De Soto, Kans. D9, m16   61
De Soto, Mo. C7   69
De Soto, Tex. *C4   84
De Soto, co., Fla. E5   54
De Soto, co., Miss. A3   68
De Soto, co., par.,La. B2   63
Des Peres, Mo. f13   69
Des Plaines, Ill. A6, h9   58
Dessau, Ger. Dem. Rep. C6   6
Destin, Fla. u15   54
Detmold, Ger., Fed. Rep of C4   6
Detroit, Mich. F7, p15   66
Detroit Beach, Mich. *G7   66
Detroit Lakes, Minn. D3   67
Detva, Czech. D5   71
Deuel, co.,Nebr. C3   71
Deuel, co., S. Dak. F9   77
Deurne, Bel. B6   5
Deux-Montagnes, Que.,Can. p19   42
Deux-Sèvres, dept., Fr. *D3   5
Deva, Rom. C6   10
Dévaványa, Hung. B5   10
Deventer, Neth. A7   5
Devils Lake, N. Dak. B7   76
Devine, Tex. E3   84
De Vola, Ohio C4   84
Devon, Alta., Can. C4   38
Devon, Pa. *G10   81
Devon, co., Eng. *E5   4
Devon, isl.,Can. *A15   36
Devonport, Austl. o15   25
Devonport, N.Z. L15   26
Dewar, Okla. B6   79
Dewey, Okla. A6   79
Dewey, co., Okla. B2   79
Dewey, co., S.C. E5   77
De Witt, Ark. C4   49
De Witt, Iowa C7   60
De Witt, Mich. F6   66
De Witt, N.Y. *B4   75
De Witt, co., Ill. C5   58
De Witt, co., Tex. E4   84
Dewsbury, Eng. A6   4
Dexter, Maine C3   64
Dexter, Mich. F7   66
Dexter, Mo. E8   69
Dexter, N.Y. A4   75
Dezful, Iran C4   15
Dezhou, China D8   17
Dhahran (Az Zahran), Sau. Ar. D5   15
Dhamar, Yemen *G3   15
Dhanbad, India *D8   20
Dharamjaygarh, India D7   20
Dharmapuri, India F6   20
Dharmsala, India B6   20
Dharwar, India E6   20
Dhaulagiri, peak, Nep. C7   20
Dhidhimótikhon, Grc. E8   10
Dhule, India D5   20
Diablo, Calif. *D2   50
Diablo,mtn.,Calif. h9   50
Diablo Heights, Pan. *B2   32
Diamante, Arg. A4   28
Diamantina, Braz. E6   27
Diamantina, Braz. B4   30
Diamond, peak, Oreg. D4   80
Diamond Springs, Calif. C3   50

Diber (Dibra), pref., Alb. *E5 10
D'Iberville, Miss. E5, f8 68
Diboll, Tex. D5 84
Dickens, co., Tex. C2 84
Dickenson, co., Va. e9 85
Dickey, co., N. Dak. D7 77
Dickinson, N. Dak. D3 77
Dickinson, Tex. *E5 84
Dickinson, co., Iowa A2 60
Dickinson, co., Kans. D6 61
Dickinson, co., Mich. B3 66
Dickson, Tenn. A4 83
Dickson, co., Tenn. A4 83
Dickson City, Pa. D10, m18 81
Didsbury, Alta., Can. D3 38
Dien Bien Phu, Viet *A2 19
Diepholz, Ger., Fed. Rep. of B4 6
Dieppe, N.B., Can. C5 43
Dieppe, Fr. C4 5
Dierks, Ark. C1 49
Digboi, India C10 20
Digby, N.S., Can. E4 43
Digby, co., N.S., Can. E4 43
Dighton, Kans. D3 61
Digne, Fr. E7 5
Digoin, Fr. D5 5
Dijon, Fr. D6 5
Dikson, Sov. Un. B11 16
Dili, Indon. G7 19
Dilley, Tex. E3 84
Dilligen an der Donau,
    Ger., Fed. Rep. of D5 6
Dillon, Mont. E4 70
Dillon, S.C. C9 82
Dillon, co., S.C. C9 82
Dillonvale, Ohio B5 78
Dillsburg, Pa. F7 81
Dilworth, Minn. D2 67
Dimitrovgrad, Bul. D7 10
Dimmit, co., Tex. E3 84
Dimmitt, Tex. E3 84
Dimona, Isr. C3 15
Dimondale, Mich. F6 66
Dinan, Fr C3 5
Dinant, Bel. B6 5
Dinard, Fr. C2 5
Dindigul, India F6 20
Dingwall, Scot. B4 4
Dinh Lap, Viet. *G6 17
Dinuba, Calif. D4 50
Dinwiddie, co., Va. C5 85
Diourbel, Sen. F1 22
Dipolog, Phil *D6 19
Dire Dawa, Eth. G6 23
Diriamba, Nic. E7 34
Dirranbandi, Austl. E8 25
Dishman, Wash. g14 86
Dismal, peak, Va. C2 85
Disraéli, Que. D6 42
District Heights, Md. *C4 53
District of Columbia, U.S. C3, f8 53
Distrito Federal, fed. dist.,
    Mex. D5 34
Distrito Federal, fed. dist.,
    Ven. A4 32
Disūq, Eg. *G8 14
Diu, India D5 20
Divernon, Ill. D4 58
Dives-sur-Mer, Fr. C3 5
Divide, co., N. Dak. B2 77
Divide, peak, Wyo. E5 89
Divinópolis, Braz. C4 30
Divnoye, Sov. Un. I14 12
Dix, mtn., N.Y. A7 75
Dixfield, Maine D2 64
Dixiana, Ala. B3 46
Dixie, co., Fla. C3 54
Dixmoor, Ill. *B6 58
Dixon, Calif. C3 50
Dixon, Ill. B4 58
Dixon, Mo. D5 69
Dixon, co., Nebr. B9 71
Dixonville, Pa. E3 81
Diyarbakir, Tur. D13 14
Djajapura, see Jayapura, Indon.
Djakarta, see Jakarta, Indon.
Djakovica, Yugo. D5 10
Djakovo, Yugo. D4 10
Djibouti, Dji. F6 23
Djibouti, country, Afr. F6 23
Djombang, Indon. *G4 19
Djurdjevac, Yugo. B3 10
Djursholm, Swe. t36 11
Dmitriyevka, Sov. Un. H12, r21 12
Dmitrov, Sov. Un. C11 12
Dmitrovsk-Orlovskiy, Sov. Un. ... E10 12
Dnepr, riv., Sov. Un. H9 12
Dneprodzerzhinsk, Sov. Un. G10 12
Dnepropetrovsk, Sov. Un. G10 12
Dnestr, riv., Sov. Un. H7 12
Dno, Sov. Un. C7 12
Dobbs Ferry, N.Y. g13 75
Döbeln, Ger. Dem. Rep. C6 6

Doboj, Yugo. C4 10
Dobrich, see Tolbukhin, Bul.
Dobrogea, reg., Rom. *C9 10
Dobruja, reg., Bul. C9 10
Dobruja, reg., Rom. D9 10
Docena, Ala. f7 46
Doddridge, co., W. Va. B4 87
Dodge, co., Ga. D3 55
Dodge, co., Minn. G6 67
Dodge, co., Nebr. C9 71
Dodge, co., Wis. E5 88
Dodge Center, Minn. F6 67
Dodge City, Kans. E3 61
Dodgeville, Wis. F3 88
Dodoma, Tan. B7 24
Doerun, Ga. E3 55
Doe Run, Mo. D7 69
Doha (Ad Dawḩah), Qatar D5 15
Doi Inthanon, mtn., Thai E10 20
Dolbeau, Que., Can. G19 36
Dôle, Fr. D6 5
Dolgeville, N.Y. B6 75
Dolina, Sov. Un. D8 7
Dolinsk (Ochiai), Sov. Un. C11 18
Dolomite, Ala. B3, g7 46
Dolores, Arg. B5 28
Dolores, Ur. E1 30
Dolores, co., Colo. D2 51
Dolores Hidalgo, Mex. m13 34
Dolton, Ill. k9 58
Dolzhanskaya, Sov. Un. q22 12
Domažlice, Czech. D2 7
Dominguez, Calif. *F4 50
Dominica, country, N.A. I14 35
Dominican Republic,
    country, N.A. E8 35
Dominion, N.S., Can. C9 43
Domodossola, It. A2 9
Dom Pedrito, Braz. E2 30
Don, riv., Sov. Un. H13 12
Dona Ana, co., N. Mex. C5 48
Donaghadee, N. Ire. C4 4
Donaldsonville, La. D4, h10 63
Donalsonville, Ga F2 55
Don Benito, Sp. C3 8
Doncaster, Eng. D6 4
Donegal, co., Ire. *C2 4
Doneraile, S.C. C8 82
Donets, riv., Sov. Un. G13 12
Donetsk, Sov. Un. H11, r20 12
Dongchuan, China F5 17
Donggala, Indon. F5 19
Dong Hoi, Viet. B3 19
Doniphan, Mo. E7 69
Doniphan, co., Kans. C8 61
Donkin, N.S., Can. C10 43
Donley, co., Tex. B2 84
Donna, Tex. F3 84
Donnacona, Que., Can. C6, o16 42
Donora, Pa. F2 81
Donzère, Fr. E6 5
Doolittle, Mo. D6 69
Dooly, co., Ga. D3 55
Door, co., Wis. D6 88
Dora, Ala. B2 46
Doraville, Ga. h8 55
Dorbod, China C2 18
Dorchester, N.B., Can. D5 43
Dorchester, Eng. E5 4
Dorchester, co., Que., Can. C7 42
Dorchester, co., Md. D5 53
Dorchester, co., S.C. E6 82
Dordogne, dept., Fr. *E4 5
Dordrecht, Neth. B6 5
Dores do Indaiá, Braz. B3 30
Dorgali, It. D2 9
Dorion-Vaudreuil, Que., Can. q18 42
Dorking, Eng. m12 4
Dormont, Pa. k13 81
Dornbirn, Aus. E4 6
Dornoch, Scot. B4 4
Dorohoi, Rom. B8 10
Dorris, Calif. B3 50
Dorset, co., Eng. *F5 4
Dortmund, Ger., Fed. Rep. of C3 6
Dorton, Ky. C7 62
Dörtyol, Tur. D11 14
Dorval, Que., Can. q19 42
Dos Hermanas, Sp. D3 8
Dos Palos, Calif. D3 50
Dothan, Ala. D4 46
Douai, Fr. B5 5
Douala, Cam. H6 22
Douarnenez, Fr. C1 5
Doubletop, peak, Wyo. C2 89
Doubs, dept., Fr. *D7 5
Dougherty, co., Ga. E2 55
Douglas, Alsk. D13, k22 47
Douglas, Ariz. D4 48
Douglas, Ga. E4 55
Douglas, I. of Man C4 4
Douglas, Wyo. *D7 89
Douglas, co., Colo. B6 51

Douglas, co., Ga. C2 55
Douglas, co., Ill. D5 58
Douglas, co., Kans. D8 61
Douglas, co., Minn. E3 67
Douglas, co., Mo. E5 69
Douglas, co., Nebr. C9 71
Douglas, co., Nev. B2 72
Douglas, co., Oreg. D3 80
Douglas, co., S. Dak. G7 77
Douglas, co., Wash. B6 86
Douglas, co., Wis. B1 88
Douglass, Kans. E7 61
Douglasville, Ga. C2 55
Doullens, Fr. B5 5
Douro Litoral, prov., Port. *B1 8
Dove Creek, Colo. D2 51
Dover, Del. B6 53
Dover, Eng. E7 4
Dover, Fla. D4 54
Dover, Mass. h10 65
Dover, N.H. E6 73
Dover, N.J. B3 74
Dover, Ohio B4 78
Dover, Pa. F8 81
Dover, Tenn. A4 83
Dover-Foxcroft, Maine C3 64
Dover Plains, N.Y. D7 75
Dowagiac, Mich. G4 66
Down, co., N. Ire. *C4 4
Downers Grove, Ill. B5, k8 58
Downey, Calif. n12 50
Downington, Pa. F10 81
Downpatrick, N. Ire. C4 4
Downs, Kans. C5 61
Downs, mtn., Wyo. C3 89
Downton, mtn., B.C., Can. C5 37
Dows, Iowa B4 60
Doylestown, Ohio B4 78
Doylestown, Pa. F11 81
Doyline, La. B2 63
Dracut, Mass. A5 65
Draganovo, Bul. D7 10
Drăgăsani, Rom. C7 10
Dragerton, Utah *B6 72
Draguignan, Fr. F7 5
Drain, Oreg. D3 80
Drake, peak, Oreg. E6 80
Drakesboro, Ky. C2 62
Drama, Grc. B5 14
Drama, prov., Grc. *B5 14
Drammen, Nor. H4, p28 11
Drancy, Fr. g10 5
Draper, Utah A6, D2 72
Dravosburg, Pa. *E1 81
Drayton, N. Dak. A8 77
Drayton, S.C. B4 82
Drayton Plains, Mich. F7 66
Drayton Valley, Alta., Can. C3 38
Drenthe, prov., Neth. *A7 5
Dresden, Ont., Can. E2 41
Dresden, Ger. Dem. Rep. C6 6
Dresden, Ohio B3 78
Dresden, Tenn. A3 83
Dreux, Fr. C4 5
Drew, Miss. B3 68
Drew, co., Ark. D4 49
Drexel, N.C. B1 76
Drexel, Ohio C1 78
Drexel Hill, Pa. *G11 81
Drift, Ky. C7 62
Drifton, Pa. D10 81
Driggs, Idaho F7 57
Driskill, mtn., La. B3 63
Drissa, Sov. Un. D6 12
Drogheda, Ire. D3 4
Drogobych, Sov. Un. G4 12
Druid Hills, N.C. *f10 76
Drumheller, Alta., Can. D4 38
Drummond, co., Que., Can. D5 42
Drummond Range, mts., Austl. D8 25
Drummondville, Que., Can. D3 42
Drummondville Ouest, Que., Can. . *D5 42
Drumright, Okla. B5 79
Druzhkovka, Sov. Un. q20 12
Dryden, Ont., Can. o16 41
Dryden, N.Y. C4 75
Duarte, Calif. *E5 50
Duarte, peak, Dom. Rep. E8 35
Dubach, La. B3 63
Dubai (Dubayy), U.A.E. D6 15
Dubawnt, lake, N.W. Ter., Can. .. D13 36
Dubbo, Austl. F8 25
Dublin, Ga. D4 55
Dublin, Ind. E7 59
Dublin (Baile Átha Cliath),
    Ire. D3 4
Dublin, Tex. C3 84
Dublin, Va. C2 85
Dublin, co. Ire. D3 4
Dubois, co., Ind. H4 59
Du Bois, Pa. D4 81
Duboistown, Pa. D7 81
Dubossary, Sov. Un. H7 12

Dubovka, Sov. Un. G15 12
Dubrovnik, Yugo. D4 10
Dubuque, Iowa B7 60
Dubuque, co., Iowa B7 60
Duchesne, co., Utah A6 72
Duchov, Czech. C2 7
Duck, mtn., Man., Can. D1 40
Ducktown, Tenn. D9 83
Dudinka, Sov. Un. C11 13
Dudley, Eng. D5 4
Dudley, Mass. B4 65
Due West, S.C. D3 82
Dufferin, co., Ont., Can. C4 41
Dugger, Ind. F3 59
Duisburg, Ger., Fed. Rep. of C3 6
Duitama, Col. B3 32
Dukes, co., Mass. B6 65
Dulawan, Phil. *D6 19
Duluth, Ga. B2, g8 55
Duluth, Minn. D6 67
Dumaguete, Phil. D6 19
Dumas, Ark. D4 49
Dumas, Tex. B2 84
Dumfries, Scot. C5 4
Dumfries, Va. B5 85
Dumfries, co., Scot. *C5 4
Dumont, N.J. B5, h9 74
Dumyāt (Damietta), Eg. G8 14
Dunaföldvár, Hung. B4 10
Dunapataj, Hung. B4 10
Dunaujváros, Hung. B4 10
Dunayevsty, Sov. Un. G6 12
Dunbar, Pa. G2 81
Dunbar, Scot. B5 4
Dunbar, W. Va. C3, m12 87
Dunbarton, co., Scot. *B4 4
Duncan, Ariz. C4 48
Duncan, B.C., Can. E6, g12 37
Duncan, Okla. C4 79
Duncan, S.C. B3 82
Duncannon, Pa. F7 81
Duncansville, Pa. F5 81
Duncanville, Tex. n10 84
Dundalk, Ont., Can. C4 41
Dundalk, Ire. C3 4
Dundalk, Md. B4, g11 53
Dundas, Ont., Can. D5 41
Dundas, co., Ont., Can. B9 41
Dundee, Ill. A5, h6 58
Dundee, Fla. D5 54
Dundee, Mich. G7 66
Dundee, N.Y. C4 75
Dundee, Scot. B5 4
Dundee, S. Afr. F6 24
Dundy, co., Nebr. D4 71
Dunean, S.C. *B3 82
Dunedin, Fla. D4, o10 54
Dunedin, N.Z. P13 26
Dunellen, N.J. B4 74
Dunfermline, Scot. B5 4
Dungannon, N. Ire. C3 4
Dungarvan, Ire. D3 4
Dungulah, Sud. E4 23
Dunhua, China C10 17
Dunkerque, Fr. B5 5
Dunkirk, Ind. D7 59
Dunkirk, N.Y. C1 75
Dunkirk, Ohio B2 78
Dunkirk, see Dunkerque, Fr.
Dunklin, co., Mo. E7 69
Dun Laoghaire, Ire. D3 4
Dunlap, Ind. A6 59
Dunlap, Iowa C2 60
Dunlap, Tenn. D8 83
Dunlo, Pa. F4 81
Dunmore, Pa. D10, m18 81
Dunn, N.C. B4 76
Dunn, co., N. Dak. C3 77
Dunn, co., Wis. D2 88
Dunnellon, Fla. C4 54
Dunn Loring, Va. *B5 85
Dunnville, Ont., Can. E5 41
Dunoon, Scot. C4 4
Dunseith, N. Dak. A5 77
Dunsmuir, Calif. B2 50
Dunville, Newf., Can. E5 44
Du Page, co., Ill. A5 58
Duparquet, Que., Can. *D3 42
Duplin, co., N.C. C5 76
Dupnitsa, see Stanke Dimitrov, Bul.
Dupo, Ill. E3 58
Dupont, Pa. n18 81
Duque de Caxais, Braz. *C4 30
Duquesne, Pa. F2, k14 81
Du Quoin, Ill. E4 58
Dūra, Jordan C3 15
Durand, Mich. F6 66
Durand, Wis. D2 88
Durango, Colo. D3 51
Durango, Mex. C4 34
Durango, state, Mex. C4 34
Durant, Iowa C7 60
Durant, Miss. B4 68

Durant, Okla. ... D5 79
Durazno, Ur. ... E1 30
Durazno, dept., Ur. ... *E1 30
Durban, S. Afr. ... F6 24
Düren, Ger., Fed. Rep. of ... *C3 6
Durg, India ... *D7 20
Durham, Calif. ... C3 50
Durham, Maine ... g7 64
Durham, Ont., Can. ... C4 41
Durham, Eng. ... C6 4
Durham, N.H. ... E6 73
Durham, N.C. ... B4 76

Durham, co., Ont., Can. ... C6 41
Durham, co., Eng. ... *C6 4
Durham, co., N.C. ... A4 76
Durres, Alb. ... *B2 14
Duryea, Pa. ... D10, m17 81
Dushanbe, Sov. Un. ... F9 13
Duson, La. ... D3 63
Düsseldorf, Ger., Fed. Rep. of ... C3 6
Dutchess, co., N.Y. ... D7 75
Dutton, Ont., Can. ... E3 41
Duval, co., Fla. ... B5 54
Duval, co., Tex. ... F3 84

Duvergé, Dom. Rep. ... E8 35
Duxbury, Mass. ... B6 65
Duyun, China ... F6 17
Düzce, Tur. ... B8 14
Dvůr Králové *nad Labem*, Czech. ... C3 7
Dwight, Ill. ... B5 58
Dyer, Ind. ... A2 59
Dyer, Tenn. ... A3 83
Dyer, co., Tenn. ... A3 83
Dyersburg, Tenn. ... A2 83
Dyersville, Iowa ... B6 60
Dyrlow, see Darlowo, Pol.

Dysart, Iowa ... B5 60
Dzaudzhikau, see
  Ordzhonikidze, Sov. Un.
Dzerzhinsk, Sov. Un. ... q20 12
Dzerzhinsk, Sov. Un. ... C14, d7 12
Dzhambul, Sov. Un. ... E10 13
Dzhankoy, Sov. Un. ... I1 12
Dzialdowo, Pol. ... B6 7
Dzeirzlow, see Darlowo, Pol.
Dzierżoniów, Pol. ... C4 7
Dzilam Gonzáles, Mex. ... C7 34
Dzitbalché, Mex. ... C6 34

E

Eads, Colo. ... C8 51
Eagan, Tenn. ... C10 83
Eagle, W. Va. ... C3, m13 87
Eagle, co., Colo. ... B4 51
Eagle, mtn., Tex. ... o12 84
Eagle, peak, Calif. ... B3 50
Eagle Grove, Iowa ... B4 60
Eagle Lake, Fla. ... *E5 54
Eagle Lake, Maine ... A4 64
Eagle Lake, Tex. ... E4 84
Eagle Pass, Tex. ... E2 84
Eagle River, Wis. ... C4 88
Eagleton Village, Tenn. ... *D10 83
Eagleville, Pa. ... o20 81
Earle, Ark. ... B5 49
Earlimart, Calif. ... E4 50
Earlington, Ky. ... C2 62
Earlville, Ill. ... B5 58
Earlville, N.Y. ... C5 75
Early, Iowa ... B2 60
Early, co., Ga. ... E2 55
Earth, Tex. ... B1 84
Easley, S.C. ... B2 82
East, div., Ice. ... *n15 11
East Alamosa, Colo. ... D5 51
East Alliance, Ohio ... *B5 78
East Alton, Ill. ... E3 58
East Angus, Que., Can. ... D6 42
East Aurora, N.Y. ... C2 75
East Bangor, Pa. ... E11 81
East Bank, La. ... k7 63
Eastbank, W. Va. ... m13 87
East Bathurst, N.B., Can. ... B4 43
East Baton Rouge, par., La. ... D4 63
East Berlin, Pa. ... G8 81
East Bernstadt, Ky. ... C5 62
East Berwick, Pa. ... *D9 81
East Bethel, Minn. ... *E5 67
East Billerica, Mass. ... f11 65
Eastborough, Kans. ... g12 61
Eastbourne, Eng. ... E7 4
East Brady, Pa. ... E2 81
East Brewton, Ala. ... D2 46
East Bridgewater, Mass. ... B6 65
East Brookfield, Mass. ... B3 65
East Brooklyn, Conn. ... *B9 52
East Broughton Station,
  Que., Can. ... C6 42
East Brunswick, N.J. ... C4 74
East Butler, Pa. ... E2 81
East Canon, Colo. ... C5 51
East Canton, Ohio ... *B4 78
East Carroll, par., La. ... B4 63
East Chelmsford, Mass. ... f10 65
Eastchester, N.Y. ... *E7 75
East Chicago, Ind. ... A3 59
East Chicago Heights, Ill. ... *B6 58
East China, sea, China ... F9 17
East Cleveland, Ohio ... g9 78
East Conemaugh
  (Conemaugh), Pa. ... *E4 81
East Coulée, Alta., Can. ... D4 38
East Detroit, Mich. ... p16 66
East Douglas, Mass. ... B4 65
East Dubuque, Ill. ... A3 58
East Dundee, Ill. ... *A5 58
East Ely, Nev. ... D7 72
Eastern, reg., Nig. ... G6 22
Eastern Valley, Ala. ... *f6 46
East Falmouth, Mass. ... C6 65
East Farmington Heights, Conn. ... *B6 52
East Faxon, Pa. ... *D7 81
East Fayetteville, N.C. ... *B3 76
East Feliciana, par., La. ... D4 63
East Flanders, prov., Bel. ... *B5 5
East Flat Rock, N.C. ... f10 76
East Gaffney, S.C. ... A4 82
Eastgate, Wash. ... *B3 86

East Glenville, N.Y. ... *C7 75
East Grand Forks, Minn. ... C2 67
East Grand Rapids, Mich. ... F5 66
East Greenbush, N.Y. ... *C7 75
East Greenville, Pa. ... F10 81
East Greenwich, R.I. ... C11 52
East Hampden, Maine ... *D4 64
East Hampton, Conn. ... C6 52
Easthampton, Mass. ... B2 65
East Hampton, N.Y. ... m16 75
East Hartford, Conn. ... B6 52
East Haven, Conn. ... D5 52
East Hazelcrest, Ill. ... *B6 58
East Helena, Mont. ... D5 70
East Herkimer, N.Y. ... *B6 75
East Hickory, N.C. ... *B1 76
East Hills, N.Y. ... *E7 75
East Islip, N.Y. ... *G4 52
East Jordan, Mich. ... C5 66
East Keansburg, N.J. ... *C4 74
East Kingsford, Mich. ... *C2 66
Eastlake, Ohio ... A4 78
Eastland, Tex. ... C3 84
Eastland, co., Tex. ... C3 84
East Lansdowne, Pa. ... *G11 81
East Lansing, Mich. ... F6 66
East Liverpool, Ohio ... B5 78
East London, S. Afr. ... G5 24
East Longmeadow, Mass. ... B2 65
East Los Angeles, Calif. ... m12 50
East Lothian, co., Scot. ... *C5 4
East McKeesport, Pa. ... *F2 81
Eastman, Ga. ... D3 55
East Marietta, Ohio ... *A5 55
East Meadow, N.Y. ... n15 75
East Millbury, Mass. ... *B4 65
East Millinockot, Maine ... C4 64
East Moline, Ill. ... B3 58
East Moriches, N.Y. ... F5 52
East Naples, Fla. ... F5 54
East Newark, N.J. ... k8 74
East Newnan, Ga. ... C2 55
East Northport, N.Y. ... *F3 52
East Norwich, N.Y. ... *F2 52
Easton, Calif. ... *D4 50
Easton, Maine ... B5 64
Easton, Md. ... C5 53
Easton, Pa. ... E11 81
East Orange, N.J. ... B4, h8 74
East Palatka, Fla. ... C5 54
East Palestine, Ohio ... B5 78
East Palo Alto, Calif. ... *D2 50
East Patchogue, N.Y. ... G5 52
East Peoria, Ill. ... C4 58
East Pepperell, Mass. ... A4 65
East Petersburg, Pa. ... F9 81
East Pines, Md. ... *C4 53
East Pittsburgh, Pa. ... *k14 81
East Point, Ga. ... C2, h8 55
Eastport, Newf., Can. ... D5 44
Eastport, Maine ... D6 64
Eastport, N.Y. ... n16 75
East Prairie, Mo. ... E8 69
East Pryor, mtn., Mont. ... E8 70
East Providence, R.I. ... B11 52
East Quincy, Calif. ... *C3 50
East Quogue, N.Y. ... *n16 75
East Richmond, Calif. ... *D2 50
East Ridge, Tenn. ... h11 83
East Rochester, N.Y. ... B3 75
East Rochester, Pa. ... *E1 81
East Rockaway, N.Y. ... G2 52
East Rockingham, N.C. ... C3 76
East Rockwood, Mich. ... *F7 66
East Rutherford, N.J. ... h8 74
East St. John, N.B., Can. ... D3 43
East St. Louis, Ill. ... E3 58
East Setauket, N.Y. ... F4 52

Eastside, Oreg. ... D2 80
East Sparta, Ohio ... B4 78
East Spencer, N.C. ... B2 76
East Stroudsburg, Pa. ... D11 81
East Sudbury, Mass. ... g10 65
East Syracuse, N.Y. ... B4 75
East Tawas, Mich. ... D7 66
East Templeton, Mass. ... A3 65
East Troy, Wis. ... F5 88
East Uniontown, Pa. ... *G2 81
East Vandergrift, Pa. ... *F2 81
East Walpole, Mass. ... D2 65
East Wareham, Mass. ... C6 65
East Washington, Pa. ... F1 81
East Wenatchee, Wash. ... B5 86
East Whittier, Calif. ... *F4 50
East Williston, N.Y. ... G2 52
Eastwood, Mich. ... *E5 66
East York, Ont., Can. ... *m15 41
East York, Pa. ... *G8 81
Eaton, Colo. ... A6 51
Eaton, Ind. ... D7 59
Eaton, Ohio ... C1 78
Eaton, co., Mich. ... F6 66
Eaton Rapids, Mich. ... F6 66
Eatonton, Ga. ... C3 55
Eatontown, N.J. ... C4 74
Eatonville, Wash. ... C3 86
Eau Claire, Wis. ... D2 88
Eau Claire, co., Wis. ... D2 88
Ebensburg, Pa. ... F4 81
Eberswalde, Ger. Dem. Rep. ... B6 6
Ebetsu, Jap. ... E10 18
Ebingen, Ger., Fed. Rep. of ... D4 6
Eboli, It. ... D5 9
Eccles, W. Va. ... D3, n13 87
Eceabat (Maydos), Tur. ... B6 14
Ech Cheliff, Alg. ... A5 22
Echigawa, Jap. ... n15 18
Echols, co., Ga. ... F3 55
Echuca, Austl. ... G7 25
Écija, Sp. ... D3 8
Eckernförde, Ger., Fed.
  Rep. of ... A4 6
Eckert, Colo. ... C3 51
Eckhart Mines, Md. ... k13 53
Eckman, W. Va. ... *D3 87
Eclectic, Ala. ... C3 46
Economy, Pa. ... *E1 81
Ecorse, Mich. ... p15 66
Ector, co., Tex. ... D1 84
Ecuador, country, S.A. ... 31
Edcouch, Tex. ... F4 84
Eddiceton, Miss. ... D3 68
Eddy, co., N. Mex. ... C6 48
Eddy, co., N. Dak. ... C7 77
Eddystone, Pa. ... p20 81
Eddyville, Iowa ... C5 60
Eddyville, Ky. ... e9 62
Ede, Neth. ... A6 5
Ede, Nig. ... *G5 22
Edea, Cam. ... H7 22
Eden, N.Y. ... C2 75
Eden, N.C. ... A3 76
Eden, Tex. ... D3 84
Edenborn, Pa. ... G2 81
Edenton, N.C. ... A6 76
Edgar, Wis. ... D4 88
Edgar, co., Ill. ... D6 58
Edgartown, Mass. ... D6 65
Edgecombe, co., N.C. ... B5 76
Edgefield, S.C. ... D4 82
Edgefield, co., S.C. ... D3 82
Edgeley, N. Dak. ... D7 77
Edgely, Pa. ... *F11 81
Edgemere, Md. ... *B5 53
Edgemont, Calif. ... *F5 50
Edgemont, S. Dak. ... G2 77

Edgerton, Minn. ... G2 67
Edgerton, Ohio ... A1 78
Edgerton, Wis. ... F4 88
Edgewater, Ala. ... f7 46
Edgewater, Colo. ... B5 51
Edgewater, Fla. ... D6 54
Edgewater, Md. ... C4 53
Edgewater, N.J. ... h9 74
Edgewater Park, N.J. ... C3 74
Edgewood, Ind. ... D6 59
Edgewood, Ky. ... A7 62
Edgewood, Md. ... B5 53
Edgewood, Ohio ... A5 78
Edgewood, Pa. ... k14 81
Edgeworth, Pa. ... h13 81
Edgewood, Pa. ... *D8 81
Edhessa, Grc. ... B4 14
Edina, Minn. ... n12 67
Edoma, Mo. ... A5 69
Edinboro, Pa. ... C1 81
Edinburg, Ill. ... D4 58
Edinburg, Ind. ... F6 59
Edinburg, Miss. ... C4 68
Edinburg, Tex. ... F3 84
Edinburg, Scot. ... C5 4
Edirne, Tur. ... B6 14
Edison, Ga. ... E2 55
Edison, N.J. ... B4 74
Edisto Island, S.C. ... F7, k11 82
Edith, mtn., Mont. ... D5 70
Edmeston, N.Y. ... C5 75
Edmond, Okla. ... B4 79
Edmonds, Wash. ... B3 86
Edmonson, co., Ky. ... C3 62
Edmonston, Md. ... *C4 53
Edmonton, Alta., Can. ... C4, g8 38
Edmonton, Eng. ... K12 4
Edmore, Mich. ... E5 66
Edmunds, co., S. Dak. ... E6 77
Edmundson, Mo. ... *C7 69
Edmundston, N.B., Can. ... B1 43
Edna, Tex. ... E4 84
Edremit, Tur. ... *C6 14
Edson, Alta., Can. ... C7, g7 38
Edwards, Miss. ... C3 68
Edwards, co., Ill. ... E5 58
Edwards, co., Kans. ... E4 61
Edwards, co., Tex. ... E2 84
Edwardsburg, Mich. ... G4 66
Edwardsville, Ill. ... E4 58
Edwardsville, Pa. ... n17 81
Eferding, Aus. ... D7 6
Effingham, Ill. ... D5 58
Effingham, co., Ga. ... D5 55
Effingham, co., Ill. ... D5 58
Eganville, Ont., Can. ... B7 41
Eger, Hung. ... B5 10
Egg Harbor City, N.J. ... D3 74
Egmont, mtn. N.Z. ... M15 26
Egridir, Tur. ... D8 14
Egypt, Mass. ... B6, h12 65
Egypt, Pa. ... E10 81
Egypt, country, Afr. ... C3 23
Ehime, pref., Jap. ... *J6 18
Ehrenfeld, Pa. ... F4 81
Éibar, Sp. ... A4 8
Eichstätt, Ger., Fed. Rep. of ... D5 6
Eidsberg, Nor. ... H4, p29 11
Eidsvoll, Nor. ... G4 11
Eilenburg, Ger. Dem. Rep. ... C6 6
Einbeck, Ger., Fed. Rep. of ... C4 6
Eindhoven, Neth. ... B6 5
Eire, see Ireland, country, Eur.
Eisenach, Ger. Dem. Rep. ... C5 6
Eisenhüttenstadt, Ger.
  Dem. Rep. ... B7 6
Eisenstadt, Aus. ... E8 6
Eisleben, Ger. Dem. Rep. ... C5 6

Place	Grid	Page
Ekalaka, Mont.	E12	70
Eksjö, Swe.	I6	11
El Aaiún, W. Sah.	C2	22
El Arahal, Sp.	D3	8
Elâziğ, Tur.	C12	14
Elba, Ala.	D3	46
El Banco, Col.	B3	32
El Barco, Sp.	A2	8
Elbasan, Alb.	B3	14
Elbasan, pref., Alb.	*B3	14
Elbe, (Labe), riv., Eur.	B5	6
Elbert, Colo.	B4	51
Elbert, co., Colo.	B6	51
Elbert, co., Ga.	B4	55
Elberton, Ga.	B4	55
Elbeuf, Fr.	C4	5
Elbing, see Elblag, Pol.		
Elbistan, Tur.	C11	14
Elblag, Pol.	A5	7
El Bonillo, Sp.	C4	8
El Bordo, Col.	C2	32
El Boulaïda, Alg.	A5	22
Elbow Lake, Minn.	E3	67
Elbrus, mtn., Sov. Un.	E7	13
Elburn, Ill.	B5	58
El Cajon, Calif.	F5, o16	50
El Campo, Tex.	E4	84
El Camp South, Tex.	*E4	84
El Capitan, mtn., Mont.	D2	70
El Carmen de Bolivar, Col.	B2	32
El Carrizo, Mex.	B3	34
El Centro, Calif.	F6	50
El Cerrito, Calif.	h8	50
Elche, Sp.	C5	8
El Cocuy, Col.	B3	32
Elda, Sp.	C5	8
El Djelfa, Alg.	B5	22
Eldon, Iowa	D5	60
Eldon, Mo.	C5	69
Eldora, Iowa	B4	60
El Dorado, Ark.	D3	49
Eldorado, Ill.	F5	58
El Dorado, Kans.	E7, g13	61
Eldorado, Mex.	C3	34
Eldorado, Tex.	D2	84
El Dorado, co., Calif.	C3	50
Eldorado, peak, Wash.	A4	86
El Dorado Springs, Mo.	D3	69
Eldoret, Ken.	H5	23
Eldred, Pa.	C5	81
Eldridge, Iowa	C7, g10	60
Eleanor, W. Va.	C3	87
Electra, Tex.	C3	84
Electric, peak, Mont.	D6	70
Eleele, Haw.	B2	56
Elektrostal, Sov. Un.	n18	12
Elephant, mtn., Maine	D2	64
Elevsís (Eleusis), Grc.	g11	14
El Fasher, Sud.	F3	23
El Ferrol del Caudillo, Sp.	A1	8
El Fuerte, Mex.	B3	34
Elgin, Ill.	A5, h8	58
Elgin, Iowa	B6	60
Elgin, N. Dak.	D4	77
Elgin, Oreg.	B9	80
Elgin, Scot.	B5	4
Elgin, Tex.	D4	84
Elgin, co., Ont., Can.	E3	41
Elgon, mtn., Ken., Ug.	H4	23
El Grullo, Mex.	n11	34
Elida, Ohio	B1	78
Elim, Pa.	*E4	81
Eliot, Maine	E2	64
Elizabeth, Austl.	F6	25
Elizabeth, Ga.	C2, h7	55
Elizabeth, La.	D3	63
Elizabeth, N.J.	B4, k8	74
Elizabeth, Pa.	*E1	81
Elizabeth City, N.C.	A6	76
Elizabeth Lake Estates, Mich.	*F7	66
Elizabethton, Tenn.	C11	83
Elizabethtown, Ky.	C4	62
Elizabethtown, N.C.	C4	76
Elizabethtown, Pa.	F8	81
Elizabethville, Pa.	E8	81
El Jadida, Mor.	B3	22
Elk, Pol.	B7	7
Elk, co., Kans.	E7	61
Elk, co., Pa.	D4	81
Elk, mtn., Wyo.	E6	89
Elk, peak, Mont.	D6	70
Elkader, Iowa	B6	60
Elk City, Okla.	B2	79
El Kef, Tun.	A6	22
Elk Grove, Calif.	C3	50
Elk Grove Village, Ill.	h9	58
Elkhart, Ind.	A6	59
Elkhart, Kans.	E2	61
Elkhart, co., Ind.	A6	59
Elkhorn, W. Va.	*D3	87
Elkhorn, Wis.	F5	88
Elkhorn City, Ky.	C7	62
Elkhovo, Bul.	D8	10
Elkin, N.C.	A2	76
Elkins, W. Va.	C5	87
Elkins Park, Pa.	o21	81
Elkland, Pa.	C7	81
Elk Mountain, N.C.	f10	76
Elko, Nev.	A4	72
Elko, co., Nev.	A4	72
Elk Point, S. Dak.	H9	77
Elk Rapids, Mich.	D5	66
Elkridge, Md.	B4, h10	53
Elkridge, W. Va.	m13	87
Elk River, Idaho	C2	57
Elk River, Minn.	E5	67
Elk Run Heights, Iowa	*B5	60
Elkton, Ky.	D2	62
Elkton, Md.	A6	53
Elkton, Mich.	E7	66
Elkton, Va.	B4	85
Elkville, Ill.	F4	58
Ellaville, Ga.	D2	55
Ellendale, N. Dak.	E7	77
Ellensburg, Wash.	C5	86
Ellenton, Fla.	E4, p10	54
Ellenville, N.Y.	D6	75
Ellerbe, N.C.	B3	76
Ellesmere, isl., N.W. Ter., Can.	k34	36
Ellettsville, Ind.	F4	59
Ellicott City, Md.	B4	53
Ellicottville, N.Y.	C2	75
Ellijay, Ga.	B2	55
Ellington, Mo.	D7	69
Ellinwood, Kans.	D5	61
Elliott, co., Ky.	B6	62
Ellis, Kans.	D4	61
Ellis, co., Kans.	D4	61
Ellis, co., Okla.	A2	79
Ellis, co., Tex.	C4	84
Ellisville, Miss.	D4	68
Ellisville, Mo.	f12	69
Ellon, Scot.	B5	4
Ellport, Pa.	E1	81
Ellsworth, Kans.	D5	61
Ellsworth, Maine	D4	64
Ellsworth, Pa.	F1	81
Ellsworth, Wis.	D1	88
Ellsworth, co., Kans.	D5	61
Ellwangen, Ger., Fed. Rep. of	D5	6
Ellwood City, Pa.	E1	81
Elma, N.Y.	*C2	75
Elma, Wash.	C2	86
El Mahdia, Tun.	A7	22
Elmali, Tur.	*D7	14
Elmer, N.J.	D2	74
Elm Grove, Wis.	*m11	88
Elmhurst, Ill.	B6, k9	58
Elmira, Ont., Can.	D4	41
Elmira, N.Y.	C4	75
El Mirage, Ariz.	D1	48
Elmira Heights, N.Y.	C4	75
Elmont, N.Y.	*G2	52
El Monte, Calif.	*E4	50
Elmora, Pa.	E4	81
Elmore, Minn.	G4	67
Elmore, Ohio	A2	78
Elmore, co., Ala.	C3	46
Elmore, co., Idaho	F3	57
Elmore City, Okla.	C4	79
Elmsford, N.Y.	g13	75
Elmshorn, Ger., Fed. Rep. of	B4	6
Elmwood, Ill.	C4	58
Elmwood Park, Ill.	k9	58
Elmwood Park, N.J.	h8	74
Elmwood Place, Ohio	o13	78
El Nevado, mtn., Col.	C3	32
Elnora, Ind.	G3	59
El Obeid, Sud.	F4	23
Eloise, Fla.	E5	54
Elon College, N.C.	A3	76
Elora, Ont., Can.	D4	41
El Oro, prov., Ec.	B2	31
Eloy, Ariz.	C3	48
El Paso, Ill.	C4	58
El Paso, Tex.	o11	84
El Paso, co., Colo.	C6	51
El Paso, co., Tex.	o11	84
El Portal, Fla.	s13	54
El Porto Beach, Calif.	*F4	50
El Puerto de Santa María, Sp.	D2	8
Elrama, Pa.	F2	81
El Reno, Okla.	B4	79
El Rio, Calif.	E4	50
Elroy, Wis.	E3	88
Elsa, Tex.	F3	84
El Salto, Mex.	C3	34
El Salvador, country, N.A.	E7	34
Elsberry, Mo.	B6	69
El Segundo, Calif.	*F4	50
El Seibo, Dom. Rep.	E9	35
Elsie, Mich.	E6	66
Elsinore, Calif.	F5	50
Elsmere, Del.	A6	53
Elsmere, Ky.	B5, h13	62
El Sobrante, Calif.	*D2	50
Elsterwerda, Ger. Dem. Rep.	C6	6
El Tigre, Ven.	B5	32
El Tocuyo, Ven.	B4	32
Elton, La.	D3	63
Elûru, India	E7	20
Elvas, Port.	C2	8
El Verano, Calif.	*C2	50
Elverum, Nor.	G4	11
El Viejo, mtn., Col.	B3	32
Elvins, Mo.	D7	69
Elwood, Ind.	D6	59
Elwood, Kans.	C9	61
Elwood, N.Y.	n15	75
Elwyn, Pa.	*G11	81
Ely, Eng.	D7	4
Ely, Minn.	C7	67
Ely, Nev.	B4	72
Elyria, Ohio	A3	78
Elysburg, Pa.	E8	81
Emânshahr, Iran	B6	15
Emanuel, co., Ga.	D4	55
Embetsu, Jap.	E10	18
Embrun, Ont., Can.	B9	41
Emden, Ger., Fed. Rep. of	B3	6
Emerald, Austl.	D8	25
Emerson, Man., Can.	E3	40
Emerson, Nebr.	B9	71
Emerson, N.J.	H8	74
Emery, co., Utah	B6	72
Emeryville, Calif.	*D3	50
Emi Koussi, vol., Chad	E1	23
Emilia, reg., It.	B3	9
Emilia-Romagna, pol. dist., It.	B3	9
Emiliano Zapata, Mex.	D6	34
Eminence, Ky.	B4	62
Emirdağ, Tur.	C8	14
Emlenton, Pa.	D2	81
Emmaus, Pa.	E11	81
Emmen, Neth.	A7	5
Emmerich, Ger., Fed. Rep. of	C3	6
Emmet, co., Iowa	A3	60
Emmet, co., Mich.	C6	66
Emmetsburg, Iowa	A3	60
Emmett, Idaho	F2	57
Emmitsburg, Md.	A3	53
Emmons, co., N. Dak.	D5	77
Empire, Calif.	*D3	50
Empire, La.	E6	63
Empire, Nev.	A2	72
Empoli, It.	C3	9
Emporia, Kans.	D7	61
Emporia, Va.	D5	85
Emporium, Pa.	D5	81
Emsdetten, Ger., Fed. Rep. of	B3	6
Emsworth, Pa.	h13	81
Ena, Jap.	n16	18
Encarnación, Par.	E4	29
Encarnación de Díaz, Mex.	m12	34
Encinal, Tex.	E3	84
Encinitas, Calif.	F5	50
Ende, Indon.	G6	19
Enderby, B.C., Can.	D8	37
Enderlin, N. Dak.	D8	77
Endicott, N.Y.	C4	75
Endwell, N.Y.	*C4	75
Enfield, Conn.	B6	52
Enfield, Ill.	E5	58
Enfield, N.H.	D3	73
Enfield, N.C.	A5	76
Engaru, Jap.	D11	18
Engels, Sov. Un.	F16	12
Enghien, Fr.	g10	5
England, Ark.	C4, k11	49
England, reg., U.K.	D6	4
Englee, Newf., Can.	C3, h10	44
Englewood, Colo.	B6	51
Englewood, Fla.	*B5	54
Englewood, Fla.	F4	54
Englewood, Ind.	*G5	59
Englewood, N.J.	h9	74
Englewood, Ohio	C1	78
Englewood, Oreg.	*D2	80
Englewood, Tenn.	D9	83
Englewood Cliffs, N.J.	B5	74
Englishtown, N.J.	C4	74
Enguera, Sp.	C5	8
Enhaut, Pa.	*F8	81
Enid, Okla.	A4	79
Enka, N.C.	f10	76
Enköping, Swe.	H7, t35	11
Enna, It.	F5	9
Ennis, Ire.	D2	4
Ennis, Tex.	C4, n10	84
Enniscorthy, Ire.	D3	4
Enniskillen, N.Ire.	C3	4
Enns, Aus.	D7	6
Enola, Pa.	F8	81
Enon, Ohio	C2	78
Enoree, S.C.	B4	82
Enosberg Falls, Vt.	B2	73
Enriquillo, Dom. Rep.	F8	35
Enschede, Neth.	A7	5
Ensenada, Arg.	g8	28
Ensenada, Mex.	A1	34
Ensenada, P.R.	G11	35
Ensley, Fla.	u14	54
Entebbe, Ug.	H4	23
Enterprise, Ala.	D4	46
Enterprise, Calif.	*B2	50
Enterprise, Kans.	D6	61
Enterprise, Oreg.	B9	80
Entiat, mts., Wash.	B5	86
Entre Minho e Douro, reg., Port.	B1	8
Entre Ríos, prov., Arg.	A5, f7	28
Enugu, Nig.	G6	22
Enumclaw, Wash.	B4, f12	86
Enzan, Jap.	n17	18
Épernay, Fr.	C5	5
Ephraim, Utah	B6	72
Ephrata, Pa.	F9	81
Ephrata, Wash.	B6	86
Épila, Sp.	B5	8
Épinal, Fr.	C7	5
Épinay-sur-Seine, Fr.	g10	5
Epirus, reg., Grc.	*C3	14
Epping, Eng.	k13	4
Epping, N.H.	E5	73
Epsom (& Ewell) Eng.	m12	4
Epworth, Iowa	B7	60
Equatorial Guinea, country, Afr.	H6	22
Erath, La.	E3	63
Erath, co., Tex.	C3	84
Ercis, Tur.	C14	14
Erciyes Dagi, mtn., Tur.	C10	14
Érd, Hung.	B4	10
Erdek, Tur.	*B6	14
Erdenheim, Pa.	o21	81
Erding, Ger., Fed. Rep. of	D5	6
Eregli, Tur.	B8	14
Ereğli, Tur.	D10	14
Erfurt, Ger. Dem. Rep.	C5	6
Erice, It.	E4	9
Erick, Okla.	B2	79
Erickson, B.C., Can.	E9	37
Erie, Colo.	A5	51
Erie, Ill.	B3	58
Erie, Kans.	E8	61
Erie, Pa.	B1	81
Erie, co., N.Y.	C2	75
Erie, co., Ohio	A3	78
Erie, co., Pa.	C1	81
Erie, lake, Can., U.S.	B10	45
Erin, Tenn.	A4	83
Eritrea, prov., Eth.	E5	23
Erlangen, Ger., Fed. Rep. of	D5	6
Erlanger, Ky.	A5, h13	62
Ermenak, Tur.	D9	14
Ermont, Fr.	g10	5
Ernakulam, India	*G6	20
Ernest, Pa.	E3	81
Errigal, mtn., Ire.	C2	4
Errol Heights, Oreg.	*B4	80
Erstein, Fr.	C7	5
Erwin, N.C.	B4	76
Erwin, Tenn.	C11	83
Erzincan, Tur.	C12	14
Erzurum, Tur.	C13	14
Esashi, Jap.	D11	18
Esashi, Jap.	F10	18
Esbjerg, Den.	J3	11
Escada, Braz.	*D7	27
Escalante, Utah	C6	72
Escalón, Calif.	D3	50
Escalón, Mex.	B4	34
Escambia, co., Ala.	D2	46
Escambia, co., Fla.	u14	54
Escanaba, Mich.	C3	66
Escatawpa, Miss.	E5, f8	68
Esch-sur-Alzette, Lux.	C7	5
Eschwege, Ger., Fed. Rep. of	C5	6
Eschweiler, Ger., Fed. Rep. of	C3	6
Escondido, Calif.	F5	50
Escoublac-La-Baule, Fr.	D2	5
Escuinapa de Hidalgo, Mex.	C3	34
Escuintla, Guat.	E6	34
Esfahān (Isfajamn), Iran	C5	23
Esher, Eng.	m12	4
Eskdale, W. Va.	C3,m13	87
Eskilstuna, Swe.	H7, t34	11
Eskisehir, Tur.	C8	14
Esmeralda, co., Nev.	C3	72
Esmeraldas, Ec.	A2	31
Esmeraldas, prov., Ec.	A2	31
Esmond, R.I.	B10	52
Espanola, Ont., Can.	A3	41
Espanola, N. Mex.	B5	48
Esperanza, Arg.	A4	28
Espinal, Col.	C3	32
Espírito Santo, state, Braz.	C4	30
Espita, Mex.	C7	34
Espy, Pa.	D9	81
Esquel, Arg.	C2	28
Esquimalt, B.C., Can.	E6, h12	37
Essaouira, Mor.	B3	22
Essen, Ger., Fed. Rep. of	C3	6
Essendon, mtn., Austl.	D3	25

Essex, Ont., Can. E2 41
Essex, Conn. D7 52
Essex, Md. B5 52
Essex, co., Ont., Can. E2 41
Essex, co., Eng. *E7 41
Essex, co., Mass. A5 65
Essex, co., N.J. B4 74
Essex, co., N.Y. B4 75
Essex, co., Vt. B4 73
Essex, co., Va. C6 85
Essex Fells, N.J. *B4 74
Essex Junction, Vt. C1 73
Essexville, Mich. *E7 66
Essington, Pa. *G11 81
Esslingen, Ger., Fed. Rep. of D4 6
Estacada, Oreg. B4 80
Estancia, Braz. *E7 27
Estancia, N. Mex. B5 48
Este, It. B3 9
Esteli, Nic. E7 34
Estepa, Sp. D3 8
Esterhazy, Sask., Can. G4 39
Estes Park, Colo. A5 51
Estevan, Sask., Can. H4 39
Esther, Mo. *D7 69
Estherville, Iowa A3 60
Estill, S.C. F5 82
Estill, co., Ky. C5 62
Eston, Sask., Can. F1 39
Estonia (S.S.R.), rep., Sov. Un. B5 12
Estremadura, prov., Port. *C1 8
Estremadura, reg., Port. *C1 8

Estremoz, Port. C2 8
Esztergom, Hung. B4 10
Étampes, Fr. C5 5
Étaples, Fr. B4 5
Etawah, India C6 20
Ethel, W. Va. D5 87
Ethiopia (Abyssinia), country, Afr. ... G5 23
Etna, Pa. k14 41
Etna, Monte, vol., It. F5 9
Etobicoke, Ont., Can. D5, m14 41
Etowah, Tenn. D9 83
Etowah, co., Ala. A3 46
Ettrick, Va. C5, n18 85
Etzatlan, Mex. m11 34
Eu, Fr. B4 5
Euclid, Ohio A4, g9 78
Euclid Center, Mich. *F4 66
Eudora, Ark. D4 49
Eudora, Kans. D8, m15 61
Eufaula, Ala. D4 46
Eufaula, Okla. B6 79
Eugene, Oreg. C3 80
Euless, Tex. *C4 84
Eunice, La. D3 63
Eunice, N. Mex. C7 48
Eupen, Bel. B7 5
Euphrates, see Firat, riv., Asia
Eupora, Miss. B4 68
Eure, dept., Fr. *C4 5
Eure-et-Loir, dept., Fr. *C4 5
Eureka, Calif. B1 50
Eureka, Ill. C4 58

Eureka, Kans. E7 61
Eureka, Mo. f12 69
Eureka, Mont. B1 70
Eureka, S. Dak. E6 77
Eureka, Utah B5 72
Eureka, co., Nev. B3 72
Eureka Springs, Ark. A2 49
Europe, cont. 3
Euskirchen, Ger., Fed. Rep. of C3 6
Eustis, Fla. D5 54
Eutaw, Ala. C2 46
Evangeline, La. D3 63
Evangeline, par., La. D3 63
Evans, Colo. A6 51
Evans, co., Ga. D5 55
Evans, mtn., Colo. B5 51
Evans City (Evansburg), Pa. E1 81
Evansdale, Iowa B5 60
Evanston, Ill. A6, h9 58
Evanston, Wyo. E2 89
Evansville, Ill. E4 58
Evansville, Ind. I2 59
Evansville, Wis. F4 88
Evart, Mich. E5 66
Evarts, Ky. D6 62
Eveleth, Minn. C6 67
Even Yehuda, Isr. *B2 15
Everard, mtn., B.C., Can. D5 37
Everest, peak, China, Nep. C8 20
Everett, Mass. g11 65
Everett, Pa. F5 81
Everett, Wash. B3 86

Everett, mtn., Mass. B1 65
Everglades, Fla. G5 54
Evergreen, Ala. D3 46
Evergreen Park, Ill. k9 58
Everman, Tex. *C4 84
Everson, Pa. F2 81
Évora, Port. C2 8
Évreux, Fr. C4 5
Évvoia, prov., Grc. *B5 14
Evvoia (Euboea), prov., Grc. *C4 14
Ewa, Haw. B3, g9 56
Ewa Beach, Haw. g9 56
Ewing, N.J. C3 74
Ewing, Va. f8 85
Excelsior, Minn. F5, n11 67
Excelsior, mtn., Cal. n14 50
Excelsior Springs, Mo. B3, h11 69
Exeter, Calif. D4 50
Exeter, Ont., Can. D3 41
Exeter, Eng. E5 4
Exeter, N.H. F6 73
Exeter, Pa. D10, n17 81
Exira, Iowa C3 60
Exmore, Va. C7 85
Exmouth, Austl. D1 25
Exmouth, Eng. E5 4
Experiment, Ga. C2 55
Export, Pa. F2 81
Eyemouth, Scot. C5 4
Eylar, mtn., Calif. D3 50
Eyre, lake, Austl. E6 25
Ezine, Tur. C6 14

F

Fabens, Tex. o11 84
Fabriano, It. C4 9
Facatativá, Col. C3 32
Factoryville, Pa. C10 81
Fada Ngourma, Burkina Faso E6 21
Faenza, It. B3 9
Faeroe Islands, Dan. dep. Eur. C6 3
Fafe, Port. B1 8
Făgăraş, Rom. C7 10
Fagatogo, Am. Sam. *G9 2
Fagersta, Swe. G6 11
Faifo, Viet. *B3 19
Fairbank, Iowa B5 60
Fairbanks, Alsk. C10 47
Fair Bluff, N.C. C3 76
Fairborn, Ohio C1 78
Fairburn, Ga. C2, h7 55
Fairbury, Ill. C5 58
Fairbury, Nebr. D8 71
Fairchance, Pa. G2 81
Fairdale, Ky. g11 62
Fairfax, Ala. C4 46
Fairfax, Calif. C2, h7 50
Fairfax, Del. *A6 53
Fairfax, Iowa C6 60
Fairfax, Minn. F4 67
Fairfax, Mo. A2 69
Fairfax, Ohio C1 78
Fairfax, Okla. A5 79
Fairfax, S.C. F5 82
Fairfax (Independent City)
  Va. B5, g12 85
Fairfax, co., Va. B5 85
Fairfield, Ala. B3, f7 46
Fairfield, Calif. C2 50
Fairfield, Conn. E3 52
Fairfield, Ill. E5 58
Fairfield, Iowa D6 60
Fairfield, Maine D3 64
Fairfield, Mont. C5 70
Fairfield, N.J. *B4 74
Fairfield, Ohio n12 78
Fairfield, Tex. D4 84
Fairfield, co., Conn. D3 52
Fairfield, co., Ohio C3 78
Fairfield, co., S.C. C5 82
Fairgrove, Mich. E7 66
Fair Grove, N.C. *B2 76
Fairhaven, Mass. C6 65
Fair Haven, Mich. F8 66
Fair Haven, N.J. C4 74
Fair Haven, N.Y. B4 75
Fair Haven, Vt. D1 73
Fairhope, Ala. E2 46

Fairhope, Pa. *G2 81
Fairland, Ind. E6 59
Fairland, Okla. A7 79
Fair Lawn, N.J. h8 74
Fairlawn, Ohio *A4 78
Fairless Hills, Pa. *F11 81
Fairmont, Ill. k8 58
Fairmont, Minn. G4 67
Fairmont, N.C. C3 76
Fairmont, Wash. *B3 86
Fairmont, W. Va. B4, k10 87
Fairmont City, Ill. f13 69
Fairmount, Ill. C6 58
Fairmount, Ind. D6 59
Fairmount, N.Y. *B4 75
Fairmount Heights, Md. f9 53
Fair Oaks, Calif. C3 50
Fair Oaks, Calif. *E3 50
Fair Oaks, Ga. h7 55
Fairoaks, Pa. h13 81
Fair Plain, Mich. F4 66
Fairpoint, Ohio B5 78
Fairport, N.Y. B3 75
Fairport Harbor, Ohio A4 78
Fairton, N.J. E2 74
Fairvale, N.B., Can. D4 43
Fairview, Alta., Can. A1 38
Fairview, Ill. C3 58
Fairview, Mont. C12 70
Fairview, N.J. D3 74
Fairview, N.J. h8 74
Fairview, N.Y. *D7 75
Fairview, Ohio B4 78
Fairview, Okla. A3 79
Fairview, Pa. *D8 81
Fairview, Pa. *E11 81
Fairview, Pa. B1 81
Fairview, Tenn. B4 83
Fairview, Utah B6 72
Fairview, Wash. *C5 86
Fairview, peak, Oreg. D4 80
Fairview Park, Ind. E3 59
Fairview Park, Ohio h9 78
Fairview Shores, Fla. *D5 54
Fairvilla, Fla. *D5 54
Fairway, Kans. B9 61
Faisalabad, Pak. B5 20
Faizabad, Afg. A5 20
Faizābād, India C7 20
Fajardo, P.R. G12 35
Fakfak, Indon. F8 19
Fălciu, Rom. B9 10
Falxón, state, Ven. A3 32
Falconer, N.Y. C1 75

Falcon Heights, Minn. n12 67
Falconwood, N.Y. *C2 75
Faleshty, Sov. Un. B8 10
Falfurrias, Tex. F3 84
Falher, Alta., Can. B2 38
Falkirk, Scot. C5 4
Falkland Islands, Br. dep., S.A. I5 27
Falköping, Swe. H5 11
Fall Branch, Tenn. C11 83
Fallbrook, Calif. F5 50
Fallon, Nev. B2 72
Fallon, co., Mont. D12 70
Fall River, Mass. C5 65
Fall River, co., S.Dak. G2 77
Fall Rock, Ky. C6 62
Falls, co., Tex. D4 84
Falls Church (Independent
  City), Va. g12 85
Falls City, Nebr. D10 71
Falls City, Oreg. C3 80
Falls Creek, Pa. D4 81
Fallsington, Pa. *F11 81
Falmouth, Eng. E4 4
Falmouth, Jam. E5 35
Falmouth, Ky. B5 62
Falmouth, Maine E5 64
Falmouth, Mass. C6 65
Falmouth, N.S. E5 43
Falmouth, Va. B5 85
Fălticeni, Rom. B8 10
Falun, Swe. G6 11
Fannin, co., Ga. B2 55
Fannin, co., Tex. C4 84
Fanny, mtn., Oreg. B9 80
Fano, It. C4 9
Fanwood, N.J. B4 74
Faradofay, Mad. E9 24
Farafangana, Mad. E9 24
Farah, Afg. B3 20
Faranah, Guinea F2 22
Fargo, N.Dak. D9 77
Far Hills, N.J. B3 74
Faribault, Minn. F5 67
Faribault, co., Minn. G5 67
Farina, Ill. E5 58
Farley, Iowa B6 60
Farmer City, Ill. C5 58
Farmers Branch, Tex. n10 84
Farmersburg, Ind. F3 59
Farmersville, Tex. C4 84
Farmerville, La. B3 63
Farmingdale, Maine D3 64
Farmingdale, N.J. C4 74
Farmingdale, N.Y. G3 52

Farmington, Conn. C5 52
Farmington, Ill. C3 58
Farmington, Iowa D6 60
Farmington, Maine D2 64
Farmington, Mich. p15 66
Farmington, Minn. F5 67
Farmington, Mo. D7 69
Farmington, N.H. E5 73
Farmington, N. Mex. A4 48
Farmington, Utah A6, C2 72
Farmington Hills, Mich. o15 66
Farmingville, N.Y. n16 75
Farmland, Ind. D7 59
Farmville, N.C. B5 76
Farmville, Va. C4 85
Farnham, Que., Can. D5 42
Farnham, mtn., B.C. D9 37
Faro, Port. D2 8
Farrell, Pa. D1 81
Farrukhābād, India C6 20
Farwell, Mich. E6 66
Farwell, Tex. B1 84
Fasano, It. D6 9
Fastov, Sov. Un. F7 12
Fatehpur, India C7 20
Fatsa, Tur. B11 14
Faulk, co., S.Dak. E6 77
Faulkner, co., Ark. B3 49
Faulkton, S.Dak. E6 77
Fauquier, co., Va. B5 85
Faust, Alta., Can. B3 38
Favara, It. F4 9
Fawnie Nose, mtn., B.C.,
  Can. C5 37
Faxon, Pa. *D7 81
Fayette, Ala. B2 46
Fayette, Iowa B6 60
Fayette, Miss. D2 68
Fayette, Mo. B5 69
Fayette, Ohio A1 78
Fayette, co., Ala. B2 46
Fayette, co., Ga. C2 55
Fayette, co., Ill. D4 58
Fayette, co., Ind. E7 59
Fayette, co., Iowa B6 60
Fayette, co., Ky. B5 62
Fayette, co., Ohio C2 78
Fayette, co., Pa. G2 81
Fayette, co., Tenn. B2 83
Fayette, co., Tex. E4 84
Fayette, co., W.Va. C3 87
Fayette City, Pa. *G2 81
Fayetteville, Ark. A1 49
Fayetteville, Ga. C2 55

Fayetteville, N.Y. B5 75
Fayetteville, N.C. B4 76
Fayetteville, Pa. G6 81
Fayetteville, Tenn. B5 83
Fayetteville, W.Va. C3,m13 87
Fayville, Mass. g9 65
Feasterville, Pa. o21 81
Feather Falls, Calif. C3 50
Fécamp, Fr. C4 5
Federalsburg, Md. C6 53
Federal Way, Wash. *B3 86
Fedscreek, Ky C7 62
Feeding Hills, Mass. B2 65
Feilding, N.Z. N15 26
Feira de Santana, Braz. *E7 27
Fejer, co., Hung. *B4 10
Felanitx, Sp. C7 8
Feldkirch, Aus. E4 6
Felicity, Ohio D1 78
Felipe Carrillo Puerto, Mex. D7 34
Fellsmere, Fla. E6 54
Felton, Calif. D2 50
Feltre, It. A3 9
Fenelon Falls, Ont., Can. C6 41
Fengshan, Taiwan *G9 17
Fennimore, Wis. F3 88
Fennville, Mich. F4 66
Fenton, Mich. F7 66
Fenton, Mo. f13 69
Fentress, co., Tenn. C9 83
Fenyang, China D7 17
Fedosiya, Sov. Un. I10 12
Ferdinand, Ind. H4 59
Ferentino, It. D4 9
Fergana, Sov. Un. *E10 13
Fergus, Ont., Can. D4 41
Fergus, co., Mont. C7 70
Fergus Falls, Minn. D2 67
Ferguson, Mo. C7, f13 69
Fermanagh, co., N.Ire. *C3 4
Ferme-Neuve, Que., Can. C2 42
Fermo, It. C4 9
Fernandina Beach, Fla. B5, k9 54
Fern Creek, Ky. q11 62
Ferndale, Calif. B1 50
Ferndale, Md. B4 53
Ferndale, Mich. *F7 66
Ferndale, Pa. F4 81
Ferndale, Wash. A3 86
Fernie, B.C., Can. E10 37
Fern Park, Fla. D5 54
Fernwood, N.Y. B4 75
Ferrara, It. B3 9
Ferreñafe, Peru C2 31
Ferriday, La. C4 63
Ferris, Ont., Can. *A5 41
Ferris, Tex. C4, n10 84
Ferris, mts., Wyo D5 89
Ferry, co., Wash. A7 86
Ferryland, Newf., Can. E5 44
Ferrysburg, Mich. *E4 66
Ferryville, Tun. F2 9
Fertile, Minn. C2 67
Fès, Mor. B3 22
Fessenden, N. Dak. C6 77
Festus, Mo. C7, g13 69
Fetesti, Rom. C8 10
Fetters Hot Springs, Calif. *C2 50
Ffestiniog, Wales D5 4
Fianarantsoa, Malag. E9 24
Fidenza, It. B3 9
Fieldale, Va. D3 85
Fier, Alb. *B2 14
Fierro Urco, vol., Peru B2 31
Fife, co., Sask., Can. *B5 4
Fife, Wash. *B3 86
Figeac, Fr. E4 5
Figueira da Foz, Port. B1 8
Figueras, Sp. A7 8
Fiji, country, Oceania H8 2
Filer, Idaho G4 57
Filiatra, Grc. D3 14
Fillmore, Calif. E4 50
Fillmore, Utah B5 72
Fillmore, co., Minn. G6 67
Fillmore, co., Nebr. D8 71
Finderne, N.J. *B3 74
Findlay, Ohio A2 78
Findlay, Ill. D5 58
Findlay, mtn., B.C., Can. D9 37
Finistère, dept., Fr. *C2 5
Finland, country, Eur. E12 11
Finney, co., Kans. D3 61
Finneytown, Ohio *C1 78
Finnmark, co., Nor. *B13 11
Finspång, Swe. u33 11
Finsterwalde, Ger. Dem. Rep. C6 6
Firat (Euphrates), riv.,
  Asia D12 14
Fircrest, Wash. f10 86
Firebaugh, Calif. D3 50
Firenze, see Florence, It.

Firenzuola, It. B3 9
Firminy, Fr. E6 5
Firozabad, India *C6 20
Firozpur, India B5 20
Fisher, Ill. C5 58
Fisher, co., Tex. C2 84
Fisher, peak, Va. D2 85
Fishersville, Va. B4 85
Fishguard, Wales E4 4
Fishing Creek, Md. D5 53
Fishkill, N.Y. D7 75
Fiskdale, Mass. D3 65
Fitchburg, Mass. A4 65
Fitzgerald, Ga. E3 55
Fitz Roy, mtn., Arg. D2 28
Fiume, see Rijeka, Yugo.

Five Points, N.Mex. *B3 48
Flagler, co., Fla. C5 54
Flagler Beach, Fla. C5 54
Flagstaff, Ariz. B3 48
Flagtown, N.J. B3 74
Flanagan, Ill. C5 58
Flanders, N.Y. *n16 75
Flandreau, S.Dak. F9 77
Flat Creek, Ala. B2, f6 46
Flathead, co., Mont. B2 70
Flathead, mts., Mont. B2 70
Flatonia, Tex. E4 84
Flat River, Mo. D7 69
Flat Rock, Newf., Can. *E5 44
Flat Rock, Mich. F7 66
Flat Rock, N.C. f10 76
Flatwoods, Ky. B7 62
Fleetwing Estates, Pa. *F11 81
Fleetwood, Pa. F10 81
Fleming, co., Ky. B6 62
Flemingsburg, Ky. B6 62
Flemington, N.J. B3 74
Flemington, Pa. D7 81
Flensburg, Ger., Fed. Rep. of A4 6
Flers, Fr. C3 5
Fletcher, N.C. f10 76
Fletcher, Okla. C4 79
Flin Flon, Man., Can. B1, g7 40
Flint, Mich. F7 66
Flint, co., Wales *D5 4
Forest, Ont., Can. D2 41
Flintridge, Calif. *F4 50
Flomaton, Ala. D2 46
Floodwood, Minn. D6 67
Flora, Ill. E5 58
Flora, Ind. C4 59
Florala, Ala. D3 46
Floral City, Fla. D4 54
Floral Park, Mont. *D4 70
Floral Park, N.Y. k13 75
Flordell Hills, Mo. *C7 69
Florence, Ala. A2 46
Florence, Ariz. C3, D2 48
Florence, Calif. *E4 50
Florence, Colo. C5 51
Florence (Firenze), It. C3 9
Florence, Kans. D7 61
Florence, KY. B5, k13 62
Florence, N.J. C3 74
Florence, Oreg. D2 80
Florence, S.C. C8 82
Florence, Wis. C5 88
Florence, co., S.C. C8 82
Florence, co., Wis. C5 88
Florence (Firenze), It. C3 9
Florencia, Col. C2 32
Flores, Guat. H12 33
Flores, isl., Indon. G6 10
Flores, dept., Ur. *E1 30
Floresville, Tex. E3, k7 84
Florham Park, N.J. B4 74
Floriano, Braz. D6 27
Florianópolis, Braz. *D3 30
Florida, Cuba D4 35
Florida, N.Y. D6, m14 75
Florida, Ur. E1 30
Florida, dept., Ur. *E1 30
Florida, state, U.S. E10 45
Florida, bay, Fla. E10 54
Florida City, Fla. G6, t13 54
Florida Keys, is., Fla. H6 54
Florina, Grc. E5 10
Flórina, prov., Grc. *B3 14
Florissant, Mo. f13 69
Flossmoor, Ill. k9 58
Flourtown, Pa. o21 81
Flower Hill, N.Y. *E7 75
Floyd, co., Ga. B1 55
Floyd, co., Ind. H6 59
Floyd, co., Iowa A5 60
Floyd, co., Ky. C7 62
Floyd, co., Tex. B2 84
Floyd, co., Va. D2 85
Floydada, Tex. C2 84
Flushing, Mich. E7 66
Flushing, Ohio B4 78
Fluvanna, co., Va. C4 85
Foam Lake, Sask., Can. F4 39

Foard, co., Tex. B3 84
Focşani, Rom. C8 10
Foggia, It. D5 9
Fogo, Newf., Can. D4 44
Fohnsdorf, Aus. E7 6
Foix, Fr. F4 5
Folcroft, Pa. *G11 81
Foley, Ala. E2 46
Foley, Minn. E5 67
Foligno, It. C4 9
Folkestone, Eng. E7 4
Folkston, Ga. F4 55
Follansbee, W. Va. A4, f8 87
Follonica, It. C3 9
Folly Beach, S.C. F8, k12 82
Folsom, Calif. C3 50
Folsom, Pa. *G11 81
Fomento, Cuba C4 35
Fonda, Iowa B3 60
Fonda, N.Y. C6 75
Fond du Lac, Wis. E5, k9 88
Fond du Lac, co., Wis. E5 88
Fondi, It. D4 9
Fonsagrada, Sp. A2 8
Fontainebleau, Fr. C5 5
Fontana, Calif. m14 50
Fontana, Wis. F5 88
Fontanelle, Iowa C3 60
Fontenay-le-Comte, Fr. D3 5
Fontenay -sous-Bois, Fr. g10 5
Foochow, see Fuzhou, China
Footville, Wis. F4 88
Forbach, Fr. C7 5
Forbes, Austl. F8 25
Forbes, mtn., Alta., Can. D2 38
Forchheim, Ger., Fed. Rep. of D5 6
Ford, co., Ill. C5 58
Ford, co., Kans. E4 61
Ford City, Calif. E4 50
Ford City, Pa. E2 81
Fords, N.J. *B4 74
Fords Prairie, Wash. *C3 86
Fordyce, Ark. D3 49
Foreman, Ark. D1 49
Forest, Bel. B6 5
Forest, Ont., Can. D2 41
Forest, Miss. C4 68
Forest, Ohio B2 78
Forest, co., Pa. C3 81
Forest, co., Wis. C5 88
Forest Acres, S.C. C6 82
Forestburg, Alta., Can. C4 38
Forest City, Iowa A4 60
Forest City, N.C. B1, f11 76
Forest City, Pa. C11 81
Forest Grove, Oreg. B3, g11 80
Forest Heights, Md. *C4 53
Forest Hills, N.B., Can. *D4 43
Forest Hill, Tex. *C4 84
Forest Hills, Pa. k14 81
Forest Homes, Ill. *E3 58
Forest Knolls, Calif. g7 50
Forest Lake, Minn. E6 67
Forest Park, Ga. h8 55
Forest Park, Ill. K9 58
Forestview, Ill. *B6 58
Forestville, Md. *C4 53
Forestville, N.Y. C1 75
Forfar, Scot. B5 4
Forge Village, Mass. A5, f10 65
Forked River, N.J. D4 74
Forks, Wash. B1 86
Forlì, It. B4 9
Formiga, Braz. C3 30
Formosa, Arg. E4 29
Formosa, prov., Arg. E4 29
Formosa, see Taiwan, Asia
Forney, Tex. C4, n10 84
Forres, Scot. B5 4
Forrest, Ill. C5 58
Forrest, co., Miss. D4 68
Forrest City, Ark. B5 49
Forreston, Ill. A4 58
Forst, Ger. Dem. Rep. C7 6
Forster-Tuncurry,
  Austl. F9 26
Forsyth, Ga. C3 55
Forsyth, Mont. D10 70
Forsyth, co., Ga. B2 55
Forsyth, co., N.C. A2 76
Fortaleza, Braz. D7 27
Fort Atkinson, Wis. F5 88
Fort Bend, co., Tex. E5 84
Fort Benton, Mont. C6 70
Fort Bragg, Calif. C2 50
Fort Branch, Ind. H2 59
Fort Chipewyan, Alta., Can. f8 38
Fort Cobb, Okla. B3 79
Fort Collins, Colo. A5 51
Fort Collins West, Colo. *A5 51
Fort Coulonge, Que., Can. B8 41
Fort Covington, N.Y. f10 75
Fort Davis, Tex. o13 84

Fort-de France, Mart. I14 35
Fort Deposit, Ala. D3 46
Fort Dodge, Iowa B3 60
Fort Edward, N.Y. B7 75
Fort Erie, Ont., Can. E6 41
Fort Fairfield, Maine B7 64
Fort Frances, Ont., Can. o16 41
Fort Gaines, Ga. E1 55
Fort-George, Que., Can. h11 42
Fort Gibson, Okla. B6 79
Fort Hall, Idaho F6 57
Fort Hancock, Tex. o12 84
Fort Howard, Md. B5 53
Fort Johnson, N.Y. *C6 75
Fort Kent, Maine A4 64
Fort-Lamy, see Ndjamena, Chad
Fort Langley, B.C., Can. f13 37
Fort Lauderdale, Fla. F6, r13 54
Fort Lee, N.J. h9 74
Fort Levenworth, Kans. C8, k15 61
Fort-Liberté, Hai. E8 35
Fort Loramie, Ohio B1 78
Fort Lupton, Colo. A6 51
Fort Macleod, Alta.,Can. E4 38
Fort Madison, Iowa D6 60
Fort McKinley, Ohio *C1 78
Fort Meade, Fla. E5 54
Fort Mill, S.C. A6 82
Fort Morgan, Colo. A7 51
Fort Myers, Fla. F5 54
Fort Myers Beach, Fla. F5 54
Fort Nelson, B.C., Can. m18 37
Fort Oglethorpe, Ga. B1 55
Fort Payne, Ala. A4 46
Fort Peck, Mont. B10 70
Fort Pierce, Fla. E6 54
Fort Pierre, S. Dak. F5 77
Fort Plain, N.Y. C6 75
Fort Qu'Appelle, Sask., Can. G4 39
Fort Recovery, Ohio B1 78
Fort Riley, Kans. C7 61
Fort St. James, B.C., Can. B5 37
Fort St. John, B.C., Can. A7, m18 37
Fort Saskatchewan, Alta., Can. C4 38
Fort Scott, Kans. E9 61
Fort Shawnee, Ohio B1 78
Fort Smith, Ark. B1 49
Fort St. John, B.C., Can. A7, m18 37
Fort Stockton, Tex. D1 84
Fort Sumner, N. Mex. B6 48
Fort Thomas, Ky. h14 62
Fortuna, Calif. B1 50
Fortune, Newf., Can. E4 44
Fort Valley, Ga. D3 55
Fort Vermilion, Alta., Can. f7 38
Fortville, Ind. E6 59
Fort Walton Beach, Fla. u15 54
Fort Washington, Pa. o21 81
Fort Washington Forest,
  Md. C4 53
Fort Wayne, Ind. B7 59
Fort William, Scot. B4 4
Fort Worth, Tex. C4, n9 84
Fort Wright, Ky h13 62
Fort Yates, N. Dak. D5 77
Forty Fort, Pa. D10, n17 81
Fossano, It. B1 9
Fossil, Oreg. B6 80
Fossombrone, It. C4 9
Fosston, Minn. C3 67
Foster, co., N. Dak. C7 77
Foster Brook, Pa. C4 81
Foster Village, Haw. g10 56
Fostoria, Ohio A2 78
Fougères, Fr. C3 5
Foumban, Cam. G7 22
Fountain, Colo. C6 51
Fountain, co., Ind. D3 59
Fountain, peak, Calif. E6 50
Fountain City, Ind. E8 59
Fountain City, Wis. D2 88
Fountain Green, Utah B6 72
Fountain Hill, Pa. E11 81
Fountain Inn, S.C. B3 82
Fountain Place, La. *D4 63
Fountain Valley, Calif. *F5 50
Four Corners, Oreg. *C4 80
Fourmies, Fr. B6 5
Four Oaks, N.C. B4 76
Fowler, Calif. D4 50
Fowler, Colo. C6 51
Fowler, Ind. C3 59
Fowler, Kans. E3 61
Fowler, Mich. E6 66
Fowlerville, Mich. F6 66
Foxboro, Mass. B5 65
Fox Chapel, Pa. *E1 81
Fox Farm, Wyo *E8 89
Fox Harbour, Newf., Can. E5 44
Fox Lake, Ill. A5, h8 58
Fox Lake, Wis. E5 88
Fox Point, Wis. E5, m12 88
Fox River Grove, Ill. h8 58

Foxworth, Miss. ... D4 68
Frackville, Pa. ... E9 81
Fraga, Sp. ... B6 8
Framingham, Mass. ... B5, g10 65
Franca, Braz. ... C3 30
Francavilla Fontana, It. ... D6 9
France, country, Eur. ... 5
Francesville, Ind. ... C4 9
Franche-Comté reg., Fr. ... D6 5
Francistown, Bots. ... E5 24
Franconville, Fr. ... g9 5
Frankenberg, Ger., Fed. Rep. of ... C4 6
Frankenmuth, Mich. ... E7 66
Frankenthal, Ger., Fed. Rep. of ... D4 6
Frankford, Ont., Can. ... C7 41
Frankfort, Ill. ... m9 58
Frankfort, Ind. ... D4 59
Frankfort, Kans. ... C7 61
Frankfort, Ky. ... B5 62
Frankfort, Mich. ... D4 66
Frankfort, N.Y. ... B5 75
Frankfurt am Main, Ger., Fed. Rep. of ... C4 6
Frankfurt an der Oder, Ger. Dem. Rep ... B7 6
Franklin, Idaho ... *F2 57
Franklin, Ind. ... F5 59
Franklin, Kans. ... E9 61
Franklin, Ky. ... D3 62
Franklin, La. ... E4 63
Franklin, Mass. ... B5 65
Franklin, Mich. ... *F7 66
Franklin, Nebr. ... D7 71
Franklin, N.H. ... E4 73
Franklin, N.J. ... A3 74
Franklin, N.C. ... f9 76
Franklin, Ohio ... C1 78
Franklin, Pa. ... *E4 81
Franklin, Pa. ... D2 81
Franklin, Tenn. ... B5 83
Franklin, Tex. ... D4 84
Franklin (Independent City) Va. ... D6 85
Franklin, Wis. ... n11 88
Franklin, co., Ala. ... A2 46
Franklin, co., Ark. ... B2 49
Franklin, co., Fla. ... C2 54
Franklin, co., Ga. ... B3 55
Franklin, co., Idaho ... G7 57
Franklin, co., Ill. ... E5 58
Franklin, co., Ind. ... F7 59
Franklin, co. Iowa ... B4 60
Franklin, co., Kans. ... D8 61
Franklin, co., Ky. ... B5 62
Franklin, co., Maine ... C2 64
Franklin, co., Mass. ... A2 65
Franklin, co., Miss. ... D3 68
Franklin, co., Mo. ... C6 69
Franklin, co., Nebr. ... D7 71
Franklin, co., N.Y. ... A6 75
Franklin, co., N.C. ... A4 76
Franklin, co., Ohio ... B2 78
Franklin, co., Pa. ... G6 81
Franklin, co., Tenn. ... B5 83
Franklin, co., Tex. ... C5 84
Franklin, co., Vt. ... B2 73
Franklin, co., Va. ... D3 85
Franklin, co., Wash. ... C6 86
Franklin, dist., N. W. Ter., Can. ... B13 36
Franklin, par.,La. ... B4 63
Franklin Furnace, Ohio ... D3 78
Franklin Grove, Ill. ... B4 58
Franklin Lakes, N.J. ... *B4 74

Franklin Park, Ill. ... k9 58
Franklin Park, N.J. ... C3 74
Franklin Park, Va. ... *B5 85
Franklin Square, N.Y. ... G2 52
Franklinton La. ... D5 63
Franklinton, N.C. ... A4 76
Franklinville, N.J. ... D2 74
Franklinville, N.Y. ... C2 75
Franklinville, N.C. ... B3 76
Frankston, Tex. ... C5 84
Frankton, Ind. ... D6 59
Frascati, It. ... D4, h9 9
Fraser, Mich. ... *F8 66
Fraser, riv., B.C., Can. ... C6 37
Fraser, mtn., B.C., Can. ... C8 37
Fraserburgh, Scot. ... B6 4
Frauenfeld, Switz. ... E4 6
Fray Bentos, Ur. ... E1 30
Frazee, Minn. ... D3 67
Frazeyburg, Ohio ... B3 78
Frazier Park, Calif. ... E4 50
Frederic, Wis. ... C1 88
Fredericia, Den. ... J3 11
Frederick, Md. ... B3 53
Frederick, Okla. ... C2 79
Frederick, co., Md. ... B3 53
Frederick, co., Va. ... A4 85
Fredericksburg, Iowa ... B5 60
Fredericksburg, Pa. ... *F9 81
Fredericksburg, Tex. ... D3 84
Fredericksburg (Independent City), Va. ... B5 85
Fredericktown, Mo. ... D7 69
Fredericktown, Ohio ... B3 78
Fredericktown, Pa. ... F1 81
Fredericton, N.B., Can. ... D3 43
Frederiksborg, co., Den. ... *J5 11
Frederikshavn, Den. ... I4 11
Frederiksted, Vir. Is., (U.S.) ... H12 35
Fredonia, Kans. ... E8 61
Fredonia, N.Y. ... C1 75
Fredonia, Pa. ... D1 81
Fredonia, Wis. ... E6 88
Fredrikstad, Nor. ... H4, p28 11
Freeborn, co., Minn. ... G5 67
Freeburg, Ill. ... E4 58
Freedom, Calif. ... *D3 50
Freedom, Pa. ... E1 81
Freehold, N.J. ... C4 74
Freel, peak, Calif. ... C4 50
Freeland, Mich. ... E6 66
Freeland, Pa. ... D10 81
Freelandville, Ind. ... G3 59
Freeman, S. Dak. ... G8 77
Freemansburg, Pa. ... E11 81
Freeport, Fla. ... u15 54
Freeport, Ill. ... A4 58
Freeport, Maine ... E2, g7 64
Freeport ,Minn. ... E4 67
Freeport, N.Y. ... G2 52
Freeport, Pa. ... E2 81
Freeport, Tex. ... E5, s14 84
Freer, Tex. ... F3 84
Freestone, co., Tex. ... D4 84
Freetown, N.Y. ... *m16 75
Freetown, S.L. ... G2 22
Fregenal de la Sierra, Sp. ... C2 8
Freiberg, Ger. Dem. Rep ... C6 6
Freiburg im Breisgau, Ger., Fed. Rep. of ... D3 6
Freising, Ger., Fed. Rep. of ... D5 6
Freistadt, Aus. ... D7 6
Fréjus, Fr. ... F3 5

Fremantle, Austl. ... F2 25
Fremont, Calif. ... D2, h9 50
Fremont, Ind. ... A8 59
Fremont, Mich. ... E5 66
Fremont, Nebr. ... C9, g11 71
Fremont, N.C. ... B5 76
Fremont, Ohio ... A2 78
Fremont, co., Colo. ... C5 51
Fremont, co., Idaho ... E7 57
Fremont, co., Iowa ... D2 60
Fremont, co., Wyo. ... C4 89
French Camp, Calif. ... *D3 50
French Guiana, dep., S.A. ... C5 27
French Lick, Ind. ... G4 59
French Polynesia, Fr. dep., Oceania ... *H11 2
Frenchtown, N.J. ... B2 74
Frenchville, Maine ... A4 64
Freshfield, mtn., Alta., Can. ... D9 37
Freshwater, Newf., Can. ... *f9 44
Fresnillo de González Echeverría, Mex. ... C4 34
Fresno, Calif. ... D4 50
Fresno, co., Calif. ... D4 50
Freudenstadt, Ger., Fed. Rep. of ... D4 6
Frewsburg, N.Y. ... C1 75
Friant, Calif. ... D4 50
Friars Point, Miss. ... A3 68
Frias, Arg. ... E2 29
Fribourg, Switz. ... E8 6
Fribourg, canton, Switz. ... *E3 6
Friday Harbor, Wash. ... A2 86
Fridley, Minn. ... m12 67
Friedberg, Ger., Fed. Rep. of ... B6 6
Friedens, Pa. ... F4 81
Friedland, Ger. Dem. Rep. ... B6 6
Friedrichshafen, Ger., Fed. Rep. of ... E4 6
Friend, Nebr. ... D8 71
Friendship, N.Y. ... C2 75
Friern Barnet, Eng. ... k12 4
Fries, Va. ... D2 85
Friesland, prov., Neth. ... *A6 5
Frio, co., Tex. ... E3 84
Friona, Tex. ... B1 84
Frisco, Pa. ... *E1 81
Frisco, Tex. ... *C4 84
Frisco City, Ala. ... D2 46
Fritch, Tex. ... B2 84
Fritzlar, Ger., Fed. Rep. of ... C4 6
Friuli-Venezia Giulia, reg., It. ... *B4 9
Frontenac, Kans. ... E9 61
Frontenac, Mo. ... *C7 69
Frontenac, co., Ont., Can. ... C8 41
Frontenac, co., Que., Can. ... D7 42
Frontera, Mex. ... D6 34
Frontier, co., Nebr. ... D5 71
Frontignan, Fr. ... F5 5
Frontino, peak, Col. ... B2 32
Front Royal, Va. ... B4 85
Frosinone, It. ... D4 9
Frostburg, Md. ... k13 53
Frostproof, Fla. ... E5 54
Frouard, Fr. ... C7 4
Fruita, Colo. ... B2 51
Fruitdale, Oreg. ... *E3 80
Fruitland, Idaho ... F2 57
Fruitland, Ill. ... *B3 58
Fruitland, Md. ... D6 53
Fruitland Park, Fla. ... D5 54
Fruitport, Mich. ... E4 66
Fruitvale, Wash. ... *C5 86

Fruitville, Fla. ... E4, q11 54
Frunze, Sov. Un. ... E10 13
Frýdek-Mistek,Czech. ... D5 7
Fryeburg, Maine ... D2 64
Fthiotis (Phthiotis), prov., Grc. ... *C4 14
Fuchou see Fuzhou, China
Fuchu, Jap. ... *I9 18
Fuente Alamo, Sp. ... D5 8
Fuente de Cantos, Sp. ... C2 8
Fuenteovejuna, Sp. ... C3 8
Fuhai, China ... B2 17
Fuji, Jap. ... n17 18
Fuji, vol., Jap. ... I9, n17 18
Fujian, prov., China ... F8 17
Fujieda, Jap. ... o17 18
Fujimi, Jap. ... n17 18
Fujin, China ... B11 17
Fujinomiya, Jap. ... n17 18
Fujisawa, Jap. ... *I9 18
Fuji-yoshida, Jap. ... n17 18
Fukagawka, Jap. ... E10 18
Fukuchiyama, Jap. ... I7, n14 18
Fukui, Jap. ... H8 18
Fukui, pref., Jap. ... *H8 18
Fukuoka, Jap. ... F10 18
Fukuoka, Jap. ... J5 18
Fukuoka, pref., Jap. ... *J5 18
Fukushima, Jap. ... I8, n16 18
Fukushima, Jap. ... H10 18
Fukushima, pref., Jap. ... *H10 18
Fukuyama, Jap. ... I6 18
Fulda, Ger., Fed. Rep. of ... C4 6
Fulda, Minn. ... G3 67
Fullerton, Calif. ... n13 50
Fullerton, Ky. ... B7 62
Fullerton, Nebr. ... C8 71
Fulton, Ill. ... B3 58
Fulton, Ky. ... f9 62
Fulton, Miss. ... A5 68
Fulton, Mo. ... C6 69
Fulton, N.Y. ... B4 75
Fulton, co., Ark. ... A4 49
Fulton, co., Ga. ... C2 55
Fulton, co., Ill. ... C3 58
Fulton, co., Ind. ... B5 59
Fulton, co., Ky. ... B2 62
Fulton, co., N.Y. ... B6 75
Fulton, co., Ohio ... A1 78
Fulton, co., Pa. ... G5 81
Fultondale, Ala. ... f7 46
Fumay, Fr. ... C6 5
Funabashi, Jap. ... n19 18
Funchal, Port. ... h12 8
Fundación, Col. ... A3 32
Funkstown, Md. ... A2 53
Fuquay-Varina, N.C. ... *B4 76
Furano, Jap ... E11 18
Furman University,S.C. ... *B3 82
Furnas, co., Nebr. ... D6 71
Fürstenfeld, Aus. ... E8 6
Fürstenwalde, Ger. Dem. Rep. ... B7 6
Fürth, Ger., Fed. Rep. of ... D5 6
Furukawa, Jap. ... H8, m16 18
Fusagasugá, Col. ... C3 32
Fushun, China ... C9 17
Fusong, China ... E3 18
Füssen, Ger., Fed. Rep. of ... E5 6
Fuxin, China ... C9 17
Fuyang, China ... E8 17
Fuyu, China ... B9 17
Fuyuan, China ... B7 18
Fuzhou, China ... F8 17

G

Gabès, Tun. ... B7 22
Gabin, Pol. ... B5 7
Gabon (Gabun),country, Afr. ... I7 22
Gaborone, Bots. ... E5 24
Gabrovo, Bul. ... D7 10
Gadag, India ... E6 20
Gadsden, Ala. ... A3 46
Gadsden, co., Fla. ... B2 54
Gadyach, Sov.Un ... F9 12
Gäesti, Rom. ... C7 10
Gaeta, It. ... D4 9
Gaffney, S.C. ... A4 82
Gafsa, Tun. ... B6 22
Gage, co., Nebr. ... D9 71
Gages Lake, Ill. ... *A5 58

Gagnon, Que., Can. ... h13 42
Gagny, Fr. ... g11 5
Gahanna, Ohio ... k11 78
Gaillac, Fr. ... F4 5
Gaines, co., Tex. ... C1 84
Gainesboro, Tenn. ... C8 83
Gainesville, Fla. ... C4 54
Gainesville, Ga. ... B3 55
Gainesville, Tex. ... C4 84
Gainsborough, Eng. ... D6 4
Gairdner, lake, Austl. ... F6 25
Gairloch, Scot. ... B4 4
Gaithersburg, Md. ... B3 53
Gaixian, China ... C9 17
Galacz, see Galati, Rom.

Galápagos, prov., Ec. ... g5 31
Galashiels, Scot. ... C5 4
Galati, Rom. ... C8 10
Galatia, Ill. ... F5 58
Galatina, It. ... D7 9
Galax (Independent City), Va. ... D2 85
Gáldar, Sp. ... m14 8
Galeana, Mex. ... A3 34
Galena, Ill. ... A3 58
Galena, Kans. ... E9 61
Galena Park, Tex. ... r14 84
Gales, peak, Oreg. ... g11 80
Galesburg, Ill. ... C3 58
Galesburg, Mich. ... F5 66
Galesville, Md. ... C4 53

Galesville, Wis. ... D2 88
Galeton, Pa. ... C6 81
Galeville, N.Y. ... *B4 75
Galicia, reg., Pol., Sov. Un. ... D6 7
Galicia, reg., Sp. ... A1 8
Galien, Mich. ... G4 66
Galion, Ohio ... B3 78
Gallarate, It. ... B1 9
Gallatin, Mo. ... B4 69
Gallatin, Tenn. ... A5 83
Gallatin, co., Ill. ... F5 58
Gallatin, co., Ky. ... B5 62
Gallatin, co., Mont. ... E5 70
Galle, Sri Lanka ... G7 20
Gallia, co., Ohio ... D3 78

Gallipoli, It. D6 9
Gallipoli, see Gelibolu, Tur.
Gallipolis, Ohio D3 78
Gallitzin, Pa. F4 81
Gällivare, Swe. D9 11
Galloway, W. Va. B4 87
Gallup, N. Mex. B4 48
Galt, Calif. C3 50
Galt, Ont., Can. D4 41
Galty, mts., Ire. D2 4
Galva, Ill. B3 58
Galveston, Ind. C5 59
Galveston, Tex. E5, r15 84
Galveston, co., Tex. E5 84
Galway, Ire. D2 4
Galway, co., Ire. *D2 4
Gamagori, Jap. o16 18
Gamarra, Col. B3 22
Gambia, country, Afr. F1 32
Gambia, riv., Afr. F2 22
Gambier, Ohio B3 78
Gamboa, Pan. *B2 32
Gambrills, Md. B4 53
Ganado, Tex. E4 84
Gananoque, Ont., Can. C8 41
Gand, see Gent, Bel.
Gander, Newf., Can. D4 44
Gandhinager, India D5 20
Gandía, Sp. C5 8
Gangaw, Bur. D9 20
Ganges, riv., Asia D8 20
Gangtok, India C8 20
Gannat, Fr. D5 5
Gannett, peak, Wyo. C3 89
Gansu, prov., China D5 17
Gantt, S.C. B3 82
Ganzhou, China F7 17
Gao, Mali E5 22
Gap, Fr. E7 5
Gap, Pa. G9 81
Gar, China B7 20
Garanhuns, Braz. *D7 27
Garber, Okla. A4 27
Garberville, Calif. B2 50
Garça, Braz. C3 30
Garciasville, Tex. F3 84
Gard, dept., Fr. *F6 5
Gardelegen, Ger. Dem. Rep. B5 6
Garden, co., Nebr. C3 71
Gardena, Calif. n12 50
Garden City, Ga. D5 55
Garden City, Idaho *F2 57
Garden City, Kans. E3 61
Garden City, Mich. p15 66
Garden City, Mo. C3 69
Garden City, N.Y. G2 52
Garden City, Pa. *G11 81
Garden City Park, N.Y. *G2 52
Gardendale, Ala. B3, f7 46
Garden Grove, Calif. n13 50
Garden Home, Oreg. *B4 80
Garden Lakes, Ga. *B1 55
Garden View, Pa. *D7 81
Gardez, Afg. B4 20
Gardiner, Maine D3 64
Gardiner, Mont. E6 70
Gardner, Ill. B5 58
Gardner, Kans. D9 61
Gardner, Mass. A4 65
Garfield, N.J. h8 74
Garfield, Wash. B8 86
Garfield, co., Colo. B2 51
Garfield, co., Mont. C9 70
Garfield, co., Nebr. C6 71
Garfield, co., Okla. A4 79
Garfield, co., Utah C6 72
Garfield, co., Wash. C8 86
Garfield Heights, Ohio h9 78
Garfield peak, Wyo. D5 89
Gargaliánoi, Grc. D3 14
Garibaldi, Oreg. B3 80
Garibaldi, mtn., B.C., Can. E6 37
Garland, Md. *B4 53
Garland, N.C. C4 76
Garland, Tex. n10 84
Garland, Utah A5 72
Garland, co., Ark. C2 49
Garmisch-Partenkirchen,
  Ger., Fed. Rep. of E5 6
Garnavillo, Iowa B6 60
Garner, Iowa A4 60
Garner, N.C. B4 76
Garnett, Kans. D8 61
Garoua, Cam. G7 22
Garrard, co., Ky. C5 62
Garrett, Ind. B7 59
Garrett, Ky. C7 62
Garrett, co., Md. k12 53
Garrett Park, Md. B3 53
Garrett Park Estates, Md. *B3 53
Garrettsville, Ohio A4 78
Garrison, Md. B4 53
Garrison, N.Dak. *C4 77

Garrison, Tex. D5 84
Garrovillas, Sp. C2 8
Garson, Ont., Can. *p19 41
Garut, Indon. G3 19
Garvin, co., Okla. C4 79
Garwolin, Pol. C6 7
Garwood, N.J. *B4 74
Gary, Ind. A3 59
Gary, W. Va. D3 87
Garyville, La. D5, h10 63
Garza, co., Tex. C2 84
Garzón, Col. C2 32
Gas City, Ind. D6 59
Gasconade, co., Mo. C6 69
Gascony (Gascogne),
  former prov., Fr. E3 5
Gaspé, Que., Can. k14 42
Gaspe East, co., Que., Can. ... *k14 42
Gaspe West, co., Que., Can. .. *k13 42
Gasport, N.Y. B2 75
Gassaway, W. Va. C4 87
Gaston, Ind. D7 59
Gaston, N.C. A5 76
Gastonia, co., N.C. B1 76
Gastonia, N.C. B1 76
Gatchina, Sov. Un. H14, s31 11
Gate City, Va. f9 85
Gates, N.Y. *B3 75
Gates, co., N.C. A6 76
Gateshead, Eng. C6 4
Gates Mills, Ohio *A4 78
Gatesville, Tex. D4 84
Gatineau, Que., Can. D2 42
Gatineau, co., Que., Can. C2 42
Gatlinburg, Tenn. D10 83
Gatton, Austl. C9 26
Gatun, Pan. *B2 32
Gauhāti, India C9 20
Gauley Bridge, W. Va. C3, m13 87
Gävle, Swe. G7 11
Gävleborg, co., Swe. *G7 11
Gavrilovka, Sov. Un. G11 12
Gawler, Austl. G2 26
Gaya, India D7 20
Gaylord, Mich. C6 66
Gaylord, Minn. F4 67
Gaysin, Sov. Un. G7 12
Gays Mills, Wis. E3 88
Gaza (Ghazzah), Gaza Strip ... C2 15
Gaza Strip, Israeli occ., Asia ... C2 15
Gaziantep, Tur. D11 14
Gdańsk (Danzig), Pol. A5 7
Gdynia, Pol. A5 7
Gearhart, mtn., Oreg. E6 80
Geary, N.B., Can. D3 43
Geary, Okla. B3 79
Geary, co., Kans. D7 61
Geauga, co., Ohio A4 78
Gediz, Tur. C7 14
Geelong, Austl. G7, n14 25
Geislingen, Ger., Fed. Rep of .. D4 6
Geistown, Pa. F4 81
Gejiu, China G5 17
Gela, It. F5 9
Gelderland, prov., Neth. *A6 5
Gelibolu, Tur. B6 14
Gelsenkirchen,
  Ger. Fed. Rep of C3 6
Gem, co., Idaho *E2 57
Gemlik, Tur. B7 14
General Belgrano, Arg. B5 28
General Madariaga, Arg. B5 28
General Pico, Arg. B4 28
General Roca, Arg. B3 28
Genessee, Idaho C2 57
Genesee, Mich. E7 66
Genesee, co., Mich. E7 66
Genesee, co., N.Y. B2 75
Geneseo, Ill. B3 58
Geneseo, N.Y. C3 75
Geneva, Ala. D4 46
Geneva, Ill. B5 58
Geneva, Ind. C8 59
Geneva, Nebr. D8 71
Geneva, N.Y. C4 75
Geneva, Ohio A5 78
Geneva-on-the-Lake, Ohio A5 78
Geneva, co., Ala. D4 46
Genève (Geneva), Switz. E3 6
Genève, canton, Switz. *E3 6
Genevia, Ark. C3, k10 49
Genichesk, Sov. Un. H10 12
Genk, Bel. B6 5
Gennevillliers, Fr. g10 5
Genoa, Ill. A5 58
Genoa (Genova), It. B2 9
Genoa, Nebr. C8 71
Genoa, Ohio A2, e7 78
Genoa City, Wis. F5, n11 88
Genova, see Genoa, It.
Gent (Ghent), Bel. B5 5
Genthin, Ger. Dem. Rep. B6 6
Gentilly, Fr. g10 5

Gentry, co., Mo. A3 9
Genzano di Roma, It. h9 9
George, Iowa A2 60
George, S. Afr. G4 24
George, co., Miss. E5 68
George, hill, Md. k12 53
George Town, Austl. o15 25
Georgetown, Ont., Can. D5 41
Georgetown, P.E.I., Can. C7 43
Georgetown, Conn. D3 52
Georgetown, Del. C7 53
Georgetown, Guy. C5 27
Georgetown, Idaho G7 57
Georgetown, Ill. D6 58
Georgetown, Ind. H6 59
Georgetown, Ky. B5 62
Georgetown, Mass. A6 65
Georgetown, Ohio D2 78
Georgetown, S.C. E9 82
George Town (Pinang), Mala. .. D2 19
Georgetown, co., S.C. E9 82
George West, Tex. E3 84
Georgia (Georgian S.S.R.),
  rep., Sov. Un. *A3 15
Georgia, state, U.S. 55
Georgiana, Ala. D3 46
Gera, Ger. Dem. Rep. C6 6
Geraldton, Austl. E1 25
Geraldton, Ont., Can. o18 41
Gerber, Calif. B2 50
Gering, Nebr. C2 71
Gerlachovka, mtn., Czech. D6 7
German Democratic
  Republic, country, Eur. E10 6
Germantown, Ill. E4 58
Germantown, Ohio C1 78
Germantown, Tenn. B2 83
Germantown, Wis. E5, m11 88
Germany, East, see German
  Democratic Republic, country, Eur.
Germany, Federal Republic
  of, country, Eur. E9 6
Germany, West, see
  Germany, Federal
  Republic of, country, Eur.
Germiston, S. Afr. F5 24
Gero, Jap. n16 18
Gerona, Sp. B7 8
Gerona, prov., Sp. *B7 8
Gers, dept., Fr. *F4 5
Gertrudis Sánchez, Mex. h9 34
Getafe, Sp. B4, p17 8
Gettysburg, Pa. G7 81
Gettysburg, S.Dak. E6 77
Geyserville, Calif. C2 50
Ghana, country, Afr. G4 22
Gharyān, Libya B7 22
Ghazni, Afg. B4 20
Ghazzah, see
  Gaza, Gaza Strip
Ghent, see Gent, Bel.
Gheorgheni, Rom. B7 10
Gherla, Rom. B6 10
Ghilizane, Alg. A5 22
Gia Dinh, Viet. S. C3 19
Giant, mtn., N.Y. A7 75
Gibara, Cuba D5 35
Gibbon, Minn. F4 67
Gibbon, Nebr. D7 71
Gibbstown, N.J. D2 74
Gibraleón, Sp. D2 8
Gibraltar, Gib. D3 8
Gibraltar, Mich. *F7 66
Gibraltar, Br. dep., Eur. *D3 8
Gibsland, La. B2 63
Gibson, co., Ind. H2 59
Gibson, co., Tenn. A3 83
Gibsonburg, Ohio A2, e7 78
Gibson City, Ill. C5 58
Gibsonia, Pa. h14 81
Gibsons, B.C., Can. E6 37
Gibsonton, Fla. p11 54
Gibsonville, N.C. A3 76
Giddings, Tex. D4 84
Gideon, Mo. E8 69
Gien, Fr. D5 5
Giessen, Ger., Fed. Rep. of C4 6
Gifford, Fla. E6 54
Gifu, Jap. I8, n15 18
Gifu, pref., Jap. *I8 18
Gigante, Col. C2 32
Gig Harbor, Wash. B3, f10 86
Gijon, Sp. A3 8
Gila, co., Ariz. C3 48
Gila, riv., Ariz., N.Mex. D4 45
Gila Bend, Ariz. E3 48
Gilbert, Ariz. C3, D2 48
Gilbert, Minn. C6 67
Gilbert, peak, Wash. C4 86
Gilberton, Pa. *E9 81
Gilbert Plains, Man., Can. D1 40
Gilbertsville, Pa. F10 81
Gilbertville, Iowa B5 60

Gilbertville, Mass. B3 65
Gilchrist, co., Fla. C4 54
Giles, co., Tenn. B4 83
Giles, co., Va. C2 85
Gilford Park, N.J. *D4 74
Gillespie, Ill. D4 58
Gillespie, co., Tex. D3 84
Gillett, Wis. D5 88
Gillette, Wyo. B7 89
Gilliam, co., Oreg. B6 80
Gillingham, Eng. E7 4
Gilly, Bel. B6 5
Gilman, Ill. C5 58
Gilmer, Tex. C5 84
Gilmer, co., Ga. B2 55
Gilmer, co., W.Va. C4 87
Gilmore City, Iowa B3 60
Gilpin, co., Colo. B5 51
Gilroy, Calif. D3 50
Gimli, Man., Can. D3 40
Ginosa, It. D6 9
Ginzo, Sp. A2 8
Gioia del Colle, It. D6 9
Gioiosa Ionica, It. E6 9
Girard, Ill. D4 58
Girard, Kans. E9 61
Girard, Ohio A5 78
Girard, Pa. B1 81
Girardot, Col. C3 32
Girardville, Pa. E9 81
Giresun, Tur. B12 14
Giridih, India D8 20
Girishk, Afg. B3 20
Gironde, dept., Fr. *E3 5
Girvan, Scot. C4 4
Gisborne, N.Z. M17 26
Giscome, B.C., Can. B6 37
Gisors, Fr. C4 5
Giteqa, Burundi I4 23
Giulianova, It. C4 9
Giurgiu, Rom. D7 10
Giv'atayim, Isr. *B2 15
Givet, Fr. B6 5
Givors, Fr. F6 5
Gjinokaster, Alb. B3 14
Gjinokaster, pref., Alb. *B3 14
Gjövik, Nor. G4 11
Glace Bay, N.S., Can. C10 43
Glacier, co., Mont. B3 70
Glacier, peak, Wash. A4 86
Gladbrook, Iowa B5 60
Glades, co., Fla. F5 54
Glade Spring, Va. f10 85
Gladewater, Tex. C5 84
Gladstone, Austl. D9 25
Gladstone, Man., Can. D2 40
Gladstone, Mich. C4 66
Gladstone, Mo. h10 69
Gladstone, N.J. B3 74
Gladstone, Oreg. B4, h12 80
Gladwin, Mich. E6 66
Gladwin, co., Mich. D6 66
Gladwyne, Pa. *F11 81
Glamoč, Yugo. C3 10
Glamorgan, co., Wales *E5 4
Glandorf, Ohio A1 78
Glarus, Switz. E4 6
Glarus, canton, Switz. *E4 6
Glasco, Kans. C6 61
Glasco, N.Y. C7 75
Glascock, co., Ga. C4 55
Glasford, Ill. C4 58
Glasgow, Ky. C4 62
Glasgow, Mo. B5 69
Glasgow, Mont. B10 70
Glasgow, Scot. C4 4
Glasgow, Va. C3 85
Glasgow, W.Va. m13 87
Glassboro, N.J. D2 74
Glasscock, co., Tex. D2 84
Glassport, Pa. F2 81
Glastonbury, Conn. C6 52
Glauchau, Ger. Dem. Rep. C6 6
Gleason, Tenn. A3 83
Gleasondale, Mass. g9 65
Glenarden, Md. *C4 53
Glen Allen, Va. C5 85
Glen Alpine, N.C. B1, f11 76
Glen Avon Heights, Calif. *F5 50
Glenboro, Man., Can. E2 40
Glen Burnie, Md. B4 53
Glen Carbon, Ill. E4 58
Glencoe, Ala. B4 46
Glencoe, Ont., Can. E3 41
Glencoe, Ill. A6, h9 58
Glencoe, Minn. F4 67
Glen Cove, N.Y. h13 75
Glendale, Ariz. C2, D1 48
Glendale, Calif. m12 50
Glendale, Mo. *C7 69
Glendale, Ohio C1, m13 78
Glendale, S.C. B4 82
Glen Dale, W.Va. B4 87

Glendale, Wis. *E6 88
Glendive, Mont. C12 70
Glendora, Calif. m13 50
Glendora, N.J. *D2 74
Glen Ellyn, Ill. k8 58
Glen Gardner, N.J. B3 74
Glengarry, co., Ont., Can. B10 41
Glen Head, N.Y. *F2 52
Glen Innes, Austl. E9 25
Glen Jean, W.Va. D3, n13 87
Glen Lake, B.C., Can. E5 37
Glen Lyon, Pa. D9 81
Glen Moore, Pa. *G9 81
Glenmora, La. D3 63
Glenn, co., Calif. C2 50
Glenn Dale, Md. C4 53
Glenns Ferry, Idaho G3 57
Glennville, Ga. E5 55
Glenolden, Pa. p20 81
Glenorchy, Austl. o15 25
Glen Raven, N.C. A3 76
Glen Rock, Pa. G8 81
Glenrock, Wyo. D7 89
Glen Rose, Tex. C4 84
Glens Falls, N.Y. B7 75
Glenshaw, Pa. *E1 81
Glenside, Pa. o21 81
Glen Ullin, N. Dak. D4 77
Glenview, Ill. h9 58
Glenview Countryside, Ill. *E2 58
Glenville, Minn. G5 67
Glenville, W. Va. C4 87
Glenwillard, Pa. *E1 81
Glenwood, Newf., Can. D4 44
Glenwood, Iowa C2 60
Glenwood, Minn. E3 67
Glenwood, Va. *D3 85
Glenwood Landing, N.Y. *F2 52
Glenwood Springs, Colo. B3 51
Glidden, Iowa B3 60
Glidden, Wis. B3 88
Gliwice, Pol. C5, g9 7
Globe, Ariz. C3, D3 48
Globino, Sov. Un. G9 12
Glochika, Sov. Un. G9 12
Gloucester, Eng. E5 4
Gloucester, Mass. A6, f13 65
Gloucester, co., N.B., Can. B4 43
Gloucester, co.,Eng. *E5 4
Gloucester, co., N.J. D2 74
Gloucester, co., Va. C6 85
Gloucester City, N.J. D2 74
Glouster, Ohio C3 78
Gloversville, N.Y. B6 75
Glovertown, Newf., Can. D4 44
Glovertown South, Newf., Can. *D5 44
Gloverville, S.C. E4 82
Glubczyce, Pol. C4 7
Glubokoye, Sov. Un. D6 12
Głuchołazy, Pol. C4 7
Gluck, S.C. C2 82
Gluckhov, Sov. Un. F9 12
Glussk, Sov. Un. E7 12
Glyndon, Md. B4 53
Glynn, co., Ga. E5 55
Gmunden, Aus. E6 6
Gnadenhutten. Ohio B4 78
Gniezno, Pol. B4 7
Goa, Daman and Diu, ter.,
   India D5, E5 20
Goat, mtn., Mont. C3 70
Gobles, Mich. F5 66
Gobo, Jap. J7 18
Goch, Ger., Fed. Rep. of C3 6
Godāvari, riv., India E6 20
Goderich, Ont., Can. D3 41
Godfrey, Ill. E3 58
Godwin Austen, peak, Pak. A6 20
Goffstown, N.H. E4 73
Gogebic, co., Mich. n12 66
Goiânia, Braz. B3 30
Goiás, state, Braz. B2 30
Gojo, Jap. o14 18
Golan Heights, hills, Syria *B3 15
Golchika, Sov. Un. B11 13
Golconda, Ill. F5 58
Gold Beach, Oreg. E2 80
Gold Coast, see Ghana, country, Afr.
Gold Coast, see Southport, Austl.
Golden, B.C., Can. D9 37
Golden, Colo. B5 51
Golden City, Mo. D3 69
Goldendale, Wash. D5 86
Golden Hill, Minn. *F6 67
Golden Hinde, mtn., B.C., Can. E5 37
Golden Meadow, La. E5 63
Golden Valley, Minn. n12 67
Golden Valley, co., Mont. D7 70
Golden Valley, co., N. Dak. D2 77
Gold Hill, Ore. E3 80
Goldsboro, N.C. B5 76
Goldsmith, Tex. D1 84
Goldthwaite, Tex. D3 84
Goleta, Calif. E4 50

Golf Manor, Ohio o13 78
Goliad, Tex. E4 84
Goliad, co., Tex. E4 84
Golspie, Scot. A5 4
Gomel, Sov. Un. E8 12
Gómez Palacio, Mex. B4 34
Gonaïves, Hai. E7 35
Gonda, India C7 20
Gondar, Eth. F5 23
Gönen, Tur. B6 14
Gonesse, Fr. g10 5
Gongga, mtn., China F5 17
Gonzales, Calif. D3 50
Gonzales, La. D5, h10 63
Gonzales, Tex. E4 84
Gonzales, co., Tex. E4 84
Goochland, co., Va. C5 85
Goodhue, co., Minn. F6 67
Gooding, Idaho G4 57
Gooding, co., Idaho F4 57
Goodland, Ind. C3 59
Goodland, Kans. C2 61
Goodman, Miss. C4 68
Good Pine, La. C3 63
Goodsprings, Ala. B2 46
Goodview, Minn. F7 67
Goodwater, Ala. B3 46
Goodwell, Okla. e9 79
Goodyear, Ariz. C3, D2 48
Goondiwindi, Austl. E9 25
Goose Bay, Newf., Can. B1, h9 44
Goose Creek, S.C. F7, k11 82
Goppingen, Ger., Fed. Rep. of D4 6
Gorakhpur, India C7 20
Gordo, Ala. B2 46
Gordon, Ga. D3 55
Gordon, Nebr. B3 71
Gordon, Pa. *E9 81
Gordon, co., Ga. B1 55
Gordonsville, Va. B4 85
Gore, Eth. G5 23
Gore, N.Z. Q10 26
Gore Bay, Ont., Can. B2 41
Gorgan, Iran B5 15
Gorgas, Ala. B2 46
Gorham, Maine E2, g7 64
Gorham, N.H. C5 73
Gorham, N.Y. C3 75
Gorizia, It. B4 9
Gorki (Gorkiy), Sov. Un. D7 13
Gorlice, Pol. D6 7
Görlitz, Ger. Dem. Rep. C7 6
Gorlovka, Sov. Un. G12, q21 12
Gorman, Tex. C3 84
Gorna-Dzhumaya, see
   Blagoevgrad, Bul.
Gorna Oryakhovitsa, Bul. D7 10
Gorno-Altaysk, Sov. Un. *D11 12
Gorodenka, Sov. Un. G5 12
Gorodisehe, Sov. Un. q22 12
Gorodnya, Sov. Un. F8 12
Gorodok, Sov. Un. D7 12
Gorodok, Sov. Un. G4 12
Gorontalo, Indon. E6 19
Gorzów Wielkopolski, Pol. B3 7
Gosford, Austl. F8 26
Goshen, Calif. *D4 50
Goshen, Ind. A6 59
Goshen, N.Y. D6, m14 75
Goshen, Ohio C1 78
Goshen, co., Wyo. D8 89
Goshogawara, Jap. F10 18
Goslar, Ger., Fed. Rep. of C5 6
Gosper, co., Nebr. D6 71
Gospic, Yugo. C2 10
Gosport, Ind. F4 59
Gostivar, Yugo. E5 10
Gostyń, Pol. C4 7
Gostynin, Pol. B5 7
Goteborg, Swe. I4 11
Göteborg, och Bohus, co., Swe. *I4 11
Gotemba, Jap. n18 18
Gotha, Ger. Dem. Rep. C5 6
Gothenburg, Nebr. D5 71
Gotland, co., Swe. *I8 11
Göttingen, Ger., Fed. Rep. of C4 6
Gottwaldov, (Zlin), Czech. D4 7
Gouda, Neth. A6 5
Goulburn, Austl. F8 25
Gould, Ark. D4 49
Goulding, Fla. *u14 54
Goulds, Fla. s13 54
Gournay-en-Bray, Fr. C4 5
Gouverneur, N.Y. f9 75
Gove, co., Kans. D3 61
Governador Valadares, Braz. B4 30
Gowanda, N.Y. C2 75
Gowrie, Iowa B3 60
Goya, Arg. E4 29
Graat-Reinet, S. Afr. G4 24
Gračanica, Yugo. C4 10
Grace, Idaho G7 57
Grace, mtn., Mass. A3 65

Grace Park, Pa. *G11 81
Graceville, Fla. u16 54
Graceville, Minn. E2 67
Gradacac, Yugo. C4 10
Gradizhsk, Sov. Un. G9 12
Grado, Sp. A2 8
Grady, co., Ga. F2 55
Grady, co., Okla. C4 79
Graehl, Alsk. *C10 47
Graettinger, Iowa A3 60
Grafton, Austl. E9 25
Grafton, Ill. E3 58
Grafton, Mass. B4 65
Grafton, N. Dak. B8 77
Grafton, Ohio A3 78
Grafton, Va. h15 85
Grafton, W.Va. B4, k10 87
Grafton, Wis. E5, m12 88
Grafton, co., N.H. D4 73
Graham, N.C. A3 76
Graham, Tex. C3 84
Graham, co., Ariz. C3 48
Graham, co., Kans. C4 61
Graham, co., N.C. f9 76
Grahamstown, S.Afr. G5 24
Grainger, co., Tenn. C10 83
Grajewo, Pol. B7 7
Gramalote, Col. B3 32
Grambling, La. B3 63
Gramercy, La. h10 63
Grammichele, It. F5 9
Granada, Nic. E7 34
Granada, Sp. D4 8
Granada, prov., Sp. *D4 8
Granbury, Tex. C4 84
Granby, Que., Can. D5 42
Granby, Mo. E3 69
Grand, co., Colo. A4 51
Grand, co., Utah B7 72
Grand, isl., La. E6 63
Grand Bank, Newf., Can. E4 44
Grand Bassam, I.C. G4 22
Grand Bay, N.B., Can. D3 43
Grand Bend, Ont., Can. D3 41
Grand Blanc, Mich. F7 66
Grand-Bourg, Guad. I14 35
Grand Centre, Alta., Can. B5 38
Grand Coteau, La. D3 63
Grand Coulee, Wash. B6 86
Grande-Entrée, Que., Can. B8 43
Grande Prairie, Alta., Can. B1, f7 38
Grande Rivière, Que., Can. *k14 42
Grandes-Bergeronnes,
   Que., Can. A8 42
Grand Falls, N.B., Can. B2 43
Grand Falls, Newf., Can. D4 44
Grandfalls, Tex. D1 84
Grandfather, mtn., N.C. A1 76
Grandfield, Okla. C3 79
Grand Forks, B.C., Can. E8 37
Grand Forks, N. Dak. C8 77
Grand Forks, co., N.Dak. C8 77
Grand Gorge, N.Y. C6 75
Grand Haven, Mich. E4 66
Grand Island, Nebr. D7 71
Grand Island, N.Y. *B2 75
Grand Isle, La. E6 63
Grand Isle, co., Vt. B1 73
Grand Junction, Colo. B2 51
Grand Junction, Iowa B3 60
Grand Ledge, Mich. F6 66
Grand Marais, Minn. k9 67
Grand Meadow, Minn. G6 67
Grand' Mère, Que., Can. C5 42
Grand Prairie, Tex. n10 84
Grand Rapids, Man., Can. C2 40
Grand Rapids, Mich. F5 66
Grand Rapids, Minn. C5 67
Grand Rapids, Ohio A2, f6 78
Grand Saline, Tex. C5 84
Grand Terrace, Calif. *F5 50
Grand Teton, mtn., Wyo. C2 89
Grand Tower, Ill. F4 58
Grand Traverse, co., Mich. D5 66
Grand Valley, Ont., Can. D4 41
Grandview, Man., Can. D1 40
Grandview, Ill. D6 58
Grand View, Ind. I4 59
Grandview, Mo. C3, k10 69
Grandview, Tex. *C4 84
Grandview, Wash. C5 86
Grandview Heights, Ohio m10 78
Grandview Heights, Pa. *G9 81
Grandville, Mich. F5 66
Granger, Tex. D4 84
Granger, Utah *A5 72
Granger, Wash. C5 86
Grangeville, Idaho D2 57
Grangeville, Pa. *G8 81
Granite, Md. B4 53
Granite, Okla. C2 79
Granite, co., Mont. D3 70
Granite, peak, Mont. E7 70

Granite, peak, Wyo. D4 89
Granite City, Ill. E3 58
Granite Falls, Minn. F3 67
Granite Falls, N.C. B1 76
Granite Falls, Wash. A4 86
Granite Quarry, N.C. B2 76
Graniteville, Mass. f10 65
Graniteville, S.C. D4 82
Granja de Torrehermosa, Sp. C3 8
Granollers, Sp. B7 8
Grant, Mich. E5 66
Grant, Nebr. D4 71
Grant, co., Ark. C3 49
Grant, co., Ind. C6 59
Grant, co., Kans. E2 61
Grant, co., Ky. B5 62
Grant, co., Minn. E2 67
Grant, co., Nebr. C4 71
Grant, co., N. Mex. C4 48
Grant, co., N. Dak. D4 77
Grant, co., Okla. A4 79
Grant, co., Oreg. C7 80
Grant, co., S. Dak. E9 77
Grant, co., Wash. B6 86
Grant, co., W.Va. B5 87
Grant, co., Wis. F3 88
Grant, par., La. C3 63
Grant City, Mo. A3 69
Grantham, Eng. D6 4
Grant Park, Ill. B6 58
Grants, N. Mex. B5 48
Grantsboro, N.C. B6 76
Grantsburg, Wis. C1 88
Grants Pass, Oreg. E3 80
Grantsville, Utah A5, D1 72
Grantsville, W. Va. C3 87
Grant Town, W. Va. B4 h10 87
Grantville, Ga. C2 55
Granville, Fr. C3 5
Granville, Ill. B4 58
Granville, N.Y. B7 75
Granville, Ohio B3 78
Granville, W. Va. h11 87
Granville, co., N.C. A4 76
Grapeland, Tex. D5 84
Grapeville, Pa. *F2 81
Grapevine, Ky. C2 62
Grapevine, Tex. C4, n9 84
Grasonville, Md. C5 53
Grasse, Fr. F7 5
Grassflat, Pa. D5 81
Grass Lake, Mich. F6 66
Grass Valley, Calif. C3 50
Gratiot, co., Mich. E6 66
Graton, Calif. *C2 50
Graubünden, canton, Switz. *E4 6
Graulhet, Fr. F5 5
Gravatá, Braz. *D7 27
Grave, peak, Idaho C4 57
Gravelbourg, Sask., Can. H2 39
Gravenhurst, Ont., Can. C5 41
Graves, co., Ky. f9 62
Gravesend, Eng. E7, m13 4
Gravina in Puglia, It. D6 9
Gray, Ga. C3 55
Gray, Ky. D5 62
Gray, co., Kans. E3 61
Gray, co., Tex. B2 84
Grayling, Mich. D6 66
Grays, peak, Colo. B5 51
Grays Harbor, co., Wash. B2 86
Grayslake, Ill. A5, h8 58
Grayson, Ky. B7 62
Grayson, co., Ky. C3 62
Grayson, co., Tex. C4 84
Grayson, co., Va. D1 85
Graysville, Ala. f7 46
Grayville, Ill. E5 58
Graz, Aus. E7 6
Great Barrington, Mass. B1 65
Great Bear, lake, Can. C9 36
Great Bend, Kans. D5 61
Great Bend, Pa. C10 81
Great Blue, hill, Mass. B5 65
Great Divide, basin, Wyo. E4 89
Greater Antilles, is., W.I. B3 27
Great Falls, Mont. G5 70
Great Falls, S.C. B6 82
Greathouse, peak, Mont. D7 70
Great Neck, N.Y. h13 75
Great Neck Estates, N.Y. n15 75
Great Salt, lake, Utah A5 72
Great Slave, lake, Can. D11 36
Great Yarmouth, Eng. D7 4
Greece, N.Y. *B3 75
Greece, country, Eur. C4 14
Greeley, Colo. A6 51
Greeley, Nebr. C7 71
Greeley, co., Kans. D2 61
Greeley, co., Nebr. C7 71
Green, co., Ky. C4 62
Green, co., Wis. F4 88
Green, riv., U.S. B6 72

Name	Grid	Page
Greenacres, Calif.	*E4	50
Greenacres, Wash.	B8, g14	86
Greenacres City, Fla.	F6	54
Greenback, Tenn.	D9	83
Green Bay, Wis.	D6, g10	88
Greenbelt, Md.	B4	53
Greenbrae, Calif.	*D2	50
Greenbrier, co., W. Va.	D4	87
Green Brook, N.J.	*B4	74
Greenbush, Mass.	h12	65
Greenbush, Minn.	B2	67
Greencastle, Ind.	E4	59
Greencastle, Pa.	G6	81
Green City, Mo.	A5	69
Green Cove Springs, Fla.	C5, n8	54
Greendale, Ind.	F8	59
Greendale, Wis.	F6, n12	88
Greene, Iowa	B5	60
Greene, N.Y.	C5	75
Greene, co., Ala.	C1	46
Greene, co., Ark.	A5	49
Greene, co., Ga.	C3	55
Greene, co., Ill.	D3	58
Greene, co., Ind.	F4	59
Greene, co., Iowa	B3	60
Greene, co., Miss.	D5	68
Greene, co., Mo.	D4	69
Greene, co., N.Y.	D6	75
Greene, co., N.C.	B5	76
Greene, co., Ohio	C2	78
Greene, co., Pa.	G1	81
Greene, co., Tenn.	C11	83
Greene, co., Va.	B4	85
Greeneville, Tenn.	C11	83
Greenfield, Calif.	D3	50
Greenfield, Ill.	D3	58
Greenfield, Ind.	E6	59
Greenfield, Iowa	C3	60
Greenfield, Mass.	A2	65
Greenfield, Mo.	D4	69
Greenfield, Ohio	C2	78
Greenfield, Tenn.	A3	83
Greenfield, Wis.	n12	88
Greenfield Park, Que., Can.	q20	42
Green Forest, Ark.	A2	49
Green Harbor, Mass.	B6	65
Green Haven, Md.	*B2	53
Greenhills, Ohio	n12	78
Green Island, N.Y.	*C7	75
Green Lake, Sask., Can.	C2	39
Green Lake, Wis.	E5	88
Green Lake, co., Wis.	E4	88
Greenland, Dan. dep., N.A.	B16	33
Greenlawn, N.Y.	F3	52
Greenlee, co., Ariz.	C4	48
Green Lookout, mtn., Wash.	D3	86
Green Manorville, Conn.	*B6	52
Green Meadows, Md.	*C4	53
Greenock, Pa.	*E1	81
Greenock, Scot.	C4	4
Greenport, N.Y.	m16	75
Green Ridge, Pa.	*G11	81
Green River, Utah	B6	72
Green River, Wyo.	E3	89
Greensboro, Ala.	C2	46
Greensboro, Fla.	B2	54
Greensboro, Ga.	C3	55
Greensboro, Md.	C6	53
Greensboro, N.C.	A3	76
Greensburg, Ind.	F7	59
Greensburg, Kans.	E4	61
Greensburg, Ky.	C4	62
Greensburg, Pa.	F2	81
Green's Harbour, Newf., Can.	E5	44
Greenspond, Newf., Can.	D5	44
Green Springs, Ohio	A2	78
Greensville, co., Va.	D5	85
Greentown, Ind.	D6	59
Green Tree, Pa.	*E1	81
Greenup, Ill.	D5	58
Greenup, Ky.	B7	62
Greenup, co., Ky.	B6	62
Greenvale, N.Y.	*F2	52
Greenview, Ill.	C4	58
Greenville, Ala.	D3	46
Greenville, co., S.C.	A3	82
Greenville, Calif.	B3	50
Greenville, Fla.	B3	54
Greenville, Ill.	E4	58
Greenville, Ky.	C2	62
Greenville, Maine	C3	64
Greenville, Mich.	E5	66
Greenville, Miss.	B2	68
Greenville, N.H.	F4	73
Greenville, N.Y.	h13	75
Greenville, N.C.	B5	76
Greenville, Ohio	B1	78
Greenville, Pa.	D1	81
Greenville, R.I.	B10	52
Greenville, S.C.	B3	82
Greenville, Tex.	C4	84
Greenville Junction, Maine	C3	64
Greenwich, Conn.	E2	52
Greenwich, Eng., (part of London)	m13	4
Greenwich, N.Y.	B7	75
Greenwich, Ohio	A3	78
Greenwood, Ark.	B1	49
Greenwood, B.C., Can.	E8	37
Greenwood, Ind.	E5, m10	59
Greenwood, Miss.	B3	68
Greenwood, Pa.	E5	81
Greenwood, S.C.	C3	82
Greenwood, Wis.	D3	88
Greenwood, co., Kans.	E7	61
Greenwood, co., S.C.	C3	82
Greenwood Lake, N.Y.	*D6	75
Greer, S.C.	B3	82
Greer, co., Okla.	C2	79
Gregg, co., Tex.	C5	84
Gregory, S. Dak.	G6	77
Gregory, Tex.	*F4	84
Gregory, co., S. Dak.	G6	77
Greifswald, Ger. Dem. Rep.	A6	6
Greilickville, Mich.	D5	66
Greiz, Ger. Dem. Rep.	C6	6
Grenada, Miss.	B4	68
Grenada, co., Miss.	B4	68
Grenada, country, N A	J14	35
Gronfell, Sask., Can.	G4	39
Grenloch, N.J.	D2	74
Grenoble, Fr.	E6	5
Grenville, Que., Can.	D3	42
Grenville, co., Ont., Can.	C9	41
Gresham, Oreg.	B4	80
Gretna, Fla.	B2	54
Gretna, La.	E5, k11	63
Gretna, Nebr.	C9, g12	71
Gretna, Va.	D3	85
Grey, co., Ont., Can.	C4	41
Greybull, Wyo.	B4	89
Greylock, mtn., Mass.	A1	65
Greymouth, N.Z.	O13	26
Gridley, Calif.	C3	50
Gridley, Ill.	C5	58
Griffin, Ga.	C2	55
Griffing Park, Tex.	*E5	84
Griffith, Austl.	F8	25
Griffith, Ind.	A3	59
Grifton, N.C.	B5	76
Griggs, co., N. Dak.	C7	77
Griggsville, Ill.	D3	58
Grimes, co., Tex.	D4	84
Grimma, Ger. Dem. Rep.	C6	6
Grimsby, Ont., Can.	D5	41
Grimsby, Eng.	D6	4
Grimshaw, Alta., Can.	A2	38
Grindstone, Pa.	*G2	81
Grinnell, Iowa	C5	60
Griswold, Iowa	C2	60
Grodno, Sov. Un.	E4	12
Grodzisk, Pol.	B4	7
Grodzisk Mazowiecki, Pol.	m13	7
Groesbeck, Ohio	*C1	78
Groesbeck, Tex.	D4	84
Grójec, Pol.	C6	7
Grombalia, Tun.	F3	9
Gronau, Ger., Fed. Rep. of	B3	6
Groningen, Neth.	A7	5
Groningen, prov., Neth.	*A7	5
Grosse Ile, Mich.	*B7	66
Grossenhain, Ger. Dem. Rep.	C6	6
Grosse Pointe, Mich.	p16	66
Grosse Pointe Farms, Mich.	*p16	66
Grosse Pointe Park, Mich.	p16	66
Grosse Pointe Shores, Mich.	F8	66
Grosse Pointe Woods, Mich.	p16	66
Grosseto, It.	C3	9
Grossglockner, mtn., Aus.	E6	6
Grossmont, Calif.	o16	50
Gros Ventre, range, Wyo.	C2	89
Groton, Conn.	D8	52
Groton, Mass.	A4, f9	65
Groton, N.Y.	C4	75
Groton, S. Dak.	E7	77
Grottaferrata, It.	h9	9
Grottaglie, It.	D6	9
Grottoes, Va.	B4	85
Grove, Okla.	A7	79
Grove City, Ohio	C2, m10	78
Grove City, Pa.	D1	81
Grove Hill, Ala.	D2	46
Groveland, Fla.	D5	54
Groveland, Mass.	A5	65
Groveport, Ohio	C2, m11	78
Grover City, Calif.	E3	50
Groves, Tex.	E6	84
Groveton, N.H.	B4	73
Groveton, Tex.	D5	84
Groveton, Va.	g12	85
Grovetown, Ga.	C4	55
Groveville, N.J.	C3	74
Groznyy, Sov. Un.	E7	13
Grudziądz, Pol.	B5	7
Grulla, Tex.	F3	84
Grundy, Va.	e9	85
Grundy, co., Ill.	B5	58
Grundy, co., Iowa	B5	60
Grundy, co., Mo.	A4	69
Grundy, co., Tenn.	D8	83
Grundy Center, Iowa	B5	60
Gruver, Tex.	A2	84
Gruz, Yugo.	D4	10
Gryazi, Sov. Un.	E12	12
Guadalajara, Mex.	C4, m12	34
Guadalajara, Sp	B4	8
Guadalajara, prov., Sp.	*B4	8
Guadalcanal, Sp.	C3	8
Guadalupe, Ariz.	D2	48
Guadalupe, Calif.	E3	50
Guadalupe, co., N. Mex.	B6	48
Guadalupe, co., Tex.	E4	84
Guadalupe, peak, Tex.	o12	84
Guadeloupe, Fr. dep., N.A.	H14	35
Guaira, dept., Par.	E4	29
Gualeguay, Arg.	A5	28
Gualeguaychú, Arg.	A5	28
Guam, U.S., dep., Oceania	*F6	2
Guanabacoa, Cuba	C2	35
Guanacaste, prov., C.R.	*E8	34
Guanajay, Cuba	C2	35
Guanajuato, Mex.	C4, m13	34
Guanajuato, state, Mex.	C4	34
Guanare, Ven.	B4	32
Guane, Cuba	C1	35
Guangdong, prov., China	G7	17
Guangxi Zhuangzu, auton reg., China	G6	17
Guánica, P.R.	*Q11	35
Guantánamo, Cuba	D6	35
Guarabira, Braz.	*D7	27
Guaranda, Ec.	B2	31
Guarapuava, Braz.	D2	30
Guaratinguetá, Braz.	C3	30
Guarda, Port.	B2	8
Guareña, Sp.	C2	8
Guárico, state, Ven.	B4	32
Guarujá, Braz.	n8	30
Guatemala, Guat.	E6	34
Guatemala, country, N.A.	D6	34
Guavaire, comisairía, Col.	C3	32
Guaxupé, Braz.	C3, k8	30
Guayabal, Cuba	D5	35
Guayama, P.R.	n13	36
Guayaquil, Ec.	B2	31
Guayas, prov., Ec.	B1	31
Guaymas, Mex.	B2	34
Gubakha, Sov. Un.	*D8	13
Gubat, Phil.	*C6	19
Gubbio, It.	C4	9
Gūdūr, India	F6	20
Guebwiller, Fr.	D7	5
Guecho, Sp.	A4	8
Guelma, Alg.	A6	22
Guelph, Ont., Can.	D4	41
Güemes, Arg.	D2	29
Guéret, Fr.	D4	5
Guerneville, Calif.	*C2	50
Guernsey, Wyo.	D8	89
Guernsey, Br. dep., Eur.	F5	4
Guernsey, co., Ohio	B4	78
Guerrero, state, Mex.	D5	34
Gueydan, La.	D3	63
Guiana, French, see French Guiana, dep., S.A.		
Guiana, Netherlands, see Surinam, Neth. dep., S.A.		
Guidonia, It.	D4, h9	9
Guildford, Eng.	E6, m11	4
Guilford, Conn.	D6	52
Guilford, Maine	C3	64
Guilford, N.C.	*A3	76
Guilford, co., N.C.	A3	76
Guilin, China	F7	17
Guimarães, Port.	B1	8
Guin, Ala.	B2	46
Guinea, country, Afr.	F2	22
Guinea-Bissau, country, Afr.	E4	21
Güines, Cuba	C2	35
Guingamp, Fr.	C2	5
Güira de Melena, Cuba	C2	35
Güiria, Ven.	A5	32
Guise, Fr.	C5	5
Guiyang, China	F6	17
Guizhou, prov., China	F6	17
Gujarat, state, India	D5	20
Gujrānwāla, Pak.	B5	20
Gujrat, Pak.	*B5	20
Gulbarga, India	E6	20
Gulf, co., Fla.	C1	54
Gulf Hammock, Fla.	C4	54
Gulfport, Fla.	E4, p10	54
Gulfport, Miss.	E4, f7	68
Gull Lake, Sask., Can.	G1	39
Gulyay-Pole, Sov. Un.	H11	12
Gumma, pref., Jap.	*H9	18
Gummersbach, Ger., Fed. Rep. of	*C3	6
Gunnedah, Austl.	E8	26
Gunnison, Colo.	C4	51
Gunnison, Utah	B6	72
Gunnison, co., Colo.	C3	51
Guntersville, Ala.	A3	46
Guntūr, India	E7	20
Gurabo, P.R.	*G11	35
Gurdon, Ark.	D2	49
Gurnee, Ill.	E8	58
Guryev, Sov. Un.	E8	13
Gusav, Nig.	F6	22
Gusev, Sov. Un.	A7	7
Gusinje, Yugo.	D4	10
Gus-Khrustalnyy, Sov. Un.	D13	12
Gustavo A. Madero, Mex.	h9	34
Gustine, Calif.	D3	50
Güstrow, Ger. Dem. Rep.	B6	6
Gütersloh, Ger., Fed. Rep of	C4	6
Guthrie, Ky.	D2	62
Guthrie, Okla.	B4	79
Guthrie, co., Iowa	C3	60
Guthrie Center, Iowa	C3	60
Guttenberg, Iowa	B6	60
Guttenberg, N.J.	h8	74
Guyana, country, S.A.	C5	27
Guyenne, former prov., Fr.	E4	5
Guymon, Okla.	e9	79
Guysborough, co., N.S., Can.	D8	43
Gvardeysk, Sov. Un.	A6	7
Gwādar, Pak.	*C3	20
Gwalior, India	C6	20
Gweru, Zimb.	D5	24
Gwinn, Mich.	Be	66
Gwinnett, co., Ga.	C2	55
Gyangzê, China	C8	20
Gympie, Austl.	E9	25
Gyöngyös, Hung.	B4	10
Győr, Hung.	B3	10
Gyor-Sopron, co., Hung.	*B3	10
Gyula, Hung.	B5	10

H

Haakon, co., S. Dak. F4 77
Haapsalu, Sov. Un. B4 12
Haarlem, Neth. A6 5
Habersham, Ga. B3 55
Habersham, co., Ga. B3 55
Haboru, Jap. D10 18
Hachiman, Jap. n15 18
Hachinohe, Jap. F10 18
Hachioji, Jap. I9, n18 18
Hackberry, La. E2 63
Hackensack, N.J. B4, h8 74
Hackettstown, N.J. B3 74
Haddonfield, N.J. D2 74
Haddon Heights, N.J. D2 74
Hadera, Isr. B2, g5 15
Haderslev, co., Den. *J3 11
Hadramawt, reg., P.D.R. of Yem. ... G4 15
Hadley, Mass. B2 65
Haeju, Kor. G2 18
Hagaman, N.Y. *C6 75
Hagar Shores (Lake Michigan
  Beach), Mich. *F4 66
Hagen, Ger., Fed. Rep. of C3 6
Hagerman, N. Mex. C6 48
Hagerstown, Ind. E7 59
Hagerstown, Md. A2 53
Hagersville, Ont., Can. E4 41
Hagi, Jap. I5 18
Ha Giang, Viet. G6 17
Haguenau, Fr. C7 5
Hague, The ('s Gravenhage),
  see The Hague, Neth.
Hahira, Ga. F3 55
Hahnville, La. E5, k11 63
Hai Duong, Viet. *A3 19
Haifa (Hefa), Isr. B3, g5 15
Hā'il, Sau. Ar. D3 15
Hailar, China B8 17
Hailey, Idaho F4 57
Haileybury, Ont., Can. p20 41
Haileyville, Okla. C6 79
Hailong, China E2 18
Hailun, China C3 18
Hainan, isl., China B4 19
Hainaut, prov., Bel. *B5 5
Haines City, Fla. D5 54
Haines Falls, N.Y. C6 75
Hainesport, N.J. D3 74
Haiphong, Viet. A3 19
Haiti, country, N.A. E7 35
Hajdu-Bihar, co., Hung. *B5 10
Hajduhadház, Hung. B5 10
Hajdunánás, Hung. B5 10
Hajduszoboszló, Hung. B5 10
Hakalau, Haw. D6 56
Hakodate, Jap. F10 18
Halawa Heights, Haw. g10 56
Halberstadt, Ger. Dem. Rep. C5 6
Halden, Nor. H4 11
Haldensleben, Ger. Dem. Rep. B5 6
Haldimand, co., Ont., Can. E5 41
Hale, co., Ala. C2 46
Hale, co., Tex. B2 84
Haleakala, crater, Haw. C5 56
Hale Center, Tex. B2 84
Haledon, N.J. *B4 74
Haleiwa, Haw. B3, f9 56
Hales Corners, Wis. n11 88
Halesite, N.Y. *n15 75
Halethorpe, Md. B4, h10 53
Haleyville, Ala. A2 46
Half Moon Bay, Calif. k8 50
Halfway, Md. A2 53
Haliburton, Ont., Can. B6 41
Haliburton, co., Ont., Can. B6 41
Halifax, N.S., Can. E6 43
Halifax, Eng. D6 4
Halifax, N.C. A5 76
Halifax, Mass. C6 65
Halifax, Pa. F8 81
Halifax, Va. D4 85
Halifax, co., N.C. A5 76
Halifax, co., N.S., Can. E7 43
Halifax, co., Va. D4 85
Hall, Aus. E5 6
Hall, co., Ga. B3 55
Hall, co., Nebr. D7 71
Hall, co., Tex. B2 84
Halland, co., Swe. I15 11
Hallandale, Fla. G6, s13 54
Halle, Ger. Dem. Rep. C5 6
Hallein, Aus. E6 6
Hallettsville, Tex. E4 84
Hallock, Minn. B2 67
Hallowell, Maine D3 64
Halls, Tenn. B2 83
Hallstead, Pa. C10 81

Hallsville, Tex. C5 84
Halmstad, Swe. I5 11
Halstad, Minn. C2 67
Halstead, Kans. E6, g11 61
Haltia, mtn., Fin. C9 11
Haltom City, Tex. *C4 84
Halton, co., Ont., Can. D4 41
Hamada, Jap. I6 18
Hamadān, Iran F7 16
Hamāh, Syr. E11 14
Hamamatsu, Jap. I8, o16 18
Hamar, Nor. G4 11
Hama-tombetsu, Jap. D11 18
Hambantota, Sri Lanka G7 20
Hamblen, co., Tenn. C10 83
Hamburg, Ark. D4 49
Hamburg, Ger., Fed. Rep. of B5 6
Hamburg, Iowa D2 60
Hamburg, N.J. A3 74
Hamburg, N.Y. C2 75
Hamburg, Pa. E10 81
Hamburg, state, Ger. Fed.
  Rep. of *B5 6
Hamburg, mts., N.J. A3 74
Hamden, Conn. D6 52
Hamden, Ohio C3 78
Häme, prov., Fin. G11 11
Hämeenlinna, Fin. G11 11
Hamel, Minn. *E5 67
Hameln, Ger., Fed. Rep. of B4 6
Hamhung, Kor. G3 18
Hami, China C3 17
Hamilton, Ala. A2 46
Hamilton, Austl. G7 25
Hamilton, Bermuda p20 35
Hamilton, Ont., Can. D5 41
Hamilton, Ill. C2 58
Hamilton, Mass. A6, f12 65
Hamilton, Mich. F4 66
Hamilton, Mo. B3 69
Hamilton, Mont. D2 70
Hamilton, N.Y. C5 75
Hamilton, N.Z. L15 26
Hamilton, Ohio C1 78
Hamilton, Scot. C4 4
Hamilton, Tex. D3 84
Hamilton, co., Fla. B3 54
Hamilton, co., Ill. E5 58
Hamilton, co., Ind. D5 59
Hamilton, co., Iowa B4 60
Hamilton, co., Kans. E2 61
Hamilton, co., Nebr. D7 71
Hamilton, co., N.Y. C5 75
Hamilton, co., Ohio C1 78
Hamilton, co., Tenn. D8 83
Hamilton, co., Tex. D3 84
Hamilton, mtn., N.Y. B6 75
Hamilton Park, Pa. *G9 81
Hamilton Square, N.J. C3 74
Hamina, Fin. G12 11
Hamiota, Man., Can. D1 40
Hamīrpur, India C7 20
Hamlet, N.C. C3 76
Hamlin, Tex. C2 84
Hamlin, co., S. Dak. F8 77
Hamm in Westfalen, Ger.,
  Fed. Rep. of C3 6
Hammon, Okla. B2 79
Hammond, Ind. A2 59
Hammond, La. D5, h11 63
Hammond, Wis. D1 88
Hammond East, La. *D5 63
Hammondsport, N.Y. C3 75
Hammonton, N.J. D3 74
Hampden, Newf., Can. D3 44
Hampden, Maine *D4 64
Hampden, co., Mass. B2 65
Hampden Highlands, Maine D4 64
Hampshire, Ill. A5 58
Hampshire, co., Eng. *E6 4
Hampshire, co., Mass. B2 65
Hampshire, co., W.Va. B6 87
Hampstead, Que., Can. *D4 42
Hampton, Ark. D3 49
Hampton, Ga. C2 55
Hampton, Iowa B4 60
Hampton, N.H. F6 73
Hampton, N.J. B3 74
Hampton, S.C. F5 82
Hampton, Tenn. C11 83
Hampton (Independent City), Va. ... C6, h15 85
Hampton, co., S.C. F5 82
Hampton Bays, N.Y. n16 75
Hamtramck, Mich. p15 66
Hana, Haw. C6 56
Hanahan, S.C. F7, k11 82
Hanamaki, Jap. G10 18

Hanamaulu, Haw. B2 56
Hanapepe, Haw. B2 56
Hanau, Ger., Fed. Rep. of C4 6
Hanceville, Ala. A3 46
Hancock, Md. A1 53
Hancock, Mich. A2 66
Hancock, Minn. E3 67
Hancock, N.Y. D5 75
Hancock, co., Ga. C3 55
Hancock, co., Ill. C2 58
Hancock, co., Ind. E6 59
Hancock, co., Iowa A4 60
Hancock, co., Ky. C3 62
Hancock, co., Maine D4 64
Hancock, co., Miss. E4 68
Hancock, co., Ohio A2 78
Hancock, co., Tenn. C10 83
Hancock, co., W. Va. A4 87
Hand, co., S. Dak. F6 77
Handa, Jap. o15 18
Handan, China D7 17
Handley, W. Va. m13 87
Haney, B.C., Can. E6, f13 37
Hanford, Calif. D4 50
Hanford Northwest, Calif. *D4 50
Hangchou, see Hangzhou, China
Hangö, Fin. H10 11
Hangzhou, China E8 17
Hankinson, N. Dak. D9 77
Hanley Hills, Mo. *C7 69
Hanna, Alta., Can. D5 38
Hanna, Wyo. E6 89
Hanna City, Ill. C4 58
Hannibal, Mo. B6 69
Hannibal, N.Y. B4 75
Hannover (Hanover), Ger.,
  Fed. Rep. of B4 6
Hanoi, Viet. G6 17
Hanover, Ont., Can. C3 41
Hanover, Ill. A3 58
Hanover, Ind. G7 59
Hanover, Kan. C7 61
Hanover, Mass. B6, h12 65
Hanover, N.H. D3 73
Hanover, N.J. *B4 74
Hanover, Pa. G8 81
Hanover, co., Va. C5 85
Hanover, reg., Ger., Fed.
  Rep. of B4 6
Hanover Green, Pa. *D9 81
Hansford, co., Tex. A2 84
Hanson, Mass. B6 65
Hanson, co., S. Dak. G8 77
Hants, co., N.S., Can. D6 43
Hantsport, N.S., Can. D5 43
Hanzhong, China E6 17
Hapeville, Ga. C2, h8 55
Happy Valley, Newf., Can. ... B1, h9 44
Harahan, La. k11 63
Haralson, co., Ga. C1 55
Harar, Eth. G6 23
Harare, (Salisbury), Zimb. D6 24
Harbin, China B10 17
Harbor Beach, Mich. E8 66
Harborcreek, Pa. B2 81
Harbor Isle, N.Y. *E7 75
Harbor Springs, Mich. C6 66
Harbour Breton, Newf., Can. E4 44
Harbour Grace, Newf., Can. E5 44
Harbour Main, Newf., Can. E5 44
Hardee, co., Fla. E5 54
Hardeeville, S.C. G5 82
Hardeman, co., Tenn. B2 83
Hardeman, co., Tex. B3 84
Hardin, Ill. D3 58
Hardin, Mo. B4 69
Hardin, co., Ill. F5 58
Hardin, co., Iowa B4 60
Hardin, co., Ky. C3 62
Hardin, co., Mont. E9 70
Hardin, co., Ohio B2 78
Hardin, co., Tenn. B3 83
Hardin, co., Tex. D5 84
Harding, co., N. Mex. B7 48
Harding, co., S. Dak. E2 77
Hardinsburg, Ky. C3 62
Hardshell, Ky. C6 62
Hardwār, India C6 20
Hardwick, Ga. C3 55
Hardwick, Vt. B3 73
Hardy, co., W. Va. B6 87
Hare Bay, Newf., Can. D4 44
Harfleur, Fr. C4 5
Harford, co., Md. A5 53
Hargeisa, Som. G6 23
Harihar, India F6 20
Harkers Island, N.C. C6 76

Harlan, Iowa C2 60
Harlan, Ky. D6 62
Harlan, co., Ky. D6 62
Harlan, co., Nebr. D6 71
Harlem, Fla. F6 54
Harlem, Ga. C4 55
Harlem, Mont. B8 70
Harlingen, Neth. A6 5
Harlingen, Tex. F4 84
Harlow, Eng. k13 4
Harlowton, Mont. D7 70
Harmarville, Pa. h14 81
Harmon, co., Okla. C2 79
Harmony, Ind. E3 59
Harmony, Minn. G6 67
Harmony, Pa. E1 81
Harnett, co., N.C. B4 76
Harney, co., Oreg. D7 80
Harney, peak, S. Dak. F2 77
Harnösand, Swe. F8 11
Haro, Sp. A4 8
Harper, Kans. E5 61
Harper, Lib. H3 22
Harper, co., Kans. E5 61
Harper, co., Okla. A2 79
Harper Woods, Mich. *F7 66
Harrah, Okla. B4 79
Harriman, Tenn. D1 83
Harrington, Del. C6 53
Harrington Park, N.J. h9 74
Harris, co., Ga. D1 55
Harris, co., Tex. E5 84
Harris, hill, Mass. A3 65
Harrisburg, Ark. B5 49
Harrisburg, Ill. F5 58
Harrisburg, Oreg. C3 80
Harrisburg, Pa. F8 81
Harris Hill, N.Y. *C2 75
Harrison, Ark. A2 49
Harrison, Mich. D6 66
Harrison, N.J. k8 74
Harrison, N.Y. D2, h13 75
Harrison, Ohio C3 78
Harrison, co., Ind. H5 59
Harrison, co., Iowa C2 60
Harrison, co., Ky. B5 62
Harrison, co., Miss. E4 68
Harrison, co., Mo. A3 69
Harrison, co., Ohio B4 78
Harrison, co., Tex. C5 84
Harrison, co., W. Va. B4 87
Harrisonburg, La. C4 63
Harrisonburg (Independent city), Va. ... B4 85
Harrisonville, Mo. C3 69
Harriston, Ont., Can. D4 41
Harrisville, Pa. D2 81
Harrisville, R.I. B10 52
Harrisville, W. Va. B3 87
Harrisville, N.Y. A5 75
Harrodsburg, Ky. C5 62
Harrogate, Eng. C6 4
Harrow, Ont., Can. E2 41
Hart, Mich. E4 66
Hart, co., Ga. B3 55
Hart, co., Ky. C4 62
Hart, mtn. Man., Can. C1 40
Hartford, Ala. D4 46
Hartford, Conn. B6 52
Hartford, Ill. E3 58
Hartford, Ky. C3 62
Hartford, Mich. F4 66
Hartford, Wis. E5, m11 88
Hartford, co., Conn. B5 52
Hartford City, Ind. D7 59
Hartington, Nebr. B8 71
Hartland, N.B., Can. C2 43
Hartland, Maine D3 64
Hartland, Wis. E5, m11 88
Hartlepool, Eng. C6 4
Hartley, Iowa A2 60
Hartley, co., Tex. B1 84
Hartsdale, N.Y. *D7 75
Hartselle, Ala. A3 46
Hartshorne, Okla. C6 79
Hartsville, S.C. C7 82
Hartsville, Tenn. A5 83
Hartville, Ohio B4 78
Hartwell, Ga. B4 55
Hartwick, N.Y. C5 75
Harvard, Ill. A5 58
Harvard, Nebr. D7 71
Harvard, mtn., Colo. C4 51
Harvey, Ill. B6, k9 58
Harvey, La. E5, k11 63
Harvey, Mich. B3 66
Harvey, N. Dak. C6 77
Harvey, co., Kans. D6 61

Harvey, mtn., Mass. B1 65
Harwich, Eng. E7 4
Harwich, Mass. C7 65
Harwich Port, Mass. C7 65
Harwick, Pa. *E1 81
Harwood Heights, Ill. *B6 58
Haryāna, state, India C5 20
Hasbrouck Heights, N.J. h8 74
Hashimoto, Jap. o14 18
Haskell, Okla. B6 79
Haskell, Tex. C3 84
Haskell, co., Kans. E3 61
Haskell, co., Okla. B6 79
Haskell, co., Tex. C3 84
Haslett, Mich. *F6 66
Hassan, India F6 20
Hasselt, Bel. B6 5
Hässleholm, Swe. I5 11
Hastings, Ont., Can. C7 41
Hastings, Eng. E7 4
Hastings, Fla. C4 54
Hastings, Mich. F5 66
Hastings, Minn. F6 67
Hastings, Nebr. D7 71
Hastings, N.Z. M16 26
Hastings, Pa. E4 81
Hastings, co., Ont., Can. C7 41
Hastings-on-Hudson, N.Y. h13 75
Hatboro, Pa. F11 81
Hatch, N. Mex. C5 48
Hatfield, Mass. B2 65
Hatfield, Pa. F11 81
Hathras, India *C6 20
Ha Tien, Viet. C2 19
Hatteras, N.C. B7 76
Hattiesburg, Miss. D4 68
Hatton, N. Dak. C8 77
Hatton Fields, Calif. *D3 50
Hatvan, Hung. B4 10
Hatzic, B.C., Can. f13 37
Haubstadt, Ind. H2 59
Haugesund, Nor. H1 11
Hauppauge, N.Y. *D3 75
Haute-Garonne, dept., Fr. *F4 5
Haute-Loire, dept., Fr. *E5 5
Haute-Marne, dept., Fr. *C6 5
Hauterive, Que., Can. k13 42
Hautes-Alpes, dept., Fr. *E7 5
Haute-Saône, dept., Fr. *D6 5
Haute-Savoie, dept., Fr. *D7 5
Hautes-Pyrénées, dept., Fr. *F4 5
Haute-Vienne, dept., Fr. *E4 5
Hautmont, Fr. B6 5
Haut-Rhin, dept., Fr. *C7 5
Hauula, Haw. B4, f10 56
Havana (La Habana), Cuba C2 35
Havana, Fla. B2 54
Havana, Ill. C3 58
Havelock, Ont., Can. C7 41
Havelock, N.C. C6 76
Haven, Kans. E6, g11 61
Haverford, Pa. *F10 81
Haverhill, Mass. A5 65
Haverstraw, N.Y. D7, m15 75
Havertown, Pa. *G10 81
Haviland, Kans. E4 61
Havlíčkuv Brod, Czech. D3 7
Havre, Mont. B7 70
Havre, see Le Havre, Fr.
Havre-Aubert, Que., Can. B8 43
Havre de Grace, Md. A5 53
Havza, Tur. B10 14
Hawaii, co., Haw. D5 56
Hawaii, state, U.S. D5 56
Hawaii, isl., Haw. D6 56
Hawaiian Gardens, Calif. *F4 50
Hawarden, Iowa A1 60
Hawera, N.Z. M15 26
Hawesville, Ky. C3 62
Hawi, Haw. C6 56
Hawick, Scot. C5 4
Hawkesbury, Ont., Can. B10 41
Hawkins, co., Tenn. C10 83
Hawkinsville, Ga. D3 55
Hawk Run, Pa. E5 81
Hawks Bill, mtn., Va. B4 85
Hawley, Minn. D2 67
Hawley, Pa. D11 81
Haworth, N.J. h9 74
Haw River, N.C. A3 76
Hawthorne, Calif. n12 50
Hawthorne, Fla. C4 54
Hawthorne, Nev. B2 72
Hawthorne, N.J. B4 74
Hawthorne, N.Y. g13 75
Haxtun, Colo. A8 51
Hayange, Fr. C7 5
Hayden, Ariz. C3, D3 48
Hayden, Idaho B2 57
Haydenville, Mass. B2 65
Haydenville, Ohio C3 78
Hayes, La. D3 63
Hayes, co., Nebr. D4 71

Hayesville, Oreg. *C4 80
Hayfield, Minn. G6 67
Haynau, see Chojnow, Pol.
Haynesville, La. B2 63
Hay River, N. W. Ter., Can. D10 36
Hays, Kans. D4 61
Hays, Mont. C8 70
Hays, co., Tex. D3 84
Hay Springs, Nebr. B3 71
Haysville, Kans. B5 61
Hayti, Mo. E8 69
Hayward, Calif. h8 50
Hayward, Wis. B2 88
Haywood, N.C. B3 76
Haywood, co., N.C. f9 76
Haywood, co., Tenn. B2 83
Hazard, Ky. C6 62
Hazardville, Conn. B6 52
Hazebrouck, Fr. B5 5
Hazel Crest, Ill. k9 58
Hazel Dell, Wash. *D3 86
Hazel Green, Wis. F3 88
Hazel Park, Mich. p15 66
Hazelwood, Mo. *C7 69
Hazelwood, N.C. f10 76
Hazen, Ark. C4 49
Hazen, N. Dak. C4 77
Hazlehurst, Ga. E4 55
Hazlehurst, Miss. D3 83
Hazlet, N.J. C4 74
Hazleton, Iowa B6 60
Hazleton, Pa. E10 81
Hazleton, peak, Wyo. C3 89
Headland, Ala. D4 46
Healdsburg, Calif. C2 50
Healdton, Okla. C4 79
Heard, co., Ga. C1 55
Hearne, Tex. D4 84
Hearst, Ont., Can. o19 41
Heart's Content, Newf., Can. E5 44
Heart's Delight, Newf., Can. *E5 44
Heath, Ohio B3 78
Heavener, Okla. C7 79
Hebbronville, Tex. F3 84
Hebei, prov., China D8 17
Heber, Utah A6, D2 72
Heber Springs, Ark. B3 49
Hébertville, Que., Can. A6 42
Hébertville Station,
  Que., Can. *A6 42
Hebrides, sea, Scot. B3 4
Hebron, Ill. A5 58
Hebron, Ind. B3 59
Hebron, Nebr. D8 71
Hebron, N. Dak. D3 77
Hebron, Ohio C3 78
Hecelchakán, Mex. C6 34
Hechingen, Ger., Fed. Rep. of D4 6
Hechuan, China E6 17
Hector, Minn. F4 67
Hedemora, Swe. G6 11
Hedmark, co., Nor. *G4 11
Hedwing, Iowa C5 60
Hedrick Village, Tex. *E5 84
Heerlen, Neth. B6 5
Hefei, China E8 17
Heflin, Ala. B4 46
Hegang, China B11 17
Hegeler, Ill. *C6 58
Hegins, Pa. E8 81
Heide, Ger., Fed. Rep. of A4 6
Heidelberg, Ger., Fed. Rep. of D4 6
Heidelberg, Miss. D5 68
Heidelberg, Pa. *E1 81
Heidenheim, Ger., Fed. Rep. of D5 6
Heidrick, Ky. D6 62
Heilbronn, Ger., Fed. Rep. of D4 6
Heiligenstadt, Ger. Dem. Rep. C5 6
Heilongjiang, prov., China B10 17
Heislerville, N.J. E3 74
Hejaz, pol. div., Sau. Ar. D2 15
Hekla, peak, Ice. n23 11
Helena, Ark. C5 49
Helena, Ga. D4 55
Helena, Mont. D5 70
Helensburgh, Scot. B4 4
Heli, China C5 18
Hellam, Pa. G8 81
Hellertown, Pa. E11 81
Helmetta, N.J. C4 74
Helmond, Neth. B6 5
Helmstedt, Ger., Fed. Rep. of B5 6
Helper, Utah B6 72
Helsingborg, Swe. I5 11
Helsingfors, see Helsinki, Fin.
Helsingor, Den. I5 11
Helsinki, Fin. G11 11
Hemel Hempstead, Eng. k12 4
Hemet, Calif. F5 50
Hemingford, Nebr. B2 71
Hemingway, S.C. D9 82
Hemlock, Mich. E6 66
Hemlock (Eureka), S.C. B5 82

Hemmingford, Que.,Can. D4 42
Hemphill, Tex. D6 84
Hemphill, co., Tex. B2 84
Hempstead, N.Y. k13 75
Hempstead, Tex. D4 84
Hempstead, co., Ark. D2 49
Henan, prov., China E7 17
Hendaye, Fr. F3 5
Hendek, Tur. B8 14
Henderson, Ky. C2 62
Henderson, Minn. F5 67
Henderson, Nebr. D8 71
Henderson, Nev. C4 72
Henderson, N.C. A4 76
Henderson, Tenn. B3 83
Henderson, Tex. C5 84
Henderson, co., Ill. C3 58
Henderson, co., Ky. C2 62
Henderson, co., N.C. f10 76
Henderson, co., Tenn. B3 83
Henderson, co., Tex. C5 84
Hendersonville, N.C. f10 76
Hendersonville, Tenn. A5, g10 83
Hendricks, Minn. F2 67
Hendricks, co., Ind. E4 59
Hendry, co., Fla. F5 54
Hengelo, Neth. A7 5
Hengyang, China F7 17
Henlawson, W. Va. n12 87
Hennebont, Fr. D2 5
Hennepin, co., Minn. E5 67
Hennessey, Okla. A4 79
Henning, Minn. D3 67
Henrico, co., Va. C5 85
Henrietta, N.Y. B3 75
Henrietta, N.C. B2, f11 76
Henrietta, Tex. C3 84
Henry, Ill. B4 58
Henry, co., Ala. D4 46
Henry, co., Ga. C2 55
Henry, co., Ill. B3 58
Henry, co., Ind. E7 59
Henry, co., Iowa C6 60
Henry, co., Ky. B4 62
Henry, co., Mo. C4 69
Henry, co., Ohio A1 78
Henry, co., Tenn. A3 83
Henry, co., Va. D3 85
Henryetta, Okla. B6 79
Hensall, Ont., Can. D3 41
Henryville, Que., Can. D4 42
Henzada, Bur. E10 20
Heppner, Oreg. B7 80
Hepu, China G6 17
Heqing, China F5 17
Herat, Afg. B3 20
Hérault, dept., Fr. *F5 5
Herbert, Sask., Can. G2 39
Herblay, Fr. g9 5
Hercegovina, reg., Yugo. D3 10
Herculaneum, Mo. C7, g13 69
Heredia, C.R. E8 34
Heredia, prov., C.R. *E8 34
Hereford, Eng. D5 4
Hereford, Tex. B1 84
Hereford, co., Eng. *D5 4
Herencia, Sp. C4 8
Herford, Ger., Fed. Rep. of B4 6
Herington, Kans. D7 61
Herisau, Switz. E4 6
Herkimer, N.Y. B6 75
Herkimer, co., N.Y. B5 75
Herman, Minn. E2 67
Hermann, Mo. C6 69
Hermansville, Mich. C3 66
Hermantown, Minn. D6 67
Herminie, Pa. F2 81
Hermiston, Oreg. B7 80
Herman, N.Y. f9 75
Hermosa Beach, Calif. *F4 50
Hermosillo, Mex. B2 34
Hernando, Miss. A4 68
Hernando, co., Fla. D4 54
Herndon, Va. B5, g12 85
Herning, Den. I3 11
Heron Lake, Minn. G3 67
Herrin, Ill. F4 58
Hershey, Pa. F8 81
Herstal, Bel. E6, k12 4
Hertford, Eng. *E6 4
Hertford, N.C. A6 76
Hertford, co., Eng. *E6 4
Hertford, co., N.C. A5 76
Herzliyya, Isr. B2, g5 15
Hesperia, Mich. E4 66
Hesse, reg., Ger., Fed. Rep. of *C4 6
Hessen, state, Ger., Fed. Rep. of ... *C4 6
Hesston, Kans. D6 61
Hettinger, N. Dak. D3 77
Hettinger, co., N. Dak. D3 77
Heuvelton, N.Y. f9 75
Heves, Hung. B5 10
Heves, co., Hung. *B5 10

Hewitt, N.J. A4 74
Hewlett, N.Y. *G2 52
Hewlett Harbor, N.Y. *G2 52
Heyworth, Ill. C5 58
Hialeah, Fla. G6, s13 54
Hiawatha, Iowa *C6 60
Hiawatha, Kans. C8 61
Hiawatha, Utah B6 72
Hibbing, Minn. C6 67
Hibernia, N.J. B4 74
Hickman, Ky. f8 62
Hickman, co., Ky. f8 62
Hickman, co., Tenn. B4 83
Hickory, co., Mo. D4 69
Hickory Hills, Ill. *B6 58
Hicksville, N.Y. E7, n15 75
Hicksville, Ohio A1 78
Hico, Tex. D3 84
Hidalgo, Tex. F3 84
Hidalgo, co., N. Mex. D4 48
Hidalgo, co., Tex. F3 84
Hidalgo, state, Mex. C5, m14 34
Hidalgo del Parral, Mex. B3 34
Higashiizu, Jap. o18 18
Higashiosaka, Jap. I7, o14 18
Higbee, Mo. B5 69
Higgins, Tex. A2 84
Higginsville, Mo. B4 69
High Bridge, N.J. B3 74
Highgrove, Calif. *F5 50
High Knob, mtn., Va. A4 85
Highland, Calif. *E5 50
Highland, Ill. E4 58
Highland, Ind. A3 59
Highland, Kans. C8 61
Highland, Mich. o14 66
Highland, N.Y. D7 75
Highland, Wis. E3 88
Highland, co., Ohio C2 78
Highland, co., Va. B3 85
Highland City, Fla. *E5 54
Highland Creek, Ont., Can. D5 41
Highland Crest, Kans. *B8 61
Highland Falls, N.Y. *D7 75
Highland Heights, Ky. *A5 62
Highland Heights, Ohio A4 78
Highland Park, Ill. A6, h9 58
Highland Park, Mich. p15 66
Highland Park, N.J. *C4 74
Highland Park, Pa. *F6 81
Highland Park, Tex. B5 84
Highlands, Fla. *B5 54
Highlands, N.J. C5 74
Highlands, Tex. r14 84
Highlands, co., Fla. E5 54
Highland Springs, Va. C5, m18 85
Highmore, S. Dak. F6 77
High Point, N.C. B3 76
High Point, mtn., N.J. A3 74
High Prairie, Alta., Can. B2 38
High River, Alta., Can. D4 38
Highshoals, N.C. B1 76
High Spire, Pa. F8 81
High Springs, Fla. C4 54
Hightstown, N.J. C3 74
Highway City, Calif. *D4 50
Highway Village, Tex. *F4 84
Highwood, Ill. A6, h9 58
High Wycombe, Eng. E6 4
Higüey, Dom. Rep. E9 35
Hikone, Jap. n15 18
Hilbert, Wis. E3 88
Hildburghausen, Ger. Dem. Rep. C5 6
Hildesheim, Ger., Fed. Rep. of B4 6
Hill, co., Mont. B6 70
Hill, co., Tex. D4 84
Hillburn, N.Y. *D6 75
Hill City, Kans. C4 61
Hillcrest, N.J. *B2 74
Hillcrest, N.Y. *D6 75
Hillcrest Center, Calif. *E4 50
Hillcrest Heights, Md. *C3 53
Hillcrest Mines, Alta., Can. E3 38
Hiller, Pa. *G2 81
Hilliard, Fla. B4 54
Hilliard, Ohio k10 78
Hillsboro, Ill. D4 58
Hillsboro, Kans. D6 61
Hillsboro, N.H. D3 73
Hillsboro, N. Dak. C8 77
Hillsboro, Ohio *C2 78
Hillsboro, Oreg. B3, g12 80
Hillsboro, Tenn. B6 83
Hillsboro, Tex. C4 84
Hillsboro, Wis. E3 88
Hillsboro, co., N.H. F4 73
Hillsborough, Calif. *D2 50
Hillsborough, N.B., Can. D5 43
Hillsborough, N.C. A3 76
Hillsborough, co., Fla. E4 54
Hillsborough Lower Village, N.H. E3 73
Hillsborough Upper Village, N.H. E4 73
Hillsdale, Mich. G6 66

Hillsdale, Mo. *C7 69
Hillsdale, N.J. g8 74
Hillsdale, co., Mich. G6 66
Hillside, Ill. *B6 58
Hillside, N.J. k8 74
Hillside Manor, N.Y. *G2 52
Hillsville, Pa. D1 81
Hillsville, Va. D2 85
Hilltop, N.J. *D2 74
Hillwood, Va. *B5 85
Hilo, Haw. D6, n16 56
Hilton, N.Y. B3 75
Hilversum, Neth. A6 5
Himachal Pradesh, state, India *B6 20
Himalayas, mts., India C7 20
Himeji, Jap. I7 18
Himi, Jap. H8 18
Hims, (Homs), Syr. B5 23
Hinche, Hai E7 35
Hinckley, Ill. B5 58
Hinckley, Minn. D6 67
Hindenburg, see Zabrze, Pol.
Hinds, co., Miss. C3 68
Hines, Oreg. D7 80
Hinesville, Ga. D5 55
Hingham, Mass. B6, h12 65
Hinojosa del Duque, Sp. C3 8
Hinsdale, Ill. k9 58
Hinsdale, Mass. B1 65
Hinsdale, N.H. F3 73
Hinsdale, co., Colo. D3 51
Hinton, Alta., Can. C2 38
Hinton, Okla. B3 79
Hinton, W. Va. D4 87
Hirakata, Jap. *I7 18
Hiram, Ohio A4 78
Hiratsuka, Jap. n17 18
Hiroo, Jap. E11 18
Hirosaki, Jap. F10 18
Hiroshima, Jap. I6 18
Hiroshima, pref., Jap. *I6 18
Hirson, Fr. C5 5
Hisār, India. C6 20
Hispaniola, isl., N.A. D8 35
Hita, Jap. *J5 18
Hitachi, Jap. H10 18
Hitchcock, Tex. r14 84
Hitchcock, co., Nebr. D4 71
Hitchins, Ky. B7 62
Hitoyoshi, Jap. J5 18
Hixon, Tenn. D8, h11 83
Hjørring, Den. I3 11
Hjørring, co., Den. *I3 11
Hlohovec, Czech. D4 7
Hlomsak, Thai. *E11 20
Hoa Binh, Viet. *A3 19
Hobart, Austl. o15 25
Hobart, Ind. A3 59
Hobart, Okla. B2 79
Hobbs, N. Mex. C7 48
Hoboken, Bel. B6 5
Hoboken, N.J. k8 74
Ho Chi Minh City
  (Saigon), Viet. C3 19
Hocking, co., Ohio C3 78
Hockley, co., Tex. C1 84
Hoddesdon, Eng. k13 4
Hodeida, Yemen F2 23
Hodgeman, co., Kans. D4 61
Hodgenville, Ky. C4 62
Hodgkins, Ill. *B6 58
Hódmezővásárhely, Hung. B5 10
Hodonín, Czech. D4 7
Hoeryong, Kor. E4 18
Hof, Ger., Fed.,Rep of C5 6
Hoffman, Minn. E3 67
Hoffman Estates, Ill. h8 58
Hofu, Jap. I5 18
Hogansville, Ga. C2 55
Hogback, mtn., S.C. A3 82
Hohenwald, Tenn. B4 83
Hohhot, China C7 17
Ho-Ho-Kus (Hohokus) N.J. h8 74
Hoisington, Kans. D5 61
Hokah, Minn. G7 67
Hoke, co.,N.C. *B3 76
Hokendauqua, Pa. *E10 81
Hokes Bluff, Ala. B4 46
Hokkaido, pref., Jap. *E10 18
Hokkaido, isl., Jap. E10 18
Holbaek, co., Den. *J4 11
Holbrook, Ariz. B3 48
Holbrook, Mass. B5, h11 65
Holbrook N.Y. *n15 75
Holden, Mass. B4 65
Holden, Mo. C4 69
Holden, W. Va. D2 87
Holdenville, Okla. B5 79
Holdrege, Nebr. D6 71
Holgate, Ohio A1 78
Holguín, Cuba D5 35
Hollabrunn, Aus. D8 6
Holladay, Utah *C3 72

Holland, Mich. F4 66
Holland, N.Y. C2 75
Holland, Ohio A2, e6 78
Hollandale, Miss. B3 68
Holley, N.Y. B2 75
Holliday, Tex. C3 84
Hollidaysburg, Pa. F5 81
Hollins, Va. C3 85
Hollis, Alsk. n23 47
Hollis, Okla. C2 79
Hollister, Calif. D3 50
Hollister, Mo. E4 69
Holliston, Mass. h10 65
Holloway Terrace, Del. *A6 53
Hollsopple, Pa. F4 81
Holly, Colo. C8 51
Holly, Mich. F7 66
Holly Hill, Fla. C5 54
Holly Hill, S.C. E7 82
Holly Oak, Del. A7 53
Holly Ridge, N.C. C5 76
Holly Springs, Miss. A4 68
Hollywood, Fla. f6, r13 54
Hollywood, La. *D2 63
Hollywood, Pa. *F11 81
Hollywood Heights, Ill. *E3 58
Holmdel Gardens, Kans. *D6 61
Holmen, Wis. E2 88
Holmes, Pa. *G11 81
Holmes, co., Fla. u16 54
Holmes, co., Miss. B3 68
Holmes, co., Ohio B4 78
Holmes, mtn., Wyo. B2 89
Holmes Beach, Fla. *F4 54
Holmes Run Acres, Va. *B5 85
Holmes Run Park, Va. *B5 85
Holon, Isr. B2 15
Holopaw, Fla. D5 54
Holstebro, Den. I3 11
Holstein, Iowa B2 60
Holt, Ala. B2 46
Holt, Mich. F6 66
Holt, co., Mo. A2 69
Holt, co., Nebr. B7 71
Holton, Kans. C8 61
Holtville, Calif. F6 50
Holyhead, Wales. D4 4
Holyoke, Colo. A8 51
Holyoke, Mass. B2 65
Holyoke, range, Mass. B2 65
Holyrood, Kans. D5 61
Holzminden, Ger., Fed. Rep of C4 6
Homalin, Bur. D9 20
Homeacre, Ind. *E2 81
Home Corner, Ind. C6 59
Homécourt, Fr. C6 5
Homedale, Idaho F2 57
Homedale, Ohio *B2 78
Home Gardens, Calif. *F5 50
Home Hill, Austl. C8 25
Homer, Alsk. D6, h16 47
Homer, Ill. C6 58
Homer, La. B2 63
Homer, Mich. F6 66
Homer, N.Y. C4 75
Homer City, Pa. E3 81
Homerville, Ga. E4 55
Homestead, Fla. G6, t13 54
Homestead, Pa. k14 81
Homestead Valley, Calif. *C2 50
Hometown, Ill. *B6 58
Homewood, Ala. g7 46
Homewood, Calif. C3 50
Homewood, Ill. B6, k9 58
Homeworth, Ohio B4 78
Hominy, Okla. A5 79
Honaker, Va. e10 85
Honan, see Henan, China
Honda, Col. B3 32
Hondo, Tex. E3 84
Honduras, country, N.A. D7 34
Honea Path, S.C. C3 82
Honeoye Falls, N.Y. C3 75
Honesdale, Pa. C11 81
Honey Brook, Pa. F10 81
Honey Grove, Tex. C5 84
Honfleur, Fr. C4 5
Hon Gai, Viet. *A3 19
Hongwon, Kor. G3 18
Hong Kong, Br. dep.,Asia G7 17
Honokaa, Haw. C6 56
Honolulu, Haw. B4, g10 56
Honolulu, co., Haw. B3 56
Honshū, isl., Jap. H8 18
Honto, see Nevelsk, Sov. Un.
Hood, co., Tex. C4 84
Hood, mtn., Oreg. B5 80
Hoodoo, peak, Wash. A5 86
Hood River, Oreg. B5 80
Hood River, co., Oreg. B5 80
Hoodsport, Wash. B2 86
Hooghly-Chinsura, India *D8 20
Hooker, Okla. e9 79
Hooker, co., Nebr. C4 71

Hooker, mtn., B.C., Can. C8 37
Hooks, Tex. *C5 84
Hooksett, N.H. E5 73
Hoolehua, Haw. B4 56
Hooper, Nebr. C9 71
Hooper, Utah A5, C2 72
Hooper Bay, Alsk. C6 47
Hoopeston, Ill. C6 58
Hoorn, Neth. A6 5
Hoosac, range, Mass. A1 65
Hoosick Falls, N.Y. C7 75
Hooversville, Pa. F4 81
Hopatcong, N.J. B3 74
Hope, Ark. D2 49
Hope, B.C., Can. E7 37
Hope, Ind. F6 59
Hopedale, Ill. C4 58
Hopedale, La. E6 63
Hopedale, Mass. B4, h9 65
Hopedale, Ohio B5 78
Hopelawn, N.J. *B4 74
Hope Mills, N.C. C4 76
Hope Ranch, Calif. *E4 50
Hope Valley, R.I. C10 52
Hopewell, N.J. C3 74
Hopewell
  (Independent City), Va. C5, n18 85
Hopewell Junction, N.Y. D7 75
Hopkins, Minn. n12 67
Hopkins, Mo. A3 69
Hopkins, co., Ky. C2 62
Hopkins, co., Tex. C5 84
Hopkinsville, Ky. D2 62
Hopkinton, Iowa B6 60
Hopkinton, Mass. B4, h9 65
Hopland, Calif. C2 50
Hopwood, Pa. G2 81
Hoquiam, Wash. C2 86
Hordaland, co., Nor. *G1 11
Horicon, Wis. E5 88
Hornbeck, La. C2 63
Hornell, N.Y. C3 75
Hornersville, Mo. E7 69
Horní Počernice, Czech. n18 7
Hornsea, Eng. D6 4
Hornsey, Eng. k12 4
Horqueta, Par. D4 29
Horry, co., S.C. D9 82
Horseback Knob, hill, Ohio C2 78
Horse Cave, Ky. C4 62
Horseheads, N.Y. C4 75
Horsens,Den. J3 11
Horsham, Austl. G7 25
Horsham, Pa. *F11 81
Horta, Port. (Azores) k9 22
Horten, Nor. H4, p28 11
Hortonville, Wis. D5 88
Hoshiārpur, India B6 20
Hospers, Iowa A2 60
Hospitalet, Sp. B7 8
Hotan, China A6 20
Hot Springs, N.C. f10 76
Hot Springs, S. Dak. G2 77
Hot Springs, co., Ark. C2 49
Hot Springs, co., Wyo. C4 89
Hot Springs, see Truth or
  Consequences, N. Mex.
Hot Springs National Park, Ark. . . . C2, f7 49
Houghton, Mich. A2 66
Houghton, N.Y. C2 75
Houghton, Wash. e11 86
Houghton, co., Mich. B2 66
Houghton Lake, Mich. D6 66
Houghton Lake Heights, Mich. D6 66
Houilles, Fr. g9 5
Houlton, Maine B5 64
Houma, La. E5, k10 63
Housatonic, Mass. B1 65
Houston, B.C., Can. B4 37
Houston, Minn. G7 67
Houston, Miss. B4 68
Houston, Mo. D6 69
Houston, Pa. F1 81
Houston, Tex. E5, r14 84
Houston, co., Ala. D4 46
Houston, co., Ga. D3 55
Houston, co., Minn. G7 67
Houston, co., Tenn. A4 83
Houston, co., Tex. D5 84
Houtzdale,Pa. E5 81
Hove, Eng. E6 4
Howard, Kans. E7 61
Howard, S. Dak. D8 77
Howard, Wis. D5, g9 88
Howard, co., Ark. C2 49
Howard, co., Ind. C5 59
Howard, co., Iowa A5 60
Howard, co., Md. B4 53
Howard, co., Mo. B5 69
Howard, co., Nebr. C7 71
Howard, co., Tex. C2 84
Howard City, Mich. E5 66
Howard Lake, Minn. E4 67

Howe, Ind. A7 59
Howell, Mich. F7 66
Howell, co., Mo. E6 69
Howells, Nebr. C8 71
Howick, Que., Can. D4 42
Howland, Maine C4 64
Howley, mtn., Newf. Can. D2 44
Howrah, India D8 20
Howson, peak, B.C., Can. B4, n17 37
Hoxie, Ark. A5 49
Hoxie, Kans. C3 61
Hoya, Ger., Fed. Rep. of B4 6
Hoyerswerda, Ger. Dem Rep. C7 6
Hoyt Lakes, Minn. C6 67
Hradec Králové, Czech. C3 7
Hranice, Czech. D4 7
Hriňová, Czech. D5 7
Hrubieszów, Pol. C7 7
Hsinchu, Taiwan G9 17
Hsinkao, mtn., Taiwan G9 17
Hsipaw, Bur. *D10 20
Huacho, Peru D2 31
Huadian, China C10 17
Huaide, China E2 18
Huailley, Peru D2 31
Huainan, China E8 17
Hualgayoc, Peru C2 3
Hualien,Taiwan G9 17
Huamachuco, Peru C2 31
Huamantla, Mex. n15 34
Huambo, Ang. C3 24
Huancabamba, Peru C2 31
Huancané, Peru E4 31
Huancavelica, Peru D2 31
Huancavelica, dept., Peru D2 31
Huancayo, Peru D2 31
Huang He (Yellow), riv., China F13 16
Huangshi, China E8 17
Huanta, Peru D3 31
Huánuco, Peru C2 31
Huánuco, dept., Peru C2 31
Huaral, Peru D2 31
Huaráz, Peru C2 31
Huariaca, Peru D2 31
Huascaran, mtn., Peru C2 31
Huatabampo, Mex. B3 34
Huatusco de Chicuellar, Mex. n15 34
Huauchinango, Mex. m14 34
Huaytará, Peru D2 31
Hubbard, Iowa B4 60
Hubbard, Ohio A5 78
Hubbard, Tex. D4 84
Hubbard, co., Minn. C3 67
Hubbell, Mich. A2 66
Hubei, prov., China E7 17
Huberdeau, Que., Can. D3 42
Huber Heights, Ohio *C1 78
Hubli, India. E6 20
Huddersfield, Eng. D6 4
Hudiksvall, Swe. G7 11
Hudson, Que., Can. D3, q18 42
Hudson, Iowa B5 60
Hudson, Mass. B4, g9 65
Hudson, Mich. g6 66
Hudson, N.H. F5 73
Hudson, N.Y. C7 75
Hudson, N.C. B1 76
Hudson, Ohio A4 78
Hudson, Pa. *D9 81
Hudson, Wis. D1 88
Hudson, co., N.J. B4 74
Hudson, bay, Can. D16 36
Hudson, mtn., Maine B3 64
Hudson Bay, Sask., Can. E4 39
Hudson Falls, N.Y. B7 75
Hudsonville, Mich. F5 66
Hudspeth, co.,Tex. o12 84
Hue, Viet. B3 19
Hueco, mts., Tex. o11 84
Huedin, Rom. B6 10
Huehuetenango, Guat. *D6 34
Huelma, Sp. D4 8
Huelva, Sp. D2 8
Huelva, prov., Sp. *D2 8
Huércal-Overa, Sp. D5 8
Huerfano, co., Colo. C6 51
Huesca, Sp. A5 8
Huesca, prov., Sp. *A5 8
Huéscar, Sp. D4 8
Hueytown, Ala. g6 46
Hughes, Ark. C5 49
Hughes, co., Okla. B5 79
Hughes, co., S. Dak. F6 77
Hughes Springs, Tex. *C5 84
Hughestown, Pa. *D9 81
Hughesville, Pa. D8 81
Hughson, Calif. *D3 50
Hugo, Colo. B7 51
Hugo, Okla. C6 79
Hugoton, Kans. E2 61
Huguley, Ala. *C4 6
Huichon, Kor. F3 18
Huila, dept., Col. C2 32

Huixtla, Mex. D6 34
Huizhou, China G7 17
Hukou, China F8 17
Hulan, China B10 17
Hulen, Ky. D6 62
Hull, Que., Can. D2 42
Hull, Eng. D6 4
Hull, Iowa A1 60
Hull, Mass. B6, g12 65
Hull, co., Que., Can. D2 42
Hulmeville, Pa. *F11 81
Humacao, P.R. *G12 35
Humansville, Mo. D4 69
Humble, Tex. E5, q14 84
Humboldt, Sask., Can. E3 39
Humboldt, Iowa B3 60
Humboldt, Kans. E8 61
Humboldt, Nebr. D10 71
Humboldt, Tenn. B3 83
Humboldt, co., Calif. B2 50
Humboldt, co., Iowa B3 60
Humboldt, co., Nev. A2 72
Humenné, Czech. D6 7
Humeston, Iowa D4 60
Hummelstown, Pa. *F8 81
Humphrey, Nebr. C8 71
Humphreys, co., Miss. B3 68
Humphreys, co., Tenn. A4 83
Humphreys, peak, Ariz. B2 48
Humpolec, Czech. D3 7
Hunan, prov., China F7 17

Hunchun, China C11 17
Hunedoara, Rom. C6 10
Hungary, country, Eur. B4 10
Hungnam, Kor. G3 18
Hunjiang, China C10 17
Hunt, mtn., Wyo B5 89
Hunt, co., Tex. C4 84
Hunterdon, N.J. B3 74
Huntersville, N.C. B2 76
Huntingburg, Ind. H4 59
Huntingdon, Que., Can. D3 42
Huntingdon, Pa. F6 81
Huntingdon, Tenn. A3 83
Huntingdon, co., Que., Can. D3 42
Huntingdon, co., Pa. F5 81
Huntingdon & Peterborough,
    co., Eng. *D7 4
Huntington, Ind. C7 59
Huntington, Mass. B2 65
Huntington, N.J. B2 74
Huntington, N.Y. E7, n15 75
Huntington, Oreg. C9 80
Huntington, Tex. D5 84
Huntington, Utah B6 72
Huntington, W. Va. C2 87
Huntington, co., Ind. C6 59
Huntington Bay, N.Y. *G3 52
Huntington Beach, Calif. n13 50
Huntington Beach, N.Y. *D3 75
Huntington Park, Calif. F4 50
Huntington Station, N.Y. F3 52

Huntington Woods, Mich. p15 66
Huntingtown, Md. C4 53
Huntley, Ill. A5 58
Huntly, Scot. B5 4
Huntsville, Ala. A3 46
Huntsville, Ark. A2 49
Huntsville, Ont., Can. B5 41
Huntsville, Mo. B5 69
Huntsville, Tex. D5 84
Hurley, N. Mex. C4 48
Hurley, N.Y. D6 75
Hurley, Wis. B3 88
Hurleyville, N.Y. D6 75
Hurlock, Md. C3 53
Huron, Calif. *D4 50
Huron, Ohio A3 78
Huron, S. Dak. F7 77
Huron, co., Ont., Can. D3 41
Huron, co., Mich. E7 66
Huron, co., Ohio A3 78
Huron, lake, Can. B10 45
Hurricane, Utah C5 72
Hurricane, W. Va. C2 87
Hurst, Ill. F4 58
Hurst, Tex. *C4 84
Hurtsboro, Ala. C4 46
Huşi, Rom. B9 10
Hustisford, Wis. E5 88
Husum, Ger., Fed. Rep. of A4 6
Hutchins, Tex. n10 84
Hutchinson, Kans. D6, f11 61

Hutchinson, Minn. F4 67
Hutchinson, co., S. Dak. G8 77
Hutchinson, co., Tex. B2 84
Huttig, Ark. D3 49
Huxley, Iowa C4, e8 60
Huy, Bel. B6 5
Hvannadalshnúkur, mtn., Ice. o24 11
Hvittingfoss, Nor. p28 11
Hwange, Zimb. D5 24
Hyannis, Mass. C7 65
Hyannis Port, Mass. C7 65
Hyattsville, Md. C4, f9 53
Hybla Valley, Va *B5 85
Hyde, Pa. D5 81
Hyde, co., N.C. B6 76
Hyde, co., S. Dak. F6 77
Hyde Park, N.Y. D7 75
Hyde Park, Pa. *F9 81
Hyderābād, India E6 20
Hyderābād, Pak. C4 20
Hyde Villa, Pa. *F9 81
Hydro, Okla. B3 79
Hyères, Fr. F7 5
Hymera, Ind. F3 59
Hyndman, Pa. G4 81
Hyogo, pref., Jap. *I7 18
Hyopchon, Kor. I4 18
Hyrum, Utah A6 72
Hyrynsalmi, Fin. E13 11
Hythe, Alta., Can. B1 38
Hythe, Eng. E7 4

I

Iaeger, W. Va. D3 87
Iasi, Rom. B8 10
Iba, Phil. *B5 19
Ibadan, Nig. G5 22
Ibagué, Col. C2 32
Ibaraki, Jap. *o14 18
Ibaraki, pref., Jap. *H10 18
Ibarra, Ec. A2 31
Ibb, Yemen G3 15
Iberia, Mo. C5 69
Iberia, par., La. E4 63
Iberville, Que., Can. D4 42
Iberville, co.,Que.,
    Can. D4 42
Iberville, par., La. D4, h9 63
Iberville, mtn., Newf. f9 44
Ibitinga, Braz. C3 30
Ibiza, Sp. C6 8
Ica, Peru D2 31
Ica, dept., Peru D2 31
Ice, mtn., B.C., Can. B7 37
Iceland, country, Eur. n23 11
Ichihara, Jap. *n19 18
Ichikawa, Jap. n18 18
Ichinomiya, Jap. n15 18
Ichinoseki, Jap. G10 18
Ichnya, Sov. Un. F9 12
Ida, Mich. G7 66
Ida, co., Iowa B2 60
Idabel, Okla. D7 79
Ida Grove, Iowa B2 60
Idaho, co., Idaho D3 57
Idaho,state, U.S. 57
Idaho Falls, Idaho F6 67
Idaho Springs, Colo. B5 51
Idahou, Tex. C2 84
Idamay, W. VA. k10 87
Idanha-a-Nova, Port. C2 8
Idaville, Ind. C4 59
Idrija, Yugo. B2 10
Ieper (Ypres), Bel. B5 5
Ieràpetra, Grc. E5 14
Iesi, It. C4 9
Ife, Nig. G5 22
Igarapava, Braz. C3 30
Igarka, Sov. Un. C11 13
Iğdir, Tur. C15 14
Iglesias, It. E2 9
Igloo, S. Dak. G2 77
Igualada, Sp. B6 8
Iguatu, Braz. *D7 27
Iida, Jap. I8, n16 18

Iide-san, mtn., Jap. H9 18
Iijima, Jap. n16 18
Iisalmi, Fin. F12 11
Iizuka, Jap. J5 18
Ijebu Ode, Nig. G5 22
Ijuí, Braz. D2 30
Ikeda, Jap. D14 18
Ikerre, Nig. *G6 22
Ikhtiman, Bul. D6 10
Ila, Nig. E5 22
Ilagan, Phil. B6 19
Ilan, Taiwan *G9 17
Ilawe, Nig. *E6 22
Ile-a-la-Cross, Sask., Can. m7 39
Ilebo (Port-Francqui), Zaire I2 23
Ile-de-France, former
    prov., Fr. C5 5
Ile-Perrot, Que., Can. q19 42
Ilesha, Nig. G5 22
Ilford, Eng. k13 4
Ilfracombe, Eng. E4 4
Ilgin, Tur. C8 14
Ilhavo, Port. B1 8
Ilhéus, Braz. E7 27
Ilia (Elis), prov., Grc. *D3 14
Ilinskaya, Sov. Un. I13 12
Ilion, N.Y. B5 75
Illampu, mtn., Bol. C2 29
Illapel, Chile A2 28
Ille-et-Vilaine, dept., Fr. *C3 5
Illinois, state, U.S. 58
Illinois, peak, Idaho B3 57
Illinois, peak, Mont. C1 70
Illiopolis, Ill. D4 58
Illmo, Mo. D8 69
Illora, Sp. D4 8
Ilmenau, Ger. Dem. Rep. C5 6
Ilo, Peru E3 31
Ilocos Norte, prov., Phil *B6 19
Ilocos Sur, prov., Phil. C6 19
Iloilo, Phil. *C6 19
Iloilo, prov., Phil. *C6 19
Ilorin, Nig. G5 22
Ilovaysk, Sov. Un. r21 12
Imabari, Jap. I6 18
Imabetsu, Jap. F10 18
Imari, Jap. *J4 18
Imazu, Jap. n15 18
Imbabah, Eg. *G8 14
Imbabura, prov., Ec. A2 31
Imlay City, Mich. E7 66
Immenstadt, Ger., Fed. Rep. of E5 6

Immokalee, Fla. F5 54
Imola, It. B3 9
Imperia, It. C2 9
Imperial, Calif. F6 50
Imperial, Sask., Can. F3 39
Imperial, Mo. C7, g13 69
Imperial, Nebr. D4 71
Imperial, Pa. k13 81
Imperial, co., Calif. F6 50
Imperial Beach, Calif. o15 50
Imperoyal, N.S.,Can. E6 43
Imphal, India D9 20
Ina, Jap. n16 18
Inca, Sp. C7 8
Inchon, Kor. H3 18
Indaw, Bur. D10 20
Independence, Calif. D4 50
Independence, Iowa B6 60
Independence, Kans. E8 61
Independence, La. D5 63
Independence, Minn. *F5 67
Independence, Mo. B3, h11 60
Independence, Ohio h9 78
Independence, Oreg. C3, k11 80
Independence, Wis. D2 88
Independence, co., Ark. B4 49
Independence Hill, Ind. *B3 59
India, country, Asia D6 20
Indialantic, Fla. *D6 54
Indian, ocean G2 2
Indiana, Pa. E3 81
Indiana, co., Pa. E3 81
Indiana, state, U.S. 59
Indianapolis, Ind. E5, k10 59
Indian Head, Sask., Can. G4 39
Indian Head, Md. C3 53
Indian Hill, Ohio o13 78
Indian Lake, N.Y. B6 75
Indian Mound Beach, Mass. *C6 65
Indianola, Iowa C4 60
Indianola, Miss. B3 68
Indianola, Nebr. D5 71
Indianola, Pa. *E1 81
Indian, peak, Wyo. B3 89
Indian River, co., Fla. E6 54
Indian Rocks, Beach, Fla. p10 54
Indiantown, Fla. E6 54
Indio, Calif. F5 50
Indochina, reg., Asia B3 19
Indonesia, country, Asia F6 19
Indore, India D6 20
Indramayu, Indon. G3 19

Indre, dept., Fr. *D4 5
Indre-et-Loire, dept., Fr. *D4 5
Indus, riv., Asia C4 20
Industrial, S.C. B6 82
Industry, Pa. *E1 81
Ine, Jap. n14 18
Infantes, Sp. C4 8
Infiesto, Sp. A3 8
Ingalls, Ind. E6 59
Ingalls Park, Ill. B5 58
Ingersoll, Ont., Can. D4 41
Ingham, Austl. C8 25
Ingham, co., Mich. F6 66
Ingleside, Nebr. D7 71
Ingleside, Tex. F4 84
Inglewood, Calif. n12 50
Inglewood, Nebr. C9, g11 71
Ingolstadt, Ger., Fed. Rep. of D5 6
Ingomar, Pa. h13 81
Ingonish Beach, N.S., Can. C9 43
Ingram, Pa. k13 81
Inhambane, Moz. E7 24
Inharrime, Moz. E7 24
Inishbofin, isl., U.K. D1 4
Inishtrahull, isl., U.K. C3 4
Inishturk, isl., U.K. D1 4
Inkerman, Pa. *D9 81
Inkom, Idaho G6 57
Inkster, Mich. p15 66
Inman, Kans. D6 61
Inman, S.C. A3 82
Inman Mills, S.C. *A3 82
Inner Mongolia, prov., China C8 17
Innisfail, Alta., Can. C4 38
Innisfail,Austl. C8 25
Innsbruck, Aus. E5 6
Ino, Jap. J6 18
Inowroclaw, Pol. B5 7
Insein, Bur. E10 20
Institute, W. Va. C3 87
Intercesion City, Fla. D5 54
Intercity, Wash. *B3 86
Interlaken, N.J. *C4 74
International Falls, Minn. B5 67
Intersection, mtn., B.C., Can. C7 37
Invercargill, N.Z. Q12 26
Inverell, Austl. E9 25
Invermere, B.C., Can. D9 37
Inverness, Calif. C2 50
Inverness, N.S., Can. C8 43
Inverness, Fla. D4 54
Inverness, Ill. *B6 58

Inverness, Miss.	B3 68	Irondale, Ala.	f7 46
Inverness, Scot.	B4 4	Irondale, Ohio	B5 78
Inverness, co., N.S., Can.	C8 43	Irondequoit, N.Y.	B3 75
Inverness, co., Scot.	*B4 4	Ironia, N.J.	B3 74
Invisible, mtn.,Idaho	F5 57	Iron Mountain, Mich.	C2 66
Inwood, Iowa	A1 60	Iron River, Mich.	B2 66
Inwood, N.Y.	k13 75	Iron River, Wis.	B2 88
Inyan Kara, mtn., Wyo.	B8 89	Ironton, Minn.	D5 67
Inyo,co., Calif.	D5 50	Ironton, Mo.	D7 69
Inyokern, Calif.	E5 50	Ironton, Ohio	D3 78
Ioánnina, Grc.	C3 14	Ironwood, Mich.	nII 66
Ioannina, prov.,Grc.	*C3 14	Iroquois, N.B., Can.	*B1 43
Iola, Kans.	E8 61	Iroquois, Ont., Can.	C9 41
Iola, Wis.	D4 88	Iroquois, co., Ill.	C6 58
Iona, Idaho	F7 57	Iroquois Falls, Ont., Can.	*o19 41
Ione, Calif.	D3 50	Irosin, Phil.	*C6 19
Ionia, Mich.	F5 66	Irrawaddy, riv., Bur.	D10 20
Ionia, co., Mich.	F5 66	Irtysh, riv., Sov. Un.	D10 13
Iosco, co., Mich.	D7 66	Irún, Sp.	A5 8
Iota, La.	D3 63	Irvine, Ky.	C6 62
Iowa, La.	D2 63	Irvine, Scot.	C4 4
Iowa, co.,Iowa	C5 60	Irving, Tex.	n10 84
Iowa, co., Wis.	E3 88	Irvington, Ky.	C3 62
Iowa, state, U.S.	60	Irvington, N.J.	k8 74
Iowa City, Iowa	C6 60	Irvington, N.Y.	g13 75
Iowa Falls, Iowa	B4 60	Irvona, Pa.	E4 81
Iowa Park, Tex.	C3 84	Irwin, Pa.	F2 81
Ipameri, Braz.	B3 30	Irwin, S.C.	*B6 82
Ipava, Ill.	C3 58	Irwin, co., Ga.	E3 55
Ipiales, Col.	C2 32	Irwindale, Calif.	*E4 50
Ipin, China	F5 17	Isabell, mtn., Wyo.	D2 89
Ipoh, Mala.	E2 19	Isabela, P.R.	*G11 35
Ipswich, Austl.	E9 25	Isabela, prov.,Phil.	*D6 19
Ipswich, Eng.	D7 4	Isabella, Pa.	G2 81
Ipswich, Mass.	A6 55	Isabella, Tenn.	D9 83
Ipswich, S. Dak.	E6 77	Isabella, co., Mich.	E6 66
Iquique, Chile	D2 29	Isahaya, Jap.	J5 18
Iquitos, Peru	B3 31	Isanti, Minn.	E5 67
Iraan, Tex.	D2 84	Isanti,co., Minn.	E5 67
Iraklion (Candia), Grc.	E5 14	Ise (Uji-yamada), Jap.	I8, o15 18
Iraklion, prov., Grc.	*E5 14	Iselin, N.J.	B4 74
Iran, (Persia), country, Asia	F8 16	Iselin, Pa.	E3 81
Irapuato, Mex.	C4, m13 34	Isère, dept., Fr.	*E6 5
Iraq, country, Asia	C3 15	Iserlohn, Ger., Fed. Rep. of	*C3 6
Irbid, Jordan	B3, g5 15	Isernia, It.	D5 9
Irbil, Iraq	D15 14	Isesaki, Jap.	H9, m18 18
Iredell, co., N.C.	B2 76	Iseyin, Nig.	G5 22
Ireland (Eire), country, Eur.	D3 4	Ishikawa, pref., Jap.	*H8 18
Ireton, Iowa	B1 60	Ishim, Sov. Un.	D9 13
Iri, Kor.	I3 18	Ishimbay, Sov. Un.	*D8 13
Iringa, Tan.	B7 24	Ishinomaki, Jap.	G10 18
Irion, co.,Tex.	D2 84	Ishioka, Jap.	m19 18
Irkutsk, Sov. Un.	D13 13	Ishpeming, Mich.	B3 66
Iron, co., Mich.	B2 66	Isigny-sur-Mer, Fr.	C3 5
Iron, co., Mo.	D7 69	Isiro (Paulis), Zaire	H3 23
Iron, co., Utah	C5 72	Iskenderun (Alexandretta), Tur.	D11 14
Iron, co., Wis.	B3 88	Iskilip, Tur.	B10 14
Iron, mts., Va.	f10 85	Isla Cristina, Sp.	D2 8
Islāmābād, Pak.	B5 20	Itaúna, Braz.	C4 30
Islamorado,Fla.	H6 54	Itawamba, co., Miss.	A5 68
Island, co., Wash.	A3 86	Ithaca, Mich.	E6 66
Island Falls, Maine	B4 64	Ithaca, N.Y.	C4 75
Island Heights, N.J.	D4 74	Itō, Jap.	o18 18
Island Lake, Ill.	*E2 58	Itoigawa, Jap.	H8 18
Island Park, N.Y.	*E7 75	Itta Bena, Miss.	B3 68
Island Pond, Vt.	B4 73	Itu, Braz.	C3, m8 30
Islav, isl., U.K.	C3 4	Ituango, Col.	B2 32
Isle, Minn.	D5 67	Ituiutaba, Braz.	B3 30
Isle-aux-Morts, Newf., Can.	E2 44	Ituna, Sask., Can.	F4 39
Isle, of Ely, co., Eng.	*D7 4	Itzehoe, Ger.,Fed. Rep. of	B4 6
Isle of Man, Br. dep; Eur.	*C4 4	Iuka, Miss.	A4 68
Isle of Man, isl., U.K.	C4 4	Iva, S.C.	C2 82
Isle of Palms, S.C.	k12 82	Ivanhoe, Calif.	*D4 50
Isle of Wight, co., Eng.	*E6 4	Ivanhoe, Minn.	F2 67
Isle of Wight, co., Va.	D6 85	Ivanhoe, Va.	D2 85
Isle of Wight, isl., U.K.	E6 4	Ivano-Frankovsk, Sov. Un.	G5 12
Isle Royale, isl., Mich.	h9 66	Ivanovka, Sov. Un.	q21 12
Isleton, Calif.	C3 50	Ivanovo, Sov. Un.	C13 12
Isle-Verte, Que., Can.	A8 42	Ivanteyevka, Sov. Un.	n17 12
Islington, Mass.	h11 65	Ivory Coast, country, Afr.	G3 22
Islip, N.Y.	*n15 75	Ivoryton, Conn.	D7 52
Islip Terrace, N.Y.	*n15 75	Ivrea, It.	B1 9
Isola Capo Rizzuto, It.	E6 9	Ivry-sur-Seine, Fr.	g10 5
Isparta, Tur.	D8 14	Ivywild, Colo.	C6 51
Israel, country, Asia	C2 15	Iwaki (Tairi), Jap.	H10 18
Issaquah, Wash.	e11 86	Iwaki-yama, mtn., Jap.	F10 18
Issaquena, co., Miss.	C2 68	Iwakuni, Jap.	I6 18
Issoire, Fr.	E5 5	Iwamizawa, Jap.	E10 18
Issoudun, Fr.	D4 5	Iwanai, Jap.	E10 18
Issyk-kul, lake, Sov. Un.	E10 13	Iwate, pref., Jap.	*G10 18
Issy les-Moulineaux, Fr.	g10 5	Iwate-yama, mtn., Jap.	G10 18
Istanbul (Constantinople), Tur.	B7 14	Iwo, Nig.	G5 22
Istmina, Col.	B2 32	Ixmiquilpan, Mex.	m14 34
Itá, Par.	E4 29	Ixtacalco, Mex.	h9 34
Itabaiana, Braz.	*E7 27	Ixtacihuatl, mtn., Mex.	n14 34
Itabaiana, Braz.	*D7 27	Ixtapalapa, Mex.	h9 34
Itaberaba, Braz.	*E6 27	Ixtlán de Juárez, Mex.	o15 34
Itabira, Braz.	B4 30	Ixtlán del Rio, Mex.	C4, m11 34
Itabuna, Braz.	E7 27	Izamal, Mex.	C7 34
Itajaí, Braz.	D3 30	Izard, co., Ark.	A4 49
Itajubá, Braz.	C3 30	Izhevsk, see Ustinov, Sov. Un.	
Italy, Tex.	C4 84	Izmail, Sov. Un.	I7 12
Italy, country, Eur.	9	Izmir (Smyrna), Tur.	C6 14
Itami, Jap.	o14 18	Izmit (Kocaeli), Tur.	B7 14
Itaperuna, Braz.	C4 30	Izúcar de Matamoros, Mex.	n14 34
Itapetininga, Braz.	C3, m7 30	Izuhara, Jap.	I4 18
Itapeva, Braz.	C3 30	Izumo, Jap.	I6 18
Itápolis, Braz.	k7 30	Izyum, Sov. Un.	G11 12
Itapúa, dept., Par.	E4 29		
Itaqui, Braz.	D1 30		
Itararé, Braz.	C3 30		
Itasca, Ill.	k8 58		
Itasca, Tex.	C4 84		
Itasca, co., Minn.	C5 67		
Itatiba, Braz.	m8 30		

J

Jabalpur (Jubbulpore), India	D6 20	Jackson, co., Colo.	A4 51
Jaboatão, Braz.	*D7 27	Jackson, co., Fla.	B1 54
Jaboticabal, Braz.	C3, k7 30	Jackson, co., Ga.	B3 55
Jaca, Sp.	A5 8	Jackson, co., Ill.	F4 58
Jacala de Ledesma, Mex.	m14 34	Jackson, co., Ind.	G5 59
Jacarei, Braz.	m9 30	Jackson, co., Iowa	B7 60
Jacarèzinho, Braz.	C3 30	Jackson, co., Kans.	C8 61
Jáchymov, Czech.	r2 7	Jackson, co., Ky.	C5 62
Jacinto City, Tex.	r14 84	Jackson, co., Mich.	F6 66
Jack, co., Tex.	C3 84	Jackson, co., Minn.	G3 67
Jack, mtn., Mont.	D4 70	Jackson, co., Miss.	E5 68
Jack, mtn., Va.	B3 85	Jackson, co., Mo.	C3 69
Jackfork, mtn., Okla.	C6 79	Jackson, co., N.C.	f9 76
Jacks, mtn., Pa.	E6 81	Jackson, co., Ohio	C3 78
Jacksboro, Tex.	C3 84	Jackson, co., Okla.	C2 79
Jackson, Ala.	D2 46	Jackson, co., Oreg.	E3 80
Jackson, Calif.	C3 50	Jackson, co., S. Dak.	G4 77
Jackson, Ga.	C3 55	Jackson, co., Tenn.	C8 83
Jackson, Ky.	C6 62	Jackson, co., Tex.	E4 84
Jackson, La.	D4 63	Jackson, co., W. Va.	C3 87
Jackson, Mich.	F6 66	Jackson, co., Wis.	D3 88
Jackson, Minn.	G3 67	Jackson, par., La.	B3 63
Jackson, Miss.	C3 68	Jackson, mtn., Maine	D2 64
Jackson, Mo.	D8 69	Jackson Center, Ohio	B1 78
Jackson, N.C.	A5 76	Jacksonville, Ala.	B4 46
Jackson, Ohio	C3 78	Jacksonville, Ark.	C3, h10 49
Jackson, S.C.	E4 82	Jacksonville, Fla.	B5, m8 54
Jackson, Tenn.	B3 83	Jacksonville, Ill.	D3 58
Jackson, Wyo.	C2 89	Jacksonville, N.C.	C5 76
Jackson, co., Ala.	A3 46	Jacksonville, Oreg.	E4 80
Jackson, co., Ark.	B4 49	Jacksonville, Tex.	D5 84
Jacksonville Beach, Fla.	B5, m9 54	James, riv., S. Dak.	F7 77
Jacmel, Hai.	E7 35	Jamesburg, N.J.	C4 74
Jacobābād, Pak.	C4 20	James City, N.C.	B5 76
Jacobina, Braz.	*E6 27	James City, co., Va.	C6 85
Jacomino, Cuba	*C2 35	Jamesport, Mo.	B4 69
Jacques Cartier, mtn., Que., Can.	k13 42	Jamestown, Calif.	D3 50
Jaén, Sp.	D4 8	Jamestown, Ind.	E4 59
Jaén, prov., Sp.	*D4 8	Jamestown, Ky.	D4 62
Jaffna, Sri Lanka	G7 20	Jamestown, N.Y.	C1 75
Jaffrey, N.H.	F3 73	Jamestown, N.C.	B3 76
Jaguarào, Braz.	E2 30	Jamestown, N. Dak.	D7 77
Jagüey Grande, Cuba	C3 35	Jamestown, Ohio	C2 78
Jaipur, India	C6 20	Jamestown, Pa.	D1 81
Jaisalmer, India	C5 20	Jamestown, R.I.	D11 52
Jajce, Yugo.	C3 10	Jamestown, Tenn.	C9 83
Jājpur, India	D8 20	Jamesville, N.Y.	*C4 75
Jakarta (Djakarta), Indon.	G3 19	Jamiltepec, Mex.	D5 34
Jakobstad (Pietersaari), Fin.	F10 11	Jammu, India	B5 20
Jal, N. Mex.	C7 48	Jammu and Kashmir, Disputed reg., India, Pak.	B6 20
Jalalabad, Afg.	B5 20	Jāmnagar, India	D5 20
Jalapa, Guat.	*F6 34	Jamshedpur, India	D8 20
Jalapa Enriquez, Mex.	D5, n15 34	Jämtland, co., Swe.	*F6 11
Jalca Grande, Peru	C2 31	Janesville, Iowa	B5 60
Jālgaon, India	D6 20	Janesville, Minn.	F5 67
Jalisco,state, Mex.	C4, m12 34	Janesville, Wis.	F4 88
Jālna, India	E6 20	Janin, Jordan	B3 15
Jalpa, Mex.	C4, m12 34	Janos, Mex.	A3 34
Jalpan, Mex.	C5, m14 34	Jánoshalma, Hung.	B4 7
Jamaica, country, N.A.	E5 35	Janów, Lubelski, Pol.	C7 7
Jambi, Indon.	F2 19	Januária, Braz.	B4 30

Jaoho (Tuanshantzu), China B11 17
Japan, country, Asia I6 18
Japan, sea, Asia F6 18
Jaral *del Progreso*, Mex. m13 34
Jarales, N. Mex. B5 48
Jarocin, Pol. C4 7
Jaroslaw, Pol. C7 7
Jarvis, Ont., Can. E4 41
Jarvisburg, N.C. A7 76
Jasonville, Ind. F3 59
Jasper, Ala. B2 46
Jasper, Alta., Can. C1 38
Jasper, Fla. B4 54
Jasper, Ga. B2 55
Jasper, Ind. H4 59
Jasper, Minn. G2 67
Jasper, Mo. D3 69
Jasper, Tenn. D8 83
Jasper, Tex. D6 84
Jasper, co., Ga. C3 55
Jasper, co., Ill. D5 58
Jasper, co., Ind. B3 59
Jasper, co., Iowa C4 60
Jasper, co., Miss. C4 68
Jasper, co., Mo. D3 69
Jasper, co., S.C. G5 82
Jasper, co., Tex. D5 84
Jászapáti, Hung. B5 10
Jászbereny, Hung. B4 10
Jatibonico,Cuba D4 35
Játiva, Sp. C5 8
Jaú, Braz. C3, m7 30
Jauja, Peru D2 31
Jaumave, Mex. C5 34
Jaunpur, India C7 20
Java, isl., Indon. G3 19
Javellanos, Cuba C3 35
Jawor, Pol. C4 7
Jaworzno, Pol. g10 7
Jay, Fla. u14 54
Jay, N.Y. f11 75
Jay, Okla. A7 79
Jay, co., Ind. D7 59
Jayanca, Peru C2 31
Jayapura (Sukarnapura), Indon. ... F10 19
Jeanerette, La. E4 63
Jeannette, Pa. F2 81
Jeberos, Peru C2 31
Jedburgh, Scot. C5 4
Jedrzejów, Pol. C6 7
Jeff, Ky. C6 62
Jeff Davis, co., Ga. E4 55
Jeff Davis, co., Tex. o12 84
Jefferson, Ga. B3 55
Jefferson, Iowa B3 60
Jefferson, La. k11 63
Jefferson, Mass. B4 65
Jefferson, N.C. A1 76
Jefferson, Ohio A5 78
Jefferson, Oreg. C3, k11 80
Jefferson, Pa. *E1 81
Jefferson, Tex. C5 84
Jefferson, Wis. E5 88
Jefferson, co., Ala. B3 46
Jefferson, co., Ark. C3 49
Jefferson, co., Colo. B5 51
Jefferson, co., Fla. B3 54
Jefferson, co., Ga. C4 55
Jefferson, co., Idaho F6 57
Jefferson, co., Ill. E5 58
Jefferson, co., Ind. G7 59
Jefferson, co., Iowa C6 60
Jefferson, co., Kans. C8 61
Jefferson, co., Ky. B4 62
Jefferson, co., Miss. D2 68
Jefferson, co., Mo. C7 69
Jefferson, co., Mont. D4 70
Jefferson, co., Nebr. D8 71
Jefferson, co., N.Y. A5 75
Jefferson, co., Ohio B5 78
Jefferson, co., Okla. C4 79
Jefferson, co., Oreg. C5 80
Jefferson, co., Pa. D3 81
Jefferson, co., Tenn. C10 83
Jefferson, co., Tex. E5 84
Jefferson, co., Wash. B2 86
Jefferson, co., W. Va. B7 87
Jefferson, co., Wis. E5 88
Jefferson, par., La. E5 63

Jefferson City, Mo. C5 69
Jefferson City, Tenn. C10 83
Jefferson Davis, co., Miss. D4 68
Jefferson Davis, par., La. D3 63
Jeffersontown, Ky. B4, g11 62
Jefferson Village, Va. *B5 85
Jeffersonville, Ga. D3 55
Jeffersonville, Ind. H6 59
Jeffersonville, Ky. C6 62
Jeffrey City, Wyo. *D4 89
Jehossee, isl., S.C. k11 81
Jekabpils, Sov. Un. C5 12
Jelenia Góra, Pol. C3 7
Jelgava, Sov. Un. C4 12
Jellico, Tenn. C9 83
Jelm, mtn., Wyo. E7 89
Jember, Indon. G4 19
Jemison, Ala. C3 46
Jena, Ger. Dem. Rep. C5 6
Jena, La. C3 63
Jenison, Mich. *F4 66
Jenkins, Ky. C7 62
Jenkins, co., Ga. D4 55
Jenkinsville, S.C. C5 82
Jenkintown, Pa. F11, o21 81
Jenks, Okla. A6 79
Jenners, Pa. F3 81
Jennings, Fla. B3 54
Jennings, La. D3 63
Jennings, Mo. f13 69
Jennings, co., Ind. G6 59
Jennings Lodge, Oreg. *B4 80
Jensen Beach, Florida E6 54
Jenny Jump, mtn., N.J. B3 74
Jequié, Braz. *E6 27
Jerauld, co., S. Dak. F7 77
Jérémie, Hai E6 35
Jerez de García Salinas, Mex. C4 34
Jerez, de la Frontera, Sp. D2 8
Jericho, N.Y. *E7 75
Jericho, Va. *D6 85
Jermyn, Pa. C10 81
Jerome, Idaho G4 57
Jerome, Ill. *D4 58
Jerome, Pa. F4 81
Jerome, co., Idaho G4 57
Jersey, Br. dep., Eur. F5 4
Jersey, co., Ill. D3 58
Jersey City, N.J. B4, k8 74
Jersey Shore, Pa. D7 81
Jerseyside, Newf., Can. *E5 44
Jerseyville, Ill. D3 58
Jerusalem (Yerushalayim), Isr. C3, h5 15
Jerusalem, Jordan C3, h5 15
Jesenik, Czech. C4 7
Jessamine, co., Ky. C5 62
Jessup, Md. B4 53
Jessup, Pa. m18 81
Jesup, Ga. E5 55
Jesup, Iowa B5 60
Jesús Carranza, Mex. D6 34
Jesús María, Arg. A4 28
Jetmore, Kans. D4 61
Jever, Ger., Fed. Rep. of B3 6
Jewell, Iowa B4 60
Jewell, Kans. C5 61
Jewell, co., Kan. C5 61
Jewett, Ohio B4 78
Jewett City, Conn. C9 52
Jeypore, India E7 20
Jhang Maghiana, Pak. *B5 20
Jhālrapātan, India D6 20
Jhānsi, India C6 20
Jhelum, Pak. B5 20
Jiamusi, China C5 18
Ji'an, China F3 18
Jiangling, China E7 17
Jiangmen, China G7 17
Jiangsu, prov., China E9 17
Jiangxi, prov., China F9 17
Jiaoxian, China D9 17
Jiaozuo, China D7 17
Jiaxing, China E9 17
Jicín, Czech. C3 7
Jiddah, Sau. Ar. E2 15
Jieyang, China G8 17
Jihlava, Czech. D3 7
Jilin, China C10 17
Jilin, prov., China C9 17

Jima, Eth. G5 23
Jimbolia, Rom. C5 10
Jimena, Sp. D3 8
Jim Hogg, co., Tex. F3 84
Jim Thorpe, Pa. E10 81
Jim Wells, co., Tex. F3 84
Jinan, China D8 17
Jindřichuv Hradec, Czech. D3 7
Jingdezhen, China F8 17
Jining, China D8 17
Jining, China C7 17
Jinja, Ug. H4 23
Jinotepe, Nic. E7 34
Jinxian, China D9 17
Jinzhou, China C9 17
Jipijapa, Ec. B1 31
Jiquilpan de Juárez, Mex. n12 34
Jiujiang, China F8 17
Jixi, China B11 17
Joanna, S.C. C4 82
João Pessoa, Braz. D7 27
Jocobus, Pa. *G8 81
Jocotepec, Mex. m12 34
Jódar, Sp. D4 8
Jo Daviess, co., Ill. A3 58
Jodhpur, India C5 20
Joe Batt's, Arm, Newf., Can. D4 44
Joensuu, Fin. F13 11
Joeuf, Fr. C6 5
Joffre, mtn., Alta., Can. D3 38
Joffre, mtn., B.C.,Can. D10 37
Joggins, N.S., Can. D5 43
Jogjakarta, see
  Yogyakarta, Indon.
Johannesburg, S. Afr. F5 24
John Day, Oreg. C8 80
Johns Island, S.C. F7, k11 82
Johnson, Kans. E2 61
Johnson, Vt. B2 73
Johnson, co., Ark. B2 49
Johnson, co., Ga. D4 55
Johnson, co., Ill. F5 58
Johnson, co., Ind. F5 59
Johnson, co., Iowa C6 60
Johnson, co., Kans. D9 61
Johnson, co., Ky. C7 62
Johnson, co., Mo. C4 69
Johnson, co., Nebr. D9 71
Johnson, co., Tenn. C12 83
Johnson, co., Tex. C4 84
Johnson, co., Wyo. B6 89
Johnsonburg, Pa. D4 81
Johnson City, N.Y. C5 75
Johnson City, Tenn. C11 83
Johnson City, Tex. D3 84
Johnson Creek, Wis. E5 88
Johnsonville, S.C. D9 82
Johnston, Iowa E8 60
Johnston, R.I. B10 52
Johnston, S.C. D4 82
Johnston, co., N.C. B4 76
Johnston, co., Okla. C5 79
Johnston City, Ill. F5 58
Johnstown, Colo. A6 51
Johnstown, N.Y. B6 75
Johnstown, Ohio B3 78
Johnstown, Pa. F4 81
Johor, state, Mala. *E2 19
Johor Baharu, Mala. E2 19
Joigny, Fr. D5 5
Joinville, Braz. D3 30
Jojutla, Mex. n14 34
Joliet, Ill. B6, k8 58
Joliette, Que., Can. C4 42
Joliette, co., Que.,Can. C3 42
Jolo, Phil. D6 19
Jonava, Sov. Un. A8 7
Jones, Okla. B4 79
Jones, co., Ga. C3 55
Jones, co., Iowa B6 60
Jones, co., Miss. D4 68
Jones, co., N.C. B5 76
Jones, co., S. Dak. G5 77
Jones, co., Tex. C3 84
Jonesboro, Ark. B5 49
Jonesboro, Ga. C2 55
Jonesboro, Ill. F4 58
Jonesboro, Ind. D6 59
Jonesboro, La. B3 63

Jonesboro, Tenn. C11 83
Jones Mill, Ark. C3, g8 49
Jonesport, Maine D5 64
Jonesville, La. C4 63
Jonesville, Mich. G6 66
Jonesville, N.C. A2 76
Jonesville, S.C. B4 82
Jonesville, Va. f8 85
Jönköping, Swe. I6 11
Jönköping, co., Swe. *I5 11
Jonquière, Que., Can. A6 42
Jonuta, Mex. D6 34
Joplin, Mo. D3 69
Joppa, Ill. F5 58
Jordan, Minn. F5 67
Jordan, N.Y. B4 75
Jordan, country, Asia C3 15
Jorhāt, India C9 20
Jos, Nig. G6 22
José Battle y Ordóñez, Ur. E1 30
Joseph, Oreg. B9 80
Josephine, Oreg. E3 80
Joshua Tree, Calif. E5 50
Jourdanton, Tex. E3 84
Jovellanos, Cuba C3 35
Juab, co., Utah B5 72
Juana Díaz, P.R. *G11 35
Juan Aldama, Mex. C4 34
Juanita, Wash. *B3 86
Juanjui, Peru C2 31
Juárez, Arg. B5 28
Juarez, Mex. B4 34
Juàzeiro, Braz. D6 27
Juazeiro do Norte, Braz. *D7 27
Jūbā, Sud. H4 23
Júcaro, Cuba D4 35
Juchipila, Mex. m12 34
Juchitán de Zaragoza, Mex. D6 34
Jude, isl.,Newf., Can. E4 44
Judenburg, Aus. E7 6
Judith Basin, co., Mont. C6 70
Judith, mtn., Mont. C7 70
Judith, peak, Mont. C7 70
Judson, S.C. *B3 82
Judsonia, Ark. B4 49
Juiz de Fora, Braz. C4, g6 30
Jujuy, Arg. D2 29
Jujuy, prov., Arg. D2 29
Julesburg, Colo. A8 51
Juliaca, Peru E3 31
Julian, Calif. F5 50
Julianehab, Grnld. C16 33
Jullundur, India B6 20
Julimes, Mex. B3 34
Jumet, Bel. B6 5
Jumilla, Sp. C5 8
Junāgadh, India D5 20
Juncos, P.R. *G12 35
Junction, Tex. D3 84
Junction City, Ark. D3 49
Junction City, Kans. C7 61
Junction City, Ky. C5 62
Junction City, Ohio C3 78
Junction City, Oreg. C3 80
Jundiaí, Braz. C3, m8 30
Juneau, Alsk. D13, k22 47
Juneau, Wis. E5 88
Juneau, co., Wis. E3 88
Junee, Austl. F8 25
Jungfrau, mtn., Switz. E3 6
Juniata, co., Pa. F6 81
Juniata Terrace, Pa. E6 81
Junín, Arg. A4 28
Junín, Peru D2 31
Junín, dept., Peru D2 31
Juniper, N.B., Can. C2 43
Junipero Serra, peak, Calif. D3 50
Jupiter, Fla. F6 54
Jura, dept., Fr. *D6 5
Jura, isl., Scot. C4 4
Jurbarkas, Sov. Un. A7 7
Juruá, riv. C4 31
Justice, Ill. *B6 58
Jüterbog, Ger. Dem. Rep. C6 6
Jutiapa, Guat. E7 34
Juwain, Afg. B3 20
Jyvaskylä, Fin. F11 11

K

Kaala, peak, Haw. f9 56
Kaalaea, Haw. g10 56
Kabaena, isl., Mala. G6 19
Kabong, Mala. E4 19
Kabul, Afg. B4 20
Kachuga, Sov. Un. D13 13
Kadinhani, Tur. C9 14
Kadiri, India F6 20
Kadiyevka, Sov. Un. G12, o21 12
Kaduna, Nig. F6 22
Kaédi, Maur. E2 22
Kaeryong, Kor. H4 18
Kaesong, Kor. G3 18
Kāf, Sau. Ar. C2 15
Kafr az Zayyat, Eg. D2 14
Kagawa, pref., Jap. *I7 18
Kağızman, Tur. B14 14
Kagoshima, Jap. K5 18
Kagoshima, pref., Jap. *K5 18
Kagul, Sov. Un. C9 12
Kahoolawe, isl., Haw. C5 56
Kahuka, Haw. B4, f10 56
Kahului, Haw. C5 56
Kaifeng, China E7 17
Kailua, Haw. g11 56
Kaimana, Indon. F8 19
Kainan, Jap. I7 18
Kairouan, Tun. A6 22
Kaiserslautern, Ger., Fed. Rep.
 of D3 6
Kaiyuan, China E2 18
Kaizuka, Jap. o14 18
Kajaani, Fin. E12 11
Kajikazawa, Jap. n17 18
Kakegawa, Jap. o17 18
Kākināda, India E7 20
Kakogawa, Jap. *I7 18
Kālābagh, Pak. B5 20
Kalach, Sov. Un. F13 12
Kalaheo, Haw. B2 56
Kalama, Wash. C3 86
Kalamai (Kalamata), Grc. D4 14
Kalamazoo, Mich. F5 66
Kalamazoo, co., Mich. F5 66
Kalaotoa, isl., Indon. G6 19
Kalapana, Haw. D7 56
Kalemie, Zaire B5 24
Kalgoorlie, Austl. F3 25
Kálimnos, Grc. *D6 14
Kalinin, Sov. Un. C10 12
Kaliningrad, Sov. Un. n17 12
Kalingrad (Königsbert), Sov. Un. D3 12
Kalinkovichi, Sov. Un. E7 12
Kalispell, Mont. B2 70
Kalisz, Pol. C5 7
Kalkaska, Mich. D5 66
Kalkaska, co., Mich. D5 66
Kallithéa, Grc. *D4 14
Kalmar, Swe. I7 11
Kalmar, co., Swe. *I7 11
Kalocsa, Hung. B4 10
Kalona, Iowa C6 60
Kalone, peak, B.C., Can. C4 37
Kaluga, Sov. Un. D11 12
Kalush, Sov. Un. G5 12
Kama, riv., Sov. Un. D8 13
Kamaishi, Jap. G10 18
Kamakura, Jap. n18 18
Kamarhati, India *D8 20
Kamenets-Podolskiy, Sov. Un. G6 12
Kamen-na-Obi, Sov. Un. D11 13
Kamensk-Shakhtinskiy, Sov. Un. G13 12
Kamensk-Uralskiy, Sov. Un. D9 13
Kamenz, Ger. Dem. Rep. C7 6
Kameoka, Jap. o14 18
Kamiah, Idaho C2 57
Kamioka, Jap. m16 18
Kamloops, B.C., Can. D7, n18 37
Kammuri-Yama, mtn., Jap. I6 18
Kamouraska, co., Que., Can. B8 42
Kampala, Ug. H4 23
Kampen, Neth. A6 5
Kampot, Kam. C2 19
Kampuchea, country, Asia C2 19
Kamsack, Sask., Can. F5 39
Kamuela, Haw. C6 56
Kamyshin, Sov. Un. F15 12
Kanab, Utah C5 72
Kanabec, co., Minn. E5 67
Kanagawa, pref., Jap. *I9 18
Kananga (Luluabourg), Zaire B4 24
Kanash, Sov. Un. D16 12
Kanawha, Iowa B4 60
Kanawha, co., W. Va. C3 87
Kanayama, Jap. n16 18
Kanazawa, Jap. H8 18
Kanchanaburi, Thai. C1 19

Kānchenjunga, peak, Nep.,
 India C8 20
Kānchipuram, India F7 20
Kandahar, Afg. B4 20
Kandalaksha, Sov. Un. C6 13
Kandangan, Indon. F5 19
Kandira, Tur. B8 14
Kandiyohi, co., Minn. E3 67
Kandy, Sri Lanka G7 20
Kane, Pa. C4 81
Kane, co., Ill. B5 58
Kane, co., Utah C5 72
Kaneohe, Haw. B4, g10 56
Kangding, China E5 17
Kanggye, Kor. F3 18
Kangnung, Kor. H4 18
Kanjiža, Yugo. B5 10
Kankakee, Ill. B6 58
Kankakee, co., Ill. B6 58
Kankan, Guinea F3 22
Kānker, India D7 20
Kannapolis, N.C. B2 76
Kano, Nig. F6 22
Kanopolis, Kans. D5 61
Kanoya, Jap. K5 18
Kānpur, India C7 20
Kansas, Ill. D6 58
Kansas, state, U.S. 61
Kansas, riv., Kans. C7 61
Kansas City, Kans. C9, k16 61
Kansas City, Mo. B3, h10 69
Kansk, Sov. Un. D12 13
Kansong, Kor. G4 18
Kantunilkín, Mex. C7 34
Kanye, Bots. E5 24
Kaohsiung, Taiwan G9 17
Kaolack, Sen. F1 22
Kapaa, Haw. A2 56
Kapanga, Zaire B4 24
Kapfenberg, Aus. E7 6
Kapit, Mala. E4 19
Kaplan, La. D3 63
Kaposvár, Hung. B3 10
Kapuskasing, Ont., Can. o19 41
Kapuvár, Hung. B3 10
Karachev, Sov. Un. E10 12
Karāchi, Pak. D4 20
Karaga, Sov. Un. D19 13
Karaganda, Sov. Un. E10 13
Karaköse, Tur. C14 14
Karaman, Tur. D9 14
Karamay, China B1 17
Karapinar, Tur. D9 14
Karatsu, Jap. J4 18
Karbalā, Iraq C3 15
Karcag, Hung. B5 10
Kardhitsa, Grc. C3 14
Karelia (Kerelo-Finnish S.S.R.),
 former rep., Sov. Un. *C6 16
Kargil, India B6 20
Kargopol, Sov. Un. A12 12
Kariba, Zimb. D5 24
Kārikal, India F6 20
Karkaralinsk, Sov. Un. E10 13
Karl-Marx-Stadt (Chemnitz),
 Ger. Dem. Rep. C6 6
Karlovac, Yugo. C2 10
Karlóvasi, Grc. D6 14
Karlovy Vary, Czech. C2 7
Karlshamn, Swe. I6 11
Karlskoga, Swe. H6 11
Karlskrona, Swe. I6 11
Karlsruhe, Ger., Fed. Rep. of D4 6
Karlstad, Minn. B2 67
Karlstad, Swe. H5 11
Karmutzen, mtn., B.C., Can. D4 37
Karnak, Ill. F5 58
Karnataka, state, India F6 20
Karnes, co., Tex. E4 84
Karnes City, Tex. E4 84
Kars, Tur. B14 14
Karsakpay, Sov. Un. E9 13
Karshi, Sov. Un. F9 13
Kartal, Tur. *B7 14
Kartaly, Sov. Un. D9 13
Kartuzy, Pol. A5 7
Karviná, Czech. D5 7
Kārwār, India F5 20
Kāsaragod, India F6 20
Kasba Tadla, Mor. B3 22
Kāshān, Iran B8 23
Kashi, China F10 16
Kashima, Jap. n19 18
Kashira, Sov. Un. D12 12
Kashiwa, Jap. *n18 18
Kashiwazaki, Jap. H9 18
Kasimov, Sov. Un. D13 12

Kaslo, B.C., Can. E9 37
Kasota, Minn. F5 67
Kassalā, Sud. E5 23
Kassel, Ger., Fed. Rep. of C4 6
Kasson, Minn. F6 67
Kastamonu, Tur. B9 14
Kastoria, Grc. B3 14
Kasugai, Jap. *n15 18
Kasukabe, Jap. n18 18
Kasumi, Jap. I7 18
Kasur, Pak. B5 20
Katahdin, mtn., Maine C4 64
Katanga, prov., Zaire C5 24
Katanning, Austl. F2 25
Katata, Jap. (part of Otsu) n14 18
Kateríni, Grc. B4 14
Katherine, Austl. B5 25
Kathleen, Fla. D4 54
Kathmandu, Nep. C8 20
Kathwood, S.C. *D4 82
Katiola, I.C. G4 22
Katonah, N.Y. A5 75
Katoomba-Wentworth Falls, Austl. F8 26
Katowice (Stalinogród), Pol. C5, g10 7
Kātrīnā, mtn., Eg. C4 23
Katrineholm, Swe. H7, u34 11
Katsina, Nig. F6 22
Katsuyama, Jap. m15 18
Katy, Tex. r14 84
Kauai, isl., Haw. A2 56
Kauai, co., Haw. B2 56
Kaufbeuren, Ger., Fed. Rep. of E5 6
Kaufman, Tex. C4 84
Kaufman, co., Tex. C4 84
Kaukauna, Wis. D5, h9 88
Kaumakani, Haw. B2 56
Kaunakakai, Haw. B4 56
Kaunas, Sov. Un. D4 12
Kavaje, Alb. *B2 14
Kaválla, Grc. B5 14
Kaválla, prov., Grc. *B5 14
Kavarna, Bul. D9 10
Kawagoe, Jap. n18 18
Kawaguchi, Jap. n18 18
Kawaikini, peak, Haw. A2 56
Kawasaki, Jap. I9, n18 18
Kawkareik, Bur. *B1 19
Kawkawlin, Mich. E7 66
Kawn Umbū, Eg. D4 23
Kay, co., Okla. A4 79
Kayes, Mali F2 22
Kayford, W. Va. C3, m13 87
Kayseri, Tur. C10 14
Kaysville, Utah A6, C2 72
Kazachye, Sov. Un. B16 13
Kazakh S.S.R., rep., Sov. Un. *E9 16
Kazan, Sov. Un. D7 13
Kazanluk, Bul. D7 10
Keaau, Haw. D6 56
Keansburg, N.J. C4 74
Kearney, Nebr. D6 71
Kearney, Mo. B3, h11 69
Kearney, co., Nebr. D7 71
Kearns, Utah *A5 72
Kearny, N.J. h8 74
Kearny, co., Kans. D2 61
Kearsarge, Mich. A2 66
Keasbey, N.J. *B4 74
Kebnekaise, mtn., Swe. D8 11
Kecskemét, Hung. B4 10
Kedah, state, Mala. *D2 19
Kedainiai, Sov. Un. A7 7
Kedgwick, N.B., Can. B2 43
Kediri, Indon. *G4 19
Kedong, China C3 18
Keegan, Maine A5 64
Keego Harbor, Mich. o15 66
Keene, N.H. F3 73
Keene, Tex. n9 84
Keeseville, N.Y. f11 75
Keewatin, Ont., Can. E4 40
Keewatin, Minn. C5 67
Keewatin, dist., N.W. Ter., Can. D15 36
Kefallinía, prov., Grc. *C3 14
Kefar Ata, Isr. B3 15
Kefar Sava, Isr. B2 15
Keighley, Eng. D6 4
Keith, Scot. B5 4
Keith, co., Nebr. C4 71
Keithsburg, Ill. B3 58
Keizer, Oreg. *C4 80
Kekaha, Haw. B2 56
Kelang, Mala. K4 19
Kelantan, state, Mala. D2 19
Keller, Tex. n9 84
Kellerman, Ala. B2 46
Kellogg, Idaho B2 57

Kellogg, Iowa C5 60
Kelly Brook, mtn., Maine A3 64
Kelly Lake, Minn. C5 67
Kelowna, B.C., Can. E8 37
Kelseyville, Calif. C2 50
Kelso, Mo. D8 69
Kelso, Scot. C5 4
Kelso, Wash. C3 86
Keltys, Tex. *D5 84
Keluang, Mala. E2 19
Kelvington, Sask., Can. E4 39
Kem, Sov. Un. E16 11
Kemah, Tex. *E5 84
Kemerovo, Sov. Un. D11 13
Kemi, Fin. E11 11
Kemmerer, Wyo. E2 89
Kemp, Tex. C4 84
Kemper, co., Miss. C5 68
Kempsey, Austl. F9 25
Kempshall, mtn., N.Y. A6 75
Kempten, Ger., Fed. Rep. of E5 6
Kemptville, Ont., Can. B9 41
Kenansville, N.C. C4 76
Kenbridge, Va. D4 85
Kendal, Eng. C5 4
Kendall, Fla. s13 54
Kendall, co., Ill. B5 58
Kendall, co., Tex. E3 84
Kendall Park, N.J. C3 74
Kendallville, Ind. B7 59
Kendari, Indon. F6 19
Kendrāpāṛa, India D8 20
Kendrick, Fla. C4 54
Kenedy, Tex. E4 84
Kenedy, co., Tex. F4 84
Kenhorst, Pa. *F9 81
Kenilworth, Ill. H9 58
Kenilworth, N.J. *B4 74
Kenitra, Mor. B3 22
Kenly, N.C. B4 76
Kenmare, N. Dak. B3 77
Kenmawr, Pa. *E1 81
Kenmore, N.Y. C2 75
Kenmore, Wash. *B3 86
Kennaday, peak, Wyo. E6 89
Kennebec, co., Maine D3 64
Kennebunk, Maine E2 64
Kennebunkport, Maine E2 64
Kennedale, Tex. n9 84
Kennedy, N.Y. C1 75
Kenner, La. k11 63
Kennesaw, Ga. B2, g7 55
Kenneth City, Fla. *E4 54
Kennett, Mo. E7 69
Kennett Square, Pa. G10 81
Kennewick, Wash. C6 86
Kennydale, Wash. e11 86
Kénogami, Que., Can. A6 42
Kenora, Ont., Can. o16 41
Kenora, dist., Ont., Can. o16 41
Kenosha, Wis. F6, n12 88
Kenosha, co., Wis. F5 88
Kenova, W. Va. C2 87
Kensington, Calif. *D3 50
Kensington, Conn. C5 52
Kensington, Kans. C4 61
Kensington, Md. B3 53
Kensington, N.Y. *G2 52
Kensington Estates, Md. *B3 53
Kensington Park, Fla. *E4 54
Kent, Conn. C2 52
Kent, Ohio A4 78
Kent, Wash. B3, f11 86
Kent, co., N.B., Can. C4 43
Kent, co., Ont., Can. E2 41
Kent, co., Del. B6 53
Kent, co., Eng. *E7 4
Kent, co., Md. B5 53
Kent, co., Mich. E5 66
Kent, co., R.I. C10 52
Kent, co., Tex. C2 84
Kent City, Mich. E5 66
Kentfield, Calif. *C2 50
Kentland, Ind. C3 59
Kentland, Md. *C4 53
Kenton, Ohio B2 78
Kenton, Tenn. A2 83
Kenton, co., Ky. B5 62
Kentucky, state, U.S. 62
Kent Village, Md. *C4 53
Kentville, N.S., Can. D5 43
Kentwood, La. D5 63
Kentwood, Mich. F5 66
Kenvil, N.J. B3 74
Kenvir, Ky. D6 62
Kenwood, Ohio *C1 78
Kenya, country, Afr. H5 23

Kenyon, Minn. ... F6 67
Keokuk, Iowa ... D6 60
Keokuk, co., Iowa ... C5 60
Keosauqua, Iowa ... D6 60
Keota, Iowa ... C6 60
Keota, Okla. ... B7 79
Kepno, Pol. ... C5 7
Kerala, state, India ... F6 20
Kerang, Austl. ... G7 25
Kerby, Oreg. ... E3 80
Kerch, Sov. Un. ... I11 12
Keremeos, B.C., Can. ... E8 37
Kerens, Tex. ... C4 84
Kerhonkson, N.Y. ... D6 75
Kerinci, mtn., Indon. ... F2 19
Kerkhoven, Minn. ... E3 67
Kérkira, Grc. ... C2 14
Kerkira, prov., Grc. ... *C2 14
Kerkrade, Neth. ... B7 5
Kerman, Calif. ... *D4 50
Kermān, Iran ... C6 15
Kermānshāh, see Bakhtarān, Iran
Kermit, Tex. ... D1 84
Kermit, W. Va. ... D2 87
Kermode, mtn., B.C., Can. ... C2 37
Kern, co., Calif. ... E4 50
Kernersville, N.C. ... A2 76
Kernville, Calif. ... E4 50
Kerr, co., Tex. ... D3 84
Kerrobert, Sask., Can. ... F1 39
Kerrville, Tex. ... D3 84
Kerry, co., Ire. ... *D2 4
Kershaw, S.C. ... B6 82
Kershaw, co., S.C. ... C6 82
Keşan, Tur. ... B6 14
Kesennuma, Jap. ... G10 18
Keshan, China ... B10 17
Keski-Suomi, prov., Fin. ... *K5 11
Keswick, Ont., Can. ... C5 41
Keszthely, Hung. ... B3 10
Keta, Ghana ... G5 22
Ketapang, Indon. ... F3 19
Ketchikan, Alsk. ... D13, n24 47
Ketchum, Idaho ... F4 57
Ketona, Ala. ... f7 46
Ketrzyn Mazowiecki, Pol. ... A6 7
Kettering, Eng. ... D6 4
Kettering, Ohio ... C1 78
Kettle Falls, Wash. ... A7 86
Kety, Pol. ... D5, h10 7
Kewanee, Ill. ... B4 58
Kewaskum, Wis. ... E5 88
Kewaunee, Wis. ... D6 88
Kewanna, Ind. ... B5 59
Kewaunee, co., Wis. ... D6 88
Keweenaw, co., Mich. ... A2 66
Keya Paha, co., Nebr. ... B6 71
Key Biscayne, Fla. ... *G6 54
Keyes, Calif. ... *D4 50
Keyes, Okla. ... e8 79
Keyport, N.J. ... C4 74
Keyser, W. Va. ... B6 87
Keystone, Iowa ... C5 60
Keystone, W. Va. ... D3 87
Keysville, Fla. ... E2 54
Keysville, Va. ... C4 85
Keytesville, Mo. ... B5 69
Key West, Fla. ... H5 54
Kezar Falls, Maine ... E2 64
Kezhma, Sov. Un. ... D13 13
Kežmarok, Czech. ... D6 7
Khabarovsk, Sov. Un. ... E16 13
Khairpur, Pak. ... C4 20
Khalkidhikí (Chalcidice), prov., Grc. ... *B4 14
Khalkís, Grc. ... C4 14
Khalūf, Om. ... E6 15
Khambhāliya, India ... D4 20
Khanabad, Afg. ... A4 20
Khānaqīn, Iraq ... E15 15
Khandwa, India ... D6 20
Khaniá (Canea), Grc. ... E5 14
Khaniá, prov., Grc. ... *E4 14
Khānpur, Pak. ... C5 20
Khān Yūnus, Gaza Strip ... C2, h5 15
Kharagpur, India ... D8 20
Kharkov, Sov. Un. ... G11 12
Kharmanli, Bul. ... E7 10
Kharovsk, Sov. Un. ... B13 12
Khartoum (Al-Kharţūm), Sud. ... E4 23
Khartoum North, Sud. ... E4 23
Khartsyzsk, Sov. Un. ... g21 12
Khash, Afg. ... B3 20
Khaskovo, Bul. ... E7 10
Khenifra, Mor. ... B3 22
Kherson, Sov. Un. ... H9 12
Khilok, Sov. Un. ... D14 13
Khimki, Sov. Un. ... n17 12
Khíos, Grc. ... C6 14
Khíos, (Chios), prov., Grc. ... *C6 14
Khmelnik, Sov. Un. ... G6 12
Khmelnitskiy, Sov. Un. ... G6 12

Kholm, Sov. Un. ... C8 12
Khong, Laos ... C3 19
Khong Sedone, Laos ... *B3 19
Khorog, Sov. Un. ... F10 13
Khorol, Sov. Un. ... G9 12
Khorramābād, Iran ... C4 15
Khorramshahr, Iran ... C4 15
Khotin, Sov. Un. ... G6 12
Khulna, Bngl. ... D8 20
Khust, Sov. Un. ... G4 12
Kiamichi, mtn., Okla. ... C6 79
Kiangsu, prov., China ... E8 17
Kičevo, Yugo. ... E5 10
Kidder, co., N. Dak. ... C6 77
Kidderminster, Eng. ... D5 4
Kiel, Ger., Fed. Rep. of ... A5 6
Kiel, Wis. ... E5, k9 88
Kielce, Pol. ... C6 7
Kiester, Minn. ... G5 67
Kiev (Kiyev), Sov. Un. ... F8 12
Kifisiá, Grc. ... g11 14
Kigali, Rwanda ... I4 23
Kikinda, Yugo. ... C5 10
Kikladhes (Cyclades), prov., Grc. ... *D5 14
Kikwit, Zaire ... B3 24
Kilauea, crater, Haw. ... D6 56
Kilbride, Newf., Can. ... *E5 44
Kilchu, Kor. ... F4 18
Kildare, co., Ire. ... *D3 4
Kilgore, Tex. ... C5 84
Kilimanjaro, mtn., Tan. ... I5 23
Kilis, Tur. ... D11 14
Kiliya, Sov. Un. ... I7 12
Kilkenny, Ire. ... D3 4
Kilkenny, co., Ire. ... *D3 4
Kilkís, Grc. ... E6 10
Kilkís, prov., Grc. ... *B4 14
Killaloe Station, Ont., Can. ... B7 41
Killarney, Man., Can. ... E2 40
Killarney, Ire. ... D2 4
Killbuck, Ohio ... B4 78
Killeen, Tex. ... D4 84
Killian, S.C. ... C6 82
Killona, La. ... h11 63
Kilmallie, Scot. ... B4 4
Kilmarnock, Scot. ... C4 4
Kilmarnock, Va. ... C6 85
Kimball, Minn. ... E4 67
Kimball, Nebr. ... C2 71
Kimball, S. Dak. ... G7 77
Kimball, co., Nebr. ... C2 71
Kimberley, B.C., Can. ... E9 37
Kimberley, S. Afr. ... F4 24
Kimberly, Ala. ... B3 46
Kimberly, Idaho ... G4 57
Kimberly, W. Va. ... D6 87
Kimberly, Wis. ... h9 88
Kimble, co., Tex. ... D3 84
Kimry, Sov. Un. ... C11 12
Kinabalu, mtn., Mala. ... D5 19
Kincaid, Ill. ... D4 58
Kincardine, Ont., Can. ... C3 41
Kincardine, co., Scot. ... *B5 4
Kinde, Mich. ... E8 66
Kinder, La. ... D3 63
Kinderhook, N.Y. ... C7 75
Kindersley, Sask., Can. ... F1 39
Kindia, Guinea ... F2 22
Kindu, Zaire ... I3 23
Kineo, mtn., Maine ... C3 64
Kineshma, Sov. Un. ... C14 12
King, N.C. ... A2 76
King, co., Tex. ... C2 84
King, co., Wash. ... B4 86
King, mtn., Oreg. ... D8 80
King, mtn., Oreg. ... E3 80
King and Queen, co., Va. ... C6 85
Kingaroy, Austl. ... E9 25
King City, Calif. ... D3 50
King City, Ont., Can. ... k14 41
King City, Mo. ... A3 69
Kingfield, Maine ... D2 64
Kingfisher, Okla. ... B4 79
Kingfisher, co., Okla. ... B3 79
King George, co., Va. ... B5 85
King George, mtn., B.C., Can. ... D10 37
Kingman, Ariz. ... B1 48
Kingman, Kans. ... E5, g10 61
Kingman, co., Kans. ... E5 61
King of Prussia, Pa. ... *F11 81
Kings, co., Calif. ... D3 50
Kings, co., N.B., Can. ... D4 43
Kings, co., N.S., Can. ... E5 43
Kings, co., P.E.I., Can. ... C7 43
Kings (Brooklyn Borough), co., N.Y. ... E7 75
Kings, peak, Calif. ... B1 50
Kings, peak, Utah ... A6 72
Kingsburg, Calif. ... D4 50
Kingsbury, co., S. Dak. ... F7 77
Kingscote, Austl. ... G6 25
Kingsford, Mich. ... C2 66

Kingsford Heights, Ind. ... *A4 59
Kings Gardens, Kans. ... A4 61
Kingsley, Iowa ... B2 60
Kingsley, Mich. ... D5 66
King's Lynn, Eng. ... D7 4
Kings Mills, Ohio ... C1, n13 78
Kings Mountain, N.C. ... B1 76
Kings Park, N.Y. ... n15 75
King's Point, Newf., Can. ... D3 44
Kings Point, N.Y. ... F1 52
Kingsport, Tenn. ... C11 83
Kingston, Austl. ... G6 25
Kingston, Ont., Can. ... C8 41
Kingston, Idaho ... B2 57
Kingston, Jam. ... F5 35
Kingston, Mass. ... C6 65
Kingston, N.H. ... F6 73
Kingston, N.J. ... C3 74
Kingston, N.Y. ... D6 75
Kingston, Ohio ... C3 78
Kingston, Okla. ... D5 79
Kingston, Pa. ... D10, n17 81
Kingston, R.I. ... D10 52
Kingston, Tenn. ... D9 83
Kingston, W. Va. ... D3, n13 87
Kingstree, S.C. ... D8 82
Kingsville, Ont., Can. ... E2 41
Kingsville, Ohio ... A5 78
Kingsville, Tex. ... F4 84
King William, co., Va. ... C5 85
King William's Town, S. Afr. ... G5 24
Kingwood, W. Va. ... B5 87
Kinistino, Sask., Can. ... E3 39
Kinloch, Mo. ... f13 69
Kinmundy, Ill. ... E5 58
Kinnaird, B.C., Can. ... E9 37
Kinnelon, N.J. ... B4 74
Kinney, co., Tex. ... E2 84
Kinross, co., Scot. ... *B5 4
Kinshasa (Leopoldville), Zaire ... A3 24
Kinsley, Kans. ... E4 61
Kinsman, Ohio ... A5 78
Kinston, N.C. ... B5 76
Kinwood, Tex. ... *E5 84
Kiowa, Kans. ... E5 61
Kiowa, Okla. ... C6 79
Kiowa, co., Colo. ... C8 51
Kiowa, co., Kans. ... E4 61
Kiowa, co., Okla. ... C2 79
Kiparissía, Grc. ... D3 14
Kipling, Sask., Can. ... G4 39
Kipushi, Zaire ... C5 24
Kirensk, Sov. Un. ... D13 13
Kirghiz, S.S.R., rep., Sov. Un. ... E10 16
Kiribati, country, Oceania ... F8 2
Kirikkale, Tur. ... *C9 14
Kirin, prov., China ... C9 17
Kirinyaga, mts., Ken. ... I5 23
Kirkcaldy, Scot. ... B5 4
Kirkcudbright, co., Scot. ... *C4 4
Kirkland, Ill. ... A5 58
Kirkland, Wash. ... B3, e11 86
Kirkland Lake, Ont., Can. ... o19 41
Kirklareli, Tur. ... B6 14
Kirklin, Ind. ... D5 59
Kirksville, Mo. ... A5 69
Kirkūk, Iraq ... E15 14
Kirkwood, Md. ... *C3 53
Kirkwood, Mo. ... f13 69
Kirn, Ger., Fed. Rep. of ... D3 6
Kirov, Sov. Un. ... D7 13
Kirovabad, Sov. Un. ... E7 13
Kirovograd, Sov. Un. ... G9 12
Kirovsk, Sov. Un. ... C6 13
Kirsanov, Sov. Un. ... E14 12
Kirşehir, Tur. ... C10 14
Kirtland, Ohio ... *A4 78
Kiruna, Swe. ... D9 11
Kiryū, Jap. ... H9, m18 18
Kisangani (Stanleyville), Zaire ... H3 23
Kisarazu, Jap. ... n18 18
Kiselevsk, Sov. Un. ... *D11 13
Kishangarh, India ... C5 20
Kishinev, Sov. Un. ... H7 12
Kishiwada, Jap. ... o14 18
Kishorganj, Bngl. ... D9 20
Kiskoros, Hung. ... B4 10
Kiskundorozsma, Hung. ... B5 10
Kiskunfelegyháza, Hung. ... B4 10
Kiskunhalas, Hung. ... B4 10
Kiskunmajsa, Hung. ... B4 10
Kislovodsk, Sov. Un. ... *E7 13
Kiso-sammyaku, mts., Jap. ... n16 18
Kissimmee, Fla. ... D5 54
Kistler, W. Va. ... D3, D5 87
Kisújszállás, Hung. ... B5 10
Kisumu, Ken. ... I4 23
Kisvárda, Hung. ... A6 10
Kita-shin, mtn., Jap. ... I9 18
Kitakyūshū, Jap. ... J5 18
Kitale, Ken. ... H4 23
Kitami, Jap. ... E11 18

Kit Carson, co., Colo. ... B8 51
Kitchener, Ont., Can. ... D4 41
Kitimat, B.C., Can. ... B3 37
Kitsap, co., Wash. ... B3 86
Kittanning, Pa. ... E2 81
Kittery, Maine ... E2 64
Kittery Point, Maine ... E2 64
Kittitas, co., Wash. ... B5 86
Kitts, Ky. ... D6 62
Kittson, co., Minn. ... B2 67
Kitwe, Zam. ... *C5 24
Kitzbühel, Aus. ... E6 6
Kitzingen, Ger., Fed. Rep. of ... D5 6
Kitzmiller, Md. ... m12 53
Kizel, Sov. Un. ... *D8 13
Kizyl-Arvat, Sov. Un. ... F8 13
Kladno, Czech. ... C3, n17 7
Klagenfurt, Aus. ... E7 6
Klaipeda (Memel), Sov. Un. ... D3 12
Klamath, co., Oreg. ... E4 80
Klamath, mts., Calif. ... B2 50
Klamath Falls, Oreg. ... E5 80
Klamath Glen, Calif. ... B2 50
Klatovy, Czech. ... D2 7
Kleberg, Tex. ... *C4 84
Kleberg, co., Tex. ... F4 84
Klemme, Iowa ... A4 60
Kletnya, Sov. Un. ... E9 12
Kletsk, Sov. Un. ... E6 12
Kleve, Ger., Fed. Rep. of ... C3 6
Klickitat, Wash. ... D4 86
Klickitat, co., Wash. ... D5 86
Klintsy, Sov. Un. ... E9 12
Ključ, Yugo. ... C3 10
Kłobuck, Pol. ... C5 7
Kłodzko, Pol. ... C4 7
Klosterneuburg, Aus. ... D8 6
Kluczbork, Pol. ... C5 7
Klyuchevskaya, vol., Sov. Un. ... D19 13
Knezha, Bul. ... D7 10
Knightdale, N.C. ... B4 76
Knights Landing, Calif. ... C3 50
Knightstown, Ind. ... E6 59
Knightsville, Ind. ... E3 59
Knittelfeld, Aus. ... E7 6
Knob Noster, Mo. ... C4 69
Knockmealdown, mts., Ire. ... D2 4
Knollwood, Ohio ... *C2 78
Knoolwood Park, Mich. ... *F6 66
Knot, co., Ky. ... C6 62
Knox, Ind. ... B4 59
Knox, Pa. ... *E1 81
Knox, co., Ill. ... B3 58
Knox, co., Ind. ... G3 59
Knox, co., Ky. ... D6 62
Knox, co., Maine ... D4 64
Knox, co., Mo. ... A5 69
Knox, co., Nebr. ... B8 71
Knox, co., Ohio ... B3 78
Knox, co., Tenn. ... C10 83
Knox, co., Tex. ... C3 84
Knox City, Tex. ... C3 84
Knoxville, Ill. ... C3 58
Knoxville, Iowa ... C4 60
Knoxville, Tenn. ... D10, n14 83
Knysna, S. Afr. ... G4 24
Kōbe, Jap. ... o14 18
Kobelyaki, Sov. Un. ... G10 12
København, see Copenhagen, Den.
Koblenz, Ger., Fed. Rep. of ... C3 6
Kobrin, Sov. Un. ... E5 12
Kočani, Yugo. ... E6 10
Koch, mtn., Mont. ... E5 70
Kochi, Jap. ... J6 18
Kōchi, pref., Jap. ... *J6 18
Kodaira, Jap. ... *n18 18
Kodak, Ky. ... C6 62
Kodiak, Alsk. ... D9 47
Kodiak, isl., Alsk. ... D9 47
Koforidua, Ghana ... G4 22
Kofu, Jap. ... I9, n17 18
Koga, Jap. ... m18 18
Kohala, Haw. ... C6 56
Kohāt, Pak. ... B5 20
Kohler, Wis. ... E5, k10 88
Kokand, Sov. Un. ... E10 13
Kokchetav, Sov. Un. ... D9 13
Kokkola, Fin. ... F10 11
Kokomo, Ind. ... D5 59
Kokstad, S.Afr. ... G5 24
Kolar Gold Fields, India ... F6 20
Kolarovo, Bul. ... D8 10
Kolárovo, Czech. ... E4 7
Kolhapur, India ... E5 20
Kolín, Czech. ... C3 7
Köln, see Cologne, Ger.
Kolo, Pol. ... B5 7
Koloa, Haw. ... B2 56
Kolomna, Sov. Un. ... D12, n18 12
Kolomyya, Sov. Un. ... G5 12
Kolonodale, Indon. ... F6 19
Kolpino, Sov. Un. ... s31 1

Kolpino, Sov. Un. s31 11
Kolwezi, Zaire C5 24
Kolyberovo, Sov. Un. n18 12
Kolyma, riv., Sov. Un. C18 16
Komádi, Hung. B5 10
Komandorski Village, Calif. *D2 50
Komárno, Czech. E5 7
Komarno, Sov. Un. D7 7
Komárom, Hung. B4 10
Komárom, co., Hung. *B4 10
Komatsu, Jap. H8 18
Komatsushima, Jap. I7 18
Kommunarsk, Sov. Un. G12, q21 12
Komotiní, Grc. B5 14
Kompong Cham, Kam. C3 19
Kompong Chhnang, Kam. *C2 19
Kompong Kleang, Kam. *C2 19
Kompong Speu, Kam. *C2 19
Kompong Thom, Kam. C2 19
Komrat, Sov. Un. H7 12
Komsomolsk -na Amure,
  Sov. Un. D16 13
Konawa, Okla. C5 79
Kondoa, Tan. A7 24
Kondopoga, Sov. Un. F16 11
Kong, reg., I.C. G4 22
Kongju, Kor. H3 18
Kongsberg, Nor. H3 11
Konin, Pol. B5 7
Konosha, Sov. Un. A13 12
Konotop, Sov. Un. F9 12
Końskie, Pol. C6 7
Konstantinovka, Sov. Un. q20 12
Konstanz, Ger., Fed. Rep. of E4 6
Kontum, Viet. C3 19
Konya, Tur. D9 14
Konyang, Kor. I3 18
Koochiching, co., Minn. B4 67
Koontz Lake, Ind. B5 59
Kooskia, Idaho C3 57
Kootenai, co., Idaho B2 57
Kopeysk, Sov. Un. *D9 13
Köping, Swe. H6, t33 11
Kopparberg, co., Swe. *G6 11
Koppel, Pa. E1 81
Koprivnica, Yugo. B3 10
Kopychintsy, Sov. Un. G5 12
Korçë, Alb. B3 14
Korçë, pref., Alb. *B3 14
Korea, North, country, Asia F4 18
Korea, South, country, Asia H4 18
Korets, Sov. Un. F6 12
Korhogo, I.C. G3 22
Kórinthos (Corinth), Grc. D4 14
Kóriyama, Jap. H10 18
Korkino, Sov. Un. *D9 13
Korla, China C2 17
Körmend, Hung. B3 10
Korneuburg, Aus. D8 6
Koropí, Grc. h11 14
Korosten, Sov. Un. F7 12
Korsakov, Sov. Un. E17 13
Kortrijk, Bel. B5 5
Kos, Grc. D6 14
Kościan, Pol. B4 7
Kościerzyna, Pol. A4 7

Kosciusko, Miss. B4 68
Kosciusko, co., Ind. B6 59
Kosciusko, mtn., Austl. G8 25
Košice, Czech. D6 7
Kosong, Kor. G4 18
Kosove (Kosovo), pref., Alb. *A3 14
Kosovska Mitrovica, Yugo. D5 10
Kossuth, co., Iowa A3 60
Kostroma, Sov. Un. C13 12
Kostrzyn, Pol. B3 7
Koszalin, Pol. A4 7
Koszeg, Hung. B3 10
Kota, India C6 20
Kota Baharu, Mala. D2 19
Kotabaru, Indon. F5 19
Kota Kinabalu, Mala. I14 19
Kotelnikovskiy, Sov. Un. H14 12
Köthen, Ger. Dem. Rep. C5 6
Kotka, Fin. G12 11
Kotlas, Sov. Un. C7 13
Kotor, Yugo. D4 10
Kotovsk, Sov. Un. H7 12
Kotzebue, Alsk. *B7 47
Koudougou, Burkina Faso. F4 22
Kountze, Tex. D5 84
Kouts, Ind. B3 59
Kouvola, Fin. G12 11
Kovel, Sov. Un. F5 12
Kovrov, Sov. Un. C13 12
Kowa, Jap. o15 18
Kowloon, Hong Kong G7 17
Kowon, Kor. G3 18
Kozan, Tur. D10 14
Kozáni, Grc. B3 14
Kozáni, prov., Grc. *B3 14
Kozienice, Pol. C6 7
Koźle, Pol. C5 7
Kozloduy, Bul. D6 10
Kozuchów, Pol. C3 7
Kragujevac, Yugo. D5 10
Kraków, Pol. C5 7
Kraljevo, Yugo. D5 10
Kralupy nad Vltavou, Czech. n17 7
Kramatorsk, Sov. Un. G11, q20 12
Kranj, Yugo. B2 10
Kraslice, Czech. C2 7
Kraśnik Lubelski, Pol. C7 7
Krasnoarmeysk, Sov. Un. F15 12
Krasnodar, Sov. Un. I12 12
Krasnograd, Sov. Un. G10 12
Krasnoselye, Sov. Un. G9 12
Krasnoslobodsk, Sov. Un. D14 12
Krasnovodsk, Sov. Un. E8 13
Krasnoyarsk, Sov. Un. D12 13
Krasnystaw, Pol. C7 7
Krasnyy Liman, Sov. Un. q20 12
Krasnyy Luch, Sov. Un. q21 12
Krasnyy Sulin, Sov. Un. H13 12
Krasnyy Yar, Sov. Un. F15 12
Kratie, Kam. C3 19
Krebs, Okla. C6 79
Krefeld, Ger., Fed. Rep. of C3 6
Kremenchug, Sov. Un. G9 12
Kremenets, Sov. Un. F5 12
Kremennaya, Sov. Un. p21 12
Krems, Aus. D7 6

Krichev, Sov. Un. E8 12
Krishnagiri, India F6 20
Kristiansand, Nor. H2 11
Kristianstad, Swe. I6 11
Kristianstad, co., Swe. *I5 11
Kristiansund, Nor. F2 11
Krivoy Rog, Sov. Un. H9 12
Križevci, Yugo. B3 10
Krnov, Czech. C4 7
Kroměříž, Czech. D4 7
Kromy, Sov. Un. E10 12
Kronoberg, co., Swe. *I6 11
Kronshtadt, Sov. Un. B7 12
Kroonstad, S. Afr. F5 24
Kropotkin, Sov. Un. I13 12
Krosno, Pol. D6 7
Krosno Odrzańskie, Pol. B3 7
Krotoszyn, Pol. C4 7
Krotz Springs, La. D4 63
Krsko, Yugo. C2 10
Krugersdorp, S. Afr. F5 24
Krumroy, Ohio *A4 78
Kruševac, Yugo. D5 10
Krusevo, Yugo. E6 10
Krymskaya, Sov. Un. I11 12
Krynki, Pol. B7 7
Ksar el Kebir, Mor. B3 22
Ksar es Souk, Mor. B4 22
Kuala Lipis, Mala. E2 19
Kuala Lumpur, Mala. E2 19
Kuala Terengganu, Mala. D2 19
Kuantan, Mala. E2 19
Kubokawa, Jap. J6 19
Kuching, Mala. E4 19
Kudat, Mala. D5 19
Kudus, Indon. G4 19
Kufstein, Aus. E6 6
Kuji, Jap. F10 18
Kuju-San, mtn., Jap. J5 18
Kuki, Jap. m18 18
Kula, Bul. D6 10
Kula, Tur. *C7 14
Kula, Yugo. C4 10
Kula Kangri, peak, Bhutan,
  China C9 20
Kulebaki, Sov. Un. D14 12
Kulmbach, Ger., Fed. Rep. of C5 6
Kulpmont, Pa. E9 81
Kumagaya, Jap. m18 18
Kumamoto, Jap. J5 18
Kumamoto, pref., Jap. *J5 18
Kumanovo, Yugo. D5 10
Kumasi, Ghana G4 22
Kumbakonam, India F6 20
Kumchon, Kor. H4 18
Kumha, Kor. G3 18
Kumihama, Jap. n14 19
Kumla, Swe. H6, t33 11
Kumo, Nig. D7 22
Kuna, Idaho F2 57
Kuneitra (Al Qunaytirah), Syr. ... F10 14
Kunming (Yunnanfu), China F5 17
Kunsan, Kor. I3 18
Kunszentmárton, Hung. B5 10
Kuolayarvi, Sov. Un. D13 11
Kuopio, Fin. F12 11

Kuopio, prov., Fin. *F12 11
Kupang, Indon. H6 19
Kupyansk, Sov. Un. G11 12
Kura, riv., Sov. Un. I6 18
Kurashiki, Jap. I6 18
Kuraymah, Sud. E4 23
Kurdzhali, Bul. E7 10
Kure, Jap. I6 18
Kuressaare, Sov. Un. B4 12
Kurgan, Sov. Un. D9 13
Kurnool, India E6 20
Kurri Kurri-Weston, Austl. F8 26
Kursk, Sov. Un. F11 12
Kurthwood, La. C2 63
Kurtistown, Haw. D6 56
Kurume, Jap. J5 18
Kurunegala, Sri Lanka G7 20
Kusatsu, Jap. n14 18
Kushchevskaya, Sov. Un. H12 12
Kushevat, Sov. Un. C9 13
Kushimoto, Jap. J7 18
Kushiro, Jap. E12 18
Kushka, Sov. Un. F9 13
Kustanay, Sov. Un. D9 13
Kūsti, Sud. F4 23
Küstrin, see Kostrzyn, Pol.
Kütahya (Kutaiah), Tur. C7 14
Kutaisi, Sov. Un. A14 14
Kutná Hora, Czech. D3 7
Kutno, Pol. B5 7
Kutztown, Pa. E10 81
Kuwait, Kuw. D4 15
Kuwait, country, Asia D4 15
Kuwana, Jap. I8, n18 18
Kuybyshev, Sov. Un. D8 13
Kuybyshev, Sov. Un. D10 13
Kuznetsk, Sov. Un. E16 12
Kwangju, Kor. I3 18
Kwidzyń, Pol. B5 7
Kyabram, Austl. H5 26
Kyaiklat, Bur. E10 20
Kyaikto, Bur. *B1 19
Kyakhta, Sov. Un. D13 13
Kyaukse, Bur. D10 20
Kybartai, Sov. Un. A7 7
Kyje, Czech. n18 7
Kyle, Sask., Can. G1 39
Kyle, Tex. E4 84
Kylestrome, Scot. *A4 4
Kyllburg, Ger., Fed. Rep. of *C3 6
Kymi, prov., Fin. *G12 11
Kynlyn, Del. *A6 53
Kyomipo, see Songnim, Kor.
Kyongju, Kor. I4 18
Kyongsong, Kor. F4 18
Kyōto, Jap. I7, n14 18
Kyoto, pref., Jap. *I7 18
Kyritz, Ger. Dem. Rep. B6 6
Kyshtym, Sov. Un. *D9 13
Kyūshū, isl., Jap. J5 18
Kyustendil, Bul. D6 10
Kyzyl, Sov. Un. D12 13
Kzyl-Orda, Sov. Un. E9 13

L

Labadieville, La. E5, k10 63
La Barca, Mex. C4, m12 34
La Barge, Wyo. D2 89
Labe, Guinea F2 22
Labelle, Que., Can. C3 42
La Belle, Fla. F5 54
La Belle, Mo. A6 69
Labelle, co., Que., Can. C2 42
Labette, co., Kans. E8 61
Labin, Yugo. C2 10
La Boca, Pan. *B2 32
Laboulaye, Arg. A4 28
Labrador, reg., Newf., Can. g9 44
Laburnum Manor, Va. *C5 85
La Canada, Calif. m12 50
La Carlota, Phil. *C6 19
La Carolina, Sp. C4 8
Lac au Saumon, Que., Can. *k13 42

Lac-aux-Sables, Que., Can. C5 42
Lac-Beauport, Que., Can. C9 42
Lac-Bouchette, Que., Can. A5 42
Lac-Brome, Que., Can. D5 42
Laccadive, is., India F5 20
Lac-Carré, Que., Can. C3 42
Lac-du-Bonnet, Man., Can. D3 40
Lac du Flambeau, Wis. B4 88
La Ceiba, Hond. D7 34
La Ceja, Col. B2 32
Lac-Etchemin, Que., Can. C7 42
Lacey, Wash. B3 86
Lacey Park, Pa. *F11 81
La Chaux-de-Fonds, Switz. E3 6
Lachine, Que., Can. D4, q19 42
La Chorrera, Pan. B2 32
Lachute, Que., Can. D3 42
La Ciotat, Fr. F6 5

Lackawanna, N.Y. C2 75
Lackawanna, co., Pa. D10 81
Lac la Biche, Alta., Can. B5 38
Lac la Hache, B.C., Can. D7 37
Laclede, co., Mo. D5 69
Lac-Mégantic, Que., Can. D7 42
Lacolle, Que., Can. D4 42
Lacombe, Alta., Can. C4 38
Lacombe, La. D6, h12 63
Lacon, Ill. B4 58
Laconia, N.H. D5 73
La Conner, Wash. A3 86
Lacoochee, Fla. D4 54
La Coruña, Sp. A1 8
La Coruña, prov., Sp. *A1 8
La Courneuve, Fr. g10 5
Lac Qui Parle, co., Minn. F2 67
La Crescent, Minn. G7 67

La Crescenta, Calif. *F4 50
La Cresta Village, Calif. *E4 50
La Crosse, Ind. B4 59
La Crosse, Kans. D4 61
La Crosse, Va. D4 85
La Crosse, Wis. E2 88
La Crosse, co., Wis. E2 88
La Cruz, Col. C2 32
La Cruz, Mex. C3 34
Lac-St.-Jean-Est, co., Que., Can. . A6 42
Lac-St.-Jean-Ouest, co.,
  Que., Can. A5 42
La Cygne, Kans. D9 61
Lacy-Lakeview, Tex. *D4 84
Ladd, Ill. B4 58
Ladera Heights, Calif. *F4 50
Ladner, B.C., Can. E6, f12 37
Ladoga, Ind. E4 59

Ladoga, lake, Sov. Un. A8 12
Ladonia, Tex. C5 84
La Dorado, Col. B3 32
Ladue, Mo. *C7 69
Lady Laurier, mtn., B.C., Can. A6 37
Ladysmith, B.C., Can. E6, g12 37
Ladysmith, S. Afr. F5 24
Ladysmith, Wis. C2 88
Lae, Pap. N. Gui. k12 25
La Esperanza, Cuba C2 35
La Estrada, Sp. A1 8
La Farge, Wis. E3 88
Lafayette, Ala. C4 46
Lafayette, Calif. *D2 50
Lafayette, Colo. B5 51
La Fayette, Ga. B1 55
Lafayette, Ind. D4 59
Lafayette, La. D3 63
Lafayette, N.J. A3 74
Lafayette, Oreg. B3, h11 80
Lafayette, Tenn. C7 83
Lafayette, co., Ark. D2 49
Lafayette, co., Fla. C3 54
Lafayette, co., Miss. A4 68
Lafayette, co., Mo. C4 69
Lafayette, co., Wis. F3 88
Lafayette, par., La. D3 63
Lafayette Hill, Pa. *F11 81
La Feria, Tex. F4 84
La Ferté-Bernard, Fr. C4 5
Lafferty, Ohio B4 78
Lafitte, La. k11 63
Laflèche, (Mackayville),
  Que., Can. *D4 42
Laflèche, Sask., Can. H2 39
La Flèche, Fr. D3 5
La Follette, Tenn. C9 83
La Fontaine, Ind. C6 59
Lafourche, par., La. E5 63
La France, S.C. B2 82
Laghouat, Alg. B5 22
La Gloria, Col. B3 52
Lagny, Fr. C5 5
Lagos, Nig. G5 22
Lagos, Port. D1 8
Lagos, de Moreno, Mex. C4, m13 34
La Grand' Combe, Fr. E5 5
La Grande, Oreg. B8 80
La Grange, Ga. C1 55
La Grange, Ill. B6, k9 58
Lagrange, Ind. A7 59
La Grange, Ky. B4 62
La Grange, Mo. A6 69
La Grange, N.C. B5 76
Lagrange, Ohio A3 78
La Grange, Tex. E4 84
Lagrange, co., Ind. A7 59
La Grange Highlands, Ill. *B6 58
La Grange Park, Ill. k9 58
Lagro, Ind. C6 59
La Guadeloupe, Que., Can. D7 42
La Guaira, Ven. A4 32
La Guajira, intendencia, Col. A3 32
La Guardia, Sp. B1 8
Laguna, Braz. D3 30
Laguna, prov., Phil. *C6 19
Laguna Beach, Calif. F5, n13 50
Lagunas, Peru C2 31
Laguna Shores, Tex. *F4 84
La Habra, Calif. n13 50
La Habra Heights, Calif. *F4 50
Lahad Datu, Mala. D5 19
Lahaina, Haw. C5 56
La Harpe, Ill. C3 58
Lahij, P.D.R. of Yem. G3 15
Lahore, Pak. B5 20
Lahr, Ger., Fed. Rep. of D3 6
Lahti, Fin. G11 11
La Huaca, Peru B1 31
Laie, Haw. B4, f10 56
Laigle, Fr. C4 5
Laingsburg, Mich. F6 66
Lairg, Scot. A4 4
La Jara, Colo. D5 51
Lajes, Braz. D2 30
Lajosmizse, Hung. B4 10
La Joya, Mex. h9 34
La Junta, Colo. D7 51
Lake, co., Calif. C2 50
Lake, co., Colo. b4 51
Lake, co., Fla. D5 54
Lake, co., Ill. a6 58
Lake, co., Ind. B3 59
Lake, co., Mich. E3 66
Lake, co., Minn. C7 67
Lake, co., Mont. C2 70
Lake, co., Ohio A4 78
Lake, co., Oreg. E6 80
Lake, co., S. Dak. F8 77
Lake, co., Tenn. A2 83
Lake, mtn., Wyo E6 89
Lake Alfred, Fla. D5 54
Lake Andes, S. Dak. *G7 77

Lake Arrowhead, Calif. E5 50
Lake Arthur, La. D3 63
Lake Barcroft, Va. *B5 85
Lake Benton, Minn. F2 67
Lake Bluff, Ill. A6, h9 58
Lake Butler, Fla. B4 54
Lake Charles, La. D2 63
Lake City, Fla. B4 54
Lake City, Iowa B3 60
Lake City, Mich. D5 66
Lake City, Minn. F6 67
Lake City, Pa. B1 81
Lake City, S.C. D8 82
Lake City, Tenn. C9 83
Lake Cowichan, B.C., Can. g11 37
Lake Crystal, Minn. F4 67
Lake Delton, Wis. E4 88
Lake Erie Beach, N.Y. *C1 75
Lake Fenton, Mich. *F7 66
Lakefield, Ont., Can. C6 41
Lakefield, Minn. G3 67
Lake Forest, Ill. A6, h9 58
Lake Forest, S.C. *B3 82
Lake Forest Park, Wash. *B3 86
Lake Geneva, Wis. F5 88
Lake George, N.Y. B7 75
Lake Hamilton, Fla. *D5 54
Lake Harbor, Fla. *F6 54
Lake Helen, Fla. D5 54
Lake Hiawatha, N.J. B4 74
Lake Hills, Wash. *B3 86
Lake Hopatcong, N.J. *B3 74
Lakehurst, N.J. C4 74
Lake in the Hills, Ill. *A5 58
Lake Jackson, Tex. E5, r14 84
Lake James, Ind. A7 59
Lakeland, Fla. D5 54
Lakeland, Ga. E3 55
Lakeland Village, Calif. *F5 50
Lake Linden, Mich. A2 66
Lake Lotawana, Mo. *C3 69
Lake Luzerne, N.Y. B7 75
Lake Mary, Fla. D5 54
Lake Mills, Iowa A4 60
Lake Mills, Wis. E5 88
Lake Mohawk, N.J. A3 74
Lakemont, Pa. F5 81
Lakemore, Ohio A4 78
Lake Odessa, Mich. F5 66
Lake of the Woods, lake,
  Can., U.S. A4 67
Lake of the Woods, co., Minn. B3 67
Lake Orion, Mich. F7 66
Lake Orion Heights, Mich. *F7 66
Lake Oswego, Oreg. B4, h12 80
Lake Ozark, Mo. C5 69
Lake Park, Fla. F6 54
Lake Park, Iowa A2 60
Lake Park, Minn. D2 67
Lake Placid, Fla. E5 54
Lake Placid, N.Y. A7, f10 75
Lakeport, Calif. C2 50
Lake Preston, S. Dak. F8 77
Lake Providence, La. *B4 63
Lake Ronkonkoma, N.Y. F4 52
Lakeside, Calif. F5, o16 50
Lakeside, N.S., Can. E6 43
Lakeside, La. *C3 63
Lakeside, Ohio A3 78
Lakeside, Oreg. D2 80
Lakeside, Va. *C5 85
Lakeside Park, Ky. h13 62
Lake Station, Ind. A3 59
Lake Stevens, Wash. A3 86
Lake Success, N.Y. h13 75
Lake Telemark, N.J. *B3 74
Lake Toxaway, N.C. f10 76
Lake View, Iowa B2 60
Lakeview, Mich. *F5 66
Lakeview, Mich. E5 66
Lake View, N.Y. *C2 75
Lakeview, Ohio B2 78
Lakeview, Oreg. E6 80
Lake View, S.C. C9 82
Lakeview, Tex. *E6 84
Lake Villa, Ill. h8 58
Lake Village, Ark. D4 49
Lakeville, Conn. B3 52
Lakeville, Ind. A5 59
Lakeville, Minn. F5 67
Lakeville, N.Y. C3 75
Lakeville, Ohio A5 78
Lake Waccamaw, N.C. C4 76
Lake Wales, Fla. E5 54
Lakewood Calif. n12 50
Lakewood, N.B., Can. *C2 43
Lakewood, Colo. B5 51
Lakewood, N.J. C4 74
Lakewood, N.Y. C1 75
Lakewood, Ohio A4, h9 78
Lakewood, Tex. *E5 84
Lakewood Center, Wash. *B3 86
Lake Worth, Fla. *F6 54

Lake Zurich, Ill. h8 58
Lakhīmpur, India C7 20
Lakin, Kans. E2 61
Lakonia (Laconia), prov., Grc. *D4 14
Lakota, N. Dak. B7 77
Lakshadweep, ter., India *F5 20
La Laguna, Sp. m13 8
La Libertad, dept., Peru C2 31
Lalin, Sp. A1 8
La Linea, Sp. D3 8
Lalitpur, India D6 20
La Loche, Sask., Can. m7 39
La Maddalena, It. D2 9
La Malbaie, Que., Can. B7 42
Lamar, Colo. C8 51
Lamar, Mo. D3 69
Lamar, S.C. C7 82
Lamar, co., Ala. B1 46
Lamar, co., Ga. C2 55
Lamar, co., Tex. C5 84
Lamar, co., Miss. D4 68
La Marque, Tex. r15 84
Lamartine, Que., Can. B7 42
Lamas, Peru C2 31
Lamb, co., Tex. B1 84
Lamballe, Fr. C2 5
Lambayeque, Peru C2 31
Lambayeque, dept., Peru C2 31
Lambert, Miss. A3 68
Lamberton, Minn. F3 67
Lambertville, Mich. *G7 66
Lambertville, N.J. C3 74
Lambeth, Ont., Can. E3 41
Lambton, Que., Can. D6 42
Lambton, co., Ont., Can. E2 41
Lamego, Port. B2 8
Lamèque, N.B., Can. B5 43
La Mesa, Calif. o15 50
Lamesa, Tex. C2 84
Lamia, Grc. C4 14
La Mirada, Calif. *F4 50
La Moille, Ill. B4 58
Lamoille, co., Vt. B2 73
Lamoni, Iowa D4 60
Lamont, Calif. E4 50
Lamont, Alta., Can. C4 38
Lamont, Okla. A4 79
La Monte, Mo. C4 69
La Moure, N. Dak. D7 77
La Moure, co., N. Dak. D7 77
Lampa, Peru E3 31
Lampang, Thai. *B1 19
Lampasas, Tex. D3 84
Lampasas, co., Tex. D3 84
Lamphun, Thai. *B1 19
Lampman, Sask., Can. H4 39
Lanai City, Haw. C5 56
Lanao del Norte, prov., Phil. *D6 19
Lanark, Ont., Can. C8 41
Lanark, Ill. A4 58
Lanark, Scot. C5 4
Lanark, co., Ont., Can. C8 41
Lanark, co., Scot. *C5 4
Lanark Village, Fla. C2 54
Lancashire, co., Eng. *C5 4
Lancaster, Calif. E4 50
Lancaster, N.B., Can. D3 43
Lancaster, Ont., Can. B10 41
Lancaster, Eng. C5 4
Lancaster, Ky. C5 62
Lancaster, Mass. B4 65
Lancaster, Mo. A5 69
Lancaster, N.H. C4 73
Lancaster, N.Y. C2 75
Lancaster, Ohio G3 78
Lancaster, Pa. F9 81
Lancaster, S.C. B6 82
Lancaster, Tex. n10 84
Lancaster, Wis. F3 88
Lancaster, co., Nebr. D9 71
Lancaster, co., Pa. G9 81
Lancaster, co., S.C. B6 82
Lancaster, co., Va. C6 85
Lancaster Mills, S.C. *B6 82
Lancer, Ky. C7 62
Lanciano, It. C5 9
Lanćut, Pol. C7 7
Landau an der Isar, Ger
  Fed., Rep. of D6 6
Landau in der Pfalz, Ger.,
  Fed. Rep. of D4 6
Landeck, Aus. E5 6
Lander, Wyo. D4 89
Lander, co., Nev. A3 72
Landerneau, Fr. C1 5
Landes, dept., Fr. *F3 5
Landing, N.J. *B3 74
Landis, N.C. B2 76
Landisville, Pa. *F11 81
Landivisiau, Fr. C1 5
Lando, S.C. B5 82
Landover Hills, Md. *C4 53
Landrum, S.C. A3 82

Landsberg, Ger., Fed. Rep. of D5 6
Landshut, Ger., Fed. Rep of D6 6
Landskrona, Swe. J5 11
Lane, co., Kans. D3 61
Lane, co., Oreg. D4 80
Lanesboro, Mass. A1 65
Lanesboro, Minn. G7 67
Lanett, Ala. C4 46
Langadhas, Grc. *B4 14
Langdale, Ala. C4 46
Langdon, N. Dak. B7 77
L'Ange-Gardien, Que., Can. n17 42
Langeloth, Pa. F1 81
Langenburg, Sask., Can. G5 39
Langenthal, Switz. E3 6
Langesund, Nor. H3, p27 11
Langford, B.C., Can. h12 37
Langhorne, Pa. F12 81
Langlade, co., Wis. C4 88
Langley, B.C., Can. f13 37
Langley, Ky. C7 62
Langley, S.C. D4 82
Langley Park, Md. *C3 53
Langnau in Emmental, Switz. E3 6
Langon, Fr. E3 5
Langreo, Sp. A3 8
Langres, Fr. D6 5
Langsa, Indon. E1, m11 19
Lang Son, Viet. *G13 16
Langstaff, Ont., Can. k15 41
Languedoc, former prov.,Fr. F5 5
Lanham, Md. C4 53
Lanier, co., Ga. E3 55
Lannion, Fr. C2 5
Lannon, Wis. m11 88
L'Annonciation, Que., Can. C3 42
Lanoraie, Que., Can. D4 42
Lansdale, Pa. F11 81
Lansdowne, Md. B4 53
Lansdowne, Pa. G11, p20 81
Lansdowne House, Ont., Can. n18 41
L'Anse, Mich. B2 66
Lansford, Pa. E10 81
Lansing, Ill. B6, k9 58
Lansing, Iowa A6 60
Lansing, Kans. B8 61
Lansing, Mich. F6 66
Lansing, Ohio *C4 78
Lantana, Fla. F6 54
Lanús, Arg. *A5 28
Lanxi, China C3 18
Lanzhou, China D5 17
Laoag, Phil. B6 19
Laoighis, co., Ire. *D3 4
Lao Kay, Viet. *G13 16
Laon, Fr. C5 5
Laona, Wis. C5 88
La Oroya, Peru D2 31
Laos, country, Asia. B2 19
Lapa, Braz. D3 30
La Palma, Sp. D2 8
La Pampa, prov., Arg. B3 28
La Paz, Arg. A4 28
La Paz, Bol. C2 29
La Paz, Col. A3 32
La Paz, Mex. C2 34
La Paz, co., Ariz. C1 48
La Paz, dept., Bol. C2 29
Lapeer, Mich. E7 66
Lapeer, co., Mich. E7 56
Lapel, Ind. D6 59
La Piedad Cavadas Mex m12 34
Laplace, La. h11 63
Lapland, reg., Eur. C12 11
La Plata, Arg. A5, g8 28
La Plata, Col. C2 32
La Plata, Md. C4 53
La Plata, Mo. A5 69
La Plata, co., Colo. D3 51
La Pocatière, Que., Can. B7 42
La Pocatieew, Que. Can. B7 42
La Pola, Sp. A3 8
La Porte, Ind. A4 59
La Porte, Tex. r14 84
La Porte, co., Ind. A4 59
La Porte City, Iowa B5 60
Lappeenranta, Fin. G13 11
Lappi, prov., Fin. *D11 11
La Prairie, Que., Can. D4, q20 42
Laprairie, co., Que., Can. D4, q20 42
La Presa, Calif. *F5 50
La Providence, Que., Can. *D5 42
La Pryor, Tex. E3 84
La Puebla, Sp. C7 8
La Puebla de Montalbán, Sp. C3 8
La Puente, Calif. *F4 50
La Purisima, Mex. B2 34
La Quiaca, Arg. D2 29
L'Aquila, It. C4 9
Lara, state, Ven. A3 32
Larache, Mor. A3 22
Laramie, Wyo. E7 89
Laramie, co., Wyo. E8 89

Laramie, peak, Wyo. D7 89
Larchmont, N.Y. h13 75
Laredo, Sp. A4 8
Laredo, Tex. F3 84
Largo, Fla. E4, p10 54
Lariat, Colo. D4 51
La Ricamarie, Fr. E6 5
Larimer, Pa. *F2 81
Larimer, co., Colo. A5 51
Larimore, N. Dak. C8 77
Larino, It. D5 9
La Rioja, Arg. E2 29
La Rioja, prov., Arg. E2 29
La Rioja, Cuba D5 35
Lárisa (Larissa), Grc. C4 14
Lárisa (Larissa), prov., Grc. *C4 14
Lārkāna, Pak. C4 20
Larkspur, Calif. h7 50
Larksville, Pa. n17 81
Larne, N. Ire. C4 4
Larned, Kans. D4 61
La Rochelle, Fr. D3 5
La Roche-sur-Yon, Fr. D3 5
La Roda, Sp. C4 8
La Romana, Dom. Rep E9 35
La Ronge, Sask., Can. B3 39
Larose, La. E5 63
La Rue, Ohio B2 78
La Rue, co., Ky. C4 62
Larvik, Nor. H4, p28 11
Larwill, Ind. B6 59
La Salle, Que., Can. q19 42
La Salle, Colo. A6 51
La Salle, Ill. B4 58
La Salle, co., Ill. B5 58
La Salle, co. Tex. *E3 84
La Salle, par.,La. C3 63
Las Animas, Colo. C7 51
Las Animas, co., Colo. D6 51
La Sarre, Que., Can. o20 41
Lascahobas, Hai. E8 35
L'Ascension, Que., Can. A6 42
La Scie, Newf., Can. D4 44
Las Conchas, Arg. g7 28
Las Cruces, N. Mex. C5 48
La Selle, peak, Hai. E8 37
La Serena, Chile E1 29
La Seyne -sur-Mer, Fr. F6 5
Las Flores, Arg. B5 28
La Sierra, Calif. n14 50
Lasithi (Lasithion), prov., Grc. *E5 14
Las Matas de Farfan, Dom. Rep. *E8 35
La Solana, Sp. C4 8
Las Palmas de Gran Canaria, Sp. m14 8
Las Palmas, prov., Sp. m14 8
La Spezia, It. B2 9
Las Piedras, Ur. E1 30
Lassen, co., Calif. B3 50
Lassen, peak, Calif. B3 50
L'Assomption, Que., Can. D4 42
L'Assomption, co., Que., Can. D4 42
Las Varillas, Arg. A4 28
Las Vegas, Nev. C4 72
Las Vegas, N. Mex. B6, D7 48
Las Villas, prov., Cuba C3 35
Lataunga, Ec. B2 31
Latah, co., Idaho C2 57
Latakia (Al Lādhiqīyah), Syr. E10 14
Laterrière, Que., Can. A6 42
La Teste-de-Bunch, Fr. D3 5
Latham, N.Y. *C7 75
Lathrop, Calif. *D3 50
Lathrop, Mo. B3 69
Lathrup Village, Mich. *F7 66
Latimer, co.,Okla. C6 79
Latina, It. D4, k9 9
Latium, reg., It. C4 9
Laton, Calif. D4 50
Latour, peak, Idaho B2 57
La Trinité, Mart. I14 35
Latrobe, Pa. F3 81
Latta, S.C. C9 82
Lattimer Mines, Pa. E10 81
Lattingtown, N.Y. *E7 75
La Tuque, Que., Can. B5 42
Latvia (S.S.R.), rep., Sov.
  Un. C4 12
Lauderdale, Minn. n12 67
Lauderdale, co., Ala. A2 46
Lauderdale, co., Miss. C5 68
Lauderdale, co., Tenn. B2 83
Lauderdale-by-the-Sea, Fla. *F6 54
Launceston, Austl. o15 25
Launceston, Eng. E4 4
La Unión, Chile C5 28
La Unión, Col.`. C2 32
La Unión, Mex. D4, o13 34
La Unión, Peru C2 31
La Unión, Sal. E7 34
La Unión, Sp. D5 8
La Union, prov., Phil. *B6 19
Laupheim, Ger., Fed. Rep. of D4 6
Laurel, Del. C6 53

Laurel, Fla. E4 54
Laurel, Ind. F7 59
Laurel, Md. B4 53
Laurel, Miss. D4 68
Laurel, Mont. E8 70
Laurel, Nebr. B8 71
Laurel, Va. C5 85
Laurel, co., Ky. C5 62
Laurel Bay, S.C. G6 82
Laureldale, Pa. F10 81
Laurel Gardens, Pa. *E1 81
Laurel Heights, Wash. *B3 86
Laurel Hill, N.C. C3 76
Laurel Run, Pa. n17 81
Laurel Springs, N.J. *D3 74
Laurence Harbor, N.J. C4 74
Laurens, Iowa B3 60
Laurens, S.C. B3 82
Laurens, co., Ga. D3 55
Laurens, co., S.C. C3 82
Laurentides, Que., Can. D4 42
Laurier, Que., Can. C6 42
Laurierville, Que., Can. C6 42
Laurinburg, N.C. C3 76
Laurium, Mich. A2 66
Lausanne, Switz. E3 6
Lautaro, Chile B2 28
Lauzon, Que., Can. C6, n17 42
Lavaca, co., Tex. E4 84
Lava Hot Springs, Idaho G6 57
Laval, Fr. C3 5
Laval, Que., Can. D4 42
Laval-des-Rapides, Que., Can. *D4 42
La Vale, Md. k13 53
Lavalleja, dept., Ur. *E1 30
Lavallette, N.J. D4 74
Laval-Ouest, Que., Can. *p19 42
Lavaltrie, Que., Can. D4 42
Lavaur, Fr. F4 5
La Vega, Dom. Rep. E8 35
Lavello, It. D5 9
La Verne, Calif. m13 50
Laverne, Okla. A2 79
Laviania, Sp. A3 8
La Victoria, Ven. A4 32
La Villa, Tex. *F4 84
La Vista, Ga. C2 55
La Vista, Nebr. g13 71
La Viuda, mtn., Peru C2 31
Lavonia, Ga. B3 55
Lavras da Mangabeira, Braz. *D7 27
Lawn, Newf., Can. E4 44
Lawndale, Calif. *F4 50
Lawndale, N.C. B1 76
Lawnside, N.J. *D2 74
Lawnton, Pa. *F8 81
Lawrence, Ind. E5, k10 59
Lawrence, Kans. D9, m15 61
Lawrence, Mass. A5 65
Lawrence, Mich. F4 66
Lawrence, N.Y. G2 52
Lawrence, Pa. F1 81
Lawrence, co., Ala. A2 46
Lawrence, co., Ark. A4 49
Lawrence, co., Ill. E6 58
Lawrence, co., Ind. G4 59
Lawrence, co., Ky. B7 62
Lawrence, co., Miss. D3 68
Lawrence, co., Mo. D4 69
Lawrence, co., Ohio D3 78
Lawrence, co., Pa. E1 81
Lawrence, co., S. Dak. F2 77
Lawrence, co., Tenn. B4 83
Lawrenceburg, Ind. F8 59
Lawrenceburg, Ky. B5 62
Lawrenceburg, Tenn. B4 83
Lawrence Park, Pa. B1 81
Lawrenceville, Ga. C3, h9 55
Lawrenceville, Ill. E6 58
Lawrenceville, N.J. C3 74
Lawrenceville, Va. D5 85
Lawson, Mo. B3 69
Lawtey, Fla. B4 54
Lawton, Mich. F5 66
Lawton, Okla. C3 79
Layland, W. Va. n14 87
Layton, Utah C2 72
Laytonville, Calif. C2 50
Lazio, reg., It. *D4 9
Lea, co., N. Mex. C7 48
Leachville, Ark. B5 49
Lead, S. Dak. F2 77
Lead, mtn., Maine D4 64
Leader, Sask., Can. G1 39
Leadville, Colo. B4 51
Leadwood, Mo. D7 69
League City, Tex. *E5 84
Leake, co., Miss. C4 68
Leakey, Tex. E3 84
Leakville, N.C. A3 76
Leakesville, Miss. D5 68
Lealman, Fla. p10 54
Leamington, Ont., Can. E2 41

Leamington, Eng. D6 4
Leaside, Ont., Can. m15 41
Leatherhead, Eng. m12 4
Leatherwood, Ky. C6 62
Leavenworth, Kans. C9, k16 61
Leavenworth, Wash. B5 86
Leavenworth, co., Kans. C8 61
Leavittsburg, Ohio A5 78
Leawood, Kans. D9 61
Lebanon, Ill. E4 58
Lebanon, Ind. D5 59
Lebanon, Ky. C4 62
Lebanon, Mo. D5 69
Lebanon, N.H. D3 73
Lebanon, N.J. B3 74
Lebanon, Ohio G1 78
Lebanon, Oreg. C4, k12 80
Lebanon, Pa. F9 81
Lebanon, Tenn. A5 83
Lebanon, Va. f9 85
Lebanon, co., Pa. F9 81
Lebanon, country, Asia F10 14
Lebanon Junction, Ky. C4 62
Lebedyan, Sov. Un. E12 12
Le Blanc, Fr. D4 5
Le Blanc-Mesnil, Fr. g10 5
Lębork, Pol. A4 7
Le Bourget, Fr. g10 5
Le Bouscat, Fr. E3 5
Lebrija, Sp. D2 8
Le Cateau, Fr. B5 5
Lecce, It. D7 9
Lecco, It. B2 9
Le Center, Minn. F5 67
Le Chambon-Feugerolles, Fr. E6 5
Le Chesnay, Fr. g9 5
Le Claire, Iowa C7, g11 60
Lecompte, La. C3 63
Le Coteau, Fr. D6 5
Le Creusot, Fr. D6 5
Lędziyca, Pol. B5 7
Ledgewood, N.J. B3 74
Ledo, India C10 20
Leduc, Alta, Can. C4 38
Lee, Mass. B1 65
Lee, co., Ala. C4 46
Lee, co., Ark. C5 49
Lee, co., Fla. F5 54
Lee, co., Ga. E2 55
Lee, co., Ill. B4 58
Lee, co., Iowa D6 60
Lee, co., Ky. C6 62
Lee, co., Miss. A5 68
Lee, co., N.C. B3 76
Lee, co., S.C. C7 82
Lee, co., Tex. D4 84
Lee, co., Va. f8 85
Leechburg, Pa. E2 81
Leedon, Estates, Pa. *G11 81
Leeds, Ala. B3, f7 46
Leeds, Eng. D6 4
Leeds, co., Ont., Can. C8 41
Leelanau, co., Mich. D5 66
Lee Park, Pa. n17 81
Leer, Ger., Fed. Rep. of B3 6
Leesburg, Fla. D5 54
Leesburg, N.J. E3 74
Leesburg, Ohio C2 78
Leesburg, Va. A5 85
Lee's Summit, Mo. C3, k11 69
Leesville, La. C2 63
Leeville, S.C. D4 82
Leetes Island, Conn. D6 52
Leeton, Austl. G6 26
Leetonia, Ohio B5 78
Leetsdale, Pa. h13 81
Leeuwarden, Neth. A6 5
Leeward, is., see Antigua,
  Montserrat, St. Kitts-Nevis-
  Anguilla, and Virgin Islands,
  (Br.), Br. dep., N.A.
Leflore, co., Miss. B3 68
Le Flore, co., Okla. C7 79
Lefors, Tex. B2 84
Le François, Mart. I14 37
Leganés, Sp. p17 8
Legaspi, Phil. C6 19
Legion, Tex. *E3 84
Legnano, It. B2 9
Legnica, Pol. C4 7
Lago, mtn., Wash. A5 86
Le Grand, Calif. D3 50
Le Harve, Fr. C3 5
Lehi, Utah A6, D2 72
Lehigh, Iowa B3 60
Lehigh, co.,Pa. E10 81
Lehigh Acres, Fla. F5 54
Lehighton, Pa. E10 81
Lehrte, Ger., Fed. Rep of B4 6
Leiah, Pak. B5 20
Leicester, Eng. D6 4
Leicester, Mass. B4 65
Leicester, co.,Eng. *D6 4

Leiden, Neth. A6 5
Leigh Creek, Austl. F6 25
Leighton, Ala. A2 46
Leinster, prov., Ire. *D3 4
Leipsic, Ohio A2 78
Leipzig, Ger. Dem. Rep C6 6
Leira, Port. C1 8
Leisure City, Fla. s13 54
Leitchfield, Ky. C3 62
Leith, Pa. *G2 81
Leitrim, co., Ire. *D3 4
Leiva, mtn., Col. C3 32
Lejunior, Ky. D6 62
Leksand, Swe. G6 11
Leland, Miss. B3 68
Leland Grove, Ill. *D4 58
Le Locle, Switz. E3 6
Le Mans, Fr. D4 5
Le Marin, Mart. I14 35
Le Mars, Iowa B1 60
Lemay (Luxemburg), Mo. *C7 69
Leme, Braz. m8 30
Lemeta, Alsk. *C10 47
Lemgo, Ger., Fed. Rep. of B4 6
Lemhi, co., Idaho E4 57
Lemmon, S. Dak. E3 77
Lemon Grove, Calif. F5, o15 50
Lemont, Ill. B6, k9 58
Lemont, Pa. E6 81
Lemoore, Calif. D4 50
Le Moule, Guad. H14 35
Le Moyen, La. D3 63
Lemoyne, Pa. *F8 81
Le Moyne, Que., Can. *D4 42
Lena, Ill. A4 58
Lena, Sp. A3 8
Lena, riv.,Sov. Un. C15 13
Lenawee, co., Mich. G6 66
Lenexa, Kans. D9 61
Leninabad, Sov. Un. E9 13
Leninakan, Sov. Un. B14 14
Leningrad, Sov. Un. H14, s31 11
Leninogorsk, Sov. Un. D11 3
Leninsk, Sov. Un. G15 12
Leninsk-Kuznetskiy, Sov. Un. D11 13
Lenkoran, Sov. Un. F7 13
Lennox, Calif. *E4 50
Lennox, S. Dak. G9 77
Lennox & Addington, co.,
  Ont., Can. C7 41
Lennoxville, Que., Can. D6 42
Lenoir, N.C. B1 76
Lenoir, co., N.C. B5 76
Lenoir City, Tenn. D9 83
Lenox, Iowa D3 60
Lenox, Mass. B1 65
Lenox Avenue, N.Y. *C4 75
Lens, Fr. B5 5
Lenwood, Calif. *E5 50
Leo, Ind. B7 59
Leoben, Aus. E7 6
Léogâne, Hai. E7 35
Leominster, Mass. A4 65
Leon, Iowa D4 60
León (de los Aldamas), Mex. C4, m13 34
León, Nic. E7 34
León, Sp. A3 8
Leon, co., Fla. B2 54
Leon, co., Tex. D5 84
León, prov., Sp. *A3 8
León, reg., Sp. B3 8
Leonard, Tex. C4 84
Leonardo, N.J. C4 74
Leonardtown, Md. D4 53
Leonforte, It. F5 9
Leonia, N.J. h9 74
Leonora, Austl. E3 24
Leopoldina, Braz. C4, g6 30
Leoti, Kans. D2 61
Leovo,Sov. Un. H7 12
Lepanto, Ark. B5 49
Lepe, Sp. D2 8
Lepel, Sov. Un. D7 12
Le Petit-Quevilly, Fr. C4 5
L'Epiphanie, Que., Can. D4 42
Le Puy -en-Velay, Fr. E5 5
Le Raincy, Fr. g11 5
Lercara Friddi, It. F4 9
Lérida, Sp. B6 8
Lérida, prov., Sp. *B6 8
Le Roy, Ill. C5 58
Le Roy, Kans. D8 61
Le Roy, Minn. G6 67
Le Roy, N.Y. C3 75
Lerwick, Scot. g10 4
Léry, Que., Can. q19 42
Les Cayes, Hai E7 35
Les Eboulements, Que.,Can. B7 42
Lesh, Alb. B2 14
Leshan, China F5 17
Leskovac, Yugo. D5 10
Leslie, Mich. F6 66
Leslie, co.. Ky. C6 62

Les Lilas, Fr. g10   5
Lesotho, country, Afr. F5   24
Les Sables-d'Olonne, Fr. D3   5
Lesser Antilles, is., W.I. B4   27
Lester, Pa. *G11   81
Lester, W. Va. n13   87
Lester Prairie, Minn. F4   67
Le Sueur, Minn. F5   67
Le Sueur, co., Minn. F5   67
Lesvos (Lesbos), prov., Grc. *C6   14
Leszno, Pol. C4   7
Letcher, co., Ky. C7   62
Le Teil, Fr. E6   5
Lethbridge, Alta., Can. E4, h8   38
Leticia, Col. D4   32
Letpadan, Bur. *H12   16
Le Tréport, Fr. B4   5
Leucadia, Calif. *F5   50
Leuser mtn., Indon. m11   19
Leuven, Bel. B6   5
Levack, co., Ont., Can. *A3   41
Levadhia, Grc. C4   14
Levallois-Perret, Fr. C4, g10   5
Level Green, Pa. *F2   81
Levelland, Tex. C1   84
Level Park, Mich. *F5   66
Leven, Scot. B5   4
Leverkusden, Ger., Fed. Rep. of *C3   6
Levice, Czech. D5   7
Levin, N.Z. N15   26
Lévis, Que., Can. C6, n17   42
Lévis, co., Que., Can. C6   42
Levittown, N.Y. *G2   52
Levittown, Pa. *F12   81
Levkas, Grc. C3   14
Levoča, Czech. D6   7
Levy, co., Fla. C4   54
Lewes, Del. C7   53
Lewes, Eng. E7   4
Lewis, co., Idaho C2   57
Lewis, co., Ky. B6   62
Lewis, co., Mo. A6   69
Lewis, co., N.Y. B5   75
Lewis, co., Tenn. B4   83
Lewis, co., Wash. C3   86
Lewis, co., W. Va. C4   87
Lewis and Clark, co., Mont. C4   70
Lewisburg, Ohio C1   78
Lewisburg, Pa. E8   81
Lewisburg, Tenn. B5   83
Lewisburg, W. Va. D4   87
Lewisdale, Md. *C3   53
Lewis Gardens, Va. *C5   85
Lewisporte, Newf., Can. D4   44
Lewis Run, Pa. C4   81
Lewiston, Idaho C1   57
Lewiston, Maine D2, f7   64
Lewiston, Mich. D6   66
Lewiston, Minn. G7   67
Lewiston, N.Y. B1   75
Lewiston, Utah A6   72
Lewiston Orchards, Idaho C1   57
Lewiston, Ill. C3   58
Lewiston, Mont. C7   70
Lewiston, Pa. E6   81
Lewisville, Ark. D2   49
Lewisville, Ind. F7   59
Lewisville, N.B., Can. C5   43
Lewisville, Tex. C4, m10   84
Lexington, Ill. C5   58
Lexington, Ky. B5   62
Lexington, Mass. B5, g11   65
Lexington, Mich. E8   66
Lexington, Minn. *E5   67
Lexington, Miss. B3   83
Lexington, Mo. B4   69
Lexington, Nebr. D6   71
Lexington, N.C. B2   76
Lexington, Ohio B3   78
Lexington, Okla. B4   79
Lexington, S.C. D5   82
Lexington, Tenn. B3   83
Lexington (Independent city), Va. ... C3   85
Lexington, co., S.C. D5   82
Lexington Park, Md. *D5   53
Leyte, prov., Phil. *C6   19
Leyte, isl., Phil. C6   19
Leyton, Eng. k12   4
Lézignan, Fr. F5   5
Lezirias, reg., Port. f10   8
Lgov, Sov. Un. F10   12
Lhasa, China F3   17
L'Hay-les-Roses, Fr. g10   5
Lianyungang, China E8   17
Liaoning, prov., China C9   17
Liaoyang, China C9   17
Liaoyuan, China C10   17
Libano,Col. C3   32
Libby, Mont. B1   70
Liberal, Mo. D3   69
Liberec, Czech. C3   7
Liberia, country, Afr. G3   22
Liberty, Ind. E8   59

Liberty, Ky. C5   62
Liberty, Mo. B3, h11   69
Liberty, N.Y. D6   75
Liberty, N.C. B3   76
Liberty, Pa. *E1   81
Liberty, S.C. B2   82
Liberty, Tex. D5, q15   84
Liberty, co., Fla. B2   54
Liberty, co., Ga. E5   55
Liberty, co., Mont. B5   70
Liberty, co., Tex. D5   84
Liberty Acres, Calif. *E4   50
Liberty Center, Ohio A1   78
Liberty Corner, N.J. B3   74
Liberty Lake, Wash. g14   86
Liberty Plain, Mass. h12   65
Libertyville, Ill. A6, h9   58
Libourne, Fr. E3   5
Library, Pa. *E1   81
Libreville, Gabon H6   22
Libya, country, Afr. C2   22
Licata, It. F4   9
Lice, Tur. C13   14
Licking, Mo. D6   69
Licking, co., Ohio B3   78
Lida, Sov. Un. E5   12
Lidgerwood, N. Dak. D8   77
Lidice, Czech. C3, n17   7
Lidingö, Swe. H8, t36   11
Lidköping, Swe. H5   11
Liechtenstein, country, Eur. E4   6
Liège, Bel. B6   5
Liège, prov., Bel. B6   5
Lienz, Aus. E6   6
Liepāja, Sov. Un. C3   12
Lier, Bel. B6   5
Liestal, Switz. E3   6
Lighthouse Point, Fla. *F6   54
Lighthouse, point, Fla. C2   80
Lighthouse, point, Mich. C5   66
Ligonior, Ind. B6   59
Ligonier, Pa. F3   81
Liguria, pol. dist., It. *B2   9
Liguria, reg., It. B2   0
Lihue, Haw. B2   56
Likasi, Zaire C5   24
Likhoslavl, Sov. Un. C10   12
Likino-Dulevo, Sov. Un. n18   12
Lilbourn, Mo. E8   69
Lilesville, N.C. C2   76
Lille, Fr. B5   5
Lillehammer, Nor. G4   11
Lillestrøm, Nor. H4, p29   11
Lillington, N.C. B4   76
Lillooet, B.C., Can. D7   37
Lillooet, range, B.C., Can. E7   37
Lilongwe, Malawi C6   24
Lima, N.Y. C3   75
Lima, Ohio B1   78
Lima, Peru D2   31
Lima, dept., Peru D2   31
Limbé, Hai. E7   35
Limburg, Ger., Fed. Rep. of C4   6
Limburg, prov., Bel. *B6   5
Limburg, prov., Neth. *B6   5
Limeil-Brévannes, Fr. h10   5
Limeira, Braz. m8   30
Limerick, Ire. D2   4
Limerick, co., Ire. *D2   4
Limestone, Maine B5   64
Limestone, co., Ala. A2   46
Limestone, co., Tex. D4   84
Limoeiro do Norte, Braz. *D7   27
Limoges, Fr. E4   5
Limon, Colo. B7   51
Limón, C.R. F8   34
Limón, prov., C.R. *I12   33
Limousin, former prov., Fr. E4   5
Limoux, Fr. F5   5
Linares, Chile B2   28
Linares, Col. C2   32
Linares, Mex. C5   34
Linares, Sp. C4   8
Linares, prov. Chile B2   28
Linch, Wyo. *C6   89
Linchuan, China F8   17
Lincoln, Arg. A4   28
Lincoln, Calif. C3   50
Lincoln, Ont., Can. D5   41
Lincoln, Eng. D6   4
Lincoln, Ill. C4   58
Lincoln, Kans. C5   61
Lincoln, Maine C4   64
Lincoln, Mass. g10   65
Lincoln, Nebr. D9, h11   71
Lincoln, N.H. *C4   73
Lincoln, Pa. *E1   81
Lincoln, R.I. B11   52
Lincoln, co., Ark. D4   49
Lincoln, co., Colo C7   51
Lincoln, co., Eng. *D6   4
Lincoln, co., Ga. C4   55
Lincoln, co., Idaho G4   57

Lincoln, co., Kans. C5   61
Lincoln, co., Ky. C5   62
Lincoln, co., Maine D3   64
Lincoln, co., Minn. F2   67
Lincoln, co., Miss. D3   68
Lincoln, co., Mo. B6   69
Lincoln, co., Mont. B1   70
Lincoln, co., Nebr. D5   71
Lincoln, co., Nev. C4   72
Lincoln, co., N. Mex. C6   48
Lincoln, co., N.C. B1   76
Lincoln, co., Okla. B5   79
Lincoln, co., Oreg. C3   80
Lincoln, co., S. Dak. G9   77
Lincoln, co., Tenn. B5   83
Lincoln, co., Wash. B7   86
Lincoln, co., W. Va. C2   87
Lincoln, co., Wis. C4   88
Lincoln, co., Wyo. D2   89
Lincoln, par., La. B3   63
Lincoln Acres, Calif. o15   50
Lincoln City, Oreg. C3   80
Lincoln Heights, Ohio o13   78
Lincoln Highway, Nebr. *C5   71
Lincoln Park, Colo. *C5   51
Lincoln Park, Ga. D2   55
Lincoln Park, Mich. B4   74
Lincoln Park, N.J. B4   74
Lincoln Park, N.Y. *D6   75
Lincoln Park, Pa. *F9   81
Lincolnton, Ga. C4   55
Lincolnton, N.C. B1   76
Lincoln Village, Calif. *D3   50
Lincoln Village, Ohio *C3   78
Lincolnwood, Ill. h9   58
Lincroft, N.J. C4   74
Lind, Wash. D7   86
Linda, Calif. *C3   50
Lindale, Ga. B1   55
Lindale, Tex. C5   84
Lindau, Ger., Fed. Rep. of E4   6
Linden, Ala. C2   46
Linden, Ind. D4   59
Linden, Mich. F7   66
Linden, N.J. k8   74
Linden, Tenn. B4   83
Linden, Tex. C5   84
Lindenhurst, Ill. h8   58
Lindenhurst, N.Y. G3   52
Lindenwold, N.J. D3   74
Lindesberg, Swe. H6   11
Lindi, Tan. B7   24
Lindon, Utah *A6   72
Lindsay, Calif. D4   50
Lindsay, Ont., Can. C6   41
Lindsay, Okla. C4   79
Lindsborg, Kans. D6   61
Lindstrom, Minn. E6   67
Linesville, Pa. C1   81
Lineville, Ala. B4   46
Linfen, China D7   17
Lingayen, Phil. B6   19
Lingen, Ger., Fed. Rep. of B3   6
Linglestown, Pa. F8   81
Lingyuan, China C8   17
Linhai, China F9   17
Linière, Que., Can. C7   42
Linköping, Swe. H6   11
Linn, Mo. C6   69
Linn, co., Iowa B6   60
Linn, co., Kans. D9   61
Linn, co., Mo. B4   69
Linn, co., Oreg. C4   80
Linntown, Pa. *E7   81
Lino Lakes, Minn. *E5   67
Linqing, China D8   17
Lins, Braz. C3   30
Linthicum Heights, Md. B4, h11   53
Linton, Ind. F3   59
Linton, N. Dak. D5   77
Linwood, Mass. B4   65
Linwood, Mich. E7   66
Linwood, N.J. E3   74
Linwood, Pa. *G11   81
Linworth, Ohio k10   78
Linxia, China D5   17
Linyi, China D8   17
Linz, Aus. D7   6
Lipa, Phil. C6, p13   19
Lipari, It. E5   9
Lipetsk, Sov. Un. E12   12
Lipkany, Sov. Un. A8   10
Lipno, Pol. B5   7
Lipova, Rom. B5   10
Lippstadt, Ger., Fed. Rep. of C4   6
Lipscomb, Ala. B3, g7   46
Lipscomb, co., Tex. A2   84
Liria, Sp. C5   8
Lisboa, see Lisbon, Port. C6   60
Lisbon, Iowa C6   60
Lisbon, Maine D2, f7   64
Lisbon, N.H. C4   73
Lisbon, N. Dak. D8   77
Lisbon, Ohio B5   78

Lisbon (Lisboa), Port. C1, f9   8
Lisbon Falls, Maine D5, f7   64
Lisburn, N. Ire. C3   4
Lishu, China E2   18
Lisichansk, Sov. Un. q21   12
Lisieux, Fr. C4   5
Lisle, Ill. k8   58
L'Islet, co., Que., Can. B7   42
L'Islet-sur-Mer, Que.,Can. B7   42
L'isletville, Que., Can. B7   42
Lisman, Ala. C1   46
Lismore, Austl. E9   25
Listowel, Ont., Can. D4   41
Litchfield, Conn. B4   52
Litchfield, Ill. D4   58
Litchfield, Mich. F6   66
Litchfield, Minn. E4   67
Litchfield, co., Conn. B3   52
Litchfield Park, Ariz. D1   48
Lithgow, Austl. F9   25
Lithonia, Ga. C2, h8   55
Lithuania (S.S.R) rep., Sov. Un. D4   12
Lititz, Pa. F9   81
Litókhoron, Grc. *B4   14
Litoměřice, Czech. C3   7
Litomyšl, Czech. D7   7
Little, mtn., Wyo. E5   89
Little Belt, mtn., Mont. D6   70
Little Canada, Minn. *E5   67
Little Catalina, Newf. D5   44
Little Chute, Wis. D5, h9   88
Little Current, Ont., Can. B3   41
Little Falls, Minn. E4   67
Little Falls, N.J. B4   74
Little Falls, N.Y. B6   75
Little Ferry, N.J. h8   74
Littlefield, Tex. C1   84
Littlefork, Minn. B5   67
Little River, co., Ark. D1   49
Little Rock, Ark. C3, k10   49
Little Rock, river, Iowa A1   70
Little Silver, N.J. C4   74
Littletown, Pa. G7   81
Littleton, Colo. B6   51
Littleton, Mass. f9   65
Littleton, N.H. C4   73
Littleton, N.C. A5   76
Littleton Common, Mass. f10   65
Little Valley, N.Y. C2   75
Liuhe, China E2   18
Liuzhou, China G6   17
Lively, Ont., Can. A3   41
Live Oak, Calif. C3   50
Live Oak, Fla. B4   54
Live Oak, Co., Tex. E3   84
Livermore, Calif. h9   50
Livermore, Ky. C2   62
Livermore, peak, Tex. o12   84
Livermore Falls, Maine D2   64
Liverpool, N.S., Can. E5   43
Liverpool, Eng. D5   4
Liverpool, N.Y. B4   75
Liverpool, Pa. E7   81
Livingston, Ala. C1   46
Livingston, Calif. D3   50
Livingston, Guat. D7   34
Livingston, Ill. E4   58
Livingston, La. D5, g10   63
Livingston, Mont. E6   70
Livingston, N.J. B4   74
Livingston, Tenn. C8   83
Livingston, Tex. D5   84
Livingstone, Zambia D5   24
Livingston, co.,Ill. C5   58
Livingston, co., Ky. e9   62
Livingston, co., Mich. F6   66
Livingston, co., Mo. B4   69
Livingston, co., N.Y. C3   75
Livingston, par., La. D5   63
Livingston Manor, N.Y. D6   75
Livno, Yugo. D3   10
Livny, Sov. Un. E11   12
Livonia, Mich. F7   66
Livonia, N.Y. C3   75
Livorno (Leghorn), It. C3   9
Livry-Gargan, Fr. g11   5
Lizard Head, peak, Wyo. D3   89
Ljubljana, Yugo. B2   10
Ljunby, Swe. I5   11
Llandrindod Wells, Wales D5   4
Llandudno, Wales D5   4
Llanelli, Wales E4   4
Llanes, Sp. A3   8
Llano, Tex. D3   84
Llano, co.,Tex. D3   84
Llanquihue, prov.,Chile C2   28
Lloyd, Ky. B7   62
Lloyd Harbor, N.Y. *G3   52
Lloydminster, Alta., Sask., Can. D1   39
Lloyd Palce, N.Y. *D6   85
Lluchmayor, Sp. C7   8
Llullaillaco, vol., Chile D2   29
Löbau, Ger. Dem. Rep. C7   6

Lobería, Arg. B5 28
Lobito, Arg. C2 24
Lobos, Arg. B5, g7 28
Locarno, Switz. E4 6
Lochdale, B.C., Can. f12 37
Lochearn, Md. *B4 53
Loches, Fr. D4 5
Loch Raven, Md. *B4 53
Lockeport, N.S.,Can. F4 43
Lockhart, Tex. E4, h8 84
Lock Haven, Pa. D7 81
Lockland, Ohio o13 78
Lockney, Tex. B2 84
Lockport, Ill. B5, k8 58
Lockport, La. F5, k10 62
Lockport, N.Y. B2 75
Lockwood, Mo. D4 69
Locumba, Peru E3 31
Locust, N.J. C4 74
Locust Grove, Okla. A6 79
Locust Valley, N.Y. F2 52
Lod (Lydda), Isr. C2, h5 15
Lodève, Fr. F5 5
Lodeynoye Pole, Sov. Un. A9 12
Lodge Grass, Mont. E9 70
Lodhrān, Pak. C5 20
Lodi, Calif. C3 50
Lodi, N.J. h8 74
Lodi, Ohio A3 78
Lodi, Wis. E4 88
Łódź, Pol. C5 7
Loei,Thai *B2 19
Logan, Iowa C2 60
Logan, Kans. C4 61
Logan, Ohio C3 78
Logan, Utah A6 72
Logan, W. Va. D3, n12 87
Logan, co.,Ark. B2 49
Logan, co., Colo. A7 51
Logan, co., Ill. C4 58
Logan, co., Kans. D2 61
Logan, co., Ky. D3 62
Logan, co., Nebr. C5 71
Logan, co., N. Dak. D6 77
Logan, co., Ohio B2 78
Logan, co., Okla. B4 79
Logan, co., W. Va. D3 87
Logan, mtn, Yukon, Can. D6 36
Logansport, Ind. C5 59
Logansport, La. C2 63
Loganville, Ga. C3 55
Loggieville, N.C., Can. B4 43
Logroño, Sp. A4 8
Logroño, prov., Sp. *A4 8
Logrosán, Sp. C3 8
Lohārdaga, India D7 20
Lohrville, Iowa B3 60
Loire, dept., Fr. *E6 5
Loire, riv., Fr. D3 5
Loire-atlantique, dept., Fr. *D3 5
Loiret, dept., Fr. *D4 5
Loir-et-Cher, dept., Fr. *D4 5
Loja, Ec. B2 31
Loja, Sp. D3 8
Loja, prov.,Ec. B2 31
Lokhvitsa, Sov. Un. F9 12
Lom, Bul. D6 10
Loma Linda, Calif. *E5 50
Lomas de Zamora, Arg. A5, g7 28
Lombard, Ill. k8 58
Lombardia, reg., It. *B2 9
Lombardy, reg.,It. B2 9
Lomé, Togo G5 22
Lometa, Tex. D3 84
Lomira, Wis. E5 88
Lomita, Calif. *E4 50
Lomonosov, Sov. Un. s30 11
Lompoc, Calif. E3 50
Łomza, Pol. B7 7
Lonaconing, Md. k13 53
London, Ont., Can. E3 41
London, Eng. E6, k12 4
London, Ky. C5 62
London, Ohio C2 78
London, Greater, co., Eng. *E6 4
Londonderry, N. Ire. C3 4
Londonderry, co., N. Ire. *C3 4
London Mills, Ill. C3 58
Londrina, Braz. C2 30
Lone Oak, Ky. e9 62
Lone Pine, Calif. D4 50
Lone Star, Tex. *C5 84
Lone Wolf, Okla. C2 79
Lone Tree, Iowa C6 60
Long, co., Ga. E5 55
Long Beach, Calif. F4, n12 50
Long Beach, Ind. A4 59
Long Beach, Miss. E4, f7 68
Long Beach, N.Y. E7, n15 75
Long Beach, Wash. C1 86
Longboat Key, Fla. q10 54
Long Branch, Ont., Can. m14 41
Long Branch, N.J. C5 74
Long Creek, mtn., Wyo D4 89
Longford, co., Ire. *D3 4
Longhurst, N.C. A4 76
Long Island, isl, N.Y. n15 75
Long Lake, Ill. h8 58
Long Lake, Minn. *F5 67
Long Lake, N.Y. B6 75
Longleaf, La. C3 63
Long Leaf Park, N.C. *C5 76
Longmeadow, Mass. B2 65
Longmont, Colo. A5 51
Long Pond, Newf., Can. E5 44
Longport, N.J. E13 74
Long Prairie, Minn. E4 67
Longreach, Austl. D7 25
Longs, peak, Colo. A5 51
Long Range, mts., Newf., Can. E2, k10 44
Longueuil, Que.,Can. D4 42
Long Valley, N.J. B3 74
Longview, Alta, Can. D3 38
Long View, Ky. C4 62
Long View, N.C. B1 76
Longview, Tex. C5 84
Longview, Wash. C3 86
Longwood, Fla. *D4 54
Longwood Park, N.C. *B3 76
Longwy, Fr. C6 5
Long Xuyen, Viet. *C3 19
Lonoke, Ark. C4, h11 49
Lonoke, co., Ark. C4 49
Lons-le-Saunier, Fr. D6 5
Loogootee, Ind. G4 59
Lookout, Ky. C7 62
Lookout Mountain, Tenn. h11 83
Loon Lake, mtn. N.Y. f10 75
Lora, Sp. D3 8
Lorado, W. Va. D3, n12 87
Lorain, Ohio A3 78
Lorain, Pa. *E4 81
Lorain, co., Ohio A3 78
Loraine, Tex. C2 84
Lorca, Sp. D5 8
Lordsburg, N. Mex. C4 84
Loreauville, La. D4 63
Lorena, Braz. G3 30
Lorenzo, Tex. C2 84
Loreto, Mex. B2 34
Loreto, Par. D4 29
Loreto, dept., Peru C3 31
Loretteville, Que., Can. C6, n17 42
Loretto, Pa. F4 81
Loretto, Tenn. B4 83
Lorica, Col. B2 32
Lorient, Fr. D2 5
L'Orignal, Ont., Can. B10 41
Loris, S.C. C10 82
Lorne, N.B., Can. D3 43
Lorneville, N.B., Can. B3 43
Lörrach, Ger., Fed. Rep. of E3 6
Lorraine, former prov., Fr. C6 5
Los Alamitos, Calif. *F5 50
Los Alamos, N. Mex. B5 48
Los Alamos, co., N. Mex. B5 48
Los Altos, Calif. k8 50
Los Altos Hills, Calif. *D2 50
Los Andes, Chile A2 28
Los Angeles, Calif. E4, m12 50
Los Angeles, Chile B2 28
Los Angeles, co., Calif. E4 50
Los Banos, Calif. D3 50
Los Barrios, Sp. D3 8
Los Fresnos, Tex. F4 84
Los Gatos, Calif. D2 50
Los Mochis, Mex. B3 34
Los Nietos, Calif. *E4 50
Los Palacios, Cuba C2 35
Los Reyes de *Salgado*, Mex. D4, n12 34
Los Rios, prov., Ec. B2 31
Los Teques, Ven. A4 32
Lost Nation, Iowa C7 60
Lot, dept., Fr. *E4 5
Lota, Chile B2 28
Lotbinière, co., Que, Can. C6 42
Lot-et-Garonne, dept., Fr. *E4 5
Lothair, Ky. C6 62
Lott, Tex. D4 84
Loudon, Tenn. D9 83
Loudon, co., Tenn. D9 30
Loudonville, N.Y. *D6 75
Loudonville, Ohio B3 78
Loudoun, co., Va. B5 85
Loudun, Fr. D4 5
Loughborough, Eng. D6 4
Louisa, Ky. B7 62
Louisa, co., Iowa C6 60
Louisa, co., Va. C5 85
Louisbourg, N.S., Can. D10 43
Louisburg, Kans. D9 61
Louisburg, N.C. A4 76
Louisdale, N.S. D8 43
Louisiana, Mo. B6 69
Louisiana, state, U.S. 63
Louis Trichardt, S. Afr. F5 24
Louisville, Que., Can. C5 42
Louisville, Colo. B5 51
Louisville, Ga. C4 55
Louisville, Ill. E5 58
Louisville, Ky. B4, g11 62
Louisville, Miss. B4 68
Louisville, Nebr. D9, h12 71
Louisville, Ohio B4 78
Loulé, Port. D1 8
Louny, Czech. C2 7
Loup, co., Nebr. C6 71
Loup, riv., Nebr. C8 71
Loup City, Nebr. C7 71
Lourdes, Newf., Can. D2 44
Lourdes, Fr. F4 5
Lourenço Marques, see Maputo, Moz.
Loures, Port. f9 8
Louth, Eng. D7 4
Louth, co., Ire. *C3 4
Loutrá Aidhipsoú Grc. C4 14
Louvain, see Leuven, Bel.
Louviers, Fr. C4 5
Love, co., Okla. D4 79
Lovech, Bul. D7 10
Lovejoy,Ill. *E3 58
Loveland, Colo. A5 51
Loveland, Ohio C1, n12 78
Loveland Park, Ohio C1, n13 78
Lovell, Wyo. B4 89
Lovelock, Nev. A2 72
Lovely, Ky. C7 62
Loves Park, Ill. A4 58
Lovilia, Iowa C5 60
Loving, N. Mex. C6 48
Loving, co., Tex. o13 84
Lovington, Ill. D5 58
Lovington, Iowa e8 60
Lovington, N. Mex. C7 48
Lowden, Iowa C7 60
Lowell, Ind. B3 59
Lowell, Mass. A5, f10 65
Lowell, Mich. F5 66
Lowell, N.C. B1 76
Lowell, Ohio C4 78
Lowell, Wash. *B3 86
Lowellville, Ohio A5 78
Lower Burrell, Pa. *F2 81
Lower Caraquet, N.B., Can. *B5 43
Lower Hutt, N.Z. *N15 26
Lower Paia, Haw C5 56
Lower West Pubnico, N.S., Can. F4 43
Lowestoft, Eng. D7 4
Łowicz, Pol. B5 7
Lowmoore, Va. C3 85
Lowndes, co., Ala. C3 46
Lowndes, co., Ga. F3 55
Lowndes, co., Miss. B5 68
Lowville, N.Y. B5 75
Loxton, Austl. G3 26
Loyal, Wis. D3 88
Loyalhanna, Pa. *F2 81
Loyall, Ky. D6 62
Loyalton, Calif. C3 50
Loyalty, is., Pac. O. H8 2
Lozere, dept., Fr. *E5 5
Loznica, Yugo. C4 10
Lozovatka, Sov. Un. G9 12
Luanda, Ang. B2 24
Luang Prabang, Laos B2 19
Luanshya, Zambia C5 24
Lubań, Pol. C3 7
Lubango, Ang. C2 24
Lubartów, Pol. C7 7
Lübben, Ger. C6 6
Lubbock, Tex. C2 84
Lubbock, co., Tex. C2 84
Lubec, Maine D6 64
Lubeck, Ger., Fed. Rep. of B5 6
Lublin, Pol. C7 7
Lubliniec, Pol. C5 7
Lubny, Sov. Un. F9 12
Lubrin, Sp. D4 8
Lubumbashi (Elisabethville) Zaire C5 24
Lubutu, Zaire I3 23
Lucan, Ont., Can. D3 41
Lucas, Ohio B3 78
Lucas, co., Iowa C4 60
Lucas, co., Ohio A2 78
Lucasville, Ohio D3 78
Lucca, It. C3 9
Luce, co., Mich. B5 66
Lucedale, Miss. E5 68
Lucena, Phil. C6, p13 19
Lucenec, Czech. D5 7
Lucera, It. D5 9
Lucerne, see Luzern, Switz.
Lucernemines, Pa. E3 81
Luceville, Que, Can. A9 42
Luck, Wis. C1 88
Luckau, Ger. C6 6
Luckenwalde, Ger. Dem. Rep. B6 6
Luckey, Ohio A2, f7 78
Lucknow, Ont., Can. D3 41
Lucknow, India C7 20
Lucknow, Pa. *F8 81
Loçon, Fr. D3 5
Lucy, La. h10 63
Lüda, China D9 17
Lüdenscheid, Ger., Fed. Rep. of C3 6
Ludhiana, India B6 20
Ludington, Mich. E4 66
Ludlam, Fla. *G6 54
Ludlow, Eng. D5 4
Ludlow, Ky. h13 62
Ludlow, Mass. B3 65
Ludlow, Pa. C4 81
Ludlow, Vt. E2 73
Ludowici, Ga. E5 55
Ludvika, Swe. G6 11
Ludwigsburg, Ger., Fed. Rep. of D4 6
Ludwigshafen, Ger., Fed. Rep. of D4 6
Ludwigslust, Ger. Dem. Rep. B5 6
Lueders, Tex. C3 84
Lufkin, Tex. D5 84
Luga, Sov. Un. B7 12
Lugano, Switz. E4 6
Lugansk, see Voroshilovgrad Sov. Un.
Lugo, It. B3 9
Lugo, Sp. A2 8
Lugo, prov., Sp. *A2 8
Lugoff, S.C. C6 82
Lugoj, Rom. C5 10
Luján, Arg. g7 28
Lukovit, Bul. D7 10
Łuków, Pol. C7 7
Lukoyanov, Sov. Un. D15 12
Luleå, Swe. E10 11
Luling, La. k11 63
Luling, Tex. E4, h8 84
Luluabourg, see Kananga, Zaire
Lumber City, Ga. E4 55
Lumberport, W.Va. B4, k10 87
Lumberton, Miss. D4 68
Lumberton, N.J. D3 74
Lumberton, N.C. C4 76
Lumby, B.C., Can. D8 37
Lumpkin, B.C., Can. D8 37
Lumpkin, Ga. D2 55
Lumpkin, co., Ga. B2 55
Lumsden, Sask., Can. G3 39
Luna, co., N. Mex. C5 48
Luna Pier (Lakewood), Mich. G7 66
Lund, Swe. J5 11
Lundale, W. Va. D3, n12 87
Lundar, Man., Can. D2 40
Lüneburg, Ger., Fed. Rep. of B5 6
Lunel, Fr. F6 5
Lunenburg, N.S., Can. E5 43
Lunenburg, Mass. A4 65
Lunenburg, co., N.S., Can. E5 43
Lunenburg, co., Va. D4 85
Lunéville, Fr. C7 5
Lunino, Sov. Un. E15 12
Luohe, China E7 17
Luoyang, China E7 17
Lupeni, Rom. C6 10
Luque, Par. E4 29
Luray, Va. B4 85
Lure, Fr. D7 5
Luragn, N. Ire. C3 4
Lusaka, Zambia D5 24
Lusambo, Zaire I2 23
Luseland, Sask.,Can. E1 39
Lushan, China F8 17
Lüshun (Port Arthur), China D9 17
Lusk, Wyo. D8 89
Lutcher, La. D5, h10 63
Lutesville, Mo. D8 69
Lutherville-Timonium, Md. B4 53
Luton, Eng. E6 4
Lutsk, Sov. Un. F5 12
Lutugino, Sov. Un. q22 12
Lutz, Fla. D4 54
Luverne, Ala. D3 46
Luverne, Minn. G2 67
Luwuk, Indon. F6 19
Luxembourg, Lux. C7 5
Luxembourg, country, Eur. C7 5
Luxembourg, prov., Bel. *C6 5
Luxembourg, Wis. D6 88
Luxeuil-les-Bains, Fr. D7 5
Luxor, see Al Uqsur, Eg.
Luxora, Ark. B6 49
Luzern, Switz. E4 6
Luzern, canton, Switz. *E4 6
Luzerne, Pa. n17 81
Luzerne, co., Pa. D9 81
Luzhou, China F6 17
Luzon, isl., Phil. B6 19
Lvov, Sov. Un. G5 12
Lyaskovets, Bul. D7 10
Lycoming, co., Pa. D7 81
Lydia Mills, S.C. *C4 82

Lydick, Ind. *A5 59
Lyell, mtn., B.C., Can.......... D9 37
Lyford, Tex................... F4 84
Lykens, Pa.................... E8 81
Lyle, Minn.................... G6 67
Lyman, Nebr.................. C1 71
Lyman, S.C................... B3 82
Lyman, co., S. Dak............ G6 77
Lyman, N.Y................... G2 52
Lynbrook, N.Y................ G2 52
Lynch, Ky.................... D7 62
Lynchburg, Ohio.............. C2 78
Lynchburgh (Independent
   City), Va. C3 85
Lynden, Wash................. A3 86

Lyndhurst, N.J. h8 74
Lyndhurst, Ohio g9 78
Lyndon, Kans. D8 61
Lyndon, Ky. g11 62
Lyndonville, N.Y. B2 75
Lyndonville, Vt. B3 73
Lyndora, Pa. E2 81
Lynn, Ind. D8 59
Lynn, Mass. B6, g12 65
Lynn, co., Tex. C2 84
Lynnfield, Mass. f11 65
Lynn Garden, Tenn. C11 83
Lynn Haven, Fla. u16 54
Lynn Lake, Man............ A1, f7 40

Lynville, Ky. f9 62
Lynnwood, Pa. *D9 81
Lynnwood, Wash. *B3 86
Lynwood, Calif. n12 50
Lyon, Fr. E6 4
Lyon, co., Iowa A1 60
Lyon, co., Kans. D7 61
Lyon, co., Ky. C1 62
Lyon, co., Minn. F3 67
Lyon, co., Nev. B2 72
Lyon Mountain, N.Y. f11 75
Lyonnais, former prov.,Fr. E6 5
Lyons, Ga. D4 55
Lyons, Ill. k9 58

Lyons, Ind. G3 59
Lyons, Kans. D5 61
Lyons, Mich. F6 66
Lyons, Nebr. C9 71
Lyons, N.Y. B4 75
Lyons Falls, N.Y. B5 75
Lysá, Czech. n18 7
Lysaya Gora, Sov. Un. G8 12
Lysekil, Swe. H4 11
Lyster Station, Que., Can. C6 42
Lysva, Sov. Un. D8 13
Lytle, Tex. E3 84
Lyubar, Sov. Un. G6 12
Lyubertsy, Sov. Un. N17 12

M

Ma'alot Tarshiha, Isr. A3 15
Maastricht, Neth. B6 5
Mabank, Tex. C4 84
Mabel, Minn. G7 67
Mableton, Ga. h7 55
Mabscott, W. Va. D3, n13 87
Mabton, Wash. C5 86
McAdam, N.B., Can. D2 43
McAdenville, N.C. *B1 76
McAdoo, Pa. E9 81
Macaé, Braz. C4 30
McAlester, Okla. ...,.'........... C6 79
McAllen, Tex. F3 84
Macamic, Que., Can.............. *o20 41
Macao, Port. dep., Asia G7 17
Macapá, Braz. C5 27
McArthur, Ohio C3 78
Macas, Ec. D3 27
Macau, Braz. D7 27
McBee, S.C. C7 82
McBride, B.C., Can. C7 37
McCall, Idaho E2 57
McCamey, Tex. D1 84
McCarthy, mtn., Mont. E4 70
McCaysville, Ga. B2 55
McChesneytown, Pa. *F2 81
McClain, co., Okla. C4 79
McCleary, Wash. B2 86
McClenny, Fla. *B4 54
Macclesfield, Eng. D5 4
McCloud, Calif. B2 50
McClure, Ohio A2 78
McClure, Pa. E7 81
McColl, S.C. B8 82
McComas, W. Va. D3 87
McComb, Miss. D3 68
McComb, Ohio A2 78
McCone, co., Mont. C11 70
McConnellsburg, Pa. G6 81
McConnelsville, Ohio C4 78
McCook, Nebr. D5 71
McCook, co., S. Dak. G8 77
McCormick, S.C. D3 82
McCormick, co., S.C. *D3 82
McCracken, co., Ky. e9 62
McCreary, Man., Can. D2 40
McCreary, co., Ky. D5 62
McCrory, Ark. B4 49
McCulloch, co., Tex. D3 84
McCurtain, Okla. B7 79
McCurtain, co., Okla. C7 79
McDermott, Ohio D2 78
McDonald, Ohio A5 78
McDonald, Pa. k13 81
MacDonald, W. Va. D3, D7 87
McDonald, co., Mo. E3 69
McDonough, Ga. C2 55
McDonough, co., Ill. C3 58
McDowell, co., N.C. f10 76
McDowell, co., W. Va. D3 87
McDuffie, co., Ga. C4 55
Macedon, N.Y. B3 75
Macedonia, reg., Eur. *B4 14
Macedonia, rep., Yugo. *D5 10
Maceió, Braz. D7 27
Macerata, It. C4 9
McEwen, Tenn. A4 83
McFarland, Calif. E4 50
McFarland, Wis. E4 88
McGehee, Ark. *D4 49

McGill, Nev. B4 72
MacGillicuddy's Reeks, mts., Ire. E2 4
McGrann, Pa..................... *E2 81
McGraw, N.Y. C4 75
MacGregor, Man., Can. E2 40
McGregor, Iowa A6 60
McGregor, Tex. D4 84
McGuffey, Ohio B2 78
McGuire, mtn., Idaho D4 57
Machado, Braz. C3, k9 30
Machala, Ec. B2 31
McHenry, Ill A5, h8 58
McHenry, co., Ill. A5 58
McHenry, co., N. Dak. B5 77
Machias, Maine D5 64
Machida, Jap. *n18 18
Machilipatnam (Bandar),
   India E7 20
Măcin, Rom. C9 10
McIntosh, Minn. C3 67
McIntosh, co., Ga. E5 55
McIntosh, co., N. Dak. D6 77
McIntosh, co., Okla. B6 79
Mack, Ohio *D2 78
Mackay, Austl. D8 25
Mackay, Idaho F5 57
McKean, co., Pa. C4 81
McKeesport, Pa. F4, r14 81
McKees Rocks, Pa. F1, k13 81
McKenney, Va. D5 85
McKenzie, Tenn. A3 83
McKenzie, co., N. Dak. C2 77
Mackenzie, dist., N.W.
   Ter., Can. D11 36
Mackenzie, mts., Can. C7 33
Mackenzie, riv., N.W. Ter., Can. C8 36
Mackinac, co., Mich. B5 66
Mackinaw, Ill. C4 58
Mackinaw City, Mich. C6 66
McKinley, Minn. C6 67
McKinley, co., N. Mex. B4 48
McKinley, mtn., Alsk. C9 47
McKinley Heights, Ohio *A5 78
McKinleyville, Calif. B1 50
McKinney, Tex. C4 84
McKittrick Summit, mtn., Calif. E4 50
Macklin, Sask., Can. E1 39
McKnight, Pa. *E1 81
McKnownville, N.Y. *C7 75
McLaughlin, S. Dak. E5 77
McLean, Tex. B2 84
McLean, Va. g12 85
McLean, co., Ill. C5 58
McLean, co., Ky. C2 62
McLean, co., N. Dak. C4 77
McLean, co., Maine A4 64
McLeansboro, Ill. E5 58
McLennan, Alta., Can. B2 38
McLennan, co., Tex. D4 84
McLeod, co., Minn. F4 67
McLeod Lake, B.C., Can. B6, n18 37
McLoud, Okla. B4 79
McLoughlin, mtn., Oreg. E4 80
McLouth, Kans. C8, k15 61
McMasterville, Que., Can. *D4 42
McMechen, W. Va. B4, g8 87
McMillan Manor, Calif. *E4 50
McMinn, co., Tenn. D9 83
McMinnville, Oreg. B3, h11 80

McMinnville, Tenn. D8 83
McMullen, co., Tex. E3 84
McMurray, Alta., Can. A5, f8 38
McNair, Tex. E5 84
McNairy, co., Tenn. B3 83
McNary, Ariz. B4 48
McNeill, mtn., B.C., Can. B2 37
Macomb, Ill. C3 58
Macomb, co., Mich. F8 66
Macon, Fr. D6 5
Macon, Ga. D3 55
Macon, Ill. D5 58
Macon, Miss. B5 68
Macon, Mo. B5 69
Macon, co., Ala. C4 46
Macon, co., Ga. D2 55
Macon, co., Ill. D5 58
Macon, co., Mo. B5 69
Macon, co., N.C. f9 76
Macon, co., Tenn. C7 83
Macoupin, co., Ill. D4 58
McPherson, Kans. D6 61
McPherson, co., Kans. D6 61
McPherson, co., Nebr. C4 71
McPherson, co., S. Dak. E6 77
McRae, Ga. D4 55
McRoberts, Ky. C7 62
McSherrystown, Pa. G7 81
Macksville, Kans. E5 61
MacTier, Ont., Can. B5 41
Macungie, Pa. E10 81
McVeigh, Ky. C7 62
Ma'dabā, Jordan C3 15
Madagascar, country, Afr. E9 24
Madawaska, Maine A4 64
Madawaska, co., N.B. , Can. B1 43
Madeira, Ohio o13 78
Madeira Beach, Fla............... *E4 54
Madeira Is., reg., Port. B1 22
Madelia, Minn. F4 67
Madera, Calif. D3 50
Madera, Mex. B3 34
Madera, Pa. E5 81
Madera, co., Calif. D4 50
Madgaon, India E5 20
Madhya Pradesh, state, India D6 20
Madill, Okla. C5 79
Madīnat ash Sha'b, P.D.R. of
   Yem. G4 15
Madison, Ala. A3 46
Madison, Ala. C3 46
Madison, Conn. D6 52
Madison, Fla. B3 54
Madison, Ga. C3 55
Madison, Ill. E3 58
Madison, Ind. G7 59
Madison, Kans. D7 61
Madison, Maine D3 64
Madison, Minn. E2 67
Madison, Mo. B5 69
Madison, Nebr. C8 71
Madison, N.J. B4 74
Madison, N.C. A3 76
Madison, Ohio A4 78
Madison, S. Dak. G9 77
Madison, W. Va. C3, m12 87
Madison, Wis. E4 88
Madison, co., Ala. A3 46
Madison, co., Ark. B2 49
Madison, co., Fla. *B3 54

Madison, co., Ga. B3 55
Madison, co., Idaho F7 57
Madison, co., Ill. E4 58
Madison, co., Ind. D6 59
Madison, co., Iowa C3 60
Madison, co., Ky. C5 62
Madison, co., Miss. C4 68
Madison, co., Mo. D7 69
Madison, co., Mont. E4 70
Madison, co., Nebr. C8 71
Madison, co., N.Y. C5 75
Madison, co., N.C. f10 76
Madison, co., Ohio C2 78
Madison, co., Tenn. B3 83
Madison, co., Tex. D5 84
Madison, co., Va. B4 85
Madison, par., La. B4 63
Madison Heights, Mich o15 66
Madison Heights, Va. C3 85
Madisonville, Ky. C2 62
Madisonville, La. D5, h11 63
Madisonville, Tenn. D9 83
Madisonville, Tex. D5 84
Madium, Indon. *G4 19
Madoc, Ont., Can. C7 41
Madras, India F7 20
Madras, Oreg. C5 80
Madre de Dios, dept., Peru D3 31
Madrid, Iowa C4, e8 60
Madrid, N.Y. f9 75
Madrid, Sp. B4, p17 8
Madrid, prov., Sp. *B4 8
Madridejos, Phil. *C6 19
Madridejos, Sp. C4 8
Madurai, India G6 20
Maebashi, Jap. H9, m18 18
Maeser, Utah A7 72
Mafeking, S. Afr. F5 24
Mafra, Braz. D3 30
Magadan, Sov. Un. D19 13
Magallanes, prov., Chile E2, h11 28
Magangué, Col. B3 32
Magdalena, Mex. A2 34
Magdalena, N. Mex. B5 48
Magdalena, dept., Col. A3 32
Magdalena, riv., Col. C3 27
Magdalena Contreras, Mex. h9 34
Magdalen Islands, co.,
   Que., Can. B8 43
Magdeburg, Ger. Dem. Rep. B5 6
Magé, Braz. h6 30
Magee, Miss. D4 68
Magelang, Indon. G4 19
Magenta, It. B2 9
Maglie, It. D7 9
Magna, Utah A5, C2 72
Magnitogorsk, Sov. Un. D8 13
Magnolia, Ark. D2 49
Magnolia, Miss. D3 68
Magnolia, N.J. D2 74
Magnolia, N.C. C4 76
Magnolia, Ohio B4 78
Magoffin, co., Ky. C6 62
Magog, Que., Can. D5 42
Magrath, Alta., Can. E4 38
Magwe, Bur. D9 20
Mahameru, mtn., Indon. G4 19
Mahanoy City, Pa. E9 81
Maharashtra, state, India D5 20
Mahaska, co., Iowa C5 60

Mahbūbnagar, India E6 20
Mahe, India F6 20
Mahnomen, Minn. C3 67
Mahnomen, co., Minn. C2 67
Mahogany, mtn., Oreg. D9 80
Mahomet, Ill. C5 58
Mahón, Sp. C8 8
Mahone Bay, N.S., Can. E5 43
Mahoning, co., Ohio B5 78
Mahopac, N.Y. D7, m15 75
Mahtomedi, Minn. E7 67
Mahwah, N.J. A4 74
Maiden, N.C. B1 76
Maidstone, Sask., Can. D1 39
Maidstone, Eng. E7 4
Maiduguri, Nig. F7 22
Maimana, Afg. A3 20
Maine, former prov., Fr. C3 5
Maine, state, U.S. 64
Maine-et-Loire, dept., Fr. *D3 5
Maintirano, Mad. D8 24
Main Topsail, mtn., Newf., Can. ... D3 44
Mainz, Ger., Fed. Rep. of C4 6
Maipú, Arg. B5 28
Maiquetía, Ven. A4 32
Maisonette, N.B., Can. B4 43
Maisons-Alfort, Fr. g10 5
Maisons-Laffitte, Fr. g9 5
Maitland, Austl. F9 25
Maitland (Lake Maitland), Fla. *D5 54
Maize, Kans. g12 61
Maizuru, Jap. I7, n14 18
Majagual, Col. B3 32
Majestic, Ky. C7 62
Major, co., Okla. A3 79
Makaha, Haw. g9 56
Makajanga, Mad. D9 24
Makarov Shirutoru, Sov. Un. B11 18
Makarska, Yugo. D3 10
Makasar, see Ujung Pandang, Indon.
Makati, Phil. *o3 19
Makawao, Haw. C5 56
Makaweli, Haw. B2 56
Makeyevka, Sov. Un. G11, q20 12
Makhachkala, Sov. Un. E7 13
Makhlata, Bul. D7 10
Makurazaki, Jap. K5 18
Makurdi, Nig. G6 22
Malabar, Fla. D6 54
Malabo, Equat. Gui. H6 22
Malacca, state, Mala. E2 19
Malad City, Idaho G6 57
Málaga, Col. B3 32
Malaga, N.J. D2 74
Málaga, Sp. D3 8
Málaga, prov., Sp. *D3 8
Malagasy Republic, see
  Madagascar, country, Afr.
Malakāl, Sud. G4 23
Malakoff, Fr. g10 5
Malakoff, Tex. C4 84
Malang, Indon. G4 19
Malanje, Ang. B3 24
Malartic, Que., Can. k11 42
Malatya, Tur. C12 14
Malawi, country, Afr. C6 24
Malaya Vishera, Sov. Un. B9 12
Malaybalay, Phil. D7 19
Malaysia, country, Asia E4 19
Malbork, Pol. A5 7
Malchin, Ger. Dem. Rep. B6 6
Malden, Mass. B5, g11 65
Malden, Mo. E8 69
Malden, W. Va. m12 87
Maldives, country, Asia G5 20
Maldonado, Ur. E2 30
Maldonado, dept., Ur. *E2 30
Malegaon, India *D5 20
Māler Kotla, India B6 20
Malheur, co., Oreg. D9 80
Mali, country, Afr. F3 22
Malibu, Calif. m11 50
Malin, Oreg. E5 80
Malinec, Czech. D5 7
Malita, Phil. *D7 19
Malkara, Tur. B6 14
Mallawī, Eg. C4 23
Malleco, prov., Chile B2 28
Mallory, W. Va. *D3 87
Mallow, Ire. D2 4
Malmédy, Bel. B7 5
Malmö, Swe. J5 11
Malmöhus, co., Swe. *J5 11
Maloarkhangelsk, Sov. Un. E11 12
Malolos, Phil. o13 19
Malone, Fla. B1 54
Malone, N.Y. f10 75
Maloyaroslavets, Sov. Un. D11 12
Malta, Mont. B9 70
Malta, Ohio C4 78
Malta, country, Eur. A7 22
Malton, Eng. C6 4
Malvern, Ark. C3, g8 49

Malvern, Iowa D2 60
Malvern, Ohio B4 78
Malvern, Pa. F10, o19 81
Malverne, N.Y. *G2 52
Mamanguape, Braz. *D7 27
Mamaroneck, N.Y. h13 75
Mamba, Jap. m17 18
Mamers, Fr. C4 5
Mammoth, Ariz. C3 48
Mammoth, W. Va. C3, m13 87
Mamou, Guinea F2 22
Mamou, La. D3 63
Man, W. Va. D3, n12 87
Man, Isle of, see Isle of
  Man, Br. dep., Eur.
Manabi, prov., Ec. B1 31
Manacor, Sp. C7 8
Manado, Indon. E6 19
Managua, Nic. E7 34
Manahawkin, N.J. D4 74
Manakara, Mad. E9 24
Manama, Bahrain D5 15
Mananjary, Mad. E9 24
Manasquan, N.J. C4 74
Manassas, Va. B5, g12 85
Manassas Park, Va. *B5 85
Manatee, co., Fla. E4 54
Manatí, P.R. *G11 35
Manaus, Braz. D4 27
Manawa, Wis. D5 88
Mancelona, Mich. D5 66
Mancha, reg., Sp. C4 8
Mancha Real, Sp. D4 8
Manchaug, Mass. B4 65
Manche, dept., Fr. *C3 5
Manchester, Conn. B6 52
Manchester, Eng. D5 4
Manchester, Ga. D2 55
Manchester, Iowa B6 60
Manchester, Ky. C6 62
Manchester, Md. A4 53
Manchester, Mass. A6, f12 65
Manchester, Mich. F6 66
Manchester, Mo. f12 69
Manchester, N.H. F5 73
Manchester, N.Y. C3 75
Manchester, Ohio D2 78
Manchester, Pa. F8 81
Manchester, Tenn. B5 83
Manchester Depot, Vt. E1 73
Manchuria, reg., China B10 17
Mandalay, Bur. D10 20
Mandan, N. Dak. D5 77
Mandasor, India D6 20
Manderson, Wyo. B5 89
Mandeville, Jam. E5 35
Mandeville, La. D5, h11 63
Mandurah, Austl. F2 25
Manduria, It. D6 9
Māndvi, India D4 20
Manfalūṭ, Eg. C4 23
Manfredonia, It. D5 9
Mangalore, India F5 20
Mangham, La. B4 63
Mangum, Okla. C2 79
Manhasset, N.Y. *F2 52
Manhattan, Ill. *B6 58
Manhattan, Kans. C7 61
Manhattan, N.Y. *B5 75
Manhattan Beach, Calif. n12 50
Manheim, Pa. F9 81
Manhuaçu, Braz. C4 30
Manila, Ark. B5 49
Manila, Phil. o13 19
Manilla, Iowa C2 60
Manipur, state, India D9 20
Manisa, Tur. C6 14
Manistee, Mich. D4 66
Manistee, co., Mich. D4 66
Manistique, Mich. C4 66
Manito, Ill. C4 58
Manitoba, prov., Can. 40
Manitoba, lake, Man., Can. D2 40
Manitou, Man., Can. E2 40
Manitou Beach, Mich. *G6 66
Manitoulin, dist., Ont., Can. B2 41
Manitou Springs, Colo. C6 51
Manitowoc, Wis. D6, h10 88
Manitowoc, co., Wis. D6 88
Maniwaki, Que., Can. C2 42
Manizales, col. B2 32
Manjimup, Austl. F2 25
Mankato, Kans. C5 61
Mankato, Minn. F5 67
Manlius, N.Y. C5 75
Manlléu, Sp. A7 8
Manly, Iowa A4 60
Mannar, Sri Lanka G6 20
Mannheim, Ger., Fed. Rep. of D4 6
Manning, Alta., Can. A2 38
Manning, Iowa C2 60
Manning, S.C. D7 82
Mannington, W. Va. B4, h10 87

Mannum, Austl. G2 26
Mannville, Alta., Can. C5 38
Manomet, Mass. C6 65
Manomet, hill, Mass. C6 65
Manono, Zaire B5 24
Manor, Pa. *F2 81
Manorhaven, N.Y. *E7 75
Manosque, Fr. F6 5
Manresa, Sp. B6 8
Manseau, Que., Can. C5 42
Mansfield, Eng. D6 4
Mansfield Ill. C5 58
Mansfield, La. B2 63
Mansfield, Mass. B5 65
Mansfield, Ohio B3 78
Mansfield, Pa. C7 81
Mansfield, Tex. n9 84
Mansfield, mtn., Vt. B2 73
Mansfield Southeast, Ohio *B3 78
Manson, Iowa B3 60
Mansura, La. C3 63
Manta, Ec. B1 31
Manteca, Calif. D3 50
Manteno, Ill. B6 58
Mantes la-Jolie, Fr. C4 5
Manti, Utah B6 72
Manton, Mich. D5 66
Mantova, It. B3 9
Mantua, N.J. D2 74
Mantua, Ohio A4 78
Manuel Benavides, Mex. B4 34
Manuels, Newf., Can. *E5 44
Manukau, N.Z. *L15 26
Manvllle, N.J. B3 74
Manville, R.I. B11 52
Many, La. C2 63
Manzanares, Sp. C4 8
Manzanillo, Cuba D5 35
Manzanillo, Mex. D4, n11 34
Manzhouli, China B8 17
Maoming, China G7 17
Mapastepec, Mex. D6 34
Maple, Ont., Can. k14 41
Maple Bluff, Wis. E4 88
Maple Creek, Sask., Can. H1 39
Maple Heights, Ohio h9 78
Maple Lake, Minn. E4 67
Maple Lane, Ind. *A5 59
Maple Mount, Ky. C2 62
Maple Plain, Minn. m11 67
Maple Rapids, Mich. E6 66
Maple Shade, N.J. D2 74
Mapleton, Iowa B2 60
Mapleton, Maine B4 64
Mapleton, Minn. G5 67
Mapleton, Oreg. C3 80
Mapleton, Utah D2 72
Maplewood, La. D2 63
Maplewood, Minn. m12 67
Maplewood, Mo. f13 69
Maplewood, N.J. B4 74
Maplewood, N.Y. *C7 75
Maplewood Park, Pa. *G11 81
Maputo, Moz. F6 24
Maquoketa, Iowa B7 60
Marabá, Braz. D6 27
Maracaibo, Ven. A3 32
Maracaju, Braz. F5 27
Maracay, Ven. A4 32
Maradi, Niger F6 22
Marāgheh, Iran B4 15
Maragogipe, Braz. *E7 27
Marana, Ariz. C3 48
Maranguape, Braz. *D7 27
Maranhão, state, Braz. *D6 27
Marañón, riv., Peru B2 31
Maraş, Tur. D11 14
Marathon, Ont., Can. o18 41
Marathon, Fla. H5 54
Marathon, Iowa B3 60
Marathon, N.Y. C4 75
Marathon, Tex. D1, o13 84
Marathon, Wis. D4 88
Marathon, co., Wis. D4 88
Maravatío de Ocampo, Mex. n13 34
Mara Vista, Mass. C6 65
Marawi, Sud. E4 23
Marbella, Sp. D3 8
Marble, Minn. C5 67
Marble Cliff, Ohio m10 78
Marble Falls, Tex. D3 84
Marblehead, Mass. B6, f12 65
Marblehead, Ohio A3 78
Marbleton, Que., Can. D6 42
Marburg, Ger., Fed. Rep. of C4 6
Marbury, Md. C3 53
Marceline, Mo. B5 69
Marcellus, Mich. F5 66
Marcellus, N.Y. C4 75
Marche, former prov., Fr. D4 5
Marche, pol. dist., It. *C4 9
Marchena, Sp. D3 8
Marches, reg., It. C4 9

Marcola, Oreg. C4 80
Marcos Juarez, Arg. A4 28
Marcus, Iowa B2 60
Marcus Hook, Pa. G11 81
Marcy, mtn., N.Y. A7 75
Mardān, Pak. B5 20
Mar Del Plata, Arg. B5 28
Mardin, Tur. D13 14
Marechal Deodoro, Braz. *D7 27
Marengo, Ill. A5 58
Marengo, Ind. H5 59
Marengo, Iowa C5 60
Marengo, co., Ala. C2 46
Marenisco, Mich. n12 66
Marfa, Tex. o12 84
Margaret, Ala. B3 46
Margaretville, N.Y. C6 75
Margate, Eng. E7 4
Margate, Fla. *F6 54
Margate City, N.J. E3 74
Margelan, Sov. Un. E10 13
Margherita, mtn., Ug. H3 23
Maria la Baja, col. A2 32
Mariana, is., Pac. O. E6 2
Marianna, Ark. C5 49
Marianna, Fla. B1 54
Marianna, Pa. *F1 81
Mariánské Lázně, Czech. D2 7
Maribo, co., Den. *J4 11
Maribor, Yugo. B2 10
Maricopa, Calif. E4 50
Maricopa, co., Ariz. C2 48
Mariemont, Ohio o13 78
Marienville, Pa. D3 81
Maries, co., Mo. C6 69
Mariestad, Swe. H5 11
Marietta, Ga. C2, h7 55
Marietta, Ohio C4 78
Marietta, Okla. D4 79
Marietta, Pa. F8 81
Marietta, S.C. A2 82
Marieville, Que., Can. D4 42
Marília, Braz. C3 30
Marín, Sp. A1 8
Marin, co., Calif. C2 50
Marin City, Calif. *C2 50
Marinduque, prov., Phil. *C6 19
Marine, Ill. E4 58
Marine City, Mich. F8 66
Marinette, Wis. C6 88
Marinette, co., Wis. C5 88
Maringouin, La. D4 63
Marinha Grande, Port. C1 8
Marino, It. H9 9
Marion, Ala. C2 46
Marion, Ill. F5 58
Marion, Ind. C6 59
Marion, Iowa B6 60
Marion, Kans. D6 61
Marion, Ky. e9 62
Marion, La. B3 63
Marion, Mass. C6 65
Marion, Mich. D5 66
Marion, N.Y. B3 75
Marion, N.C. B1, f10 76
Marion, Ohio B2 78
Marion, S.C. C9 82
Marion, Va. f10 85
Marion, Wis. D5 88
Marion, co., Ala. A2 46
Marion, co., Ark. A3 49
Marion, co., Fla. C4 54
Marion, co., Ga. D2 55
Marion, co., Ill. E5 58
Marion, co., Ind. E5 59
Marion, co., Iowa C4 60
Marion, co., Kans. D6 61
Marion, co., Ky. C4 62
Marion, co., Miss. D4 68
Marion, co., Mo. B6 69
Marion, co., Ohio B2 78
Marion, co., Oreg. C4 80
Marion, co., S.C. C9 82
Marion, co., Tenn. D8 83
Marion, co., Tex. C5 84
Marion, co., W. Va. B4 87
Marion Heights, Pa. *D8 81
Marionville, Mo. D4 69
Mariposa, Calif. D4 50
Mariposa, co., Calif. D3 50
Marissa, Ill. E4 58
Maris Town, Miss. C3 68
Mariupol, see Zhdanov, Sov. Un.
Marka, Som. H6 23
Markdale, Ont., Can. C4 41
Marked Tree, Ark. B5 49
Markesan, Wis. E5 88
Markham, Ont., Can. D5, k15 41
Markham, Ill. k9 58
Markham, mtn., Ant. L7 2
Markle, Ind. C7 59
Markova, Sov. Un. G12 12
Marks, Miss. A3 68

Marksville, La. C3 63
Marktredwitz, Ger., Fed.
Rep. of C6 6
Marlbank, Ont., Can. C7 41
Marlboro, Mass. B4, g9 65
Marlboro, N.J. C4 74
Marlboro, N.Y. D6 75
Marlboro, co., S.C. B8 82
Marlborough, N.H. F3 73
Marlette, Mich. E7 66
Marley, Md. B4 53
Marlin, Tex. D4 84
Marlinton, W. Va. C4 87
Marlow, Okla. C4 79
Marlowe, W.Va. B7 87
Marlton, N.J. D3 74
Marmande, Fr. E4 5
Marmet, W. Va. C3, m12 87
Marmora, Ont., Can. C7 41
Marmora, N.J. E3 74
Marmora, peak, It. D2 9
Marne, Mich. E5 66
Marne, dept., Fr. *C6 5
Maroa, Ill. C5 58
Maroantsetra, Mad. D9 24
Maromokotro, mtn., Mad. C9 24
Maroochydore-Mooloolaba,
Austl. C9 26
Maroua, Cam. F7 22
Marovoay, Mad. D9 24
Marquesas, is., Fr. Polynesia G11 2
Marquette, Kans. D6 61
Marquette, Mich. B3 66
Marquette, co., Mich. B3 66
Marquette, co., Wis. E4 88
Marquette Heights, Ill. C4 58
Marrakech, Mor. B3 22
Marrero, La. k11 63
Marromeu, Moz. D7 24
Mars, Pa. E1 81
Mars, hill, Maine g7 64
Marsala, It. F4 9
Marsa Matruh, Eg. B3 23
Marseille, Fr. F6 5
Marseilles, Ill. B5 58
Marshall, Ark. B3 49
Marshall, Ill. D6 58
Marshall, Mich. F6 66
Marshall, Minn. F3 67
Marshall, Mo. B4 69
Marshall, N.C. F10 76
Marshall, Tex. C5 84
Marshall, Va. B5 85
Marshall, Wis. E4 88
Marshall, co., Ala. A3 46
Marshall, co., Ill. B4 58
Marshall, co., Ind. B5 59
Marshall, co., Iowa C4 60
Marshall, co., Kans. C7 61
Marshall, co., Ky. f9 62
Marshall, co., Minn. B2 67
Marshall, co., Miss. A4 68
Marshall, co., Okla. C5 79
Marshall, co., S. Dak. E8 77
Marshall, co., Tenn. B5 83
Marshall, co., W. Va. B4 87
Marshallberg, N.C. *C6 76
Marshall Northeast, Tex. *C5 84
Marshallton, Del. A6 35
Marshallton, Pa. *D8 81
Marshalltown, Iowa B5 60
Marshallville, Ga. D3 55
Marshallville, Ohio B4 78
Marshfield, Mass. B6, h13 65
Marshfield, Mo. D5 69
Marshfield, Wis. D3 88
Marshfield Hills, Mass. B6, h13 65
Mars Hill, Ind. E5, m10 59
Mars Hill, Maine B5 64
Mars Hill, N.C. f10 76
Marshville, N.C. C2 76
Marsing, Idaho F2 57
Marston, Mo. E8 69
Mart, Tex. D4 84
Martel, Que., Can. A6 42
Martí, Cuba D5 35
Martigues, Fr. F6 5
Martin, Ky. C7 62
Martin, Mich. F5 66
Martin, S. Dak. G4 77
Martin, Tenn. A3 83
Martin, co., Fla. E6 54
Martin, co., Ind. G4 59
Martin, co., Ky. C7 62
Martin, co., Minn. G4 67
Martin, co., N.C. B5 76
Martin, co., Tex. C2 84
Martina Franca, It. D6 9
Martinez, Calif. C2, h8 50
Martinez, Ga. C4 55
Martinique, Fr. dep., N.A. I14 35
Martinsburg, Pa. F5 81
Martinsburg, W. Va. B7 87

Martins Creek, Pa. B2 81
Martins Ferry, Ohio B5 78
Martinsville, Ill. D6 58
Martinsville, Ind. F5 59
Martinsville, N.J. B3 74
Martinsville (Independent City),
Va. D3 85
Martos, Sp. D4 8
Marudi, Mala. E5 19
Maruf, Afg. B4 20
Marugame, Jap. I6 18
Marvell, Ark. C5 49
Mary, Sov. Un. F9 13
Maryborough, Austl. E9 25
Maryborough, Austl. G7 25
Maryfield, Sask., Can. H5 39
Maryland, state, U.S. 53
Maryland Heights, Mo. f13 69
Maryport, Eng. C5 4
Marys, peak, Oreg. C3 80
Mary's Harbour, Newf., Can. B4 44
Marystown, Newf., Can. E4 44
Marysville, Calif. C3 50
Marysville, B.C., Can. E10 37
Marysville, Kans. C7 61
Marysville, Mich. F8 66
Marysville, Ohio B2 78
Marysville, Pa. F8 81
Marysville, Wash. A3 86
Maryvale, Ariz. *C2 48
Maryville, Mo. A3 69
Maryville, Tenn. D10, n14 83
Masan, Kor. I4 18
Masaya, Nic. E7 34
Masbate, Phil. C6 19
Masbate, prov., Phil. *H7 19
Mascot, Tenn. C10, m14 83
Mascota, Mex. m11 34
Mascouche, Que., Can. D4 42
Mascoutah, Ill. E4 58
Mashhad (Meshed), Iran B6 15
Masindi, Ug. H4 23
Masisea, Peru C3 31
Masjed, Soleyman, Iran C4 16
Maskinongé, Que., Can. C4 42
Maskinongé, co., Que., Can. C4 42
Mason, Mich. F6 66
Mason, Ohio C1, n13 78
Mason, Tex. D3 84
Mason, W. Va. B2 87
Mason, co., Ill. C4 58
Mason, co., Ky. B6 62
Mason, co., Mich. D4 66
Mason, co., Tex. D3 84
Mason, co., Wash. B2 86
Mason, co., W. Va. C3 87
Mason City, Ill. C4 58
Mason City, Iowa A4 60
Masontown, Pa. G2 81
Masontown, W. Va. B5 87
Mass, Mich. B1, m12 66
Massa, It. B3 9
Massac, co., Ill. F5 58
Massachusetts, state, U.S. 65
Massaemett, mtn., Mass. A2 65
Massafra, It. D6 9
Massa Marittima, It. C3 9
Massanutten, mtn., Va. B4 85
Massapequa, N.Y. G3 52
Massapequa Park, N.Y. *E7 75
Massawa, Eth. E5 23
Massena, N.Y. f10 75
Masset, B.C., Can. C1 37
Massey, Ont., Can. A2 41
Massillon, Ohio B4 78
Massive, mtn., Colo. B4 51
Masson, Que., Can. D2 42
Masterton, N.Z. N15 26
Mastic, N.Y. *n15 75
Mastic Beach, N.Y. *F4 52
Mastung, Pak. C4 20
Masuda, Jap. I5 18
Masuria, reg., Pol. B6 7
Masury, Ohio A5 78
Masvingo, Zimb. E6 24
Matachewan, Ont. Can. p19 41
Matadi, Zaire B2 24
Matador, Tex. C2 84
Matagalpa, Nic. E7 34
Matagorda, co., Tex. E5 84
Matamoras, Pa. D12 81
Matamoros, Mex. B5 34
Matamoros de la Laguna, Mex. B4 34
Matane, Que., Can. G20 36
Matane, co., Que., Can. *G20 36
Matanzas, Cuba C3 35
Matanzas, prov., Cuba C3 35
Matapedia, co., Que., Can. *G20 36
Matara, Sri Lanka G7 20
Mataram, Indon. G5 19
Mataró, Sp. B7 8
Matawan, N.J. C4 74
Matehuala, Mex. C4 34

Matera, It. D6 9
Mátészalka, Hung. B6 10
Mateur, Tun. F2 9
Matewan, W. Va. D2 87
Matfield, Mass. B6 65
Mather, Pa. G1 81
Mather, peak, Wyo. B5 89
Mathews, co., Va. C6 85
Mathis, Tex. E4 84
Mathura, India C6 20
Matoaca, Va. n18 85
Matoaka, W. Va. D3 87
Mato Grosso, state, Braz. B1 30
Matozinhos, Port. B1 8
Maţrāh, Om. E6 15
Matsudo, Jap. *I9 18
Matsue, Jap. I6 18
Matsuida, Jap. m17 18
Matsumae, Jap. F10 18
Matsumoto, Jap. H9, m16 18
Matsuyama, Jap. J6 18
Matsuzaka, Jap. I8, o15 18
Matsuzaki, Jap. o17 18
Mattapoisett, Mass. C6 65
Mattawa, Ont., Can. A6, p20 41
Mattawamkeag, Maine C4 64
Matterhorn, mtn., Switz. E3 6
Matteson, Ill. k9 58
Matthews, Ind. D7 59
Matthews, N.C. B2 76
Matthews, mtn. Mo. D7 69
Matthew Town, Ba. D7 35
Mattituck, N.Y. n16 75
Mattoon, Ill. D5 58
Mattydale, N.Y. *B4 75
Matucana, Peru D2 31
Matun, Afg. B4 20
Maturín, Ven. B5 32
Maubeuge, Fr. B5 5
Maubin, Bur. *E10 20
Mauch Chunk, see Jim Thorpe, Pa.
Maud, Ohio C1, n13 78
Maud, Okla. B5 79
Maud, Tex. C5 84
Maugansville, Md. A2 52
Maugerville, N.B., Can. D3 43
Maui (incl. Kalawao), co., Haw. B6 56
Maui, isl., Haw. C6 56
Mauldin, S.C. *B3 82
Maule, prov., Chile B2 28
Maumee, Ohio A2, e6 78
Mauna Kea, vol., Haw. D6 56
Maunaloa, Haw. B4 56
Mauna Loa, vol., Haw. D6 56
Mauritania, country, Afr. *E2 22
Mauritius, country, Afr. *H24 2
Maury, co., Tenn. B4 83
Mauston, Wis. E3 88
Maverick, co., Tex. E2 84
Maxcanú, Mex. C7 34
Max Meadows, Va. D2 85
Maxton, N.C. C3 76
Maxwell, Iowa C4, e9 60
May, mtn., Alta., Can. B1 38
Mayagüez, P.R. G11 35
Mayarí, Cuba D6 35
Maybee, Mich. F7 66
Maybeury, W.Va. *D3 87
Maybole, Scot. C4 4
Maybrook, N.Y. D6 75
Mayen, Ger., Fed. Rep of C3 6
Mayenne, Fr. C3 5
Mayenne, dept., Fr. *C3 5
Mayer, Ariz. B2 48
Mayerthorpe, Alta., Can. C3 38
Mayes, co., Okla. A6 79
Mayesville, S.C. D7 82
Mayfield, Ky. f9 62
Mayfield, N.Y. B6 75
Mayfield, Ohio *A4 78
Mayfield, Pa. C11 81
Mayfield Heights, Ohio A4 78
Mayking, Ky. C7 62
Maymyo, Bur. D10 20
Maynard, Iowa B6 60
Maynard, Mass. B5, g10 65
Mayo, Yukon, Can. D6 36
Mayo, Fla. B3 54
Mayo, Md. C4 53
Mayo, S.C. A4 82
Mayo, co., Ire. *D2 4
Mayodan, N.C. A3 76
Mayon, vol., Phil. C6 19
Mayotte, Fr. ter., Afr. C9 24
May Pen, Jam. F5 35
Mays Landing, N.J. D3 74
Maysville, Ky. B6 62
Maysville, Mo. B3 69
Maysville, N.C. C5 76
Maysville, Okla. C4 79
Mayville, Mich. E7 66
Mayville, N.J. E3 74

Mayville, N.Y. C1 75
Mayville, N. Dak. C8 77
Mayville, Wis. E5 88
Maywood, Calif. *F4 50
Maywood, Ill. k9 58
Maywood, N.J. h8 74
Maywood, N.Y. *C7 75
Mazamet, Fr. F5 5
Mazapil, Mex. C4 34
Mazara Del Vallo, It. F4 9
Mazar-I-Sharif, Afg. A4 20
Mazarrón, Sp. D5 8
Mazatenango, Guat. E6 34
Mazatlán, Mex. C3 34
Mazomanie, Wis. E4 88
Mazon, Ill. B5 58
Mazzarino, It. F5 9
Mbabane, Swaz. F6 24
Mbala, Zambia B6 24
Mbalmayo, Cam. H7 22
Mbandaka, Zaire H1 23
Mbanza-Ngungu, Zaire B2 24
Mbeya, Tan. B6 24
Mead, Wash. B8, g14 86
Meade, Kans. E3 61
Meade, co., Kans. E3 61
Meade, co., Ky. C3 62
Meade, co., S. Dak. F3 77
Meade, peak, Idaho G7 57
Meaderville, Mont. *D4 70
Meadowbrook, Ind. *B7 59
Meadowbrook, W. Va. k10 87
Meadow Lake, Sask., Can. n7 39
Meadow Lands, Pa. F1 81
Meadow Park, Fla. F6 54
Meadowview, Va. f10 85
Meadville, Pa. C1 81
Meaford, Ont., Can. C4 41
Meagher, co., Mont. D6 70
Meath, co., Ire. *D3 4
Meaux, Fr. C5 5
Mebane, N.C. A3 76
Mecca, Ind. E3 59
Mecca (Makkah), Sau. Ar. E2 15
Mechanic Falls, Maine D2 64
Mechanicsburg, Ohio B2 78
Mechanicsburg, Pa. F7 81
Mechanicsville, Iowa C6 60
Mechanicsville, Va. C5 85
Mechanicville, N Y C7 75
Mechelen, Bel. B6 5
Mecklenburg, co., N.C. B2 76
Mecklenburg, co., Va. D4 85
Mecklenburg, state, Ger.
Dem. Rep. *B6 6
Mecosta, co., Mich. E5 66
Medan, Indon. E1, m11 19
Medaryville, Ind. B4 59
Medéa, Alg. A5 22
Medellín, Col. B2 32
Medfield, Mass. h10 65
Medford, Mass. B5, g11 65
Medford, N.J. D3 74
Medford, Okla. A4 79
Medford, Oreg. E4 80
Medford, Wis. C3 88
Medford Lakes, N.J. D3 74
Medgidia, Rom. C9 10
Media, Pa. G11, p20 81
Mediapolis, Iowa C6 60
Medias, Rom. B7 10
Medical Lake, Wash. B8, g13 86
Medicine Bow, peak, Wyo. E6 89
Medicine Hat, Alta., Can. D5, g8 38
Medicine Lodge, Kans. E5 61
Medicine Park, Okla. C3 79
Medina, N.Y. B2 75
Medina, Ohio A4 78
Medina (Al Madīnah), Sau. Ar. E2 15
Medina, Wash. e11 86
Medina, co., Ohio A4 78
Medina, co., Tex. E3 84
Medina del Campo, Sp. B3 8
Medina Sidonia, Sp. D3 8
Mediterranean, sea D21 2
Medora, Ind. G5 59
Medvezhegorsk, Sov. Un. F16 11
Medway, Mass. B5, h10 65
Medzhibozh, Sov. Un. G6 12
Meekatharra, Austl. E2 25
Meeker, Colo. A3 51
Meeker, Okla. B5 79
Meeker, co., Minn. E4 67
Meerane, Ger. Dem. Rep. C6 6
Meerut, India C6 20
Mégantic, co., Que., Can. C6 42
Mégantic, mtn., Que., Can. D6 42
Megara, Grc. C4 14
Meggett, S.C. F7, k11 82
Meghalaya, state, India C9 20
Megunticook, mtn., Maine D3 64
Mehun-sur-Yèvre, Fr. D5 5
Meigs, Ga. E2 55

Meigs, co., Ohio C3 78
Meigs, co., Tenn. D9 83
Meiktila, Bur. D10 20
Meiners Oaks, Calif. *E4 50
Meiningen, Ger. Dem. C5 6
Meissen, Ger. Dem. Rep. C6 6
Meixian, China G8 17
Mejillones, Chile F3 27
Meknès, Mor. B3 22
Mekong, riv., Asia. B2 19
Melaka (Malacca), Mala. E2 19
Melbourne, Austl. G8, n15 25
Melbourne, Fla. D6 54
Melbourne, Iowa C4 60
Melbourne Beach, Fla. D6 54
Melcher, Iowa C4 60
Melfi, It. D5 9
Melfort, Sask., Can. E3 39
Melilla, Sp. dep., Afr. A4 22
Melipilla, Chile A2 28
Melita, Man., Can. E1 40
Melito di Porto Salvo, It. F5 9
Melitopol, Sov. Un. H10 12
Mellen, Wis. B3 88
Mellette, co., S. Dak. G5 77
Mělník, Czech. n18 7
Melo, Ur. E2 30
Melocheville, Que., Can. q19 42
Melouprey, Camb. *C3 19
Melrose, Fla. C4 54
Melrose, Mass. B5, g11 65
Melrose, La. E4 67
Melrose, N. Mex. B7 48
Melrose, Wis. D3 88
Melrose Park, Fla. *F6 54
Melrose Park, Ill. F2 58
Melrose Park, N.Y. *C4 75
Melrose Park, Pa. *F11 81
Melun, Fr. C5 5
Melville, Sask., Can. G4 39
Melville, La. D4 63
Melville, isl., N.W. Ter., Can. A11 36
Melvin, Ky. C7 62
Melvindale, Mich. *F7 66
Memel, see Klaipeda, Sov. Un.
Memmingen, Ger., Fed. Rep. of ... E5 6
Memphis, Fla. p10 54
Memphis, Mich. F8 66
Memphis, Mo. A5 69
Memphis, Tenn. B1, e9 83
Memphis, Tex. B2 84
Memramcook, N.B., Can. C5 43
Memramcook East, N.B., Can. ... *C5 43
Mena, Ark. C1 49
Menahga, Minn. D3 67
Menands, N.Y. C7 75
Menard, Tex. D3 84
Menard, co., Ill. C4 58
Menard, co., Tex. D3 84
Menasha, Wis. D5, h9 88
Mende, Fr. E5 5
Mendenhall, Miss. D4 68
Mendham, N.J. B3 74
Mendocino, Calif. C2 50
Mendocino, co., Calif. C2 50
Mendon, Ill. C2 58
Mendon, Mass. h9 65
Mendon, Mich. F5 66
Mendon, Ohio B1 78
Mendota, Calif. D3 50
Mendota, Ill. B4 58
Mendota Heights, Minn. *F5 67
Mendoza, Arg. A3 28
Mendoza, prov., Arg. A3 28
Menemen, Tur. *C6 14
Menfi, It. F4 9
Mengzi, China G5 17
Menifee, co., Ky. C6 62
Menindee, Austl. F7 25
Menlo Park, Calif. k8 50
Menlo Park, N.J. B4 74
Menlo Park Terrace, N.J. *B4 74
Menominee, Mich. C3 66
Menominee, co., Mich. C3 66
Menominee, co., Wis. C5 88
Menominee, riv., Mich. C3 66
Menomonee Falls, Wis. E5, m11 88
Menomonie, Wis. D2 88
Mentana, It. g9 9
Menton, Fr. F7 5
Mentone, Calif. *E5 50
Mentone, Ind. B5 59
Mentor, Ohio A4 78
Mentor Headlands, Ohio *A4 78
Mentor-on-the-Lake, Ohio A4 78
Meoqui, Mex. B3 34
Meppel, Neth. A7 5
Meppen, Ger., Fed. Rep. of B3 6
Mequon, Wis. E6, m12 88
Merano, It. A3 9
Merauke, Indon. G10 19
Mercâra, India F6 20
Merced, Calif. D3 50

Merced, co., Calif. D3 50
Mercedes, Arg. E4 29
Mercedes, Arg. A5, g7 28
Mercedes, Arg. A3 28
Mercedes, Tex. F4 84
Mercedes, Ur. E1 30
Mercer, Pa. D1 81
Mercer, Wis. B3 88
Mercer, co., Ill. B3 58
Mercer, co., Ky. C5 62
Mercer, co., Mo. A4 69
Mercer, co., N.J. C3 74
Mercer, co., N. Dak. C4 77
Mercer, co., Ohio B1 78
Mercer, co., Pa. D1 81
Mercer, co., W. Va. D3 87
Mercer Island, Wash. B3, e11 86
Mercersburg, Pa. G6 81
Mercerville, N.J. C3 74
Merchantville, N.J. *D2 74
Meredith, N.H. D4 73
Meredosia, Ill. D3 58
Merefa, Sov. Un. G11 12
Mergui, Bur. F10 20
Mérida, Mex. C7 34
Mérida, Sp. C2 8
Mérida, Ven. B3 32
Mérida, state, Ven. B3 32
Meriden, Conn. C5 52
Meridian, Idaho F2 57
Meridian, Miss. C5 68
Meridian, Pa. *E2 81
Meridian, Tex. D4 84
Merioneth, co., Wales *D5 4
Merion Park, Pa. *F11 81
Merion Station, Pa. *F11 81
Meriwether, co., Ga. C2 55
Merkel, Tex. C3 84
Merksem, Bel. B6 5
Merlin, Ont., Can. E2 41
Merlo, Arg. g7 28
Mermentau, La. D3 63
Mermentau, riv., La. E2 63
Merredin, Austl. F2 25
Merriam, Kans. B8 61
Merrick, N.Y. G2 52
Merrick, co., Nebr. C7 71
Merrickville, Ont., Can. C9 41
Merrifield, Va. g12 85
Merrill, Iowa B1 60
Merrill, Mich. E6 66
Merrill, Oreg. E5 80
Merrill, Wis. C4 88
Merrillan, Wis. D3 88
Merrillville, Ind. B3 59
Merrimac, Mass. A5 65
Merrimack, N.H. F5 73
Merrimack, co., N.H. E4 73
Merritt, B.C., Can. D7 37
Merritt Island, Fla. D6 54
Mer Rouge, La. B4 63
Merryville, La. D2 63
Merseburg, Ger. Dem. Rep. C4 6
Mersey, riv., Eng. D5 4
Mersin, Tur. D10 14
Mersing, Mala. E2 19
Merthyr Tydfil, Wales E5 4
Meru, mtn., Tan. I5 23
Merzifon, Tur. B10 14
Mesa, Ariz. C3, D2 48
Mesa, co., Colo. C2 51
Mesa de Tijuana, Mex. *A1 34
Mesagne, It. D6 9
Meshkovskaya, Sov. Un. G13 12
Mesilla, N. Mex. E3 48
Mesilla Park, N. Mex. E3 48
Mesolongion, Grc. C3 14
Mesquite, Tex. n10 84
Messina, It. E5 9
Messina, S. Afr. E6 24
Messini, Grc. D3 14
Messinia (Messenia), prov.,
  Grc. *D4 14
Mestghanem, Alg. A5 22
Mestre, It. B4 9
Meta, dept., Col. C3 32
Meta, riv., Col. B4 32
Métabetchouan, Que., Can. A6 42
Metairie, La. k11 63
Metamora, Ill. C4 58
Metamora, Ohio A2 78
Metán, Arg. E3 29
Metcalfe, co., Ky. C4 62
Meteghan, N.S., Can. E3 43
Methuen, Mass. A5 65
Metkovic, Yugo. D3 10
Metropolis, Ill. F5 58
Metter, Ga. D4 55
Metuchen, N.J. B4 74
Metz, Fr. C7 5
Metzger, Oreg. h12 80
Meudon, Fr. g9 5
Meulaboh, Indon. m11 19

Meurthe-et-Moselle, dept., Fr. *C7 5
Meuse, dept., Fr. *C6 5
Mexia, Tex. D4 84
Mexicali, Mex. A1 34
Mexico, Ind. C5 59
Mexico, Maine D2 64
Mexico, Mo. B6 69
Mexico, N.Y. B4 75
Mexico, country, N.A. G10 33
México, state, Mex. D5, n14 34
Mexico, gulf, N.A. G11 33
Mexico City, Mex. n14 34
Meyersdale, Pa. G3 81
Mezen, Sov. Un. C7 13
Mezőkövesd, Hung. B5 10
Mezőtúr, Hung. B5 10
Mglin, Sov. Un. E9 12
Miajadas, Sp. C3 8
Miami, Ariz. C3, D3 48
Miami, Fla. G6, s13 54
Miami, Okla. A7 79
Miami, W. Va. m13 87
Miami, co., Ind. C5 59
Miami, co., Kans. D9 61
Miami, co., Ohio B1 78
Miami Beach, Fla. G6, s13 54
Miamisburg, Ohio C1 78
Miami Shores, Fla. G6, s13 54
Miami Springs, Fla. G6, s13 54
Miamitown, Ohio o12 78
Miānwāli, Pak. B5 20
Mianyang, China E5 17
Miaoli, Taiwan *G9 17
Miass, Sov. Un. *D9 13
Micanopy, Fla. C4 54
Michalovce, Czech. D6 7
Michigan, lake, U.S. E12 33
Michigan, state, U.S. 66
Michigan Center, Mich. F6 66
Michigan City, Ind. A4 59
Michoacán, state, Mex. D4, n13 34
Michurinsk, Sov. Un. E13 12
Mickleyville, Ind. m10 59
Micoud, St. Lucia J14 35
Middelburg, Neth. B5 5
Middelburg, S. Afr. G5 24
Middleboro, Mass. C6 65
Middlebranch, Ohio B4 78
Middle Brook, Newf., Can. D4 44
Middleburg, Fla. B5 54
Middleburg, N.Y. C6 75
Middleburg, Pa. E7 81
Middleburg, Va. B5 85
Middleburgh Heights, Ohio h9 78
Middlebury, Conn. C4 52
Middlebury, Ind. A6 59
Middlebury, Vt. C1 73
Middle Caraquet, N.B., Can. *B5 43
Middlefield, Conn. C5 52
Middlefield, Ohio A4 78
Middle Granville, N.Y. B7 75
Middle Haddam, Conn. C5 52
Middle Musquodoboit, N.S., Can. . D6 43
Middleport, N.Y. B2 75
Middleport, Ohio C3 78
Middleport, Pa. *E9 81
Middle River, Md. *B5 53
Middlesboro, Ky. D6 62
Middlesbrough (Teesside), Eng. ... C6 4
Middlesex, N.J. B4 74
Middlesex, N.C. B4 76
Middlesex, co., Ont., Can. D3 41
Middlesex, co., Conn. D6 52
Middlesex, co., Eng. *E6 4
Middlesex, co., Mass. A5 65
Middlesex, co., N.J. C4 74
Middlesex, co., Va. C6 85
Middleton, Conn. C6 52
Middleton, N.S., Can. E4 43
Middleton, Idaho F2 57
Middleton, Mass. A5, f11 65
Middleton, Wis. E4 88
Middletown, Calif. C2 50
Middletown, Del. B6 53
Middletown, Ind. D6 59
Middletown, Ky. g11 62
Middletown, Md. B2 53
Middletown, N.J. C4 74
Middletown, N.Y. D6 75
Middletown, Ohio C1 78
Middletown, Pa. F8 81
Middletown, R.I. C11 52
Middletown Heights, Pa. *G11 81
Middleville, Mich. F5 66
Middleville, N.Y. B6 75
Midfield, Ala. g7 46
Midland, Calif. F6 50
Midland, Ont.,Can. C5 41
Midland, La. D3 63
Midland, Md. K13 53
Midland, Mich. *E6 66
Midland, N.C. B2 76

Midland, Pa. E1 81
Midland, Tex. D1 84
Midland, Wash. *D3 86
Midland, co., Mich. E6 66
Midland, co., Tex. D1 84
Midland Park, Kans. B5 61
Midland Park, N.J. B4 74
Midland Park, S.C. K11 82
Midleton, Ire. E2 4
Midlothian, Ill. k9 58
Midlothian, Tex. C4, n10 84
Midlothian, co., Scot. *C5 4
Midnapore, India D8 20
Midvale, Ohio B4 78
Midvale, Utah D2 72
Midway, Ky. B5 62
Midway, Oreg. *B4 80
Midway, Pa. G7 81
Midway City, Calif. *F5 50
Midway Park, N.C. C5 76
Midway Is., U.S. dep., Oceania ... E9 2
Midwest, Wyo. C6 89
Midwest City, Okla. B4 79
Mid-Western, reg., Nig. G6 22
Midyat, Tur. D13 14
Mie, pref., Jap. *I8 18
Miechów, Pol. C6 7
Miechowice, Pol. g9 7
Miedzyrzec, Pol. C7 7
Mielec, Pol. C6 7
Mieres, Sp. A3 8
Mifflin, co., Pa. F6 81
Mifflinburg, Pa. E7 81
Mifflintown, Pa. E7 81
Mifflinville, Pa. E9 81
Migennes, Fr. D5 5
Mignon, Ala. B3 46
Mihama, Jap. o15 18
Mihara, Jap. *I6 18
Mikhaylovgrad, Bul. D6 10
Mikhaylovka, Sov. Un. H10 12
Mikhaylovka, Sov. Un. F14 12
Mikindani, Tan. C8 24
Mikkeli, Fin. G12 11
Mikkeli, prov., Fin. *G12 11
Mikołów, Pol. g9 7
Mikulczyce, Pol. g8 7
Mikulov, Czech. D4 7
Milaca, Minn. E5 67
Milam, co., Tex. D4 84
Milan, Ill. B3 58
Milan, Ind. F7 59
Milan (Milano), It. B2 9
Milan, Mich. F7 66
Milan, Mo. A4 69
Milan, N. Mex. *B2 48
Milan, Ohio A3 78
Milan, Tenn. B3 83
Milano, see Milan, It.
Milas, Tur. *D6 14
Milazzo, It. E5 9
Milbank, S. Dak. E9 77
Milbridge, Maine D5 64
Mildmay, Ont., Can. *C3 41
Mildred, Pa. D9 81
Mildura, Austl. F7 25
Miles, Austl. *E9 25
Miles, Tex. D2 84
Miles City, Mont. D11 70
Milford, Conn. E4 52
Milford, Del. C7 53
Milford, Ill. C6 58
Milford, Ind. B6 59
Milford, Iowa A2 60
Milford, Maine D4 64
Milford, Mass. B4, h9 65
Milford, Mich. F7, o14 66
Milford, Nebr. D8 71
Milford, N.H. F4 73
Milford, N.J. B2 74
Milford, N.Y. C6 75
Milford, Ohio C1 78
Milford, Pa. D12 81
Milford, Utah B5 72
Milford Center, Ohio B2 78
Milford Haven, Wales E4 4
Milford Station, N.S., Can. D6 43
Miliana, Alg. A5 22
Milk, riv., Alta, Can. E5 38
Milk River, Alta., Can. E4 38
Mill, riv., Mass. h9 65
Millard, Nebr. g12 71
Millard, co., Utah B5 72
Millau, Fr. E5 5
Millbourne, Pa. *G11 81
Millbrae, Calif. h8 50
Millbrook, Ala. C3 46
Millbrook, Ont., Can. C6 41
Millbrook, N.J. *B3 74
Millbrook, N.Y. D7 75
Millburn, N.J. B4 74
Millbury, Mass. *B4 65
Millbury, Ohio e7 78

Place	Ref	Pg
Mill City, Oreg.	C4	80
Milldale, Conn.	C4	52
Milledgeville, Ga.	C3	55
Milledgeville, Ill.	B4	58
Mille Lacs, co., Minn.	E5	67
Mille Lacs, lake, Minn.	D5	67
Millen, Ga.	D5	55
Miller, S. Dak.	F7	77
Miller, co., Ark.	D2	49
Miller, co., Ga.	E2	55
Miller, co., Mo.	C5	69
Millerovo, Sov. Un.	G13	12
Millersburg, Ky.	B5	62
Millersburg, Ohio	B4	78
Millersburg, Pa.	E8	81
Millers Falls, Mass.	A3	65
Millersport, Ohio	C3	78
Millersville, Pa.	F9	81
Millerton, N.Y.	D7	75
Mill Hall, Pa.	D7	81
Millicent, Austl.	G7	25
Milligan, Fla.	u15	54
Millington, Mich.	E7	66
Millington, N.J.	*B3	74
Millington, Tenn.	B2	83
Millinocket, Maine	C4	64
Millis, Mass.	B5, h10	65
Millport, Ala.	B1	46
Mills, Wyo.	D6	89
Mills, co., Iowa	C2	60
Mills, co., Tex.	D3	84
Millsboro, Del.	C2	53
Millsboro, Pa.	G1	81
Millside, Del.	*A6	53
Millstadt, Ill.	E3	58
Milltown, N.B., Can.	D2	43
Milltown, Ind.	H5	59
Milltown, Mont.	D3	70
Milltown, N.J.	C4	74
Milltown, Wis.	C1	88
Millvale, Pa.	k14	81
Mill Valley, Calif.	D2, h7	50
Millville, Mass.	B4	65
Millville, N.J.	E2	74
Millville, Ohio	n12	78
Millville, Pa.	D9	81
Millwood, Wash.	g14	86
Milmont Park, Pa.	*G11	81
Milo, Maine	C4	64
Milpitas, Calif.	*D3	50
Milroy, Ind.	F7	59
Milroy, Pa.	E6	81
Milstead, Ga.	C3, h8	55
Milton, N.S., Can.	E5	43
Milton, Ont., Can.	D5	41
Milton, Del.	C7	53
Milton, Fla.	u14	54
Milton, Ind.	E7	59
Milton, Iowa	D5	60
Milton, Mass.	B5, g11	65
Milton, N.H.	D5	73
Milton, N.J.	A3	74
Milton, N.Y.	D7	75
Milton, Pa.	D8	81
Milton, Wash.	f11	86
Milton, W. Va.	C2	87
Milton, Wis.	F5	88
Milton-Freewater, Oreg.	B8	80
Milton Junction, Wis.	F5	88
Miltonvale, Kans.	C6	61
Milverton, Ont., Can.	D4	41
Milwaukee, Wis.	E6, m12	88
Milwaukee, co., Wis.	E6	88
Milwaukie, Oreg.	B4, h12	80
Mims, Fla.	D6	54
Minamata, Jap.	J5	18
Minas, Ur.	E1	30
Minas de Riotinto, Sp.	D2	8
Minas Gerais, state, Braz.	B4	30
Minatare, Nebr.	C2	71
Minatitlán, Mex.	D6	34
Minato, Jap.	m19	18
Minbu, Bur.	D9	20
Minco, Okla.	B4	79
Mindanao, isl., Phil.	D6	19
Minden, Ont., Can.	C6	41
Minden, Ger., Fed. Rep. of	B4	6
Minden, La.	B2	63
Minden, Nebr.	D7	71
Minden, W. Va.	D3, n13	87
Mindoro, isl., Phil.	C6	19
Minechoag, mtn.,Mass.	B3	65
Minehead, Eng.	E5	4
Mine Hill, N.J.	*B3	74
Mineola, N.Y.	E7, n15	75
Mineola, Tex.	C5	84
Miner, Mo.	E8	69
Miner, co., S. Dak.	G8	77
Mineral, co., Colo.	D4	51
Mineral, co., Mont.	C1	70
Mineral, co., Nev.	B2	72
Mineral, co., W. Va.	B6	87
Mineral City, Ohio	B4	78
Mineral del Oro, Mex.	n13	34
Mineral Point, Wis.	F3	88
Mineral Ridge, Ohio	*A5	78
Mineral Wells, Tex.	C3	84
Minersville, Pa.	E9	81
Minerva, Ohio	B4	78
Minerva Park, Ohio	*C3	78
Minervino Murge, It.	D6	9
Minetto, N.Y.	B4	75
Mineville, N.Y.	A7	75
Mingenew, Austl.	E2	25
Mingo, co., W. Va.	D2	87
Mingo Junction, Ohio	B5	78
Mingshul, China	C2	18
Minho, prov., Port.	*B1	8
Minidoka, co., Idaho	G5	57
Minier, Ill.	C4	58
Minitonas, Man., Can.	C1	40
Minna, Nig.	G6	22
Minneapolis, Kans.	C6	61
Minneapolis, Minn.	F5, n12	67
Minnedosa, Man., Can.	D2	40
Minnehaha, Wash.	*D3	86
Minnehaha, co., S. Dak.	G9	77
Minneola, Kans.	E3	61
Minneota, Minn.	F3	67
Minnesota, state, U.S.		67
Minnesota, riv., Minn.	F3	67
Minnesota Lake, Minn.	G5	67
Minnetonka, Minn.	*F5	67
Minnetrista, Minn.	*E5	67
Mino, Jap.	n15	18
Minoa, N.Y.	*B4	75
Minocqua, Wis.	C4	88
Minokamo, Jap.	n15	18
Minonk, Ill.	C4	58
Minot, N. Dak.	B4	77
Minquadale, Del.	*A6	53
Minsk, Sov. Un.	E6	12
Minster, Ohio	B1	78
Minturno, It.	D4	9
Minūf, Eg.	*G8	14
Minusinsk, Sov. Un.	D12	13
Miraflores, Col.	C3	32
Miraflores, Peru	A3	31
Miraj, Indai	E5	20
Mira Loma, Calif.	*E5	50
Miramar, Fla.	s13	54
Miranda, state, Ven.	A4	32
Miranda de Ebro, Sp.	A4	8
Mirassol, Braz.	C3	30
Mirebalais, Hai.	E7	35
Mirecourt, Fr.	C7	5
Mirgorod, Sov. Un.	G9	12
Miri, Mala.	E4	19
Mirpur-Khas, Pak.	*C4	20
Mirror, Alta., Can.	C4	38
Mirzāpur, India	C7	20
Misakubo, Jap.	n16	18
Misamis Occidental, prov., Phil.	*D6	19
Misamis Oriental, prov., Phil.	*D7	19
Misantla, Mex.	D5, h15	34
Misenheimer, N.C.	B2	76
Mishan, China	D6	18
Mishawaka, Ind.	A5	59
Mishicot, Wis.	D6, h10	88
Mishima, Jap.	I9, h17	18
Misiones, dept., Par.	E4	19
Misiones, prov., Arg.	E4	29
Miskolc, Hung.	A5	10
Misrātah, Libya	B8	22
Missaukee, co., Mich.	D5	66
Mission, Kans.	*D9	61
Mission, Tex.	F3	84
Mission City, B.C., Can.	E6, f13	37
Mission Hills, Kans.	B9	61
Missisquoi, co., Que., Can.	D4	42
Mississauga, Ont., Can.	D5, m14	41
Mississippi, co., Ark.	B5	49
Mississippi, co., Mo.	E8	69
Mississippi, state, U.S.		68
Mississippi, riv., U.S.	D8	45
Mississippi City, Miss.	E4, f7	68
Missoula, Mont.	D2	70
Missoula, co., Mont.	D2	70
Missoula Southwest, Mont.	*D2	70
Missouri, state, U.S.		69
Missouri, riv., U.S.	B7	45
Missouri Valley, Iowa	C2	60
Mistelbach an der Zaya, Aus.	D8	6
Misti, vol., Peru	E3	31
Mistretta, It.	F5	9
Mitaka, Jap.	*I9	18
Mitchell, Austl.	E8	25
Mitchell, Ont., Can.	D3	41
Mitchell, Ind.	G5	59
Mitchell, Nebr.	C2	71
Mitchell, S. Dak.	G7	77
Mitchell, co., Ga.	E2	55
Mitchell, co., Iowa	A5	60
Mitchell, co., Kans.	C5	61
Mitchell, co., N.C.	e10	76
Mitchell, co., Tex.	C2	84
Mitchell, mtn., N.C.	f10	76
Mitchellsberg, Ky.	C5	62
Mitchellville, Iowa	C4	60
Mitilíni (Mytilene), Grc.	C6	14
Mito, Jap.	H10, m19	18
Mittagong, Austl.	*F9	25
Mitterteich, Ger., Fed. Rep. of	C6	6
Mittweida, Ger. Dem. Rep.	C6	6
Mitú, Col.	C3	32
Miura, Jap.	n18	18
Mixquiahuala, Mex.	m13	34
Miyagi, pref., Jap.	*G10	18
Miyako, Jap.	G10	18
Miyakonojo, Jap.	K5	18
Miyazaki, Jap.	K5	18
Miyazaki, pref., Jap.	*K5	18
Miyazu, Jap.	n14	18
Mizil, Rom	C8	10
Mizoram, ter., India	D9	20
Mjölby, Swe	H6	11
Mlada Boleslav, Czech.	C3, n18	7
Mława, Pol.	B6	7
Moab, Utah	B7	72
Mobara, Jap.	n19	18
Moberly, Mo.	B5	69
Mobile, Ala.	E1	46
Mobile, co., Ala.	E1	46
Mobridge, S. Dak.	E5	77
Moca, mun., P.R.	E8	35
Mocanaqua, Pa.	D9	81
Mochudi, Bots.	E5	24
Mocksville, N.C.	B2	76
Moclips, Wash.	B1	86
Mocoa, Col.	C2	32
Mococa, Braz.	C3, k8	30
Mocorito, Mex.	B3	34
Moctezuma, Mex.	B3	34
Modena, It.	B3	9
Modesto, Calif.	D3	50
Modica, It.	F5	9
Modjokerto, Indon.	*G4	19
Modlin, Pol.	B6, k13	7
Mödling, Aus.	D8	6
Modoc, co.,Calif.	B3	50
Modřany, Czech.	o17	7
Moeo-Yallourn, Austl.	I6	26
Moffat, co., Colo.	A2	51
Mogadishu, Som.	H7	23
Mogadore, Ohio	A4	78
Mogaung, Bur.	C10	20
Mogi das Cruzes, Braz.	C3, m8	30
Mogilev, Sov. Un.	E8	12
Mogilev-Podolskiy, Sov. Un.	G6	12
Mogilno, Pol.	B4	7
Mogi Mirim, Braz.	C3, m8	30
Mogocha, Sov. Un.	D14	13
Mogok, Bur.	D10	20
Mohács, Hung.	C4	10
Mohall, N. Dak.	B4	77
Mohammedia, Mor.	B3	22
Mohave, co., Ariz.	B1	48
Mohawk, Mich.	A2	66
Mohawk, N.Y.	C5	75
Mohnton, Pa.	F10	81
Moinesti, Rom.	B8	10
Moissac, Fr.	E4	5
Mojave, Calif.	E4	50
Mokleumne Hill, Calif.	C3	50
Mokena, Ill.	k9	58
Mokpo, Kor.	I3	18
Mol, Yugo	C5	10
Mola de Bari, It.	D6	9
Molalla, Oreg.	B4	80
Mold, Wales	*D5	4
Moldavia, reg., Rom.	B8	10
Moldavia (S.S.R.), rep., Sov. Un.	H7	12
Molepolole, Bots.	E5	24
Molfetta, It.	D6	9
Molina, Chile	B2	28
Molina de Segura, Sp.	C5	8
Moline, Ill.	B3	58
Moline, Kans.	E7	61
Moline, Mich.	F5	66
Moline Acres, Mo.	*C7	69
Molino, Fla.	u14	54
Molino de Rosas, Mex.	h9	34
Moliterno, It.	D5	9
Mollendo, Peru	E3	31
Mölndal, Swe	I5	11
Molodechno, Sov. Un.	D6	12
Molotovsk, Sov. Un.	E18	11
Molotovskoye, Sov. Un.	I13	12
Molus, Ky.	D6	62
Mombasa, Ken.	I5	23
Mombetsu, Jap.	D11	18
Momence, Ill.	B6	58
Momostenango, Guat.	*D6	34
Mompós, Col.	B3	32
Monaca, Pa.	E1	81
Monaco, country, Eur.	F7	5
Monagas, state, Ven.	B5	32
Monaghan, S.C.	B5	82
Monaghan, co., Ire.	*C3	4
Monahans, Tex.	D1	84
Monarch, S.C.	B4	82
Monarch, mtn., B.C., Can.	D5, n17	37
Monashee, mts., B.C., Can.	D8	37
Monastir, Tur.	A7	22
Monchegorsk, Sov. Un.	D15	11
Mönchengladbach, Ger., Fed. Rep. of	C3	6
Moncks Corner, S.C.	E7	82
Monclova, Mex.	B4	34
Moncton, N.B., Can.	C5	43
Mondoñedo, Sp.	A2	8
Mondoví, It.	B1	9
Mondovi, Wis.	D2	88
Monessen, Pa.	F2	81
Monett, Mo.	E4	69
Monette, Ark.	B4	49
Monfalcone, It.	B4	9
Monforte de Lemos, Sp.	A2	8
Monfort Heights, Ohio	*C1	78
Monghyr, India	C8	20
Mong Mit, Bur.	D10	20
Mongolia, country, Asia	B4	17
Moniquirá, Col.	B3	32
Moniteau, co., Mo.	C5	69
Monmouth, Ill.	C3	58
Monmouth, Oreg.	C3, k11	80
Monmouth, co., N.J.	C4	74
Monmouth, co., Wales	*E5	4
Monmouth, mtn., B.C., Can.	D6	37
Monmouth Beach, N.J.	C5	74
Monmouth Junction, N.J.	C3	74
Mono, co., Calif.	D4	50
Monon, Ind.	C4	59
Monona, Iowa	A6	60
Monona, Wis.	E4	88
Monona, co., Iowa	B1	60
Monongah, W. Va.	B4, k10	87
Monongahela, Pa.	F2	81
Monongahela, riv., Pa.	G2	81
Monongalia, co., W. Va.	B4	87
Monopoli, It.	D6	9
Monor, Hung.	B4	10
Monóvar, Sp.	C5	8
Monponsett, Mass.	B9	65
Monreale, It.	E4	9
Monroe, Conn.	D3	52
Monroe, Ga.	C3	55
Monroe, Iowa	C4	60
Monroe, La.	B3	63
Monroe, Mich.	G7	66
Monroe, N.Y.	D6, m14	75
Monroe, N.C.	C2	76
Monroe, Ohio	*C1	78
Monroe, Utah	B5	72
Monroe, Va.	C3	85
Monroe, Wash.	B4	86
Monroe, Wis.	F4	88
Monroe, co., Ala.	D2	46
Monroe, co., Ark.	C4	49
Monroe, co., Fla.	G5	54
Monroe, co., Ga.	D3	55
Monroe, co., Ill.	E3	58
Monroe, co., Ind.	F4	59
Monroe, co., Iowa	D5	60
Monroe, co., Ky.	D4	62
Monroe, co., Mich.	G7	66
Monroe, co., Miss.	B5	68
Monroe, co., Mo.	B5	69
Monroe, co., N.Y.	B3	75
Monroe, co., Ohio	C4	78
Monroe, co., Pa.	D11	81
Monroe, co., Tenn.	D9	83
Monroe, co., W. Va.	D4	87
Monroe, co., Wis.	E3	88
Monroe City, Mo.	B6	69
Monroeville, Ala.	D2	46
Monroeville, Ind.	C8	59
Monroeville, Ohio	A3	78
Monroeville, Pa.	*E1	81
Monrovia, Calif.	m13	50
Monrovia, Lib.	G2	22
Mons, Bel.	B5	5
Monson, Maine	C3	64
Monson, Mass.	B2	65
Montague, Calif.	B2	50
Montague, P.E.I., Can.	C7	43
Montague, Mass.	A2	65
Montague, Mich.	E4	66
Montague, co., Tex.	C4	84
Montague City, Mass.	A2	65
Mont Alto, Pa.	G6	81
Montalvo, Calif.	*E4	50
Montana, state, U.S.		70
Montánchez, Sp.	C2	8
Montargis, Fr.	D5	5
Montauban, Que., Can.	C5	42
Montauban, Fr.	E4	5
Montauk, N.Y.	m17	75

Monta Vista, Calif. *B3 50
Monta Vista, Wash. *B33 86
Montbeliard, Fr. D7 5
Mont Belvieu, Tex. E5, r15 84
Montbrison, Fr. E6 5
Montcalm, co., Que., Can. C3 42
Montcalm, co., Mich. E5 66
Mont-Carmel, Que., Can. B8 42
Montceau-les-Mines, Fr. D6 5
Montchanin -les-Mines, Fr. D6 5
Montclair (Monte Vista), Calif. .. m13 50
Montclair, N.J. B4 74
Mont Clare, Pa. o19 81
Montcoal, W. Va. D3, n12 87
Mont-De-Marsan, Fr. F3 5
Montebello, Calif. m12 50
Montebello, Que., Can. D3 42
Monte Caseros, Arg. A5 28
Montecelio, It. g9 9
Montecristi, Dom. Rep. E8 35
Montefrio, Sp. D3 8
Montego Bay, Jam. E5 35
Montegut, La. E5 63
Monteith, mtn., B.C., Can. B6 38
Montélimar, Fr. E6 5
Montellano, Sp. D3 8
Montello, Wis. E4 88
Montemorelos, Mex. B5 34
Montemor-o-Novo, Port. C1 8
Montenegro, Braz. D2 30
Montenegro (Crna Gora),
 rep., Yugo. *D4 10
Monte Plata, Dom. Rep. E9 35
Montepulciano, It. C3 9
Montereau, Fr. C5 5
Monterey, Calif. D3 50
Monterey, Ohio *C1 78
Monterey, Tenn. C8 83
Monterey, co., Calif. D3 50
Monterey Park, Calif. m12 50
Monteria, Col. B2 32
Monteros, Arg. E2 29
Monterotondo, It. g9 9
Monterrey, Mex. B4 34
Montesano, Wash. C2 86
Monte Sant' Angelo, It. D5 9
Montes Claros, Braz. B4 30
Monte Sereno, Calif. *D3 50
Montevallo, Ala. B3 46
Montevarchi, It. C3 9
Montevideo, Minn. F3 67
Montevideo, Ur. E1 30
Montevideo, dept., Ur. *E1 30
Monte Vista, Colo. D4 51
Montezuma, Ga. D2 55
Montezuma, Ind. E3 59
Montezuma, Iowa C5 60
Montezuma, co., Colo. D2 51
Montfort, Wis. F3 88
Montgomery, Ala. C3 46
Montgomery, Ill. B5, k8 58
Montgomery, La. C3 63
Montgomery, Minn. F5 67
Montgomery, N.Y. D6 75
Montgomery, Ohio *C1 78
Montgomery, Pa. D8 81
Montgomery, W. Va. C3, m13 87
Montgomery, co., Ala. C3 46
Montgomery, co., Ark. C2 49
Montgomery, co., Ga. D4 55
Montgomery, co., Ill. D4 58
Montgomery, co., Ind. D4 59
Montgomery, co., Iowa C2 60
Montgomery, co., Kans. E8 61
Montgomery, co., Ky. B6 62
Montgomery, co., Md. B3 53
Montgomery, co., Miss. B4 68
Montgomery, co., Mo. C6 69
Montgomery, co., N.Y. C6 75
Montgomery, co., N.C. B3 76
Montgomery, co., Ohio C1 78
Montgomery, co., Pa. F11 81
Montgomery, co., Tenn. A4 83
Montgomery, co., Tex. D5 84
Montgomery, co., Va. C2 85
Montgomery, co., Wales *D5 4
Montgomery City, Mo. C6 69
Monticello, Ark. D4 49
Monticello, Fla. B3 54
Monticello, Ga. C3 55
Monticello, Ill. C5 58
Monticello, Ind. C4 59
Monticello, Iowa B6 60
Monticello, Ky. D5 62
Monticello, Maine B5 64
Monticello, Minn. E5 67
Monticello, Miss. D3 68
Monticello, N.Y. D6 75
Monticello, Utah C7 72
Monticello, Wis. F4 88
Montigny -lès-Metz, Fr. C7 5
Montijo, Port. C1, f10 8
Montijo, Sp. C2 8

Montilla, Sp. D3 8
Montivilliers, Fr. C4 5
Mont-Joli, Que., Can. G20 36
Mont-Laurier, Que., Can. C2 42
Montluçon, Fr. D5 5
Montmagny, Que., Can. C7 42
Montmagny, co., Que., Can. C7 42
Montmartre, Sask., Can. G4 39
Montmorenci, S.C. D4 82
Montmorency, Fr. g10 5
Montmorency, co., Mich. C6 66
Montmorency No. 1, co.,
 Que., Can. B6 42
Montmorency No. 2, co.,
 Que., Can. C7 42
Montmorillon, Fr. D4 5
Montoro, Sp. C3 8
Montour, co., Pa. D8 81
Montour Falls, N.Y. C4 75
Montoursville, Pa. D8 81
Montpelier, Idaho G7 57
Montpelier, Ind. C7 59
Montpelier, Ohio A1 78
Montpelier, Vt. C2 73
Montpellier, Fr. F5 5
Montréal, Que., Can. D4, q19 42
Montreal, Wis. *B3 88
Montréal West, Que., Can. *D4 42
Montreuil-sous-Bois, Fr. C5 5
Montreux, Switz. E3 6
Mont-Rolland, Que., Can. D3 42
Montrose, Ala. E2 46
Montrose, Calif. *E4 50
Montrose, B.C., Can. E9 37
Montrose, Colo. C3 51
Montrose, Iowa D6 60
Montrose, Mich. E7 66
Montrose, Pa. *F10 81
Montrose, Pa. C10 81
Montrose, Scot. B5 4
Montrose, co., Colo. C2 51
Montrose Hill, Pa. *E1 81
Montrouge, Fr. g10 5
Mont-Royal, Que., Can. p19 42
Montserrat, Br. dep., N.A. H13 35
Montvale, N.J. g8 74
Montville, Conn. D8 52
Montville, N.J. B4 74
Monument, peak, Idaho G4 57
Monument Beach, Mass. C6 65
Monywa, Bur. D10 20
Monza, It. B2 9
Monzón, Peru C2 31
Monzón, Peru C2 31
Moodus, Conn. D7 52
Moody, Tex. D4 84
Moody, co., S. Dak. F9 77
Mooers, N.Y. f11 75
Moonachie, N.J. *B4 74
Moon Crest, Pa. *E1 81
Moon Run, Pa. k13 81
Moonta, Austl. F6 25
Moora, Austl. F2 25
Moorcraft, Wyo. B8 89
Moore, Okla. B4 79
Moore, co., N.C. B3 76
Moore, co., Tenn. B5 83
Moore, co., Tex. B2 84
Moorefield, W. Va. B6 87
Moore Haven, Fla. F5 54
Mooreland, Okla. A2 79
Moorestown, N.J. D3 74
Mooresville, Ind. E5 59
Mooresville, N.C. B2 76
Moorhead, Minn. D2 67
Moorhead, Miss. B3 83
Mooringsport, La. B2 63
Moorpark, Calif. E4 50
Moose, mtn., Sask., Can. H4 39
Mooseheart, Ill. B5, k8 58
Moose Jaw, Sask., Can. G3, n7 39
Moose Lake, Minn. D6 67
Moosic, Pa. m18 81
Moosic, mts., Pa. m18 81
Moosomin, Sask., Can. G5 39
Moosonee, Ont., Can. o19 41
Moosup, Conn. C9 52
Mopti, Mali F4 22
Moquegua, Peru E3 31
Moquegua, dept., Peru E3 31
Mor, Hung. B4 10
Mora, Minn. E5 67
Mora, N. Mex. B6 48
Mora, Sp. C4 8
Mora Swe. G6 11
Mora, co., N. Mex. A6 48
Morada, Calif. *D3 50
Morādābād, India C6 20
Moraine, Ohio *C1 78
Moramanga, Mad. D9 24
Moran, Kans. E8 61
Morant Bay, Jam. F5 35
Moratalla, Sp. C5 8
Moratuwa, Sri Lanka *G6 20

Moravia, Iowa D5 60
Moravia, N.Y. C4 75
Moravia (Morava), reg., Czech. .. D4 7
Moray, co., Scot. *B5 4
Morbihan, dept., Fr. *D2 5
Morden, Man., Can. E2 40
Moreauville, La. C4 63
Moree, Austl. E8 25
Morehead, Ky. B6 62
Morehead City, N.C. C6 76
Morehouse, par., La. B4 63
Morehouse, Mo. E8 69
Moreland Hills, Ohio *A4 78
Morelia, Mex. D4, n13 34
Morelos, state, Mex. D5, n14 34
Morenci, Ariz. C4 48
Morenci, Mich. G6 66
Moreno, Arg. g7 28
Morón, Arg. g7 28
Morón, Cuba C4 35
Morona-Santiago, prov., Ec. B3 31
Morondava, Mad. E8 24
Moroni, Utah B6 72
Morón de la Frontera, Sp. ...... C4 8 [note: appears as Morozovsk below? see image]
Morón, Cuba
Morozovsk, Sov. Un. G13 12
Morrill, Nebr. C2 71
Morrill, co., Nebr. C2 71
Morrilton, Ark. B3 49
Morris, Ala. B3 46
Morris, Man., Can. E3 40
Morris, Ill. B5 58
Morris, Minn. E3 67
Morris, N.Y. C5 75
Morris, Okla. B6 79
Morris, co., Kans. D7 61
Morris, co., N.J. B3 74
Morris, co., Tex. C5 84
Morris, mtn., N.Y. A6 75
Morrisburg, Ont., Can. C9 41
Morrisdale, Pa. E5 81
Morrison, Ill. B4 58
Morrison, Tenn. D8 83
Morrison, co., Minn. D4 67
Morrisonville, Ill. D4 58
Morris Plains, N.J. B4 74
Morristown, Ind. E6 59
Morristown, Minn. F5 67
Morristown, N.J. B4 74
Morristown, N.Y. f9 75
Morristown, Tenn. C10 83
Morrisville, N.Y. C5 75
Morrisville, Vt. B2 73
Morro Bay, Calif. E3 50
Morro do Chapéu, Braz. E6 27
Morropón, Peru C2 31
Morrow, Ohio *C1 78
Morrow, co., Ohio B3 78
Morrow, co., Oreg. B7 80
Morse, La. D3 63
Morshansk, Sov. Un. E13 12
Mortara, It. B2 9
Morteros, Arg. A4 28
Morton, Ill. C4 58
Morton, Minn. F4 67
Morton, Miss. C4 68
Morton, Pa. *G11 81
Morton, Tex. C1 84
Morton, Wash. C3 86

Morton, co., Kans. E2 61
Morton, co., N. Dak. D4 77
Morton Grove, Ill. h9 58
Mortons Gap, Ky. C2 62
Moruya, Austl. G8 26
Morven, N.C. C2 76
Morwell, Austl. G8, n15 25
Moscow, Idaho C2 57
Moscow, Pa. m18 81
Moscow (Moskva), Sov. Un. .. D11, n17 12
Moselle, dept., Fr. *C7 5
Moses Lake, Wash. B6 86
Moshi, Tan. I5 23
Mosinee, Wis. D4 88
Mosjoen, Nor. E5 11
Moskva, see Moscow, Sov. Un.
Mosonmagyaróvár, Hung. B3 10
Mosquera, Col. C2 32
Moss, Nor. H4, p28 11
Mossbank, Sask., Can. H3 39
Mosselbaai, S. Afr. G4 24
Mossman, Austl. C8 25
Mossoro, Braz. *D7 27
Moss Point, Miss. E5, f8 68
Moss Vale, Austl. *F9 25
Most, Czech. C2 7
Mostar, Yugo. D3 10
Mosul (Al Mawsil), Iraq D14 14
Motala, Swe. H6 11
Motherwell & Wishaw, Scot. C5 4
Motley, co., Tex. B2 84
Motomachi, Jap. o18 18
Motril, Sp. D4 8
Mott, N. Dak. D3 77
Motul de Felipe Carrillo
 Puerto, Mex. C7 34
Motupe, Peru C2 31
Mouaskar, Alg. A5 22
Moulins, Fr. D5 5
Moulmein, Bur. E10 20
Moulton, Ala. A2 46
Moulton, Iowa D5 60
Moultrie, Ga. E3 55
Moultrie, co., Ill. D5 58
Mound, Minn. n11 67
Mound Bayou, Miss. B3 68
Mound City, Ill. F4 58
Mound City, Kans. D9 61
Mound City, Mo. A2 69
Moundridge, Kans. D6 61
Mounds, Ill. F4 58
Mounds, Okla. B5 79
Mounds View, Minn. *F5 67
Moundsville, W. Va. B4, g8 87
Moundville, Ala. C2 46
Mountain, prov., Phil. *B6 19
Mountainair, N. Mex. B5 48
Mountain Brook, Ala. g7 46
Mountain City, Tenn. C12 83
Mountain Dale, N.Y. D6 75
Mountain Grove, Mo. D5 69
Mountain Home, Ark. A3 49
Mountain Home, Idaho F3 57
Mountain Iron, Minn. C6 67
Mountain Lake, Minn. G4 67
Mountain Lake Park, Mo. m12 53
Mountain Lakes, N.J. B4 74
Mountain Pine, Ark. C2, f7 49
Mountainside, N.J. *B4 74
Mountain View, Ark. B3 49
Mountain View, Calif. k8 50
Mountainview, Haw. D6 56
Mountain View, Idaho *F2 57
Mountain View, Mo. D6 69
Mountain View, Okla. B3 79
Mountain View, Wyo. E3 89
Mount Airy, Md. B3 53
Mount Airy, N.C. A2 76
Mount Angel, Oreg. B4, h12 80
Mount Arlington, N.J. B3 74
Mount Ayr, Iowa D3 60
Mount Berry, Ga. B1 55
Mount Bethel, N.J. B3 74
Mount Brydges, Ont., Can. E3 41
Mount Carmel, Newf., Can. E5 44
Mount Carmel, Ill. E6 58
Mount Carmel, Ohio o13 78
Mount Carmel, Pa. E9 81
Mount Carroll, Ill. A4 58
Mount Clare, W. Va. B4 87
Mount Clemens, Mich. F8, o16 66
Mount Dora, Fla. D5 54
Mount Edgecumbe, Alsk. m22 47
Mount Ephraim, N.J. *D2 74
Mount Forest, Ont., Can. D4 41
Mount Gambier, Austl. G7 25
Mount Gilead, N.C. B3 76
Mount Gilead, Ohio B3 78
Mount Healthy, Ohio o12 78
Mount Hermon, Mass. A3 65
Mount Holly, N.J. C3 74
Mount Holly, N.C. B1 76
Mount Holly Springs, Pa. F7 81

Mount Hope, Ont., Can. D5 42
Mount Hope, Kans. E6, g11 61
Mount Hope, N.J. B3 74
Mount Hope, W. Va. D3, n13 87
Mount Horeb, Wis. E4 88
Mount Houston, Tex. *E5 84
Mount Isa, Austl. D6 25
Mount Jackson, Va. B4 85
Mount Jewett, Pa. C4 81
Mount Joy, Pa. F9 81
Mount Kisco, N.Y. D7, m15 75
Mountlake Terrace, Wash. *B3 86
Mount Lebanon, Pa. F1 81
Mount Magnet, Austl. E2 25
Mount Morgan, Austl. D9 25
Mount Moriah, Newf., Can. *D2 44
Mount Morris, Ill. A4 58
Mount Morris, Mich. E7 66
Mount Morris, N.Y. C3 75
Mount Olive, Ala. B3, f7 46
Mount Olive, Ill. D4 58
Mount Olive, N.C. B4 76
Mount Oliver, Pa. k14 81
Mount Orab, Ohio C2 78
Mount Pearl Park, Newf., Can. f9 44
Mount Penn, Pa. *F10 81
Mount Pleasant, Iowa D6 60
Mount Pleasant, Mich. E6 66
Mount Pleasant, N.C. B2 76
Mount Pleasant, Pa. F2 81
Mount Pleasant, S.C. F8, k12 82
Mount Pleasant, Tenn. B4 83
Mount Pleasant, Tex. C5 84
Mount Pleasant, Utah B6 72
Mount Pocono, Pa. D11 81
Mount Prospect, Ill. A6, h9 58
Mount Pulaski, Ill. C4 58
Mountrail, co., N. Dak. B3 77
Mount Rainier, Md. f9 53
Mount Royal, N.J. D2 74
Mount Savage, Md. k13 53
Mount Shasta, Calif. B2 50
Mount Sterling, Ill D3 58
Mount Sterling, Ky. B6 62
Mount Sterling, Ohio C2 78
Mount Union, Pa. F6 81
Mount Vernon, Ala. D1 46
Mount Vernon, Ga. D4 55
Mount Vernon, Ill. E5 58
Mount Vernon, Ind. I2 59
Mount Vernon, Iowa C6 60
Mount Vernon, Ky. C5 62
Mount Vernon, Md. D6 53
Mount Vernon, Mo. D4 69
Mount Vernon, N.Y. *C2 75
Mount Vernon, N.Y. h13 75
Mount Vernon, Ohio B3 78
Mount Vernon, Tex. C5 84
Mount Vernon, Wash. A3 86
Mount Victory, Ohio B2 78

Mountville, Pa. *G9 81
Mount Washington, Ky. B4, g11 62
Mount Wolf, Pa. F8 81
Mount Zion, Ill. D5 58
Moura, Port. C2 8
Mourne, mts., N. Ire. C3 4
Mouscron, Bel. B5 5
Mousie, Ky. C7 62
Moville, Iowa B1 60
Moweaqua, Ill. D4 58
Mower, co., Minn. G6 67
Moyeuvre -Grande, Fr. C7 5
Moyobamba, Peru C2 31
Mozambique, country, Afr. D7 24
Mozhaysk, Sov. Un. D11 12
Mozyr, Sov. Un. E7 12
Mtsensk, Sov. Un. E11 12
Muang Hot, Thai. *B1 19
Muang Nan, Thai. *B2 19
Muar (Bandar Maharani), Mala. ... *E2 19
Muchkap, Sov. Un. F14 12
Mucuri, Braz. E7 27
Mudanjiang, China C10 17
Mudanya, Tur. *B7 14
Mudgee, Austl. F7 26
Muenster, Tex. C4 84
Mufulira, Zambia C5 24
Mugía, Sp. A1 8
Muğla, Tur. D7 14
Mühldorf, Ger., Fed. Rep. of D6 6
Muhlenberg, co., Ky. C2 62
Muhlenberg Park, Pa. *F9 81
Mühlhausen, Ger. Dem. Rep. C5 6
Muir, Mich. E6 66
Mukachevo, Sov. Un. G4 12
Mukden, see Shenyang, China
Mukilteo, Wash. B3 86
Mukwonago, Wis. F5, n11 88
Mula, Sp. C5 8
Mulberry, Ark. B1 49
Mulberry, Fla. E5 54
Mulberry, Ind. D4 59
Mulberry, Kans. E9 61
Mulchén, Chile B2 28
Muldraugh, Ky. C4 26
Muldrow, Okla. B7 79
Mulege, Mex. B2 34
Muleshoe, Tex. B1 84
Mulga, Ala. B3, f7 46
Mulgrave, N.S., Can. D8 43
Mulhacén, mtn., Sp. D4 8
Mülheim an der Ruhr, Ger.
  Fed. Rep. of C3 6
Mulhouse, Fr. D7 5
Muling, China D5 18
Mullan, Idaho B3 57
Mullens, W. Va. D3 87
Mullewa, Austl. E2 25
Mullica Hill, N.J. D2 74
Mullingar, Ire. D3 4
Mullins, S.C. C9 82

Mūltan, Pak. B5 20
Multnomah, co., Oreg. B4 80
Mulvane, Kans. E6 61
Muna, Mex. C7 34
München, see Munich, Ger.,
  Fed. Rep. of
Munchon, Kor. G3 18
Muncie, Ind. D7 59
Muncy, Pa. D8 81
Mundare, Alta., Can. C4 38
Munday, Tex. C3 84
Mundelein, Ill. A5, h9 58
Münden, Ger., Fed. Rep. of C4 6
Munford, Tenn. B2 83
Munfordville, Ky. C4 62
Mungindi, Austl. E8 25
Munhall, Pa. k14 81
Munich (München), Ger.,
  Fed. Rep. of C5 6
Munising, Mich. B4 66
Munroe Falls, Ohio *A4 78
Munsan, Kor. H3 18
Munsey Park, N.Y. *E7 75
Munster, Fr. C7 5
Munster, Ind. A2 59
Münster in Westfalen, Ger.
  Fed. Rep. of C3 6
Munster, prov., Ire. *D2 4
Muntenia, prov., Rom. *C8 10
Muntenia, reg., Rom. C7 10
Muntok, Indon. F3 19
Muong Hou Nua, Laos, ... *D11 20
Muong Sing, Laos D11 20
Murakami, Jap. G9 18
Murcia, Sp. C5 8
Murcia, reg., Sp. C5 8
Murfreesboro, Ark. C2 49
Murfreesboro, N.C. A5 76
Murfreesboro, Tenn. B5 83
Murgon, Austl. E9 25
Muriae, Braz. C4 30
Murmansk, Sov. Un. C15 11
Murom, Sov. Un. D13 11
Muroran, Jap. C10 17
Muroto, Jap. J7 18
Murphy, Mo. g13 69
Murphy, N.C. F8 76
Murphysboro, Ill. F4 58
Murray, Iowa C4 60
Murray, Ky. f9 62
Murray, Utah A6, C2 72
Murray, co., Ga. B2 55
Murray, co., Minn. F3 67
Murray, co., Okla. C4 79
Murray, riv., Austl. G7 25
Murray Bridge, Austl. G6 25
Murray City, Ohio C3 78
Murrells Inlet, S.C. D9 82
Murrysville, Pa. k15 81
Murud, India E5 20
Murwāra, India D7 20

Murwillumbah, Austl. D9 26
Mürzzuschlag, Aus. E7 6
Mus, Tur. C13 14
Musala, peak, Bul. D6 10
Musan, Kor. E4 18
Musashino, Jap. *I9 18
Muscat, Om. D2 20
Muscat & Oman, see Oman,
  country, Asia.
Muscatine, Iowa C6 60
Muscatine, co., Iowa C6 60
Muscle Shoals, Ala. A2 46
Musclow, mtn., B.C., Can. C4 37
Muscoda, Wis. E3 88
Musconetcong, mtn., N.J. B2 74
Muse, Pa. F1 81
Musgravetown, Newf., Can. D5 44
Mushketovo, Sov. Un. r20 12
Muskego, Wis. F5, n11 88
Muskegon, Mich. E4 66
Muskegon, co., Mich. E4 66
Muskegon Heights, Mich. E4 66
Muskigum, co., Ohio B3 78
Muskö, Swe. u36 11
Muskogee, Okla. B6 79
Muskogee, co., Okla. B6 79
Muskoka, dist., Ont., Can. B5 41
Musquash, mtn., Maine C5 64
Musquodoboit Harbour, N.S., Can. .. E6 43
Musselburgh, Scot. C5 4
Musselshell, co., Mont. D8 70
Mustafakemalpasa, Tur. B7 14
Muswellbrook, Austl. F9 25
Mutare, Zimb. D6 24
Mutsu, Jap. F10 18
Mutton, mts., Oreg. C5 80
Muttontown, N.Y. *E7 75
Muzaffarnagar, India *C6 20
Muzaffarpur, India C8 20
Muzambinho, Braz. k8 30
Muztag, mtn., Braz. A7 20
Muztag, mtn., China A8 20
Mvuma, Zimb. D6 24
Mwanza, Tan. I4 23
Myers, S.C. k12 02
Myerstown, Pa. F9 81
Myingyan, Bur. D10 20
Myitkyina, Bur. C10 20
Myjava, Czech. D4 7
Myrtle Beach, S.C. D10 82
Myrtle Creek, Oreg. D3 80
Myrtle Grove, Fla. u14 54
Myrtle Point, Oreg. D2 80
Mysen, Nor. p29 11
Myślenice, Pol. D5 7
Mysłowice, Pol. g10 7
Mysore, India F6 20
Mysore, see Karnataka, state, India
Mystic, Conn. D9 52
Mystic, Iowa D5 60
My Tho, Viet. C3 19
Mytishchi, Sov. Un. n17 12

N

Naalehu, Haw. D6 56
Nabadwip, India *D8 20
Nabeul, Tun. A7 22
Nabnasset, Mass. A5 65
Nābulus, Jordan B3, g5 15
Naches, Wash. C5 86
Náchod, Czech. C4 7
Nacogdoches, Tex. D5 84
Nacogdoches, co., Tex. D5 84
Nacozari de García, Mex. A3 34
Nadiad, India *D5 20
Nădlac, Rom. B5 10
Nadvornaya, Sov. Un. G5 12
Naesong, Kor. H4 18
Naestved, Den. J4 11
Naga, Phil. C6 19
Nagaland, state, India *C9 20
Nagano, Jap. H9 18
Nagano, pref., Jap. *H9 18
Nagaoka, Jap. H9 18
Nagappattinam, India F6 20
Nagasaki, Jap. J4 18

Nagasaki, pref., Jap. *J4 18
Nāgercoil, India *G6 20
Nagoya, Jap. J8, n15 18
Nāgpur, India D6 20
Nags Head, N.C. B7 76
Nagua, Dom. Rep. E9 35
Nagykanizsa, Hung. B3 10
Nagykőrös, Hung. B4 10
Naha, Jap. F10 17
Nahant, Mass. g10 65
Nahariyya, Isr. A3 15
Nahunta, Ga. E5 55
Naicam, Sask., Can. E3 39
Nairn, Scot. B5 4
Nairn, co., Scot. *B5 4
Nairobi, Ken. I5 23
Najin, Kor. E5 18
Nakaminato, Jap. m19 18
Nakamura, Jap. J6 18
Nakatsu, Jap. J5 18
Nakhichevan na Arakse,
  Sov. Un. F7 16

Nakhon Ratchasima, Thai. C2 19
Nakina, Ont., Can. o18 41
Nakło, Pol. B4 7
Nakskov, Den. J4 11
Nakuru, Ken. I5 23
Nakusp, B.C., Can. D9 37
Nalchik, Sov. Un. *E7 13
Namangan, Sov. Un. E10 12
Nambour, Austl. E9 25
Namcha Barwa, mtn., China F4 17
Nam Dinh, Viet. A3 19
Namibia (South West Africa),
  country, Afr. E3 24
Namiquipa, Mex. B3 34
Nampa, Idaho F2 57
Nampo (Chinnampo), Kor. G2 18
Namur, Bel. B6 5
Namur, prov., Bel. *B6 5
Namwŏn, Kor. I3 18
Nanaimo, B.C., Can. E5, f12 37
Nanakuli, Haw. B3, g9 56
Nanam, Kor. F4 18

Nanao, Jap. H8 18
Nance, co., Nebr. C7 71
Nanchang, China F8 17
Nanchong, China E6 17
Nancy, Fr. C7 5
Nanda Devi, peak, India B7 20
Nanded, India *E6 20
Nānga Parbat, peak, Pak. A5 20
Nanjing, China E8 17
Nanju, Kor. I3 18
Nanking, see Nanjing, China
Nanning, China G6 17
Nanping, China F8 17
Nanterre, Fr. g9 5
Nantes, Fr. D3 5
Nanticoke, Md. D6 53
Nanticoke, Pa. D10, n16 81
Nanton, Alta., Can. D4 38
Nantong, China E9 17
Nantucket, Mass. D7 65
Nantucket, co., Mass. D7 65
Nanty Glo, Pa. F4 81

Nanuet, N.Y. g12 75
Nanyang, China E7 17
Naoma, W. Va. n13 87
Naousa, Grc. B4 14
Napa, Calif. C2 50
Napa, co., Calif. C2 50
Napanee, Ont., Can. C8 41
Napanoch, N.Y. D5 75
Naperville, Ill. B5, k8 58
Napier, N.Z. M16 26
Napierville, Que., Can. D4 42
Napierville, co., Que., Can. D4 42
Naples, Fla. F5 54
Naples (Napoli), It. D5 9
Naples, N.Y. C3 75
Naples, Tex. C5 84
Napo, riv., Ec., Peru B2 31
Napoleon, N. Dak. D6 77
Napoleon, Ohio A1 78
Napoleonville, La. E4, k9 63
Napoli, see Naples, It.
Nappanee, Ind. B5 59
Naqadeh, Iran D15 14
Nara, Jap. o14 18
Naracoorte, Austl. G7 25
Naranja, Fla. G6, s13 54
Nārāyanganj, Bngl. D9 20
Narberth, Pa. o20 81
Narbonne, Fr. F5 5
Nardó, It. D7 9
Nariño, dept., Col. C2 32
Narita, Jap. n19 18
Narmada, riv., India D6 20
Narodnaya, mtn., Sov. Un. C9 13
Naro-Fominsk, Sov. Un. D11 12
Narol, Man., Can. D3 40
Narrabri, Austl. F8 25
Narragansett, R.I. D11 52
Narrandera, Austl. F8 25
Narrogin, Austl. F2 25
Narrows, Va. C2 85
Narrowsburg, N.Y. D5 75
Narva, Sov. Un. B7 12
Narvik, Nor. C7 11
Naryan-Mar, Sov. Un. C8 13
Nash, Tex. C5 84
Nash, co., N.C. A4 76
Nashua, Iowa B5 60
Nashua, Mont. B10 70
Nashua, N.H. F5 73
Nashville, Ark. D2 49
Nashville, Ga. E3 55
Nashville, Ill. E4 58
Nashville, Mich. F5 66
Nashville, N.C. B5 76
Nashville, Tenn. A5, g10 83
Nashwauk, Minn. C5 67
Našice, Yugo. C4 10
Nāsik, India E5 20
Nasirābād, Bngl. D9 20
Nassau, Ba. B5, m17 35
Nassau, N.Y. C7 75
Nassau, co., Fla. B5 54
Nassau, co., N.Y. E7 75
Nassawadox, Va. C7 85
Nässjö, Swe. I6 11
Nasukoin, mtn., Mont. B2 70
Natagaima, Col. C2 32
Natal, Braz. D7 27
Natal, B.C., Can. E10 37
Natal, prov., S. Afr. F6 24
Natalia, Tex. E3 84
Natchez, Miss. D2 68
Natchitoches, La. C2 63
Natchitoches, par., La. C2 63
Nathanya, Isr. B2 15
Natick, Mass. B5, g10 65
National City, Calif. F5, o15 50
National Park, N.J. *D2 74
Natívitas, Mex. h9 34
Natoma, Kans. C4 61
Natrona, co., Wyo. D6 89
Natrona Heights, Pa. E2, h15 81
Natural Bridge, N.Y. A5 75
Naturita, Colo. C2 51
Nauen, Ger. Dem. Rep. B6 6
Naugatuck, Conn. D4 52
Naughton, Ont., Can. A3 41
Naumburg an der Saale,
    Ger. Dem. Rep. C5 6
Nauru, country, Oceania G8 2
Nauta, Peru B3 31
Nautla, Mex. C5, m15 34
Nauvoo, Ill. C2 58
Navajo, co., Ariz. B3 48
Navalmoral de la Mata, Sp. C3 8
Navarre, Ohio B4 78
Navarre, reg., Sp. A5 8
Navarro, co., Tex. C4 84
Navasota, Tex. D4 84
Navassa, N.C. C4 76
Navesink, N.J. C4 74
Navojoa, Mex. B3 34

Navolato, Mex. C3 34
Navplion, Grc. D4 14
Navy Yard City, Wash. *B3 86
Nayarit, state, Mex. C4, m11 34
Nayoro, Jap. D11 18
Nazaré, Braz. *E7 27
Nazaré, Port. C1 8
Nazareth, Ky. C4 62
Nazareth, Pa. E11 81
Nazas, Mex. B4 34
Nazca, Peru D3 31
Nazerat (Nazareth), Isr. B3, g5 15
Nazilli, Tur. D7 14
Ndjemena, Chad. F8 22
Ndola, Zambia C5 24
Neah Bay, Wash. A1 86
Neath, Wales E5 4
Nebraska, state, U.S. 71
Nebraska City, Nebr. D10, h13 71
Necedah, Wis. D3 88
Nechako, mts., B.C., Can. C5 37
Necochea, Arg. B5 28
Nedede, Tex. *E6 84
Nederland, Tex. *E6 84
Nedrow, N.Y. *C4 75
Needham, Mass. g11 65
Needle,mtn., Wyo. B3 89
Needles, Calif. E6 50
Needville, Tex. r14 84
Neembucu, dept., Par. E4 29
Neenah, Wis. D5, h9 88
Neepawa, Man., Can. D2 40
Neffs, Ohio B5 78
Neffsville, Pa. F9 81
Negaunee, Mich. *B3 66
Negley, Ohio B5 78
Negotin, Yugo. C6 10
Negra, mts., Peru C2 31
Negreira, Sp. A1 8
Negro, riv., S.A. D4 27
Negro, riv., S.A. D6 19
Negros, isl., Phil. D6 19
Negros Occidental, prov., Phil. *C6 19
Negros Oriental, prov., Phil. *D6 19
Neguac, N.B., Can. B4 43
Neiba, Dom. Rep. E8 35
Neijiang, China F6 17
Neillsville, Wis. D3 88
Neiva, Col. C2 32
Nejd, pol. div., Sau. Ar. D3 15
Nekoosa, Wis. D4 88
Neligh, Nebr. B7 71
Nellore, India F6 20
Nelson, B.C., Can. E9 37
Nelson, Nebr. D7 71
Nelson, N.Z. N14 26
Nelson, co., Ky. C4 62
Nelson, co., N. Dak. C7 77
Nelson, co., Va. C4 85
Nelsonville, Ohio C3 78
Nemacolin, Pa. G2 81
Nemaha, co., Kans. C7 61
Nemaha, co., Nebr. D10 71
Nemunas (Niemen), riv., Sov. Un. ... D3 12
Nemuro, Jap. E12 18
Nenagh, Ire. D5 88
Neoga, Ill. D5 58
Neola, Iowa C2 60
Neon, Ky. C7 62
Neopit, Wis. D5 88
Neosho, Mo. E3 69
Neosho, co., Kans. E8 61
Nepal, country, Asia C7 20
Nephi, Utah B6 72
Neptune, N.J. C4 74
Neptune Beach, Fla. B5, m9 54
Neptune City, N.J. *C4 74
Nerchinsk, Sov. Un. D14 13
Nerekhta, Sov. Un. C13 12
Nerja, Sp. D4 8
Nerva, Sp. D2 8
Nesconset, N.Y. F4 52
Nescopeck, Pa. D9 81
Neshoba, co., Miss. C4 68
Nesquehoning, Pa. E10 81
Ness, co., Kans. D3 61
Ness City, Kans. D4 61
Nes Ziyyona, Isr. C2 15
Netarts, Oreg. B3 80
Netcong, N.J. B3 74
Netherlands, country, Eur. A6 5
Netherlands Antilles, dep., N.A. *A4 32
Nettleton, Miss. A5 68
Nettuno, It. k9 9
Neubrandenburg, Ger. Dem. Rep. ... B6 6
Neuburg, Ger., Fed. Rep. of D5 6
Neuchâtel, Switz. E3 6
Neuchâtel, canton, Switz. E3 6
Neufchâtel-en-Bray, Fr. C4 5
Neuilly sur-Marne, Fr. g11 5
Neuilly -sur-Seine, Fr. g10 5
Neumarkt, Ger., Fed. Rep. of D5 6
Neumünster, Ger., Fed. Rep. of A4 6
Neunkirchen, Aus. E8 6

Neunkirchen, Ger., Fed. Rep. of ... *D3 6
Neuquén, Arg. B3 28
Neuquén, prov., Arg. B3 28
Neuruppin, Ger. Dem. Rep. B6 6
Neuss, Ger., Fed. Rep. of *C3 6
Neustadt, Ont., Can. C4 41
Neustadt an der Aisch,
    Ger., Fed. Rep. of C5 6
Neustadt an der Weinstrasse,
    Ger., Fed. Rep. of D4 6
Neustadt bei Coburg,
    Ger., Fed. Rep. of D4 6
Neustadt im Schwarzwald,
    Ger., Fed. Rep. of A5 6
Neustadt in Holstein,
    Ger., Fed. Rep. of C5 6
Neustrelitz, Ger. Dem. Rep. B6 6
Neu-Ulm, Ger., Fed. Rep. of D5 6
Neuville, Que., Can. C6, o16 42
Neuwied, Ger., Fed. Rep. of C3 6
Nevada, Iowa B4 60
Nevada, Mo. D3 69
Nevada, Ohio B2 78
Nevada, co., Ark. D2 49
Nevada, co., Calif. C3 50
Nevada, state, U.S. 72
Nevada City, Calif. C3 50
Nevada de Colima, mtn., Mex. n12 34
Nevada de Toluca, mtn., Mex. n14 34
Nevado del Huilo, peak, Col. C2 32
Nevelsk, Sov. Un. C10 18
Nevers, Fr. D5 5
Nevesinje, Yugo. D4 10
Neville Island, Pa. *E1 81
Nevşehir, Tur. C10 14
New Albany, Ind. H6 59
New Albany, Miss. A4 68
New Albin, Iowa A6 60
New Alexandria, Va. *B5 85
New Amsterdam, Guy. C5 27
Newark, Ark. B4 49
Newark, Calif. h8 50
Newark, Del. A6 53
Newark, Eng. D6 4
Newark, N.J. B4, k8 74
Newark, N.Y. B3 75
Newark, Ohio B3 78
Newark Valley, N.Y. C4 75
New Athens, Ill. E4 58
Newaygo, Mich. E5 66
Newaygo, co., Mich. E5 66
New Baden, Ill. E4 58
New Baltimore, Mich. F8 66
New Baltimore, N.Y. C7 75
New Beaver, Pa. *E1 81
New Bedford, Mass. C6 65
Newberg, Oreg. B4, h12 80
New Berlin, Ill. D4 58
New Berlin, N.Y. C5 75
New Berlin, Wis. n11 88
New Berlinville, Pa. *F9 81
New Bern, N.C. B5 76
Newbern, Tenn. A2 83
Newberry, Fla. C4 54
Newberry, Mich. B5 66
Newberry, S.C. C4 82
Newberry, co., S.C. C4 82
New Bethlehem, Pa. D3 81
New Bloomfield (Bloomfield),
    Pa. F7 81
New Boston, Ill. B3 58
New Boston, Mich. p15 66
New Boston, Ohio D3 78
New Boston, Tex. C5 84
New Braunfels, Tex. E3, h7 84
New Bremen, Ohio B1 78
New Brighton, Minn. *E5 67
New Brighton, Pa. E1 81
New Britain, Conn. C5 52
New Britain, Isl., Pap. N. Gui. G7 2
New Brockton, Ala. D4 46
New Brunswick, N.J. C4 74
New Brunswick, prov., Can. C3 43
New Brunswick Heights, N.J. *C4 74
New Buffalo, Mich. G4 66
Newburg, Mo. D6 69
Newburgh, Ont., Can. C8 41
Newburgh, Ind. I3 59
Newburgh, N.Y. D6 75
Newburgh Heights, Ohio h12 78
Newbury, Eng. E6 4
Newbury, Mass. A6 65
Newburyport, Mass. A6 65
New Caledonia, Fr., dep., Oceania ... H7 2
New Canaan, Conn. E3 52
New Carlisle, Que., Can. A4 43
New Carlisle, Ind. A4 59
New Carlisle, Ohio C1 78
New Cassel, N.Y. *E7 75
New Castle, reg., Sp. C4 8
New Castle, Ala. B3, f7 46
Newcastle, Austl. F9 25
Newcastle, Calif. C3 50

Newcastle, N.B., Can. B4 43
Newcastle, Ont., Can. D6 41
New Castle, Del. A6 53
New Castle, Ind. E7 59
New Castle, Pa. D1 81
Newcastle, Tex. C3 84
Newcastle, Wyo. C8 89
New Castle, co., Del. A6 53
Newcastle Bridge, N.B., Can. C3 43
Newcastle Mine, Alta., Can. D4 38
New Castle Northwest, Pa. *E1 81
Newcastle-on-Tyne, Eng. C6 4
Newcomerstown, Ohio B4 78
New Concord, Ohio C4 78
New Cumberland, Pa. F8 81
New Cumberland, W. Va. A4, f8 87
New Cumnock, Scot. C4 4
New Delhi, India C6 20
New Denver, B.C., Can. D9 37
New Eagle, Pa. *F1 81
Newell, Iowa B2 60
Newell, W. Va. A4, e8 87
New Ellenton, S.C. E4 82
Newellton, La. B4 63
New England, N. Dak. D3 77
Newfane, N.Y. B2 75
Newfield, N.J. D2 74
New Florence, Mo. C6 69
New Florence, Pa. F3 81
Newfoundland, prov., Can. 44
Newfoundland, N.J. A4 74
New Franklin, Mo. B5 69
New Freedom, Pa. G8 81
New Germany, N.S., Can. E5 43
New Glarus, Wis. F4 88
New Glasgow, N.S., Can. D7 43
New Gretna, N.J. D4 74
New Guinea, isl., Oceania G6 2
New Guinea, Territory of, see
    Papua New Guinea, country, Oceania
Newgulf, Tex. *E5 84
Newhall, Calif. E4 50
Newhall, Iowa C6 60
New Hamburg, Ont., Can. D4 41
New Hampshire, state, U.S. 73
New Hampton, Iowa A5 60
New Hanover, co., N.C. C5 76
New Harbour, Newf., Can. E5 44
New Harmony, Ind. H2 59
New Hartford, Conn. B5 52
New Hartford, Iowa B5 60
New Hartford, N.Y. *B5 75
New Haven, Conn. D5 52
New Haven, Ill. F5 58
New Haven, Ind. B7 59
New Haven, Ky. C4 62
New Haven, Mich. F8 66
New Haven, Mo. C6 69
New Haven, W. Va. C3 87
New Haven, co., Conn. D4 52
New Hebrides, see Vanuatu,
    country, Oceania
New Holland, Ga. B3 55
New Holland, Ohio C2 78
New Holland, Pa. F9 81
New Holstein, Wis. E5, k9 88
New Hope, Ala. A3 46
New Hope, Minn. *E5 67
New Hope, Pa. F12 81
New Hudson, Mich. o14 66
New Hyde Park, N.Y. G2 52
New Iberia, La. D4 63
Newington, Conn. C6 52
New Jersey, state, U.S. 74
New Kensington, Pa. E2, h14 81
New Kent, co., Va. C6 85
Newkirk, Okla. A4 79
New Knoxville, Ohio B1 78
New Kowloon, Hong Kong *G7 17
Newland, N.C. A1, e11 76
New Lebanon, Ohio *C1 78
New Lenox, Ill. B6, k9 58
New Lexington, Ohio C3 78
New Lisbon, Wis. E3 88
New Liskeard, Ont. Can. p20 41
New London, Conn. C8 52
New London, Iowa D6 60
New London, Minn. E4 67
New London, Mo. B6 69
New London, N.H. E4 73
New London, Ohio A3 78
New London, Wis. D5 88
New London, co., Conn. D8 52
New Madison, Ohio C1 78
New Madrid, Mo. E8 69
New Madrid, co., Mo. E8 69
New Malden, Eng. m11 4
Newman, Calif. D3 50
Newman, Ill. D6 58

Newman Grove, Nebr.	C8	71
Newmanstown, Pa.	F9	81
Newmarket, Ont., Can.	C5	41
New Market, Ind.	E4	59
Newmarket, N.H.	E6	73
New Market, N.J.	*B4	74
New Market, Va.	B4	85
New Martinsville, W. Va.	B4	87
New Matamoras, Ohio	C4	78
New Meadows, Idaho	E2	57
New Mexico, state, U.S.		48
New Miami, Ohio	C1, n12	78
New Milford, Conn.	C3	52
New Milford, N.J.	h8	74
New Milford, Ohio	A4	78
New Milford, Pa.	C10	81
New Monmouth, N.J.	C4	74
Newnan, Ga.	C2	55
New Norfolk, Austl.	o15	25
New Orleans, La.	E5, h11	63
New Oxford, Pa.	G7	81
New Palestine, Ind.	E6	59
New Paltz, N.Y.	D6	75
New Paris, Ind.	B6	59
New Paris, Ohio	C1	78
New Philadelphia, Ohio	B4	78
New Philadelphia, Pa.	E9	81
New Plymouth, Idaho	F2	57
New Plymouth, N.Z.	M15	26
Newport, Ark.	B4	49
Newport, Del.	A6	53
Newport, Eng.	E6	4
New Port, Ind.	E3	59
Newport, Ky.	A5, h14	62
Newport, Maine	D3	64
Newport, Mich.	G7	66
Newport, Minn.	n13	67
Newport, N.H.	E3	73
Newport, N.J.	F2	74
New Port, N.Y.	B5	75
New Port, N.C.	C6	76
Newport, Ohio	C4	78
Newport, Oreg.	C2	80
Newport, Pa.	F7	81
Newport, R.I.	D11	52
Newport, Tenn.	D10	83
Newport, Vt.	B3	73
Newport, Wales	E5	4
Newport, Wash.	A8	86
Newport, co., R.I.	C11	52
Newport Beach, Calif.	F5, n13	50
Newport News (Independent City), Va.	D6, k15	85
New Port Richey, Fla.	D4	54
Newportville, Pa.	*F11	81
New Prague, Minn.	F5	67
New Providence, N.J.	B4	74
New Providence, isl., Ba.	B5, m17	35
Newquay, Eng.	E4	4
New Richland, Minn.	G5	67
New Richmond, Que., Can.	A4	43
New Richmond, Ohio	D1	78
New Richmond, Wis.	C1	88
New Road, N.S., Can.	E6	43
New Roads, La.	D4	63
New Rochelle, N.Y.	h13, n15	75
New Rockford, N. Dak.	C6	77
Newry, N. Ire.	C3	4
Newry, S.C.	B2	82
New Salem, N. Dak.	D4	77
New Salem, Pa.	*G2	81
New Sarpy, La.	k11	63
New Sharon, Iowa	C5	60
New Shrewsbury, N.J.	C4	74
New Smyrna Beach, Fla.	C6	54
New South Wales, state, Austl.	F8	25
New Straitsville, Ohio	C3	78
New Tazewell, Tenn.	C10	83
Newton, Ala.	D4	46
Newton, Ill.	E5	58
Newton, Iowa	C4	60
Newton, Kans.	D6, f12	61
Newton, Mass.	B5, g11	65
Newton, Miss.	C4	68
Newton, N.J.	A3	74
Newton, N.C.	B1	76
Newton, Tex.	D6	84
Newton, co., Ark.	B2	49
Newton, co., Ga.	C3	55
Newton, co., Ind.	B3	59
Newton, co., Miss.	C4	68
Newton, co., Mo.	E3	69
Newton, co., Tex.	D6	84
Newton Falls, N.Y.	A6, f9	75
Newton Falls, Ohio	A5	78
Newtonville, N.Y.	*C7	75
Newtown, Newf., Can.	D5	44
Newtown, Conn.	D3	52
New Town, N. Dak.	C3	77
Newtown, Ohio	C1, o13	78
Newtown, Pa.	F12	81
Newtown & *Llanllwchaiarn*, Wales	D5	4
Newtownards, N. Ire.	C4	4

Newtown Square, Pa.	p20	81
New Ulm, Minn.	F4	67
New Vienna, Ohio	C2	78
Newville, Pa.	F7	81
New Washington, Ohio	B3	78
New Waterford, N.S., Can.	C9	43
New Waterford, Ohio	B5	78
New Westminster, B.C., Can.	E6, f13	37
New Whiteland, Ind.	E5	59
New Wilmington, Pa.	D1	81
New Windsor, Ill.	B3	58
New Windsor, Md.	A3	53
New Windsor, N.Y.	*D6	75
New York, N.Y.	E7, h13	75
New York, co., N.Y.	k13	75
New York, state, U.S.		75
New York Mills, Minn.	D3	67
New York Mills, N.Y.	*B5	75
New Zealand, country, Oceania	N15	26
Nezhin, Sov. Un.	F8	12
Nez Perce, Idaho	C2	57
Nez Perce, co., Idaho	C2	57
Ngaoundéré, Cam	G7	22
Nha Trang, Viet.	C3	19
Niagara, Wis.	C6	88
Niagara, co., Ont., Can.	D5	41
Niagara, co., N.Y.	B2	75
Niagara, co., Ohio	C4	78
Niagara Falls, Ont., Can.	D5	41
Niagara Falls, N.Y.	B1	75
Niagara-on-the-Lake, Ont., Can.	D5	41
Niagara University, N.Y.	*B1	75
Niamey, Niger	F5	22
Niantic, Conn.	D8	52
Niantic, Ill.	D4	58
Nicaragua, country, N.A.	E7	34
Nicaragua, lake, Nic.	E7	34
Nicastro (Lamezia Terme), It.	E6	9
Nice, Fr.	F7	5
Niceville, Fla	u15	54
Nichinan, Jap.	K5	18
Nicholas, co., Ky.	B5	62
Nicholas, co., W. Va.	C4	87
Nicholasville, Ky.	C5	62
Nicholls, Ga.	E4	55
Nichols, N.Y.	C4	75
Nichols, S.C.	C9	82
Nichols Hills, Okla.	B4	79
Nicholson, Pa.	C10	81
Nickerson, Kans.	D5	61
Nicolet, Que., Can.	C5	42
Nicolet, co., Que., Can.	C5	42
Nicollet, Minn.	F4	67
Nicollet, co., Minn.	F4	67
Nicoma Park, Okla.	B4	79
Nicosia (Levkosía), Cyp.	A4	23
Nicosia, It.	F5	9
Nicotera, It.	E5	9
Nicoya, C.R.	E7	34
Niedersachsen (Lower Saxony), state, Ger., Fed. Rep. of	*B4	6
Nienburg, Ger., Fed. Rep. of	B4	6
Nievre, dept., Fr.	*D5	5
Niğde, Tur.	D10	14
Niger, country, Afr.	F6	22
Niger, riv., Afr.	F5	22
Nigeria, country, Afr.	G6	22
Nigrita, Grc.	B4	14
Niigata, Jap.	H9	18
Niigata, pref., Jap.	*H9	18
Niihama, Jap.	J6	18
Niihau, isl., Haw.	B1	56
Niimi, Jap.	J6	18
Níjar, Sp.	D4	8
Nijmegen, Neth.	B6	5
Nikitovka, Sov. Un.	q21	12
Nikko, Jap.	H9	18
Nikolayev, Sov. Un.	H9	12
Nikopol, Sov. Un.	H10	12
Niland, Calif.	F6	50
Nile, riv., Afr.	C4	23
Niles, Ill.	h9	58
Niles, Mich.	G4	66
Niles, Ohio	A5	78
Nîmes, Fr.	F6	5
Ninette, Man., Can.	E2	40
Ninety Six, S.C.	C3	82
Ning'an, China	D4	18
Ningbo, China	F9	17
Ningde, China	F8	17
Ningxia, Huizu, auton. reg., China	D6	17
Ningxian, China	D6	17
Ninh Binh, Viet.	A3	19
Niobrara, Nebr.	B7	71
Niobrara, co., Wyo.	C8	89
Niort, Fr.	D3	5
Niota, Tenn.	D9	83
Nipawin, Sask., Can.	D5	39
Nipigon, lake, Ont., Can.	o17	41
Nipissing, dist., Ont., Can.	A5	41
Nipomo, Calif.	E3	50
Niquero, Cuba	D5	35
Nirasaki, Jap.	n17	18
Nis, Yugo.	D5	10

Nisa, Port.	C2	8
Nishinomiya, Jap.	*I7	18
Nishio, Jap.	o16	18
Nisko, Pol.	C7	7
Nisswa, Minn.	D4	67
Niterói, Braz.	C4, h6	30
Nitra, Czech.	D5	7
Nitro, W. Va.	C3	87
Niue, N.Z., dep., Oceania	*H9	2
Nivelles, Bel.	B6	5
Nivernais, former prov., Fr.	D5	5
Niverville, Man., Can.	E3	40
Nixa, Mo.	D4	69
Nixon, N.J.	B4	74
Nixon, Tex.	E4, k8	84
Nizāmābād, India	*E6	20
Nizhneudinsk, Sov. Un.	D12	13
Nizhneye, Sov. Un.	q21	12
Nizhniy Tagil, Sov. Un.	D9	13
Nkangsamba, Cam.	H6	22
Noank, Conn.	D9	52
Nobel, Ont., Can.	B4	41
Noble, Ill.	E5	58
Noble, Okla.	B4	79
Noble, co., Ind.	B7	59
Noble, co., Ohio	C4	78
Noble, co., Okla.	A4	79
Nobles, co., Minn.	G3	67
Noblesville, Ind.	D6	59
Noboribetsu, Jap.	E10	18
Nocatee, Fla.	E5	54
Nochixtán, Mex.	o15	34
Nocona, Tex.	C4	84
Nodaway, co., Mo.	A3	69
Noel, Mo.	E3	69
Nogales, Ariz.	D3	48
Nogales, Mex.	A2	34
Nogales, Mex.	n15	34
Nogata, Jap.	J5	18
Nogent-le-Rotrou, Fr.	C4	18
Nogent *sur-Marne*, Fr.	g10	5
Noginsk, Sov. Un.	D12, n18	12
Nogoyá, Arg.	A5	20
Nógrád, co., Hung.	*A4	10
Nohar, India	C5	20
Noheji, Jap.	F10	18
Noisy-le-Sec, Fr.	g10	5
Nokomis, Sask., Can.	F3	39
Nokomis, Fla.	E4	54
Nokomis, Ill.	D4	58
Nola, It.	D5	9
Nolan, co., Tex.	C2	84
Nome, Alsk.	C6	47
Nominingue, Que., Can.	C2	42
Nomme, Sov. Un.	*B5	12
Nong'an, China	C10	17
Nonoava, Mex.	B3	34
Noranda, Que., Can.	*o20	41
Nora Springs, Iowa	A5	60
Norborne, Mo.	B4	69
Norco, Calif.	*F5	50
Norco, La.	D5, h11	63
Nord, dept., Fr.	*B5	5
Nordegg, Alta., Can.	C2, g7	38
Norden, Ger., Fed. Rep. of	B3	6
Nordenham, Ger., Fed. Rep. of	B4	6
Nordhausen, Ger. Dem. Rep.	C5	6
Nordhorn, Ger., Fed. Rep. of	B3	6
Nordland, co., Nor.	*D6	11
Nördlingen, Ger., Fed. Rep. of	D5	6
Nordrhein-Westfalen, state, Ger., Fed. Rep. of	*C3	6
Nord-Tröndelag, co., Nor.	*E4	11
Nordvik, Sov. Un.	B14	13
Norfolk, Nebr.	B8	71
Norfolk, N.Y.	f9	75
Norfolk (Independent City), Va.	D6, k15	85
Norfolk, co., Ont., Can.	E4	41
Norfolk, co., Eng.	*D7	4
Norfolk, co., Mass.	B5	65
Norilsk, Sov. Un.	C11	13
Norlina, N.C.	A4	76
Norma, N.J.	E2	74
Normal, Ala.	*A3	46
Normal, Ill.	C5	58
Norman, co., Minn.	C2	67
Norman, Okla.	B4	79
Normandin, Que., Can.	*G19	36
Normandy, Fla.	*B5	54
Normandy, Mo.	f13	69
Normandy, former prov., Fr.	C4	5
Normandy Heights, Ohio	n12	78
Normandy Park, Wash.	*B4	86
Norman's Cove, Newf.	*D5	44
Norquay, Sask., Can.	F4	39
Norridge, Ill.	k9	58
Norridgewock, Maine	D3	64
Norris, S.C.	B2	82
Norris, Tenn.	C9	83

Norris Arm, Newf., Can.	D4	44
Norris City, Ill.	F5	58
Norris Point, Newf., Can.	D3	44
Norristown, Pa.	F11, o20	81
Norrköping, Swe.	H7, u34	11
Norrtälje, Swe.	H8, t36	11
Norseman, Austl.	F3	25
Norte de Santander, dept., Col.	B3	32
North, S.C.	D5	82
North, isl., N.Z.	L14	26
North, sea, Eur.	D8	3
North Abington, Mass.	B6, h12	65
North Adams, Mass.	A1	65
North Adams, Mich.	G6	66
North Albany, Oreg.	k11	80
Northam, Austl.	F2	25
North America, cont.		33
North Amherst, Mass.	B2	65
North Amityville, N.Y.	*E7	75
Northampton, Austl.	E1	25
Northampton, Eng.	D6	4
Northampton, Mass.	B2	65
Northampton, Pa.	E11	81
Northampton, co., Eng.	*D6	4
Northampton, co., N.C.	A5	76
Northampton, co., Pa.	E11	81
Northampton, co., Va.	C7	85
North Andover, Mass.	A5	65
North Anson, Maine	D3	64
North Apollo, Pa.	E2	81
North Arlington, N.J.	h8	74
North Asheboro, N.C.	*B3	76
North Atlanta, Ga.	h8	55
North Attleboro, Mass.	C5	65
North Augusta, S.C.	E3	82
North Aurora, Ill.	k8	58
North Babylon, N.Y.	*n15	75
North Baltimore, Ohio	A2	78
North Bangor, N.Y.	f10	75
North Battleford, Sask., Can.	E1, n7	39
North Bay, Ont., Can.	A5, p20	41
North Bay, Fla.	*G6	54
North Beach, Md.	C4	53
North Belle Vernon, Pa.	*F2	81
North Bellmore, N.Y.	*E7	75
North Bellport, N.Y.	n15	75
North Belmont, N.C.	B1	76
North Bend, Nebr.	C9	71
North Bend, Ohio	o12	78
North Bend, Oreg.	D2	80
North Bend, Pa.	D6	81
North Bend, Wash.	B4	86
North Bennington, Vt.	F1	73
North Bergen, N.J.	h8	74
North Berwick, Maine	E2	64
North Billerica, Mass.	A5, f10	65
North Bonneville, Wash.	D4	86
Northboro, Mass.	B4	65
North Brabant, prov., Neth.	*B6	5
North Braddock, Pa.	k14	81
North Branch, Mich.	E7	66
North Branch, Minn.	E6	67
North Branch, N.J.	B3	74
Northbridge, Mass.	B4	65
Northbrook, Ill.	h9	58
North Brookfield, Mass.	B3	65
North Brother, mtn., Maine	C4	64
North Brunswick, N.J.	*C4	74
North Caldwell, N.J.	B4	74
North Canton, Ga.	B2	55
North Canton, Ohio	B4	78
North Carolina, state, U.S.		76
North Catasauqua, Pa.	*E11	81
North Cedar, Iowa	*B5	60
North Charleroi, Pa.	*F1	81
North Charleston, S.C.	F8, k12	82
North Chelmsford, Mass.	A5	65
North Chicago, Ill.	A6, h9	58
North Chili, N.Y.	*B3	75
North Chillicothe, Ill.	C4	58
North City, Wash.	*B3	86
Northcliffe, Austl.	F2	25
North Cohasset, Mass.	h12	65
North College Hill, Ohio	o12	78
North Collins, N.Y.	C2	75
North Conway, N.H.	B4	73
North Corbin, Ky.	D5	62
North Creek, N.Y.	B7	75
Northcrest, Calif.	*B1	50
North Dakota, state, U.S.		77
North Dartmouth, Mass.	C6	65
North Decatur, Ga.	*C2	55
North Dighton, Mass.	C5	65
North East, Md.	A6	53
North East, Nor.	E5	13
North East, Pa.	B2	81
Northeastern Polder, prov., Neth.	*A6	5
Northeast Harbor, Maine	D4	64
North Easton, Mass.	B5	65
Northeim, Ger., Fed. Rep. of	C4	6
North English, Iowa	C5	60
Northern Arm, Newf., Can.	D4	44

Northern, reg., Nig. *F6 22
Northern Ireland, reg., U.K. C3   4
Northern Territory, ter., Austl. C5 25
North Fairfield, Ohio A3 78
North Falmouth, Mass. C6 65
Northfield, B.C., Can. f2 37
Northfield, Ill. *B6 58
Northfield, Mass. A3 65
Northfield, Minn. F5 67
Northfield, N.H. E4 73
Northfield, N.J. E3 74
Northfield, Ohio h9 78
Northfield, Vt. C2 73
North Fond du Lac, Wis. E5, k9 88
North Fork, Calif. D4 50
North Freedom, Wis. E4 88
North Glen Ellyn, Ill. *B5 58
Northglenn, Colo. B6 51
North Grafton, Mass. B4 65
North Great River, N.Y. n15 75
North Grosvenor Dale, Conn. B9 52
North Haledon, N.J. *B4 74
North Hampton, Ohio C2 78
North Hartsville, S.C. *C7 82
North Hatley, Que., Can. D6 42
North Haven, Conn. D5 52
North Head, N.S., Can. E3 43
North Henderson, N.C. *A4 76
North Highlands, Calif. *C3 50
North Holland (Noordholland), prov.,
   Neth. *A6   5
North Hornell, N.Y. *C3 75
North Hudson, Wis. *D1 88
North Industry, Ohio B4 78
North Irwin, Pa. *F2 81
North Judson, Ind. B4 59
North Kamloops, B.C., Can. D7 37
North Kansas City, Mo. h10 69
North Kingstown, R.I. C11 52
North Kingsville, Ohio A5 78
North La Junta, Colo. C7 51
Northlake, Ill. K9 58
North Larchmont, N.Y. *D2 75
North Las Vegas, Nev. C4 72
North Lewisburg, Ohio B2 78
North Liberty, Ind. A5 59
North Lima, Ohio B5 78
North Lindenhurst, N.Y. n15 75
North Little Rock, Ark. C3, h10 49
North Manchester, Ind. C6 59
North Mankato, Minn. F4 67
North Massapequa, N.Y. *E7 75
North Merrick, N.Y. *E7 75
North Miami, Fla. G6, s13 54
North Miami Beach, Fla. s13 54
Northmoor, Mo. h10 69
North Muskegon, Mich. E4 66
North New Hyde Park, N.Y. *E7 75
North Norwich, N.Y. C5 75
North Ogden, Utah A6, C2 72
North Olmsted, Ohio h9 78
North Oxford, Mass. B4 65
North Palisade, mtn., Calif. D4 50
North Palm Beach, Fla. *F6 54
North Park, Ill. A4 58
North Patchogue, N.Y. n14 75
North Pembroke, Mass. C6 65
North Perkin, Ill. *C4 58
North Pelham, N.Y. h13 75
North Plainfield, N.J. B4 74
North Plains, Oreg. B4, g12 80
North Platte, Nebr. C5 71
North Platte, riv., U.S. B6 45
North Pleasanton, Tex. *E3 84

Northport, Ala. B2 46
Northport, Mich. C5 66
Northport, N.Y. n15 75
Northport, Wash. A8 86
North Prairie, Wis. F5 88
North Providence, R.I. B11 52
North Quincy, Ill. D2 58
North Reading, Mass. f11 65
North Richland Hills, Tex. C4 84
Northridge, Ohio *C1 78
North Riverside, Ill. *B6 58
North Rockville Centre, N.Y. *E7 75
North Rose, N.Y. B4 75
North Royalton, Ohio h9 78
North Sacramento, Calif. *C3 50
North Salem, Ind. E4 59
North Salt Lake, Utah *A6 72
North Seaford, N.Y. *E7 75
North Scituate, Mass. h12 65
North Shreveport, La. *B2 63
North Springfield, Va. *B5 85
North St. Paul, Minn. m13 67
North Sudbury, Mass. g10 65
North Swansea, Mass. C5 65
North Sydney, N.S., Can. C9 43
North Syracuse, N.Y. B4 75
North Tarrytown, N.Y. g13, m15 75
North Terre Haute, Ind. E3 59
North Tewksbury, Mass. A5 65
North Tonawanda, N.Y. B2 75
North Troy, Vt. B3 73
North Turlock, Calif. *D3 50
North Turner, mtn., Mass. C4 65
Northumberland, Pa. E8 81
Northumberland, co., N.B., Can. B3 43
Northumberland, co., Ont., Can. C6 41
Northumberland, co., Eng. *C6   4
Northumberland, co., Pa. D8 81
Northumberland, co., Va. C6 85
North Uxbridge, Mass. B4 65
Northvale, N.J. g9 74
North Valley Stream, N.Y. *E7 75
North Vancouver, B.C., Can. E6, f12 37
North Vandergrift, Pa. *E2 81
North Vassalboro, Maine D3 64
North Vernon, Ind. F6 59
Northville, Mich. p15 66
Northville, N.Y. B6 75
North Wales, Pa. F11 81
North Walsham, Eng. D7   4
North Warren, Pa. C3 81
Northwest Park, Md. *B3 53
North Westport, Mass. C5 65
North West River, Newf., Can. B1, h9 44
Northwest Territories, ter.,
   Can. C10 36
North Wilbraham, Mass. B3 65
North Wildwood, N.J. E3 74
North Wilkesboro, N.C. A1 76
Northwood, Iowa A4 60
Northwood, Mich. *E5 66
Northwood, N.H. E5 73
Northwood, N. Dak. C8 77
Northwoods, Mo. *C7 69
North York, Pa. G8 81
North York, Ont., Can. D5, k15 41
Norton, N.S., Can. D4 43
Norton, Kans. C4 61
Norton, Mass. C5 65
Norton, Ohio A4 78
Norton (Independent City), Va. f9 85
Norton, co., Kans. C4 61
Norton Shores, Mich. E4 66
Nortonville, Kans. C8, k15 61

Nortonville, Ky. C2 62
Norvelt, Pa. *F2 81
Norwalk, Calif. n12 50
Norwalk, Conn. E3 52
Norwalk, Iowa C4, f8 60
Norwalk, Ohio A3 78
Norwalk, Wis. E3 88
Norway, Iowa C6 60
Norway, Maine D2 64
Norway, Mich. C3 66
Norway, S.C. E5 82
Norway, country, Eur. E5 11
Norway House, Man., Can. C3 40
Norwayne, Mich. *F7 66
Norwell, Mass. h12 65
Norwich, Ont., Can. E4 41
Norwich, Conn. C8 52
Norwich, Eng. D7   4
Norwich, N.Y. C5 75
Norwood, Ont., Can. C7 41
Norwood, Mass. B5, h11 65
Norwood, Minn. F5 67
Norwood, N.J. h9 74
Norwood, N.Y. f10 75
Norwood, N.C. B2 76
Norwood, Ohio o13 78
Norwood, Pa. p20 81
Norwood, Tenn. *D10 83
Norwottock, mtn., Mass. B2 65
Noshiro, Jap. F10 18
Nossa Senhora das Dores,
   Braz. *E7 27
Notch, mtn., Mass. A3 65
Noto, It. F5   9
Notodden, Nor. H3 11
Notre Dame, Ind. *A5 59
Notre-Dame-de-Lourdes,
   Man., Can. E2 40
Notre Dame du Lac, Que., Can. B9 42
Notre-Dame-du-Laus, Que., Can. C2 42
Nottingham, Eng. D6   4
Nottingham, Pa. *F11 81
Nottingham, co., Eng. *D6   4
Nottoway, co., Va. C4 85
Nouadhibou, Maur. D4 21
Nouakchott, Maur. E1 22
Nouméa, N. Cal. *H8   2
Nova Cruz, Braz. *D7 27
Nova Friburgo, Braz. C4, h6 30
Nova Iguaçu, Braz. h6 30
Nova Lima, Braz. C4 30
Nova Lisboa, see Huambo, Ang.
Novara, It. B2   9
Nova Scotia, prov., Can. D6 43
Novato, Calif. C2 50
Nova Varos, Yugo. D4 10
Novaya Ladoga, Sov. Un. A9 12
Novaya Zemlya, isl., Sov. Un. B8 16
Nova Zagora, Bul. D8 10
Nové Zámky, Czech. E5   7
Novgorod, Sov. Un. B8 12
Novgorod-Severskiy, Sov. Un. E9 12
Novi, Mich. p15 66
Novigrad, Yugo. C2 10
Novi Ligure, It. B2   9
Novi Pazar, Bul. D8 10
Novi Pazar, Yugo. D5 10
Novi Sad, Yugo. C4 10
Novoaydar, Sov. Un. G12, q21 12
Novocherkassk, Sov. Un. H13 12
Novoekonomicheskoye, Sov. Un. ... q20 12
Novogrudok, Sov. Un. E5 12
Novo-Kazalinsk, Sov. Un. E9 16
Novokuznetsk, Sov. Un. D11 13

Novomoskovsk, Sov. Un. G10 12
Novomoskovsk, Sov. Un. D12 12
Novorossiysk, Sov. Un. I11 12
Novoshakhtinsk, Sov. Un. H12 12
Novosibirsk, Sov. Un. D11 13
Novosil, Sov. Un. E11 12
Novoukrainka, Sov. Un. G8 12
Nový Bohumín, Czech. D5   7
Nový Bydžov, Czech. C3   7
Nový Jičín, Czech. D5   7
Novyye Senzhary, Sov. Un. G10 12
Novyy Oskol, Sov. Un. F11 12
Nowa Sól, Pol. C3   7
Nowata, Okla. A6 79
Nowata, co., Okla. A6 79
Nowra-Bomaderry, Austl. G8 26
Nowshera, Pak. B5 20
Nowy Dwór, Pol. k13   7
Nowy Sacz, Pol. D6   7
Nowy Targ, Pol. D6   7
Noxen, Pa. D9, m16 81
Noxubee, co., Miss. B5 68
Noya, Sp. A1   8
Noyon, Fr. C5   5
Nsawam, Ghana G4 22
Nuble, prov., Chile B2 28
Nuckolls, co., Nebr. D7 71
Nucla, Colo. C2 51
Nueces, co., Tex. F4 84
Nueva Atzacoálco, Mex. *D5 34
Nueva Casas Grandes, Mex. A3 34
Nueva Ecija, prov., Phil. *C6 19
Nueva Esparta, state, Ven. A5 32
Nueva Gerona, Cuba D2 35
Nueva Imperial, Chile B2 28
Nueva Rosita, Mex. B4 34
Neuva San Salvador, Sal. *E7 34
Neuva Vizcaya, prov., Phil. *B6 19
Nueve de Julio, Arg. B4 28
Nuevitas, Cuba D5 35
Nuevo Laredo, Mex. B5 34
Nuevo León, state, Mex. B5 34
Nukualofa, Tonga *H9   2
Nules, Sp. C5   8
Numazu, Jap. I9, n17 18
Nu Mine, Pa. E3 81
Nunda, N.Y. C3 75
Nuoro, It. D2   9
Nuquí, Col. C3 27
Nuremberg, Pa. E9 81
Nuri, Mex. B3 34
Nürnberg (Nuremberg), Ger.,
   Fed. Rep. of D5   6
Nushki, Pak. C4 20
Nutley, N.J. B4, h8 74
Nutter Fort, W. Va. B4, k10 87
Nutting Lake, Mass. f10 65
Nuwara Eliya, Sri Lanka G7 20
Nyack, N.Y. D7, m15 75
Nyamandhlovu, Zimb. D5 24
Nyandoma, Sov. Un. A13 12
Nyasa, lake, Afr. C6 24
Nybro, Swe. I6 11
Nye, co., Nev. B3 72
Nyíregyháza, Hung. B5 10
Nykobing Falster, Den. A1   7
Nykøbing Mors, Den. I3 11
Nyköping, Swe. H7, u34 11
Nyland Acres, Calif. *E4 50
Nymburk, Czech. C3, n19   7
Nynäshamn, Swe. H7, u35 11
Nyngan, Austl. F8 25
Nysa, Pol. C4   7
Nyssa, Oreg. D10 80

O

Oahu, isl., Haw. B4, g9 56
Oak Bay, B.C., Can. h12 37
Oak Bluffs, Mass. D6 65
Oakbrook Terrace, Ill. *F2 58
Oak Creek, Colo. A4 51
Oak Creek, Wis. n12 88
Oakdale, Calif. D3 50
Oakdale, La. D3 63
Oakdale, Mass. B4 65
Oakdale, N.Y. *n16 75
Oakdale, Pa. k13 81
Oakes, N. Dak. D7 77

Oakfield, Maine B4 64
Oakfield, N.Y. B2 75
Oakford, Pa. F12, o22 81
Oak Forest, Ill. k9 58
Oak Grove, Ga. *C2 55
Oak Grove, La. B4 63
Oak Grove, Oreg. B4, h12 80
Oakharbor, Ohio A2 78
Oak Harbor, Wash. A3 86
Oak Hill, Fla. D6 54
Oak Hill, Mich. D4 66
Oak Hill, Ohio D3 78

Oak Hill, Tenn. *A5 83
Oak Hill, W. Va. D3, n13 87
Oakhurst, N.J. C4 74
Oakhurst, Okla. A5 79
Oakland, Calif. D2, h8 50
Oakland, Ill. D5 58
Oakland, Iowa C2 60
Oakland, Maine D3 64
Oakland, Md. m12 53
Oakland, Mo. *C7 69
Oakland, Nebr. C9 71
Oakland, N.J. A4 74

Oakland, Oreg. D3 80
Oakland, Pa. *D1 81
Oakland, co., Mich. F7 66
Oakland City, Ind. H3 59
Oaklandon, Ind. k11 59
Oakland Park, Fla. F6, r13 54
Oak Lawn, Ill. B6, k9 58
Oaklawn, Kans. B5 61
Oakley, Idaho G5 57
Oakley, Kans. C3 61
Oakley Park, Mich. *F7 66
Oaklyn, N.J. *D2 74

Oakman, Ala. ... B2 46
Oakmont, Pa. ... E2, h14 81
Oak Park, Ill. ... B6, k9 58
Oak Park, Mich. ... p15 66
Oak Ridge, N.C. ... A3 76
Oakridge, Oreg. ... D4 80
Oak Ridge, Tenn. ... C9 83
Oak Ridges, Ont., Can. ... k15 41
Oaks, Pa. ... o20 81
Oaktown, Ind. ... G3 59
Oak View, Calif. ... *E4 50
Oak View, Md. ... *C3 53
Oakville, Ont., Can. ... D5 41
Oakville, Conn. ... C4 52
Oakville, Mo. ... g13 69
Oakwood, Ill. ... C6 58
Oakwood, Ohio ... A1 78
Oakwood (Oakwood Village), Ohio ... *A4 78
Oakwood (Far Hills), Ohio ... C1 78
Oakwood, Pa. ... *E1 81
Oakwood, Tex. ... D5 84
Oakwood Beach, N.J. ... D1 74
Oakwood Villa, Fla. ... *B5 54
Oamaru, N.Z. ... P13 26
Oamishirasato, Jap. ... n19 18
Oaxaca de Juarez, Mex. ... D5 34
Oaxaca, state, Mex. ... D5 34
Ob, riv., Sov. Un. ... C9 13
Obama, Jap. ... n14 18
Oban, Scot. ... B4 4
Oberhausen, Ger., Fed. Rep. of ... C3 6
Oberlin, Kans. ... C3 61
Oberlin, La. ... D3 63
Oberlin, Ohio ... A3 78
Oberlin, Pa. ... *F8 81
Oberstdorf, Ger., Fed. Rep. of ... E5 6
Obetz, Ohio ... C3, m11 78
Obihiro, Jap. ... E11 18
Obion, Tenn. ... A2 83
Obion, co., Tenn. ... A2 83
Oblong, Ill. ... D6 58
Obluchye, Sov. Un. ... E16 13
O'Brien, co., Iowa ... A2 60
Observation, peak, Calif. ... B3 50
Obuasi, Ghana ... G4 22
Ocala, Fla. ... C4 54
Ocaña, Col. ... B3 32
Ocaña, Sp. ... C4 8
Occidental, mts., Peru ... D2 31
Ocean, co., N.J. ... D4 74
Oceana, W. Va. ... D3 87
Oceana, co., Mich. ... E4 66
Ocean Bluff, Mass. ... B6, h13 65
Ocean City, Md. ... D7 53
Ocean City, N.J. ... E3 74
Ocean Falls, B.C., Can. ... C4 37
Ocean Gate, N.J. ... D4 74
Ocean Grove, Mass. ... C5 65
Ocean Grove, N.J. ... C4 74
Oceanlake, Oreg. ... *C3 80
Oceano, Calif. ... *E3 50
Ocean Park, Wash. ... C1 86
Oceanport, N.J. ... C4 74
Oceanside, Calif. ... F5 50
Oceanside, N.Y. ... *G2 52
Ocean Springs, Miss. ... E5, f8 68
Oceanville, N.J. ... E4 74
Ocheyedan, Iowa ... A2 60
Ochiltree, co., Tex. ... A2 84
Ocilla, Ga. ... E3 55
Ockelbo, Swe. ... G7 11
Ocenle Mari, Rom. ... C7 10
Ocho Rios, Jam. ... E5 35
Ocoee, Fla. ... D5 54
Ocoña, Peru ... E3 31
Oconee, co., Ga. ... C3 55
Oconee, co., S.C. ... B1 82
Oconomowoc, Wis. ... E5 88
Oconto, Wis. ... D6 88
Oconto Falls, Wis. ... D5 88
Oconto, co., Wis. ... D6 88
Ocotlán, Mex. ... C4, m12 34
Ocracoke, N.C. ... B7 76
Ocros, Peru ... D2 31
Oda, Ghana ... G4 22
Ōdate, Jap. ... F10 18
Odawara, Jap. ... I9, n18 18
Odda, Nor. ... G2 11
Odebolt, Iowa ... B2 60
Odell, Ill. ... B5 58
Odem, Tex. ... F4 84
Ödemiş, Tur. ... C7 14
Odendaalsrus, S. Afr. ... F5 24
Odense, Den. ... J4 11
Odense, co., Den. ... *J4 11
Odenton, Md. ... B4 53
Oder (Odra), riv., Eur. ... B7 6
Odessa, Ont., Can. ... C8 41
Odessa, Mo. ... B4 69
Odessa, N.Y. ... C4 75
Odessa, Sov. Un. ... H8 12
Odessa, Tex. ... D1 84

Odessa, Wash. ... B7 86
Odin, Ill. ... E4 58
Odin, mtn., B.C., Can. ... D8 37
Odon, Ind. ... G4 59
O'Donnell, Tex. ... C2 84
Odorhei, Rom. ... B7 10
Oella, Md. ... B4 53
Oelsnitz, Ger. Dem. Rep. ... C6 6
Oelwein, Iowa ... B6 60
O'Fallon, Ill. ... E4 58
O'Fallon, Mo. ... f12 69
Offaly, co., Ire. ... *D3 4
Offenbach, Ger., Fed. Rep. of ... C4 6
Offenburg, Ger., Fed. Rep. of ... D3 6
Ōfunato, Jap. ... G10 18
Oga, Jap. ... G9 18
Ōgaki, Jap. ... I8, n15 18
Ogallala, Nebr. ... C4 71
Ogbomosho, Nig. ... G5 22
Ogden, Iowa ... B3 60
Ogden, Kans. ... C7 61
Ogden, Pa. ... *G11 81
Ogden, Utah ... A6, C2 72
Ogden Dunes, Ind. ... *A3 59
Ogdensburg, N.J. ... A3 74
Ogdensburg, N.Y. ... f9 75
Ogemaw, co., Mich. ... D6 66
Ogle, co., Ill. ... A4 58
Ogles, Ill. ... *E4 58
Oglesby, Ill. ... B4 58
Oglethorpe, Ga. ... D2 55
Oglethorpe, co., Ga. ... C3 55
Ogletown, Del. ... *A6 53
Ogoamas, mtn., Indon. ... E6 19
Ogulin, Yugo. ... C2 10
Ogunquit, Maine ... E2 64
Ōhara, Jap. ... n19 18
O'Higgins, prov., Chile ... A2 28
Ohio, co., Ind. ... G7 59
Ohio, co., Ky. ... C2 62
Ohio, co., W. Va. ... A4 87
Ohio, state, U.S. ... 78
Ohio, river, U.S. ... C10 45
Ohio City, Ohio ... B1 78
Ohioville, Pa. ... *E1 81
Ohrid, Yugo. ... E5 10
Oil City, La. ... B2 63
Oil City, Pa. ... D2 81
Oildale, Calif. ... E4 50
Oilton, Okla. ... A5 79
Oise, dept., Fr. ... *C5 5
Ōita, Jap. ... J5 18
Oita, pref., Jap. ... *J5 18
Ojai, Calif. ... E4 50
Ojinaga, Mex. ... B4 34
Ojocaliente, Mex. ... D4 34
Ojos del Salado, mtn., Arg., Chile ... F4 27
Ojus, Fla. ... G6, s13 54
Oka, Que., Can. ... D3, q18 42
Oka, Nig. ... E6 22
Oka, river, Sov. Un. ... D11, o18 12
Okaloosa, co., Fla. ... u15 54
Okanagan Landing, B.C., Can. ... D8 37
Okanogan, Wash. ... A6 86
Okanogan, co., Wash. ... A6 86
Okara, Pak. ... *B5 20
Okarche, Okla. ... B4 79
Okauchee, Wis. ... *E5 88
Okawville, Ill. ... E4 58
Okaya, Jap. ... H9, m17 18
Okayama, Jap. ... I6 18
Okayama, pref., Jap. ... *I6 18
Okazaki, Jap. ... o16 18
Okecie, Pol. (part of Warsaw) ... B6, m13 7
Okeechobee, Fla. ... E6 54
Okeechobee, co., Fla. ... E5 54
Okeene, Okla. ... A3 79
Okehampton, Eng. ... E4 4
Okemah, Okla. ... B5 79
Okfuskee, co., Okla. ... B5 79
Okha, Sov. Un. ... D17 13
Okhotsk, Sov. Un. ... D17 13
Okhotsk, sea, Sov. Un. ... D17 13
Oklahoma, Pa. ... *F2 81
Oklahoma, co., Okla. ... B4 79
Oklahoma, state, U.S. ... 79
Oklahoma City, Okla. ... B4 79
Oklawaha, Fla. ... C5 54
Oklee, Minn. ... C3 67
Okmulgee, Okla. ... B6 79
Okmulgee, co., Okla. ... B5 79
Okolona, Ky. ... g11 62
Okolona, Miss. ... B5 68
Okotoks, Alta., Can. ... D4 38
Oktibbeha, co., Miss. ... B5 68
Okushiri, Jap. ... E9 18
Olancha, peak, Calif. ... D4 50
Olanta, S.C. ... D8 82
Olathe, Kans. ... D9 61
Olavarriá, Arg. ... B4 28
Oława, Pol. ... C4 7

Olbia, It. ... D2 9
Olcott, N.Y. ... B2 75
Old Bethpage, N.Y. ... *E7 75
Old Bridge, N.J. ... C4 74
Old Brookville, N.Y. ... *E7 75
Old Castile, reg., Sp. ... B4 8
Oldenburg in Holstein, Ger., Fed. Rep. of ... A5 6
Oldenburg, Ger., Fed. Rep. of ... B4 6
Oldenburg, Ind. ... F7 59
Old Forge, N.Y. ... B6 75
Old Forge, Pa. ... D10, m17 81
Old Fort, N.C. ... F10 76
Oldham, Eng. ... D5 4
Oldham, co., Ky. ... B4 62
Oldham, co., Tex. ... B1 84
Oldham Village, Mass. ... *B6 65
Old Hometown, Tenn. ... *B1 83
Old Man, mtn., Newf., Can. ... D3 44
Old Orchard Beach, Maine ... E2, g7 64
Old Perlican, Newf., Can. ... D5 44
Olds, Alta., Can. ... D3 38
Old Saybrook, Conn. ... *D7 52
Oldsmar, Fla. ... o10 54
Old Speck, mtn., Maine ... D2 64
Old Tappan, N.J. ... *B4 74
Old Town, Maine ... D4 64
Oldtown, N.C. ... *A2 76
Old Westbury, N.Y. ... *E7 75
Olean, N.Y. ... C2 75
O'Leary Station, P.E.I., Can. ... C5 43
Oleiros, Sp. ... A1 8
Olekminsk, Sov. Un. ... C15 13
Olesno, Pol. ... C5 7
Olhão, Port. ... D2 8
Olimpia, Braz. ... C3 30
Olimpo, dept., Par. ... D4 29
Olin, Iowa ... B6 60
Olinda, Braz. ... *D7 27
Oliva, Sp. ... C5 8
Oliva de la Frontera, Sp. ... C2 8
Olive Hill, Ky. ... B6 62
Olivehurst, Calif. ... C3 50
Oliveira, Braz. ... C4 30
Olivenza, Sp. ... C2 8
Oliver, B.C., Can. ... E8 37
Oliver, Pa. ... G2 81
Oliver, co., N. Dak. ... C4 77
Oliver Springs, Tenn. ... C9 83
Olivet, Mich. ... F6 66
Olivette, Mo. ... *C7 69
Olivia, Minn. ... F4 67
Olkusz, Pol. ... g11 7
Olla, La. ... C3 63
Olmos, Peru ... C2 31
Olmos Park, Tex. ... k7 84
Olmsted, Ohio ... *A4 78
Olmsted, co., Minn. ... G6 67
Olmsted Falls, Ohio ... h9 78
Olney, Md. ... B3 53
Olney, Tex. ... C3 84
Olomouc, Czech. ... D4 7
Oloron-Ste. Marie, Fr. ... F3 5
Olot, Sp. ... A7 8
Olpe, Kans. ... D7 61
Olshany, Sov. Un. ... F10 12
Olsztyn, Pol. ... B6 7
Olten, Switz. ... E3 6
Oltenia, prov., Rom. ... *C6 10
Oltenia, reg., Rom. ... C6 10
Oltenita, Rom. ... C8 10
Olton, Tex. ... B1 84
Olvera, Sp. ... D3 8
Olympia, Wash. ... B3 86
Olympia Fields, Ill. ... *B6 58
Olympus, mtn., Grc. ... B4 14
Olympus, mtn., Wash. ... B2 86
Olyphant, Pa. ... D10, m18 81
Omagh, N. Ire. ... C3 4
Omaha, Nebr. ... C10, g13 71
Omak, Wash. ... A6 86
Oman, country, Asia ... F6 15
Omar, W. Va. ... D3, n12 87
Omdurman (Umm Durmān), Sud. ... E4 23
Omega, Ga. ... E3 55
Omemee, Ont., Can. ... C6 41
Omerville, Que., Can. ... D5 42
Ometepec, Mex. ... D5 34
Omigawa, Jap. ... n19 18
Omiya, Jap. ... I9, n18 18
Omro, Wis. ... D5 88
Omsk, Sov. Un. ... D10 13
Ōmuta, Jap. ... J5 18
Onalaska, Wis. ... E2 88
Onamia, Minn. ... D5 67
Onancock, Va. ... C7 85
Onarga, Ill. ... C5 58
Onawa, Iowa ... B1 60
Onaway, Mich. ... C6 66
Ondör Haan, Mong. ... B7 17
Oneco, Fla. ... E4, q10 54
Onega, Sov. Un. ... C6 13
Onega, lake, Sov. Un. ... G16 11

Oneida, Ill. ... B3 58
Oneida, N.Y. ... B5 75
Oneida, Ohio ... C1 78
Oneida, Tenn. ... C9 83
Oneida, co., Idaho ... G6 57
Oneida, co., N.Y. ... B5 75
Oneida, co., Wis. ... C4 88
O'Neill, Nebr. ... B7 71
Oneonta, Ala. ... B3 46
Oneonta, N.Y. ... C5 75
Ongjin, Kor. ... H2 18
Onitsha, Nig. ... G6 22
Ono, Jap. ... n15 18
Onoda, Jap. ... *J15 18
Onomichi, Jap. ... I6 18
Onondaga, N.Y. ... *C4 75
Onondaga, co., N.Y. ... C4 75
Onset, Mass. ... C6 65
Onslow, co., N.C. ... C5 76
Onsong, Kor. ... E4 18
Onsted, Mich. ... F6 66
Ontake-san, mtn., Jap. ... n16 18
Ontario, Calif. ... E5, m13 50
Ontario, N.Y. ... B3 75
Ontario, Ohio ... B3 78
Ontario, Oreg. ... C10 80
Ontario, co., Ont., Can. ... C5 41
Ontario, co., N.Y. ... C3 75
Ontario, prov., Can. ... 41
Onteniente, Sp. ... C5 8
Ontonagon, Mich. ... B1, m12 66
Ontonagon, co., Mich. ... m12 66
Oolitic, Ind. ... G4 59
Oostburg, Wis. ... E6 88
Oostende, Bel. ... B5 5
Ootacamund, India ... F6 20
Oot Park, N.Y. ... *B4 75
Opal Cliffs, Calif. ... *D2 50
Opa-Locka, Fla. ... s13 54
Opatów, Pol. ... C6 7
Opava, Czech. ... D4 7
Opelika, Ala. ... C4 46
Opelousas, La. ... D3 63
Opochka, Sov. Un. ... C7 12
Opoczno, Pol. ... C6 7
Opole, Pol. ... C5 7
Opole Lubelskie, Pol. ... C6 7
Opp, Ala. ... D3 46
Oppdal, Nor. ... F3 11
Oppeln see Opole, Pol.
Oppland, co., Nor. ... *G4 11
Opportunity, Wash. ... B8, g14 86
Oquawka, Ill. ... C3 58
Oradea, Rom. ... B5 10
Oradell, N.J. ... h8 74
Oran (Wahran), Alg. ... A4 22
Oran, Mo. ... D8 69
Oran, dept., Alg. ... *B5 22
Orange, Austl. ... F8 25
Orange, Calif. ... n13 50
Orange, Conn. ... D4 52
Orange, Fr. ... E6 5
Orange, Mass. ... A3 65
Orange, N.J. ... B4 74
Orange, Ohio ... *A4 78
Orange, Tex. ... D6 84
Orange, Va. ... B4 85
Orange, co., Calif. ... F5 50
Orange, co., Fla. ... D5 54
Orange, co., Ind. ... G4 59
Orange, co., N.Y. ... D6 75
Orange, co., N.C. ... A3 76
Orange, co., Tex. ... D6 84
Orange, co., Vt. ... D3 73
Orange, co., Va. ... B4 85
Orange, riv., Afr. ... F3 24
Orangeburg, N.Y. ... *D6 75
Orangeburg, S.C. ... E6 82
Orangeburg, co., S.C. ... E6 82
Orange City, Fla. ... D5 54
Orange City, Iowa ... A1 60
Orange Cove, Calif. ... *D4 50
Orange Free State, prov., S. Afr. ... F5 24
Orange Grove, Tex. ... F4 84
Orange Park, Fla. ... B5, m8 54
Orangevale, Calif. ... *C3 50
Orangeville, Ont., Can. ... D4 41
Oranienburg, Ger. Dem. Rep. ... B6 6
Oras, Phil. ... *C7 19
Orăstie, Rom. ... C6 10
Oravita, Rom. ... C5 10
Orchard Avenue, Wash. ... *B8 86
Orchard Beach, Md. ... *B4 53
Orchard Homes, Mont. ... D2 70
Orchard Lake, Mich. ... *F7 66
Orchard Park, N.Y. ... C2 75
Orchard Valley, Wyo. ... E8 89
Orchards, Wash. ... D3 86
Orcotuna, Peru ... D2 31
Orcutt, Calif. ... E3 50
Ord, Nebr. ... C7 71
Ördenes, Sp. ... A1 8
Ordu, Tur. ... B11 14

Orduña, Sp. A4   8
Ordville, Nebr. *C2   71
Ordway, Colo. C7   51
Ordzhonikidze, Sov. Un. E7   13
Örebro, Swe. H6, t33   11
Örebro, co., Swe. *H6   11
Oregon, Ill. A4   58
Oregon, Mo. B2   69
Oregon, Ohio A2, e7   78
Oregon, Wis. F4   88
Oregon, co., Mo. E6   69
Oregon, state, U.S.   80
Oregon City, Oreg. B4, h12   80
Orehov, Sov. Un. H10   12
Orekhovo-Zuyevo,
   Sov. Un. D12, n18   12
Orel, Sov. Un. E11   12
Oreland, Pa. *F11   81
Orem, Utah A6   72
Orenburg, Sov. Un. D8   13
Orense, prov., Sp. *A2   8
Orestes, Ind. D6   59
Orestiás, Grc. B6   14
Orford, mtn., Que., Can. D5   42
Orfordville, Wis. F4   88
Orgeyev, Sov. Un. H7   12
Orick, Calif. B1   50
Orient, Ill. F5   58
Orient, N.Y. m16   75
Oriental, N.C. B6   76
Oriente, prov., Cuba D6   35
Orihuela, Sp. C5   8
Orillia, Ont., Can. C5   41
Orinda, Calif. *D2   50
Orinoco, river, Ven. B5   32
Orion, Ill. B3   58
Oriskany, N.Y. B5   75
Oriskany Falls, N.Y. C5   75
Orissa, state, India E7   20
Oristano, It. E2   9
Orizaba, Mex. D5, n15   34
Orkney, co., Scot. *A5   4
Orkney, isl., Scot. *A5   4
Orland, Calif. C2   50
Orlando, Fla. D5   54
Orland Park, Ill. k9   58
Orleanais, former prov., Fr. D4   5
Orleans, Calif. B2   50
Orléans, Ont., Can. h12   41
Orléans, Fr. D4   5
Orleans, Ind. G5   59
Orleans, Mass. C7   65
Orleans, Nebr. D6   71
Orleans, Vt. B3   73
Orleans, co., N.Y. B2   75
Orleans, co., Vt. B3   73
Orleans, par., La. E6   63
Orlovista, Fla. *D5   54
Ormoc, prov., Phil. *C6   19
Ormond Beach, Fla. C5   54
Ormstown, dept., Que., Can. D3   42
Orne, dept., Fr. *C3   5
Örnsköldsvik, Swe. F8   11
Orocué, Col. C3   32
Orofino, Idaho C2   57
Oro Grande, Calif. E5   50
Oromocto, N.B., Can. D3   43
Orono, Ont., Can. D6   41
Orono, Maine D4   64
Orono, Minn. *E5   67
Oronogo, Mo. D3   69
Oroquieta, Phil. *D6   19
Oroshàza, Hung. B5   10
Oroville, Calif. C3   50
Oroville, Wash. A6   86
Orpington, Eng. m13   4
Orrick, Mo. B3   69
Orrville, Ohio B4   78
Orsha, Sov. Un. D8   12
Orsk, Sov. Un. D8   13
Orsova, Rom. C6   10

Orthez, Fr. F3   5
Ortigueria, Sp. A2   8
Orting, Wash. B3   86
Ortiz, Mex. B2   34
Ortona a Mare, It. C5   9
Ortonville, Mich. F7   66
Ortonville, Minn. E2   67
Orumiyeh (Urmia), Iran B4   15
Oruro, Bol. C2   29
Oruro, dept., Bol. C2   29
Orvieto, It. C4   9
Orwell, Ohio A5   78
Orwigsburg, Pa. E9   81
Oryakhovo, Bul. D6   10
Osage, Iowa A5   60
Osage, co., Kans. D8   61
Osage, co., Mo. C6   69
Osage Beach, Mo. C5   69
Osage City, Kans. D8   61
Ōsaka, Jap. I7, o14   18
Ōsaka, Jap. n16   18
Ōsaka, pref., Jap. *I7   18
Osakis, Minn. E3   67
Osawatomie, Kans. D9   61
Osborne, Kans. C5   61
Osborne, co., Kans. C5   61
Osbornsville, N.J. *C4   74
Osburn, Idaho B3   57
Osceola, Ark. B6   49
Osceola, Ind. A5   59
Osceola, Iowa C4   60
Osceola, Mo. C4   69
Osceola, Nebr. C8   71
Osceola, Wis. C1   88
Osceola, co., Fla. E5   54
Osceola, co., Iowa A2   60
Osceola, co., Mich. E5   66
Osceola Mills, Pa. E5   81
Oschatz, Ger. Dem. Rep. C6   6
Oschersleben, Ger. Dem. Rep. B5   6
Oscoda, Mich. D7   66
Oscoda, co., Mich. D6   66
Osgoode, Ont., Can. B9   41
Osgood, Ind. F7   59
Osh, Sov. Un. E10   13
Oshamambe, Jap. E10   18
Oshawa, Ont., Can. D6   41
Oshkosh, Nebr. C3   71
Oshkosh, Wis. D5, h8   88
Oshogbo, Nig. G5   22
Osijek, Yugo. C4   10
Osinniki, Sov. Un. *D11   13
Oskaloosa, Iowa C5   60
Oskaloosa, Kans. C8, k15   61
Oskarshamm, Swe. I7   11
Oslo, Nor. G4, p28   11
Oslo, co., Nor. *H4   11
Osmaniye, Tur. D11   14
Osmond, Nebr. B8   71
Osnabrück, Ger. Fed. Rep. of B4   6
Osorno, Chile C2   28
Osorno, prov., Chile C2   28
Osoyoos, B.C., Can. E8   37
Osprey, Fla. E4   54
Oss, Neth. B6   5
Ossa, mtn., Austl. o15   25
Osseo, Minn. m12   67
Osseo, Wis. D2   88
Ossian, Ind. C7   59
Ossian, Iowa A6   60
Ossining, N.Y. D7, m15   75
Ostashkov, Sov. Un. C9   12
Osteen, Fla. D5   54
Östergötland, co., Swe. *H6   11
Östersund, Swe. F6   11
Osterville, Mass. C7   65
Ostfold, co., Nor. *H4   11
Ostrava, Czech. D5   7
Ostróda, Pol. B5   7
Ostrogozhsk, Sov. Un. F12   12
Ostrołeka, Pol. B6   7

Ostrov, Czech. C2   7
Ostrov, Sov. Un. C7   12
Ostrowiec *Swietokrzyski*, Pol. C6   7
Ostrów Mazowiecka, Pol. B6   7
Ostrów Wielkopolski, Pol. C4   7
Ostrzeszów, Pol. C4   7
Ostuni, It. D6   9
Ōsuka, Jap. o16   18
Osuna, Sp. D3   8
Oswego, Ill. B5, k8   58
Oswego, Kans. E8   61
Oswego, N.Y. B4   75
Oswego, co., N.Y. B4   75
Oswestry, Eng. D5   4
Oświecim, Pol. C5, g10   7
Ota, Jap. *m18   18
Otaki, Jap. n19   18
Otaré, mtn., Col. C3   32
Otaru, Jap. E10   18
Otavalo, Ec. A2   31
Otay, Calif. *F5   50
Oteen, N.C. f10   76
Otego, N.Y. C5   75
Otero, co., Colo. D7   51
Otero, co., N. Mex. C6   48
Othello, Wash. C6   86
Otho, Iowa B3   60
Otis Orchards, Wash. g14   86
Otisville, Mich. E7   66
Otisville, N.Y. *D6   75
Otoe, co., Nebr. D9   71
Otsego, Mich. F5   66
Otsego, co., Mich. C6   66
Otsego, co., N.Y. C5   75
Ōtsu, Jap. o14   18
Otsuki, Jap. n17   18
Ottawa, Ont., Can. B9, h12   41
Ottawa, Ill. B5   58
Ottawa, Kans. D8   61
Ottawa, Ohio A1   78
Ottawa, co., Kans. C6   61
Ottawa, co., Mich. F4   66
Ottawa, co., Ohio A2   78
Ottawa, co., Okla. A7   79
Ottawa, river, Ont., Que., Can. E18   36
Ottawa-Carleton, co.,
   Ont., Can. B9   41
Ottawa Hills, Ohio A2, e6   78
Otterbien, Ind. D3   59
Otter Lake, Mich. E7   66
Otter River, Mass. A3   65
Otter Tail, co., Minn. D3   67
Otterville, Ont., Can. E4   41
Ottoville, Ohio B1   78
Ottumwa, Iowa C5   60
Otuzco, Peru C2   31
Otwell, Ind. H3   59
Otwock, Pol. m14   7
Ouachita, co., Ark. D3   49
Ouachita, par., La. B3   63
Ouachita, river, U.S. D8   45
Ouagadougou, Burkina Faso. F4   22
Ouahigouya, Burkina Faso. F4   22
Oudtshoorn, S. Afr. G4   24
Ouezzane, Mor. B3   22
Ouidah, Benin G5   22
Oujda, Mor. C5   21
Oullins, Fr. E6   5
Oulu, Fin. E11   11
Oulu, prov., Fin. *E11   11
Ouray, Colo. C3   51
Ouray, co., Colo. C3   51
Ourinhos, Braz. C3   30
Ouro Fino, Braz. C3, m8   30
Ouro Prêto, Braz. C4   30
Outagamie, co., Wis. D5   88
Outes, Sp. A1   8
Outlook, Sask., Can. F2   39
Outreau, Fr. B4   5
Outremont, Que., Can. p19   42
Ovada, It. B2   9

Ovalle, Chile A2   28
Ovar, Port. B1   8
Overbrook, Kans. D8   61
Overijssel, prov., Neth. *A7   5
Overland, Mo. f13   69
Overland Park, Kans. m16   61
Overlea, Md. B4, g11   53
Overton, Nebr. D6   71
Overton, Nev. C4   72
Overton, Tex. C5   84
Overton, co., Tenn. C8   83
Ovid, Mich. E6   66
Ovid, N.Y. C4   75
Oviedo, Fla. D5   54
Oviedo, Sp. A3   8
Oviedo, prov., Sp. *A3   8
Ovruch, Sov. Un. F7   12
Owasso, Okla. A6   79
Owatonna, Minn. F5   67
Owego, N.Y. C4   75
Owen, Wis. D3   88
Owen, co., Ind. F4   59
Owen, co., Ky. B5   62
Owens, N.C. *C4   76
Owensboro, Ky. C2   62
Owen Sound, Ont., Can. C4   41
Owensville, Ind. H2   59
Owensville, Mo. C6   69
Owensville, Ohio C1   78
Owenton, Ky. B5   62
Owings Mills, Md. *B4   53
Owingsville, Ky. B6   62
Owl Creek, mts., Wyo. C4   89
Owosso, Mich. E6   66
Owsley, co., Ky. C6   62
Owyhee, co., Idaho G2   57
Oxbow, Sask., Can. H4   39
Oxbow, Mich. *F6   66
Oxelösund, Swe. o35   11
Oxford, Ala. B4   46
Oxford, N.S., Can. D6   43
Oxford, Eng. E6   4
Oxford, Ga. C3   55
Oxford, Ind. C3   59
Oxford, Iowa C6   60
Oxford, Kans. E6   61
Oxford, Maine D2   64
Oxford, Md. C5   53
Oxford, Mass. B4   65
Oxford, Mich. F7   66
Oxford, Miss. A4   68
Oxford, Nebr. D6   71
Oxford, N.J. B3   74
Oxford, N.Y. C5   75
Oxford, N.C. A4   76
Oxford, Ohio C1   78
Oxford, Pa. G10   81
Oxford, co., Ont., Can. D4   41
Oxford, co., Eng. *E6   4
Oxford, co., Maine D2   64
Oxnard, Calif. E4   50
Oxnard Beach, Calif. *E4   50
Oyama, Jap. m18   18
Oyo, Nig. G5   22
Oyonnax, Fr. D6   5
Oyster Bay, N.Y. E7, n15   75
Oyster Bay Cove, N.Y. *E7   75
Ozamiz, Phil. D6   19
Ozark, Ala. D4   46
Ozark, Ark. B2   49
Ozark, Mo. D4   69
Ozark, co., Mo. E5   69
Ozaukee, co., Wis. E6   88
Ozd, Hung. A5   10
Ozieri, It. D2   9
Ozona, Fla. o10   54
Ozona, Tex. D2   84
Ozorków, Pol. C5   7
Ozu, Jap. J6   18

P

Paarl, S. Afr. G3   24
Paauilo, Haw. C6   56
Pabianice, Pol. C5   7
Pābna, Bngl. D8   20
Pacasmayo, Peru C2   31
Pace, Fla. u14   54
Pacheco, Calif. *C2   50

Pachuca *de Soto*, Mex. C5, m14   34
Pacific, Mo. C7, g12   69
Pacific, Wash. f11   86
Pacific, co., Wash. C2   86
Pacific, ocean F6   2
Pacifica, Calif. h8   50
Pacific Grove, Calif. D3   50

Packard, mtn., Mass. B3   65
Pacolet, S.C. B4   82
Pacolet Mills, S.C. B4   82
Paczkow, Pol. C4   7
Padang, Indon. F2   19
Padangpanjang, Indon. F2   19
Padangsidempuan, Indon. E1, m11   19

Paddock Lake, Wis. n11   88
Paden City, W. Va. B4   87
Paderborn, Ger., Fed. Rep. of C4   6
Padova (Padua), It. B3   9
Paducah, Ky. A2   62
Paducah, Tex. B2   84
Paektu-san, mtn., Kor. F4   18

Pagadian, Phil. *D6 19
Page, Ariz. A4 48
Page, W. Va. C3, m13 87
Page, co., Iowa D2 60
Page, co., Va. B4 85
Pagedale, Mo. *C7 69
Pageland, S.C. B7 82
Page Manor, Ohio *C1 78
Pago Pago, Am. Sam. *G9 2
Pagosa Springs, Colo. D3 51
Pahala, Haw. D6 56
Pahang, state, Mala. E2 19
Pahoa, Haw. D7 56
Pahokee, Fla. F6 54
Paia, Haw. C5 65
Painesdale, Mich. A2 66
Painesville, Ohio A4 78
Paint, Pa. *F4 81
Painted Post, N.Y. C3 75
Paintsville, Ky. C7 62
Paisley, Ont., Can. C3 41
Paisley, Scot. C4 4
Paita, Peru C1 31
Pajaro, Calif. *D3 50
Pakanbaru, Indon. E2 19
Pakistan, country, Asia C4 20
Pakistan, East, see
  Bangladesh, country, Asia
Pakokku, Bur. D10 20
Paks, Hung. B4 10
Pakse, Laos B3 19
Palacios, Tex. E4 84
Palafrugell, Sp. B7 8
Palaiseau, Fr. h9 5
Palamós, Sp. B7 8
Palana, Sov. Un. D18 13
Pālanpur, India D5 20
Palas de Rey, Sp. A2 8
Palatine, Ill. A5, h8 58
Palatka, Fla. C5 54
Palawan, prov., Phil. C5 19
Palawan, isl., Phil. C5 19
Palayankottai, India *G6 20
Palazzolo Acreide, It. F6 9
Palembang, Indon. F2 19
Palencia, Sp. A3 8
Palencia, prov., Sp. *A3 8
Palermo, It. E4 9
Palestine, Ill. D6 58
Palestine, Tex. D5 84
Palestine, reg., Asia D2 15
Palestrina, It. h9 9
Pālghāt, India F6 20
Palisades, Idaho *F7 57
Palisades Park, N.J. h8 74
Palma de Mallorca, Sp. C7 8
Palmares, Braz. *D7 27
Palma Soriano, Cuba D5 35
Palm Bay, Fla. D6 54
Palm Beach, Fla. F6 54
Palm Beach, co., Fla. F6 54
Palmdale, Calif. E4 50
Palm Desert, Calif. *F5 50
Palmeira dos Indios, Braz. *D7 27
Palmer, Alsk. C10, g17 47
Palmer, Mass. B3 65
Palmer, Mich. B3 66
Palmer, Tenn. D8 83
Palmer Heights, Pa. *E11 81
Palmer Park, Md. *C4 53
Palmerston, Ont., Can. D3 41
Palmerston North, N.Z. N15 26
Palmerton, Pa. E10 81
Palmetto, Fla. E4, p10 54
Palmetto, Ga. C2 55
Palm Harbor, Fla. o10 54
Palmi, It. E5 9
Palmira, Col. C2 32
Palmira, Cuba C3 35
Palm Springs, Calif. F5 50
Palm Springs, Fla. *F6 54
Palmyra, Ill. D4 58
Palmyra, Mo. B6 69
Palmyra, N.J. C2 74
Palmyra, N.Y. B3 75
Palmyra, Pa. F8 81
Palmyra, Wis. F5 88
Palo Alto, Calif. D2, k8 50
Palo Alto, Pa. *E9 81
Palo Alto, co., Iowa A3 60
Pálomar, mtn., Calif. F5 50
Palombara Sabina, It. g9 9
Palo Pinto, co., Tex. C3 84
Palopo, Indon. F6 19
Palos Heights, Ill. *B6 58
Palos Hills, Ill. *B6 58
Palos Park, Ill. k9 58
Palos Verdes Estates, Calif. n12 50
Palouse, Wash. C8 86
Palpa, Peru D3 31
Pamekasan, Indon. G4 19
Pamiers, Fr. F4 5
Pamlico, co., N.C. B6 76

Pampa, Tex. B2 84
Pampanga, prov., Phil. *B6 19
Pampas, Peru D3 31
Pampas, reg., Arg. *G4 27
Pamplico, S.C. C8 82
Pamplona, Col. B3 32
Pamplona, Sp. A5 8
Pana, Ill. D4 58
Panagyurishte, Bul. D7 10
Panaji (Panjim), India E5 20
Panama, Okla. B7 79
Panamá, Pan. B2 32
Panama, country, N.A. B2 32
Panama City, Fla. u16 54
Panao, Peru C2 31
Panay, isl., Phil. C6 19
Pancevo, Yugo. C5 10
Pandharpur, India E6 20
Pando, Ur. E1 30
Pando, dept., Bol. B2 29
Pandora, Ohio B2 78
Panevėžys, Sov. Un. D5 12
Panfilov, Sov. Un. E10 13
Pangasinan, prov., Phil. *B6 19
Pangkalpinang, Indon. F3 19
Panguitch, Utah C5 72
Panhandle, Tex. B2 84
Pānipat, India *C6 20
Panna, India D7 20
Panola, co., Miss. A3 68
Panola, co., Tex. C5 84
Panora, Iowa C3 60
Pantelleria, It. F3 9
Pantin, Fr. g10 5
Pánuco, Mex. C5, k14 34
Paola, It. E6 9
Paoli, Ind. G5 59
Paoli, Pa. o20 81
Paonia, Colo. C3 51
Pápa, Hung. B3 10
Papaikou, Haw. D6 56
Papantla de Olarte, Mex. C5, m15 34
Papeete, Fr. Polynesia H11 2
Papenburg, Ger., Fed. Rep. of B3 6
Papillion, Nebr. C9, g12 71
Papineau, co., Que., Can. D2 42
Papineauville, Que., Can. D2 42
Papua New Guinea,
  country, Oceania h11 25
Para, state, Braz. A4 29
Paracatu, Braz. B3 30
Paracin, Yugo. D5 10
Paradis, La. k11 63
Paradise, Calif. C3 50
Paradise Valley, Ariz. D2 48
Paragould, Ark. A5 49
Paraguaçu Paulista, Braz. C2 30
Paraguarí, Par. E4 29
Paraguarí, dept., Par. E4 29
Paraguay, country, S.A. D4 29
Paraguay, riv., Braz., Par. F5 27
Paraíba do Sul, Braz. h6 30
Paraíba do Sul, riv., Braz. F6 27
Paraíso, Pan. *B2 32
Paraiso, Mex. D6 34
Paraisópolis, Braz. C3 30
Parakhino-Padduybe, Sov. Un. B9 12
Paramaribo, Sur. C5 27
Paramount, Calif. *F4 50
Paramus, N.J. h8 74
Paraná, Arg. A4 28
Paraná, state, Braz. C2 30
Paraná, riv., S.A. E4 29
Paranaguá, Braz. D3 30
Paray-Le-Monial, Fr. D6 5
Parchim, Ger. Dem. Rep. B5 6
Parchment, Mich. F5 66
Pardeeville, Wis. E4 88
Pardes Hanna, Isr. B2 15
Pardubice, Czech. C3 7
Parecis, mts., Braz. E5 27
Parent, Que., Can. k12 42
Parepare, Indon. F5 19
Paricutín, vol., Mex. n12 34
Parintins, Braz. *D5 27
Paris, Ark. B2 49
Paris, Ont., Can. D4 41
Paris, Fr. C5, g10 5
Paris, Idaho G7 57
Paris, Ill. D6 58
Paris, Ky. B5 62
Paris, Mo. B6 69
Paris, S.C. *B3 82
Paris, Tenn. A3 83
Paris, Tex. C5 84
Paris, peak, Idaho G7 57
Park, co., Colo. B5 51
Park, co., Mont. E6 70
Park, co., Wyo. B3 89
Park City, Ill. *A6 58
Park City, Kans. B5 61
Park City, Utah A6, D2 72
Parkdale, P.E.I., Can. C6 43

Parke, co., Ind. E3 59
Parker, Ariz. B1 48
Parker, Fla. u16 54
Parker, Pa. D2 81
Parker, S. Dak. G8 77
Parker, co., Tex. C4 84
Parker City, Ind. D7 59
Parkersburg, Iowa B5 60
Parkersburg, W. Va. B3 87
Parkers Prairie, Minn. D3 67
Parkes, Austl. F7 26
Parkesburg, Pa. G10 81
Park Falls, Wis. C3 88
Park Forest, Ill. B6, m9 58
Parkhill, Ont., Can. D3 41
Park Hills, Ky. A7 62
Parkin, Ark. B5 49
Parkland, Pa. *F11 81
Parkland, Wash. f11 86
Parklawn, Va. *B5 85
Park Place, Pa. *B3 81
Park Rapids, Minn. D3 67
Park Ridge, Ill. B6, h9 58
Park Ridge N.J. g8 74
Park Ridge Manor, Ill. *B6 58
Park River, N. Dak. B8 77
Parkrose, Oreg. *B4 80
Parkside, Pa. *G11 81
Parksley, Va. C7 85
Parkston, S. Dak. G8 77
Parksville, B.C., Can. E5 37
Parksville, N.Y. D6 75
Parkton, N.C. C3 76
Parkview, Ohio *A4 78
Parkview, Pa. *E2 81
Parkville, Md. C3 53
Parkville, Mo. B3, h10 69
Parkville, Pa. *G8 81
Parkwood, Md. *B3 53
Parlier, Calif. D4 50
Parma, Idaho F2 57
Parma, It. B3 9
Parma, Mich. F6 66
Parma, Mo. E8 69
Parma, Ohio A4, h9 78
Parma Heights, Ohio h9 78
Parmer, co., Tex. B1 84
Parnaíba, Braz. D6 27
Parnaíba, riv., Braz. D6 27
Pärnu, Sov. Un. B5 12
Parowan, Utah C5 72
Parral, Chile B2 28
Parramatta, Austl. *F8 26
Parras de la Fuente, Mex. B4 34
Parrish, Ala. B2 46
Parrish, Fla. E4, p11 54
Parrsboro, N.S., Can. D5 43
Parry, isl., N.W. Ter., Can. m28 36
Parry, mtn., B.C., Can. C3 37
Parry Sound, Ont., Can. B4, p20 41
Parry Sound, dist., Ont., Can. B4 41
Parshall, N. Dak. C3 77
Parsippany, N.J. B4 74
Parsons, Kans. E8 61
Parsons, Tenn. B3 83
Parsons, W. Va. B5 87
Parthenay, Fr. D3 5
Partinico, It. E4 9
Partizansk, Sov. Un. E16 13
Pasadena, Calif. E4, m12 50
Pasadena, Md. B4 53
Pasadena, Tex. r14 84
Pasadena Hills, Mo. *C7 69
Pasadena Park, Wash. *B8 86
Pasay, Phil. C6, o13 19
Pascagoula, Miss. E5, f8 68
Pascani -Gara, Rom. B8 10
Pasco, Wash. C6 86
Pasco, co., Fla. D4 54
Pasco, dept., Peru D2 31
Pascoag, R.I. B2 52
Pas-de-Calais, dept., Fr. B5 5
Pasewalk, Ger. Dem. Rep. B7 6
Pasig, Phil. o13 19
Paso de los Libres, Arg. E4 29
Paso Robles, Calif. E3 50
Pasquotank, co., N.C. A6 76
Pasrur, Pak. B5 20
Passadumkeag, mtn., Maine C4 64
Passaic, N.J. B4, h8 74
Passaic, co., N.J. A4 74
Passau, Ger., Fed. Rep. of D6 6
Pass Christian, Miss. E4, g7 68
Passo Fundo, Braz. D2 30
Passos, Braz. C3 30
Pastaza, prov., Ec. B2 32
Pasto, Col. C2 32
Pasuruan, Indon. G4 19
Pataskala, Ohio C3 78
Paternó, It. F5 9
Paterson, N.J. B4, h8 74
Pathankot, India B6 20

Pathfork, Ky. D6 62
Patiāla, India B6 20
Patna, India C8 20
Patos, Braz. *D7 27
Patos de Minas, Braz. B3 30
Patrai, Grc. C3 14
Patrick, co., Va. D2 85
Patrocinio, Braz. B3 30
Pattani, Thai. D2 19
Patten, Maine C4 64
Patterson, Calif. *D3 50
Patterson, La. E4 63
Patterson, N.Y. D7 75
Patterson Gardens, Mich. *G7 66
Patton, Pa. E4 81
Pattonsburg, Mo. A3 69
Pattullo, mtn., B.C., Can. A3 37
Pátzcuaro, Mex. D4, n13 34
Patzicia, Guat. *E6 34
Patzún, Guat. *E6 34
Pau, Fr. F3 5
Paucarbamba, Peru D3 31
Paudalho, Braz. *D7 27
Pauk, Bur. D9 20
Paulding, Ohio A1 78
Paulding, co., Ga. C2 55
Paulding, co., Ohio A1 78
Paulina (Remy), La. D5, h10 63
Paulina, mts., Oreg. D5 80
Paulina, peak, Oreg. D5 80
Pauline, mtn., B.C., Can. C8 37
Paullina, Iowa B2 60
Paulsboro, N.J. D2 74
Pauls Valley, Okla. C4 79
Paungde, Bur. E10 20
Pavia, It. B2 9
Pavlodar, Sov. Un. D10 13
Pavlograd, Sov. Un. G10 12
Pavlovo, Sov. Un. D14 12
Pavlovsk, Sov. Un. F13 12
Pavlovskiy Posad, Sov. Un. n18 12
Pawcatuck, Conn. D9 52
Paw Creek, N.C. B2 76
Pawhuska, Okla. A5 79
Pawling, N.Y. D7 75
Pawnee, Ill. D4 58
Pawnee, Okla. A5 79
Pawnee, co., Kans. D4 61
Pawnee, co., Nebr. D9 71
Pawnee, co., Okla. A5 79
Pawnee City, Nebr. D9 71
Paw Paw, Mich. F5 66
Paw Paw, W. Va. B6 87
Paw Paw Lake, Mich. *F4 66
Pawtucket, R.I. B11 52
Paxtang, Pa. *F8 81
Paxton, Ill. C5 58
Payette, Idaho E2 57
Payette, co., Idaho E2 57
Payne, Ohio A1 78
Payne, co., Okla. A4 79
Paynesville, Minn. E4 67
Paysandú, Ur. *E1 30
Paysandú, dept., Ur. *E1 30
Payson, Utah A6, D2 72
Pazardzhik, Bul. D7 10
Pazin, Yugo. C1 10
Peabody, Kans. D6 61
Peabody, Mass. A6, f12 65
Peace, riv., Alta., B.C., Can. E10 36
Peace Dale, R.I. D11 52
Peace River, Alta., Can. A2, f7 38
Peach, co., Ga. D3 55
Peach Creek, W. Va. n12 87
Peaked, mtn., Maine B4 64
Pearisburg, Va. C2 85
Pearl, Miss. C3 68
Pearland, Tex. r14 84
Pearl Beach, Mich. *F8 66
Pearl City, Haw. B4, g10 56
Pearl River, La. D6 63
Pearl River, N.Y. g12 75
Pearl River, co., Miss. D6 63
Pear Ridge, Tex. E2 63
Pearsall, Tex. E3 84
Pearsall, peak, Oreg. E3 80
Pearson, Ga. E4 55
Pebane, Moz. D7 24
Peć, Yugo. D5 10
Peçanha, Braz. B4 30
Pecatonica, Ill. A4 58
Pechenga, Sov. Un. C6 13
Pechora, riv., Sov. Un. C8 13
Peckville (Blakely), Pa. A9 81
Pecos, N. Mex. *B6 48
Pecos, Tex. D1, o13 84
Pecos, co., Tex. D1 84
Pecos, riv., N. Mex., Tex. D6 45
Pécs, Hung. B4 10
Pedley, Calif. *F5 50
Pedreiras, Braz. *D6 27
Pedricktown, N.J. *D2 74
Pedro Juan Caballero, Par. D4 29

Pedro Velho, Braz. *D7 27
Peebles, Ohio D2 78
Peebles, Scot. C5 4
Peebles, co., Scot. *C5 4
Peekaboo, mtn., Maine C5 64
Peekskill, N.Y. D7, m15 75
Peel, co., Ont., Can. D5 41
Pego, Sp. C5 8
Pegu, Bur. E10 20
Pehuajó, Arg. B4 28
Peine, Ger., Fed. Rep. of B5 6
Pekalongan, Indon. G3 19
Pekan, Mala. E2 19
Pekin, Ill. C4 58
Peking (Beijing), China D8 17
Pelahatchie, Miss. C4 68
Pelée, mtn., Mart. I14 35
Pelham, Ont., Can. D5 41
Pelham, Ga. E2 55
Pelham, N.Y. *D7 75
Pelham Manor, N.Y. h13 75
Pelhrimov, Czech. D3 7
Pelican Rapids, Minn. D2 67
Pelican, mtn., Alta., Can. B4 38
Pell Lake, Wis. n11 88
Pella, Iowa C5 60
Pella, prov., Grc. *B4 14
Pell City, Ala. B3 46
Peloponnesos (Peloponnesus), reg., Grc. D4 14
Pelotas, Braz. E2 30
Pelzer North, S.C. *B2 82
Pematangsiantar, Indon. m11 19
Pemba, Moz. C8 24
Pemberton, N.J. D3 74
Pemberville, Ohio A4 78
Pembina, co., N. Dak. B8 77
Pembroke, Ont., Can. B7, p20 41
Pembroke, Ga. D5 55
Pembroke, Mass. B6 65
Pembroke, N.C. C3 76
Pembroke, Va. C2 85
Pembroke, Wales E4 4
Pembroke, co., Wales *E4 4
Pembroke Pines, Fla. *F6 54
Pemiscot, co., Mo. E8 69
Penápolis, Braz. C2 30
Pen Argyl, Pa. E11 81
Peñarroya-Pueblonuevo, Sp. C3 8
Penbrook, Pa. F8 81
Pender, Nebr. B9 71
Pender, co., N.C. C4 76
Pendleton, Ind. E6 59
Pendleton, Oreg. B8 80
Pendleton, S.C. B2 82
Pendleton, co., Ky. B5 62
Pendleton, co., W. Va. C5 87
Pend Oreille, co., Wash. A8 86
Penedo, Braz. E7 27
Penetanguishene, Ont., Can. C5 41
Penfield, N.Y. *B3 75
Penfield Junction, Ohio *A3 78
Peniche, Port. C1 8
Peninsula, Ohio A4 78
Penn, Pa. *F3 81
Pennask, mtn., B.C., Can. E7 37
Penndel, Pa. *F12 81
Penne, It. C4 9
Penn Hills, Pa. F2 81
Pennines, mts., Eng. C5 4
Pennington, Ala. C1 46
Pennington, N.J. C3 74
Pennington, co., Minn. B2 67
Pennington, co., S. Dak. G3 77
Pennington Gap, Va. f8 85
Pennsauken, N.J. D2 74
Pennsboro, W. Va. B4 87
Pennsburg, Pa. F11 81
Penns Grove, N.J. D2 74
Pennside, Pa. *F10 81
Pennsville, N.J. D1 74
Pennsylvania, state, U.S. 81
Penn Valley, Pa. *F11 81
Penn Wynne, Pa. *C11 81
Penn Yan, N.Y. C3 75
Penny Hill, Del. *A6 53
Penobscot, co., Maine C4 64
Pensacola, Fla. u14 54
Pentecost, Miss. B3 68
Penticton, B.C., Can. E8 37
Penton, Miss. A3 68
Pentwater, Mich. E4 66
Penza, Sov. Un. D7 13
Penzance, Eng. E4 4
Penzberg, Ger., Fed. Rep. of E5 6
Penzhino, Sov. Un. C19 13
Peoria, Ariz. C2, D1 48
Peoria, Ill. C4 58
Peoria, co., Ill. C4 58
Peoria Heights, Ill. C4 58
Peotone, Ill. B6 58
Pepin, Wis. D1 88
Pepin, co., Wis. D2 88
Pepper Pike, Ohio *A4 78

Pequannock, N.J. B4 74
Perak, state, Mala. *E2 19
Percy, Ill. E4 58
Perdido, mtn., Sp. A6 8
Pereira Barreto, Braz. C2 30
Pereira, Col. C2 32
Perekop, Sov. Un. H9 12
Pereslavl-Zalesskiy, Sov. Un. C12 12
Pereyaslav-Khmelnitskiy, Sov. Un. F8 12
Pergamino, Arg. A4 28
Perham, Minn. D3 67
Périgueux, Fr. E4 5
Perija, mts.,Col. B3 32
Perkasie, Pa. F11 81
Perkins, co., Nebr. D4 71
Perkins, co., S. Dak. E3 77
Perleberg, Ger. Dem. Rep. B5 6
Perlis, state, Mala. *D2 19
Perl-Mack, Colo. *B6 51
Perm, Sov. Un. D8 13
Përmet, Alb. B3 14
Pernambuco, state, Braz. *D7 27
Pernik, Bul. D6 10
Perpignan, Fr. F5 5
Perquimans, co., N.C. A6 76
Perrine, Fla. G6, s13 54
Perris, Calif. F5 50
Perry, Fla. B3 54
Perry, Ga. D3 55
Perry, Iowa C3 60
Perry, Mich. F6 66
Perry, Mo. B6 69
Perry, N.Y. C3 75
Perry, Ohio A4 78
Perry, Okla. A4 79
Perry, co., Ala. C2 46
Perry, co., Ark. C3 49
Perry, co., Ill. E4 58
Perry, co., Ind. H4 59
Perry, co., Ky. C6 62
Perry, co., Miss. D4 68
Perry, co., Mo. D8 69
Perry, co., Ohio C3 78
Perry, co., Pa. F7 81
Perry, co., Tenn. B4 83
Perry, peak, Mass. B1 65
Perry Hall (Fullerton), Md. B5 53
Perry Heights, Ohio *B4 78
Perryman, Md. B5 53
Perryopolis, Pa. *F2 81
Perrysburg, Ohio A2, e6 78
Perryton, Tex. A2 84
Perryville, Mo. D8 69
Pershing, co., Nev. A2 72
Persia, see Iran, country, Asia
Persimmon Grove, Ky. k14 62
Person, co., N.C. A3 76
Perth, Austl. F2 25
Perth, N.S., Can. C2 43
Perth, Ont., Can. C8 41
Perth, Scot. B5 4
Perth, co., Ont., Can. D3 41
Perth, co., Scot. *B5 4
Perth Amboy, N.J. B4, k7 74
Pertuis, Fr. F6 5
Peru, Ill. B4 58
Peru, Ind. C5 59
Peru, Nebr. D10 71
Peru, country, S.A. D3 31
Perugia, It. C4 9
Pervomaysk, Sov. Un. G8 12
Pervomaysk, Sov. Un. q21 12
Pervouralsk, Sov. Un. D8 13
Pesaro, It. C4 9
Pescara, It. C5 9
Peshawar, Pak. B5 20
Peshtera, Bul. D7 10
Peshtigo, Wis. C6 88
Peski, Sov. Un. F14 12
Peso da Régua, Port. B2 8
Pesqueira, Braz. *D7 27
Pest, co., Hung. *B4 10
Petacas, mtn., Col. C2 32
Petah Tiqwa, Isr. B2 15
Petal, Miss. D4 68
Petaling Jaya, Mala. *E2 19
Petaluma, Calif. C2 50
Petatlán, Mex. D4 34
Peterborough, Ont., Can. C6 41
Peterborough, Eng. D6 4
Peterborough (Peterboro), N.H. F4 73
Peterborough, co., Ont., Can. C6 41
Peterhead, Scot. B6 4
Petermann, ranges, Austl. D4 25
Peters, mtn., Va. C2 85
Petersburg, Alsk. D13, m23 47
Petersburg, Ill. C4 58
Petersburg, Ind. H3 59
Petersburg, Mich. G7 66
Petersburg, Tex. C2 84
Petersburg (Independent City), Va. C5, n18 85

Petersburg, W. Va. B5 87
Pétionville, Hai. E7 35
Petite-de Grat, N.S., Can. D9 43
Petite-Rivière-de-l'Artibonite, Hai. E7 35
Petit-Goâve, Hai. E7 35
Peto, Mex. C7 34
Petoskey, Mich. C6 66
Petrich, Bul. E6 10
Petrikov, Sov. Un. E7 12
Petrinja, Yugo. C3 10
Petrodvorets, Sov. Un. s30 11
Petrokrepost, Sov. Un. s32 11
Petroleum, co., Mont. C8 70
Petrolia, Ont., Can. E2 41
Petrolina, Braz. *D6 27
Petropavlovsk, Sov. Un. D9 13
Petropavlovsk-Kamchatskiy, Sov. Un. D18 13
Petrópolis, Braz. C4, h6 30
Petros, Tenn. C9 83
Petroseni, Rom. C6 10
Petrovgrad, see Zrenjanin, Yugo.
Petrovsk, Sov. Un. E15 12
Petrovskoye, Sov. Un. I14 12
Petrovsk-Zabaykalskiy, Sov. Un. D13 13
Petrozavodsk, Sov. Un. A10 12
Pettis, co., Mo. C4 49
Petty Harbour, Newf., Can. E5 44
Pewaukee, Wis. E5, m11 88
Pézenas, Fr. F5 5
Pforzheim, Ger., Fed. Rep. of D4 6
Phalodi, India C5 20
Phan Rang, Viet. C3 19
Phan Thiet, Viet. C3 19
Pharr, Tex. F3 84
Phelps, Ky. C7 62
Phelps, N.Y. C3 75
Phelps, co., Mo. D6 69
Phelps, co., Nebr. D6 71
Phenix City, Ala. C4 46
Phet Buri, Thai. C1 19
Phetchabun, Thai. B2 19
Phichit, Thai. *B2 19
Philadelphia, Miss. C4 68
Philadelphia, N.Y. A5 75
Philadelphia, Pa. G11, p21 81
Philadelphia, co., Pa. G11 81
Phil Campbell, Ala. A2 46
Philip, S. Dak. C4 77
Philippeville, Bel. *B6 5
Philippi, W. Va. B4 87
Philippines, country, Asia B6 19
Philippolis, S. Afr. G5 24
Philipsburg, Mont. D3 70
Philipsburg, Pa. E5 81
Phillips, Tex. B2 84
Phillips, Wis. C3 88
Phillips, co., Ark. C5 49
Phillips, co., Colo. A8 51
Phillips, co., Kans. C4 61
Phillips, co., Mont. B8 70
Phillipsburg, Kans. C4 61
Phillipsburg, N.J. B2 74
Phillipsville, N.C. *f9 76
Philmont, N.Y. C7 75
Philo, Ohio C4 78
Philomath, Ga. C4 55
Philomath, Oreg. C3 80
Phitsanulok, Thai. B2 19
Phnom Penh, Kam. C2 19
Phoenix, Ariz. C2, D2 48
Phoenix, Ill. k9 58
Phoenix, N.Y. B4 75
Phoenixville, Pa. F10, o19 81
Phong Saly, Laos G5 17
Phrae, Thai. *B2 19
Phucket, Thai. D1 19
Piacenza, It. B2 9
Pialba, Austl. B9 26
Piaseczno, Pol. m14 7
Piatra-Neamt, Rom. B8 10
Piatt, co., Ill. D5 58
Piauí, state, Braz. *D6 27
Piazza Armerina, It. F5 9
Picardy (Picardie), former prov., Fr. C5 5
Picayune, Miss. E4 68
Picher, Okla. A7 79
Pichincha, prov., Ec. B2 31
Pickaway, co., Ohio C2 78
Pickens, S.C. B2 82
Pickens, co., Ala. B1 46
Pickens, co., Ga. B2 55
Pickens, co., S.C. B2 82
Pickering, Ont., Can. D5 41
Pickett, co., Tenn. C8 83
Pickstown, S. Dak. H7 77
Pico Duarte, peak, Dom. Rep. E8 35
Pico Rivera, Calif. N12 50
Picton, Ont., Can. D7 41
Pictou, N.S., Can. D7 43

Pidurutalagala, peak, Sri Lanka G7 20
Piedmont, Ala. B4 46
Piedmont, Calif. h8 50
Piedmont, Mo. D7 69
Piedmont, S.C. B3 82
Piedmont, W. Va. B5 87
Piedmont, reg., It. B1 9
Piedrabuena, Sp. C3 8
Piedras Negras, Mex. B4 34
Pieksämäki, Fin. F12 11
Piélagos, Sp. A4 8
Piemonte, pol. dist., It. *B1 9
Piendamó, Col. C2 32
Pierce, Fla. E5 54
Pierce, Nebr. B8 71
Pierce, co., Ga. E4 55
Pierce, co., Nebr. B8 71
Pierce, co., N. Dak. B5 77
Pierce, co., Wash. C3 86
Pierce, co., Wis. D1 88
Pierce City, Mo. E3 69
Pierceton, Ind. B6 59
Piermont, N.Y. D7 75
Pierre, S. Dak. F5 77
Pierrefitte sur-Seine, Fr. g10 5
Pierrefonds, Que.,Can. q19 42
Pierreville, Que., Can. C5 42
Pierz, Minn. E4 67
Piešt'any, Czech. D4 7
Pietermaritzburg, S. Afr. F6 24
Pietersburg, S. Afr. E5 24
Pigeon, Mich. E7 66
Pigeon Cove, Mass. A6 65
Piggott, Ark. A5 49
Pigüé, Arg. B4 28
Pike, co., Ala. D4 46
Pike, co., Ark. C2 49
Pike, co., Ga. C2 55
Pike, co., Ill. D3 58
Pike, co., Ind. H3 59
Pike, co., Ky. C7 62
Pike, co., Miss. D3 68
Pike, co., Mo. B6 69
Pike, co., Ohio C2 78
Pike, co., Pa. D11 81
Pikes, peak, Colo. C5 51
Piketon, Ohio C2 78
Pikeville, Ky. C7 62
Pikesville, Md. B4, g10 53
Pikeville, Tenn. D8 83
Piła, Pol. B4 7
Pilar, Braz. *D7 27
Pilar, Par. E4 29
Pilcomayo, riv., S.A. D3 29
Pilgrim Gardens, Pa. *B11 81
Pilot Mound, Man., Can. E2 40
Pilot Mountain, N.C. A2 76
Pilot, peak, Wyo. B3 89
Pilot Point, Tex. C4 84
Pilot Rock, Oreg. B8 80
Pima, co., Ariz. C2 48
Pimmit Hills, Va. *B5 85
Pinal co., Ariz. C3 48
Pinang, see George Town, Mala.
Pinang, state, Mal. D2 19
Pinar del Río, Cuba C2 35
Pinar del Río, prov., Cuba C2 35
Pinardville, N.H. *E4 73
Pincher Creek, Alta., Can. E4 38
Pinckneyville, Ill. E4 58
Pinconning, Mich. E7 66
Pindamonhangaba, Braz. C3 30
Pine, co., Minn. D6 67
Pine, riv., Mich. D5 66
Pine Beach, N.J. *D4 74
Pine Bluff, Ark. C3 49
Pine Bluffs, Wyo. E8 89
Pine Bush, N.Y. D6 75
Pine Castle, Fla. D5 54
Pine City, Minn. E6 67
Pineda, Fla. D6 54
Pinedale, Ariz. B3 48
Pinedale, Wyo. D3 89
Pine Falls, Man., Can. D3 40
Pine Grove, Pa. E9 81
Pine Hill, N.J. D3 74
Pine Hills, Fla. *D5 54
Pinehurst, Idaho B2 57
Pinehurst, Mass. f11 65
Pinehurst, N.C. B3 76
Pinehurst, Wash. *B3 86
Pine Island, Minn. F6 67
Pine Island, N.Y. D6 75
Pine Knot, Ky. D5 62
Pine Lake, Ind. *A4 59
Pine Lake, Mass. g10 65
Pineland, Tex. D6 84
Pine Lawn, Mo. f13 69
Pinellas, co., Fla. D4 54
Pinellas Park, Fla. E4, p10 54
Pine Ridge, S. Dak. G3 77
Pinerolo, It. B1 9
Pinetops, N.C. B5 76

Pineville., Ky.	D6	62
Pineville, La.	C3	63
Pineville, N.C.	B2	76
Pineville, W. Va.	D3	87
Piney Point, Tex.	*E5	84
Piney View, W. Va.	D7	87
Pingliang, China	D6	17
Pingtung, Taiwan	*G9	17
Pingxiang, China	F7	17
Pinhal, Braz.	C3, m8	30
Pinkney (South Gastonia), N.C.	*B1	76
Pinole, Calif.	h8	50
Pinon, Ariz.	A3	48
Pinos, Mex.	C4	34
Pinoso, Sp.	C5	8
Pinos-Puente, Sp.	D4	8
Pinsk, Sov. Un.	E6	12
Pinson, Ala.	f7	46
Pioche, Nev.	C4	72
Piombino, It.	C3	9
Piotrków *Trybunalski*, Pol.	C5	7
Piper City, Ill.	C5	58
Pipestone, Minn.	G2	67
Pipestone, co., Minn.	F2	67
Piqua, Ohio	B1	78
Piracicaba, Braz.	C3, m8	30
Piraçununga, Braz.	C3, k8	30
Piraeus, see Piraievs, Grc.		
Piraiévs (Piraeus), Grc.	D4	14
Pirajú, Braz.	C3	30
Pirajui, Braz.	C3	30
Piran, Yugo.	B4	9
Pirapóra, Braz.	B4	30
Pirgos, Grc.	D3	14
Piriápolis, Ur.	E1	30
Pirmasens, Ger., Fed. Rep. of	D3	6
Pirna, Ger. Dem. Rep.	C6	6
Pirot, Yugo	D6	10
Piryatin, Sov. Un.	F9	12
Pisa, It.	C3	9
Piscataquis, co., Maine	C3	64
Piscataway, N.J.	B4	74
Pisco, Peru	D2	31
Pisek, Czech.	D3	7
Pisinimo, Ariz.	C2	48
Pismo Beach, Calif.	E3	50
Pissis, mtn., Arg.	E2	29
Pisticci, It.	D6	9
Pistoia, It.	C3	9
Pitalito, Col.	C2	32
Pitangui, Braz.	B4	30
Pitcairn, Pa.	k14	81
Piteå, Swe.	E9	11
Pitesti, Rom.	C7	10
Pith'iviers, Fr.	C5	5
Pitkin, co., Colo.	B4	51
Pitlochry, Scot.	B5	4
Pitman, N.J.	D2	74
Pitrufquén, Chile	B2	28
Pitt, co., N.C.	B5	76
Pittsboro, N.C.	B3	76
Pittsboro, Ind.	E5	59
Pittsburg, Calif.	g9	50
Pittsburg, Kans.	E9	61
Pittsburg, Tex.	C5	84
Pittsburg, co., Okla.	C6	79
Pittsburgh, Pa.	F1, k13	81
Pittsfield, Ill.	D3	58
Pittsfield, Maine	D3	64
Pittsfield, Mass.	B1	65
Pittsfield, Mich.	*F7	66
Pittsfield, N.H.	E5	73
Pittsford, N.Y.	B3	75
Pittston, Pa.	D10, n17	81
Pittsylvania, co., Va.	D3	85
Piura, Peru	C1	31
Piura, dept., Peru	C1	31
Piute, co., Utah	B5	72
Pixley, Calif.	E4	50
Pizzo, It.	E6	9
Placentia, Calif.	*F5	50
Placentia, Newf., Can.	E5	44
Placer, co., Calif.	C3	50
Placerville, Calif.	C3	50
Placetas, Cuba	C4	35
Placida, Fla.	F4	54
Plain City, Ohio	B2	78
Plain Dealing, La.	B2	63
Plainfield, Conn.	C9	52
Plainfield, Ill.	B5, k8	58
Plainfield, Ind.	E5	59
Plainfield, N.J.	B4	74
Plainfield, Tenn.	*D10	83
Plainfield Heights, Mich.	*F5	66
Plainsboro, N.J.	C3	74
Plainsville, Pa.	*D10	81
Plainview, Minn.	F6	67
Plainview, Nebr.	B8	71
Plainview, N.Y.	*G3	52
Plainview, Tex.	*B2	84
Plainville, Conn.	C5	52
Plainville, Kans.	C4	61
Plainwell, Mich.	F5	66
Plaisance, Hai.	E7	35
Plaistow, N.H.	F5	73
Planada, Calif.	*D3	50
Plandome, N.Y.	*E7	75
Plandome Heights, N.Y.	*E7	75
Plano, Calif.	*D4	50
Plano, Ill.	B5	58
Plano, Tex.	C4, m10	84
Plantagenet, Ont., Can.	B9	41
Plantation, Fla.	r13	54
Plant City, Fla.	D4	54
Plantsite, Ariz.	*D6	48
Plantsville, Conn	C5	52
Plaquemine, La.	D4, h9	63
Plaquemines, par., La.	*D4	63
Plasencia, Sp.	B2	8
Plaster Rock, N.B., Can.	C2	43
Plato, Col.	B3	32
Platón, Sánchez, Mex.	m14	34
Platte, S. Dak.	G7	77
Platte, co., Mo.	B3	69
Platte, co., Nebr.	C8	71
Platte, co., Wyo.	D7	89
Platte City, Mo.	B3, h10	69
Platteville, Wis.	F3	88
Plattsburg, Mo.	B3	69
Plattsburgh, N.Y.	f11	75
Plattsmouth, Nebr.	D10, h13	71
Plauen, Ger. Dem. Rep.	C6	6
Pleasant Dale, Nebr.	D9	71
Pleasant Gap, Pa.	E6	81
Pleasant Grove, Ala.	g7	46
Pleasant Grove, Utah	A6, D2	72
Pleasant Hill, Calif.	h8	50
Pleasant Hill, Ill.	D3	58
Pleasant Hill, Iowa	e8	60
Pleasant Hill, La.	C2	63
Pleasant Hill, Mo.	C3	69
Pleasant Hill, Ohio	B1	78
Pleasant Hill, Pa.	*F9	81
Pleasant Hill, Va.	*D6	85
Pleasant Hills, Pa.	*F2	81
Pleasanton, Calif.	h9	50
Pleasanton, Kans	D9	61
Pleasanton, Tex.	E3	84
Pleasant Ridge, Mich.	*F7	66
Pleasants, co., W. Va.	B3	87
Pleasant Valley, Mo.	h11	69
Pleasant Valley, N.Y.	D7	75
Pleasant View, Colo.	*B5	51
Pleasant View, Utah	A5	72
Pleasantville, Iowa	C4	60
Pleasantville, N.J.	E3	74
Pleasantville, N.Y.	m15	75
Pleasantville, Pa.	C2	81
Pleasure Beach, Conn.	*E4	52
Pleasure Ridge Park, Ky.	g11	62
Pleasureville, Pa.	*G8	81
Pleiku, Viet.	*C3	19
Plenita, Rom.	C6	10
Plentywood, Mont.	B12	70
Plesetsk, Sov. Un.	C7	13
Plessisville, Que., Can.	C6	42
Pleszew, Pol.	C4	7
Pleven, Bul.	D7	10
Pleven, co., Bul.	*D7	10
Pljevlja, Yugo.	D4	10
Plock, Pol.	B5	7
Ploërmel, Fr.	D2	5
Ploiesti, Rom.	C8	10
Plomarion, Grc.	C6	14
Plonsk, Pol.	B6	7
Plovdiv, Bul.	D7	10
Plovdiv, co., Bul.	*D7	10
Plum, Pa.	*E1	81
Plumas, co., Calif.	B3	50
Plymouth, Conn.	C4	52
Plymouth, Eng.	E4	4
Plymouth, Ind.	B5	59
Plymouth, Mass.	C6	65
Plymouth, Mich.	F7, p15	66
Plymouth, Minn.	*F5	67
Plymouth, Mont.	H13	35
Plymouth, N.H.	D4	73
Plymouth, N.C.	B6	76
Plymouth, Ohio	B3	78
Plymouth, Pa.	D10, n17	81
Plymouth, Wis.	E6, k10	88
Plymouth, co., Iowa	B1	60
Plymouth, co., Mass.	C6	65
Plymouth Meeting, Pa.	*F11	81
Plymouth Valley, Pa.	*F11	81
Plymptonville, Pa.	D5	81
Plzeň, Czech.	D2	7
Pobedy, peak, Asia	E11	13
Pocahontas, Ark.	A5	49
Pocahontas, Iowa	B3	60
Pocahontas, Va.	e10	85
Pocahontas, co., Iowa	B3	60
Pocahontas, co., W. Va.	C4	87
Pocatello, Idaho	G6	57
Pochep, Sov. Un.	E9	12
Pochutla, Mex.	D5	34
Pocomoke City, Md.	D6	53
Poços de Caldas, Braz.	C3, k8	30
Podgorica, see Titograd, Yugo.		
Podolsk, Sov. Un.	D11, n17	12
Podor, Sen.	E2	22
Poe, S.C.	*B3	82
Poggibonsi, It.	C3	9
Pohang, Kor.	H4	18
Pohjois-Karjala, prov., Fin.	*F13	11
Poinsett, co., Ark.	B5	49
Point Comfort, Tex.	*E4	84
Pointe-à-Pitre, Guad.	H14	35
Pointe-au-Pic, Que., Can.	B7	42
Pointe-aux-Trembles, Que., Can.	p20	42
Pointe-Claire, Que., Can.	D4, q19	42
Pointe Coupee, par., La.	D4	63
Pointe-du-Lac, Que., Can.	C5	42
Point Edward, Ont., Can.	D2	41
Pointe-Gatineau, Que., Can.	D2	42
Pointe-Noire, Con.	I7	22
Point Leamington, Newf., Can.	D4	44
Point Lookout, Mo.	E4	69
Point Marion, Pa.	F2	81
Point Pleasant, N.J.	C4	74
Point Pleasant Beach, N.J.	C4	74
Poissy, Fr.	C4	5
Poitiers, Fr.	D4	5
Poitou, former prov., Fr.	D3	5
Pokaran, India	C5	20
Pokrovskoye, Sov. Un.	H12	12
Poland, Ohio	*A5	78
Poland, country, Eur.	C5	7
Polgár, Hung.	B5	10
Polikhnitos, Grc.	C6	14
Polk, Pa.	D2	81
Polk, co., Ark.	C1	49
Polk, co., Fla.	E5	54
Polk, co., Ga.	C1	55
Polk, co., Iowa	C4	60
Polk, co., Minn.	C2	67
Polk, co., Mo.	D4	69
Polk, co., Nebr.	C8	71
Polk, co., N.C.	f10	76
Polk, co., Oreg.	C3	80
Polk, co., Tenn.	D9	83
Polk, co., Tex.	D5	84
Polk, co., Wis.	C1	88
Pollensa, Sp.	C7	8
Pollocksville, N.C.	C5	76
Polo, Ill.	B4	58
Polotsk, Sov. Un.	D7	12
Polson, Mont.	C2	70
Poltava, Sov. Un.	G10	12
Pomabamba, Peru	C2	31
Pombal, Braz.	*D7	27
Pomerania, reg., Pol.	B4	7
Pomeroy, Iowa	B3	60
Pomeroy, Ohio	C3	78
Pomeroy, Pa.	*G10	81
Pomeroy, Wash.	C8	86
Pomoho, Haw.	f9	56
Pomona, Calif.	E5, m13	50
Pompano Beach, Fla.	F6, r13	54
Pompton Lakes, N.J.	A4	74
Pompton Plains, N.J.	B4	74
Ponca, Nebr.	B9	71
Ponca City, Okla.	A4	79
Ponce, P.R.	*G11	35
Ponchatoula, La.	D5, h11	63
Pondera, co., Mont.	B4	70
Pondicherry, India	F6	20
Pondicherry, ter., India	*F6	20
Ponferrada, Sp.	A2	8
Ponoka, Alta., Can.	C4	38
Ponorogo, Indon.	*G4	19
Ponta Delgada (Azores Is.), Port.	m10	22
Ponta Grossa, Braz.	D2	30
Pont-A-Mousson, Fr.	C7	5
Ponta Porã, Braz.	C1	30
Pontarlier, Fr.	D7	5
Pontedera, It.	C3	9
Ponteix, Sask., Can.	H2	39
Ponte Nova, Braz.	C4	30
Pontevedra, Sp.	A1	8
Pontevedra, prov., Sp.	*A1	8
Pontiac, Ill.	C5	58
Pontiac, Mich.	F7, o15	66
Pontiac, co., Que., Can.	A7	41
Pontianak, Indon.	F3	19
Pontivy, Fr.	C2	5
Pont-l'-Abbé, Fr.	D1	5
Pontoise, Fr.	C4	5
Pontotoc, Miss.	A4	68
Pontotoc, co., Miss.	A4	68
Pontotoc, co., Okla.	C5	79
Pontremoli, It.	B2	9
Pont-Rouge, Que., Can.	C6, n16	42
Pont-Vieu, Que., Can.	*D4	42
Poole, Eng.	E5	4
Pooler, Ga.	D5	55
Popasnaya, Sov. Un.	q21	12
Popayán, Col.	C2	32
Pope, co., Ark.	B2	49
Pope, co., Ill.	F5	58
Pope, co., Minn.	E3	67
Poplar, Calif.	*D4	50
Poplar, Mont.	B11	70
Poplar Bluff, Mo.	E7	69
Poplar Heights, Va.	*B5	85
Poplarville, Miss.	E4	68
Popocatepetl, vol., Mex.	n14	34
Popovka, Sov. Un.	H11	12
Popovo, Bul.	D8	10
Poquonock, Conn.	B6	52
Poquonock Bridge, Conn.	D8	52
Poquoson, Va.	h15	85
Porbandar, India	D4	20
Porcuna, Sp.	D3	8
Pordenone, It.	B4	9
Porec, Yugo.	C1	10
Pori, Fin.	G9	11
Porlamar, Ven.	A5	32
Poronaysk Shikuka, Sov. Un.	E17	13
Porrentruy, Switz.	C3	4
Porsgrunn, Nor.	p27	11
Portadown, N. Ire.	C3	4
Portage, Ind.	A3	59
Portage, Mich.	F5	66
Portage, Pa.	F4	81
Portage, Wis.	E4	88
Portage, co., Ohio	A4	78
Portage, co., Wis.	D4	88
Portage Lakes, Ohio	*A4	78
Portage-la-Prairie, Man., Can.	E2, h8	40
Portageville, Mo.	E8	69
Port Alberni, B.C., Can.	E5	37
Portalegre, Port.	C2	8
Portales, N. Mex.	B7	48
Port Alfred, S. Afr.	G5	24
Port Alice, B.C., Can.	D4	37
Port Allegany, Pa.	C5	81
Port Allen, La.	D4, h9	63
Port Angles, Wash.	*A2	86
Port Angles East, Wash.	*A2	86
Port Antonio, Jam.	E5	35
Port Arthur, see Lushun, China		
Port Arthur, Tex.	E6	84
Port Augusta, Austl.	F6	25
Port-au-Prince, Hai.	E7	35
Port Barre, La.	D4	63
Port Blair, India	F9	20
Port Byron, Ill.	B3	58
Port Byron, N.Y.	B4	75
Port Carbon, Pa.	E9	81
Port-Cartier-Ouest, Que., Can.	k13	42
Port Charlotte, Fla.	F4	54
Port Chester, N.Y.	E7, n15	75
Port Chicago, Calif.	G8	50
Port Clinton, Ohio	A3	78
Port Colborne, Ont., Can.	E5	41
Port Coquitlam, B.C., Can.	E6, f13	37
Port Crane, N.Y.	C5	75
Port Credit, Ont., Can.	D5, m14	41
Port-de-Bouc, Fr.	F6	5
Port-de-Paix, Hai.	E7	35
Port Deposit, Md.	A5	53
Port Dickinson, N.Y.	C5	75
Port Dickson, Mala.	E2	19
Port Dover, Ont., Can.	E4	41
Port Edward, B.C., Can.	B2	37
Port Edwards, Wis.	D4	88
Port Elgin, N.B., Can.	C5	43
Port Elgin, Ont., Can.	C3	41
Port Elizabeth, S. Afr.	G5	24
Porter, Ind.	A3	59
Porter, co., Ind.	B3	59
Porterdale, Ga.	C3	55
Porterville, Calif.	D4	50
Port Ewen, N.Y.	D7	75
Port-Francqui, see Ilebo, Zaire		
Port-Gentil, Gabon	I6	22
Port Gibson, Miss.	D3	68
Port Hammond, B.C., Can.	f13	37
Port Harcourt, Nig.	H6	22
Port Hawkesbury, N.S., Can.	D8	43
Port Hedland, Austl.	D2	25
Port Henry, N.Y.	A7	75
Port Hope, Ont., Can.	D6	41
Port Hueneme, Calif.	E4	50
Port Huron, Mich.	F8	66
Portimão, Port.	D1	8
Port Isabel, Tex.	F4	84
Port Jefferson, N.Y.	F4	52
Port Jefferson Station, N.Y.	n15	75
Port Jervis, N.Y.	D6	75
Portland, Austl.	G7	25
Portland, Conn.	C6	52
Portland, Ind.	D8	59
Portland, Maine	E2, g7	64
Portland, Mich.	F6	66
Portland, Oreg.	B4, g12	80
Portland, Tenn.	A5	83
Port Lavaca, Tex.	E4	84
Port Leyden, N.Y.	B5	75

Port Lincoln, Austl. F6 25
Port Louis, Mau. *H24 2
Port McNicoll, Ont., Can. C5 41
Port Macquarie, Austl. F9 25
Port Monmouth, N.J. C4 74
Port Moody, B.C., Can. E6, f13 37
Port Moresby, Pap. k12 25
Port Neches, Tex. E6 84
Portneuf, Que., Can. C5 42
Portneuf, co., Que., Can. C5 42
Port Norris, N.J. E2 74
Pôrto (Oporto), Port. B1 8
Pôrto Alegre, Braz. E2 30
Porto Alexandre, Ang. D2 24
Porto de Moz, Braz. D5 27
Pôrto Feliz, Braz. C3, m8 30
Portoferraio, It. C3 9
Port of Spain, Trin. K14 35
Portogruaro, It. B4 9
Portomaggiore, It. B3 9
Porto Nacional, Braz. E6 27
Port-Novo, Benin G5 22
Port Orange, Fla. C6 54
Port Orchard, Wash. B3, e10 86
Port Orford, Oreg. E2 80
Portolo, Calif. C3 50
Porto Torres, It. D2 9
Pôrto União, Braz. D2 30
Porto Velho, Braz. D4 27
Portovlejo, Ec. B1 31
Portpatrick, Scot. C4 4
Port Perry, Ont., Can. C6 41
Port Pirie, Austl. F6 25
Port Reading, N.J. k8 74
Port Richey, Fla. D4 54
Port Said (Būr Sa'īd), Eg. G9 14
Port Saint Joe, Fla. C1, v16 54
Port St. Lucie, Fla. E6 54
Port Sewall, Fla. E6 54
Portsmouth, Eng. E6 4
Portsmouth, N.H. E6 73
Portsmouth, Ohio D3 78
Portsmouth, R.I. C12 52
Portsmouth, (Independent City),
Va. D6, k15 85
Port Stanley, Ont., Can. E3 41
Port Sudan, Sud. E5 23
Port Sulphur, La. E6 63
Port Talbot, Wales *E5 4
Port Townsend, Wash. A3 86
Portugal, country, Eur. C1 8
Portugal Cove, Newf., Can. *E5 44
Portugalete, Sp. A4 8
Portuguesa, state, Ven. B4 32
Portuguese Guinea, see Guinea-
Bissau, country, Afr.
Port Vue, Pa. *F2 81
Port Wakefield, Austl. *F6 25
Port Washington, N.Y. h13 75
Port Washington, Wis. E6 88
Port Wentworth, Ga. D5 55
Posadas, Arg. E4 29
Posadas, Sp. D3 8
Posen, Ill. k9 58
Posen, see Poznan, Pol.
Posey, co., Ind. H2 59
Poseyville, Ind. H2 59
Poso, Indon. F6 19
Post, Tex. C2 84
Poste-de-la-Baleine, Que.,
Can. g11 42
Poste-Mistassini, Que., Can. h12 42
Post Falls, Idaho B2 57
Postojna, Yugo. C2 10
Poston, S.C. D9 82
Postville, Iowa A6 60
Potchefstroom, S. Afr. F5 24
Poteau, Okla. B7 79
Poteet, Tex. E3 84
Potenza, It. D5 9
Potgietersrus, S. Afr. E5 24
Poth, Tex. E3 84
Potlatch, Idaho C2 57
Potomac, Md. B3 53
Potomac Heights, Md. C3 53
Potomac Park, Md. k13 53
Potosí, Bol. C2 29
Potosi, Mo. D7 69
Potosí, dept., Bol. C2 29
Pototan, Phil. *C6 19
Potsdam, Ger. Dem. Rep. B6 6
Potsdam, N.Y. f10 75
Pottawatomie, co., Kans. C7 61
Pottawatomie, co., Okla. B5 79
Pottawattamie, co., Iowa C2 60
Potter, co., Pa. C6 81
Potter, co., S. Dak. F5 77
Potter, co., Tex. B2 84
Potterville, Mich. *F6 66
Pottstown, Pa. F10 81
Pottsville, Pa. E9 81
Pouch Cove, Newf., Can. E5 44
Poughkeepsie, N.Y. D7 75

Poulsbo, Wash. B3 86
Poultney, Vt. D1 73
Pound, Va. e9 85
Pouso Alegre, Braz. C3 30
Póvoa, de Varzim, Port. B1 8
Powassan, Ont., Can. A5 41
Poway, Calif. F5 50
Powder River, co., Mont. E11 70
Powell, Mo. E3 69
Powell, Wyo. B4 89
Powell, co., Ky. C6 62
Powell, co., Mont. D4 70
Powell River, B.C., Can. E5 37
Powellton, W. Va. C3 87
Power, co., Idaho G6 57
Powers, Oreg. E2 80
Poweshiek, co., Iowa C5 60
Powhatan, co., Va. C5 85
Powhatan Point, Ohio C5 78
Poynette, Wis. E4 88
Požarevac, Yugo. C5 10
Poza Rica de Hidalgo, Mex. m15 34
Poznań, Pol. B4 7
Pozoblanco, Sp. C3 8
Pozzallo, It. F5 9
Pozzuoli, It. D5 9
Prachin Buri, Thai. C2 19
Prachuap Khiri Khan, Thai. *C1 19
Praco, Ala. f6 46
Prades, Fr. F5 5
Praestö, co., Den. *J5 11
Prague (Praha), Czech. C3, n17 7
Prague, Okla. B5 79
Praha, see Prague, Czech.
Prairie, co., Ark. C4 49
Prairie, co., Mont. D11 70
Prairie City, Iowa C4 60
Prairie du Chien, Wis. E2 88
Prairie du Sac, Wis. E4 88
Prairie Grove, Ark. B1 49
Prairie Village, Kans. *B9 61
Pran Buri, Thai. C1 19
Prato, It. C3 9
Pratt, Kans. E5 61
Pratt, Minn. *C6 87
Pratt, co., Kans. E5 61
Prattville, Ala. C3 46
Prattville, Okla. *A5 79
Pravdinsk (Friedland), Sov. Un. ... A6 7
Pravia, Sp. A2 8
Preble, co., Ohio C1 78
Premont, Tex. F3 84
Prentiss, Miss. D4 68
Prentiss, co., Miss. A5 68
Prenzlau, Ger. F6 6
Přerov, Czech. D4 7
Prescott, Ariz. B2 48
Prescott, Ark. D2 49
Prescott, Ont., Can. C9 41
Prescott, Wis. D1 88
Prescott, co., Ont., Can. B10 41
Presidencia Roque Sáenz Peña,
Arg. E3 29
Presidente Hayes, dept., Par. D4 29
Presidente Prudente, Braz. C2 30
Presidio, Tex. p12 84
Presidio, co., Tex. o12 84
Prešov, Czech. D6 7
Presque Isle, Maine B4 64
Presque Isle, co., Mich. C6 66
Preston, Eng. D5 4
Preston, Idaho G7 57
Preston, Ky. B6 62
Preston, Minn. G6 67
Preston, co., W. Va. B5 87
Preston, peak, Calif. B2 50
Prestonburg, Ky. C7 62
Prestonville, Ky. B4 62
Prestwick, Scot. C4 4
Pretoria, S. Afr. F5 24
Préveza, Grc. C3 14
Préveza, prov., Grc. *C3 14
Prey Veng, Camb. *C3 19
Pribram, Czech. D3 7
Price, Que., Can. *G20 36
Price, Utah B6 72
Price, co., Wis. C3 88
Pricedale, Pa. *F2 81
Prichard, Ala. E1 46
Priestly, mtn., B.C., Can. B3 37
Priest River, Idaho A2 57
Prilep, Yugo. E5 10
Priluki, Sov. Un. F9 12
Primera, Tex. *F4 84
Primghar, Iowa A2 60
Primorsk, Sov. Un. A6 7
Primorsk-Akhtarsk, Sov. Un. H12 12
Primos, Pa. *G11 81
Primrose, Pa. *E9 81
Prince, co., P.E.I., Can. C5 43
Prince Albert, Sask., Can. D3, n7 39
Prince Edward, co., Ont., Can. C7 41

Prince Edward, co., Va. C4 85
Prince Edward Island, prov., Can. .. C6 43
Prince George, B.C., Can. C6, n18 37
Prince George, co., Va. C5 85
Prince Georges, co., Md. C4 53
Prince of Wales, isl., N.W. Ter.,
Can. B14 36
Prince Rupert, B.C., Can. B2, n16 37
Princess Anne, Md. D6 53
Princeton, Ala. A3 46
Princeton, B.C., Can. E7 37
Princeton, Fla. G6, s13 54
Princeton, Ill. B4 58
Princeton, Ind. H2 59
Princeton, Ky. C2 62
Princeton, Minn. E5 67
Princeton, Mo. A4 69
Princeton, N.J. C3 74
Princeton, N.C. B4 76
Princeton, W. Va. D3 87
Princeton, Wis. E4 88
Princeville, Que., Can. C6 42
Princeville, Ill. C4 58
Princeville, N.C. B5 76
Prince William, co., Va. B5 85
Prineville, Oreg. C6 80
Prineville Southeast, Oreg. *C6 80
Pringle, Pa. *D10 81
Prinsburg, Minn. *F3 67
Priozersk, Sov. Un. G14 11
Pristina, Yugo. D5 10
Pritzwalk, Ger. Dem. Rep. B6 6
Privas, Fr. E6 5
Privolnoye, Sov. Un. H9 12
Prizren, Yugo. D5 10
Prizzi, It. F4 9
Probolinggo, Indon. G4 19
Proctor, Minn. D6 67
Proctor, Vt. D1 73
Proctorville, Ohio D3 78
Progreso, Hond. *D7 34
Progreso, Mex. C7 34
Progress, Pa. *F8 81
Prokopyevsk, Sov. Un. D11 13
Prokuplje, Yugo. D5 10
Proletarskaya, Sov. Un. H13 12
Prome, Bur. E10 20
Prophetstown, Ill. B4 58
Propriá, Braz. *D7 27
Proserpine, Austl. D8 25
Prosotsáni, Grc. *B4 14
Prospect, Conn. C5 52
Prospect, Ohio B2 78
Prospect, Pa. E1 81
Prospect Heights, Ill. *B6 58
Prospect Park, N.J. B4 74
Prospect Park, Pa. p20 81
Prosser, Wash. C6 86
Prostějov, Czech. D4 7
Provadiya, Bul. D8 10
Provence, former prov., Fr. F7 5
Providence, Ky. C2 62
Providence, R.I. B11 52
Providence, Tenn. *A5 83
Providence, Utah *A6 72
Providence, co., R.I. B10 52
Provincetown, Mass. B7 65
Provins, Fr. C5 5
Provo, Utah A6, D2 72
Provost, Alta., Can. C5 38
Prowers, co., Colo. D8 51
Prozor, Yugo. D3 10
Prudnik, Pol. C4 7
Pruszków, Pol. B6, m13 7
Pruzhany, Sov. Un. E5 12
Pryor, Okla. A6 79
Pryor, mts., Mont. E8 70
Przasnysz, Pol. B6 7
Przemyśl, Pol. D7 7
Przeworsk, Pol. C7 7
Pskov, Sov. Un. C7 12
Pszczyna, Pol. D5, h9 7
Ptolemaís, Grc. *B3 14
Ptuj, Yugo. B2 10
Puebla, state, Mex. D5, n14 34
Puebla de Don Fadrique, Sp. D4 8
Puebla del Caramiñal, Sp. A1 8
Puebla de Zaragoza, Mex. D5, n14 34
Pueblo, Colo. C6 51
Pueblo, co., Colo. C6 51
Puenteareas, Sp. A1 8
Puente Ceso, Sp. A1 8
Puentedeume, Sp. A2 8
Puente-Genil, Sp. D3 8
Puerto Alvaro Obregón, Mex. *D6 34
Puerto Armuelles, Pan. *B1 32
Puerto Barrios, Guat. D7 34
Puerto Berrio, Col. B3 32
Puerto Cabello, Ven. A4 32
Puerto Casado, Par. D4 29
Puerto Cortés, Hond. D7 34
Puerto de la Cruz, Sp. m13 8
Puerto Eten, Peru C2 31

Puerto La Cruz, Ven. A5 32
Puertollano, Sp. C3 8
Puerto Maldonado, Peru D4 31
Puerto Montt, Chile C2 28
Puerto Padre, Cuba D5 35
Puerto Peñasco, Mex. A2 34
Puerto Pinasco, Par. D4 29
Puerto Plata, Dom. Rep. E8 35
Puerto Rico, U.S., dep., N.A. G11 35
Puerto Sastre, Par. D4 29
Puerto Supe, Peru D2 31
Puerto Tejada, Col. C2 32
Puerto Vallarto, Mex. C3, m11 34
Puerto Wilches, Col. B3 32
Puglia, pol. dist., It. *D6 9
Pugwash, N.S., Can. D6 43
Puhi, Haw. B2 56
Puhsi, China B2 18
Pukchong, Kor. F4 18
Puksubaek-san, mtn., Kor. F3 18
Pula, Yugo. C1 10
Pulaski, Miss. C4 68
Pulaski, N.Y. B4 75
Pulaski, Tenn. B4 83
Pulaski, Va. C2 85
Pulaski, Wis. D5 88
Pulaski, co., Ark. C3 49
Pulaski, co., Ga. D3 55
Pulaski, co., Ill. F4 58
Pulaski, co., Ind. B4 59
Pulaski, co., Ky. C5 62
Pulaski, co., Mo. D5 69
Pulaski, co., Va. C2 85
Pulawy, Pol. C6 7
Pul-I-Khumri, Afg. A4 20
Pullman, Wash. C8 86
Pulog, mtn., Phil. n13 19
Pultusk, Pol. B6 7
Pune (Poona), India E5 20
Pungsan, Kor. F4 18
Punjab, state, India B5 20
Puno, Peru E3 31
Puno, dept., Peru E3 31
Punta Alta, Arg. B4 28
Punta Arenas, Chile h11 28
Punta Gorda, Fla. F4 54
Puntarenas, C.R. *F8 34
Puntarenas, prov., C.R. *F8 34
Punxsutawney, Pa. E4 81
Puquio, Peru D3 31
Purcell, Mo. D3 69
Purcell, Okla. B4 79
Purcellville, Va. A5 85
Purèpero, Mex. n12 34
Puri, India E8 20
Purnea, India C8 20
Pursat, Kam. C2 19
Pursglove, W. Va. B4 87
Purūlia, India D8 20
Purús, riv., Peru D3 31
Purvis, Miss. D4 68
Purwokerto, Indon. *G3 19
Pusan, Kor. I4 18
Pushkin, Sov. Un. B8 12
Pushkino, Sov. Un. C11, m17 12
Pushmataha, Ala. C1 46
Pushmataha, co., Okla. C6 79
Püspökladány, Hung. B5 10
Pustelnik, Pol. k14 7
Putao, Bur. C10 20
Puteaux, Fr. g9 5
Putivl, Sov. Un. F9 12
Putnam, Conn. B9 52
Putnam, co., Fla. C5 54
Putnam, co., Ga. C3 55
Putnam, co., Ill. B4 58
Putnam, co., Ind. E4 59
Putnam, co., Mo. A4 69
Putnam, co., N.Y. D7 75
Putnam, co., Ohio B1 78
Putnam, co., Tenn. C8 83
Putnam, co., W. Va. C3 87
Puttalam, Sri Lanka G6 20
Putumayo, comisaría, Col. C2 32
Puukolii, Haw. C5 56
Puunene, Haw. C5 56
Puxico, Mo. E7 69
Puyallup, Wash. B3, f11 86
Puy-de-Dôme, dept., Fr. *E5 5
Puyo, Ec. B2 31
Pwllheli, Wales D4 4
Pyapon, Bur. E10 20
Pyatigorsk, Sov. Un. *E7 13
Pyinmana, Bur. E10 20
Pyŏngchang, Kor. H4 18
Pyongtaek, Kor. H3 18
Pyongyang, Kor. G2 18
Pyrénées-Orientales, dept., Fr. *F5 5
Pyskowice, Pol. g9 7
Pyu, Bur. E10 20

Q

Qamdo, China...........................E4 17
Qāna, Leb..............................A3 15
Qaṣr al Farāfirah, Eg..................C3 23
Qatar, country, Asia...................D5 15
Qazvin, Iran...........................B5 15
Qiemo, China...........................A8 20
Qina, Eg...............................C4 23
Qingdao, China.........................D9 17
Qinghai, prov., China..................D4 17
Qinghai, lake, China...................D4 17
Qingjiang, China.......................E8 20
Qinhuangdao, China.....................D8 17
Qiqihar, China.........................B9 17
Qitai, China...........................C2 17
Qiryat Shemona, Isr....................A3 15
Qiryat Yam, Isr........................B3 15
Qom, Iran..............................C5 15
Quakenbruck, Ger., Fed. Rep. of........B3 6
Quaker Hill, Conn......................D8 52
Quakertown, Pa.........................F11 81
Quanah, Tex............................B3 84
Quang Ngai, Viet.......................B3 19
Quang Tri, Viet........................B3 19

Quantico, Va...........................B5 85
Quanzhou, China........................G8 17
Quapaw, Okla...........................A7 79
Quarai, Braz...........................E1 30
Quarryville, Pa........................G9 81
Quartu Sant' Elena, It.................E2 9
Quartz Hill, Calif.....................*E4 50
Quay, co., N. Mex......................B7 48
Québec., Que., Can................C6, n17 42
Québec, co., Que., Can.................B5 42
Québec, prov., Can.....................42
Québec-Quest, Que., Can................*C6 42
Quedlinburg, Ger. Dem. Rep.............C5 6
Queen Annes, co., Md...................B5 53
Queen Bess, mtn., B.C., Can............D5 37
Queen City, Tex........................*C5 84
Queen Elizabeth. is., N.W. Ter.,
Can................................m31 36
Queens, borough and co., N.Y...........E7 75
Queens, co., N.B., Can.................D4 43
Queens, co., N.S., Can.................E4 43
Queens, co., P.E.I., Can...............C6 43
Queensland, state, Austl...............D7 25

Queenstown, S. Afr.....................G5 24
Quelimane, Moz.........................D7 24
Querétaro, Mex.....................C4, m13 34
Querétaro, state, Mex..............C4, m13 34
Quesada, Sp............................D4 8
Quesnel, B.C., Can.....................C6 37
Questa, N. Mex.........................A6 48
Quetta, Pak............................B4 20
Quezaltenango, Guat....................E6 34
Quezaltepeque, Sal.....................*E7 34
Quezon, prov., Phil....................*C6 19
Quezon City, Phil......................C6 19
Quibdó, Col............................B2 32
Quidnessett, R.I.......................C11 52
Quidnick, R.I..........................C10 52
Quiindy, Par...........................E4 29
Quilá, Mex.............................C3 34
Quillota, Chile........................A2 28
Quilmes, Arg...........................g7 28
Quilon, India..........................G6 20
Quilpie, Austl.........................E7 25
Quilpué, Chile.........................A2 28
Quimper, Fr............................C2 5

Quimperlé, Fr..........................D2 5
Quincy, Calif..........................C3 50
Quincy, Fla............................B2 54
Quincy, Ill............................D2 58
Quincy, Mass...........................h11 65
Quincy, Mich...........................G6 66
Quincy, Wash...........................B6 86
Qui Nhon, Viet.........................C3 19
Quinnville, R.I........................B11 52
Quintana de la Serena, Sp..............C3 8
Quintanar, Sp..........................C4 8
Quintana Roo, state, Mex...............D7 34
Quinter, Kans..........................C3 61
Quinton, Okla..........................B6 79
Quiroga, Sp............................A2 8
Quitman, Ga............................F3 55
Quitman, Miss..........................C5 68
Quitman, Tex...........................C5 84
Quitman, co., Ga.......................E1 55
Quitman, co., Miss.....................A3 68
Quito, Ec..............................B2 31
Quixadá, Braz..........................*D7 27
Quxian, China..........................F8 17

R

Raba, Indon. G5 19
Rabat, Mor............................B3 22
Rabaul, Pap. N. Gui...................h13 25
Rabun, Ala............................D2 46
Rabun, co., Ga........................B3 55
Raceland, Ky..........................B7 62
Raceland, La......................E5, k10 63
Rach Gia, Viet........................*C2 19
Raciborz, Pol.........................C5 7
Racine, Wis.......................F6, n12 88
Racine, co., Wis......................F5 88
Radauti, Rom..........................B7 10
Radcliff, Ky..........................C4 62
Radeberg, Ger. Dem. Rep...............C6 6
Radford (Independent City), Va........C2 85
Radiant Valley, Md....................C4 53
Radnor, Pa............................*G11 81
Radnor, co., Wales....................*D5 4
Radom, Pol............................C6 7
Radomir, Bul..........................D6 10
Radomsko, Pol.........................C5 7
Radville, Sask., Can..................H3 39
Radzionków, Pol.......................g9 7
Rae Bareli, India.....................C7 20
Raeford, N.C..........................C3 76
Rafaela, Arg..........................A4 28
Rafah, Gaza Strip.....................C2 15
Ragland, Ala..........................B3 46
Ragusa, It............................F5 9
Rahīmyār-Khān, Pak....................C5 20
Rahway, N.J........................B4, k7 74
Rāichūr, India........................E6 20
Raigarh, India........................D7 20
Rainbow City, Ala.....................*A3 46
Rainbow City, Pan.....................*B2 32
Rainier, Oreg.........................A4 80
Rainier, mtn., Wash...................C4 86
Rains, co., Tex.......................C5 84
Rainsville, Ala.......................A4 46
Rainy River, Ont., Can................*o16 41
Rainy River, dist., Ont., Can.........o16 41
Raipur, India.........................D7 20
Rājahmundry, India....................E7 20
Rajapalaiyam, India...................*G6 20
Rājasthān, state, India...............C5 20
Rājkot, India.........................D5 20
Rājshāhi, Bngl........................D8 20

Rakovnik, Czech.......................C2 · 7
Rakvere, Sov. Un......................B6 12
Raleigh, N.C..........................B4 76
Raleigh, W. Va........................n13 87
Raleigh, co., W. Va...................D3 87
Ralls, Tex............................C2 84
Ralls, co., Mo........................B6 69
Ralston, Nebr.........................g12 71
Rām Allāh, Jordan.....................*C3 15
Ramat Gan, Isr........................B2 15
Ramat HaSharon, Isr...................*B2 15
Rambervillers, Fr.....................C7 5
Ramea, Newf, Can......................E3 44
Ramenskoye, Sov. Un...............D12, n18 12
Ramla, Isr............................C2 15
Ramleh, Eg............................*G8 14
Ramona, Calif.........................F5 50
Rāmpur, India.........................C6 20
Ramsay, Mich..........................n12 66
Ramseur, N.C..........................B3 76
Ramsey, N.J...........................A4 74
Ramsey, co. Minn......................E5 67
Ramsey, co., N. Dak...................B7 77
Ramsgate, Eng.........................E7 4
Rancagua, Chile.......................A2 28
Ranches of Taos, N. Mex...............A6 48
Rānchī, India.........................D8 20
Rancho Cordova, Calif.................*C3 50
Rand, W. Va...........................m12 87
Randall, co., Tex.....................B2 84
Randallstown, Md......................B4 53
Randers, Den..........................I4 11
Randers, co., Den.....................*I4 11
Randleman, N.C........................B3 76
Randolph, Maine.......................D3 64
Randolph, Mass.....................B5, h11 65
Randolph, Nebr........................B8 71
Randolph, Vt..........................D2 73
Randolph, Wis.........................E4 88
Randolph, co., Ala....................B4 46
Randolph, co., Ark....................A4 49
Randolph, co., Ga.....................E2 55
Randolph, co., Ill....................E4 58
Randolph, co., Ind....................D7 59
Randolph, co., Mo.....................B5 69
Randolph, co., N.C....................B3 76
Randolph, co., W. Va..................C5 87

Randolph Hills, Md....................*B3 53
Rangely, Colo.........................A2 51
Ranger, Tex...........................C3 84
Rangoon, Bur..........................E10 20
Rangpur, Bngl.........................C8 20
Rāniganj, India.......................D8 20
Rankin, Pa............................k14 81
Rankin, Tex...........................D2 84
Rankin, co., Miss.....................C4 68
Ranlo, N.C............................*B1 76
Ranshaw, Pa...........................*E9 81
Ransom, co., N. Dak...................D8 77
Ranson, W. Va.........................B7 87
Rantoul, Ill..........................C5 58
Rapallo, It...........................B2 9
Rapid City, S. Dak....................F2 77
Rapides, par., La.....................C3 63
Rappahannock, co., Va.................B4 85
Raritan, N.J..........................B3 74
Raseiniai, Sov. Un....................A7 12
Rashīd (Rosetta), Eg..................G8 14
Rasht, Iran...........................A7 23
Rasskazovo, Sov. Un...................E13 12
Rastatt, Ger. Dem. Rep. of............D4 6
Rat Buri, Thai........................C1 19
Rathenow, Ger. Dem. Rep...............B6 6
Ratibor, see Raciborz, Pol.
Ratlām, India.........................*D6 20
Ratnāgiri, India......................E5 20
Raton, N. Mex.........................A6 48
Rauch, Arg............................B5 28
Rauma, Fin............................G9 11
Raurkela, India.......................*D7 20
Ravalli, co., Mont....................D2 70
Rava-Russkaya, Sov. Un................F4 12
Raven, Va.............................e10 85
Ravena, N.Y...........................C7 75
Ravenna, It...........................B4 9
Ravenna, Ky...........................C6 62
Ravenna, Nebr.........................C7 71
Ravenna, Ohio.........................A4 78
Ravensburg, Ger. Fed. Rep. of.........E4 6
Ravenswood, W. Va.....................C3 87
Rāwalpindi, Pak.......................B5 20
Rawa Mazowiecka, Pol..................C6 7
Rawdon, Que., Can.....................C4 42
Rawicz, Pol...........................C4 7

Rawlins, Wyo..........................E5 89
Rawlins, co.,Kans.....................C2 61
Rawlins, co., Kan.....................C2 61
Ray, Ariz.........................C3, D3 48
Ray, N. Dak...........................B2 77
Ray, co., Mo..........................B3 69
Raybon, Ga............................E5 55
Raychikhinsk, Sov. Un.................B4 18
Raymond, Alta, Can....................E4 38
Raymond, Miss.........................C3 68
Raymond, Wash.........................C2 86
Raymond Terrace, Austl................F8 26
Raymondville, Tex.....................F4 84
Rayne, La.............................D3 63
Raynham Center, Mass..................C5 65
Rayong, Thai..........................*C2 19
Raytown, Ga...........................C4 55
Raytown, Mo...........................h11 69
Rayville, La..........................B4 63
Razgrad, Bul..........................D8 10
Razlog, Bul...........................E6 10
Reading, Eng..........................E6 4
Reading, Mass......................A5, f11 65
Reading, Mich.........................G6 66
Reading, Ohio......................C1, o13 78
Reading, Pa...........................F10 81
Reagan, co., Tex......................D2 84
Real, co., Tex........................E3 84
Ream, Camb............................*C2 19
Ream, W. Va...........................*D3 87
Reamstown, Pa.........................F9 81
Recanati, It..........................C4 9
Rechitsa, Sov. Un.....................E8 12
Recife (Pernambuco), Braz.............D7 27
Recklinghausen, Ger. Fed.
Rep. of...........................C3 6
Reconquista, Arg......................E4 29
Rector, Ark...........................A5 49
Red, riv., U.S........................D8 45
Red, sea, Afr.........................D9 21
Red, sea, Asia........................D9 21
Red Bank, N.J.........................C4 74
Red Bank, Tenn........................D8 83
Red Bay, Ala..........................A1 46
Red Bluff, Calif......................B2 50
Red Boiling Springs, Tenn.............C8 83
Red Bud, Ill..........................E4 58

Redcliff, Alta, Can. D5 38
Red Cloud, Nebr. D7 71
Red Deer, Alta, Can. C4, g8 38
Reddell, La. D3 63
Redding, Calif. B2 50
Redfield, Iowa C3 60
Redfield, S. Dak. F7 77
Redford Township, Mich. p15 66
Red Hill, Pa. *F11 81
Red Hook, N.Y. D7 75
Redington, Beach, Fla. *E4 54
Redington Shores, Fla. *E4 54
Red Jacket, W. Va. D2 87
Red Key, Ind. D7 59
Red Lake, Ont., Can. o16 41
Red Lake, co., Minn. C2 67
Red Lake Falls, Minn. C2 67
Redlands, Calif. E5 50
Red Lion, Pa. G8 81
Red Lodge, Mont. E7 70
Redmond, Oreg. C5 80
Redmond, Wash. e11 86
Red Oak, Ga. h7 55
Redon, Fr. D3 5
Redondela, Sp. A1 8
Redondo Beach, Calif. n12 50
Redore, Minn. C6 67
Red River, co., Tex. C5 84
Red River, par., La. *B2 63
Red Springs, N.C. C3 76
Redstown, Colo. B3 51
Red Tank, C.Z. *B2 32
Redtop, Mo. D4 69
Redwater, Alta, Can. C4 38
Red Willow, co., Nebr. D5 71
Red Wing, Minn. F6 67
Redwood, co., Minn. F3 67
Redwood City, Calif. D2 k8 50
Redwood Estates, Calif. *D3 50
Redwood Falls, Minn. *F3 67
Reed City, Mich. E5 66
Reedley, Calif. D4 50
Reedsburg, Wis. E3 88
Reeds Lake, Mich. *F5 66
Reedsport, Oreg. D2 80
Reedsville, Pa. E6 81
Reese Village, Tex. *C2 84
Reeves, co., Tex. o13 84
Reform, Ala. B1 46
Refuge, Tex. D5 84
Refugio, co., Tex. E4 84
Regensburg, Ger., Fed. Rep. of D6 6
Reggio di Calabria, It. E5 9
Reggio nell 'Emilia, It. B3 9
Reghin, Rom. B7 10
Regina, Sask., Can. G3, n8 39
Region Occidental
  (Chaco), dept., Par. *D3 29
Regla, Cuba, (part of Havanna) C2 35
Rehoboth Beach, Del. C7 53
Rehovot, Isr. C2 15
Reichenbach, Ger. Dem. Rep. C6 6
Reidsville, Ga. D4 55
Reidsville, N.C. A3 76
Reigate, Eng. E6, m12 4
Reims, Fr. C6 5
Reinbeck, Iowa B5 60
Reindeer, lake, Can. E13 36
Reinosa, Sp. A3 8
Reisterstown, Md. B4 53
Rembertów, Pol., (part of
  Warsaw) B6, k14 7
Remedios, Cuba C4 35
Remerton, Ga. F3 55
Remington, Ind. C3 59
Remiremont, Fr. C7 5
Remscheid, Ger., Fed. Rep. of C3 6
Remsen, Iowa B2 60
Rendsburg, Ger., Fed. Rep. of A4 6
Renfrew, Ont., Can. B8 41
Renfrew, co., Ont., Can. B7 41
Renfrew, co., Scot. *C4 4
Rengo, Chile A2 28
Rennes, Fr. C3 5
Reno, Nev. B2 72
Reno, co., Kans. E5 61
Renovo, Pa. D6 81
Rensselaer, Ind. C3 59
Rensselaer, N.Y. C6 75
Rensselaer, co., N.Y. C7 75
Renton, Wash. B3, f11 86
Renville, Minn. F3 67
Renville, co., Minn. F3 67
Renville, co., N. Dak. B4 77
Republic, Mich. B3 66
Republic, Mo. D4 69
Republic, Pa. G2 81
Republic, Wash. A7 86
Republic, co., Kans. C7 61
Requena, Sp. C5 8
Reserve, La. h10 63
Resistencia, Arg. E4 29
Resita, Rom. C5 10

Restigouche, co., N.B., Can. B2 43
Reston, Va. B5 85
Reszel, Pol. A6 7
Retalhuleu, Guat. E6 34
Rethimni (Rhethymnon), prov.,
  Grc. *E5 14
Réthimnon, Grc. E5 14
Reus, Sp. B6 8
Reutlingen, Ger., Fed. Rep. of D4 6
Revel, Fr. F5 5
Revelo, Ky. D5 62
Revelstoke, B.C., Can. D8 37
Revere, Mass. g11 65
Revere, Minn. F3 67
Revin, Fr. C6 5
Revloc, Pa. F4 81
Rewa, India D7 20
Rewâri, India C6 20
Rexburg, Idaho F7 57
Rey, Iran C5 15
Reykjavik, Ice. n22 11
Reynolds, Ga. D2 55
Reynolds, co., Mo. D6 69
Reynoldsburg, Ohio C3, m11 78
Reynoldsville, Pa. D4 81
Reynosa (Reinosa), Mex. B5 34
Rezé, Fr. D3 5
Rezekne, Sov. Un. C6 12
Rhea, co., Tenn. D9 83
Rheden, Neth. A7 5
Rhein (Rhine), riv., Eur. C3 6
Rheine, Ger., Fed. Rep. of B3 6
Rheinland-Pfalz, state, Ger.,
  Fed. Rep. of C3 6
Rheydt, Ger., Fed. Rep. of *C3 6
Rhinebeck, N.Y. D7 75
Rhineland, reg., Ger., Fed.
  Rep. of C3 6
Rhinelander, Wis. C4 88
Rhode Island, state, U.S. 52
Rhodesia, see Zimbabwe, Afr.
Rhodhiss, N.C. B1 76
Rhondda, Wales E5 4
Rhône, dept., Fr. *E6 5
Rhyl, Wales D5 4
Rialto, Calif. m14 50
Rianjo, Sp. A1 8
Ribadavia, Sp. A1 8
Ribadeo, Sp. A2 8
Ribadesella, Sp. A3 8
Ribatejo, prov., Port. *C1 8
Ribe, co., Den. *J3 11
Ribeirào Prêto, Braz. C3, k8 30
Ribera, It. F4 9
Ričany, Czech. o18 7
Rice, co., Kans. D5 61
Rice, co., Minn. F5 67
Rice Lake, Wis. C2 88
Riceville, Iowa A5 60
Rich, Miss. A3 68
Rich, co., Utah A6 72
Richardson, Tex. n10 84
Richardson, co., Nebr. D10 71
Richelieu, co., Que., Can. D4 42
Richfield, Calif. C2 50
Richfield, Minn. n12 67
Richfield, Utah B5 72
Richfield Springs, N.Y. C6 75
Richford, Vt. B3 73
Rich Hill, Mo. C3 69
Richibucto, N.B., Can. C5 43
Richland, Ga. D2 55
Richland, Mo. D5 69
Richland, Pa. *F9 81
Richland, Wash. C6 86
Richland, co., Ill. E5 58
Richland, co., Mont. C12 70
Richland, co., N. Dak. D9 77
Richland, co., Ohio B3 78
Richland, co., S.C. D6 82
Richland, co., Wis. E3 88
Richland, par., La. B4 63
Richland Center, Wis. E3 88
Richland Hills, Tex. *C4 84
Richlands, N.C. C5 76
Richlands, Va. e10 85
Richmond, Calif. D2, h8 50
Richmond, Que., Can. D5 42
Richmond, Ind. E8 59
Richmond, Ky. C5 62
Richmond, Maine D3, f8 64
Richmond, Mich. F8 66
Richmond, Mo. B4 69
Richmond, Tex. E5, r14 84
Richmond, Utah A6 72
Richmond (Independent City),
  Va. C5, m18 85
Richmond (Staten Island), borough
  and co., N.Y. E6 75
Richmond, co., N.S., Can. D9 43
Richmond, co., Que., Can. D5 42
Richmond, co., Ga. C4 55
Richmond, co., N.C. B3 76

Richmond, co., Va. C6 85
Richmond Beach, Wash. B3 86
Richmond Heights, Fla. s13 54
Richmond Heights, Mo. f13 69
Richmond Highlands, Wash. *B3 86
Richmond Hill, Ont., Can. D5, k15 41
Richmond Hill, N.C. *B3 76
Richmond-Windsor, Austl. F8 26
Rich Square, N.C. A5 76
Richton, Miss. D5 68
Richwood, Ohio B2 78
Richwood, W. Va. C4 87
Riddle, Oreg. E3 80
Ridge, Va. *C5 85
Ridgecrest, Calif. *E5 50
Ridgecrest, Wash. *B3 86
Ridgedale, Mo. E4 69
Ridgedale, Tenn. C10 83
Ridge Farm, Ill. D6 58
Ridgefield, Conn. D3 52
Ridgefield, N.J. h8 74
Ridgefield Park, N.J. B4, h8 74
Ridgeland, S.C. G6 82
Ridgeley, W.Va. B6 87
Ridgely, Tenn. A2 83
Ridgetown, Ont., Can. E3 41
Ridgeville, Ga. E5 55
Ridgeville, Ind. D7 59
Ridgewood, Ill. B5 58
Ridgewood, N.J. B4 74
Ridgewood Heights, Ohio *C1 78
Ridgway, Ill. F5 58
Ridgway, Pa. D4 81
Ridley Farms, Pa. *G11 81
Ridley Park, Pa. p20 81
Ried, Aus. D6 6
Riegelsville, Pa. B2 81
Riesa, Ger. Dem. Rep. C6 6
Rieti, It. C4 9
Rifle, Colo. B3 51
Rïga, Sov. Un. C5 12
Rigaud, Que., Can. D3 42
Rigby, Idaho F7 57
Riihimäki, Fin. G11 11
Rijeka (Fiume), Yugo. C2 10
Riley, co., Kans. C7 61
Rimbey, Alta., Can. C3 38
Rimersburg, Pa. D2 81
Rimini, It. B4 9
Rîmnicu-Sărat, Rom. C8 10
Rîmnicu-Vîlcea, Rom. C7 10
Rimouski, Que., Can. A9 42
Rimouski, co., Que., Can. A9 42
Rincon, Ga. D5 55
Ringgold, Ga. B1 55
Ringgold, La. B2 63
Ringgold, co., Iowa D3 60
Ringkobing, co., Den. *I3 11
Ringling, Okla. C4 79
Ringsaker, Nor. G4 11
Ringsted, Den. A1 7
Ringwood, N.J. A4 74
Rinjani, peak, Indon. G5 19
Rio Arriba, co., N.Mex. A5 48
Riobamba, Ec. B2 31
Rio Blanco, co., Colo. B2 51
Rio Branco, Braz. C4 31
Rio Caribe, Ven. A5 32
Rio Claro, Braz. C3, m8 30
Rio Cuarto, Arg. A4 28
Rio de Janeiro, Braz. C4, h6 30
Rio de Janeiro, state, Braz. C4, h6 30
Rio Dell, Calif. B1 50
Rio Gallegos, Arg. E3, h12 28
Rio Grande, Braz. E2 30
Rio Grande, Mex. C4 34
Rio Grande, N.J. E3 74
Rio Grande, co., Colo. D4 51
Rio Grande (Rio Bravo del Norte),
  river, Mex., U.S. E6 45
Rio Grande do Norte, state, Braz. *D7 30
Rio Grande do Sul, state, Braz. E2 30
Riohacha, Col. A3 32
Rio Hondo, Tex. F4 84
Rio Linda, Calif. *C3 50
Hıom, Fr. E5 5
Rio Muni, reg., Equat. Gui. H7 22
Rio Negro, Braz. D3 30
Rio Negro, dept. Ur. *E1 30
Rio Negro, prov., Arg. C3 28
Rionero in Vulture, It. D5 9
Rio Pardo, Braz. D2 30
Rio Piedras, P.R. *G11 35
Rio Tercero, Arg. A4 28
Rio Verde, Braz. B2 30
Rio Verde (Rioverde), Mex. m13 34
Rio Vista, Calif. C3 50
Ripley, Miss. A5 68
Ripley, N.Y. C1 75
Ripley, Ohio D2 78
Ripley, Tenn. B2 83
Ripley, W. Va. C3 87
Ripley, co., Ind. F7 59

Ripley, co., Mo. E7 69
Ripoll, Sp. A7 8
Ripon, Calif. *D3 50
Ripon, Eng. C6 4
Ripon, Wis. E5 88
Rishon leZiyyon, Isr. C2 15
Rising Star, Tex. C3 84
Rising Sun, Ind. G8 59
Rison, Ark. D3 49
Ritchey, Mo. E3 69
Ritchie, co., W. Va. B3 87
Rittman, Ohio B4 78
Ritzville, Wash. B7 86
Riva, It. B3 9
Rivadavia, Arg. A3 28
Rive-de-Gier, Fr. E6 5
Rivera, Ur. E1 30
Rivera, dept., Ur. *E1 30
Riverbank, Calif. D3 50
Riverdale, Calif. D4 50
Riverdale, Ill. k9 58
Riverdale, Md. C4, f9 53
Riverdale, N.J. B4 74
Riverdale, N. Dak. C4 77
Riverdale, Oreg. *B4 80
Riverdale, Utah *A6 72
Riverdale Heights, Md. *C4 53
River Edge, N.J. h8 74
River Falls, Wis. D1 88
River Forest, Ill. k9 58
River Grove, Ill. k9 58
Riverhead, N.Y. n15 75
River Hebert, N.S., Can. D5 43
River Hills, Wis. m12 88
Riverina, reg., Austl. F7 25
Riverland Terrace, S.C. k12 82
River Pines, Mass. *A5 65
River Plaza, N.J. *C4 74
River Rouge, Mich. F7, p15 66
Rivers, Man., Can. D1 40
Riverside, Calif. F5, n14 50
Riverside, Ont., Can. E2 41
Riverside, Colo. B5 51
Riverside, Ill. k9 58
Riverside, Mich. *F6 66
Riverside, Mo. *B3 69
Riverside, N.J. C3 74
Riverside, N.Y. *C3 75
Riverside, Pa. E8 81
Riverside, S.C. *B3 82
Riverside, co., Calif. F5 50
Riverton, Ill. D4 58
Riverton, N.J. C3 74
Riverton, Utah D2 72
Riverton, Wyo. C4 89
Riverton Heights, Wash. *B3 86
River Vale, N.J. *A5 74
River View, Ala. C4 46
Riverview, Fla. p11 54
Riverview, Mich. p15 66
Riverview, Mo. *C7 69
Riverview (Pasco West), Wash. *C6 86
Rives, Fr. E7 69
Rivesville, W. Va. B4, h10 87
Riviera Beach, Fla. F6 54
Riviera Beach, Md. *B4 53
Rivière-Bleue, Que., Can. B8 42
Rivière-du-Loup, Que., Can. B8 42
Rivière-du-Loup, co., Que., Can. B9 42
Riyadh (Ar Riyāḍ), Sau. Ar. E4 15
Rizal, Prov., Phil. *B6 19
Rize, Tur. B13 14
Rjukan, Nor. H3 11
Roachdale, Ind. E4 59
Roane, co., Tenn. D9 83
Roane, co., W. Va. C3 87
Roan Mountain, Tenn. C11 83
Roanne, Fr. D5 5
Roanoke, Ala. B4 46
Roanoke, Ill. C4 58
Roanoke, Ind. C7 59
Roanoke (Independent City), Va. C3 85
Roanoke, co., Va. C2 85
Roanoke Rapids, N.C. A5 76
Roanoke Rapids West, N.C. *A5 76
Roaring Springs, Pa. F5 81
Robbins, Ill. k9 58
Robbins, N.C. B3 76
Robbinsdale, Minn. E5, m12 67
Robersonville, N.C. B5 76
Robert Lee, Tex. D2 84
Roberts, co., S. Dak. E9 77
Roberts, co., Tex. B2 84
Robertsdale, Pa. F5 81
Robertsdale, Ala. E2 46
Robertson, co., Ky. B5 62
Robertson, co., Tenn. A5 83
Robertson, co., Tex. D4 84
Robertsonville, Que., Can. C6 42
Roberval, Que., Can. A5 42
Robeson, co., N.C. C3 76
Robesonia, Pa. *F9 81
Robinson, Ill. D6 58

Robinson, Pa. F3 81
Robinson, Tex. *D4 84
Robinsonville, Miss. A3 68
Roblin, Man., Can. D1 40
Robson, mtn., Can. C1 38
Robstown, Tex. F4 84
Roby, Mo. D5 69
Roby, Tex. C2 84
Roccastrada, It. C3 9
Rocha, Ur. E2 30
Rocha, dept., Ur. *E2 30
Rochdale, Eng. D5 4
Rochdale, Mass. B4 65
Rochefort, Fr. E3 5
Rochelle, Ga. E3 55
Rochelle, Ill. B4 58
Rochelle Park, N.J. h8 74
Rochester, Ind. B5 59
Rochester, Mich. F7 66
Rochester, Minn. F6 67
Rochester, N.H. E6 73
Rochester, N.Y. B3 75
Rochester, Pa. E1 81
Rock, co., Minn. G2 67
Rock, co., Nebr. B6 71
Rock, co., Wis. F4 88
Rockaway, N.J. B3 74
Rockaway, Oreg. B3 80
Rockbridge, co., Va. C3 85
Rockcastle, co., Ky. C5 62
Rockcliffe Park, Ont., Can. *B9 41
Rock Creek Hills, Md. *B3 53
Rockdale, Ill. B5, m8 58
Rockdale, Md. *B4 53
Rockdale, Tex. D4 84
Rockdale, co., Ga. C2 55
Rock Falls, Ill. B4 58
Rockford, Ill. A4 58
Rockford, Iowa A5 60
Rockford, Mich. E5 66
Rockford, Ohio B1 78
Rockford, Tenn. D10, n14 83
Rock Hall, Md. B5 53
Rockhampton, Austl. D9 25
Rock Hill, Mo. *C7 69
Rock Hill, S.C. B5 82
Rockingham, N.C. C3 76
Rockingham, co., N.H. E5 73
Rockingham, co., N.C. A3 76
Rockingham, co., Va. B4 85
Rock Island, Que., Can. D5 42
Rock Island, Ill. B3 58
Rock Island, co., Ill. B3 58
Rockland, Ont., Can. B9 41
Rockland, Maine B3 64
Rockland, Mass. B6, h12 65
Rockland, co., N.Y. D6 75
Rockledge, Fla. D6 54
Rockledge, Pa. o21 81
Rocklin, Calif. *C3 50
Rockmart, Ga. B1 55
Rockport, Ind. I3 59
Rockport, Maine D3 64
Rockport, Mass. A6 65
Rock Port, Mo. A2 69
Rockport, Tex. F4 84
Rock Rapids, Iowa A1 60
Rocksprings, Tex. D2 84
Rock Springs, Wyo. E3 89
Rockton, Ill. A4 58
Rock Valley, Iowa A1 60
Rockville, Conn. B7 52
Rockville, Ind. E3 59
Rockville, Md. B3 53
Rockville Center, N.Y. n15 75
Rockwall, Tex. C4, n10 84
Rockwall, co., Tex. C4 84
Rockwell City, Iowa B3 60
Rockwood, Mich. F7 66
Rockwood, Pa. F3 81
Rockwood, Tenn. D9 83
Rocky Ford, Colo. C7 51
Rocky Grove, Pa. D2 81
Rocky Hill, Conn. C6 52
Rocky Mount, N.C. B5 76
Rocky Mount, Va. C3 85
Rocky Mountain House,
 Alta., Can. C3 38
Rocky Point, N.Y. *n15 75
Rocky Point, Wash. *B3 86
Rocky Ripple, Ind. k10 59
Rocky River, Ohio A4, h9 78
Roddickton, Newf., Can. C3, h10 44
Rodeo, Calif. *D3 50
Roderfield, W. Va. D3 87
Rodessa, La. B1 63
Rodez, Fr. E5 5
Rodgers Forge, Md. *B4 53
Rodhópi (Rhodope), prov., Grc. .. *B5 14
Ródhos, Grc. D7 14
Rodney, Ont., Can. E3 41
Rodney Village, Del. B6 53
Roebling, N.J. C3 74

Roeland Park, Kans. B9 61
Roermond, Neth. B6 5
Roeselare, Bel. B5 5
Roessleville, N.Y. *C7 75
Rogachev, Sov. Un. E8 12
Rogaland, co., Nor. *H1 11
Rogatica, Yugo. D4 10
Roger Mills, co., Okla. B2 79
Rogers, Ark. A1 49
Rogers, Tex. D4 84
Rogers, Va. f10 85
Rogers, co., Okla. A6 79
Rogers City, Mich. C7 66
Rogers Heights, Md. *C4 53
Rogersville, Tenn. C10 83
Rogoźno, Pol. B4 7
Rohnerville, Calif. *B1 50
Rohtak, India *C6 20
Roi Et, Thai. B2 19
Rojas, Arg. A4 28
Rokitno, Sov. Un. F6 12
Rokycany, Czech. D2 7
Roland Terrace, Md. *B4 53
Rolette, co., N. Dak. B6 77
Rolfe, Iowa B3 60
Rolla, Mo. D6 69
Rolla, N. Dak. A6 77
Rolling Fork, Miss. C3 68
Rolling Hills, Kans. B5 61
Rolling Hills Estates, Calif. .. *F4 50
Rolling Meadows, Ill. h8 58
Rollingwood, Calif. *D2 50
Roma, Austl. E8 25
Roma, Tex. F3 84
Roma, see Rome, It.
Roman, Rom. B8 10
Romania, country, Eur. B7 10
Romans -sur-Isère, Fr. E6 5
Romblon, Phil. *C6 19
Romblon, prov., Phil. *C6 19
Rome, Ga. B1 55
Rome, Ill. C4 58
Rome (Roma), It. D4, h8 9
Rome, N.Y. B5 75
Rome, Ohio *A5 78
Romeo, Ill. *B5 58
Romeo, Mich. F7 66
Romilly -sur-Seine, Fr. C5 5
Romita, Mex. m11 34
Romney, W.Va. B6 87
Romny, Sov. Un. F9 12
Romorantin, Fr. D4 5
Romulus, Mich. p15 66
Ronan, Mont. C2 70
Roncerverte, W. Va. D4 87
Ronciglione, It. C4 9
Ronda, Sp. D3 8
Rondôia, ter., Braz. B3 29
Ronkonkoma, N.Y. F4 52
Rønne, Den. A3 7
Ronse, Bel. B5 5
Roodhouse, Ill. D3 58
Rooks, co., Kans. C4 61
Roosendaal, Neth. B6 5
Roosevelt, N.Y. G2 52
Roosevelt, Utah A6 72
Roosevelt, co., Mont. B11 70
Roosevelt, co., N. Mex. B7 48
Roosevelt, riv., Braz. B3 29
Roosevelt Park, Mich. E4 66
Roquetas, Sp. B6 8
Roquevaire, Ky. E4 62
Rorschach, Switz. E4 6
Rosa, mtn., It., Switz. B2 9
Roraima, ter., Braz. C5 32
Rosario, Arg. A4 28
Rosário, Braz. *D6 27
Rosario, Mex. C3 34
Rosario, Par. D4 29
Rosario, Ur. E1 30
Rosário do Sul, Braz. E2 30
Rosario Tala, Arg. A5 28
Rosburg, Wash. B5 89
Roscoe, N.Y. D6 75
Roscoe, Pa. F2 81
Roscoe, Tex. C2 84
Roscommon, co., Ire. *D2 4
Roscommon, co., Mich. D6 66
Roseau, Dominica I14 35
Roseau, Minn. B3 67
Roseau, co., Minn. B3 67
Roseboro, N.C. C4 76
Rosebud, Tex. D4 84
Rosebud, co., Mont. D10 70
Roseburg, Oreg. D3 80
Rosedale, Fla. *E4 54
Rosedale, Miss. B2 68
Rosedale Station, Alta., Can. ... D4 38
Rose Hill, Kans. E6 61
Rose Hill, N.C. C4 76
Roseland, Fla. E6 54
Roseland, Ind. A5 59
Roseland, La. *D5 63
Roseland, N.J. *B4 74

Roseland, Ohio B3 78
Roselle, Ill. k8 58
Roselle, N.J. k7 74
Roselle Park, N.J. k7 74
Rosemead, Calif. *F4 50
Rosemère, Que., Can. p19 42
Rosemont, Ill. *E3 58
Rosemont, Pa. *F11 81
Rosemount, Minn. F5 67
Rosenberg, Tex. E5, r14 84
Rosendael, Fr. B5 5
Rosendale, N.Y. *C6 75
Rosenheim, Ger., Fed. Rep of E6 6
Roseto, Pa. E11 81
Rosetown, Sask., Can. F1, n7 39
Roseville, Calif. C3 50
Roseville, Ill. C3 58
Roseville, Mich. o16 66
Roseville, Minn. m12 67
Roseville, Ohio C3 78
Rosewood, Calif. *B1 50
Rosewood Heights, Ill. *E3 58
Rosiclare, Ill. F5 58
Rosiorii-de-Vede, Rom. C7 10
Roskilde, co., Den. *J5 11
Roslavl, Sov. Un. E9 12
Roslyn, N.Y. *E7 75
Roslyn, Pa. *F11 81
Roslyn, Wash. B4 86
Roslyn Estates, N.Y. *G2 52
Roslyn Harbor, N.Y. *E7 75
Roslyn Heights, N.Y. D2, h13 75
Rosny-sous-Bois, Fr. g10 5
Ross, Calif. *C2 50
Ross, co., Ohio C2 78
Ross and Cromarty, co., Scot. .. *B4 4
Rossano, It. E6 9
Rossford, Ohio A2, e6 78
Rossiter, Pa. E4 81
Rossland, B.C., Can. E9 37
Rossmoor, Calif. *F5 50
Rossmoyne, Ohio *C1 78
Rossosh, Sov. Un. F12 12
Rossville, Ga. B1 55
Rossville, Ill. C6 58
Rossville, Kan. C8 61
Rosthern, Sask., Can. E2 39
Rostock, Ger. Dem. Rep. A6 6
Rostov, Sov. Un. C12 12
Rostov -na-Donu, Sov. Un. H12 12
Roswell, Ga. B2 55
Roswell, N. Mex. C6 40
Rotan, Tex. C2 84
Rotenburg an der Fulda,
 Ger., Fed. Rep of B4 6
Rothenburg ob der Tauber
 Ger., Fed. Rep of D5 6
Rothesay, Scot. C4 4
Rothschild, Wis. D4 88
Rothsville, Pa. F9 81
Rotondella, It. D6 9
Rotorua, N.Z. M16 26
Rotterdam, Neth. B6 5
Rotterdam, N.Y. *C6 75
Rottweil, Ger., Fed. Rep of D4 6
Roubaix, Fr. B5 5
Roudnice ned Labem, Czech. n7 17
Rouen, Fr. C4 5
Roulette, Pa. C5 81
Round Lake, Ill. h8 58
Roundlake, Miss. A3 68
Round Lake Beach, Ill. h8 58
Round Lake Heights, Ill. *h8 58
Round Lake Park, Ill. *h8 58
Round Pond, Ark. *B5 49
Round Rock, Tex. D4 84
Roundup, Mont. D8 70
Rouses Point, N.Y. f11 75
Rouseville, Pa. D2 81
Routt, co., Colo. A3 51
Rouville, co., Que., Can. D4 42
Rouzerville, Pa. G7 81
Rovaniemi, Fin. D11 11
Rovato, It. B2 9
Rovenki, Sov. Un. G12, q22 12
Rovereto, It. B3 9
Rovigo, It. B3 9
Rovinj, Yugo. C1 10
Rovno, Sov. Un. F6 12
Rovnoye, Sov. Un. F16 12
Rowan, co., Ky. B6 62
Rowan, co., N.C. B2 76
Rowan Mill, N.C. B2 76
Rowes Run, Pa. *F2 81
Rowland, N.C. C3 76
Rowland, Pa. D11 81
Rowlesburg, W. Va. B5 87
Rowlett, Tex. *C4 84
Rowley, Mass. A6 65
Roxana, Ill. f13 69
Roxas (Capiz), Phil. C6 19
Roxboro, N.C. A4 76
Roxburgh, co., Scot. *C5 4
Roxton Falls, Que., Can. D5 42

Roy, N. Mex. B6 48
Roy, Utah A5, C2 72
Royal, Fla. D4 54
Royal Center, Ind. C4 59
Royal Mills, N.C. A4 76
Royal Oak, Mich. F7, o15 66
Royal Oak, Township,
 Mich. *F7 66
Royalton, Ill. F4 58
Royalton, Pa. *F8 81
Royan, Fr. E3 5
Royersford, Pa. F10 81
Royse City, Tex. C4 84
Royston, Ga. B3 55
Rožňava, Czech. D6 7
Rtishchevo, Sov. Un. E14 12
Ruapehu, mtn., N.Z. M15 26
Rubezhnoye, Sov. Un. p21 12
Rubidoux, Calif. n14 50
Ruda Slaska, Pol. *C5 7
Rudbar, Afg. B3 20
Rudolf, lake, Afr. F9 21
Rudolstadt, Ger. Dem. Rep. C5 6
Rueil-Malmaison, Fr. g9 5
Rufino, Arg. A4 28
Rufisque, Sen. F1 22
Rugby, Eng. D6 4
Rugby, N. Dak. B6 77
Ruidoso, N. Mex. C6 48
Rule, Tex. C3 84
Ruleville, Miss. B3 68
Ruma, Yugo. C4 10
Rumford, Maine D2 64
Rumoi, Jap. E10 18
Rumson, N.J. C4 74
Runge, Tex. E4 84
Runnels, co., Tex. D3 84
Runnemede, N.J. D2 74
Rupert, Idaho G5 57
Rupert, W. Va. D4 87
Rural Hall, N.C. A2 76
Ruse (Ruschuk), Bul. *D7 10
Ruse (Ruschuk), co., Bul. *D8 10
Rush, co., Ind. E7 59
Rush City, Minn. E6 67
Rush, co., Kan. D4 61
Rushford, Minn. G7 67
Rush Springs, Okla. C4 79
Rushville, Ill. C3 58
Rushville, Ind. E7 59
Rushville, Nebr. B3 71
Rusk, Tex. D5 84
Rusk, co.,Tex. C5 84
Rusk, co., Wis. C2 88
Ruskin, Fla. E4, p11 54
Russas, Braz. *D7 27
Russell (Russell City), Calif. . *D3 50
Russell, Man., Can. D1 40
Russell, Kans. D5 61
Russell, Ky. B7 62
Russell, co., Ala. C4 46
Russell, co., Ont. Can. B9 41
Russell, co., Kans. D5 61
Russell, co., Ky. C4 62
Russell, co., Va. f9 85
Russell Gardens, N.Y. *E7 75
Russells Point, Ohio *B2 78
Russell Springs, Ky. C4 62
Russellton, Pa. E2 81
Russellville, Ala. A2 46
Russellville, Ark. B2 49
Russellville, Ky. D3 62
Russian Soviet Federated Socialist
 Republic, rep., Sov. Un. C8 12
Russiaville, Ind. D5 59
Rustavi, Sov. Un. B15 14
Ruston, La. B3 63
Rutchenkovo, Sov. Un. r20 12
Rute, Sp. D3 8
Ruteng, Indon. G6 19
Ruth, Miss. D3 68
Ruth, Nev. B4 72
Ruthenia, reg., Sov. Un. D7 7
Rutherford, N.J. B4, h8 74
Rutherford, Tenn. A3 83
Rutherford, co., N.C. B1 76
Rutherford, co., Tenn. B5 83
Rutherford Heights, Pa. *F8 81
Rutherfordton, N.C. B1, f11 76
Rutland, Mass. B4 65
Rutland, Vt. D2 73
Rutland, co., Eng. *D6 4
Rutland, co., Vt. D1 73
Rutledge, Pa. *G11 81
Ruvo di Puglia, It. D6 9
Ruxton, Md. *B4 53
Ruzayevka, Sov. Un. D15 12
Ružomberok, Czech. D5 7
Rwanda, country, Afr. I3 23
Ryazan, Sov. Un. D12 12
Rybink, Pol. C5, g9 7
Rydal, Pa. *F11 81
Ryde, Eng. E6 4

Rye, N.Y. ... h13, n15 75
Rylsk, Sov. Un. ... F10 12
Ryotsu, Jap. ... G9 18
Rypin, Pol. ... B5 7
Ryukyu Islands, Jap. ... F10 7
Rzeszów, Po. ... C6 7
Rzhev, Sov. Un. ... C10 12

S

Saalfeld, Ger. Dem Rep. ... C5 6
Saar, state, Ger. Fed. Rep. of ... D3 6
Saarbrüken, Ger., Fed. Rep. of ... D3 6
Saarlouis, Ger., Fed. Rep. of ... D3 6
Sabac, Yugo. ... C4 10
Sabadell, Sp. ... B7 8
Sabae, Jap. ... n15 18
Sabah (North Borneo), reg., Mala. ... D5 19
Sabana de la Mar, Dom. Rep. ... E9 35
Sabana Grande, P.R. ... *G11 35
Sabanalarga, Col. ... A3 32
Sabang, Indon. ... k11 19
Sabará, Braz. ... B4 30
Sabaudia, It. ... D4 9
Sabetha, Kans. ... C8 61
Sabina, Ohio ... C2 78
Sabinal, Tex. ... E3 84
Sabinas, Mex. ... B4 34
Sabinas Hidalgo, Mex. ... B4 34
Sabine, co., Tex. ... D6 84
Sabine, par., La. ... C2 63
Sablé -sur-Sarthe, Fr. ... D3 5
Sabzawar, Afg. ... B3 20
Sac, co., Iowa ... B2 60
Sac City, Iowa ... B2 60
Sache, China ... F10 16
Sachsen, former state, Ger. Dem. Rep. ... *C6 6
Sachsen-Anhalt (Saxony-Anhalt), former state, Ger. Dem. Rep. ... *C5 6
Sackets Harbor, N.Y. ... B4 75
Sackets Harbor, N.Y. ... B4 75
Sackville, N.B., Can. ... D5 43
Saco, Maine ... E2, g7 64
Sacramento, Calif. ... A6 50
Sacramento, co., Calif. ... C3 50
Sacré-Coeur Saguenay, Que., Can. ... A8 42
Sa'dah, Yemen ... *F3 15
Saddle Brook, N.J. ... *A4 74
Saddle River, N.J. ... *A4 74
Saddle Rock, N.Y. ... *G2 52
Saegertown, Pa. ... C1 81
Saeki, Jap. ... J5 18
Safety Harbor, Fla. ... D4, p10 54
Safford, Ariz. ... C4 48
Safi, Mor. ... B3 22
Safranbolu, Tur. ... B9 14
Saga, China ... C8 20
Saga, Jap. ... J5 18
Saga, pref., Jap. ... *J5 18
Sagadahoc, co., Maine ... E3 64
Sagaing, Bur. ... D10 20
Sagamihara, Jap. ... *I9 18
Sagamore, Pa. ... E3 81
Sagamore Hills, Ohio ... h9 78
Sāgar, India ... D6 20
Sagara, Jap. ... o17 18
Sag Harbor, N.Y. ... n16 75
Saginaw, Mich. ... E7 66
Saginaw, Tex. ... n9 84
Saginaw, co., Mich. ... E6 66
Sagle, Idaho ... A2 57
Saguache, Colo. ... C4 51
Saguache, co., Colo. ... C4 51
Sagua de Tánamo, Cuba ... D6 35
Sagua la Grande, Cuba ... C3 35
Saguenay, co., Que., Can. ... A8 42
Sagunto, Sp. ... C5 8
Sahagún, Col. ... B2 32
Sahāranpur, India ... C6 20
Sahiwal, Pak. ... B5 20
Sahuaripa, Mex. ... B3 34
Sahuayo de Díaz, Mex. ... m12 34
Saida (Sidon), Leb. ... F10 14
Saidpur, Bngl. ... C8 20
Saigo, Jap. ... H6 18
Saigon, see Ho Chi Minh City, Viet.
Saijo, Jap. ... *I6 18
Saiki, Jap. ... J5 18
St. Affrique, Fr. ... F5 5
St. Agapit, Que., Can. ... C6 42
Ste. Agathe-des-Monts, Que., Can. ... C3 42
St. Alban, Que., Can. ... C5 42
St. Alban's, Newf., Can. ... E4 44
St. Albans, Eng. ... h6, k12 4
St. Albans, W. Va. ... C3 87
St. Albans, Vt. ... B1 73
St. Albans Bay, Vt. ... B1 73
St. Albert, Alta., Can. ... C4 38

St. Alexandre -de-Kamouraska, Que., Can. ... B8 42
St. Alexis-des-Monts, Que., Can. ... C3 42
St. Armand-Mont-Rond, Fr. ... D5 5
St. Ambroise-de-Chicoutimi, Que., Can. ... A6 42
St. André-Avellin, Que., Can. ... D2 42
St. Andrews, N.B., Can. ... D2 43
St. Andrews, Scot. ... B5 4
St. Andrews, S.C. ... F7, k11 82
St. Andrews East, Que., Can. ... D3 42
St. Ann, Mo. ... *C7 69
Ste. Anne, Que., Can. ... D4 42
Ste. Anne, Guad. ... H14 35
St. Anne, Ill. ... D6 58
Ste. Anne-de-Beaupré, Que., Can. ... B7 42
Ste. Anne -de-Bellevue, Que., Can. ... q10 42
Ste. Anne-de-la-Pérade, Que., Can. ... C5 42
St. Anselme, Que., Can. ... C7 42
St. Ansgar, Iowa ... A5 60
St. Anthony, Newf., Can. ... C4 44
St. Anthony, Minn. ... *F5 67
St. Antoine des Laurentides, Que., Can. ... *D3 42
St. Apollinaire, Que., Can. ... C6, o16 42
St. Aubert, Que., Can. ... B7 42
St. Augustine, Fla. ... C5, n9 54
St. Avold, Fr. ... C7 5
St. Barthélémy, Que., Can. ... C4 42
St. Basile -de-Portneuf, Que., Can. ... C6 42
St. Bernard, Ohio ... o12 78
St. Bernard, par., La. ... E6 63
St. Bernice, Ind. ... E2 59
St. Bonaventure, N.Y. ... *C2 75
St. Bride, mtn., Alta., Can. ... D3 88
St. Brieuc, Fr. ... C2 5
St. Bruno-Lac-St. Jean, Que., Can. ... A6 42
St. Camille -de-Belle-chasse, Que., Can. ... C7 42
St. Casimir, Que., Can. ... C5 42
St. Catharines, Ont., Can. ... D5 41
Ste. Catherine, Que., Can. ... C6, n16 42
St. Césaire, Que., Can. ... D4 42
St. Chamond, Fr. ... E6 5
St. Charles, Ill. ... B5 58
St. Charles, Mich. ... E6 66
St. Charles, Minn. ... G6 67
St. Charles, Mo. ... C7, f12 69
St. Charles, co., Mo. ... C7 69
St. Charles, par., La. ... E5 63
St. Charles -de-Bellechasse, Que., Can. ... C7 42
St. Christopher-Nevis, country, N.A. ... H13 35
St. Chrysostome, Que., Can. ... D4 42
St. Clair, Mich. ... F8 66
St. Clair, Mo. ... C6 69
St. Clair, Pa. ... E9 81
St. Clair, co., Ala. ... B3 46
St. Clair, co., Ill. ... E3 58
St. Clair, co., Mich. ... F8 66
St. Clair, co., Mo. ... C4 69
Ste. Clair, Que., Can. ... C7 42
St. Clair Haven, Mich. ... *F8 66
St. Clair Shores, Mich. ... *F8 66
St. Clairsville, Ohio ... B5 78
St. Claude, Man., Can. ... E2 40
St. Claude -sur-Bienne, Fr ... D6 5
St. Cloud, Fla. ... D5 54
St. Cloud, Fr. ... g9 5
St. Cloud, Minn. ... E4 67
St. Constant, Que., Can. ... q19 42
St. Croix, Que., Can. ... C6, o16 42
St. Croix, co., Wis. ... C1 88
St. Croix Falls, Wis. ... C1 88
St. Cyrille -de-L'Islet, Que., Can. ... B7 42
St. Cyrille -de-Wendover, Que., Can. ... D5 42
St. Damase, Que., Can. ... D4 42
St. Davids, Pa. ... *G11 81
St. Denis, Fr. ... C5, g10 5
St. Denis, Reunion ... *H24 2
St. Denis -de-la-Bouteillerie, Que., Can. ... B8 42
St. Denis, River Richelieu, Que., Can. ... D4 42

St. Dié, Fr. ... C7 5
St. Dizier, Fr. ... C6 5
St. Donat-de-Mont-calm, Que., Can. ... C3 42
St. Edward, Nebr. ... C8 71
St. Eleuthère, Que., Can. ... B8 42
St. Elias, mts., N.A. ... C11 47
St. Elmo, Ill. ... D5 58
Ste. Emélie-de-l'Energie, Que., Can. ... C4 42
St. Ephrem, Que., Can. ... C7 42
St. Esprit, Que., Can. ... D4 42
St. Etienne, Fr. ... E6 5
St. Eustache, Que., Can. ... D4, p19 42
St. Fabien, Que., Can. ... A9 42
St. Felicien, Que., Can. ... A5 42
St. Félix-de-Valois, Que., Can. ... C4 42
St. Ferdinand, Que., Can. ... C6 42
St. Flavien, Que., Can. ... C6 42
St. Flour, Fr. ... E5 5
Ste. Foy, Que., Can. ... c6 42
St. Francis, Kans. ... C2 61
St. Francis, Wis. ... E2 88
St. Francis, co., Ark. ... B4 49
St. François -de-Lac, Que., Can. ... C5 42
St. Francisville, Ill. ... E6 58
St. Francisville, La. ... D4 63
St. Francois, co., Mo. ... D7 69
St. Fulgence, Que., Can. ... A7 42
St. Gabriel -de-Brandon, Que., Can. ... C4 42
St. Gallen, see Sankt Gallen, Switz.
St. Gaudens, Fr. ... F4 5
Ste. Genevieve, Mo. ... D7 69
Ste. Genevieve, co., Mo. ... D7 69
Ste. Geneviève-de-Pierrefonds, Que., Can. ... *D4 42
St. George, Austl. ... E8 25
St. George, N.B., Can. ... D3 43
St. George, Ont., Can. ... D4 41
St. George, Mo. ... *C7 69
St. George, S.C. ... E6 82
St. Georges, Que., Can. ... C5 42
St. George's, Grenada ... J14 35
St. Georges -de-Windsor Que., Can. ... D6 42
St. Georges-Ouest, Que., Can. ... *C7 42
St. Gérard, Que., Can. ... D6 42
St. Germain -de-Grantham, Que., Can. ... D5 42
St. Germain-en-Laye, Fr. ... g9 5
St. Gervais, Que., Can. ... C7 42
St. Gilles, Que., Can. ... C6 42
St. Gilles-du-Gard, Fr. ... F6 5
St. Girons, Fr. ... F4 5
St. Helena, Calif. ... A5 50
St. Helena, Br. dep., Afr. ... H20 2
St. Helena, par., La. ... D5 63
St. Helens, Eng. ... *D5 4
St. Helens, Oreg. ... B4 80
St. Helier, Jersey ... F5 4
St. Henry, Ohio ... B1 78
St. Hilaire Est, Que., Can. ... D4 42
St. Hyacinthe, Que., Can. ... D5 42
St. Hyacinthe, co., Que., Can. ... D4 42
St. Ignace, Mich. ... C6 66
St. Jacobs, Ont., Can. ... D4 41
St. Jacques, Que., Can. ... D4 42
St. James, Man., Can. ... E3 40
St. James, Minn. ... G4 67
St. James, Mo. ... D6 69
St. James, N.Y. ... *F4 75
St. James, par., La. ... D5 63
St. Jean, Que., Can. ... D4 42
St. Jean, co., Que., Can. ... D4 42
St. Jean-Baptiste, Man., Can. ... E3 40
St. Jean-D'Angély, Fr. ... E3 5
St. Jean-de-Dieu, Que., Can. ... A9 42
St. Jean-de-Luz, Fr. ... F3 5
St. Jean-de-Matha, Que., Can. ... C4 42
St. Jean-Eudes, Que., Can. ... *A7 42
St. Jéôme, Que., Can. ... D3 42
St. John, N.B., Can. ... D3 43
St. John, Ind. ... B3 59
St. John, Kans. ... E5 61
St. John, co., N.B., Can. ... D4 43
St. John's, Antigua and Barbuda ... H14 35
St. Johns, Ariz. ... B4 48
St. John's, Newf., Can. ... E5 44

St. Johns, Mich. ... F6 66
St. Johns, Mo. ... *C7 69
St. Johns, co., Fla. ... B5 54
St. Johnsbury, Vt. ... C3 73
St. Johnsville, N.Y. ... *B6 75
St. John the Baptist, par., La. ... D5 63
St. Joseph, Ill. ... C5 58
St. Joseph, La. ... C4 63
St. Joseph, Mich. ... F4 66
St. Joseph, Minn. ... E4 67
St. Joseph, Mo. ... B3 69
St. Joseph, co., Ind. ... A5 59
St. Joseph, co., Mich. ... G5 66
St. Joseph-de-Beauce, Que., Can. ... C7 42
St. Joseph-de-Sorel, Que., Can. ... *D4 42
St. Joseph-de-St. Hyacinthe Que., Can. ... *D5 42
St. Jovite, Que., Can. ... C3 42
St. Junien, Fr. ... E4 5
St. Kitts-Nevis,see St. Christopher-Nevis, N.A.
St. Lambert, Que., Can. ... p19 42
St. Landry, par., La. ... D3 63
St. Laurent, Man., Can. ... D3 40
St. Laurent, Que., Can. ... p19 42
St. Lawrence, Newf., Can. ... E4 44
St. Lawrence, i., N.A. ... *F10 81
St.Lawrence, co., N.Y. ... A6 75
St. Lawrence, riv., N.A. ... G20 36
St. Léonard, N.B., Can. ... B2 43
St. Léonard -de-Noblat, Fr. ... E4 5
St. Lô, Fr. ... C3 5
St. Louis, Mich. ... E6 66
St.-Louis, Sen. ... E1 22
St. Louis (Independent City), Mo. ... C37 69
St. Louis, co., Minn. ... C6 67
St. Louis, co., Mo. ... C7 69
St. Louis Park, Minn. ... n12 67
St. Lucia, country, N.A. ... J14 35
St. Lucie, co., Fla. ... E6 54
St. Maixent-l' Ecole, Fr. ... D3 5
St. Malo, Fr. ... C2 5
St. Mandé, Fr. ... g10 5
St. Marc, Hai. ... E7 35
St. Marc -des-Carrières, Que., Can. ... C5 42
Ste. Maire-Beauce, Que., Can. ... C6 42
St. Maries, Idaho ... B2 57
St. Martin, par., La. ... D4 63
St. Martinville, La. ... D4 63
St. Mary, par., La. ... E4 63
St. Mary, peak, Austl. ... *F6 25
St. Mary-of-the-woods, Ind. ... E3 59
St. Mary's, Ont., Can. ... D3 41
St. Marys, Ga. ... F5 55
St. Marys, Ind. ... A5 59
St. Marys, Kans. ... C7 61
St. Marys, Ohio ... B3 78
St. Marys, Pa. ... D4 81
St. Marys, W. Va. ... B3 87
St. Marys, co., Md. ... D4 53
St. Matthews, Ky. ... B4, g11 62
St. Matthews, S.C. ... D6 82
St. Maur-des-Fossés, Fr. ... g10 5
St. Maurice, co., Que., Can. ... C4 42
St. Michael, Minn. ... E5 67
St. Michael, Pa. ... *E4 81
St. Michaels, Md. ... C5 53
St. Nazaire, Fr. ... D2 5
St. Noël, Que., Can. ... *G20 36
St. Norbert, Man., Can. ... E3 40
St. Omer, Fr. ... B5 5
St. Ouen, Fr. ... g10 5
St. Pacôme, Que., Can. ... B8 42
St. Pamphile, Que., Can. ... C8 42
St. Paris, Ohio ... B2 78
St. Pascal, Que., Can. ... B8 42
St. Paul, Alta., Can. ... B5 38
St. Paul, Minn. ... E5, n12 67
St. Paul, Nebr. ... C7 71
St. Paul, Va. ... f9 85
St. Paulin, Que., Can. ... C4 42
St. Paul Park, Minn. ... *F5, n12 67
St. Pauls, N.C. ... C4 76
St. Peter, Minn. ... F5 67
St. Peter Port, Guernsey ... F5 4
St. Petersburg, Fla. ... E4, p10 54

St. Petersburg Beach, Fla. ... p10 54
St. Pie, Que., Can. ... D5 42
St. Pierre, Mart. ... I14 35
St. Pierre-Jolys, Man., Can. ... E3 40
St. Pierre & Miquelon, Fr. Dep., N.A. ... E3 44
St. Pol-de-Léon, Fr. ... C2 5
St. Pourçain, -sur-Sioule, Fr. ... D5 5
St. Prosper, Que., Can. ... C7 42
St. Quentin, N.B., Can. ... B2 43
St. Quentin, Fr. ... C5 5
St. Raphaël, Que., Can. ... C7 42
St. Raphaël, Fr. ... F7 5
St. Raymond, Que., Can. ... C6 42
St. Rémi, Que., Can. ... D4, q19 42
St. Romuald, Que., Can. ... C6, n17 42
Ste. Rose, Que., Can. ... D4 42
Ste. Rose, Guad. ... H14 35
St. Rose, La. ... k11 63
Ste. Rose-du-Dégelé, Que., Can. ... B9 42
St. Rose-du-Lac, Man., Can. ... D2 40
Saintes, Fr. ... E3 5
St. Sauveur-des-Monts, Que., Can. ... D3 42
Ste. Savine, Fr. ... C5 5
St. Siméon, Que., Can. ... B8 42
St. Simons Island, Ga. ... E5 55
St. Stephen, N.B., Can. ... D2 43
St. Stephen, S.C. ... E8 82
St. Tammany, par., La. ... D5 63
Ste. Thérèse-de-Blainville, Que., Can. ... D4, p19 42
St. Thomas, Ont., Can. ... E3 41
St. Tite, Que., Can. ... C5 42
St. Ulric, Que., Can. ... *K13 52
St. Vincent and the Grenadines, country, N.A. ... J9 35
St. Vincent-de-Paul, Que., Can. ... *D4 42
St. Walburg, Sask., Can. ... D1 39
St. Yrieix-la-Perche, Fr. ... E4 5
Saintonge, former prov., Fr. ... E3 5
Saitama, pref., Jap. ... *I9 18
Sajama, mtn., Bol. ... C2 29
Sakai, Jap. ... o14 18
Çakākah, Sau. Ar. ... D3 15
Sakania, Zaire ... C5 24
Sakashita, Jap. ... n16 18
Sakata, Jap. ... G9 18
Sakchu, Kor. ... F2 18
Sakhalin, isl., Sov. Un. ... D17 16
Sakon Nakhon, Thai. ... B2 19
Sakti, India ... D7 20
Sala, Swe. ... H7, t34 11
Sala Consilina, It. ... D5 9
Saladillo, Arg. ... B5 28
Salado, riv., Arg. ... A3 28
Salamá, Guat. ... *D7 34
Salamanca, Mex. ... m13 34
Salamanca, N.Y. ... C2 75
Salamanca, Sp. ... B3 8
Salamanca, prov., Sp. ... *B3 8
Salamina, Col. ... B2 32
Salamis, Grc. ... D4 14
Salas, Sp. ... A2 8
Salatiga, Indon. ... *G4 19
Salavat, Sov. Un. ... *D8 13
Salaverry, Peru ... C2 31
Saldanha, S. Afr. ... G3 24
Saldus, Sov. Un. ... C4 12
Sale, Austl. ... I6 26
Salé, Mor. ... B3 22
Salekhard, Sov. Un. ... C9 13
Salem, Ill. ... E5 58
Salem, India ... F6 20
Salem, Ind. ... G5 59
Salem, Mass. ... A6, f12 65
Salem, Mo. ... D6 69
Salem, N.H. ... F5 73
Salem, N.J. ... D2 74
Salem, N.Y. ... B7 75
Salem, Ohio ... B5 78
Salem, Oreg. ... C4, k12 80
Salem, S. Dak. ... G8 77
Salem, Utah ... D2 72
Salem, Va. (Independent City) ... C2 85
Salem, W. Va. ... B4, k9 87
Salem, co., N.J. ... D2 74
Salem Depot, N.H. ... F5 73
Salemi, It. ... F4 9
Salerno, It. ... D5 9
Salford, Eng. ... D5 4
Salgótarján Hung. ... A4 10
Salida, Calif. ... *D3 50
Salida, Colo. ... C5 51
Salies-de-Béarn, Fr. ... F3 5
Salihli, Tur. ... *C7 4
Salin, Bur. ... *D9 20
Salina, Kans. ... D6 61
Salina, Okla. ... A6 79
Salina, Utah ... B6 72
Salinas, Calif. ... D3 50
Salinas, P.R. ... *G11 35

Salina Springs, Ariz. ... A4 48
Saline, Mich. ... F7 66
Saline, co., Ark. ... C3 49
Saline, co., Ill. ... F5 58
Saline, co., Kans. ... D6 61
Saline, co., Mo. ... B4 69
Saline, co., Nebr. ... D8 71
Salineville, Ohio ... B5 78
Salisbury, Eng. ... E6 4
Salisbury, Md. ... D6 53
Salisbury, Mass. ... A6 65
Salisbury, Mo. ... B5 69
Salisbury, N.C. ... B2 76
Salisbury, see Harare, Zimb.
Salisbury West, N.C. ... *B2 76
Sallisaw, Okla. ... B7 79
Salmon, Idaho ... D5 57
Salmon Arm, B.C., Can. ... D8 37
Salmon Falls, N.H. ... E6 73
Salo, Fin. ... G10 11
Salon-de-Provence, Fr. ... F6 5
Salonta, Rom. ... B5 10
Salsk, Sov. Un. ... H13 12
Salsomaggiore, It. ... B2 9
Salta, Arg. ... D2 29
Salta, prov., Arg. ... D2 29
Saltillo, Mex. ... B4 34
Salt Lake, co., Utah ... A5 72
Salt Lake City, Utah ... A6, C2 72
Salto, Braz. ... m8 30
Salto, Ur. ... E1 30
Salto, dept., Ur. ... *E1 30
Saltpond, Ghana ... G4 22
Salt River, Ky. ... C4 62
Saltsburg, Pa. ... E2 81
Salt Springs, Fla. ... C5 54
Saltville, Va. ... f10 85
Saluda, co., S.C. ... C4 82
Saluda, co., S.C. ... C4 82
Saluda Gardens, S.C. ... *D5 82
Sālūr, India ... E7 20
Saluzzo, It. ... B1 9
Salvador, Braz. ... E7 27
Salvatierra, Mex. ... m13 34
Salween, riv., Asia ... D10 20
Salyersville, Ky. ... C6 62
Salzburg, Aus. ... E6 6
Saltzburg, state, Aus. ... E6 6
Salzgitter, Ger., Fed. Rep. of ... B5 6
Salzwedel, Ger. Dem Rep. ... B5 6
Samani, Jap. ... F11 18
Samaniego, Col. ... C2 32
Samar, prov., Phil. ... C7 19
Samar, isl.,Phil. ... C7 19
Samarinda, Indon. ... F5 19
Samarkand, Sov. Un. ... F9 13
Sāmarrā', Iraq ... E14 14
Sambalpur, India ... D7 20
Sambas, Indon. ... E3 19
Sambhal, India ... *C6 20
Sambor, Sov. Un. ... G4 12
Samchŏk, Kor. ... H4 18
Samchonpo, Kor. ... I4 18
Samokov, Bul. ... D6 10
Samos, prov., Grc. ... *D6 14
Samoset, Fla. ... q10 54
Sampson, co., N.C. ... B4 76
Samson, Ala. ... D3 46
Samsun, Tur. ... B11 14
Samtown, La. ... *C3 63
San'ā', Yemen ... F3 15
San Agustín, Col. ... C2 32
Sanandaj, Iran ... B4 15
San Andreas, Calif. ... C3 50
San Andrés de Giles, Arg. ... g7 28
San Andre's Tuxtla, Mex. ... D5 34
San Angelo, Tex. ... D2 84
San Anselmo, Calif. ... h7 50
San Antonio, Chile ... A2 28
San Antonio, Tex. ... E3, k7 84
San Antonio de Areco, Arg. ... g7 28
San Antonio de los Baños, Cuba ... C2 35
San Antonio Heights, Calif. ... *E5 50
San Augustine, Tex. ... D5 84
San Augustine, co., Tex. ... D5 84
San Bartolomeo in Galdo, It. ... D5 9
San Benedetto del Tronto, It. ... C4 9
San Benito, Tex. ... F4 84
San Benito, co., Calif. ... D3 50
San Bernardino, Calif. ... E5, m14 50
San Bernardino, co., Calif. ... E5 50
San Bernardo, Chile ... A2 28
Sanborn, Iowa ... A2 60
Sanborn, co., S. Dak. ... G7 77
San Bruno, Calif. ... D2, h8 50
San Carlos, Arg. ... C2 28
San Carlos, Calif. ... k8 51
San Carlos, Chile ... B2 28
San Carlos, Phil. ... o13 19
San Carlos, Ur. ... E2 30
San Carlos de Bariloche, Arg. ... C2 28
San Cataldo, It. ... F4 9
Sanch'ung, Tai. ... *G9 17

San Clemente, Calif. ... F5 50
San Clemente, Sp. ... C4 8
San Cristóbal, Dom Rep. ... E8 35
San Cristóbal, Ven. ... B3 22
San Cristóbal Las Casas, Mex. ... D6 34
Sancti-Spíritus, Cuba ... D4 35
Sanda, Jap. ... o14 18
Sandakan, Mala. ... D5 19
Sandefjord, Nor. ... p28 11
Sanders, co., Mont. ... C1 70
Sanderville, Ga. ... D4 55
Sandia, Peru ... D4 31
San Diego, Calif. ... F5, o15 50
San Diego, Tex. ... F3 84
San Diego, co., Calif. ... F5 50
Sandīkli, Tur. ... C8 14
Sandila, India ... C7 20
San Dimas, Calif. ... *F4 50
Sandoa, Zaire ... B4 24
Sandomierz, Pol. ... C6 7
Sandoná, Col. ... C2 32
San Doná di Piave, It. ... B4 9
Sandoval, Ill. ... E4 58
Sandoval, co., N. Mex. ... B5 48
Sandpoint, Idaho ... A2 57
Sandpit, B.C., Can. ... C2 37
Sands Point, N.Y. ... *G2 52
Sand Springs, Okla. ... A5 79
Sandstone, Minn. ... D6 67
Sandusky, Mich. ... E8 66
Sandusky, Ohio ... A3 78
Sandusky, co., Ohio ... A2 78
Sandusky South, Ohio ... *A3 78
Sandviken, Swe. ... G7 11
Sandwich, Ill. ... B5 58
Sandwich, Mass. ... C7 65
Sandy, Oreg. ... B4 80
Sandy, Pa. ... *D4 81
Sandy, Utah ... D2 72
Sandy Beach, N.Y. ... *C2 75
Sandy Hook, Conn. ... D3 52
Sandy Springs, Ga. ... h8 55
San Elizario, Tex. ... o11 84
San Estanislao, Par. ... D4 29
San Felipe, Chile ... A2 28
San Felipe, N. Mex. ... B5, D6 48
San Felipe, Ven. ... A4 32
San Felipe de Jesus, Mex. ... *D5 34
San Feliu de Guixols, Sp. ... B7 8
San Fernando, Arg. ... A5, g7 28
San Fernando, Calif. ... m12 50
San Fernando, Chile ... A2 28
San Fernando, Phil. ... B6, n13 19
San Fernando, Phil. ... o13 19
San Fernando, Sp. ... D2 8
San Fernando, Trin. ... A5 32
San Fernando de Apure, Ven. ... B4 32
San Fernando de Atabapo, Ven. ... C4 32
Sanford, Fla. ... D5 54
Sanford, Maine ... E4 64
Sanford, N.C. ... B3 76
San Francisco, Arg. ... A4 28
San Francisco, Calif. ... D2, h8 50
San Francisco, co., Calif. ... C2 32
San Fransico del Oro, Mex. ... B3 34
San Fransico del Rincón, Mex. ... m13 34
San Francisco de Macorís, Dom. Rep. ... E8 35
San Gabriel, Calif. ... m12 50
San Gabriel, Ec. ... A2 31
San Gabriel Chilac, Mex. ... D5, n15 34
Sangamon, co., Ill. ... D4 58
Sanger, Calif. ... D4 50
Sanger, Tex. ... C4 84
Sangerhausen, Ger. Dem Rep. ... C5 6
San Germán, P.R. ... *G11 35
San Gil, Col. ... B3 32
San Giovanni in Fiore, It. ... E6 9
Sangju, Kor. ... H4 18
Sāngli, India ... *E5 20
San Gorgonio, mtn., Calif. ... E5 50
San Ignacio, Pr. ... E4 29
San Isidro, Arg. ... g7 28
San Jacinto, Calif. ... F5 50
San Jacinto, co., Tex. ... D5 84
San Javier, Chile ... B2 28
Sanjo, Jap. ... H9 18
San Joaquin, co., Calif. ... C3 50
San Jose, Ariz. ... C4 48
San Jose, Calif. ... D3, k9 50
San José, C.R. ... F8 34
San Jose, Ill. ... C4 58
San José, Ur. ... E1 30
San José, dept. Ur. ... *E1 30
San José, prov., C.R. ... *F8 34
San José de Feliciano, Arg. ... A5 28
San José de los Molinos, Peru ... D2 31
San Juan, Arg. ... A3 29
San Juan, Colo. ... D6 51
San Juan, Dom. Rep. ... E8 25
San Juan, P.R. ... *G11 35
San Juan, Tex. ... G2 84
San Juan, co., Colo. ... D3 51

San Juan, co., N. Mex. ... A4 28
San Juan, co., Utah ... C6 72
San Juan, co., Wash. ... A2 86
San Juan, prov., Arg. ... A3 28
San Juan Bautista, Calif. ... *D3 50
San Juan Bautista, Par. ... E4 29
San Juan Capistrano, Calif. ... F5 50
San Juan de los Lagos, Mex. ... m12 34
San Juan de los Morros, Ven. ... B4 32
San Juan del Rio, Mex. ... m13 34
San Julián, Arg. ... D3 28
San Justo, Arg. ... *B5 28
Sankt Gallen, Switz. ... E4 6
Sankt Gallen, canton, Switz. ... *E4 6
Sankt Pölten, Aus. ... D7 6
Sankt Veit an der Glan, Aus. ... E7 6
San Leandro, Calif. ... h8 50
San Lorenzo, Art. ... A4 28
San Lorenzo, Calif. ... *D2 50
San Lorenzo, P.R. ... *G12 35
San Lorenzo del Escorial, Sp. ... B3, 016 8
Sanlúcar, Sp. ... D2 8
San Luis, Arg. ... A3 28
San Luis, Colo. ... D5 51
San Luis, Cuba ... D6 35
San Luis, prov., Arg. ... A3 28
San Luis de la Paz, Mex. ... m13 34
San Luis Obispo, Calif. ... E3 50
San Luis Obispo, co., Calif. ... E3 50
San Luis Potosí, Mex. ... C4, k13 34
San Luis Potosí, state, Mex. ... C4, k13 34
San Manuel, Ariz. ... *C3 48
San Marco in Lamis, It. ... D5 9
San Marcos, Tex. ... E4, h8 84
San Marino, Calif. ... m12 50
San Marino, country, Eur. ... C4 9
San Martín, Arg. ... A3 28
San Martin (General San Martin) Arg. ... g7 28
San Martin, Calif. ... *D3 50
San Martin, dept., Peru ... C2 31
San Mateo, Calif. ... h8 50
San Mateo, Ven. ... B5 32
San Mateo, co., Calif. ... D2 50
Sanmenxia, China ... E7 17
San Miguel, Sal. ... D4 34
San Miguel, co., Colo. ... D2 51
San Miguel, co., N. Mex. ... B6 48
San Miguel de Allende, Mex. ... m13 34
San Miguel del Padrón, Cuba ... *C2 35
San Miguel de Tucumán, Arg. ... F4 27
San Nicolás, Arg. ... A4 28
San Nicolás Totolapan, Mex. ... h9 34
Sannois, Fr. ... g10 5
Sano, Jap. ... m18 18
Sanok, Pol. ... D7 7
San Onofre, Col. ... B2 32
San Pablo, Calif. ... *D2 50
San Patricio, co., Tex. ... E4 84
San Pedro, Arg. ... D3 29
San Pedro, Arg. ... A5, f7 28
San Pedro, Par. ... D4 29
San Pedro, Tex. ... *F4 84
San Pedro, dept., Par. ... D4 29
San Pedro de las Colonias, Mex. ... B4 34
San Pedro de Lloc, Peru ... C2 31
San Pedro de Macorís, Dom Rep. ... E9 35
San Pedro Mártir, mts., Mex. ... A1 34
San Pedro Sula, Hond. ... D7 34
Sanpete, co., Utah ... B6 72
San Rafael, Arg. ... A3 28
San Rafael, Calif. ... D2, h7 50
San Rafael, mts., Calif. ... E4 50
San Ramon, Peru ... D2 31
San Ramon, Ur. ... g9 28
San Remo, It. ... C1 9
San Roque, Sp. ... D3 8
San Saba, Tex. ... D3 84
San Saba, co., Tex. ... D3 84
San Salvador, Sal. ... E7 34
San Salvador de Jujuy, Arg. ... F4 27
San Sebastián, P.R. ... *G11 35
San Sebastián, Sp. ... A4 8
San Sepolcro, It. ... C4 9
San Severo, It. ... D5 9
Sansom Park Village, Tex. ... *C4 84
Sans Souci, S.C. ... *B3 82
Santa, Peru ... C2 31
Santa Ana, Calif. ... F5, n13 50
Santa Ana, Ven. ... A2 32
Santa Ana, Sal. ... E7 34
Santa Ana, mts., Calif. ... n13 50
Santa Antia, Mex. ... h9 34
Santa Anna, Tex. ... D3 84
Santa Bárbara d'Oeste, Braz. ... m8 30
Santa Barbara, Calif. ... E4 50
Santa Bárbara, Mex. ... B3 34
Santa Barbara, co., Calif. ... E3 50
Santa Catalina, isl., Calif. ... F4 50
Santa Catarina, state, Braz. ... D2 30
Santa Clara, Calif. ... D2, k9 50
Santa Clara, Cuba ... C4 35
Santa Clara, Ur. ... E2 30

Santa Clara, co., Calif. D3 50
Santa Cruz, Bol. C3 29
Santa Cruz, Calif. D2 50
Santa Cruz, C.R. E7 34
Santa Cruz, co., Ariz. D3 48
Santa Cruz, co., Calif. D2 50
Santa Cruz, prov., Arg. D3 28
Santa Cruz de la Palma, Sp. m13 8
Santa Cruz de la Zarza, Sp. C4 8
Santa Cruz del Sur. D5 35
Santa Cruz de Tenerife, Sp. m13 8
Santa Cruz de Tenerife, prov., Sp. . *m13 8
Santa Cruz do Rio Pardo, Braz. C3 30
Santa Cruz do Sul., Braz. D2 30
Santa Elena, Tex. F3 84
Santa Eugenia de Ribeira, Sp. A1 8
Santa Eulalia del Río, Sp. C6 8
Santa Fe, Arg. A4 28
Santa Fé, Cuba, (part of Havanna) ... D2 35
Santa Fe, Mex. h9 34
Santa Fe, N. Mex. B6, D6 48
Santafé, Sp. D4 8
Santa Fe, co., N. Mex. B5 48
Santa Fe. prov., Arg. A4 28
Santa Fe Springs, Calif. F4 50
Santai, China E6 17
Santa Inés, Ahuatempan, Mex. n14 34
Santa Isabel, P.R. *G11 22
Santa Lucia, Cuba D6 35
Santa Lucia, Ur. E1 30
Santa Margarita, Calif. E3 50
Santa Maria, Braz. D2 30
Santa Maria, Calfi. E3 50
Santa Maria Capua Vetere, It. D5 9
Santa Maria Colotepec, Mex. D5 34
Santa María del Oro, Mex. B3 34
Santa Marta, Col. A3 32
Santa Marta, Sp. C2 8
Santa Monica, Calif. m12 50
Santana, Port. h12 8
Santana do Livramento, Braz. E1 30
Santander, Col. C2 32
Santander, Sp. A4 8
Santander, dept., Col. B3 32
Santander, prov., Sp. *A4 8
Santanoni, peak, N.Y. A6 75
Santañy, Sp. C7 8
Santa Paula, Calif. E4 50
Santaquin, Utah B6 72
Santarém, Braz. D5 27
Santarém, Port. C1 8
Santa Rita, Braz. *D7 27
Santa Rita, Guam. *F6 2
Santa Rita, N. Mex. C4 48
Santa Rosa, Arg. B4 28
Santa Rosa, Calif. C2 50
Santa Rosa, N. Mex. B6 48
Santa Rosa, co., Fla. G2 54
Santa Rosa de Copán, Hond. *E7 34
Santa Rosa, de Osos, Col. B2 32
Santa Rosalia, Mex. B2 34
Santa Susana, Calif. *E4 50
Santa Tomé de Guayana, Ven. B5 32
Santa Ursula Coapa, Mex. h9 34
Santa Venetia, Calif. *D2 50
Santa Vitória do Palmar, Braz. E2 30
Santee, Calif. o16 50
Santiago, Braz. D2 30
Santiago, Chile A2 28
Santiago, Dom. Rep. E8 35
Santiago, Mex. C3 34
Santiago, Pan. B1 32
Santiago, Par. E4 29
Santiago, Sp. A1 8
Santiago, prov., Chile A2 28
Santiago, mts., Tex. D1 84
Santiago, peak, Calif. n14 50
Santiago, peak, Tex. p13 84
Santiago de Cao, Peru C2 31
Santiago de Cuba, Cuba D6 35
Santiago del Estero, Arg. E3 29
Santiago del Estero, prov., Arg. E3 29
Santiago Ixcuintla, Mex. C3, m11 34
Santiago Tepalcatlalpan, Mex. h9 34
Santisteban, del Puerto, Sp. C4 8
Santo Amaro, Braz. *E7 27
Santo Andre, Braz. *m8 30
Santo Ângelo, Braz. D2 30
Santo Antônio, Braz. *E7 27
Santo Domingo, Dom. Rep. E9 35
Santo Domingo Pueblo, N. Mex. B5 48
San Tomas, Calif. *D3 50
Santoña, Sp. A4 8
Santos, Braz. C3, m8 30
Santos Dumont, Braz. C4, g6 30
Santo Tomás, Peru D3 31
Santo Tomas, Ven. B5 32
Santo Tomé de Guayana, Ven. B5 22
San Valentín, mtn., Chile H3 27
San Vicente, Sal. E7 34
San Vicente de Alcántara, Sp. C2 8
San Vicente del Caguán, Col. C3 32
San Vito al Tagliamento, It. B4 9

San Ygnacio, Tex. F3 84
São Bernardo do Campo,
  Braz. C3, m8 30
São Borja, Braz. D1 30
São Carlos, Braz. C3, m8 30
São Caetano do sul, Braz. *m8 30
São Cristovão, Braz. *E7 27
São Francisco, riv., Braz. A4 30
São Francisco do Sul, Braz. D3 30
São Gabriel, Braz. E2 30
São João da Boa Vista, Braz. C3, k8 30
São João del Rei, Braz. C4, g5 30
São João de Meriti, Braz. C4, *h6 30
São Joao do Rio Pardo, Braz. k8 30
São José do Rio Prêto, Braz. C3 30
São José dos Campos, Braz. C3, m9 30
São Leopoldo, Braz. D2 30
São Lourenço, Braz. C3 30
São Luís, Braz. D6 27
São Luís Gonzaga, Braz. D2 30
São Manuel, Braz. C3, m7 30
Saône-et-Loire, dept., Fr. *D6 5
São Paulo, Braz. C3, m8 30
São Paulo, state, Braz. C3, m8 30
São Roque, Braz. m8 30
São Sebastião do Paraíso, Braz. C3 30
São Tomé, São Tomé
  & Principe H6 22
Sao Tome & Principe, country, Afr. .. H5 22
São Vicente, Port. h11 8
São Vincente, Braz. C3 30
Sapai, Grc. B5 14
Sapele, Nig. G6 22
Saposoa, Peru C2 31
Sapozhok, Sov. Un. E13 12
Sappington, Mo. f13 69
Sapporo, Jap. E10 18
Sapri, It. D5 9
Sapulpa, Okla. B5 79
Sara Buri, Thai. *C2 19
Sarah, Miss. A3 68
Sarajevo, Yugo. D4 10
Sara Kaeo, Thai. *C2 19
Saraland, Ala. E1 46
Saranac, Mich. F5 66
Saranac, N.Y. f11 75
Saranac Lake, N.Y. B3 75
Saranap, Calif. *D2 50
Sarandí del Yí, Ur. E1 30
Sarandi Grande, Ur. E1 30
Saransk, Sov. Un. D15 12
Sarapul, Sov. Un. D8 12
Sarasota, Fla. E4, q10 54
Sarasota, co., Fla. E4 54
Saratoga, Calif. *D3 50
Saratoga, Tex. D5 84
Saratoga, Wyo. E6 89
Saratoga, co., N.Y. B7 75
Saratoga Place, Va. *D6 85
Saratoga Springs, N.Y. B7 75
Saratov, Sov. Un. F15 12
Saravane, Laos *B3 19
Sarawak, reg., Mala. E4 19
Sarayköy, Tur. D7 14
Sarcelles, Fr. g10 5
Sarcoxie, Mo. D3 69
Sardegna, pol. dist., It. *E2 9
Sardinia, Ohio C2 78
Sardinia, isl., It. D2 9
Sardis, Ala. C3 46
Sardis, B.C., Can. f14 37
Sardis, Miss. A4 68
Sardis, Ohio C5 78
Sarepta, La. B2 63
Sargent, Nebr. C6 71
Sargent, co., N. Dak. D8 77
Sargodha, Pak. *B5 20
Sarh, Chad G1 23
Sarikamiş, Tur. B14 14
Sarina, Austl. D8 25
Sariwon, Kor. G2 18
Sarlat, Fr. E4 5
Sarmiento, mtn., Chile I3 27
Sarnia, Ont., Can. E2 41
Sarny, Sov. Un. F6 12
Saronno, It. B2 9
Sárospatak, Hung. A5 10
Sarpsborg, Nor. p29 11
Sarpy, co., Nebr. C9 71
Sarreguemines, Fr. C7 5
Sartell, Minn. E4 67
Sartène, Fr. D2 9
Sarthe, dept., Fr. *D4 5
Sartrouville, Fr. g9 5
Sarufutsu, Jap. D11 18
Sárvár, Hung. B3 10
Sarzana, It. B2 9
Sāsarām, India D7 20
Sasebo, Jap. J4 18
Saskatchewan, prov., Can. 39
Saskatchewan, riv., Can. F13 36
Saskatoon, Sask., Can. E2, n7 39

Sasovo, Sov. Un. D13 12
Sassafras, mtn., S.C. A2 82
Sassari, It. D2 9
Satah, mtn., B.C., Can. C5 37
Satanta, Kans. E3 61
Saticoy, Calif. E4 50
Satka, Sov. Un. D8 13
Satsuma, Ala. E1 46
Sattahip, Thai. *C2 19
Satu-Mare, Rom. B6 10
Saucillo, Mex. B3 34
Sauda, Nor. H2 11
Saudi Arabia, country, Asia D3 15
Saugatuck, Mich. F4 66
Saugerties, N.Y. C7 75
Saugus, Mass. B5, g11 65
Sauk, co., Wis. E4 88
Sauk Centre, Minn. E4 67
Sauk City, Wis. E4 88
Sauk Rapids, Minn. E4 67
Sauk Village, Ill. *B6 58
Saukville, Wis. E6 88
Sault-au-Mouton, Que., Can. A8 42
Sault Ste. Marie, Mich. B6 66
Sault Ste. Marie, Ont., Can. p18 41
Saumur, Fr. D4 5
Saunders, co., Nebr. C9 71
Sauquoit, N.Y. *B5 75
Sausalito, Calif. D2, h8 50
Sava, Yugo. C4 10
Savage, Md. B4 53
Savage, Minn. F5, n11 67
Savanna, Ill. A3 58
Savanna, Okla. C6 79
Savanna-la-Mar, Jam. E4 35
Savannah, Ga. D5 55
Savannah, Mo. B3 69
Savannah, N.Y. B4 75
Savannah, Tenn. B3 83
Savannah Beach, Ga. D6 55
Saveni, Rom. B8 10
Saverne, Fr. C7 5
Savigliano, It. D7 5
Savona, B.C., Can. D7 37
Savona, It. B2 9
Savona, N.Y. C3 75
Savonlinna, Fin. G13 11
Savoy (Savoie), former prov., Fr. ... E7 5
Savran, Sov. Un. G8 12
Sawahlunto, Indon. F2 19
Sawakin, Sud. E5 23
Sawan Khalok, Thai. B1 19
Sawbill Landing, Minn. C7 67
Sawhāj, Eg. C4 23
Sawtooth, mts., Idaho E3 57
Sawyer, Mich. G4 66
Sawyer, co., Wis. C2 88
Sawyerville, Que., Can. D6 42
Sawyerwood, Ohio *A4 78
Saxapahaw, N.C. B3 78
Saxis, Va. C7 85
Saxon, S.C. B4 82
Saxony, reg., Ger. Dem. Rep. C6 6
Saxonburg, Pa. E2 81
Saxton, Pa. F5 81
Sayabec, Que., Can. *G19 36
Sayán, Peru D2 31
Saybrook, Ill. C5 58
Sahyūt, P.D.R. of Yem F5 15
Sayre, Ala. B3 46
Sayre, Okla. B2 79
Sayre, Pa. C9 81
Sayreton, Ala. B3, f7 46
Sayreville, N.J. C4 74
Sayula, Mex. D4, n12 34
Sayville, N.Y. G4 52
Scafell Pikes, mtn., Eng. C4 4
Scalp Level, Pa. F4 81
Scandia, Kans. C6 61
Scanlon, Minn. D6 67
Scansano, It. C3 9
Scapegoat, mtn., Mont. C4 70
Scappoose, Oreg. B4 80
Scarboro, Maine E2, g7 64
Scarborough, Ont., Can. m15 41
Scarborough, Eng. C6 4
Scarborough, Trin. K14 35
Scarbro, W. Va. n13 87
Scarsdale, N.Y. h13 75
Sceaux, Fr. g10 5
Schaefferstown, Pa. F9 81
Schaerbeek, Bel. *B6 5
Schaffhausen, Switz. E4 6
Schaffhausen, canton, Switz. *E4 6
Schaghticoke, N.Y. C7 75
Schaller, Iowa B2 60
Schaumburg, Ill. h8 58
Schefferville, Que., Can. h13 42
Schenectady, N.Y. C7 75
Schenectady, co., N.Y. C6 75
Schererville, Ind. B3 59

Schertz., Tex. h7 84
Schiedam, Neth. B6 5
Schiller Park, Ill. k9 58
Schiltigheim, Fr. C7 5
Schio, It. B3 9
Schivelbein, see Swidwin, Pol.
Schleicher, co., Tex. D2 84
Schleswig, Ger., Fed. Rep. of A4 6
Schleswig, Iowa B2 60
Schleswig-Holstein, reg., Ger.,
  Fed. Rep. of A4 6
Schleswig-Holstein, state, Ger.,
  Fed. Rep. of A4 6
Schley, co., Ga. D2 55
Schlüchtern, Ger., Fed. Rep. of C4 6
Schmalkalden, Ger. Dem. Rep. C5 6
Schneidemuhl, see Pila, Pol.
Schofield, Wis. D4 88
Schoharie, N.Y. C6 75
Schoharie, co., N.Y. C6 75
Schönebeck, Ger. Dem. Rep. B5 6
Schongau, Ger., Fed. Rep. of E5 6
Schoolcraft, Mich. F5 66
Schoolcraft, co., Mich. B4 66
Schooley, mtn., N.J. B3 74
Schramberg, Ger., Fed. Rep. of D4 6
Schram City, Ill. D4 58
Schriever, La. E5, k10 63
Schrobenhausen, Ger.,
  Fed. Rep. of D5 6
Schroon Lake, N.Y. B7 75
Schulenburg, Tex. E4 84
Schuyler, Nebr. C8 71
Schuyler, co., Ill. C3 58
Schuyler, co., Mo. A5 69
Schuyler, co., N.Y. C4 75
Schuylerville, N.Y. B7 75
Schuylkill, co., Pa. E9 81
Schuylkill Haven, Pa. E9 81
Schwabach, Ger., Fed. Rep. of D5 6
Schwäbisch Gmünd, Ger., Fed.
  Rep. of D4 6
Schwäbisch Hall, Ger., Fed.
  Rep. of D4 6
Schwandorf, Ger., Fed. Rep. of D6 6
Schwaner, mts., Indon. F4 19
Schwaz, Aus. E5 6
Schwedt, Ger. Dem. Rep. B7 6
Schweinfurt, Ger., Fed. Rep. of C5 6
Schwerin, Ger. Dem. Rep. B5 6
Schwyz, Switz. E4 6
Schwyz, canton, switz. *E4 6
Sciacca, It. F4 9
Scio, Ohio B4 78
Scioto, co., Ohio D2 78
Sciotodale, Ohio *D2 78
Scituate, Mass. B6, h13 65
Scobey, Mont. B11 70
Scone, Austl. F8 26
Scotch Plains, N.J. B4 74
Scotia, Calif. B1 50
Scotia, N.Y. C7 75
Scotland, Ont., Can. D4 41
Scotland, S. Dak. C8 77
Scotland, co., Mo. A5 69
Scotland, co., N.C. C3 76
Scotland, reg., U.K. B4 4
Scotland Neck, N.C. A5 76
Scotlandville, La. D4, g9 63
Scotstown, Que., Can. D6 42
Scott, La. D3 63
Scott, co., Ark. C1 49
Scott, co., Ill. D3 58
Scott, co., Ind. G6 59
Scott, co., Iowa C7 60
Scott, co., Kans. D3 61
Scott, co., Ky. B5 62
Scott, co., Minn. F5 67
Scott, co., Miss. C4 68
Scott, co., Mo. D8 69
Scott, co., Tenn. C9 83
Scott, co., Va. f9 85
Scott, mtn., Idaho E3 57
Scott, mtn., Okla. C3 79
Scott, mtn., Oreg. E4 80
Scott, peak, Idaho E6 57
Scott City, Kans. D3 61
Scott City, Mo. D8 69
Scottdale, Ga. h8 55
Scottdale, Pa. F2 81
Scotts, mtn., N.J. B2 74
Scottsbluff, Nebr. C2 71
Scotts Bluff, co., Nebr. C2 71
Scottsboro, Ala. A3 46
Scottsburg, Ind. G6 59
Scottsdale, Ariz. C3, D2 48
Scottsville, Ky. D3 62
Scottsville, N.Y. B3 75
Scottville, Mich. E4 66
Scranton, Iowa B3 60
Scranton, Kans. D8 61
Scranton, Pa. D10, m18 81
Scranton, S.C. D8 82

Screven, Ga. E4 55
Screven, co., Ga. D5 55
Scribner, Nebr. C9 71
Scunthorpe, Eng. D6 4
Scurry, co., Tex. C2 84
Seaboard, N.C. A5 76
Sea Bright, N.J. C5 74
Seabrook, Md. *C4 53
Seabrook, N.J. E2 74
Seabrook, Tex. r14 84
Sea Cliff, N.Y. F2 52
Seadrift, Tex. E4 84
Seaford, Del. C6 53
Seaford, N.Y. G3 52
Seaford, Va. h15 85
Seaforth, Ont., Can. D3 41
Sea Girt, N.J. C4 74
Seagoville, Tex. n10 84
Seagraves, Tex. C1 84
Sea Isle City, N.J. E3 74
Seal Beach, Calif. *F5 50
Seal Cove, N.B., Can. E3 43
Sealevel, N.C. C6 76
Sealy, Tex. E4 84
Seaman, Ohio D2 78
Searcy, Ark. B4 49
Searsport, Maine D4 64
Seaside, Calif. *D3 50
Seaside, Oreg. B3 80
Seaside Heights, N.J. D4 74
Seaside Park, N.J. D4 74
Seat Pleasant, Md. C4, f9 53
Seattle, Wash. B3, e11 86
Seaview, Wash. C1 86
Sebastian, Fla. E6 54
Sebastian, co., Ark. B1 49
Sebastopol, Calif. C2 50
Sebeka, Minn. D3 67
Sebeș, Rom. C6 10
Sebewaing, Mich. E7 66
Şebinkarahisar, Tur. B12 14
Sebnitz, Ger. Dem. Rep. C7 6
Sebree, Ky. C2 62
Sebring, Fla. E5 54
Sebring, Ohio B4 78
Sebring, Ont., Can. D3 41
Secane, Pa. *B11 81
Secaucus, N.J. h8 74
Sechura, Peru C1 31
Sector Popular, Mex. h9 34
Security, Colo. C6 51
Sedalia, Mo. C4 69
Sedan, Fr. C6 5
Sedan, Kans. E7 61
Sedgefield, N.C. *A3 76
Sedgwick, Alta., Can. C5 38
Sedgwick, Kans. E6, g12 61
Sedgwick, co., Colo. A8 51
Sedgwick, co., Kans. E6 61
Sedro Woolley, Wash. A3 86
Seekonk, Mass. C5 65
Seeley, Calif. F6 50
Seeley Lake, Mont. C3 70
Seelyville, Ind. F3 59
Segorbe, Sp. C5 8
Ségou, Mali F3 22
Segovia, Sp. B3 8
Segovia, prov., Sp. *B3 8
Segré, Fr. D3 5
Seguin, Tex. E4, h8 84
Sehwān, Pak. C4 20
Seiling, Okla. A3 79
Seinäjoki, Fin. F10 11
Seine, dept., Fr. C5, g1 5
Seine-et-Marne, dept., Fr. *C5 5
Seine-et-Oise, dept., Fr. *C5 5
Seine-Maritime, dept., Fr. C4 5
Seixal, Port. f9 8
Seki, Jap. o15 18
Sekondi-Takoradi, Ghana H4 22
Selah, Wash. C5 86
Selangor, state, Mala. E2 19
Selanovtsi, Bul. D7 10
Selb, Ger., Fed. Rep. of C6 6
Selby, S. Dak. E5 77
Selbyville, Del. D7 53
Selden, N.Y. *E3 75
Sélestat, Fr. C7 5
Selidovka, Sov. Un. q20 12
Selinsgrove, Pa. E8 81
Selkirk, Man., Can. D3 40
Selkirk, Scot. C5 4
Selkirk, co., Scot. *C5 4
Selle, Pic la, peak, Hai. E8 35
Sellersburg, Ind. H6 59
Sellersville, Pa. F11 81
Selma, Ala. C2 46
Selma, Calif. D4 50
Selma, Ind. D7 59
Selma, N.C. B4 76
Selmer, Tenn. B3 83
Selvas, reg., Braz. *D4 27

Selwyn, mtn., B.C., Can. B6 37
Semarang, Indon. G4 19
Sembilan, state, Mala. *E2 19
Semenovka, Sov. Un. E9 12
Semeru, mtn., Indon. G4 19
Seminoe, mts., Wyo. D6 89
Seminole, Ala. E2 46
Seminole, Fla. *E4 54
Seminole, Okla. B5 79
Seminole, Tex. C1 84
Seminole, co., Fla. D5 54
Seminole, co., Ga. F2 55
Seminole, co., Okla. B5 79
Semipalatinsk, Sov. Un. D11 13
Semnān, Iran A8 23
Senador Pompeu, Braz. *D7 27
Senath, Mo. F7 69
Senatobia, Miss. A4 68
Sendai, Jap. G10 18
Sendai (Kagoshima, Perf.), Jap. ... K5 18
Seneca, Ill. B5 58
Sececa, Kans. C7 61
Seneca, Mo. E3 69
Seneca, Pa. D2 81
Seneca, S.C. B2 82
Seneca, co., N.Y. C4 75
Seneca, co., Ohio A2 78
Seneca Falls, N.Y. C4 75
Senegal, country, Afr. F2 22
Senftenberg, Ger. Dem. Rep. C6 6
Senhor do Bonfim, Braz. *E7 27
Senigallia, It. C4 9
Senlis, Fr. C5 5
Senneterre, Que., Can. B2 42
Sens, Fr. C5 42
Senta, Yugo. C5 10
Sentinel, Okla. B2 79
Sentinel, peak, B.C., Can. B6 37
Seoul (Soul), Kor. H3 18
Sept Iles (Seven Islands),
  Que., Can. h13 42
Sequatchie, co., Tenn. D8 83
Sequim, Wash. A2 86
Sequoia, Calif. D4 50
Sequoyah, co., Okla. B7 79
Serafimovich, Sov. Un. G14 12
Seraing, Bel. B6 5
Serampore, India *D8 20
Serang, Indon. G3 19
Serbia, reg., Yugo. D5 10
Serbia, rep., Yugo. *D5 10
Serdobsk, Sov. Un. E15 12
Sered, Czech. D4 7
Seremban, Mala. E2 19
Sergeant Bluff, Iowa B1 60
Sergipe, state, Braz. *E7 27
Seria, Bru. E4 19
Seringapatam, India F6 20
Serón, Sp. D4 8
Serov, Sov. Un. D9 13
Serowe, Bots. E5 24
Serpa, Port. D2 8
Serpukhov, Sov. Un. D11 12
Sérrai, Grc. B4 14
Sérrai, prov., Grc. *B4 14
Serra Talhada, Braz. *D7 27
Serrinha, Braz. *E7 27
Sêrxü, China E4 17
Sesser, Ill. E4 58
Sesto Fiorentino, It. C3 9
Sestri Levante, It. B2 9
Sestroretck, Sov. Un. A8 12
Setana, Jap. F9 18
Setauket, N.Y. F4 52
Sète, Fr. F5 5
Sete Lagoas, Braz. B4 30
Seth, W. Va. C3, m12 87
Seth Ward, Tex. *B2 84
Seto, Jap. I8, n16 18
Settat, Mor. B3 22
Setúbal, Port. C1 8
Sevastopol, Sov. Un. I9 12
Seven Devils, mts., Idaho D2 57
Seven Hills, Ohio *A4 78
Seven Mile, Ohio C1 78
Sevenoaks, Eng. m13 4
Severn, Md. B4 53
Severna Park, Md. B4 53
Sevier, co., Ark. D1 49
Sevier, co., Tenn. D10 83
Sevier, co., Utah B6 72
Sevierville, Tenn. D10 83
Sevilla, Col. C2 32
Sevilla (Seville), Sp. D3 8
Sevilla (Seville), prov., Sp. *D3 8
Seville, Fla. C5 54
Seville, Ohio A4 78
Sevlievo, Bul. D7 10
Sevran, Fr. g11 5
Sèvres, Fr. g9 5
Sewanee, Tenn. B6 83

Seward, Alsk. C10, g17 47
Seward, Nebr. D8 71
Seward, co., Kans. E3 61
Seward, co., Nebr. D8 71
Sewaren, N.J. k7 74
Sewell, N.J. D2 74
Sewickley, Pa. E1, h13 81
Sewickley Heights, Pa. *E1 81
Sexsmith, Alta., Can. B1 38
Seychelles, Br. dep., Afr. G24 2
Seymour, Conn. D4 52
Seymour, Ind. G6 59
Seymour, Iowa D4 60
Seymour, Mo. D5 69
Seymour, Tex. C3 84
Seymour, Wis. D5, g9 88
Seymourville, La. h9 63
Sezimbra, Port. C1 8
Sezze, It. D4 9
Sfax, Tun. B7 22
Sfîntul-Gheorghe, Rom. C7 10
's Gravenhage, see The Hague, Neth.
Shaanxi, prov., China D6 17
Shabbona, Ill. B5 58
Shache, China F10 16
Shackelford, co., Tex. C3 84
Shady Cove, Oreg. E4 80
Shady Side, Md. C4 53
Shadyside, Ohio C5 78
Shaft (William Penn), Pa. *E9 81
Shafter, Calif. E4 50
Shāhjahanpur, India C7 20
Shaker Heights, Ohio A4, h9 78
Shakhty, Sov. Un. H13 12
Shaki, Nig. G5 22
Shakopee, Minn. F5, n11 67
Shalimar, Fla. u15 54
Shallowater, Tex. C2 84
Sham, Jabal ash, mtn., Om. D2 20
Shamokin, Pa. E8 81
Shamokin Dam, Pa. E8 81
Shamrock, Fla. C3 54
Shamrock, Tex. B2 84
Shandaken, N.Y. C6 75
Shandi, Sud. C4 23
Shandong, prov., China D8 17
Shanghai, China E9 17
Shangqui, China D8 17
Shangshui, China E7 17
Shangzhi, China D3 18
Shanhaiguan, China C8 17
Shannon, Ga. B1 55
Shannon, Ill. A4 58
Shannon, co., Mo. D6 69
Shannon, co., S. Dak. G3 77
Shannontown, S.C. *D7 82
Shansi, see Shanxi, China
Shantou, China G8 17
Shanxi, prov., China D7 17
Shaoguan, China G7 17
Shaoxing, China E9 17
Shaoyang, China F7 17
Shari, Jap. E12 18
Sharkey, co., Miss. C3 68
Sharon, Mass. B5, h11 65
Sharon, Pa. D1 81
Sharon, Tenn. A3 83
Sharon, Wis. F5 88
Sharon Hill, Pa. p20 81
Sharon Park, Ohio n12 78
Sharon Springs, Kans. D2 61
Sharonville, Ohio n13 78
Sharp, co., Ark. A4 49
Sharpes, Fla. D6 54
Sharpsburg, Md. B2 53
Sharpsburg, Pa. k14 81
Sharpsville, Ind. D5 59
Sharpsville, Pa. D1 81
Sharptown, Md. C6 53
Shashi, China E7 17
Shasta, co., Calif. B3 50
Shasta, mtn., Calif. B2 50
Shastsk, Sov. Un. D13 12
Shattuck, Okla. A2 79
Shaunavon, Sask., Can. H1 39
Shavertown, Pa. *B8 81
Shaw, Miss. B3 68
Shawano, Wis. D5 88
Shawano, co., Wis. D5 88
Shawbridge, Que., Can. D3 43
Shawinigan, Que., Can. C5 42
Shawinigan-Sud, Que., Can. C5 43
Shawmut, Ala. C4 46
Shawnee, Kans. k16 61
Shawnee, Ohio C3 78
Shawnee, Okla. B5 79
Shawnee, co., Kans. D8 61
Shawneetown, Ill. F5 58
Shawville, Que., Can. D3 41
Shchelkovo, Sov. Un. n18 12
Shchetovo, Sov. Un. q22 12
Shchigry, Sov. Un. F11 12

Shchors, Sov. Un. F8 12
Sheartown, Newf., Can. *E5 44
Sheboygan, Wis. E5, k10 88
Sheboygan, co., Wis. E6 88
Sheboygan Falls, Wis. E5, k10 88
Shediac, N.B., Can. C5 43
Sheep, mtn., Wyo. B5 89
Sheep, mtn., Wyo. C2 89
Sheeps Heaven, mtn., Mass. A1 65
Sheet Harbour, N.S., Can. E7 43
Sheffield, Ala. A2 46
Sheffield, Eng. D6 4
Sheffield, Ill. B4 58
Sheffield, Iowa B4 60
Sheffield, Ohio A3 78
Sheffield, Pa. C3 81
Sheffield Lake, Ohio *A3 78
Shefford, co., Que., Can. D5 42
Sheila, N.B., Can. B5 43
Shelagyote, Ky. C7 62
Shelagyote, peak, B.C., Can. B4 37
Shelbiana, Ky. C7 62
Shelbina, Mo. B5 69
Shelburn, Ind. F3 59
Shelburne, N.S., Can. F4 43
Shelburne, Ont., Can. C4 41
Shelburne, co., N.S., Can. F4 43
Shelburne Falls, Mass. A2 65
Shelby, Ind. B3 59
Shelby, Iowa C2 60
Shelby, Mich. E4 66
Shelby, Miss. B3 68
Shelby, Mont. B5 70
Shelby, Nebr. C8 71
Shelby, N.C. B1 76
Shelby, Ohio B3 78
Shelby, co., Ala. B3 46
Shelby, co., Ill. D5 58
Shelby, co., Ind. E6 59
Shelby, co., Iowa C2 60
Shelby, co., Ky. B4 62
Shelby, co., Mo. B5 69
Shelby, co., Ohio B1 78
Shelby, co., Tenn. B2 83
Shelby, co., Tex. D5 84
Shelby City, Ky. C5 62
Shelby Village, Mich. *F7 66
Shelbyville, Ill. D5 58
Shelbyville, Ind. F6 59
Shelbyville, Ky. B4 62
Shelbyville, Mo. B5 69
Shelbyville, Tenn. B5 83
Sheldon, Ill. C6 58
Sheldon, Iowa A2 60
Shell Beach, Calif. *E3 50
Shellbrook, Sask., Can. D2 39
Shell Camp, Tex. *C5 84
Shelley, Idaho F6 57
Shell Lake, Wis. C2 88
Shellman, Ga. E2 55
Shellman Bluff, Ga. E5 55
Shell Rock, Iowa B5 60
Shellsburg, Iowa B6 60
Shelter Island, N.Y. m16 75
Shelton, Conn. D4 52
Shelton, Nebr. D7 71
Shelton, Wash. B2 86
Shenandoah, Iowa D2 60
Shenandoah, Pa. E9 81
Shenandoah, Va. B4 85
Shenandoah, co., Va. B4 85
Shenandoah, mtn., Va. B3 85
Shenandoah Heights, Pa. *E9 81
Shenorock, N.Y. *D7 75
Shensi, see Shaanxi, China
Shenyang, China C9 17
Shepetovka, Sov. Un. F6 12
Shepherd, Mich. E6 66
Shepherd Brook, mtn., Maine B3 64
Shepherdstown, W.Va. B7 87
Shepherdsville, Ky. C4, g11 62
Shepparton, Austl. H5 26
Sheppton, Pa. E9 81
Sherborn, Mass. h10 65
Sherbrooke, Que., Can. D6, k12 42
Sherbrooke, co., Que., Can. D5 42
Sherburn, Minn. G4 67
Sherburne, N.Y. C5 75
Sherburne, co., Minn. E5 67
Shereshevo, Sov. Un. B8 7
Sheridan, Ark. C3 49
Sheridan, Colo. B6 51
Sheridan, Ind. D5 59
Sheridan, Mich. E5 66
Sheridan, Mont. E4 70
Sheridan, Oreg. B3 80
Sheridan, Wyo. B8 89
Sheridan, co., Kans. C3 61
Sheridan, co., Mont. B12 70
Sheridan, co., Nebr. B3 71
Sheridan, co., N.Dak. C5 77
Sheridan, co., Wyo. B5 89

Sheridan, mtn., Wyo. ... B2 89
Sheridan Beach, Wash. ... *B3 86
Sheringham, Eng. ... D7 4
Sherman, N.Y. ... C1 75
Sherman, Tex. ... C4 84
Sherman, co., Kans. ... C2 61
Sherman, co., Nebr. ... C6 71
Sherman, co., Oreg. ... B6 80
Sherman, co., Tex. ... A2 84
Sherridon, Man., Can. ... B1 40
Sherrill, N.Y. ... B5 75
's Hertogenbosch, Neth. ... B6 5
Sherwood, Ark. ... C3, h10 49
Sherwood, Ohio ... A1 78
Sherwood, Oreg. ... h12 80
Sherwood, Tenn. ... B6 83
Sherwood Park, Alta., Can. ... C4 38
Sheshebee, Minn. ... D5 67
Shetland, co., Scot. ... *g10 4
Shetland, is., Scot. ... g1 4
Shiawassee, co., Mich. ... F6 66
Shibām, P.D.R. of Yem. ... F4 15
Shibarghan (Shibargan), Afg. ... A4 20
Shibata, Jap. ... H9 18
Shibecha, Jap. ... E12 18
Shibetsu, Jap. ... D11 18
Shibetsu, Jap. ... E12 18
Shibīn al Kawm, Eg. ... G8 14
Shickshinny, Pa. ... D9 81
Shidler, Okla. ... A5 79
Shiga, pref., Jap. ... *I8 18
Shijiazhuang, China ... D7 17
Shikārpur, Pak. ... C4 20
Shikoku, isl., Jap. ... J6 18
Shilka, Sov. Un. ... D14 13
Shillington, Pa. ... F10 81
Shillong, India ... C9 20
Shiloh, Ohio ... B3 78
Shiloh, Ohio ... C1 78
Shimabara, Jap. ... J5 18
Shimada, Jap. ... o17 18
Shimane, pref., Jap. ... *I16 18
Shimanovsk, Sov. Un. ... D15 13
Shimizu, Jap. ... I9, n17 18
Shimoda, Jap. ... o17 18
Shimodate, Jap. ... m18 18
Shimoga, India ... F6 20
Shimonoseki, Jap. ... I5 18
Shimotsuma, Jap. ... m18 18
Shiner, Tex. ... E4 84
Shinglehouse, Pa. ... C5 81
Shingu, Jap. ... J7 18
Shinjo, Jap. ... G10 18
Shinkolobwe, Zaire ... C5 24
Shinnston, W. Va. ... B4, k10 87
Shinshiro, Jap. ... o16 18
Shiocton, Wis. ... D5, h8 88
Shiogama, Jap. ... G10 18
Shiojiri, Jap. ... m16 18
Ship Bottom, N.J. ... D4 74
Shipman, Va. ... C4 85
Shippegan, N.B., Can. ... B5 43
Shippegan Gully, N.B., Can. ... *B5 43
Shippensburg, Pa. ... F7 81
Shirane-san, mtn., Jap. ... H9 18
Shīrāz, Iran ... G8 16
Shirbin, Eg. ... G8 14
Shiremanstown, Pa. ... *F8 81
Shiribeshi-yama, mtn., Jap. ... E10 18
Shirley, Ind. ... E6 59
Shirley, Mass. ... A4 65
Shirley, Mont. ... D11 70
Shirley, N.Y. ... *n15 75
Shirley, mtn., Wyo. ... D6 89
Shirntoru, see Makarov, Sov. Un.
Shiroishi, Jap. ... G10 18
Shirotori, Jap. ... n15 18
Shitara, Jap. ... n16 18
Shively, Ky. ... B4, g11 62
Shizuoka, Jap. ... I9, o17 18
Shizuoka, pref., Jap. ... *I9 18
Shkodër (Scutari), Alb. ... A2 14
Shkodër (Scutari), pref., Alb. ... *A2 14
Shoal Lake, Man., Can. ... D1 40
Shoals, Ind. ... G4 59
Shoemakersville, Pa. ... E10 81
Sholāpur, India ... E6 20
Shore Acres, Calif. ... *D2 50
Shore Acres, Mass. ... h13 65
Shoreview, Minn. ... *F5 67
Shorewood, Minn. ... *F5 67
Shorewood, Wis. ... E6, m12 88
Shorewood Hills, Wis. ... *E4 88
Short Beach, Conn. ... D5 52
Shortsville, N.Y. ... C3 75
Shoshone, Idaho ... G4 57
Shoshone, co., Idaho ... B3 57
Shoshoni, Wyo. ... C4 89
Show Low, Ariz. ... B3 48
Shpola, Sov. Un. ... G8 12
Shreve, Ohio ... *B3 78
Shreveport, La. ... B2 63

Shrewsbury, Eng. ... D5 4
Shrewsbury, Mass. ... B4 65
Shrewsbury, Mo. ... *C7 69
Shrewsbury, N.J. ... C4 74
Shrewsbury, Pa. ... G8 81
Shropshire, co., Eng. ... *D5 4
Shrub Oak, N.Y. ... *D7 75
Shuangcheng, China ... D3 18
Shuangliao, China ... C9 17
Shuangshan, China ... E1 18
Shuangyang, China ... E2 18
Shuangyashan, China ... C5 18
Shubenacadie, N.S., Can. ... D6 43
Shubrā al Khaymah, Eg. ... *G8 14
Shuksan, mtn., Wash. ... A4 86
Shulan, China ... D3 18
Shulaps, peak, B.C., Can. ... D6 37
Shullsburg, Wis. ... F3 88
Shumen, Bul. ... D8 10
Shumen, co., Bul. ... *D8 10
Shumerlya, Sov. Un. ... D16 12
Shuya, Sov. Un. ... C13 12
Shuzenji, Jap. ... o17 18
Shwebo, Bur. ... D10 20
Shwegyin, Bur. ... *B1 19
Siālkot, Pak. ... B5 20
Siam, see Thailand, Asia
Sian see Xi'an, China
Siauliai, Sov. Un. ... D4 12
Sibenik, Yugo. ... D2 10
Sibert, Ky. ... C6 62
Sibi, Pak. ... C4 20
Sibiu, Rom. ... C7 10
Sibley, Iowa ... A2 60
Sibley, La. ... B2 63
Sibley, co., Minn. ... F4 67
Sibolga, Indon. ... E1 19
Sibsagar, India ... C9 20
Sibu, Mala. ... E4 19
Sicard, La. ... B3 63
Sichuan, prov., China ... E5 17
Sicilia, pol. dist., It. ... *F4 9
Sicily, isl., It. ... F4 9
Sicily Island, La. ... C4 63
Sicklerville, N.J. ... D3 74
Sicuani, Peru ... D3 31
Siderno Marina, It. ... E6 9
Sidhirokastron, Grc. ... B4 14
Sidi bel Abbès, Alg. ... A4 22
Sidi Ifni, Mor. ... C2 22
Sidmouth, Eng. ... E5 4
Sidney, B.C., Can. ... E6, g12 37
Sidney, Iowa ... D2 60
Sidney, Mont. ... C12 70
Sidney, Nebr. ... C3 71
Sidney, N.Y. ... C5 75
Sidney, Ohio ... B1 78
Sidney Center, N.Y. ... C5 75
Siedlce, Pol. ... B7 7
Siegburg, Ger., Fed. Rep. of ... C3 6
Siegen, Ger., Fed. Rep. of ... C4 6
Siemianowice Slaskie, Pol. ... g10 7
Siem Reap, Kam. ... C2 19
Siena, It. ... C3 9
Sieradz, Pol. ... C5 7
Siero, Sp. ... A3 8
Sierpc, Pol. ... B5 7
Sierra, co., Calif. ... C3 50
Sierra, co., N.Mex. ... C5 48
Sierra Blanca, Tex. ... o12 84
Sierra Leone, country, Afr. ... G2 22
Sierra Madre, Calif. ... m12 50
Sierra Nevada, mts., Calif. ... C3 50
Sierraville, Calif. ... C3 50
Sierra Vieja, mts., Tex. ... o12 84
Sierra Vista, Ariz. ... *D3 48
Sifton, Man., Can. ... D1 40
Sighet, Rom. ... B6 10
Sighişoara, Rom. ... B7 10
Sigli, Indon. ... k11 19
Signal, mtn., Va. ... g11 85
Signal Hill, Calif. ... *F4 50
Signal Hill, Ill. ... *E3 58
Signal Mountain, Tenn. ... D8, h11 83
Sigourney, Iowa ... C5 60
Siguiri, Guinea ... F3 22
Sihaus, Peru ... C2 31
Siirt, Tur. ... D13 14
Sīkar, India ... C6 20
Sikasso, Mali ... F3 22
Sikeston, Mo. ... E8 69
Sikionia, Grc. ... C4 14
Silao, Mex. ... m13 34
Silchar, India ... D9 20
Siler City, N.C. ... B3 76
Silesia, reg., Pol. ... C4 7
Siletz, Oreg. ... C3 80
Silifke, Tur. ... D9 14
Silīguri, India ... C8 20
Silistra, Bul. ... C8 10
Sillery, Que., Can. ... n17 42
Siloam Springs, Ark. ... A1 49

Silsbee, Tex. ... D5 84
Siluria, Ala. ... B3 46
Silva, Mo. ... D7 69
Silva Jardim, Braz. ... h6 30
Silver Bay, Minn. ... C7 67
Silver Bow, co., Mont. ... E4 70
Silver Bow Park, Mont. ... D4 70
Silver City, N. Mex. ... C4 48
Silver Creek, N.Y. ... C1 75
Silverdale, Wash. ... B3, e10 86
Silver Grove, Ky. ... h14 62
Silver Hill, Md. ... f9 53
Silver Lake, Ind. ... B6 59
Silver Lake, Mass. ... f11 65
Silver Lake, Minn. ... F4 67
Silver Lake, Ohio ... *A4 78
Silver Lake, Wis. ... F5, n11 88
Silver Spring, Md. ... C3, f8 53
Silver Springs, N.Y. ... C2 75
Silverthrone, mtn., B.C., Can. ... D4 37
Silvertip, mtn., Mont. ... C3 70
Silverton, Colo. ... D3 51
Silverton, Idaho ... B3 57
Silverton, Ohio ... o13 78
Silverton, Oreg. ... B4, h12 80
Silverton, Tex. ... B2 84
Silvia, Col. ... C2 32
Silvis, Ill. ... B3 58
Silvis Heights, Ill. ... *B3 58
Silwān, Jordan ... *C3 15
Simav, Tur. ... C7 14
Simcoe, Ont., Can. ... E4 41
Simcoe, co., Ont., Can. ... C4 41
Simferopol, Sov. Un. ... I10 12
Simi, Calif. ... m11 50
Simiti, Col. ... B3 32
Simla, India ... B6 20
Simleul-Silvaniei, Rom. ... B6 10
Simmesport, La. ... D4 63
Simpson, N.C. ... B5 76
Simpson, Pa. ... C11 81
Simpson, co., Ky. ... D3 62
Simpson, co., Miss. ... D4 68
Simpsonville, S.C. ... B3 82
Simsbury, Conn. ... B5 52
Sinaia, Rom. ... C7 10
Sinajana, Guam ... *F6 2
Sinaloa de Leyva, Mex. ... B3 34
Sinaloa, state, Mex. ... C3 34
Sinanju, Kor. ... G2 18
Sincé, Col. ... B2 32
Sincelejo, Col. ... B2 32
Sinclair, Wyo. ... E5 89
Sinclairville, N.Y. ... C1 75
Sind, reg., Pak. ... C4 20
Sinelnikovo, Sov. Un. ... G10 12
Sines, Port. ... D1 8
Singapore, Singapore ... E2 19
Singapore, country, Asia ... E2 19
Singaraja, Indon. ... G5 19
Singkawang, Indon. ... E3 19
Singleton, Austl. ... *F9 25
Sinhung, Kor. ... F3 18
Siniscola, It. ... D2 9
Sinj, Yugo. ... D3 10
Sinjah, Sud. ... F4 23
Sinking Spring, Pa. ... *F9 81
Šinnicolau-Mare, Rom. ... B5 10
Sinnūris, Eg. ... H8 14
Sinpo, Tur. ... A10 14
Sinpo, Kor. ... F4 18
Sintang, Indon. ... E4 19
Sint-Niklaas, Bel. ... B6 5
Sinton, Tex. ... E4 84
Sintra, Port. ... f9 8
Sinuiju, Kor. ... F2 18
Sion, Switz. ... E3 6
Sioux, co., Iowa ... A1 60
Sioux, co., Nebr. ... B2 71
Sioux, co., N. Dak. ... D5 77
Sioux Center, Iowa ... A1 60
Sioux City, Iowa ... B1 60
Sioux Falls, S. Dak. ... G9 77
Sioux Lookout, Ont., Can. ... o17 41
Sioux Rapids, Iowa ... B2 60
Sipes (Midway), Fla. ... *D5 54
Siping, China ... C9 17
Sipsey, Ala. ... B2 46
Siracusa, It. ... F5 9
Sirājganj, Bngl. ... D8 20
Siren, Wis. ... C1 88
Siret, Rom. ... B8 10
Siros, Grc. ... D5 14
Sirpur, India ... E6 20
Sirsa, India ... C6 20
Sir Wilfrid, mtn., Que., Can. ... C2 42
Sisak, Yugo. ... C3 10
Siskiyou, co., Calif. ... B2 50
Sisseton, S.Dak. ... E9 77
Sister Bay, Wis. ... C6 88
Sisters, Oreg. ... C5 80
Sistersville, W. Va. ... B4 87

Sītāpur, India ... C7 20
Sitionuevo, Col. ... A3 32
Sitka, Alsk. ... D12 47
Sittwe, Burma ... D9 20
Sivas, Tur. ... C11 14
Siverek, Tur. ... D12 14
Sivrihisar, Tur. ... C8 14
Skagit, co., Wash. ... A4 86
Skamania, co., Wash. ... D3 86
Skanderborg, co., Den. ... *I3 11
Skaneateles, N.Y. ... C4 75
Skara, Swe. ... H5 11
Skegness, Eng. ... D7 4
Skellefteå, Swe. ... E9 11
Skidmore, Tex. ... E4 84
Skien, Nor. ... H3, p27 11
Skierniewice, Pol. ... C6 7
Skihist, mtn., B.C., Can. ... D7 37
Skikda (Phillippeville), Alg. ... A6 22
Skokie, Ill. ... A6, h9 58
Skole, Sov. Un. ... D7 7
Skopin, Sov. Un. ... E13 12
Skopje (Skoplje), Yugo. ... D5 10
Skövde, Swe. ... H5 11
Skovorodino, Sov. Un. ... D15 13
Skowhegan, Maine ... D3 64
Skradin, Yugo. ... D2 10
Skvira, Sov. Un. ... G7 12
Skyland, N.C. ... f10 76
Sky Manor, N.J. ... C4 74
Slagelse, Den. ... A1 7
Slamet, mtn., Indon. ... G3 19
Slănic, Rom. ... C7 10
Slany, Czech. ... n17 7
Slater, Iowa ... C4, e8 60
Slater, Mo. ... B4 69
Slater, S.C. ... A3 82
Slatersville, R.I. ... B10 52
Slatina, Rom. ... C7 10
Slatington, Pa. ... E10 81
Slaton, Tex. ... C2 48
Slavgorod, Sov. Un. ... D10 13
Slavonia, reg., Yugo. ... C3 10
Slavonska Pozega, Yugo. ... C3 10
Slavonska Pozega, Yugo. ... C3 10
Slavyanoserbsk, Sov. Un. ... q21 12
Slavyansk, Sov. Un. ... G11, q20 12
Slavyanskaya, Sov. Un. ... I12 12
Slayton, Minn. ... G3 67
Sleepy Eye, Minn. ... F4 67
Sleepy Hollow, Calif. ... *D2 50
Sleepy Hollow, Va. ... *B5 85
Slickville, Pa. ... F2 81
Slidell, La. ... D6, h12 63
Slide, mtn. ... C6 75
Sliderock, mtn., Mont. ... D3 70
Slieve Donard, mtn., N. Ire. ... C3 4
Sligo, Ire. ... C2 4
Sligo, Pa. ... D3 81
Sligo, co., Ire. ... *C2 4
Slinger, Wis. ... E5 88
Slingerlands, N.Y. ... *C7 75
Slippery Rock, Pa. ... D1 81
Sliven, Bul. ... D8 10
Sloan, Iowa ... B1 60
Sloan, N.Y. ... C2 75
Sloatsburg, N.Y. ... A4 75
Slobozia, Rom. ... C8 10
Slocomb, Ala. ... D4 46
Slonim, Sov. Un. ... E5 12
Slope, co., N. Dak. ... D2 77
Slough, Eng. ... k11 4
Slovakia (Slovensko), reg., Czech. ... D5 7
Slovan, Pa. ... F1 81
Slovenia, reg., Yugo. ... C2 10
Slovenia, rep., Yugo. ... *C2 10
Słupca, Pol. ... B4 7
Słupsk, Pol. ... A4 7
Slutsk, Sov. Un. ... s31 11
Slyudyanka, Sov. Un. ... D13 13
Smackover, Ark. ... D3 49
Smederevo, Yugo. ... C5 10
Smela, Sov. Un. ... G8 12
Smelterville, Idaho ... B2 57
Smethport, Pa. ... C5 81
Smethwick (Warley), Eng. ... D5 4
Smidovich, Sov. Un. ... B6 18
Smith, co., Kans. ... C5 61
Smith, co., Miss. ... C4 68
Smith, co., Tenn. ... C8 83
Smith, co., Tex. ... C5 84
Smith, peak, Idaho ... A2 57
Smith Center, Kans. ... C5 61
Smithers, B.C., Can. ... B4 37
Smithers, W. Va. ... C3, m13 87
Smithfield, N.C. ... B4 76
Smithfield, Ohio ... B5 78
Smithfield, Pa. ... *E5 81
Smithfield, Pa. ... G2 81
Smithfield, Utah ... A6 72
Smithfield, Va. ... k14 85
Smithmill, Pa. ... E5 81
Smith River, Calif. ... B1 50

Smithsburg, Md. A2 53
Smiths Falls, Ont., Can. C8 41
Smithton, Austl. o15 25
Smithtown, N.Y. F4 52
Smithville, Mo. B3, h10 69
Smithville, Ohio B4 78
Smithville, Tenn. D8 83
Smithville, Tex. D4 84
Smock, Pa. *G2 81
Smokey Dome, mtn., Idaho F4 57
Smoky, mts., Idaho F4 57
Smoky Lake, Alta, Can. B4 38
Smolensk, Sov. Un. D8 12
Smooth Rock Falls, Ont., Can. o19 41
Smyre, N.C. *B1 76
Smyrna, Del. B6 53
Smyrna, Ga. C2, h7 55
Smyrna, Tenn. B5 83
Smyrna, see Izmir, Tur.
Smyth, co., Va. f10 85
Snake, riv., U.S. B3 45
Sneads, Fla. B2 54
Sneads Ferry, N.C. C5 76
Sneek, Neth. A6 5
Snezhnoye, Sov. Un. q21 12
Snohomish, Wash. B3 86
Snohomish, co., Wash. A4 86
Snoqualmie, Wash. B4 86
Snow, mtn., Calif. C2 50
Snow, mtn., Maine C2 64
Snow, peak, Wash. A7 86
Snowdon, mtn., Wales D4 4
Snowflake, Ariz. B3 48
Snow Hill, Md. D7 53
Snow Hill, N.C. B5 76
Snow Lake, Man., Can. B1 40
Snowshoe, peak, Mont. B1 70
Snowyside, peak, Idaho F4 57
Snyatyn, Sov. Un. A7 10
Snyder, Okla. C3 79
Snyder, Tex. C2 84
Snyder, co., Pa. E7 81
Soap Lake, Wash. B6 86
Soatá, Col. B3 32
Sobinka, Sov. Un. D13 12
Sobota Rimavská, Czech. D6 7
Sobral, Braz. *D6 27
Socaste, S.C. D9 82
Sochaczew, Pol. B6 7
Sochi, Sov. Un. *E6 13
Society, is., Fr. Polynesia H10 2
Society Hill, S.C. B8 82
Socorro, Col. B3 32
Socorro, N. Mex. B5 48
Socorro, co., N. Mex. C5 48
Soc Trang, Viet. D3 19
Socuéllamos, Sp. C4 8
Soda Springs, Idaho G7 57
Soddy-Daisy, Tenn. D8, h11 83
Söderhamn, Swe. G7 11
Södertälje, Swe. t35 11
Sodus, N.Y. B3 75
Soest, Ger., Fed. Rep. of C4 6
Sofia (Sofiya), Bul. D6 10
Sofiya, see Sofia, Bul.
Sofiya, co., Bul. *D6 10
Sofiyevka, Sov. Un. G9 12
Sogamoso, Col. B3 32
Sogn og Fjordane, co., Nor. *G1 11
Sointula, B.C., Can. D4 37
Soissons, Fr. C5 5
Sokal, Sov. Un. F5 12
Sokcho, Kor. G4 18
Söke, Tur. *D6 14
Soke of Peterborough, co., Eng. .. *D6 4
Sokol, Sov. Un. B13 12
Sokołow, Pol. B7 7
Sokoto, Nig. F6 22
Solana, Fla. F5 54
Solana Beach, Calif. *F5 50
Solano, Phil. *B6 19
Solano, co., Calif. C2 50
Soldiers Grove, Wis. E3 88
Soledad, Calif. D3 50
Soledad, Col. A3 32
Solihull, Eng. *D6 4
Solikamsk, Sov. Un. D8 13
Soliman, Tun. F3 9
Solingen, Ger., Fed. Rep. of C3 6
Solleftea, Swe. F7 11
Söller, Sp. C7 8
Solna, Swe. H7 11
Solomon, Kans. D6 61
Solomon Is., country, Oceania G7 2
Solon, Iowa C6 60
Solon, Maine D3 64
Solon, Ohio A4 78
Solonika, see Thessaloniki, Grc.
Solon Springs, Wis. B2 88
Solothurn, Switz. E3 6
Solothurn, canton, Switz. E3 6
Solovyevsk, Sov. Un. D15 13
Soltau, Ger., Fed. Rep. of B4 6

Solvang, Calif. *E3 50
Solvay, N.Y. B4 75
Soma, Tur. *C6 14
Somalia, country, Afr. H6 23
Sombor, Yugo. C4 10
Sombra, Ont., Can. E2 41
Sombrerete, Mex. C4 34
Somerdale, N.J. D2 74
Somers, Conn. B7 52
Somers, Mont. B2 70
Somers, Man., Can. E2 40
Somerset, Ky. C5 62
Somerset, Md. *C3 53
Somerset, Mass. C5 65
Somerset, Ohio C3 78
Somerset, Pa. F3 81
Somerset, Wis. C1 88
Somerset, co., Eng. *E5 4
Somerset, co., Maine C2 64
Somerset, co., Md. D6 53
Somerset, co., N.J. C3 74
Somerset, co., Pa. G3 81
Somerset, isl., N.W. Ter., Can. B15 36
Somerset East, S.Afr. G5 24
Somers Point, N.J. E3 74
Somersworth, N.H. E6 73
Somerton, Ariz. C1 48
Somervell, co., Tex. C4 84
Somerville, Mass. B5, g11 65
Somerville, N.J. B3 74
Somerville, Tenn. B2 83
Somerville, Tex. D4 84
Somme, dept., Fr. C5 5
Somogy, co., Hung. *B3 10
Somonauk, Ill. B5 58
Sonchon, Kor. G2 18
Sønderborg, Den. A4 6
Sønderborg, co., Den. *A4 6
Sondershausen, Ger. Dem. Rep. ... C5 6
Sondrio, It. A2 9
Sonepur, India D7 20
Songjiang, China E9 17
Songjin, see Kimchaek, Kor.
Songkhla, Thai. D2 19
Songnim (Kyomipo), Kor. G2 18
Son La, Viet. G5 17
Sonneberg, Ger. Dem. Rep. C5 6
Sonobe, Jap. n14 18
Sonoma, Calif. C2 50
Sonoma, co., Calif. C2 50
Sonora, Ariz. C3, D3 48
Sonora, Calif. D3 50
Sonora, Tex. D2 84
Sonora, state, Mex. B2 34
Sonsón, Col. B2 32
Sonsonate, Sal. E7 34
Son Tay, Viet. G6 17
Soperton, Ga. D4 55
Sophia, W.Va. D3 87
Sopot, Pol. A5 7
Sopron, Hung. B3 10
Sora, It. D4 9
Sorbas, Sp. D4 8
Sorel, Que., Can. C4 42
Sorento, Ill. E4 58
Soresina, It. B2 9
Soria, Sp. B4 8
Soria, prov., Sp. *B4 8
Soriano, dept., Ur. *E1 30
Søro, coba, Den. *J4 11
Sorocaba, Braz. C3, m8 30
Soroki, Sov. Un. G7 12
Sorong, Indon. F8 19
Soroti, Ug. H4 23
Sorrento, It. D5 9
Sorrento, La. D5, h10 63
Sorrento, Maine *D5 64
Sorsogon, Phil. C6 19
Sorsogon, prov., Phil. *C6 19
Sortavala, Sov. Un. G14 11
Sor Trondelag, co., Nor. *F4 11
Sosnovka, Sov. Un. E13 12
Sosnowiec, Pol. C5, g10 7
Sotteville-lès-Rouen, Fr. C4 5
Soudan, Minn. C6 67
Souderton, Pa. F11 81
Souflion, Grc. B6 14
Soufriere, St. Lucia J14 35
Souk-el Arba, Tun. F2 9
Soul, see Seoul, Kor.
Soulanges, co., Que., Can. D3 42
Sound Beach, N.Y. *n15 75
Soure, Braz. *D6 27
Souris, Man., Can. E1 40
Souris East, P.E.I., Can. C7 43
Sourlake, Tex. D5 84
Sousse, Tun. F3 9
South, div., Ice. *n21 11
South, isl., N.Z. O12 26
South Acton, Mass. g10 65
South Africa, country, Afr. F5 24
South Amboy, N.J. C4, m7 74
South America, cont. 27

South Amherst, Mass. B2 65
South Amherst, Ohio A3 78
Southampton, Ont., Can. C3 42
Southampton, Eng. E6 4
Southampton, N.Y. n16 75
Southampton, Pa. *F11 81
Southampton, co., Va. D5 85
Southampton Island, Can. D16 36
South Apopka, Fla. *D5 54
South Arabia, see Yemen, People's
  Democratic Republic of, country, Asia
South Ashburnham, Mass. A4 65
South Australia, state, Austl. E5 25
South Barre, Mass. B3 65
South Bathurst, N.S., Can. *B4 43
South Bay, Fla. F6 54
South Bellingham, Mass. B5 65
South Belmar, N.J. C4 74
South Belmont, N.C. *B1 76
South Beloit, Ill. A4 58
South Bend, Ind. A5 59
South Bend, Wash. C2 86
South Bennettsville, S.C. *B8 82
South Berwick, Maine E2 64
South Boise, Idaho *F2 57
Southboro, Mass. B4, g9 65
South Boston (Independent City),
  Va. *D4 85
South Bound Brook, N.J. B3 74
Southbridge, Mass. B3 65
South Broadway, Wash. *C5 86
South Brook, Newf., Can. *D3 44
South Burlington, Vt. *C1 73
South Carolina, state, U.S. 82
South Charleston, Ohio C2 78
South Charleston, W.Va. m12 87
South Chelmsford, Mass. C1 65
South Chicago Heights, Ill. m9 58
South China, sea, Asia H14 16
South Cleveland, Tenn. *D9 83
South Clinton, Tenn. *C9 83
South Coatesville, Pa. *G10 81
South Coffeyville, Okla. A6 79
South Congaree, S.C. D5 82
South Connellsville, Pa. G2 81
South Corning, N.Y. *C3 75
South Dakota, state, U.S. 77
South Dartmouth, Mass. C6 65
South Dayton, N.Y. C1 75
South Daytona, Fla. C5 54
South Decatur, Ga. *C2 55
South Deerfield, Mass. B2 65
South Dennis, Mass. C7 65
South Dum-Dum, India *D8 20
South Duxbury, Mass. B6 65
South Easton, Mass. B5 65
South Elgin, Ill. B5, h8 58
South El Monte, Calif. *E5 50
Southend-on-Sea, Eng. E7 4
Southern Cross, Austl. F2 25
Southern Pines, N.C. B3 76
Southern Shops, S.C. *B4 82
Southern View, Ill. *D4 58
Southern Yemen, see Yemen, Peoples
  Democratic Republic of, country, Asia
South Essex, Mass. A6 65
South Euclid, Ohio g9 78
South Fallsburg, N.Y. D6 75
South Farmingdale, N.Y. *E7 75
South Fayetteville, N.C. *B3 76
Southfield, Mass. B1 65
Southfield, Mich. o15 66
South Floral Park, N.Y. *E7 75
South Fork, Pa. F4 81
South Fort George, B.C., Can. C6 37
South Fulton, Tenn. A3 83
South Fulton, Tenn. A3 83
South Gate, Calif. n12 50
Southgate, Ky. h14 62
Southgate, Mich. p15 66
South Glastonbury, Conn. C6 52
South Glens Falls, N.Y. *B7 75
South Grafton, Mass. B4 65
South Greensburg, Pa. *F2 81
South Greenwood, S.C. C3 82
South Hackensack, N.J. *B4 74
South Hadley, Mass. B2 65
South Hadley Falls, Mass. B3 65
South Hamilton, Mass. A6, f12 65
South Hanover, Mass. h12 65
South Harriman, Tenn. *D9 83
South Harwich, Mass. C7 65
South Haven, Mich. F4 66
South Hempstead, N.Y. *E7 75
South Henderson, N.C. *A4 76
South Hill, Va. D4 85
South Holland, Ill. k9 58
South Holland (Zuid-Holland),
  prov., Neth. *A6 5
South Hooksett, N.H. D4 73
South Houston, Tex. r14 84
South Huntington, N.Y. *D3 75
South Hutchinson, Kans. f11 61

Southington, Conn. C5 52
South International Falls, Minn. ... B5 67
South Jacksonville, Ill. D3 58
South Jordan, Utah *A6 72
Southkent, Mich. *F5 50
South Laguna, Calif. *F5 50
Southlake, Tex. *C4 84
South Lake Tahoe, Calif. C4 50
South Lancaster, Mass. B4 65
Southland, Mich. *F6 66
Southlawn, Ill. *D4 58
South Lebanon, Ohio C1 78
South Lyon, Mich. F7, p14 66
South Mansfield, La. B2 63
South Miami, Fla. G6, s13 54
South Milwaukee, Wis. F6, n12 88
South Modesto, Calif. *D3 50
South Monroe, Mich. *G7 66
Southmont, N.C. B2 76
Southmont, Pa. *F4 81
South Montrose, Pa. C10 81
South Mt. Vernon, Ohio *B3 78
South Nelson, N.S., Can. *C4 43
South Nelson Village, B.C., Can. .. *E9 37
South New Castle, Pa. *D1 81
South Nyack, N.Y. g9 75
South Ogden, Utah A6, C2 72
Southold, N.Y. m16 75
South Orange, N.J. B4 75
South Oroville, Calif. *C3 50
South Paris, Maine D2 64
South Park, Ill. *B5 58
South Pasadena, Calif. *E4 50
South Patrick Shores, Fla. D6 54
South Pekin, Ill. C4 58
South Pittsburg, Tenn. D8 83
South Plainfield, N.J. B4 74
South Point, Ohio D3 78
South Porcupine, Ont., Can. o19 41
Southport, Austl. E9 25
Southport, Eng. D5 4
Southport, Fla. u16 54
Southport, Ind. E5, m10 59
Southport, N.Y. *C4 75
Southport, N.C. D4 76
South Portland, Maine E2, g7 64
South Pottstown, Pa. *F10 81
South Range, Mich. A2 66
South Renovo, Pa. D6 81
South Revelstoke, B.C., Can. D8 37
South River, Ont., Can. B5 42
South River, N.J. C4 74
South Rockwood, Mich. *F7 66
South Roxana, Ill. *E4 58
South Russell, Ohio *A4 78
South St. Paul, Minn. F5, n12 67
South Salisbury, N.C. *B2 76
South Salt Lake, Utah C2 72
South San Francisco, Calif. h8 50
South San Gabriel, Calif. *F4 50
South Shields, Eng. C6 4
South Shore, Mo. *f12 69
Southside Estates, Fla. *B5 54
South Side Place, Tex. r14 84
South Sioux City, Nebr. B9 71
South Stickney, Ill. k9 58
South Streator, Ill. *B5 58
South Swansea, Mass. C5 65
South Taft, Calif. *E4 50
South Temple, Pa. *F10 81
South Toms River, N.J. D4 74
South Torrington, Wyo. D8 89
South Trail, Fla. q10 54
South Tucson, Ariz. C3 48
South Uniontown, Pa. *G2 81
South Walpole, Mass. h10 65
South Waverly, Pa. C8 81
South Webster, Ohio D3 78
Southwest, Mo. F2 81
South West Africa, see Namibia,
  country, Afr.
South Westbury, N.Y. *E7 75
Southwestern Dillon, S.C. *C9 82
Southwestern, mts., Va. B4 85
South West Fargo, N.Dak. D9 77
Southwest Greensburg, Pa. *F2 81
Southwest Harbor, Maine D4 64
South Whitley, Ind. B6 59
Southwick, Mass. B2 65
South Williamson, Ky. C7 62
South Williamsport, Pa. D7 81
South Wilmington, Ill. B5 58
South Windermere, S.C. *F8 82
South Windham, Maine E2, g7 64
South Windsor, Conn. B6 52
Southwood Acres, Conn. *B6 52
South Yarmouth, Mass. C7 65
South Zanesville, Ohio C3 78
Sovetsk (Tilsit), Sov. Un. A6 7
Sovetskaya Gavan, Sov. Un. E17 13
Soviet Union (U.S.S.R.), country,
  Eur. Asia 13

Place	Grid	Page
Spa, Bel.	B6	5
Spain, country, Eur.		8
Spalding, Eng.	D6	4
Spalding, Nebr.	C7	71
Spalding, co., Ga.	C2	55
Spanaway, Wash.	B3	86
Spangler, Pa.	E4	81
Spaniard's Bay, Newf., Can.	E5	44
Spanish, Ont., Can.	A2	41
Spanish Fork, Utah	A6, D2	72
Spanish Sahara, see Western Sahara, Afr.		
Spanish Town, Jam.	F5	35
Sparkill, N.Y.	*D6	75
Sparkman, Ark.	D3	49
Sparks, Ga.	E3	55
Sparks, Nev.	B2	72
Sparlingville, Mich.	*F8	66
Sparrows Point, Md.	B5	53
Sparta, Ga.	C4	55
Sparta, Ill.	E4	58
Sparta, Mich.	E5	66
Sparta, N.J.	A3	74
Sparta, N.C.	A1	76
Sparta, Tenn.	D8	83
Sparta, Wis.	E3	88
Sparta, mtn., N.J.	B3	74
Spartanburg, S.C.	B4	82
Spartanburg, co., S.C.	B3	82
Sparti (Sparta), Grc.	D4	14
Spassk-Dalniy, Sov. Un.	E16	13
Spearfish, S.Dak.	F2	77
Spearman, Tex.	A2	84
Spearville, Kans.	E4	61
Speed, Ind.	H6	59
Speedway, Ind.	E5, k10	59
Speers, Pa.	*F2	81
Speight, Ky.	C7	62
Spenard, Alsk.	*C10	47
Spencer, Ind.	F4	59
Spencer, Iowa	A2	60
Spencer, Mass.	B4	65
Spencer, Nebr.	B7	71
Spencer, N.Y.	C4	75
Spencer, N.C.	B2	76
Spencer, Ohio	A3	78
Spencer, Okla.	*B4	79
Spencer, W.Va.	C3	87
Spencer, Wis.	D3	88
Spencer, co., Ind.	H4	59
Spencer, co., Ky.	B4	62
Spencerport, Ky.	B3	75
Spencerville, Ohio	B1	78
Sperry, Okla.	A6	79
Speyer, Ger., Fed. Rep. of	D4	6
Spiceland, Ind.	E7	59
Spinazzola, It.	D6	9
Spindale, N.C.	B1	76
Spink, co., S. Dak.	F7	77
Spirit Lake, Idaho	B3	57
Spirit Lake, Iowa	A2	60
Spirit River, Alta., Can.	B1	38
Spiro, Okla.	B7	79
Spišská Nová Ves, Czech.	D6	7
Spittal an der Drau, Aus.	E6	6
Split, Yugo.	D3	10
Spokane, Wash.	B8, g14	86
Spokane, co., Wash.	B8	86
Spoleto, It.	C4	9
Spooner, Wis.	C2	88
Spotswood, N.J.	C4	74
Spotsylvania, co., Va.	B5	85
Sprague, W.Va.	n13	87
Spray, N.C.	A3	76
Spreckels, Calif.	*D3	50
Spreckelsville, Haw.	*C5	56
Spremberg, Ger. Dem. Rep.	C7	6
Spring, Tex.	q14	84
Spring Arbor, Mich.	F6	66
Springboro, Ohio	C1	78
Spring City, Pa.	F10	81
Spring City, Tenn.	D9	83
Springdale, Ark.	A1	49
Springdale, Newf., Can.	D3	44
Springdale, Ohio	n13	78
Springdale, Pa.	E2, h14	81
Springdale, S.C.	*D5	82
Springer, N. Mex.	A6	48
Springfield, Colo.	D8	51
Springfield, Fla.	v16	54
Springfield, Ill.	D4	58
Springfield, Ky.	C4	62
Springfield, Mass.	B2	65
Springfield, Minn.	F4	67
Springfield, Mo.	D4	69
Springfiled, Nebr.	C9, g12	71
Springfield, N.J.	B4	74
Springfield, Ohio	C2	78
Springfield, Oreg.	C4	80
Springfield, Pa.	*B11	81
Springfield, S.C.	E5	82
Springfield, S.Dak.	H8	77
Springfield, Tenn.	A5	83
Springfield, Vt.	E3	73
Springfield, Va.	g12	85
Springfield Place, Mich.	*F5	66
Spring Glen, Fla.	*B5	54
Spring Green, Wis.	E3	88
Spring Grove, Minn.	G7	67
Spring Grove, Pa.	G8	81
Springhill, N.S., Can.	D6	43
Spring Hill, Kans.	D9	61
Springhill, La.	A2	63
Spring Hill Pa.	*F4	81
Spring Hope, N.C.	B4	76
Spring Lake, Mich.	E4	66
Spring Lake, N.J.	C4	74
Spring Lake, N.C.	B3	76
Spring Lake Heights, N.J.	C4	74
Spring Lake Park, Minn.	*E5	67
Springlee, Ky.	*H6	62
Spring Mills, S.C.	*B6	82
Springmont, Pa.	*F10	81
Springport, Mich.	F6	66
Springs, S. Afr.	*F5	24
Springsure, Aust.	B8	25
Springvale, Maine	E2	64
Spring Valley, Calif.	o16	50
Spring Valley, Ill.	B4	58
Spring Valley, Minn.	G6	67
Spring Valley, N.Y.	g12	75
Spring Valley, Ohio	C1	78
Spring Valley, Tex.	*E5	84
Springville, Iowa	B6	60
Springville, N.Y.	C2	75
Springville, Utah	A6, D2	72
Spruce Knob, mtn., W.Va.	C5	87
Spruce Pine, N.C.	f10	76
Spur, Tex.	C2	84
Squamish, B.C., Can.	E6	37
Squatteck, Que., Can.	B9	42
Squaw Lake, Minn.	C4	67
Squaw Rapids, Sask., Can.	D4	39
Srbobran, Yugo.	C4	10
Sredne-Kolymsk, Sov. Un.	C18	13
Sremska Mitrovica, Yugo.	C4	10
Sretensk, Sov. Un.	D14	13
Sri Lanka, country, Asia	G7	20
Srinagar, India	B6	20
Staatsburg, N.Y.	D7	75
Stade, Ger., Fed. Rep. of	B4	6
Stafford, Eng.	D5	4
Stafford, Kans.	E5	61
Stafford, Tex.	*E5	84
Stafford, co., Eng.	*D5	4
Stafford, co., Kans.	D5	61
Stafford, co., Va.	B5	85
Stafford Springs, Conn.	B7	52
Staffordsville, Ky.	C7	62
Staines, Eng.	m11	4
Stains, Fr.	g10	5
Stambaugh, Mich.	B2	66
Stamford, Conn.	E2	52
Stamford, N.Y.	C6	75
Stamford, Tex.	C3	84
Stamps, Ark.	D2	49
Stanaford, W.Va.	D3, n13	87
Stanberry, Mo.	A3	69
Standale, Mich.	*F5	66
Standerton, S. Afr.	F5	24
Standish, Mich.	E7	66
Stanfield, Oreg.	B7	80
Stanford, Calif.	*D2	50
Stanford, Ky.	C5	62
Stanford, Mont.	C6	70
Stanhope, N.J.	B3	74
Stanislaus, co., Calif.	D3	50
Stanke Dimitrov, Bul.	D6	10
Stanley, Falk. Is.	I5	27
Stanley, N.C.	B1	76
Stanley, N.Dak.	B3	77
Stanley, Va.	B4	85
Stanley, Wis.	D3	88
Stanley, co., S.Dak.	F5	77
Stanleytown, Va.	D3	85
Stanleyville, N.C.	*A2	76
Stanly, co., N.C.	B2	76
Stanstead, Que., Can.	D5	42
Stanstead, co., Que., Can.	D5	42
Stanthorpe, Austl.	E9	25
Stanton, Calif.	*F5	50
Stanton, Del.	*A6	53
Stanton, Mich.	E5	66
Stanton, Nebr.	C8	71
Stanton, Tex.	C2	84
Stanton, co., Kans.	E2	61
Stanton, co., Nebr.	C8	71
Stantonsburg, N.C.	B5	76
Stanwood, Wash.	A3	86
Staples, Minn.	D4	67
Star, N.C.	B3	76
Starachowice, Pol.	C6	7
Staraya Russa, Sov. Un.	C8	12
Stara Zagora, Bul.	D7	10
Stara-Zagora, co., Bul.	*D7	10
Starbuck, Minn.	E3	67
Star City, Ark.	D4	49
Star City, W.Va.	B5	87
Stargard, Pol.	B3	7
Stargo, Ariz.	C4	48
Starjunction, Pa.	*F2	81
Stark, co., Ill.	B4	58
Stark, co., N.Dak.	D3	77
Stark, co., Ohio	B4	78
Starke, Fla.	C4	54
Starke, co., Ind.	B4	59
Starkey, Va.	C3	85
Starkville, Miss.	B5	68
Starobelsk, Sov. Un.	G12	12
Starodub, Sov. Un.	E9	12
Starogard, Pol.	B5	7
Starr, co., Tex.	F3	84
Startex, S.C.	B3	82
Staryy Oskol, Sov. Un.	F11	12
Stassfurt, Ger. Dem. Rep.	C5	6
State Center, Iowa	B4	60
State College, Miss.	B5	68
State College, Pa.	E6	81
State Road, N.C.	A2	76
Statesboro, Ga.	D5	55
Statesville, N.C.	A2	76
Staunton, Ill.	D4	58
Staunton (Independent City), Va.	B3	85
Stavanger, Nor.	H1	11
Stavropol, Sov. Un.	I13	12
Stawell, Austl.	H4	26
Stayner, Ont., Can.	C4	41
Stayton, Oreg.	C4, k12	80
Steamboat Springs, Colo.	A4	51
Stearns, Ky.	D5	62
Stearns, co., Minn.	E4	67
Steblev, Sov. Un.	G8	12
Steele, Mo.	E8	69
Steele, co., Minn.	F5	67
Steele, co., N.Dak.	C8	77
Steeleville, Ill.	E4	58
Steelton, Pa.	F8	81
Steelville, Mo.	D6	69
Steep Rock Lake, Ont., Can.	o17	41
Stefanesti, Rom.	B8	10
Steger, Ill.	B6, m9	58
Steiermark (Styria), state, Aus.	*E7	6
Steilacoom, Wash.	B3, f10	86
Steinbach, Man., Can.	E3	40
Stellarton, N.S., Can.	D7	43
Stendal, Ger. Dem. Rep.	B5	6
Stephen, Minn.	B2	67
Stephens, Ark.	D2	49
Stephens, co., Ga.	B3	55
Stephens, co., Okla.	C4	79
Stephens, co., Tex.	C3	84
Stephens City, Va.	A4	85
Stephenson, Mich.	C3	66
Stephenson, co., Ill.	A4	58
Stephenville, Newf., Can.	D2	44
Stephenville, Tex.	C3	84
Stephenville Crossing, Newf., Can.	D2	44
Sterling, Colo.	A7	51
Sterling, Ill.	B4	58
Sterling, Kans.	D5	61
Sterling, Mass.	B4	65
Sterling, co., Tex.	D2	84
Sterling City, Tex.	D2	84
Sterling Heights, Mich.	o15	66
Sterlington, La.	B3	63
Sterlitamak, Sov. Un.	D8	13
Sternberk, Czech.	D4	7
Stettin, see Szczecin, Pol.		
Stettler, Alta., Can.	C4	38
Stetson, mtn., Maine	C4	64
Steuben, co., Ind.	A7	59
Steuben, co., N.Y.	C3	75
Steubenville, Ohio	B5	78
Stevenage, Eng.	*E6	4
Stevens, co., Kans.	E3	61
Stevens, co., Minn.	E2	67
Stevens, co., Wash.	A7	86
Stevenson, Ala.	A4	46
Stevenson, Wash.	D4	86
Stevens Point, Wis.	D4	88
Stevensville, Mich.	F4	66
Stevensville, Mont.	D2	70
Steveston, B.C., Can.	F12	37
Stewardson, Ill.	D5	58
Stewart, Minn.	F4	67
Stewart, co., Ga.	D2	55
Stewart, co., Tenn.	A4	83
Stewart Manor, N.Y.	*E7	75
Stewartstown, Pa.	G8	81
Stewartsville, N.J.	B2	74
Stewartville, Minn.	G6	67
Stewiacke, N.S., Can.	D6	43
Steyr, Aus.	D7	6
Stickney, Ill.	*B6	58
Stif, Alg.	A6	22
Stigler, Okla.	B6	79
Stillwater, Minn.	E6	67
Stillwater, N.Y.	C7	75
Stillwater, Okla.	A4	79
Stillwater, co., Mont.	E7	70
Stilwell, Okla.	B7	79
Stinnett, Tex.	B2	84
Štip, Yugo.	E6	10
Stirling, Ont., Can.	C7	41
Stirling, N.J.	B4	74
Stirling, Scot.	B5	4
Stirling, co., Scot.	*B5	4
Stittsville, Ont., Can.	B9	41
Stockbridge, Ga.	C2	55
Stockbridge, Mass.	B1	65
Stockbridge, Mich.	F6	66
Stockdale, Tex.	E4, k8	84
Stockerau, Aus.	D8	6
Stockholm, Swe.	H8, t36	11
Stockholm, co., Swe.	*H8	11
Stockport, Eng.	D5	4
Stockton, Ala.	E2	46
Stockton, Calif.	D3, h10	50
Stockton, Ill.	A3	58
Stockton, Kans.	C4	61
Stockton, Mo.	D4	69
Stoddard, co., Mo.	E8	69
Stoke-on-Trent, Eng.	D5	4
Stokes, co., N.C.	A2	76
Stokesdale, N.C.	A3	76
Stokke, Nor.	p28	11
Stolberg, Ger., Fed. Rep. of	C3	6
Stone, Ky.	C7	62
Stone, co., Ark.	B3	49
Stone, co., Miss.	E4	68
Stone, co., Mo.	E4	69
Stoneboro, Pa.	D1	81
Stonega, Va.	f9	85
Stoneham, Mass.	g11	65
Stone Harbor, N.J.	E3	74
Stonehaven, Scot.	B5	4
Stoneleigh, Md.	*B4	53
Stone Mountain, Ga.	C2, h8	55
Stone Park, Ill.	*B6	58
Stones River Homes, Tenn.	*B5	83
Stoneville, N.C.	A3	76
Stonewall, Man., Can.	D3	40
Stonewall, Miss.	C5	68
Stonewall, co., Tex.	C2	84
Stoney Creek, Ont., Can.	D5	41
Stonington, Conn.	D9	52
Stonington, Ill.	D4	58
Stonington, Maine	D4	64
Stony Brook, N.Y.	*n15	75
Stony Creek Mills, Pa.	*F10	81
Stony Mountain, Can.	D3	40
Stony Plain, Alta., Can.	C3	38
Stony Point, N.Y.	A5	75
Stony Point, N.C.	B1	76
Stony Prairie, Ohio	*A2	78
Storey, co., Nev.	B2	72
Storm Lake, Iowa	B2	60
Stormont, co., Ont., Can.	B9	41
Stornoway, Scot.	A3	4
Storozhinets, Sov. Un.	G5	12
Storrs, Conn.	B7	52
Story, co., Iowa	B4	60
Story City, Iowa	B4	60
Stottville, N.Y.	C7	75
Stoughton, Sask., Can.	H4	39
Stoughton, Mass.	B5, h11	65
Stoughton, Wis.	F4	88
Stovall, Miss.	A3	68
Stover, Mo.	C4	69
Stow, Ohio	A4	78
Stowe, Pa.	F10	81
Stowe Township, Pa.	*E2	81
Stoyoma, mtn., B.C., Can.	E7	37
Strabane, N. Ire.	C3	4
Strabane, Pa.	F1	81
Strafford, Mo.	D4	69
Strafford, Pa.	*G10	81
Strafford, co., N.H.	E5	73
Strakonice, Czech.	D2	7
Straldzha, Bul.	D8	10
Stralsund, Ger. Dem. Rep.	A6	6
Strängnäs, Swe.	t35	11
Stranraer, Scot.	C4	4
Strasbourg, Sask., Can.	F3	39
Strasbourg, Fr.	D3	6
Strasburg, N.Dak.	D5	77
Strasburg, Ohio	B4	78
Strasburg, Pa.	G9	81
Strasburg, Va.	B4	85
Stratford, Calif.	D4	50
Stratford, Ont., Can.	D3	41
Stratford, Conn.	E4	52
Stratford, Iowa	B4	60
Stratford, N.J.	D2	74
Stratford, Okla.	C5	79
Stratford, Tex.	A1	84
Stratford, Wis.	D3	88
Stratford Hills, Va.	*C5	85
Stratford-on-Avon, Eng.	D6	4
Strathmore, Calif.	D4	50
Strathmore, Alta., Can.	D4	38
Strathroy, Ont., Can.	E3	41
Straubing, Ger., Fed. Rep. of	D6	6
Strawberry, mts., Oreg.	C8	80

Strawberry Point, Calif. *C2 50
Strawberry Point, Iowa B6 60
Strawn, Tex. C3 84
Strážnice, Czech. D4 7
Streamwood, Ill. *A5 58
Streator, Ill. B5 58
Streetsboro, Ohio *A4 78
Streetsville, Ont., Can. m14 41
Strehaia, Rom. C6 10
Stringtown, Ky. B5 62
Stromsburg, Nebr. C8 71
Strong City, Kans. D7 61
Stronghurst, Ill. C3 58
Strongsville, Ohio A4 78
Stroud, Okla. B5 79
Stroudsburg, Pa. E11 81
Stroudsburg West, Pa. *E11 81
Struer, Den. I3 11
Strum, Wis. D2 88
Strumica, Yugo. E6 10
Struthers, Ohio A5 78
Stryker, Ohio A1 78
Stryy, Sov. Un. G4 12
Strzegom, Pol. C4 7
Strzelce, Pol. C5 7
Strzelin, Pol. C4 7
Strzelno, Pol. B5 7
Strzemieszyce, Pol. g10 7
Stuart, Fla. E6 54
Stuart, Iowa C3 60
Stuart, Nebr. B6 71
Stuart, Va. D2 85
Stuarts Draft, Va. B3 85
Stung Treng, Kam. C3 19
Sturbridge, Mass. B3 65
Sturgeon, Mo. D6 69
Sturgeon, Pa. *F1 81
Sturgeon Bay, Wis. D6 88
Sturgeon Falls, Ont., Can. A5 41
Sturgis, Sask., Can. F4 39
Sturgis, Ky. C2 62
Sturgis, Mich. G5 66
Sturgis, S.Dak. F2 77
Sturtevant, Wis. F6, n12 88
Stutsman, co., N. Dak. C7 77
Stuttgart, Ark. C4 49
Stuttgart, Ger., Fed. Rep. of D4 6
Styria, reg., Aus. E7 6
Suao, Taiwan *G9 17
Sublette, Kans. E3 61
Sublette, co., Wyo. D2 89
Subotica, Yugo. B4 10
Succasunna, N.J. B3 74
Suceava, Rom. B8 10
Sucha, Pol. D5 7
Suchitoto, Sal. *E7 34
Suchow see Xuzhou China
Sucre, Bol. C2 29
Sucre, state, Ven. A5 32
Sucy-en-Brie, Fr. g11 5
Sudan, Tex. B1 84
Sudan, country, Afr. E8 21
Sudan, reg., Afr. E7 21
Sudbury, Ont., Can. A4, p19 41
Sudbury, Mass. B5, g10 65
Sudbury, dist., Ont., Can. A3 41
Sudbury Center, Mass. *B5 65
Sudirman, mts., Indon. F9 19
Sudzha, Sov. Un. F10 12
Sueca, Sp. C5 8
Suez, Eg. H9 14
Suffern, N.Y. D6, m14 75
Suffield, Conn. B6 52
Suffolk (Independent City), Va. .. D6, k14 85
Suffolk, co., Eng. *D7 4
Suffolk, co., Mass. B5 65
Suffolk, co., N.Y. n15 75
Sugar, mtn., Mich. k9 66
Sugar Creek, Mo. h11 69
Sugarcreek, Ohio *B4 78
Sugar Grove, Va. D1, f10 85
Sugar Hill, Ga. B2 55
Sugar Land, Tex. E5, r14 84
Sugarloaf, mtn., Maine C2 64
Sugar Notch, Pa. n17 81
Şuḥār, Om. E6 15
Suhl, Ger. Dem. Rep. C5 6
Suibin, China C5 18
Suihua, China B10 18
Suileng, China C3 18
Suining, China E6 17
Suita, Jap. *I7 18
Suitland, Md. f9 53
Suixian, China E7 17
Sukabumi, Indon. G3 19
Sukaraja, Indon. F4 19

Sukarnapura, see Jayapura, Indon.
Sukhumi, Sov. Un. A13 14
Sukumo, Jap. J6 18
Sukkur, Pak. C4 20
Sulawesi, see Celebes, isl., Indon.
Sullana, Peru B1 31
Sulligent, Ala. B1 46
Sullivan, Ill. D5 58
Sullivan, Ind. F3 59
Sullivan, Mo. C6 69
Sullivan, co., Ind. F3 59
Sullivan, co., Mo. A4 69
Sullivan, co., N.H. E3 73
Sullivan, co., N.Y. D6 75
Sullivan, co., Pa. D8 81
Sullivan, co., Tenn. C11 83
Sullivans Island, S.C. k12 82
Sully, Iowa C5 60
Sully, co., S. Dak. F5 77
Sulmona, It. C4 9
Sulphur, La. D2 63
Sulphur, Okla. C5 79
Sulphur South, La. *D2 63
Sulphur Springs, Tex. C5 84
Sultan, Wash. B4 86
Sulu, prov., Phil. *D6 19
Sumach, Wash. *C5 86
Sumas, Wash. A3 86
Sumatra, isl., Indon. F2 19
Sumenep, Indon. G4 19
Sumiton, Ala. B2 46
Summerdale, Pa. *F8 81
Summerfield, N.C. A3 76
Summerland, B.C., Can. E8 37
Summers, co., W. Va. D4 87
Summerside, P.E.I., Can. C6 43
Summersville, W. Va. C4, m14 87
Summerton, S.C. D7 82
Summerville, Ga. B1 55
Summerville, Pa. D3 81
Summerville, S.C. E7, h11 82
Summit, Ill. k9 58
Summit, Miss. D3 68
Summit, N.J. B4 74
Summit, co., Colo. B4 51
Summit, co., Ohio A4 78
Summit, co., Utah A6 72
Summit Hill, Pa. E10 81
Summitville, Ind. D6 59
Sumner, Ill. E6 58
Sumner, Iowa B5 60
Sumner, Wash. B3 86
Sumner, co., Kans. E6 61
Sumner, co., Tenn. A5 83
Sumoto, Jap. I7 18
Šumperk, Czech. D4 7
Sumter, S.C. D7 82
Sumter, co., Ala. C1 46
Sumter, co., Fla. D4 54
Sumter, co., Ga. D2 55
Sumter, co., S.C. D7 82
Sumy, Sov. Un. F10 12
Sun, La. D6 63
Sunburst, Mont. B5 70
Sunbury, Ohio B3 78
Sunbury, Pa. E8 81
Sunbury, co., N.B., Can. D3 43
Sunchŏn, Kor. I3 18
Sunchŏn, Kor. G2 18
Sun City, Ariz. D1 48
Suncook, N.H. E5 73
Sun Crest, Calif. *F5 50
Sundance, Wyo. B8 89
Sundance, mtn., Wyo. B8 89
Sundbyberg, Swe. t35 11
Sunderland, Ont., Can. C5 41
Sunderland, Eng. C6 4
Sundown, Tex. C1 84
Sundre, Alta., Can. D3 38
Sundsvall, Swe. F7 11
Sunfield, Mich. F5 66
Sunflower, co., Miss. B3 68
Sungari, riv., China C5 18
Sungchiang, China E7 17
Sungurlu, Tur. B10 14
Suniland, Fla. *G6 54
Sunman, Ind. F7 59
Sunnyland, Fla. q11 54
Sunnyland, Ill. *C4 58
Sunnymead, Calif. *F5 50
Sunnyside, Utah B6 72
Sunnyside, Wash. C5 86
Sunnyvale, Calif. k8 50
Sunol, Calif. h9 50
Sun Prairie, Wis. E4 88
Sunray, Tex. B2 84

Sunridge, Ont., Can. B5 41
Sunrise Heights, Mich. *F5 66
Sunset, La. D3 63
Sunset, Utah *A5 72
Sunset Beach, Calif. *F5 50
Sunset Hills, Mo. *C7 69
Sunset Park, Kans. *B5 61
Superior, Ariz. C3, D3 48
Superior, Mont. C2 70
Superior, Nebr. E7 71
Superior, W.Va. *D3 87
Superior, Wis. B1 88
Superior, Wyo. E4 89
Superior, lake, Can., U.S. A9 45
Suquamish, Wash. B3 86
Şuʼ (Tyre), Leb. F10 14
Şur, Om. E6 15
Surabaja, see Surabaya, Indon.
Surabaya, Indon. G4 19
Surakarta, Indon. G4 19
Šurany, Czech. D5 7
Surat, India D5 20
Suresnes, Fr. g9 5
Surfside, Fla. s13 54
Surgoinsville, Tenn. C11 83
Surgut, Sov. Un. C10 13
Suri, India D8 20
Surigao, Phil. D7 19
Surigao del Norte, prov., Phil. *D7 19
Surigao del sur, prov., Phil. *D7 19
Suriname, dep., S.A. C5 27
Suriname, riv., Sur. C5 27
Surrey, co., Eng. *E6 4
Surry, N.H. E3 73
Surry, co., N.C. A2 76
Surry, co., Va. C6 85
Susa, It. B1 9
Susana Knolls, Calif. *E4 50
Susanville, Calif. B3 50
Sušice, Czech. D2 7
Susquehanna, Pa. C10 81
Susquehanna, co., Pa. C10 81
Sussex, N.B., Can. D4 43
Sussex, N.J. A3 74
Sussex, Wis. m11 88
Sussex, co., Del. C6 53
Sussex, co., Eng. *E7 4
Sussex, co., N.J. A3 74
Sussex, co., Va. D5 85
Susurluk, Tur. C7 14
Sutersville, Pa. *F2 81
Sutherland, Iowa B2 60
Sutherland, Nebr. C4 71
Sutherland, co., Scot. *B4 4
Sutherlin, Oreg. D3 80
Sutter, Calif. *C3 50
Sutter, co., Calif. C3 50
Sutter Creek, Calif. C3 50
Sutton, Que., Can. D5 42
Sutton, Nebr. D8 71
Sutton, W. Va. C4 87
Sutton, co., Tex. D2 84
Sutton-in-Ashfield, Eng. D6 4
Sutton West, Ont., Can. C5 41
Suttsu, Jap. E10 18
Suva, Fiji H8 2
Suwa, Jap. m17 18
Suwalki, Pol. A7 7
Suwannee, Fla. C3 54
Suwannee, co., Fla. B3 54
Suwŏn, S. Kor. H3 18
Suyo, Peru B1 31
Suzhou, China E9 17
Suzuka, Jap. o15 18
Svalbard (Spitzbergen),
   Nor., dep. B5 13
Svedala, Swe. A2 7
Swendborg, co., Den. *J4 11
Sverdlovsk, Sov. Un. D9 13
Sverdrup, is., Can. m30 36
Svetlaya, Sov. Un. C9 18
Svilajnac, Yugo. C5 10
Svilengrad, Bul. E8 10
Svirstroy, Sov. Un. A9 12
Svishtov, Bul. D7 10
Svitavy, Czech. D4 7
Svobodnyy, Sov. Un. D15 13
Swain, co., N.C. f9 76
Swainsboro, Ga. D4 55
Swampscott, Mass. B6, g12 65
Swan Hill, Aust. G7 25
Swan Hills, Alta., Can. B3 38
Swanlake, Idaho G6 57
Swan Lake, Miss. B3 68
Swannanoa, N.C. f10 76
Swan River, Man., Can. C1 40

Swansboro, N.C. C5 76
Swansea, Ill. f14 69
Swansea, Mass. C5 65
Swansea, S.C. D5 82
Swansea, Wales E5 4
Swansea Center, Mass. *C5 65
Swanton, Ohio A2 78
Swanton, Vt. B1 73
Swarthmore, Pa. q20 81
Swartz Creek, Mich. F7 66
Swayzee, Ind. C6 59
Swaziland, country, Afr. F6 24
Swea City, Iowa A3 60
Swedeborg, Mo. D5 59
Swedeland, Pa. o20 81
Sweden, country, Eur. F7 11
Swedesboro, N.J. D2 74
Sweeny, Tex. r14 84
Sweet, Idaho F2 57
Sweet Briar, Va. C3 85
Sweet Grass, co., Mont. E7 70
Sweet Home, Oreg. C4 80
Sweetsburg, Que., Can. D5 42
Sweetsers, Ind. C6 59
Sweet Springs, Mo. C4 69
Sweetwater, Tenn. D8 83
Sweetwater, Tex. C2 84
Sweetwater, co., Wyo. E3 89
Swepsonville, N.C. A3 76
Swidnica, Pol. C4 7
Swidwin, Pol. B3 7
Swiebodzice, Pol. C4 7
Swiebodzin, Pol. B3 7
Swiecie, Pol. B5 7
Swiętochlowice, Pol. g9 7
Swift, co., Minn. E3 67
Swift Current, Sask., Can. G2, n7 39
Swindon, Eng. E6 4
Swinemünde, see
   Swinoujscie, Pol.
Świnoujście, Pol. B3 7
Swisher, co., Tex. B2 84
Swissvale, Pa. k14 81
Switzer, W. Va. D3 87
Switzerland, co., Ind. G7 59
Switzerland, country, Eur. E4 6
Swoyerville, Pa. D10, n17 81
Sycamore, Ill. B5 58
Sycamore, Ohio B2 78
Sycamore Hills, Mo. *C7 69
Sydenham, Ont., Can. C8 41
Sydney, Austl. F9 25
Sydney, N.S., Can. C9 43
Sydney Mines, N.S., Can. C9 43
Sykesville, Md. B4 53
Sykesville, Pa. D4 81
Syktyvkar, Sov. Un. C8 13
Sylacauga, Ala. B3 46
Sylhet, Bngl. D9 20
Sylva, N.C. f9 76
Sylvan, Oreg. f12 80
Sylvan Beach, N.Y. B5 75
Sylvania, Ala. A4 46
Sylvania, Ga. D5 55
Sylvania, Ky. g11 62
Sylvania, Ohio A2, e6 78
Sylvan Lake, Alta., Can. C3 38
Sylvester, Ga. E3 55
Syosset, N.Y. F2 52
Syracuse, Ind. B6 59
Syracuse, Kans. E2 61
Syracuse, Nebr. D9, h12 71
Syracuse, N.Y. B4 75
Syracuse, Ohio D4 78
Syracuse, Utah C2 72
Syr Darya, riv., Sov. Un. E9 13
Syria, country, Asia F6 16
Syriam, Bur. *B1 19
Syzran, Sov. Un. D7 13
Szabadszállás, Hung. B4 10
Szabolcs-Szatmár, co., Hung. *B5 10
Szamotuly, Pol. B4 7
Szarvas, Hung. B5 10
Szczebrzeszyn, Pol. C7 7
Szczecin (Stettin), Pol. B3 7
Szczecinek, Pol. B4 7
Szechwan, see Sichuan, China
Szeged, Hung. B5 10
Székesfehérvár, Hung. B4 10
Szekszárd, Hung. B4 10
Szentendre, Hung. B4 10
Szentes, Hung. B5 10
Szolnok, Hung. B5 10
Szolnok, co., Hung. *B5 10
Szombathely, Hung. B3 10

T

Tabaco, Phil.	*C6	19
Tabasco, state, Mex.	D6	34
Taber, Alta., Can.	E4	38
Taboada, Sp.	A2	8
Tábor, Czech.	D3	7
Tabor, Iowa	D2	60
Tabor, N.J.	*B4	74
Tabora, Tan.	B6	24
Tabor City, N.C.	C4	76
Tabrīz, Iran	B4	15
Tabūk, Sau. Ar.	D2	15
Tachikawa, Jap.	n18	18
Táchira, state, Ven.	B3	32
Tacloban, Phil.	C6	19
Tacna, Peru	E5	31
Tacna, dept., Peru	E3	31
Tacoma, Wash.	B3, f11	86
Tacuarembó, Ur.	E1	30
Tacuarembó, dept., Ur.	*E1	30
Tadoussac, Que., Can.	A8	42
Tadzhik, rep., Sov. Un.	F9	16
Taegu, Kor.	I4	18
Taejon, Kor.	H3	18
Tafalla, Sp.	A5	8
Taff Viejo, Arg.	E2	29
Tafí Viejo, Arg.	E2	29
Taft, Calif.	E4	50
Taft, Fla.	D5	54
Taft, Tex.	F4	84
Taft Heights, Calif.	*E4	50
Taft Southwest, Tex.	*F4	84
Taganrog, Sov. Un.	H12	12
Tahāt, mtn., Alg.	D6	22
Tahlequah, Okla.	B7	79
Tahoka, Tex.	C2	84
Tahoua, Niger	F6	22
T'aichung, Taiwan	G9	17
Tailai, China	C1	18
T'ainan, Taiwan	G9	17
Taipei, Taiwan	G9	17
Taiping, Mala.	E2	19
T'aitung, Taiwan	G9	17
Taiwan (Formosa), country		
(Nationalist China), Asia	G9	17
Taiyuan, China	D7	17
Taizz, Yemen	G3	15
Tajimi, Jap.	I8, n16	18
Tajrīsh, Iran	*B5	15
Tājūrā, Libya	B7	22
Tak, Thai.	*B1	19
Takada, Jap.	H9	18
Takamatsu, Jap.	I7	18
Takaoka, Jap.	H8	18
Takasaki, Jap.	H9, m17	18
Takatsuki, Jap.	o14	18
Takawa, Jap.	*J5	18
Takayama, Jap.	H8, m16	18
Takefu, Jap.	n15	18
Takeo, Kam.	*C2	19
Takingeun, Indon.	*m11	19
Takoma Park, Md.	f8	53
Takut, Bur.	*D10	20
Talā, Eg.	*G8	14
Tala, Mex.	m12	34
Tala, Ur.	E1	30
Talagante, Chile	A2	28
Talara, Peru	B1	31
Talavera de la Reina, Sp.	C3	8
Talbert, Ky.	C6	62
Talbot, co., Ga.	D2	5
Talbot, co., Md.	C5	53
Talbotton, Ga.	D2	55
Talca, Chile	B2	28
Talca, prov., Chile	B2	28
Talcahuano, Chile	B2	28
Tālcher, India	D8	20
Talco, Tex.	C5	84
Taliaferro, co., Ga.	C4	55
Talihina, Okla.	C6	79
Talisayan, Phil.	*D6	19
Talladega, Ala.	B3	46
Talladega, co., Ala.	B3	46
Tallahassee, Fla.	B2	54
Tallahatchie, co., Miss.	B3	68
Tallapoosa, Ga.	C1	55
Tallapoosa, co., Ala.	C4	46
Tallassee, Ala.	C4	46
Talleyville, Del.	*A6	53
Tallinn, Sov. Un.	B5	12
Tallmadge, Ohio	A4	78
Tallulah, La.	B4	63
Talnoye, Sov. Un.	G8	12
Talsi, Sov. Un.	C4	12
Taltal, Chile	E1	29
Tama, Iowa	C5	60
Tama, co., Iowa	B5	60
Tamale, Ghana	G4	22
Taman, Sov. Un.	I11	12
Tamano, Jap.	I6	18
Tamanrasset, Alg.	D6	22
Tamaqua, Pa.	E10	81
Tamaulipas, state, Mex.	C5	34
Tamazula de Gordiano, Mex.	n12	34
Tambov, Sov. Un.	E13	12
Tamil Nadu, state, India	F6	20
Tampa, Fla.	E4, p11	54
Tampere, Fin.	G10	11
Tampico, Mex.	C5, k15	34
Tams, W.Va.	D3	87
Tamworth, Austl.	F9	25
Tanabe, Jap.	J7	18
Tananarive, see Antananarive, Mad.		
Tanchon, Kor.	F4	18
Tandag, Phil.	*D7	19
Tândárei, Rom.	C8	10
Taney, co., Mo.	E4	69
Taneytown, Md.	A3	53
Tanga, Tan.	B7	24
Tanganyika, lake, Afr.	C6	24
Tanger (Tangier), Mor.	A3	22
Tangermünde, Ger. Dem. Rep.	B5	6
Tangier, Va.	C7	85
Tangipahoa, par., La.	D5	63
Tangshan, China	D8	17
Tangyuan, China	C4	18
Tanjay, Phil.	*D6	19
Tanjore, see Thanjavūr, India		
Tanjungkarang-Telukbetung,		
Indon.	G3	19
Tanjungpandan, Indon.	F3	19
Tānk, Pak.	B5	20
Tanque Verde, Ariz.	*C4	48
Tanshui, Taiwan	*F9	17
Tanţā, Eg.	G8	14
Tanzania, country, Afr.	B6	24
Tao'an, China	B9	17
Taormina, It.	F5	9
Taos, N.Mex.	A6	48
Taos, co., N.Mex.	A6	48
Tapachula, Mex.	E6	34
Tappahannock, Va.	C6	85
Tappan, N.Y.	g13	75
Taquara, Braz.	D2	30
Taquaritinga, Braz.	k7	30
Tara, Mo.	*C7	69
Tara, Sov. Un.	D10	13
Tarābulus, see Tripoli, Leb.		
Tarakan, Laos	*B2	19
Tarancon, Sp.	B4	8
Taranto, It.	D6	9
Tarapacá, prov., Chile	D1	29
Tarapoto, Peru	C2	31
Tarare, Fr.	E6	5
Tarascon-sur-Ariège, Fr.	F6	5
Tarazona, Sp.	B5	8
Tarbes, Fr.	F4	5
Tarboro, N.C.	B5	76
Taree, Austl.	E9	26
Tarentum, Pa.	E2, h14	81
Tarfaya, Mor.	C2	22
Tarifa, Sp.	D3	8
Tarija, Bol.	D3	29
Tarija, dept., Bol.	D3	29
Tarkio, Mo.	A2	69
Tarkwa, Ghana	G4	22
Tarlac, Phil.	B6, o13	19
Tarlac, prov., Phil.	*B6	19
Tarma, Peru	D2	31
Tarn, dept., Fr.	*F5	5
Tarn-et-Garonne, dept., Fr.	*E4	5
Tarnobrzeg, Pol.	C6	7
Tarnów, Pol.	C6	7
Tarnowskie Góry, Pol.	g9	7
Taroudant, Mor.	B3	22
Tarpon Springs, Fla.	D4	54
Tarquinia, It.	C3	9
Tarragona, Sp.	B6	8
Tarragona, prov., Sp.	*B6	8
Tarrant, Ala.	B3, f7	46
Tarrant, co., Tex.	C4	84
Tarrasa, Sp.	B7	8
Tarrytown, N.Y.	D7, m15	75
Tarsney, Mo.	k11	69
Tarsus, Tur.	D10	14
Tartu, Sov. Un.	B6	12
Tashkent, Sov. Un.	E9	1
Tashkurghan, Afg.	A4	20
Taskmalaya, Indon.	*G3	19
Tasmania, state, Austl.	o14	25
Tatabánya, Hun.	B4	10
Tatamagouche, N.S., Can.	D6	43
Tatarbunary, Sov. Un.	C9	10
Tate, Ga.	B2	55
Tate, co., Miss.	A4	68
Tateville, Ky.	D5	62
Tateyama, Jap.	I9, n18	18
Tatta, Pak.	D4	20
Tattnall, co., Ga.	D4	55
Tatuí, Braz.	C3, m8	30
Tatum, N.Mex.	C7	48
Taubaté, Braz.	C3	30
Taung, S.Afr.	F4	24
Taungdwingyi, Bur.	D10	20
Taunggyi, Bur.	D10	20
Taunton, Eng.	E5	4
Taunton, Mass.	C5	65
Taurage, sov. Un.	D4	12
Tauranga, N.Z.	L16	26
Taurianova, It.	E6	9
Tauste, Sp.	B5	8
Tavares, Fla.	D5	54
Tavas, Tur.	*D7	14
Tavda, Sov. Un.	D9	13
Tavira, Port.	D2	8
Tavistock, Ont., Can.	D4	41
Tavoy, Bur.	F10	20
Tavşanli, Tur.	*C7	14
Tawas City, Mich.	D7	66
Taylor, Mich.	p15	66
Taylor, Pa.	D10, m18	81
Taylor, Tex.	D4	84
Taylor, co., Fla.	B3	54
Taylor, co., Ga.	D2	55
Taylor, co., Iowa	D3	60
Taylor, co., Ky.	C4	62
Taylor, co., Tex.	C3	84
Taylor, co., W.Va.	B4	87
Taylor, co., Wis.	C3	88
Taylor Mill, Ky.	k14	62
Taylors, S.C.	B3	82
Taylorsport, Ky.	h13	62
Taylorsville, Ky.	B4	62
Taylorsville, Miss.	D4	68
Taylorsville, N.C.	B1	76
Taylorville, Ill.	D4	58
Tayshet, Sov. Un.	D12	13
Taza, Mor.	B4	22
Tazewell, Tenn.	C10	83
Tazewell, Va.	e10	85
Tazewell, co., Ill.	C4	58
Tazewell, co., Va.	e10	85
Tbilisi, Sov. Un.	E7	13
Tchula, Miss.	B3	68
Tczew, Pol.	A5	7
Teague, Tex.	D4	84
Teaneck, N.J.	h8	74
Tecuala, Mex.	C3	34
Tecuci, Rom.	C8	10
Tecumseh, Ont., Can.	E2	41
Tecumseh, Mich.	F7	66
Tecumseh, Nebr.	D9	71
Tecumseh, Okla.	B5	79
Tegal, Indon.	*G3	19
Tegucigalpa, Hond.	E7	34
Teguise, sp.	m15	8
Tehachapi, Calif.	E4	50
Tehama, co., Calif.	B2	50
Tehrān, Iran	B5	15
Tehuacan, Mex.	D5, n15	34
Tehuantepec, Mex.	D5	34
Teide, Pico de, peak, Sp. (Can.Is.)	m13	8
Tejo (Tagus), riv., Eur.	C1	8
Tekamah, Nebr.	C9	71
Tekax de Alvaro Obregón, Mex.	C7	34
Tekirdag, Tur.	B6	14
Tekoa, Wash.	B8	86
Tela, Hond.	*D7	34
Tel Aviv-Yafo (Tel Aviv Jaffa),		
Isr.	B2, g5	15
Telde, Sp.	m14	8
Telemark, co., Nor.	*H3	11
Telfair, co., Ga.	E3	55
Telford, Pa.	F11	81
Tell, Wis.	I4	59
Tell City, Ind.	I4	59
Teller, co., Colo.	C5	51
Telluride, Colo.	D3	51
Telok Anson, Mala.	E2	19
Teloloapan, Mex.	D5, n14	34
Temirtau, Sov. Un.	*D10	13
Témiscouata, co., Que., Can.	B9	42
Temora, Austl.	*F8	25
Tempe, Ariz.	C3, D2	48
Temperance, Mich.	G7	66
Tempio Pausania, It.	D2	9
Temple, Okla.	C3	79
Temple, Pa.	F10	81
Temple, Tex.	D4	84
Temple City, Calif.	*F5	50
Temple Hill, Ky.	D4	62
Temple Terrace, Fla.	o11	54
Templeton, Que., Can.	D2	42
Templeton, Mass.	A3	65
Templin, Ger. Dem. Rep.	B6	6
Temryuk, Sov. Un.	I11	12
Temuco, Chile	B2	28
Tenafly, N.J.	B5, h9	74
Tenaha, Tex.	D5	84
Tenāli, India	*E7	20
Tenancingo, de Degollado, Mex.	D5, n14	34
Tenango del Valle, Mex.	n14	34
Tenasserim, Bur.	F10	20
Tenchong, China	F4	17
Tenino, Wash.	C3	86
Tennessee, state, U.S.		83
Tennessee, riv., U.S.	D9	45
Tensas, par., La.	B4	63
Teocaltiche, Mex.	C4, m12	34
Teófilo Otoni, Braz.	B4	30
Tepatitán de Morelos, Mex.	C4, m12	34
Tepic, Mex.	C4, m11	34
Teplice, Czech.	C2	7
Teramo, It.	C4	9
Teresina, Braz.	D6	27
Teresópolis, Braz.	C4, h6	30
Termez, Sov. Un.	F9	13
Termini Imerese, It.	F4	9
Termoli, It.	C5	9
Ternate, Indon.	E7	19
Terneuzen, Neth.	B5	5
Terney, Sov. Un.	D8	18
Terni, It.	C4	9
Ternopol, Sov. Un.	G5	12
Terra Alta, W.Va.	B5	87
Terrace, B.C., Can.	B3	37
Terrace Park, Ohio	*C1	78
Terracina, It.	D4	9
Terra Linda, Calif.	*D2	50
Terrebonne, Que., Can.	D4, p19	42
Terrebonne, co., Que., Can.	D3	42
Terrebonne, par., La.	E5	63
Terre Haute, Ind.	F3	59
Terre Hill, Pa.	F9	81
Terrell, Tex.	C4	84
Terrell, co., Ga.	E2	55
Terrell, co., Tex.	D1	84
Terrell Hills, Tex.	k7	84
Terry, Mont.	D11	70
Terry, co., Tex.	C1	84
Terrytown, La.	*k11	63
Terrytown, Nebr.	C2	71
Terryville, Conn.	C4	52
Teruel, Sp.	B5	8
Teruel, prov., Sp.	*B5	8
Tesanj, Yugo.	C3	10
Teterow, Ger. Dem. Rep.	B6	6
Teton, co., Idaho	F7	57
Teton, co., Mont.	C4	70
Teton, co., Wyo.	C2	89
Tétouan, Mor.	A3	22
Tetovo, Yugo.	D5	10
Teutopolis, Ill.	D5	58
Teverya (Tiberias), Isr.	B3, g5	15
Tewantin-Noosa, Austl.	C9	26
Tewksbury, Mass.	A5, f11	65
Texarkana, Ark.	D1	49
Texarkana, Tex.	C5	84
Texas, Md.	B4	53
Texas, co., Mo.	D5	69
Texas, co., Okla.	e9	79
Texas, state, U.S.		84
Texas City, Tex.	E5, r15	84
Texhoma, Okla.	e9	79
Teziutlán, Mex.	D5, n15	34
Thailand (Siam), country, Asia	B2	19
Thames, N.Z.	L15	26
Thamesville, Ont., Can.	E3	41
Thāna, India	*E5	20
Thanh Hoa, Viet.	B3	19
Thanjāvūr (Tanjore), India	F6	20
Thann, Fr.	D7	5
Thaon -les-Vosges, Fr.	C7	5
Tharptown, Pa.	*E8	81
Tharrawaddy, Bur.	E10	20
Thatcher, Ariz.	C4	48
Thatcher, Idaho	G7	57
Thaton, Bur.	E10	20
Thayer, Mo.	E6	69
Thayer, co., Nebr.	D8	71
Thayetmyo, Bur.	*E10	20
The Dalles, Oreg.	B5	80
The Entrance, Austl.	F8	26
The Father, mtn., N.Gui.	k13	25
The Hague ('s Gravenhage), Neth.	A6	5
The Pas, Man., Can.	C1, g7	40
The Plains, Ohio	C3	78
Theresa, N.Y.	A5, f9	75
Thermalito, Calif.	*C3	50

Thermopolis, Wyo. ... C4 89
Thesprotia, prov., Grc. ... *C3 14
Thessalon, Ont., Can. ... p19 41
Thessaloniki (Salonika), Grc. ... B4 14
Thessaloniki (Salonika),
  prov., Grc. ... *B4 14
Thessaly, reg., Grc. ... C4 14
Thetford Mines, Que., Can. ... C6 42
The Village, Okla. ... *B4 79
Thibodaux, La. ... E5, k10 63
Thief River Falls, Minn. ... B2 67
Thiensville, Wis. ... E6, m12 88
Thiers, Fr. ... E5 5
Thiès, Sen ... F1 22
Thimbu, Bhu ... C8 20
Thionville, Fr. ... C7 5
Thisted, co., Den. ... *I3 11
Thivai (Thebes), Grc. ... C4 14
Thomas, Okla. ... B3 79
Thomas, W.Va. ... B5 87
Thomas, co., Ga. ... F3 55
Thomas, co., Kans. ... C2 61
Thomas, co., Nebr. ... C5 71
Thomason, Ga. ... D2 55
Thomaston, Ala. ... C2 46
Thomaston, Conn. ... C4 52
Thomaston, Maine ... D3 64
Thomaston, N.Y. ... *E7 75
Thomasville, Ala. ... D2 46
Thomasville, Ga. ... F3 55
Thomasville, N.C. ... B2 76
Thompson, Conn. ... B9 52
Thompson Falls, Mont. ... C1 70
Thompsonville, Conn. ... A6 52
Thomson, Ga. ... C4 55
Thon Buri, Thai. ... *C2 19
Thorburn, N.S., Can. ... D7 43
Thornbury, Ont., Can. ... C4 41
Thorndale, Tex. ... D4 84
Thornton, Colo. ... *B6 51
Thornton, Idaho ... F7 57
Thornton, Ill. ... *B6 58
Thornton, Miss. ... B3 68
Thorntown, Ind. ... D4 59
Thornwood, N.Y. ... *D7 75
Thorofare, N.J. ... D2 74
Thorold, Ont., Can. ... D5 41
Thorp, Wis. ... D3 88
Thorpe, W.Va. ... D3 87
Thorsby, Ala. ... C3 46
Thorshavn, Faer. Is. ... C6 3
Thouars, Fr. ... D3 5
Thousand Oaks, Calif. ... *E4 50
Three Forks, Mont. ... E5 70
Three Hills, Alta., Can. ... D4 38
Three Oaks, Mich. ... G4 66
Three Rivers, Mass. ... B3 65
Three Rivers, Mich. ... G5 66
Three Rivers, Miss. ... E5 68
Three Rivers, Tex. ... E3 84
Throckmorton, Tex. ... C3 84
Throckmorton, co., Tex. ... C3 84
Throop, Pa. ... m18 81
Thule, Grnld. ... *B14 33
Thun, Switz. ... E3 6
Thunder Bay, Ont., Can. ... o17 41
Thunder Bay, dist., Ont., Can. ... o17 41
Thunderbolt, Ga. ... D5 55
Thurgau, canton, Switz. ... *E4 6
Thüringia, former state, Ger. Dem.
  Rep. ... *C5 6
Thüringia, reg., Ger. Dem. Rep. ... *C5 6
Thurles, Ire. ... D3 4
Thurmont, Md. ... A3 53
Thurrock, Eng. ... *E7 4
Thursday Island, Austl. ... B7 25
Thurso, Que., Can. ... D2 42
Thurso, Scot. ... A5 4
Thurston, co., Nebr. ... B9 71
Thurston, co., Wash. ... C3 86
Tianjin, China ... D8 17
Tianshui, China ... E6 17
Tibet, auton., reg., China ... B8 20
Tiburon, Calif. ... *C2 50
Tice, Fla. ... F5 54
Ticino, canton, Switz. ... *E4 6
Tickfaw, La. ... D5 63
Ticonderoga, N.Y. ... B7 75
Ticul, Mex. ... C7 34
Tidioute, Pa. ... C3 81
Tieling, China ... C9 17
Tienen, Bel. ... B6 5
Tientsin, see Tianjin, China
Tie Plant, Miss. ... B4 68
Tierra Blanca, Mex. ... D5, n15 34
Tierra del Fuego, isl., Chile ... h12 28
Tietê, Braz. ... C3, m8 30
Tiff City, Mo. ... E3 69
Tiffin, Ohio ... A2 78
Tiflis, see Tbilisi, Sov. Un.
Tift, co., Ga. ... E3 55
Tifton, Ga. ... *E3 55
Tiftona, Tenn. ... *D8 83

Tigard, Oreg. ... h12 80
Tigil, Sov. Un. ... D18 13
Tignish, P.E.I., Can. ... C6 43
Tigre, Arg. ... g7 28
Tigris, riv., Asia ... F7 13
Tijuana, Mex. ... A1 34
Tikhvin, Sov. Un. ... B9 12
Tiksi, Sov. Un. ... B15 13
Tilburg, Neth. ... B6 5
Tilbury, Ont., Can. ... E2 41
Tilden, Ill. ... E4 58
Tilden, Nebr. ... B8 71
Tilghman, Md. ... C5 53
Tilimsen, Alg. ... B4 22
Tiline, Ky. ... e9 62
Tillamook, Oreg. ... B3 80
Tillamook, co., Oreg. ... B3 80
Tillicum, Wash. ... *B2 86
Tillman, Okla. ... C2 79
Tillman, co., Okla. ... C2 79
Tillsonburg, Ont., Can. ... E4 41
Tilton, Ill. ... C6 58
Tilton, N.H. ... E4 73
Tiltonsville, Ohio ... B5 78
Timaru, N.Z. ... P13 26
Timbaúba, Braz. ... *D7 27
Times Beach, Mo. ... *C7 69
Timiskaming, dist., Ont., Can. ... O19 41
Timisoara, Rom. ... C5 10
Timmins, Ont., Can. ... o19 41
Timmonsville, S.C. ... C8 82
Timoneng, Guam ... *F6 2
Timor, isl., Indon. ... G6 19
Timpson, Tex. ... D5 84
Tineo, Sp. ... A2 8
Tinley Park, Ill. ... k9 58
Tinsley, Miss. ... C3 68
Tioga, N. Dak. ... B2 77
Tioga, co., N.Y. ... C4 75
Tioga, co., Pa. ... C7 81
Tippah, co., Miss. ... A5 68
Tipp City, Ohio ... C1 78
Tippecanoe, co., Ind. ... D4 59
Tipperary, Ire. ... D2 4
Tipperary, co., Ire. ... *D3 4
Tipton, Calif. ... D4 50
Tipton, Ind. ... D5 59
Tipton, Iowa ... C6 60
Tipton, Mo. ... C5 69
Tipton, Okla. ... C2 79
Tipton, co., Ind. ... D5 59
Tipton, co., Tenn. ... B2 83
Tiptonville, Tenn. ... A2 83
Tiranë (Tirana), Alb. ... B2 14
Tiranë (Tirana), pref., Alb. ... *B2 14
Tirano, It. ... A3 9
Tiraspol, Sov. Un. ... H7 12
Tire, Tur. ... C6 14
Tirgoviste, Rom. ... C7 10
Tirgu-jiu, Rom. ... C6 10
Tirgul-Neamt, Rom. ... B8 10
Tirgul-Ocna, Rom. ... B8 10
Tirgu-Mures, Rom. ... B7 10
Tirgu-Sacuesc, Rom. ... B8 10
Tirnaveni, Rom. ... B7 10
Tirnavos, Grc. ... *C4 14
Tirol, state, Aus. ... E5 6
Tirol, reg., Aus. ... E5 6
Tiruchchirappalli, India ... F6 20
Tirunelveli, India ... G6 20
Tiruppur, India ... *F6 20
Tisdale, Sask., Can. ... E3 39
Tishomingo, Okla. ... C5 79
Tishomingo, co., Miss. ... A6 68
Tiskilwa, Ill. ... B4 58
Tisza, riv., Hung., Yugo. ... B5 10
Tiszafüred, Hung. ... B5 10
Tiszakécske, Hung. ... B5 10
Titicaca, lake, Bol., Peru ... C2 29
Titograd, Yugo. ... D4 10
Titovo Užice, Yugo. ... D4 10
Titov Veles, Yugo. ... E5 10
Titus, co., Tex. ... C5 84
Titusville, Fla. ... D6 54
Titusville, N.J. ... C3 74
Titusville, Pa. ... C2 81
Tiverton, Eng. ... E5 4
Tiverton, R.I. ... *C12 52
Tivoli, It. ... D4, h9 9
Tivoli, Tex. ... E4 84
Tixtla, Mex. ... p14 34
Tizapán, Mex. ... h9 34
Tizimin, Mex. ... C7 34
Tizi-Ouzou, Alg. ... A5 22
Tiznit, Mor. ... C3 22
Tjiandjur, Indon. ... *G3 19
Tjimahi, Indon. ... *G3 19
Tlalpan, Mex. ... h9 34
Tlaxcala, state, Mex. ... D5 34
Tlaxiaco, Mex. ... D5 34
Toamasina, Mad. ... D9 24
Toast, N.C. ... A2 76
Toba, Jap. ... o15 18

Tobarra, Sp. ... C5 8
Tobol, riv., Sov. Un. ... D9 13
Tobolsk, Sov. Un. ... D9 13
Tobyhanna, Pa. ... D11 81
Tocantins, riv., Braz. ... D6 27
Toccoa, Ga. ... B3 55
Toccoa Falls, Ga. ... B3 55
Tochigi, Jap. ... H9, m18 18
Tochigi, pref., Jap. ... *H9 18
Tocopilla, Chile ... D1 29
Todd, co., Ky. ... D2 62
Todd, co., Minn. ... D4 67
Todd, co., S. Dak. ... G5 77
Togo, country, Afr. ... G5 22
Tokat, Tur. ... B11 14
Tokenon, Kor. ... G2 18
Toki, Jap. ... *n16 18
Tokorozawa, Jap. ... n18 18
Tokushima, Jap. ... I7 18
Tokushima, pref., Jap. ... *I7 18
Tokuyama, Jap. ... I5 18
Tōkyō, Jap. ... I9, n18 18
Tokyo, pref., Jap. ... *I9 18
Tolbukhin (Dobrich), Bul. ... D8 10
Toledo, Ill. ... D5 58
Toledo, Iowa ... B5 60
Toledo, Ohio ... A2, e6 78
Toledo, Oreg. ... C3 80
Toledo, Sp. ... C3 8
Toledo, prov., sp. ... *C3 8
Toler, Ky. ... C7 62
Toliara, Mad. ... E8 24
Tolima, Dept., Col. ... C2 32
Tolland, co., Conn. ... B7 52
Tolleson, Ariz. ... D1 48
Tolmin, Yugo. ... B1 10
Tolna, Hung. ... B4 10
Tolna, co., Hung. ... *B4 10
Tolono, Ill. ... D5 58
Tolosa, Sp. ... A4 8
Toluca, Ill. ... B4 58
Toluca de Lerdo, Mex. ... D5, n14 34
Tolyatti, Sov. Un. ... *D7 13
Tomah, Wis. ... E3 88
Tomahawk, Wis. ... C4 88
Tomakomai, Jap. ... E10 18
Tomakovka, Sov. Un. ... H10 12
Tomar, Port. ... C1 8
Tomari, Sov. Un. ... E17 13
Tomaszow Lubelski, Pol. ... C7 7
Tomaszow Mazowiecki, Pol. ... C6 7
Tomball, Tex. ... D5 84
Tombouctou (Timbuktu), Mali ... E4 22
Tombstone, Ariz. ... D4 48
Tomé, Chile ... B2 28
Tomelloso, Sp. ... C4 8
Tom Green, co., Tex. ... D2 84
Tomkins Cove, N.Y. ... D7, m14 75
Tommot, Sov. Un. ... D15 13
Tompkins, co., N.Y. ... C4 75
Tompkinsville, Ky. ... D4 62
Tom Price, Austl. ... D2 25
Tomsk, Sov. Un. ... D11 13
Toms River, N.J. ... D4 74
Tonalá, Mex. ... D6 34
Tonasket, Wash. ... A6 86
Tonawanda, N.Y. ... B2 75
Tondano, Indon. ... E6 19
Tønder, Den. ... A4 6
Tønder, co., Den. ... *J3 11
Tonga, Br. dep., Oceania ... H9 2
Tonganoxie, Kans. ... C8, k15 61
Tonghua, China ... F2 18
Tongliao, China ... C9 17
Tongling, China ... E8 17
Tonk, India ... C6 20
Tonka Bay, Minn. ... *F5 67
Tonkawa, Okla. ... A4 79
Tonkin, reg., Viet. ... A3 19
Tonopah, Nev. ... B3 72
Tönsberg, Nor. ... H4, p28 11
Tooele, Utah ... A5, D2 72
Tooele, co., Utah ... A5 72
Toole, co., Mont. ... B5 70
Toombs, co., Ga. ... D4 55
Toowoomba, Austl. ... E9 25
Topanga, Calif. ... *F4 50
Topeka, Kans. ... C8, k13 61
Topol'cany, Czech. ... D5 7
Topolovgrad, Bul. ... D8 10
Toppenish, Wash. ... C5 86
Topsfield, Mass. ... A6 65
Topsham, Maine ... E3, g8 64
Topton, Pa. ... F10 81
Torbay, Newf., Can. ... E5 44
Torez, Sov. Un. ... q21 12
Torhout, Bel. ... B5 5
Toride, Jap. ... n19 18
Torino, see Turin, It.
Toro, Sp. ... B3 8
Törökszentmiklós, Hung. ... B5 10
Toronto, Ont., Can. ... D5, m15 41

Toronto, Ohio ... B5 78
Toropets, Sov. Un. ... C8 12
Topquay (Torbay), Eng. ... E5 4
Torrance, Calif. ... n12 50
Torrance, co., N. Mex. ... B5 48
Torre Annunziata, It. ... D5 9
Torre del Greco, It. ... D5 9
Torredonjimeno, Sp. ... D4 8
Torrelavega, Sp. ... A3 8
Torremaggiore, It. ... D5 9
Torrens, lake, Austl. ... F6 25
Torrente, Sp. ... C5 8
Torreón, Mex. ... B4 34
Torre Pacheco, Sp. ... D5 8
Torres Novas, Port. ... C1 8
Torrevieja, Sp. ... D5 8
Torrington, Conn. ... B4 52
Torrington, Wyo. ... D8 89
Torrox, Sp. ... D4 8
Tortilla Flat, Ariz. ... C3 48
Tortona, It. ... B2 9
Tortosa, Sp. ... B6 8
Toruń, Pol. ... B5 7
Torzhok, Sov. Un. ... C10 12
Toscana, pol. dist., It. ... *C3 9
Tosno, Sov. Un. ... C10 12
Tosya, Tur. ... B10 14
Totana, Sp. ... D5 8
Totkomlós, Hung. ... B5 10
Totonicapán, Guat. ... D6 34
Totowa, N.J. ... B4 74
Tottori, Jap. ... I7 18
Tottori, pref., Jap. ... *I7 18
Totz, Ky. ... D6 62
Toubkal, Jbel, mtn., Mor. ... B3 22
Tougaloo, Miss. ... C3 68
Touggourt, Alg. ... B6 22
Toul, Fr. ... C3 68
Toulon, Fr. ... F6 5
Toulon, Ill. ... B4 58
Toulouse, Fr. ... F4 5
Toungoo, Bur. ... E10 20
Touraine, former prov., Fr. ... D4 5
Tourcoing, Fr. ... B5 5
Tourlaville, Fr. ... C3 5
Tours, Fr. ... D4 5
Towaco, N.J. ... B4 74
Towanda, Kans. ... E7, k12 61
Towanda, Pa. ... C9 81
Tower City, Pa. ... E8 81
Town and Country, Mo. ... *C7 69
Towner, N. Dak. ... B5 77
Towner, co., N. Dak. ... B6 77
Townley, Ala. ... B2 46
Town of Pines, Ind. ... *A4 59
Town of Tonawanda, N.Y. ... *B2 75
Towns, co., Ga. ... B3 55
Townsend, Mass. ... A4 65
Townsend, Mont. ... D5 70
Townsville, Austl. ... C8 25
Towson, Md. ... B4, g11 53
Toyama, Jap. ... H8 18
Toyama, pref., Jap. ... *H8 18
Toyohashi, Jap. ... I8, o16 18
Toyokawa, Jap. ... *I8 18
Toyonaka, Jap. ... o14 18
Toyota, Jap. ... n16 18
Tozeur, Tun. ... B6 22
Trabzon, Tur. ... B12 14
Tracadie, N.B., Can. ... B5 43
Tracy, Calif. ... D3, h10 50
Tracy, Minn. ... F3 67
Tracy City, Tenn. ... D7 83
Traer, Iowa ... B5 60
Trafford, Pa. ... k14 81
Traiguén, Chile ... B2 28
Trail, B.C., Can. ... E9, o19 37
Trail Creek, Ind. ... A4 59
Trailer Estates, Fla. ... *E4 54
Traill, co., N. Dak. ... C8 77
Trainer, Pa. ... *G11 81
Tralee, Ire. ... D2 4
Tranås, Swe. ... H6 11
Trani, It. ... D6 9
Transilvania, prov., Rom. ... *B6 10
Transvaal, prov., S. Afr. ... E5 24
Transylvania, co., N.C. ... f10 76
Transylvania, reg., Rom. ... B6 10
Trapani, It. ... E4 9
Trappe, Pa. ... *F11 81
Traralgon, Austl. ... I6 26
Trás-os-Montes, reg., Port. ... B2 8
Trás-os-Montes e Alto Douro,
  prov., Port. ... *B2 8
Traunstein, Ger. Fed. Rep. of ... E6 6
Travelers Rest, S.C. ... B3 82
Traverse, co., Minn. ... E2 67
Traverse City, Mich. ... D5 66
Travis, co., Tex. ... D4 84
Travnik, Yugo. ... C3 10
Treasure, co., Mont. ... D9 70
Treasure Island, Fla. ... *E4 54

Trebič, Czech.	D3	7
Trebinje, Yugo.	D4	10
Trebišov, Czech.	D6	7
Trego, co., Kans.	D4	61
Treinta y Tres, Ur.	E2	30
Treinta y Tres, dept., Ur.	*E2	30
Trélazé, Fr.	D3	5
Trelew, Arg.	C3	28
Trelleborg, Swe.	J5	11
Tremont, Ill.	C4	58
Tremont, Pa.	E9	81
Tremonton, Utah	A5	72
Trempealeau, co., Wis.	D2	88
Trenčín, Czech.	D5	7
Trengganu, state, Mala.	*D2	19
Trenque Lauquén, Arg.	B4	28
Trentino-Alto-Adige, pol. dist., It.	*A3	9
Trento, It.	A3	9
Trenton, N.S., Can.	D7	43
Trenton, Ont., Can.	C7	41
Trenton, Fla.	C4	54
Trenton, Ga.	B1	55
Trenton, Ill.	E4	58
Trenton, Mich.	F7, p15	66
Trenton, Mo.	A4	69
Trenton, Nebr.	D4	71
Trenton, N.J.	C3	74
Trenton, Ohio	C1	78
Trenton, Tenn.	B3	83
Trentwood, Wash.	*B8	86
Tres Arroyos, Arg.	B4	28
Tresckow, Pa.	E10	81
Três Corações, Braz.	C3	30
Três Lagoas, Braz.	C2	30
Treutlen, co., Ga.	D4	55
Treviglio, It.	B2	9
Treviso, It.	B4	9
Trevorton, Pa.	E8	81
Trevose, Pa.	*F12	81
Trevose Heights, Pa.	*F12	81
Treynor, Iowa	C2	60
Trezevant, Tenn.	A3	83
Triangle, Va.	B5	85
Tribbett, Miss.	B3	68
Tribune, Kans.	D2	61
Trichinopoly, see Tiruchchirāppalli, India		
Trichūr, India	F6	20
Trier, Ger., Fed. Rep. of	D3	6
Trieste, It.	B4	9
Trigg, co., Ky.	D2	62
Triglav, mtn., Yugo.	B1	10
Trigueros, Sp.	D2	8
Trikkala, Grc.	C3	14
Trikkala, prov., Grc.	*C3	14
Tri Lakes, Ind.	*B7	59
Trimble, co., Ky.	B4	62
Trimont, Minn.	G4	67
Trincomalee, Sri Lanka	G7	20
Tring-Jonction, Que., Can.	C6	42
Trinidad, Bol.	B3	29
Trinidad, Colo.	D6	51
Trinidad, Cuba	D4	35
Trinidad, Tex.	C4	84
Trinidad, Ur.	E1	30
Trinidad & Tobago, country, N.A.	A5	32
Trinité, Mart.	I14	35
Trinity, Tex.	D5	84
Trinity, co., Calif.	B2	50
Trinity, co., Tex.	D5	84
Trinity, mts., Calif.	B2	50
Trino, It.	B2	9
Trion, Ga.	B1	55
Tripoli, Iowa	B5	60
Tripolis, Grc.	D4	14
Tripoli (Tarābulus), Leb.	f5	15
Tripoli (Tarābulus), Libya	B7	22
Tripp, S. Dak.	G8	77
Tripp, co., S. Dak.	G6	77
Tripura, state, India	D9	20
Tristate Village, Ill.	*B5	58
Triumph, La.	E6	63
Trivandrum, India	G6	20
Trnava, Czech.	D4	7
Trois-Pistoles, Que., Can.	A8	42
Trois-Rivières, Que., Can.	C5	42
Troitsk, Sov. Un.	D9	13
Trollhättan, Swe.	H5	11
Troms, co., Nor.	C8	11
Tromsö, Nor.	*C8	11
Trona, Calif.	E5	50
Trondheim, Nor.	F4	11
Troodos, mtn., Cyp.	E9	14
Tropea, It.	E5	9
Trotwood, Ohio	C1	78
Troup, Tex.	C5	84
Troup, co., Ga.	C1	55
Trousdale, co., Tenn.	A5	83
Trouville, Fr.	C3	5
Trowbridge, Eng.	E5	4
Troy, Ala.	D4	46
Troy, Ill.	E4	58
Troy, Kans.	C8	61
Troy, Mich.	o15	66
Troy, Mo.	C7	69
Troy, N.Y.	C7	75
Troy, N.C.	B3	76
Troy, Ohio	B1	78
Troy, Pa.	C8	81
Troyes, Fr.	C6	5
Trubchevsk, Sov. Un.	E9	12
Trucial States, see United Arab Emirates, country, Asia		
Trucksville, Pa.	*D10	81
Trujillo, Peru	C2	31
Trujillo, Sp.	C3	8
Trujillo, Ven.	B3	32
Trujillo, state, Ven.	B3	32
Truman, Minn.	G4	67
Trumann, Ark.	B5	49
Trumansburg, N.Y.	C4	75
Trumbull, Conn.	E4	52
Trumbull, co., Ohio	A5	78
Truro, N.S., Can.	D6	43
Truro, Eng.	E4	4
Trussville, Ala.	B3, f7	46
Truth or Consequences, N. Mex.	C5	48
Trutnov, Czech.	C3	7
Tryon, N.C.	f10	76
Trysil, Nor.	G5	11
Tselinograd, Sov. Un.	D10	13
Tsitsihar, see Qiqhar, China		
Tskhinvali, Sov. Un.	A14	14
Tsu, Jap.	I8, o15	18
Tsuchiura, Jap.	H10, m19	18
Tsun Wan, Hong Kong	*G7	17
Tsuruga, Jap.	I8, n15	18
Tsuruoka, Jap.	G9	18
Tsushima, Jap.	n15	18
Tsuyama, Jap.	I7	18
Tubarão, Braz.	D3	30
Tübingen, Ger., Fed. Rep. of	*D4	6
Tubruq, (Tobruk), Libya	B2	23
Tuchola, Pol.	B4	7
Tuckahoe, N.Y.	h13	75
Tucker, Ga.	h8	55
Tucker, co., W. Va.	B5	87
Tuckerman, Ark.	B4	49
Tuckerton, N.J.	D4	74
Tucson, Ariz.	C3	48
Tucumán, Arg.	E2	29
Tucumán, prov., Arg.	E2	29
Tucumcari, N. Mex.	B7	48
Tudela, Sp.	A5	8
Tuguegarao, Phil.	B6	19
Tuktoyaktuk, N.W. Ter., Can.	C7	36
Tukwila, Wash.	f11	86
Tula, Sov. Un.	D11	12
Tulancingo, Mex.	C5, m14	34
Tulare, Calif.	D4	50
Tulare, co., Calif.	D4	50
Tularosa, N. Mex.	C5	48
Tulcán, Ec.	A2	31
Tulcea, Rom.	C9	10
Tulelake, Calif.	B3	50
Tulia, Tex.	B2	84
Tūlkarm, Jordan	B3	15
Tullahoma, Tenn.	B5	83
Tullamore, Ire.	D3	4
Tulle, Fr.	E4	5
Tullytown, Pa.	*F12	81
Tulsa, Okla.	A6	79
Tulsa, co., Okla.	B6	79
Tuluá, Col.	C2	32
Tulun, Sov. Un.	D13	13
Tulungagung, Indon.	G4	19
Tumaco, Col.	C2	32
Tumbarumba, Austl.	G7	26
Tumbes, Peru	B1	31
Tumen, China	C10	17
Tumkūr, India	F6	20
Tumuti, Austl.	*G8	25
Tumwater, Wash.	B3	86
Tunbridge Wells, Eng.	E7	4
Tungurahua, prov., Ec.	B2	31
Tunica, Miss.	A3	68
Tunica, co., Miss.	A3	68
Tunis, Tun.	A7	22
Tunisia, country, Afr.	A6	22
Tunja, Col.	B3	32
Tunkhannock, Pa.	C10	81
Tuntutuliak, Alsk.	C7	47
Tunxi, China	F8	17
Tuolumne, Calif.	D3	50
Tuolumne, co., Calif.	C4	50
Tupelo, Miss.	A5	68
Tupper Lake, N.Y.	A6, f10	75
Tupungato, mtn., Arg.	A3	28
Tura, Sov. Un.	C13	13
Turbaco, Col.	A2	32
Turčiansky Svaty Martin, Czech.	D5	7
Turda, Rom.	B6	10
Tuerk, Pol.	B5	7
Turgay, Sov. Un.	E9	13
Turgovishte, Bul.	D8	10
Turgutlu, Tur.	C6	14
Turin (Torino), It.	B1	9
Turka, Sov. Un.	G4	12
Turkestan, Sov. Un.	E9	13
Túrkeve, Hung.	B5	10
Turkey, Tex.	B2	84
Turkey, country, Asia, Eur.	C9	14
Turkmen, S.S.R., rep., Sov. Un.	*F8	16
Turks & Caicos Islands, Br. dep., N.A.	D8	35
Turku (Abo), Fin.	G10	11
Turku-Pori, prov., Fin.	*G10	11
Turley, Okla.	A6	79
Turlock, Calif.	D3	50
Turner, Kans.	B8	61
Turner, co., Ga.	E3	55
Turner, co., S. Dak.	G8	77
Turners Falls, Mass.	A2	65
Turner Valley, Alta., Can.	D3	38
Turnhout, Bel.	B6	5
Turnov, Czech.	C3	7
Turnovo, Bul.	D7	10
Turnu Măgurele, Rom.	D7	10
Turnu Severin, Rom.	C6	10
Turquino, peak, Cuba	D5	35
Turtkul, Sov. Un.	E9	13
Turtle Creek, Pa.	k14	81
Tuscaloosa, Ala.	B2	46
Tuscaloosa, co., Ala.	B2	46
Tuscany, reg., It.	C3	9
Tuscarawas, co., Ohio	B4	78
Tuscola, Ill.	D5	58
Tuscola, co., Mich.	E7	66
Tusculum College, Tenn.	*C5	83
Tuscumbia, Ala.	A2	46
Tuskegee, Ala.	C4	46
Tuskegee Institute, Ala.	C4	46
Tustin, Calif.	*F5	50
Tuticorin, India	G6	20
Tutrakan, Bul.	C8	10
Tuttlingen, Ger., Fed. Rep. of	E4	6
Tutwiler, Miss.	A3	68
Tuvalu, country, Oceania	G8	2
Tuxedo, Md.	C4	53
Tuxedo Park, N.Y.	D6, m14	75
Tuxpan, Mex.	C3, m11	34
Tuxpan, Mex.	n12	34
Tuxpan de Rodriguez Cano, Mex.	C5, m15	34
Tuxtla Gutiérrez, Mex.	D6	34
Tuy, Sp.	A1	8
Tuzla, Yugo.	C4	10
Tweed, Ont., Can.	C7	41
Twenty-Nine Palms, Calif.	E5	50
Twig, Minn.	D6	67
Twiggs, co., Ga.	D3	55
Twillingate, Newf., Can.	D4	44
Twin City, Ga.	D4	55
Twin Falls, Idaho	G4	57
Twin Falls, co., Idaho	G4	57
Twin Lakes, Calif.	*D2	50
Twin Lakes, Ohio	*A4	78
Twin Lakes, Wis.	F5, n11	88
Twin Oaks, Pa.	*G11	81
Twin Orchards, N.Y.	*C5	75
Twin Rocks, Pa.	F4	81
Twinsburg, Ohio	A4	78
Two Harbors, Minn.	C7	67
Two Rivers, Wis.	D6, h10	88
Tyler, Minn.	F2	67
Tyler, Tex.	C5	84
Tyler, co., Tex.	D5	84
Tyler, co., W. Va.	B4	87
Tyler Park, Va.	*B5	85
Tylertown, Miss.	D3	68
Tyndall, S. Dak.	H8	77
Tynemouth, Eng.	C6	4
Tyre, see Sūr, Leb.		
Tyrrell, co., N.C.	B6	76
Tyrone, Pa.	E5	81
Tyrone, co., N. Ire.	*C3	4
Tyumen, Sov. Un.	D9	13

U

Ubá, Braz.	C4, g6	30
Ube, Jap.	J5	18
Ubeda, Sp.	C4	8
Uberaba, Braz.	B3	30
Uberlândia, Braz.	B3	30
Ubon Ratchathani, Thai.	B2	19
Uccle, Bel.	B6	5
Udaipur, India	D5	20
Uddevalla, Swe.	H4	11
Udine, It.	A4	9
Udon Thani, Thai.	B2	19
Ueda, Jap.	H9, m17	18
Uelen, Sov. Un.	C21	13
Uelkal, Sov. Un.	C21	13
Uelzen, Ger., Fed. Rep. of	B5	6
Ueno, Jap.	o15	18
Ufa, Sov. Un.	D8	13
Uganda, country, Afr.	H4	23
Uglegorsk (Esutoru), Sov. Un.	B11	18
Uglich, Sov. Un.	C12	12
Uherské Hradiště, Czech.	D4	7
Uhrichsville, Ohio	B4	78
Uijongbu, Kor.	H3	18
Uinta, co., Wyo.	E2	89
Uintah, co., Utah	B7	72
Uitenhage, S. Afr.	G5	24
Uji, Jap.	*o14	18
Ujjain, India	D6	20
Ujung Pandang, Indon.	G5	19
Ukhta, Sov. Un.	C8	13
Ukiah, Calif.	C2	50
Ukraine (S.S.R.), rep., Sov. Un.	*E6	16
Ulan Bator, Mong.	B6	17
Ulan-Ude, Sov. Un.	D13	13
Ulhasnagar, India	*E5	20
Uliastay, Mong.	B4	17
Ulla, Sov. Un.	D7	12
Ulm, Ger., Fed. Rep. of	D4	6
Ulman, Mo.	C5	69
Ulsan, Kor.	I4	18

Ulster, co., N.Y.	D6 75	Union, co., Pa.	E7 81
Ulster, prov., Ire.	*C3 4	Union, co., S.C.	B4 82
Ulverston, Eng.	C5 4	Union, co., S. Dak.	H9 77
Ulyanovsk, Sov. Un.	D7 13	Union, co., Tenn.	C10 83
Ulysses, Kans.	E2 61	Union, par., La.	B3 63
Uman, Sov. Un.	G8 12	Union Beach, N.J.	C4 74
Umatilla, Fla.	D5 54	Union City, Calif.	h8 50
Umatillia, co., Oreg.	B7 80	Union City, Ga.	C2 55
Umbria, pol. dist., It.	*C4 9	Union City, Ind.	D8 59
Umbria, reg., It.	C4 9	Union City, Mich.	F5 66
Umeå, Swe.	F9 11	Union City, N.J.	h8 74
Umm Durmān, see Omdurman, Sud.		Union City, Ohio	B1 78
Umm Ruwābah, Sud.	F4 23	Union City, Pa.	C2 81
'Umrān, Yemen	F3 15	Union City, Tenn.	A2 83
Una, S.C.	*B4 82	Uniondale, N.Y.	*G2 52
Unadilla, Ga.	D3 55	Unión de Reyes, Cuba	C3 35
Unadilla, N.Y.	C5 75	Union Gap, Wash.	C5 86
'Unayzah, Sua., Ar.	D3 15	Union Grove, Wis.	F5, n11 88
Uncasville, Conn.	D8 52	Union Lake, Mich.	*F7 66
Uncompahgre, mts., Colo.	C3 51	Union of Soviet Socialist Republics, country, Europe, Asia	13
Underwood, N. Dak.	C4 77	Union Park Fla.	*D5 54
Unecha, Sov. Un.	E9 12	Union Point, Ga.	C3 55
Unggi, Kor.	E5 18	Union Springs, Ala.	C4 46
Unicoi, co., Tenn.	C11 83	Union Springs, N.Y.	*C4 75
Unidad de San Juan de Aragón, Mex.	*D5 34	Uniontown, Ala.	C2 46
Union, Miss.	C4 68	Uniontown, Ky.	C2 62
Union, Mo.	C6 69	Uniontown, Ohio	B4 78
Union, N.J.	B4 74	Uniontown, Pa.	G2 81
Union, Ohio	C1 78	Union Village, R.I.	B10 52
Union, Oreg.	B9 80	Unionville, Conn.	B5 52
Union, S.C.	B4 82	Unionville, Mo.	A4 69
Union, co., Ark.	D3 49	United, Pa.	F3 81
Union, co., Fla.	B4 54	United Arab Emirates, country, Asia	E5 15
Union, co., Ga.	B2 55	United Arab Republic, see Egypt, country, Afr.	
Union, co., Ill.	F4 58	United Kingdom of Great Britain and Northern Ireland, country, Eur.	4
Union, co., Ind.	E8 59	United States, country, N.A.	45
Union, co., Iowa	C3 60	United States Air Force Acad., Colo.	C6 51
Union, co., Ky.	C1 62	Unity, Sask., Can.	E1 39
Union, co., Miss.	A4 68	University, Miss.	A4 68
Union, co., N.J.	B4 74	University City, Mo.	C7, f13 69
Union, co., N.Mex.	A7 48	University Gardens, Md.	*C4 53
Union, co., N.C.	B2 76	University Heights, Ohio	h9 78
Union, co., Ohio	B2 78	University Hills, Md.	*C4 53
Union, co., Oreg.	B8 80		

University Park, Md.	*C4 53	Urusha, Sov. Un.	D15 13
University Park, N. Mex.	*C5 48	Uryupinsk, Sov. Un.	F14 12
University Park, Tex.	n10 84	Uşak, Tur.	C7 14
University View, Ohio	*C3 78	Üsküdar, Tur.	B7 14
Unterwalden, canton, Switz.	*E4 6	Usman, Sov. Un.	E12 12
Ünye, Tur.	B11 14	Usolye-Sibirskoye, Sov. Un.	D13 13
Upington, S. Afr.	F4 24	Ussuriysk, Sov. Un.	E16 13
Upland, Calif.	E5, m13 50	Ústi nad Labem, Czech.	C3 7
Upland, Ind.	D7 59	Ustinov, Sov. Un.	D8 13
Upland, Pa.	*G10 81	Ust-Kamenogorsk, Sov. Un.	E11 13
Upper Arlington, Ohio	B3, k10 78	Ust-Kut, Sov. Un.	D13 13
Upper Brookville, N.Y.	*E7 75	Ust-Maya, Sov. Un.	C16 13
Upper Darby, Pa.	G11, p20 81	Ust-Srednikan, Sov. Un.	C18 13
Upper Nyack, N.Y.	*D7 75	Ust-Tsilma, Sov. Un.	C8 13
Upper Saddle River, N.J.	A4 74	Ust-Usa, Sov. Un.	C8 13
Upper Sandusky, Ohio	B2 78	Ustyuzhna, Sov. Un.	B11 12
Upper Silesia, reg., Pol.	g9 7	Usu, China	C1 17
Uppsala, Swe.	H7, t35 11	Usumbura, see Bujumbura, Burundi	
Uppsala, co., Swe.	*H7 11	Utah, co., Utah	A6 72
Upshur, co., Tex.	C5 84	Utah, state, U.S.	72
Upshur, co., W. Va.	C4 87	Utica, Ill.	B4 58
Upson, co., Ga.	D2 55	Utica, Mich.	F7, o15 66
Upton, Mass.	B4, h9 65	Utica, N.Y.	B5 75
Upton, Wyo.	B8 89	Utica, Ohio	B3 78
Upton, co., Tex.	D2 84	Utica, S.C.	*B1 82
Ural, riv., Sov. Un.	E8 13	Utica Heights, Mich.	*F8 66
Uralsk, Sov. Un.	D8 13	Utiel, Sp.	C5 8
Urania, La.	C3 63	Utrecht, Neth.	A6 5
Uranium City, Sask., Can.	E12 36	Utrecht, prov., Neth.	*A6 5
Uravan, Colo.	C2 51	Utrera, Sp.	D3 8
Urawa, Jap.	I9, n18 18	Utsunomiya, Jap.	H9 18
Urbana, Ill.	C5 58	Uttaradit, Thai.	*B2 19
Urbana, Ohio	B2 78	Uttar Pradesh, state, India	C6 20
Urbancrest, Ohio	m10 78	Utuado, P.R.	*G11 35
Urbandale, Iowa	C4, e8 60	Uusimaa, prov., Fin.	*G11 11
Urbino, It.	C4 9	Uvalde, Tex.	E3 84
Urfa, Tur.	D12 14	Uvalde, co., Tex.	E3 84
Uri, canton, Switz.	E4 6	Uvaly, Czech.	n18 7
Urla, Tur.	*C6 14	Uwajima, Jap.	J6 18
Urmia, salt lake, Iran	D15 14	Uxbridge, Ont., Can.	C5 41
Urupan del Progresso, Mex.	D4, n13 34	Uxbridge, Mass.	B4 65
Uruguaiana, Braz.	D1 30	Uzbek S.S.R., rep., Sov. Un.	*E9 16
Uruguay, country, S.A.	E1 30	Uzhgorod, Sov. Un.	G4 12
Uruguay, riv., Arg., Ur.	E1 30	Uzunköprü, Tur.	B6 14
Urumqi, China	C2 17		

V

Vaasa, Fin.	F9 11	Valley, co., Idaho	E3 57
Vaasa, prov., Fin.	*F9 11	Valley, co., Mont.	B10 70
Vác, Hung.	B4 10	Valley, co., Nebr.	C6 71
Vacaville, Calif.	C3 50	Valley Brook, Okla.	*B4 79
Vacherie, La.	h10 63	Valley Center, Kans.	E6, g12 61
Vadnais Heights, Minn.	*F5 67	Valley City, N. Dak.	D7 77
Vaduz, Liech.	E4 6	Valley Cottage, N.Y.	g13 75
Vail Homes, N.J.	*C4 74	Valleydale, Calif.	*F4 50
Valais, canton, Switz.	E3 6	Valley Falls, Kans.	C8, k15 61
Valatie, N.Y.	C7 75	Valleyfield, Que., Can.	D3, q18 42
Val-Barrette, Que., Can.	*G20 36	Valley Mills, Tex.	D4 84
Val-David, Que., Can.	C3 42	Valley Park, Miss.	C3 68
Valdepeñas, Sp.	C4 8	Valley Park, Mo.	f12 69
Valdese, N.C.	B1 76	Valley Station, Ky.	g11 62
Valdivia, Chile	B2 28	Valley Stream, N.Y.	k13 75
Valdivia, prov., Chile	B2 28	Valley View, Ill.	*B5 58
Val-d' Or, Que., Can.	o20 41	Valley View, Ohio	*A4 78
Valdosta, Ga.	F3 55	Valley View, Pa.	E9 81
Vale, Oreg.	D9 80	Valmiera, Sov. Un.	C5 12
Valença, Braz.	E7 27	Valparai, India	*F6 20
Valence, Fr.	E6 5	Valparaíso, Chile	A2 28
Valencia, Sp.	C2 8	Valparaiso, Fla.	u15 54
Valencia, Sp.	C5 8	Valparaiso, Ind.	B3 59
Valencia, Ven.	A4 32	Valparaíso, prov., Chile	A2 28
Valencia, co., N. Mex.	B4 48	Valverde, Dom. Rep.	E8 35
Valencia, prov., Sp.	*C2 8	Val Verde, co., Tex.	E2 84
Valenciennes, Fr.	B5 5	Van, Tex.	C5 84
Valentine, Nebr.	B5 71	Van, Tur.	C14 14
Valera, Ven.	B3 32	Van, prov., Tur.	*C14 14
Valhalla, N.Y.	D7, m15 75	Van Alstyne, Tex.	C4 84
Valjevo, Yugo.	C4 10	Van Buren, Ark.	B1 49
Valka, Sov. Un.	C6 12	Van Buren, Ind.	C6 59
Valki, Sov. Un.	G10 12	Van Buren, Maine	A5 64
Valladolid, Sp.	B3 8	Van Buren, co., Ark.	B3 49
Valladolid, prov., Sp.	*B3 8	Van Buren, co., Iowa	D5 60
Valle d' Aosta, pol. dist., It.	*B1 9	Van Buren, co., Mich.	F4 66
Valle de la Pascua, Ven.	B4 32	Van Buren, co., Tenn.	D8 83
Valle del Cauca, dept., Col.	C2 32	Vance, co., N.C.	A4 76
Valle de Santiago, Mex.	m13 34	Vanceburg, Ky.	B6 62
Valledupar, Col.	A3 32	Vancouver, B.C., Can.	E6, f12 37
Vallée-Jonction, Que., Can.	C7 42	Vancouver, Wash.	D3 86
Vallejo, Calif.	C2 50	Vancouver, isl., B.C., Can.	G8 36
Valletta, Malta	A7 22	Vandalia, Ill.	E4 58
Valley, Nebr.	C9, g12 71	Vandalia, Mo.	B6 69

Vandalia, Ohio	*C1 78	Vatican City, country, Eur.	D4, h8 9
Vanderbilt, Pa.	F2 81	Vaucluse, dept., Fr.	*F6 5
Vanderburgh, co., Ind.	H2 59	Vaud, canton, Switz.	*E2 6
Vandercook Lake, Mich.	*F6 66	Vaudreuil, Que., Can.	D3, a18 42
Vandergrift, Pa.	E2 81	Vaudreuil, co., Que., Can.	D3 42
Vanderhoof, B.C., Can.	C5 37	Vaughan, Ont., Can.	D5, k14 41
Vandling, Pa.	C11 81	Vaughn, N. Mex.	B6 48
Vänern (Väner), lake, Swe.	H5 11	Vaupés, comisaría, Col.	C3 32
Vänersborg, Swe.	H5 11	Växjö, Swe.	I6 11
Van Horn, Tex.	o12 84	Veachland, Ky.	B4 62
Vankleek Hill, Ont., Can.	B10 41	Veazie, Maine	*D4 64
Van Lear, Ky.	C7 62	Vecsés, Hung.	B4 10
Vannes, Fr. 	D2 6	Veedersburg, Ind.	D3 60
Vanuatu, country, Oceania	H8 2	Vegas Heights, Nev.	*G6 72
Vanves, Fr.	g10 5	Vegreville, Alta., Can.	C4 38
Van Wert, Ohio	B1 78	Vejle, Den.	J3 11
Van Wert, co., Ohio	B1 78	Vejle, co., Den.	*J3 11
Van Winkle, Miss.	C3 68	Velbert, Ger., Fed. Rep. of	*C3 6
Van Yen, Viet.	*G5 17	Velda Village Hills, Mo.	*C7 69
Van Zandt, co., Tex.	C5 84	Vélez-Rubio, Sp.	D4 8
Var, dept., Fr.	*F7 5	Velikiye Luki, Sov. Un.	C8 12
Vārānasi (Benares), India	C7 20	Velikiy Ustyug, Sov. Un.	C7 13
Varaždin, Yugo.	B3 10	Velizh, Sov. Un.	D8 12
Varazze, It.	B2 9	Velletri, It.	D4, h9 9
Varberg, Swe.	I5 11	Vellore, India	F6 20
Varel, Ger., Fed. Rep. of	B4 6	Velma, Okla.	C4 79
Varese, It.	B2 9	Velsen, Neth.	B2 6
Varginha, Braz.	C3 30	Velsk, Sov. Un.	C7 13
Varkaus, Fin.	F12 11	Velva, N. Dak.	B5 77
Varmland, co., Swe.	*H5 11	Venado Tuerto, Arg.	A4 28
Värnamo, Swe.	I6 11	Venango, co., Pa.	D2 81
Varna (Stalin), Bul.	D8 10	Vendée, hills, Fr.	*D3 5
Varnsdorf, Czech.	C3 7	Venetian Village, Ill.	*A6 58
Varnville, S.C.	F5 82	Veneto, pol. dist., It.	*B4 9
Vas, co., Hung.	*B3 10	Veneto, reg., It.	A3 9
Vasilkov, Sov. Un.	F8 12	Venezia, see Venice, It.	B4 9
Vaslui, Rom.	B8 10	Venezuela, country, S.A.	C4 27
Vassar, Mich.	E7 66	Venice, Fla.	E4 54
Västerås, Swe.	H7, t34 11	Venice, Ill.	E3 58
Västerbotten, co., Swe.	*F9 11	Venice (Venezia), It.	B4 9
Västernörrland, co., Swe.	*F8 11	Vénissieux, Fr.	E6 5
Västervik, Swe.	I7 11	Venlo, Neth.	B7 5
Västmanland, co., Swe.	*H7 11	Ventimiglia, It.	C1 9
Vasto, It.	C5 9	Ventnor City, N.J.	E4 74

Ventspils, Sov. Un.	C3 12	Viborg, co., Den.	*I3 11
Ventura, Calif.	E4 50	Vibo Valentia, It.	E6 9
Ventura, co., Calif.	E4 50	Vicco, Ky.	C6 62
Ventura North (Chrisman), Calif.	*E4 50	Vicente López, Arg.	*g7 28
Veracruz *Llave*, Mex.	D5, n15 34	Vicenza, It.	B3 9
Veracruz, state, Mex.	D5, n15 34	Vichada, comisaria, Col.	C3 32
Veradale, Wash.	*B8 86	Vichy, Fr.	D5 5
Verâval, India	D5 20	Vicksburg, Mich.	F5 66
Vercelli, It.	B2 9	Vicksburg, Miss.	C3 68
Verchères, Que., Can.	D4 42	Victor, N.Y.	C3 75
Verchères, Que., Can.	D9 42	Victor Harbour, Austl.	G2 26
Verden, Ger., Fed. Rep. of	B4 6	Victoria, Arg.	A4 28
Verdun, Que., Can.	g19 42	Victoria, B.C., Can.	E6, f12 37
Verdun -*Sur-Meuse*, Fr.	C6 5	Victoria, Newf., Can.	E5 44
Verdunville, W.Va.	D2 87	Victoria, Chile	B2 28
Vereeniging, S.Afr.	F5 24	Victoria, Hong Kong	G7 17
Verga, N.J.	*D2 74	Victoria, Kans.	D4 61
Vergennes, Vt.	C1 73	Victoria, Tex.	E4 84
Verkhneye, Sov. Un.	G12, q21 12	Victoria, Va.	D4 85
Verkhoyansk, Sov. Un.	C16 13	Victoria, co., N.B., Can.	B2 43
Vermilion, Alta., Can.	C5 38	Victoria, co., N.S., Can.	C9 43
Vermilion, Ohio	A3 78	Victoria, co., Ont., Can.	C6 43
Vermilion, co., Ill.	C6 58	Victoria, co., Tex.	E4 84
Vermilion, co., La.	E3 63	Victoria, state, Austl.	G7 25
Vermilion, par.,La.	E3 63	Victoria, isl., Can.	B11 36
Vermilion Heights, Ill.	*C6 58	Victoria, lake, Afr.	I4 23
Vermillion, S. Dak.	H9 77	Victoria de las Tunas, Cuba	D5 35
Vermillion, co., Ind.	E3 59	Victoria Harbour, Ont., Can.	C5 41
Vermilion Heights, Ill.	*C6 58	Victoriaville, Que., Can.	C6 42
Vermont, state, U.S.	73	Victor Mills, S.C.	*B3 82
Vernal, Utah	A7 72	Victorville, Calif.	E5 50
Vernon, Ala.	B1 46	Victory Gardens, N.J.	*B3 74
Vernon, B.C., Can.	D8, n19 37	Victory Heights, N.Y.	*C4 75
Vernon, Fr.	C4 5	Vidalia, Ga.	D4 55
Vernon, N.Y.	*B5 75	Vidalia, La.	C4 63
Vernon, Tex.	B3 84	Vidin, Bul.	D6 10
Vernon, co., Mo.	D3 69	Vidor, Tex.	D6 84
Vernon, co., Wis.	E3 88	Vienna (Wien), Aus.	D8 6
Vernon, par., La.	C2 63	Vienna, Ga.	D3 55
Vernonia, Oreg.	B3 80	Vienna, Ill.	F5 58
Vernon Valley, N.Y.	n15 75	Vienna, Va.	B5, g12 85
Vernona, N.J.	B4 74	Vienna, W. Va.	B3 87
Vernona, Pa.	k14 81	Vienne, Fr.	E6 5
Vernona, Wis.	E4 88	Vienne, dept., Fr.	*D4 5
Vero Beach, Fla.	E6 54	Vierzon, Fr.	D5 5
Véroia, Grc.	B4 14	Vieste, It.	D6 9
Verona, It.	B3 9	Vietnam, country, Asia	B3 19
Verona Park, Mich.	*F5 66	View Park, Calif.	*E4 50
Verplanck, N.Y.	*D7 75	Vigan, Phil.	B6 19
Versailles, Fr.	C4, g9 5	Vigevano, It.	B2 9
Versailles, Ind.	F7 59	Vigo, Sp.	A1 8
Versailles, Ky.	B5 62	Vigo, co., Ind.	F3 59
Versailles, Mo.	C5 69	Vijayawāda, India	E7 20
Versailles, Ohio	B1 78	Vila Nova de Gaia, Port.	B1 8
Versailles, Pa.	*F2 81	Vilas, co., Wis.	B4 88
Verviers, Bel.	B6 5	Vila Velha, Braz.	C4 30
Veseloye, Sov. Un.	H10 12	Vieleyka, Sov. Un.	D6 12
Vesoul, Fr.	D7 5	Viljandi, Sov. Un.	B5 12
Vest-Agder, co., Nor.	*H2 11	Vilkovo, Sov. Un.	I7 12
Vestal, N.Y.	C4 75	Villacarrillo, Sp.	C4 8
Vestavia Hills, Ala.	g7 46	Villach, Aus.	E6 6
Vestfold, co., Nor.	*H4 11	Villa Dolores, Arg.	A3 28
Vestry, Miss.	E5 68	Villafranca, It.	B3 9
Vesuvius, vol., It.	D5 9	Villafranca de los Barros, Sp.	C2 8
Veszprém, Hung.	B3 10	Villafranca del Panadés, Sp.	B6 8
Veszprem, co., Hung.	*B3 10	Villafranca di Verona, It.	B3 9
Veszto, Hung.	B5 10	Villagarcía, de Arosa, Sp.	A1 8
Vevay, Ind.	G7 59	Village-Richelieu, Que., Can.	*D4 42
Vevey, Switz.	E3 6	Villa Grove, Ill.	D5 58
Vezirköprü, Tur.	B10 14	Villaguay, Arg.	A5 28
Viadana, It.	B3 9	Villa Heights, Md.	*C4 53
Vian, Okla.	B7 79	Villahermosa, Mex.	D6 34
Viangchan, Laos	B2 19		
Viareggio, It.	C3 9		

Villa María, Arg.	A4 28	Vista, Calif.	F5 50
Villanova, Pa.	*G11 81	Vista Park, Calif.	*E4 50
Villanueva de Córdoba, Sp.	C3 8	Vitanovak, Yugo.	D5 10
Villanueva del Arzobispo, Sp.	C4 8	Vitebsk, Sov. Un.	D8 12
Villanueva de La Serena, Sp.	C3 8	Viterbo, It.	C4 9
Villanueva y Geltrú, Sp.	B6 8	Vitim, Sov. Un.	D14 13
Villa Obregón, Mex.	h9 34	Vitória, Braz.	C4 30
Villa Park, Ill.	k8 58	Vitoria, Sp.	A4 8
Villa Rica, Ga.	C2 55	Vitória da Conquista, Braz.	A4 30
Villarreal, Sp.	C5 8	Vitry -*sur-Seine*, Fr.	g10 5
Villarrica, Par.	E4 29	Vittoria, It.	F5 9
Villarrobledo, Sp.	C4 8	Vittorio Veneto, It.	B4 9
Villas, N.J.	E3 74	Vivian, La.	B2 63
Villavicencio, Col.	C3 32	Vizcaya, prov., Sp.	*A4 8
Villefranche-sur-Saône, Fr.	E6 5	Vizianagaram, India	E7 20
Villejuif, Fr.	g10 5	Vizzini, It.	F5 9
Villemomble, Fr.	g10 5	Vlaardingen, Neth.	B6 5
Villeneuve-le-Roi, Fr.	h10 5	Vladimir, Sov. Un.	C13 12
Villeneuve-St. Georges, Fr.	h10 5	Vladimiro Aleksandrovskoye,	
Villeneuve-sur-Lot, Fr.	E4 5	Sov. Un.	E6 18
Ville Platte, La.	D3 63	Vladimir Volynskiy, Sov. Un.	F5 12
Ville St. Georges, Que., Can.	C7 42	Vladivostok, Sov. Un.	E5 18
Villeta, Par.	E4 29	Vlasotince, Yugo.	D6 10
Villeurbanne, Fr.	E6 5	Vlissingen, Neth.	B5 5
Villigen-Schwenningen, Ger.,		Vlonë, pref., Alb.	*B2 14
Fed. Rep. of	*D4 6	Vlorë, Alb.	B2 14
Villisca, Iowa	D3 60	Vodnany, Czech.	*D3 7
Vilnius, Sov. Un.	D5 12	Voeune Sai, Camb.	F7 22
Vilvoorde, Bel.	B6 5	Voghera, It.	B2 9
Vilyuy, riv., Sov. Un.	C15 13	Voiron, Fr.	E6 5
Vilyuysk, Sov. Un.	C15 13	Volga, Sov. Un.	E7 13
Vimianzo, Sp.	A1 8	Volgograd, Sov. Un.	G14 12
Viña del Mar, Chile	A2 28	Volkhov, Sov. Un.	B9 12
Vinalhaven, Maine	D4 64	Volkovysk, Sov. Un.	E5 12
Vincennes, Fr.	g10 5	Vologda, Sov. Un.	B12 12
Vincennes, Ind.	G3 59	Volokolamsk, Sov. Un.	C10 12
Vincent, Ala.	B3 46	Volos, Grc.	C4 14
Vincent, Ohio	*A3 78	Volsk, Sov. Un.	*D7 13
Vindeln, Swe.	E8 11	Volta Redonda, Braz.	C4, h5 30
Vine Grove, Ky.	C4 62	Volterra, It.	C3 9
Vine Hill (Martinez East), Calif.	*C2 50	Volusia, co., Fla.	C5 54
Vineland, N.J.	E2 74	Volzhskiy, Sov. Un.	G15 12
Vineyard Haven (Tisbury), Mass.	D6 65	Voorheesville, N.Y.	*C7 75
Vinh Yen, Viet.	G6 17	Vorarlberg, state, Aus.	E4 6
Vinita, Okla.	A6 79	Vordingborg, Den.	A1 7
Vinita Park, Mo.	*C7 69	Vorkuta, Sov. Un.	C9 13
Vinkovci, Yugo.	C4 10	Voronezh, Sov Un.	F12 12
Vinnitsa, Sov. Un.	G7 12	Voroshilovgrad (Lugansk),	
Vinson Massif, mtn., Ant.	L15 2	Sov. Un.	G12, q22 12
Vinton, Iowa	B5 60	Vosges, dept., Fr.	*C7 5
Vinton, La.	D2 63	Votkinsk, Sov. Un.	*D8 13
Vinton, Va.	C3 85	Voznesensk, Sov. Un.	H8 12
Vinton, co., Ohio	C3 78	Vranje, Yugo.	D5 10
Vintondale, Pa.	F4 81	Vratsa, Bul.	D6 10
Virden, Man., Can.	E1 40	Vratsa, co., Bul.	D6 10
Virden, Ill.	D4 58	Vršac, Yugo.	C5 10
Virginia, Ill.	D3 58	Vsetín, Czech.	D5 7
Virginia, Minn.	C6 67	Vukovar, Yugo.	C4 10
Virginia, state, U.S.	85	Vulcan, Alta., Can.	D4 38
Virginia Beach		Vulcan, Mo.	D7 69
(Independent City), Va.	D7, k16 85	Vung Tau, Viet.	*C3 19
Virginia City, Nev.	B2 72	Vyazma, Sov. Un.	D10 12
Virginia Gardens, Fla.	*G6 54	Vyazniki, Sov. Un.	C14 12
Virgin Islands, Br. dep., N.A.	G12 35	Vyborg, Sov. Un.	A7 12
Virgin Islands of the U.S.,		Vyksa, Sov. Un.	D14 12
dep., N.S.	G12 35	Vyshniy Volochek, Sov. Un.	C10 12
Viroflay, Fr.	g9 5	Vysoké Tatry, Czech.	D6 7
Viroqua, Wis.	E3 88	Vytegra, Sov. Un.	A11 12
Virovitica, Yugo.	C3 10		
Visalia, Calif.	D4 50		
Visby, Swe.	I8 11		
Vishākhapatnam, India	E7 20		

W

Wabana (Bell Island), Newf., Can.	E5 44	Wadesboro, N.C.	C2 76
Wabash, Ind.	C6 59	Wadley, Ga.	D4 55
Wabash, co., Ill.	E6 58	Wad Madanī, Sud.	F4 23
Wabash, co., Ind.	C6 59	Wadsworth, Ohio	A4 78
Wabasha, Minn.	F6 67	Waelder, Tex.	E4 84
Wabasha, co., Minn.	F6 67	Wagga Wagga, Austl.	G8 25
Wabasso, Fla.	E6 54	Wagner, S.Dak.	G7 77
Wabaunsee, co., Kans.	D7 61	Wagoner, Okla.	B6 79
Wacissa, Fla.	*B3 54	Wagoner, co., Okla.	B6 79
Waco, Tex.	D4 84	Wagon Mound, N.Mex.	B6 48
Waconia, Minn.	F5 67	Wagrowiec, Pol.	B4 7
Waddington, B.C., Can.	F8 36	Wah Cantonment, Pak.	*B5 20
Waddington, N.Y.	f9 75	Wahiawa, Haw.	B3, f9 56
Wadena, Sask., Can.	F4 39	Wahkiakum, co., Wash.	*C2 86
Wadena, Minn.	D3 67	Wahneta, Fla.	*E5 54
Wadena, co., Minn.	D4 67	Wahoo, Nebr.	C9, g11 71

Wahpeton, N.Dak.	D9 77	Wakaw, Sask., Can.	E3 39
Waialua, Haw.	B3, f9 56	Wakayama, Jap.	I7, o14 18
Waianae, Haw.	B3, g9 56	Wakayama, pref., Jap.	*I7 18
Waikabubak, Indon.	G5 19	Wake, co., N.C.	B4 76
Wailua, Haw.	A2 56	WaKeeney, Kans.	C4 61
Wailuku, Haw.	C5 56	Wakefield, Mass.	B5, f11 65
Waimanalo, Haw.	B4, g11 56	Wakefield, Mich.	n12 66
Waimea, Haw.	B2 56	Wakefield, Nebr.	B9 71
Waimea, Haw.	f9 56	Wakefield, R.I.	D11 52
Wainwright, Alta., Can.	C5 38	Wakefield, Va.	D6 85
Waipahu, Haw.	B3, g9 56	Wake Forest, N.C.	B4 76
Waipio Acres, Haw.	g9 56	Wakkanai, Jap.	D10 18
Waite Park, Minn.	E4 67	Wakulla, co., Fla.	B2 54
Waitsburg, Wash.	*C7 86	Walbridge, Ohio	e6 78
Wajima, Jap.	H8 18	Walbrzych, Pol.	C4 7
Wakarusa, Ind.	A5 59	Walden, N.Y.	D6 75

Waldo, Ark. ... D2 49
Waldo, co., Maine. ... D3 64
Waldorf, Md. ... C4 53
Waldron, Ark. ... C1 49
Waldwick, N.J. ... A4 74
Wales, reg., U.K. ... D5 4
Walhalla, N.Dak. ... A8 77
Walhalla, S.C. ... B1 82
Walker, La. ... g10 63
Walker, Mich. ... E5 66
Walker, Minn. ... C4 67
Walker, co., Ala. ... B2 46
Walker, co., Ga. ... B1 55
Walker, co., Tex. ... D5 84
Walkersville, Md. ... B3 53
Walkerton, Ont., Can. ... C3 41
Walkerton, Ind. ... B5 59
Walkertown, N.C. ... A2 76
Walkerville, Mont. ... D4 70
Wall, Pa. ... *F2 81
Wallace, Idaho ... B3 57
Wallace, N.C. ... C4 76
Wallace, co., Kans. ... D2 61
Wallaceburg, Ont., Can. ... E2 41
Wallasey, Eng. ... D5 4
Walla Walla, Wash. ... C7 86
Walla Walla, co., Wash. ... C7 86
Walled Lake, Mich. ... o15 66
Waller, Tex. ... D5 84
Waller, co., Tex. ... E4 84
Wallingford, Conn. ... D5 52
Wallingford, Vt. ... E2 73
Wallington, Eng. ... m12 4
Wallington, N.J. ... h8 74
Wallis, Tex. ... E4 84
Wallkill, N.Y. ... D6 75
Wallowa, Oreg. ... B9 80
Wallowa, co., Oreg. ... B9 80
Wallsend, Eng. ... C6 4
Walnut, Calif. ... *F4 50
Walnut, Ill. ... B4 58
Walnut Cove, N.C. ... A2 76
Walnut Creek, Calif. ... h8 50
Walnut Heights, Calif. ... *D2 50
Walnut Park, Calif. ... *F4 50
Walnutport, Pa. ... E10 81
Walnut Ridge, Ark. ... A5 49
Walpole, Mass. ... B5, h10 65
Walsall, Eng. ... D6 4
Walsenburg, Colo. ... D6 51
Walsh, co., N.Dak. ... B8 77
Walterboro, S.C. ... F6 82
Walters, Okla. ... C3 79
Walthall, co., Miss. ... D3 68
Waltham, Mass. ... B5, g11 65
Walthill, Nebr. ... B9 71
Walton, Ind. ... C5 59
Walton, Ky. ... B5, k13 62
Walton, N.Y. ... C5 75
Walton, co., Fla. ... u15 54
Walton, co., Ga. ... C3 55
Walton Hills, Ohio ... *A4 78
Walvisbaai, S.Afr. ... E2 24
Walworth, Wis. ... F5 88
Walworth, co., S.Dak. ... E5 77
Walworth, co., Wis. ... F5 88
Wamac, Ill. ... E4 58
Wamego, Kans. ... C7 61
Wampum, Pa. ... E1 81
Wanamassa, N.J. ... C4 74
Wanaque, N.J. ... A4 74
Wanganui, N.Z. ... M15 26
Wangaratta, Austl. ... H6 26
Wangqing, China ... C10 17
Wantagh, N.Y. ... G2 52
Wanxian, China ... E6 17
Wapakoneta, Ohio ... B1 78
Wapato, Wash. ... C5 86
Wapello, Iowa ... C6 60
Wapello, co., Iowa ... C5 60
Wappingers Falls, N.Y. ... D7 75
War, W.Va. ... D3 87
Warangal, India ... E6 20
Ward, W. Va. ... m13 87
Ward, co., N. Dak. ... B4 77
Ward, co., Tex. ... D1 84
Warden, Wash. ... C6 86
Ward Ridge, Fla. ... *C1 54
Wardville, La. ... *C3 63
Ware, Mass. ... B3 65
Ware, co., Ga. ... E4 55
Wareham, Mass. ... C6 65
Warehouse Point, Conn. ... B6 52
Waren, Ger. Dem. Rep. ... B6 6
Ware Shoals, S.C. ... C3 82
Warfield, B.C., Can. ... E9 37
Wargla, Alg. ... B6 22
Warner Robins, Ga. ... D3 55
Warr Acres, Okla. ... B4 79
Warragul, Austl. ... *G8 25
Warren, Ark. ... D3 49
Warren, Ill. ... A4 58
Warren, Ind. ... C7 59

Warren, Mass. ... B3 65
Warren, Mich. ... *F7, p16 66
Warren, Minn. ... B2 67
Warren, Ohio ... A5 78
Warren, Pa. ... C3 81
Warren, R.I. ... C11 52
Warren, co., Ga. ... C4 55
Warren, co., Ill. ... C3 58
Warren, co., Ind. ... D3 59
Warren, co., Iowa ... C4 60
Warren, co., Ky. ... C3 62
Warren, co., Miss. ... C3 68
Warren, co., Mo. ... C6 69
Warren, co., N.J. ... B3 74
Warren, co., N.Y. ... B7 75
Warren, co., N.C. ... A4 76
Warren, co., Ohio ... C1 78
Warren, co., Pa. ... C3 81
Warren, co., Tenn. ... D8 83
Warren, co., Va. ... B4 85
Warrensburg, Mo. ... C4 69
Warrensburg, N.Y. ... B7 75
Warrensville Heights, Ohio ... h9 78
Warrenton, Ga. ... C4 55
Warrenton, Mo. ... C6 69
Warrenton, N.C. ... A4 76
Warrenton, Oreg. ... A3 80
Warrenton, Va. ... B5 85
Warrenville, Ill. ... k8 58
Warrenville, S.C. ... D4 82
Warri, Nig. ... G6 22
Warrick, co., Ind. ... H3 59
Warrington, Eng. ... D5 4
Warrington, Fla. ... u14 54
Warrior, Ala. ... B3 46
Warrnambool, Austl. ... G7, n14 25
Warroad, Minn. ... B3 67
Warsaw, Ill. ... C2 58
Warsaw, Ind. ... B6 59
Warsaw, Mo. ... C4 69
Warsaw, N.Y. ... C2 75
Warsaw, N.C. ... B4 76
Warsaw (Warszawa), Pol. ... B6, m14 7
Warson Woods, Mo. ... *C7 69
Warwick, Qué., Can. ... D6 42
Warwick, Eng. ... D6 4
Warwick, N.Y. ... D6, m14 75
Warwick, R.I. ... C10 52
Warwick, co., Eng. ... *D6 4
Wasatch, co., Utah ... A6 72
Wasco, Calif. ... E4 50
Wasco, co., Oreg. ... B5 80
Waseca, Minn. ... F5 67
Waseca, co., Minn. ... F5 67
Washakie, co., Wyo. ... C5 89
Washburn, Ill. ... C4 58
Washburn, Maine ... B4 64
Washburn, Wis. ... B3 88
Washburn, co., Wis. ... C2 88
Washington, D.C. ... C3, f8 53
Washington, Ga. ... C4 55
Washington, Ill. ... C4 58
Washington, Ind. ... G3 59
Washington, Iowa ... C6 60
Washington, Kans. ... C6 61
Washington, La. ... D3 63
Washington, Mo. ... C6 69
Washington, N.J. ... B3 74
Washington, N.C. ... B5 76
Washington, Pa. ... F1 81
Washington, co., Ala. ... D1 46
Washington, co., Ark. ... A1 49
Washington, co., Colo. ... B7 51
Washington, co., Fla. ... u16 54
Washington, co., Ga. ... C3 55
Washington, co., Idaho ... E2 57
Washington, co., Ill. ... E4 58
Washington, co., Ind. ... G5 59
Washington, co., Iowa ... C6 60
Washington, co., Kans. ... C6 61
Washington, co., Ky. ... C4 62
Washington, co., Maine ... D5 64
Washington, co., Md. ... A2 53
Washington, co., Minn. ... E6 67
Washington, co., Miss. ... B3 66
Washington, co., Mo. ... D7 69
Washington, co., Nebr. ... C9 71
Washington, co., N.Y. ... B7 75
Washington, co., N.C. ... B6 76
Washington, co., Ohio ... C4 78
Washington, co., Okla. ... A6 79
Washington, co., Oreg. ... B3 80
Washington, co., Pa. ... F1 81
Washington, co., R.I. ... D10 52
Washington, co., Tenn. ... C10 83
Washington, co., Tex. ... D4 84
Washington, co., Utah ... C5 72
Washington, co., Vt. ... C2 73
Washington, co., Va. ... f9 85
Washington, co., Wis. ... E5 88
Washington, par., La. ... D5 63
Washington, state, U.S. ... 86
Washington, mtn., N.H. ... C5 73

Washington Court House, Ohio ... C2 78
Washington Heights, N.Y. ... *D6 75
Washington North, Pa. ... *F1 81
Washington Park, Ill. ... E3 58
Washington Terrace, Utah ... *A5 72
Washingtonville, N.Y. ... *D6 75
Washington West, Pa. ... *F1 81
Washita, co., Okla. ... B2 79
Washoe, co., Nev. ... A2 72
Washougal, Wash. ... D3 86
Washtenaw, co., Mich. ... F7 66
Waskom, Tex. ... C5 84
Watauga, co., N.C. ... A1 76
Watchung, N.J. ... *B4 74
Waterbury, Conn. ... C4 52
Waterbury, Vt. ... C2 73
Waterford, Calif. ... *D3 50
Waterford, Ont., Can. ... E4 41
Waterford, Conn. ... D8 52
Waterford, Ire. ... D3 4
Waterford, N.Y. ... C7 75
Waterford, Pa. ... C1 81
Waterford, Wis. ... F5, n11 88
Waterford, co., Ire. ... *D3 4
Waterloo, Ont., Can. ... D4 41
Waterloo, Que., Can. ... D5 42
Waterloo, Ill. ... E3 58
Waterloo, Ind. ... B7 59
Waterloo, Iowa ... B5 60
Waterloo, N.Y. ... C4 75
Waterloo, Wis. ... E5 88
Waterloo, co., Ont., Can. ... D4 41
Waterman, Ill. ... B5 58
Waterproof, La. ... C4 63
Watertown, Conn. ... C4 52
Watertown, Fla. ... B4 54
Watertown, Mass. ... g11 65
Watertown, Minn. ... *F5 67
Watertown, N.Y. ... B5 75
Watertown, S. Dak. ... F8 77
Watertown, Tenn. ... A5 83
Watertown, Wis. ... E5 88
Water Valley, Miss. ... A4 68
Waterville, Que., Can. ... D6 42
Waterville, Que., Can. ... D6 42
Waterville, Maine ... D3 64
Waterville, Minn. ... F5 67
Waterville, N.Y. ... C5 75
Waterville, Ohio ... A2, f6 78
Waterville, Wash. ... B5 86
Watervliet, Mich. ... F4 66
Watervliet, N.Y. ... C7 75
Watford, Ont., Can. ... E3 41
Watford City, N. Dak. ... C2 77
Watkins Glen, N.Y. ... C4 75
Watonga, Okla. ... B3 79
Watonwan, co., Minn. ... F4 67
Watrous, Sask., Can. ... F3 39
Watseka, Ill. ... C6 58
Watsontown, Pa. ... D8 81
Watsonville, Calif. ... D3 50
Wattrelos, Fr. ... B5 5
Wattsville, S.C. ... B4 82
Wauchope, Austl. ... E9 26
Wauchula, Fla. ... E5 54
Wauconda, Ill. ... h8 58
Waukegan, Ill. ... A6, h9 58
Waukesha, Wis. ... E5 88
Waukesha, co., Wis. ... E5 88
Waukon, Iowa ... A6 60
Waunakee, Wis. ... E4 88
Waupaca, Wis. ... D4 88
Waupaca, co., Wis. ... D5 88
Waupun, Wis. ... E5 88
Waurika, Okla. ... C4 79
Wausau, Wis. ... D4 88
Wauseon, Ohio ... A1 78
Waushara, co., Wis. ... D4 88
Wautoma, Wis. ... D4 88
Wauwatosa, Wis. ... m11 88
Waverly, Ill. ... D4 58
Waverly, Iowa ... B5 60
Waverly, N.Y. ... C4 75
Waverly, Ohio ... C3 78
Waverly, Tenn. ... A4 83
Waverly, Va. ... C5 85
Waxahachie, Tex. ... C4, n10 84
Waycross, Ga. ... E4 55
Wayland, Ky. ... C7 62
Wayland, Mass. ... g10 65
Wayland, Mich. ... F5 66
Wayland, N.Y. ... C3 75
Waymart, Pa. ... C11 81
Wayne, Mich. ... p15 66
Wayne, Nebr. ... B8 71
Wayne, N.J. ... B4 74
Wayne, Pa. ... F11, o20 81
Wayne, W. Va. ... C2 87
Wayne, co., Ga. ... E4 55
Wayne, co., Ill. ... E5 58
Wayne, co., Ind. ... *E5 59
Wayne, co., Iowa ... *D4 60
Wayne, co., Ky. ... D5 62

Wayne, co., Mich. ... F7 66
Wayne, co., Miss. ... D5 68
Wayne, co., Mo. ... D7 69
Wayne, co., Nebr. ... B8 71
Wayne, co., N.Y. ... B3 75
Wayne, co., N.C. ... B4 76
Wayne, co., Ohio ... B4 78
Wayne, co., Pa. ... C11 81
Wayne, co., Tenn. ... B4 83
Wayne, co., Utah ... B6 72
Wayne, co., W. Va. ... C2 87
Waynesboro, Ga. ... C4 55
Waynesboro, Miss. ... D5 68
Waynesboro, Pa. ... G6 81
Waynesboro, Tenn. ... B4 83
Waynesboro (Independent City), Va. ... B4 85
Waynesburg, Ohio ... B4 78
Waynesburg, Pa. ... G1 81
Waynesville, Mo. ... D5 69
Waynesville, N.C. ... f10 76
Waynesville, Ohio ... C1 78
Waynoka, Okla. ... A3 79
Wayzata, Minn. ... *F5 67
Weakley, co., Tenn. ... A3 83
Weatherford, Okla. ... B3 79
Weatherford, Tex. ... C4 84
Weatherly, Pa. ... E10 81
Weaver, Ala. ... B4 46
Weaverville, Calif. ... B2 50
Weaverville, N.C. ... f10 76
Webb, co., Tex. ... F3 84
Webb City, Mo. ... D3 69
Weber, co., Utah ... A6 72
Weber City, Va. ... *f9 85
Webster, Mass. ... B4 65
Webster, N.Y. ... B3 75
Webster, S. Dak. ... E8 77
Webster, co., Ga. ... D2 55
Webster, co., Iowa ... B3 60
Webster, co., Ky. ... C2 62
Webster, co., Miss. ... B4 68
Webster, co., Mo. ... D5 69
Webster, co., Nebr. ... D7 71
Webster, co., W. Va. ... C4 87
Webster, par., La. ... B2 63
Webster City, Iowa ... B4 60
Webster Groves, Mo. ... f13 69
Webster Springs (Addison), W. Va. ... C4 87
Wedgeport, N.S., Can. ... F4 43
Wedowee, Ala. ... B4 46
Weed, Calif. ... B2 50
Weed Heights, Nev. ... *B2 72
Weedon, Que., Can. ... D6 42
Weedsport, N.Y. ... B4 75
Weehawken, N.J. ... h8 79
Weeks, La. ... E4 63
Weeping Water, Nebr. ... D9, h12 71
Weert, Neth. ... B6 5
Weiden, Ger., Fed. Rep. of ... D6 6
Weifang, China ... D8 17
Weihai, China ... D9 17
Weilheim, Ger., Fed. Rep. ... E5 6
Weimar, Ger. Dem. Rep. ... C5 6
Weimar, Tex. ... E4 84
Weinan, China ... E6 17
Weinheim, Ger., Fed. Rep. of ... D4 6
Weippe, Idaho ... C3 57
Weirton, W. Va. ... A4, f8 87
Weiser, Idaho ... E2 57
Weissenburg in Bayern, Ger., Fed. Rep. of ... D5 6
Weissenfels, Ger. Dem. Rep. ... *C5 6
Wejherowo, Pol. ... A5 7
Welborn, Kans. ... B8 61
Welch, W. Va. ... D3 87
Welcome, S.C. ... *B3 82
Weld, co., Colo. ... A6 51
Weldon, N.C. ... A5 76
Weleetka, Okla. ... B5 79
Welkom, S. Afr. ... *F5 24
Welland, Ont., Can. ... E5 41
Wellesley, Mass. ... B5, g10 65
Wellford, S.C. ... B3 82
Wellington, Austl. ... F7 26
Wellington, Ont., Can. ... D7 41
Wellington, Kans. ... E6 61
Wellington, N.Z. ... N15 26
Wellington, Ohio ... A3 78
Wellington, Tex. ... B2 84
Wellington, Utah ... B6 72
Wellington, co., Ont., Can. ... D4 41
Wellman, Iowa ... C6 60
Wells, B.C., Can. ... C7 37
Wells, Minn. ... G5 67
Wells, Nev. ... A7 72
Wells, co., Ind. ... C7 59
Wells, co., N.Dak. ... C6 77
Wellsboro, Pa. ... C7 81
Wellsburg, W. Va. ... A4, f8 87
Wellston, Mo. ... f13 69
Wellston, Ohio ... C3 78
Wellsville, Kans. ... D8 61

222 **Wel-Wil**

Wellsville, Mo. B6 69
Wellsville, N.Y. C3 75
Wellsville, Ohio B5 78
Wellsville, Utah A6 72
Wels, Aus. D7 6
Welsh, La. D3 63
Wembley, Eng. k11 4
Wenatche, Wash. B5 86
Wenatche, Wash. B5 86
Wenzhou, China F9 17
Wendell, Idaho G4 57
Wendell, N.C. B4 76
Wenham, Mass. A6, f12 65
Wenona, Ill. *B4 58
Wenonah, N.J. D2 74
Wentworth, co., Ont., Can. D4 41
Wentzville, Mo. C7 67
Werdau, Ger. Dem. Rep. C6 6
Wernersville, Pa. *F9 81
Wernigerode, Ger. Dem. Rep. C5 6
Wesel, Ger., Fed. Rep. of C3 6
Weslaco, Tex. F3 84
Weslaco North, Tex. *F3 84
Wesleyville, Newf., Can. D5 44
Wesleyville, Pa. B2 81
Wessington Springs, S. Dak. F7 77
Wesson, Miss. D3 68
West, Tex. D4 84
West Alexandria, Ohio C1 78
West Allis, Wis. m12 88
West Amityville, N.Y. *E7 75
West Babylon, N.Y. *n15 75
West Baden Springs, Ind. G4 59
West Barrington, R.I. B11 52
West Baton Rouge, par., La. D4 63
West Belmar, N.J. *C4 74
West Bend, Iowa B3 60
West Bend, Wis. E5 88
West Bengal, state, India *D8 20
West Berlin, N.J. D3 74
West Blocton, Ala. B2 46
West Bountiful, Utah *A6 72
West Boylston, Mass. B4 65
West Branch, Iowa C6 60
West Branch, Mich. D6 66
West Bridgewater, Mass. B5 65
West Bridgewater, Pa. *E1 81
West Bromwich, Eng. D6 4
Westbrook, Maine E2, g7 64
Westbrook, Minn. F3 67
West Brookfield, Mass. B3 65
Westbrook Park, Pa. *B11 81
West Brownsville, Pa. *F2 81
West Brunswick, N.J. *C4 74
West Burlington, Iowa D6 60
Westbury, N.Y. E7 75
Westby, Wis. E3 88
West Caldwell, N.J. *B4 74
West Cape May, N.J. F3 74
West Carroll, par., La. B4 63
West Carrollton, Ohio C1 78
West Carthage, N.Y. B5 75
Westchester, Ill. k9 58
West Chester, Pa. G10 81
Westchester, co., N.Y. D7 75
West Chicago, Ill. k8 58
West City, Ill. F8 58
West Clarkston, Wash. *C8 86
West Collingswood, N.J. *D2 74
West Collingswood Heights, N.J. *D2 74
West Columbia, S.C. D5 82
West Columbia, Tex. E5, r14 84
West Concord, Mass. B5, g10 65
West Concord, N.C. *B2 76
West Conshohocken, Pa. o20 81
West Corners, N.Y. *C5 75
West Covina, Calif. m13 50
Westdale, Ill. *B6 58
West Decatur, Pa. E5 81
West Derry, Pa. *F3 81
West Des Moines, Iowa C4, e8 60
West Easton, Pa. *E11 81
West Elizabeth, Pa. *F2 81
West Elkton, Ohio *C1 75
West Elmira, N.Y. *C4 75
West End, Fla. *C4 54
West End, N.Y. *C5 75
West End Anniston, Ala. *B4 46
West Endicott, N.Y. *C5 75
Westerly, R.I. D9 52
Western, reg., Nig. G5 22
Western Australia, state, Austl. D3 25
Western Hills, Colo. *B6 51
Western Peninsula, div., Ice. *m21 11
Westernport, Md. m12 53
Western Sahara, country, Afr. D2 22
Western Samoa, country, Oceania G9 2
Western Springs, Ill. k9 58
Westerville, Ohio B3, k11 78
West Fairview, Pa. F8 81
West Farmington, Maine D2 64
West Feliciana, par., La. D4 63
Westfield, Ind. D5 59
Westfield, Mass. B2 65
Westfield, N.J. B4 74
Westfield, N.Y. C1 75
Westfield, Pa. C6 81
Westfield, Wis. E4 88
West Flanders, prov., Bel. *B5 5
West Frankfort, Ill. F5 58
Westgate, Fla. F6 54
West Glens Falls, N.Y. *B7 75
West Grove, Pa. G10 81
Westhampton Beach, N.Y. n16 75
West Hartford, Conn. B6 52
West Hartsville, S.C. *C7 82
West Haven, Conn. D5 52
West Haverstraw, N.Y. *D7 75
West Hazleton, Pa. E9 81
West Helena, Ark. C5 49
West Hempstead, N.Y. *G2 52
West Hillsboro, N.C. *A3 76
West Hollywood, Calif. *E4 50
West Hollywood, Fla. r13 54
West Homestead, Pa. *F2 81
West Indies,
reg., Atl. O. 35
West Islip, N.Y. *n15 75
West Jefferson, N.C. A1 76
West Jefferson, Ohio C2, m10 78
West Jordan, Utah A5, D2 78
West Kingston, R.I. D10 52
West Kittanning, Pa. *E3 81
West Lafayette, Ind. D4 59
West Lafayette, Ohio B4 78
Westlake, La. D2 63
Westlake, Ohio h9 78
Westland, Mich. p15 66
Westlands, Mass. f10 65
West Lanham Hills, Md. *C4 53
West Lawn, Pa. F10 81
West Lebanon, Pa. *F9 81
West Leechburg, Pa. *E2 81
West Leisenring, Pa. G2 81
West Liberty, Iowa C6 60
West Liberty, Ky. C6 62
West Liberty, Ohio B2 78
West Liberty, W. Va. f8 87
West Linn, Oreg. B4, h12 80
Westlock, Alta., Can. B4 38
West Long Branch, N.J. C4 74
West Lorne, Ont., Can. E3 41
West Lothian, Scot. *C5 4
West Manayunk, Pa. *F11 81
West Marion, N.C. *f10 76
West Mayfield, Pa. *E1 81
Westmeath, co., Ire. *D3 4
West Medway, Mass. B5, h10 65
West Melbourne, Fla. *D6 54
West Memphis, Ark. B5 49
West Miami, Fla. s13 54
West Middlesex, Pa. D1 81
West Mifflin, Pa. F2 81
West Milton, Ohio C1 78
West Milwaukee, Wis. m12 88
Westminster, Calif. n12 50
Westminster, Colo. A6 51
Westminster, Md. A4 53
Westminster, Mass. A4 65
Westminster, S.C. B1 82
West Monroe, La. B3 63
Westmont, Ill. k9 58
Westmont, N.J. D2 74
Westmont, Pa. F4 81
Westmoreland, co., Pa. F2 81
Westmoreland, co., Va. B6 85
Westmoreland City, Pa. *F2 81
Westmorland, Calif. F6 50
Westmorland, co., N.B., Can. C5 43
Westmorland, co., Eng. *C5 4
Westmount, Que., Can. *D4 42
West Mystic, Conn. D9 52
West Newton, Pa. F2 81
West New York, N.J. h8 74
West Nyack, N.Y. *D7 75
Weston, Ont., Can. m14 41
Weston, Conn. E3 52
Weston, Mass. g10 65
Weston, Mo. B3, h10 69
Weston, Ohio A2 78
Weston, W. Va. B4 87
Weston, co., Wyo. C8 89
Weston-Super-Mare, Eng. E5 4
West Orange, N.J. B4 74
West Orange, Tex. *D6 84
Westover, W.Va. B5, h11 87
West Palm Beach, Fla. F6 54
West Paterson, N.J. *B4 74
West Pensacola, Fla. v14 54
West Pittston, Pa. m17 81
West Plains, Mo. E6 69
West Point, Ga. D1 55
West Point, Ky. C4 62
West Point, Miss. B5 68
West Point, Nebr. C9 71
West Point, N.Y. D7, m15 75
West Point, Va. C6 85
Westport, Conn. E3 52
West Portland, Oreg. *B4 80
West Portland Park, Oreg. *B4 80
West Portsmouth, Ohio D2 78
West Pueblo, Colo. *C6 51
West Rockingham, N.C. *B3 76
West Rutland, Vt. D1 73
West Sacramento, Calif. *C3 50
West Salem, Ill. E5 58
West Salem, Ohio B3 78
West Salem, Wis. E2 88
West Sayville, N.Y. G4 52
West Seneca, N.Y. *C2 75
West Slope, Oreg. g12 80
West Spitsbergen, isl., Nor. A21 2
West Springfield, Mass. B2 65
West St. Paul, Minn. n12 67
West Terre Haute, Ind. F3 59
West Union, Iowa B6 60
West Union, Ohio D2 78
West Union, W.Va. B4, k9 87
West Unity, Ohio A1 78
West University Place, Tex. r14 84
West Van Lear, Ky. C7 62
West View, Ohio h9 78
West View, Pa. h13 81
Westville, Ill. C6 58
Westville, N.J. D2 74
Westville Grove, N.J. *D2 74
West Virginia, state, U.S. 87
West Warren, Mass. B3 65
West Warwick, R.I. C10 52
Westwego, La. k11 63
West Wenatchee, Wash. *B5 86
West Winfield, N.Y. C5 75
West Winter Haven, Fla. *D5 54
Westwood, Calif. B3 50
Westwood, Kans. k16 61
Westwood, Ky. B7 62
Westwood, Mass. B5, h11 65
Westwood, Mich. *F5 66
Westwood, N.J. D5, h8 74
Westwood Lakes, Fla. s13 54
Westworth Village, Tex. *C4 84
West Wyalong, Austl. F6 26
West Wyoming, Pa. n17 81
West Wyomissing, Pa. *F9 81
West Yarmouth, Mass. C7 65
West York, Pa. G8 81
West Yuma, Ariz. *C1 48
Wetaskiwin, Alta., Can. C4 38
Wethersfield, Conn. C6 52
Wetumka, Okla. B5 79
Wetumpka, Ala. C3 46
Wetzel, co., W. Va. B4 87
Wetzlar, Ger., Fed. Rep. of C4 6
Wewahitchka, Fla. B1 54
Wewoka, Okla. B5 79
Wexford, Ire. D3 4
Wexford, co., Ire. *D3 4
Wexford, co., Mich. D5 66
Weyauwega, Wis. D5 88
Weyburn, Sask., Can. H4, o8 39
Weymouth, N.S., Can. E4 43
Weymouth, Mass. B6, h12 65
Weymouth & *Melcombe Regis*, Eng. E5 4
Whangarei, N.Z. K15 26
Wharton, N.J. B3 74
Wharton, Tex. E4 84
Wharton, W. Va. D6 87
Wharton, co., Tex. E4 84
Wharton West, Tex. *E4 84
What Cheer, Iowa C5 60
Whatcom, co., Wash. A4 86
Wheatland, Wyo. D8 89
Wheatland, co., Mont. D7 70
Wheatley, Ont., Can. E2 41
Wheaton, Ill. B5, k8 58
Wheaton, Md. *B3 53
Wheaton, Minn. E2 67
Wheat Ridge, Colo. *B5 51
Wheeler, Tex. B2 84
Wheeler, co., Ga. D4 55
Wheeler, co., Nebr. C7 71
Wheeler, co., Oreg. C6 80
Wheeler, co., Tex. B2 84
Wheeler, peak, N. Mex. A6 48
Wheelersburg, Ohio D3 78
Wheeling, Ill. h9 58
Wheeling, W.Va. A4, f8 87
Wheelwright, Ky. C7 62
Whippany, N.J. B4 74
Whitaker, Pa. *F2 81
Whitakers, N.C. A5 76
Whitby, Ont., Can. D6 41
Whitby, Eng. C6 4
Whitchurch-Stouffville,
Ont., Can. D5, k15 41
White, co., Ark. B4 49
White, co., Ga. B3 55
White, co., Ill. E5 58
White, co., Ind. C4 59
White, co., Tenn. D8 83
White Bear Lake, Minn. E5, m12 67
White Castle, La. D4, h9 63
White City, Fla. C1 54
White Cloud, Mich. E5 66
White Deer, Tex. B2 84
Whitefield, N.H. C4 73
Whitefish, Mont. B2 70
Whitefish Bay, Wis. *E6 88
White Hall, Ill. D3 58
Whitehall, Mich. E4 66
Whitehall, Mont. E4 70
Whitehall, N.Y. B7 75
Whitehall, Ohio m11 78
Whitehall, Pa. *F1 81
Whitehall, Wis. D2 88
Whitehaven, Eng. C5 4
White Haven, Pa. D10 81
Whitehorse, Yukon, Can. D6 36
Whitehouse, Ohio A2, e6 78
White Lake, Mich. *F7 66
Whiteland, Ind. *E5 59
White Oak, N.C. C4 76
White Oak, Ohio o12 78
White Oak, Pa. *F2 81
White Oak, Tex. *C5 84
White Pigeon, Mich. G5 66
White Pine, co., Nev. B4 72
White Pine, Tenn. C10 83
White Plains, N.Y. D7, m15 75
White River Junction, Vt. D3 73
White Rock, B.C., Can. E6, f13 37
White Salmon, Wash. D4 86
Whitesboro, N.Y. *B5 75
Whitesboro, Tex. C4 84
Whitesburg, Ky. C7 62
Whites Creek, Tenn. g10 83
White Settlement, Tex. *B5 84
Whiteside, co., Ill. B3 58
White Stone, Va. C6 85
White Sulphur Springs, Mont. D6 70
White Sulphur Springs, W.Va. D4 87
Whitesville, W.Va. n12 87
Whiteville, N.C. C4 76
Whitewright, Tex. C4 84
Whitfield, co., Ga. B1 55
Whiting, Ind. A3 59
Whiting, Wis. D4 88
Whitinsville, Mass. B4 65
Whitley, co., Ind. B6 59
Whitley, co., Ky. D5 62
Whitley City, Ky. D5 62
Whitman, Mass. B6, h12 65
Whitman, co., Wash. B8 86
Whitmire, S.C. N4 82
Whitmore City, Haw. f9 56
Whitnel, N.C. B1 76
Whitney, Idaho F2 57
Whitney, S.C. B4 82
Whitney, Tex. D4 84
Whitney, mtn., Calif. D4 50
Whitney Point, N.Y. C5 75
Whittier, Calif. F4, n12 50
Whitwell, Tenn. D8 83
Wiarton, Ont., Can. C3 41
Wibaux, co., Mont. D12 70
Wichita, Kans. E6, g12 61
Wichita, Oreg. *B4 80
Wichita, co., Kans. D2 61
Wichita, co., Tex. B3 84
Wichita Falls, Tex. C3 84
Wickenburg, Ariz. C2 48
Wickett, Tex. D1 84
Wickliffe, Ky. A2 62
Wickliffe, Ohio A4, g9 78
Wickliffe, Ohio *A5 78
Wicklow, co., Ire. *D3 4
Wicomico, co., Md. D6 53
Wiconisco, Pa. E8 81
Widnes, Eng. *D5 4
Wieluń, Pol. C6 7
Wiener Neustadt, Aus. E8 6
Wiesbaden, Ger., Fed. Rep. of C4 6
Wiggins, Miss. E4 68
Wigtown, co., Scot. *C4 4
Wilbarger, co., Tex. B3 84
Wilber, Nebr. D9 71
Wilberforce, Ohio C2 78
Wilbur, Wash. B7 86
Wilburton, Okla. C6 79
Wilcox, co., Ala. D2 46
Wilcox, co., Ga. E3 55
Wilder, Vt. D3 73
Wildwood, Fla. D4 54
Wildwood, N.J. F3 74
Wildwood, Pa. *E2 81
Wildwood Crest, N.J. F3 74
Wilhelm, mtn., N.Gui. k12 25
Wilhelmina, mtn., Indon. F9 19
Wilhelm-Pieck-Stadt Guben,
Ger. Dem. Rep. C7 6
Wilhelmshaven, Ger., Fed. Rep. of B4 6
Wilkes, co., Ga. C4 55
Wilkes, co., N.C. A1 76
Wilkes-Barre, Pa. D10, n17 81
Wilkesboro, N.C. A1 76
Wilkie, Sask., Can. E1 39

Wilkin, co., Minn. D2 67
Wilkinsburg, Pa. F2, k14 81
Wilkinson, co., Ga. D3 55
Wilkinson, co., Miss. D2 68
Will, co., Ill. B6 58
Willacoochee, Ga. E3 55
Willacy, co., Tex. F4 84
Willamina, Oreg. B3 80
Willard, Ohio A3 78
Willcox, Ariz. C4 48
Willemstad, Neth. Antilles A4 32
Williams, Ariz. B2 48
Williams, Calif. C2 50
Williams, co., N.Dak. D2 77
Williams, co., Ohio A1 78
Williams Bay, Wis. F5 88
Williamsburg, Iowa C5 60
Williamsburg, Ky. D5 62
Williamsburg, Ohio C1 78
Williamsburg, Pa. F5 81
Williamsburg (Independence City),
  Va. C6 85
Williamsburg, co., S.C. D8 82
Williams Lake, B.C., Can. C6, n18 37
Williamson, N.Y. B3 75
Williamson, W.Va. D2 87
Williamson, co., Ill. F4 58
Williamson, co., Tenn. A5 83
Williamson, co., Tex. D4 84
Williamsport, Ind. D3 59
Williamsport, Md. A2 53
Williamsport, Pa. D7 81
Williamston, Mich. F6 66
Williamston, N.C. B5 76
Williamston, S.C. B3 82
Williamstown, Ky. B5 62
Williamstown, Mass. A1 65
Williamstown, N.J. D3 74
Williamstown, Pa. E8 81
Williamstown, W. Va. B3 87
Williamsville, N.Y. C2 75
Willimantic, Conn. C8 52
Willingboro (Levittown), N.J. *C3 74
Willis Beach, Nebr. B9 71
Willioton, Fla. C4 54
Williston, N.Dak. B2 77
Williston, S.C. E5 82
Williston Park, N.Y. G2 52
Willits, Calif. C2 50
Willmar, Minn. E3 67
Willoughby, Ohio A4 78
Willow Brook, Calif. *F4 50
Willow Grove, Pa. F11 021 81
Willowick, Ohio A4, g9 78
Willow Run, Mich. p14 66
Willows, Calif. C2 50
Willow Springs, Ill. k9 58
Willow Springs, Mo. E6 69
Wills Point, Tex. *C5 84
Wilmer, Tex. n10 84
Wilmerding, Pa. B6 81
Wilmette, Ill. A6, h9 58
Wilmington, Del. A6 53
Wilmington, Ill. B5 58
Wilmington, Mass. A5, f11 65
Wilmington, N.C. C5 76
Wilmington, Ohio C2 78
Wilmington Manor, Del. *A6 53
Wilmore, Ky. C5 62
Wilson, Ark. B5 49
Wilson, Conn. B6 52
Wilson, Kans. D5 61
Wilson, N.Y. B2 75
Wilson, N.C. B5 76
Wilson, Okla. C4 79
Wilson, Pa. E11 81
Wilson, co., Kans. E8 61
Wilson, co., N.C. B5 76
Wilson, co., Tenn. A5 83
Wilson, co., Tex. E3 84
Wilton, Conn. E3 52
Wilton, Maine D2 64
Wilton, N.H. F4 73
Wilton Junction (Wilton), Iowa C6 60
Wilton Manors, Fla. *F6 54
Wiltshire, co., Eng. *F6 4
Winamac, Ind. B4 59
Winchendon, Mass. A3 65
Winchester, Ont., Can. B9 41
Winchester, Eng. E6 4
Winchester, Ill. D3 58
Winchester, Ind. D8 59
Winchester, Ky. C5 62
Winchester, Mass. g11 65
Winchester, Mo. *C7 69
Winchester, Tenn. B5 83

Winchester (Independent City),
  Va. A4 85
Windber, Pa. F4 81
Winder, Ga. C3 55
Windfall, Ind. D6 59
Windgap, Pa. E11 81
Windham, Ohio A4 78
Windham, co., Conn. B8 52
Windham, co., Vt. F3 73
Windhoek, Namibia E3 24
Wind Lake, Wis. F5 88
Windom, Minn. G3 67
Windsor, Newf., Can. D4 44
Windsor, N.S., Can. E5 43
Windsor, Ont., Can. E1 41
Windsor, Que., Can. D5 42
Windsor, Colo. *A6 51
Windsor, Conn. B6 52
Windsor, Ill. D5 58
Windsor, Mo. C4 69
Windsor, N.C. B6 76
Windsor, Pa. G8 81
Windsor, Vt. E3 73
Windsor, co., Vt. D2 73
Windsor Heights, Iowa e8 60
Windsor Hills, Calif. *F4 50
Windsor Locks, Conn. B6 52
Windward Islands, see Dominica, Grenada,
St Lucia and St. Vincent, Br. dep., N.A.
Windy Hill, S.C. *C8 82
Windy Hills, Ky. *H6 62
Winfield, Ala. B2 46
Winfield, Ill. *B5 58
Winfield, Kans. E7 61
Winfield, N.J. k7 74
Wingate, N.C. C2 76
Wingham, Ont., Can. D3 41
Wink, Tex. D1 84
Winkelman, Ariz. C3 48
Winkler, Man., Can. E3 40
Winkler, co., Tex. D1 84
Winn, par., La. C3 63
Winneab, Ghana G4 22
Winnebago, Ill. A4 58
Winnebago, Minn. G4 67
Winnebago, co., Ill. A4 58
Winnebago, co., Iowa A4 60
Winnebago, co., Wis. H9 88
Winneconne, Wis. D5 88
Winnemucca, Nev. A3 72
Winner, S Dak. G6 77
Winneshiek, co., Iowa A6 60
Winnetka, Ill. A6, h9 58
Winnfield, La. C3 63
Winnie, Tex. *E5 84
Winnipeg, Man., Can. E3, h8 40
Winnipeg, lake, Man., Can. C2 40
Winnipegosis, Man., Can. D2 40
Winnipegosis, lake,
  Man. Can. C2 40
Winnsboro, La. B4 63
Winnsboro, S.C. C5 82
Winnsboro, Tex. C5 84
Winnsboro Mills, S.C. *C5 82
Winona, Minn. F7 67
Winona, Miss. B4 68
Winona, co., Minn. F7 67
Winona Lake, Ind. B6 59
Winooski, Vt. C1 73
Winschoten, Neth. A7 5
Winslow, Ariz. B3 48
Winslow, Ind. H3 59
Winslow, Maine D3 64
Windslow, Wash. e10 86
Winsted, Conn. B4 52
Winsted, Minn. F4 67
Winston, Fla. D4 54
Winston, Oreg. *D3 80
Winston, co., Ala. A2 46
Winston, co., Miss. B4 68
Winston-Salem, N.C. A2 76
Winter Garden, Fla. D5 54
Winter Haven, Fla. D5 54
Winter Park, Fla. D5 54
Winters, Calif. C2 50
Winters, Tex. D3 84
Winterset, Iowa *C4 60
Wintersville, Ohio B5 78
Winterthur, Switz. E4 6
Winterton, Newf., Can. E5 44
Winterville, N.C. B5 76
Winthrop, Maine D3 64
Winthrop, Mass. B6, g12 65
Winthrop, Minn. F4 67
Winthrop Harbor, Ill. A6, h9 58
Wirt, co., W. Va. B3 87

Wisbech, Eng. D7 4
Wiscasset, Maine D3 64
Wisconsin, state, U.S. B8 45
Wisconsin Dells, Wis. E4 88
Wisconsin Rapids, Wis. D4 88
Wise, Va. f9 85
Wise, co., Tex. C4 84
Wise, co., Va. e9 85
Wishek, N.Dak. D6 77
Wisla, riv., Pol. B5 7
Wismar, Ger. Dem. Rep. B5 6
Wisner, La. C4 63
Wisner, Nebr. C9 71
Withamsville, Ohio C1 78
Witt, Ill. D4 58
Wittenberg, Ger. Dem. Rep. C6 6
Wittenberge, Ger. Dem. Rep. B5 6
Wixom, Mich. o14 66
Wloclawek, Pol. B5 7
Woburn, Mass. B5, g11 65
Wolcott, Conn. C5 52
Wolcott, N.Y. B4 75
Wolfe, co., Que., Can. D6 42
Wolfe, co., Ky. C6 62
Wolfeboro, N.H. D5 73
Wolfe City, Tex. C4 84
Wolfenbüttel, Ger., Fed. Rep. of B5 6
Wolf Lake, Mich. E4 66
Wolf Point, Mont. B11 70
Wolfsburg, Ger., Fed. Rep. of B5 6
Wolfville, N.S., Can. D5 43
Wollongong, Austl. F9 25
Wolseley, Sask., Can. G4 39
Wolverhampton, Eng. D5 4
Wolverine Lake, Mich. *F7 66
Wolverton, Eng. D6 4
Womelsdrof, Pa. F9 81
Wonder Lake, Ill. A5, h8 58
Wònju, Kor. H3 18
Wonsan, Kor. G3 18
Wood, co., Ohio A2 78
Wood, co., Tex. C5 84
Wood, co., W.Va. B3 87
Wood, co., Wis. D3 88
Woodbine, Iowa C2 60
Woodbine, N.J. E3 74
Woodbourne, N.Y. D6 75
Woodbridge, Conn. D4 52
Woodbridge, N.J. B4, k7 74
Woodbridge, Va. B5 85
Woodburn, Oreg. D4, h12 80
Woodbury, Conn. C4 52
Woodbury, Ga. D2 55
Woodbury, N.J. D2 74
Woodbury, N.Y. *E7 75
Woodbury, Tenn. B5 83
Woodbury, co., Iowa B1 60
Woodbury Heights, N.J. *D2 74
Woodcliff Lake, N.J. g8 74
Woodcroft, Ind. *E5 59
Wood Dale, Ill. k9 58
Woodford, Eng. k13 4
Woodford, co., Ill. C4 58
Woodford, co., Ky. B5 62
Wood Green, Eng. k12 4
Woodlake, Calif. D4 50
Woodland, Calif. C3 50
Woodland, Maine C5 64
Woodland, Pa. E5 81
Woodland, Wash. D3 86
Woodland Beach, Mich. *G7 66
Woodlawn, Ky. A2 62
Woodlawn, Md. *B4 53
Woodlawn, Md. *C4 53
Woodlawn, Ohio n13 78
Woodlawn Beach, N.Y. C2 75
Woodlawn Orchards, Mich. *F6 66
Woodley Hills, Va. *B5 85
Woodlyn, Pa. *B10 81
Wood Lynne, N.J. *D2 74
Woodmere, N.Y. G2 52
Wood-Ridge, N.J. h8 74
Woodridge, N.Y. *D6 75
Wood River, Ill. E3 58
Woodroffe, mtn., Austl. E5 25
Woodruff, S.C. B3 82
Woodruff, co., Ark. B4 49
Woodruff Place, Ind. *E5 59
Woods, co., Okla. A3 79
Woodsboro, Tex. E4 84
Woods Cross, Utah C2 72
Woodsfield, Ohio C4 78
Woodside, Calif. *D2 50
Woodson, co., Kans. E8 61
Woodson Terrace, Mo. *C7 69
Woodstock, N.B., Can. C2 43

Woodstock, Ont., Can. D4 41
Woodstock, Ill. A5 58
Woodstock, Vt. D2 73
Woodstock, Va. B4 85
Woodstown, N.J. D2 74
Woodsville, N.H. C3 73
Woodville, Calif. *D4 50
Woodville, Miss. D2 68
Woodville, Ohio A2, f7 78
Woodville, Tex. D5 84
Woodward, Ala. B3, g7 46
Woodward, Iowa C4 60
Woodward, Okla. A2 79
Woodward, co., Okla. A2 79
Woodway, Tex. *D4 84
Woolwich, Eng. m13 4
Woonsocket, R.I. A10 52
Woonsocket, S.Dak. F7 77
Wooster, Ohio B4 78
Worcester, Eng. D5 4
Worcester, Mass. B4 65
Worcester, N.Y. C6 75
Worcester, S.Afr. G3 24
Worchester, co., Eng. *D5 4
Worcester, co., Md. D7 53
Worcester, co., Mass. A3 65
Worden, Ill. E4 58
Workington, Eng. C5 4
Worland, Wyo. B5 89
World .... 2.
Wormleysburg, Pa. *F8 81
Worms, Ger., Fed. Rep. of D4 6
Worth, Ill. k9 58
Worth, co., Ga. E3 55
Worth, co., Iowa A4 60
Worth, co., Mo. A3 69
Wortham, Tex. D4 84
Worthing, Eng. E6 4
Worthington, Ind. F4 59
Worthington, Ky. B7 62
Worthington, Minn. G3 67
Worthington, Ohio B2, k10 78
Wrangel, isl., Sov. Un. B21 13
Wrangell, Alsk. D13, m23 47
Wrangell, mtn., Alsk. f19 47
Wray, Colo. A8 51
Wrens, Ga. C4 55
Wrentham, Mass. B5 65
Wrexham, Wales D5 4
Wright, co., Iowa B4 60
Wright, co., Minn. E4 67
Wright, co., Mo. D5 69
Wright City, Okla. C6 79
Wrightstown, N.J. C3 74
Wrightsville, Ga. D4 55
Wrightsville, Pa. F8 81
Wroclaw (Breslau), Pol. C4 7
Wuhan, China E7 17
Wuhu, China E8 17
Wuppertal, Ger., Fed. Rep. of C3 6
Württemberg, reg., Ger.,
  Rep. of D4 6
Würzburg, Ger., Fed. Rep. of D4 6
Wurzen, Ger. Dem. Rep. C6 6
Wutongqiao, China F5 17
Wuxi, China E9 17
Wuxing, China E9 17
Wuzhou, China G7 17
Wyandanch, N.Y. *n15 75
Wyandot, co., Ohio B2 78
Wyandotte, Mich. F7, p15 66
Wyandotte, co., Kans. C9 61
Wyckoff, N.J. *A4 74
Wymore, Nebr. D9 71
Wyncote, Pa. *F11 81
Wyndmoor, Pa. *F11 81
Wynne, Ark. B5 49
Wynnewood, Okla. C4 79
Wynnewood, Pa. *F11 81
Wynyard, Austl. o15 25
Wynyard, Sask., Can. F3, n8 39
Wyoming, Del. B6 53
Wyoming, Ill. B4 58
Wyoming, Mich. F5 66
Wyoming, Minn. E6 67
Wyoming, Ohio c13 78
Wyoming, Pa. n17 81
Wyoming, co., N.Y. C2 75
Wyoming, co., Pa. D9 81
Wyoming, co., W. Va. D3 87
Wyoming, state, U.S. 89
Wyomissing, Pa. *F10 81
Wythe, co., Va. D1 85
Wytheville, Va. D1 85

X

Xánthi, Grc. B5 14
Xavier, Kans. B8 61
Xenia, Ohio C2 78
Xiamen, China G8 17
Xi'an, China E6 17
Xiangtan, China F7 17

Xianyang, China E6 17
Xichang, China F5 17
Xigazê, China C8 20
Xi Jiang, riv., China G7 17
Xilitla, Mex. m14 34
Xingú, riv., Braz. D5 27

Xining, China D5 17
Xinjiang Uygur, auton. reg.
China F11 13
Xinmin, China C9 17
Xinxiang, China D7 17
Xinyang, China E7 17

Xixabangma, mtn., China C8 20
Xochimilco, Mex. h9 34
Xuanhua, China C8 17
Xuchang, China E7 17
Xuzhou, China E8 17

Y

Ya'an, China F5 17
Yadkin, co., N.C. A2 76
Yadkinville, N.C. A2 76
Yaizu, Jap. o17 18
Yakima, Wash. C5 86
Yakima, co., Wash. C5 86
Yakutsk, Sov. Un. C15 13
Yalobusha, co., Miss. A4 68
Yalta, Sov. Un. I10 12
Yalu, China B9 17
Yalvaç, Tur. C8 14
Yamachiche, Que., Can. C5 42
Yamagata, Jap. G10 18
Yamagata, pref.,Jap. *G10 18
Yamaguchi, Jap. I5 18
Yamaguchi, pref., Jap. *I5 18
Yamanashi, pref., Jap. *I9 18
Yamaska, co., Que., Can. C5 42
Yambol, Bul. D8 10
Yamethin, Bur. D10 20
Yamhill, co., Oreg. B3 80
Yamoussoukro, I.C. G3 22
Yanam, India E7 20
Yanbu', Sau. Ar. E2 15
Yancey, co., N.C. f10 76
Yanceyville, N.C. A3 76
Yangquan, China D7 17
Yangtze, riv., China E8 17
Yangzhou, China E8 17
Yankton, S. Dak. H8 77
Yankton, co., S. Dak. G8 77
Yanji, China C10 17
Yanqi, China C2 17
Yantai, China D9 17
Yao, Jap. *I7 18
Yaoundé, Cam. H7 22
Yaracuy, state, Ven. A4 32
Yardley, Pa. F12 81
Yarīm, Yemen G3 15
Yarmouth, N.S., Can. F3 43.
Yarmouth, Maine E2, g7 64
Yarmouth, co., N.S., Can. F4 43
Yaroslavl, Sov. Un. C12 12
Yartseveo, Sov. Un. D9 12
Yarumal, Col. B2 32

Yasinovataya, Sov. Un. q20 12
Yass, Austl. G7 26
Yates, co., N.Y. C3 75
Yates Center, Kans. E8 61
Yatsushiro, Jap. J5 18
Yauco, P.R. *G11 35
Yavapai, co., Ariz. B2 48
Yavorov, Sov. Un. G4 12
Yawatahama, Jap. J6 18
Yazd (Yezd), Iran B8 23
Yazoo, co., Miss. C3 68
Yazoo City, Mis. C3 68
Yeadon, Pa. q20 81
Yeagertown, Pa. E6 81
Yecla, Sp. C5 8
Yefremov, Sov. Un. E12 12
Yegoryevsk, Sov. Un. D12, n19 12
Yelan, Sov. Un. F14 12
Yelets, Sov. Un. E12 12
Yell, co,.Ark. B2 49
Yellow, see Huang He, riv., China
Yellow, sea, China D9 17
Yellowknife, N.W. Ter. Can. D11 36
Yellow Medicine, co., Minn. F2 67
Yellow Springs, Ohio C2 78
Yellowstone, co., Mont. D8 70
Yellowstone, riv., U.S. B2 89
Yellowstone National Park (part),
co., Wyo. B2 89
Yemen, country, Asia F3 15
Yemen, People's Democratic
Republic of, country, Asia H7 16
Yenakiyevo, Sov. Un. q20 12
Yenangyaung, Bur. *G4 17
Yenisey, riv., Sov. Un. C11 16
Yeniseysk, Sov. Un. D12 13
Yeovil, Eng. E5 4
Yeppoon, Austl. D9 25
Yerevan, Sov. Un. E7 13
Yerupaja, mtn., Peru D2 31
Yessey, Sov. Un. C13 13
Yevpatoriya, Sov. Un. I9 12
Yeysk, Sov. Un. H12 12
Yiannitsá, Grc. *B4 14
Yibin, China F5 17

Yichang, China E7 17
Yichun, China C4 18
Yilan, China B10 17
Yiliang, China G5 17
Yinchuan, China D6 17
Yingkou, China C9 17
Yiyang, China F7 17
Yoakum, Tex. E4 84
Yoakum, co., Tex. C1 84
Yogyakarta, Indon., G4 9
Yoichi, Jap. E10 18
Yokkaichi, Jap. I8, o15 18
Yokohama, Jap. I9, n18 18
Yokosuka, Jap I9, n18 18
Yokote, Jap. G10 8
Yolo, co., Calif. C2 50
Yolyn, W. Va. D5 87
Yonago, Jap. I6 18
Yonezawa, Jap. H10 18
Yonghung, Kor. G3 18
Yonkers, N.Y. E7, n15 75
Yonne, dept., Fr. *D5 5
Yorba Linda, Calif. *F5 50
York, Ala. C1 46
York, Ont., Can. *m15 41
York, Eng. D6 4
York, Maine E1 64
York, Nebr. D8 71
York, Pa. G8 81
York, S.C. B5 82
York, co., N.B., Can. C3 43
York, co., Ont., Can. D5 43
York, co., Eng. *D6 4
York, co., Maine E2 64
York, co., Nebr. D8 71
York, co., Pa. G8 81
York, co., S.C. A5 82
York, co., Va. C6 85
Yorkshire, N.Y. C2 75
Yorkton, Sask.,Can. F4, n8 39
Yorktown, Ind. D6 59
Yorktown, N.Y. *D7 75
Yorktown, Tex. E4 84
Yorktown Heights, N.Y. *D7 75
Yorktown Manor, R.I. C11 52

Yorkville, Ill. B5 58
Yorkville, N.Y. B5 75
Yorkville, Ohio B5 78
Yoshkar-Ola, Sov. Un. *D7 13
Yōsu, Kor. I3 18
Young, Austl. *F8 25
Young, co., Tex. C3 84
Youngstown, N.Y. B2 75
Youngstown, Ohio A5 78
Youngsville, La. D3 63
Youngsville, Pa. C3 81
Youngtown, Ariz. D1 48
Youngwood, Pa. F2 81
Yozgat, Tur. C10 14
Ypacaraí, Par. E4 29
Ypsilanti, Mich. *F7, p4 66
Yreka, Calif. B2 50
Ystad, Swe. J5 11
Yuanling, China F7 17
Yuba, co., Calif. C3 50
Yuba City, Calif. C3 50
Yuba City South, Calif. *C3 50
Yūbari, Jap. E10 18
Yucatán, state, Mex. C7 34
Yueyang, China F7 17
Yugoslavia, country, Eur. C3 10
Yukon, Okla. B4 79
Yukon, ter., Can. D6 36
Yukon, riv., N.A. C9 47
Yuma, Ariz. C1 48
Yuma, Colo. A8 51
Yuma, co., Ariz. C2 48
Yuma, co., Colo. A8 51
Yumen, China D4 17
Yumenzhen, China C4 17
Yunnan, prov., China G5 17
Yurécuaro, Mex. m12 34
Yuryevets, Sov. Un. C14 12
Yuryev-Polskiy, Sov. Un. C12 12
Yuty, Par. E4 29
Yuzha, Sov. Un. C13 12
Yuzhno-Sakhalinsk, Sov. Un. E17 13
Yverdon, Switz. E3 6

Z

Zabkowice, Pol. C4 7
Zabrze, Pol. C5, g9 7
Zacatecas, Mex. C4 34
Zacatecas, state, Mex. C4, m12 34
Zachary, La. D4 63
Zadar, Yugo. C2 10
Zagorsk, Sov. Un. C12 12
Zagreb, Yugo. C2 10
Zāhedān, Iran G9 16
Zaḥlah, Leb. F10 14
Zaire, country, Afr. B4 24
Zaječar, Yugo. D6 10
Zákinthos, Grc. D3 14
Zákinthos (Zante), prov., Grc. *D3 14
Zakopane, Pol. D5 7
Zala, co., Hung. *B3 10
Zalaegerszeg, Hung. B3 10
Zalău, Rom. B6 10
Zambales, prov., Phil. *B5 19
Zambezi, riv., Afr. H8 21
Zambia (Northern Rhodesia),
country, Afr. D5 24
Zamboanga, Phil. D6 19
Zamboanga del Norte, prov.,
Phil. *D6 19
Zamboanga del Sur.,
prov., Phil. *D6 19
Zamora, Sp. B3 8
Zamora, prov., Sp. *B3 8
Zamora de Hidalgo, Mex. C4, m12 34
Zamośc, Pol. C7 7

Zanesville, Ohio C4 78
Zanjān, Iran A7 23
Zanzibar, Tan. B7 24
Zapata, Tex. F3 84
Zapata, co., Tex. F3 84
Zaporozhye, Sov. Un. H10 12
Zaragoza, Sp. B5 8
Zaragoza, prov., Sp. *B5 8
Zárate, Arg. A5, g7 28
Zaraysk, Sov. Un. D12 12
Zaria, Nig. F6 22
Zashiversk, Sov. Un. C17 13
Žatec, Czech. C2 7
Zavala, co., Tex. E3 84
Zavitaya, Sov. Un. D15 13
Zawiercie, Pol. C5, g10 7
Zaysan, Sov. Un. E11 13
Zdolbunov, Sov. Un. F6 12
Zduńska Wola, Pol. C5 7
Zebulon, N.C. B4 76
Zeeland, Mich. F5 66
Zeeland, prov., Neth. B5 5
Zefat (Safad), Isr. B3, g5 15
Zehdenick, Ger. Dem. Rep. B6 6
Zeigler, Ill. F4 58
Zeist, Neth. A6 5
Zeitz, Ger. Dem. Rep. C6 6
Zelienople, Pa. E1 81
Zella-Mehlis, Ger. Dem. Rep. C5 6
Zemetchino, Sov. Un. E14 12
Zenica, Yugo. C3 10

Zephyrhills, Fla. D4 54
Zerbst, Ger. Dem. Rep. C6 6
Zeya, Sov. Un. D15 13
Zgierz, Pol. C5 7
Zhangjiakou, China C7 17
Zhangzhou, China G8 17
Zhanjiang, China G7 17
Zhaoqing, China G7 17
Zhaoxing, China C5 18
Zhaozhou, China D2 18
Zhdanov, Sov. Un. H11 12
Zhejiang, prov., China F9 17
Zhengzhou, China E7 17
Zhenjiang, China E8 17
Zhitomir, Sov. Un. F7 12
Zhizdra, Sov. Un. E10 12
Zhmerinka, Sov. Un. G7 12
Zhongba, China C7 20
Zhuzhou, China F7 17
Zibo, China D8 17
Ziebach, co., S. Dak. F4 77
Zielona Gora, Pol. C3 7
Zigong, China F5 17
Ziguinchor, Sen. F1 22
Zile, Tur. B10 14
Zilina, Czech. D5 7
Zilwaukee, Mich. E7 66
Zimbabwe, country, Afr. D6 24
Zimnicea, Rom. D7 10
Zinder, Niger. F6 22
Zion, Ill. A6, h9 58

Zionsville, Ind. E5, k9 59
Zipaquirá, Col. B3 32
Zitácuaro, Mex. n13 34
Zittau, Ger. Dem. Rep. C7 6
Zlatoust, Sov. Un. D8 13
Zlynka, Sov. Un. E8 12
Znamenka, Sov. Un. G9 12
Znojmo, Czech. D4 7
Zolochev, Sov. Un. G5 12
Zolotonosha, Sov. Un. G9 12
Zomba, Malawi D7 24
Zonguldak, Tur. B8 14
Zrejanin (Petrovgrad), Yugo. C5 10
Zug, Switz. E4 6
Zug, canton, Switz. *E4 6
Zulia, state, Ven. B3 32
Zumbrota, Minn. F6 67
Zuni, N. Mex. B4 48
Zunyi, China F6 17
Zürich, Switz. *E4 6
Zürich, canton, Switz. *E4 6
Zutphen, Neth. A7 5
Zvenigorodka, Sov. Un. G8 12
Zvolen, Czech. D5 7
Zweibrücken, Ger., Fed. Rep. of D3 6
Zwickau, Ger. Dem. Rep. C6 6
Zwolle, La. C2 63
Zwolle, Neth. A7 5
Zyrardów, Pol. B6, m12 7